BASIC WRITINGS OF
SAINT AUGUSTINE

THE RANDOM HOUSE

Lifetime Library

BASIC WRITINGS OF

SAINT

AUGUSTINE

EDITED, WITH AN INTRODUCTION AND NOTES BY

WHITNEY J. OATES

Ewing Professor of Greek Languages and Literature, Chairman
of the Department of Classics, Chairman of the Special Program
in the Humanities, Princeton University

VOLUME ONE

RANDOM HOUSE *Publishers* NEW YORK

281.1
A923

149334

PREFACE

IT IS a matter of common agreement among historians and students of culture that the Western civilization in which we live derives from a fusion of the Hebraic and Christian on the one hand and the Greek and the Roman on the other. If this interpretation be sound, then there can be no more important figure to understand than Saint Augustine. The present edition of his basic writings has been prepared in order to provide the modern reader with a comprehensive book in which a rounded portrait of his thought may be presented. Also, and no less important, has been the objective to provide students of Christian theology with the most important writings of Saint Augustine which have done so much to shape its subsequent development both in its Protestant and Catholic forms. The present edition, it is hoped, will take its place beside the companion volumes, published some years ago in the Random House Lifetime Library, which contain the basic writings of Saint Thomas Aquinas.

With the exception of the treatises *On the Immortality of the Soul* and *Concerning the Teacher* which have been translated by G. C. Leckie, the remaining texts which have been used are those to be found in *A Select Library of the Nicene and Post-Nicene Fathers of the Christian Church* published under the general editorship of Philip Schaff. These versions which are in general of the highest order of excellence have been checked against the original Latin and have been modified in certain respects either to make the version in question more accurate or to modernize the translations where this seemed to be desirable. The notes which appear in Dr. Schaff's edition, which contain references to the Bible and the Apocrypha, have been reproduced in their entirety. A selection has been made from the remaining notes in order that the reader may have the necessary information in order to understand any passage which might otherwise be obscure. A small number of other notes has been added with the same purpose in view.

In addition to brief introductory notes on the several treatises, a general introduction has been prepared which, it is hoped, will give the reader the necessary background on Saint Augustine's life and religion as well as an indication of a sound method of approaching and interpreting the complex thought of the author. Indexes to the three treatises, *The Confessions, The City of God,* and *On the Trinity* will be found at the end of Volumes I and II.

Grateful acknowledgment must be made to various individuals whose penetrating advice and criticism have been available in the preparation of this edition. Professors George Thomas, Theodor Mommsen and Paul Ramsey of Princeton University were most helpful in making the final selection of those treatises which were to be included. Father William Lynch, S.J., gave invaluable criticism to the general introduction. Profound acknowledgment also should be made to Professor Carlos Baker, Professor E. Harris Harbison, and Professor Paul Ramsey for their help in preparing the introductory essay and to Mrs. J. S. Finch for her assistance in preparing the manuscript. Random House and its able editor, Mr. Saxe Commins, have given unstinting attention to the production of this edition. It is hoped that it may take its place along with the other volumes in the Lifetime Library and that it will carry on the high ideals which sustain that series.

Princeton, New Jersey   Whitney J. Oates
June, 1948

CONTENTS

VOLUME ONE

VOLUME TWO

INTRODUCTION

THE LIFE AND RELIGION OF SAINT AUGUSTINE

IMPLICIT in the immense variety of Saint Augustine's writings is an organic wholeness of attitude. This simultaneity of his thinking, or if you choose, the "all-togetherness," accounts for many of his strengths as well as his weaknesses. The first essential for one who embarks upon a study of this great man is an awareness of the total unity in the vast multiplicity of his works. It is no wonder that the critical interpreter, who must proceed from aspect to aspect, who must compartmentalize his analysis, finds himself face to face with a task of grave complexity. He cannot, for example, satis-factorily expound "the philosophy" of Saint Augustine, for if he does, he may be forced to accept a definition of philosophy as that which proceeds only from reason, and such a definition would be utterly unacceptable to Saint Augustine himself.[1] Philosophy, theology, religion, in his thought, are all deeply interfused, their functional relations so clearly felt, that for him it is futile to talk of any one of these apart from the context of the others. For him, data derived from reason are only half alive unless they are viewed in the perspective of faith and revelation, and the converse likewise is true.

This prime characteristic of Augustinian thought has exposed it to the attack of precise philosophical criticism which can point up with relative ease places where the rational defense may be weak. The same charac-teristic also makes the individual treatises difficult to read, for the main line of an argument may be blurred or obscured by the powerful associative memory of Saint Augustine. He may choose at any moment to develop a point tangential to the major question at issue, and can do so with com-plete justification and without irrelevance if, as he believes, all things are so closely interrelated. But as a consequence the effect of logical articula-tion is often lost. On the other hand, it would be the height of absurdity to deny logical power to Saint Augustine. It is revealed clearly in many individual passages, such as his proof for the existence of God in Book II of the treatise *On Free Will*, as well as in the over-arching logic of his great works, such as *The City of God*. A synoptic view of this masterwork discloses an architectonic skill which few can rival in the Western tradition.

Saint Augustine's thought cannot strictly be called a "system." It is rather a world view or a "universe view," one which comprehends God and all of reality from the highest order down to its most insignificant details in their manifold and complex inter-connections. In contrast, there have been many philosophers who have constructed "systems" from the time of the earliest Greeks on down through the nineteenth century, from the predecessors of Socrates through Hegel and his followers. Epicurus, for example, by blending the atomism of Democritus with an ethic of pleasure, forged an almost water-tight rationalistic materialism, which is systematic in the highest degree. In fact, so carefully wrought, so "closed" is his system, that his followers, and of course notably Lucretius, had only to invoke the *ipse dixit* of the master's authority to settle any debatable issue.

Aristotle also provides an illustration of the systematic thinker with whom Saint Augustine may be contrasted. The "master of them that know" had supreme confidence in reason plus a superb analytical insight into the nature of logical relations, as well as an insatiable eagerness to absorb, organize and understand all that the world of sense experience could offer. From these elements he erected a philosophical structure, logically coherent and so all-inclusive that, as everyone knows, it dominated the intellectual life of even more than the Western world for centuries. But Aristotelianism too, generally speaking, is a "closed" system, and, as such, it has tended to beget continuators and commentators. In a sense, Aristotle set for himself a task upon which he labored until it was completed. Similarly, Saint Thomas Aquinas undertook his enterprise of forging a Christian metaphysic, and to all intents and purposes, he finished his project in such a way that, in the opinion of many Catholic thinkers, it will never be necessary to attempt it again. It, too, can be called a "closed" system. For the most part the Thomist annotators have ramified and interpreted the thought of their master, since they have not felt the need to take their start from him and embark on new voyages of philosophical discovery.

In distinction to these creators of "closed" systems, there have been philosophers whose thought has been "open." Let it be understood, as a general definition, that an "open" system is one which comprehends within it all aspects of reality, one which recognizes the principle that "life runs beyond logic," and above all, admits the fact that human speculation on ultimate questions is always in process, and cannot in any final sense ever be completed. It is "germinal" and at the same time peculiarly vulnerable to strict rational attack. Plato perhaps is the most notable example of this second type. Any attentive reader of the *Dialogues* can observe that Plato wished more than anything else to prevent his thought from congealing. The very dialogue form or the principles underlying his dialectic convey his intense desire to keep his philosophical inquiry alive and not permit it to crystallize into a series of verbal formulae. This attitude is perhaps most clearly evident in the closing section of the *Phaedrus*, where Socrates insists that only the actual conversations of men, only the real contact of mind with mind, genuinely lives, while anything that is written partakes inevitably of a certain kind of death. Plato knows the terrible finality of words.

If it be fair to call Plato the creator of an "open system," it is interesting to observe the kind of influence he has tended to exert. Whereas the "closed system" stimulates the continuator and commentator, the "open system," with its wholeness of attitude or way of looking at things, tempts either those who undertake to complete the system—*i.e.*, to change it from an "open" to a "closed system"—or those who are inspired by the general attitude and hence are led on to creative philosophical speculation of their own. Plotinus and the Neo-Platonists were convinced that they were completing Platonism, and yet this so-called logical conclusion is a "closed system," marked by a dogmatism and an abandonment of radical dualism with which Plato himself would never have concurred. The other type of influence can be seen not only in philosophers from the Stoics on down through the centuries to such men as Alfred North Whitehead, but also in the poets and artists whose creative imaginations have been stirred by the Platonic vision.

Saint Augustine must be numbered among those whose thought is "open." Surely many an Augustinian has attempted the task of completion. Almost without exception the effort has only produced a strange variant of the original, and their labors bear the same relation to Saint Augustine as the Neo-Platonists do to Plato. In fact, since in the course of time many and often conflicting Augustinianisms have appeared, depending upon the particular aspect of the original view which has been selected for emphasis, Saint Augustine has now and again been partially "exiled" by some elements in the Catholic Church. Actually he has never been an "official" philosopher of the Church in the sense that Saint Thomas is. Indeed, it may be impossible that an "open system" can ever validly achieve such an official role. Yet the dynamic vitality of Saint Augustine's whole and "open" view, and its potential as a source of inspiration, has constituted one of the Church's greatest assets throughout its history. As for the conflicts which are possible outgrowths of any "open system," M. Etienne Gilson has succinctly suggested the solution: "The difficulties which at the present time beset Augustinianism are not an ill for which we need to find remedies, for Saint Augustine is not affected by any ill; all that is needed is to return from the Augustinianism of the Augustinians to that of Saint Augustine himself." [2]

The foregoing observations which contrast the "open" with the "closed system" are offered as generalizations to which exceptions may well be taken. Yet the basic distinction appears sound and should be particularly helpful in dealing with a figure like Saint Augustine. Furthermore, in contemplating the broad sweep of Western philosophy or the development of the Christian religion, it is not too difficult to observe how the "open" and the "closed system" complement each other. To designate a system as "closed" does not mean to derogate from its value or importance. Actually each has its distinctive philosophical and religious function; each fulfills a different need. In the Roman Catholic Church, no one can take the place of Saint Thomas, but as M. Gilson has remarked, "But to be Christian *qua* philosophy a philosophy must be Augustinian or nothing . . . [Saint Augustine is] at the very heart of Christian thought, side by side with Saint Thomas Aquinas, who may have differed from him, but has never left him." [3]

Christianity by its very nature has needed and needs now a spokesman of Saint Augustine's quality. What must be stressed in Christianity is its insistence that "all things are together." If reason runs riot, or if emotionalism gets out of hand, Christianity in its essence cries out—or at least should, to restore the balance. Early twentieth-century Protestantism illustrates a serious departure from the central insights of the religion envisioned by Saint Augustine. Somehow, under the influence of a naïve optimism and trapped in the contradiction that God could be removed from Christianity without undue loss, this deviation in the name of Protestantism propounded a Christian social ethics which liquidated its spiritual inheritance. Faced with the world cataclysm of our time it merely evaporated.

Reinhold Niebuhr, with a profound sense of the comprehensiveness of Christianity, has reacted vigorously against this modern version of Protestantism. His whole analysis sees both the human predicament and the Christian answers in terms of a series of closely interconnected paradoxes, and his development of these paradoxes reveals at every step that he recognizes fundamentally the "all-togetherness" of the Christian position. In fact, it would not be too much to say that his recognition of this basic quality of Christianity has given him his stature as a leading Protestant theologian. Yet another imbalance in its turn tends to vitiate Niebuhr's position. Planted squarely as he is in the prophetic tradition, he has concentrated too exclusively on the fallen state of man, or to put it somewhat facetiously, has been so busy rehabilitating sin as a fact of man's nature that other and equally important aspects of Christianity suffer from underemphasis.

Even these two illustrations, however random they may appear, should suffice to point out what Saint Augustine's balanced view can contribute to twentieth-century Christianity. But note, this is not to suggest a mere repetition or a slavish parroting of the Augustinian position. Rather, since it is an "open system," the suggestion is that Christian thinkers expose themselves to the stimulus of its balance, absorb the spirit of its comprehensiveness, and be encouraged thereby to reinterpret afresh the inclusive unity of Christianity. That our time is ready for such a revivification of the Augustinian attitude is indicated by the recent widespread and renewed interest in Augustinian studies. Why is it that now both Protestant and Catholic alike claim Saint Augustine as their own? Can it be too much to hope that somehow, via increasing familiarity with his insights into the nature of Christianity, men can come more fully to a sense of the abiding unity which underlies sectarian difference?

Saint Augustine's monumental figure appears at that point in history when finally all the diverse forces of the ancient world had come together into a cultural amalgam which was destined to disintegrate, or at least to be transmuted, almost at the moment of its formation. In the amalgam are to be found the elements of the Hebraic and Christian traditions deriving from the nearer East. Greek culture had developed independently of its neighbor to the west in Italy, and these two cultural strains began to be consolidated into their Graeco-Roman form in the first two centuries before the Christian era. The "world state" forged by the Emperor Augustus provided a period of relative peace and security which endured for approximately two hundred years and thus afforded an opportunity to the infant religion of Christianity to grow and develop with actually less opposition than is commonly supposed.

But in the third century the manifold forces of disintegration, which had been held in precarious check by the moribund splendor of the Antonines, broke loose with terrifying violence. Barbarian pressure existed on the frontiers. The economic stability under the early emperors proved to be specious. Imperial authority came more and more to rest upon military power, with "the consent of the governed" less and less a factor in the political structure. It is a miracle that out of this third-century chaos any kind of order was restored. By radically altering many of the traditional features of the Roman imperial organization, Diocletian was able to reintroduce a modicum of stability into the situation, though at the price of establishing a more or less oriental despotism. Many of the time-honored freedoms had forever disappeared, but still there remained a few important vestiges of the best that Rome had created, sufficient at least to permit the Empire to continue with some vitality.

Strangely enough, during the years of chaos and partial rehabilitation, Christianity had grown with astonishing speed. The new religion, whose members in small numbers puzzled and irritated the Roman administrators early in the second century, had become at the beginning of the fourth century a force of such proportions that the Emperor Constantine (whatever else may have been his motive) found it expedient to recognize Christianity as one of the official religions of the Roman state. Some years later Julian the Apostate made the last and futile effort to eradicate Christianity and re-establish the paganism of Greece and Rome. Thus actually it was not until midway in the fourth century after Christ that all the cultural elements of that world were fused, when at last appropriate recognition was given to the Hebraic and Christian constituents. But all was not well with the imperial central government. Its hold on the social, political and economic organism was at best tenuous. Nothing seemed able to stem the moral decadence and the collapse of morale in the body social. No doubt many a prophetic eye could see the inevitable end of Eternal Rome.

It was into this world of the mid-fourth century that Saint Augustine was born. No one of his contemporaries realized more fully the challenge of that age, nor did any one produce a more fundamental response to that challenge. For the matter of that, the challenge of our own time has not infrequently been compared with the epoch of Rome's decline. The combined concept of Challenge-and-Response, so brilliantly delineated by Arnold Toynbee in his *Study of History,* applies with peculiar pertinence to the life and work of Saint Augustine. As Toynbee discusses the different kinds of challenges, he distinguishes between those of a lower order, such as the external challenge of a geographic environment, and those of a higher order, which are inner and moral. These can only be met by a process of interiorization, which in turn will lead to the "etherialization" of man. This attainment of a spiritual dimension by man, Toynbee believes, constitutes the next major step in his evolution and can be accomplished by continually recognizing that challenges are inner, and must be met successively by inner responses. Such almost exactly was Saint Augustine's reading of the challenge of his time, and in a way all his writing is devoted to clarifying what the nature of man's inner response to that challenge should be. In fact, all his characteristic doctrines of God, human nature, the will, grace, time, the city of earth and the City of God, formulate what, according to Christianity, man's inner response to the challenge of the human predicament should *always* be.

Tagaste, a small town in North Africa, not far to the west of Carthage and some fifty miles south of the Mediterranean, witnessed the birth of Saint Augustine in 354 A.D.[4] The North Africa of this period preserved perhaps more than any other area of the Roman World the characteristic features of the earlier Empire, removed as it was from the storm centers of political and social unrest. Thus the boyhood of Saint Augustine was passed in the more or less normal environment of a family of modest circumstances in a small Roman provincial community. His mother, Monnica, had been reared in a Christian family and apparently exhibited early in life those virtues which marked her later career. She was married on her coming of age to Patricius, a local Roman official of good standing in the community. He was not a Christian, and owing to his somewhat uneven disposition, the relations between the two were not always as pleasant as they might have been. Shortly after Saint Augustine's birth, Monnica enrolled him as a catechumen in the Catholic Church, but decided to postpone the sacrament of baptism, which according to Christian practice in those times, took place upon the attainment of adulthood.

The biography of Saint Augustine can, and indeed should, only be sketched briefly here. The major sources for it consist of a contemporary life by Possidius and the great autobiography, the *Confessions,* wherein the whole man is recreated for us. In the present discussion it is only necessary to point to those aspects of his life which are most significant prior to his assumption of the Bishopric in 395-396 A.D. In his earliest boyhood (fortunately for his future career) he picked up enough of the native Punic language to enable him to be as much at home in it as he was in his own Latin. While Monnica was introducing him to the elements of Christianity, at school he was receiving a standard education. Unhappily, he conceived a hearty dislike for the Greek language, and, amazing as it may seem, never really mastered it. However, in spite of the early resistance to schooling as shown by any normal boy, he soon gave signs of becoming a brilliant student. His parents wisely determined, after he completed his elementary education in Tagaste, to send him to the advanced schools in Madaura, a center of pagan culture some miles south of Tagaste.

Saint Augustine departed for Madaura when he was about twelve and remained there for approximately four years. During this period he received his first broad grounding in Latin literature and thought, and at the same time was exposed thoroughly to the seamier side of life. At sixteen, he returned to Tagaste. Patricius and Monnica had developed further plans for his future education, since all indications reinforced their belief that a distinguished career, perhaps as a lawyer, lay ahead of him. However, a temporary lack of funds made it necessary to postpone his training, and the youth consequently spent a year of enforced idleness in his native village. An unoccupied sixteen-year-old lad is little if any comfort to his parents, and Saint Augustine proved no exception. In his *Confessions* he recalls with sorrow his abandoned life at that time, referring to it somewhat extravagantly in these words, "Behold with what companions I walked the streets of Babylon, in whose filth I was rolled, as if in cinnamon and precious ointments." [5]

One particular and seemingly insignificant episode left a lasting impression on his mind: the theft of some pears by a gang of youths of which he was an active member. Saint Augustine's references to the occasion in the *Confessions* perhaps appear out of proportion, yet in a way nothing could be more characteristic of his method of dealing with his own experience. The theft itself amounted to little more than a boyish prank of shaking down the fruit, stealing it, discovering that it was not particularly good, and giving what was left untasted to the pigs. This event, paralleled and forgotten in the life of practically every youth, fascinated and puzzled Saint Augustine. It presented a problem to him, and in the *Confessions* he gets it between his teeth, he worries it, and almost despite himself he cannot let it go. As he ponders it, he asks himself why he did it. Was it because the fruit was good? No. He had plenty of his own of far better quality. Was it because the companionship of his fellows was peculiarly pleasant?

No. Apparently he did not think well enough of them to explain the phenomenon on that ground. In the last analysis he could only conclude that there was an overpowering attraction in the evil deed itself. As a consequence this episode takes on a pervasive symbolic significance for Saint Augustine, since the problem "Whence evil," in one form or another, preoccupied his attention until the day of his death.

The following year, his seventeenth, saw Saint Augustine beginning the study of rhetoric in the city of Carthage. The immediately succeeding years followed the regular post-adolescent pattern of the time. One of his first acts was to take a mistress with whom he lived for the next thirteen years, and who bore him a son, Adeodatus. In his education he continued his brilliant record. Of all the works that he studied, the one which really captured his imagination was the *Hortensius* of Cicero, and Saint Augustine more than once acknowledges the debt he owed to its inspiration. At this time, too, he first came in contact with the Manichaean religion and enrolled as an "auditor," the technical name for anyone who wished to apprentice himself to that sect.

It is not difficult to see why the Manichaean religion would have appealed to Saint Augustine. With its very concrete tenet, expressed in a very concrete mythology, that the universe is a battleground between two opposing principles of Good and Evil, two co-eternal causes of Light and Darkness, Manicheism not only had the attraction of offering a simple answer to the problem of evil, but also one in terms of which individual men are relieved of all the inconveniences of moral responsibility. It was no doubt comforting for Saint Augustine at this time to be told that whatever evil he did was not his own responsibility, but that of an evil principle.

Beginning with the autumn of 373 A.D., Saint Augustine embarked upon a career as a teacher. First in Tagaste, then in Carthage, and next in Rome he forged ahead with great success. Before he left Carthage, he had become increasingly dissatisfied with Manicheism, especially because he was never able to discover among its devotees an individual who could answer the difficulties which inhered in the system. In Rome finally he abandoned the religion, and in turn more or less assumed the skeptical attitude of the Platonic New Academy. This shift in attitude, as students of Saint Augustine have frequently noted, was of major importance. Prior to this time and in particular under the influence of Manicheism, Saint Augustine's thought had been inveterately concrete. It was difficult for him to conceive of existence apart from material embodiments, or to move easily on a level of abstraction. But as he associated more closely with the Platonic tradition and its postulates concerning the existence and greater reality of that which is non-material, his habit of thought changed. During the Manichaean period, God to Saint Augustine could only exist in some kind of material terms. The Platonic tradition unquestionably prepared the way for him to accept and realize the meaning of Christianity's doctrine of God as Spirit.

Apparently the conditions for teaching rhetoric at Rome were not entirely satisfactory to Saint Augustine. Consequently when he heard that the city of Milan wanted to appoint a "professor" of rhetoric to be maintained at public expense, he applied for the position, was given a formal hearing, and received the appointment. In the autumn of 384 A.D. Saint Augustine moved his household to the North Italian city. With him went his mistress and son, a few close friends, and his mother, Monnica, who, long since a widow, had followed her brilliant son from North Africa to Rome. Monnica had only one firm aim in view and that was to see him embrace the Church. As Saint Augustine's autobiography records, her days were filled with tears and ceaseless prayers that he would abandon his life of unchastity and return to the faith into which he had been born. She believed that a legitimate marriage might provide the means to this end, but, so far as the record goes, never suggested that he formalize the union with his mistress.

Though deeply troubled in mind and heart, Saint Augustine went to Milan with the desire to win new glory in his profession, to gain wealth, and to marry a rich wife. He still was deeply entangled with the seductions of the material world and the pride which they inevitably engendered in him. But a new influence came into his life in the person of Saint Ambrose, the great Bishop of Milan, whose sermons and methods of interpreting the Scriptures had not a little to do with Saint Augustine's subsequent acceptance of Christianity. But the time was not yet ripe. Monnica busied herself in finding a suitable wife for her son, and finally discovered a fitting partner in a girl who would not reach the marriageable age for another two years. Saint Augustine acquiesced in this arrangement and, apparently without much ado, dismissed the woman whose name he never records and with whom he had lived for so many years. His reference to the separation in the *Confessions* is stark in its brevity: "My mistress being torn from my side as an impediment to my marriage, my heart which clave to her, was racked, and wounded, and bleeding. And she went back to Africa, making a vow unto Thee never to know another man, leaving with me my natural son by her." [6] It is difficult not to be shocked by this episode. Though there is no explicit evidence, it is natural to suppose that Saint Augustine reports the event to show clearly the extent of his own degradation at the time. In fact, he does not hesitate to add that, so great was his enslavement to the habit of sexual lust, immediately after the dismissal he took another mistress.

Saint Augustine's period of inner conflict continued for another two years. Intellectually he began to respond more and more to the preaching of Saint Ambrose and to further study of the Neo-Platonists. Finally in 386 he reached the decision, at least on intellectual grounds, to become a catechumen of the Catholic Church, and it was in the summer of that year when he had the decisive inner experience of his conversion, which is recorded in the famous Eighth Book of the *Confessions*. All doubt was now gone and his only desire was to prepare himself for baptism.

In order not to make an over-dramatic display of his new commitment to Christianity, Saint Augustine kept up his teaching obligations during the summer of 386, and withdrew quietly in the autumn with his few faithful friends to the famous retreat in Cassiciacum. It was there that he realized for the first time his idea of a community of scholars living together.[6a] From the conversations of this group of Christian scholars in Cassiciacum derive Saint Augustine's first great writings, the *Contra Academicos, De Vita Beata*, and *De Ordine*. In the spring of 387 Saint Ambrose administered to him the sacrament of baptism. Saint Augustine's life as a Christian began. The faithful Monnica, her life's dream finally realized, started the journey back to Africa with her son. On reaching Ostia, the two had their famous joint mystical experience recounted so beautifully in the Ninth Book of the *Confessions*. Shortly thereafter Monnica died in great peace of soul.

Saint Augustine and his friends stayed in Rome for about two years and then returned to Tagaste, where they established a monastery. It was not long before his unusual powers began to make themselves felt among the Christians of North Africa. In 391 he was ordained a priest in the community of Hippo Regius. Four years later he became auxiliary Bishop of the same community, and upon the death of the Bishop, Valerius, he succeeded to the charge of the diocese. Here begins his life of incredible activity. Not only was he fulfilling his duties as a diocesan administrator, but also he was an indefatigable preacher and writer of letters. He also became a leader in the general affairs of the Church and was its ardent advocate in the face of any heresy which he might deem dangerous. In addition, he saturated himself in minute study of the Holy Scriptures and became one of the most powerful exegetes in the history of the Church. And, as though this were not enough, he composed among other treatises the immortal masterpieces, *The Confessions, On the Trinity*, and *The City of God*.

In many ways, the activity of the thirty-five years until his death was dominated by Saint Augustine's desire to defeat heresy. Hence he devoted his boundless energy first against the proponents of the Manichaean religion. For this task he was singularly well fitted because of the many years when he himself had espoused the sect and made a genuine effort to commit himself whole-heartedly to it. Next he turned the fire of his polemic against the Donatists. This heretical group split from the Church largely over a dispute concerning the question whether a priest's sins as a fallible human being impaired the validity of his acts when he was functioning as a priest. The Donatists maintained that a priest must be sinless, while the Church held that, since all men are sinners, the priest shares the common lot of man, must accept it, but must be regarded as the valid, though imperfect, human instrument through which God does His work in the world. Actually, the doctrinal issue in the Donatist controversy soon became buried deep in a welter of political maneuvers, so that by and large Saint Augustine's anti-Donatist writings are perhaps more rewarding to those who are specialists in this aspect of the history of the Church, than to the modern general reader. It must be added, however, that Saint Augustine himself never lost sight of the basic theological issue at stake.

Saint Augustine's greatest efforts were turned against the most subtle and most dangerous heresy of them all, which was developed by his contemporary, the monk Pelagius. Beyond any question, the anti-Pelagian treatises of Saint Augustine deserve close attention not only because they contain a rounded statement of his mature position, but also because in them he develops specifically his argument concerning the crucial problem of the relation between sin, free will and the grace of God. Pelagius argued, and with a power which convinced many in the Christian community, that man can by the effort and initiative of his own free will bring about his own salvation. Furthermore, he maintained that God's grace was granted to men according to their merits. Pelagius thus raised one of the most difficult problems which the Church has ever had to face. Indeed, it is fair to say that in one guise or another it has faced Pelagianism throughout its entire history. In one way, the answer to Pelagianism is simple. If you accept its thesis, you turn man into God. You automatically arrogate to him that which is God's, in view of His omnipotence. You effectively invalidate the prime Christian virtue of humility, and, by the same token, seductively invite man to commit the deadliest of all the sins, the sin of spiritual pride. On the other hand, to deny the position of Pelagianism has profound implications for the concept of man's free will. If man's salvation comes from the grace of God, with the merits of man being at bottom irrelevant, what becomes of man's free will? In what sense is it valid, and what finally is the meaning of human freedom, which man values so highly, if his will is not genuinely free? These are the questions which Saint Augustine undertook to resolve when he accepted on behalf of the Church the challenge of Pelagius. He fought against the Pelagian heresy with a vigor equal to or greater than the zeal with which he opposed the Manichaeans and the Donatists.

Since the promulgation of the Darwinian hypothesis, it has been the fashion of the Western World to see evolution in everything. This pronounced trend has induced scholars very often to approach the masters of thought in the Western tradition with the purpose of demonstrating how their positions evolved. In certain cases this purpose cannot be realized without doing violence to the evidence. After all, there are some thinkers who arrive at a basic philosophy relatively early in life to which they adhere without any appreciable modification. Such men rather strive to work out ever more thoroughly the implications and ramifications of their initial views. Plato presents a good instance of this type of thinker. Despite the large amount of scholarly opinion to the contrary, the root philosophical view expressed in his early dialogues seems to be identical with that of the *Timaeus* and the *Laws*, the works of Plato's old age.

This point is particularly significant in the case of Saint Augustine. But the problem is not simplified by the fact of his enormous productivity, his seemingly incurable repetitiousness, and the prolixity of which he is aware and for which he often apologizes. A satisfactory interpretive point of departure appears to lie first in keeping distinct the two phases of his life and thought which are separated sharply from each other by the experience of his conversion. Prior to that event, Saint Augustine's thought "evolved" through several stages marked successively by Manicheism, skepticism, and Neo-Platonism. However, after the conversion, Saint Augustine reached a position which cannot in any genuine sense be said to evolve. At the moment of conversion, Christianity in its wholeness came to him in such a form as to preclude any "evolution." To be sure, there are considerable variations in emphasis in the vast Augustinian corpus which derives entirely from the post-conversion period. The influence of Neo-Platonism looms large at the outset. In the earlier works, likewise, not so much attention is devoted to the doctrine of grace. In fact, as time goes on, the shifts in emphasis are determined in general by the nature of the opposition which Saint Augustine might be attacking at any given moment. Thus, for example, under the pressure of the Pelagian heresy, he works out in its fullest detail the doctrine of grace.

M. Gilson in his excellent book, *Introduction à l'étude de saint Augustin,* has devoted his exclusive attention to the identification and interpretation of the major theses of the Augustinian position. In the conclusion, Gilson remarks that it has been his particular purpose throughout to discuss the "stable element" of Augustinianism. In this connection he recalls that in a review of Boyer, *L'Idée de vérité dans la philosophie de saint Augustin,* he took the author to task for not having approached the problem from an evolutionary point of view. Gilson here hastens to retract this criticism, and insists that even among the many variations in detail in the position of Saint Augustine, he has never been able to discover the slightest variation in its essential nature.[7] After all, if it is correct to contend that Saint Augustine's doctrine is an organic compound in the highest degree, and if it is correct to assert that this compound soundly reflects at once the inner coherence and the comprehensiveness of Christianity, Gilson's conclusion concerning the stable essence of Augustinianism must be accepted.

The origins out of which Saint Augustine developed his major theses have already been indicated in part. Among the pagan sources the most important is Plato. No one can fail to notice the affinity in temperament and attitude which obtains between the two. In view of the inherent com-

patibility of much of Plato's philosophy with Christianity, it is not surprising that Saint Augustine regarded him as the greatest of the Greek and
Roman thinkers. It may be doubted that Saint Augustine knew Plato thoroughly at first hand, but it is absolutely clear that the essential nature of
the Platonic philosophy had been mediated through to him not only by
the Neo-Platonists but also by the Christian Platonists of Alexandria, who
had done much to make explicit the kinship between Platonism and Christianity.

Saint Augustine apparently was not attracted to Aristotle. The evidence
of his influence is rather to be felt implicitly in the tone of individual passages in the Augustinian corpus. From time to time Saint Augustine exhibits great sympathy for the Stoic position, as for example when, in *The
City of God*, he devotes a chapter to the Stoic attitude toward the "perturbations" of the soul.[8] In addition to his Roman favorite Cicero, Saint
Augustine quotes frequently from Virgil, Horace and others. Also, he uses
the encyclopaedic information of M. Terentius Varro, who supplies him
with a large amount of data on Roman antiquities and pagan theology.

Saint Augustine's detailed knowledge of the Holy Scriptures is overwhelming. Whether it be for the infusion of a devotional spirit into a passage, or for the advancement of an argument, or to cite a clinching authority for a hard-won point, or to unravel a knotty theological problem, Saint
Augustine always has a scriptural reference ready to hand. *Genesis*, the
Psalms, Job, and *Isaiah* of the *Old Testament* are perhaps the most frequently cited, and in the *New Testament* he turns most often to *Matthew,
Luke, John*, and, of course, the Pauline Epistles, which shape more than
any other influence the character of Saint Augustine's Christianity. And
obviously, in addition, there are the long, specifically exegetical works such
as the commentaries on *Genesis* and the *Psalms*, which bespeak a familiarity with the sacred writings both incredibly broad and deep.

The reader should never forget, when he is considering the major theses
of Saint Augustine's Christianity, that his writing is all created in the light
of his own intense mystical experience upon conversion. The inner conviction of its validity colors in one way or another everything he does and
everything he says. In this respect he is to be found in the company of
such men as Saint Paul, Saint Francis, Martin Luther, Pascal, and even,
in a curious way, Descartes, all of whom enjoyed their greatest creative
activity under the impulse of an extraordinary inner experience. With Saint
Augustine, the primary result of *his* experience, which in turn produces the
first and most important of the major strands in his thought, is his conviction that all things must be and are God-centered.

To illustrate this point, the very texture and attitude of the *Confessions*
are more than sufficient. Take the opening words: first the quotation from
the *Psalms*, "Great art Thou, O Lord, and greatly to be praised; great is
Thy power, and of Thy wisdom there is no end"; and then a little later

Saint Augustine's own words, "Thou movest us to delight in praising Thee; for Thou hast formed us for Thyself, *and our hearts are restless till they find rest in Thee.*" [9] In a sense, the phrase which has been italicized provides the central clue to this first and all-important Augustinian theme. A recent critic, C. C. Martindale, S.J., in commenting on the fact that Saint Augustine feels no difficulty in exhibiting his emotions, remarks, ". . . the whole of the *Confessions* is an outpouring of his soul to God—God is the immediate audience; and only now and again does the author look aside (and down) towards his human hearers." [10]

Rarely if ever has a Christian thinker kept the focus of his attention so unwaveringly upon God. This is true not only in the obvious case of the *Confessions,* but also in works on rather specific subjects such as *Concerning the Teacher.* It makes no difference whether he is enunciating the principle, *pondus meum amor meus,* "My weight is my love," [11] as the fundamental condition of man's activity of will, or whether he expounds at length the very difficult Christian dogma of the Trinity as he does in *On the Trinity.* In each instance there is always the explicit orientation to God.

According to Saint Augustine, the gravest possible error arises when God is conceived as any other than omnipotent, omniscient and perfectly good. From this initial conviction, supported as it is by faith in the Biblical revelation as well as by reason, he develops his analysis of all created things. In the first place, he submits his doctrine of "natures." God is infinitely good and infinitely wise, and thus everything which He creates, by the very fact that He is the source of all existence, has a "nature" which is good. In other words, He cannot, since He is perfect good, create any "nature" that is not intrinsically good. These "natures" are not all on the same plane or level of existence. In fact, Saint Augustine consistently recognizes their hierarchic order. In the treatise *On Free Will,* for example, when he examines the universe of space and time, he distinguishes between three categories of things: first, that which *is, i.e.,* mere bodies in the physical universe; second, that which both *is* and *lives,* the class which comprises plants and animals; and third, that which *is, lives* and *knows,* in other words, man, who shares *existence* with mere physical bodies, *existence* and *life* with plants and animals, but who alone of created things, by virtue of his reason, is capable of *knowledge.* That there are different degrees of importance, Saint Augustine attributes to the infinite wisdom of God, who desired to create the universe in a majestic harmony in which things more valuable and important could not exist, if they cannot be compared with the less valuable. In the argument, harmony in this way depends upon the hierarchic ordering of things in creation. In other contexts, when Saint Augustine is not confining his analysis to the universe of space and time, but rather has total Reality within his purview, he recognizes three planes of being: body, soul and God. As soul controls body, so does God control the soul, to which He is in the closest proximity. [12]

Saint Augustine's doctrine of "natures," as can readily be seen, has important implications for the problem which modern philosophy sees in the "fact-value" relation. If a "nature" has its existence, *i.e.*, its "factuality," from a creative act of God, and if at the same time its goodness or "value" derives from the same source of creation, it becomes quite impossible to contemplate a "nature" without considering simultaneously its "existence-and-goodness." To put it in another way, a thinker does violence to the objective character of a "nature" if he attempts solely to analyze its being, as though its being could be abstracted validly from its goodness. This Augustinian attitude towards the relation of fact and value appears also when he considers the highest level of Reality, God. At one point in his treatise, *On the Trinity,* he writes, "But as He (*i.e.*, the Holy Spirit) is a substance together with the Father and the Son, so that substance is together with them great, and together with them good, and together with them holy, and whatsoever else is said in reference to substance; since it is not one thing to God to be, and another to be great or to be good, and the rest." [13]

Saint Augustine's theory of knowledge likewise is God-centered, as is his doctrine of "natures." Whereas Aristotle and, following him, Saint Thomas Aquinas, are empiricists in their theories of knowledge, always taking their start from the data provided to the knowing subject by the senses, and proceeding via a method of abstraction from them, Saint Augustine starts from within and from the illumination in man's soul which God has planted there. Hence his epistemology or theory of knowledge is regularly called one of Divine illumination. However, man's evidence for knowing that he himself exists functions in a way as a pre-condition for Saint Augustine's whole theory of knowledge. According to him, man can soundly affirm his own existence on the ground of the famous formula, repeated in one form or another in several of his works, *si fallor, sum,* "If I am deceived, I exist." Critics regularly cite this Augustinian principle as the forerunner of Descartes' *Cogito, ergo sum.* On the problem of the relation of these two formulae, Gilson has some very discerning remarks to make: "By placing the *cogito* at the beginning of his metaphysics as fundamental basis of the entire edifice, Descartes is committed beforehand, in the name of his mathematical method, to attributing to thought whatever is contained in his clear and distinct idea, and, correlatively, to attribute to it only what is thus contained in it.—The *cogito*—is but the first of that series of conceptual snippets which substitutes progressively a mosaic of abstractions for the continuity of reality. . . . Instead of being a method practiced upon ideas, Augustinianism is an enquiry concerning the concrete content of thought." [14]

As the statement of Gilson may perhaps suggest, the theory of Divine illumination rests ultimately upon Saint Augustine's adoption of an inner empiricism. What he experiences within his own mind, not what pours into it through the avenues of the senses, constitutes his point of departure. Always he gives the impression that this inner experience is a continuum, with no segment of it to be scrutinized apart from the context of the rest. The Augustinian procedure can be seen in his proof for the existence of God. In summary it runs as follows: Through the inner empirical method, man can realize that he possesses reason and that this possession makes him superior to inorganic beings, plants and animals. Also through inner empiricism man can recognize his own mutability, but can as well realize the existence of the immutable and unchanging, that which is superior to himself. Grounds for this latter realization appear when the mind in its inner experience grasps the immutability of mathematical relations, and in turn comes to grasp the concept of Truth itself. Having reached this point by the inner empirical method, Saint Augustine cannot see in this Truth anything other than God, who has granted men these inner powers, this Divine illumination, whereby God himself can be known, and all the complex relations of the creation can be understood. Thus the mind can know that God is the Creator of the "natures" which can be perceived in the world of sense experience, and they in turn can be dealt with in their true character, because inner experience with its guarantee of Divine illumination makes it possible for the mind to view them in their proper light.

The Augustinian metaphysics of knowledge then really begins with God and what God has planted in man's mind. Here perhaps lies the basic and irreconcilable difference between Saint Augustine and Saint Thomas, though the two views insofar as they are both genuine "philosophies" of Christianity are, as has been already indicated, ultimately complementary. Saint Thomas begins with outer experience and through a rational process reaches God. Saint Augustine begins with inner experience *and* God, and in these terms investigates and analyzes the content of thought. And it should be noted that the Augustinian approach to the problem is thoroughly in accord with the "fact-value" relation which is implicit in his doctrine of "natures." As Gilson has clearly pointed out, "The intelligibility of a concept resides less in the generality of its extension (*i.e.*, the Aristotelian and Thomistic attitude) than in the normative character which its necessity itself confers upon it." [15] The latter is of course the Augustinian attitude, which does not admit of isolating the capacity of forming concepts, but rather insists that the formation of a concept implicitly and inevitably involves the judgment of that which is conceived.

Gilson elsewhere has described Saint Augustine's theory of knowledge and its concomitant ground for his proof for the existence of God, as both the central and the vulnerable point of the Augustinian metaphysics. "The essential feature of such a position, whatever its ultimate interpretation, is a definition of the human intellect which leaves us nothing wherewith to account for the existence of truth. If Saint Augustine had simply held that man cannot know truth without an intellectual light given him by God, his analysis of the contingency and insufficiency of human thought would be lacking in a precise object; but if, as the consensus of the most important texts shows, this is the point on which his proof rests, it must necessarily follow that Divine illumination (to give it its traditional name) must reach thought directly. For either it reaches it directly, and in that case we grasp at the same time the sufficient reason of truth and God who is its foundation; or it reaches it indirectly, and in that case we are equally incapable of attaining to the existence of God and of accounting for truth." [16]

Obviously, no epistemology or theory of knowledge is totally without its dilemmas. But at the same time the reader should remember that Saint Augustine is not operating in a context bounded by limits within which reason alone can effectively operate. For him faith always precedes intelligence, but with the important proviso that faith and intelligence cannot be disjoined. Saint Augustine insists that man should begin with faith. "If you cannot understand, believe in order that you may understand." [17] Such is his spirit in the opening chapter of the treatise *On the Trinity,* "The following dissertation concerning the Trinity, as the reader ought to be informed, has been written in order to guard against the sophistries of those who disdain to begin with faith, and are deceived by a crude and perverse love of reason." [18] "Faith seeking understanding" is the hall-mark of Saint Augustine's view of the relation between faith and reason. Gilson well recognizes the profundity of this view when he says, *"Nisi credideritis, non intelligetis* is and will always remain the charter of every Christian philosophy." [19] Saint Augustine's faith rests upon the revelation of the Holy Scriptures and the Incarnation of Christ, powerfully bulwarked by his own experience of conversion.

From his early manhood Saint Augustine had always been preoccupied with the problem of evil, and, as has already been suggested, probably was attracted to the Manichaean position because, whatever may have been its weaknesses, at least it presented a readily intelligible though not profound solution to the question. Hence it is not surprising that he turned his mature attention to the search for the nature of evil and grappled with it in terms of his Christian position. It is needless here to point out the stupendous difficulty of the problem. Suffice it to say that thinkers have speculated most fruitfully about it in the light of the distinction between cosmic evil and moral evil, a distinction to which Saint Augustine consistently adheres. So far as cosmic evil is concerned, he does not produce any unusual contribution, and it is fair to add that this aspect of evil did not capture his imagination. The theory which he adopts is Neo-Platonic in character, and is developed in accordance with his doctrine of "natures." As things are created by God, they are therefore good, and hence no intrinsic evil can be attributed to them. What we call evil in them is merely a want or failure or defect of goodness. On this ground, Saint Augustine can explain the superiority of certain things over others, and can account for the gradations in goodness as the result of the harmony which God chose to introduce into His creation. Whatever else which man may consider in the category of cosmic evil, Saint Augustine generally explains by assigning it to the infinite wisdom and goodness of God, who ordains all and whose ways are beyond human understanding.

In contrast, in connection with the problem of moral evil, Saint Augustine makes a creative contribution unrivaled in Christian thought. He did so by isolating the inner fact of the human will and seeing in it the ultimate source of moral evil. It is generally true that in the Greek philosophical tradition, the phenomenon of the will had never been explored with any great degree of systematic rigor. Plato, for example, to the extent to which he took seriously the Socratic paradox that knowledge is virtue, would not be expected to approach the moral problem through an analysis of the will. Indeed, in Plato, an awareness of the will is implicit rather than explicit. It appears in such places as the myth in the *Phaedrus* where the will is at least suggested when the inner struggle of the soul is prefigured in the image of the charioteer (reason) who endeavors to drive successfully an ill-matched team: the noble white horse which represents man's higher emotions, and the ugly mean black horse which represents man's baser desires. Or again, a notion of the will is not entirely absent, when in the *Republic* Socrates insists that a man can only achieve moral excellence by turning away from absorption in the material world and orienting himself towards the eternal and unchanging realm of Ideas, and the supreme Idea, the Good. And furthermore, the earlier Greek tradition as well as Plato himself cannot be said to be totally unaware of the will, when *sophrosyne*, self-control or temperance, is singled out as one of the four cardinal virtues.

Aristotle, particularly in the *Nicomachean Ethics,* made a considerable advance in studying the will more explicitly. Among the Stoics, the will plays a larger part than in any other system in Graeco-Roman culture. The Stoic would insist that, by combining a volitional act with the reason, man can discriminate between what is in his power and what is not, and thus fit himself into his proper position in the cosmic scheme. "Lead me, O Zeus, and Thou, O Destiny," the Stoic cries, and then concludes, "If with will recreant I falter, I will follow still."

The Ovidian phrase, "I know the right, and yet the wrong pursue," sums up the problem more succinctly than can be found elsewhere in the Graeco-Roman tradition. And yet the Hebrews knew it and threw much light upon it when, from the earliest days as a "stiff-necked folk," they refused to obey the commands of Yahweh. Saint Augustine, therefore, has this twofold background—the pregnant suggestions of the Greeks and Romans, plus the experience of the Hebrews down to Saint Paul—to bring to bear in his investigation of the will. But most important of all is his experience of conversion. The intensity of this event for Saint Augustine places beyond all doubt both the factuality and the ultimacy of the will. In the light of this spiritual climax, he looks back in his *Confessions* at many episodes in his earlier life and can understand them the better. He can now distinguish between acts of mere volition and acts undertaken with genuine liberty or freedom of will.

So he develops his famous analysis of the three states in which the will operates. The first exists when man through his will is only able to sin (*posse peccare*). This means that, though he has the illusion of freedom of will, the only alternatives available to him are those which involve sin. Such, according to Saint Augustine, is man's condition after Adam's fall before the grace of God has been visited upon him. All his acts prior to the advent of grace are merely volitional, since their purview is so severely limited. But in the second stage after grace has come, man is able not to sin (*posse non peccare*). This is the state of the first man Adam before the fall, and the one which Saint Augustine recognizes in himself after his conversion. Before that fateful event, he was totally absorbed in the things of this world. Possessed as he was of a brilliant mind, he advanced speedily to the heights in his profession. He knew and loved the adulation of the crowd. He knew and loved the pleasures of the flesh. He knew pride and was a victim of it. But at the same time he had an insatiable urge to get at the truth of things. When he followed along this path and became convinced intellectually that the Christian answer was correct, even then he only experienced a paralysis of the will. He wanted to become a Christian, but yet he could not, so deep was his entanglement in his worldly desires and passions. In his *Confessions* he records how he prayed to God, "Grant me chastity and continency, but not yet." [20] Then suddenly came the mysterious incident in the garden at Milan. Swept with overwhelming misery at his wretched state, he withdrew even from his faithful friend, Alypius, weeping in his sorrow and praying "How long, how long? Tomorrow and tomorrow? Why not now? Why is there not this hour an end to my uncleanness?" [21] Then he heard a child's voice, presumably chanting a refrain of some children's game, saying, "Take up and read, take up and read." He returned to the house, picked up the Holy Scriptures, opened the volume at random and read, "Not in rioting and drunkenness, not in chambering and wantonness, not in strife and envying; but put ye on the Lord Jesus Christ, and make not provision for the flesh, to fulfil the lusts thereof." [22] The miracle happened. Saint Augustine was now free to act righteously.

The third state of the will brings with it the inability to sin (*non posse peccare*). This is the final condition of beatitude, the ultimate happiness of those who have died their mortal death, and through the grace and salvation of God have attained to eternal life.

But in examining this profound analysis of the will with its three clearly identifiable states, it is impossible to dissociate from one another the Augustinian theories of the will itself, its freedom, the origin of moral evil, and of God's grace. In the treatise *On Free Will,* written not long after the conversion, Saint Augustine argues that the will is the source of moral evil. He can see no other more ultimate source, but the evidence for this conclusion lies mainly in Saint Augustine's immediate experience, and is of course completely in accord with his characteristic inner empirical method. But the next question naturally to arise is: Whence comes this will in man? If it comes from God, and if it is the source of moral evil, why then is God not ultimately the source of that evil? Is the will then to be considered a human good? Saint Augustine's answer is the Christian answer. The main tradition of the Christian Church has never deviated from it in any essential respect.

Simply stated, the will is a good which does come from God, for without it man would be unable to act rightly. Suppose man did not have a will. Under these conditions, he could not act rightly, for the concept of righteous action would have no meaning. But to be able to act rightly carries with it inevitably the possibility of acting wrongly. Presumably God could have created man without a will, but if He had done so, God would have taken from man the capacity for righteous action, a circumstance which is unthinkable. God therefore gave man a will, so that he could act rightly, but this involves also the capacity for wrong action. So, Saint Augustine contends, since God is supremely good, He cannot in any sense be considered as the source of evil or responsible for it. Therefore, man is the only other possible source, and through the operation of his will becomes responsible for moral evil.

Whatever may be the inadequacies of this theory of moral evil when it is subjected to rational analysis, it constitutes a powerful answer and one which is consistent with man's deepest inner experience of the fact that he possesses a will. Perhaps Dr. Johnson did say a final word on the problem of free will in his often repeated remark, "All theory is against the freedom of the will, all experience for it." But so far as the Augustinian doctrine of the will is concerned, it is important to keep in mind the distinction between the simple operation of the will as it exercises choice among alternative courses of action and genuine freedom of the will which can exist only if the individual has an alternative choice of both right action and wrong action. In this latter case, curiously enough, the choice is free, in the full sense of the word, only if right action is chosen. If wrong action is elected or if the will is in the state of *posse peccare* (*i.e.,* being able to sin), it can be called free only in a somewhat superficial sense. In other words, the concept of freedom in the full sense implies that the action chosen be good. If the action chosen is evil, then proper analysis shows that the will has not been really free, but rather has been enslaved by that which is not good.

In any discussion of freedom, two senses of the concept are present. One can be called "negative freedom," indicating freedom from restraint of any sort or order. All too frequently, thinking on this all-important human value has stopped at the negative level, and has failed to realize that there is always in freedom a positive aspect without which the concept itself loses a major portion of its meaning. The distinction between positive and negative freedom, *i.e.*, "freedom from" against "freedom for," is present in Saint Augustine's analysis of the will. Both in the case of mere volition as well as in the operation of a genuinely free will, negative freedom is assumed. Also neither type is dealt with without reference to the end result, but the designation of free will in the fullest sense is reserved for an operation of positive freedom, where the answer to the question "Freedom for what?" is unmistakably clear. It is freedom for the pursuit of God, God's Truth and God's Will. It is freedom that tears man away from slavery, from the seductions of worldly goods and desires, and leads him to the happiness which can only be found in God. Such, Saint Augustine insists, is the real meaning of Christ's words, "If ye continue in my word, then are ye my disciples indeed; and ye shall know the truth and the truth shall make you free." [23]

This, in substance, is Saint Augustine's account of the origin and character of moral evil. Sin comes from a perverted will, man's will that has lost touch with God. But how does man's will become rightly oriented towards God? Saint Augustine repeats the Pauline reply: by the grace of God, which is the grace revealed in Jesus Christ. The Pelagians charged that Saint Augustine, notably in his treatise *On Free Will*, had in effect expressed a position no different from their own. Unquestionably, at that moment in his career he was absorbed in the problem of the will, and consequently did not emphasize grace. Yet however much he concentrates upon the will, the presence of grace is never absent from his thought. Saint Augustine unwaveringly maintains that man is saved by grace and only by grace. The first man, Adam, was created with a will which was able not to sin. But Adam sinned and the taint of his sin was transmitted to his progeny so that all men since Adam have wills which are only able to sin. But God in his infinite mercy has seen fit to save men from this bondage to sin, and has done so by the free gift of grace. In order that man should know precisely the nature of grace, God sent His Son to become man. In the life and teaching of the Son, this knowledge becomes available to man. The wills of those to whom God elects to give grace are changed from the state of being only able to sin to the state of being able not to sin.

But to whom does God elect to grant His grace? Saint Augustine is lost in mystery in the face of this question. If grace is only given to those who by virtue of their right actions deserve it, then it cannot be given to any of Adam's descendants, as Saint Augustine sees it, for they are only able to sin, and therefore do not deserve it. Hence sinners are the only possible recipients. But why does God select one and not another? In God's infinite wisdom lies the answer, which human wisdom cannot penetrate. However,

Saint Augustine is certain that the great majority of men are not chosen, and hence are to endure everlasting punishment in eternal death. This "pitiless theology," as Bishop Welldon has pointed out, "rests upon no sure Scriptural base," [24] but the fact remains that it is Saint Augustine's position, and one, as will be seen, which served to make the whole problem more difficult for him. In any event, in the Augustinian doctrine of grace, man's good works do not, and indeed cannot, precede its gift. Good works are possible after the gift of grace, for then man's will has been transformed to the state of being able not to sin. To look at it in another way, grace is given so that good works may be performed.

The theological dilemma inherent in this position perhaps can never be solved by the human intellect. Obviously, the Christian Church must reject the Pelagian thesis that man can work out without God's help his own salvation. Man, in Christian doctrine, cannot have this power without overstepping the limits marked out for him by the fact that God created him. Yet if this is the case, what can man's will actually accomplish when he is in a state of sin? Perhaps he can try to prepare himself by acts of faith to receive God's grace, but even in this situation, may not the very will to prepare himself by faith be the first indication that God has actually given him grace? After grace has in fact been granted, then the problem is less difficult, for man now knows that he is capable of right action, and by the same token knows that it is still possible for him to sin. In this state the virtue of humility becomes of crucial importance, because if a man believes that he has received the gift of grace and therefore will not sin, he actually sins in the highest degree, for he has become a victim of the sin of spiritual pride. But if he always remembers that every action he undertakes may be a wrong action, or may carry in it the taint of imperfection which is his because he is a man, then his humility will be preserved.

Even though the doctrine of grace appears on rational grounds to diminish the significance of the will and the validity of man's initiative, even though grace and free will appear to be in certain respects mutually exclusive, still it is true that Saint Augustine espoused both doctrines with equal fervor. And as the struggle against the Pelagians grew more intense, the more vigorously he asserted their simultaneous validity. Yet whatever may have been the rational consequences for the doctrine of the will, any conclusion other than that man is saved only by God's grace was unthinkable to Saint Augustine. If man can save himself, then God can no longer be conceived as omnipotent. Moreover, God's goodness and mercy are really not possible without the doctrine of grace in its Augustinian and substantially Pauline form. For if grace comes, as the Pelagians would have it, after the performance of good works, there is no room for God's mercy, which by its very nature must go to the sinner.

A real remaining difficulty concerns God's justice. In the Pelagian view, God, though not finally omnipotent, is just in that He rewards the righteous and punishes the sinner. In the Augustinian view, God's justice can be seen in the case of those to whom He has granted grace, but who though able not to sin, still are able to sin. But the puzzle lies in discerning God's justice in the selection of those to whom He will grant grace. In this connection, Saint Augustine can only remind man that his understanding is desperately limited and that it is no little thing for him to impugn in any way God's justice. Perhaps Saint Augustine's problem would have been less difficult had he not assumed that the great majority of men were doomed to eternal damnation. Certainly the New Testament notion that God's love, grace and redemption are somehow available to all sinners implies that the category of those who are able not to sin should be comparably conceived.

In order to understand why Saint Augustine saw no incompatibility between his doctrine of the will and the doctrine of grace, it is best, as M. Gilson has suggested,[25] to approach the problem not by attempting to establish a rational harmony between the two, but rather to try to see them as they were co-present in Saint Augustine's own inner life. Following his own method of inner empiricism, he could no more deny the existence of his will than he could the very existence of himself. Nor, by using the same method, could he deny the existence of grace. His conversion at bottom supplied him with the decisive evidence in the case of both doctrines. Prior to the conversion, he could see his will at work, but only within a limited sphere. Just before the event, he "wanted to will" a certain action, *viz.*, the acceptance of Christianity, but he could not. His will was powerless. Then, suddenly, the powerless will was transmuted into a powerful will. There could be for Saint Augustine only one explanation for this phenomenon: God's grace had come to him. Something had been done for him which he could not do for himself. So through God's grace, the will which he always possessed became a free will. Viewed in the perspective of this experience, the compatibility of the will and grace is established in the mind of Saint Augustine beyond any question.

But where in this tangled theological enigma can a place be found for God's foreknowledge? Saint Augustine was thoroughly aware of this problem as well, and again the God-centered nature of his thought is apparent. God must be omniscient, as well as omnipotent and perfect Good. If He is omniscient, it follows that He knows all that has been, is, and will be. Therefore He knows who will be saved, and who will be damned. But if He foreknows these things, why then does not this situation reduce man to a complete condition of automatism, by removing every vestige of free initiative from him? Saint Augustine by no means attempts to evade the difficulty of the problem. One characteristic solution which he offers maintains that man is not coerced to perform a certain act just because God accurately foreknows the act which will ensue. God foreknows it, yet man does it through an act of volition on his own part. Saint Augustine introduces a human illustration to clarify the nature of his argument. If, for example, one individual accurately predicts that another man will cross a road, this does not mean that the accurate prediction compelled the following action.

Though this argument is not without its value, Saint Augustine's more profound thought on the question involves a consideration of his views on the nature of time. His thought concerning time is always marked by excessive humility, but at the same time he faces the problem squarely. He will not offer a facetious solution, he remarks in the *Confessions*, as a certain person did, when asked what God was doing before the creation, by replying, "He was preparing hell for those who pry into mysteries." [26] Rather, Saint Augustine's attitude is typified by the frequently quoted remark, "What, then, is time? If no one ask of me, I know; if I wish to explain to him who asks, I know not." [27] Or again, in *The City of God*, when he is discussing the problem of the creation of the angels and their temporal relation, if any, to God, after offering a tentative theory, he says, "If I make this reply . . . I fear I may be accused of recklessly affirming what I know not, instead of teaching what I know." [28] Yet despite his modesty, Saint Augustine's speculation concerning time is one of his outstanding contributions to Western thought.

In the discussion of time, his indebtedness to Plato is particularly evident. In the myth of creation contained in the *Timaeus*, Plato distinguishes between time and eternity.[29] He asserts that time came into being with the creation, and consequently it is only accurate to speak of past, present and future in connection with things found in the physical universe. It is incorrect to say that God, or the Demiurge, the Master Craftsman, as He is called in the *Timaeus*, has been or will be. The only proper assertion which can be made is that God *is*. He, like a Platonic Idea, *is*, immutable, unchanging, outside of space and time. Saint Augustine adopts this Platonic analysis in its essence.[30] He asserts that for God there is no such thing as temporal sequence. Temporal sequence is a distinguishing feature of the created universe, whereas in God's mind, since He eternally *is*, with no past or future, all things are present simultaneously. If, for example, man says that God will be, he really is speaking metaphorically, and in effect is transferring and applying to God his own spatial and temporal condition.

The application of Saint Augustine's philosophy of time to the problem of God's foreknowledge should be clear. If God is in an eternal present, then all knowledge is present to Him. From God's point of view, it would not be precise to say that He foreknows, for actually, by virtue of His eternal nature, He simply *knows*. Foreknowledge, since it itself is a temporal concept, is therefore a concept which is produced by the human mind, which is itself a temporal entity. Man, to be sure, uses the term God's foreknowledge, but this tends to confuse him, since the term implies that God, like man, is a Being in whom knowledge is characterized by temporal sequence. Though perhaps this type of thinking on time and eternity may fall far short of solving the problem of the relation of the will to God's "foreknowledge," at least it suggests that the two fall into separate categories, and that no investigation of the problem can be fruitful if this notion is neglected. The will is in the category of time. God's knowledge, or "fore-knowledge," is in the category of eternity. The real question then becomes: Does an all-inclusive eternally present knowledge in God necessarily mean that that knowledge exercises absolute coercive control over the human will which is in time? Saint Augustine would reply in the negative, because he will never deny the reality of the will. If we are puzzled by the dilemma, he would admit freely that to understand the nature of God's knowledge lies infinitely beyond human power.[31]

Saint Augustine's thinking on the question of time and eternity is absolutely fundamental for his philosophy of history contained in his greatest work, *The City of God*.[32] This masterpiece, composed over a period of about fourteen years from 413-426 A.D., elaborates certainly the first Christian philosophy of history, if not, as many would maintain, the first genuine philosophy of history ever to appear. The initial stimulus for the composition of *The City of God* arose from the shattering event of the sack of Rome by Alaric and the Goths in 410 A.D. It is impossible to imagine the impact of this catastrophe upon the minds of the Empire's citizens at the time. That the Eternal City was at the mercy of barbarians was inconceivable. As the significance of the event penetrated more deeply into the mind of Saint Augustine, he saw new meaning in human history, and therefore undertook to explain the phenomenon in the light of the Christian interpretation of Reality.

The vast work which resulted falls into two main sections. The first, comprising Books One to Ten, begins with an attack upon those pagans who assigned the Christian religion as the cause for the calamities of the times, and in particular the sack of Rome. They vigorously maintained that the gods, deserted by men under the persuasion of Christianity, were wreaking their vengeance on the Empire. By passing in review the events of Roman history, pagan theology and philosophy, Saint Augustine delineates what men normally would call an "earthly city," indeed the greatest earthly city the world had ever known. In the second part of the work, Books Eleven to Twenty-two, he introduces at the outset the concept of the City of God with which the earthly city may be contrasted. He then proceeds to outline the creation of the universe, of the angels and the first man Adam, his sin and the penalty of death. Next he describes the evidences of the earthly and the heavenly cities and their histories as they are to be found in sacred writings, followed by a more detailed analysis of the City of God through the times of Noah, the kings of Israel and the prophets, on down to the time of Christ. The earthly and the heavenly cities are then viewed in their respective courses to the end of the world. The closing portion is apocalyptic in character and looks at all of history in the perspective of the last judgment, the punishment of the wicked and the eternal blessedness of the saints.

Apparently the dualism of the "two cities" was suggested to Saint Augustine by a rather obscure African writer of the fourth century, named Tyconius, who used the notion symbolically in a commentary on the Apocalypse.[33] Saint Augustine, however, sees in the "two cities" a principle in terms of which time and human history can be understood in relation to eternity. But who are the members or the citizens of these two cities? Saint Augustine makes this beautifully clear in one short statement: "Accordingly, two cities have been formed by two loves: the earthly by the love of self, even to the contempt of God; the heavenly by the love of God, even to the contempt of self. The former, in a word, glories in itself, the latter in the Lord. For the one seeks glory from men; but the greatest glory of the other is God, the witness of conscience. The one lifts up its head in its own glory; the other says to its God, 'Thou art my glory, and the lifter up of mine head.' "[34] One city is self-oriented, the other is God-oriented. If this is the distinction between the two, then it is apparent that no specifically human or historical institution can be cited as a precise illustration. For example, Saint Augustine would deny that the Church in its external and physical manifestations is coextensive with the City of God, since there are many individuals within the Church who are obviously devoted to self. Nor, on the other hand, can Rome absolutely be equated with the earthly city, for among the citizens of Rome are to be found those whose glory is God. The true citizens of the City of God are those in this life who have received the gift of God's grace, plus those who have gone and will go to eternal glory with the saints. The remainder, who have never deviated in their love of self and the goods of this world, make up the citizenry of the earthly city. Their destiny in turn will be everlasting punishment.

Saint Augustine's estimate of the Roman state is in accord with his analysis of the two cities. In the famous nineteenth book of *The City of God,* he offers his illuminating definition of a people and a republic: "But if . . . we say that a people is an assemblage of reasonable beings bound together by a common agreement as to the objects of their love, then, in order to discover the character of any people, we have only to observe what they love . . . and it will be a superior people in proportion as it is bound together by higher interests, inferior as it is bound together by lower. According to this definition of ours, the Roman people is a people, and its weal is without doubt a commonwealth or republic. But what its tastes were in its early and subsequent days, and how it declined into sanguinary seditions and then to social and civil wars, and so burst asunder and rotted off the bond of concord in which the health of a people consists, history shows. And yet I would not on this account say either that it was not a people, or that its administration was not a republic, so long as there remains an assemblage of reasonable beings bound together by a common agreement as to the objects of love. But what I say of this people and of this republic I must be understood to think and say of the Athenians or any Greek state, of the Egyptians, of the early Assyrian Babylon, and of every other nation, great or small, which had a public government. For, in general, the city of the ungodly, which did not obey the command of God that it should offer no sacrifice save to Him alone, and which, therefore, could not give to the soul its proper command over the body, nor to the reason its just authority over the vices, is void of true justice." [35]

With this definition before him, Saint Augustine goes on to argue that without true religion there can be no true virtues, along with the implication that no society or state can be truly just without a proper orientation towards God. Yet the Roman state, particularly in the earlier stages of its development, remains most impressive to Saint Augustine. He sees that its success arose from its devotion to a certain kind of justice, and that the peace which it produced from time to time was indeed a peace of a certain sort. Because a degree of justice and virtue did exist, he can explain why the Roman state endured for so long a time, but also he can understand why with all its strength it began to disintegrate. The entire attitude is summed up in the well-known Augustinian observation that the Roman virtues were but "splendid vices." So long as Roman justice, for example, was motivated by national pride, or a desire for imperial power or glory, it could only be a spurious virtue, majestic, powerful, "splendid" indeed, but it inevitably falls short of being a true virtue, and becomes "vicious" because it has not been inspired by the love of God. At bottom, Saint Augustine in his analysis of society and history is applying again in these fields the principle already mentioned, *pondus meum, amor meus.*

Critics have frequently noted that the Greeks and the Greek philosophers were prevented from developing any thoroughgoing philosophy of history because their thought was dominated by a cyclical conception of time. Greek mythology, for example, repeats again and again the theme of the deterioration from the Golden Age on down through the various stages to the Age of Iron, followed by a return to the Golden Age and repetition of the cycle. The Stoic theory, that the universe goes through an everlastingly repeated process of mechanical involution and evolution to and from the primordial element of fire, is likewise a case in point. In terms of Christianity it is impossible to find meaning in history, if time is cyclical. But the Hebraic and Christian tradition had always proclaimed that time is linear. It begins with the creation and pursues its straight-line course on through till the millennium, the day of the last judgment and the end of the world.

Saint Augustine realized the full implications of this view of time for the philosophy of history. He sees in history the profound evidence that man is and must be God-centered, that his virtues, if they are to be really such, must derive from the love of God, and that his will must be oriented accordingly. All these ideas are finally sanctioned by the belief that man has an ultimate destiny, the destiny of an immortal life. As the desire for happiness is seen to be that which dominates the wills of men in this mortal life, so is the eternal happiness of an immortal life with God man's final purpose or goal. The nature of this supreme and final value therefore determines and orders the values which man seeks in this life. In other words, that which comes at the end of time provides the ultimate criterion by which all that happens in time must be judged. Saint Augustine further contends that these principles which are valid in the life of the individual human being are equally valid for society. In this perspective of time, eternity and ultimate destiny, he can understand, first, why the Roman state was as strong as it was, and why, in turn, it could never endure without end. *The City of God* presents the full-length argument for this conclusion.

The task of selecting a series of basic writings from the vast works of Saint Augustine is, to say the least, overwhelming. The nature of the problem itself carries with it the inevitable result that no selection will please everyone. Furthermore, the simultaneous presence of all his complex thought in the mind of Saint Augustine surely does not make the question of choice any the less difficult, for many of the most concise expressions of his central views are to be found in widely scattered individual places, in his sermons, or letters, or in the extended exegetical commentaries. On the other hand, the Augustinian compresence of thought can be viewed legitimately as an asset for one who seeks to bring together a collection of writings which will portray fully the entire position. As a consequence it is perhaps more than a pious hope that the present group of treatises will not have omitted anything of importance.

In making a selection from the Augustinian corpus, the first essential works are clearly *The Confessions, The City of God* and *On the Trinity*. *The Confessions* has been included in its entirety, but certain portions of the other two have been omitted. Because of the limited available space, the alternatives were either to print the three works complete and virtually eliminate the minor treatises, or, on the other hand, to eliminate the less essential parts of *The City of God* and *On the Trinity*, and consequently be able to include a far more extensive and representative collection from the minor writings. The second alternative, for good or ill, has been adopted. Certain books and chapters from the first ten books of *The City of God* have therefore not been included. The omitted sections contain much that is less significant and which most bear the marks of Saint Augustine's tendency to be repetitious and over-wordy. The second half of the work appears complete, since it contains the pulling together and interpretation of the evidence which has been amassed in the earlier books. The architecture of the whole should be readily discernible, and in order that no important detail be wanting, synopses of the omitted sections have been prepared. The books of the treatise *On the Trinity* which are included have been selected in accordance with the same general principles, with those omitted likewise covered in outline. For an edition of "basic writings," the presentation of these two great masterpieces in a somewhat abbreviated form has certain signal advantages. Everything possible has been done to prepare a text which will be easily apprehendable without, because of the repetitious elements, damaging in any significant particular the nature of the whole. Saint Augustine's habits of composition being what they are, it is even possible to argue that the shortened forms are superior for all but the most specialized student.

In choosing the block of minor treatises or selections from the remainder of the works of Saint Augustine, certain writings almost automatically suggested their exclusion. The commentaries, such as those on *Genesis, Job* and *The Psalms,* as well as the homilies on the *Gospel According to Saint John,* fall into this category. The sermons have also not been included, though there are a number whose absence may be keenly felt. This is also true of the letters, particularly the famous correspondence with Saint Jerome. In view of this genuinely embarrassing embarrassment of riches,[36] the decision was reached to include as many *complete* shorter treatises as the limitations of space would permit which would contain a fully rounded expression of Saint Augustine's mature thought. For this reason, the anti-Donatist writings, with their particular air of doctrinal dispute against the background of ecclesiastical politics, have not found their way into the collection. Instead, it seemed better to present with reasonable thoroughness the period immediately following the conversion (when the influence of Greek thought was strong), the attack upon the Manichaeans, and most important of all, the great writings directed against the Pelagians. If this objective has in some measure been achieved, this edition will have fulfilled its legitimate function.

In addition to the treatise *On Free Will,* a detailed analysis of which, but not the full text, is included, twelve essays comprise the group of selections. The first of these, *The Soliloquies* and *On the Immortality of the Soul,* reflect the times when Saint Augustine was moving from his Platonism into his more completely Christian mode of thought. The essay *On the Morals of the Catholic Church* (to which he wrote a sequel *On the Morals of the Manichaeans,* not here included) is typical of the anti-Manichaean writing. *On the Teacher* throws important light on Saint Augustine's theory of knowledge, while *On the Profit of Believing* continues the attack upon the Manichaeans, as does the short essay *On the Nature of the Good. On the Spirit and the Letter* illustrates well the Augustinian method of dealing with the Holy Scriptures. *On Nature and Grace, On the Grace of Christ and Original Sin,* and *On Grace and Free Will* contain the best of Saint Augustine's arguments against the Pelagians. The *Enchiridion*, written nine years before his death, is the most complete short statement of Augustinian Christianity, an expository essay unrivaled in its depth and clarity in Christian literature. *On the Predestination of the Saints*, composed within two years of Saint Augustine's death, rounds out the picture of his version of Christianity, which ranges from the simplicity of the deepest spiritual insights to the complexity of the most profound and baffling theological dilemmas.[37]

Not infrequently public lecturers have found it effective to close a speech or a series of addresses with the final words of *The City of God*, "Let those who think I have said too little, or those who think I have said too much, forgive me; and let those who think I have said just enough join me in giving thanks to God." In one way these words let us know the spirit of the man. But Saint Augustine's God-centered soul is revealed in all its illumination in the great prayer with which he concludes his work *On the Trinity:* "O Lord our God, we believe in Thee, the Father and the Son and the Holy Spirit. . . . Directing my purpose by this rule of faith, so far as I have been able, so far as Thou hast made me to be able, I have sought Thee, and have desired to see with my understanding what I believed; and I have argued and labored much. O Lord, my God, my one hope, hearken to me, lest through weariness I be unwilling to seek Thee, 'but that I may always seek Thy face.'[38] Do Thou give strength to seek, who has made me find Thee, and hast given the hope of finding Thee more and more. My strength and infirmity are in Thy sight: preserve the one and heal the other. My knowledge and my ignorance are in Thy sight; where Thou hast opened to me, receive me as I enter; where Thou hast closed, open to me as I knock. May I remember Thee, understand Thee, love Thee. . . . Set me free, O God, from that multitude of speech which I suffer inwardly in my soul, wretched as it is in Thy sight, and flying for refuge to Thy mercy; for I am not silent in thoughts, even when silent in words. And if, indeed, I thought of nothing save what pleased Thee, certainly I would not ask Thee to set me free from such multitude of speech. But many are my thoughts, such as Thou knowest, 'thoughts of man, since they are vain.'[39] Grant to me not to consent to them; and if ever they delight me, nevertheless to condemn them, and not to dwell in them, as though I slumbered. Nor let them so prevail in me, as that anything in my acts should proceed from them. . . . When, therefore, we shall have come to Thee, these very many things that we speak, and yet come short, will cease; and Thou, as One, will remain 'all in all.'[40] And we shall say one thing without end, in praising Thee in One, ourselves also made one in Thee. O Lord, the one God, God the Trinity, whatever I have said in these books that is of Thine, may they acknowledge who are Thine; if anything of my own, may it be pardoned both by Thee and by those who are Thine. Amen."

Whitney J. Oates

NOTES FOR INTRODUCTION

[1] Cf. the excellent discussion of this point by E. Gilson, "The Future of Augustinian Metaphysics," in *A Monument to Saint Augustine* (London, Sheed and Ward, 1930) pp. 289 ff.

[2] *Ibid.*, p. 300. In his essay, E. Gilson delineates clearly what I have called the "openness" of Saint Augustine's position. He also gives a splendid statement of the relation between Saint Augustine and Saint Thomas from the Roman Catholic point of view.

[3] *Ibid.*, p. 308

[4] For convenient reference and general information concerning the life and writings of Saint Augustine, cf. V. J. Bourke, *Augustine's Quest of Wisdom* (Milwaukee, The Bruce Publishing Co., 1945)

[5] *Conf.*, Bk. II, chap. 3

[6] *Conf.*, Bk. VI, chap. 15

[6a] Saint Augustine, with his conversion, decided upon a life of celibacy, and the formation of the group at Cassiciacum contributed greatly to the influence which he exerted later in the development of monasticism.

[7] *Introduction à l'étude de saint Augustin* (Paris, Librairie Philosophique, J. Vrin, 1929) p. 293, note 1

[8] *City of God*, Bk. XIV, chap. 8

[9] *Conf.*, Bk. I, chap. 1

[10] C. C. Martindale, S.J., "A Sketch of the Life and Character of Saint Augustine," in *A Monument to Saint Augustine*, p. 84

[11] *Conf.*, Bk. XIII, chap. 9

[12] Cf. Bourke, *Augustine's Quest of Wisdom*, p. 112, and the references there cited.

[13] *On the Trinity*, Bk. VI, chap. 5

[14] "The Future of Augustinian Metaphysics," in *A Monument to Saint Augustine*, pp. 301-302

[15] *Introduction à l'étude de saint Augustin*, p. 124. The translation from the French is mine.

[16] "The Future of Augustinian Metaphysics," in *A Monument to Saint Augustine*, pp. 298-299

[17] Cf. M. C. D'Arcy, S.J., "The Philosophy of Saint Augustine," in *A Monument to Saint Augustine*, pp. 159 ff.

[18] *On the Trinity*, Bk. I, chap. 1

[19] "The Future of Augustinian Metaphysics," in *A Monument to Saint Augustine*, p. 290

[20] *Conf.*, Bk. VIII, chap. 7

[21] *Conf.*, Bk. VIII, chap. 12

[22] Rom. xiii. 13, 14

[23] John viii. 31, 32

[24] *De Civitate Dei*, edited by J. E. C. Welldon (London, Society for Promoting Christian Knowledge, 1924) Bk. XIII, chap. 23, vol. II, p. 74, note 20

[25] *Introduction à l'étude de saint Augustin*, Deuxième Partie, chap. III

[26] *Conf.*, Bk. XI, chap. 12

[27] *Conf.*, Bk. XI, chap. 14

[28] *City of God*, Bk. XII, chap. 15

[29] Cf. *Timaeus*, 37 c 6 ff.

[30] Cf. *Conf.*, Bk. XI, chaps. 10-21, where Saint Augustine discusses at length the nature of time.

[31] Cf. the interesting treatment of this problem in Boethius, *The Consolation of Philosophy*, Bk. V

[32] For the best Latin text and commentary in English on *The City of God,* see the edition of Welldon, referred to in note 24 above.

[33] Cf. the excellent discussion of the question by Christopher Dawson, "Saint Augustine and His Age," in *A Monument to Saint Augustine,* pp. 58 ff.

[34] *City of God,* Bk. XIV, chap. 28. The scriptural reference is to *Psalms,* iii. 3.

[35] *City of God,* Bk. XIX, Chap. 24

[36] Apart from letters and sermons, Saint Augustine composed 232 books.

[37] For the reader who wishes to explore the minor treatises further, the following are suggested: *Contra Academicos, De Vita Beata, De Musica, De Quantitate Animae, De Vera Religione,* and *De Doctrina Christiana.* For Saint Augustine's views of the creation of the world, cf. *De Genesi ad Litteram.* Also of great interest is the *Retractationes,* written late in his life, in which he goes over carefully and modifies the detail of many passages in his preceding works.

[38] *Ps.* cv. 4

[39] *Ps.* xciv. 11

[40] *I Cor.* xv. 28

THE CONFESSIONS

THE CONFESSIONS

Introductory Note

The Confessions is easily the best known of all the works of Saint Augustine. Written in the closing years of the fourth century and published probably about 400 or 401 A.D., it contains a powerful and intimate self-portrait of the great Doctor of Grace. The work is self-explanatory and should be read first in any comprehensive study of Saint Augustine. In his own earlier life he saw above all the incontrovertible evidence of the operation of God's grace and it was primarily to make this experience widely available that he undertook the composition of the work. The first nine books comprise the autobiographical material while in the last four he turns to a discussion of such questions as the nature of our knowledge of God, the mysterious character of the memory, and the nature of time. It should be noted that his speculations concerning time are remarkable not only for their profundity but also because they really provide the context in which the full meaning of his personal experience can be understood. But above and beyond the light which this book throws upon Saint Augustine, his thought and work, *The Confessions* is a monument of spiritual literature and will never fail the reader who seeks in it devotional inspiration.

THE THIRTEEN BOOKS
OF THE
CONFESSIONS OF SAINT AUGUSTINE

BOOK ONE

Commencing with the invocation of God, Augustine relates in detail the beginning of his life, his infancy and boyhood, up to his fifteenth year; at which age he acknowledges that he was more inclined to all youthful pleasures and vices than to the study of letters.

CHAPTER I

HE PROCLAIMS THE GREATNESS OF GOD, WHOM HE DESIRES TO SEEK AND INVOKE, BEING AWAKENED BY HIM

GREAT art Thou, O Lord, and greatly to be praised; great is Thy power, and of Thy wisdom there is no end.[1] And man, being a part of Thy creation, desires to praise Thee—man, who bears about with him his mortality, the witness of his sin, even the witness that Thou resistest the proud [2]—yet man, this part of Thy creation, desires to praise Thee. Thou movest us to delight in praising Thee; for Thou hast formed us for Thyself, and our hearts are restless till they find rest in Thee. Lord, teach me to know and understand which of these should be first, to call on Thee, or to praise Thee; and likewise to know Thee, or to call upon Thee. But who is there that calls upon Thee without knowing Thee? For he that knows Thee not may call upon Thee as other than Thou art. Or perhaps we call on Thee that we may know Thee. But how shall they call on Him in whom they have not believed? or how shall they believe without a preacher?[3] And those who seek the Lord shall praise Him.[4] For those who seek shall find Him,[5] and those who find Him shall praise Him. Let me seek Thee, Lord, in calling on Thee, and call on Thee in believing in Thee; for Thou hast been preached unto us. O Lord, my faith calls on Thee—that faith which Thou hast imparted to me, which Thou hast breathed into me through the incarnation of Thy Son, through the ministry of Thy preacher.[6]

---

[1] Ps. cxlv. 3, and cxlvii. 5   [2] Jas. iv. 6, and 1 Pet. v. 5   [3] Rom. x. 14   [4] Ps. xxii.
26   [5] Matt. vii. 7   [6] That is, Ambrose, Bishop of Milan

CHAPTER II

THAT THE GOD WHOM WE INVOKE IS IN US, AND WE IN HIM

And how shall I call upon my God—my God and my Lord? For when I call on Him I ask Him to come into me. And what place is there in me into which my God can come—into which God can come, even He who made heaven and earth? Is there anything in me, O Lord my God, that can contain Thee? Do indeed the very heaven and the earth, which Thou hast made, and in which Thou hast made me, contain Thee? Or, as nothing could exist without Thee, doth whatever exists contain Thee? Why, then, do I ask Thee to come into me, since I indeed exist, and could not exist if Thou wert not in me? Because I am not yet in hell, though Thou art even there; for if I go down into hell Thou art there.[7] I could not therefore exist, could not exist at all, O my God, unless Thou wert in me. Or should I not rather say, that I could not exist unless I were in Thee from whom are all things, by whom are all things, in whom are all things? [8] Even so, Lord; even so. Where do I call Thee to, since Thou art in me, or whence canst Thou come into me? For where outside heaven and earth can I go that from thence my God may come into me who has said, I fill heaven and earth? [9]

CHAPTER III

EVERYWHERE GOD WHOLLY FILLETH ALL THINGS, BUT NEITHER HEAVEN NOR EARTH CONTAINETH HIM

Since, then, Thou fillest heaven and earth, do they contain Thee? Or, as they contain Thee not, dost Thou fill them, and yet there remains something over? And where dost Thou pour forth that which remaineth of Thee when the heaven and earth are filled? Or, indeed, is there no need that Thou who containest all things shouldest be contained of any, since those things which Thou fillest Thou fillest by containing them? For the vessels which Thou fillest do not sustain Thee, since should they even be broken Thou wilt not be poured forth.   And when Thou art poured forth on us,[10] Thou art not cast down, but we are uplifted; nor art Thou dissipated, but we are drawn together. But, as Thou fillest all things, dost Thou fill them with Thy whole self, or, as even all things cannot altogether contain Thee, do they contain a part, and do all at once contain the same part? Or has each its own proper part—the greater more, the smaller less? Is, then, one part of Thee greater, another less? Or is it that Thou art wholly everywhere whilst nothing altogether contains Thee?

[7] Ps. cxxxix. 8   [8] Rom. xi. 36   [9] Jer. xxiii. 24   [10] Acts ii. 18

CHAPTER IV

THE MAJESTY OF GOD IS SUPREME, AND HIS VIRTUES INEXPLICABLE

What, then, art Thou, O my God—what, I ask, but the Lord God? For who is Lord but the Lord? or who is God save our God? [11] Most high, most excellent, most potent, most omnipotent; most merciful and most just; most hidden and most near; most beauteous and most strong, stable, yet contained of none; unchangeable, yet changing all things; never new, never old; making all things new, yet bringing old age upon the proud and they know it not; always working, yet ever at rest; gathering, yet needing nothing; sustaining, pervading, and protecting; creating, nourishing, and developing; seeking, and yet possessing all things. Thou lovest, and burnest not; art jealous, yet free from care; repentest, and hast no sorrow; art angry, yet serene; changest Thy ways, leaving unchanged Thy plans; recoverest what Thou findest, having yet never lost; art never in want, whilst Thou rejoicest in gain; never covetous, though requiring usury.[12] That Thou mayest owe, more than enough is given to Thee; yet who hath anything that is not Thine? Thou payest debts while owing nothing; and when Thou forgivest debts, losest nothing. Yet, O my God, my life, my holy joy, what is this that I have said? And what saith any man when he speaks of Thee? Yet woe to them that keep silence, seeing that even they who say most are as the dumb.

CHAPTER V

HE SEEKS REST IN GOD, AND PARDON OF HIS SINS

Oh! how shall I find rest in Thee? Who will send Thee into my heart to inebriate it, so that I may forget my woes, and embrace Thee, my only good? What art Thou to me? Have compassion on me, that I may speak. What am I to Thee that Thou demandest my love, and unless I give it to Thee art angry, and threatenest me with great sorrows? Is it, then, a light sorrow not to love Thee? Alas! alas! tell me of Thy compassion, O Lord my God, what Thou art to me. Say unto my soul, I am thy salvation.[13] So speak that I may hear. Behold, Lord, the ears of my heart are before Thee; open Thou them, and say unto my soul, I am thy salvation. When I hear, may I run and lay hold on Thee. Hide not Thy face from me. Let me die, lest I die, if only I may see Thy face.

Cramped is the dwelling of my soul; do Thou expand it, that Thou mayest enter in. It is in ruins, restore Thou it. There is that about it which must offend Thine eyes; I confess and know it, but who will cleanse it? or to whom shall I cry but to Thee? Cleanse me from my secret sins,[14] O

---

[11] Ps. xviii. 31   [12] Matt. xxv. 27   [13] Ps. xxxv. 3   [14] Ps. xix. 12, 13

Lord, and keep Thy servant from those of other men. I believe, and therefore do I speak;[15] Lord, Thou knowest. Have I not confessed my transgressions unto Thee, O my God; and Thou hast put away the iniquity of
my heart? [16] I do not contend in judgment with Thee,[17] who art the Truth;
and I would not deceive myself, lest my iniquity lie against itself. I do not,
therefore, contend in judgment with Thee, for if Thou, Lord, shouldest
mark iniquities, O Lord, who shall stand?[18]

CHAPTER VI

HE DESCRIBES HIS INFANCY, AND LAUDS THE PROTECTION
AND ETERNAL PROVIDENCE OF GOD

Still suffer me to speak before Thy mercy—me, dust and ashes.[19] Suffer
me to speak, for, behold, it is Thy mercy I address, and not derisive man.
Yet perhaps even Thou deridest me; but when Thou art turned to me Thou
wilt have compassion on me.[20] For what do I wish to say, O Lord my God,
but that I know not whence I came hither into this—shall I call it dying
life or living death? Yet, as I have heard from my parents, from whose
substance Thou didst form me—for I myself cannot remember it—Thy
merciful comforts sustained me. Thus it was that the comforts of a
woman's milk entertained me; for neither my mother nor my nurses filled
their own breasts, but Thou by them didst give me the nourishment of
infancy according to Thy ordinance and that bounty of Thine which
underlieth all things. For Thou didst cause me not to want more than
Thou gavest, and those who nourished me willingly to give me what Thou
gavest them. For they, by an instinctive affection, were anxious to give me
what Thou hadst abundantly supplied. It was, in truth, good for them that
my good should come from them, though, indeed, it was not from them,
but by them; for from Thee, O God, are all good things, and from my God
is all my safety.[21] This is what I have since discovered, as Thou hast declared Thyself to me by the blessings both within me and without me
which Thou hast bestowed upon me. For at that time I knew how to suck,
to be satisfied when comfortable, and to cry when in pain—nothing beyond.

Afterwards I began to laugh—at first in sleep, then when waking. For
this I have heard mentioned of myself, and I believe it (though I cannot
remember it), for we see the same in other infants. And now little by little
I realized where I was, and wished to tell my wishes to those who might
satisfy them, but I could not; for my wants were within me, while they
were without, and could not by any faculty of theirs enter into my soul. So
I cast about limbs and voice, making the few and feeble signs I could, like,
though indeed not much like what I wished; and when I was not satisfied—
either not being understood, or because it would have been injurious to

[15] Ps. cxvi. 10   [16] Ps. xxxii. 5   [17] Job ix. 3   [18] Ps. cxxx. 3   [19] Gen. xviii. 27
[20] Jer. xii. 15   [21] Prov. xxi. 31

me—I grew indignant that my elders were not subject to me, and that those on whom I had no claim did not wait on me, and avenged myself on them by tears. That infants are such I have been able to learn by watching them; and they, though unknowing, have better shown me that I was such a one than my nurses who knew it.

And, behold, my infancy died long ago, and I live. But Thou, O Lord, who ever livest, and in whom nothing dies (since before the world was, and indeed before all that can be called "before," Thou existest, and art the God and Lord of all Thy creatures; and with Thee fixedly abide the causes of all unstable things, the unchanging sources of all things changeable, and the eternal reasons of all things unreasoning and temporal), tell me, Thy suppliant, O God; tell, O merciful One, Thy miserable servant—tell me whether my infancy succeeded another age of mine which had at that time perished. Was it that which I passed in my mother's womb? For of that something has been made known to me, and I have myself seen women with child. And what, O God, my joy, preceded that life? Was I, indeed, anywhere, or anybody? For no one can tell me these things, neither father nor mother, nor the experience of others, nor my own memory. Dost Thou laugh at me for asking such things, and command me to praise and confess Thee for what I know?

I give thanks to Thee, Lord of heaven and earth, giving praise to Thee for my first being and infancy, of which I have no memory; for Thou hast granted to man that from others he should come to conclusions as to himself, and that he should believe many things concerning himself on the authority of feeble women. Even then I had life and being; and as my infancy closed I was already seeking for signs by which my feelings might be made known to others. Whence could such a creature come but from Thee, O Lord? Or shall any man be skilful enough to fashion himself? Or is there any other vein by which being and life runs into us save this, that Thou, O Lord, hast made us,[22] with whom being and life are one, because Thou Thyself art being and life in the highest? Thou art the highest, Thou changest not,[23] neither in Thee doth this present day come to an end, though it doth end in Thee, since in Thee all such things are; for they would have no way of passing away unless Thou sustainedst them. And since Thy years shall have no end,[24] Thy years are an ever present day. And how many of ours and our fathers' days have passed through this Thy day, and received from it their measure and fashion of being, and others yet to come shall so receive and pass away! But Thou art the same,[25] and all the things of to-morrow and the days yet to come, and all of yesterday and the days that are past, Thou wilt do to-day, Thou hast done to-day. What is it to me if any understand not? Let him still rejoice and say What is this? [26] Let him rejoice even so, and rather love to discover in failing to discover, than in discovering not to discover Thee.

[22] Ps. c. 3   [23] Mal. iii. 6   [24] Ps. cii. 27   [25] *Ibid.*   [26] Ex. xvi. 15

CHAPTER VII

HE SHOWS BY EXAMPLE THAT EVEN INFANCY IS PRONE TO SIN

Hearken, O God! Alas for the sins of men! Man saith this, and Thou dost have mercy on him; for Thou didst create him, but didst not create the sin that is in him. Who bringeth to my remembrance the sin of my infancy? For before Thee none is free from sin, not even the infant which has lived but a day upon the earth. Who bringeth this to my remembrance? Doth not each little one, in whom I behold that which I do not remember of myself? In what, then, did I sin? Is it that I cried for the breast? If I should now so cry—not indeed for the breast, but for the food suitable to my years—I should be most justly laughed at and rebuked. What I then did deserved rebuke; but as I could not understand those who rebuked me, neither custom nor reason suffered me to be rebuked. For as we grow we root out and cast from us such habits. I have not seen any one who is wise, when purging[27] anything cast away the good. Or was it good, even for a time, to strive to get by crying that which, if given, would be hurtful—to be bitterly indignant that those who were free and its elders, and those to whom it owed its being, besides many others wiser than it, who would not give way to the nod of its good pleasure, were not subject to it—to endeavor to harm, by struggling as much as it could, because those commands were not obeyed which only could have been obeyed to its hurt? Then, in the weakness of the infant's limbs, and not in its will, lies its innocency. I myself have seen and known an infant to be jealous though it could not speak. It became pale, and cast bitter looks on its foster-brother. Who is ignorant of this? Mothers and nurses tell us that they appease these things by I know not what remedies; and may this be taken for innocence, that when the fountain of milk is flowing fresh and abundant, one who has need should not be allowed to share it, though needing that nourishment to sustain life? Yet we look leniently on these things, not because they are not faults, nor because the faults are small, but because they will vanish as age increases. For although you may allow these things now, you could not bear them with equanimity if found in an older person.

Thou, therefore, O Lord my God, who gavest life to the infant, and a frame which, as we see, Thou hast endowed with senses, compacted with limbs, beautified with form, and, for its general good and safety, hast introduced all vital energies—Thou commandest me to praise Thee for these things, to give thanks unto the Lord, and to sing praise unto Thy name, O Most High;[28] for Thou art a God omnipotent and good, though Thou hadst done nought but these things, which none other can do but Thou, who alone madest all things, O Thou most fair, who madest all things fair,

[27] John xv. 2   [28] Ps. xcii. I

and orderest all according to Thy law. This period, then, of my life, O Lord, of which I have no remembrance, which I believe on the word of others, and which I guess from other infants, it displeases me—true though the guess be—to add it to this life of mine which I lead in this world; inasmuch as, in the darkness of my forgetfulness, it is like that which I passed in my mother's womb. But if I was conceived in iniquity, and in sin did my mother nourish me in the womb,[29] where, I pray thee, O my God, where, Lord, or when was I, Thy servant, innocent? But behold, I pass by that time, for what have I to do with that, the memories of which I cannot recall?

CHAPTER VIII

THAT WHEN A BOY HE LEARNED TO SPEAK, NOT BY ANY SET METHOD, BUT FROM THE ACTS AND WORDS OF HIS PARENTS

Did I not, then, growing out of the state of infancy, come to boyhood, or rather did it not come to me, and succeed to infancy? Nor did my infancy depart (for whither went it?); and yet it did no longer abide, for I was no longer an infant that could not speak, but a chattering boy. I remember this, and I afterwards observed how I first learned to speak, for my elders did not teach me words in any set method, as they did letters afterwards; but I myself, when I was unable to say all I wished and to whomsoever I desired, by means of the whimperings and broken utterances and various motions of my limbs, which I used to enforce my wishes, repeated the sounds in my memory by the mind, O my God, which Thou gavest me. When they called anything by name, and moved the body towards it while they spoke, I saw and gathered that the thing they wished to point out was called by the name they then uttered; and that they did mean this was made plain by the motion of the body, even by the natural language of all nations expressed by the countenance, glance of the eye, movement of other members, and by the sound of the voice indicating the affections of the mind, as it seeks, possesses, rejects, or avoids. So it was that by frequently hearing words, in duly placed sentences, I gradually gathered what things they were the signs of; and having formed my mouth to the utterance of these signs, I thereby expressed my will. Thus I exchanged with those about me the signs by which we express our wishes, and advanced deeper into the stormy fellowship of human life, depending the while on the authority of parents, and the beck of elders.

[29] Ps. li. 5

CHAPTER IX

CONCERNING THE HATRED OF LEARNING, THE LOVE OF PLAY, AND
THE FEAR OF BEING WHIPPED NOTICEABLE IN BOYS: AND OF THE
FOLLY OF OUR ELDERS AND MASTERS

O my God! what miseries and mockeries did I then experience, when obedience to my teachers was set before me as proper to my boyhood, that I might flourish in this world, and distinguish myself in the science of speech, which should get me honor amongst men, and deceitful riches! After that I was put to school to get learning, of which I (worthless as I was) knew not what use there was; and yet, if slow to learn, I was flogged! For this was deemed praiseworthy by our forefathers; and many before us, passing the same course, had appointed beforehand for us these troublesome ways by which we were compelled to pass, multiplying labor and sorrow upon the sons of Adam. But we found, O Lord, men praying to Thee, and we learned from them to conceive of Thee, according to our ability, to be some Great One, who was able (though not visible to our senses) to hear and help us. For as a boy I began to pray to Thee, my help and my refuge,[30] and in invoking Thee broke the bands of my tongue, and entreated Thee though little, with no little earnestness, that I might not be beaten at school. And when Thou heardest me not, giving me not over to folly thereby, my elders, yea, and my own parents too, who wished me no ill, laughed at my stripes, my then great and grievous ill.

Is there any one, Lord, with so high a spirit, cleaving to Thee with so strong an affection—for even a kind of obtuseness may do that much—but is there, I say, any one who, by cleaving devoutly to Thee, is endowed with so great a courage that he can esteem lightly those racks and hooks, and varied tortures of the same sort, against which, throughout the whole world, men supplicate Thee with great fear, deriding those who most bitterly fear them, just as our parents derided the torments with which our masters punished us when we were boys? For we were no less afraid of our pains, nor did we pray less to Thee to avoid them; and yet we sinned, in writing, or reading, or reflecting upon our lessons less than was required of us. For we wanted not, O Lord, memory or capacity—of which, by Thy will, we possessed enough for our age—but we delighted only in play; and we were punished for this by those who were doing the same things themselves. But the idleness of our elders they call business, while boys who do the like are punished by those same elders, and yet neither boys nor men find any pity. For will any one of good sense approve of my being whipped because, as a boy, I played ball, and so was hindered from learning quickly those lessons by means of which, as a man, I should play more unbecom-

[30] Ps. ix. 9, xlvi. 1, and xlviii. 3

ingly? And did he by whom I was beaten do other than this, who, when he was overcome in any little controversy with a co-tutor, was more tormented by anger and envy than I when beaten by a playfellow in a match at ball?

CHAPTER X

THROUGH A LOVE OF BALL-PLAYING AND SHOWS, HE NEGLECTS HIS STUDIES AND THE INJUNCTIONS OF HIS PARENTS

And yet I erred, O Lord God, the Creator and Disposer of all things in Nature—but of sin the Disposer only—I erred, O Lord my God, in doing contrary to the wishes of my parents and of those masters; for this learning which they (no matter for what motive) wished me to acquire, I might have put to good account afterwards. For I disobeyed them not because I had chosen a better way, but from a fondness for play, loving the honor of victory in the matches, and to have my ears tickled with lying fables, in order that they might itch the more furiously—the same curiosity beaming more and more in my eyes for the shows and sports of my elders. Yet those who give these entertainments are held in such high repute, that almost all desire the same for their children, who they are still willing should be beaten, if these same games keep them from the studies by which they desire them to arrive at being the givers of them. Look down upon these things, O Lord, with compassion, and deliver us who now call upon Thee; deliver those also who do not call upon Thee, that they may call upon Thee, and that Thou mayest deliver them.

CHAPTER XI

SEIZED BY DISEASE, HIS MOTHER BEING TROUBLED, HE EARNESTLY DEMANDS BAPTISM, WHICH ON RECOVERY IS POSTPONED—HIS FATHER NOT AS YET BELIEVING IN CHRIST

Even as a boy I had heard of eternal life promised to us through the humility of the Lord our God condescending to our pride, and I was signed with the sign of the cross, and was seasoned with His salt even from the womb of my mother, who greatly trusted in Thee. Thou sawest, O Lord, how at one time, while yet a boy, being suddenly seized with pains in the stomach, and being at the point of death—Thou sawest, O my God, for even then Thou wast my keeper, with what emotion of mind and with what faith I solicited from the piety of my mother, and of Thy Church, the mother of us all, the baptism of Thy Christ, my Lord and my God. On which, the mother of my flesh being much troubled—since she, with a heart pure in Thy faith, travailed in birth[31] more lovingly for my eternal salvation— would, had I not quickly recovered, have without delay provided for my

[31] Gal. iv. 19

initiation and washing by Thy life-giving sacraments, confessing Thee, O Lord Jesus, for the remission of sins. So my cleansing was deferred, as if I must needs, should I live, be further polluted; because, indeed, the guilt contracted by sin would, after baptism, be greater and more perilous. Thus I at that time believed with my mother and the whole house, except my father; yet he did not overcome the influence of my mother's piety in me so as to prevent my believing in Christ, as he had not yet believed in Him. For she was desirous that Thou, O my God, shouldest be my Father rather than he; and in this Thou didst aid her to overcome her husband, to whom, though the better of the two, she yielded obedience, because in this she yielded obedience to Thee, who dost so command.

I beseech Thee, my God, I would gladly know, if it be Thy will, to what end my baptism was then deferred? Was it for my good that the reins were slackened, as it were, upon me for me to sin? Or were they not slackened? If not, whence comes it that it is still dinned into our ears on all sides, "Let him alone, let him act as he likes, for he is not yet baptized"? But as regards bodily health, no one exclaims, "Let him be more seriously wounded, for he is not yet cured!" How much better, then, had it been for me to have been cured at once; and then, by my own and my friends' diligence, my soul's restored health had been kept safe in Thy keeping, who gavest it! Better, in truth. But how numerous and great waves of temptation appeared to hang over me after my childhood! These were foreseen by my mother; and she preferred that the unformed clay should be exposed to them rather than the image itself.

CHAPTER XII

BEING COMPELLED, HE GAVE HIS ATTENTION TO LEARNING; BUT
FULLY ACKNOWLEDGES THAT THIS WAS THE WORK OF GOD

But in this my childhood (which was far less dreaded for me than youth) I had no love of learning, and hated to be forced to it, yet was I forced to it notwithstanding; and this was well done towards me, but I did not well, for I would not have learned had I not been compelled. For no man does well against his will, even if that which he does be good. Neither did they who forced me do well, but the good that was done to me came from Thee, my God. For they considered not what way I should employ what they forced me to learn, unless to satisfy the inordinate desires of a rich beggary and a shameful glory. But Thou, by whom the very hairs of our heads are numbered,[32] didst use for my good the error of all who pressed me to learn; and my own error in willing not to learn, didst Thou make use of for my punishment—of which I, being so small a boy and so great a sinner, was not unworthy. Thus by the instrumentality of those who did not well didst

[32] Matt. x. 30

Thou well for me; and by my own sin didst Thou justly punish me. For it is even as Thou has appointed, that every inordinate affection should bring its own punishment.

CHAPTER XIII

HE DELIGHTED IN LATIN STUDIES AND THE EMPTY FABLES OF THE POETS, BUT HATED THE ELEMENTS OF LITERATURE AND THE GREEK LANGUAGE

But what was the cause of my dislike of Greek literature, which I studied from my boyhood, I cannot even now understand. For the Latin I loved exceedingly—not what our first masters, but what the grammarians teach; for those primary lessons of reading, writing, and ciphering, I considered no less of a burden and a punishment than Greek. Yet whence was this unless from the sin and vanity of this life? for I was but flesh, a wind that passeth away and cometh not again.[33] For those primary lessons were better, assuredly, because more certain; seeing that by their agency I acquired, and still retain, the power of reading what I find written, and writing myself what I will; whilst in the others I was compelled to learn about the wanderings of a certain Aeneas, oblivious of my own, and to weep for Dido dead, because she slew herself for love; while at the same time I brooked with dry eyes my wretched self dying far from Thee, in the midst of those things, O God, my life.

For what can be more wretched than the wretch who pities not himself shedding tears over the death of Dido for love of Aeneas, but shedding no tears over his own death in not loving Thee, O God, light of my heart, and bread of the inner mouth of my soul, and the power that weddest my mind with my innermost thoughts? I did not love Thee, and committed fornication against Thee; and those around me thus sinning cried, "Well done! Well done!" For the friendship of this world is fornication against Thee;[34] and "Well done! Well done!" is cried until one feels ashamed not to be such a man. And for this I shed no tears, though I wept for Dido, who sought death at the sword's point, myself the while seeking the lowest of Thy creatures—having forsaken Thee—earth tending to the earth; and if forbidden to read these things, how grieved would I feel that I was not permitted to read what grieved me. This sort of madness is considered a more honorable and more fruitful learning than that by which I learned to read and write.

But now, O my God, cry unto my soul; and let Thy Truth say unto me, "It is not so; it is not so; better much was that first teaching." For behold, I would rather forget the wanderings of Aeneas, and all such things, than how to write and read. But it is true that over the entrance of the grammar

[33] Ps. lxxviii. 39, and Jas. iv. 14   [34] Jas. iv. 4

school there hangs a vail; but this is not so much a sign of the majesty
of the mystery, as of a covering for error. Let not them exclaim against me
of whom I am no longer in fear, whilst I confess to Thee my God, that
which my soul desires, and acquiesce in reprehending my evil ways, that
I may love Thy good ways. Neither let those cry out against me who
buy or sell grammar-learning. For if I ask them whether it be true, as the
poet says, that Aeneas once came to Carthage, the unlearned will reply
that they do not know, the learned will deny it to be true. But if I ask with
what letters the name Aeneas is written, all who have learnt this will answer
truly, in accordance with the conventional understanding men have arrived
at as to these signs. Again, if I should ask which, if forgotten, would cause
the greatest inconvenience in our life, reading and writing, or these poetical
fictions, who does not see what every one would answer who had not entirely forgotten himself? I erred, then, when as a boy I preferred those vain
studies to those more profitable ones, or rather loved the one and hated
the other. "One and one are two, two and two are four," this was then in
truth a hateful song to me; while the wooden horse full of armed men,
and the burning of Troy, and the "spectral image" of Creusa were a most
pleasant spectacle of vanity.[35]

CHAPTER XIV

WHY HE DESPISED GREEK LITERATURE, AND EASILY LEARNED LATIN

But why, then, did I dislike Greek learning, which was full of like tales?
For Homer also was skilled in inventing similar stories, and is most sweetly
vain, yet was he disagreeable to me as a boy. I believe Virgil, indeed, would
be the same to Greek children, if compelled to learn him, as I was Homer.
The difficulty, in truth, the difficulty of learning a foreign language mingled
as it were with gall all the sweetness of those fabulous Grecian stories. For
not a single word of it did I understand, and to make me do so, they vehemently urged me with cruel threatenings and punishments. There was a
time also when (as an infant) I knew no Latin; but this I acquired without
any fear or tormenting, by merely taking notice, amid the blandishments
of my nurses, the jests of those who smiled on me, and the sportiveness of
those who toyed with me. I learnt all this, indeed, without being urged
by any pressure of punishment, for my own heart urged me to bring forth
its own conceptions, which I could not do unless by learning words, not of
those who taught me, but of those who talked to me; into whose ears, also,
I brought forth whatever I discerned. From this it is sufficiently clear that
a free curiosity has more influence in our learning these things than a necessity full of fear. But this last restrains the overflowings of that freedom,
through Thy laws, O God—Thy laws, from the ferule of the schoolmaster

[35] *Aen.* ii. 772

to the trials of the martyr, being effective to mingle for us a salutary bitterness, calling us back to Thyself from the pernicious delights which allure us from Thee.

CHAPTER XV

HE ENTREATS GOD, THAT WHATEVER USEFUL THINGS HE LEARNED AS A BOY MAY BE DEDICATED TO HIM

Hear my prayer, O Lord; let not my soul faint under Thy discipline, nor let me faint in confessing unto Thee Thy mercies, whereby Thou hast saved me from all my most mischievous ways, that Thou mightest become sweet to me beyond all the seductions which I used to follow; and that I may love Thee entirely, and grasp Thy hand with my whole heart, and that Thou mayest deliver me from every temptation, even unto the end. For lo, O Lord, my King and my God, for Thy service be whatever useful thing I learnt as a boy—for Thy service what I speak, and write, and count. For when I learned vain things, Thou didst grant me Thy discipline; and my sin in taking delight in those vanities, Thou hast forgiven me. I learned, indeed, in them many useful words; but these may be learned in things not vain, and that is the safe way for youths to walk in.

CHAPTER XVI

HE DISAPPROVES OF THE MODE OF EDUCATING YOUTH, AND HE POINTS OUT WHY WICKEDNESS IS ATTRIBUTED TO THE GODS BY THE POETS

But woe unto thee, thou stream of human custom! Who shall stay thy course? How long shall it be before thou art dried up? How long wilt thou carry down the sons of Eve into that huge and formidable ocean, which even they who are embarked on the cross can scarce pass over? Do I not read in thee of Jove the thunderer and adulterer? And the two verily he could not be; but it was that, while the fictitious thunder served as a cloak, he might have warrant to imitate real adultery. Yet which of our gowned masters can lend a temperate ear to a man of his school who cries out and says: "These were Homer's fictions; he transfers things human to the gods. I could have wished him to transfer divine things to us." [36] But it would have been more true had he said: "These are, indeed, his fictions, but he attributed divine attributes to sinful men, that crimes might not be accounted crimes, and that whosoever committed any might appear to imitate the celestial gods and not abandoned men."

And yet, thou stream of hell, into thee are cast the sons of men, with rewards for learning these things; and much is made of it when this is going on in the forum in the sight of laws which grant a salary over and

[36] Cic. *Tusc.* i. 26

above the rewards. And thou beatest against thy rocks and roarest, saying, "Hence words are learnt; hence eloquence is to be attained, most necessary to persuade people to your way of thinking, and to unfold your opinions." So, in truth, we should never have understood these words, "golden shower," "bosom," "intrigue," "highest heavens," and other words written in the same place, unless Terence had introduced a good-for-nothing youth upon the stage, setting up Jove as his example of lewdness:—

> Viewing a picture, where the tale was drawn,
> Of Jove's descending in a golden shower
> To Danaë's bosom . . . with a woman to intrigue.

And see how he excites himself to lust, as if by celestial authority, when he says:—

> Great Jove,
> Who shakes the highest heavens with his thunder,
> And I, poor mortal man, not do the same!
> I did it, and with all my heart I did it.[37]

Not one whit more easily are the words learnt for this vileness, but by their means is the vileness perpetrated with more confidence. I do not blame the words, they being, as it were, choice and precious vessels, but the wine of error which was drunk in them to us by inebriated teachers; and unless we drank, we were beaten, without liberty of appeal to any sober judge. And yet, O my God—in whose presence I can now with security recall this—did I, unhappy one, learn these things willingly, and with delight, and for this was I called a boy of good promise.

CHAPTER XVII

HE CONTINUES ON THE UNHAPPY METHOD OF TRAINING YOUTH IN LITERARY SUBJECTS

Bear with me, my God, while I speak a little of those talents Thou hast bestowed upon me, and on what follies I wasted them. For a lesson sufficiently disquieting to my soul was given me, in hope of praise, and fear of shame or stripes, to speak the words of Juno, as she raged and sorrowed that she could not

> Latium bar
> From all approaches of the Dardan king,[38]

---

[37] Terence, *Eun.* 584 *ff.*   [38] Virgil, *Aen.* i. 38

which I had heard Juno never uttered. Yet were we compelled to stray in the footsteps of these poetic fictions, and to turn that into prose which the poet had said in verse. And his speaking was most applauded in whom, according to the reputation of the persons delineated, the passions of anger and sorrow were most strikingly reproduced, and clothed in the most suitable language. But what is it to me, O my true Life, my God, that my declaiming was applauded above that of many who were my contemporaries and fellow-students? Behold, is not all this smoke and wind? Was there nothing else, too, on which I could exercise my wit and tongue? Thy praise, Lord, Thy praises might have supported the tendrils of my heart by Thy Scriptures; so had it not been dragged away by these empty trifles, a shameful prey of the fowls of the air. For there is more than one way in which men sacrifice to the fallen angels.

CHAPTER XVIII

MEN DESIRE TO OBSERVE THE RULES OF LEARNING, BUT NEGLECT THE ETERNAL RULES OF EVERLASTING SAFETY

But what matter of surprise is it that I was thus carried towards vanity, and went forth from Thee, O my God, when men were proposed to me to imitate, who, should they in relating any acts of theirs—not in themselves evil—be guilty of a barbarism or solecism, when censured for it became confounded; but when they made a full and ornate oration, in well-chosen words, concerning their own licentiousness, and were applauded for it, they boasted? Thou seest this, O Lord, and keepest silence, long-suffering, and plenteous in mercy and truth,[39] as Thou art. Wilt Thou keep silence for ever? And even now Thou drawest out of this vast deep the soul that seeketh Thee and thirsteth after Thy delights, whose heart said unto Thee, I have sought Thy face, Thy face, Lord, will I seek.[40] For I was far from Thy face, through my darkened[41] affections. For it is not by our feet, nor by change of place, that we either turn from Thee or return to Thee. Or, indeed, did that younger son look out for horses, or chariots, or ships, or fly away with visible wings, or journey by the motion of his limbs, that he might, in a far country, prodigally waste all that Thou gavest him when he set out? A kind Father when Thou gavest, and kinder still when he returned destitute![42] So, then, in wanton, that is to say, in darkened affections, lies distance from Thy face.

Behold, O Lord God, and behold patiently, as Thou art wont to do, how diligently the sons of men observe the conventional rules of letters and syllables, received from those who spoke prior to them, and yet neglect the eternal rules of everlasting salvation received from Thee, insomuch that he who practices or teaches the hereditary rules of pronunciation, if,

[39] Ps. lxxxvi. 15   [40] Ps. xxvii. 8   [41] Rom. i. 21   [42] Luke xv. 11-32

contrary to grammatical usage, he should say, without aspirating the first letter a *uman* being, will offend men more than if, in opposition to Thy commandments, he, a human being, were to hate a human being. As if, indeed, any man should feel that an enemy could be more destructive to him than that hatred with which he is excited against him, or that he could destroy more utterly him whom he persecutes than he destroys his own soul by his enmity. And of a truth, there is no science of letters more innate than the writing of conscience—that he is doing unto another when he himself would not suffer. How mysterious art Thou, who in silence dwellest on high,[43] Thou God, the only great, who by an unwearied law dealest out the punishment of blindness to illicit desires! When a man seeking for the reputation of eloquence stands before a human judge while a thronging multitude surrounds him, inveighs against his enemy with the fiercest hatred, he takes most vigilant heed that his tongue slips not into grammatical error, but takes no heed lest through the fury of his spirit he cut off a man from his fellow-men.

These were the customs in the midst of which I, unhappy boy, was cast, and on that arena it was that I was more fearful of perpetrating a barbarism than, having done so, of envying those who had not. These things I declare and confess unto Thee, my God, for which I was applauded by them whom I then thought it my whole duty to please, for I did not perceive the gulf of infamy wherein I was cast away from Thine eyes.[44] For in Thine eyes what was more infamous than I was already, displeasing even those like myself, deceiving with innumerable lies both tutor, and masters, and parents, from love of play, a desire to see frivolous spectacles, and a stage-struck restlessness, to imitate them? Pilferings I committed from my parents' cellar and table, either enslaved by gluttony, or that I might have something to give to boys who sold me their play, who, though they sold it, liked it as well as I. In this play, likewise, I often sought dishonest victories, I myself being conquered by the vain desire of pre-eminence. And what could I so little endure, or, if I detected it, censured I so violently, as the very things I did to others, and, when myself detected I was censured, preferred rather to quarrel than to yield? Is this the innocence of childhood? Nay, Lord, nay, Lord; I entreat Thy mercy, O my God. For these same sins, as we grow older, are transferred from governors and masters, from nuts, and balls, and sparrows, to magistrates and kings, to gold, and lands, and slaves, just as the rod is succeeded by more severe chastisements. It was, then, the stature of childhood that Thou, O our King, didst approve of as an emblem of humility when Thou saidst, Of such is the kingdom of heaven.[45]

But yet, O Lord, to Thee, most excellent and most good, Thou Architect and Governor of the universe, thanks had been due unto Thee, our God,

[43] Isa. xxxiii. 5   [44] Ps. xxxi. 22   [45] Matt. xix. 14

even hadst Thou willed that I should not survive my boyhood. For I existed even then; I lived, and felt, and was solicitous about my own well-being— a trace of that most mysterious unity from whence I had my being; I kept watch by my inner sense over the wholeness of my senses, and in these insignificant pursuits, and also in my thoughts on things insignificant, I learnt to take pleasure in truth. I was averse to being deceived, I had a vigorous memory, was provided with the power of speech, was softened by friendship, shunned sorrow, meanness, ignorance. In such a being what was not wonderful and praiseworthy? But all these are gifts of my God; I did not give them to myself; and they are good, and all these constitute myself. Good, then, is He that made me, and He is my God; and before Him will I rejoice exceedingly for every good gift which, as a boy, I had. For in this lay my sin, that not in Him, but in His creatures—myself and the rest—I sought for pleasures, honors, and truths, falling thereby into sorrows, troubles, and errors. Thanks be to Thee, my joy, my pride, my confidence, my God—thanks be to Thee for Thy gifts; but preserve Thou them to me. For thus wilt Thou preserve me; and those things which Thou hast given me shall be developed and perfected, and I myself shall be with Thee, for from Thee is my being.

BOOK TWO

He advances to puberty, and indeed to the early part of the sixteenth year of his age, in which, having abandoned his studies, he indulged in lustful pleasures, and, with his companions, committed theft.

CHAPTER I

HE DEPLORES THE WICKEDNESS OF HIS YOUTH

I WILL now call to mind my past foulness, and the carnal corruptions of my soul, not because I love them, but that I may love Thee, O my God. For love of Thy love I do it, recalling, in the very bitterness of my remembrance, my most vicious ways, that Thou mayest grow sweet to me—Thou sweetness without deception! Thou sweetness happy and assured!—and re-collecting myself out of my dissipation, in which I was torn to pieces, while, turned away from Thee the One, I lost myself among many vanities. For I even longed in my youth formerly to be satisfied with worldly things, and I dared to grow wild again with various and shadowy loves; my form consumed away,[1] and I became corrupt in Thine eyes, pleasing myself, and eager to please in the eyes of men.

CHAPTER II

STRICKEN WITH EXCEEDING GRIEF, HE REMEMBERS THE DISSOLUTE PASSIONS IN WHICH, IN HIS SIXTEENTH YEAR, HE USED TO INDULGE

But what was it that I delighted in save to love and to be beloved? But I held it not in moderation, mind to mind, the bright path of friendship, but out of the dark concupiscence of the flesh and the effervescence of youth exhalations came forth which obscured and overcast my heart, so that I was unable to discern pure affection from unholy desire. Both boiled confusedly within me, and dragged away my unstable youth into the rough places of unchaste desires, and plunged me into a gulf of infamy. Thy anger had overshadowed me, and I knew it not. I became deaf by the rattling of the chains of my mortality, the punishment for my soul's pride; and I wandered farther from Thee, and Thou didst suffer[2] me; and I was tossed to and fro, and wasted, and poured out, and boiled over in my fornications, and Thou didst hold Thy peace, O Thou my tardy joy! Thou then didst hold Thy peace, and I wandered still farther from Thee, into more and

[1] Ps. xxxix. 11   [2] Matt. xvii. 17

20

more barren seed-plots of sorrows, with proud dejection and restless lassitude.

Oh for one to have regulated my disorder, and turned to my profit the fleeting beauties of the things around me, and fixed a bound to their sweetness, so that the tides of my youth might have spent themselves upon the conjugal shore, if so be they could not be tranquillized and satisfied within the object of a family, as Thy law appoints, O Lord—who thus formest the offspring of our death, being able also with a tender hand to blunt the thorns which were excluded from Thy paradise! For Thy omnipotency is not far from us even when we are far from Thee, else in truth ought I more vigilantly to have given heed to the voice from the clouds: "Nevertheless, such shall have trouble in the flesh, but I spare you;" [3] and, "It is good for a man not to touch a woman;" [4] and, "He that is unmarried careth for the things that belong to the Lord, how he may please the Lord; but he that is married careth for the things that are of the world, how he may please his wife." [5] I should, therefore, have listened more attentively to these words, and, being severed for the kingdom of heaven's sake,[6] I would with greater happiness have expected Thy embraces.

But I, poor fool, seethed as does the sea, and, forsaking Thee, followed the violent course of my own stream, and exceeded all Thy limitations; nor did I escape Thy scourges.[7] For what mortal can do so? But Thou wert always by me, mercifully angry, and dashing with the bitterest vexations all my illicit pleasures, in order that I might seek pleasures free from vexation. But where I could meet with such except in Thee, O Lord, I could not find—except in Thee, who teachest by sorrow,[8] and woundest us to heal us, and killest us that we may not die from Thee. Where was I, and how far was I exiled from the delights of Thy house, in that sixteenth year of the age of my flesh, when the madness of lust—to which human shamelessness granted full freedom, although forbidden by Thy laws—held complete sway over me, and I resigned myself entirely to it? Those about me meanwhile took no care to save me from ruin by marriage, their sole care being that I should learn to make a powerful speech, and become a persuasive orator.

CHAPTER III

CONCERNING HIS FATHER, A FREEMAN OF THAGASTE, THE ASSISTER OF HIS SON'S STUDIES, AND ON THE ADMONITIONS OF HIS MOTHER ON THE PRESERVATION OF CHASTITY

And for that year my studies were intermitted, while after my return from Madaura (a neighboring city, whither I had begun to go in order to learn grammar and rhetoric), the expenses for a further residence at Carthage

[3] I Cor. vii. 28   [4] I Cor. vii. I   [5] I Cor. vii. 32, 33   [6] Matt. xix. 12   [7] Isa. x. 26   [8] Deut. xxxii. 39

were provided for me; and that was rather by the determination than the means of my father, who was but a poor freeman of Thagaste. To whom do I narrate this? Not unto Thee, my God; but before Thee unto my own kind, even to that small part of the human race who may chance to light upon these my writings. And to what end? That I and all who read the same may reflect out of what depths we are to cry unto Thee.[9] For what cometh nearer to Thine ears than a confessing heart and a life of faith? For who did not extol and praise my father, in that he went even beyond his means to supply his son with all the necessaries for a far journey for the sake of his studies? For many far richer citizens did not the like for their children. But yet this same father did not trouble himself how I grew towards Thee, nor how chaste I was, so long as I was skilful in speaking— however barren I was to Thy tilling, O God, who art the sole true and good Lord of my heart, which is Thy field.

But while, in that sixteenth year of my age, I resided with my parents, having holiday from school for a time (this idleness being imposed upon me by my parents' necessitous circumstances), the thorns of lust grew rank over my head, and there was no hand to pluck them out. Moreover when my father, seeing me at the baths, perceived that I was becoming a man, and was stirred with a restless youthfulness, he, as if from this anticipating future descendants, joyfully told it to my mother; rejoicing in that intoxication wherein the world so often forgets Thee, its Creator, and falls in love with Thy creature instead of Thee, from the invisible wine of its own perversity turning and bowing down to the most infamous things. But in my mother's breast Thou hadst even now begun Thy temple, and the commencement of Thy holy habitation, whereas my father was only a catechumen as yet, and that but recently. She then started up with a pious fear and trembling; and, although I had not yet been baptized, she feared those crooked ways in which they walk who turn their back to Thee, and not their face.[10]

Woe is me! and dare I affirm that Thou heldest Thy peace, O my God, while I strayed farther from Thee? Didst Thou then hold Thy peace to me? And whose words were they but Thine which by my mother, Thy faithful handmaid, Thou pouredst into my ears, none of which sank into my heart to make me do it? For she desired, and I remember privately warned me, with great solicitude, not to commit fornication; but above all things never to defile another man's wife. These appeared to me but womanish counsels, which I should blush to obey. But they were Thine, and I knew it not, and I thought that Thou heldest Thy peace, and that it was she who spoke, through whom Thou heldest not Thy peace to me, and in her person wast despised by me, her son, the son of Thy handmaid, Thy servant.[11] But this I knew not; and rushed on headlong with such blindness, that amongst my equals I was ashamed to be less shameless,

[9] Ps. cxxx. 1   [10] Jer. ii. 27   [11] Ps. cxvi. 16

when I heard them pluming themselves upon their disgraceful acts, and glorying all the more in proportion to the greatness of their baseness; and I took pleasure in doing it, not for the pleasure's sake only, but for the praise. What is worthy of dispraise but vice? But I made myself out worse than I was, in order that I might not be dispraised; and when in anything I had not sinned as the abandoned ones, I would affirm that I had done what I had not, that I might not appear abject for being more innocent, or of less esteem for being more chaste.

Behold with what companions I walked the streets of Babylon, in whose filth I was rolled, as if in cinnamon and precious ointments. And that I might cleave the more tenaciously to its very centre, my invisible enemy trod me down, and seduced me, I being easily seduced. Nor did the mother of my flesh, although she herself had ere this fled out of the midst of Babylon[12]—progressing, however, but slowly in the skirts of it—in counselling me to chastity, so bear in mind what she had been told about me by her husband as to restrain in the limits of conjugal affection (if it could not be cut away to the quick) what she knew to be destructive in the present and dangerous in the future. But she took no heed of this, for she was afraid lest a wife should prove a hindrance and a clog to my hopes. Not those hopes of the future world, which my mother had in Thee; but the hope of learning, which both my parents were too anxious that I should acquire—he, because he had little or no thought of Thee, and but vain thoughts for me—she, because she calculated that those usual courses of learning would not only be no drawback, but rather a furtherance towards my attaining Thee. For thus I conjecture, recalling as well as I can the dispositions of my parents. The reins, meantime, were slackened towards me beyond the restraint of due severity, that I might play even to dissoluteness, in whatsoever I fancied. And in all there was a mist, shutting out from my sight the brightness of Thy truth, O my God; and my iniquity displayed itself as from very fatness.[13]

CHAPTER IV

HE COMMITS THEFT WITH HIS COMPANIONS, NOT URGED ON BY POVERTY, BUT FROM A CERTAIN DISTASTE OF WELL-DOING

Theft is punished by Thy law, O Lord, and by the law written in men's hearts, which iniquity itself cannot blot out. For what thief will suffer a thief? Even a rich thief will not suffer him who is driven to it by want. Yet had I a desire to commit robbery, and did so, compelled neither by hunger, nor poverty, but through a distaste for well-doing, and a lustiness of iniquity. For I pilfered that of which I had already sufficient, and much better. Nor did I desire to enjoy what I pilfered, but the theft and sin itself.

---

[12] Jer. li. 6   [13] Ps. lxxiii. 7

There was a pear-tree close to our vineyard, heavily laden with fruit, which was tempting neither for its color nor its flavor. To shake and rob this some of us wanton young fellows went, late one night (having, according to our disgraceful habit, prolonged our games in the streets until then), and carried away great loads, not to eat ourselves, but to fling to the very swine, having only eaten some of them; and to do this pleased us all the more because it was not permitted. Behold my heart, O my God; behold my heart, which Thou hadst pity upon when in the bottomless pit. Behold, now, let my heart tell Thee what it was seeking there, that I should be gratuitously wanton, having no inducement to evil but the evil itself. It was foul, and I loved it. I loved to perish. I loved my own error—not that for which I erred, but the error itself. Base soul, falling from Thy firmament to utter destruction—not seeking aught through the shame but the shame itself!

CHAPTER V

CONCERNING THE MOTIVES TO SIN, WHICH ARE NOT IN THE LOVE OF EVIL, BUT IN THE DESIRE OF OBTAINING THE PROPERTY OF OTHERS

There is a desirableness in all beautiful bodies, and in gold, and silver, and all things; and in bodily contact sympathy is powerful, and each other sense has its proper adaptation of body. Worldly honor has also its glory, and the power of command, and of overcoming; whence proceeds also the desire for revenge. And yet to acquire all these, we must not depart from Thee, O Lord, nor deviate from Thy law. The life which we live here has also its peculiar attractiveness, through a certain measure of comeliness of its own, and harmony with all things here below. The friendships of men also are endeared by a sweet bond, in the oneness of many souls. On account of all these, and such as these, is sin committed; while through an inordinate preference for these goods of a lower kind, the better and higher are neglected—even Thou, our Lord God, Thy truth, and Thy law. For these meaner things have their delights, but not like unto my God, who hath created all things; for in Him doth the righteous delight, and He is the sweetness of the upright in heart.[14]

When, therefore, we inquire why a crime was committed, we do not believe it, unless it appear that there might have been the wish to obtain some of those which we designated meaner things, or else a fear of losing them. For truly they are beautiful and comely, although in comparison with those higher and celestial goods they are abject and contemptible. A man murdered another; what was his motive? He desired his wife or his estate; or would steal to support himself; or he was afraid of losing something of the kind by him; or, being injured, he was burning to be revenged. Would he

[14] Ps. lxiv. 10

commit murder without a motive, taking delight simply in the act of murder? Who would credit it? For as for that savage and brutal man, of whom it is declared that he was gratuitously wicked and cruel, there is yet a motive assigned. "Lest through idleness," he says, "hand or heart should grow inactive." [15] And to what purpose? Why, even that, having once got possession of the city through that practice of wickedness, he might attain honors, empire, and wealth, and be exempt from the fear of the laws, and his difficult circumstances from the needs of his family, and the consciousness of his own wickedness. So it seems that even Catiline himself loved not his own villainies, but something else, which gave him the motive for committing them.

CHAPTER VI

WHY HE DELIGHTED IN THAT THEFT, WHEN ALL THINGS WHICH UNDER THE APPEARANCE OF GOOD INVITE TO VICE ARE TRUE AND PERFECT IN GOD ALONE

What was it, then, that I, miserable one, so doted on in thee, thou theft of mine, thou deed of darkness, in that sixteenth year of my age? Beautiful thou wert not, since thou wert theft. But art thou anything, that so I may argue the case with thee? Those pears that we stole were fair to the sight, because they were Thy creation, Thou fairest [16] of all, Creator of all, Thou good God—God, the highest good, and my true good. Those pears truly were pleasant to the sight; but it was not for them that my miserable soul lusted, for I had abundance of better, but those I plucked simply that I might steal. For, having plucked them, I threw them away, my sole gratification in them being my own sin, which I was pleased to enjoy. For if any of these pears entered my mouth, the sweetener of it was my sin in eating it. And now, O Lord my God, I ask what it was in that theft of mine that caused me such delight; and behold it has no beauty in it—not such, I mean, as exists in justice and wisdom; nor such as is in the mind, memory, senses, and animal life of man; nor yet such as is the glory and beauty of the stars in their courses; or the earth, or the sea, teeming with incipient life, to replace, as it is born, that which decays; nor, indeed, that false and shadowy beauty which pertains to deceptive vices.

For thus pride imitates high estate, whereas Thou alone art God, high above all. And what does ambition seek but honors and renown, whereas Thou alone art to be honored above all, and renowned for evermore? The cruelty of the powerful wishes to be feared; but who is to be feared but God only,[17] out of whose power what can be forced away or withdrawn—when, or where, or whither, or by whom? The enticements of the wanton would fain be deemed love; and yet is naught more enticing than Thy

---

[15] Sallust, *De Bello Catil.* c. 9   [16] Ps. xlv. 2   [17] Ps. lxxvi. 7

charity, nor is aught loved more healthfully than that, Thy truth, bright and beautiful above all. Curiosity affects a desire for knowledge, whereas it is Thou who supremely knowest all things. Ignorance and foolishness themselves are concealed under the names of ingenuousness and harmlessness, because nothing can be found more ingenuous than Thou; and what is more harmless, since it is a sinner's own works by which he is harmed? [18] And sloth seems to long for rest; but what sure rest is there besides the Lord? Luxury would fain be called plenty and abundance; but Thou art the fulness and unfailing plenteousness of unfading joys. Prodigality presents a shadow of liberality; but Thou art the most lavish giver of all good. Covetousness desires to possess much; and Thou art the Possessor of all things. Envy contends for excellence; but what so excellent as Thou? Anger seeks revenge; who avenges more justly than Thou? Fear starts at unwonted and sudden chances which threaten things beloved, and is wary for their security; but what can happen that is unwonted or sudden to Thee? or who can deprive Thee of what Thou lovest? or where is there unshaken security save with Thee? Grief languishes for things lost in which desire had delighted itself, even because it would have nothing taken from it, as nothing can be from Thee.

Thus the soul commits fornication when she turns away from Thee, and seeks without Thee what she cannot find pure and untainted until she returns to Thee. Thus all pervertedly imitate Thee who separate themselves far from Thee and raise themselves up against Thee. But even by thus imitating Thee they acknowledge Thee to be the Creator of all nature, and so that there is no place whither they can altogether retire from Thee.[19] What, then, was it that I loved in that theft? And wherein did I, even corruptedly and pervertedly, imitate my Lord? Did I wish, if only by artifice, to act contrary to Thy law, because by power I could not, so that, being a captive, I might imitate an imperfect liberty by doing with impunity things which I was not allowed to do, in obscured likeness of Thy omnipotence? Behold this servant of Thine, fleeing from his Lord, and following a shadow![20] O rottenness! O monstrosity of life and profundity of death! Could I like that which was unlawful only because it was unlawful?

CHAPTER VII

HE GIVES THANKS TO GOD FOR THE REMISSION OF HIS SINS, AND REMINDS
EVERY ONE THAT THE SUPREME GOD MAY HAVE PRESERVED US
FROM GREATER SINS

What shall I render unto the Lord,[21] that while my memory recalls these things my soul is not appalled at them? I will love Thee, O Lord, and thank Thee, and confess unto Thy name,[22] because Thou hast put away from me

[18] Ps. vii. 15   [19] Ps. cxxxix. 7, 8   [20] Jonah i. and iv   [21] Ps. cxvi. 12   [22] Rev. iii.

these so wicked and nefarious acts of mine. To Thy grace I attribute it, and to Thy mercy, that Thou hast melted away my sin as it were ice. To Thy grace also I attribute whatsoever of evil I have not committed; for what might I not have committed, loving as I did the sin for the sin's sake? All I confess to have been pardoned me, both those which I committed by my own perverseness, and those which, by Thy guidance, I committed not. Where is he who, reflecting upon his own infirmity, dares to ascribe his chastity and innocency to his own strength, so that he should love Thee the less, as if he had been in less need of Thy mercy, whereby Thou dost forgive the transgressions of those that turn to Thee? For whosoever, called by Thee, obeyed Thy voice, and shunned those things which he reads me recalling and confessing of myself, let him not despise me, who, being sick, was healed by that same Physician[23] by whose aid it was that he was not sick, or rather was less sick. And for this let him love Thee as much, even all the more, since by whom he sees me to have been restored from so great a feebleness of sin, by Him he sees himself from a like feebleness to have been preserved.

CHAPTER VIII

IN HIS THEFT HE LOVED THE COMPANY OF HIS FELLOW-SINNERS

What fruit had I then,[24] wretched one, in those things which, when I remember them, cause me shame—above all in that theft, which I loved only for the theft's sake? And as the theft itself was nothing, all the more wretched was I who loved it. Yet by myself alone I would not have done it—I recall what my heart was—alone I could not have done it. I loved, then, in it the companionship of my accomplices with whom I did it. I did not, therefore, love the theft alone—rather, it was that alone that I loved, for the companionship was nothing. What is the fact? Who is it that can teach me, but He who illuminateth mine heart and searcheth out the dark corners thereof? What is it that has come into my mind to inquire about, to discuss, and to reflect upon? For had I at that time loved the pears I stole, and wished to enjoy them, I might have done so alone, if I could have been satisfied with the mere commission of the theft by which my pleasure was secured; nor needed I have provoked that itching of my own passions, by the encouragement of accomplices. But as my enjoyment was not in those pears, it was in the crime itself, which the company of my fellow-sinners produced.

[23] Luke iv. 23   [24] Rom. vi. 21

CHAPTER IX

IT WAS A PLEASURE TO HIM ALSO TO LAUGH WHEN SERIOUSLY DECEIVING OTHERS

By what feelings, then, was I animated? For it was in truth too shameful; and woe was me who had it. But still what was it? Who can understand his errors? [25] We laughed, because our hearts were tickled at the thought of deceiving those who little imagined what we were doing, and would have vehemently disapproved of it. Yet, again, why did I so rejoice in this, that I did it not alone? Is it that no one readily laughs alone? No one does so readily; but yet sometimes, when men are alone by themselves, nobody being by, a fit of laughter overcomes them when anything very droll presents itself to their senses or mind. Yet alone I would not have done it— alone I could not at all have done it. Behold, my God, the lively recollection of my soul is laid bare before Thee—alone I had not committed that theft, wherein what I stole pleased me not, but rather the act of stealing; nor to have done it alone would I have liked so well, neither would I have done it. O Friendship too unfriendly! thou mysterious seducer of the soul, thou greediness to do mischief out of mirth and wantonness, thou craving for others' loss, without desire for my own profit or revenge; but when they say, "Let us go, let us do it," we are ashamed not to be shameless.

CHAPTER X

WITH GOD THERE IS TRUE REST AND LIFE UNCHANGING

Who can unravel that twisted and tangled knottiness? It is foul. I hate to reflect on it. I hate to look on it. But thee do I long for, O righteousness and innocency, fair and comely to all virtuous eyes, and of a satisfaction that never palls! With thee is perfect rest, and life unchanging. He who enters into thee enters into the joy of his Lord,[26] and shall have no fear, and shall do excellently in the most Excellent. I sank away from Thee, O my God, and I wandered too far from Thee, my stay, in my youth, and became to myself an unfruitful land.

[25] Ps. xix. 12   [26] Matt. xxv. 21

BOOK THREE

Of the seventeenth, eighteenth, and nineteenth years of his age, passed at Carthage, when, having completed his course of studies, he is caught in the snares of a licentious passion, and falls into the errors of the Manichaeans.

CHAPTER I

DELUDED BY AN INSANE LOVE, HE, THOUGH FOUL AND DISHONORABLE, DESIRES TO BE THOUGHT ELEGANT AND URBANE

To CARTHAGE I came, where a cauldron of unholy loves bubbled up all around me. I loved not as yet, yet I loved to love; and, with a hidden want, I abhorred myself that I wanted not. I searched about for something to love, in love with loving, and hating security, and a way not beset with snares. For within me I had a dearth of that inward food, Thyself, my God, though that dearth caused me no hunger; but I remained without all desire for incorruptible food, not because I was already filled thereby, but the more empty I was the more I loathed it. For this reason my soul was far from well, and, full of ulcers, it miserably cast itself forth, craving to be excited by contact with objects of sense. Yet, had these no soul, they would not surely inspire love. To love and to be loved was sweet to me, and all the more when I succeeded in enjoying the person I loved. I befouled, therefore, the spring of friendship with the filth of concupiscence, and I dimmed its lustre with the hell of lustfulness; and yet, foul and dishonorable as I was, I craved, through an excess of vanity, to be thought elegant and urbane. I fell precipitately, then, into the love in which I longed to be ensnared. My God, my mercy, with how much bitterness didst Thou, out of Thy infinite goodness, besprinkle for me that sweetness! For I was both beloved, and secretly arrived at the bond of enjoying; and was joyfully bound with troublesome ties, that I might be scourged with the burning iron rods of jealousy, suspicion, fear, anger, and strife.

CHAPTER II

IN PUBLIC SPECTACLES HE IS MOVED BY AN EMPTY COMPASSION. HE IS ATTACKED BY A TROUBLESOME SPIRITUAL DISEASE

Stage-plays also drew me away, full of representations of my miseries and of fuel to my fire. Why does man like to be made sad when viewing doleful and tragical scenes, which yet he himself would by no means suffer? And yet he wishes, as a spectator, to experience from them a sense of grief, and in this very grief his pleasure consists. What is this but wretched insanity? For a man is more affected with these actions, the less free he is from such affections. Howsoever, when he suffers in his own person, it is the custom to style it "misery;" but when he feels pity for others, then it is styled "mercy." But what kind of mercy is it that arises from fictitious and scenic passions? The hearer is not expected to relieve, but merely invited to grieve; and the more he grieves, the more he applauds the actor of these fictions. And if the misfortunes of the characters (whether of olden times or merely imaginary) be so represented as not to touch the feelings of the spectator, he goes away disgusted and censorious; but if his feelings be touched, he sits it out attentively, and sheds tears of joy.

Are sorrows, then, also loved? Surely all men desire to rejoice? Or, as man wishes to be miserable, is he, nevertheless, glad to be merciful, which, because it cannot exist without passion, for this cause alone are passions loved? This also is from that vein of friendship. But whither does it go? Whither does it flow? Wherefore runs it into that torrent of pitch, seething forth those huge tides of loathsome lusts into which it is changed and transformed, being of its own will cast away and corrupted from its celestial clearness? Shall, then, mercy be repudiated? By no means. Let us, therefore, love sorrows sometimes. But beware of uncleanness, O my soul, under the protection of my God, the God of our fathers, who is to be praised and exalted above all for ever, beware of uncleanness. For I have not now ceased to have compassion; but then in the theatres I sympathized with lovers when they sinfully enjoyed one another, although this was done fictitiously in the play. And when they lost one another, I grieved with them, as if pitying them, and yet had delight in both. But now-a-days I feel much more pity for him who delights in his wickedness, than for him who is counted as enduring hardships by failing to obtain some pernicious pleasure, and the loss of some miserable felicity. This, surely, is the truer mercy, but grief has no delight in it. For though he that condoles with the unhappy be approved for his office of charity, yet would he who had real compassion rather there were nothing for him to grieve about. For if goodwill be ill-willed (which it cannot), then can he who is truly and sincerely commiserating wish that there should be some unhappy ones, that he might commiserate them. Some grief may then be justified, none loved. For thus dost Thou, O Lord God, who lovest souls far more purely than do we, and art more incorruptibly compassionate, although Thou art wounded by no sorrow. And who is sufficient for these things? [1]

But I, wretched one, then loved to grieve, and sought out what to grieve at, as when, in another man's misery, though feigned and counterfeited, that delivery of the actor best pleased me, and attracted me the most powerfully, which moved me to tears. What marvel was it that an unhappy sheep,

[1] Cor. ii. 16

straying from Thy flock, and impatient of Thy care, I became infected with a foul disease? And hence came my love of griefs—not such as should probe me too deeply, for I loved not to suffer such things as I loved to look upon, but such as, when hearing their fictions, should lightly affect the surface; upon which, like as with empoisoned nails, following burning, swelling, putrefaction, and horrible corruption. Such was my life! But was it life, O my God?

CHAPTER III

NOT EVEN WHEN AT CHURCH DOES HE SUPPRESS HIS DESIRES. IN THE SCHOOL OF RHETORIC HE ABHORS THE ACTS OF THE SUBVERTERS

And Thy faithful mercy hovered over me afar. Upon what unseemly iniquities did I wear myself out, following a sacrilegious curiosity, that, having deserted Thee, it might drag me into the treacherous abyss, and to the beguiling obedience of devils, unto whom I immolated my wicked deeds, and in all which Thou didst scourge me! I dared, even while Thy solemn rites were being celebrated within the walls of Thy church, to desire, and to plan a business sufficient to procure me the fruits of death; for which Thou chastisedst me with grievous punishments, but nothing in comparison with my fault, O Thou my greatest mercy, my God, my refuge from those terrible hurts, among which I wandered with presumptuous neck, receding farther from Thee, loving my own ways, and not Thine—loving a vagrant liberty.

Those studies, also, which were accounted honorable, were directed towards the courts of law; to excel in which, the more crafty I was, the more I should be praised. Such is the blindness of men, that they even glory in their blindness. And now I was head in the School of Rhetoric, whereat I rejoiced proudly, and became inflated with arrogance, though more sedate, O Lord, as Thou knowest, and altogether removed from the subvertings of those "subverters" [a] (for this stupid and diabolical name was held to be the very brand of gallantry) amongst whom I lived, with an impudent shamefacedness that I was not even as they were. And with them I was, and at times I was delighted with their friendship whose acts I ever abhorred, that is, their "subverting," wherewith they insolently attacked the modesty of strangers, which they disturbed by uncalled for jeers, gratifying thereby their mischievous mirth. Nothing can more nearly resemble the actions of devils than these. By what name, therefore, could they be more truly called than "subverters"?—being themselves subverted first, and altogether perverted—being secretly mocked at and seduced by the deceiving spirits, in what they themselves delight to jeer at and deceive others.

[a] These appear to have been Carthaginian students.—Ed.

CHAPTER IV

IN THE NINETEENTH YEAR OF HIS AGE (HIS FATHER HAVING DIED TWO YEARS BEFORE) HE IS LED BY THE "HORTENSIUS" OF CICERO TO "PHILOSO-PHY," TO GOD, AND A BETTER MODE OF THINKING

Among such as these, at that unstable period of my life, I studied books of eloquence, wherein I was eager to be eminent from a damnable and inflated purpose, even a delight in human vanity. In the ordinary course of study, I lighted upon a certain book of Cicero, whose language, though not his heart, almost all admire. This book of his contains an exhortation to philosophy, and is called *Hortensius*. This book, in truth, changed my affections, and turned my prayers to Thyself, O Lord, and made me have other hopes and desires. Worthless suddenly became every vain hope to me; and, with an incredible warmth of heart, I yearned for an immortality of wisdom, and began now to arise[2] that I might return to Thee. Not, then, to improve my language—which I appeared to be purchasing with my mother's means, in my nineteenth year, my father having died two years before —not to improve my language did I have recourse to that book; nor did it persuade me by its style, but its matter.

How ardent was I then, my God, how ardent to fly from earthly things to Thee! Nor did I know how Thou wouldst deal with me. For with Thee is wisdom. In Greek the love of wisdom is called philosophy, with which that book inflamed me. There are some who seduce through philosophy, under a great, and alluring, and honorable name coloring and adorning their own errors. And almost all who in that and former times were such, are in that book censured and pointed out. There is also disclosed that most salutary admonition of Thy Spirit, by Thy good and pious servant: "Beware lest any man spoil you through philosophy and vain deceit, after the tradition of men, after the rudiments of the world, and not after Christ: for in Him dwelleth all the fulness of the Godhead bodily." [3] And since at that time (as Thou, O Light of my heart, knowest) the words of the apostle were unknown to me, I was delighted with that exhortation, in so far only as I was thereby stimulated, and enkindled, and inflamed to love, seek, obtain, hold, and embrace, not this or that sect, but wisdom itself, whatever it were; and this alone checked me thus ardent, that the name of Christ was not in it. For this name, according to Thy mercy, O Lord, this name of my Saviour Thy Son, had my tender heart piously drunk in, deeply treasured even with my mother's milk; and whatsoever was without that name, though never so erudite, polished, and truthful, took not complete hold of me.

[2] Luke xv. 18   [3] Col. ii. 8, 9

CHAPTER V

HE REJECTS THE SACRED SCRIPTURES AS TOO SIMPLE, AND AS NOT TO BE COMPARED WITH THE DIGNITY OF TULLY

I resolved, therefore, to direct my mind to the Holy Scriptures, that I might see what they were. And behold, I perceive something not comprehended by the proud, not disclosed to children, but lowly as you approach, sublime as you advance, and veiled in mysteries; and I was not of the number of those who could enter into it, or bend my neck to follow its steps. For not as when now I speak did I feel when I turned towards those Scriptures, but they appeared to me to be unworthy to be compared with the dignity of Tully; for my inflated pride shunned their style, nor could the sharpness of my wit pierce their inner meaning. Yet, truly, were they such as would develop in little ones; but I scorned to be a little one, and, swollen with pride, I looked upon myself as a great one.

CHAPTER VI

DECEIVED BY HIS OWN FAULT, HE FALLS INTO THE ERRORS OF THE MANICHAEANS, WHO GLORIED IN THE TRUE KNOWLEDGE OF GOD AND IN A THOROUGH EXAMINATION OF THINGS

Therefore I fell among men proudly raving, very carnal, and voluble, in whose mouths were the snares of the devil—the birdlime being composed of a mixture of the syllables of Thy name, and of our Lord Jesus Christ, and of the Paraclete, the Holy Ghost, the Comforter. These names departed not out of their mouths, but so far forth as the sound only and the clatter of the tongue, for the heart was empty of truth. Still they cried, "Truth, Truth," and spoke much about it to me, yet was it not in them;[4] but they spake falsely not of Thee only—who, verily, art the Truth—but also of these elements of this world, Thy creatures. And I, in truth, should have passed by philosophers, even when speaking truth concerning them, for love of Thee, my Father, supremely good, beauty of all things beautiful! O Truth, Truth! how inwardly even then did the marrow of my soul pant after Thee, when they frequently, and in a multiplicity of ways, and in numerous and huge books, sounded out Thy name to me, though it was but a voice![5] And these were the dishes in which to me, hungering for Thee, they, instead of Thee, served up the sun and moon, Thy beauteous works—but yet Thy works, not Thyself, nay, nor Thy first works. For before these

[4] 1 John ii. 4

[5] There was something peculiarly enthralling to an ardent mind like Augustine's in the Manichaean system. That system was kindred in many ways to modern Rationalism. Reason was exalted at the expense of faith. Nothing was received on mere authority, and the disciple's inner consciousness was the touchstone of truth.

corporeal works are Thy spiritual ones, celestial and shining though they be. But I hungered and thirsted not even after those first works of Thine, but after Thee Thyself, the Truth, with whom is no variableness, neither shadow of turning;[6] yet they still served up to me in those dishes glowing phantasies, than which better were it to love this very sun (which, at least, is true to our sight), than those illusions which deceive the mind through the eye. And yet, because I supposed them to be Thee, I fed upon them; not with avidity, for Thou didst not taste to my mouth as Thou art, for Thou wast not these empty fictions; neither was I nourished by them, but was rather exhausted. Food in our sleep appears like our food awake; yet the sleepers are not nourished by it, for they are asleep. But those things were not in any way like unto Thee as Thou hast now spoken unto me, in that those were corporeal phantasies, false bodies, than which these true bodies, whether celestial or terrestrial, which we perceive with our fleshly sight, are much more certain. These things the very beasts and birds perceive as well as we, and they are more certain than when we imagine them. And again, we do with more certainty imagine them, than by them conceive of other greater and infinite bodies which have no existence. With such empty husks was I then fed, and was not fed. But Thou, my Love, in looking for whom I fail [7] that I may be strong, art neither those bodies that we see, although in heaven, nor art Thou those which we see not there; for Thou hast created them, nor dost Thou reckon them amongst Thy greatest works. How far, then, art Thou from those phantasies of mine, phantasies of bodies which are not at all, than which the images of those bodies which are, are more certain, and still more certain the bodies themselves, which yet Thou are not; nay, nor yet the soul, which is the life of the bodies. Better, then, and more certain is the life of bodies than the bodies themselves. But Thou art the life of souls, the life of lives, having life in Thyself; and Thou changest not, O Life of my soul.

Where, then, wert Thou then to me, and how far from me? Far, indeed, was I wandering away from Thee, being even shut out from the very husks of the swine, whom with husks I fed.[8] For how much better, then, are the fables of the grammarians and poets than these snares! For verses, and poems, and Medea flying, are more profitable truly than these men's five elements, variously painted, to answer to the five caves of darkness, none of which exist, and which slay the believer. For verses and poems I can turn into true food, but the "Medea flying," though I sang, I maintained it not; though I heard it sung, I believed it not; but those things I did believe. Woe, woe, by what steps was I dragged down to the depths of hell! [9]— toiling and turmoiling through want of Truth, when I sought after Thee, my God—to Thee I confess it, who hadst mercy on me when I had not yet confessed—sought after Thee not according to the understanding of the mind, in which Thou desiredst that I should excel the beasts, but according

---

[6] Jas. i. 17　　[7] Ps. lxix. 3　　[8] Luke xv. 16　　[9] Prov. ix. 18

to the sense of the flesh! Thou wert more inward to me than my most inward part; and higher than my highest. I came upon that bold woman,[10] who is simple, and knoweth nothing,[11] the enigma of Solomon, sitting at the door of the house on a seat, and saying, "Stolen waters are sweet, and bread eaten in secret is pleasant." [12] This woman seduced me, because she found my soul beyond its portals, dwelling in the eye of my flesh, and thinking on such food as through it I had devoured.

CHAPTER VII

HE ATTACKS THE DOCTRINE OF THE MANICHAEANS CONCERNING EVIL, GOD, AND THE RIGHTEOUSNESS OF THE PATRIARCHS

For I was ignorant as to that which really is, and was, as it were, violently moved to give my support to foolish deceivers, when they asked me, "Whence is evil?"—and, "Is God limited by a bodily shape, and has He hairs and nails?"—and, "Are they to be esteemed righteous who had many wives at once, and did kill men, and sacrificed living creatures?" [13] At which things I, in my ignorance, was much disturbed, and, retreating from the truth, I appeared to myself to be going towards it; because as yet I knew not that evil was naught but a privation of good, until in the end it ceases altogether to be; which how should I see, the sight of whose eyes saw no further than bodies, and of my mind no further than a phantasm? And I knew not God to be a Spirit,[14] not one who hath parts extended in length and breadth, nor whose being was bulk; for every bulk is less in a part than in the whole, and, if it be infinite, it must be less in such part as is limited by a certain space than in its infinity; and cannot be wholly everywhere, as Spirit, as God is. And what that should be in us, by which we were like unto God, and might rightly in Scripture be said to be after the image of God,[15] I was entirely ignorant.

Nor had I knowledge of that true inner righteousness, which doth not judge according to custom, but out of the most perfect law of God Almighty, by which the manners of places and times were adapted to those places and times—being itself the while the same always and everywhere, not one thing in one place, and another in another; according to which Abraham, and Isaac, and Jacob, and Moses, and David, and all those commended by the mouth of God were righteous,[16] but were judged unrighteous by foolish men, judging out of man's judgment,[17] and gauging by the petty standard of their own manners the manners of the whole human race. Like as if in an armory, one knowing not what were adapted to the several members should put greaves on his head, or boot himself with a helmet, and then complain because they would not fit. Or as if, on some day when in

---

[10] *i.e.,* folly   [11] Prov. ix. 13   [12] Prov. ix. 14, 17   [13] 1 Kings xviii. 40   [14] John iv. 24   [15] Gen. i. 27   [16] Heb. xi. 8-40   [17] 1 Cor. iv. 3

the afternoon business was forbidden, one were to fume at not being allowed to sell as it was lawful to him in the forenoon. Or when in some house he sees a servant take something in his hand which the butler is not permitted to touch, or something done behind a stable which would be prohibited in the dining-room, and should be indignant that in one house, and one family, the same thing is not distributed everywhere to all. Such are they who cannot endure to hear something to have been lawful for righteous men in former times which is not so now; or that God, for certain temporal reasons, commanded them one thing, and these another, but both obeying the same righteousness; though they see, in one man, one day, and one house, different things to be fit for different members, and a thing which was formerly lawful after a time unlawful—that permitted or commanded in one corner, which done in another is justly prohibited and punished. Is justice, then, various and changeable? Nay, but the times over which she presides are not all alike, because they are times. But men, whose days upon the earth are few,[18] because by their own perception they cannot harmonize the causes of former ages and other nations, of which they had no experience, with these of which they have experience, though in one and the same body, day, or family, they can readily see what is suitable for each member, season, part, and person—to the one they take exception, to the other they submit.

These things I then knew not, nor observed. They met my eyes on every side, and I saw them not. I composed poems, in which it was not permitted me to place every foot everywhere, but in one metre one way, and in another another, nor even in any one verse the same foot in all places. Yet the art itself by which I composed had not different principles for these different cases, but comprised all in one. Still I saw not how that righteousness, which good and holy men submitted to, far more excellently and sublimely comprehended in one all those things which God commanded, and in no part varied, though in varying times it did not prescribe all things at once, but distributed and enjoined what was proper for each. And I, being blind, blamed those pious fathers, not only for making use of present things as God commanded and inspired them to do, but also for foreshowing things to come as God was revealing them.

CHAPTER VIII

HE ARGUES AGAINST THE SAME AS TO THE REASON OF OFFENCES

Can it at any time or place be an unrighteous thing for a man to love God with all his heart, with all his soul, and with all his mind, and his neighbor as himself?[19] Therefore those offences which are contrary to nature are everywhere and at all times to be held in detestation and punished; such

---

[18] Job xiv. 1   [19] Deut. vi. 5, and Matt. xxii. 37-39

were those of the Sodomites, which should all nations commit, they should all be held guilty of the same crime by the divine law, which has not so made men that they should in that way abuse one another. For even that fellowship which should be between God and us is violated, when that same nature of which He is author is polluted by the perversity of lust. But those offences which are contrary to the customs of men are to be avoided according to the customs severally prevailing; so that an agreement made, and confirmed by custom or law of any city or nation, may not be violated at the lawless pleasure of any, whether citizen or stranger. For any part which is not consistent with its whole is unseemly. But when God commands anything contrary to the customs or compacts of any nation to be done, though it were never done by them before, it is to be done; and if intermitted it is to be restored, and, if never established, to be established. For if it be lawful for a king, in the state over which he reigns, to command that which neither he himself nor any one before him had commanded, and to obey him cannot be held to be inimical to the public interest—nay, it were so if he were not obeyed (for obedience to princes is a general compact of human society)—how much more, then, ought we unhesitatingly to obey God, the Governor of all His creatures! For as among the authorities of human society the greater authority is obeyed before the lesser, so must God above all.

So also in deeds of violence, where there is a desire to harm, whether by contumely or injury; and both of these either by reason of revenge, as one enemy against another; or to obtain some advantage over another, as the highwayman to the traveller; or for the avoiding of some evil, as with him who is in fear of another; or through envy, as the unfortunate man to one who is happy; or as he that is prosperous in anything to him who he fears will become equal to himself, or whose equality he grieves at; or for the mere pleasure in another's pains, as the spectators of gladiators, or the deriders and mockers of others. These are the chief iniquities which spring forth from the lust of the flesh, of the eye, and of power, whether singly, or two together, or all at once. And so do men live in opposition to the three and seven, that psaltery of ten strings,[20] Thy ten commandments, O God most high and most sweet. But what foul offences can there be against Thee who canst not be defiled? Or what deeds of violence against Thee who canst not be harmed? But Thou avengest that which men perpetrate against themselves, seeing also that when they sin against Thee, they do wickedly against their own souls; and iniquity gives itself the lie, either by corrupting or perverting their nature, which Thou hast made and ordained, or by an immoderate use of things permitted, or in burning in things forbidden to that use which is against nature;[21] or when convicted, raging with heart and voice against Thee, kicking against the pricks;[22] or when, breaking through the pale of human society, they audaciously rejoice in private com-

[20] Ps. cxliv. 9   [21] Rom. i. 24-29   [22] Acts ix. 5

binations or divisions, according as they have been pleased or offended. And these things are done whenever Thou art forsaken, O Fountain of Life, who art the only and true Creator and Ruler of the universe, and by a self-willed pride any one false thing is selected therefrom and loved. So, then, by a humble piety we return to Thee; and Thou purgest us from our evil customs, and art merciful unto the sins of those who confess unto Thee, and dost hear the groaning of the prisoner,[23] and dost loosen us from those fetters which we have forged for ourselves, if we lift not up against Thee the horns of a false liberty—losing all through craving more, by loving more our own private good than Thee, the good of all.

CHAPTER IX

THAT THE JUDGEMENT OF GOD AND MEN, AS TO HUMAN ACTS OF VIOLENCE, IS DIFFERENT

But amidst these offences of infamy and violence, and so many iniquities, are the sins of men who are, on the whole, making progress; which, by those who judge rightly, and after the rule of perfection, are censured, yet commended withal, upon the hope of bearing fruit, like as in the green blade of the growing corn. And there are some which resemble offences of infamy or violence, and yet are not sins, because they neither offend Thee, our Lord God, nor social custom: when, for example, things suitable for the times are provided for the use of life, and we are uncertain whether it be out of a lust of having; or when acts are punished by constituted authority for the sake of correction, and we are uncertain whether it be out of a lust of hurting. Many a deed, then, which in the sight of men is disapproved, is approved by Thy testimony; and many a one who is praised by men is, Thou being witness, condemned; because frequently the view of the deed, and the mind of the doer, and the hidden exigency of the period, severally vary. But when Thou unexpectedly commandest an unusual and unthought-of thing—yea, even if Thou has formerly forbidden it, and still for the time keepest secret the reason of Thy command, and it even be contrary to the ordinance of some society of men, who doubts but it is to be done, inasmuch as that society is righteous which serves Thee? But blessed are they who know Thy commands! For all things were done by them who served Thee either to exhibit something necessary at the time, or to foreshow things to come.

[23] Ps. cii. 20

CHAPTER X

HE REPROVES THE TRIFLINGS OF THE MANICHAEANS
AS TO THE FRUITS OF THE EARTH

Of these things being ignorant, I derided those holy servants and prophets of Thine. And what did I gain by deriding them but to be derided by Thee, being insensibly, and little by little, led on to those follies, as to credit that a fig-tree wept when it was plucked, and that the mother-tree shed milky tears? Which fig notwithstanding, plucked not by his own but another's wickedness, had some "saint" [24] eaten and mingled with his entrails, he should breathe out of it angels; yea, in his prayers he shall assuredly groan and sigh forth particles of God, which particles of the most high and true God should have remained bound in that fig unless they had been set free by the teeth and belly of some "elect saint"! [25] And I, miserable one, believed that more mercy was to be shown to the fruits of the earth than unto men, for whom they were created; for if a hungry man—who was not a Manichaean—should beg for any, that morsel which should be given him would appear, as it were, condemned to capital punishment.

CHAPTER XI

HE REFERS TO THE TEARS, AND THE MEMORABLE DREAM CONCERNING
HER SON, GRANTED BY GOD TO HIS MOTHER

And Thou sendedst Thine hand from above,[26] and drewest my soul out of that profound darkness, when my mother, Thy faithful one, wept to Thee on my behalf more than mothers are wont to weep the bodily deaths of their children. For she saw that I was dead by that faith and spirit which she had from Thee, and Thou heardest her, O Lord. Thou heardest her, and despisedst not her tears, when, pouring down, they watered the earth under her eyes in every place where she prayed; yea, Thou heardest her. For whence was that dream with which Thou consoledst her, so that she permitted me to live with her, and to have my meals at the same table in the house, which she had begun to avoid, hating and detesting the blasphemies of my error? For she saw herself standing on a certain wooden rule, and a bright youth advancing towards her, joyous and smiling upon

[24] *i.e.*, Manichaean saint.

[25] According to this extraordinary system, it was the privilege of the "elect" to set free in eating such parts of the divine substance as were imprisoned in the vegetable creation. They did not marry or work in the fields, and led an ascetic life, the "hearers" or catechumens being privileged to provide them with food. The "elect" passed immediately on dying into the realm of light, while, as a reward for their service, the souls of the "hearers" after death transmigrated into plants (from which they might be most readily freed), or into the "elect," so as, in their turn, to pass away into the realm of light.   [26] Ps. cxliv. 7

her, whilst she was grieving and bowed down with sorrow. But he having inquired of her the cause of her sorrow and daily weeping (he wishing to teach, as is their wont, and not to be taught), and she answering that it was my perdition she was lamenting, he bade her rest contented, and told her to behold and see that where she was, there was I also. And when she looked she saw me standing near her on the same rule. Whence was this, unless that Thine ears were inclined towards her heart? O Thou Good Omnipotent, who so carest for every one of us as if Thou caredst for him only, and so for all as if they were but one!

Whence was this, also, that when she had narrated this vision to me, and I tried to put this construction on it, that she rather should not despair of being some day what I was, she immediately, without hesitation, replied, "No; for it was not told me that 'where he is, there shalt thou be,' but 'where thou art, there shall he be' "? I confess to Thee, O Lord, that, to the best of my remembrance (and I have oft spoken of this), Thy answer through my watchful mother—that she was not disquieted by the speciousness of my false interpretation, and saw in a moment what was to be seen, and which I myself had not in truth perceived before she spake—even then moved me more than the dream itself, by which the happiness to that pious woman, to be realized so long after, was, for the alleviation of her present anxiety, so long before predicted. For nearly nine years passed in which I wallowed in the slime of that deep pit and the darkness of falsehood, striving often to rise, but being all the more heavily dashed down. But yet that chaste, pious, and sober widow (such as Thou lovest), now more buoyed up with hope, though no whit less zealous in her weeping and mourning, desisted not, at all the hours of her supplications, to bewail my case unto Thee. And her prayers entered into Thy presence,[27] and yet Thou didst still suffer me to be involved and re-involved in that darkness.

CHAPTER XII

THE EXCELLENT ANSWER OF THE BISHOP WHEN REFERRED TO BY HIS MOTHER AS TO THE CONVERSION OF HER SON

And meanwhile Thou grantedst her another answer, which I recall; for much I pass over, hastening on to those things which the more strongly impel me to confess unto Thee, and much I do not remember. Thou didst grant her then another answer, by a priest of Thine, a certain bishop, reared in Thy Church and well versed in Thy books. He, when this woman had entreated that he would vouchsafe to have some talk with me, refute my errors, unteach me evil things, and teach me good (for this he was in the habit of doing when he found people fitted to receive it), refused, very prudently as I afterwards came to see. For he answered that I was still un-

27 Ps. lxxxviii. 1

teachable, being inflated with the novelty of that heresy, and that I had already perplexed divers inexperienced persons with vexatious questions, as she had informed him. "But leave him alone for a time," said he, "only pray God for him; he will of himself, by reading, discover what that error is, and how great its impiety." He disclosed to her at the same time how he himself, when a little one, had, by his misguided mother, been given over to the Manichaeans, and had not only read, but even written out almost all their books, and had come to see (without argument or proof from any one) how much that sect was to be shunned, and had shunned it. Which when he had said, and she would not be satisfied, but repeated more earnestly her entreaties, shedding copious tears, that he would see and discourse with me, he, a little vexed at her importunity, exclaimed, "Go thy way, and God bless thee, for it is not possible that the son of these tears should perish." Which answer (as she often mentioned in her conversations with me) she accepted as though it were a voice from heaven.

BOOK FOUR

Then follows a period of nine years from the nineteenth year of his age, during which having lost a friend, he followed the Manichaeans—and wrote books on the fair and fit, and published a work on the liberal arts, and the categories of Aristotle.

CHAPTER I

CONCERNING THAT MOST UNHAPPY TIME IN WHICH HE, BEING DECEIVED, DECEIVED OTHERS; AND CONCERNING THE MOCKERS OF HIS CONFESSION

DURING this space of nine years, then, from my nineteenth to my eight and twentieth year, we went on seduced and seducing, deceived and deceiving, in divers lusts; publicly, by sciences which they style "liberal"—secretly, with a falsity called religion. Here proud, there superstitious, everywhere vain! Here, striving after the emptiness of popular fame, even to theatrical applauses, and poetic contests, and strifes for grassy garlands, and the follies of shows and the intemperance of desire. There, seeking to be purged from these our corruptions by carrying food to those who were called "elect" and "holy," out of which, in the laboratory of their stomachs, they should make for us angels and gods, by whom we might be delivered. These things did I follow eagerly, and practise with my friends—by me and with me deceived. Let the arrogant, and such as have not been yet savingly cast down and stricken by Thee, O my God, laugh at me; but notwithstanding I would confess to Thee mine own shame in Thy praise. Bear with me, I beseech Thee, and give me grace to retrace in my present remembrance the circlings of my past errors, and to offer to Thee the sacrifice of thanksgiving.[1] For what am I to myself without Thee, but a guide to mine own downfall? Or what am I even at the best, but one sucking Thy milk,[2] and feeding upon Thee, the meat that perisheth not?[3] But what kind of man is any man, seeing that he is but a man? Let, then, the strong and the mighty laugh at us, but let us who are poor and needy[4] confess unto Thee.

CHAPTER II

HE TEACHES RHETORIC, THE ONLY THING HE LOVED, AND SCORNS THE SOOTHSAYER, WHO PROMISED HIM VICTORY

In those years I taught the art of rhetoric, and, overcome by cupidity, put to sale a loquacity by which to overcome. Yet I preferred—Lord, Thou

---

[1] Ps. cxvi. 17   [2] 1 Pet. ii. 2   [3] John vi. 27   [4] Ps. lxxiv. 21

knowest—to have honest scholars (as they are esteemed); and these I, without artifice, taught artifices, not to be put in practise against the life of the guiltless, though sometimes for the life of the guilty. And Thou, O God, from afar sawest me stumbling in that slippery path, and amid much smoke[5] sending out some flashes of fidelity, which I exhibited in my guidance of such as loved vanity and sought after leasing,[6] I being their companion. In those years I had one (whom I knew not in what is called lawful wedlock, but whom my wayward passion, void of understanding, had discovered), yet one only, remaining faithful even to her; in whom I found out truly by my own experience what difference there is between the restraints of the marriage bonds, contracted for the sake of issue, and the compact of a lustful love, where children are born against the parents' will, although, being born, they compel love.

I remember, too, that when I decided to compete for a theatrical prize, a soothsayer demanded of me what I would give him to win; but I, detesting and abominating such foul mysteries, answered, that if the garland were of imperishable gold, I would not suffer a fly to be destroyed to secure it for me. For he was to slay certain living creatures in his sacrifices, and by those honors to invite the devils to give me their support. But this ill thing I also refused, not out of a pure love for Thee, O God of my heart; for I knew not how to love Thee, knowing not how to conceive aught beyond corporeal brightness. And doth not a soul, sighing after such-like fictions, commit fornication against Thee, trust in false things, and nourish the wind?[7] But I would not, forsooth, have sacrifices offered to devils on my behalf, though I myself was offering sacrifices to them by that superstition. For what else is nourishing the wind but nourishing them, that is, by our wanderings to become their enjoyment and derision?

CHAPTER III

NOT EVEN THE MOST EXPERIENCED MEN COULD PERSUADE HIM OF THE VANITY OF ASTROLOGY, TO WHICH HE WAS DEVOTED

Those impostors, then, whom they designate Mathematicians, I consulted without hesitation, because they used no sacrifices, and invoked the aid of no spirit for their divinations, which art Christian and true piety fitly rejects and condemns. For good it is to confess unto Thee, and to say, "Be merciful unto me, heal my soul, for I have sinned against Thee;"[8] and not to abuse Thy goodness for a license to sin, but to remember the words of the Lord, "Behold, thou are made whole; sin no more, lest a worse thing come unto thee."[9] All of which salutary advice they endeavor to destroy when they say, "The cause of thy sin is inevitably determined in heaven;" and, "This did Venus, or Saturn, or Mars;" in order that man, forsooth,

[5] Isa. xlii. 3, and Matt. xii. 20   [6] Ps. iv. 2   [7] Hosea xii. 1   [8] Ps. xii. 4
[9] John v. 14

flesh and blood, and proud corruption, may be blameless, while the Creator and Ordainer of heaven and stars is to bear the blame. And who is this but Thee, our God, the sweetness and well-spring of righteousness, who renderest to every man according to his deeds,[10] and despisest not a broken and a contrite heart! [11]

There was in those days a wise man, very skilful in medicine, and much renowned therein, who had with his own proconsular hand put the Agonistic garland upon my distempered head, not, though, as a physician; for this disease Thou alone healest, who resistest the proud, and givest grace to the humble.[12] But didst Thou fail me even by that old man, or forbear from healing my soul? For when I had become more familiar with him, and hung assiduously and fixedly on his conversation (for though couched in simple language, it was replete with vivacity, life, and earnestness), when he had perceived from my discourse that I was given to books of the horoscope-casters, he, in a kind and fatherly manner, advised me to throw them away and not vainly bestow the care and labor necessary for useful things upon these vanities; saying that he himself in his earlier years had studied that art with a view to gaining his living by following it as a profession, and that, as he had understood Hippocrates, he would soon have understood this, and yet he had given it up, and followed medicine, for no other reason than that he discovered it to be utterly false, and he, being a man of character, would not gain his living by beguiling people. "But thou," said he, "who hast rhetoric to support thyself by, so that thou followest this of free will, not of necessity—all the more, then, oughtest thou to give me credit herein, who labored to attain it so perfectly, as I wished to gain my living by it alone." When I asked him to account for so many true things being foretold by it, he answered me (as he could) "that the force of chance, diffused throughout the whole order of nature, brought this about. For if when a man by accident opens the leaves of some poet, who sang and intended something far different, a verse oftentimes fell out wondrously apposite to the present business, it were not to be wondered at," he continued, "if out of the soul of man, by some higher instinct, not knowing what goes on within itself, an answer should be given by chance, not art, which should coincide with the business and actions of the questioner."

And thus truly, either by or through him, Thou didst look after me. And Thou didst delineate in my memory what I might afterwards search out for myself. But at that time neither he, nor my most dear Nebridius, a youth most good and most circumspect, who scoffed at that whole stock of divination, could persuade me to forsake it, the authority of the authors influencing me still more; and as yet I had lighted upon no certain proof—such as I sought—whereby it might without doubt appear that what had been truly foretold by those consulted was by accident or chance, not by the art of the star-gazers.

[10] Rom. ii. 6, and Matt. xvi. 27   [11] Ps. li. 17   [12] 1 Pet. v. 5, and Jas. iv. 6

CHAPTER IV

SORELY DISTRESSED BY WEEPING AT THE DEATH OF HIS FRIEND, HE
PROVIDES CONSOLATION FOR HIMSELF

In those years, when I first began to teach rhetoric in my native town, I had acquired a very dear friend, from association in our studies, of my own age, and, like myself, just rising up into the flower of youth. He had grown up with me from childhood, and we had been both school-fellows and play-fellows. But he was not then my friend, nor, indeed, afterwards, as true friendship is; for true it is not but in such as Thou bindest together, cleaving unto Thee by that love which is shed abroad in our hearts by the Holy Ghost, which is given unto us.[13] But yet it was sweet, being ripened by the fervor of similar studies. For, from the true faith (which he, as a youth, had not soundly and thoroughly become master of), I had turned him aside towards those superstitious and pernicious fables which my mother mourned in me. With me this man's mind now erred, nor could my soul exist without him. But behold, Thou wert close behind Thy fugitives—at once God of vengeance[14] and Fountain of mercies, who turnest us to Thyself by wondrous means. Thou removedst that man from this life when he had scarce completed one whole year of my friendship, sweet to me above all the sweetness of my life.

Who can show forth all Thy praise[15] which he hath experienced in himself alone? What was it that Thou didst then, O my God, and how unsearchable are the depths of Thy judgments! [16] For when, sore sick of a fever, he long lay unconscious in a death-sweat, and all despaired of his recovery, he was baptized without his knowledge; myself meanwhile little caring, presuming that his soul would retain rather what it had imbibed from me, than what was done to his unconscious body. Far different, however, was it, for he was revived and restored. Straightway, as soon as I could talk to him (which I could as soon as he was able, for I never left him, and we hung too much upon each other), I attempted to jest with him, as if he also would jest with me at that baptism which he had received when mind and senses were in abeyance, but had now learnt that he had received. But he shuddered at me, as if I were his enemy; and, with a remarkable and unexpected freedom, admonished me, if I desired to continue his friend, to desist from speaking to him in such a way. I, confounded and confused, concealed all my emotions, till he should get well, and his health be strong enough to allow me to deal with him as I wished. But he was withdrawn from my frenzy, that with Thee he might be preserved for my comfort. A few days after, during my absence, he had a return of the fever, and died.

At this sorrow my heart was utterly darkened, and whatever I looked upon was death. My native country was a torture to me, and my father's house a wondrous unhappiness; and whatsoever I had participated in with him, wanting him, turned into a frightful torture. My eyes sought him everywhere, but he was not granted them; and I hated all places because he was not in them; nor could they now say to me, "Behold, he is coming," as they did when he was alive and absent. I became a great puzzle to myself, and asked my soul why she was so sad, and why she so exceedingly disquieted me;[17] but she knew not what to answer me. And if I said, "Hope thou in God,"[18] she very properly obeyed me not; because that most dear friend whom she had lost was, being man, both truer and better than that phantasm she was bid to hope in. Naught but tears were sweet to me, and they succeeded my friend in the dearest of my affections.

CHAPTER V

WHY WEEPING IS PLEASANT TO THE WRETCHED

And now, O Lord, these things are passed away, and time hath healed my wound. May I learn from Thee, who art Truth, and apply the ear of my heart unto Thy mouth, that Thou mayest tell me why weeping should be so sweet to the unhappy. Hast Thou—although present everywhere—cast away far from Thee our misery? And Thou abidest in Thyself, but we are disquieted with divers trials; and yet, unless we wept in Thine ears, there would be no hope for us remaining. Whence, then, is it that such sweet fruit is plucked from the bitterness of life, from groans, tears, sighs, and lamentations? Is it the hope that Thou hearest us that sweetens it? This is true of prayer, for therein is a desire to approach unto Thee. But is it also in grief for a thing lost, and the sorrow with which I was then overwhelmed? For I had neither hope of his coming to life again, nor did I seek this with my tears; but I grieved and wept only, for I was miserable, and had lost my joy. Or is weeping a bitter thing, and for distaste of the things which aforetime we enjoyed before, and even then, when we are loathing them, does it cause us pleasure?

CHAPTER VI

HIS FRIEND BEING SNATCHED AWAY BY DEATH, HE IMAGINES THAT HE REMAINS ONLY AS HALF

But why do I speak of these things? For this is not the time to question, but rather to confess unto Thee. Miserable I was, and miserable is every soul fettered by the friendship of perishable things—he is torn to pieces when he loses them, and then is sensible of the misery which he had before ever he lost them. Thus was it at that time with me; I wept most bitterly,

---

[17] Ps. xlii. 5   [18] *Ibid.*

and found rest in bitterness. Thus was I miserable, and that life of misery I accounted dearer than my friend. For though I would willingly have changed it, yet I was even more unwilling to lose it than him; I knew not whether I was willing to lose it even for him, as is handed down to us (if not an invention) of Pylades and Orestes, that they would gladly have died one for another, or both together, it being worse than death to them not to live together. But there had sprung up in me some kind of feeling, too, contrary to this, for both exceedingly wearisome was it to me to live, and dreadful to die. I suppose, the more I loved him, so much the more did I hate and fear, as a most cruel enemy, that death which had robbed me of him; and I imagined it would suddenly annihilate all men, as it had power over him. Thus, I remember, it was with me. Behold my heart, O my God! Behold and look into me, for I remember it well, O my Hope! who cleansest me from the uncleanness of such affections, directing mine eyes towards Thee, and plucking my feet out of the net.[19] For I was astonished that other mortals lived, since he whom I loved, as if he would never die, was dead; and I wondered still more that I, who was to him a second self, could live when he was dead. Well did one say of his friend, "Thou half of my soul,"[20] for I felt that my soul and his soul were but one soul in two bodies;[21] and, consequently, my life was a horror to me, because I would not live in half. And therefore, perchance, was I afraid to die, lest he should die wholly whom I had so greatly loved.

CHAPTER VII

TROUBLED BY RESTLESSNESS AND GRIEF, HE LEAVES HIS COUNTRY A SECOND TIME FOR CARTHAGE

O madness, which knowest not how to love men as men should be loved! O foolish man that I then was, enduring with so much impatience the lot of man! So I fretted, sighed, wept, tormented myself, and took neither rest nor advice. For I bore about with me a rent and polluted soul, impatient of being borne by me, and where to repose it I found not. Not in pleasant groves, not in sport or song, not in fragrant spots, nor in magnificent banquetings, nor in the pleasures of the bed and the couch, nor, finally, in books and songs did it find repose. All things looked terrible, even the very light itself; and whatsoever was not what he was, was repulsive and hateful, except groans and tears, for in those alone I found a little repose. But when my soul was withdrawn from them, a heavy burden of misery weighed me down. To Thee, O Lord, should it have been raised, for Thee to lighten and avert it. This I knew, but was neither willing nor able; all the more since, in my thoughts of Thee, Thou wert not any solid or substantial thing to me. For Thou wert not Thyself, but an empty phantasm,

---

[19] Ps. xxv. 15   [20] Horace, *Carm.* i. ode 3   [21] Ovid, *Trist.* iv. eleg. iv. 72

and my error was my god. If I attempted to discharge my burden thereon, that it might find rest, it sank into emptiness, and came rushing down again upon me, and I remained to myself an unhappy spot, where I could neither stay nor depart from. For whither could my heart fly from my heart? Whither could I fly from my own self? Whither not follow myself? And yet fled I from my country; for so should my eyes look less for him where they were not accustomed to see him. And thus I left the town of Thagaste, and came to Carthage.

CHAPTER VIII

THAT HIS GRIEF CEASED BY TIME, AND THE CONSOLATION OF FRIENDS

Times lose no time, nor do they idly roll through our senses. They work strange operations on the mind. Behold, they came and went from day to day, and by coming and going they disseminated in my mind other ideas and other remembrances, and by little and little patched me up again with the former kind of delights, to which that sorrow of mine yielded. But yet there succeeded, not certainly other sorrows, yet the causes of other sorrows. For whence had that former sorrow so easily penetrated to the quick, but that I had poured out my soul upon the dust, in loving one who must die as if he were never to die? But what revived and refreshed me especially was the consolations of other friends, with whom I did love what instead of Thee I loved. And this was a monstrous fable and protracted lie, by whose adulterous contact our soul, which lay itching in our ears, was being polluted. But that fable would not die to me so oft as any of my friends died. There were other things in them which did more lay hold of my mind— to discourse and jest with them; to indulge in an interchange of kindnesses; to read together pleasant books; together to trifle, and together to be earnest; to differ at times without ill-humor, as a man would do with his own self; and even by the infrequency of these differences to give zest to our more frequent consentings; sometimes teaching, sometimes being taught; longing for the absent with impatience, and welcoming the coming with joy. These and similar expressions, emanating from the hearts of those who loved and were beloved in return, by the countenance, the tongue, the eyes, and a thousand pleasing movements, were so much fuel to melt our souls together, and out of many to make but one.

CHAPTER IX

THAT THE LOVE OF A HUMAN BEING, HOWEVER CONSTANT IN LOV-
ING AND RETURNING LOVE, PERISHES; WHILE HE WHO LOVES GOD
NEVER LOSES A FRIEND

This is it that is loved in friends; and so loved that a man's conscience accuses itself if he love not him by whom he is beloved, or love not again him that loves him, expecting nothing from him but indications of his love. Hence that mourning if one die, and gloom of sorrow, that steeping of the heart in tears, all sweetness turned into bitterness, and upon the loss of the life of the dying, the death of the living. Blessed be he who loveth Thee, and his friend in Thee, and his enemy for Thy sake. For he alone loses none dear to him to whom all are dear in Him who cannot be lost. And who is this but our God, the God that created heaven and earth,[22] and filleth them,[23] because by filling them He created them? None loseth Thee but he who leaveth Thee. And he who leaveth Thee, whither goeth he, or whither fleeth he, but from Thee well pleased to Thee angry? For where doth not he find Thy law in his own punishment? And Thy law is the truth,[24] and truth Thou.[25]

CHAPTER X

THAT ALL THINGS EXIST THAT THEY MAY PERISH, AND THAT WE
ARE NOT SAFE UNLESS GOD WATCHES OVER US

Turn us again, O Lord God of Hosts, cause Thy face to shine; and we shall be saved.[26] For whithersoever the soul of man turns itself, unless towards Thee, it is affixed to sorrows, yea, though it is affixed to beauteous things without Thee and without itself. And yet they were not unless they were from Thee. They rise and set; and by rising, they begin as it were to be; and they grow, that they may become perfect; and when perfect, they wax old and perish; and all wax not old, but all perish. Therefore when they rise and tend to be, the more rapidly they grow that they may be, so much the more they hasten not to be. This is the way of them. Thus much hast Thou given them, because they are parts of things, which exist not all at the same time, but by departing and succeeding they together make up the universe, of which they are parts. And even thus is our speech accomplished by signs emitting a sound; but this, again, is not perfected unless one word pass away when it has sounded its part, in order that another may succeed it. Let my soul praise Thee out of all these things, O God, the Creator of all; but let not my soul be affixed to these things by the glue of love,

[22] Gen. i. 1   [23] Jer. xxiii. 24   [24] Ps. cxix. 142, and John xvii. 17   [25] John xiv. 6
[26] Ps. lxxx. 19

through the senses of the body. For they go whither they were to go, that they might no longer be; and they rend her with pestilent desires, because she longs to be, and yet loves to rest in what she loves. But in these things no place is to be found; they stay not—they flee; and who is he that is able to follow them with the senses of the flesh? Or who can grasp them, even when they are near? For tardy is the sense of the flesh, because it is the sense of the flesh, and its boundary is itself. It suffices for that for which it was made, but it is not sufficient to stay things running their course from their appointed starting-place to the end appointed. For in Thy word, by which they were created, they hear the fiat, Hence and hitherto.

CHAPTER XI

THAT PORTIONS OF THE WORLD ARE NOT TO BE LOVED; BUT THAT GOD, THEIR AUTHOR, IS IMMUTABLE, AND HIS WORD ETERNAL

Be not foolish, O my soul, and deaden not the ear of thine heart with the tumult of thy folly. Hearken thou also. The word itself invokes thee to return; and there is the place of rest imperturbable, where love is not abandoned if itself abandoneth not. Behold, these things pass away, that others may succeed them, and so this lower universe be made complete in all its parts. But do I depart anywhere, saith the word of God? There fix thy habitation. There commit whatsoever thou hast thence, O my soul; at all events now thou art tired out with deceits. Commit to truth whatsoever thou hast from the truth, and nothing shalt thou lose; and thy decay shall flourish again, and all thy diseases be healed,[27] and thy perishable parts shall be re-formed and renovated, and drawn together to thee; nor shall they put thee down where themselves descend, but they shall abide with thee, and continue for ever before God, who abideth and continueth for ever.[28]

Why, then, be perverse and follow thy flesh? Rather let it be converted and follow thee. Whatever by her thou feelest, is but in part; and the whole, of which these are portions, thou art ignorant of, and yet they delight thee. But had the sense of thy flesh been capable of comprehending the whole, and not itself also, for thy punishment, been justly limited to a portion of the whole, thou wouldest that whatsoever existeth at the present time should pass away, that so the whole might please thee more. For what we speak, also by the same sense of the flesh thou hearest; and yet wouldest not thou that the syllables should stay, but fly away, that others may come, and the whole be heard. Thus it is always, when any single thing is composed of many, all of which exist not together, all together would delight more than they do simply, could all be perceived at once. But far better than these is He who made all; and He is our God, and He passeth not

---

[27] Ps. ciii. 3   [28] 1 Pet. i. 23

away, for there is nothing to succeed Him. If bodies please thee, praise God for them, and turn back thy love upon their Creator, lest in those things which please thee thou displease.

CHAPTER XII

LOVE IS NOT CONDEMNED, BUT LOVE IN GOD, IN WHOM THERE IS REST THROUGH JESUS CHRIST, IS TO BE PREFERRED

If souls please thee, let them be loved in God; for they also are mutable, but in Him are they firmly established, else would they pass, and pass away. In Him, then, let them be beloved; and draw unto Him along with thee as many souls as thou canst, and say to them, "Him let us love; He created these, nor is He far off. For He did not create them, and then depart; but they are of Him, and in Him. Behold, there is He wherever truth is known. He is within the very heart, but yet hath the heart wandered from Him. Return to your heart, O ye transgressors,[29] and cleave fast unto Him that made you. Stand with Him, and you shall stand fast. Rest in Him, and you shall be at rest. Whither go ye in rugged paths? Whither go ye? The good that you love is from Him; and as it has respect unto Him it is both good and pleasant, and justly shall it be embittered, because whatsoever cometh from Him is unjustly loved if He be forsaken for it. Why, then, will ye wander farther and farther in these difficult and toilsome ways? There is no rest where ye seek it. Seek what ye seek; but it is not there where ye seek. Ye seek a blessed life in the land of death; it is not there. For could a blessed life be where life itself is not?

"But our very Life descended hither, and bore our death, and slew it, out of the abundance of His own life; and thundering He called loudly to us to return hence to Him into that secret place whence He came forth to us—first into the Virgin's womb, where the human creature was married to Him—our mortal flesh, that it might not be for ever mortal—and thence as a bridegroom coming out of his chamber, rejoicing as a strong man to run a race.[30] For He tarried not, but ran crying out by words, deeds, death, life, descent, ascension, crying aloud to us to return to Him. And He departed from our sight, that we might return to our heart, and there find Him. For He departed, and behold, He is here. He would not be long with us, yet left us not; for He departed thither, whence He never departed, because the world was made by Him.[31] And in this world He was, and into this world He came to save sinners,[32] unto whom my soul doth confess, that He may heal it, for it hath sinned against Him.[33] O ye sons of men, how long so slow of heart?[34] Even now, after the Life is descended to you, will ye not ascend and live? But whither ascend ye, when ye are on high, and

[29] Isa. lvi. 8   [30] Ps. xix. 5   [31] John i. 10   [32] 1 Tim. i. 15   [33] Ps. xli. 4
[34] Luke xxiv. 25

set your mouth against the heavens? Descend that ye may ascend, and ascend to God. For ye have fallen by ascending against Him." Tell them this, that they may weep in the valley of tears,[35] and so draw them with thee to God, because it is by His Spirit that thou speakest thus unto them, if thou speakest burning with the fire of love.

CHAPTER XIII

LOVE ORIGINATES FROM GRACE AND BEAUTY ENTICING US

These things I knew not at that time, and I loved these lower beauties, and I was sinking to the very depths; and I said to my friends, "Do we love anything but the beautiful? What, then, is the beautiful? And what is beauty? What is it that allures and unites us to the things we love; for unless there were a grace and beauty in them, they could by no means attract us to them?" And I marked and perceived that in bodies themselves there was a beauty from their forming a kind of whole, and another from mutual fitness, as one part of the body with its whole, or a shoe with a foot, and so on. And this consideration sprang up in my mind out of the recesses of my heart, and I wrote books (two or three, I think) "on the fair and fit." Thou knowest, O Lord, for it has escaped me; for I have them not, but they have strayed from me, I know not how.

CHAPTER XIV

CONCERNING THE BOOKS WHICH HE WROTE "ON THE FAIR AND FIT," DEDICATED TO HIERIUS

But what was it that prompted me, O Lord my God, to dedicate these books to Hierius, an orator of Rome, whom I knew not by sight, but loved the man for the fame of his learning, for which he was renowned, and some words of his which I had heard, and which had pleased me? But the more did he please me in that he pleased others, who highly extolled him, astonished that a native of Syria, instructed first in Greek eloquence, should afterwards become a wonderful Latin orator, and one so well versed in studies pertaining to wisdom. Thus a man is commended and loved when absent. Does this love enter into the heart of the hearer from the mouth of the commender? Not so. But through one who loves is another inflamed. For hence he is loved who is commended when the commender is believed to praise him with an unfeigned heart; that is, when he that loves him praises him.

Thus, then, I loved men upon the judgment of men, not upon Thine, O my God, in which no man is deceived. But yet why not as the renowned charioteer, as the huntsman, known far and wide by a vulgar popularity—

[35] Ps. lxxxiv. 6

but far otherwise, and seriously, and so as I would desire to be myself commended? For I would not that they should commend and love me as actors are—although I myself did commend and love them—but I would prefer being unknown than so known, and even being hated than so loved. Where now are these influences of such various and divers kinds of loves distributed in one soul? What is it that I am in love with in another, which, if I did not hate, I should not detest and repel from myself, seeing we are equally men? For it does not follow that because a good horse is loved by him who would not, though he might, be that horse, the same should therefore be affirmed by an actor, who partakes of our nature. Do I then love in a man that which I, who am a man, hate to be? Man himself is a great deep, whose very hairs Thou numberest, O Lord, and they fall not to the ground without Thee.[36] And yet are the hairs of his head more readily numbered than are his affections and the movements of his heart.

But that orator was of the kind that I so loved as I wished myself to be such a one; and I erred through an inflated pride, and was carried about with every wind,[37] but yet was piloted by Thee, though very secretly. And whence know I, and whence confidently confess I unto Thee that I loved him more because of the love of those who praised him, than for the very things for which they praised him? Because had he been upraised, and these self-same men had dispraised him, and with dispraise and scorn told the same things of him, I should never have been so inflamed and provoked to love him. And yet the things had not been different, nor he himself different, but only the affections of the narrators. See where lies the impotent soul that is not yet sustained by the solidity of truth! Just as the blasts of tongues blow from the breasts of conjecturers, so is it tossed this way and that, driven forward and backward, and the light is obscured to it and the truth not perceived. And behold it is before us. And to me it was a great matter that my style and studies should be known to that man; if he approved them, I were the more stimulated, but if he disapproved, this vain heart of mine, void of Thy solidity, had been offended. And yet that "fair and fit," about which I wrote to him, I reflected on with pleasure, and contemplated it, and admired it, though none joined me in doing so.

CHAPTER XV

WHILE WRITING, BEING BLINDED BY CORPOREAL IMAGES, HE FAILED TO RECOGNIZE THE SPIRITUAL NATURE OF GOD

But not yet did I perceive the hinge on which this impotent matter turned in Thy wisdom, O Thou Omnipotent, who alone does great wonders;[38] and my mind ranged through corporeal forms, and I defined and distinguished as "fair," that which is so in itself, and "fit," that which is beautiful as it

---

[36] Matt. x. 29, 30   [37] Eph. iv. 14   [38] Ps. cxxxvi. 4

corresponds to some other thing; and this I supported by corporeal examples. And I turned my attention to the nature of the mind, but the false opinions which I entertained of spiritual things prevented me from seeing the truth. Yet the very power of truth forced itself on my gaze, and I turned away my throbbing soul from incorporeal substance, to lineaments, and colors, and bulky magnitudes. And not being able to perceive these in the mind, I thought I could not perceive my mind. And whereas in virtue I loved peace, and in viciousness I hated discord, in the former I distinguished unity, but in the latter a kind of division. And in that unity I conceived the rational soul and the nature of truth and of the chief good to consist. But in this division I, unfortunate one, imagined there was I know not what substance of irrational life, and the nature of the chief evil, which should not be a substance only, but real life also, and yet not emanating from Thee, O my God, from whom are all things. And yet the first I called a Monad, as if it had been a soul without sex, but the other a Duad—anger in deeds of violence, in deeds of passion, lust—not knowing of what I talked. For I had not known or learned that neither was evil a substance, nor our soul that chief and unchangeable good.

For even as it is in the case of deeds of violence, if that emotion of the soul from whence the stimulus comes be depraved, and carry itself insolently and mutinously; and in acts of passion, if that affection of the soul whereby carnal pleasures are imbibed is unrestrained—so do errors and false opinions contaminate the life, if the reasonable soul itself be depraved, as it was at that time in me, who was ignorant that it must be enlightened by another light that it may be partaker of truth, seeing that itself is not that nature of truth. For Thou wilt light my candle; the Lord my God will enlighten my darkness;[39] and of His fulness have all we received,[40] for that was the true Light which lighted every man that cometh into the world;[41] for in Thee there is no variableness, neither shadow of turning.[42]

But I pressed towards Thee, and was repelled by Thee that I might taste of death, for Thou resistest the proud.[43] But what prouder than for me, with a marvellous madness, to assert myself to be that by nature which Thou art? For whereas I was mutable—so much being clear to me, for my very longing to become wise arose from the wish from worse to become better— yet chose I rather to think Thee mutable, than myself not to be that which Thou art. Therefore was I repelled by Thee, and Thou resistedst my changeable stiffneckedness; and I imagined corporeal forms, and, being flesh, I accused flesh, and, being a wind that passeth away,[44] I returned not

[39] Ps. xviii. 28. Augustine constantly urges our recognition of the truth that God is the "Father of lights." From Him as our central sun, all light, whether of wisdom or knowledge, proceedeth, and if, changing the figure, our candle which He hath lighted be blown out, He again must light it. Compare *Enar. in Ps.* xciii. 147; and *Sermons*, 67 and 341. [40] John i. 16 [41] John i. 9 [42] Jas. i. 17 [43] Jas. iv. 6, and 1 Pet. v. 5 [44] Ps. lxxviii. 39

to Thee, but went wandering and wandering on towards those things that have no being, neither in Thee, nor in me, nor in the body. Neither were they created for me by Thy truth, but conceived by my vain conceit out of corporeal things. And I used to ask Thy faithful little ones, my fellow-citizens—from whom I unconsciously stood exiled—I used flippantly and foolishly to ask, "Why, then, does the soul which God created err?" But I would not permit any one to ask me, "Why, then, does God err?" And I contended that Thy immutable substance erred of constraint, rather than admit that my mutable substance had gone astray of free will, and erred as a punishment.

I was about six or seven and twenty years of age when I wrote those volumes—meditating upon corporeal fictions, which clamored in the ears of my heart. These I directed, O sweet Truth, to Thy inward melody, pondering on the "fair and fit," and longing to stay and listen to Thee, and to rejoice greatly at the Bridegroom's voice,[45] and I could not; for by the voices of my own errors was I driven forth, and by the weight of my own pride was I sinking into the lowest pit. For Thou didst not make me to hear joy and gladness; nor did the bones which were not yet humbled rejoice.

CHAPTER XVI

HE VERY EASILY UNDERSTOOD THE LIBERAL ARTS AND THE CATEGORIES OF ARISTOTLE, BUT WITHOUT TRUE FRUIT

And what did it profit me that, when scarce twenty years old, a book of Aristotle's, entitled *The Ten Categories*,[b] fell into my hands—on whose very name I hung as on something great and divine, when my rhetoric master of Carthage, and others who were esteemed learned, referred to it with cheeks swelling with pride—I read it alone and understood it? And on my conferring with others, who said that with the assistance of very able masters—who not only explained it orally, but drew many things in the dust—they scarcely understood it, and could tell me no more about it than I had acquired in reading it by myself alone? And the book appeared to me to speak plainly enough of substances, such as man is, and of their qualities—such as the figure of a man, of what kind it is; and his stature, how many feet high; and his relationship, whose brother he is; or where placed, or when born; or whether he stands or sits, or is shod or armed, or does or suffers anything; and whatever innumerable things might be classed under these nine categories—of which I have given some examples—or under the chief category of substance.

What did all this profit me, seeing it even hindered me, when, imagining

---

[45] John iii. 29
[b] Aristotle's categories are: substance, quantity, quality, relation, place, time, position, possession, activity, and passivity.—Ed.

that whatsoever existed was comprehended in those ten categories, I tried so to understand, O my God, Thy wonderful and unchangeable unity as if Thou also hadst been subjected to Thine own greatness or beauty, so that they should exist in Thee as their subject, like as in bodies, whereas Thou Thyself art Thy greatness and beauty? But a body is not great or fair because it is a body, seeing that, though it were less great or fair, it should nevertheless be a body. But that which I had conceived of Thee was falsehood, not truth—fictions of my misery, not the supports of Thy blessedness. For Thou hadst commanded, and it was done in me, that the earth should bring forth briars and thorns to me,[46] and that with labor I should get my bread.[47]

And what did it profit me that I, the base slave of vile affections, read unaided, and understood, all the books that I could get of the so-called liberal arts? And I took delight in them, but knew not whence came whatever in them was true and certain. For my back then was to the light, and my face towards the things enlightened; whence my face, with which I discerned the things enlightened, was not itself enlightened. Whatever was written either on rhetoric or logic, geometry, music, or arithmetic, did I, without any great difficulty, and without the teaching of any man, understand, as Thou knowest, O Lord my God, because both quickness of comprehension and acuteness of perception are Thy gifts. Yet did I not thereupon sacrifice to Thee. So, then, it served not to my use, but rather to my destruction, since I went about to get so good a portion of my substance[48] into my own power; and I kept not my strength for Thee, but went away from Thee into a far country, to waste it upon harlotries.[49] For what did good abilities profit me, if I did not employ them to good uses? For I did not perceive that those arts were acquired with great difficulty, even by the studious and those gifted with genius, until I endeavored to explain them to such; and he was the most proficient in them who followed my explanations not too slowly.

But what did this profit me, supposing that Thou, O Lord God, the Truth, wert a bright and vast body, and I a piece of that body? Perverseness too great! But such was I. Nor do I blush, O my God, to confess to Thee Thy mercies towards me, and to call upon Thee—I, who blushed not then to avow before men my blasphemies, and to bark against Thee. What profited me then my nimble wit in those sciences and all those knotty volumes, disentangled by me without help from a human master, seeing that I erred so odiously, and with such sacrilegious baseness, in the doctrine of piety? Or what impediment was it to Thy little ones to have a far slower wit, seeing that they departed not far from Thee, that in the nest of Thy Church they might safely become fledged, and nourish the wings of charity by the food of a sound faith? O Lord our God, under the shadow of Thy

---

[46] Isa. xxxii. 13   [47] Gen. iii. 19   [48] Luke xv. 12   [49] Luke xv. 13

wings let us hope,[50] defend us, and carry us. Thou wilt carry us both when little, and even to grey hairs wilt Thou carry us;[51] for our firmness, when it is Thou, then is it firmness; but when it is our own, then it is infirmity. Our good lives always with Thee, from which when we are averted we are perverted. Let us now, O Lord, return, that we be not overturned, because with Thee our good lives without any eclipse—which good Thou Thyself art. And we need not fear lest we should find no place unto which to return because we fell away from it; for when we were absent, our home —Thy Eternity—fell not.

[50] Ps. xxxvi. 7   [51] Isa. xlvi. 4

BOOK FIVE

He describes the twenty-ninth year of his age, in which, having discovered the fallacies of the Manichaeans, he professed rhetoric at Rome and Milan. Having heard Ambrose, he begins to come to himself.

CHAPTER I

THAT IT BECOMES THE SOUL TO PRAISE GOD, AND TO CONFESS UNTO HIM

ACCEPT the sacrifice of my confessions by the agency of my tongue, which Thou hast formed and quickened, that it may confess to Thy name; and heal Thou all my bones, and let them say, "Lord, who is like unto Thee?"[1] For neither does he who confesses to Thee teach Thee what may be passing within him, because a closed heart does not exclude Thine eye, nor does man's hardness of heart repulse Thine hand, but Thou dissolvest it when Thou willest, either in pity or in vengeance, and there is no one who can hide himself from Thy heat.[2] But let my soul praise Thee, that it may love Thee; and let it confess Thine own mercies to Thee, that it may praise Thee. Thy whole creation ceaseth not, nor is it silent in Thy praises— neither the spirit of man, by the voice directed unto Thee, nor animal nor corporeal things, by the voice of those meditating thereon; so that our souls may from their weariness arise towards Thee, leaning on those things which Thou hast made, and passing on to Thee, who hast made them wonderfully; and there is there refreshment and true strength.

CHAPTER II

ON THE VANITY OF THOSE WHO WISHED TO ESCAPE THE OMNIPOTENT GOD

Let the restless and the unjust depart and flee from Thee. Thou both seest them and distinguishest the shadows. And lo! all things with them are fair, yet are they themselves foul. And how have they injured Thee? Or in what have they disgraced Thy government, which is just and perfect from heaven even to the lowest parts of the earth. For whither fled they when they fled from Thy presence?[3] Or where dost Thou not find them? But they fled that they might not see Thee seeing them, and blinded might stumble against Thee,[4] since Thou forsakest nothing that Thou hast made—that

---

[1] Ps. xxxv. 10   [2] Ps. xix. 6   [3] Ps. cxxxix. 7   [4] Gen. xvi. 13, 14

the unjust might stumble against Thee, and justly be hurt, withdrawing themselves from Thy gentleness, and stumbling against Thine uprightness, and falling upon thy wrath. Forsooth, they know not that Thou art every-where whom no place encompasseth, and that Thou alone art near even to those that remove far from Thee.[5] Let them, then, be converted and seek Thee; because not as they have forsaken their Creator hast Thou forsaken Thy creature. Let them be converted and seek Thee; and behold, Thou art there in their hearts, in the hearts of those who confess to Thee, and cast themselves upon Thee, and weep on Thy bosom after their obdurate ways, even Thou gently wiping away their tears. And they weep the more, and rejoice in weeping, since Thou, O Lord, not man, flesh and blood, but Thou, Lord, who didst make, remakest and comfortest them. And where was I when I was seeking Thee? And Thou wert before me, but I had gone away even from myself; nor did I find myself, much less Thee!

CHAPTER III

HAVING HEARD FAUSTUS, THE MOST LEARNED BISHOP OF THE MANI-
CHAEANS, HE DISCERNS THAT GOD, THE AUTHOR BOTH OF THINGS
ANIMATE AND INANIMATE, CHIEFLY HAS CARE FOR THE HUMBLE

Let me lay bare before my God that twenty-ninth year of my age. There had at this time come to Carthage a certain bishop of the Manichaeans, by name Faustus, a great snare of the devil, and many were entangled by him through the allurement of his smooth speech; which, although I did com-mend it, yet could I separate from the truth of those things which I was eager to learn. Nor did I esteem the small dish of oratory so much as the science, which this their so praised Faustus placed before me to feed upon. Fame, indeed, had before spoken of him to me, as most skilled in all be-coming learning, and pre-eminently skilled in the liberal sciences. And as I had read and retained in memory many injunctions of the philosophers, I used to compare some teachings of theirs with those long fables of the Manichaeans; and the former things which they declared, who could only prevail so far as to estimate this lower world, while its lord they could by no means find out,[6] seemed to me the more probable. For Thou art great, O Lord, and hast respect unto the lowly, but the proud Thou knowest afar off.[7] Nor dost Thou draw near but to the contrite heart,[8] nor art Thou found by the proud—not even could they number by cunning skill the stars and the sand, and measure the starry regions, and trace the courses of the planets.

For with their understanding and the capacity which Thou hast be-stowed upon them they search out these things; and much have they found out, and foretold many years before—the eclipses of those luminaries,

---

[5] Ps. lxxiii. 27   [6] Wisd. xiii. 9   [7] Ps. cxxxviii. 6   [8] Ps. xxxiv, and cxlv. 18

the sun and moon, on what day, at what hour, and from how many particular points they were likely to come. Nor did their calculation fail them; and it came to pass even as they foretold. And they wrote down the rules found out, which are read at this day; and from these others foretell in what year, and in what month of the year, and on what day of the month, and at what hour of the day, and at what quarter of its light, either moon or sun is to be eclipsed, and thus it shall be even as it is foretold. And men who are ignorant of these things marvel and are amazed, and they that know them exult and are exalted; and by an impious pride, departing from Thee, and forsaking Thy light, they foretell a failure of the sun's light which is likely to occur so long before, but see not their own, which is now present. For they seek not religiously whence they have the ability wherewith they seek out these things. And finding that Thou hast made them, they give not themselves up to Thee, that Thou mayest preserve what Thou hast made, nor sacrifice themselves to Thee, even such as they have made themselves to be; nor do they slay their own pride, as fowls of the air, nor their own curiosities, by which (like the fishes of the sea) they wander over the unknown paths of the abyss, nor their own extravagance, as the beasts of the field,[9] that Thou, Lord, a consuming fire,[10] mayest burn up their lifeless cares and renew them immortally.

But the way—Thy Word,[11] by whom Thou didst make these things which they number, and themselves who number, and the sense by which they perceive what they number, and the judgment out of which they number—they knew not, and that of Thy wisdom there is no number. But the Only-begotten has been made unto us wisdom, and righteousness, and sanctification,[12] and has been numbered amongst us, and paid tribute to Caesar.[13] This way, by which they might descend to Him from themselves, they knew not; nor that through Him they might ascend unto Him. This way they knew not, and they think themselves exalted with the stars[14] and shining, and lo! they fell upon the earth,[15] and their foolish heart was darkened. They say many true things concerning the creature; but Truth, the Artificer of the creature, they seek not with devotion, and hence they find Him not. Or if they find Him, knowing that He is God, they glorify Him not as God, neither are they thankful,[16] but become vain in their imaginations, and say that they themselves are wise,[17] attributing to themselves what is their own, forging lies against Thee who art the Truth, and changing the glory of the incorruptible God into an image made like corruptible man, and to birds, and four-footed beasts, and creeping things[18]—changing Thy truth into a lie, and worshipping and serving the creature more than the Creator.[19]

Many truths, however, concerning the creature did I retain from these

[9] Ps. viii. 7, 8   [10] Deut. iv. 24   [11] John i. 3   [12] 1 Cor. i. 30   [13] Matt. xvii. 27
[14] Isa. xiv. 13   [15] Rev. xii. 4   [16] Rom. i. 21   [17] Rom. i. 22   [18] Rom. i. 23
[19] Rom. i. 25

men, and the cause appeared to me from calculations, the succession of seasons, and the visible manifestations of the stars; and I compared them with the sayings of Manichaeus, who in his frenzy has written most extensively on these subjects, but discovered not any account either of the solstices, or the equinoxes, the eclipses of the luminaries, or anything of the kind I had learned in the books of secular philosophy. But therein I was ordered to believe, and yet it corresponded not with those rules acknowledged by calculation and my own sight, but was far different.

CHAPTER IV

THAT THE KNOWLEDGE OF TERRESTRIAL AND CELESTIAL THINGS DOES NOT GIVE HAPPINESS, BUT THE KNOWLEDGE OF GOD ONLY

Doth, then, O Lord God of truth, whosoever knoweth those things therefore please Thee? For unhappy is the man who knoweth all those things, but knoweth Thee not; but happy is he who knoweth Thee, though these he may not know. But he who knoweth both Thee and them is not the happier on account of them, but is happy on account of Thee only, if knowing Thee he glorify Thee as God, and gives thanks, and becomes not vain in his thoughts.[20] But as he is happier who knows how to possess a tree, and for the use thereof renders thanks to Thee, although he may not know how many cubits high it is, or how wide it spreads, than he that measures it and counts all its branches, and neither owns it nor knows or loves its Creator; so a just man, whose is the entire world of wealth, and who, as having nothing, yet possesseth all things[21] by cleaving unto Thee, to whom all things are subservient, though he know not even the circles of the Great Bear, yet it is foolish to doubt but that he may verily be better than he who can measure the heavens, and number the stars, and weigh the elements, but is forgetful of Thee, who hast set in order all things in number, weight, and measure.[22]

CHAPTER V

OF MANICHAEUS PERTINACIOUSLY TEACHING FALSE DOCTRINES, AND PROUDLY ARROGATING TO HIMSELF THE HOLY SPIRIT

But yet who was it that ordered Manichaeus to write on these things likewise, skill in which was not necessary to piety? For Thou hast told man to behold piety and wisdom,[23] of which he might be in ignorance although having a complete knowledge of these other things; but since, knowing not these things, he yet most impudently dared to teach them, it is clear that he had no acquaintance with piety. For even when we have a knowledge of these worldly matters, it is folly to make a profession of them; but confes-

---

[20] Rom. i. 21   [21] 2 Cor. vi. 10   [22] Wisd. xi. 20   [23] Job xxviii. 28

sion to Thee is piety. It was therefore with this view that this straying one spake much of these matters, that, standing convicted by those who had in truth learned them, the understanding that he really had in those more difficult things might be made plain. For he wished not to be lightly esteemed, but went about trying to persuade men that the Holy Ghost, the Comforter and Enricher of Thy faithful ones, was with full authority personally resident in him. When, therefore, it was discovered that his teaching concerning the heavens and stars, and the motions of sun and moon, was false, though these things do not relate to the doctrine of religion, yet his sacrilegious arrogance would become sufficiently evident, seeing that not only did he affirm things of which he knew nothing, but also perverted them, and with such egregious vanity of pride as to seek to attribute them to himself as to a divine being.

For when I hear a Christian brother ignorant of these things, or in error concerning them, I can bear with patience to see that man hold to his opinions; nor can I apprehend that any want of knowledge as to the situation or nature of this material creation can be injurious to him, so long as he does not entertain belief in anything unworthy of Thee, O Lord, the Creator of all. But if he conceives it to pertain to the form of the doctrine of piety, and presumes to affirm with great obstinacy that whereof he is ignorant, therein lies the injury. And yet even a weakness such as this in the dawn of faith is borne by our Mother Charity, till the new man may grow up unto a perfect man, and not be carried about with every wind of doctrine.[24] But in him who thus presumed to be at once the teacher, author, head, and leader of all whom he could induce to believe this, so that all who followed him believed that they were following not a simple man only, but Thy Holy Spirit, who would not judge that such great insanity, when once it stood convicted of false teaching, should be abhorred and utterly cast off? But I had not yet clearly ascertained whether the changes of longer and shorter days and nights, and day and night itself, with the eclipses of the greater lights, and whatever of the like kind I had read in other books, could be expounded consistently with his words. Should I have found myself able to do so, there would still have remained a doubt in my mind whether it were so or no, although I might, on the strength of his reputed godliness, rest my faith on his authority.

CHAPTER VI

FAUSTUS WAS INDEED AN ELEGANT SPEAKER, BUT KNEW NOTHING OF THE LIBERAL SCIENCES

And for nearly the whole of those nine years during which, with unstable mind, I had been their follower, I had been looking forward with but too

[24] Eph. iv. 13, 14

great eagerness for the arrival of this same Faustus. For the other members of the sect whom I had chanced to light upon, when unable to answer the questions I raised, always bade me look forward to his coming, when, by discoursing with him, these, and greater difficulties if I had them, would be most easily and amply cleared away. When at last he did come, I found him to be a man of pleasant speech, who spoke of the very same things as they themselves did, although more fluently, and in better language. But of what profit to me was the elegance of my cup-bearer, since he offered me not the more precious draught for which I thirsted? My ears were already satiated with similar things; neither did they appear to me more conclusive, because better expressed; nor true, because oratorical; nor the spirit necessarily wise, because the face was comely and the language eloquent. But they who extolled him to me were not competent judges; and therefore, as he was possessed of suavity of speech, he appeared to them to be prudent and wise. Another sort of persons, however, was, I was aware, suspicious even of truth itself, if enunciated in smooth and flowing language. But me, O my God, Thou hadst already instructed by wonderful and mysterious ways, and therefore I believe that Thou instructedst me because it is truth; nor of truth is there any other teacher—where or whencesoever it may shine upon us—but Thee. From Thee, therefore, I had now learned, that because a thing is eloquently expressed, it should not of necessity seem to be true; nor, because uttered with stammering lips, should it be false; nor, again, perforce true, because unskilfully delivered; nor consequently untrue, because the language is fine; but that wisdom and folly are as food both wholesome and unwholesome, and courtly or simple words as town-made or rustic vessels—and both kinds of food may be served in either kind of dish.

That eagerness, therefore, with which I had so long waited for this man was in truth delighted with his action and feeling when disputing, and the fluent and apt words with which he clothed his ideas. I was therefore filled with joy, and joined with others (and even exceeded them) in exalting and praising him. It was, however, a source of annoyance to me that I was not allowed at those meetings of his auditors to introduce and impart any of those questions that troubled me in familiar exchange of arguments with him. When I might speak, and began, in conjunction with my friends, to engage his attention at such times as it was not inappropriate for him to enter into a discussion with me, and had posed such questions as perplexed me, I discovered him first to know nothing of the liberal sciences save grammar, and that only in an ordinary way. Having, however, read some of Tully's *Orations*, a very few books of Seneca, and some of the poets, and such few volumes of his own sect as were written coherently in Latin, and being day by day practised in speaking, he so acquired a sort of eloquence, which proved the more delightful and enticing in that it was under the control of ready tact, and a sort of native grace. Is it not even as I recall, O

Lord my God, Thou judge of my conscience? My heart and my memory are laid before Thee, who didst at that time direct me by the inscrutable mystery of Thy Providence, and didst set before my face those vile errors of mine, in order that I might see and loathe them.

CHAPTER VII

CLEARLY SEEING THE FALLACIES OF THE MANICHAEANS, HE RETIRES FROM THEM, BEING REMARKABLY AIDED BY GOD

For when it became plain to me that he was ignorant of those arts in which I had believed him to excel, I began to despair of his clearing up and explaining all the perplexities which harassed me: though ignorant of these, however, he might still have held the truth of piety, had he not been a Manichaean. For their books are full of lengthy fables concerning the heaven and stars, the sun and moon, and I had ceased to think him able to decide in a satisfactory manner what I ardently desired—whether, on comparing these things with the calculations I had read elsewhere, the explanations contained in the works of Manichaeus were preferable, or at any rate equally sound? But when I proposed that these subjects should be deliberated upon and reasoned out, he very modestly did not dare to endure the burden. For he was aware that he had no knowledge of these things, and was not one of those loquacious persons, many of whom I had been troubled with, who attempted to teach me these things, and said nothing; but this man possessed a heart, which, though not right towards Thee, yet was not altogether false towards himself. For he was not altogether ignorant of his own ignorance, nor would he without due consideration be inveigled in a controversy, from which he could neither draw back nor extricate himself fairly. And for that I was even more pleased with him, for more beautiful is the modesty of an ingenuous mind than the acquisition of the knowledge I desired—and such I found him to be in all the more abstruse and subtle questions.

My eagerness after the writings of Manichaeus having thus received a check, and despairing even more of their other teachers—seeing that in sundry things which puzzled me, he, so famous amongst them, had thus turned out—I began to occupy myself with him in the study of that literature which he also much affected, and which I, as Professor of Rhetoric, was then engaged in teaching the young Carthaginian students, and in reading with him either what he expressed a wish to hear, or I deemed suited to his bent of mind. But all my endeavors by which I had concluded to improve in that sect, by acquaintance with that man, came completely to an end; not that I separated myself altogether from them, but, as one who could find nothing better, I determined in the meantime upon contenting myself with what I had in any way lighted upon, unless, by chance, something more desirable should present itself. Thus that Faustus, who had entrapped so many to their death—neither willing nor witting it—now began to loosen the snare in which I had been taken. For Thy hands, O my God, in the hidden design of Thy Providence, did not desert my soul; and out of the blood of my mother's heart, through the tears that she poured out by day and by night, was a sacrifice offered unto Thee for me; and by marvellous ways didst Thou deal with me.[25] It was Thou, O my God, who didst it, for the steps of a man are ordered by the Lord, and He shall dispose his way.[26] Or how can we procure salvation but from Thy hand, remaking what it hath made?

CHAPTER VIII

HE SETS OUT FOR ROME, HIS MOTHER IN VAIN LAMENTING IT

Thou dealedst with me, therefore, that I should be persuaded to go to Rome, and teach there rather what I was then teaching at Carthage. And how I was persuaded to do this, I will not fail to confess unto Thee; for in this also the profoundest workings of Thy wisdom, and Thy ever present mercy to me, must be pondered and avowed. It was not my desire to go to Rome because greater advantages and dignities were guaranteed me by the friends who persuaded me into this—although even at this period I was influenced by these considerations—but my principal and almost sole motive was, that I had been informed that the youths studied more quietly there, and were kept under by the control of more rigid discipline, so that they did not capriciously and impudently rush into the school of a master not their own, into whose presence they were forbidden to enter unless with his consent. At Carthage, on the contrary, there was amongst the scholars a shameful and intemperate license. They burst in rudely, and, with almost furious gesticulations, interrupt the system which any one may have instituted for the good of his pupils. Many outrages they perpetrate with astounding stupidity, which would be punishable by law were they not sustained by custom; that custom showing them to be the more worthless, in that they now do, as according to law, what by Thy unchangeable law will never be lawful. And they fancy they do it with impunity, whereas the very blindness whereby they do it is their punishment, and they suffer far greater things than they do. The manners, then, which as a student I would not adopt, I was compelled as a teacher to submit to from others; and so I was too glad to go where all who knew anything about it assured me that similar things were not done. But Thou, my refuge and my portion in the land of the living,[27] didst while at Carthage goad me, so that I might thereby be withdrawn from it, and exchange my worldly habitation for the preservation of my soul; whilst at Rome Thou didst offer me enticements by which to attract me there; by men enchanted with this dying life—the one

[25] Joel ii. 26 [26] Ps. xxxvii. 23 [27] Ps. cxlii. 5

doing insane actions, and the other making assurances of vain things; and, in order to correct my footsteps, didst secretly employ their and my perversity. For both they who disturbed my tranquillity were blinded by a shameful madness, and they who allured me elsewhere smacked of the earth. And I, who hated real misery here, sought fictitious happiness there.

But the cause of my going thence and going thither, Thou, O God, knewest, yet revealedst it not, either to me or to my mother, who grievously lamented my journey, and went with me as far as the sea. But I deceived her, when she violently restrained me either that she might retain me or accompany me, and I pretended that I had a friend whom I could not quit until he had a favorable wind to set sail. And I lied to my mother—and such a mother!—and got away. For this also Thou hast in mercy pardoned me, saving me, thus replete with abominable pollutions, from the waters of the sea, for the water of Thy grace, whereby, when I was purified, the fountains of my mother's eyes should be dried, from which for me she day by day watered the ground under her face. And yet, refusing to go back without me, it was with difficulty I persuaded her to remain that night in a place quite close to our ship, where there was an oratory in memory of the blessed Cyprian. That night I secretly left, but she was not backward in prayers and weeping. And what was it, O Lord, that she, with such an abundance of tears, was asking of Thee, but that Thou wouldest not permit me to sail? But Thou, mysteriously counselling and hearing the real purpose of her desire, granted not what she then asked, in order to make me what she was ever asking. The wind blew and filled our sails, and withdrew the shore from our sight; and she, wild with grief, was there on the morrow, and filled Thine ears with complaints and groans, which Thou didst disregard; whilst, by the means of my longings, Thou wert hastening me on to the cessation of all longing, and the gross part of her love to me was whipped out by the just lash of sorrow. But, like all mothers—though even more than others—she loved to have me with her, and knew not what joy Thou wert preparing for her by my absence. Being ignorant of this, she did weep and mourn, and in her agony was seen the inheritance of Eve—seeking in sorrow what in sorrow she had brought forth. And yet, after accusing my perfidy and cruelty, she again continued her intercessions for me with Thee, returned to her accustomed place, and I to Rome.

CHAPTER IX

BEING ATTACKED BY FEVER, HE IS IN GREAT DANGER

And behold, there I was received by the scourge of bodily sickness, and I was descending into hell burdened with all the sins that I had committed, both against Thee, myself, and others, many and grievous, over and above that bond of original sin whereby we all die in Adam.[28] For none of these

[28] I Cor. xv. 22

things hadst Thou forgiven me in Christ, neither had He abolished by His cross the enmity[29] which, by my sins, I had incurred with Thee. For how could He, by the crucifixion of a phantasm, which I supposed Him to be? As true, then, was the death of my soul, as that of His flesh appeared to me to be untrue; and as true the death of His flesh as the life of my soul, which believed it not, was false. The fever increasing, I was now passing away and perishing. For had I then gone hence, whither should I have gone but into the fiery torments meet for my misdeeds, in the truth of Thy ordinance? She was ignorant of this, yet, while absent, prayed for me. But Thou, everywhere present, hearkened to her where she was, and hadst pity upon me where I was, that I should regain my bodily health, although still frenzied in my sacrilegious heart. For all that peril did not make me wish to be baptized, and I was better when, as a lad, I entreated it of my mother's piety, as I have already related and confessed. But I had grown up to my own dishonor, and all the purposes of Thy medicine I madly derided, who wouldst not suffer me, though such a one, to die a double death. Had my mother's heart been smitten with this wound, it never could have been cured. For I cannot sufficiently express the love she had for me, nor how she now travailed for me in the spirit with a far keener anguish than when she bore me in the flesh.

I cannot conceive, therefore, how she could have been healed if such a death of mine had transfixed the bowels of her love. Where then would have been her so earnest, frequent, and unintermitted prayers to Thee alone? But couldst Thou, most merciful God, despise the contrite and humble heart [30] of that pure and prudent widow, so constant in alms-deeds, so gracious and attentive to Thy saints, not permitting one day to pass without oblation at Thy altar, twice a day, at morning and even-tide, coming to Thy church without intermission—not for vain gossiping, nor old wives' fables,[31] but in order that she might listen to Thee in Thy sermons, and Thou to her in her prayers? Couldst Thou—Thou by whose gift she was such—despise and disregard without succoring the tears of such a one, wherewith she entreated Thee not for gold or silver, nor for any changing or fleeting good, but for the salvation of the soul of her son? By no means, Lord. Assuredly Thou wert near, and wert hearing and doing in that method in which Thou hadst predetermined that it should be done. Far be it from Thee that Thou shouldst delude her in those visions and the answers she had from Thee—some of which I have spoken of, and others not—which she kept [32] in her faithful breast, and, always petitioning, pressed them upon Thee as though they were Thine own bond. For Thou, because Thy mercy endureth for ever,[33] condescendest to those whose debts Thou hast pardoned, to become likewise a debtor by Thy promises.

[29] Eph. ii. 15, and Col. i. 20   [30] Ps. li. 19   [31] 1 Tim. v. 10   [32] Luke ii. 19
[33] Ps. cxviii. 1

CHAPTER X

WHEN HE HAD LEFT THE MANICHAEANS, HE RETAINED HIS DEPRAVED
OPINIONS CONCERNING SIN AND THE ORIGIN OF THE SAVIOUR

Thou restoredst me then from that illness, and made sound the son of Thy handmaid meanwhile in body, that he might live for Thee, to endow him with a higher and more enduring health. And even then at Rome I joined those deluding and deluded "saints"; not their "hearers" only—of the number of whom was he in whose house I had fallen ill, and had recovered—but those also whom they designate "The Elect." [34] For it still seemed to me that it was not we that sin, but that I know not what other nature sinned in us. And it gratified my pride to be free from blame, and, after I had committed any fault, not to acknowledge that I had done any —that Thou mightest heal my soul because it had sinned against Thee;[35] but I loved to excuse it, and to accuse something else (I wot not what) which was with me, but was not I. But assuredly it was wholly I, and my impiety had divided me against myself; and that sin was all the more incurable in that I did not deem myself a sinner. And execrable iniquity it was, O God omnipotent, that I would rather have Thee to be overcome in me to my destruction, than myself of Thee to salvation! Not yet, therefore, hadst Thou set a watch before my mouth, and kept the door of my lips, that my heart might not incline to wicked speeches, to make excuses of sins, with men that work iniquity[36]—and, therefore, was I still united with their "Elect."

But now, hopeless of becoming proficient in that false doctrine, even those things with which I had decided upon contenting myself, providing that I could find nothing better, I now held more loosely and negligently. For I was half inclined to believe that those philosophers whom they call "Academics" were more sagacious than the rest, in that they held that we ought to doubt everything, and ruled that man had not the power of comprehending any truth; for so, not yet realizing their meaning, I also was fully persuaded that they thought just as they are commonly held to do. And I did not fail frankly to restrain in my host that assurance which I observed him to have in those fictions of which the works of Manichaeus are full. Notwithstanding, I was on terms of more intimate friendship with them than with others who were not of this heresy. Nor did I defend it with my former ardor; still my familiarity with that sect (many of them being concealed in Rome) made me slower to seek any other way—particularly since I was hopeless of finding the truth, from which in Thy Church, O Lord of heaven and earth, Creator of all things visible and invisible, they had turned me aside—and it seemed to me most unbecoming

[34] See iv. 1   [35] Ps. xli. 4   [36] Ps. cxli. 3, 4

to believe Thee to have the form of human flesh, and to be bounded by the bodily lineaments of our members. And because, when I desired to meditate on my God, I knew not what to think of but a mass of bodies (for what was not such did not seem to me to be), this was the greatest and almost sole cause of my inevitable error.

For hence I also believed evil to be a similar sort of substance, and to be possessed of its own foul and misshapen mass—whether dense, which they denominated earth, or thin and subtle, as is the body of the air, which they fancy some malignant spirit crawling through that earth. And because a piety—such as it was—compelled me to believe that the good God never created any evil nature, I conceived two masses, the one opposed to the other, both infinite, but the evil the more contracted, the good the more expansive. And from this mischievous commencement the other profanities followed on me. For when my mind tried to revert to the Catholic faith, I was cast back, since what I had held to be the Catholic faith was not so. And it appeared to me more devout to look upon Thee, my God—to whom I make confession of Thy mercies—as infinite, at least, on other sides, although on that side where the mass of evil was in opposition to Thee I was compelled to confess Thee finite, than if on every side I should conceive Thee to be confined by the form of a human body. And better did it seem to me to believe that no evil had been created by Thee—which to me in my ignorance appeared not only some substance, but a bodily one, because I had no conception of the mind excepting as a subtle body, and that diffused in local spaces—than to believe that anything could emanate from Thee of such a kind as I considered the nature of evil to be. And our very Saviour Himself, also, Thine only-begotten, I believed to have been reached forth, as it were, for our salvation out of the lump of Thy most effulgent mass, so as to believe nothing of Him but what I was able to imagine in my vanity. Such a nature, then, I thought could not be born of the Virgin Mary without being mingled with the flesh; and how that which I had thus figured to myself could be mingled without being contaminated, I saw not. I was afraid, therefore, to believe Him to be born in the flesh, lest I should be compelled to believe Him contaminated by the flesh. Now will Thy spiritual ones blandly and lovingly smile at me if they shall read these my confessions; yet such was I.

CHAPTER XI

HELPIDIUS DISPUTED WELL AGAINST THE MANICHAEANS AS TO THE AUTHENTICITY OF THE NEW TESTAMENT

Furthermore, whatever they had censured in Thy Scriptures I thought impossible to be defended; and yet sometimes, indeed, I desired to confer on these several points with some one well learned in those books, and to try what he thought of them. For at this time the words of one Helpidius, speaking and disputing face to face against the said Manichaeans, had begun to move me even at Carthage, in that he brought forth things from the Scriptures not easily withstood, to which their answer appeared to me feeble. And this answer they did not give forth publicly, but only to us in private—when they said that the writings of the New Testament had been tampered with by I know not whom, who were desirous of ingrafting the Jewish law upon the Christian faith; but they themselves did not bring forward any uncorrupted copies. But I, thinking of corporeal things, very much ensnared and in a measure stifled, was oppressed by those masses; panting under which for the breath of Thy Truth, I was not able to breathe it pure and undefiled.

CHAPTER XII

PROFESSING RHETORIC AT ROME, HE DISCOVERS THE FRAUD OF HIS SCHOLARS

Then I began assiduously to practise that for which I came to Rome— the teaching of rhetoric; and first to bring together at my home some to whom, and through whom, I had begun to be known; when, behold, I learnt that other offences were committed in Rome which I had not to bear in Africa. For those subvertings by abandoned young men were not practised here, as I had been informed; yet, suddenly, said they, to evade paying their master's fees, many of the youths conspire together, and remove themselves to another—breakers of faith, who, for the love of money, set a small value on justice. These also my heart hated, though not with a perfect hatred;[37] for, perhaps, I hated them more in that I was to suffer by them, than for the illicit acts they committed. Such of a truth are base persons, and they are unfaithful to Thee, loving these transitory mockeries of temporal things, and vile gain, which begrimes the hand that lays hold on it; and embracing the fleeting world, and scorning Thee, who abidest, and invitest to return, and pardonest the prostituted human soul when it returneth to Thee. And now I hate such crooked and perverse men, although I love them if they are to be corrected so as to prefer the learning they obtain to money, and to learning Thee, O God, the truth and fulness of certain good and most chaste peace. But then was the wish stronger in me for my own sake not to suffer them evil, than was the wish that they should become good for Thine.

CHAPTER XIII

HE IS SENT TO MILAN, THAT HE, ABOUT TO TEACH RHETORIC,
MAY BE KNOWN BY AMBROSE

When, therefore, they of Milan had sent to Rome to the prefect of the city, to provide them with a teacher of rhetoric for their city, and to des-

[37] Ps. cxxxix. 22

patch him at the public expense, I made solicitations through those identical persons, drunk with Manichaean vanities, to be freed from whom I was going away—neither of us, however, being aware of it—that Symmachus, the then prefect, having proved me by proposing a subject, would send me. And to Milan I came, to Ambrose the bishop, known to the whole world as among the best of men, Thy devout servant; whose eloquent discourse did at that time strenuously dispense unto Thy people the flour of Thy wheat, the gladness of Thy oil, and the sober intoxication of Thy wine.[38] To him was I unknowingly led by Thee, that by him I might knowingly be led to Thee. That man of God received me like a father, and looked with a benevolent and episcopal kindliness on my change of abode. And I began to love him, not at first, indeed, as a teacher of the truth—which I entirely despaired of in Thy Church—but as a man friendly to myself. And I studiously hearkened to him preaching to the people, not with the motive I should, but, as it were, trying to discover whether his eloquence came up to the fame thereof, or flowed fuller or lower than was asserted; and I hung on his words intently, but of the matter I was but as a careless and contemptuous spectator; and I was delighted with the pleasantness of his speech, more erudite, yet less cheerful and soothing in manner, than that of Faustus. Of the matter, however, there could be no comparison; for the latter was straying amid Manichaean deceptions, while the former was teaching salvation most soundly. But salvation is far from the wicked,[39] such as I then stood before him; and yet I was drawing nearer gradually and unconsciously.

CHAPTER XIV

HAVING HEARD THE BISHOP, HE PERCEIVES THE FORCE OF THE CATHOLIC FAITH, YET DOUBTS, AFTER THE MANNER OF THE MODERN ACADEMICS

For although I took no trouble to learn what he spoke, but only to hear how he spoke (for that empty care alone remained to me, despairing of a way accessible for man to Thee), yet, together with the words which I prized, there came into my mind also the things about which I was careless; for I could not separate them. And whilst I opened my heart to admit how skilfully he spoke, there also entered with it, but gradually, and how truly he spoke! For first, these things also had begun to appear to me to be defensible; and the Catholic faith, for which I had fancied nothing could be said against the attacks of the Manichaeans, I now conceived might be maintained without presumption; especially after I had heard one or two parts of the Old Testament explained, and often allegorically—which when I accepted literally, I was killed spiritually.[40] Many places, then, of those books having been expounded to me, I now blamed my despair in having

---

[38] Ps. iv. 7, and civ. 15   [39] Ps. cxix. 155   [40] 1 Cor. xiii. 12, and 2 Cor. iii. 6

believed that no reply could be made to those who hated and derided the Law and the Prophets. Yet I did not then see that for that reason the Catholic way was to be held because it had its learned advocates, who could at length, and not irrationally, answer objections; nor that what I held ought therefore to be condemned because both sides were equally defensible. For that way did not appear to me to be vanquished; nor yet did it seem to me to be victorious.

Hereupon did I earnestly bend my mind to see if in any way I could possibly prove the Manichaeans guilty of falsehood. Could I have realized a spiritual substance, all their strongholds would have been beaten down, and cast utterly out of my mind; but I could not. But yet, concerning the body of this world, and the whole of nature, which the senses of the flesh can attain unto, I, now more and more considering and comparing things, judged that the greater part of the philosophers held much the more probable opinions. So, then, after the manner of the Academics (as they are supposed), doubting of everything and fluctuating between all, I decided that the Manichaeans were to be abandoned; judging that, even while in that period of doubt, I could not remain in a sect to which I preferred some of the philosophers; to which philosophers, however, because they were without the saving name of Christ, I utterly refused to commit the cure of my fainting soul. I resolved, therefore, to be a catechumen in the Catholic Church, which my parents had commended to me, until something settled should manifest itself to me whither I might steer my course.

BOOK SIX

Attaining his thirtieth year, he, under the admonition of the discourses of Ambrose, discovered more and more the truth of the Catholic doctrine, and deliberates as to the better regulation of his life.

CHAPTER I

HIS MOTHER HAVING FOLLOWED HIM TO MILAN, DECLARES THAT SHE WILL NOT DIE BEFORE HER SON SHALL HAVE EMBRACED THE CATHOLIC FAITH

O Thou, my hope from my youth,[1] where wert Thou to me, and whither hadst Thou gone? For in truth, hadst Thou not created me, and made a difference between me and the beasts of the field and fowls of the air? Thou hadst made me wiser than they, yet did I wander about in dark and slippery places, and sought Thee abroad out of myself, and found not the God of my heart; and had entered the depths of the sea, and distrusted and despaired finding out the truth. By this time my mother, made strong by her piety, had come to me, following me over sea and land, in all perils feeling secure in Thee. For in the dangers of the sea she comforted the very sailors (to whom the inexperienced passengers, when alarmed, were wont rather to go for comfort), assuring them of a safe arrival, because she had been so assured by Thee in a vision. She found me in grievous danger, through despair of ever finding truth. But when I had disclosed to her that I was now no longer a Manichaean, though not yet a Catholic Christian, she did not leap for joy as at what was unexpected; although she was now reassured as to that part of my misery for which she had mourned me as one dead, but who would be raised to Thee, carrying me forth upon the bier of her thoughts, that Thou mightest say unto the widow's son, "Young man, I say unto thee, arise," and he should revive, and begin to speak, and Thou shouldest deliver him to his mother.[2] Her heart, then, was not agitated with any violent exultation, when she had heard that to be already in so great a part accomplished which she daily, with tears, entreated of Thee might be done—that though I had not yet grasped the truth, I was rescued from falsehood. Rather, for that she was fully confident that Thou, who hadst promised the whole, wouldst give the rest, most calmly, and with a breast full of confidence, she replied to me that she believed in Christ, that before she departed this life, she would see me a Catholic believer. And thus much said she to me; but to Thee, O Fountain of mercies, poured

---

[1] Ps. lxxi. 5   [2] Luke vii. 12-15

she out more frequent prayers and tears, that Thou wouldest hasten Thy aid, and enlighten my darkness; and she hurried all the more assiduously to the church, and hung upon the words of Ambrose, praying for the fountain of water that springeth up into everlasting life.[3] For she loved that man as an angel of God, because she knew that it was by him that I had been brought, for the present, to that perplexing state of agitation I was now in, through which she was fully persuaded that I should pass from sickness unto health, after an excess, as it were, of a sharper fit, which doctors term the crisis.

CHAPTER II

SHE, ON THE PROHIBITION OF AMBROSE, ABSTAINS FROM HONORING THE MEMORY OF THE MARTYRS

When, therefore, my mother had at one time—as was her custom in Africa—brought to the oratories built in the memory of the saints certain cakes, and bread, and wine, and was forbidden by the door-keeper, so soon as she learnt that it was the bishop who had forbidden it, she so piously and obediently acceded to it, that I myself marvelled how readily she could bring herself to accuse her own custom, rather than question his prohibition. For wine-bibbing did not take possession of her spirit, nor did the love of wine stimulate her to hatred of the truth, as it does too many, both male and female, who nauseate at a song of sobriety, as men well drunk at a draught of water. But she, when she had brought her basket with the festive meats, of which she would taste herself first and give the rest away, would never allow herself more than one little cup of wine, diluted according to her own temperate palate, which, out of courtesy, she would taste. And if there were many oratories of departed saints that ought to be honored in the same way, she still carried round with her the selfsame cup, to be used everywhere; and this, which was not only very much watered, but was also very tepid with carrying about, she would distribute by small sips to those around; for she sought their devotion, not pleasure. As soon, therefore, as she found this custom to be forbidden by that famous preacher and most pious prelate, even to those who would use it with moderation, lest thereby an occasion of excess might be given to such as were drunken, and because these, so to say, festivals in honor of the dead were very like the superstition of the Gentiles, she most willingly abstained from it. And in lieu of a basket filled with fruits of the earth, she had learned to bring to the oratories of the martyrs a heart full of more purified petitions, and to give all that she could to the poor; that so the communion of the Lord's body might be rightly celebrated there, where, after the example of His passion, the martyrs had been sacrificed and crowned. But yet it seems to

[3] John iv. 14

me, O Lord my God, and thus my heart thinks of it in Thy sight, that my mother perhaps would not so easily have given way to the relinquishment of this custom had it been forbidden by another whom she loved not as Ambrose, whom, out of regard for my salvation, she loved most dearly; and he loved her truly, on account of her most religious conversation, whereby, in good works so fervent in spirit,[4] she frequented the church; so that he would often, when he saw me, burst forth into her praises, congratulating me that I had such a mother—little knowing what a son she had in me, who was in doubt as to all these things, and did not imagine the way of life could be found out.

CHAPTER III

AS AMBROSE WAS OCCUPIED WITH BUSINESS AND STUDY, AUGUSTINE COULD SELDOM CONSULT HIM CONCERNING THE HOLY SCRIPTURES

Nor did I now groan in my prayers that Thou wouldest help me; but my mind was wholly intent on knowledge, and eager to dispute. And Ambrose himself I esteemed a happy man, as the world counted happiness, in that such great personages held him in honor; only his celibacy appeared to me a painful thing. But what hope he cherished, what struggles he had against the temptations that beset his very excellences, what solace in adversities, and what savory joys Thy bread possessed for the hidden mouth of his heart when ruminating on it, I could neither conjecture, nor had I experienced. Nor did he know my embarrassments, nor the pit of my danger. For I could not request of him what I wished as I wished, in that I was debarred from hearing and speaking to him by crowds of busy people, whose infirmities he devoted himself to. With whom when he was not engaged (which was but a little time), he either was refreshing his body with necessary sustenance, or his mind with reading. But while reading, his eyes glanced over the pages, and his heart searched out the sense, but his voice and tongue were silent. Ofttimes, when we had come (for no one was forbidden to enter, nor was it his custom that the arrival of those who came should be announced to him), we saw him thus reading to himself, and never otherwise; and, having long sat in silence (for who would dare interrupt one so intent?), we were fain to depart, inferring that in the little time he secured for the recruiting of his mind, free from the clamor of other men's business, he was unwilling to be taken off. And perchance he was fearful lest, if the author he studied should express aught vaguely, some doubtful and attentive hearer should ask him to expound it, or to discuss some of the more abstruse questions, as that, his time being thus occupied, he could not turn over as many volumes as he wished; although the preservation of his voice, which was very easily weakened, might be

[4] Rom. xii. 11

the truer reason for his reading to himself. But whatever was his motive in so doing, doubtless in such a man was a good one.

But truly no opportunity could I find of ascertaining what I desired from Thy so holy oracle, his breast, unless the thing might be entered into briefly. But those surgings in me required to find him at full leisure, that I might pour them out to him, but never were they able to find him so; and I heard him, indeed, every Lord's day, rightly dividing the word of truth[5] among the people; and I was all the more convinced that all those knots of crafty calumnies, which those deceivers of ours had knit against the divine books, could be unravelled. But so soon as I understood, withal, that man made after the image of Him that created him[6] was not so understood by Thy spiritual sons (whom of the Catholic mother Thou hadst begotten again through grace), as though they believed and imagined Thee to be bounded by human form—although what was the nature of a spiritual substance I had not the faintest or dimmest suspicion—yet rejoicing, I blushed that for so many years I had barked, not against the Catholic faith, but against the fables of carnal imaginations. For I had been both impious and rash in this, that what I ought inquiring to have learnt, I had pronounced on condemning. For Thou, O most high and most near, most secret, yet most present, who hast not limbs some larger some smaller, but art wholly everywhere, and nowhere in space, nor art Thou of such corporeal form, yet hast Thou created man after Thine own image, and, behold, from head to foot is he confined by space.

CHAPTER IV

HE RECOGNISES THE FALSITY OF HIS OWN OPINIONS, AND COMMITS TO MEMORY THE SAYING OF AMBROSE

As, then, I knew not how this image of Thine should subsist, I should have knocked and propounded the doubt how it was to be believed, and not have insultingly opposed it, as if it were believed. Anxiety, therefore, as to what to retain as certain, did all the more sharply gnaw into my soul, the more shame I felt that, having been so long deluded and deceived by the promise of certainties, I had, with puerile error and petulance, prated of so many uncertainties as if they were certainties. For that they were falsehoods became apparent to me afterwards. However, I was certain that they were uncertain, and that I had formerly held them as certain when with a blind contentiousness I accused Thy Catholic Church, which though I had not yet discovered to teach truly, yet not to teach that of which I had so vehemently accused her. In this manner was I confounded and converted, and I rejoiced, O my God, that the one Church, the body of Thine only Son (wherein the name of Christ had been set upon me when an

[5] 2 Tim. ii. 15   [6] Col. iii. 10, and Gen. i. 26, 27

infant), did not appreciate these infantile trifles, nor maintained, in her sound doctrine, any tenet that would confine Thee, the Creator of all, in space—though ever so great and wide, yet bounded on all sides by the restraints of a human form.

I rejoiced also that the old Scriptures of the law and the prophets were laid before me, to be perused, not now with that eye to which they seemed most absurd before, when I censured Thy holy ones for so thinking, whereas in truth they thought not so; and with delight I heard Ambrose, in his sermons to the people, oftentimes most diligently recommend this text as a rule—"The letter killeth, but the Spirit giveth life;"[7] while, drawing aside the mystic veil, he spiritually laid open that which, accepted according to the "letter," seemed to teach perverse doctrines—teaching herein nothing that offended me, though he taught such things as I knew not as yet whether they were true. For all this time I restrained my heart from assenting to anything, fearing to fall headlong; but by hanging in suspense I was the worse killed. For my desire was to be as well assured of those things that I saw not, as I was that seven and three are ten. For I was not so insane as to believe that this could not be comprehended; but I desired to have other things as clear as this, whether corporeal things, which were not present to my senses, or spiritual, whereof I knew not how to conceive except corporeally. And by believing I might have been cured, that so the sight of my soul being cleared, it might in some way be directed towards Thy truth, which abideth always, and faileth in naught. But as it happens that he who has tried a bad physician fears to trust himself with a good one, so was it with the health of my soul, which could not be healed but by believing, and, lest it should believe falsehoods, refused to be cured—resisting Thy hands, who hast prepared for us the medicaments of faith, and hast applied them to the maladies of the whole world, and hast bestowed upon them so great authority.

CHAPTER V

FAITH IS THE BASIS OF HUMAN LIFE; MAN CANNOT DISCOVER THAT TRUTH WHICH HOLY SCRIPTURE HAS DISCLOSED

From this, however, being led to prefer the Catholic doctrine, I felt that it was with more moderation and honesty that it commanded things to be believed that were not demonstrated (whether it was that they could be demonstrated, but not to any one, or could not be demonstrated at all), than was the method of the Manichaeans, where our credulity was mocked by audacious promise of knowledge, and then so many most fabulous and absurd things were forced upon belief because they were not capable of demonstration. After that, O Lord, Thou, by little and little, with most

[7] 2 Cor. iii. 6

gentle and most merciful hand, drawing and calming my heart, didst persuade me—taking into consideration what a multiplicity of things which I had never seen, nor was present when they were enacted, like so many of the things in secular history, and so many accounts of places and cities which I had not seen; so many of friends, so many of physicians, so many now of these men, now of those, which unless we should believe, we should do nothing at all in this life; lastly, with how unalterable an assurance I believed of what parents I was born, which it would have been impossible for me to know otherwise than by hearsay—taking into consideration all this, Thou persuadest me that not they who believed Thy books (which, with so great authority, Thou hast established among nearly all nations), but those who believed them not were to be blamed; and that those men were not to be listened to who should say to me, "How do you know that those Scriptures were imparted to mankind by the Spirit of the one true and most true God?" For it was the same thing that was most of all to be believed, since no wranglings of blasphemous questions, whereof I had read so many amongst the self-contradicting philosophers, could once wring the belief from me that Thou art—whatsoever Thou wert, though what I knew not—or that the government of human affairs belongs to Thee.

Thus much I believed, at one time more strongly than another, yet did I ever believe both that Thou wert, and hadst a care of us, although I was ignorant both what was to be thought of Thy substance, and what way led, or led back to Thee. Seeing, then, that we were too weak by unaided reason to find out the truth, and for this cause needed the authority of the holy writings, I had now begun to believe that Thou wouldest by no means have given such excellency of authority to those Scriptures throughout all lands, had it not been Thy will thereby to be believed in, and thereby sought. For now those things which heretofore appeared incongruous to me in the Scripture, and used to offend me, having heard many of them expounded reasonably, I referred to the depth of the mysteries, and its authority seemed to me all the more venerable and worthy of religious belief, in that, while it was visible for all to read it, it reserved the majesty of its secret within its profound significance, stooping to all in the great plainness of its language and lowliness of its style, yet exercising the application of such as are not light of heart; that it might receive all into its common bosom, and through narrow passages waft over some few towards Thee, yet many more than if it did not stand upon such a height of authority, nor allured multitudes within its bosom by its holy humility. These things I meditated upon, and Thou wert with me; I sighed, and Thou heardest me; I vacillated, and Thou didst guide me; I roamed through the broad way[8] of the world, and Thou didst not desert me.

[8] Matt. vii. 13

CHAPTER VI

ON THE SOURCE AND CAUSE OF TRUE JOY—THE EXAMPLE
OF THE JOYOUS BEGGAR BEING ADDUCED

I longed for honors, gains, wedlock; and Thou mockedst me. In these desires I underwent most bitter hardships, Thou being the more gracious the less Thou didst suffer anything which was not Thou to grow sweet to me. Behold my heart, O Lord, who wouldest that I should recall all this, and confess unto Thee. Now let my soul cleave to Thee, which Thou hast freed from that fast-holding bird-lime of death. How wretched was it! And Thou didst irritate the feeling of its wound, that, forsaking all else, it might be converted unto Thee—who art above all, and without whom all things would be naught—be converted and be healed. How wretched was I at that time, and how didst Thou deal with me, to make me sensible of my wretchedness on that day when I was preparing to recite a panegyric on the Emperor, wherein I was to deliver many a lie, and lying was to be applauded by those who knew I lied; and my heart panted with these cares, and boiled over with the feverishness of consuming thoughts. For, while walking along one of the streets of Milan, I observed a poor mendicant—then, I imagine, with a full belly—joking and joyous; and I sighed, and spake to the friends around me of the many sorrows resulting from our madness, for that by all such exertions of ours—as those in which I then labored, dragging along, under the spur of desires, the burden of my own unhappiness, and by dragging increasing it—we yet aimed only to attain that very joyousness which that mendicant had reached before us, who, perchance, never would attain it! For what he had obtained through a few begged pence, the same was I scheming for by many a wretched and tortuous turning—the joy of a temporary felicity. For he possessed not true joy, but yet I, with these my ambitions, was seeking one much more untrue. And in truth he was joyous, I anxious; he free from care, I full of alarms. But should any one inquire of me whether I would rather be merry or fearful, I would reply, Merry. Again, were I asked whether I would rather be such as he was, or as I myself then was, I should elect to be myself, though beset with cares and alarms, but out of perversity; for was it so in truth? For I ought not to prefer myself to him because I happened to be more learned than he, seeing that I took no delight therein, but sought rather to please men by it; and that not to instruct, but only to please. Wherefore also didst Thou break my bones with the rod of Thy correction.[9]

Away with those, then, from my soul, who say unto it, "It makes a difference from whence a man's joy is derived. That mendicant rejoiced in drunkenness; thou longedst to rejoice in glory." What glory, O Lord? That

[9] Prov. xxii. 15

which is not in Thee. For even as his was no true joy, so was mine no true glory; and it subverted my soul more. He would digest his drunkenness that same night, but many a night had I slept with mine, and risen again with it, and was to sleep again and again to rise with it, I know not how often. It does indeed make a difference whence a man's joy is derived. I know it is so, and that the joy of a faithful hope is incomparably beyond such vanity. And even at that time was he beyond me, for he truly was the happier man; not only because he was thoroughly steeped in mirth, I torn to pieces with cares, but he, by giving good wishes, had gotten wine, I, by lying, was following after pride. Much to this effect I then said to my dear friends, and I often marked in them how it fared with me; and I found that it went ill with me, and fretted, and doubled that very ill. And if any prosperity smiled upon me, I loathed to seize it, for almost before I could grasp it it flew away.

CHAPTER VII

HE LEADS TO REFORMATION HIS FRIEND ALYPIUS, SEIZED WITH MADNESS FOR THE CIRCENSIAN GAMES

These things we, who lived like friends together, jointly deplored, but chiefly and most familiarly did I discuss them with Alypius and Nebridius, of whom Alypius was born in the same town as myself, his parents being of the highest rank there, but he being younger than I. For he had studied under me, first, when I taught in our own town, and afterwards at Carthage, and esteemed me highly, because I appeared to him good and learned; and I esteemed him for his innate love of virtue, which, in one of no great age, was sufficiently eminent. But the vortex of Carthaginian customs (amongst whom these frivolous spectacles are hotly followed) had inveigled him into the madness of the Circensian games. But while he was miserably involved in them, I was professing rhetoric there, and had a public school. As yet he did not give ear to my teaching, on account of some ill-feeling that had arisen between me and his father. I had then found how fatally he doted upon the circus, and was deeply grieved that he seemed likely—if, indeed, he had not already done so—to cast away his great promise. Yet had I no means of advising, or by a sort of restraint reclaiming him, either by the kindness of a friend or by the authority of a master. For I imagined that his sentiments towards me were the same as his father's; but he was not such. Disregarding, therefore, his father's will in that matter, he commenced to salute me, and, coming into my lecture-room, to listen for a little and depart.

But it slipped my memory to deal with him, so that he should not, through a blind and headstrong desire of empty pastimes, undo so great a wit. But Thou, O Lord, who governest the helm of all Thou hast created, hadst not forgotten him, who was one day to be amongst Thy sons, the President of Thy sacrament; and that his amendment might plainly be attributed to Thyself, Thou broughtest it about through me, but I knowing nothing of it. For one day, when I was sitting in my accustomed place, with my scholars before me, he came in, saluted me, sat himself down, and fixed his attention on the subject I was then handling. It so happened that I had a passage in hand, which while I was explaining, a simile borrowed from the Circensian games occurred to me, as likely to make what I wished to convey pleasanter and plainer, imbued with a biting jibe at those whom that madness had enthralled. Thou knowest, O our God, that I had no thought at that time of curing Alypius of that plague. But he took it to himself, and thought that I would not have said it but for his sake. And what any other man would have made a ground of offence against me, this worthy young man took as a reason for being offended at himself, and for loving me more fervently. For Thou hast said it long ago, and written in Thy book, "Rebuke a wise man, and he will love thee." [10] But I had not rebuked him, but Thou, who makest use of all consciously or unconsciously, in that order which Thyself knowest (and that order is right), wroughtest out of my heart and tongue burning coals, by which Thou mightest set on fire and cure the hopeful mind thus languishing. Let him be silent in Thy praises who meditates not on Thy mercies, which from my inmost parts confess unto Thee. For he upon that speech rushed out from that deep pit, wherein he was wilfully plunged, and was blinded by its miserable pastimes; and he roused his mind with a resolute moderation; whereupon all the filth of the Circensian pastimes flew off from him, and he did not approach them further. Upon this, he prevailed with his reluctant father to let him be my pupil. He gave in and consented. And Alypius, beginning again to hear me, was involved in the same superstition as I was, loving in the Manichaeans that ostentation of continency which he believed to be true and unfeigned. It was, however, a senseless and seducing continency, ensnaring precious souls, not able as yet to reach the height of virtue, and easily beguiled with the veneer of what was but a shadowy and feigned virtue.

CHAPTER VIII

THE SAME WHEN AT ROME, BEING LED BY OTHERS INTO THE AMPHITHEATRE, IS DELIGHTED WITH THE GLADIATORIAL GAMES

He, not relinquishing that worldly way which his parents had bewitched him to pursue, had gone before me to Rome, to study law, and there he was carried away in an extraordinary manner with an incredible eagerness after the gladiatorial shows. For, being utterly opposed to and detesting

[10] Prov. ix. 8

such spectacles, he was one day met by chance by certain of his acquaintance and fellow-students returning from dinner, and they with a friendly
violence drew him, vehemently objecting and resisting, into the amphi-
theatre, on a day of those cruel and deadly shows, he thus protesting:
"Though you drag my body to that place, and there place me, can you
force me to give my mind and lend my eyes to these shows? Thus shall I be
absent while present, and so shall overcome both you and them." They
hearing this, dragged him on nevertheless, desirous, perchance, to see
whether he could do as he said. When they had arrived thither, and had
taken their places as they could, the whole place became excited with the
inhuman sports. But he, shutting up the doors of his eyes, forbade his mind
to roam abroad after such evil; and would that he had shut his ears also!
For, upon the fall of one in the fight, a mighty cry from the whole audience stirring him strongly, he, overcome by curiosity, and prepared as it
were to despise and rise superior to it, no matter what it were, opened his
eyes, and was struck with a deeper wound in his soul than the other, whom
he desired to see, was in his body; and he fell more miserably than he on
whose fall that mighty clamor was raised, which entered through his ears,
and unlocked his eyes, to make way for the striking and beating down of
his soul, which was bold rather than valiant hitherto; and so much the
weaker in that it presumed on itself, which ought to have depended on
Thee. For, directly he saw that blood, he therewith imbibed a sort of sav-
ageness; nor did he turn away, but fixed his eye, drinking in madness unconsciously, and was delighted with the guilty contest, and drunken with
the bloody pastime. Nor was he now the same as he came in, but was one
of the throng he came to, and a true companion of those who had brought
him thither. Why need I say more? He looked, shouted, was excited, carried away with him the madness which would stimulate him to return, not
only with those who first enticed him, but also before them, and to draw
in others. And from all this didst Thou, with a most powerful and most
merciful hand, pluck him, and taughtest him not to repose confidence in
himself, but in Thee—but not till long after.

CHAPTER IX

INNOCENT ALYPIUS, BEING APPREHENDED AS A THIEF, IS SET
AT LIBERTY BY THE CLEVERNESS OF AN ARCHITECT

But this was all being stored up in his memory for a medicine hereafter.
As was that also, when he was yet studying under me at Carthage, and was
meditating at noonday in the market-place upon what he had to recite (as
scholars are wont to be exercised), Thou sufferedst him to be apprehended
as a thief by the officers of the market-place. For no other reason, I apprehend, didst Thou, O our God, suffer it, but that he who was in the future to

prove so great a man should now begin to learn that, in judging of causes, man should not with a reckless credulity readily be condemned by man. For as he was walking up and down alone before the judgment-seat with his tablets and pen, a young man, one of the scholars, the real thief, privily bringing a hatchet, got in without Alypius' seeing him as far as the leaden bars which protect the silversmiths' shops, and began to cut away the lead. But the noise of the hatchet being heard, the silversmiths below began to make a stir, and sent to take in custody whomsoever they should find. But the thief, hearing their voices, ran away, leaving his hatchet, fearing to be taken with it. Now Alypius, who had not seen him come in, caught sight of him as he went out, and noted with what speed he made off. And, being curious to know the reasons, he entered the place, where, finding the hatchet, he stood wondering and pondering, when behold, those that were sent caught him alone, hatchet in hand, the noise of which had startled them and brought them thither. They lay hold of him and drag him away, and, gathering the tenants of the market-place about them, boast of having taken a notorious thief, and thereupon he was being led away to appear before the judge.

But thus far was he to be instructed. For immediately, O Lord, Thou camest to the succor of his innocency, whereof Thou wert the sole witness. For, as he was being led either to prison or to punishment, they were met by a certain architect, who had the chief charge of the public buildings. They were specially glad to come across him, by whom they used to be suspected of stealing the goods lost out of the market-place, as though at last to convince him by whom these thefts were committed. He, however, had often seen Alypius at the house of a certain senator, whom he was wont to visit to pay his respects; and, recognising him at once, he took him aside by the hand, and inquiring of him the cause of so great a misfortune, heard the whole affair, and commanded all the rabble then present (who were very uproarious and full of threatenings) to go with him. And they came to the house of the young man who had committed the deed. There, before the door, was a lad so young as not to refrain from disclosing the whole through the fear of injuring his master. For he had followed his master to the market-place. So soon as Alypius recognised him, he intimated it to the architect; and he, showing the hatchet to the lad, asked him to whom it belonged. "To us," said he immediately; and on being further interrogated, he disclosed everything. Thus, the crime being transferred to that house, and the rabble shamed, which had begun to triumph over Alypius, he, the future dispenser of Thy word, and an examiner of numerous causes in Thy Church,[11] went away better experienced and instructed.

[11] Alypius became Bishop of Thagaste.

CHAPTER X

THE WONDERFUL INTEGRITY OF ALYPIUS IN JUDGMENT. THE LASTING
FRIENDSHIP OF NEBRIDIUS WITH AUGUSTINE

Him, therefore, had I lighted upon at Rome, and he clung to me by a most strong tie, and accompanied me to Milan, both that he might not leave me, and that he might practise something of the law he had studied, more with a view of pleasing his parents than himself. There had he thrice sat as assessor with an uncorruptness wondered at by others, he rather wondering at those who could prefer gold to integrity. His character was tested, also, not only by the bait of covetousness, but by the spur of fear. At Rome, he was assessor to the Count of the Italian Treasury. There was at that time a most potent senator, to whose favors many were indebted, of whom also many stood in fear. He would fain, by his usual power, have a thing granted him which was forbidden by the laws. This Alypius resisted; a bride was promised, he scorned it with all his heart; threats were employed, he trampled them under foot—all men being astonished at so rare a spirit, which neither coveted the friendship nor feared the enmity of a man at once so powerful and so greatly famed for his innumerable means of doing good or ill. Even the judge whose councillor Alypius was, although also unwilling that it should be done, yet did not openly refuse it, but put the matter off upon Alypius, alleging that it was he who would not permit him to do it; for in fact, had the judge done it, Alypius would have decided otherwise. With this one thing in the way of learning was he very nearly led away—that he might have books copied for him at praetorian prices.[12] But, consulting justice, he changed his mind for the better, esteeming equity, whereby he was hindered, more gainful than the power whereby he was permitted. These are little things, but He that is faithful in that which is least, is faithful also in much.[13] Nor can that possibly be void which proceedeth out of the mouth of Thy Truth. If, therefore, ye have not been faithful in the unrighteous mammon, who will commit to your trust the true riches? And if ye have not been faithful in that which is another man's, who shall give you that which is your own? [14] He, being such, did at that time cling to me, and wavered in purpose, as I did, what course of life was to be taken.

Nebridius also, who had left his native country near Carthage, and Carthage itself, where he had usually lived, leaving behind his fine paternal estate, his house, and his mother, who intended not to follow him, had come to Milan, for no other reason than that he might live with me in a most ardent search after truth and wisdom. Like me he sighed, like me he wavered, an ardent seeker after true life, and a most acute examiner of the

---

[12] *i.e.*, at a lower price   [13] Luke xvi. 10   [14] Luke xvi. 11, 12

most abstruse questions. So were there three begging mouths, sighing out their wants one to the other, and waiting upon Thee, that Thou mightest give them their meat in due season.[15] And in all the bitterness which by Thy mercy followed our worldly pursuits, as we contemplated the end, why this suffering should be ours, darkness came upon us; and we turned away groaning and exclaiming, "How long shall these things be?" And this we often said; and saying so, we did not relinquish them, for as yet we had discovered nothing certain to which, when relinquished, we might betake ourselves.

CHAPTER XI

BEING TROUBLED BY HIS GRIEVOUS ERRORS, HE MEDITATES ENTERING ON A NEW LIFE

And I, puzzling over and reviewing these things, most marvelled at the length of time from my nineteenth year, when I began to be inflamed with the desire of wisdom, resolving, when I had found her, to forsake all the empty hopes and lying insanities of vain desires. And behold, I was now getting on to my thirtieth year, sticking in the same mire, eager for the enjoyment of things present, which fly away and destroy me, whilst I say, "To-morrow I shall discover it; behold, it will appear plainly, and I shall seize it; behold, Faustus will come and explain everything! O ye great men, ye Academicians, it is then true that nothing certain for the ordering of life can be attained! Nay, let us search the more diligently, and let us not despair. Lo, the things in the ecclesiastical books, which appeared to us absurd, do not appear so now, and may be otherwise and honestly interpreted. I will set my feet upon that step, where, as a child, my parents placed me, until the clear truth be discovered. But where and when shall it be sought? Ambrose has no leisure—we have no leisure to read. Where are we to find the books? Whence or when procure them? From whom borrow them? Let set times be appointed, and certain hours be set apart for the health of the soul. Great hope has risen upon us, the Catholic faith does not teach what we conceived, and vainly accused it of. Her learned ones hold it as an abomination to believe that God is limited by the form of a human body. And do we doubt to 'knock,' in order that the rest may be 'opened'? [16] The mornings are taken up by our scholars; how do we employ the rest of the day? Why do we not set about this? But when, then, pay our respects to our great friends, of whose favors we stand in need? When prepare what our scholars buy from us? When recreate ourselves, relaxing our minds from the pressure of care?

"Perish everything, and let us dismiss these empty vanities, and betake ourselves solely to the search after truth! Life is miserable, death uncertain.

[15] Ps. cxlv. 15   [16] Matt. vii. 7

If it creeps upon us suddenly, in what state shall we depart hence, and where shall we learn what we have neglected here? Or rather shall we not suffer the punishment of this negligence? What if death itself should cut off and put an end to all care and feeling? This also, then, must be inquired into. But God forbid that it should be so. It is not without reason, it is no empty thing, that the so eminent height of the authority of the Christian faith is diffused throughout the entire world. Never would such and so great things be wrought for us, if, by the death of the body, the life of the soul were destroyed. Why, therefore, do we delay to abandon our hopes of this world, and give ourselves wholly to seek after God and the blessed life? But stay! Even those things are enjoyable; and they possess some and no little sweetness. We must not abandon them lightly, for it would be a shame to return to them again. Behold, now is it a great matter to obtain some post of honor! And what more could we desire? We have crowds of influential friends, though we have nothing else, and if we make haste a presidentship may be offered us; and a wife with some money, that she increase not our expenses; and this shall be the height of desire. Many men, who are great and worthy of imitation, have applied themselves to the study of wisdom in the marriage state."

While I talked of these things, and these winds veered about and tossed my heart hither and thither, the time passed on; but I was slow to turn to the Lord, and from day to day deferred to live in Thee, and deferred not daily to die in myself. Being enamored of a happy life, I yet feared it in its own abode, and, fleeing from it, sought after it. I conceived that I should be too unhappy were I deprived of the embracements of a woman; and of Thy merciful medicine to cure that infirmity I thought not, not having tried it. As regards continency, I imagined it to be under the control of our own strength (though in myself I found it not), being so foolish as not to know what is written, that none can be continent unless Thou give it;[17] and that Thou wouldst give it, if with heartfelt groaning I should knock at Thine ears, and should with firm faith cast my care upon Thee.

CHAPTER XII

DISCUSSION WITH ALYPIUS CONCERNING A LIFE OF CELIBACY

It was in truth Alypius who prevented me from marrying, alleging that thus we could by no means live together, having so much undistracted leisure in the love of wisdom, as we had long desired. For he himself was so chaste in this matter that it was wonderful—all the more, too, that in his early youth he had entered upon that path, but had not clung to it; rather had he, feeling sorrow and disgust at it, lived from that time to the present most continently. But I opposed him with examples of those who as

17 Wisd. viii. 2

married men had loved wisdom, found favor with God, and walked faithfully and lovingly with their friends. From the greatness of whose spirit I fell far short, and, enthralled with the disease of the flesh and its deadly sweetness, dragged my chain along, fearing to be loosed, and, as if it pressed my wound, rejected his kind expostulations, as it were the hand of one who would unchain me. Moreover, it was by me that the serpent spoke to Alypius himself, weaving and laying in his path, by my tongue, pleasant snares, wherein his honorable and free feet might be entangled.

For when he wondered that I, for whom he had no slight esteem, stuck so fast in the bird-lime of that pleasure as to affirm whenever we discussed the matter that it would be impossible for me to lead a single life, and urged in my defence when I saw him wonder that there was a vast difference between the life that he had tried by stealth and snatches (of which he had now but a faint recollection, and might therefore, without regret, easily despise), and my sustained acquaintance with it, whereto if but the honorable name of marriage were added, he would not then be astonished at my inability to contemn that course—then he began also to wish to be married, not as if overpowered by the lust of such pleasure, but from curiosity. For, as he said, he was anxious to know what that could be without which my life, which was so pleasing to him, seemed to me not life but a penalty. For his mind, free from that chain, was astounded at my slavery, and through that astonishment was going on to a desire of trying it, and from it to the trial itself, and thence, perchance, to fall into that bondage whereat he was so astonished, seeing he was ready to enter into a covenant with death;[18] and he that loves danger shall fall into it.[19] For whatever the conjugal honor be in the office of well-ordering a married life, and sustaining children, influenced us but slightly. But that which did for the most part afflict me, already made a slave to it, was the habit of satisfying an insatiable lust; an admiring wonder drew him on as he was about to be enslaved. In this state were we, until Thou, O most High, not forsaking our lowliness, commiserating our misery, didst come to our rescue by wonderful and secret ways.

CHAPTER XIII

BEING URGED BY HIS MOTHER TO TAKE A WIFE, HE SOUGHT A MAIDEN THAT WAS PLEASING TO HIM

Active efforts were made to get me a wife. I wooed. I was engaged, my mother taking the greatest pains in the matter, that when I was once married, the health-giving baptism might cleanse me; for which she rejoiced that I was being daily fitted, remarking that her desires and Thy promises were being fulfilled in my faith. At this time, indeed, both at my

---

[18] Isa. xxviii. 15   [19] Ecclus. iii. 27

request and her own desire, with strong heartfelt cries did we daily beg of Thee that Thou wouldest by a vision disclose unto her something concerning my future marriage; but Thou wouldest not. She saw indeed certain vain and fantastic things, such as the earnestness of a human spirit, bent thereon, conjured up; and these she told me of, not with her usual confidence when Thou hadst shown her anything, but slighting them. For she could, she declared, through some feeling which she could not express in words, discern the difference between Thy revelations and the dreams of her own spirit. Yet the affair was pressed on, and a maiden sued who wanted two years of the marriageable age; and, as she was pleasing, she was waited for.

CHAPTER XIV

THE DESIGN OF ESTABLISHING A COMMON HOUSEHOLD WITH HIS FRIENDS IS SPEEDILY HINDERED

And many of us friends, consulting on and abhorring the turbulent vexations of human life, had considered and now almost determined upon living at ease and separate from the turmoil of men. And this was to be obtained in this way; we were to bring whatever we could severally procure, and make a common household, so that, through the sincerity of our friendship, nothing should belong more to one than the other; but the whole, being derived from all, should as a whole belong to each, and the whole to all. It seemed to us that this society might consist of ten persons, some of whom were very rich, especially Romanianus,[20] our townsman, an intimate friend of mine from his childhood, whom grave business matters had then brought up to Court; who was the most earnest of us all for this project, and whose voice was of great weight in commending it, because his estate was far more ample than that of the rest. We had arranged, too, that two officers should be chosen yearly, for the providing of all necessary things, while the rest were left undisturbed. But when we began to reflect whether the wives which some of us had already, and others hoped to have, would permit this, all that plan, which was being so well framed, broke to pieces in our hands, and was utterly wrecked and cast aside. Thence we fell again to sighs and groans, and our steps to follow the broad and beaten ways[21] of the world; for many thoughts were in our heart, but Thy counsel standeth for ever.[22] Out of which counsel Thou didst mock ours, and preparedst Thine own, purposing to give us meat in due season, and to open Thy hand, and to fill our souls with blessing.[23]

[20] Romanianus was a relation of Alypius. [21] Matt. vii. 13 [22] Ps. xxxiii. 11
[23] Ps. cxlv. 15, 16

CHAPTER XV

HE DISMISSES ONE MISTRESS, AND CHOOSES ANOTHER

Meanwhile my sins were being multiplied, and my mistress being torn from my side as an impediment to my marriage, my heart, which clung to her, was racked, and wounded, and bleeding. And she went back to Africa, making a vow unto Thee never to know another man, leaving with me my natural son by her. But I, unhappy one, who could not imitate a woman, impatient of delay, since it was not until two years' time I was to obtain her I sought—being not so much a lover of marriage as a slave to lust—procured another (not a wife, though), that so by the bondage of a lasting habit the disease of my soul might be nursed up, and kept up in its vigor, or even increased into the kingdom of marriage. Nor was that wound of mine as yet cured which had been caused by the separation from my former mistress, but after inflammation and most acute anguish it mortified, and the pain became numbed, but more desperate.

CHAPTER XVI

THE FEAR OF DEATH AND JUDGMENT CALLED HIM, BELIEVING IN THE IMMORTALITY OF THE SOUL, BACK FROM HIS WICKEDNESS WHO BEFORE BELIEVED IN THE OPINIONS OF EPICURUS

Unto Thee be praise, unto Thee be glory, O Fountain of mercies! I became more wretched, and Thou nearer. Thy right hand was ever ready to pluck me out of the mire, and to cleanse me, but I was ignorant of it. Nor did anything recall me from a yet deeper abyss of carnal pleasures, but the fear of death and of Thy future judgment, which, amid all my fluctuations of opinion, never left my breast. And in disputing with my friends, Alypius and Nebridius, concerning the nature of good and evil, I held that Epicurus had, in my judgment, won the palm, had I not believed that after death there remained a life for the soul, and places of recompense, which Epicurus would not believe. And I demanded, "Supposing us to be immortal, and to be living in the enjoyment of perpetual bodily pleasure, and that without any fear of losing it, why, then, should we not be happy, or why should we search for anything else"—not knowing that even this very thing was a part of my great misery, that, being thus sunk and blinded, I could not discern that light of honor, and beauty to be embraced for its own sake, which cannot be seen by the eye of the flesh, it being visible only to the inner man. Nor did I, unhappy one, consider out of what vein it emanated, that even these things, loathsome as they were, I with pleasure discussed with my friends. Nor could I, even in accordance with my then notions of happiness, make myself happy without friends, amid no matter how great abundance of carnal pleasures. And these friends assuredly I loved for their own sakes, and I knew myself to be loved of them again for my own sake. O crooked ways! Woe to the audacious soul which hoped that, if it forsook Thee, it would find some better thing! It hath turned and re-turned, on back, sides, and belly, and all was hard, and Thou alone rest. And behold, Thou are near, and deliverest us from our wretched wanderings, and stablishest us in Thy way, and dost comfort us, and say, "Run; I will carry you, yea, I will lead you, and there also will I carry you."

BOOK SEVEN

He recalls the beginning of his youth, i.e. the thirty-first year of his age, in which very grave errors as to the nature of God and the origin of evil being distinguished, and the sacred books more accurately known, he at length arrives at a clear knowledge of God, not yet rightly apprehending Jesus Christ.

CHAPTER I

HE REGARDED NOT GOD INDEED UNDER THE FORM OF A HUMAN BODY, BUT AS A CORPOREAL SUBSTANCE DIFFUSED THROUGH SPACE

DEAD now was that evil and abominable youth of mine, and I was passing into early manhood: as I increased in years, the fouler I became in vanity, who could not conceive of any substance but such as I saw with my own eyes. I thought not of Thee, O God, under the form of a human body. Since the time I began to hear something of wisdom, I always avoided this; and I rejoiced to have found the same in the faith of our spiritual mother, Thy Catholic Church. But what else to imagine Thee I knew not. And I, a man, and such a man, sought to conceive of Thee, the sovereign and only true God; and I did in my inmost heart believe that Thou wert incorruptible, and inviolable, and unchangeable; because, not knowing whence or how, yet most plainly did I see and feel sure that that which may be corrupted must be worse than that which cannot, and what cannot be violated did I without hesitation prefer before that which can, and deemed that which suffers no change to be better than that which is changeable. Violently did my heart cry out against all my phantasms, and with this one blow I endeavored to beat away from the eye of my mind all that unclean crowd which fluttered around it. And lo, being scarce put off, they, in the twinkling of an eye, pressed in multitudes around me, dashed against my face, and beclouded it; so that, though I thought not of Thee under the form of a human body, yet was I constrained to image Thee to be something corporeal in space, either infused into the world, or infinitely diffused beyond it—even that incorruptible, inviolable, and unchangeable, which I preferred to the corruptible, and violable, and changeable; since whatsoever I conceived, deprived of this space, appeared as nothing to me, yes, altogether nothing, not even a void, as if a body were removed from its place and the place should remain empty of any body at all, whether earthy, terrestrial, watery, aerial, or celestial, but should remain a void place—a spacious nothing, as it were.

I therefore being thus gross-hearted, nor clear even to myself, whatso-

ever was not stretched over certain spaces, nor diffused, nor crowded together, nor swelled out, or which did not or could not receive some of these
dimensions, I judged to be altogether nothing. For over such forms as my
eyes are wont to range did my heart then range; nor did I see that this
same observation, by which I formed those same images, was not of this
kind, and yet it could not have formed them had not itself been something
great. In like manner did I conceive of Thee, Life of my life, as vast through
infinite spaces, on every side penetrating the whole mass of the world, and
beyond it, all ways, through immeasurable and boundless spaces; so that
the earth should have Thee, the heaven have Thee, all things have Thee,
and they bounded in Thee, but Thou nowhere. For as the body of this air
which is above the earth does not prevent the light of the sun from passing
through it, penetrating it, not by bursting or by cutting, but by filling it
entirely, so I imagined the body, not of heaven, air, and sea only, but of
the earth also, to be pervious to Thee, and in all its greatest parts as well as
smallest penetrable to receive Thy presence, by a secret inspiration, both
inwardly and outwardly governing all things which Thou hast created. So
I conjectured, because I was unable to think of anything else; for it was
untrue. For in this way would a greater part of the earth contain a greater
portion of Thee, and the less a lesser; and all things should so be full of
Thee, as that the body of an elephant should contain more of Thee than
that of a sparrow by how much larger it is, and occupies more room; and
so shouldest Thou make the portions of Thyself present unto the several
portions of the world, in pieces, great to the great, little to the little. But
Thou art not such a one; nor hadst Thou as yet enlightened my darkness.

CHAPTER II

THE DISPUTATION OF NEBRIDIUS AGAINST THE MANICHAEANS, ON THE QUESTION WHETHER GOD BE CORRUPTIBLE OR INCORRUPTIBLE

It was sufficient for me, O Lord, to oppose to those deceived deceivers and
dumb praters (dumb, since Thy word sounded not forth from them) that
which a long while ago, while we were at Carthage, Nebridius used to pro-
pound, at which all we who heard it were disturbed: "What could that reputed nation of darkness, which the Manichaeans are in the habit of setting
up as a mass opposed to Thee, have done unto Thee hadst Thou objected to
fight with it? For had it been answered. 'It would have done Thee some injury,' then shouldest Thou be subject to violence and corruption; but if the
reply were: 'It could do Thee no injury,' then was no cause assigned for
Thy fighting with it; and so fighting as that a certain portion and member
of Thee, or offspring of Thy very substance, should be blended with adverse
powers and natures not of Thy creation, and be by them corrupted and
deteriorated to such an extent as to be turned from happiness into misery,

and need help whereby it might be delivered and purged; and that this off-spring of Thy substance was the soul, to which, being enslaved, contaminated, and corrupted, Thy word, free, pure, and entire, might bring succor; but yet also the word itself being corruptible, because it was from one and the same substance. So that should they affirm Thee, whatsoever Thou art, that is, Thy substance whereby Thou art, to be incorruptible, then were all these assertions false and execrable; but if corruptible, then that were false, and at the first utterance to be abhorred." This argument, then, was enough against those who wholly merited to be vomited forth from the surfeited stomach, since they had no means of escape without horrible sacrilege, both of heart and tongue, thinking and speaking such things of Thee

CHAPTER III

THAT THE CAUSE OF EVIL IS THE FREE JUDGMENT OF THE WILL

But I also, as yet, although I said and was firmly persuaded, that Thou our Lord, the true God, who madest not only our souls but our bodies, and not our souls and bodies alone, but all creatures and all things, wert uncontaminable and inconvertible, and in no part mutable; yet understood I not readily and clearly what was the cause of evil. And yet, whatever it was, I perceived that it must be so sought out as not to constrain me by it to believe that the immutable God was mutable, lest I myself should become the thing that I was seeking out. I sought, therefore, for it free from care, certain of the untruthfulness of what these asserted, whom I shunned with my whole heart; for I perceived that through seeking after the origin of evil, they were filled with malice, in that they liked better to think that Thy Substance did suffer evil than that their own did commit it.

And I directed my attention to discern what I now heard, that free will was the cause of our doing evil, and Thy righteous judgment of our suffering it. But I was unable clearly to discern it. So, then, trying to draw the eye of my mind from that pit, I was plunged again therein, and trying often, was as often plunged back again. But this raised me towards Thy light, that I knew as well that I had a will as that I had life: when, therefore, I was willing or unwilling to do anything, I was most certain that it was none but myself that was willing and unwilling; and immediately I perceived that there was the cause of my sin. But what I did against my will I saw that I suffered rather than did, and that I judged not to be my fault, but my punishment; whereby, believing Thee to be most just, I quickly confessed myself to be not unjustly punished. But again I said: "Who made me? Was it not my God, who is not only good, but goodness itself? Whence came I then to will to do evil, and to be unwilling to do good, that there might be cause for my just punishment? Who was it that put this in me, and implanted in me the root of bitterness, seeing I was altogether made by my most sweet God? If the devil were the author, whence is that devil? And if he also, by his own perverse will, of a good angel became a devil, whence also was the evil will in him whereby he became a devil, seeing that the angel was made altogether good by that most good Creator?" By these reflections was I again cast down and stifled; yet not plunged into that hell of error (where no man confesseth unto Thee),[1] to think that Thou dost suffer evil, rather than that man doth it.

CHAPTER IV

THAT GOD IS NOT CORRUPTIBLE, WHO, IF HE WERE, WOULD NOT BE GOD AT ALL

For I was so struggling to find out the rest, as having already found that what was incorruptible must be better than the corruptible; and Thee, therefore, whatsoever Thou wert, did I acknowledge to be incorruptible. For never yet was, nor will be, a soul able to conceive of anything better than Thou, who art the highest and best good. But whereas most truly and certainly that which is incorruptible is to be preferred to the corruptible (as I myself did now prefer it), then, if Thou wert not incorruptible, I could in my thoughts have reached unto something better than my God. Where, then, I saw that the incorruptible was to be preferred to the corruptible, there ought I to seek Thee, and there observe whence evil itself was, that is, whence comes the corruption by which Thy substance can by no means be profaned. For corruption, truly, in no way injures our God —by no will, by no necessity, by no unforeseen chance—because He is God, and what He wills is good, and Himself is that good; but to be corrupted is not good. Nor art Thou compelled to do anything against Thy will in that Thy will is not greater than Thy power. But greater should it be wert Thou Thyself greater than Thyself; for the will and power of God is God Himself. And what can be unforeseen by Thee, who knowest all things? Nor is there any sort of nature but Thou knowest it. And why should we say more concerning why that substance which God is should not be corruptible, seeing that if it were so it could not be God?

CHAPTER V

QUESTIONS CONCERNING THE ORIGIN OF EVIL IN REGARD TO GOD, WHO, SINCE HE IS THE CHIEF GOOD, CANNOT BE THE CAUSE OF EVIL

And I sought "whence is evil?" And sought in an evil way; nor did I see the evil in my very search. And I set in order before the view of my spirit the whole creation, and whatever we can discern in it, such as earth,

[1] Ps. vi. 5

sea, air, stars, trees, living creatures; and whatever in it we do not see, as the firmament of heaven, all the angels, too, and all the spiritual inhabitants thereof. But these very beings, as though they were bodies, my fancy disposed in such and such places, and I made one huge mass of all Thy creatures, distinguished according to the kinds of bodies—some of them being real bodies, some what I myself had feigned for spirits. And this mass I made huge—not as it was, which I could not know, but as large as I thought well, yet in every way finite. But Thee, O Lord, I imagined on every part environing and penetrating it, though in every way infinite; as if there were a sea everywhere, and on every side through immensity nothing but an infinite sea; and it contained within itself some sponge, huge, though finite, so that the sponge would in all its parts be filled from the immeasurable sea. So I conceived Thy creation to be itself finite, and filled by Thee, the Infinite. And I said, Behold God, and behold what God hath created; and God is good, most mightily and incomparably better than all these; but yet He, who is good, hath created them good, and behold how He encircleth and filleth them. Where, then, is evil, and whence, and how crept it in hither? What is its root, and what its seed? Or has it no being at all? Why, then, do we fear and shun that which has no being? Or if we fear it needlessly, then surely is that fear evil whereby the heart is unnecessarily pricked and tormented—and so much a greater evil, as we have naught to fear, and yet do fear. Therefore either that is evil which we fear, or the act of fearing is in itself evil. Whence, therefore, is it, seeing that God, who is good, has made all these things good? He, indeed, the greatest and chiefest Good, has created these lesser goods; but both Creator and created are all good. Whence is evil? Or was there some evil matter of which He made and formed and ordered it, but left something in it which He did not convert into good? But why was this? Was He powerless to change the whole lump, so that no evil should remain in it, seeing that He is omnipotent? Lastly, why would He make anything at all of it, and not rather by the same omnipotency cause it not to be at all? Or could it indeed exist contrary to His will? Or if it were from eternity, why did He permit it so to be for infinite spaces of times in the past, and was pleased so long after to make something out of it? Or if He wished now all of a sudden to do something, this rather should the Omnipotent have accomplished, that this evil matter should not be at all, and that He only should be the whole, true, chief, and infinite Good. Or if it were not good that He, who was good, should not also be the framer and creator of what was good, then that matter which was evil being removed, and brought to nothing, He might form good matter, whereof He might create all things. For He would not be omnipotent were He not able to create something good without being assisted by that matter which had not been created by Himself. Such things did I revolve in my miserable breast, overwhelmed with most gnawing cares lest I should die ere I discovered the truth; yet was the faith of Thy Christ, our Lord and Saviour, as held in the Catholic Church, fixed firmly in my heart, unformed, indeed, as yet upon many points, and diverging from doctrinal rules, but yet my mind did not utterly leave it, but every day rather drank in more and more of it.

CHAPTER VI

HE REFUTES THE DIVINATIONS OF THE ASTROLOGERS, DEDUCED FROM THE CONSTELLATIONS

Now also had I repudiated the lying divinations and impious absurdities of the astrologers. Let Thy mercies, out of the depth of my soul, confess unto thee for this also, O my God. For Thou, Thou altogether—for who else is it that calls us back from the death of all errors, but that Life which knows not how to die, and the Wisdom which, requiring no light, enlightens the minds that do, whereby the universe is governed, even to the fluttering leaves of trees?—Thou providedst also for my obstinacy wherewith I struggled with Vindicianus,[2] an acute old man, and Nebridius, a young one of remarkable talent; the former vehemently declaring, and the latter frequently, though with a certain measure of doubt, saying, That no art existed by which to foresee future things, but that men's surmises had oftentimes the help of luck, and that of many things which they foretold some came to pass unawares to the predicters, who lighted on it by their frequent speaking." Thou, therefore, didst provide a friend for me, who was no negligent consulter of the astrologers, and yet not thoroughly skilled in those arts, but, as I said, a curious consulter with them; and yet knowing somewhat, which he said he had heard from his father, which, how far it would tend to overthrow the estimation of that art, he knew not. This man, then, by name Firminius, having received a liberal education, and being well versed in rhetoric, consulted me, as one very dear to him, as to what I thought on some affairs of his, wherein his worldly hopes had risen, viewed with regard to his so-called constellations; and I, who had now begun to lean in this particular towards Nebridius' opinion, did not indeed decline to speculate about the matter, and to tell him what came into my irresolute mind, but still added that I was now almost persuaded that these were but empty and ridiculous follies. Upon this he told me that his father had been very curious in such books, and that he had a friend who was as interested in them as he was himself, who, with combined study and consultation, fanned the flame of their affection for these toys, so much that they would observe the moment when the very dumb animals which bred in their houses brought forth, and then observed the position of the heavens with regard to them, so as to gather fresh proofs of this so-called art. He said, moreover, that his father had told him, that at the time his mother

[2] cf. IV, 5 above

was about to give birth to him (Firminius), a female servant of that friend of his father's was also great with child, which could not be hidden from her master, who took care with most diligent exactness to know of the birth of his very dogs. And so it happened that (the one for his wife, and the other for his servant, with the most careful observation, calculating the days and hours, and the smaller divisions of the hours) both were delivered at the same moment, so that both were compelled to allow the very self-same constellations, even to the minutest point, the one for his son, the other for his young slave. For as soon as the women began to be in travail, they each gave notice to the other of what was fallen out in their respective houses, and had messengers ready to despatch to one another as soon as they had information of the actual birth, of which they had easily provided, each in his own province, to give instant intelligence. Thus, then, he said, the messengers of the respective parties met one another in such equal distances from either house, than neither of them could discern any difference either in the position of the stars or other most minute points. And yet Firminius, born in a high estate in his parents' house, ran his course through the prosperous paths of this world, was increased in wealth, and elevated to honors; whereas that slave—the yoke of his condition being unrelaxed—continued to serve his masters, as Firminius, who knew him, informed me.

Upon hearing and believing these things, related by so reliable a person, all that resistance of mine melted away; and first I endeavored to reclaim Firminius himself from that curiosity, by telling him, that upon inspecting his constellations, I ought, were I to foretell truly, to have seen in them parents eminent among their neighbors, a noble family in its own city, good birth, becoming education, and liberal learning. But if that servant had consulted me upon the same constellations, since they were his also, I ought again to tell him, likewise truly, to see in them the meanness of his origin, the abjectness of his condition, and everything else altogether removed from and at variance with the former. Whence, then, looking upon the same constellations, I should, if I spoke the truth, speak diverse things, or if I spoke the same, speak falsely; thence assuredly was it to be gathered, that whatever, upon consideration of the constellations, was foretold truly, was not by art, but by chance; and whatever falsely, was not from the unskilfulness of the art, but the error of chance.

An opening being thus made, I ruminated within myself on such things, that no one of those dotards (who followed such occupations, and whom I longed to assail, and with derision to confute) might urge against me that Firminius had informed me falsely, or his father him: I turned my thoughts to those that are born twins, who generally come out of the womb so near one to another, that the small distance of time between them—how much force soever they may contend that it has in the nature of things—cannot be noted by human observation, or be expressed in those figures which the astrologer is to examine that he may pronounce the truth. Nor can they be true; for, looking into the same figures, he must have foretold the same of Esau and Jacob, whereas the same did not happen to them. He must therefore speak falsely; or if truly, then, looking into the same figures, he must not speak the same things. Not then by art, but by chance, would he speak truly. For Thou, O Lord, most righteous Ruler of the universe, the inquirers and inquired of knowing it not, workest by a hidden inspiration that the consulter should hear what, according to the hidden deservings of souls, he ought to hear, out of the depth of Thy righteous judgment, to whom let not man say, "What is this?" or "Why that?" Let him not say so, for he is man.

CHAPTER VII

HE IS SEVERELY EXERCISED AS TO THE ORIGIN OF EVIL

And now, O my Helper, hadst Thou freed me from those fetters; and I inquired, "Whence is evil?" and found no result. But Thou sufferedst me not to be carried away from the faith by any fluctuations of thought, whereby I believed Thee both to exist, and Thy substance to be unchangeable, and that Thou hadst a care of and wouldest judge men; and that in Christ, Thy Son, our Lord, and the Holy Scriptures, which the authority of Thy Catholic Church pressed upon me, Thou hadst planned the way of man's salvation to that life which is to come after this death. These things being safe and immovably settled in my mind, I eagerly inquired, "Whence is evil?" What torments did my travailing heart then endure! What sighs, O my God! Yet even there were Thine ears open, and I knew it not; and when in stillness I sought earnestly, those silent contritions of my soul were strong cries unto Thy mercy. No man knoweth, but only Thou, what I endured. For what was that which was thence through my tongue poured into the ears of my most familiar friends? Did the whole tumult of my soul, for which neither time nor speech was sufficient, reach them? Yet went the whole into Thine ears, all of which I bellowed out from the sighings of my heart; and my desire was before Thee, and the light of mine eyes was not with me; for that was within, I without. Nor was that in place, but my attention was directed to things contained in place; but there did I find no resting-place, nor did they receive me in such a way as that I could say, "It is sufficient, it is well;" nor did they let me turn back, where it might be well enough with me. For to these things was I superior, but inferior to Thee; and Thou art my true joy when I am subjected to Thee, and Thou hadst subjected to me what Thou createdst beneath me. And this was the true temperature and middle region of my safety, to continue in Thine image, and by serving Thee to have dominion over the body. But when I lifted myself proudly against Thee, and ran against the Lord, even on His neck, with the thick bosses of my buckler,[3] even these

___
[3] Job xv. 26

inferior things were placed above me, and pressed upon me, and nowhere was there alleviation or breathing space. They encountered my sight on every side in crowds and troops, and in thought the images of bodies obtruded themselves as I was returning to Thee, as if they would say unto me, "Whither goest thou, unworthy and base one?" And these things had sprung forth out of my wound; for Thou humblest the proud like one that is wounded, and through my own swelling was I separated from Thee; yea, my too much swollen face closed up mine eyes.

CHAPTER VIII

BY GOD'S ASSISTANCE HE BY DEGREES ARRIVES AT THE TRUTH

But Thou, O Lord, shalt endure for ever,[4] yet not for ever art Thou angry with us, because Thou dost commiserate our dust and ashes; and it was pleasing in Thy sight to reform my deformity, and by inward stings didst Thou disturb me, that I should be dissatisfied until Thou wert made sure to my inward sight. And by the secret hand of Thy remedy was my swelling lessened, and the disordered and darkened eyesight of my mind, by the sharp anointings of healthful sorrows, was from day to day made whole.

CHAPTER IX

HE COMPARES THE DOCTRINE OF THE PLATONISTS CONCERNING THE Λόγος WITH THE MUCH MORE EXCELLENT DOCTRINE OF CHRISTIANITY

149334

And Thou, willing first to show me how Thou resistest the proud, but givest grace unto the humble,[5] and by how great an act of mercy Thou hadst pointed out to men the path of humility, in that Thy Word was made flesh and dwelt among men—Thou procuredst for me, by the instrumentality of one inflated with most monstrous pride, certain books of the Platonists, translated from Greek into Latin. And therein I read, not indeed in the same words, but to the selfsame effect, enforced by many and varied reasons, that, In the beginning was the Word, and the Word was with God, and the Word was God. The same was in the beginning with God. All things were made by Him; and without Him was not any thing made that was made. That which was made by Him is life; and the life was the light of men. And the light shineth in darkness; and the darkness comprehendeth it not.[6] And that the soul of man, though it bears witness of the light,[7] yet itself is not that light; but the Word of God, being God, is that true light that lighteth every man that cometh into the world.[8] And that He was in the world, and the world was made by Him, and the world knew Him not.[9]

---

[4] Ps. cii. 12   [5] Jas. iv. 6, and 1 Pet. v. 5   [6] John i. 1-5   [7] *Ibid*. i. 7, 8   [8] John i. 9   [9] *Ibid*. i. 10

But that He came unto His own, and His own received Him not.[10] But as many as received Him, to them gave He power to become the sons of God, even to them that believe on His name.[11] This I did not read there.

In like manner, I read there that God the Word was born not of flesh, nor of blood, nor of the will of man, nor of the will of the flesh, but of God. But that the Word was made flesh, and dwelt among us,[12] I read not there. For I discovered in those books that it was in many and varied ways said, that the Son was in the form of the Father, and thought it not robbery to be equal with God, for that naturally He was the same substance. But that He emptied Himself, and took upon Him the form of a servant, and was made in the likeness of men: and being found in fashion as a man, He humbled Himself, and became obedient unto death, even the death of the cross. Wherefore God also hath highly exalted Him from the dead, and given Him a name above every name; that at the name of Jesus every knee should bow, of things in heaven, and things in earth, and things under the earth; and that every tongue should confess that Jesus Christ is Lord, to the glory of God the Father;[13] those books have not. For that before all times, and above all times, Thy only-begotten Son remaineth unchangeably co-eternal with Thee; and that of His fulness souls receive,[14] that they may be blessed; and that by participation of the wisdom remaining in them they are renewed, that they may be wise, is there. But that in due time Christ died for the ungodly,[15] and that Thou sparedst not Thine only Son, but deliveredst Him up for us all,[16] is not there. Because Thou hast hid these things from the wise and prudent, and hast revealed them unto babes;[17] that they that labor and are heavy laden might come unto Him and He might refresh them,[18] because He is meek and lowly in heart.[19] The meek will He guide in judgment; and the meek will He teach His way;[20] looking upon our humility and our distress, and forgiving all our sins.[21] But such as are puffed up with the elation of would-be sublimer learning, do not hear Him saying, Learn of Me; for I am meek and lowly in heart: and ye shall find rest unto your souls.[22] Because that, when they knew God, they glorified Him not as God, neither were thankful; but became vain in their imaginations, and their foolish heart was darkened. Professing themselves to be wise, they became fools.[23]

And therefore also did I read there, that they had changed the glory of Thy incorruptible nature into idols and varied forms—into an image made like to corruptible man, and to birds, and four-footed beasts, and creeping things,[24] namely, into that Egyptian food for which Esau lost his birthright;[25] for that Thy first-born people worshipped the head of a four-footed beast instead of Thee, turning back in heart towards Egypt, and prostrat-

[10] *Ibid.* i. 11   [11] *Ibid.* i. 12   [12] *Ibid.* i. 14   [13] Phil. ii. 6-11   [14] John i. 16
[15] Rom. v. 6   [16] Rom. viii. 32   [17] Matt. xi. 25   [18] *Ibid.* ver. 28   [19] *Ibid.* ver. 29
[20] Ps. xxv. 9   [21] *Ibid.* ver. 18   [22] Matt. xi. 29   [23] Rom. i. 21, 22   [24] *Ibid.* i. 23
[25] Gen. xxv. 33, 34

ing Thy image—their own soul—before the image of an ox that eateth grass.[26] These things found I there; but I fed not on them. For it pleased Thee, O Lord, to take away the reproach of diminution from Jacob, that the elder should serve the younger;[27] and Thou hast called the Gentiles into Thine inheritance. And I had come unto Thee from among the Gentiles, and I strained after that gold which Thou willedst Thy people to take from Egypt, seeing that wheresoever it was it was Thine. And to the Athenians Thou saidst by Thy apostle, that in Thee we live, and move, and have our being; as one of their own poets has said.[28] And verily these books came from thence. But I set not my mind on the idols of Egypt, whom they ministered to with Thy gold,[29] who changed the truth of God into a lie, and worshipped and served the creature more than the Creator.[30]

CHAPTER X

DIVINE THINGS ARE THE MORE CLEARLY MANIFESTED TO HIM WHO WITHDRAWS INTO THE RECESSES OF HIS HEART

And being thence warned to return to myself, I entered into my inward self, Thou leading me on; and I was able to do it, for Thou wert become my helper. And I entered, and with the eye of my soul (such as it was) saw above the same eye of my soul, above my mind, the Unchangeable Light. Not this common light, which all flesh may look upon, nor, as it were, a greater one of the same kind, as though the brightness of this should be much more resplendent, and with its greatness fill up all things. Not like this was that light, but different, very different from all these. Nor was it above my mind as oil is above water, nor as heaven above earth; but above it was, because it made me, and I below it, because I was made by it. He who knows the Truth knows that Light; and he that knows it knoweth eternity. Love knoweth it. O Eternal Truth, and true Love, and loved Eternity! Thou art my God; to Thee do I sigh both night and day. When I first knew Thee, Thou liftedst me up, that I might see there was that which I might see, and that yet it was not I that did see. And Thou didst beat back the infirmity of my sight, pouring forth upon me most strongly Thy beams of light, and I trembled with love and fear; and I found myself to be far off from Thee, in the region of dissimilarity, as if I heard this voice of Thine from on high: "I am the food of strong men; grow, and thou shalt feed upon me; nor shalt thou convert me, like the food of thy flesh, into thee, but thou shalt be converted into me." And I learned that Thou for iniquity dost correct man, and Thou dost make my soul to consume away like a spider.[31] And I said, "Is Truth, therefore, nothing because it is neither diffused through space, finite, nor infinite?"

[26] Ps. cvi. 20; Ex. xxxii. 1-6   [27] Rom. ix. 12   [28] Acts xvii. 28   [29] Hosea ii. 8
[30] Rom. i. 25   [31] Ps. xxxix. 11

And Thou criedst to me from afar, "Yea, verily, 'I am that I am.' "[32] And I heard this, as things are heard in the heart, nor was there room for doubt; and I should more readily doubt that I live than that Truth is not, which is clearly seen, being understood by the things that are made.[33]

CHAPTER XI

THAT CREATURES ARE MUTABLE AND GOD ALONE IMMUTABLE

And I viewed the other things below Thee, and perceived that they neither altogether are, nor altogether are not. They are, indeed, because they are from Thee; but are not, because they are not what Thou art. For that truly is which remains immutably. It is good, then, for me to cleave unto God,[34] for if I remain not in Him, neither shall I in myself; but He, remaining in Himself, reneweth all things.[35] And Thou art the Lord my God, since Thou standest not in need of my goodness.[36]

CHAPTER XII

WHATEVER THINGS THE GOOD GOD HAS CREATED ARE VERY GOOD

And it was made clear to me that those things are good which yet are corrupted, which, neither were they supremely good, nor unless they were good, could be corrupted; because if supremely good, they were incorruptible, and if not good at all, there was nothing in them to be corrupted. For corruption harms, but, unless it could diminish goodness, it could not harm. Either, then, corruption harms not, which cannot be; or, what is most certain, all which is corrupted is deprived of good. But if they be deprived of all good, they will cease to be. For if they be, and cannot be at all corrupted, they will become better, because they shall remain incorruptibly. And what more monstrous than to assert that those things which have lost all their goodness are made better? Therefore, if they shall be deprived of all good, they shall no longer be. So long, therefore, as they are, they are good; therefore whatsoever is, is good. That evil, then, which I sought whence it was, is not any substance; for were it a substance, it would be good. For either it would be an incorruptible substance, and so a chief good, or a corruptible substance, which unless it were good it could not be corrupted. I perceived, therefore, and it was made clear to me, that Thou didst make all things good, nor is there any substance at all that was not made by Thee; and because all that Thou hast made are not equal, therefore all things are; because individually they are good, and altogether very good, because our God made all things very good.[37]

---

[32] Ex. iii. 14　　[33] Rom. i. 20　　[34] Ps. lxxiii. 28　　[35] Wisd. vii. 27　　[36] Ps. xvi. 2
[37] Gen. i. 31, and Ecclus. xxxix. 21. Evil, with Augustine, is a "privation of good."

CHAPTER XIII

IT IS MEET TO PRAISE THE CREATOR FOR THE GOOD THINGS WHICH
ARE MADE IN HEAVEN AND EARTH

And to Thee is there nothing at all evil, and not only to Thee, but to Thy whole creation; because there is nothing without which can break in, and mar that order which Thou hast appointed it. But in the parts thereof, some things, because they harmonize not with others, are considered evil; whereas those very things harmonize with others, and are good, and in themselves are good. And all these things which do not harmonize together harmonize with the inferior part which we call earth, having its own cloudy and windy sky concordant to it. Far be it from me, then, to say, "These things should not be." For should I see nothing but these, I should indeed desire better; but yet, if only for these, ought I to praise Thee; for that Thou art to be praised is shown from the earth, dragons, and all deeps; fire, and hail; snow, and vapors; stormy winds fulfilling Thy word; mountains, and all hills; fruitful trees, and all cedars; beasts, and all cattle; creeping things, and flying fowl; kings of the earth, and all people; princes, and all judges of the earth; both young men and maidens; old men and children, praise Thy name. But when, from the heavens, these praise Thee, praise Thee, our God, in the heights, all Thy angels, all Thy hosts, sun and moon, all ye stars and light, the heavens of heavens, and the waters that be above the heavens, praise Thy name.[38] I did not now desire better things, because I was thinking of all; and with a better judgment I reflected that the things above were better than those below, but that all were better than those above alone.

CHAPTER XIV

BEING DISPLEASED WITH SOME PART OF GOD'S CREATION, HE
CONCEIVES OF TWO ORIGINAL SUBSTANCES

There is no wholeness in them whom aught of Thy creation displeaseth; no more than there was in me, when many things which Thou madest displeased me. And, because my soul dared not be displeased at my God, it would not suffer aught to be Thine which displeased it. Hence it had gone into the opinion of two substances, and resisted not, but talked foolishly. And, returning thence, it had made to itself a god, through infinite measures of all space; and imagined it to be Thee, and placed it in its heart, and again had become the temple of its own idol, which was to Thee an abomination. But after Thou hadst fomented the head of me unconscious of it, and closed mine eyes lest they should behold vanity,[39] I ceased from myself

---

[38] Ps. cxlviii. 1-12   [39] Ps. cxix. 37

a little, and my madness was lulled to sleep; and I awoke in Thee, and saw Thee to be infinite, though in another way; and this sight was not derived from the flesh.

CHAPTER XV

WHATEVER IS, OWES ITS BEING TO GOD

And I looked back on other things, and I perceived that it was to Thee they owed their being, and that they were all bounded in Thee; but in another way, not as being in space, but because Thou holdest all things in Thine hand in truth: and all things are true so far as they have a being; nor is there any falsehood, unless that which is not is thought to be. And I saw that all things harmonized, not with their places only, but with their seasons also. And that Thou, who only art eternal, didst not begin to work after innumerable spaces of times; for all spaces of times, both those which have passed and which shall pass, neither go nor come, save through Thee, working and abiding.

CHAPTER XVI

EVIL ARISES NOT FROM A SUBSTANCE, BUT FROM THE PERVERSION OF THE WILL

And I discerned and found it no marvel, that bread which is distasteful to an unhealthy palate is pleasant to a healthy one; and that the light, which is painful to sore eyes, is delightful to sound ones. And Thy righteousness displeaseth the wicked; much more the viper and little worm, which Thou hast created good, fitting in with inferior parts of Thy creation; with which the wicked themselves also fit in, the more in proportion as they are unlike Thee, but with the superior creatures, in proportion as they become like to Thee. And I inquired what iniquity was, and ascertained it not to be a substance, but a perversion of the will, bent aside from Thee, O God, the Supreme Substance, towards these lower things, and casting out its bowels,[40] and swelling outwardly.

CHAPTER XVII

ABOVE HIS CHANGEABLE MIND, HE DISCOVERS THE UNCHANGEABLE AUTHOR OF TRUTH

And I marvelled that I now loved Thee, and no phantasm instead of Thee. And yet I did not merit to enjoy my God, but was transported to Thee by Thy beauty, and presently torn away from Thee by mine own weight, sinking with grief into these inferior things. This weight was carnal

[40] Ecclus. x. 9

custom. Yet was there a remembrance of Thee with me; nor did I any way doubt that there was one to whom I might cleave, but that I was not yet one who could cleave unto Thee; for the body which is corrupted presseth down the soul, and the earthly dwelling weigheth down the mind which thinketh upon many things.[41] And most certain I was that Thy invisible things from the creation of the world are clearly seen, being understood by the things that are made, even Thy eternal power and Godhead.[42] For, inquiring whence it was that I admired the beauty of bodies whether celestial or terrestrial, and what supported me in judging correctly on things mutable, and pronouncing, "This should be thus, this not,"—inquiring, then, whence I so judged, seeing I did so judge, I had found the unchangeable and true eternity of Truth, above my changeable mind. And thus, by degrees, I passed from bodies to the soul, which makes use of the senses of the body to perceive; and thence to its inward faculty, to which the bodily senses represent outward things, and up to which reach the capabilities of beasts; and thence, again, I passed on to the reasoning faculty, to which whatever is received from the senses of the body is referred to be judged, which also, finding itself to be variable in me, raised itself up to its own intelligence, and from habit drew away my thoughts, withdrawing itself from the crowds of contradictory phantasms; that so it might find out that light by which it was besprinkled, when, without all doubting, it cried out, that the unchangeable was to be preferred before the changeable; whence also it knew that unchangeable, which, unless it had in some way known, it could have had no sure ground for preferring it to the changeable. And thus, with the flash of a trembling glance, it arrived at that which is. And then I saw Thy invisible things understood by the things that are made.[43] But I was not able to fix my gaze thereon; and my infirmity being beaten back, I was thrown again on my accustomed habits, carrying along with me naught but a loving memory thereof, and an appetite for what I had, as it were, smelt the odor of, but was not yet able to eat.

CHAPTER XVIII

JESUS CHRIST, THE MEDIATOR, IS THE ONLY WAY OF SAFETY

And I sought a way of acquiring strength sufficient to enjoy Thee; but I found it not until I embraced that Mediator between God and man, the man Christ Jesus,[44] who is over all, God blessed for ever,[45] calling unto me, and saying, I am the way, the truth, and the life,[46] and mingling that food which I was unable to receive with our flesh. For the Word was made flesh,[47] that Thy wisdom, by which Thou createdst all things, might provide milk for our infancy. For I did not grasp my Lord Jesus—I, though humbled, grasped not the humble One; nor did I know what lesson that in-

---

[41] Wisd. ix. 15   [42] Rom. i. 20   [43] Rom. i. 20   [44] 1 Tim. ii. 5   [45] Rom. ix. 5
[46] John xiv. 6   [47] John i. 14

firmity of His would teach us. For Thy Word, the Eternal Truth, pre-eminent above the higher parts of Thy creation, raises up those that are subject unto Itself; but in this lower world built for Itself a humble habitation of our clay, whereby He intended to abase from themselves such as would be subjected and bring them over unto Himself, allaying their swelling, and fostering their love; to the end that they might go on no further in self-confidence, but rather should become weak, seeing before their feet the Divinity weak by taking our coats of skins;[48] and wearied, might cast themselves down upon It, and It rising, might lift them up.

CHAPTER XIX

HE DOES NOT YET FULLY UNDERSTAND THE SAYING OF JOHN, THAT THE WORD WAS MADE FLESH

But I thought differently, thinking only of my Lord Christ as of a man of excellent wisdom, to whom no man could be equalled; especially since, being wonderfully born of a virgin. He seemed, through the divine care for us, to have attained so great authority of leadership—for an example of contemning temporal things for the obtaining of immortality. But what mystery there was in The Word was made flesh, I could not even imagine. Only I had learnt out of what is delivered to us in writing of Him, that He did eat, drink, sleep, walk, rejoice in spirit, was sad, and discoursed; that flesh alone did not cleave unto Thy Word, but with the human soul and body. All know thus who know the unchangeableness of Thy Word, which I now knew as well as I could, nor did I at all have any doubt about it. For, now to move the limbs of the body at will, now not; now to be stirred by some affection, now not; now by signs to enunciate wise sayings, now to keep silence, are properties of a soul and mind subject to change. And should these things be falsely written of Him, all the rest would risk the imputation, nor would there remain in those books any saving faith for the human race. Since, then, they were written truthfully, I acknowledged a perfect man to be in Christ—not the body of a man only, nor with the body a sensitive soul without a rational, but a very man; who, not only as being a form of truth, but for a certain great excellency of human nature and a more perfect participation of wisdom, I decided was to be preferred before others. But Alypius imagined the Catholics to believe that God was so clothed with flesh, that, besides God and flesh, there was no soul in Christ, and did not think that a human mind was ascribed to Him. And, because He was thoroughly persuaded that the actions which were recorded of Him could not be performed except by a vital and rational creature, he moved the more slowly towards the Christian faith. But, learning afterwards that this was the error of the Apollinarian heretics, he rejoiced

[48] Gen. iii. 21

in the Catholic faith, and was conformed to it. But somewhat later it was, I confess, that I learned how in the sentence, The Word was made flesh, the Catholic truth can be distinguished from the falsehood of Photinus. For the disapproval of heretics makes the tenets of Thy Church and sound doctrine to stand out boldly. For there must be also heresies, that the approved may be made manifest among the weak.[49]

CHAPTER XX

HE REJOICES THAT HE PROCEEDED FROM PLATO TO THE HOLY SCRIPTURES, AND NOT THE REVERSE

But having then read those books of the Platonists, and being admonished by them to search for incorporeal truth, I saw Thy invisible things, understood by those things that are made,[50] and though repulsed, I perceived what that was, which through the darkness of my mind I was not allowed to contemplate—assured that Thou wert, and wert infinite, and yet not diffused in space finite or infinite; and that Thou truly art, who art the same ever, varying neither in part nor motion; and that all other things are from Thee, on this most sure ground alone, that they are. Of these things was I indeed assured, yet too weak to enjoy Thee. I chattered as one well skilled; but had I not sought Thy way in Christ our Saviour, I would have proved not skilful, but ready to perish. For now, filled with my punishment, I had begun to desire to seem wise; yet mourned I not, but rather was puffed up with knowledge.[51] For where was that charity building upon the foundation of humility, which is Jesus Christ?[52] Or, when would these books teach me it? Upon these, therefore, I believe, it was Thy pleasure that I should fall before I studied Thy Scriptures, that it might be impressed on my memory how I was affected by them; and that afterwards when I was subdued by Thy books, and when my wounds were touched by Thy healing fingers, I might discern and distinguish what a difference there is between presumption and confession—between those who saw whither they were to go, yet saw not the way, and the way which leadeth not only to behold but to inhabit the blessed country. For had I first been moulded in Thy Holy Scriptures, and hadst Thou, in the familiar use of them, grown sweet unto me, and had I afterwards fallen upon those volumes, they might perhaps have withdrawn me from the solid ground of piety; or, had I stood firm in that wholesome disposition which I had thence imbibed, I might have thought that it could have been attained by the study of those books alone.

[49] 1 Cor. xi. 19   [50] Rom. i. 20   [51] 1 Cor. viii. 1   [52] 1 Cor. iii. 11

CHAPTER XXI

WHAT HE FOUND IN THE SACRED BOOKS WHICH ARE NOT TO BE FOUND IN PLATO

Most eagerly, then, did I seize that venerable writing of Thy Spirit, but more especially the Apostle Paul; and those difficulties vanished away, in which he at one time appeared to me to contradict himself, and the text of his discourse not to agree with the testimonies of the Law and the Prophets. And the face of that pure speech appeared to me one and the same; and I learned to rejoice with trembling.[53] So I commenced, and found that whatsoever truth I had there read was declared here with the recommendation of Thy grace; that he who sees may not so glory as if he had not received [54] not only that which he sees, but also that he can see (for what hath he which he hath not received?); and that he may not only be admonished to see Thee, who art ever the same, but also may be healed, to hold Thee; and that he who from afar off is not able to see, may still walk on the way by which he may reach, behold, and possess Thee. For though a man delight in the law of God after the inward man,[55] what shall he do with that other law in his members which warreth against the law of his mind, and bringeth him into captivity to the law of sin, which is in his members? [56] For Thou art righteous, O Lord, but we have sinned and committed iniquity, and have done wickedly, and Thy hand is grown heavy upon us, and we are justly delivered over unto that ancient sinner, the governor of death; for he induced our will to be like his will, whereby he remained not in Thy truth. What shall wretched man do? Who shall deliver him from the body of this death, but Thy grace only, through Jesus Christ our Lord,[57] whom Thou hast begotten co-eternal, and createdst in the beginning of Thy ways, in whom the Prince of this world found nothing worthy of death,[58] yet killed he Him, and the handwriting which was contrary to us was blotted out? [59] This those writings contain not. Those pages contain not the expression of this piety—the tears of confession, Thy sacrifice, a troubled spirit, a broken and a contrite heart,[60] the salvation of the people, the espoused city,[61] the earnest of the Holy Ghost,[62] the cup of our redemption.[63] No man sings there, Shall not my soul be subject unto God? For of Him cometh my salvation, for He is my God and my salvation, my defender, I shall not be further moved.[64] No one there hears Him calling, "Come unto me all ye that labor." They scorn to learn of Him, because He is meek and lowly of heart;[65] for Thou hast hid those things from the wise and prudent, and hast revealed them unto babes.[66] For it

[53] Ps. ii. 11   [54] 1 Cor. iv. 7   [55] Rom. vii. 22   [56] Rom. vii. 23   [57] Rom. vii. 24, 25   [58] John xviii. 38   [59] Col. ii. 14   [60] Ps. li. 17   [61] Rev. xxi. 2   [62] 2 Cor. v. 5   [63] Ps. cxvi. 13   [64] Ps. lxii. 1, 2   [65] Matt. xi. 28, 29   [66] Matt. xi. 25

is one thing, from the mountain's wooded summit to see the land of peace,[67] and not to find the way thither—in vain to attempt impassable ways, opposed and waylaid by fugitives and deserters, under their captain the lion[68] and the dragon;[69] and another to keep to the way that leads thither, guarded by the host of the heavenly general, where they rob not who have deserted the heavenly army, which they shun as torture. These things did in a wonderful manner sink into my bowels, when I read that least of Thy apostles,[70] and had reflected upon Thy works, and feared greatly.

[67] Deut. xxxii. 49   [68] 1 Pet. v. 8   [69] Rev. xii. 3   [70] 1 Cor. xv. 9

BOOK EIGHT

He finally describes the thirty-second year of his age, the most memorable of his whole life, in which, being instructed by Simplicianus concerning the conversion of others, and the manner of acting, he is, after a severe struggle, renewed in his whole mind, and is converted unto God.

CHAPTER I

HE, NOW GIVEN TO DIVINE THINGS, AND YET ENTANGLED BY THE LUSTS OF LOVE, CONSULTS SIMPLICIANUS IN REFERENCE TO THE RENEWING OF HIS MIND

O MY God, let me with gratitude remember and confess unto Thee Thy mercies bestowed upon me. Let my bones be steeped in Thy love, and let them say, Who is like unto Thee, O Lord? [1] Thou hast loosed my bonds, I will offer unto Thee the sacrifice of thanksgiving.[2] And how Thou hast loosed them I will declare; and all who worship Thee when they hear these things shall say: "Blessed be the Lord in heaven and earth, great and wonderful is His name." Thy words had stuck fast into my breast, and I was hedged round about by Thee on every side.[3] Of Thy eternal life I was now certain, although I had seen it through a glass darkly.[4] Yet I no longer doubted that there was an incorruptible substance, from which was derived all other substance; nor did I now desire to be more certain of Thee, but more stedfast in Thee. As for my temporal life, all things were uncertain, and my heart had to be purged from the old leaven.[5] The Way,[6] the Saviour Himself, was pleasant unto me, but as yet I disliked to pass through its straightness. And Thou didst put into my mind, and it seemed good in my eyes, to go unto Simplicianus,[7] who appeared to me a faithful servant of Thine, and Thy grace shone in him. I had also heard that from his very youth he had lived most devoted to Thee. Now he had grown into years, and by reason of so great age, passed in such zealous following of Thy ways, he appeared to me likely to have gained much experience; and so in truth he had. Out of this experience I desired him to tell me (setting before him my griefs) which would be the most fitting way for one afflicted as I was to walk in Thy way.

For the Church I saw to be full, and one went this way, and another that. But it was displeasing to me that I led a secular life; and now that

---

[1] Ps. xxxv. 10   [2] Ps. cxvi. 16, 17   [3] Job. i. 10   [4] 1 Cor. xiii. 12   [5] 1 Cor. v. 7
[6] John xiv. 6   [7] Successor of Ambrose as Bishop of Milan

my passions had ceased to excite me as of old with hopes of honor and wealth, a very grievous burden it was to undergo so great a servitude. For, compared with Thy sweetness, and the beauty of Thy house, which I loved,[8] those things delighted me no longer. But still very tenaciously was I held by the love of women; nor did the apostle forbid me to marry, although he exhorted me to something better, especially wishing that all men were as he himself was.[9] But I, being weak, chose the more agreeable place, and because of this alone was tossed up and down in all beside, faint and languishing with withering cares, because in other matters I was compelled, though unwilling, to agree to a married life, to which I was given up and enthralled. I had heard from the mouth of truth that there be eunuchs, which have made themselves eunuchs for the kingdom of heaven's sake; but, saith He, "he that is able to receive it, let him receive it." [10] Vain, assuredly, are all men in whom the knowledge of God is not, and who could not, out of the good things which are seen, find out Him who is good.[11] But I was no longer in that vanity; I had surmounted it, and by the united testimony of Thy whole creation had found Thee, our Creator, and Thy Word, God with Thee, and together with Thee and the Holy Ghost one God, by whom Thou createdst all things. There is yet another kind of impious men, who when they knew God, they glorified Him not as God, neither were thankful.[12] Into this also had I fallen; but Thy right hand held me up,[13] and bore me away, and Thou placedst me where I might recover. For Thou hast said unto man, "Behold, the fear of the Lord, that is wisdom;[14] and desire not to seem wise,[15] because, professing themselves to be wise, they became fools.[16] But I had now found the goodly pearl, which, selling all that I had,[17] I ought to have bought; and I hesitated.

CHAPTER II

THE PIOUS OLD MAN REJOICES THAT HE READ PLATO AND THE
SCRIPTURES, AND TELLS HIM OF THE RHETORICIAN VICTORINUS
HAVING BEEN CONVERTED TO THE FAITH THROUGH THE
READING OF THE SACRED BOOKS

To Simplicianus then I went—the father of Ambrose (at that time a bishop) in receiving Thy grace,[18] and whom he truly loved as a father. To him I narrated the windings of my error. But when I mentioned to him that I had read certain books of the Platonists, which Victorinus, sometime Professor of Rhetoric at Rome (who died a Christian, as I had been told), had translated into Latin, he congratulated me that I had not fallen upon

[8] Ps. xxvi. 8   [9] 1 Cor. vii. 7   [10] Matt. xix. 12   [11] Wisd. xiii. 1   [12] Rom. i. 21
[13] Ps. xviii. 35   [14] Job xxviii. 28   [15] Prov. iii. 7   [16] Rom. i. 22   [17] Matt. xiii. 46
[18] This is doubtless a reference to his having been instrumental in Ambrose's conversion, Simplicianus having "begotten" him "through the Gospel" (1 Cor. iv. 15).

the writings of other philosophers, which were full of fallacies and deceit, after the rudiments of the world,[19] whereas they,[20] in many ways, led to the belief in God and His word. Then, to exhort me to the humility of Christ, hidden from the wise, and revealed to little ones,[21] he spoke of Victorinus himself, whom, while he was at Rome, he had known very intimately; and of him he related that about which I will not be silent. For it contains great praise of Thy grace, which ought to be confessed unto Thee, how that most learned old man, highly skilled in all the liberal sciences, who had read, criticised, and explained so many works of the philosophers; the teacher of so many noble senators; who also, as a mark of his excellent discharge of his duties, had (which men of this world esteem a great honor) both merited and obtained a statue in the Roman Forum, he—even to that age a worshipper of idols, and a participator in the sacrilegious rites to which almost all the nobility of Rome were wedded, and had inspired the people with the love of

> The dog Anubis, and a medley crew
> Of monster gods [who] 'gainst Neptune stand in arms,
> 'Gainst Venus and Minerva, steel-clad Mars,[22]

whom Rome once conquered, now worshipped, all which old Victorinus had with thundering eloquence defended so many years—he now blushed not to be the child of Thy Christ, and an infant at Thy fountain, submitting his neck to the yoke of humility, and subduing his forehead to the reproach of the Cross.

O Lord, Lord, who has bowed the heavens and come down, touched the mountains and they did smoke,[23] by what means didst Thou convey Thyself into that bosom? He used to read, as Simplicianus said, the Holy Scripture, most studiously sought after and searched into all the Christian writings, and said to Simplicianus—not openly, but secretly, and as a friend—"Know thou that I am a Christian." To which he replied, "I will not believe it, nor will I rank you among the Christians unless I see you in the Church of Christ." Whereupon he replied derisively, "Is it then the walls that make Christians?" And this he often said, that he already was a Christian; and Simplicianus making the same answer, the conceit of the walls was by the other as often renewed. For he was fearful of offending his friends, proud demon-worshippers, from the height of whose Babylonian dignity, as from cedars of Lebanon which had not yet been broken by the Lord,[24] he thought a storm of enmity would descend upon him. But after that, from reading and inquiry, he had derived strength, and feared lest he should be denied by Christ before the holy angels if he now was afraid to confess Him before men,[25] and appeared to himself guilty of a great fault

[19] Col. ii. 8   [20] *i.e.* the Platonists   [21] Matt. xi. 25   [22] *Aeneid,* viii. 698-9   [23] Ps. cxliv. 5   [24] Ps. xxix. 5   [25] Luke ix. 26

in being ashamed of the sacraments of the humility of Thy word, and not being ashamed of the sacrilegious rites of those proud demons, whose pride he had imitated and their rites adopted, he became bold-faced against vanity, and shame-faced toward the truth, and suddenly and unexpectedly said to Simplicianus—as he himself informed me—"Let us go to the church; I wish to be made a Christian." But he, not containing himself for joy, accompanied him. And having been admitted to the first sacraments of instruction, he not long after gave in his name, that he might be regenerated by baptism—Rome marvelling, and the Church rejoicing. The proud saw, and were enraged; they gnashed with their teeth, and melted away! [26] But the Lord God was the hope of Thy servant, and He regarded not vanities and lying madness.[27]

Finally, when the hour arrived for him to make profession of his faith (which at Rome they who are about to approach Thy grace are wont to deliver from an elevated place, in view of the faithful people, in a set form of words learnt by heart), the presbyters, he said, offered Victorinus to make his profession more privately, as the custom was to do to those who were likely, through bashfulness, to be afraid; but he chose rather to profess his salvation in the presence of the holy assembly. For it was not salvation that he taught in rhetoric, and yet he had publicly professed that. How much less, therefore, ought he, when pronouncing Thy word, to dread Thy meek flock, who, in the delivery of his own words, had not feared the mad multitudes! So, then, when he ascended to make his profession, all, as they recognised him, whispered his name one to the other, with a voice of congratulation. And who was there amongst them that did not know him? And there ran a low murmur through the mouths of all the rejoicing multitude, "Victorinus! Victorinus!" Sudden was the burst of exultation at the sight of him; and suddenly were they hushed, that they might hear him. He pronounced the true faith with an excellent boldness, and all desired to take him to their very heart—by their love and joy they took him thither; such were the hands with which they took him.

CHAPTER III

THAT GOD AND THE ANGELS REJOICE MORE ON THE RETURN OF ONE SINNER THAN OF MANY JUST PERSONS

Good God, what passed in man to make him rejoice more at the salvation of a soul despaired of, and delivered from greater danger, than if there had always been hope of him, or the danger had been less? For so Thou also, O merciful Father, dost joy over one sinner that repenteth, more than over ninety and nine just persons that need no repentance. And with much joyfulness do we hear, whenever we hear, how the lost sheep is

[26] Ps. cxii. 10   [27] Ps. xxxi. 6, 14, 18

brought home again on the Shepherd's shoulders, while the angels rejoice, and the drachma is restored to Thy treasury, the neighbors rejoicing with the woman who found it;[28] and the joy of the solemn service of Thy house constraineth to tears, when in Thy house it is read of Thy younger son that he was dead, and is alive again, and was lost, and is found.[29] For Thou rejoicest both in us and in Thy angels, holy through holy charity. For Thou art ever the same; for all things which abide neither the same nor for ever, Thou ever knowest after the same manner.

What, then, passes in the soul when it more delights at finding or having restored to it the thing it loves than if it had always possessed them? Yea, and other things bear witness hereunto; and all things are full of witnesses, crying out, "So it is." The victorious commander triumphs; yet he would not have conquered had he not fought, and the greater the peril of the battle, the more the rejoicing of the triumph. The storm tosses the voyagers, threatens shipwreck, and every one waxes pale at the approach of death; but sky and sea grow calm, and they rejoice much, as they feared much. A loved one is sick, and his pulse indicates danger; all who desire his safety are at once sick at heart; he recovers, though not able as yet to walk with his former strength, and there is such joy as was not before when he walked sound and strong. The very pleasures of human life—not those only which rush upon us unexpectedly, and against our wills, but those that are voluntary and designed—do men obtain by difficulties. There is no pleasure at all in eating and drinking unless the pains of hunger and thirst go before. And drunkards eat certain salt meats with the view of creating a troublesome heat, which the drink allaying causes pleasure. It is also the custom that the affianced bride should not immediately be given up, that the husband may not less esteem her whom, as betrothed, he longed not for.

This law obtains in base and accursed joy; in that joy also which is permitted and lawful; in the sincerity of honest friendship; and in Him who was dead, and lived again, had been lost, and was found.[30] The greater joy is everywhere preceded by the greater pain. What meaneth this, O Lord my God, when Thou art an everlasting joy unto Thine own self, and some things about Thee are ever rejoicing in Thee? What meaneth this, that this portion of things thus ebbs and flows, alternately offended and reconciled? Is this the fashion of them, and is this all Thou hast allotted to them, whereas from the highest heaven to the lowest earth, from the beginning of the world to its end, from the angel to the worm, from the first movement unto the last, Thou settedst each in its right place, and appointedst each its proper seasons, everything good after its kind? Woe is me! How high art Thou in the highest, and how deep in the deepest! Thou withdrawest no whither, and scarcely do we *return* to Thee.

[28] Luke xv. 4-10   [29] Luke xv. 32   [30] Luke xv. 32

CHAPTER IV

HE SHOWS BY THE EXAMPLE OF VICTORINUS THAT THERE IS MORE
JOY IN THE CONVERSION OF NOBLES

Haste, Lord, and act; stir us up, and call us back; inflame us, and draw us to Thee; stir us up, and grow sweet unto us; let us now love Thee, let us run after Thee.[31] Do not many men, out of a deeper hell of blindness than that of Victorinus, return unto Thee, and approach, and are enlightened, receiving that light, which they that receive, receive power from Thee to become Thy sons?[32] But if they be less known among the people, even they that know them joy less for them. For when many rejoice together, the joy of each one is the fuller, in that they are incited and inflamed by one another. Again, because those that are known to many influence many towards salvation, and take the lead with many to follow them. And, therefore, do they also who preceded them much rejoice in regard to them, because they rejoice not in them alone. May it be averted that in Thy tabernacle the persons of the rich should be accepted before the poor, or the noble before the ignoble; since rather Thou hast chosen the weak things of the world to confound the things which are mighty; and base things of the world, and things which are despised, hast Thou chosen, yea, and things which are not, to bring to naught things that are.[33] And yet, even that least of the apostles,[34] by whose tongue Thou soundest out these words, when Paulus the proconsul[35]—his pride overcome by the apostle's warfare—was made to pass under the easy yoke[36] of Thy Christ, and became a provincial of the great King—he also, instead of Saul, his former name, desired to be called Paul, in testimony of so great a victory. For the enemy is more overcome in one of whom he hath more hold, and by whom he hath hold of more. But the proud hath he more hold of by reason of their nobility; and by them of more, by reason of their authority. By how much the more welcome, then, was the heart of Victorinus esteemed, which the devil had held as an unassailable retreat, and the tongue of Victorinus, with which mighty and cutting weapon he had slain many; so much the more abundantly should Thy sons rejoice, seeing that our King hath bound the strong man,[37] and they saw his vessels taken from him and cleansed,[38] and made meet for Thy honor, and become serviceable for the Lord unto every good work.[39]

[31] Cant. i. 4   [32] John i. 12   [33] 1 Cor. i. 27, 28   [34] 1 Cor. xv. 9   [35] Acts xiii. 12
[36] Matt. xi. 30   [37] Matt. xii. 29   [38] Luke xi. 22, 25   [39] 2 Tim. ii. 21

CHAPTER V

OF THE CAUSES WHICH ALIENATE US FROM GOD

But when that man of Thine, Simplicianus, related this to me about Victorinus, I burned to imitate him; and it was for this end he had related it. But when he had added this also, that in the time of the Emperor Julian, there was a law made by which Christians were forbidden to teach grammar and oratory, and he, in obedience to this law, chose rather to abandon the wordy school than Thy word, by which Thou makest eloquent the tongues of the dumb[40]—he appeared to me not more brave than happy, in having thus discovered an opportunity of waiting on Thee only, which thing I was sighing for, thus bound, not with the irons of another, but my own iron will. My will was the enemy master of, and thence had made a chain for me and bound me. Because of a perverse will was lust made; and lust indulged in became custom; and custom not resisted became necessity. By which links, as it were, joined together (whence I term it a "chain"), did a hard bondage hold me enthralled. But that new will which had begun to develop in me, freely to worship Thee, and to wish to enjoy Thee, O God, the only sure enjoyment, was not able as yet to overcome my former wilfulness, made strong by long indulgence. Thus did my two wills, one old and the other new, one carnal, the other spiritual, contend within me; and by their discord they unstrung my soul.

Thus came I to understand, from my own experience, what I had read, how the flesh lusteth against the Spirit, and the Spirit against the flesh.[41] I lusted both ways; yet more in that which I approved in myself, than in that which I disapproved in myself. For in this last it was now rather not "I,"[42] because in much I rather suffered against my will than did it willingly. And yet it was through me that custom became more combative against me, because I had come willingly whither I willed not. And who, then, can with any justice speak against it, when just punishment follows the sinner? Nor had I now any longer my wonted excuse, that as yet I hesitated to be above the world and serve Thee, because my perception of the truth was uncertain; for now it was certain. But I, still bound to the earth, refused to be Thy soldier; and was as much afraid of being freed from all embarrassments, as we ought to fear to be embarrassed.

Thus with the baggage of the world was I sweetly burdened, as when in slumber; and the thoughts wherein I meditated upon Thee were like the efforts of those desiring to awake, who, still overpowered with a heavy drowsiness, are again steeped therein. And as no one desires to sleep always, and in the sober judgment of all waking is better, yet does a man generally defer to shake off drowsiness, when there is a heavy lethargy in all his limbs,

[40] Wisd. x. 21   [41] Gal. v. 17   [42] Rom. vii. 20

and, though displeased, yet even after it is time to rise with pleasure yields to it, so was I assured that it were much better for me to give up myself to Thy charity, than to yield myself to my own cupidity; but the former course satisfied and vanquished me, the latter pleased me and fettered me. Nor had I aught to answer Thee calling to me, "Awake, thou that sleepest, and arise from the dead, and Christ shall give thee light." [43] And to Thee showing me on every side, that what Thou saidst was true, I, convicted by the truth, had nothing at all to reply, but the drawling and drowsy words: "Presently, lo, presently;" "Leave me a little while." But "presently, presently," had no present; and my "leave me a little while" went on for a long while. In vain did I delight in Thy law after the inner man, when another law in my members warred against the law of my mind, and brought me into captivity to the law of sin which is in my members. For the law of sin is the violence of custom, whereby the mind is drawn and held, even against its will; deserving to be so held in that it so willingly falls into it. O wretched man that I am! who shall deliver me from the body of this death but Thy grace only, through Jesus Christ our Lord? [44]

CHAPTER VI

PONTITIANUS' ACCOUNT OF ANTONY, THE FOUNDER OF MONACHISM, AND OF SOME WHO IMITATED HIM

And how, then, Thou didst deliver me out of the bonds of carnal desire, wherewith I was most firmly fettered, and out of the drudgery of worldly business, will I now declare and confess unto Thy name, O Lord, my strength and my Redeemer.[45] Amid increasing anxiety, I was transacting my usual affairs, and daily sighing unto Thee. I resorted as frequently to Thy church as the business, under the burden of which I groaned, left me free to do. Alypius was with me, being after the third sitting disengaged from his legal occupation, and awaiting further opportunity of selling his counsel, as I was wont to sell the power of speaking, if it can be supplied by teaching. But Nebridius had, on account of our friendship, consented to teach under Verecundus, a citizen and a grammarian of Milan, and a very intimate friend of us all; who vehemently desired, and by the right of friendship demanded from our company, the faithful aid he greatly stood in need of. Nebridius, then, was not drawn to this by any desire of gain (for he could have made much more of his learning had he been so inclined), but, as a most sweet and kindly friend, he would not be wanting in an office of friendliness, and slight our request. But in this he acted very discreetly, taking care not to become known to those personages whom the world esteems great; thus avoiding distraction of mind, which he desired to have free and at leisure as many hours as possible, to search, or read, or hear something concerning wisdom.

[43] Eph. v. 14   [44] Rom. vii. 22-24   [45] Ps. xix. 14

Upon a certain day, then, Nebridius being away (why, I do not remember), there came to the house to see Alypius and me, Pontitianus, a countryman of ours, in so far as he was an African, who held high office in the emperor's court. What he wanted with us I know not, but we sat down to talk together, and it fell out that upon a table before us, used for games, he noticed a book; he took it up, opened it, and, contrary to his expectation, found it to be the Apostle Paul—for he imagined it to be one of those books which I was wearing myself out in teaching. At this he looked up at me smilingly, and expressed his delight and wonder that he had so unexpectedly found this book, and this only, before my eyes. For he was both a Christian and baptized, and often prostrated himself before Thee our God in the church, in constant and daily prayers. When, then, I had told him that I bestowed much pains upon these writings, a conversation ensued on his speaking of Antony, the Egyptian monk, whose name was in high repute among Thy servants, though up to that time not familiar to us. When he came to know this, he lingered on that topic, imparting to us a knowledge of this man so eminent, and marvelling at our ignorance. But we were amazed, hearing Thy wonderful works most fully manifested in times so recent, and almost in our own, wrought in the true faith and the Catholic Church. We all wondered—we, that they were so great, and he, that we had never heard of them.

From this his conversation turned to the companies in the monasteries, and their manners so fragrant unto Thee, and of the fruitful deserts of the wilderness, of which we knew nothing. And there was a monastery at Milan full of good brethren, without the walls of the city, under the fostering care of Ambrose, and we were ignorant of it. He went on with his relation, and we listened intently and in silence. He then related to us how on a certain afternoon, at Triers, when the emperor was taken up with seeing the Circensian games, he and three others, his comrades, went out for a walk in the gardens close to the city walls, and there, as they chanced to walk two and two, one strolled away with him, while the other two went by themselves; and these, in their rambling, came upon a certain cottage inhabited by some of Thy servants, poor in spirit, of whom is the kingdom of heaven,[46] where they found a book in which was written the life of Antony. This one of them began to read, marvel at, and be inflamed by it; and in the reading, to meditate on embracing such a life, and giving up his worldly employments to serve Thee. And these were of the body called Agents for Public Affairs. Then, suddenly being overwhelmed with a holy love and a sober sense of shame, in anger with himself, he cast his eyes upon his friend, exclaiming, "Tell me, I entreat thee, what end we are striving for by all these labors of ours. What is our aim? What is our motive in doing service? Can our hopes in court rise higher than to be ministers of the emperor? And in such a position, what is there not brittle, and

[46] Matt. v. 3

fraught with danger, and by how many dangers arrive we at greater danger? And when arrive we thither? But if I desire to become a friend of God, behold, I am even now made it." Thus he spoke, and in the pangs of the travail of the new life, he turned his eyes again upon the page and continued reading, and was inwardly changed where Thou sawest, and his mind was divested of the world, as soon became evident; for as he read, and the surging of his heart rolled along, he raged awhile, discerned and resolved on a better course, and now, having become Thine, he said to his friend, "Now have I broken loose from those hopes of ours, and am determined to serve God; and this, from this hour, in this place, I enter upon. If thou art reluctant to imitate me, hinder me not." The other replied that he would cleave to him, to share in so great a reward and so great a service. Thus both of them, being now Thine, were building a tower at the necessary cost [47]—of forsaking all that they had and following Thee. Then Pontitianus, and he who had walked with him through other parts of the garden, came in search of them to the same place, and having found them, reminded them to return as the day had declined. But they, making known to him their resolution and purpose, and how such a resolve had sprung up and become confirmed in them, entreated them not to molest them, if they refused to join themselves to them. But the others, no whit changed from their former selves, did yet (as he said) bewail themselves, and piously congratulated them, recommending themselves to their prayers; and with their hearts inclining towards earthly things, returned to the palace. But the other two, setting their affections upon heavenly things, remained in the cottage. And both of them had affianced brides, who, when they heard of this, dedicated also their virginity to Thee.

CHAPTER VII

HE DEPLORES HIS WRETCHEDNESS, THAT HAVING BEEN BORN
THIRTY-TWO YEARS, HE HAD NOT YET FOUND OUT
THE TRUTH

Such was the story of Pontitianus. But Thou, O Lord, whilst he was speaking, didst turn me towards myself, taking me from behind my back, where I had placed myself while unwilling to exercise self-scrutiny; and Thou didst set me face to face with myself, that I might behold how foul I was, and how crooked and sordid, bespotted and ulcerous. And I beheld and loathed myself; and whither to fly from myself I discovered not. And if I sought to turn my gaze away from myself, he continued his narrative, and Thou again opposedst me unto myself, and thrustedst me before my own eyes, that I might discover my iniquity, and hate it.[48] I had known it, but acted as though I knew it not—winked at it, and forgot it.

[47] Luke xiv. 26-35   [48] Ps. xxxvi. 2

But now, the more ardently I loved those whose healthful affections I heard of, that they had given up themselves wholly to Thee to be cured, the more did I abhor myself when compared with them. For many of my years (perhaps twelve) had passed away since my nineteenth, when, on the reading of Cicero's *Hortensius*,[49] I was roused to a desire for wisdom; and still I was delaying to reject mere worldly happiness, and to devote myself to search out that of which not the finding alone, but the bare search, ought to have been preferred before the treasures and kingdoms of this world, though already found, and before the pleasures of the body, though encompassing me at my will. But I, miserable young man, supremely miserable even in the very outset of my youth, had entreated chastity of Thee, and said, "Grant me chastity and continency, but not yet." For I was afraid lest Thou shouldest hear me soon, and soon deliver me from the disease of concupiscence, which I desired to have satisfied rather than extinguished. And I had wandered through perverse ways in a sacrilegious superstition; not indeed assured thereof, but preferring that to the others, which I did not seek religiously, but opposed maliciously.

And I had thought that I delayed from day to day to reject worldly hopes and follow Thee only, because there did not appear anything certain whither to direct my course. And now had the day arrived in which I was to be laid bare to myself, and my conscience was to chide me. "Where art thou, O my tongue? Thou saidst that for an uncertain truth thou wert not willing to cast off the baggage of vanity. Behold, now it is certain, and yet doth that burden still oppress thee; whereas they who neither have so worn themselves out with searching after it, nor yet have spent ten years and more in thinking thereon, have had their shoulders unburdened, and gotten wings to fly away." Thus was I inwardly consumed and mightily confounded with a horrible shame, while Pontitianus was relating these things. And he, having finished his story, and the business he came for, went his way. And to myself, what said I not within myself? With what scourges of rebuke lashed I not my soul to make it follow me, struggling to go after Thee! Yet it drew back; it refused, and exercised not itself. All its arguments were exhausted and confuted. There remained a silent trembling; and it feared, as it would death, to be restrained from the flow of that custom whereby it was wasting away even to death.

CHAPTER VIII

THE CONVERSATION WITH ALYPIUS BEING ENDED, HE RETIRES TO THE GARDEN, WHITHER HIS FRIEND FOLLOWS HIM

In the midst, then, of this great strife of my inner dwelling, which I had strongly raised up against my soul in the chamber of my heart,[50] troubled

---

[49] Cf. iii. 7   [50] Isa. xxvi. 20, and Matt. vi. 6

both in mind and countenance, I seized upon Alypius, and exclaimed: "What is wrong with us? What is this? What heardest thou? The unlearned start up and 'take' heaven,[51] and we, with our learning, but wanting heart, see where we wallow in flesh and blood! Because others have preceded us, are we ashamed to follow, and not rather ashamed at not following?" Some such words I uttered, and in my excitement flung myself from him, while he gazed upon me in silent astonishment. For I spoke not in my wonted tone, and my brow, cheeks, eyes, color, tone of voice, all expressed my emotion more than the words. There was a little garden belonging to our lodging, of which we had the use, as of the whole house; for the master, our landlord, did not live there. Thither had the tempest within my breast hurried me, where no one might impede the fiery struggle in which I was engaged with myself, until it came to the issue that Thou knewest, though I did not. But I was mad that I might be whole, and dying that I might have life, knowing what evil thing I was, but not knowing what good thing I was shortly to become. Into the garden, then, I retired, Alypius following my steps. For his presence was no bar to my solitude; or how could he desert me so troubled? We sat down at as great a distance from the house as we could. I was disquieted in spirit, being most impatient with myself that I entered not into Thy will and covenant, O my God, which all my bones cried out to me to enter, extolling it to the skies. And we enter not therein by ships, or chariots, or feet, no, nor by going so far as I had come from the house to that place where we were sitting. For not to go only, but to enter there, was naught else but to will to go, but to will it resolutely and thoroughly; not to stagger and sway about this way and that, a changeable and half-wounded will, wrestling, with one part falling as another rose.

Finally, in the very fever of my irresolution, I made many of those motions with my body which men sometimes desire to do, but cannot, if either they have not the limbs, or if their limbs be bound with fetters, weakened by disease, or hindered in any other way. Thus, if I tore my hair, struck my forehead, or if, entwining my fingers, I clasped my knee, this I did because I willed it. But I might have willed and not done it, if the power of motion in my limbs had not responded. So many things, then, I did, when to have the will was not to have the power, and I did not that which both with an unequalled desire I longed more to do, and which shortly when I should will I should have the power to do; because shortly when I should will, I should will thoroughly. For in such things the power was one with the will, and to will was to do, and yet was it not done; and more readily did the body obey the slightest wish of the soul in the moving its limbs at the order of the mind, than the soul obeyed itself to accomplish in the will alone this its great will.

[51] Matt. xi. 12

CHAPTER IX

THAT THE MIND COMMANDS THE MIND, BUT IT WILLS NOT ENTIRELY

Whence is this monstrous thing? And why is it? Let Thy mercy shine on me, that I may inquire, if the hiding-places of man's punishment and the darkest contritions of the sons of Adam may perhaps answer me. Whence is this monstrous thing? and why is it? The mind commands the body, and it obeys forthwith; the mind commands itself, and is resisted. The mind commands the hand to be moved, and such readiness is there that the command is scarce to be distinguished from the obedience. Yet the mind is mind, and the hand is body. The mind commands the mind to will, and yet, though it be itself, it obeys not. Whence this monstrous thing? and why is it? I repeat, it commands itself to will, and would not give the command unless it willed; yet is not that done which it commands. But it wills not entirely; therefore it commands not entirely. For so far forth it commands, as it wills; and so far forth is the thing commanded not done, as it wills not. For the will commands that there be a will—not another, but itself. But it does not command entirely, therefore that is not which it commands. For were it entire, it would not even command it to be, because it would already be. It is, therefore, no monstrous thing partly to will, partly to be unwilling, but an infirmity of the mind, that it does not wholly rise, sustained by truth, pressed down by custom. And so there are two wills, because one of them is not entire; and the one is supplied with what the other needs.

CHAPTER X

HE REFUTES THE OPINION OF THE MANICHAEANS AS TO TWO KINDS OF MINDS—ONE GOOD AND THE OTHER EVIL

Let them perish from Thy presence,[52] O God, as vain talkers and deceivers[53] of the soul do perish, who, observing that there were two wills in deliberating, affirm that there are two kinds of minds in us—one good, the other evil. They themselves truly are evil when they hold these evil opinions, and they shall become good when they hold the truth, and shall consent unto the truth, that Thy apostle may say unto them, "Ye were sometimes darkness, but now are ye light in the Lord."[54] But they, desiring to be light, not in the Lord, but in themselves, conceiving the nature of the soul to be the same as that which God is, are made more gross darkness; since through a shocking arrogance they went farther from Thee, the true Light, which lighteth every man that cometh into the world.[55] Take heed what you say, and blush for shame; draw near unto Him and be lightened,

[52] Ps. lxviii. 2   [53] Titus i. 10   [54] Eph. v. 8   [55] John i. 9

and your faces shall not be ashamed.[56] I, when I was deliberating upon serving the Lord my God now, as I had long purposed—I it was who willed, I who was unwilling. It was I, even I myself. I neither willed entirely, nor was entirely unwilling. Therefore I was at war with myself, and destroyed by myself. And this destruction overtook me against my will, and yet showed not the presence of another mind, but the punishment of my own. Now, then, it is no more I that do it, but sin that dwelleth in me[57] —the punishment of a more unconfined sin, in that I was a son of Adam.

For if there be as many contrary natures as there are conflicting wills, there will not now be two natures only, but many. If any one deliberate whether he should go to their conventicle, or to the theatre, those men[58] at once cry out, "Behold, here are two natures—one good, drawing this way, another bad, drawing back that way; for whence else is this indecision between conflicting wills?" But I reply that both are bad—that which draws to them, and that which draws back to the theatre. But they believe not that will to be other than good which draws to them. Supposing, then, one of us should deliberate, and through the conflict of his two wills should waver whether he should go to the theatre or to our church, would not these also waver what to answer? For either they must confess, which they are not willing to do, that the will which leads to our church is good, as well as that of those who have received and are held by the mysteries of theirs, or they must imagine that there are two evil natures and two evil minds in one man, at war one with the other; and that will not be true which they say, that there is one good and another bad; or they must be converted to the truth, and no longer deny that where any one deliberates, there is one soul fluctuating between conflicting wills.

Let them no more say, then, when they perceive two wills to be antagonistic to each other in the same man, that the contest is between two opposing minds, of two opposing substances, from two opposing principles, the one good and the other bad. For Thou, O true God, dost disprove, check, and convince them; as when both wills are bad, one deliberates whether he should kill a man by poison, or by the sword; whether he should take possession of this or that estate of another's, when he cannot both; whether he should purchase pleasure by prodigality, or retain his money by covetousness; whether he should go to the circus or the theatre, if both are open on the same day; or thirdly, whether he should rob another man's house, if he have the opportunity; or, fourthly, whether he should commit adultery, if at the same time he have the means of doing so—all these things concurring in the same point of time, and all being equally longed for, although impossible to be enacted at one time. For they rend the mind amid four, or even (among the vast variety of things men desire) more antagonistic wills, nor do they yet affirm that there are so many different

---

[56] Ps. xxxiv. 5   [57] Rom. vii. 17   [58] The Manichaeans

substances. Thus also is it in wills which are good. For I ask them, is it a good thing to have delight in reading the apostle, or good to have delight in a sober psalm, or good to discourse on the gospel? To each of these they will answer, "It is good." What, then, if all equally delight us, and all at the same time? Do not different wills distract the mind, when a man is deliberating which he should rather choose? Yet are they all good, and are at variance until one be fixed upon, whither the whole united will may be borne, which before was divided into many. Thus, also, when eternity delights us above, and the pleasure of temporal good holds us down below, it is the same soul which wills not that or this with an entire will, and is therefore torn asunder with grievous perplexities, while out of truth it prefers that, but out of custom does not lay aside this.

CHAPTER XI

IN WHAT MANNER THE SPIRIT STRUGGLED WITH THE FLESH, THAT IT MIGHT BE FREED FROM THE BONDAGE OF VANITY

Thus was I sick and tormented, accusing myself far more severely than was my wont, tossing and turning me in my chain till that was utterly broken, whereby I now was but slightly, but still was held. And Thou, O Lord, pressedst upon me in my inward parts by a severe mercy, redoubling the lashes of fear and shame, lest I should again give way, and that same slender remaining tie not being broken off, it should recover strength, and enchain me the faster. For I said mentally, "Lo, let it be done now, let it be done now." And as I spoke, I all but came to a resolve. I all but did it, yet I did it not. Yet I fell not back to my old condition, but took up my position hard by, and drew breath. And I tried again, and wanted but very little of reaching it, and somewhat less, and then all but touched and grasped it; and yet came not at it, nor touched, nor grasped it, hesitating to die to death, and to live to life; and the worse, to which I had been habituated, prevailed more with me than the better, which I had not tried. And the very moment in which I was to become another man, the nearer it approached me, the greater horror did it strike into me; but it did not strike me back, nor turn me aside, but kept me in suspense.

The very toys of toys, and vanities of vanities, my old mistresses, still enthralled me; they shook my fleshly garment, and whispered softly, "Dost thou part with us? And from that moment shall we no more be with thee for ever? And from that moment shall not this or that be lawful for thee for ever?" And what did they suggest to me in the words "this or that?" What is it that they suggested, O my God? Let Thy mercy avert it from the soul of Thy servant. What impurities did they suggest! What shame! And now I far less than half heard them, not openly showing themselves and contradicting me, but muttering, as it were, behind my back, and furtively plucking me as I was departing, to make me look back upon them.

Yet they did delay me, so that I hesitated to burst and shake myself free from them, and to leap over whither I was called—an unruly habit saying to me, "Dost thou think thou canst live without them?"

But now it said this very faintly; for on that side towards which I had set my face, and whither I trembled to go, did the chaste dignity of Continence appear to me, cheerful, but not dissolutely gay, honestly alluring me to come and doubt nothing, and extending her holy hands, full of a multiplicity of good examples, to receive and embrace me. There were there so many young men and maidens, a multitude of youth and every age, grave widows and ancient virgins, and Continence herself in all, not barren, but a fruitful mother of children of joys, by Thee, O Lord, her Husband. And she smiled on me with an encouraging mockery, as if to say, "Canst not thou do what these youths and maidens can? Or can one or other do it of themselves, and not rather in the Lord their God? The Lord their God gave me to them. Why standest thou in thine own strength, and so standest not? Cast thyself upon Him; fear not, He will not withdraw that thou shouldest fall; cast thyself upon Him without fear, He will receive thee, and heal thee." And I blushed beyond measure, for I still heard the muttering of those toys, and hung in suspense. And she again seemed to say, "Shut up thine ears against those unclean members of thine upon the earth, that they may be mortified.[59] They tell thee of delights, but not as doth the law of the Lord thy God." This controversy in my heart was naught but self against self. But Alypius, sitting close by my side, awaited in silence the result of my unwonted emotion.

CHAPTER XII

HAVING PRAYED TO GOD, HE POURS FORTH A SHOWER OF TEARS, AND, ADMONISHED BY A VOICE, HE OPENS THE BOOK AND READS THE WORDS IN ROM. XIII. 13; BY WHICH, BEING CHANGED IN HIS WHOLE SOUL, HE DISCLOSES THE DIVINE FAVOR TO HIS FRIEND AND HIS MOTHER

But when a profound reflection had, from the secret depths of my soul, drawn together and heaped up all my misery before the sight of my heart, there arose a mighty storm, accompanied by as mighty a shower of tears. Which, that I might pour forth fully, with its natural expressions, I stole away from Alypius; for it suggested itself to me that solitude was fitter for the business of weeping. So I retired to such a distance that even his presence could not be oppressive to me. Thus it was with me at that time, and he perceived it; for something, I believe, I had spoken, wherein the sound of my voice appeared choked with weeping, and in that state had I risen up. He then remained where we had been sitting, most completely astonished. I flung myself down, how, I know not, under a certain fig-tree, giv-

[59] Col. iii. 5

ing free course to my tears, and the streams of mine eyes gushed out, an acceptable sacrifice unto Thee.[60] And, not indeed in these words, yet to this effect, spake I much unto Thee—"But Thou, O Lord, how long?" [61] "How long, Lord? Wilt Thou be angry for ever? Oh, remember not against us former iniquities;" [62] for I felt that I was enthralled by them. I sent up these sorrowful cries—"How long, how long? To-morrow, and to-morrow? Why not now? Why is there not this hour an end to my uncleanness?"

I was saying these things and weeping in the most bitter contrition of my heart, when, lo, I heard the voice as of a boy or girl, I know not which, coming from a neighboring house, chanting, and oft repeating, "Take up and read; take up and read." Immediately my countenance was changed, and I began most earnestly to consider whether it was usual for children in any kind of game to sing such words; nor could I remember ever to have heard the like. So, restraining the torrent of my tears, I rose up, interpreting it no other way than as a command to me from Heaven to open the book, and to read the first chapter I should light upon. For I had heard of Antony, that, accidentally coming in while the gospel was being read, he received the admonition as if what was read were addressed to him, "Go and sell that thou hast, and give to the poor, and thou shalt have treasure in heaven; and come and follow me." [63] And by such oracle was he forthwith converted unto Thee. So quickly I returned to the place where Alypius was sitting; for there had I put down the volume of the apostles, when I rose thence. I grasped, opened, and in silence read that paragraph on which my eyes first fell—"Not in rioting and drunkenness, not in chambering and wantonness, not in strife and envying; but put ye on the Lord Jesus Christ, and make not provision for the flesh, to fulfil the lusts thereof." [64] No further would I read, nor did I need; for instantly, as the sentence ended—by a light, as it were, of security infused into my heart—all the gloom of doubt vanished away.

Closing the book, then, and putting either my finger between, or some other mark, I now with a tranquil countenance made it known to Alypius. And he thus disclosed to me what was wrought in him, which I knew not. He asked to look at what I had read. I showed him; and he looked even further than I had read, and I knew not what followed. This it was, "Him that is weak in the faith, receive ye;" [65] which he applied to himself, and discovered to me. By this admonition was he strengthened; and by a good resolution and purpose, very much in accord with his character (in which, for the better, he was always far different from me), without any restless delay he joined me. Thence we go in to my mother. We make it known to her—she rejoices. We relate how it came to pass—she leaps for joy, and triumphs, and blesses Thee, who art able to do exceeding abundantly above all that we ask or think;[66] for she perceived Thee to have given her more

---

[60] I Pet. ii. 5   [61] Ps. vi. 3   [62] Ps. lxxix. 5, 8   [63] Matt. xix. 21   [64] Rom. xiii. 13, 14   [65] Rom. xiv. 1   [66] Eph. iii. 20

for me than she used to ask by her pitiful and most doleful groanings. For Thou didst so convert me unto Thyself, that I sought neither a wife, nor any other of this world's hopes—standing in that rule of faith in which Thou, so many years before, had showed me unto her in a vision. And thou didst turn her grief into a gladness,[67] much more plentiful than she had desired, and much dearer and chaster than she used to crave, by having grandchildren of my body.

[67] Ps. xxx. 11

BOOK NINE

He speaks of his design of forsaking the profession of rhetoric; of the death of his friends, Nebridius and Verecundus; of having received baptism in the thirty-third year of his age; and of the virtues and death of his mother, Monica.

CHAPTER I

HE PRAISES GOD, THE AUTHOR OF SAFETY, AND JESUS CHRIST, THE
REDEEMER, ACKNOWLEDGING HIS OWN WICKEDNESS

O LORD, truly I am Thy servant; I am Thy servant, and the son of Thine handmaid: Thou hast loosed my bonds. I will offer to Thee the sacrifice of thanksgiving.[1] Let my heart and my tongue praise Thee, and let all my bones say, "Lord, who is like unto Thee?"[2] Let them so say, and answer Thou me, and say unto my soul, I am Thy salvation.[3] Who am I, and what is my nature? How evil have not my deeds been; or if not my deeds, my words; or if not my words, my will? But Thou, O Lord, art good and merciful, and Thy right hand had respect unto the profoundness of my death, and removed from the bottom of my heart that abyss of corruption. And this was the result, that I willed not to do what I willed, and willed to do what thou willedst. But where, during all those years, and out of what deep and secret retreat was my free will summoned forth in a moment, whereby I gave my neck to Thy easy yoke, and my shoulders to Thy light burden,[4] O Christ Jesus, my strength and my Redeemer?[5] How sweet did it suddenly become to me to be without the delights of trifles! And what at one time I feared to lose, it was now a joy to me to put away. For Thou didst cast them away from me, Thou true and highest sweetness. Thou didst cast them away, and instead of them didst enter in Thyself—sweeter than all pleasure, though not to flesh and blood; brighter than all light, but more veiled than all mysteries; more exalted than all honor, but not to the exalted in their own conceits. Now was my soul free from the gnawing cares of seeking and getting, and of wallowing and exciting the itch of lust. And I babbled unto Thee my brightness, my riches, and my health, the Lord my God.

[1] Ps. cxvi. 16, 17   [2] *Ibid.* xxxv. 10   [3] *Ibid.* xxxv. 3   [4] Matt. xi. 30   [5] Ps. xix. 14

CHAPTER II

AS HIS LUNGS WERE AFFECTED, HE MEDITATES WITHDRAWING HIMSELF FROM PUBLIC FAVOR

And it seemed good to me, as before Thee, not tumultuously to snatch away, but gently to withdraw the service of my tongue from the talker's trade; that the young, who thought not on Thy law, nor on Thy peace, but on mendacious follies and forensic strifes, might no longer purchase at my mouth equipments for their vehemence. And opportunity there wanted but a few days until the Vacation of the Vintage; and I determined to endure them, in order to leave in the usual way, and, being redeemed by Thee, no more to return for sale. Our intention then was known to Thee; but to men —excepting our own friends—was it not known. For we had determined among ourselves not to let it get abroad to any; although Thou hadst given to us, ascending from the valley of tears,[6] and singing the song of degrees, sharp arrows, and destroying coals, against the deceitful tongue,[7] which in giving counsel opposes, and in showing love consumes, as it is wont to do with its food.

Thou hadst penetrated our hearts with Thy charity, and we carried Thy words fixed, as it were, in our bowels; and the examples of Thy servant, whom of black Thou hadst made bright, and of dead, alive, crowded in the bosom of our thoughts, burned and consumed our heavy torpor, that we might not topple into the abyss; and they enkindled us exceedingly, that every breath of the deceitful tongue of the gainsayer might inflame us the more, not extinguish us. Nevertheless, because for Thy name's sake which Thou hast sanctified throughout the earth, this, our vow and purpose, might also find commenders, it looked like a vaunting of oneself not to wait for the vacation, now so near, but to leave beforehand a public profession, and one, too, under general observation; so that all who looked on this act of mine, and saw how near was the vintage-time I desired to anticipate, would talk of me a great deal as if I were trying to appear to be a great person. And what purpose would it serve that people should consider and dispute about my intention, and that our good should be evil spoken of?[8]

Furthermore, this very summer, from too great literary labor, my lungs began to be weak, and with difficulty to draw deep breaths; showing by the pains in my chest that they were affected, and refusing too loud or prolonged speaking. This had at first been a trial to me, for it compelled me almost of necessity to lay down that burden of teaching; or, if I could be cured and become strong again, at least to leave it off for a while. But when the full desire for leisure, that I might see that Thou art the Lord,[9] arose, and was confirmed in me, my God, Thou knowest I even began to

---

[6] Ps. lxxxiv. 6   [7] Ps. cxx. 3, 4   [8] Rom. xiv. 16   [9] Ps. xlvi. 10

rejoice that I had this excuse ready—and that not a feigned one—which might somewhat temper the offence taken by those who for their sons' good wished me never to have the freedom of sons. Full, therefore, with such joy, I bore it till that period of time had passed—perhaps it was some twenty days—yet they were bravely borne; for the cupidity which was wont to sustain part of this weighty business had departed, and I had remained overwhelmed had not its place been supplied by patience. Some of Thy servants, my brethren, may perchance say that I sinned in this, in that having once fully, and from my heart, entered on Thy warfare, I permitted myself to sit a single hour in the seat of falsehood. I will not contend. But hast not Thou, O most merciful Lord, pardoned and remitted this sin also, with my others, so horrible and deadly, in the holy water?

CHAPTER III

HE RETIRES TO THE VILLA OF HIS FRIEND VERECUNDUS, WHO WAS NOT YET A CHRISTIAN, AND REFERS TO HIS CONVERSION AND DEATH, AS WELL AS THAT OF NEBRIDIUS

Verecundus was wasted with anxiety at our happiness, since he, being most firmly held by his bonds, saw that he would lose our fellowship. For he was not yet a Christian, though his wife was one of the faithful; and yet hereby, being more firmly enchained than by anything else, was he held back from that journey which we had commenced. Nor, he declared, did he wish to be a Christian on any other terms than those that were impossible. However, he invited us most courteously to make use of his country house so long as we should stay there. Thou, O Lord, wilt recompense him for this at the resurrection of the just,[10] seeing that Thou hast already given him the lot of the righteous.[11] For although, when we were absent at Rome, he, being overtaken with bodily sickness, and therein being made a Christian, and one of the faithful, departed this life, yet hadst Thou mercy on him, and not on him only, but on us also;[12] lest, thinking on the exceeding kindness of our friend to us, and unable to count him in Thy flock, we should be tortured with intolerable grief. Thanks be unto Thee, our God, we are Thine. Thy exhortations, consolations, and faithful promises assure us that Thou now repayest Verecundus for that country house at Cassiciacum where from the fever of the world we found rest in Thee, with the perpetual freshness of Thy Paradise, in that Thou hast forgiven him his earthly sins, in that mountain flowing with milk, that fruitful mountain—Thine own.

He then was at that time full of grief; but Nebridius was joyous. Although he also, not being yet a Christian, had fallen into the pit of that most pernicious error of believing Thy Son to be a phantasm, yet, coming

[10] Luke xiv. 14   [11] Ps. cxxv. 2   [12] Phil. ii. 27

out thence, he held the same belief that we did; not as yet initiated in any of the sacraments of Thy Church, but a most earnest inquirer after truth. Him, not long after our conversion and regeneration by Thy baptism, he being also a faithful member of the Catholic Church, and serving Thee in perfect chastity and continency amongst his own people in Africa, when his whole household had been brought to Christianity through him, didst Thou release from the flesh; and now he lives in Abraham's bosom. Whatever that may be which is signified by that bosom, there lives my Nebridius, my sweet friend, Thy son, O Lord, adopted of a freedman; there he liveth. For what other place could there be for such a soul? There liveth he, concerning which he used to ask me much—me, an inexperienced, feeble one. Now he puts not his ear unto my mouth, but his spiritual mouth unto Thy fountain, and drinketh as much as he is able, wisdom according to his desire—happy without end. Nor do I believe that he is so inebriated with it as to forget me, seeing Thou, O Lord, whom he drinketh, art mindful of us. Thus, then, were we comforting the sorrowing Verecundus (our friendship being untouched, concerning our conversion) and exhorting him to a faith according to his condition, I mean, his married state. And tarrying for Nebridius to follow us, which, being so near, he was just about to do, when, behold, those days passed over at last; for long and many they seemed, on account of my love of easeful liberty, that I might sing unto Thee from my very marrow. My heart said unto Thee—I have sought Thy face; Thy face, Lord, will I seek.[13]

CHAPTER IV

IN THE COUNTRY HE GIVES HIS ATTENTION TO LITERATURE, AND EXPLAINS
THE FOURTH PSALM IN CONNECTION WITH THE HAPPY CONVERSION
OF ALYPIUS. HE IS TROUBLED WITH TOOTHACHE

And the day arrived on which, in very deed, I was to be released from the Professorship of Rhetoric, from which in intention I had been already released. And it was done; and Thou didst deliver my tongue whence Thou hadst already delivered my heart; and full of joy I blessed Thee for it, and retired with all mine to the villa. What I accomplished here in writing, which was now wholly devoted to Thy service, though still, in this pause as it were, panting from the school of pride, my books testify—those in which I disputed with my friends, and those with myself alone before Thee; and what with the absent Nebridius, my letters testify. And when can I find time to recount all Thy great benefits which Thou bestowedst upon us at that time, especially as I am hasting on to still greater mercies? For my memory calls upon me, and pleasant it is to me, O Lord, to confess unto Thee, by what inward goads Thou didst subdue me, and how Thou

[13] Ps. xxvii. 8

didst make me low, bringing down the mountains and hills of my imaginations, and didst straighten my crookedness, and smooth my rough ways;[14]
and by what means Thou also didst subdue that brother of my heart,
Alypius, unto the name of Thy only-begotten, our Lord and Saviour Jesus
Christ, which he at first refused to have inserted in our writings. For he
rather desired that they should savor of the "cedars" of the schools, which
the Lord hath now broken down,[15] than of the wholesome herbs of the
Church, hostile to serpents.

What utterances sent I up unto Thee, my God, when I read the Psalms
of David, those faithful songs and sounds of devotion which exclude all
swelling of spirit, when new to Thy true love, at rest in the villa with
Alypius, a catechumen like myself, my mother cleaving unto us—in woman's
garb truly, but with a man's faith, with the peacefulness of age, full of
motherly love and Christian piety! What utterances I used to send up unto
Thee in those Psalms, and how was I inflamed towards Thee by them, and
burned to rehearse them, if it were possible, throughout the whole world,
against the pride of the human race! And yet they are sung throughout
the whole world, and none can hide himself from Thy heat.[16] With what
vehement and bitter sorrow was I indignant at the Manichaeans; whom
yet again I pitied, for they were ignorant of those sacraments, those medicaments, and were mad against the antidote which might have made them
sane! I wished that they had been somewhere near me then, and, without
my being aware of their presence, could have beheld my face, and heard
my words, when I read the fourth Psalm in that time of my leisure—how
that Psalm wrought upon me. When I called upon Thee, Thou didst hear
me, O God of my righteousness; Thou hast enlarged me when I was in
distress; have mercy upon me, and hear my prayer.[17] Oh that they might
have heard what I uttered on these words, without my knowing whether
they heard or no, lest they should think that I spake it because of them!
For, of a truth, neither should I have said the same things, nor in the way
I said them, if I had perceived that I was heard and seen by them; and
had I spoken them, they would not so have received them as when I spoke
by and for myself before Thee, out of the private feelings of my soul.

I alternately quaked with fear, and warmed with hope, and with rejoicing
in Thy mercy, O Father. And all these passed forth, both by mine eyes and
voice, when Thy good Spirit, turning unto us, said, O ye sons of men, how
long will ye be slow of heart? How long will ye love vanity, and seek after
leasing?[18] For I had loved vanity, and sought after leasing. And Thou, O
Lord, hadst already magnified Thy Holy One, raising Him from the dead,
and setting Him at Thy right hand,[19] whence from on high He should send
His promise,[20] the Paraclete, the Spirit of Truth.[21] And He had already
sent Him,[22] but I knew it not; He had sent Him, because He was now

[14] Luke iii. 5   [15] Ps. xxix. 5   [16] Ps. xix. 6   [17] Ps. iv. 1   [18] *Ibid.* 23   [19] Eph.
i. 20   [20] Luke xxiv. 49   [21] John xiv. 16, 17   [22] Acts ii. 1-4

magnified, rising again from the dead, and ascending into heaven. For till then the Holy Ghost was not yet given, because that Jesus was not yet glorified.[23] And the prophet cries out, How long will ye be slow of heart? How long will ye love vanity, and seek after leasing? Know this, that the Lord hath magnified His Holy One. He cries out, "How long?" He cries out, "Know this," and I, so long ignorant, loved vanity, and sought after leasing. And therefore I heard and trembled, because these words were spoken unto such as I remembered that I myself had been. For in those phantasms which I once held for truths was there vanity and leasing. And I spoke many things loudly and earnestly, in the sorrow of my remembrance, which, would that they who yet love vanity and seek after leasing had heard! They would perchance have been troubled, and have vomited it forth, and Thou wouldest hear them when they cried unto Thee;[24] for by a true death in the flesh He died for us, who now maketh intercession for us[25] with Thee.

I read further, "Be ye angry, and sin not." [26] And how was I moved, O my God, who had now learned to be angry with myself for the things past, so that in the future I might not sin! Yea, to be justly angry; for it was not another nature of the race of darkness which sinned for me, as they affirm it to be who are not angry with themselves, and who treasure up to themselves wrath against the day of wrath, and of the revelation of Thy righteous judgment.[27] Nor were my good things[28] now without, nor were they sought after with eyes of flesh in that sun; for they that would have joy from without easily sink into oblivion, and are wasted upon those things which are seen and temporal, and in their starving thoughts do lick their very shadows. Oh, if only they were wearied out with their fasting, and said, "Who will show us any good?" [29] And we would answer, and they hear, O Lord. The light of Thy countenance is lifted up upon us.[30] For we are not that Light, which lighteth every man,[31] but we are enlightened by Thee, that we, who were sometimes darkness, may be light in Thee.[32] Oh that they could behold the internal Eternal, which having tasted I gnashed my teeth that I could not show It to them, while they brought me their heart in their eyes, roaming abroad from Thee, and said, "Who will show us any good?" But there, where I was angry with myself in my chamber, where I was inwardly pricked, where I had offered my sacrifice, slaying my old man, and beginning the resolution of a new life, putting my trust in Thee[33]—there hadst Thou begun to grow sweet unto me, and to put gladness in my heart.[34] And I cried out as I read this outwardly, and felt it inwardly. Nor would I be increased with worldly goods, wasting time and being wasted by time; whereas I possessed in Thy eternal simplicity other corn, and wine, and oil.[35]

[23] John vii. 39   [24] Ps. iv. 1   [25] Rom. viii. 34   [26] Eph. iv. 26   [27] Rom. ii. 5
[28] Ps. iv. 6   [29] Ps. iv. 6   [30] Ibid.   [31] John i. 9   [32] Eph. v. 8   [33] Ps. iv. 5
[34] Ps. iv. 7   [35] Ps. iv. 7

And with a loud cry from my heart, I called out in the following verse,
Oh, in peace! and the self-same! Oh, what said he, I will lay me down and
sleep! [36] For who shall hinder us, when shall be brought to pass the saying
that is written, Death is swallowed up in victory? [37] And Thou are in the
highest degree[38] the self-same, who changest not; and in Thee is the rest
which forgetteth all labor, for there is no other beside Thee, nor ought we
to seek after those many other things which are not what Thou art; but
Thou, Lord, only makest me to dwell in hope. These things I read, and
was inflamed; but discovered not what to do with those deaf and dead, of
whom I had been a pestilent member—a bitter and a blind declaimer
against the writings be-honied with the honey of heaven and luminous with
Thine own light; and I was consumed on account of the enemies of this
Scripture.

When shall I call to mind all that took place in those holidays? Yet
neither have I forgotten, nor will I be silent about the severity of Thy
scourge, and the amazing quickness of Thy mercy. Thou didst at that time
torture me with toothache; and when it had become so exceeding great that
I was not able to speak, it came into my heart to urge all my friends who
were present to pray for me to Thee, the God of all manner of health. And
I wrote it down on wax, and gave it to them to read. Presently, as with submissive desire we bowed our knees, that pain departed. But what pain?
Or how did it depart? I confess to being much afraid, my Lord my God,
seeing that from my earliest years I had not experienced such pain. And
Thy purposes were profoundly impressed upon me; and, rejoicing in faith,
I praised Thy name. And that faith suffered me not to be at rest in regard
to my past sins, which were not yet forgiven me by Thy baptism.

CHAPTER V

AT THE RECOMMENDATION OF AMBROSE, HE READS THE PROPHECIES OF ISAIAH, BUT DOES NOT UNDERSTAND THEM

The vintage vacation being ended, I gave the citizens of Milan notice
that they might provide their scholars with another seller of words; because
both of my election to serve Thee, and my inability, by reason of the difficulty of breathing and the pain in my chest, to continue the Professorship.
And by letters I notified Thy bishop, the holy man Ambrose, of my former
errors and present resolutions, with a view to his advising me which of
Thy books it was best for me to read, so that I might be readier and fitter
for the reception of such great grace. He recommended Isaiah the Prophet;
I believe, because he foreshows more clearly than others the gospel, and the
calling of the Gentiles. But I, not understanding the first portion of the
book, and imagining the whole to be like it, laid it aside, intending to take
it up hereafter, when better practised in our Lord's words.

[36] Ps. iv. 8   [37] 1 Cor. xv. 54   [38] Ps. iv. 9

CHAPTER VI

HE IS BAPTIZED AT MILAN WITH ALYPIUS AND HIS SON ADEODATUS. THE BOOK "DE MAGISTRO"

Thence, when the time had arrived at which I was to give in my name, having left the country, we returned to Milan. Alypius also was pleased to be born again with me in Thee, being now clothed with the humility appropriate to Thy sacraments, and being so brave a tamer of the body, as with unusual fortitude to tread the frozen soil of Italy with his naked feet. We took into our company the boy Adeodatus, born of me carnally, of my sin. Well hadst Thou made him. He was barely fifteen years, yet in wit excelled many grave and learned men. I confess unto Thee Thy gifts, O Lord my God, Creator of all, and of exceeding power to reform our deformities; for of me was there naught in that boy but the sin. For we fostered him in Thy discipline, Thou inspiredst us, none other—Thy gifts I confess unto Thee. There is a book of ours, which is entitled *The Master*. It is a dialogue between him and me. Thou knowest that all things there put into the mouth of the person in argument with me were his thoughts in his sixteenth year. Many others more wonderful did I find in him. That talent was a source of awe to me. And who but Thou could be the worker of such marvels? Quickly didst Thou remove his life from the earth; and now I recall him to mind with a sense of security, in that I fear nothing for his childhood or youth, or for his whole self. We took him of equal age with us in Thy grace, to be educated in Thy discipline; and we were baptized, and solicitude about our past life left us. Nor was I satiated in those days with the wondrous sweetness of considering the depth of Thy counsels concerning the salvation of the human race. How greatly did I weep in Thy hymns and canticles, deeply moved by the voices of Thy sweet-speaking Church! The voices flowed into mine ears, and the truth was poured forth into my heart, whence the agitation of my piety overflowed, and my tears ran over, and blessed was I therein.

CHAPTER VII

OF THE CHURCH HYMNS INSTITUTED AT MILAN; OF THE AMBROSIAN PERSECUTION RAISED BY JUSTINA; AND OF THE DISCOVERY OF THE BODIES OF TWO MARTYRS

Not long had the Church of Milan begun to employ this kind of consolation and exhortation, the brethren singing together with great earnestness of voice and heart. For it was about a year, or not much more, since Justina, the mother of the boy-Emperor Valentinian, persecuted Thy servant Ambrose in the interest of her heresy, to which she had been seduced by the Arians. The pious people kept guard in the church, prepared to die with their bishop, Thy servant. There my mother, Thy handmaid, bearing a chief part of those cares and watchings, lived in prayer. We, still unmelted by the heat of Thy Spirit, were yet moved by the astonished and disturbed city. At this time it was instituted that, after the manner of the Eastern Church, hymns and psalms should be sung, lest the people should pine away in the tediousness of sorrow; this custom, retained from then till now, is imitated by many, by almost all of Thy congregations throughout the rest of the world.

Then didst Thou by a vision make known to Thy renowned bishop the spot where lay the bodies of Gervasius and Protasius, the martyrs (whom Thou hadst in Thy secret storehouse preserved uncorrupted for so many years), whence Thou mightest at the fitting time produce them to repress the feminine but royal fury. For when they were revealed and dug up and with due honor transferred to the Ambrosian Basilica, not only they who were troubled with unclean spirits (the devils confessing themselves) were healed, but a certain man also, who had been blind many years, a well-known citizen of that city, having asked and been told the reason of the people's tumultuous joy, rushed forth, asking his guide to lead him thither. Arrived there, he begged to be permitted to touch with his handkerchief the bier of Thy saints, whose death is precious in Thy sight.[39] When he had done this, and put it to his eyes, they were forthwith opened. Thence did the fame spread; thence did Thy praises burn—shine; thence was the mind of that enemy, though not yet enlarged to the wholeness of believing, restrained from the fury of persecuting. Thanks be to Thee, O my God. Whence and whither hast Thou thus led my remembrance, that I should confess these things also unto Thee—great, though I, forgetful, had passed them over? And yet then, when the savor of Thy ointments was so fragrant, did we not run after Thee?[40] And so I did the more abundantly weep at the singing of Thy hymns, formerly panting for Thee, and at last breathing in Thee, as far as the air can play in this house of grass.

CHAPTER VIII

OF THE CONVERSION OF EVODIUS, AND THE DEATH OF HIS MOTHER WHEN RETURNING WITH HIM TO AFRICA; AND WHOSE EDUCATION HE TENDERLY RELATES

Thou, who makest men to dwell of one mind in a house,[41] didst associate with us Evodius also, a young man of our city, who, when serving as an agent for Public Affairs, was converted unto Thee and baptized prior to us; and relinquishing his secular service, prepared himself for Thine. We were together, and together were we about to dwell with a holy purpose.

[39] Ps. cxvi. 15   [40] Cant. i. 3, 4   [41] Ps. lxviii. 6

We sought for some place where we might be most useful in our service to Thee, and were going back together to Africa. And when we were at the Tiberine Ostia my mother died. Much I omit, having much to hasten. Receive my confessions and thanksgivings, O my God, for innumerable things concerning which I am silent. But I will not omit anything that my soul has brought forth as to Thy handmaid who brought me forth—in her flesh, that I might be born to this temporal light, and in her heart, that I might be born to life eternal. I will speak not of her gifts, but Thine in her; for she neither made herself nor educated herself. Thou createdst her, nor did her father nor her mother know what a being was to proceed from them. And it was the rod of Thy Christ, the discipline of Thine only Son, that trained her in Thy fear, in the house of one of Thy faithful ones, who was a sound member of Thy Church. Yet this good discipline she did not so much attribute to the diligence of her mother, as that of a certain decrepit maid-servant, who had carried about her father when an infant, as little ones are wont to be carried on the backs of elder girls. For this reason, and on account of her extreme age and very good character, was she much respected by the heads of that Christian house. Whence also was committed to her the care of her master's daughters, which she with diligence performed, and was earnest in restraining them when necessary, with a holy severity, and instructing them with a sober sagacity. For, excepting at the hours in which they were very temperately fed at their parents' table, she used not to permit them, though parched with thirst, to drink even water; thereby taking precautions against an evil custom, and adding the wholesome advice, "You drink water only because you have not control of wine; but when you have come to be married, and made mistresses of storeroom and cellar, you will despise water, but the habit of drinking will remain." By this method of instruction, and power of command, she restrained the longing of their tender age, and regulated the very thirst of the girls to such a becoming limit, as that what was not seemly they did not long for.

And yet—as Thine handmaid related to me, her son—there had stolen upon her a love of wine. For when she, as a sober maiden, was as usual bidden by her parents to draw wine from the cask, the vessel being held under the opening, before she poured the wine into the bottle, she would wet the tips of her lips with a little, for more than that her inclination refused. For this she did not from any craving for drink, but out of the overflowing buoyancy of her time of life, which bubbles up with sportiveness, and is, in youthful spirits, wont to be repressed by the gravity of elders. And so to that little, adding daily littles (for "he that contemneth small things shall fall by little and little"),[42] she contracted such a habit as to drink off eagerly her little cup nearly full of wine. Where, then, was the sagacious old woman with her earnest restraint? Could anything prevail

[42] Ecclus. xix. 1

against a secret disease if Thy medicine, O Lord, did not watch over us? Father, mother, and nurturers absent, Thou present, who hast created, who callest, who also by those who are set over us workest some good for the salvation of our souls, what didst Thou at that time, O my God? How didst Thou heal her? How didst Thou make her whole? Didst Thou not out of another woman's soul evoke a hard and bitter insult, as a surgeon's knife from Thy secret store, and with one thrust remove all that putrefaction? For the maid-servant who used to accompany her to the cellar, falling out, as it happens, with her little mistress, when she was alone with her, cast in her teeth this vice, with very bitter insult, calling her a wine-bibber. Stung by this taunt, she perceived her foulness, and immediately condemned and renounced it. Even as friends by their flattery pervert, so do enemies by their taunts often correct us. Yet Thou renderest not unto them what Thou dost by them, but what was proposed by them. For she, being angry, desired to irritate her young mistress, not to cure her; and did it in secret, either because the time and place of the dispute found them thus, or perhaps lest she herself should be exposed to danger for disclosing it so late. But Thou, Lord, Governor of heavenly and earthly things, who convertest to Thy purposes the deepest torrents, and disposest the turbulent current of the ages, healest one soul by the unsoundness of another; lest any man, when he remarks this, should attribute it to his own power if another, whom he wishes to be reformed, is so through a word of his.

CHAPTER IX

HE DESCRIBES THE PRAISEWORTHY HABITS OF HIS MOTHER; HER KINDNESS TOWARDS HER HUSBAND AND HER SONS

Being thus modestly and soberly trained, and rather made subject by Thee to her parents, than by her parents to Thee, when she had arrived at a marriageable age, she was given to a husband whom she served as her lord. And she busied herself to gain him to Thee, preaching Thee unto him by her behavior; by which Thou madest her fair, and reverently amiable, and admirable to her husband. For she so bore the wronging of her bed as never to have any dissension with her husband on account of it. For she waited for Thy mercy upon him, that by believing in Thee he might become chaste. And besides this, as he was earnest in friendship, so was he violent in anger; but she had learned that an angry husband should not be resisted, neither in deed, nor even in word. But so soon as he was grown calm and tranquil, and she saw a fitting moment, she would give him a reason for her conduct, should he have been excited without cause. In short, while many matrons, whose husbands were more gentle, carried the marks of blows on their dishonored faces, and would in private conversation blame the lives of their husbands, she would blame their tongues, monishing them gravely, as if in jest that from the hour they heard what are called the matrimonial tablets read to them, they should think of them as instruments whereby they were made servants; so, being always mindful of their condition, they ought not to set themselves in opposition to their lords. And when they, knowing what a furious husband she endured, marvelled that it had never been reported, nor appeared by any indication, that Patricius had beaten his wife, or that there had been any domestic strife between them, even for a day, and asked her in confidence the reason of this, she taught them her rule, which I have mentioned above. They who observed it experienced the wisdom of it, and rejoiced; those who observed it not were kept in subjection, and suffered.

Her mother-in-law, also, being at first prejudiced against her by the whisperings of evil-disposed servants, she so conquered by submission, persevering in it with patience and meekness, that she voluntarily disclosed to her son the tongues of the meddling servants, whereby the domestic peace between herself and her daughter-in-law had been agitated, begging him to punish them for it. When, therefore, he had—in conformity with his mother's wish, and with a view to the discipline of his family, and to ensure the future harmony of its members—corrected with stripes those discovered, according to the will of her who had discovered them, she promised a similar reward to any who, to please her, should say anything evil to her of her daughter-in-law. And, none now daring to do so, they lived together with a wonderful sweetness of mutual good-will.

This great gift Thou bestowedst also, my God, my mercy, upon that good handmaid of Thine, out of whose womb Thou createdst me, even that, whenever she could, she showed herself such a peacemaker between any differing and discordant spirits, that when she had heard on both sides most bitter things, such as swelling and undigested discord is wont to give vent to, when the crudities of enmities are breathed out in bitter speeches to a present friend against an absent enemy, she would disclose nothing about the one to the other, save what might avail to their reconcilement. A small good this might seem to me, did I not know to my sorrow countless persons, who, through some horrible and far-spreading infection of sin, not only disclose to enemies mutually enraged the things said in passion against each other, but add some things that were never spoken at all; whereas, to a generous man, it ought to seem a small thing not to incite or increase the enmities of men by ill-speaking, unless he endeavor likewise by kind words to extinguish them. Such a one was she—Thou, her most intimate Instructor, teaching her in the school of her heart.

Finally, her own husband, now towards the end of his earthly existence, did she gain over unto Thee; and she had not to complain of that in him, as one of the faithful, which, before he became so, she had endured. She was also the servant of Thy servants. Whosoever of them knew her, did in her much magnify, honor, and love Thee; for through the testimony of the fruits of a holy conversation, they perceived Thee to be present in her heart. For she had been the wife of one man, had requited her parents, had guided her house piously, was well-reported of for good works, had brought up children,[43] as often travailing in birth of them[44] as she saw them swerving from Thee. Lastly, to all of us, O Lord (since of Thy favor Thou sufferest Thy servants to speak), who, before her sleeping in Thee,[45] lived associated together, having received the grace of Thy baptism, did she devote care such as she might if she had been mother of us all; served us as if she had been child of all.

CHAPTER X

A CONVERSATION HE HAD WITH HIS MOTHER
CONCERNING THE KINGDOM OF HEAVEN

As the day now approached on which she was to depart this life (which day Thou knewest, we did not), it fell out—Thou, as I believe, by Thy secret ways arranging it—that she and I stood alone, leaning in a certain window, from which the garden of the house we occupied at Ostia could be seen; at this place, removed from the crowd, we were resting ourselves for the voyage, after the fatigues of a long journey. We then were conversing alone very pleasantly; and, forgetting those things which are behind, and reaching forth unto those things which are before,[46] we were seeking between ourselves in the presence of the Truth, which Thou art, of what nature the eternal life of the saints would be, which eye hath not seen, nor ear heard, neither hath entered into the heart of man.[47] But yet we opened wide the mouth of our heart, after those supernal streams of Thy fountain, the fountain of life, which is with Thee;[48] that being sprinkled with it according to our capacity, we might in some measure weigh so high a mystery.

And when our conversation had arrived at that point, that the very highest pleasure of the carnal senses, and that in the very brightest material light, seemed by reason of the sweetness of that life not only not worthy of comparison, but not even of mention, we, lifting ourselves with a more ardent affection towards the Selfsame, did gradually pass through all corporeal things, and even the heaven itself, whence sun, and moon, and stars shine upon the earth; yea, we soared higher yet by inward musing, and discoursing, and admiring Thy works; and we came to our own minds, and went beyond them, that we might advance as high as that region of unfailing plenty, where Thou feedest Israel [49] for ever with the food of truth, and where life is that Wisdom by whom all these things are made, both which have been, and which are to come; and she is not made, but is as she hath been, and so shall ever be; yea, rather, to have been, and to be hereafter, are not in her, but only to be, seeing she is eternal, for to have

[43] 1 Tim. v. 4, 9, 10, 14   [44] Gal. iv. 19   [45] I Thess. iv. 14   [46] Phil. iii. 13
[47] 1 Cor. ii. 9; Isa. lxiv. 4   [48] Ps. xxxvi. 9   [49] Ps. lxxx. 5

been and to be hereafter are not eternal. And while we were thus speaking, and straining after her, we slightly touched her with the whole effort of our heart; and we sighed, and there left bound the first-fruits of the Spirit;[50] and returned to the noise of our own mouth, where the word uttered has both beginning and end. And what is like unto Thy Word, our Lord, who remaineth in Himself without becoming old, and maketh all things new? [51]

We were saying, then, If to any man the tumult of the flesh were silenced —silenced the phantasies of earth, waters, and air—silenced, too, the poles; yea, the very soul be silenced to herself, and go beyond herself by not thinking of herself—silenced fancies and imaginary revelations, every tongue, and every sign, and whatsoever exists by passing away, since, if any could hearken, all these say, "We created not ourselves, but were created by Him who abideth for ever:" If, having uttered this, they now should be silenced, having only quickened our ears to Him who created them, and He alone speak not by them, but by Himself, that we may hear His word, not by fleshly tongue, nor angelic voice, nor sound of thunder, nor the obscurity of a similitude, but might hear Him—Him whom in these we love—without these, as we two now strained ourselves, and with rapid thought touched on that Eternal Wisdom which remaineth over all. If this could be sustained, and other visions of a far different kind be withdrawn, and this one ravish, and absorb, and envelope its beholder amid these inward joys, so that his life might be eternally like that one moment of knowledge which we now sighed after, were not this "Enter thou into the joy of Thy Lord"? [52] And when shall that be? When we shall all rise again; but all shall not be changed.[53]

Such things was I saying; and if not after this manner, and in these words, yet, Lord, Thou knowest, that in that day when we were talking thus, this world with all its delights grew contemptible to us, even while we spake. Then my mother said, "Son, for myself, I have no longer any pleasure in aught in this life. What I want here further, and why I am here, I know not, now that my hopes in this world are satisfied. There was indeed one thing for which I wished to tarry a little in this life, and that was that I might see thee a Catholic Christian before I died. My God has exceeded this abundantly, so that I see thee despising all earthly felicity, made His servant—what do I here?"

CHAPTER XI

HIS MOTHER, ATTACKED BY FEVER, DIES AT OSTIA

What reply I made to her to these things I do not well remember. However, scarcely five days after, or not much more, she was prostrated by

---

[50] Rom. viii. 23   [51] Wisd. vii. 27   [52] Matt. xxv. 21   [53] I Cor. xv. 51

fever; and while she was sick, she one day sank into a swoon, and was for a short time unconscious of visible things. We hurried up to her; but she soon regained her senses, and gazing on me and my brother as we stood by her, she said to us inquiringly, "Where was I?" Then looking intently at us stupefied with grief, "Here," said she, "shall you bury your mother." I was silent, and refrained from weeping; but my brother said something, wishing her, as the happier lot, to die in her own country and not abroad. She, when she heard this, with anxious countenance arrested him with her eye, as savoring of such things, and then gazing at me, "Behold," said she, "what he said;" and soon after to us both she said, "Lay this body anywhere, let not the care for it trouble you at all. This only I ask, that you will remember me at the Lord's altar, wherever you be." And when she had given forth this opinion in such words as she could, she was silent, being in pain with her increasing sickness.

But, as I reflected on Thy gifts, O thou invisible God, which Thou instillest into the hearts of Thy faithful ones, whence such marvellous fruits do spring, I did rejoice and give thanks unto Thee, calling to mind what I knew before, how she had ever burned with anxiety respecting her burial-place, which she had provided and prepared for herself by the body of her husband. For as they had lived very peacefully together, her desire had also been (so little is the human mind capable of grasping things divine) that this should be added to that happiness, and be talked of among men, that after her wandering beyond the sea, it had been granted her that they both, so united on earth, should lie in the same grave. But when this uselessness had, through the bounty of Thy goodness, begun to be no longer in her heart, I knew not, and I was full of joy admiring what she had thus disclosed to me; though indeed in our conversation in the window also, when she said, "What do I here any longer?" she appeared not to desire to die in her own country. I heard afterwards, too, that at the time we were at Ostia, with a maternal confidence she one day, when I was absent, was speaking with certain of my friends on the contemning of this life, and the blessing of death; and when they—amazed at the courage which Thou hadst given to her, a woman—asked her whether she did not dread leaving her body at such a distance from her own city, she replied, "Nothing is far to God; nor need I fear lest He should be ignorant at the end of the world of the place whence He is to raise me up." On the ninth day, then, of her sickness, the fifty-sixth year of her age, and the thirty-third of mine, was that religious and devout soul set free from the body.

CHAPTER XII

HOW HE MOURNED HIS DEAD MOTHER

I closed her eyes; and there flowed a great sadness into my heart, and it was passing into tears, when mine eyes at the same time, by the violent control of my mind, sucked back the fountain dry, and woe was me in such a struggle! But, as soon as she breathed her last, the boy Adeodatus burst out into wailing, but, being checked by us all, he became quiet. In like manner also my own childish feeling, which was, through the youthful voice of my heart, finding escape in tears, was restrained and silenced. For we did not consider it fitting to celebrate that funeral with tearful plaints and groanings; for on such wise are they who die unhappy, or are altogether dead, wont to be mourned. But she neither died unhappy, nor did she altogether die. For of this were we assured by the witness of her good conversation, her faith unfeigned,[54] and other sufficient grounds.

What, then, was that which did grievously pain me within, but the newly-made wound, from having that most sweet and dear habit of living together suddenly broken off? I was full of joy indeed in her testimony, when, in her last illness, flattering my dutifulness, she called me kind, and recalled, with great affection of love, that she had never heard any harsh or reproachful sound come out of my mouth against her. But yet, O my God, who madest us, how can the honor which I paid to her be compared with her slavery for me? As, then, I was left destitute of so great comfort in her, my soul was stricken, and that life torn apart as it were, which, of hers and mine together, had been made but one.

The boy then being restrained from weeping, Evodius took up the Psalter, and began to sing—the whole house responding—the Psalm, "I will sing of mercy and judgment: unto Thee, O Lord." But when they heard what we were doing, many brethren and religious women came together; and whilst they whose office it was were, according to custom, making ready for the funeral, I, in a part of the house where I conveniently could, together with those who thought that I ought not to be left alone, discoursed on what was suited to the occasion; and by this alleviation of truth mitigated the anguish known unto Thee—they being unconscious of it, listened intently, and thought me to be devoid of any sense of sorrow. But in Thine ears, where none of them heard, did I blame the softness of my feelings, and restrained the flow of my grief, which yielded a little unto me; but the paroxysm returned again, though not so as to burst forth into tears, nor to a change of countenance, though I knew what I repressed in my heart. And as I was exceedingly annoyed that these human things had such power over me, which in the due order and destiny of our natural condition must of necessity come to pass, with a new sorrow I sorrowed for my sorrow, and was wasted by a twofold sadness.

So, when the body was carried forth, we both went and returned without tears. For neither in those prayers which we poured forth unto Thee when the sacrifice of our redemption was offered up unto Thee for her—the dead body being now placed by the side of the grave, as the custom there is, prior to its being laid therein—neither in their prayers did I shed tears:

[54] I Tim. i. 5

yet I was most grievously sad in secret all the day, and with a troubled mind entreated Thee, as I was able, to heal my sorrow, but Thou didst not; fixing, I believe, in my memory by this one lesson the power of the bonds of all habit, even upon a mind which now feeds not upon a fallacious word. It appeared to me also a good thing to go and bathe, I having heard that the bath [*balneum*] took its name from the Greek βαλανεῖον, because it drives trouble from the mind. Lo, this also I confess unto Thy mercy, Father of the fatherless,[55] that I bathed, and felt the same as before I had done so. For the bitterness of my grief exuded not from my heart. Then I slept, and on awaking found my grief not a little mitigated; and as I lay alone upon my bed, there came into my mind those true verses of Thy Ambrose, for Thou art—

> Deus creator omnium,
> Polique rector, vestiens
> Diem decora lumine,
> Noctem sopora gratia;
>   Artus solutos ut quies
> Reddat laboris usui,
> Mentesque fessas allevet,
> Luctusque solvat anxios.

> O God, the world's great Architect,
> Who dost heaven's rowling orbs direct;
> Cloathing the day with beauteous light,
> And with sweet slumbers silent night;
> When wearied limbs new vigour gain
> From rest, new labours to sustain;
> When hearts oppressed do meet relief,
> And anxious minds forget their grief.

And then little by little did I bring back my former thoughts of Thine handmaid, her devout conversation towards Thee, her holy tenderness and attentiveness towards us, which was suddenly taken away from me; and it was pleasant to me to weep in Thy sight, for her and for me, concerning her and concerning myself. And I set free the tears which before I repressed, that they might flow at their will, spreading them beneath my heart; and it rested in them, for Thy ears were nigh me—not those of man, who would have put a scornful interpretation on my weeping. But now in writing I confess it unto Thee, O Lord! Read it who will, and interpret how he will; and if he finds me to have sinned in weeping for my mother during so small a part of an hour—that mother who was for a while dead to mine eyes, who had for many years wept for me, that I might live in Thine eyes —let him not laugh at me, but rather, if he be a man of a noble charity,

[55] Ps. lxviii. 5

let him weep for my sins against Thee, the Father of all the brethren of Thy Christ.

CHAPTER XIII

HE ENTREATS GOD FOR HER SINS, AND ADMONISHES HIS READERS TO REMEMBER HER PIOUSLY

But—my heart being now healed of that wound, in so far as it could be convicted of a carnal [56] affection—I pour out unto Thee, O our God, on behalf of Thine handmaid, tears of a far different sort, even that which flows from a spirit broken by the thoughts of the dangers of every soul that dieth in Adam. And although she, having been made alive in Christ [57] even before she was freed from the flesh, had so lived as to praise Thy name both by her faith and conversation, yet dare I not say that from the time Thou didst regenerate her by baptism, no word went forth from her mouth against Thy precepts.[58] And it hath been declared by Thy Son, the Truth, that whosoever shall say to his brother, Thou fool, shall be in danger of hell fire.[59] And woe even unto the praiseworthy life of man, if, putting away mercy, Thou shouldest investigate it. But because Thou dost not narrowly inquire after sins, we hope with confidence to find some place of indulgence with Thee. But whosoever recounts his true merits to Thee, what is it that he recounts to Thee but Thine own gifts? Oh, if men would know themselves to be men; and that he that glorieth would glory in the Lord! [60]

I then, O my Praise and my Life, Thou God of my heart, putting aside for a little her good deeds, for which I joyfully give thanks to Thee, do now beseech Thee for the sins of my mother. Hearken unto me, through that Medicine of our wounds who hung upon the tree, and who, sitting at Thy right hand, maketh intercession for us.[61] I know that she acted mercifully, and from the heart [62] forgave her debtors their debts; do Thou also forgive her debts,[63] whatever she contracted during so many years since the water of salvation. Forgive her, O Lord, forgive her, I beseech Thee; enter not into judgment with her.[64] Let Thy mercy be exalted above Thy justice,[65] because Thy words are true, and Thou hast promised mercy unto the merciful;[66] which Thou gavest them to be who wilt have mercy on whom Thou wilt have mercy, and wilt have compassion on whom Thou hast had compassion.[67]

And I believe Thou hast already done that which I ask Thee; but accept the freewill offerings of my mouth, O Lord.[68] For she, when the day of her dissolution was near at hand, took no thought to have her body sumptuously covered, or embalmed with spices; nor did she covet a choice monu-

[56] Rom. viii. 7   [57] 1 Cor. xv. 22   [58] Matt. xii. 36   [59] Matt. v. 22   [60] 2 Cor. x. 17   [61] Rom. viii. 34   [62] Matt. xviii. 35   [63] Matt. vi. 12   [64] Ps. cxliii. 2   [65] Jas. ii. 13   [66] Matt. v. 7   [67] Rom. ix. 15   [68] Ps. cxix. 108

ment, or desire her paternal burial-place. These things she entrusted not to us, but only desired to have her name remembered at Thy altar, which she had served without the omission of a single day; whence she knew that the holy sacrifice was dispensed, by which the handwriting that was against us is blotted out;[69] by which the enemy was triumphed over, who, summing up our offences, and searching for something to bring against us, found nothing in Him[70] in whom we conquer. Who will restore to Him the innocent blood? Who will repay Him the price with which He bought us, so as to take us from Him? Unto the sacrament of our ransom did Thy handmaid bind her soul by the bond of faith. Let none separate her from Thy protection. Let not the lion or the dragon[71] introduce himself by force or fraud. For she will not reply that she owes nothing, lest she be convicted and got the better of by the wily deceiver; but she will answer that her sins are forgiven[72] by Him to whom no one is able to repay that price which He, owing nothing, laid down for us.

May she therefore rest in peace with her husband, before or after whom she married none; whom she obeyed, with patience bringing forth fruit [73] unto Thee, that she might gain him also for Thee. And inspire, O my Lord my God, inspire Thy servants my brethren, Thy sons my masters, who with voice and heart and writings I serve, that so many of them as shall read these confessions may at Thy altar remember Monnica, Thy handmaid, together with Patricius, her sometime husband, by whose flesh Thou introducedst me into this life, in what manner I know not. May they with pious affection be mindful of my parents in this transitory light, of my brethren that are under Thee our Father in our Catholic mother, and of my fellow-citizens in the eternal Jerusalem, which the wandering of Thy people sigheth for from their departure until their return. That so my mother's last entreaty to me may, through my confessions more than through my prayers, be more abundantly fulfilled to her through the prayers of many.

[69] Col. ii. 14   [70] John xiv. 30   [71] Ps. xci. 13   [72] Matt. ix. 2   [73] Luke viii. 15

BOOK TEN

Having manifested what he was and what he is, he shows the great fruit of his confession; and being about to examine by what method God and the happy life may be found, he enlarges on the nature and power of memory. Then he examines his own acts, thoughts and affections, viewed under the threefold division of temptation; and commemorates the Lord, the one Mediator of God and men.

CHAPTER I

IN GOD ALONE IS THE HOPE AND JOY OF MAN

LET me know Thee, O Thou who knowest me; let me know Thee, as I am known.[1] O Thou strength of my soul, enter into it, and prepare it for Thyself, that Thou mayest have and hold it without spot or wrinkle.[2] This is my hope, therefore have I spoken;[3] and in this hope do I rejoice, when I rejoice soberly. Other things of this life ought the less to be sorrowed for, the more they are sorrowed for; and ought the more to be sorrowed for, the less men do sorrow for them. For behold, Thou desirest truth,[4] seeing that he who does it cometh to the light.[5] This I wish to do in confession in my heart before Thee, and in my writing before many witnesses.

CHAPTER II

THAT ALL THINGS ARE MANIFEST TO GOD. THAT CONFESSION UNTO HIM IS NOT MADE BY THE WORDS OF THE FLESH, BUT OF THE SOUL, AND THE CRY OF REFLECTION

And from Thee, O Lord, unto whose eyes the depths of man's conscience are naked,[6] what in me could be hidden though I were unwilling to confess to Thee? For so should I hide Thee from myself, not myself from Thee. But now, because my groaning witnesseth that I am dissatisfied with myself, Thou shinest forth, and satisfiest, and art beloved and desired; that I may blush for myself, and renounce myself, and choose Thee, and may neither please Thee nor myself, except in Thee. To Thee, then, O Lord, am I manifest, whatever I am, and with what fruit I may confess unto Thee I have spoken. Nor do I do it with words and sounds of the flesh, but with the words of the soul, and that cry of reflection which Thine ear knoweth. For when I am wicked, to confess to Thee is naught but to

[1] I Cor. xiii. 12   [2] Eph. v. 27   [3] Ps. cxvi, 10   [4] Ps. li. 6   [5] John iii. 20
[6] Heb. iv. 13

be dissatisfied with myself; but when I am truly devout, it is naught but
not to attribute it to myself, because Thou, O Lord, dost bless the righteous;[7] but first Thou justifiest him ungodly.[8] My confession, therefore, O
my God, in Thy sight, is made unto Thee silently, and yet not silently.
For in noise it is silent, in affection it cries aloud. For neither do I give
utterance to anything that is right unto men which Thou hast not heard
from me before, nor dost Thou hear anything of the kind from me which
Thyself saidst not first unto me.

CHAPTER III

HE WHO CONFESSETH RIGHTLY UNTO GOD BEST KNOWETH HIMSELF

What then have I to do with men, that they should hear my confessions,
as if they were going to cure all my diseases? [9] A people curious to know
the lives of others, but slow to correct their own, why do they desire to
hear from me what I am, who are unwilling to hear from Thee what they
are? And how can they tell, when they hear from me of myself, whether I
speak the truth, seeing that no man knoweth what is in man, save the
spirit of man which is in him? [10] But if they hear from Thee aught concerning themselves, they will not be able to say, "The Lord lieth." For
what is it to hear from Thee of themselves, but to know themselves? And
who is he that knoweth himself and saith, "It is false," unless he himself
lieth? But because charity believeth all things[11] (amongst those at all
events whom by union with itself it maketh one), I too, O Lord, also so
confess unto Thee that men may hear, to whom I cannot prove whether I
confess the truth, yet do they believe me whose ears charity openeth
unto me.

But yet do Thou, my most secret Physician, make clear to me what fruit
I may reap by doing it. For the confessions of my past sins—which Thou
hast forgiven and covered,[12] that Thou mightest make me happy in Thee,
changing my soul by faith and Thy sacrament—when they are read and
heard, stir up the heart, that it sleep not in despair and say, "I cannot;"
but that it may awake in the love of Thy mercy and the sweetness of Thy
grace, by which he that is weak is strong,[13] if by it he is made conscious of
his own weakness. As for the good, they take delight in hearing of the past
errors of such as are now freed from them; and they delight, not because
they are errors, but because they have been and are so no longer. For what
fruit, then, O Lord my God, to whom my conscience maketh her daily confession, more confident in the hope of Thy mercy than in her own innocence—for what fruit, I beseech Thee, do I confess even to men in Thy
presence by this book what I am at this time, nor what I have been? For
that fruit I have both seen and spoken of, but what I am at this time, at

---

[7] Ps. v. 12   [8] Rom. iv. 5   [9] Ps. ciii. 3   [10] I Cor. ii. 11   [11] I Cor. xiii. 7
[12] Ps. xxxii. 1   [13] 2 Cor. xii. 10

the very moment of making my confessions, divers people desire to know, both who knew me and who knew me not—who have heard of or from me —but their ear is not at my heart, where I am whatsoever I am. They are desirous, then, of hearing me confess what I am within, where they can neither stretch eye, nor ear, nor mind; they desire it as those willing to believe—but will they understand? For charity, by which they are good, says unto them that I do not lie in my confessions, and she in them believes me.

CHAPTER IV

THAT IN HIS CONFESSIONS HE MAY DO GOOD, HE CONSIDERS OTHERS

But for what fruit do they desire this? Do they wish me happiness when they learn how near, by Thy gift, I come unto Thee; and to pray for me, when they learn how much I am kept back by my own weight? To such will I declare myself. For it is no small fruit, O Lord my God, that by many thanks should be given to Thee on our behalf,[14] and that by many Thou shouldest be entreated for us. Let the fraternal soul love that in me which Thou teachest should be loved, and lament that in me which Thou teachest should be lamented. Let a fraternal and not an alien soul do this, nor that of strange children, whose mouth speaketh vanity, and their right hand is a right hand of falsehood,[15] but that fraternal one which, when it approves me, rejoices for me, but when it disapproves me, is sorry for me; because whether it approves or disapproves it loves me. To such will I declare myself; let them breathe freely at my good deeds, and sigh over my evil ones. My good deeds are Thy institutions and Thy gifts, my evil ones are my delinquencies and Thy judgments. Let them breathe freely at the one, and sigh over the other; and let hymns and tears ascend into Thy sight out of the fraternal hearts—Thy censers.[16] And do Thou, O Lord, who takest delight in the incense of Thy holy temple, have mercy upon me according to Thy great mercy,[17] for Thy name's sake,[18] and on no account leaving what Thou hast begun in me, do Thou complete what is imperfect in me.

This is the fruit of my confessions, not of what I was, but of what I am, that I may confess this not before Thee only, in a secret exultation with trembling,[19] and a secret sorrow with hope, but in the ears also of the believing sons of men—partakers of my joy, and sharers of my mortality, my fellow-citizens and the companions of my pilgrimage, those who are gone before, and those that are to follow after, and the comrades of my way. These are Thy servants, my brethren, those whom Thou wishest to be Thy sons; my masters, whom Thou hast commanded me to serve, if I desire to

---

[14] 2 Cor. i. 11   [15] Ps. cxliv. 11   [16] Rev. viii. 3   [17] Ps. li. 1   [18] Ps. xxv. 11
[19] Ps. ii. 11

live with and of Thee. But this Thy word were little to me did it command in speaking, without going before in acting. This then I do both in deed and word, this I do under Thy wings, in too great danger, were it not that my soul, under Thy wings, is subject unto Thee, and my weakness known unto Thee. I am a little one, but my Father liveth for ever, and my Defender is sufficient [20] for me. For He is the same who begat me and who defends me; and Thou Thyself art all my good; even Thou, the Omnipotent, who art with me, and that before I am with Thee. To such, therefore, whom Thou commandest me to serve will I declare, not what I was, but what I now am, and what I still am. But neither do I judge myself.[21] Thus then I would be heard.

CHAPTER V

THAT MAN KNOWETH NOT HIMSELF WHOLLY

For it is Thou, Lord, that judgest me;[22] for although no man knoweth the things of a man, save the spirit of man which is in him,[23] yet is there something of man which the spirit of man which is in him itself knoweth not. But Thou, Lord, who hast made him, knowest him wholly. I indeed, though in Thy sight I despise myself, and reckon myself but dust and ashes,[24] yet know something concerning Thee, which I know not concerning myself. And assuredly now we see through a glass darkly, not yet face to face.[25] So long, therefore, as I be absent from Thee, I am more present with myself than with Thee;[26] and yet know I that Thou canst not suffer violence; but for myself I know not what temptations I am able to resist, and what I am not able. But there is hope, because Thou art faithful, who wilt not suffer us to be tempted above that we are able, but wilt with the temptation also make a way to escape, that we may be able to bear it.[27] I would therefore confess what I know concerning myself; I will confess also what I know not concerning myself. And because what I do know of myself, I know by Thee enlightening me; and what I know not of myself, so long I know not until the time when my darkness be as the noonday[28] in Thy sight.

CHAPTER VI

THE LOVE OF GOD, IN HIS NATURE SUPERIOR TO ALL CREATURES, IS ACQUIRED BY THE KNOWLEDGE OF THE SENSES AND THE EXERCISE OF REASON

Not with uncertain, but with assured consciousness do I love Thee, O Lord. Thou hast stricken my heart with Thy word, and I loved Thee. And

[20] 2 Cor. xii. 9   [21] 1 Cor. iv. 3   [22] 1 Cor. iv. 4   [23] 1 Cor. ii. 11   [24] Gen. xviii.
27   [25] 1 Cor. xiii. 12   [26] 2 Cor. v. 6   [27] 1 Cor. x. 13   [28] Isa. lviii. 10

also the heaven, and earth, and all that is therein, behold, on every side they say that I should love Thee; nor do they cease to speak unto all, so that they are without excuse? [29] But more profoundly wilt Thou have mercy on whom Thou wilt have mercy, and compassion on whom Thou wilt have compassion,[30] otherwise do both heaven and earth tell forth Thy praises to deaf ears. But what is it that I love in loving Thee? Not corporeal beauty, nor the splendor of time, nor the radiance of the light, so pleasant to our eyes, nor the sweet melodies of songs of all kinds, nor the fragrant smell of flowers, and ointments, and spices, not manna and honey, not limbs pleasant to the embracements of flesh. I love not these things when I love my God; and yet I love a certain kind of light, and sound, and fragrance, and food, and embracement in loving my God, who is the light, sound, fragrance, food, and embracement of my inner man—where that light shineth unto my soul which no place can contain, where that soundeth which time snatcheth not away, where there is a fragrance which no breeze disperseth, where there is a food which no eating can diminish, and where that clingeth which no satiety can sunder. This is what I love, when I love my God.

And what is this? I asked the earth; and it answered, "I am not He;" and whatsoever are therein made the same confession. I asked the sea and the deeps, and the creeping things that lived, and they replied, "We are not thy God, seek higher than we." I asked the breezy air, and the universal air with its inhabitants answered, "Anaximenes[c] was deceived, I am not God." I asked the heavens, the sun, moon, and stars: "Neither," say they, "are we the God whom thou seekest." And I answered unto all these things which stand about the door of my flesh, "Ye have told me concerning my God, that ye are not He; tell me something about Him." And with a loud voice they exclaimed, "He made us." My questioning was my observing of them; and their beauty was their reply. And I directed my thoughts to myself, and said, "Who art thou?" And I answered, "A man." And lo, in me there appear both body and soul, the one without, the other within. By which of these should I seek my God, whom I had sought through the body from earth to heaven, as far as I was able to send messengers—the beams of mine eyes? But the better part is that which is inner; for to it, as both president and judge, did all my corporeal messengers render the answers of heaven and earth and all things therein, who said, "We are not God, but He made us." These things my inner man knew by the ministry of the outer; I, the inner man, knew all this—I, the soul, through the senses of my body. I asked the vast bulk of the earth of my God, and it answered me, "I am not He, but He made me."

Is not this beauty visible to all whose senses are unimpaired? Why then doth it not speak the same things unto all? Animals, the very small and the

---

[29] Rom. i. 20   [30] Rom. ix. 15
    [c] A Pre-Socratic philosopher who held that air was the first principle of all things.—Ed.

great, see it, but they are unable to question it, because their senses are not endowed with reason to enable them to judge on what they report. But men can question it, so that the invisible things of Him . . . are clearly seen, being understood by the things that are made;[31] but by loving them, they are brought into subjection to them; and subjects are not able to judge. Neither do the creatures reply to such as question them, unless they can judge; nor will they alter their voice (that is, their beauty), if so be one man only sees, another both sees and questions, so as to appear one way to this man, and another to that; but appearing the same way to both, it is mute to this, it speaks to that—nay, rather it speaks to all; but they only understand it who compare that voice received from without with the truth within. For the truth declareth unto me, "Neither heaven, nor earth, nor any body is thy God." This, their nature declareth unto him that beholdeth them. "They are a mass; a mass is less in part than in the whole." Now, O my soul, thou art my better part, unto thee I speak; for thou animatest the mass of thy body, giving it life, which no body furnishes to a body; but thy God is even unto thee the Life of life.

CHAPTER VII

THAT GOD IS TO BE FOUND NEITHER FROM THE POWERS OF THE BODY NOR OF THE SOUL

What then is it that I love when I love my God? Who is He that is above the head of my soul? By my soul itself will I mount up unto Him. I will soar beyond that power of mine whereby I cling to the body, and fill the whole structure of it with life. Not by that power do I find my God; for then the horse and the mule, which have no understanding,[32] might find Him, since it is the same power by which their bodies also live. But there is another power, not that only by which I quicken, but that also by which I endow with sense my flesh, which the Lord hath made for me; bidding the eye not to hear, and the ear not to see; but that, for me to see by, and this, for me to hear by; and to each of the other senses its own proper seat and office, which being different, I, the single mind, do through them govern. I will soar also beyond this power of mine; for this the horse and mule possess, for they too discern through the body.

CHAPTER VIII

OF THE NATURE AND THE AMAZING POWER OF MEMORY

I will soar, then, beyond this power of my nature also, ascending by degrees unto Him who made me. And I enter the fields and roomy chambers

---

[31] Rom. i. 20   [32] Ps. xxxii. 9

[d] With this chapter, cf. Plato, *Theaetetus,* and Aristotle, *Metaphysics,* I. i.—Ed.

of memory, where are the treasures of countless images, imported into it from all manner of things by the senses. There is treasured up whatsoever likewise we think, either by enlarging or diminishing, or by varying in any way whatever those things which the sense hath arrived at; and whatever else hath been entrusted to it and stored up, which oblivion hath not yet engulfed and buried. When I am in this storehouse, I demand that what I wish should be brought forth, and some things immediately appear; others require to be longer sought after, and are dragged, as it were, out of some hidden receptacle; others, again, hurry forth in crowds, and while another thing is sought and inquired for, they leap into view, as if to say, "Is it not we, perchance?" These I drive away with the hand of my heart from before the face of my remembrance, until what I wish be discovered making its appearance out of its secret cell. Other things suggest themselves without effort, and in continuous order, just as they are called for—those in front giving place to those that follow, and in giving place are treasured up again to be forthcoming when I wish it. All of which takes place when I repeat a thing from memory.

All these things, each of which entered by its own avenue, are distinctly and under general heads there laid up: as, for example, light, and all colors and forms of bodies, by the eyes; sounds of all kinds by the ears; all smells by the passage of the nostrils; all flavors by that of the mouth; and by the sensation of the whole body is brought in what is hard or soft, hot or cold, smooth or rough, heavy or light, whether external or internal to the body. All these does that great receptacle of memory, with its many and indescribable departments, receive, to be recalled and brought forth when required; each, entering by its own door, is laid up in it. And yet the things themselves do not enter it, but only the images of the things perceived are there ready at hand for thought to recall. And who can tell how these images are formed, notwithstanding that it is evident by which of the senses each has been fetched in and treasured up? For even while I live in darkness and silence, I can bring out colors in memory if I wish, and discern between black and white, and what others I wish; nor yet do sounds break in and disturb what is drawn in by mine eyes, and which I am considering, seeing that they also are there, and are concealed—laid up, as it were, apart. For these too I can summon if I please, and immediately they appear. And though my tongue be at rest, and my throat silent, yet can I sing as much as I will; and those images of colors, which notwithstanding are there, do not interpose themselves and interrupt when another treasure is under consideration which flowed in through the ears. So the remaining things carried in and heaped up by the other senses, I recall at my pleasure. And I discern the scent of lilies from that of violets while smelling nothing; and I prefer honey to grape-syrup, a smooth thing to a rough, though then I neither taste nor handle, but only remember.

These things I do within, in that vast chamber of my memory. For there are nigh me heaven, earth, sea, and whatever I can think upon in them, besides those which I have forgotten. There also do I meet with myself, and recall myself—what, when, or where I did a thing, and how I was affected when I did it. There are all which I remember, either by personal experience or on the faith of others. Out of the same supply do I myself with the past construct now this, now that likeness of things, which either I have experienced, or, from having experienced, have believed; and thence again future actions, events, and hopes, and upon all these again do I meditate as if they were present. "I will do this or that," I say to myself in that vast womb of my mind, filled with the images of things so many and so great, "and this or that shall follow upon it." "Oh that this or that might come to pass!" "God avert this or that!" Thus I speak to myself; and when I speak, the images of all I speak about are present, out of the same treasury of memory; nor could I say anything at all about them were the images absent.

Great is this power of memory, exceeding great, O my God—an inner chamber large and boundless! Who has plumbed its depths? Yet it is a power of mine, and appertains unto my nature; nor do I myself grasp all that I am. Therefore is the mind too narrow to contain itself. And where should that be which it does not contain of itself? Is it outside and not in itself? How is it, then, that it does not grasp itself? A great admiration rises upon me; astonishment seizes me. And men go forth to wonder at the heights of mountains, the huge waves of the sea, the broad flow of the rivers, the extent of the ocean, and the courses of the stars, and omit to wonder at themselves; nor do they marvel that when I spoke of all these things, I was not looking on them with my eyes, and yet could not speak of them unless those mountains, and waves, and rivers, and stars which I saw, and that ocean which I believe in, I saw inwardly in my memory, and with the same vast spaces between as when I saw them abroad. But I did not by seeing appropriate them when I looked on them with my eyes; nor are the things themselves with me, but their images. And I knew by what corporeal sense each made impression on me.

CHAPTER IX

NOT ONLY THINGS, BUT ALSO LITERATURE AND IMAGES, ARE TAKEN FROM THE MEMORY, AND ARE BROUGHT FORTH BY THE ACT OF REMEMBERING

And yet are not these all that the illimitable capacity of my memory retains. Here also is all that is apprehended of the liberal sciences, and not yet forgotten—removed as it were into an inner place, which is not a place; nor are they the images which are retained, but the things themselves. For what is literature, what skill in disputation, whatsoever I know of all the many kinds of questions there are, is so in my memory, that I have not taken in the image and left the thing without, or that it should have sounded and passed away like a voice imprinted on the ear by that trace, whereby it might be recorded, as though it sounded when it no longer did so; or as an odor while it passes away, and vanishes into wind, affects the sense of smell, whence it conveys the image of itself into the memory, which we realize in recollecting; or like food, which assuredly in the belly has now no taste, and yet has a kind of taste in the memory, or like anything that is by touching felt by the body, and which even when removed from us is imagined by the memory. For these things themselves are not put into it, but the images of them only are caught up, with a marvellous quickness, and laid up, as it were, in most wonderful cabinets, and wonderfully brought forth when we remember.

CHAPTER X

LITERATURE IS NOT INTRODUCED TO THE MEMORY THROUGH THE SENSES, BUT IS BROUGHT FORTH FROM ITS MORE SECRET PLACES

But truly when I hear that there are three kinds of questions, "Whether a thing is—what it is—of what kind it is?" I do indeed hold fast the images of the sounds of which these words are composed, and I know that those sounds passed through the air with a noise, and now are not. But the things themselves which are signified by these sounds I never arrived at by any sense of the body, nor ever perceived them otherwise than by my mind; and in my memory have I laid up not their images, but themselves, which, how they entered into me, let them tell if they are able. For I examine all the gates of my flesh, but find not by which of them they entered. For the eyes say, "If they were colored, we announced them." The ears say, "If they sounded, we gave notice of them." The nostrils say, "If they smell, they passed in by us." The sense of taste says, "If they have no flavor, ask not me." The touch says, "If it have not body, I handled it not, and if I never handled it, I gave no notice of it." Whence and how did these things enter into my memory? I know not how. For when I learned them, I gave not credit to the heart of another man, but perceived them in my own; and I approved them as true, and committed them to it, laying them up, as it were, whence I might fetch them when I willed. There, then, they were, even before I learned them, but were not in my memory. Where were they, then, or wherefore, when they were spoken, did I acknowledge them, and say, "So it is, it is true," unless as being already in the memory, though so put back and concealed, as it were, in more secret caverns, that had they not been drawn forth by the advice of another I would not, perchance, have been able to conceive of them?

CHAPTER XI

WHAT IT IS TO LEARN AND TO THINK

Wherefore we find that to learn these things, whose images we drink not in by our senses, but perceive within as they are by themselves, without images, is nothing else but by meditation as it were to concentrate, and by observing to take care that those notions which the memory did before contain scattered and confused, he laid up at hand, as it were, in that same memory, where before they lay concealed, scattered and neglected, and so the more easily present themselves to the mind well accustomed to observe them. And how many things of this sort does my memory retain which have been found out already, and, as I said, are, as it were, laid up ready to hand, which we are said to have learned and to have known; which, should we for small intervals of time cease to recall, they are again so submerged and slide back, as it were, into the more remote chambers, that they must be evolved thence again as if new (for other sphere they have none), and must be marshalled [*cogenda*] again that they may become known; that is to say, they must be collected [*colligenda*], as it were, from their dispersion; whence we have the word *cogitare*. For *cogo* [*I collect*] and *cogito* [*I re-collect*] have the same relation to each other as *ago* and *agito, facio* and *factito*. But the mind has appropriated to itself this word [cogitation], so that not that which is collected anywhere, but what is collected,[33] that is marshalled,[34] in the mind, is properly said to be cogitated.[35]

CHAPTER XII

ON THE RECOLLECTION OF THINGS MATHEMATICAL

The memory contains also the reasons and innumerable laws of numbers and dimensions, none of which has any sense of the body impressed, seeing they have neither color, nor sound, nor taste, nor smell, nor sense of touch. I have heard the sound of the words by which these things are signified when they are discussed; but the sounds are one thing, the things another. For the sounds are one thing in Greek, another in Latin; but the things themselves are neither Greek, nor Latin, nor any other language. I have seen the lines of the craftsmen, even the finest, like a spider's web; but these are of another kind, they are not the images of those which the eye of my flesh showed me; he knows them who, without any idea whatsoever of a body, perceives them within himself. I have also observed the numbers of the things with which we number all the senses of the body; but those by which we number are of another kind, nor are they the images of these, and therefore they certainly are. Let him who sees not these things mock me for saying them; and I will pity him, while he mocks me.

[33] Colligitur   [34] Cogitur   [35] Cogitari

CHAPTER XIII

MEMORY RETAINS ALL THINGS

All these things I retain in my memory, and how I learnt them I retain. I retain also many things which I have heard most falsely objected against them, which though they be false, yet is it not false that I have remembered them; and I remember, too, that I have distinguished between those truths and these falsehoods uttered against them; and I now see that it is one thing to distinguish these things, another to remember that I often distinguished them, when I often reflected upon them. I both remember, then, that I have often understood these things, and what I now distinguish and comprehend I store away in my memory, that hereafter I may remember that I understood it now. Therefore also I remember that I have remembered; so that if afterwards I shall call to mind that I have been able to remember these things, it will be through the power of memory that I shall call it to mind.

CHAPTER XIV

CONCERNING THE MANNER IN WHICH JOY AND SADNESS MAY BE BROUGHT BACK TO THE MIND AND MEMORY

This same memory contains also the affections of my mind; not in the manner in which the mind itself contains them when it suffers them, but very differently according to a power peculiar to memory. For without being joyous, I remember myself to have had joy; and without being sad, I call to mind my past sadness; and that of which I was once afraid, I remember without fear; and without desire recall a former desire. Again, on the contrary, I at times remember when joyous my past sadness, and when sad my joy. Which is not to be wondered at as regards the body; for the mind is one thing, the body another. If I, therefore, when happy, recall some past bodily pain, it is not so strange a thing. But now, as this very memory itself is mind (for when we give orders to have a thing kept in memory, we say, "See that you bear this in mind;" and when we forget a thing, we say, "It did not enter my mind," and, "It slipped from my mind," thus calling the memory itself mind), as this is so, how comes it to pass that when being joyful I remember my past sorrow, the mind has joy, the memory sorrow—the mind, from the joy that is in it, is joyful, yet the memory, from the sadness that is in it, is not sad? Does not the memory perchance belong to the mind? Who will say so? The memory doubtless is, so to say, the belly of the mind, and joy and sadness like sweet and bitter food, which, when entrusted to the memory, are, as it were, passed into the belly, where they can be reposited, but cannot taste. It is ridiculous to imagine these to be alike; and yet they are not utterly unlike.

But behold, out of my memory I educe it, when I affirm that there be four perturbations of the mind—desire, joy, fear, sorrow; and whatsoever I shall be able to dispute on these, by dividing each into its peculiar species, and by defining it, there I find what I may say, and thence I educe it; yet I am not disturbed by any of these perturbations when by remembering them I call them to mind; and before I recollected and reviewed them, they were there; wherefore by remembrance could they be brought thence. Perchance, then, even as meat is in ruminating brought up out of the belly, so by calling to mind are these educed from the memory. Why, then, does not the disputant, thus recollecting, perceive in the mouth of his meditation the sweetness of joy or the bitterness of sorrow? Is the comparison unlike in this because not like in all points? For who would willingly discourse on these subjects, if, as often as we name sorrow or fear, we should be compelled to be sorrowful or fearful? And yet we could never speak of them, did we not find in our memory not merely the sounds of the names according to the images imprinted on it by the senses of the body, but the notions of the things themselves, which we never received by any door of the flesh, but which the mind itself, recognising by the experience of its own passions, entrusted to the memory, or else which the memory itself retained without their being entrusted to it.

CHAPTER XV

IN MEMORY THERE ARE ALSO IMAGES OF THINGS WHICH ARE ABSENT

But whether by images or no, who can well affirm? For I name a stone, I name the sun, and the things themselves are not present to my senses, but their images are near to my memory. I name some pain of the body, yet it is not present when there is no pain; yet if its image were not in my memory, I should be ignorant what to say concerning it, nor in arguing be able to distinguish it from pleasure. I name bodily health when sound in body; the thing itself is indeed present with me, but unless its image also were in my memory, I could by no means call to mind what the sound of this name signified. Nor would sick people know, when health was named, what was said, unless the same image were retained by the power of memory, although the thing itself were absent from the body. I name numbers whereby we enumerate; and not their images, but they themselves are in my memory. I name the image of the sun, and this, too, is in my memory. For I do not recall the image of that image, but itself, for the image itself is present when I remember it. I name memory, and I know what I name. But where do I know it, except in the memory itself? Is it also present to itself by its image, and not by itself?

CHAPTER XVI

THE PRIVATION OF MEMORY IS FORGETFULNESS

When I name forgetfulness, and know, too, what I name, whence should I know it if I did not remember it? I do not say the sound of the name, but the thing which it signifies; which, had I forgotten, I could not know what that sound signified. When, therefore, I remember memory, then is memory present with itself, through itself. But when I remember forgetfulness, there are present both memory and forgetfulness—memory, whereby I remember, forgetfulness, which I remember. But what is forgetfulness but the privation of memory? How, then, is that present for me to remember, since, when it is so, I cannot remember? But if what we remember we retain in memory, yet, unless we remembered forgetfulness, we could never at the hearing of the name know the thing meant by it, then is forgetfulness retained by memory. Present, therefore, it is, lest we should forget it; and being so, we do forget. Is it to be inferred from this that forgetfulness, when we remember it, is not present to the memory through itself, but through its image; because, were forgetfulness present through itself, it would not lead us to remember, but to forget? Who will now investigate this? Who shall understand how it is?

Truly, O Lord, I labor therein, and labor in myself. I am become a troublesome soil that requires overmuch labor. For we are not now searching out the tracts of heaven, or measuring the distance of the stars, or inquiring about the weight of the earth. It is I myself, I, the mind—who remember. It is not much to be wondered at, if, what I myself am not, be far from me. But what is nearer to me than myself. And, behold, I am not able to comprehend the force of my own memory, though I cannot name myself without it. For what shall I say when it is plain to me that I remember forgetfulness? Shall I affirm that that which I remember is not in my memory? Or shall I say that forgetfulness is in my memory with the view of my not forgetting? Both of these are most absurd. What third view is there? How can I assert that the image of forgetfulness is retained by my memory, and not forgetfulness itself, when I remember it? And how can I assert this, seeing that when the image of anything is imprinted on the memory, the thing itself must of necessity be present first by which that image may be imprinted? For thus do I remember Carthage; thus, all the places to which I have been; thus, the faces of men whom I have seen, and things reported by the other senses; thus, the health or sickness of the body. For when these objects were present, my memory received images from them, which, when they were present, I might gaze on and reconsider in my mind, as I remembered them when they were absent. If, therefore, forgetfulness is retained in the memory through its image, and not through itself, then itself was once present, that its image might be taken. But when it was present, how did it write its image on the memory, seeing that forgetfulness by its presence bolts out even what it finds already noted? And yet, in whatever way, though it be incomprehensible and inexplicable, yet I am most certain that I remember also forgetfulness itself, whereby what we do remember is blotted out.

CHAPTER XVII

GOD CANNOT BE ATTAINED BY THE POWER OF MEMORY, WHICH BEASTS AND BIRDS POSSESS

Great is the power of memory; very wonderful is it. O my God, a profound and infinite manifoldness; and this thing is the mind, and this I myself am. What then am I, O my God? Of what nature am I? A life various and manifold, and exceeding vast. Behold, in the numberless fields, and caves, and caverns of my memory, full without number of numberless kinds of things, either through images, as all bodies are; or by the presence of the things themselves, as are the arts; or by some notion or observation, as the affections of the mind are, which, even though the mind does not suffer, the memory retains, while whatsoever is in the memory is also in the mind: through all these do I run to and fro, and fly; I penetrate on this side and that, as far as I am able, and nowhere is there an end. So great is the power of memory, so great the power of life in man, whose life is mortal. What then shall I do, O Thou my true life, my God? I will pass even beyond this power of mine which is called memory—I will pass beyond it, that I may proceed to Thee, O Thou sweet Light. What sayest Thou to me? Behold, I am soaring by my mind towards Thee who remainest above me. I will also pass beyond this power of mine which is called memory, wishful to reach Thee whence Thou canst be reached, and to cleave unto Thee whence it is possible to cleave unto Thee. For even beasts and birds possess memory, else could they never find their lairs and nests again, nor many other things to which they are used; neither indeed could they become used to anything, but by their memory. I will pass, then, beyond memory also, that I may reach Him who has separated me from the four-footed beasts and the fowls of the air, making me wiser than they. I will pass beyond memory also, but where shall I find Thee, O Thou truly good and assured sweetness? But where shall I find Thee? If I find Thee without memory, then am I unmindful of Thee. And how now shall I find Thee, if I do not remember Thee?

CHAPTER XVIII

A THING WHEN LOST COULD NOT BE FOUND UNLESS IT WERE RETAINED IN THE MEMORY

For the woman who lost her drachma, and searched for it with a lamp,[36] unless she had remembered it, would never have found it. For when it was found, whence could she know whether it were the same, had she not remembered it? I remember to have lost and found many things; and this I know thereby, that when I was searching for any of them, and was asked, "Is this it?" "Is that it?" I answered "No," until such time as that which I sought were offered to me. Which had I not remembered—whatever it were —though it were offered me, yet would I not find it, because I could not recognise it. And thus it is always, when we search for and find anything that is lost. Notwithstanding, if anything be by accident lost from the sight, not from the memory—as any visible body—the image of it is retained within, and is searched for until it be restored to sight; and when it is found, it is recognised by the image which is within. Nor do we say that we have found what we had lost unless we recognise it; nor can we recognise it unless we remember it. But this, though lost to the sight, was retained in the memory.

CHAPTER XIX

WHAT IT IS TO REMEMBER

But how is it when the memory itself loses anything, as it happens when we forget anything and try to recall it? Where finally do we search, but in the memory itself? And there, if perchance one thing be offered for another, we refuse it, until we meet with what we seek; and when we do, we exclaim, "This is it!" which we should not do unless we knew it again, nor should we recognise it unless we remembered it. Assuredly, therefore, we had forgotten it. Or, had not the whole of it slipped our memory, but by the part by which we had hold was the other part sought for; since the memory perceived that it did not revolve together as much as it was accustomed to do, and halting, as if from the mutilation of its old habit, demanded the restoration of that which was wanting. For example, if we see or think of some man known to us, and, having forgotten his name, endeavor to recover it, whatsoever other thing presents itself is not connected with it; because it was not used to be thought of in connection with him, and is consequently rejected, until that is present on which the knowledge reposes fittingly as its accustomed object. And whence, save from the memory itself, does that present itself? For even when we recognise it as put in mind of it by an-

[36] Luke xv. 8

other, it is thence it comes. For we do not believe it as something new, but, as we recall it, admit what was said to be correct. But if it were entirely blotted out of the mind, we should not, even when put in mind of it, recollect it. For we have not as yet entirely forgotten what we remember that we have forgotten. A lost notion, then, which we have entirely forgotten, we cannot even search for.

CHAPTER XX

WE SHOULD NOT SEEK FOR GOD AND THE HAPPY LIFE UNLESS WE HAD KNOWN IT

How, then, do I seek Thee, O Lord? For when I seek Thee, my God, I seek a happy life. I will seek Thee, that my soul may live.[37] For my body liveth by my soul, and my soul liveth by Thee. How, then, do I seek a happy life, seeing that it is not mine till I can say, "It is enough!" in that place where I ought to say it? How do I seek it? Is it by remembrance, as though I had forgotten it, knowing too that I had forgotten it? or, longing to learn it as a thing unknown, which either I had never known, or had so forgotten it as not even to remember that I had forgotten it? Is not a happy life the thing that all desire, and is there any one who altogether desires it not? But where did they acquire the knowledge of it, that they so desire it? Where have they seen it, that they so love it? Truly we have it, but how I know not. And there is another way in which, when any one has it, he is happy; and some there be that are happy in hope. These have it in an inferior kind to those that are happy in fact; and yet are they better off than they who are happy neither in fact nor in hope. And even these, had they it not in some way, would not so much desire to be happy—that they do desire it is most certain. How they come to know it, I cannot tell, but they have it by some kind of knowledge unknown to me, who am in much doubt as to whether it be in the memory; for if it be there, then have we been happy once; whether all individually, or as in that man who first sinned, in whom also we all died,[38] and from whom we are all born with misery, I do not now ask; but I ask whether the happy life be in the memory? For did we not know it, we should not love it. We hear the name, and we all acknowledge that we desire the thing; for we are not delighted with the sound only. For when a Greek hears it spoken in Latin, he does not feel delighted, for he knows not what is spoken; but we are delighted, as he too would be if he heard it in Greek; because the thing itself is neither Greek nor Latin, which Greeks and Latins, and men of all other tongues, long so earnestly to obtain. It is then known to all, and could they with one voice be asked whether they wished to be happy, without doubt they would all answer that they would. And

[37] Amos v. 4   [38] 1 Cor. xv. 22

this could not be unless the thing itself, of which it is the name, were retained in their memory.

CHAPTER XXI

HOW A HAPPY LIFE MAY BE RETAINED IN THE MEMORY

But is it so as one who has seen Carthage remembers it? No. For a happy life is not visible to the eye, because it is not a body. Is it, then, as we remember numbers? No. For he that hath these in his knowledge strives not to attain further; but a happy life we have in our knowledge, and, therefore, do we love it, while yet we wish further to attain it that we may be happy. Is it, then, as we remember eloquence? No. For although some, when they hear this name, call the thing to mind, who, indeed, are not yet eloquent, and many who wish to be so, whence it appears to be in their knowledge; yet have these by their bodily perceptions noticed that others are eloquent, and been delighted with it, and long to be so—although they would not be delighted save for some interior knowledge, nor desire to be so unless they were delighted—but a happy life we can by no bodily perception experience in others. Is it, then, as we remember joy? It may be so; for my joy I remember, even when sad, as I do a happy life when I am miserable. Nor did I ever with perception of the body either see, hear, smell, taste, or touch my joy; but I experienced it in my mind when I rejoiced; and the knowledge of it clung to my memory, so that I can call it to mind, sometimes with disdain and at others with desire, according to the difference of the things in which I now remember that I rejoiced. For even from unclean things have I been bathed with a certain joy, which now calling to mind, I detest and execrate; at other times, from good and honest things, which, with longing, I call to mind, though perchance they be not near at hand, and then with sadness do I call to mind a former joy.

Where and when, then, did I experience my happy life, that I should call it to mind, and love and long for it. Nor is it I alone or a few others who wish to be happy, but truly all; which, unless by certain knowledge we knew, we should not wish with so certain a will. But how is this, that if two men be asked whether they would wish to serve as soldiers, one, it may be, would reply that he would, the other that he would not; but if they were asked whether they would wish to be happy, both of them would unhesitatingly say that they would; and this one would wish to serve, and the other not, from no other motive but to be happy? Is it, perchance, that as one joys in this, and another in that, so do all men agree in their wish for happiness, as they would agree, were they asked, in wishing to have joy—and this joy they call a happy life? Although, then, one pursues joy in this way, and another in that, all have one goal, which they strive to attain, namely, to have joy. This life being a thing which no one can say he has not experienced, it is on that account found in the memory, and recognised whenever the name of a happy life is heard.

CHAPTER XXII

A HAPPY LIFE IS TO REJOICE IN GOD, AND FOR GOD

Let it be far, O Lord—let it be far from the heart of Thy servant who confesseth unto Thee; let it be far from me to think myself happy, be the joy what it may. For there is a joy which is not granted to the wicked [39] but to those who worship Thee thankfully, whose joy Thou Thyself art. And the happy life is this—to rejoice unto Thee, in Thee, and for Thee; this it is, and there is no other. But those who think there is another, follow after another joy, and that not the true one. Their will, however, is not turned away from some shadow of joy.

CHAPTER XXIII

ALL WISH TO REJOICE IN THE TRUTH

It is not, then, certain that all men wish to be happy, since those who wish not to rejoice in Thee, which is the only happy life, do not certainly desire the happy life. Or do all desire this, but because the flesh lusteth against the spirit, and the spirit against the flesh, so that they cannot do the things that they would,[40] they fall upon that which they are able to do, and with that are content; because that which they are not able to do, they do not so will as to make them able? For I ask of every man, whether he would rather rejoice in truth or in falsehood. They will no more hesitate to say, "in truth," than to say that they wish to be happy. For a happy life is joy in the truth. For this is joy in Thee, who art the truth,[41] O God, my light,[42] the health of my countenance, and my God.[43] All wish for this happy life, this life do all wish for, which is the only happy one; joy in the truth do all wish for. I have had experience of many who wished to deceive, but not one who wished to be deceived. Where, then, did they know this happy life, save where they knew also the truth. For they love it, too, since they would not be deceived. And when they love a happy life, which is nothing else but joy in the truth, assuredly they love also the truth; which yet they would not love were there not some knowledge of it in the memory. Wherefore, then, do they not rejoice in it? Why are they not happy? Because they are most entirely occupied with other things which rather make them miserable, than that which would make them happy, which they remember so little of. For there is yet a little light in men; let them walk— let them walk, that the darkness seize them not.[44]

[39] Isa. xlviii. 22   [40] Gal. v. 17   [41] John xiv. 6   [42] Ps. xxvii. 1   [43] Ps. xlii. 2
[44] John xii. 35

Why, then, doth truth beget hatred,[45] and that man of thine,[46] preaching the truth, become an enemy to them, whereas a happy life is loved, which is nothing else but joy in the truth; unless that truth is loved in such a sort as those who love anything else wish that to be the truth which they love, and, as they are willing to be deceived, are unwilling to be convinced that they are so? Therefore they hate the truth for the sake of that thing which they love instead of the truth. They love truth when she shines on them, and hate her when she rebukes them. For, because they are not willing to be deceived, and wish to deceive, they love her when she reveals herself, and hate her when she reveals them. On that account shall she so requite them, that those who were unwilling to be discovered by her she both discovers against their will, and discovers not herself to them. Thus, thus, truly thus does the human mind, so blind and sick, so base and unseemly, desire to lie concealed, but wishes not that anything should be concealed from it. But the opposite is rendered to it—that itself is not concealed from the truth, but the truth is concealed from it. Yet, even while thus wretched, it prefers to rejoice in truth rather than in falsehood. Happy then will it be, when, no trouble intervening, it shall rejoice in that only truth by whom all things else are true.

CHAPTER XXIV

HE WHO FINDS TRUTH, FINDS GOD

Behold how I have enlarged in my memory seeking Thee, O Lord; and out of it have I not found Thee. Nor have I found aught concerning Thee, but what I have retained in memory from the time I learned Thee. For from the time I learned Thee have I never forgotten Thee. For where I found truth, there I found my God, who is the Truth itself, which from the time I learned it have I not forgotten. And thus since the time I learned Thee, Thou abidest in my memory; and there do I find Thee whensoever I call Thee to remembrance, and delight in Thee. These are my holy delights, which Thou hast bestowed upon me in Thy mercy, having respect unto my poverty.

CHAPTER XXV

HE IS GLAD THAT GOD DWELLS IN HIS MEMORY

But where in my memory abidest Thou, O Lord, where dost Thou there abide? What manner of chamber hast Thou there formed for Thyself? What sort of sanctuary hast Thou erected for Thyself? Thou hast granted this honor to my memory, to take up Thy abode in it; but in what quarter of it Thou abidest, I am considering. For in calling Thee to mind, I

---

[45] Terence, *Andria,* i. 1, 41   [46] John viii. 40

soared beyond those parts of it which the beasts also possess, since I found Thee not there amongst the images of corporeal things; and I arrived at those parts where I had committed the affections of my mind, nor there did I find Thee. And I entered into the very seat of my mind, which it has in my memory, since the mind remembers itself also—nor wert Thou there. For as Thou art not a bodily image, nor the affection of a living creature, as when we rejoice, condole, desire, fear, remember, forget, or aught of the kind; so neither art Thou the mind itself, because Thou art the Lord God of the mind; and all these things are changed, but Thou remainest unchangeable over all, yet vouchsafest to dwell in my memory, from the time I learned Thee. But why do I now seek in what part of it Thou dwellest, as if truly there were places in it? Thou dost dwell in it assuredly, since I have remembered Thee from the time I learned Thee, and I find Thee in it when I call Thee to mind.

CHAPTER XXVI

GOD EVERYWHERE ANSWERS THOSE WHO TAKE COUNSEL OF HIM

Where, then, did I find Thee, so as to be able to learn Thee? For Thou wert not in my memory before I learned Thee. Where, then, did I find Thee, so as to be able to learn Thee, but in Thee above me? Place there is none; we go both backward and forward,[47] and there is no place. Everywhere, O Truth, dost Thou direct all who consult Thee, and dost at once answer all, though they consult Thee on divers things. Clearly dost Thou answer, though all do not with clearness hear. All consult Thee upon whatever they wish, though they hear not always that which they wish. He is Thy best servant who does not so much look to hear that from Thee which he himself wisheth, as to wish that which he heareth from Thee.

CHAPTER XXVII

HE GRIEVES THAT HE WAS SO LONG WITHOUT GOD

Too late did I love Thee, O Fairness, so ancient, and yet so new! Too late did I love Thee! For behold, Thou wert within, and I without, and there did I seek Thee; I, unlovely, rushed heedlessly among the things of beauty Thou madest. Thou wert with me, but I was not with Thee. Those things kept me far from Thee, which, unless they were in Thee, were not. Thou calledst, and criedst aloud, and forcedst open my deafness. Thou didst gleam and shine, and chase away my blindness. Thou didst exhale odors, and I drew in my breath and do pant after Thee. I tasted, and do hunger and thirst. Thou didst touch me, and I burned for Thy peace.

[47] Job xxiii. 8

CHAPTER XXVIII

ON THE MISERY OF HUMAN LIFE

When I shall cleave unto Thee with all my being, then shall I in nothing have pain and labor; and my life shall be a real life, being wholly full of Thee. But now since he whom Thou fillest is the one Thou liftest up, I am a burden to myself, as not being full of Thee. Joys of sorrow contend with sorrows of joy; and on which side the victory may be I know not. Woe is me! Lord, have pity on me. My evil sorrows contend with my good joys; and on which side the victory may be I know not. Woe is me! Lord, have pity on me. Woe is me! Lo, I hide not my wounds; Thou art the Physician, I the sick; Thou merciful, I miserable. Is not the life of man upon earth a temptation? [48] Who is he that wishes for vexations and difficulties? Thou commandest them to be endured, not to be loved. For no man loves what he endures, though he may love to endure. For notwithstanding he rejoices to endure, he would rather there were nothing for him to endure. In adversity, I desire prosperity; in prosperity, I fear adversity. What middle place, then, is there between these, where human life is not a temptation? Woe unto the prosperity of this world, once and again, from fear of misfortune and a corruption of joy! Woe unto the adversities of this world, once and again, and for the third time, from the desire of prosperity; and because adversity itself is a hard thing, and makes shipwreck of endurance! Is not the life of man upon earth a temptation, and that without intermission?

CHAPTER XXIX

ALL HOPE IS IN THE MERCY OF GOD

And my whole hope is only in Thy exceeding great mercy. Give what Thou commandest, and command what Thou wilt. Thou imposest continency upon us, "nevertheless, when I perceived," says one, "that I could not otherwise obtain it, except God gave it me; . . . that was a point of wisdom also to know whose gift it was." [49] For by continency are we bound up and brought into one, whence we were scattered abroad into many. For he loves Thee too little who loves aught with Thee, which he loves not for Thee, O love, who ever burnest, and art never quenched! O charity, my God, kindle me! Thou commandest continency; give what Thou commandest, and command what Thou wilt.

[48] Job vii. 1   [49] Wisd. viii, 21

CHAPTER XXX

OF THE PERVERSE IMAGES OF DREAMS, WHICH HE WISHES
TO HAVE TAKEN AWAY

Verily, Thou commandest that I should be continent from the lust of the flesh, and the lust of the eyes, and the pride of life.[50] Thou hast commanded me to abstain from concubinage; and as to marriage itself, Thou hast advised something better than Thou hast allowed. And because Thou didst give it, it was done; and that before I became a dispenser of Thy sacrament. But there still exist in my memory—of which I have spoken much—the images of such things as my habits had fixed there; and these rush into my thoughts, though strengthless, when I am awake; but in sleep they do so not only so as to give pleasure, but even to obtain consent, and what very nearly resembles reality. And to such an extent prevails the illusion of the image, both in my soul and in my flesh, that the false persuade me, when sleeping, to that which the true are not able when waking. Am I not myself at that time, O Lord my God? And there is yet so much difference between myself and myself, in that instant when I pass back from waking to sleeping, or return from sleeping to waking! Where, then, is the reason which when waking resists such suggestions? And if the things themselves be forced on it, I remain unmoved. Is it shut up with the eyes? Or is it put to sleep with the bodily senses? But whence, then, comes it to pass, that even in slumber we often resist, and, bearing our purpose in mind, and continuing most chastely in it, yield no assent to such allurements? And there is yet so much difference that, when it happens otherwise, upon awaking we return to peace of conscience; and by this same diversity do we discover that it was not we that did it, while we still feel sorry that in some way it was done in us.

Is not Thy hand able, O Almighty God, to heal all the diseases of my soul,[51] and by Thy more abundant grace to quench even the lascivious motions of my sleep? Thou wilt increase in me, O Lord, Thy gifts more and more, that my soul may follow me to Thee, disengaged from the bird-lime of concupiscence; that it may not be in rebellion against itself, and even in dreams not simply not, through sensual images, commit those deformities of corruption, even to the pollution of the flesh, but that it may not even consent to them. For it is no great thing for the Almighty, who is able to do . . . above all that we ask or think,[52] to bring it about that no such influence—not even so slight a one as a sign might restrain—should afford gratification to the chaste affection even of one sleeping; and that not only in this life, but at my present age. But what I still am in this species of my ill, have I confessed unto my good Lord; rejoicing with trembling[53] in

[50] I John ii. 16   [51] Ps. ciii. ?   [52] Eph. iii. 20   [53] Ps. ii. 11

that which Thou hast given me, and bewailing myself for that wherein I am still imperfect; trusting that Thou wilt perfect Thy mercies in me, even to the fulness of peace, which both that which is within and that which is without shall have with Thee, when death is swallowed up in victory.[54]

CHAPTER XXXI

ABOUT TO SPEAK OF THE TEMPTATIONS OF THE LUST OF THE FLESH, HE FIRST COMPLAINS OF THE LUST OF EATING AND DRINKING

There is another evil of the day that I would were sufficient unto it.[55] For by eating and drinking we repair the daily decays of the body, until Thou destroyest both food and stomach, when Thou shalt destroy my want with an amazing satiety, and shalt clothe this corruptible with an eternal incorruption.[56] But now is necessity sweet to me, and against this sweetness I fight, lest I be enthralled; and I carry on a daily war by fastings, oftentimes bringing my body into subjection,[57] and my pains are expelled by pleasure. For hunger and thirst are in some sort pains; they consume and destroy like a fever, unless the medicine of nourishment relieve us. This, since it is at hand through the comfort we receive of Thy gifts, with which land and water and air serve our infirmity, our calamity is called pleasure.

This much hast Thou taught me, that I should bring myself to take food as medicine. But during the time that I am passing from the uneasiness of want to the calmness of satiety, even in the very passage that snare of concupiscence lies in wait for me. For the passage itself is pleasure, nor is there any other way of passing thither, whither necessity compels us to pass. And whereas health is the reason of eating and drinking, there joins itself as a handmaid a perilous delight, which mostly tries to precede it, in order that I may do for her sake what I say I do, or desire to do, for health's sake. Nor have both the same limit; for what is sufficient for health is too little for pleasure. And oftentimes it is doubtful whether it be the necessary care of the body which still asks nourishment, or whether a sensual snare of desire offers its ministry. In this uncertainty does my unhappy soul rejoice, and therein prepares an excuse as a defence, glad that it does not appear what may be sufficient for the moderation of health, that so under the pretence of health it may conceal the business of pleasure. These temptations do I daily endeavor to resist, and I summon Thy right hand to my help, and refer my excitements to Thee, because as yet I have no resolve in this matter.

I hear the voice of my God commanding, let not your hearts be overcharged with surfeiting and drunkenness.[58] Drunkenness is far from me; Thou wilt have mercy, that it approach not near unto me. But surfeiting

[54] 1 Cor. xv. 54　　[55] Matt. vi. 34　　[56] 1 Cor. xv. 54　　[57] 1 Cor. ix. 27　　[58] Luke xxi. 34

sometimes creepeth upon Thy servant; Thou wilt have mercy, that it may be far from me. For no man can be continent unless Thou give it.[59] Many things which we pray for dost Thou give us; and what good soever we receive before we prayed for it, do we receive from Thee, and that we might afterwards know this did we receive it from Thee. Drunkard was I never, but I have known drunkards to be made sober men by Thee. Thy doing, then, was it, that they who never were such might not be so, as from Thee it was that they who have been so heretofore might not remain so always; and from Thee, too, was it, that both might know from whom it was. I heard another voice of Thine, "Go not after thy lusts, but refrain thyself from thine appetites." [60] And by Thy favor have I heard this saying likewise, which I have much delighted in, "Neither if we eat, are we the better; neither if we eat not, are we the worse;" [61] which is to say, that neither shall the one make me to abound, nor the other to be wretched. I heard also another voice, "For I have learned, in whatsoever state I am, therewith to be content, I know both how to be abased, and I know how to abound. . . . I can do all things through Christ which strengtheneth me." [62] Lo! a soldier of the celestial camp—not dust as we are. But remember, O Lord, that we are dust,[63] and that of dust Thou hast created man,[64] and he was lost, and is found.[65] Nor could he do this of his own power, seeing that he whom I so loved, saying these things through the afflatus of Thy inspiration, was of that same dust. "I can," said he, "do all things through Him which strengtheneth me." [66] Strengthen me, that I may be able. Give what Thou commandest, and command what Thou wilt. He confesses to have received, and when he glorieth, he glorieth in the Lord.[67] Another have I heard entreating that he might receive—"Take from me," said he, "the greediness of the belly;" [68] by which it appeareth, O my holy God, that Thou givest when what Thou commandest to be done is done.

Thou hast taught me, good Father, that unto the pure all things are pure;[69] but it is evil for that man who eateth with offence;[70] and that every creature of Thine is good, and nothing to be refused, if it be received with thanksgiving;[71] and that meat commendeth us not to God;[72] and that no man should judge us in meat or in drink;[73] and that he that eateth, let him not despise him that eateth not; and let not him that eateth not judge him that eateth.[74] These things have I learned, thanks and praise be unto Thee, O my God and Master, who dost knock at my ears and enlighten my heart; deliver me out of all temptation. It is not the uncleanness of meat that I fear, but the uncleanness of lusting. I know that permission was granted unto Noah to eat every kind of flesh that was good for food;[75] that Elias was fed with flesh;[76] that John, endued with a wonderful abstinence, was

---

[59] Wisd. viii. 21 [60] Ecclus. xviii. 30 [61] 1 Cor. viii. 8 [62] Phil. iv. 11-14 [63] Ps. ciii. 14 [64] Gen. iii. 19 [65] Luke xv. 32 [66] Phil. iv. 13 [67] 1 Cor. i. 31 [68] Ecclus. xxiii. 6 [69] Titus i. 15 [70] Rom. xiv. 20 [71] 1 Tim. iv. 4 [72] 1 Cor. viii. 8 [73] Col. ii. 16 [74] Rom. xiii. 23 [75] Gen. ix. 3 [76] 1 Kings xvii. 6

not polluted by the living creatures (that is, the locusts[77]) which he fed on. I know, too, that Esau was deceived by a longing for lentiles,[78] and that David took blame to himself for desiring water,[79] and that our King was tempted not by flesh but bread.[80] And the people in the wilderness, therefore, also deserved reproof, not because they desired flesh, but because, in their desire for food, they murmured against the Lord.[81]

Placed, then, in the midst of these temptations, I strive daily against longing for food and drink. For it is not of such a nature as that I am able to resolve to cut it off once for all, and not touch it afterwards, as I was able to do with concubinage. The bridle of the throat, therefore, is to be held in the mean of slackness and tightness. And who, O Lord, is he who is not in some degree carried away beyond the bounds of necessity? Whoever he is, he is great; let him magnify Thy name. But I am not such a one, for I am a sinful man.[82] Yet do I also magnify Thy name; and He who hath overcome the world [83] maketh intercession to Thee for my sins,[84] accounting me among the feeble members of His body,[85] because Thine eyes saw that of him which was imperfect; and in Thy book all shall be written.[86]

CHAPTER XXXII

OF THE CHARMS OF PERFUMES WHICH ARE MORE EASILY OVERCOME

With the attractions of odors I am not much troubled. When absent I do not seek them; when present I do not refuse them; and am prepared ever to be without them. At any rate thus I appear to myself; perchance I am deceived. For that also is a lamentable darkness in which my capacity that is in me is concealed, so that my mind, making inquiry into herself concerning her own powers, ventures not readily to credit herself; because that which is already in it is, for the most part, concealed, unless experience reveal it. And no man ought to feel secure in this life, the whole of which is called a temptation, that he, who could be made better from worse, may not also from better be made worse. Our sole hope, our sole confidence, our sole assured promise, is Thy mercy.

CHAPTER XXXIII

HE OVERCAME THE PLEASURES OF THE EAR, ALTHOUGH IN THE CHURCH HE FREQUENTLY DELIGHTED IN THE SONG, NOT IN THE THING SUNG

The delights of the ear had more powerfully inveigled and conquered me, but Thou didst unbind and liberate me. Now, in those airs which Thy

---

[77] Matt. iii. 4   [78] Gen. xxv. 34   [79] 2 Sam. xxiii. 15-17   [80] Matt. iv. 3   [81] Num. xi.   [82] Luke v. 8   [83] John xvi. 33   [84] Rom. viii. 34   [85] 1 Cor. xii. 22   [86] Ps. cxxxix. 16

words breathe soul into, when sung with a sweet and trained voice, do I somewhat repose; yet not so as to cling to them, but so as to free myself when I wish. But with the words which are their life do they, that they may gain admission into me, strive after a place of some honor in my heart; and I can hardly assign them a fitting one. Sometimes I appear to myself to give them more respect than is fitting, as I perceive that our minds are more devoutly and earnestly elevated into a flame of piety by the holy words themselves when they are thus sung, than when they are not; and that all affections of our spirit, by their own diversity, have their appropriate measures in the voice and singing, wherewith by I know not what secret relationship they are stimulated. But the gratification of my flesh, to which the mind ought never to be given over to be enervated, often beguiles me, while the sense does not so attend on reason as to follow her patiently; but having gained admission merely for her sake, it strives even to run on before her, and be her leader. Thus in these things do I sin unknowing, but afterwards I know it.

Sometimes, again, avoiding very earnestly this same deception, I err out of too great preciseness; and sometimes so much as to desire that every air of the pleasant songs to which David's Psalter is often used, be banished both from my ears and those of the Church itself; and that way seemed to me safer which I remembered to have been often related to me of Athanasius, Bishop of Alexandria, who obliged the reader of the psalm to give utterance to it with so slight an inflection of voice, that it was more like speaking than singing. Notwithstanding, when I call to mind the tears I shed at the songs of Thy Church, at the outset of my recovered faith, and how even now I am moved not by the singing but by what is sung, when they are sung with a clear and skilfully modulated voice, I then acknowledge the great utility of this custom. Thus vacillate I between dangerous pleasure and tried soundness; being inclined rather (though I pronounce no irrevocable opinion upon the subject) to approve of the use of singing in the church, that so by the delights of the ear the weaker minds may be stimulated to a devotional frame. Yet when it happens to me to be more moved by the singing than by what is sung, I confess myself to have sinned criminally, and then I would rather not have heard the singing. See now the condition I am in! Weep with me, and weep for me, you who so control your inward feelings that good results ensue. As for you who do not thus act, these things concern you not. But Thou, O Lord my God, give ear, behold and see, and have mercy upon me, and heal me[87]—Thou, in whose sight I am become a puzzle to myself; and this is my infirmity.[88]

[87] Ps. vi. 2   [88] Ps. lxxvii. 1c

CHAPTER XXXIV

OF THE VERY DANGEROUS ALLUREMENTS OF THE EYES; ON ACCOUNT
OF BEAUTY OF FORM, GOD, THE CREATOR, IS TO BE PRAISED

There remain the delights of these eyes of my flesh, concerning which to make my confessions in the hearing of the ears of Thy temple, those fraternal and devout ears; and so to conclude the temptations of the lust of the flesh [89] which still assail me, groaning and desiring to be clothed upon with my house from heaven.[90] The eyes delight in fair and varied forms, and bright and pleasing colors. Suffer not these to take possession of my soul; let God rather possess it, He who made these things very good [91] indeed; yet is He my good, not these. And these move me while awake, during the day; nor is rest from them granted me, as there is from the voices of melody, sometimes, in silence, from them all. For that queen of colors, the light, flooding all that we look upon, wherever I am during the day, gliding past me in manifold forms, soothes me when busied about other things, and not noticing it. And so strongly does it insinuate itself, that if it be suddenly withdrawn it is looked for longingly, and if long absent saddens the mind.

O Thou Light, which Tobias saw,[92] when, his eyes being closed, he taught his son the way of life; himself going before with the feet of charity, never going astray. Or that which Isaac saw, when his fleshly eyes were dim, so that he could not see[93] by reason of old age; it was permitted him, not knowingly to bless his sons, but in blessing them to know them. Or that which Jacob saw, when he too, blind through great age, with an enlightened heart, in the persons of his own sons, threw light upon the races of the future people, presignified in them; and laid his hands, mystically crossed, upon his grandchildren by Joseph, not as their father, looking outwardly, corrected them, but as he himself distinguished them.[94] This is the light, the only one, and all those who see and love it are one. But that corporeal light of which I was speaking seasons the life of the world for her blind lovers, with a tempting and fatal sweetness. But they who know how to praise Thee for it, "O God, the world's great Architect," [95] take it up in Thy hymn, and are not taken up with it in their sleep. Such I desire to be. I resist seductions of the eyes, lest my feet with which I advance on Thy way be entangled; and I raise my invisible eyes to Thee, that Thou wouldst be pleased to pluck my feet out of the net.[96] Thou dost continually pluck them out, for they are ensnared. Thou never ceasest to pluck them out, but I constantly remain fast in the snares set all around me; because Thou that keepest Israel shall neither slumber nor sleep.[97]

What numberless things, made by various arts and manufactures, both in

[89] 1 John ii. 16   [90] 2 Cor. v. 2   [91] Gen. i. 31   [92] Tobit iv.   [93] Gen. xxvii. 1
[94] Gen. xlviii. 13-19   [95] Cf. ix. 32   [96] Ps. xxv. 15   [97] Ps. cxxi. 4

our apparel, shoes, vessels, and every kind of work, in pictures, too, and sundry images, and these going far beyond necessary and moderate use and holy signification, have men added for the enthralment of the eyes; following outwardly what they make, forsaking inwardly Him by whom they were made, and destroying that which they themselves were made! But I, O my God and my Joy, do hence also sing a hymn unto Thee, and offer a sacrifice of praise to Thee who dost sacrifice for me,[98] because those beautiful patterns, which through the medium of men's souls are conveyed into their artistic hands, emanate from that Beauty which is above our souls, which my soul sigheth after day and night. But as for the makers and followers of those outward beauties, they from thence derive the way of approving them, but not of using them. And though they see Him not, yet is He there, that they might not go astray, but keep their strength for Thee, and not dissipate it upon delicious lassitudes. And I, though I both say and perceive this, impede my course with such beauties, but Thou dost rescue me, O Lord, Thou dost rescue me; for Thy loving-kindness is before mine eyes.[99] For I am taken miserably, and Thou rescuest me mercifully; sometimes not perceiving it, in that I had come upon them hesitatingly; at other times with pain, because I was held fast by them.

CHAPTER XXXV

ANOTHER KIND OF TEMPTATION IS CURIOSITY, WHICH IS STIMULATED BY THE LUST OF THE EYES

In addition to this there is another form of temptation, more complex in its peril. For besides that concupiscence of the flesh which lies in the gratification of all senses and pleasures, wherein its slaves who are far from Thee perish,[100] there pertains to the soul, through the same senses of the body, a certain vain and curious longing, cloaked under the name of knowledge and learning, not of having pleasure in the flesh, but of making experiments through the flesh. This longing, since it originates in an appetite for knowledge, and the sight being the chief amongst the senses in the acquisition of knowledge, is called in divine language, the lust of the eyes.[101] For seeing belongs properly to the eyes; yet we apply this word to the other senses also, when we exercise them in the search after knowledge. For we do not say, Listen how it glows, smell how it glistens, taste how it shines, or feel how it flashes, since all these are said to be seen. And yet we say not only, See how it shines, which the eyes alone can perceive; but also, See how it sounds, see how it smells, see how it tastes, see how hard it is. And thus the general experience of the senses, as was said before, is termed the lust of the eyes, because the function of seeing, wherein the eyes hold

---

[98] *Sanctificatori meo*, but some MSS. have *sacrificatori*.   [99] Ps. xxvi. 3   [100] Ps. lxiii.
27   [101] 1 John ii. 16

the pre-eminence, the other senses by way of similitude take possession of, whenever they seek any knowledge.

But by this is it more clearly discerned, when pleasure and when curiosity is pursued by the senses; for pleasure follows after objects that are beautiful, melodious, fragrant, savory, soft; but curiosity, for experiment's sake, seeks the contrary of these—not with a view of undergoing uneasiness, but from the passion of experimenting upon and knowing them. For what pleasure is there to see, in a lacerated corpse, that which makes you shudder? And yet if it lie near, we flock thither, to be made sad, and to turn pale. Even in sleep they fear lest they should see it. Just as if when awake any one compelled them to go and see it, or any report of its beauty had attracted them! Thus also is it with the other senses, which it were tedious to pursue. From this malady of curiosity are all those strange sights exhibited in the theatre. Hence do we proceed to search out the secret powers of nature (which is beside our end), which to know profits not, and wherein men desire nothing but to know. Hence, too, with that same end of perverted knowledge we consult magical arts. Hence, again, even in religion itself, is God tempted, when signs and wonders are eagerly asked of Him—not desired for any saving end, but to make trial only.

In this vast wilderness, replete with snares and dangers, lo, many of them have I lopped off, and expelled from my heart, as Thou, O God of my salvation, hast enabled me to do. And yet when dare I say, since so many things of this kind buzz around our daily life—when dare I say that no such thing makes me intent to see it, or creates in me vain solicitude? It is true that the theatres never now carry me away, nor do I now care to know the courses of the stars, nor has my soul at any time consulted departed spirits; all sacrilegious oaths I abhor. O Lord my God, to whom I owe all humble and single-hearted service, with what subtlety of suggestion does the enemy influence me to require some sign from Thee! But by our King, and by our pure and chaste country Jerusalem, I beseech Thee, that as any consenting to such thoughts is far from me, so may it always be farther and farther. But when I entreat Thee for the salvation of any, the end I aim at is far otherwise, and Thou who doest what Thou wilt, givest and wilt give me willingly to follow Thee.[102]

Nevertheless, in how many most minute and contemptible things is our curiosity daily tempted, and who can number how often we succumb? How often, when people are narrating idle tales, do we begin by tolerating them, lest we should give offence to the weak; and then gradually we listen willingly! I do not now-a-days go to the circus to see a dog chasing a hare; but if by chance I pass such a coursing in the fields, it possibly distracts me even from some serious thought, and draws me after it—not that I turn the body of my beast aside, but the inclination of my mind. And except Thou, by demonstrating to me my weakness, dost speedily warn me, either

[102] John xxi. 22

through the sight itself, by some reflection to rise to Thee, or wholly to despise and pass it by, I, vain one, am absorbed by it. How is it, when sitting at home, a lizard catching flies, or a spider entangling them as they rush into her nets, oftentimes arrests me? Is the feeling of curiosity not the same because these are such tiny creatures? From them I proceed to praise Thee, the wonderful Creator and Disposer of all things; but it is not this that first attracts my attention. It is one thing to get up quickly, and another not to fall, and of such things is my life full; and my only hope is in Thy exceeding great mercy. For when this heart of ours is made the receptacle of such things, and bears crowds of this abounding vanity, then are our prayers often interrupted and disturbed thereby; and while in Thy presence we direct the voice of our heart to Thine ears, this so great a matter is broken off by the influx of I know not what idle thoughts.

CHAPTER XXXVI

A THIRD KIND IS PRIDE, WHICH IS PLEASING TO MAN, NOT TO GOD

Shall we, then, account this too amongst such things as are to be lightly esteemed, or shall anything restore us to hope, save Thy complete mercy, since Thou hast begun to change us? And Thou knowest to what extent Thou hast already changed me, Thou who first healest me of the lust of vindicating myself, that so Thou mightest forgive all my remaining iniquities, and heal all my diseases, and redeem my life from corruption, and crown me with loving-kindness and tender mercies and satisfy my desire with good things;[103] who didst restrain my pride with Thy fear, and subdue my neck to Thy yoke. And now I bear it, and it is light [104] unto me, because so hast Thou promised, and made it, and so in truth it was, though I knew it not, when I feared to take it up. But, O Lord—Thou who alone reignest without pride, because Thou art the only true Lord, who hast no lord—hath this third kind of temptation left me, or can it leave me during this life?

The desire to be feared and loved of men, with no other view than that I may experience a joy therein which is no joy, is a miserable life, and unseemly ostentation. Hence especially it arises that we do not love Thee, nor devoutly fear Thee. And therefore dost Thou resist the proud, but givest grace unto the humble,[105] and Thou thunderest upon the ambitious designs of the world, and the foundations of the hills tremble.[106] Because now certain offices of human society render it necessary to be loved and feared of men, the adversary of our true blessedness presses hard upon us, everywhere scattering his snares of "well done, well done;" that while acquiring them eagerly, we may be caught unawares, and disunite our joy from Thy truth, and fix it on the deceits of men; and take pleasure in being

[103] Ps. ciii. 3-5   [104] Matt. xi. 30   [105] Jas. iv. 6   [106] Ps. xviii. 7

loved and feared, not for Thy sake, but in Thy stead, by which means, being made like unto him, he may have them as his, not in harmony of love, but in the fellowship of punishment; who aspired to exalt his throne in the north,[107] that dark and cold they might serve him, imitating Thee in perverse and distorted ways. But we, O Lord, lo, we are Thy little flock;[108] do Thou possess us, stretch Thy wings over us, and let us take refuge under them. Be Thou our glory; let us be loved for Thy sake, and Thy word feared in us. They who desire to be commended of men when Thou blamest, will not be defended of men when Thou judgest; nor will they be delivered when Thou condemnest. But when not the sinner is praised in the desires of his soul, nor he blessed who does unjustly, but a man is praised for some gift that Thou hast bestowed upon him, and he is more gratified at the praise for himself, than that he possesses the gift for which he is praised, such a one is praised while Thou blamest. And better truly is he who praised than the one who was praised. For the gift of God in man was pleasing to the one, while the other was better pleased with the gift of man than that of God.

CHAPTER XXXVII

HE IS FORCIBLY GOADED ON BY THE LOVE OF PRAISE

By these temptations, O Lord, are we daily tried; unceasingly are we tried. Our daily furnace[109] is the human tongue. And in this respect also dost Thou command us to be continent. Give what Thou commandest, and command what Thou wilt. Regarding this matter, Thou knowest the groans of my heart, and the rivers[110] of mine eyes. For I am not able to ascertain how far I am clean of this plague, and I stand in great fear of my secret faults,[111] which Thine eyes perceive, though mine do not. For in other kinds of temptations I have some sort of power of examining myself; but in this, hardly any. For, both as regards the pleasures of the flesh and an idle curiosity, I see how far I have been able to hold my mind in check when I do without them, either voluntarily or by reason of their not being at hand; for then I inquire of myself how much more or less troublesome it is to me not to have them. Riches truly which are sought for in order that they may minister to some one of these three lusts,[112] or to two, or the whole of them, if the mind be not able to see clearly whether, when it hath them, it despises them, they may be cast on one side, that so it may prove itself. But if we desire to test our power of doing without praise, need we live ill, and that so desperately and immoderately that every one who knows us shall detest us? What greater madness than this can be either said or conceived? But if praise both is wont and ought to be the companion of a good life and of good works, we should as little forego its com-

---

[107] Isa. xiv. 13, 14   [108] Luke xii. 32   [109] Isa. xlviii. 10, and Prov. xxvii. 21
[110] Lam. iii. 48   [111] Ps. xix. 12   [112] 1 John ii. 16

panionship as a good life itself. But unless a thing be absent, I do not know whether I shall be contented or troubled at being without it.

What, then, do I confess unto Thee, O Lord, in this kind of temptation? What, save that I am delighted with praise, but more with the truth itself than with praise? For were I to have my choice, whether I had rather, being mad, or astray on all things, be praised by all men, or, being firm and well-assured in the truth, be blamed by all, I see which I should choose. Yet would I be unwilling that the approval of another should even add to my joy for any good I have. Yet I admit that it does increase it, and, more than that, that dispraise does diminish it. And when I am disquieted at this misery of mine, an excuse presents itself to me, the value of which Thou, God, knowest, for it renders me uncertain. For since it is not continency alone that Thou hast enjoined upon us, that is, from what things to hold back our love, but righteousness also, that is, upon what to bestow it, and hast wished us to love not Thee only, but also our neighbor[113]— often, when gratified by intelligent praise, I appear to myself to be gratified by the proficiency or promise of my neighbor, and again to be sorry for evil in him when I hear him dispraise either that which he understands not, or is good. For I am sometimes grieved at mine own praise, either when those things which I am displeased at in myself be praised in me, or even lesser and trifling goods are more valued than they should be. But, again, how do I know whether I am thus affected, because I am unwilling that he who praises me should differ from me concerning myself—not as moved with consideration for him, but because the same good things which please me in myself are more pleasing to me when they also please another? For, in a sort, I am not praised when my judgment of myself is not praised; since either those things which are displeasing to me are praised, or those more so which are less pleasing to me. Am I then uncertain of myself in this matter?

Behold, O Truth, in Thee do I see that I ought not to be moved at my own praises for my own sake, but for my neighbor's good. And whether it be so, in truth I know not. For concerning this I know less of myself than dost Thou. I beseech Thee now, O my God, to reveal to me myself also, that I may confess unto my brethren, who are to pray for me, what I find in myself weak. Once again let me more diligently examine myself. If, in mine own praise, I am moved with consideration for my neighbor, why am I less moved if some other man be unjustly dispraised than if it be myself? Why am I more irritated at that reproach which is cast upon myself, than at that which is with equal injustice cast upon another in my presence? Am I ignorant of this also? or does it remain that I deceive myself,[114] and do not the truth[115] before Thee in my heart and tongue? Put such madness far from me, O Lord, lest my mouth be to me the oil of sinners, to anoint my head.

[113] Lev. xix. 18   [114] Gal. vi. 3   [115] 1 John i. 8

CHAPTER XXXVIII

VAIN-GLORY IS THE HIGHEST DANGER

I am poor and needy,[116] yet better am I while in secret groanings I displease myself, and seek for Thy mercy, until what is lacking in me be renewed and made complete, even up to that peace of which the eye of the proud is ignorant. Yet the word which proceeds out of the mouth, and actions known to men, have a most dangerous temptation from the love of praise, which, for the establishing of a certain excellency of our own, gathers together praise that is begged for. It tempts, even when within I reprove myself for it, on the very ground that it is reproved; and often man glories more vainly of the very scorn of vain-glory; wherefore it is not any longer scorn of vain-glory whereof it glories, for he does not truly contemn it when he inwardly glories.

CHAPTER XXXIX

OF THE VICE OF THOSE WHO, WHILE PLEASING THEMSELVES, DISPLEASE GOD

Within also, within is another evil, arising out of the same kind of temptation; whereby they become empty who please themselves in themselves, although they please not, or displease, or aim at pleasing others. But in pleasing themselves, they much displease Thee, not merely taking pleasure in things not good as if they were good, but in Thy good things as though they were their own; or even as if in Thine, yet as though of their own merits; or even as if though of Thy grace, yet not with friendly rejoicings, but as envying that grace to others. In all these and similar perils and labors Thou perceivest the trembling of my heart, and I rather feel my wounds to be cured by Thee than not inflicted by me.

CHAPTER XL

THE ONLY SAFE RESTING-PLACE FOR THE SOUL IS TO BE FOUND IN GOD

Where hast Thou not accompanied me, O Truth, teaching me both what to avoid and what to desire, when I submitted to Thee what I could perceive of things here below and asked Thy counsel? With my external senses, as I could, I viewed the world, and noted the life which my body derives from me, and these my senses. Thence I advanced inwardly into the recesses of my memory—the manifold rooms, wondrously full of multitudinous wealth; and I considered and was afraid, and could discern none of these things without Thee, and found none of them to be Thee. Nor was

---

[116] Ps. cix. 22

I myself the discoverer of these things—I, who went over them all, and labored to distinguish and to value everything according to its dignity, accepting some things upon the report of my senses, and questioning about others which I felt to be mixed up with myself, distinguishing and numbering the reporters themselves, and in the vast storehouse of my memory investigating some things, laying up others, taking out others. Neither was I myself when I did this (that is, that ability of mine whereby I did it), nor was it Thou, for Thou art that never-failing light which I took counsel of as to them all, whether they were what they were, and what was their worth; and I heard Thee teaching and commanding me. And this I do often; this is a delight to me, and, as far as I can get relief from necessary duties, to this gratification I resort. Nor in all these which I review when consulting Thee, find I a secure place for my soul, save in Thee, into whom my scattered members may be gathered together, and nothing of me depart from Thee. And sometimes Thou dost introduce me to a most rare affection, inwardly, to an inexplicable sweetness, which, if it should be perfected in me, I know not to what point that life might not arrive. But by these wretched weights[117] of mine do I relapse into these things, and am sucked in by my old customs, and am held, and sorrow much, yet am much held. To such an extent does the burden of habit press us down. In this way I can be, but will not; in that I will, but cannot—on both ways miserable.

CHAPTER XLI

HAVING CONQUERED HIS TRIPLE DESIRE, HE ARRIVES AT SALVATION

And thus have I reflected upon the wearinesses of my sins, in that threefold lust, and have invoked Thy right hand to my aid. For with a wounded heart have I seen Thy brightness, and being beaten back I exclaimed, "Who can attain unto it?" I am cut off from before Thine eyes.[118] Thou art the Truth, who presidest over all things, but I, through my covetousness, wished not to lose Thee, but with Thee wished to possess a lie; as no one wishes so to speak falsely as himself to be ignorant of the truth. So then I lost Thee, because Thou deignest not to be enjoyed with a lie.

CHAPTER XLII

IN WHAT MANNER MANY SOUGHT THE MEDIATOR

Whom could I find to reconcile me to Thee? Was I to solicit the angels? By what prayer? By what sacraments? Many striving to return unto Thee, and not able of themselves, have, as I am told, tried this, and have fallen into a longing for curious visions, and were held worthy to be deceived.

---

[117] Heb. xii. 1   [118] Ps. xxxi. 22

For they, being exalted, sought Thee by the pride of learning, thrusting themselves forward rather than beating their breasts, and so by correspondence of heart drew unto themselves the princes of the air,[119] the conspirators and companions in pride, by whom, through the power of magic, they were deceived, seeking a mediator by whom they might be cleansed; but none was there. For the devil it was, transforming himself into an angel of light.[120] And he much allured proud flesh, in that he had no fleshly body. For they were mortal, and sinful; but Thou, O Lord, to whom they arrogantly sought to be reconciled, art immortal, and sinless. But a mediator between God and man ought to have something like unto God, and something like unto man; lest being in both like unto man, he should be far from God; or if in both like unto God, he should be far from man, and so should not be a mediator. That deceitful mediator, then, by whom in Thy secret judgments pride deserved to be deceived, hath one thing in common with man, that is, sin; another he would appear to have with God, and, not being clothed with mortality of flesh, would boast that he was immortal. But since the wages of sin is death,[121] this hath he in common with men, that together with them he should be condemned to death.

CHAPTER XLIII

THAT JESUS CHRIST, AT THE SAME TIME GOD AND MAN, IS THE TRUE AND MOST EFFICACIOUS MEDIATOR

But the true Mediator, whom in Thy secret mercy Thou hast pointed out to the humble, and didst send, that by His example also they might learn the same humility—that Mediator between God and men, the man Christ Jesus,[122] appeared between mortal sinners and the immortal Just One— mortal with men, just with God; that because the reward of righteousness is life and peace, He might, by righteousness conjoined with God, cancel the death of justified sinners, which He willed to have in common with them. Hence He was pointed out to holy men of old; to the intent that they, through faith in His Passion to come, even as we through faith in that which is past, might be saved. For as man He was Mediator; but as the Word He was not between, because equal to God, and God with God, and together one God.

How hast Thou loved us, O good Father, who sparedst not Thine only Son, but deliveredst Him up for us wicked ones.[123] How hast Thou loved us, for whom He, who thought it no robbery to be equal with Thee, became obedient unto death, even the death of the cross;[124] He alone free among the dead,[125] that had power to lay down His life, and power to take it again;[126] for us was He unto Thee both Victor and Victim, and the Victor as being the Victim; for us was He unto Thee both Priest and Sacrifice,

[119] Eph. ii. 2   [120] 2 Cor. xi. 14   [121] Rom. vi. 23   [122] 1 Tim. ii. 5   [123] Rom. viii.
34   [124] Phil. ii. 6, 8   [125] Ps. lxxxviii. 5   [126] John x. 18

and Priest as being the Sacrifice; of slaves making us Thy sons, by being born of Thee, and serving us. Rightly, then, is my hope strongly fixed on Him, that Thou wilt heal all my diseases[127] by Him who sitteth at Thy right hand and maketh intercession for us;[128] else should I utterly despair. For numerous and great are my infirmities, yea, numerous and great are they; but Thy medicine is greater. We might think that Thy Word was removed from union with man, and despair of ourselves had He not been made flesh and dwelt among us.[129]

Terrified by my sins and the load of my misery, I had resolved in my heart, and meditated flight into the wilderness;[130] but Thou didst forbid me, and didst strengthen me, saying, therefore, Christ died for all, that they which live should not henceforth live unto themselves, but unto Him which died for them.[131] Behold, O Lord, I cast my care upon Thee,[132] that I may live, and behold wondrous things out of Thy law.[133] Thou knowest my unskilfulness and my infirmities; teach me, and heal me. Thine only Son— He in whom are hid all the treasures of wisdom and knowledge[134]—hath redeemed me with His blood. Let not the proud speak evil of me,[135] because I consider my ransom, and eat and drink, and distribute; and poor, desire to be satisfied from Him, together with those who eat and are satisfied, and they praise the Lord that seek him.[136]

[127] Ps. ciii. 3   [128] Rom. viii. 34   [129] John i. 14   [130] Ps. iv. 7   [131] 2 Cor. v. 15
[132] Ps. lv. 22   [133] Ps. cxix. 18   [134] Col. ii. 3   [135] Ps. cxix. 122   [136] Ps. xxii. 26

BOOK ELEVEN

The design of his confessions being declared, he seeks from God the knowledge of the Holy Scriptures, and begins to expound the words of Genesis i. 1, concerning the creation of the world. The questions of rash disputers being refuted, "What did God before He created the world?" that He might the better overcome His opponents, he adds a copious disquisition concerning time.

CHAPTER I

BY CONFESSION HE DESIRES TO STIMULATE TOWARDS GOD HIS OWN LOVE AND THAT OF HIS READERS

O LORD, since eternity is Thine, art Thou ignorant of the things which I say unto Thee? Or seest Thou at the time that which cometh to pass in time? Why, therefore, do I place before Thee so many relations of things? Not surely that Thou mightest know them through me, but that I may awaken my own love and that of my readers towards Thee, that we may all say, "Great is the Lord, and greatly to be praised." [1] I have already said, and shall say, for the love of Thy love I do this. For we also pray, and yet Truth says, "Your Father knoweth what things ye have need of before ye ask Him." [2] Therefore do we make known unto Thee our love, in confessing unto Thee our own miseries and Thy mercies upon us, that Thou mayest free us altogether, since Thou hast begun, that we may cease to be wretched in ourselves, and that we may be blessed in Thee; since Thou hast called us, that we may be poor in spirit, and meek, and mourners, and hungering and athirst after righteousness, and merciful, and pure in heart, and peacemakers.[3] Behold, I have told unto Thee many things, which I could and which I would, for Thou first wouldest that I should confess unto Thee, the Lord my God, for Thou art good, since Thy mercy endureth for ever.[4]

CHAPTER II

HE BEGS OF GOD THAT THROUGH THE HOLY SCRIPTURES HE MAY BE LED TO TRUTH

But when shall I suffice with the tongue of my pen to express all Thy exhortations, and all Thy terrors, and comforts, and guidances, whereby Thou hast led me to preach Thy Word and to dispense Thy Sacrament

---

[1] Ps. xcvi. 4   [2] Matt. vi. 8   [3] Matt. v. 3-9   [4] Ps. cxviii. 1

unto Thy people? And if I suffice to utter these things in order, the drops of time are dear to me. Long time have I burned to meditate in Thy law, and in it to confess to Thee my knowledge and ignorance, the beginning of Thine enlightening, and the remains of my darkness, until infirmity be swallowed up by strength. And I would not that to aught else those hours should flow away, which I find free from the necessities of refreshing my body, and the care of my mind, and of the service which we owe to men, and which, though we owe not, even yet we pay.

O Lord my God, hear my prayer, and let Thy mercy regard my longing, since it burns not for myself alone, but because it desires to benefit brotherly charity; and Thou seest into my heart, that so it is. I would sacrifice to Thee the service of my thought and tongue; and do Thou give what I may offer unto Thee. For I am poor and needy,[5] Thou rich unto all that call upon Thee,[6] who free from care carest for us. Circumcise from all rashness and from all lying my inward and outward lips.[7] Let Thy Scriptures be my chaste delights. Neither let me be deceived in them, nor deceive out of them. Lord, hear and pity, O Lord my God, light of the blind, and strength of the weak; even also light of those that see, and strength of the strong, hearken unto my soul, and hear it crying out of the depths.[8] For unless Thine ears be present in the depths also, whither shall we go? whither shall we cry? The day is Thine, and the night also is Thine.[9] At Thy nod the moments flee by. Grant thereof space for our meditations amongst the hidden things of Thy law, nor close it against us who knock. For not in vain hast Thou willed that the obscure secret of so many pages should be written. Nor is it that those forests have not their harts,[10] betaking themselves therein, and ranging, and walking, and feeding, lying down, and ruminating. Perfect me, O Lord, and reveal them unto me. Behold, Thy voice is my joy, Thy voice surpasseth the abundance of pleasures. Give that which I love, for I do love; and this hast Thou given. Abandon not Thine own gifts, nor despise Thy grass that thirsteth. Let me confess unto Thee whatsoever I shall have found in Thy books, and let me hear the voice of praise, and let me imbibe Thee, and reflect on the wonderful things of Thy Law;[11] even from the beginning, wherein Thou madest the heaven and the earth, unto the everlasting kingdom of Thy holy city that is with Thee.

Lord, have mercy on me and hear my desire. For I think that it is not of the earth, nor of gold and silver, and precious stones, nor gorgeous apparel, nor honors and powers, nor the pleasures of the flesh, nor necessaries for the body, and this life of our pilgrimage; all which are added to those that seek Thy kingdom and Thy righteousness.[12] Behold, O Lord my God, whence is my desire. The unrighteous have told me of delights, but

---

[5] Ps. lxxxvi. 1   [6] Rom. x. 12   [7] Ex. vi. 12   [8] Ps. cxxx. 1   [9] Ps. lxxiv. 16
[10] Ps. xxix. 9. The hart was supposed to be invulnerable to snake-bites. They thus signify those who can resist temptation.—Ed.   [11] Ps. xxvi. 7   [12] Matt. vi. 33

not such as Thy law, O Lord.[13] Behold whence is my desire. Behold, Father, look and see, and approve; and let it be pleasing in the sight of Thy mercy, that I may find grace before Thee, that the secret things of Thy Word may be opened unto me when I knock. I beseech, by our Lord Jesus Christ, Thy Son, the Man of Thy right hand, the Son of man, whom Thou madest strong for Thyself,[14] as Thy Mediator and ours, through whom Thou hast sought us, although not seeking Thee, but didst seek us that we might seek Thee—Thy Word through whom Thou hast made all things,[15] and amongst them me also—Thy Only-begotten, through whom Thou hast called to adoption the believing people, and therein me also. I beseech Thee through Him, who sitteth at Thy right hand, and maketh intercession for us,[16] in whom are hid all treasures of wisdom and knowledge.[17] These do I seek in Thy books. Of Him did Moses write;[18] this saith Himself; this saith the Truth.

CHAPTER III

HE BEGINS FROM THE CREATION OF THE WORLD—
NOT UNDERSTANDING THE HEBREW TEXT

Let me hear and understand how in the beginning Thou didst make the heaven and the earth.[19] Moses wrote this; he wrote and departed—passed hence from Thee to Thee. Nor now is he before me; for if he were I would hold him, and ask him, and would adjure him by Thee that he would open to me these things, and I would lend the ears of my body to the sounds bursting forth from his mouth. And should he speak in the Hebrew tongue, in vain would it beat on my senses, nor would aught touch my mind; but if in Latin, I should know what he said. But whence should I know whether he said what was true? But if I knew this even, should I know it from him? Surely within me, within in the chamber of my thought, Truth, neither Hebrew, nor Greek, nor Latin, nor barbarian, without the organs of voice and tongue, without the sound of syllables, would say, "He speaks the truth," and I, forthwith assured of it, confidently would say to that man of Thine, "Thou speakest the truth." As, then, I cannot inquire of him, I beseech Thee—Thee, O Truth, full of whom he spoke truth—Thee, my God, I beseech, forgive my sins; and do Thou, who didst give to Thy servant to speak these things, grant to me also to understand them.

CHAPTER IV

HEAVEN AND EARTH CRY OUT THAT THEY HAVE BEEN CREATED BY GOD

Behold, the heaven and earth are; they proclaim that they were made, for they are changed and varied. Whereas whatsoever has not been made,

[13] Ps. cxix. 85   [14] Ps. lxxx. 17   [15] John i. 3   [16] Rom. viii. 34   [17] Col. ii. 3
[18] John v. 4-6   [19] Gen. i. 1

and yet has being, has nothing in it which there was not before; this is what it is to be changed and varied. They also proclaim that they made not themselves; "therefore we are, because we have been made; we were not therefore before we were, so that we could have made ourselves." And the voice of those that speak is in itself an evidence. Thou, therefore, Lord, didst make these things; Thou who art beautiful, for they are beautiful; Thou who art good, for they are good; Thou who art, for they are. Nor even so are they beautiful, nor good, nor are they, as Thou their Creator art; compared with whom they are neither beautiful, nor good, nor are at all. These things we know, thanks be to Thee. And our knowledge, compared with Thy knowledge, is ignorance.

CHAPTER V

GOD CREATED THE WORLD NOT FROM ANY CERTAIN MATTER, BUT IN HIS OWN WORD

But how didst Thou make the heaven and the earth, and what was the instrument of Thy so mighty work? For it was not as a human worker fashioning body from body, according to the fancy of his mind, in somewise able to assign a form which it perceives in itself by its inner eye. And whence should he be able to do this, hadst not Thou made that mind? And he assigns to it already existing, and as it were having a being, a form, as clay, or stone, or wood, or gold, or such like. And whence should these things be, hadst not Thou appointed them? Thou didst make for the workman his body—Thou the mind commanding the limbs—Thou the matter whereof he makes anything—Thou the capacity whereby he may apprehend his art, and see within what he may do without—Thou the sense of his body, by which, as by an interpreter, he may from mind to matter convey that which he does, and report to his mind what may have been done, that it within may consult the truth, presiding over itself, whether it be well done. All these things praise Thee, the Creator of all. But how dost Thou make them? How, O God, didst Thou make heaven and earth? Truly, neither in the heaven nor in the earth didst Thou make heaven and earth; nor in the air, nor in the waters, since these also belong to the heaven and the earth; nor in the whole world didst Thou make the whole world; because there was no place wherein it could be made before it was made, that it might be; nor didst Thou hold anything in Thy hand wherewith to make heaven and earth. For whence couldest Thou have what Thou hadst not made, whereof to make anything? For what is, save because Thou art? Therefore Thou didst speak and they were made,[20] and in Thy Word Thou madest these things.[21]

[20] Ps. xxxiii. 9   [21] *Ibid.* 6

CHAPTER VI

HE DID NOT, HOWEVER, CREATE IT BY A SOUNDING AND PASSING WORD

But how didst Thou speak? Was it in that manner in which the voice came from cloud, saying, "This is my beloved Son"? [22] For that voice was uttered and passed away, began and ended. The syllables sounded and passed by, the second after the first, the third after the second, and thence in order, until the last after the rest, and silence after the last. Hence it is clear and plain that the motion of a creature expressed it, itself temporal, obeying Thy Eternal will. And these thy words formed at the time, the outer ear conveyed to the intelligent mind, whose inner ear lay attentive to Thy eternal word. But it compared these words sounding in time with Thy eternal word in silence, and said, "It is different, very different. These words are far beneath me, nor are they, since they flee and pass away`, but the Word of my Lord remaineth above me for ever." If, then, in sounding and fleeting words Thou didst say that heaven and earth should be made, and didst thus make heaven and earth, there was already a corporeal creature before heaven and earth by whose temporal motions that voice might take its course in time. But there was nothing corporeal before heaven and earth; or if there were, certainly Thou without a transitory voice hadst created that whence Thou wouldest make the passing voice, by which to say that the heaven and the earth should be made. For whatsoever that were of which such a voice was made, unless it were made by Thee, it could not be at all. By what word of Thine was it decreed that a body might be made, whereby these words might be made?

CHAPTER VII

BY HIS CO-ETERNAL WORD HE SPEAKS, AND ALL THINGS ARE DONE

Thou callest us, therefore, to understand the Word, God with Thee, God,[23] which is spoken eternally, and by it are all things spoken eternally. For what was spoken was not finished, and another spoken until all were spoken; but all things at once and for ever. For otherwise have we time and change, and not a true eternity, nor a true immortality. This I know, O my God, and give thanks. I know, I confess to Thee, O Lord, and whosoever is not unthankful to certain truth, knows and blesses Thee with me. We know, O Lord, we know; since in proportion as anything is not what it was, and is what it was not, in that proportion does it die and arise. Not anything, therefore, of Thy Word giveth place and cometh into place again, because it is truly immortal and eternal. And, therefore, unto the Word co-eternal with Thee, Thou dost at once and for ever say all that Thou

[22] Matt. xvii. 5   [23] John i. 1

dost say; and whatever Thou sayest shall be made, is made; nor dost Thou make otherwise than by speaking; yet all things are not made both together and everlasting which Thou makest by speaking.

CHAPTER VIII

THAT WORD ITSELF IS THE BEGINNING OF ALL THINGS, IN WHICH WE ARE INSTRUCTED AS TO EVANGELICAL TRUTH

Why is this, I beseech Thee, O Lord my God? I see it, however; but how I shall express it, I know not, unless that everything which begins to be and ceases to be, then begins and ceases when in Thy eternal Reason it is known that it ought to begin or cease where nothing beginneth or ceaseth. The same is Thy Word, which is also the Beginning, because also it speaketh unto us.[24] Thus, in the gospel He speaketh through the flesh; and this sounded outwardly in the ears of men, that it might be believed and sought inwardly, and that it might be found in the eternal Truth, where the good and only Master teacheth all His disciples. There, O Lord, I hear Thy voice, the voice of one speaking unto me, since He speaketh unto us who teacheth us. But He that teacheth us not, although He speaketh, speaketh not to us. Moreover, who teacheth us, unless it be the immutable Truth? For even when we are admonished through a changeable creature, we are led to the Truth immutable. There we learn truly while we stand and hear Him, and rejoice greatly because of the Bridegroom's voice,[25] restoring us to that whence we are. And, therefore, the Beginning, because unless It remained, there would not, where we strayed, be whither to return. But when we return from error, it is by knowing that we return. But that we may know, He teacheth us, because He is the Beginning and speaketh unto us.

CHAPTER IX

WISDOM AND THE BEGINNING

In this Beginning, O God, hast Thou made heaven and earth—in Thy Word, in Thy Son, in Thy Power, in Thy Wisdom, in Thy Truth, wondrously speaking and wondrously making. Who shall comprehend? who shall relate it? What is that which shines through me, and strikes my heart without injury, and I both shudder and burn? I shudder inasmuch as I am unlike it; and I burn inasmuch as I am like it. It is Wisdom itself that shines through me, clearing my cloudiness, which again overwhelms me, fainting from it, in the darkness and amount of my punishment. For my strength is brought down in need,[26] so that I cannot endure my blessings, until Thou, O Lord, who hast been gracious to all mine iniquities,

[24] John viii. 25   [25] John iii. 29   [26] Ps. xxxi. 10

heal also all mine infirmities; because Thou shalt also redeem my life from corruption, and crown me with Thy loving-kindness and mercy, and shalt satisfy my desire with good things, because my youth shall be renewed like the eagle's.[27] For by hope we are saved; and through patience we await Thy promises.[28] Let him that is able hear Thee discoursing within. I will with confidence cry out from Thy oracle, How wonderful are Thy works, O Lord, in Wisdom hast Thou made them all.[29] And this Wisdom is the Beginning, and in that Beginning hast Thou made heaven and earth.

CHAPTER X

THE RASHNESS OF THOSE WHO INQUIRE WHAT GOD DID BEFORE HE CREATED HEAVEN AND EARTH

Lo, are they not full of their ancient way, who say to us, "What was God doing before He made heaven and earth? For if," say they, "He were unoccupied, and did nothing, why does He not for ever also, and from henceforth, cease from working, as in times past He did? For if any new motion has arisen in God, and a new will, to form a creature which He had never before formed, however can that be a true eternity where there ariseth a will which was not before? For the will of God is not a creature, but before the creature; because nothing could be created unless the will of the Creator were before it. The will of God, therefore, pertains to His very Substance. But if anything has arisen in the Substance of God which was not before, that Substance is not truly called eternal. But if it was the eternal will of God that the creature should be, why was not the creature also from eternity?"

CHAPTER XI

THEY WHO ASK THIS HAVE NOT AS YET KNOWN THE ETERNITY OF GOD, WHICH IS EXEMPT FROM THE RELATION OF TIME

Those who say these things do not as yet understand Thee, O Thou Wisdom of God, Thou light of souls; not as yet do they understand how these things be made which are made by and in Thee. They even endeavor to comprehend things eternal; but as yet their heart flieth about in the past and future motions of things, and is still wavering. Who shall hold it and fix it, that it may rest a little, and by degrees catch the glory of that ever-standing eternity, and compare it with the times which never stand, and see that it is incomparable; and that a long time cannot become long, save from the many motions that pass by, which cannot at the same instant be prolonged; but that in the Eternal nothing passeth away, but that the whole is present; but no time is wholly present; and let him see that

[27] Ps. ciii. 3-5   [28] Rom. viii. 24, 25   [29] Ps. civ. 24

all time past is forced on by the future, and that all the future follows from the past, and that all, both past and future, is created and issues from that which is always present? Who will hold the heart of man, that it may stand still, and see how the still-standing eternity, itself neither future nor past, utters the times future and past? Can my hand accomplish this, or the hand of my mouth by persuasion bring about a thing so great?

CHAPTER XII

WHAT GOD DID BEFORE THE CREATION OF THE WORLD

Behold, I answer to him who asks, "What was God doing before He made heaven and earth?" I answer not, as a certain person is reported to have done facetiously (avoiding the pressure of the question), "He was preparing hell," said he, "for those who pry into mysteries." It is one thing to perceive, another to laugh—these things I answer not. For more willingly would I have answered, "I know not what I know not," than that I should make him a laughing-stock who asks deep things, and gain praise as one who answers false things. But I say that Thou, our God, art the Creator of every creature; and if by the term "heaven and earth" every creature is understood, I boldly say that before God made heaven and earth, He made not anything. For if He did, what did He make unless the creature? And would that I knew whatever I desire to know to my advantage, as I know that no creature was made before any creature was made.

CHAPTER XIII

BEFORE THE TIMES CREATED BY GOD, TIMES WERE NOT

But if the roving thought of any one should wander through the images of bygone time, and wonder that Thou, the God Almighty, and All-creating, and All-sustaining, the Architect of heaven and earth, didst for innumerable ages refrain from so great a work before Thou wouldst make it, let him awake and consider that he wonders at false things. For whence could innumerable ages pass by which Thou didst not make, since Thou art the Author and Creator of all ages? Or what times should those be which were not made by Thee? Or how should they pass by if they had not been? Since, therefore, Thou art the Creator of all times, if any time was before Thou madest heaven and earth, why is it said that Thou didst refrain from working? For that very time Thou madest, nor could times pass by before Thou madest times. But if before heaven and earth there was no time, why is it asked, What didst Thou then? For there was no "then" when time was not.

Nor dost Thou by time precede time; else wouldest not Thou precede all times. But in the excellency of an ever-present eternity, Thou precedest all times past, and survivest all future times, because they are future, and when they have come they will be past; but Thou art the same, and Thy years shall have no end.[30] Thy years neither go nor come; but ours both go and come, that all may come. All Thy years stand at once since they do stand; nor were they when departing excluded by coming years, because they pass not away; but all these of ours shall be when all shall cease to be. Thy years are one day, and Thy day is not daily, but to-day; because Thy to-day yields not with to-morrow, for neither doth it follow yesterday. Thy to-day is eternity; therefore didst Thou beget the Co-eternal, to whom Thou saidst, "This day have I begotten Thee."[31] Thou hast made all time; and before all times Thou art, nor in any time was there not time.

CHAPTER XIV

NEITHER TIME PAST NOR FUTURE, BUT THE PRESENT ONLY, REALLY IS

At no time, therefore, hadst Thou not made anything, because Thou hadst made time itself. And no times are co-eternal with Thee, because Thou remainest for ever; but should these continue, they would not be times. For what is time? Who can easily and briefly explain it? Who even in thought can comprehend it, even to the pronouncing of a word concerning it? But what in speaking do we refer to more familiarly and knowingly than time? And certainly we understand when we speak of it; we understand also when we hear it spoken of by another. What, then, is time? If no one ask of me, I know; if I wish to explain to him who asks, I know not. Yet I say with confidence, that I know that if nothing passed away, there would not be past time; and if nothing were coming, there would not be future time; and if nothing were, there would not be present time. Those two times, therefore, past and future, how are they, when even the past now is not, and the future is not as yet? But should the present be always present, and should it not pass into time past, truly it could not be time, but eternity. If, then, time present—if it be time—only comes into existence because it passes into time past, how do we say that even this is, whose cause of being is that it shall not be—namely, so that we cannot truly say that time is, unless because it tends not to be?

CHAPTER XV

THERE IS ONLY A MOMENT OF PRESENT TIME

And yet we say that time is long and time is short; nor do we speak of this save of time past and future. A long time past, for example, we call a hundred years ago; in like manner a long time to come, a hundred years

[30] Ps. cii. 27   [31] Ps. ii. 7, and Heb. v. 5

hence. But a short time past we call, say, ten days ago: and a short time to come, ten days hence. But in what sense is that long or short which is not? For the past is not now, and the future is not yet. Therefore let us not say, "It is long;" but let us say of the past, "It has been long," and of the future, "It will be long." O my Lord, my light, shall not even here Thy truth deride man? For that past time which was long, was it long when it was already past, or when it was as yet present? For then it might be long when there was that which could be long, but when past it no longer was; wherefore that could not be long which was not at all. Let us not, therefore, say, "Time past has been long;" for we shall not find what may have been long, seeing that since it was past it is not; but let us say that present time was long, because when it was present it was long. For it had not as yet passed away so as not to be, and therefore there was that which could be long. But after it passed, that ceased also to be long which ceased to be.

Let us therefore see, O human soul, whether present time can be long; for to thee is it given to perceive and to measure periods of time. What wilt thou reply to me? Is a hundred years when present a long time? See, first, whether a hundred years can be present. For if the first year of these is current, that is present, but the other ninety and nine are future, and therefore they are not as yet. But if the second year is current, one is already past, the other present, the rest future. And thus, if we fix on any middle year of this hundred as present, those before it are past, those after it are future; wherefore a hundred years cannot be present. See at least whether that year itself which is current can be present. For if its first month be current, the rest are future; if the second, the first has already passed, and the remainder are not yet. Therefore neither is the year which is current as a whole present; and if it is not present as a whole, then the year is not present. For twelve months make the year, of which each individual month which is current is itself present, but the rest are either past or future. Although neither is that month which is current present, but one day only: if the first, the rest being to come, if the last, the rest being past; if any of the middle, then between past and future.

Behold, the present time, which alone we found could be called long, is abridged to the space scarcely of one day. But let us discuss even that, for there it not one day present as a whole. For it is made up of four-and-twenty hours of night and day, of which the first has the rest future, the last has them past, but any one of the intervening has those before it past, those after it future. And that one hour passes away in fleeting particles. Whatever of it has flown away is past, whatever remains is future. If any portion of time be conceived which cannot now be divided into even the minutest particles of moments, this only is that which may be called present; which, however, flies so rapidly from future to past, that it cannot be extended by any delay. For if it be extended, it is divided into the past and future; but the present has no space. Where, therefore, is the time which we may call long? Is it future? Indeed we do not say, "It is long," because it is not yet, so as to be long; but we say, "It will be long." When, then, will it be? For if even then, since as yet it is future, it will not be long, because what may be long is not as yet; but it shall be long, when from the future, which as yet is not, it shall already have begun to be, and will have become present, so that there could be that which may be long; then does the present time cry out in the words above that it cannot be long.

CHAPTER XVI

TIME CAN ONLY BE PERCEIVED OR MEASURED WHILE IT IS PASSING

And yet, O Lord, we perceive intervals of times, and we compare them with themselves, and we say some are longer, others shorter. We even measure by how much shorter or longer this time may be than that; and we answer That this is double or treble, while that is but once, or only as much as that. But we measure times passing when we measure them by perceiving them; but past times, which now are not, or future times, which as yet are not, who can measure them? Unless, perchance, any one will dare to say, that that can be measured which is not. When, therefore, time is passing, it can be perceived and measured; but when it has passed, it cannot, since it is not.

CHAPTER XVII

NEVERTHELESS THERE IS TIME PAST AND FUTURE

I ask, Father, I do not affirm. O my God, rule and guide me. Who is there who can say to me that there are not three times (as we learned when boys, and as we have taught boys), the past, present, and future, but only present, because these two are not? Or are they also; but when from future it becomes present, comes it forth from some secret place, and when from the present it becomes past, does it retire into anything secret? For where have they, who have foretold future things, seen these things, if as yet they are not? For that which is not cannot be seen. And they who relate things past could not relate them as true, did they not perceive them in their mind. Which things, if they were not, they could in no wise be discerned. There are therefore things both future and past.

CHAPTER XVIII

PAST AND FUTURE TIMES CANNOT BE THOUGHT OF BUT AS PRESENT

Suffer me, O Lord, to seek further; O my Hope, let not my purpose be confounded. For if there are times past and future, I desire to know where they are. But if as yet I do not succeed, I still know, wherever they are, that they are not there as future or past, but as present. For if there also they be future, they are not as yet there; if even there they be past, they are no longer there. Wheresoever, therefore, they are, whatsoever they are, they are only so as present. Although past things are related as true, they are drawn out from the memory—not the things themselves, which have passed, but the words conceived from the images of the things which they have formed in the mind as footprints in their passage through the senses. My childhood, indeed, which no longer is, is in time past, which now is not; but when I call to mind its image, and speak of it, I behold it in the present, because it is as yet in my memory. Whether there be a like cause of foretelling future things, that of things which as yet are not the images may be perceived as already existing, I confess, my God, I know not. This certainly I know, that we generally think before on our future actions, and that this premeditation is present; but that the action on which we premeditate is not yet, because it is future; which when we shall have entered upon, and have begun to do that which we were premeditating, then shall that action be, because then it is not future, but present.

In whatever manner, therefore, this secret preconception of future things may be, nothing can be seen, save what is. But what now is is not future, but present. When, therefore, they say that things future are seen, it is not themselves, which as yet are not (that is, which are future); but their causes or their signs perhaps are seen, which already are. Therefore, to those already beholding them, they are not future, but present, from which future things conceived in the mind are foretold. These conceptions again now are, and they who foretell those things behold these conceptions present before them. Let now so multitudinous a variety of things afford me some example. I behold daybreak; I foretell that the sun is about to rise. That which I behold is present; what I foretell is future—not that the sun is future, which already is; but his rising, which is not yet. Yet even its rising I could not predict unless I had an image of it in my mind, as now I have while I speak. But that dawn which I see in the sky is not the rising of the sun, although it may go before it, nor that imagination in my mind; which two are seen as present, that the other which is future may be foretold. Future things, therefore, are not as yet; and if they are not as yet, they are not. And if they are not, they cannot be seen at all; but they can be foretold from things present which now are, and are seen.

CHAPTER XIX

WE ARE IGNORANT IN WHAT MANNER GOD TEACHES FUTURE THINGS

Thou, therefore, Ruler of Thy creatures, what is the method by which Thou teachest souls those things which are future? For Thou hast taught

Thy prophets. What is that way by which Thou, to whom nothing is future, dost teach future things; or rather of future things dost teach present? For what is not, of a certainty cannot be taught. Too far is this way from my view; it is too mighty for me, I cannot attain unto it;[32] but by Thee I shall be enabled, when Thou shalt have granted it, sweet light of my hidden eyes.

CHAPTER XX

IN WHAT MANNER TIME MAY PROPERLY BE DESIGNATED

But what now is manifest and clear is, that neither are there future nor past things. Nor is it fitly said, "There are three times, past, present and future;" but perchance it might be fitly said, "There are three times; a present of things past, a present of things present, and a present of things future." For these three do somehow exist in the soul, and otherwise I see them not: present of things past, memory; present of things present, sight; present of things future, expectation. If of these things we are permitted to speak, I see three times, and I grant there are three. It may also be said, "There are three times, past, present and future," as usage falsely has it. See, I trouble not, nor gainsay, nor reprove; provided always that which is said may be understood, that neither the future, nor that which is past, now is. For there are but few things which we speak properly, many things improperly; but what we may wish to say is understood.

CHAPTER XXI

HOW TIME MAY BE MEASURED

I have just now said, then, that we measure times as they pass, that we may be able to say that this time is twice as much as that one, or that this is only as much as that, and so of any other of the parts of time which we are able to tell by measuring. Wherefore, as I said, we measure times as they pass. And if any one should ask me, "Whence dost thou know?" I can answer, "I know, because we measure; nor can we measure things that are not; and things past and future are not." But how do we measure present time, since it has not space? It is measured while it passes; but when it shall have passed, it is not measured; for there will not be aught that can be measured. But whence, in what way, and whither does it pass while it is being measured? Whence, but from the future? Which way, save through the present? Whither, but into the past? From that, therefore, which as yet is not, through that which has no space, into that which now is not. But what do we measure, unless time in some space? For we say not single, and double, and triple, and equal, or in any other way in which

[32] Ps. cxxxix. 6

we speak of time, unless with respect to the spaces of times. In what space, then, do we measure passing time? Is it in the future, whence it passes over? But what yet we measure not, is not. Or is it in the present, by which it passes? But no space we do not measure. Or in the past, whither it passes? But that which is not now, we measure not.

CHAPTER XXII

HE PRAYS GOD THAT HE WOULD EXPLAIN THIS MOST ENTANGLED ENIGMA

My soul yearns to know this most entangled enigma. Forbear to shut up, O Lord my God, good Father—through Christ I beseech Thee—forbear to shut up these things, both usual and hidden, from my desire, that it may be hindered from penetrating them; but let them dawn through Thy enlightening mercy, O Lord. Of whom shall I inquire concerning these things? And to whom shall I with more advantage confess my ignorance than to Thee to whom these my studies, so vehemently kindled towards Thy Scriptures, are not troublesome? Give that which I love; for I do love, and this hast Thou given me. Give, Father, who truly knowest to give good gifts unto Thy children.[33] Give, since I have undertaken to know, and trouble is before me until Thou dost open it.[34] Through Christ, I beseech Thee, in His name, Holy of Holies, let no man interrupt me. For I believed, and therefore do I speak.[35] This is my hope; for this do I live, that I may contemplate the delights of the Lord.[36] Behold, Thou hast made my days old,[37] and they pass away, and in what manner I know not. And we speak as to time and time, times and times—"How long is the time since he said this?" "How long the time since he did this?" and, "How long the time since I saw that?" and, "This syllable has double the time of that single short syllable." These words we speak, and these we hear; and we are understood, and we understand. They are most manifest and most usual, and the same things again lie hid too deeply, and the discovery of them is new.

CHAPTER XXIII

THAT TIME IS A CERTAIN EXTENSION

I have heard from a learned man that the motions of the sun, moon, and stars constituted time, and I assented not. For why should not rather the motions of all bodies be time? What if the lights of heaven should cease, and a potter's wheel run round, would there be no time by which we might measure those revolutions, and say either that it turned with equal pauses, or, if it were moved, at one time more slowly, at another more quickly, that some revolutions were longer, others less so? Or while we were saying

---

[33] Matt. vii. 11   [34] Ps. lxxiii. 16   [35] Ps. cxvi. 10   [36] Ps. xxvii. 4   [37] Ps. xxxix. 5

this, should we not also be speaking in time? Or should there in our words be some syllables long, others short, but because those sounded in a longer time, these in a shorter? God grant to men to see in a small thing ideas common to things great and small. Both the stars and luminaries of heaven are for signs and for seasons, and for days and years.[38] No doubt they are; but neither should I say that the circuit of that wooden wheel was a day, nor yet should he say that therefore there was no time.

I desire to know the power and nature of time, by which we measure the motions of bodies, and say (for example) that this motion is twice as long as that. For, I ask, since "day" declares not the stay only of the sun upon the earth, according to which day is one thing, night another, but also its entire circuit from east even to east—according to which we say, "So many days have passed" (the nights being included when we say "so many days," and their spaces not counted apart)—since, then, the day is finished by the motion of the sun, and by his circuit from east to east, I ask, whether the motion itself is the day, or the period in which that motion is completed, or both? For if the first be the day, then would there be a day although the sun should finish that course in so small a space of time as an hour. If the second, then that would not be a day if from one sunrise to another there were but so short a period as an hour, but the sun must go round four-and-twenty times to complete a day. If both, neither could that be called a day if the sun should run his entire round in the space of an hour; nor that, if, while the sun stood still, so much time should pass as the sun is accustomed to accomplish his whole course in from morning to morning. I shall not therefore now ask, what that is which is called day, but what time is, by which we, measuring the circuit of the sun, should say that it was accomplished in half the space of time it was wont, if it had been completed in so small a space as twelve hours; and comparing both times, we should call that single, this double time, although the sun should run his course from east to east sometimes in that single, sometimes in that double time. Let no man then tell me that the motions of the heavenly bodies are times, because, when at the prayer of one the sun stood still in order that he might achieve his victorious battle, the sun stood still, but time went on. For in such space of time as was sufficient was that battle fought and ended.[39] I see that time, then, is a certain extension. But do I see it, or do I seem to see it? Thou, O Light and Truth, wilt show me.

CHAPTER XXIV

THAT TIME IS NOT A MOTION OF A BODY WHICH WE MEASURE BY TIME

Dost Thou command that I should assent, if any one should say that time is the motion of a body? Thou dost not command me. For I hear that

[38] Gen. i. 14   [39] Josh. x. 12-14

no body is moved but in time. This Thou sayest; but that the very motion of a body is time, I hear not; Thou sayest it not. For when a body is moved, I by time measure how long it may be moving from the time in which it began to be moved till it left off. And if I saw not whence it began, and it continued to be moved, so that I see not when it leaves off, I cannot measure unless, perchance, from the time I began until I cease to see. But if I look long, I only proclaim that the time is long, but not how long it may be; because when we say, "How long," we speak by comparison, as, "This is as long as that," or, "This is double as long as that," or any other thing of the kind. But if we were able to note down the distances of places whence and whither comes the body which is moved, or its parts, if it moved as in a wheel, we can say in how much time the motion of the body or its part, from this place to that, was performed. Since, then, the motion of a body is one thing, that by which we measure how long it is another, who cannot see which of these is rather to be called time? For, although a body be sometimes moved, sometimes stand still, we measure not its motion only, but also its standing still, by time; and we say, "It stood still as much as it moved;" or, "It stood still twice or thrice as long as it moved;" and if any other space which our measuring has either determined or imagined, more or less, as we are accustomed to say. Time, therefore, is not the motion of a body.

CHAPTER XXV

HE CALLS ON GOD TO ENLIGHTEN HIS MIND

And I confess unto Thee, O Lord, that I am as yet ignorant as to what time is, and again I confess unto Thee, O Lord, that I know that I speak these things in time, and that I have already long spoken of time, and that very "long" is not long save by the stay of time. How, then, know I this, when I know not what time is? Or is it, perchance, that I know not in what wise I may express what I know? Alas for me, that I do not at least know the extent of my own ignorance! Behold, O my God, before Thee I lie not. As I speak, so is my heart. Thou shalt light my candle; Thou, O Lord my God, wilt enlighten my darkness.[40]

CHAPTER XXVI

WE MEASURE LONGER EVENTS BY SHORTER IN TIME

Doth not my soul pour out unto Thee truly in confession that I do measure times? But do I thus measure, O my God, and know not what I measure? I measure the motion of a body by time; and the time itself do I not measure? But, in truth, could I measure the motion of a body, how

---

[40] Ps. xviii. 28

long it is, and how long it is in coming from this place to that, unless I should measure the time in which it is moved? How, therefore, do I measure this very time itself? Or do we by a shorter time measure a longer, as by the space of a cubit the space of a crossbeam? For thus, indeed, we seem by the space of a short syllable to measure the space of a long syllable, and to say that this is double. Thus we measure the spaces of stanzas by the spaces of the verses, and the spaces of the verses by the spaces of the feet, and the spaces of the feet by the spaces of the syllables, and the spaces of long by the spaces of short syllables; not measuring by pages (for in that manner we measure spaces, not times), but when in uttering the words they pass by, and we say, "It is a long stanza because it is made up of so many verses; long verses, because they consist of so many feet; long feet, because they are prolonged by so many syllables; a long syllable, because double a short one." But neither thus is any certain measure of time obtained; since it is possible that a shorter verse, if it be pronounced more fully, may take up more time than a longer one, if pronounced more hurriedly. Thus for a stanza, thus for a foot, thus for a syllable. Whence it appeared to me that time is nothing else than extension; but of what I know not. It is wonderful to me, if it be not of the mind itself. For what do I measure, I beseech Thee, O my God, even when I say either indefinitely, "This time is longer than that;" or even definitely, "This is double that?" That I measure time, I know. But I measure not the future, for it is not yet; nor do I measure the present, because it is extended by no space; nor do I measure the past, because it no longer is. What, therefore, do I measure? Is it times passing, not past? For thus had I said.

CHAPTER XXVII

TIMES ARE MEASURED IN PROPORTION AS THEY PASS BY

Persevere, O my mind, and give earnest heed. God is our helper; He made us, and not we ourselves.[41] Give heed, where truth dawns. Lo, suppose the voice of a body begins to sound, and does sound, and sounds on, and lo! it ceases—it is now silence, and that voice is past and is no longer a voice. It was future before it sounded, and could not be measured, because as yet it was not; and now it cannot, because it no longer is. Then, therefore, while it was sounding, it might, because there was then that which might be measured. But even then it did not stand still, for it was going and passing away. Could it, then, on that account be measured the more? For, while passing, it was being extended into some space of time, in which it might be measured, since the present has no space. If, therefore, then it might be measured, lo! suppose another voice has begun to sound, and still sounds, in a continued tenor without any interruption, we

---

[41] Ps. c. 3

can measure it while it is sounding; for when it shall have ceased to sound, it will be already past, and there will not be that which can be measured. Let us measure it truly, and let us say how much it is. But as yet it sounds, nor can it be measured, save from that instant in which it began to sound, even to the end in which it left off. For the interval itself we measure from some beginning to some end. On which account, a voice which is not yet ended cannot be measured, so that it may be said how long or how short it may be; nor can it be said to be equal to another, or single or double in respect of it, or the like. But when it is ended, it no longer is. In what manner, therefore, may it be measured? And yet we measure times; still not those which as yet are not, nor those which no longer are, nor those which are protracted by some delay, nor those which have no limits. We, therefore, measure neither future times, nor past, nor present, nor those passing by; and yet we do measure times.

Deus Creator omnium; this verse of eight syllables alternates between short and long syllables. The four short, then, the first, third, fifth and seventh, are single in respect of the four long, the second, fourth, sixth, and eighth. Each of these has a double time to every one of those. I pronounce them, report on them, and thus it is, as is perceived by common sense. By common sense, then, I measure a long by a short syllable, and I find that it has twice as much. But when one sounds after another, if the former be short the latter long, how shall I hold the short one, and how measuring shall I apply it to the long, so that I may find out that this has twice as much, when indeed the long does not begin to sound unless the short leaves off sounding? That very long one I measure not as present, since I measure it not save when ended. But its ending is its passing away. What, then, is it that I can measure? Where is the short syllable by which I measure? Where is the long one which I measure? Both have sounded, have flown, have passed away, and are no longer; and still I measure, and I confidently answer (so far as is trusted to a practised sense), that as to space of time this syllable is single, that double. Nor could I do this, unless because they have past, and are ended. Therefore do I not measure themselves, which now are not, but something in my memory, which remains fixed.

In thee, O my mind, I measure times. Do not overwhelm me with thy clamor. That is, do not overwhelm thyself with the multitude of thy impressions. In thee, I say, I measure times; the impression which things as they pass by make on Thee, and which, when they have passed by, remains, that I measure as time present, not those things which have passed by, that the impression should be made. This I measure when I measure times. Either, then, these are times, or I do not measure times. What when we measure silence, and say that this silence has lasted as long as that voice lasts? Do we not extend our thought to the measure of a voice, as if it sounded, so that we may be able to declare something concerning the intervals of silence in a given space of time? For when both the voice and tongue are still, we go over in thought poems and verses, and any discourse, or dimensions of motions; and declare concerning the spaces of times, how much this may be in respect of that, not otherwise than if uttering them we should pronounce them. Should any one wish to utter a lengthened sound, and had with forethought determined how long it should be, that man has in silence surely gone through a space of time, and, committing it to memory, he begins to utter that speech, which sounds until it be extended to the end proposed; truly it has sounded, and will sound. For what of it is already finished has surely sounded, but what remains will sound; and thus does it pass on, until the present intention carry over the future into the past; the past increasing by the diminution of the future, until, by the consumption of the future, all be past.

CHAPTER XXVIII

TIME IN THE HUMAN MIND, WHICH EXPECTS,
CONSIDERS, AND REMEMBERS

But how is that future diminished or consumed which as yet is not? Or how does the past, which is no longer, increase, unless in the mind which enacts this there are three things done? For it both expects, and considers, and remembers, that that which it expects, through that which it considers may pass into that which it remembers. Who, therefore, denies that future things as yet are not? But yet there is already in the mind the expectation of things future. And who denies that past things are now no longer? But, however, there is still in the mind the memory of things past. And who denies that time present wants space, because it passes away in a moment? But yet our consideration endures, through which that which may be present may proceed to become absent. Future time, which is not, is not therefore long; but a "long future" is "a long expectation of the future." Nor is time past, which is now no longer, long; but a long past is "a long memory of the past."

I am about to repeat a psalm that I know. Before I begin, my attention is extended to the whole; but when I have begun, as much of it as becomes past by my saying it is extended in my memory; and the life of this action of mine is extended both ways between my memory, on account of what I have repeated, and my expectation, on account of what I am about to repeat; yet my consideration is present with me, through which that which was future may be carried over so that it may become past. The more this is done and repeated, by so much (expectation being shortened) the memory is enlarged, until the whole expectation be exhausted, when that whole action being ended shall have passed into memory. And what takes place in the entire psalm, takes place also in each individual part of it, and in each individual syllable: this holds in the longer action, of which that psalm is perchance a portion; the same holds in the whole life of man, of which all the actions of man are parts; the same holds in the whole age of the sons of men, of which all the lives of men are parts.

CHAPTER XXIX

THAT HUMAN LIFE IS A DISTRACTION, BUT THAT THROUGH THE MERCY OF GOD HE WAS INTENT ON THE PRIZE OF HIS HEAVENLY CALLING

But because Thy loving-kindness is better than life,[42] behold, my life is but a distraction,[43] and Thy right hand upheld me[44] in my Lord, the Son of man, the Mediator between Thee,[45] The One, and us the many—in many distractions amid many things—that through Him I may apprehend in whom I have been apprehended, and may be re-collected from my old days, following The One, forgetting the things that are past; and not distracted, but drawn on,[46] not to those things which shall be and shall pass away, but to those things which are before,[47] not distractedly, but intently, I follow on for the prize of my heavenly calling,[48] where I may hear the voice of Thy praise, and contemplate Thy delights,[49] neither coming nor passing away. But now are my years spent in mourning.[50] And Thou, O Lord, art my comfort, my Father everlasting. But I have been divided amid times, the order of which I know not; and my thoughts, even the inmost bowels of my soul, are mangled with tumultuous varieties, until I flow together unto Thee, purged and molten in the fire of Thy love.[51]

CHAPTER XXX

AGAIN HE REFUTES THE EMPTY QUESTION, "WHAT DID GOD BEFORE THE CREATION OF THE WORLD?"

And I will be immovable, and fixed in Thee, in my mould, Thy truth; nor will I endure the questions of men, who by a penal disease thirst for more than they can hold, and say, "What did God make before He made heaven and earth?" Or, "How came it into His mind to make anything when He never before made anything?" Grant to them, O Lord, to think well what they say, and to see that where there is no time, they cannot say "never." What, therefore, He is said "never to have made," what else is it but to say, that in no time was it made? Let them therefore see that there could be no time without a created being, and let them cease to speak that vanity. Let them also be extended unto those things which are

---

[42] Ps. lxiii. 3

[43] *Distentio.* It will be observed that there is a play on the word throughout the section. [44] Ps. lxiii. 8 [45] 1 Tim. ii. 5 [46] *Non distentus sed extentus* [47] Phil. iii. 13 [48] Phil. iii. 14 [49] Ps. xxvi. 7 [50] Ps. xxvii. 4 [51] Ps. xxxi. 10

before,[52] and understand that thou, the eternal Creator of all times, art before all times, and that no times are co-eternal with Thee, nor any creature, even if there be any creature beyond all times.

CHAPTER XXXI

HOW THE KNOWLEDGE OF GOD DIFFERS FROM THAT OF MAN

O Lord my God, what is that secret place of Thy mystery, and how far thence have the consequences of my transgressions cast me? Heal my eyes, that I may enjoy Thy light. Surely, if there be a mind, so greatly abounding in knowledge and foreknowledge, to which all things past and future are so known as one psalm is well known to me, that mind is exceedingly wonderful, and very astonishing; because whatever is so past, and whatever is to come of after ages, is no more concealed from Him than was it hidden from me when singing that psalm, what and how much of it had been sung from the beginning, what and how much remained unto the end. But far be it that Thou, the Creator of the universe, the Creator of souls and bodies—far be it that Thou shouldest know all things future and past. Far, far more wonderfully, and far more mysteriously, Thou knowest them. For it is not as the feelings of one singing known things, or hearing a known song, are—through expectation of future words, and in remembrance of those that are past—varied, and his senses divided, that anything happeneth unto Thee, unchangeably eternal, that is, the truly eternal Creator of minds. As, then, Thou in the Beginning knewest the heaven and the earth without any change of Thy knowledge, so in the Beginning didst Thou make heaven and earth without any distraction of Thy action. Let him who understandeth confess unto Thee; and let him who understandeth not, confess unto Thee. Oh, how exalted art Thou, and yet the humble in heart are Thy dwelling-place; for Thou raisest up those that are bowed down,[53] and they whose exaltation Thou art fall not.

[52] Phil. iii. 13   [53] Ps. cxlvi. 8

BOOK TWELVE

He continues his explanation of the first chapter of Genesis according to the Septuagint, and by its assistance he argues, especially, concerning the double heaven, and the formless matter out of which the whole world may have been created; afterwards of the interpretations of others not disallowed, and sets forth at great length the sense of the Holy Scripture.

CHAPTER I

THE DISCOVERY OF TRUTH IS DIFFICULT, BUT GOD HAS PROMISED THAT HE WHO SEEKS SHALL FIND

MY HEART, O Lord, affected by the words of Thy Holy Scripture, is much busied in this poverty of my life; and therefore, for the most part, is the want of human intelligence copious in language, because inquiry speaks more than discovery, and because demanding is longer than obtaining, and the hand that knocks is more active than the hand that receives. We hold the promise; who shall break it? If God be for us, who can be against us? [1] Ask, and ye shall have; seek, and ye shall find; knock, and it shall be opened unto you: for every one that asketh receiveth; and he that seeketh findeth; and to him that knocketh it shall be opened.[2] These are Thine own promises; and who need fear to be deceived where the Truth promiseth?

CHAPTER II

OF THE DOUBLE HEAVEN—THE VISIBLE, AND THE HEAVEN OF HEAVENS

The weakness of my tongue confesseth unto Thy Highness, seeing that Thou madest heaven and earth. This heaven which I see, and this earth upon which I tread (from which is this earth that I carry about me), Thou hast made. But where is that heaven of heavens, O Lord, of which we hear in the words of the Psalm, The heaven of heavens are the Lord's, but the earth hath He given to the children of men? [3] Where is the heaven, which we behold not, in comparison of which all this, which we behold, is earth? For this corporeal whole, not as a whole everywhere, has thus received its beautiful figure in these lower parts, of which the bottom is our earth; but compared with that heaven of heavens, even the heaven of our earth is but earth; yea, each of these great bodies is not absurdly called earth, as com-

---

[1] Rom. viii. 31   [2] Matt. vii. 7, 8   [3] Ps. cxv. 16

pared with that, I know not what manner of heaven, which is the Lord's, not the sons' of men.

CHAPTER III

OF THE DARKNESS UPON THE DEEP, AND OF THE INVISIBLE AND FORMLESS EARTH

And truly this earth was invisible and formless,[4] and there was I know not what profundity of the deep upon which there was no light, because it had no form. Therefore didst Thou command that it should be written, that darkness was upon the face of the deep; what else was it than the absence of light? For had there been light, where should it have been save by being above all, showing itself aloft, and enlightening? Where, therefore, light was as yet not, why was it that darkness was present, unless because light was absent? Darkness therefore was upon it, because the light above was absent; as silence is there present where sound is not. And what is it to have silence there, but not to have sound there? Hast not Thou, O Lord, taught this soul which confesseth unto Thee? Hast not Thou taught me, O Lord, that before Thou didst form and separate this formless matter, there was nothing, neither color, nor figure, nor body, nor spirit? Yet not altogether nothing; there was a certain formlessness without any shape.

CHAPTER IV

FROM THE FORMLESSNESS OF MATTER, THE BEAUTIFUL WORLD HAS ARISEN

What, then, should it be called, that even in some ways it might be conveyed to those of duller mind, save by some conventional word? But what, in all parts of the world, can be found nearer to a total formlessness than the earth and the deep? For, from their being of the lowest position, they are less beautiful than are the higher parts, all transparent and shining. Why, therefore, may I not consider the formlessness of matter—which Thou hadst created without shape, whereof to make this shapely world— to be fittingly intimated unto men by the name of earth invisible and formless?

CHAPTER V

WHAT MAY HAVE BEEN THE FORM OF MATTER

So that when herein thought seeks what the sense may arrive at, and says to itself, "It is no intelligible form, such as life or justice, because it is the matter of bodies; nor perceptible by the senses, because in the invisi-

---

[4] Gen. i. 2

ble and formless there is nothing which can be seen and felt—while human thought says these things to itself, it may endeavor either to know it by being ignorant, or by knowing it to be ignorant.

CHAPTER VI

HE CONFESSES THAT AT ONE TIME HE HIMSELF THOUGHT ERRONEOUSLY OF MATTER

But were I, O Lord, by my mouth and by my pen to confess unto Thee the whole, whatever Thou hast taught me concerning that matter, the name of which hearing beforehand, and not understanding (they who could not understand it telling me of it), I conceived it as having innumerable and varied forms. And therefore did I not conceive it; my mind revolved in disturbed order foul and horrible "forms," but yet "forms;" and I called it formless, not that it lacked form, but because it had such as, did it appear, my mind would turn from, as unwonted and incongruous, and at which human weakness would be disturbed. But even that which I did conceive was formless, not by the privation of all form, but in comparison of more beautiful forms; and true reason persuaded me that I ought altogether to remove from it all remnants of any form whatever, if I wished to conceive matter wholly without form; and I could not. For sooner could I imagine that that which should be deprived of all form was not at all, than conceive anything between form and nothing—neither formed, nor nothing, formless, nearly nothing. And my mind hence ceased to question my spirit, filled (as it was) with the images of formed bodies, and changing and varying them according to its will; and I applied myself to the bodies themselves, and looked more deeply into their mutability, by which they cease to be what they had been, and begin to be what they were not; and this same transit from form to form I have looked upon to be through some formless condition, not through a very nothing; but I desired to know, not to guess. And if my voice and my pen should confess the whole unto Thee, whatsoever knots Thou hast untied for me concerning this question, who of my readers would endure to take in the whole? Nor yet, therefore, shall my heart cease to give Thee honor, and a song of praise, for those things which it is not able to express. For the mutability of mutable things is itself capable of all those forms into which mutable things are changed. And this mutability, what is it? Is it soul? Is it body? Is it the outer appearance of soul or body? Could it be said, "Nothing were something," and "That which is, is not," I would say that this were it; and yet in some manner was it already, since it could receive these visible and compound shapes.

CHAPTER VII

OUT OF NOTHING GOD MADE HEAVEN AND EARTH

And whence and in what manner was this, unless from Thee, from whom are all things, in so far as they are? But by how much the farther from Thee, so much the more unlike unto Thee; for it is not distance of place. Thou, therefore, O Lord, who art not one thing in one place, and otherwise in another, but the Self-same, and the Self-same, and the Self-same, Holy, Holy, Holy, Lord God Almighty, didst in the beginning, which is of Thee, in Thy Wisdom, which was born of Thy Substance, create something, and that out of nothing. For Thou didst create heaven and earth, not out of Thyself, for then they would be equal to Thine Only-begotten, and thereby even to Thee; and in no wise would it be right that anything should be equal to Thee which was not of Thee. And aught else except Thee there was not whence Thou mightest create these things, O God, One Trinity, and Trine Unity; and, therefore, out of nothing didst Thou create heaven and earth—a great thing and a small— because Thou art Almighty and Good, to make all things good, even the great heaven and the small earth. Thou wast, and there was nought else from which Thou didst create heaven and earth; two such things, one near unto Thee, the other near to nothing—one to which Thou shouldest be superior, the other to which nothing should be inferior.

CHAPTER VIII

HEAVEN AND EARTH WERE MADE "IN THE BEGINNING;" AFTERWARDS THE WORLD, DURING SIX DAYS, FROM SHAPELESS MATTER

But that heaven of heavens was for Thee, O Lord; but the earth, which Thou hast given to the sons of men,[5] to be seen and touched, was not such as now we see and touch. For it was invisible and without form,[6] and there was a deep over which there was not light; or, darkness was over the deep, that is, more than in the deep. For this deep of waters, now visible, has, even in its depths, a light suitable to its nature, perceptible in some manner to fishes and creeping things in the bottom of it. But the entire deep was almost nothing, since hitherto it was altogether formless; yet there was then that which could be formed. For Thou, O Lord, hast made the world of a formless matter, which matter, out of nothing, Thou hast made almost nothing, out of which to make those great things which we, sons of men, wonder at. For very wonderful is this corporeal heaven, of which firmament, between water and water, the second day after the creation of light, Thou saidst, Let it be made, and it was made.[7] Which firmament Thou calledst heaven, that is, the heaven of this earth and sea, which Thou madest on the

[5] Ps. cxv. 16   [6] Gen. i. 2   [7] Gen. i. 6-8

third day, by giving a visible shape to the formless matter which Thou madest before all days. For even already hadst Thou made a heaven before all days, but that was the heaven of this heaven; because in the beginning Thou hadst made heaven and earth. But the earth itself which Thou hadst made was formless matter, because it was invisible and without form, and darkness was upon the deep. Of which invisible and formless earth, of which formlessness, of which almost nothing, Thou mightest make all these things of which this changeable world consists, and yet consisteth not; whose very changeableness appears in this, that times can be observed and numbered in it. Because times are made by the changes of things, while the shapes, whose matter is the invisible earth aforesaid, are varied and turned.

CHAPTER IX

THAT THE HEAVEN OF HEAVENS WAS AN INTELLECTUAL CREATURE, BUT THAT THE EARTH WAS INVISIBLE AND FORMLESS BEFORE THE DAYS THAT IT WAS MADE

And therefore the Spirit, the Teacher of Thy servant,[8] when He relates that Thou didst in the Beginning create heaven and earth, is silent as to times, silent as to days. For, doubtless, that heaven of heavens, which Thou in the Beginning didst create, is some intellectual creature, which, although in no wise co-eternal unto Thee, the Trinity, is yet a partaker of Thy eternity, and by reason of the sweetness of that most happy contemplation of Thyself, doth greatly restrain its own mutability, and without any failure, from the time in which it was created, in clinging unto Thee, surpasses all the rolling change of times. But this shapelessness—this earth invisible and without form—has not itself been numbered among the days. For where there is no shape nor order, nothing either cometh or goeth; and where this is not, there certainly are no days, nor any vicissitude of spaces of times.

CHAPTER X

HE BEGS OF GOD THAT HE MAY LIVE IN THE TRUE LIGHT, AND MAY BE INSTRUCTED AS TO THE MYSTERIES OF THE SACRED BOOKS

Oh, let Truth, the light of my heart, not my own darkness, speak unto me! I have descended to that, and am darkened. But thence, even thence, did I love Thee. I went astray, and remembered Thee. I heard Thy voice behind me bidding me return, and scarcely did I hear it for the tumults of the unquiet ones. And now, behold, I return burning and panting after Thy fountain. Let no one prohibit me; of this will I drink, and so have life. Let me not be my own life; from myself have I badly lived—death was I unto

[8] Moses

myself; in Thee do I revive. Do Thou speak unto me; do Thou discourse unto me. In Thy books have I believed, and their words are very deep.

CHAPTER XI

WHAT MAY BE DISCOVERED TO HIM BY GOD

Already hast Thou told me, O Lord, with a strong voice, in my inner ear, that Thou art eternal, having alone immortality.[9] Since Thou art not changed by any shape or motion, nor is Thy will altered by times, because no will which changes is immortal. This in Thy sight is clear to me, and let it become more and more clear, I beseech Thee; and in that manifestation let me abide more soberly under Thy wings. Likewise hast Thou said to me, O Lord, with a strong voice, in my inner ear, that Thou hast made all natures and substances, which are not what Thou Thyself art, and yet they are; and that only is not from Thee which is not, and the motion of the will from Thee who art, to that which in a less degree is, because such motion is guilt and sin; and that no one's sin doth either hurt Thee, or disturb the order of Thy rule, either first or last. This, in Thy sight, is clear to me, and let it become more and more clear, I beseech Thee; and in that manifestation let me abide more soberly under Thy wings.

Likewise hast Thou said to me, with a strong voice in my inner ear, that that creature, whose will Thou alone art, is not co-eternal unto Thee, and which, with a most persevering purity drawing its support from Thee, doth, in place and at no time, put forth its own mutability; and Thyself being ever present with it, unto whom with its entire affection it holds itself, having no future to expect nor conveying into the past what it remembereth, is varied by no change, nor extended into any times. O blessed one—if any such there be—in clinging unto Thy Blessedness; blest in Thee, its everlasting Inhabitant and its Enlightener! Nor do I find what the heaven of heavens, which is the Lord's, can be better called than Thine house, which contemplateth Thy delight without any defection of going forth to another; a pure mind, most peacefully one, by that stability of peace of holy spirits, the citizens of Thy city in the heavenly places, above these heavenly places which are seen.[10]

Whence the soul, whose wandering has been made far away, may understand, if now she thirsts for Thee, if now her tears have become bread to her, while it is daily said unto her "Where is thy God?" [11] if she now seeketh of Thee one thing, and desireth that she may dwell in Thy house all the days of her life.[12] And what is her life but Thee? And what are Thy days but Thy eternity, as Thy years which fail not, because Thou art the same? Hence, therefore, can the soul, which is able, understand how far beyond all times Thou art eternal; when Thy house, which has not wandered

---

[9] I Tim. vi. 16   [10] Eph. i. 20   [11] Ps. xlii. 2, 3, 10   [12] Ps. xxvii. 4

from Thee, although it be not co-eternal with Thee, yet by continually and unfailingly clinging unto Thee, suffers no vicissitude of times. This in Thy sight is clear unto me, and may it become more and more clear unto me, I beseech Thee; and in this manifestation may I abide more soberly under Thy wings.

Behold, I know not what shapelessness there is in those changes of these last and lowest creatures. And who shall tell me, unless it be some one who, through the emptiness of his own heart, wanders and is staggered by his own fancies? Who, unless such a one, would tell me that (all figure being diminished and consumed), if the formlessness only remain, through which the thing was changed and was turned from one figure into another, that that can exhibit the changes of times? For surely it could not be, because without the change of motions times are not, and there is no change where there is no figure.

CHAPTER XII

FROM THE FORMLESS EARTH GOD CREATED ANOTHER HEAVEN AND A VISIBLE AND FORMED EARTH

Which things considered as much as Thou givest, O my God, as much as Thou excitest me to knock, and as much as Thou openest unto me when I knock,[13] two things I find which Thou hast made, not within the compass of time, since neither is co-eternal with Thee. One, which is so formed that, without any failing of contemplation, without any interval of change, although changeable, yet not changed, it may fully enjoy Thy eternity and unchangeableness; the other, which was so formless, that it had not that by which it could be changed from one form into another, either of motion or of repose, whereby it might be subject unto time. But this Thou didst not leave to be formless, since before all days, in the beginning Thou createdst heaven and earth—these two things of which I spoke. But the earth was invisible and without form, and darkness was upon the deep.[14] By which words its shapelessness is conveyed to us—that by degrees those minds may be drawn on which cannot wholly conceive the privation of all form without coming to nothing—whence another heaven might be created, and another earth visible and well-formed, and water beautifully ordered, and whatever besides is, in the formation of this world, recorded to have been, not without days, created; because such things are so that in them the vicissitudes of times may take place, on account of the appointed changes of motions and of forms.

[13] Matt. vii. 7   [14] Gen. i. 2

CHAPTER XIII

OF THE INTELLECTUAL HEAVEN AND FORMLESS EARTH, OUT OF WHICH, ON ANOTHER DAY, THE FIRMAMENT WAS FORMED

Meanwhile I conceive this, O my God, when I hear Thy Scripture speak, saying, In the beginning God made heaven and earth; but the earth was invisible and without form, and darkness was upon the deep, and not stating on what day Thou didst create these things. Thus, meanwhile, do I conceive, that it is on account of that heaven of heavens, that intellectual heaven, where to understand is to know all at once—not in part, not darkly, not through a glass,[15] but as a whole, in manifestation, face to face; not this thing now, that anon, but (as has been said) to know at once without any change of times; and on account of the invisible and formless earth, without any change of times; which change is wont to have this thing now, that anon, because, where there is no form there can be no distinction between this or that—it is, then, on account of these two—a primitively formed, and a wholly formless; the one heaven, but the heaven of heavens, the other earth, but the earth invisible and formless—on account of these two do I meanwhile conceive that Thy Scripture said without mention of days, "In the beginning God created the heaven and the earth." For immediately it added of what earth it spake. And when on the second day the firmament is recorded to have been created, and called heaven, it suggests to us of which heaven He spoke before without mention of days.

CHAPTER XIV

OF THE DEPTH OF THE SACRED SCRIPTURE, AND ITS ENEMIES

Wonderful is the depth of Thy oracles, whose surface is before us, inviting the little ones; and yet wonderful is the depth, O my God, wonderful is the depth. It is awe to look into it; and awe of honor, and a tremor of love. The enemies thereof I hate vehemently.[16] Oh, if Thou wouldest slay them with Thy two-edged sword,[17] that they be not its enemies! For thus do I love, that they should be slain unto themselves that they may live unto Thee. But behold others not reprovers, but praisers of the book of Genesis —"The Spirit of God," they say, "Who by His servant Moses wrote these things, willed not that these words should be thus understood. He willed not that it should be understood as Thou sayest, but as we say." Unto whom, O God of us all, Thyself being Judge, do I thus answer.

---

[15] 1 Cor. xiii. 12   [16] Ps. cxxxix. 21
[17] Ps. cxlix. 6. He refers to the Manichaeans. In his comment on this place, he interprets the "two-edged sword" to mean the Old and New Testament, called two-edged, he says, because it speaks of things temporal and eternal

CHAPTER XV

HE ARGUES AGAINST ADVERSARIES CONCERNING THE HEAVEN OF HEAVENS

Will you say that these things are false, which, with a strong voice, Truth tells me in my inner ear, concerning the very eternity of the Creator, that His substance is in no wise changed by time, nor that His will is separate from His substance? Wherefore, He wills not one thing now, another anon, but once and for ever He wills all things that He wills; not again and again, nor now this, now that; nor wills afterwards what He wills not before, nor wills not what before He willed. Because such a will is mutable, and no mutable thing is eternal; but our God is eternal. Likewise He tells me, tells me in my inner ear, that the expectation of future things is turned to sight when they have come; and this same sight is turned to memory when they have passed. Moreover, all thought which is thus varied is mutable, and nothing mutable is eternal; but our God is eternal. These things I sum up and put together, and I find that my God, the eternal God, has not made any creature by any new will, nor that His knowledge suffers anything transitory.

What, therefore, will ye say, ye objectors? Are these things false? "No," they say. "What is this? Is it false, then, that every nature already formed, or matter formable, is only from Him who is supremely good, because He is supreme?" "Neither do we deny this," they say. "What then? Do you deny this, that there is a certain sublime creature, clinging with so chaste a love with the true and truly eternal God, that although it be not co-eternal with Him, yet it separates itself not from Him, nor flows into any variety and vicissitude of times, but rests in the truest contemplation of Him only?" Since Thou, O God, showest Thyself unto him, and sufficest him, who loveth Thee as much as Thou commandest, and, therefore, he declineth not from Thee, nor toward himself. This is the house of God, not earthly, nor of any celestial bulk corporeal, but a spiritual house and a partaker of Thy eternity, because without blemish for ever. For Thou hast made it fast for ever and ever; Thou hast given it a law, which it shall not pass.[18] Nor yet is it co-eternal with Thee, O God, because not without beginning, for it was made.

For although we find no time before it, for wisdom was created before all things[19]—not certainly that Wisdom manifestly co-eternal and equal unto Thee, our God, His Father, and by Whom all things were created, and in Whom, as the Beginning, Thou createdst heaven and earth; but truly that wisdom which has been created, namely, the intellectual nature, which, in the contemplation of light, is light. For this, although created, is also called wisdom. But as great as is the difference between the Light which

---

[18] Ps. cxlviii. 6   [19] Ecclus. i. 4

enlighteneth and that which is enlightened, so great is the difference between the Wisdom that createth and that which hath been created; as between the Righteousness which justifieth, and the righteousness which has been made by justification. For we also are called Thy righteousness; for thus saith a certain servant of Thine: "That we might be made the righteousness of God in Him." [20] Therefore, since a certain created wisdom was created before all things, the rational and intellectual mind of that chaste city of Thine, our mother which is above, and is free,[21] and eternal in the heavens[22] (in what heavens, unless in those that praise Thee, the heaven of heavens, because this also is the heaven of heavens,[23] which is the Lord's)—although we find not time before it, because that which hath been created before all things also precedeth the creature of time, yet is the Eternity of the Creator Himself before it, from Whom, having been created, it took the beginning, although not of time—for time as yet was not —yet of its own very nature.

Hence comes it so to be of Thee, our God, as to be manifestly another than Thou, and not the Self-same. Since, although we find time not only not before it, but not in it (it being proper ever to behold Thy face, nor is ever turned aside from it, wherefore it happens that it is varied by no change), yet is there in it that mutability itself whence it would become dark and cold, but that, clinging unto Thee with sublime love, it shineth and gloweth from Thee like a perpetual noon. O house, full of light and splendor! I have loved thy beauty, and the place of the habitation of the glory of my Lord,[24] thy builder and owner. Let my wandering sigh after thee; and I speak unto Him that made thee, that He may possess me also in thee, seeing He hath made me likewise. I have gone astray, like a lost sheep;[25] yet upon the shoulders of my Shepherd,[26] thy builder, I hope that I may be brought back to thee.

What say ye to me, O ye objectors whom I was addressing, and who yet believe that Moses was the holy servant of God, and that his books were the oracles of the Holy Ghost? Is not this house of God, not indeed co-eternal with God, yet, according to its measure, eternal in the heavens,[27] where in vain you seek for changes of times, because you will not find them? For that surpasseth all extension, and every revolving space of time, to which it is ever good to cleave fast to God.[28] "It is," say they. What, therefore, of those things which my heart cried out unto my God, when within it heard the voice of His praise, what then do you contend is false? Or is it because the matter was formless, wherein, as there was no form, there was no order? But where there was no order there could not be any change of times; and yet this "almost nothing," inasmuch as it was not altogether nothing, was verily from Him, from Whom is whatever is, in what state soever anything is. "This also," say they, "we do not deny."

[20] 2 Cor. v. 21   [21] Gal. iv. 26   [22] 2 Cor. v. 1   [23] Ps. cxlviii. 4   [24] Ps. xxvi. 8
[25] Ps. cxix. 176   [26] Luke xv. 5   [27] 2 Cor. v. 1   [28] Ps. lxxiii. 28

CHAPTER XVI

With such as grant that all these things which Thy truth indicates to my mind are true, I desire to confer a little before Thee, O my God. For let those who deny these things bark and drown their own voices with their clamor as much as they please; I will endeavor to persuade them to be quiet, and to suffer Thy word to reach them. But should they be unwilling, and should they repel me, I beseech, O my God, that Thou be not silent to me.[29] Do Thou speak truly in my heart, for Thou only so speakest, and I will send them away blowing upon the dust from without, and raising it up into their own eyes; and I will myself enter into my chamber,[30] and sing there unto Thee songs of love—groaning with groaning unutterable[31] in my pilgrimage, and remembering Jerusalem, with heart raised up towards it, Jerusalem my country, Jerusalem my mother, and Thyself, the Ruler over it, the Enlightener, the Father, the Guardian, the Husband, the chaste and strong delight, the solid joy, and all good things ineffable, even all at the same time, because the one supreme and true Good. And I will not be turned away until Thou collect all that I am, from this dispersion and deformity, into the peace of that very dear mother, where are the first-fruits of my spirit, whence these things are assured to me, and Thou conform and confirm it for ever, my God, my Mercy. But with reference to those who say not that all these things which are true and false, who honor Thy Holy Scripture set forth by holy Moses, placing it, as with us, on the summit of an authority to be followed, and yet who contradict us in some particulars, I thus speak: Be Thou, O our God, judge between my confessions and their contradictions.

CHAPTER XVII

For they say, "Although these things be true, yet Moses regarded not those two things, when by divine revelation he said, 'In the beginning God created the heaven and the earth.' [32] Under the name of heaven he did not indicate that spiritual or intellectual creature which always beholds the face of God; nor under the name of earth, that shapeless matter." "What then?" "That man," they say, "meant as we say; this it is that he declared by those words." "What is that?" "By the name of heaven and earth," they say, "did he first wish to set forth, universally and briefly, all this visible world, that afterwards by the enumeration of the days he might distribute, as

---

[29] Ps. xxviii. 1   [30] Isa. xxvi. 20   [31] Rom. viii. 26   [32] Gen. i. 1

if in detail, all those things which it pleased the Holy Spirit thus to reveal. For such men were that rude and carnal people to which he spoke, that he judged it prudent that only those works of God as were visible should be entrusted to them." They agree, however, that the earth invisible and formless, and the darksome deep (out of which it is subsequently pointed out that all these visible things, which are known to all, were made and set in order during those "days"), may not unsuitably be understood of this formless matter.

What, now, if another should say that this same formlessness and confusion of matter was first introduced under the name of heaven and earth, because out of it this visible world, with all those natures which most manifestly appear in it, which is wont to be called by the name of heaven and earth, was created and perfected? But what if another should say, that that invisible and visible nature is not inaptly called heaven and earth; and that consequently the universal creation, which God in His wisdom hath made—that is, in the beginning—was comprehended under these two words. Yet, since all things have been made, not of the substance of God, but out of nothing (because they are not that same thing that God is, and there is in them all a certain mutability, whether they remain, as does the eternal house of God, or be changed, as are the soul and body of man), therefore, that the common matter of all things invisible and visible—as yet shapeless, but still capable of form—out of which was to be created heaven and earth (that is, the invisible and visible creature already formed), was spoken of by the same names by which the earth invisible and formless and the darkness upon the deep would be called; with this difference, however, that the earth invisible and formless is understood as corporeal matter, before it had any manner of form, but the darkness upon the deep as spiritual matter, before it was restrained at all of its unlimited fluidity, and before the enlightening of wisdom.

Should any man wish, he may still say that the already perfected and formed natures, invisible and visible, are not signified under the name of heaven and earth when it is read, "In the beginning God created the heaven and the earth;" but that the yet same formless beginning of things, the matter capable of being formed and made, was called by these names, because contained in it there were these confused things not as yet distinguished by their qualities and forms, which now being digested in their own orders, are called heaven and earth, the former being the spiritual, the latter the corporeal creature.

CHAPTER XVIII

WHAT ERROR IS HARMLESS IN SACRED SCRIPTURE

All these things having been heard and considered, I am unwilling to contend about words, for that is profitable to nothing but to the subverting of the hearers.[33] But the law is good to edify, if a man use it lawfully;[34] for the end of it is charity out of a pure heart, and of a good conscience, and of faith unfeigned.[35] And well did our Master know, upon which two commandments He hung all the Law and the Prophets.[36] And what doth it hinder me, O my God, Thou light of my eyes in secret, while ardently confessing these things—since by these words many things may be understood, all of which are yet true—what, I say, doth it hinder me, should I think otherwise of what the writer thought than some other man thinketh? Indeed, all of us who read endeavor to trace out and to understand that which he whom we read wished to convey; and as we believe him to speak truly, we dare not suppose that he has spoken anything which we either know or suppose to be false. Since, therefore, each person endeavors to understand in the Holy Scriptures that which the writer understood, what hurt is it if a man understand what Thou, the light of all true-speaking minds, dost show him to be true although he whom he reads understood not this, seeing that he also understood a Truth, not, however, this Truth?

CHAPTER XIX

HE ENUMERATES THE THINGS CONCERNING WHICH ALL AGREE

For it is true, O Lord, that Thou hast made heaven and earth; it is also true, that the Beginning is Thy Wisdom, in Which Thou hast made all things.[37] It is likewise true, that this visible world has its own great parts, the heaven and the earth, which in a short compass comprehends all made and created natures. It is also true, that everything mutable sets before our minds a certain want of form, whereof it takes a form, or is changed and turned. It is true, that that is subject to no times which so cleaves to the changeless form as that, though it be mutable, it is not changed. It is true, that the formlessness, which is almost nothing, cannot have changes of times. It is true, that that of which anything is made may by a certain mode of speech be called by the name of that thing which is made of it; whence that formlessness of which heaven and earth were made might be called "heaven and earth." It is true, that of all things having form, nothing is nearer to the formless than the earth and the deep. It is true, that not only every created and formed thing, but also whatever is capable of creation and of form, Thou hast made, by whom are all things.[38] It is true, that everything that is formed from that which is formless was formless before it was formed.

[33] 2 Tim. ii. 14   [34] 1 Tim. i. 8   [35] *Ibid.* 5   [36] Matt. xxii. 40   [37] Ps. civ. 24
[38] 1 Cor. viii. 6

CHAPTER XX

OF THE WORDS, "IN THE BEGINNING," VARIOUSLY UNDERSTOOD

From all these truths, of which they doubt not whose inner eye Thou hast granted to see such things, and who immovably believe Moses, Thy servant, to have spoken in the spirit of truth; from all these, then, he taketh one who saith, "In the beginning God created the heaven and the earth"—that is, "In His Word, co-eternal with Himself, God made the intelligible and the sensible, or the spiritual and corporeal creature." He taketh another, who saith, "In the beginning God created the heaven and the earth" —that is, "In His Word, co-eternal with Himself, God made the universal mass of this corporeal world, with all those manifest and known natures which it containeth." He, another, who saith, "In the beginning God created the heaven and the earth"—that is, "In His Word, co-eternal with Himself, God made the formless matter of the spiritual and corporeal creature." He, another, who saith, "In the beginning God created the heaven and the earth"—that is, "In His Word, co-eternal with Himself, God made the formless matter of the corporeal creature, wherein heaven and earth lay as yet confused, which being now distinguished and formed, we, at this day, see in the mass of this world." He, another, who saith, "In the beginning God created heaven and earth"—that is, "In the very beginning of creating and working, God made that formless matter confusedly containing heaven and earth, out of which, being formed, they now stand out, and are manifest, with all the things that are in them."

CHAPTER XXI

OF THE EXPLANATION OF THE WORDS, "THE EARTH WAS INVISIBLE"

And as concerns the understanding of the following words, out of all those truths he selected one to himself, who saith, "But the earth was invisible and without form, and darkness was upon the deep"—that is, "That corporeal thing, which God made, was as yet the formless matter of corporeal things, without order, without light." He taketh another, who saith, "But the earth was invisible and without form, and darkness was upon the deep"—that is, "This whole, which is called heaven and earth, was as yet formless and darksome matter, out of which the corporeal heaven and the corporeal earth were to be made, with all things therein which are known to our corporeal senses." He, another, who saith, "But the earth was invisible and without form, and darkness was upon the deep"—that is, "This whole, which is called heaven and earth, was as yet a formless and darksome matter, out of which were to be made that intelligible heaven, which is otherwise called the heaven of heavens, and the earth, namely, the whole corporeal nature, under which name may also be comprised this corporeal heaven—that is, from which every invisible and visible creature would be created." He, another, who saith, "But the earth was invisible and without form, and darkness was upon the deep"—"The Scripture called not that formlessness by the name of heaven and earth, but that formlessness itself," saith he, "already was, which he named the earth invisible and formless and the darksome deep, of which he had said before, that God had made the heaven and the earth, namely, the spiritual and corporeal creature." He, another, who saith, "But the earth was invisible and formless, and darkness was upon the deep"—that is, "There was already a formless matter, whereof the Scripture before said, that God had made heaven and earth, namely, the entire corporeal mass of the world, divided into two very great parts, the superior and the inferior, with all those familiar and known creatures which are in them."

CHAPTER XXII

HE DISCUSSES WHETHER MATTER WAS FROM ETERNITY, OR WAS MADE BY GOD[39]

For, should any one endeavor to contend against these last two opinions, thus—"If you will not admit that this formlessness of matter appears to be called by the name of heaven and earth, then there was something which God had not made out of which He could make heaven and earth; for Scripture has not told us that God made this matter, unless we understand it to be implied in the term of heaven and earth, or of earth only, when it is said, 'In the beginning God created heaven and earth,' as that which follows, but the earth was invisible and formless, although it was pleasing to him so to call the formless matter, we may not yet understand any but that which God made in that text which has been already written, 'God made heaven and earth.' " The maintainers of either one or the other of these two opinions which we have put last will, when they have heard these things, answer and say, "We deny not indeed that this formless matter was created by God, the God of whom are all things, very good; for, as we say that that is a greater good which is created and formed, so we acknowledge that that is a minor good which is capable of creation and form, but yet good. But yet the Scripture has not declared that God made this formlessness, any more than it has declared many other things; as the 'Cherubim,' and 'Seraphim,' [40] and those of which the apostle distinctly speaks, 'Thrones,' 'Dominions,' 'Principalities,' 'Powers,' [41] all of which it is manifest God

---

[39] See xi. sec. 7, and note, above; and xii. sec. 33, and note, below. See also the subtle reasoning of Dean Mansel (*Bampton Lectures*, lect. ii.), on the inconsequence of receiving the idea of the creation out of nothing on other than Christian principles. And compare Coleridge, *The Friend*, iii. 213

[40] Isa. vi. 2, and xxxvii. 16   [41] Col. i. 16

made. Or if in that which is said, 'He made heaven and earth,' all things are comprehended, what do we say of the waters upon which the Spirit of God moved? For if they are understood as incorporated in the word earth, how then can formless matter be meant in the term earth when we see the waters so beautiful? Or if it be so meant, why then is it written that out of the same formlessness the firmament was made and called heaven, and yet it is not written that the waters were made? For those waters, which we perceive flowing in so beautiful a manner, remain not formless and invisible. But if, then, they received that beauty when God said, Let the water which is under the firmament be gathered together,[42] so that the gathering be the very formation, what will be answered concerning the waters which are above the firmament, because if formless they would not have deserved to receive a seat so honorable, nor is it written by what word they were formed? If, then, Genesis is silent as to anything that God has made, which, however, neither sound faith nor unerring understanding doubts that God has made, let not any sober teaching dare to say that these waters were co-eternal with God because we find them mentioned in the book of Genesis; but when they were created, we find not. Why—truth instructing us—may we not understand that that formless matter, which the Scripture calls the earth invisible and without form, and the darksome deep, have been made by God out of nothing, and therefore that they are not co-eternal with Him, although that narrative has failed to tell when they were made?"

CHAPTER XXIII

TWO KINDS OF DISAGREEMENTS IN THE BOOKS TO BE EXPLAINED

These things, therefore, being heard and perceived according to my weakness of apprehension, which I confess unto Thee, O Lord, who knowest it, I see that two sorts of differences may arise when by signs anything is related, even by true reporters—one concerning the truth of the things, the other concerning the meaning of him who reports them. For in one way we inquire, concerning the forming of the creature, what is true; but in another, what Moses, that excellent servant of Thy faith, would have wished that the reader and hearer should understand by these words. As for the first kind, let all those depart from me who imagine themselves to know as true what is false. And as for the other also, let all depart from me who imagine Moses to have spoken things that are false. But let me be united in Thee, O Lord, with them, and in Thee delight myself with them that feed on Thy truth, in the breadth of charity; and let us approach together the words of Thy book, and in them make search for Thy will, through the will of Thy servant by whose pen Thou hast dispensed them.

[42] Gen. i. 9

CHAPTER XXIV

OUT OF THE MANY TRUE THINGS, IT IS NOT ASSERTED CONFIDENTLY
THAT MOSES UNDERSTOOD THIS OR THAT

But which of us, amid so many truths which occur to inquirers in these
words, understood as they are in different ways, shall so discover that one
interpretation as to say confidently that Moses thought this, and that in
that narrative he wished this to be understood, as confidently as he says
that this is true, whether he thought this thing or the other? For behold,
O my God, I Thy servant, who in this book have vowed unto Thee a
sacrifice of confession, and beseech Thee that of Thy mercy I may pay my
vows unto Thee,[43] behold, can I, as I confidently assert that Thou in Thy
immutable word hast created all things, invisible and visible, with equal
confidence assert that Moses meant nothing else than this when he wrote,
"In the beginning God created the heaven and the earth." No. Because it
is not as clear to me that this was in his mind when he wrote these things,
as I see it to be certain in Thy truth. For his thoughts might be set upon
the very beginning of the creation when he said, "In the beginning;" and
he might wish it to be understood that, in this place, the heaven and the
earth were no formed and perfected nature, whether spiritual or corporeal,
but each of them newly begun, and as yet formless. Because I see, that
whichsoever of these had been said, it might have been said truly; but
which of them he may have thought in these words, I do not so perceive.
Although, whether it were one of these, or some other meaning which
has not been mentioned by me, that this great man saw in his mind when
he used these words, I make no doubt but that he saw it truly, and expressed it suitably.

CHAPTER XXV

IT BEHOVES INTERPRETERS, WHEN DISAGREEING CONCERNING OBSCURE
PLACES, TO REGARD GOD THE AUTHOR OF TRUTH, AND THE
RULE OF CHARITY

Let no one now trouble me by saying, "Moses thought not as you say,
but as I say." For should he ask me, "Whence knowest thou that Moses
thought this which you deduce from his words?" I ought to take it con-
tentedly, and reply perhaps as I have before, or somewhat more fully
should he be obstinate. But when he says, "Moses meant not what you say,
but what I say," and yet denies not what each of us says, and that both are
true, O my God, life of the poor, in whose bosom there is no contradiction,
pour down into my heart Thy soothings, that I may patiently bear with

[43] Ps. xxii. 25

such as say this to me; not because they are divine, and because they have seen in the heart of Thy servant what they say, but because they are proud, and have not known the opinion of Moses, but love their own— not because it is true, but because it is their own. Otherwise they would equally love another true opinion, as I love what they say when they speak what is true; not because it is theirs, but because it is true, and therefore now not theirs because true. But if they therefore love that because it is true, it is now both theirs and mine, since it is common to all the lovers of truth. But because they contend that Moses meant not what I say, but what they themselves say, this I neither like nor love; because, though it were so, yet that rashness is not of knowledge, but of audacity; and not vision, but vanity brought it forth. And therefore, O Lord, are Thy judgments to be dreaded, since Thy truth is neither mine, nor his, nor another's, but of all of us, whom Thou publicly callest to have it in common, warning us terribly not to hold it as specially for ourselves, lest we be deprived of it. For whosoever claims to himself as his own that which Thou appointed to all to enjoy, and desires that to be his own which belongs to all, is forced away from what is common to all to that which is his own—that is, from truth to falsehood. For he that speaketh a lie, speaketh of his own.[44]

Hearken, O God, Thou best Judge! Truth itself, hearken to what I shall say to this objector; hearken, for before Thee I say it, and before my brethren who use Thy law lawfully, to the end of charity;[45] hearken and behold what I shall say to him, if it be pleasing unto Thee. For this brotherly and peaceful word do I return unto him: "If we both see that that which thou sayest is true, and if we both see that what I say is true, where, I ask, do we see it? Certainly not I in thee, nor thou in me, but both in the unchangeable truth itself, which is above our minds." When, therefore, we may not contend about the very light of the Lord our God, why do we contend about the thoughts of our neighbor, which we cannot so see as incommutable truth is seen; when, if Moses himself had appeared to us and said, "This I meant," not so should we see it, but believe it? Let us not, then, be puffed up for one against the other,[46] above that which is written; let us love the Lord our God with all our heart, with all our soul, and with all our mind, and our neighbor as ourself.[47] As to which two precepts of charity, unless we believe that Moses meant whatever in these books he did mean, we shall make God a liar when we think otherwise concerning our fellow-servants' mind than He has taught us. Behold, now, how foolish it is, in so great an abundance of the truest opinions which can be extracted from these words, rashly to affirm which of them Moses particularly meant; and with pernicious contentions to offend charity itself, on account of which he has spoken all the things whose words we endeavor to explain!

[44] John viii. 44   [45] 1 Tim. i. 8   [46] 1 Cor. iv. 6   [47] Mark xii. 30, 31

CHAPTER XXVI

WHAT HE MIGHT HAVE ASKED OF GOD HAD HE BEEN ENJOINED TO WRITE THE BOOK OF GENESIS

And yet, O my God, Thou exaltation of my humility, and rest of my labor, who hearest my confessions, and forgivest my sins, since Thou commandest me that I should love my neighbor as myself, I cannot believe that Thou gavest to Moses, Thy most faithful servant, a less gift than I should wish and desire for myself from Thee, had I been born in his time, and hadst Thou placed me in that position that through the service of my heart and of my tongue those books might be distributed, which so long after were to profit all nations, and through the whole world, from so great a pinnacle of authority, were to surmount the words of all false and proud teachings. I should have wished truly had I then been Moses (for we all come from the same mass; and what is man, saving that Thou art mindful of him? [48]). I should then, had I been at that time what he was, and enjoined by Thee to write the book of Genesis, have wished that such a power of expression and such a method of arrangement should be given me, that they who cannot as yet understand how God creates might not reject the words as surpassing their powers; and they who are already able to do this, would find, in what true opinion soever they had by thought arrived at, that it was not passed over in the few words of Thy servant; and should another man by the light of truth have discovered another, neither should that fail to be found in those same words.

CHAPTER XXVII

THE STYLE OF SPEAKING IN THE BOOK OF GENESIS IS SIMPLE AND CLEAR

For as a fountain in a limited space is more plentiful, and affords supply for more streams over larger spaces than any one of those streams which, after a wide interval, is derived from the same fountain; so the narrative of Thy dispenser, destined to benefit many who were likely to discourse thereon, does, from a limited measure of language, overflow into streams of clear truth, whence each one may draw out for himself that truth which he can concerning these subjects—this one that truth, that one another, by larger circumlocutions of discourse. For some, when they read or hear these words, think that God as a man or some mass gifted with immense power, by some new and sudden resolve, had, outside itself, as if at distant places, created heaven and earth, two great bodies above and below, wherein all things were to be contained. And when they hear, God said, Let it be

[48] Ps. vii. 8

made, and it was made, they think of words begun and ended, sounding in times and passing away, after the departure of which that came into being which was commanded to be; and whatever else of the kind their familiarity with the world would suggest. In whom, being as yet little ones, while their weakness by this humble kind of speech is carried on as if in a mother's bosom, their faith is healthfully built up, by which they have and hold as certain that God made all natures, which in wondrous variety their senses perceive on every side. Which words, if any one despising them, as if trivial, with proud weakness shall have stretched himself beyond his fostering cradle, he will, alas, fall miserably. Have pity, O Lord God, lest they who pass by trample on the unfledged bird; and send Thine angel, who may restore it to its nest, that it may live until it can fly.[49]

CHAPTER XXVIII

THE WORDS, "IN THE BEGINNING," AND, "THE HEAVEN AND THE EARTH," ARE DIFFERENTLY UNDERSTOOD

But others, to whom these words are no longer a nest, but shady fruit-bowers, see the fruits concealed in them, fly around rejoicing, and chirpingly search and pluck them. For they see when they read or hear these words, O God, that all times past and future are surmounted by Thy eternal and stable abiding, and still that there is no temporal creature which Thou hast not made. And by Thy will, because it is that which Thou art, Thou hast made all things, not by any changed will, nor by a will which before was not—not out of Thyself, in Thine own likeness, the form of all things, but out of nothing, a formless unlikeness which should be formed by Thy likeness (having recourse to Thee the One, after their settled capacity, according as it has been given to each thing in his kind), and might all be made very good; whether they remain around Thee, or, being by degrees removed in time and place, make or undergo beautiful variations. These things they see, and rejoice in the light of Thy truth, in the little degree they here may.

Again, another of these directs his attention to that which is said, "In the beginning God made the heaven and the earth," and beholdeth Wisdom—the Beginning, because It also speaketh unto us.[50] Another likewise directs his attention to the same words, and by "beginning" understands the commencement of things created; and receives it thus—In the beginning He made, as if it were said, He at first made. And among those who understand "In the beginning" to mean, that "in Thy Wisdom Thou hast created heaven and earth," one believes the matter out of which the heaven and earth were to be created to be there called "heaven and earth;" another, that they are natures already formed and distinct; another, one formed

---

[49] In allusion, perhaps, to Prov. xxvii. 8: "As a bird that wandereth from her nest, so is a man that wandereth from his place"   [50] John viii. 23

nature, and that a spiritual, under the name of heaven, the other formless, of corporeal matter, under the name of earth. But they who under the name of "heaven and earth" understand matter as yet formless, out of which were to be formed heaven and earth, do not themselves understand it in one manner; but one, that matter out of which the intelligible and the sensible creature were to be completed; another, that only out of which this sensible corporeal mass was to come, holding in its vast bosom these visible and prepared natures. Nor are they who believe that the creatures already set in order and arranged are in this place called heaven and earth of one accord; but the one, both the invisible and visible; the other, the visible only, in which we admire the luminous heaven and darksome earth, and the things that are therein.

CHAPTER XXIX

CONCERNING THE OPINION OF THOSE WHO EXPLAIN IT "AT FIRST HE MADE"

But he who does not otherwise understand, "In the beginning He made," than if it were said, "At first He made," can only truly understand heaven and earth of the matter of heaven and earth, namely, of the universal, that is, intelligible and corporeal creation. For if he would have it of the universe, as already formed, it might rightly be asked of him: "If at first God made this, what made He afterwards?" And after the universe he will find nothing; thereupon must he, though unwilling, hear, "How is this first, if there is nothing afterwards?" But when he says that God made matter first formless, then formed, he is not absurd if he be but able to discern what precedes by eternity, what by time, what by choice, what by origin. By eternity, as God is before all things; by time, as the flower is before the fruit; by choice, as the fruit is before the flower; by origin, as sound is before the tune. Of these four, the first and last which I have referred to are with much difficulty understood; the two middle very easily. For an uncommon and too lofty vision it is to behold, O Lord, Thy Eternity, immutably making things mutable, and thereby before them. Who is so acute of mind as to be able without great labor to discover how the sound is prior to the tune, because a tune is a formed sound; and a thing not formed may exist, but that which exists not cannot be formed? So is the matter prior to that which is made from it; not prior because it makes it, since itself is rather made, nor is it prior by an interval of time. For we do not as to time first utter formless sounds without singing, and then adapt or fashion them into the form of a song, just as wood or silver from which a chest or vessel is made. Because such materials do by time also precede the forms of the things which are made from them; but in singing this is not so. For when it is sung, its sound is heard at the same time; seeing there is not first a formless sound, which is afterwards formed into a song. For as soon as it shall have first sounded it passes away; nor can you find anything of it, which being recalled you can by art compose. And, therefore, the song is absorbed in its own sound, which sound of it is its matter. Because this same is formed that it may be a tune; and therefore, as I was saying, the matter of the sound is prior to the form of the tune, not before through any power of making it a tune; for neither is a sound the composer of the tune, but is sent forth from the body and is subjected to the soul of the singer, that from it he may form a tune. Nor is it first in time, for it is given forth together with the tune; nor first in choice, for a sound is not better than a tune, since a tune is not merely a sound, but a beautiful sound. But it is first in origin, because the tune is not formed that it may become a sound, but the sound is formed that it may become a tune. By this example, let him who is able understand that the matter of things was first made, and called heaven and earth, because out of it heaven and earth were made. Not that it was made first in time, because the forms of things give rise to time, but that was formless; but now, in time, it is perceived together with its form. Nor yet can anything be related concerning that matter, unless as if it were prior in time, while it is considered last (because things formed are assuredly superior to things formless), and is preceded by the Eternity of the Creator, so that there might be out of nothing that from which something might be made.

CHAPTER XXX

IN THE GREAT DIVERSITY OF OPINIONS, IT BECOMES ALL TO UNITE CHARITY AND DIVINE TRUTH

In this diversity of true opinions let Truth itself beget concord; and may our God have mercy upon us, that we may use the law lawfully,[51] the end of the commandment, pure charity. And by this if any one asks of me, "Which of these was the meaning of Thy servant Moses?" these were not the utterances of my confessions, should I not confess unto Thee, "I know not;" and yet I know that those opinions are true, with the exception of those carnal ones concerning which I have spoken what I thought well. However, these words of Thy Book affright not those little ones of good hope, treating few of high things in a humble fashion, and few things in varied ways. But let all, whom I acknowledge to see and speak the truth in these words, love one another, and equally love Thee, our God, fountain of truth—if we thirst not for vain things, but for it; let us so honor this servant of Thine, the dispenser of this Scripture, full of Thy Spirit, as to believe that when Thou revealedst Thyself to him, and he wrote these things, he intended that which in them chiefly excels both for light of truth and fruitfulness of profit.

[51] I Tim. i. 8

CHAPTER XXXI

MOSES IS SUPPOSED TO HAVE PERCEIVED WHATEVER OF TRUTH CAN BE DISCOVERED IN HIS WORDS

Thus, when one shall say, "He [Moses] meant as I do," and another, "Nay, but as I do," I suppose that I am speaking more religiously when I say, "Why not rather as both, if both be true?" And if there be a third truth, or a fourth, and if any one seek any truth altogether different in those words, why may not he be believed to have seen all these, through whom one God hath tempered the Holy Scriptures to the senses of many, about to see therein things true but different? I certainly—and I fearlessly declare it from my heart—were I to write anything to have the highest authority, should prefer so to write, that whatever of truth any one might apprehend concerning these matters, my words should re-echo, rather than that I should set down one true opinion so clearly on this as that I should exclude the rest, that which was false in which could not offend me. Therefore am I unwilling, O my God, to be so headstrong as not to believe that from Thee this man [Moses] hath received so much. He, surely, when he wrote those words, perceived and thought whatever of truth we have been able to discover, and whatever we have not been able, nor yet are able, though still it may be found in them.

CHAPTER XXXII

FIRST, THE SENSE OF THE WRITER IS TO BE DISCOVERED, THEN THAT IS TO BE BROUGHT OUT WHICH DIVINE TRUTH INTENDED

Finally, O Lord, who art God, and not flesh and blood, if man doth see anything less, can anything lie hid from Thy good Spirit, who shall lead me into the land of uprightness,[52] which Thou Thyself, by those words, wert about to reveal to future readers, although he through whom they were spoken, amid the many interpretations that might have been found, fixed on but one? Which, if it be so, let that which he thought on be more exalted than the rest. But to us, O Lord, either point out the same, or any other true one which may be pleasing unto Thee; so that whether Thou makest known to us that which Thou didst to that man of Thine, or some other by occasion of the same words, yet Thou mayest feed us, not error deceive us. Behold, O Lord my God, how many things we have written concerning a few words—how many, I beseech Thee! What strength of ours, what ages would suffice for all Thy books after this manner? Permit me, therefore, in these more briefly to confess unto Thee, and to select some one true, certain, and good sense, that Thou shalt inspire, although many senses offer

---

[52] Ps. cxliii. 10

themselves, where many, indeed, may; this being the faith of my confession that if I should say that which Thy minister felt, rightly and profitably, this I should strive for; if I shall not attain this, yet I may say that which Thy Truth willed through Its words to say unto me, which said also unto him what It willed.

BOOK THIRTEEN

Of the goodness of God explained in the creation of things, and of the Trinity as found in the first words of Genesis. The story concerning the origin of the world (Gen. i.) is allegorically explained, and he applies it to those things which God works for sanctified and blessed man. Finally, he makes an end of this work, having implored eternal rest from God.

CHAPTER I

HE CALLS UPON GOD, AND PROPOSES TO HIMSELF TO WORSHIP HIM

I CALL upon Thee, my God, my mercy, who madest me, and who didst not forget me, though forgetful of Thee. I call Thee into my soul, which by the desire which Thou inspirest in it Thou preparest for Thy reception. Do not Thou forsake me calling upon Thee, who didst anticipate me before I called, and didst importunately urge with manifold calls that I should hear Thee from afar, and be converted, and call upon Thee who calledst me. For Thou, O Lord, hast blotted out all my evil deserts, that Thou mightest not repay into my hands wherewith I have fallen from Thee, and Thou hast anticipated all my good deserts, that Thou mightest repay into Thy hands wherewith Thou madest me; because before I was, Thou wast, nor was I [anything] to which Thou mightest grant being. And yet behold, I am, out of Thy goodness, anticipating all this which Thou hast made me, and of which Thou hast made me. For neither hadst Thou stood in need of me, nor am I such a good as to be helpful unto Thee, my Lord and God; not that I may so serve Thee as though Thou wert fatigued in working, or lest Thy power may be less if lacking my assistance; nor that, like the land, I may so cultivate Thee that Thou wouldest be uncultivated did I cultivate Thee not; but that I may serve and worship Thee, to the end that I may have well-being from Thee, from whom it is that I am one susceptible of well-being.

CHAPTER II

ALL CREATURES SUBSIST FROM THE PLENITUDE OF DIVINE GOODNESS

For of the plenitude of Thy goodness Thy creature subsists, that a good, which could profit Thee nothing, nor though of Thee was equal to Thee, might yet be, since it could be made of Thee. For what did heaven and earth, which Thou madest in the beginning, deserve of Thee? Let those spiritual and corporeal natures, which Thou in Thy wisdom madest, declare what they deserve of Thee to depend thereon—even the inchoate and formless, each in its own kind, either spiritual or corporeal, going into excess, and into remote unlikeness unto Thee (the spiritual, though formless, more excellent than if it were a formed body; and the corporeal, though formless, more excellent than if it were altogether nothing), and thus they as formless would depend upon Thy Word, unless by the same Word they were recalled to Thy Unity, and endued with form, and from Thee, the one sovereign Good, were all made very good. How have they deserved of Thee, that they should be even formless, since they would not be even this except from Thee?

How has corporeal matter deserved of Thee, to be even invisible and formless,[1] since it were not even this hadst Thou not made it; and therefore since it was not, it could not deserve of Thee that it should be made? Or how could the inchoate spiritual creature deserve of Thee, that even it should flow darksomely like the deep—unlike Thee, had it not been by the same Word turned to that by Whom it was created, and by Him so enlightened become light, although not equally, yet conformably to that Form which is equal unto Thee? For as to a body, to be is not all one with being beautiful, for then it could not be deformed; so also to a created spirit, to live is not all one with living wisely, for then it would be wise unchangeably. But it is good [2] for it always to hold fast unto Thee, lest, in turning from Thee, it lose that light which it hath obtained in turning to Thee, and relapse into a light resembling the darksome deep. For even we ourselves, who in respect of the soul are a spiritual creature, having turned away from Thee, our light, were in that life sometimes darkness;[3] and do labor amidst the remains of our darkness, until in Thy Only One we become Thy righteousness, like the mountains of God. For we have been Thy judgments, which are like the great deep.[4]

CHAPTER III

GENESIS I. 3—OF "LIGHT"—HE UNDERSTANDS AS IT IS SEEN IN THE SPIRITUAL CREATURE

But what Thou saidst in the beginning of the creation, "Let there be light, and there was light," [5] I do not unfitly understand of the spiritual creature; because there was even then a kind of life, which Thou mightest illuminate. But as it had not deserved of Thee that it should be such a life as could be enlightened, so neither, when it already was, hath it deserved of Thee that it should be enlightened. For neither could its formlessness be pleasing unto Thee, unless it became light—not by merely existing, but by beholding the illuminating light, and cleaving unto it; so also, that it lives,

---

[1] Gen. i. 2   [2] Ps. lxxiii. 28   [3] Eph. v. 8   [4] Ps. xxxvi. 6   [5] Gen. i. 3

and lives happily, it owes to nothing whatsoever but to Thy grace; being converted by means of a better change unto that which can be changed neither into better nor into worse; which Thou only art because Thou only simply art, to whom it is not one thing to live, another to live blessedly, since Thou art Thyself Thine own Blessedness.

CHAPTER IV

ALL THINGS HAVE BEEN CREATED BY THE GRACE OF GOD, AND ARE NOT OF HIM AS STANDING IN NEED OF CREATED THINGS

What, therefore, could there be wanting unto Thy good, which Thou Thyself art, although these things had either never been, or had remained formless—which Thou madest not out of any want, but out of the plenitude of Thy goodness, restraining them and converting them to form not as though Thy joy were perfected by them? For to Thee, being perfect, their imperfection is displeasing, and therefore were they perfected by Thee, and were pleasing unto Thee; but not as if Thou wert imperfect, and wert to be perfected in their perfection. For Thy good Spirit was borne over the waters,[6] not borne up by them as if He rested upon them. For those in whom Thy good Spirit is said to rest,[7] He causes to rest in Himself. But Thy incorruptible and unchangeable will, which in itself is all-sufficient for itself, was borne over that life which Thou hadst made, to which to live is not all one with living happily, since, flowing in its own darkness, it liveth also; for which it remaineth to be converted unto Him by whom it was made, and to live more and more by the fountain of life, and in His light to see light,[8] and to be perfected, and enlightened, and made happy.

CHAPTER V

HE RECOGNIZES THE TRINITY IN THE FIRST TWO VERSES OF GENESIS

Behold now, the Trinity appears unto me in an enigma, which Thou, O my God, art, since Thou, O Father, in the Beginning of our wisdom— Which is Thy Wisdom, born of Thyself, equal and co-eternal unto Thee— that is, in Thy Son, hast created heaven and earth. Many things have we said of the heaven of heavens, and of the earth invisible and formless, and of the darksome deep, in reference to the wandering defects of its spiritual deformity, were it not converted unto Him from whom was its life, such as it was, and by His enlightening became a beauteous life, and the heaven of that heaven which was afterwards set between water and water. And under the name of God, I now held the Father, who made these things; and under the name of the Beginning, the Son, in whom He made these

---

[6] Gen. i. 2   [7] Num. xi. 25   [8] Ps. xxxvi. 9

things; and believing, as I did, that my God was the Trinity, I sought further in His holy words, and behold, Thy Spirit was borne over the waters. Behold the Trinity, O my God, Father, Son, and Holy Ghost—the Creator of all creation.

CHAPTER VI

WHY THE HOLY GHOST SHOULD HAVE BEEN MENTIONED AFTER THE MENTION OF HEAVEN AND EARTH

But what was the cause, O Thou true-speaking Light? Unto Thee do I lift up my heart, let it not teach me vain things; disperse its darkness, and tell me, I beseech Thee, by our mother charity, tell me, I beseech Thee, the reason why, after the mention of heaven, and of the earth invisible and formless, and darkness upon the deep, Thy Scripture should then at length mention Thy Spirit? Was it because it was meet that it should be spoken of Him that He was "borne over," and this could not be said, unless that were first mentioned "over" which Thy Spirit may be understood to have been "borne?" For neither was He "borne over" the Father, nor the Son, nor could it rightly be said that He was "borne over" if He were "borne over" nothing. That, therefore, was first to be spoken of "over" which He might be "borne;" and then He, whom it was not meet to mention otherwise than as having been "borne." Why, then, was it not meet that it should otherwise be mentioned of Him, than as having been "borne over?"

CHAPTER VII

THAT THE HOLY SPIRIT BRINGS US TO GOD

Hence let him that is able now follow Thy apostle with his understanding where he thus speaks, because Thy love is shed abroad in our hearts by the Holy Ghost, which is given unto us;[9] and where, concerning spiritual gifts, he teacheth and showeth unto us a more excellent way of charity;[10] and where he bows his knees unto Thee for us, that we may know the super-eminent knowledge of the love of Christ.[11] And, therefore, from the beginning was He super-eminently "borne above the waters." To whom shall I tell this? How speak of the weight of lustful desires, pressing downwards to the steep abyss? and how charity raises us up again, through Thy Spirit which was "borne over the waters?" To whom shall I tell it? How tell it? For neither are there places in which we are merged and emerge. What can be more like, and yet more unlike? They be affections, they be loves; the filthiness of our spirit flowing away downwards with the love of cares, and the sanctity of Thine raising us upwards by the love of freedom from care; that we may lift our hearts unto Thee where Thy Spirit is "borne

[9] Rom. v. 5   [10] I Cor. xii. 1, 31   [11] Eph. iii. 14-19

over the waters;" and that we may come to that pre-eminent rest, when our soul shall have passed through the waters which have no substance.

CHAPTER VIII

THAT NOTHING WHATEVER, SHORT OF GOD, CAN YIELD TO THE RATIONAL CREATURE A HAPPY REST

The angels fell, the soul of man fell, and they have thus indicated the abyss in that dark deep, ready for the whole spiritual creation, unless Thou hadst said from the beginning, "Let there be light," and there had been light, and every obedient intelligence of Thy celestial City had cleaved to Thee, and rested in Thy Spirit, which unchangeably is "borne over" everything changeable. Otherwise, even the heaven of heavens itself would have been a darksome deep, whereas now it is light in the Lord. For even in that wretched restlessness of the spirits who fell away, and, when unclothed of the garments of Thy light, discovered their own darkness, dost Thou sufficiently disclose how noble Thou hast made the rational creature; to which nought which is inferior to Thee will suffice to yield a happy rest, and so not even herself. For Thou, O our God, shalt enlighten our darkness;[12] from Thee are derived our garments of light,[13] and then shall our darkness be as the noonday.[14] Give Thyself unto me, O my God, restore Thyself unto me; behold, I love Thee, and if it be too little, let me love Thee more strongly. I cannot measure my love, so that I may come to know how much there is yet wanting in me, ere my life run into Thy embracements, and not be turned away until it be hidden in the secret place of Thy Presence.[15] This only I know, that woe is me except in Thee—not only without, but even also within myself; and all plenty which is not my God is poverty to me.

CHAPTER IX

WHY THE HOLY SPIRIT WAS ONLY "BORNE OVER" THE WATERS

But was not either the Father or the Son "borne over the waters?" If we understand this to mean in space, as a body, then neither was the Holy Spirit; but if the incommutable super-eminence of Divinity above everything mutable, then both Father, and Son, and Holy Ghost were borne "over the waters." Why, then, is this said of Thy Spirit only? Why is it said of Him alone? As if He had been in place who is not in place, of whom only it is written, that He is Thy gift? In Thy gift we rest; there we enjoy Thee. Our rest is our place. Love lifts us up thither, and Thy good Spirit lifteth our lowliness from the gates of death.[16] In Thy good pleasure lies

---

[12] Ps. xviii. 28   [13] Ps. civ. 2   [14] Ps. cxxxix. 12   [15] Ps. xxxi. 20   [16] Ps. ix. 13

our peace.[17] The body by its own weight gravitates towards its own place.[e] Weight goes not downward only, but to its own place. Fire tends upwards, a stone downwards. They are propelled by their own weights, they seek their own places. Oil poured under the water is raised above the water; water poured upon oil sinks under the oil. They are propelled by their own weights, they seek their own places. Out of order, they are restless; restored to order, they are at rest. My weight is my love; by it am I borne whithersoever I am borne. By Thy Gift we are inflamed, and are borne upwards; we wax hot inwardly, and go forwards. We ascend Thy ways that be in our heart,[18] and sing a song of degrees; we glow inwardly with Thy fire, with Thy good fire, and we go, because we go upwards to the peace of Jerusalem; for glad was I when they said unto me, "Let us go into the house of the Lord." [19] There hath Thy good pleasure placed us, that we may desire no other thing than to dwell there for ever.

CHAPTER X

THAT NOTHING AROSE SAVE BY THE GIFT OF GOD

Happy creature, which, though in itself it was other than Thou, hath known no other state than that as soon as it was made, it was, without any interval of time, by Thy Gift, which is borne over everything mutable, raised up by that calling whereby Thou saidst, "Let there be light, and there was light." Whereas in us there is a difference of times, in that we were darkness, and are made light;[20] but of that it is only said what it would have been had it not been enlightened. And this is so spoken as if it had been fleeting and darksome before; that so the cause whereby it was made to be otherwise might appear—that is to say, being turned to the unfailing Light it might become light. Let him who is able understand this; let him ask of Thee. Why should he trouble me, as if I could enlighten any man that cometh into the world? [21]

CHAPTER XI

THAT THE SYMBOLS OF THE TRINITY IN MAN, TO BE, TO KNOW, AND TO WILL, ARE NEVER THOROUGHLY EXAMINED

Which of us understands the Almighty Trinity? And yet which speaks not of It, if indeed it be It? Rare is that soul which, while it speaks of It, knows what it speaks of. And they contend and strive, but no one without peace sees that vision. I could wish that men would consider these three things that are in themselves. These three are far other than the Trinity; but I speak of things in which they may exercise and prove themselves, and

---

[e] This is the characteristic Aristotelian theory concerning this problem.—Ed.

[17] Luke ii. 14   [18] Ps. lxxxiv. 5   [19] Ps. cxxii. 1   [20] Eph. v. 8   [21] John i. 9

feel how far other they be. But the three things I speak of are, To Be, to Know, and to Will. For I Am, and I Know, and I Will; I Am Knowing and Willing; and I Know myself to Be and to Will; and I Will to Be and to Know. In these three, therefore, let him who can see how inseparable a life there is—even one life, one mind, and one essence; finally, how inseparable is the distinction, and yet a distinction. Surely a man has it before him; let him look into himself, and see, and tell me. But when he discovers and can say anything of these, let him not then think that he has discovered that which is above these Unchangeable, which Is unchangeably, and Knows unchangeably, and Wills unchangeably. And whether on account of these three there is also, where they are, a Trinity; or whether these three be in Each, so that the three belong to Each; or whether both ways at once, wondrously, simply, and yet diversely, in Itself a limit unto Itself, yet illimitable; whereby It is, and is known unto Itself, and suffices to Itself, unchangeably the Self-same, by the abundant magnitude of its Unity —who can readily conceive? Who in any wise express it? Who in any way rashly pronounce on it?

CHAPTER XII

ALLEGORICAL EXPLANATION OF GENESIS, CHAP. I., CONCERNING THE ORIGIN OF THE CHURCH AND ITS WORSHIP

Proceed in thy confession, say to the Lord thy God, O my faith, Holy, Holy, Holy, O Lord my God, in Thy name have we been baptized, Father, Son, and Holy Ghost, in Thy name do we baptize, Father, Son, and Holy Ghost,[22] because among us also in His Christ did God make heaven and earth, namely, the spiritual and carnal people of His Church. Yea, and our earth, before it received the form of doctrine,[23] was invisible and formless, and we were covered with the darkness of ignorance. For Thou correctest man for iniquity,[24] and Thy judgments are a great deep.[25] But because Thy Spirit was borne over the waters,[26] Thy mercy forsook not our misery, and Thou saidst, "Let there be light," "Repent ye, for the kingdom of heaven is at hand." [27] Repent ye, let there be light. And because our soul was troubled within us,[28] we remembered Thee, O Lord, from the land of Jordan, and that mountain[29] equal unto Thyself, but little for our sakes; and upon our being displeased with our darkness, we turned unto Thee, and there was light. And, behold, we were sometimes darkness, but now light in the Lord.[30]

[22] Matt. xxviii. 19   [23] Rom. vi. 17   [24] Ps. xxxix. 11   [25] Ps. xxxvi. 6   [26] Gen. i. 3   [27] Matt. iii. 2   [28] Ps. xlii. 6   [29] That is, Christ   [30] Eph. v. 8

CHAPTER XIII

THAT THE RENEWAL OF MAN IS NOT COMPLETED IN THIS WORLD

But as yet by faith, not by sight,[31] for we are saved by hope; but hope that is seen is not hope.[32] As yet deep calleth unto deep but in the noise of Thy waterspouts.[33] And as yet doth he that saith, I could not speak unto you as unto spiritual, but as unto carnal,[34] even he, as yet, doth not count himself to have apprehended, and forgetteth those things which are behind, and reacheth forth to those things which are before,[35] and groaneth being burdened;[36] and his soul thirsteth after the living God, as the hart after the water-brooks, and saith, "When shall I come?"[37] desiring to be clothed upon with his house which is from heaven;[38] and calleth upon this lower deep, saying, "Be not conformed to this world, but be ye transformed by the renewing of your mind."[39] And, "Be not children in understanding, howbeit in malice be ye children," that in understanding ye may be perfect;[40] and "O foolish Galatians, who hath bewitched you?"[41] But now not in his own voice, but in Thine who sentest Thy Spirit from above;[42] through Him who ascended up on high,[43] and set open the flood-gates of His gifts,[44] that the force of His streams might make glad the city of God.[45] For, for Him doth the friend of the bridegroom[46] sigh, having now the first-fruits of the Spirit laid up with Him, yet still groaning within himself, waiting for the adoption, to wit, the redemption of his body;[47] to Him he sighs, for he is a member of the Bride; for Him is he jealous, for he is the friend of the Bridegroom;[46] for Him is he jealous, not for himself; because in the voice of Thy waterspouts,[33] not in his own voice, doth he call on that other deep, for whom being jealous he feareth, lest that, as the serpent beguiled Eve through his subtilty, so their minds should be corrupted from the simplicity that is in our Bridegroom, Thine only Son.[48] What a light of beauty will that be when we shall see Him as He is,[49] and those tears be passed away which have been my meat day and night, while they continually say unto me, Where is thy God?[50]

CHAPTER XIV

THAT OUT OF THE CHILDREN OF THE NIGHT AND OF THE DARKNESS, CHILDREN OF THE LIGHT AND OF THE DAY ARE MADE

And so say I too, O my God, where art Thou? Behold where Thou art! In Thee I breathe a little, when I pour out my soul by myself in the voice

---

[31] 2 Cor. v. 7   [32] Rom. viii. 24   [33] Ps. xlii. 7   [34] 1 Cor. iii. 1   [35] Phil. iii. 13
[36] 2 Cor. v. 2, 4   [37] Ps. xlii. 1, 2   [38] 2 Cor. v. 2   [39] Rom. xii. 2   [40] 1 Cor. xiv. 20
[41] Gal. iii. 1   [42] Acts ii. 19   [43] Eph. iv. 8   [44] Mal. iii. 10   [45] Ps. xlvi. 4   [46] John
iii. 29   [47] Rom. viii. 23   [48] 2 Cor. xi. 3, and 1 John iii. 3   [49] *Ibid.* 2   [50] Ps.
xlii. 3

of joy and praise, the sound of him that keeps holy-day.[51] And yet it is cast down, because it relapses and becomes a deep, or rather it feels that it is still a deep. Unto it doth my faith speak which Thou hast kindled to enlighten my feet in the night. Why art thou cast down, O my soul? and why art thou disquieted in me? hope thou in God;[52] His word is a lamp unto my feet.[53] Hope and endure until the night—the mother of the wicked —until the anger of the Lord be overpast,[54] whereof we also were once children who were sometimes darkness,[55] the remains whereof we carry about us in our body, dead on account of sin,[56] until the day break and the shadows flee away.[57] Hope thou in the Lord. In the morning I shall stand in Thy presence, and contemplate Thee;[58] I shall for ever confess unto Thee.[59] In the morning I shall stand in Thy presence, and shall see the health of my countenance,[60] my God, who also shall quicken our mortal bodies by the Spirit that dwelleth in us,[61] because in mercy He was borne over our inner darksome and floating deep. Whence we have in this pilgrimage received an earnest [62] that we should now be light, whilst as yet we are saved by hope,[63] and are the children of light, and the children of the day—not the children of the night nor of the darkness, which yet we have been.[64] Betwixt whom and us, in this as yet uncertain state of human knowledge, Thou only dividest, who provest our hearts[65] and callest the light day, and the darkness night.[66] For who discerneth us but Thou? But what have we that we have not received of Thee? [67] Out of the same lump vessels unto honor, of which others also are made to dishonor.[68]

CHAPTER XV

ALLEGORICAL EXPLANATION OF THE FIRMAMENT AND UPPER WORKS, VER. 6

Or who but Thou, our God, made for us that firmament [69] of authority over us in Thy divine Scripture? As it is said, For heaven shall be folded up like a scroll;[70] and now it is extended over us like a skin.[71] For Thy divine Scripture is of more sublime authority, since those mortals through whom Thou didst dispense it unto us underwent mortality. And Thou knowest, O Lord, Thou knowest, how Thou with skins didst clothe men[72] when by sin they became mortal. Whence as a skin hast Thou stretched out the firmament of Thy Book; that is to say, Thy harmonious words, which by the ministry of mortals Thou hast spread over us. For by their very death is that solid firmament of authority in Thy discourses set forth by them more sublimely extended above all things that are under it, which, while they were living here, was not so eminently extended. Thou hadst

[51] *Ibid.* 4   [52] *Ibid.* 5   [53] Ps. cxix. 105   [54] Job xiv. 13   [55] Eph. ii. 3, and v. 8   [56] Rom. viii. 10   [57] Cant. ii. 17   [58] Ps. v. 3   [59] Ps. xxx. 12   [60] Ps. xliii. 5   [61] Rom. viii. 11   [62] 2 Cor. i. 22   [63] Rom. viii. 24   [64] Eph. v. 8, and 1 Thess. v. 5   [65] Ps. viii. 9   [66] Gen. i. 5   [67] 1 Cor. iv. 7   [68] Rom. ix. 21   [69] Gen. i. 6   [70] Isa. xxxiv. 4, and Rev. vi. 14   [71] Ps. civ. 2   [72] Gen. iii. 21

not as yet spread abroad the heaven like a skin; Thou hadst not as yet noised everywhere the report of their deaths.

Let us look, O Lord, upon the heavens, the work of Thy fingers;[73] clear from our eyes that mist with which Thou hast covered them. There is that testimony of Thine which giveth wisdom unto the little ones.[74] Perfect, O my God, Thy praise out of the mouth of babes and sucklings.[75] Nor have we known any other books so destructive to pride, so destructive to the enemy and the defender,[76] who resisteth Thy reconciliation in defence of his own sins. I know not, O Lord, I know not other such pure[77] words which so persuade me to confession, and make my neck submissive to Thy yoke, and invite me to serve Thee for nought. Let me understand these things, good Father. Grant this to me, placed under them; because Thou hast established these things for those placed under them.

Other waters there be above this firmament, I believe immortal, and removed from earthly corruption. Let them praise Thy Name—those super-celestial people, Thine angels, who have no need to look up at this firmament, or by reading to attain the knowledge of Thy Word—let them praise Thee. For they always behold Thy face,[78] and therein read without any syllables in time what Thy eternal will willeth. They read, they choose, they love. They are always reading; and that which they read never passeth away. For, by choosing and by loving, they read the very unchangeableness of Thy counsel. Their book is not closed, nor is the scroll folded up,[79] because Thou Thyself art this to them, yea, and art so eternally; because Thou hast appointed them above this firmament, which Thou hast made firm over the weakness of the lower people, where they might look up and learn Thy mercy, announcing in time Thee who hast made times. For Thy mercy, O Lord, is in the heavens, and Thy faithfulness reacheth unto the clouds.[80] The clouds pass away, but the heaven remaineth. The preachers of Thy Word pass away from this life into another; but Thy Scripture is spread abroad over the people, even to the end of the world. Yea, both heaven and earth shall pass away, but Thy Words shall not pass away.[81] Because the scroll shall be rolled together,[79] and the grass over which it was spread shall with its goodliness pass away; but Thy Word remaineth for ever,[82] which now appeareth unto us in the dark image of the clouds, and through the glass of the heavens, not as it is;[83] because we also, although we be the well-beloved of Thy Son, yet it hath not yet appeared what we shall be.[84] He looketh through the lattice[85] of our flesh, and He is fair-speaking, and hath inflamed us, and we run after His odors.[86] But when He shall appear, then shall we be like Him, for we shall see Him as He is.[84] As He is, O Lord, shall we see Him, although the time be not yet.

---

[73] Ps. viii. 3　　[74] Ps. xix. 7　　[75] Ps. viii. 2　　[76] He alludes to the Manichaeans [77] Ps. xix. 8　　[78] Matt. xviii. 10　　[79] Isa. xxxiv. 4　　[80] Ps. xxxvi. 5　　[81] Matt. xxiv. 35　　[82] Isa. xl. 6-8　　[83] 1 Cor. xiii. 12　　[84] 1 John iii. 2　　[85] Cant. ii. 9　　[86] Cant. i. 3

CHAPTER XVI

THAT NO ONE BUT THE UNCHANGEABLE LIGHT KNOWS HIMSELF

For altogether as Thou art, Thou only knowest, Who art unchangeably, and knowest unchangeably, and willest unchangeably. And Thy Essence Knoweth and Willeth unchangeably; and Thy Knowledge Is, and Willeth unchangeably; and Thy Will Is, and Knoweth unchangeably. Nor doth it appear just to Thee, that as the Unchangeable Light knoweth Itself, so should It be known by that which is enlightened and changeable. Therefore unto Thee is my soul as land where no water is,[87] because as it cannot of itself enlighten itself, so it cannot of itself satisfy itself. For so is the fountain of life with Thee, like as in Thy light we shall see light.[88]

CHAPTER XVII

ALLEGORICAL EXPLANATION OF THE SEA AND THE FRUIT-BEARING EARTH—VERSES 9 AND 11

Who hath gathered the embittered together into one society? For they have all the same end, that of temporal and earthly happiness, on account of which they do all things, although they may fluctuate with an innumerable variety of cares. Who, O Lord, unless Thou, saidst, Let the waters be gathered together into one place, and let the dry land appear,[89] which thirsteth after Thee? [90] For the sea also is Thine, and Thou hast made it, and Thy hands prepared the dry land.[91] For neither is the bitterness of men's wills, but the gathering together of waters called sea; for Thou even curbest the wicked desires of men's souls, and fixest their bounds, how far they may be permitted to advance,[92] and that their waves may be broken against each other; and thus dost Thou make it a sea, by the order of Thy dominion over all things.

But as for the souls that thirst after Thee, and that appear before Thee (being by other bounds divided from the society of the sea), them Thou waterest by a secret and sweet spring, that the earth may bring forth her fruit,[93] and, Thou, O Lord God, so commanding, our soul may bud forth works of mercy according to their kind [94]—loving our neighbor in the relief of his bodily necessities, having seed in itself according to its likeness, when from our infirmity we compassionate even to the relieving of the needy; helping them in a like manner as we would that help should be brought unto us if we were in a like need; not only in the things that are easy, as in herb yielding seed, but also in the protection of our assistance, in our very strength, like the tree yielding fruit; that is, a good turn in

---

[87] Ps. lxiii. 1   [88] Ps. xxxvi. 9   [89] Gen. i. 9   [90] Ps. cxliii. 6, and lxiii. 1   [91] Ps. xcv. 5   [92] Ps. civ. 9, and Job xxxviii. 11, 12   [93] Gen. i. 11   [94] Ps. lxxxv. 11

delivering him who suffers an injury from the hand of the powerful, and in furnishing him with the shelter of protection by the mighty strength of just judgment.

CHAPTER XVIII

Thus, O Lord, thus I beseech Thee, let there arise, as Thou makest, as Thou givest joy and ability—let truth spring out of the earth, and right-eousness look down from heaven,[94] and let there be lights in the firma-ment.[95] Let us break our bread to the hungry, and let us bring the house-less poor to our house.[96] Let us clothe the naked, and despise not those of our own flesh.[96] These fruits having sprung forth from the earth, behold, because it is good;[97] and let our temporary light burst forth;[98] and let us, from this inferior fruit of action, possessing the delights of contemplation and of the Word of Life above, let us appear as lights in the world,[99] clinging to the firmament of Thy Scripture. For therein Thou makest it plain unto us, that we may distinguish between things intelligible and things of sense, as if between the day and the night; or between souls, given, some to things intellectual, others to things of sense; so that now not Thou only in the secret of Thy judgment, as before the firmament was made, dividest between the light and the darkness, but Thy spiritual chil-dren also, placed and ranked in the same firmament (Thy grace being manifest throughout the world), may give light upon the earth, and divide between the day and night, and be for signs of times; because old things have passed away, and behold all things are become new;[100] and because our salvation is nearer than when we believed;[101] and because the night is far spent, the day is at hand;[101] and because Thou wilt crown Thy year with blessing,[102] sending the laborers of Thy goodness into Thy harvest,[103] in the sowing of which others have labored, sending also into another field, whose harvest shall be in the end.[104] Thus Thou grantest the prayers of him that asketh, and blessest the years of the just;[105] but Thou art the same, and in Thy years which fail not [106] Thou preparest a garner for our passing years. For by an eternal counsel Thou dost in their proper seasons bestow upon the earth heavenly blessings.

For, indeed, to one is given by the Spirit the word of wisdom, as if the greater light, on account of those who are delighted with the light of mani-fest truth, as in the beginning of the day; but to another the word of knowledge by the same Spirit, as if the lesser light; to another faith; to another the gift of healing; to another the working of miracles; to another prophecy; to another the discerning of spirits; to another divers kinds of

---

[95] Gen. i. 14   [96] Isa. lviii. 7   [97] Gen. i. 12   [98] Isa. lviii. 8   [99] Phil. ii. 15
[100] 2 Cor. v. 17   [101] Rom. xiii. 11, 12   [102] Ps. lxv. 11   [103] Matt. ix. 38   [104] Matt. xiii. 39   [105] Prov. x. 6   [106] Ps. cii. 27

tongues. And all these as stars. For all these worketh the one and self-same Spirit, dividing to every man his own as He willeth;[107] and making stars appear manifestly, to profit withal.[108] But the word of knowledge, wherein are contained all sacraments,[109] which are varied in their periods like the moon, and the other conceptions of gifts, which are successively reckoned up as stars, inasmuch as they come short of that splendor of wisdom in which the fore-mentioned day rejoices, are only for the beginning of the night. For they are necessary to such as he Thy most prudent servant could not speak unto as unto spiritual, but as unto carnal [110]—even he who speaketh wisdom among those that are perfect.[111] But the natural man, as a babe in Christ—and a drinker of milk—until he be strengthened for solid meat,[112] and his eye be enabled to look upon the Sun, let him not dwell in his own deserted night, but let him be contented with the light of the moon and the stars. Thou reasonest these things with us, our All-wise God, in Thy Book, Thy firmament, that we may discern all things in an admirable contemplation, although as yet in signs, and in times, and in days, and in years.

CHAPTER XIX

ALL MEN SHOULD BECOME LIGHTS IN THE FIRMAMENT OF HEAVEN

But first, Wash you, make you clean; put away iniquity from your souls, and from before mine eyes, that the dry land may appear. Learn to do well; judge the fatherless; plead for the widow,[113] that the earth may bring forth the green herb for meat, and the tree bearing fruit;[114] and come let us reason together, saith the Lord,[115] that there may be lights in the firmament of heaven, and that they may shine upon the earth.[116] That rich man asked of the good Master what he should do to attain eternal life.[117] Let the good Master, whom he thought a man, and nothing more, tell him (but He is good because He is God)—let Him tell him, that if he would enter into life he must keep the commandments;[118] let him banish from himself the bitterness of malice and wickedness;[119] let him not kill, nor commit adultery, nor steal, nor bear false witness; that the dry land may appear, and bud forth the honoring of father and mother, and the love of our neighbor.[120] All these, saith he, have I kept.[121] Whence, then, are there so many thorns, if the earth be fruitful? Go, root up the woody thicket of avarice; sell that thou hast, and be filled with fruit by giving to the poor, and thou shalt have treasure in heaven; and follow the Lord if thou wilt be perfect,[122] coupled with those amongst whom He speaketh wisdom, Who knoweth what to distribute to the day and to the night, that

---

[107] I Cor. xii. 8-11   [108] I Cor. xii. 7   [109] I Cor. xiii. 2   [110] I Cor. iii. 1
[111] I Cor. ii. 6   [112] I Cor. iii. 2, and Heb. v. 12   [113] Isa. i. 16, 19   [114] Gen. i. II, 30
[115] Isa. i. 18   [116] Gen. i. 15   [117] Matt. xix. 16   [118] Ibid. 17   [119] I Cor. v. 8
[120] Matt. xix. 16-19   [121] Ibid. 20   [122] Ibid. 21

thou also mayest know it, that for thee also there may be lights in the firmament of heaven, which will not be unless thy heart be there;[123] which likewise also will not be unless thy treasure be there, as thou hast heard from the good Master. But the barren earth was grieved,[124] and the thorns choked the word.[125]

But you, chosen generation,[126] you weak things of the world, who have forsaken all things that you might follow the Lord, go after Him, and confound the things which are mighty;[127] go after Him, ye beautiful feet,[128] and shine in the firmament,[129] that the heavens may declare His glory, dividing between the light of the perfect, though not as of the angels, and the darkness of the little, though not despised ones. Shine over all the earth, and let the day, lightened by the sun, utter unto day the word of wisdom; and let night, shining by the moon, announce unto night the word of knowledge.[130] The moon and the stars shine for the night, but the night obscureth them not, since they illumine it in its degree. For behold God (as it were) saying, "Let there be lights in the firmament of the heaven." There came suddenly a sound from heaven, as it had been the rushing of a mighty wind, and there appeared cloven tongues like as of fire, and it sat upon each of them.[131] And there were made lights in the firmament of heaven, having the word of life.[132] Run ye to and fro everywhere, ye holy fires, ye beautiful fires; for ye are the light of the world, nor are ye put under a bushel.[133] He to whom ye cleave is exalted, and hath exalted you. Run ye to and fro, and be known unto all nations.

CHAPTER XX

CONCERNING REPTILES AND FLYING CREATURES (VER. 20)— THE SACRAMENT OF BAPTISM BEING REGARDED

Let the sea also conceive and bring forth your works, and let the waters bring forth the moving creatures that have life.[134] For ye, who take forth the precious from the vile,[135] have been made the mouth of God, through which He saith, "Let the waters bring forth," not the living creature which the earth bringeth forth, but the moving creature having life, and the fowls that fly above the earth. For Thy sacraments, O God, by the ministry of Thy holy ones, have made their way amid the billows of the temptations of the world, to instruct the Gentiles in Thy Name, in Thy Baptism. And amongst these things, many great works of wonder have been wrought, like great whales; and the voices of Thy messengers flying above the earth, near to the firmament of Thy Book; that being set over them as an authority, under which they were to fly whithersoever they were to go. For there is no speech, nor language, where their voice is not heard;

---

[123] Matt. vi. 21   [124] Matt. xix. 22   [125] Matt. xiii. 7, 22   [126] I Pet. ii. 9   [127] I Cor. i. 27   [128] Isa. lii. 7   [129] Dan. xii. 3   [130] Ps. xix.   [131] Acts ii. 3   [132] I John i. 1   [133] Matt. v. 14   [134] Gen. i. 20   [135] Jer. xv. 19

seeing their sound [136] hath gone through all the earth, and their words to the end of the world, because Thou, O Lord, hast multiplied these things by blessing.[137]

Whether do I lie, or do I mingle and confound, and not distinguish between the clear knowledge of these things that are in the firmament of heaven, and the corporeal works in the undulating sea and under the firmament of heaven? For of those things whereof the knowledge is solid and defined, without increase by generation, as it were lights of wisdom and knowledge, yet of these self-same things the material operations are many and varied; and one thing in growing from another is multiplied by Thy blessing, O God, who hast refreshed the fastidiousness of mortal senses; so that in the knowledge of our mind, one thing may, through the motions of the body, be in many ways set out and expressed. These sacraments have the waters brought forth; but through Thy Word. The wants of the people estranged from the eternity of Thy truth have produced them, but through Thy Gospel; because the waters themselves have cast them forth, the bitter weakness of which was the cause of these things being sent forth in Thy Word.

Now all things are fair that Thou hast made, but behold, Thou art inexpressibly fairer who hast made all things; from whom had not Adam fallen, the saltness of the sea would never have flowed from him—the human race so profoundly curious, and boisterously swelling, and restlessly moving; and thus there would be no need that Thy dispensers should work in many waters, in a corporeal and sensible manner, mysterious doings and sayings. For so these creeping and flying creatures now present themselves to my mind, whereby men, instructed, initiated, and subjected by corporeal sacraments, should not further profit, unless their soul had a higher spiritual life, and unless, after the word of admission, it looked forwards to perfection.

CHAPTER XXI

CONCERNING THE LIVING SOUL, BIRDS, AND FISHES (VER. 24)— THE SACRAMENT OF THE EUCHARIST BEING REGARDED

And hereby, in Thy Word, not the depth of the sea, but the earth parted from the bitterness of the waters, bringeth forth not the creeping and flying creature that hath life,[134] but the living soul itself.[138] For now hath it no longer need of baptism, as the heathen have, and as itself had when it was covered with the waters—for no other entrance is there into the kingdom of heaven,[139] since Thou hast appointed that this should be the entrance—nor does it seek great works of miracles by which to cause faith; for it is not such that, unless it shall have seen signs and wonders, it will not believe,[140] when now the faithful earth is separated from the waters of

[136] Ps. xix. 3, 4   [137] Gen. i. 4   [138] Gen. ii. 7   [139] John iii. 5   [140] John iv. 48

the sea, rendered bitter by infidelity; and tongues are for a sign, not to those that believe, but to those that believe not.[141] Nor then doth the earth, which Thou hast founded above the waters,[142] stand in need of that flying kind which at Thy word the waters brought forth. Send Thy word forth into it by Thy messengers. For we relate their works, but it is Thou who workest in them, that in it they may work out a living soul. The earth bringeth it forth, because the earth is the cause that they work these things in the soul; as the sea has been the cause that they wrought upon the moving creatures that have life, and the fowls that fly under the firmament of heaven, of which the earth hath now no need; although it feeds on the fish which was taken out of the deep, upon that table which Thou hast prepared in the presence of those that believe.[143] For therefore He was raised from the deep, that He might feed the dry land; and the fowl, though bred in the sea, is yet multiplied upon the earth. For of the first preachings of the Evangelists, the infidelity of men was the prominent cause; but the faithful also are exhorted, and are manifoldly blessed by them day by day. But the living soul takes its origin from the earth, for it is not profitable, unless to those already among the faithful, to restrain themselves from the love of this world, that so their soul may live unto Thee, which was dead while living in pleasures[144]—in death-bearing pleasures, O Lord, for Thou art the vital delight of the pure heart.

Now, therefore, let Thy ministers work upon the earth—not as in the waters of infidelity, by announcing and speaking by miracles, and sacraments, and mystic words; in which ignorance, the mother of admiration, may be intent upon them, in fear of those hidden signs. For such is the entrance unto the faith for the sons of Adam forgetful of Thee, while they hide themselves from Thy face,[145] and become a darksome deep. But let Thy ministers work even as on the dry land, separated from the whirlpools of the great deep; and let them be an example unto the faithful, by living before them, and by stimulating them to imitation. For thus do men hear not with an intent to hear merely, but to act also. Seek the Lord, and your soul shall live,[146] that the earth may bring forth the living soul. Be not conformed to this world.[147] Restrain yourselves from it; the soul lives by avoiding those things which it dies by affecting. Restrain yourselves from the unbridled wildness of pride, from the indolent voluptuousness of luxury, and from the false name of knowledge;[148] so that wild beasts may be tamed, the cattle subdued, and serpents harmless. For these are the motions of the mind in allegory; that is to say, the haughtiness of pride, the delight of lust, and the poison of curiosity are the motions of the dead soul; for the soul dies not so as to lose all motion, because it dies by forsaking the fountain of life,[149] and so is received by this transitory world, and is conformed unto it.

---

[141] 1 Cor. xiv. 22   [142] Ps. cxxxvi. 6   [143] Ps. xxiii. 5   [144] 1 Tim. v. 6   [145] Gen. iii. 8   [146] Ps. lxix. 32   [147] Rom. xii. 2   [148] 1 Tim. vi. 20   [149] Jer. ii. 13

But Thy Word, O God, is the fountain of eternal life, and passeth not away; therefore this departure is kept in check by Thy word when it is said unto us, "Be not conformed unto this world," [150] so that the earth may bring forth a living soul in the fountain of life—a soul restrained in Thy Word, by Thy Evangelists, by imitating the followers of Thy Christ.[151] For this is after his kind; because a man is stimulated to emulation by his friend. "Be ye," saith he, "as I am, for I am as you are." [152] Thus in the living soul shall there be good beasts, in gentleness of action. For Thou hast commanded, saying, Go on with thy business in meekness, and thou shalt be beloved by all men;[153] and good cattle, which neither if they eat, shall they over-abound, nor if they do not eat, have they any want;[154] and good serpents, not destructive to do hurt, but wise[155] to take heed; and exploring only so much of this temporal nature as is sufficient that eternity may be clearly seen, being understood by the things that are.[156] For these animals are subservient to reason, when, being kept in check from a deadly advance, they live, and are good.

CHAPTER XXII

HE EXPLAINS THE DIVINE IMAGE (VER. 26) OF THE RENEWAL OF THE MIND

For behold, O Lord our God, our Creator, when our affections have been restrained from the love of the world, by which we died by living ill, and began to be a living soul by living well; and Thy word which Thou spakest by Thy apostle is made good in us, "Be not conformed to this world;" next also follows that which Thou presently subjoinedst, saying, "But be ye transformed by the renewing of your mind" [150]—not now after your kind, as if following your neighbor who went before you, nor as if living after the example of a better man (for Thou hast not said, "Let man be made after his kind," but, "Let us make man in our image, after our like-ness"),[157] that we may prove what Thy will is. For to this purpose said that dispenser of Thine—begetting children by the gospel [158]—that he might not always have them babes, whom he would feed on milk, and cherish as a nurse;[159] "be ye transformed," saith He, "by the renewing of your mind, that he may prove what is that good, and acceptable, and per-fect will of God." [160] Therefore Thou sayest not, "Let man be made," but, "Let us make man." Nor sayest Thou, "after his kind," but, after "our image" and "likeness." Because, being renewed in his mind, and beholding and apprehending Thy truth, man needeth not man as his director[161] that he may imitate his kind; but by Thy direction proveth what is that good, and acceptable, and perfect will of Thine. And Thou teachest him, now made capable, to perceive the Trinity of the Unity, and the Unity of the

---

[150] Rom. xii. 2   [151] I Cor. xi. I   [152] Gal. iv. 12   [153] Ecclus. iii. 17   [154] I Cor. viii. 8   [155] Matt. x. 16   [156] Rom. i. 20   [157] Gen. i. 26   [158] I Cor. iv. 15   [159] I Thess. ii. 7   [160] Rom. xii. 2   [161] Jer. xxxi. 34

Trinity. And therefore this being said in the plural, "Let us make man," it is yet subjoined in the singular, "and God made man;" and this being said in the plural, "after our likeness," is subjoined in the singular, "after the image of God." [162] Thus is man renewed in the knowledge of God, after the image of Him that created him; [163] and being made spiritual, he judgeth all things—all things that are to be judged—yet he himself is judged of no man.[164]

CHAPTER XXIII

THAT TO HAVE POWER OVER ALL THINGS (VER. 26)
IS TO JUDGE SPIRITUALLY OF ALL

But that he judgeth all things answers to his having dominion over the fish of the sea, and over the fowls of the air, and over all cattle and wild beasts, and over all the earth, and over every creeping thing that creepeth upon the earth. For this he doth by the discernment of his mind, whereby he perceiveth the things of the Spirit of God; [165] whereas, otherwise, man being placed in honor, had no understanding, and is compared unto the brute beasts, and is become like unto them.[166] In Thy Church, therefore, O our God, according to Thy grace which Thou hast accorded unto it, since we are Thy workmanship created in good works,[167] there are not only those who are spiritually set over, but those also who are spiritually subjected to those placed over them; for in this manner hast Thou made man, male and female,[162] in Thy grace spiritual, where, according to the sex of body, there is not male and female, because neither Jew nor Greek, nor bond nor free.[168] Spiritual persons, therefore, whether those that are set over, or those who obey, judge spiritually; not of that spiritual knowledge which shines in the firmament, for they ought not to judge as to an authority so sublime, nor doth it behove them to judge of Thy Book itself, although there be something that is not clear therein; because we submit our understanding unto it, and esteem as certain that even that which is shut up from our sight is rightly and truly spoken. For thus man, although now spiritual and renewed in the knowledge of God after His image that created him, ought yet to be the doer of the law, not the judge.[169] Neither doth he judge of that distinction of spiritual and carnal men, who are known to Thine eyes, O our God, and have not as yet made themselves manifest unto us by works, that by their fruits we may know them; [170] but Thou, O Lord, dost already know them, and Thou hast divided and hast called them in secret, before the firmament was made. Nor doth that man, though spiritual, judge the restless people of this world; for what hath he to do to judge them that are without,[171] knowing not which of

---

[162] Gen. i. 27   [163] Col. iii. 10   [164] 1 Cor. ii. 15   [165] 1 Cor. ii. 14   [166] Ps. xlix. 20
[167] Eph. ii. 10   [168] Gal. iii. 28   [169] Jas. iv. 11   [170] Matt. viii. 20   [171] 1 Cor. v. 12

them may afterwards come into the sweetness of Thy grace, and which continue in the perpetual bitterness of impiety?

Man, therefore, whom Thou hast made after Thine own image, received not dominion over the lights of heaven, nor over the hidden heaven itself, nor over the day and the night, which Thou didst call before the foundation of the heaven, nor over the gathering together of the waters, which is the sea; but he received dominion over the fishes of the sea, and the fowls of the air, and over all cattle, and over all the earth, and over all creeping things which creep upon the earth. For He judgeth and approveth what He findeth right, but disapproveth what He findeth amiss, whether in the celebration of those sacraments by which are initiated those whom Thy mercy searches out in many waters; or in that in which the Fish[f] Itself is exhibited, which, being raised from the deep, the devout earth feedeth upon; or in the signs and expressions of words, subject to the authority of Thy Book—such signs as burst forth and sound from the mouth, as it were flying under the firmament, by interpreting, expounding, discoursing, disputing, blessing, calling upon Thee, so that the people may answer, *Amen.* The vocal pronunciation of all these words is caused by the deep of this world, and the blindness of the flesh, by which thoughts cannot be seen, so that it is necessary to speak aloud in the ears; thus, although flying fowls be multiplied upon the earth, yet they derive their beginning from the waters. The spiritual man judges also by approving what is right and reproving what he finds amiss in the works and morals of the faithful, in their alms, as if in the earth bringing forth fruit; and he judges of the living soul, rendered living by softened affections, in chastity, in fastings, in pious thoughts; and of those things which are perceived through the senses of the body. For it is now said, that he should judge concerning those things in which he has also the power of correction.

CHAPTER XXIV

WHY GOD HAS BLESSED MEN, FISHES, FLYING CREATURES, AND NOT HERBS AND THE OTHER ANIMALS (VER. 28)

But what is this, and what kind of mystery is it? Behold, Thou blessest men, O Lord, that they may be fruitful and multiply, and replenish the earth;[172] in this dost Thou not make a sign unto us that we may understand something? Why hast Thou not also blessed the light, which Thou calledst day, nor the firmament of heaven, nor the lights, nor the stars, nor the earth, nor the sea? I might say, O our God, that Thou, who hast created us after Thine Image—I might say, that Thou hast willed to bestow

---

[f] The Greek word ἰχθύς, meaning fish, is made up of the first letters of 'Ιησοῦς Χριστὸς Θεοῦ Υἱὸς Σωτήρ, which means, Jesus Christ the Son of God, the Saviour.—Ed.
[172] Gen. i. 28

this gift of blessing especially upon man, hadst Thou not in like manner blessed the fishes and the whales, that they should be fruitful and multiply, and replenish the waters of the sea, and that the fowls should be multiplied upon the earth. Likewise might I say, that this blessing belonged properly unto such creatures as are propagated from their own kind, if I had found it in the shrubs, and the fruit trees, and beasts of the earth. But now is it not said either unto the herbs, or trees, or beasts, or serpents, "Be fruitful and multiply;" since all these also, as well as fishes, and fowls, and men, do by propagation increase and preserve their kind.

What, then, shall I say, O Thou Truth, my Light—that it was idly and vainly said? Not so, O Father of piety; far be it from a minister of Thy word to say this. But if I understand not what Thou meanest by that phrase, let my betters—that is, those more intelligent than I—use it better, in proportion as Thou, O my God, hast given to each to understand. But let my confession be also pleasing before Thine eyes, in which I confess to Thee that I believe, O Lord, that Thou hast not thus spoken in vain; nor will I be silent as to what this lesson suggests to me. For it is true, nor do I see what should prevent me from thus understanding the figurative sayings of Thy books. For I know a thing may be manifoldly signified by bodily expression which is understood in one manner by the mind; and that that may be manifoldly understood in the mind which is in one manner signified by bodily expression. Behold, the single love of God and of our neighbor, by what manifold sacraments and innumerable languages, and in each several language in how innumerable modes of speaking, it is bodily expressed. Thus do the young of the waters increase and multiply. Observe again, whosoever thou art who readest; behold what Scripture delivers, and the voice pronounces in one only way, "In the beginning God created heaven and earth;" is it not manifoldly understood, not by any deceit of error, but by divers kinds of true senses? Thus are the offspring of men "fruitful" and do "multiply."

If, therefore, we conceive of the natures of things, not allegorically, but properly, then does the phrase, "be fruitful and multiply," correspond to all things which are begotten of seed. But if we treat those words as taken figuratively (the which I rather suppose the Scripture intended, which does not superfluously attribute this benediction to the offspring of marine animals and man only), then do we find that "multitude" belongs also to creatures both spiritual and corporeal, as in heaven and in earth; and to souls both righteous and unrighteous, as in light and darkness; and to holy authors, through whom the law has been furnished unto us, as in the firmament which has been firmly placed betwixt waters and waters; and to the society of people yet endued with bitterness, as in the sea; and to the desire of holy souls, as in the dry land; and to works of mercy pertaining to this present life, as in the seed-bearing herbs and fruit-bearing trees; and to spiritual gifts shining forth for edification, as in the lights of heaven;

and to affections formed unto temperance, as in the living soul. In all these cases we meet with multitudes, abundance, and increase; but what shall thus "be fruitful and multiply," that one thing may be expressed in many ways, and one expression understood in many ways, we discover not, unless in signs corporeally expressed, and in things mentally conceived. We understand the signs corporeally pronounced as the generations of the waters, necessarily occasioned by carnal depth; but things mentally conceived we understand as human generations, on account of the fruitfulness of reason. And therefore do we believe that to each kind of these it has been said by Thee, O Lord, "Be fruitful and multiply." For in this blessing I acknowledge that a power and faculty has been granted unto us, by Thee, both to express in many ways what we understand but in one, and to understand in many ways what we read as obscurely delivered but in one. Thus are the waters of the sea replenished, which are not moved but by various significations; thus even with the human offspring is the earth also replenished, the dryness whereof appeareth in its desire, and reason ruleth over it.

CHAPTER XXV

HE EXPLAINS THE FRUITS OF THE EARTH
(VER. 29) OF WORKS OF MERCY

I would also say, O Lord my God, what the following Scripture reminds me of; and I will say it without fear. For I will speak the truth, Thou inspiring me as to what Thou willest that I should say out of these words. For by none other than Thy inspiration do I believe that I can speak the truth, since Thou art the Truth, but every man a liar.[173] And therefore he that speaketh a lie, he speaketh of his own;[174] therefore that I may speak the truth, I will speak of Thine. Behold, Thou hast given unto us for food every herb bearing seed, which is upon the face of all the earth, and every tree in which is the fruit of a tree yielding seed.[175] Nor to us only, but to all the fowls of the air, and to the beasts of the earth, and to all creeping things;[176] but unto the fishes, and great whales, Thou hast not given these things. Now we were saying, that by these fruits of the earth works of mercy were signified and figured in an allegory, which are provided for the necessities of this life out of the fruitful earth. Such an earth was the godly Onesiphorus, unto whose house Thou didst give mercy, because he frequently refreshed Thy Paul, and was not ashamed of his chain.[177] This did also the brethren, and such fruit did they bear, who out of Macedonia supplied what was wanting unto him.[178] But how doth he grieve for certain trees, which did not afford him the fruit due unto him, when he saith, "At my first answer no man stood with me, but all men forsook me: I pray

---

[173] Rom. iii. 4, and Ps. cxvi. 11   [174] John viii. 44   [175] Gen. i. 29   [176] *Ibid.* 30
[177] 2 Tim. i. 16   [178] 2 Cor. xi. 9

God that it may not be laid to their charge." [179] For these fruits are due to those who minister spiritual doctrine, through their understanding of the divine mysteries; and they are due to them as men. They are due to them, too, as to the living soul, supplying itself as an example in all continency; and due unto them likewise as flying creatures, for their blessings which are multiplied upon the earth, since their sound went out into all lands.[180]

CHAPTER XXVI

IN THE CONFESSING OF BENEFITS, COMPUTATION IS MADE NOT AS TO THE "GIFT," BUT AS TO THE "FRUIT"—THAT IS, THE GOOD AND RIGHT WILL OF THE GIVER

But they who are delighted with them are fed by those fruits; nor are they delighted with them whose god is their belly.[181] For neither in those that yield them are the things given the fruit, but in what spirit they give them. Therefore he who serves God and not his own belly,[182] I plainly see why he may rejoice; I see it, and I rejoice with him exceedingly. For he hath received from the Philippians those things which they had sent from Epaphroditus;[183] but yet I see why he rejoiced. For whereat he rejoices, upon that he feeds; for speaking in truth, "I rejoiced," saith he, "in the Lord greatly, that now at the last your care of me hath flourished again, wherein ye were also careful," [184] but it had become wearisome unto you. These Philippians, then, by protracted wearisomeness, had become enfeebled, and as it were dried up, as to bringing forth this fruit of a good work; and he rejoiceth for them, because they flourished again, not for himself, because they ministered to his wants. Therefore, adds he, "not that I speak in respect of want, for I have learned in whatsoever state I am therewith to be content. I know both how to be abased, and I know how to abound; everywhere and in all things I am instructed both to be full and to be hungry, both to abound and to suffer need. I can do all things through Christ which strengtheneth me." [185]

Whereat, then, dost thou rejoice in all things, O great Paul? Whereat dost thou rejoice? Whereon dost thou feed, O man, renewed in the knowledge of God, after the image of Him that created thee, thou living soul of so great continency, and thou tongue like flying fowls, speaking mysteries—for to such creatures is this food due—what is that which feeds thee? Joy. Let us hear what follows. "Notwithstanding," saith he, "ye have well done that ye did communicate with my affliction." [186] Hereat doth he rejoice, hereon doth he feed; because they have well done, not because his strait was relieved, who saith unto thee, "Thou hast enlarged me when I was in dis-

---

[179] 2 Tim. iv. 16   [180] Ps. xix. 4   [181] Phil. iii. 19   [182] Rom. xvi. 18   [183] Phil. iv. 18   [184] *Ibid.* 10   [185] *Ibid.* 11-13   [186] Phil. iv. 14

tress;" [187] because he knew both to abound and to suffer need, in Thee Who strengthenest him. For, saith he, "ye Philippians know also that in the beginning of the gospel, when I departed from Macedonia, no Church communicated with me as concerning giving and receiving, but ye only. For even in Thessalonica ye sent once and again unto my necessity." [188] Unto these good works he now rejoiceth that they have returned; and is made glad that they flourished again, as when a fruitful field recovers its greenness.

Was it on account of his own necessities that he said, "Ye have sent unto my necessity"? Rejoiceth he for that? Verily not for that. But whence know we this? Because he himself continues, "Not because I desire a gift, but I desire fruit." [189] From Thee, O my God, have I learned to distinguish between a "gift" and "fruit." A gift is the thing itself which he gives who bestows these necessaries, as money, food, drink, clothing, shelter, aid; but the fruit is the good and right will of the giver. For the good Master saith not only, "He that receiveth a prophet," but addeth, "in the name of a prophet." Not saith He only, "He that receiveth a righteous man," but addeth, "in the name of a righteous man." So, verily, the former shall receive the reward of a prophet, the latter that of a righteous man. Nor saith He only, "Whosoever shall give to drink unto one of these little ones a cup of cold water," but addeth, "in the name of a disciple;" and so concludeth, "Verily I say unto you, he shall in no wise lose his reward." [190] The gift is to receive a prophet, to receive a righteous man, to hand a cup of cold water to a disciple; but the fruit is to do this in the name of a prophet, in the name of a righteous man, in the name of a disciple. With fruit was Elijah fed by the widow, who knew that she fed a man of God, and on this account fed him; but by the raven was he fed with a gift. Nor was the inner man[191] of Elijah fed, but the outer only, which might also from want of such food have perished.

CHAPTER XXVII

MANY ARE IGNORANT AS TO THIS, AND ASK FOR MIRACLES, WHICH ARE SIGNIFIED UNDER THE NAMES OF "FISHES" AND "WHALES"

Therefore will I speak before Thee, O Lord, what is true, when ignorant men and infidels (for the initiating and gaining of whom the sacraments of initiation and great works of miracles are necessary, which we believe to be signified under the name of "fishes" and "whales") undertake that Thy servants should be bodily refreshed, or should be otherwise succored for this present life, although they may be ignorant wherefore this is to be done, and to what end; neither do the former feed the latter, nor the latter the former; for neither do the one perform these things through a holy and

[187] Ps. iv. 1   [188] Phil. iv. 15, 16   [189] *Ibid.* 17   [190] Matt. x. 41, 42   [191] 1 Kings xvii.

right intent, nor do the other rejoice in the gifts of those who behold not as yet the fruit. For on that is the mind fed wherein it is gladdened. And, therefore, fishes and whales are not fed on such food as the earth bringeth not forth until it had been separated and divided from the bitterness of the waters of the sea.

CHAPTER XXVIII

HE PROCEEDS TO THE LAST VERSE, "ALL THINGS ARE VERY GOOD"— THAT IS, THE WORK BEING ALTOGETHER GOOD

And Thou, O God, sawest everything that Thou hadst made, and behold it was very good.[192] So we also see the same, and behold all are very good. In each particular kind of Thy works, when Thou hadst said, "Let them be made," and they were made, Thou sawest that it was good. Seven times have I counted it written that Thou sawest that that which Thou madest was "good;" and this is the eighth, that Thou sawest all things that Thou hadst made, and behold they are not only good, but also "very good," as being now taken together. For individually they were only good, but all taken together they were both good and very good. All beautiful bodies also express this; for a body which consists of members, all of which are beautiful, is by far more beautiful than the several members individually are by whose well-ordered union the whole is completed, though these members also be severally beautiful.

CHAPTER XXIX

ALTHOUGH IT IS SAID EIGHT TIMES THAT "GOD SAW THAT IT WAS GOOD," YET TIME HAS NO RELATION TO GOD AND HIS WORD

And I looked attentively to find whether seven or eight times Thou sawest that Thy works were good, when they were pleasing unto Thee; but in Thy seeing I found no times, by which I might understand that thou sawest so often what Thou madest. And I said, "O Lord, is not this Thy Scripture true, since Thou art true, and being Truth hast set it forth? Why, then, dost Thou say unto me that in Thy seeing there are no times, while this Thy Scripture telleth me that what Thou madest each day, Thou sawest to be good; and when I counted them I found how often?" Unto these things Thou repliest unto me, for Thou art my God, and with strong voice tellest unto Thy servant in his inner ear, bursting through my deafness, and crying, "O man, that which My Scripture saith, I say; and yet doth that speak in time; but time has no reference to My Word, because My Word existeth in equal eternity with Myself. Thus those things which ye see through My Spirit, I see, just as those things which ye speak through My Spirit, I speak.

[192] Gen. i. 31

And so when ye see those things in time, I see them not in time; as when ye speak them in time, I speak them not in time."

CHAPTER XXX

HE REFUTES THE OPINIONS OF THE MANICHAEANS AND THE GNOSTICS CONCERNING THE ORIGIN OF THE WORLD

And I heard, O Lord my God, and drank up a drop of sweetness from Thy truth, and understood that there are certain men to whom Thy works are displeasing, who say that many of them Thou madest being compelled by necessity—such as the fabric of the heavens and the courses of the stars, and that Thou madest them not of what was Thine, but, that they were elsewhere and from other sources created; that Thou mightest bring together and compact and interweave, when from Thy conquered enemies Thou raisedst up the walls of the universe, that they, bound down by this structure, might not be able a second time to rebel against Thee. But, as to other things, they say Thou neither madest them nor compactedst them—such as all flesh and all very minute creatures, and whatsoever holdeth the earth by its roots; but that a mind hostile unto Thee, and another nature not created by Thee, and in everywise contrary unto Thee, did, in these lower places of the world, beget and frame these things.[193] Infatuated are they who speak thus, since they see not Thy works through Thy Spirit, nor recognise Thee in them.

CHAPTER XXXI

WE DO NOT SEE "THAT IT WAS GOOD" BUT THROUGH THE SPIRIT OF GOD, WHICH IS IN US

But as for those who through Thy Spirit see these things, Thou seest in them. When, therefore, they see that these things are good, Thou seest that they are good; and whatsoever things for Thy sake are pleasing, Thou art pleased in them; and those things which through Thy Spirit are pleasing unto us, are pleasing unto Thee in us. "For what man knoweth the things of a man, save the spirit of ·a man which is in him? Even so the things of God knoweth no man, but the Spirit of God. Now we," saith he, "have received not the spirit of the world, but the Spirit which is of God, that we might know the things that ·are freely given to us of God." [194] And I am reminded to say, "Truly, the things of God knoweth no man, but the Spirit of God; how, then, do we also know what things are given us by God?" It is answered unto me, "Because the things which we know by His Spirit, even these knoweth no man, but the Spirit of God. For, as it is rightly said

[193] He alludes in the above statement to the heretical notions of the Manichaeans.
[194] I Cor. ii. 12

unto those who were to speak by the Spirit of God, 'It is not ye that speak,' [195] so is it rightly said to them who know by the Spirit of God, 'It is not ye that know.' None the less, then, is it rightly said to those that see by the Spirit of God, 'It is not ye that see;' so whatever they see by the Spirit of God that it is good, it is not they, but God who 'sees that it is good.' " It is one thing, then, for a man to suppose that to be bad which is good, as the fore-named do; another, that what is good a man should see to be good (as Thy creatures are pleasing unto many, because they are good, whom, however, Thou pleasest not in them when they wish to enjoy them rather than enjoy Thee); and another, that when a man sees a thing to be good, God should in him see that it is good—that in truth He may be loved in that which He made, who cannot be loved unless by the Holy Ghost, which He hath given. Because the love of God is shed abroad in our hearts by the Holy Ghost which is given unto us;[196] by whom we see that whatsoever in any degree is, is good. Because it is from Him who Is not in any degree, but He Is that He Is.

CHAPTER XXXII

OF THE PARTICULAR WORKS OF GOD, MORE ESPECIALLY OF MAN

Thanks to Thee, O Lord. We behold the heaven and the earth, whether the corporeal part, superior and inferior, or the spiritual and corporeal creature; and in the embellishment of these parts, whereof the universal mass of the world or the universal creation consists, we see light made, and divided from the darkness. We see the firmament of heaven, whether the primary body of the world between the spiritual upper waters and the corporeal lower waters, or—because this also is called heaven—this expanse of air, through which wander the fowls of heaven, between the waters which are in vapors borne above them, and which in clear nights drop down in dew, and those which being heavy flow along the earth. We behold the waters gathered together through the plains of the sea; and the dry land both void and formed, so as to be visible and compact, and the matter of herbs and trees. We behold the lights shining from above—the sun to serve the day, the moon and the stars to cheer the night; and that by all these, times should be marked and noted. We behold on every side a humid element, fruitful with fishes, beasts, and birds; because the density of the air, which bears up the flights of birds, is increased by the exhalation of the waters. We behold the face of the earth furnished with terrestrial creatures, and man, created after Thy image and likeness, in that very image and likeness of Thee (that is, the power of reason and understanding) on account of which he was set over all irrational creatures. And as in his soul there is one power which rules by directing, another made subject that it

---

[195] Matt. x. 20   [196] Rom. v. 5

might obey, so also for the man a woman was corporeally made, who, in the mind of her rational understanding should also have a like nature, in the sex, however, of her body should be in like manner subject to the sex of her husband, as the appetite of action is subjected by reason of the mind, to conceive the skill of acting rightly. These things we behold, and they are severally good, and all very good.

CHAPTER XXXIII

THE WORLD WAS CREATED BY GOD OUT OF NOTHING

Let Thy works praise Thee, that we may love Thee; and let us love Thee, that Thy works may praise Thee, which have beginning and end from time—rising and setting, growth and decay, form and privation. They have therefore their successions of morning and evening, partly hidden, partly apparent; for they were made from nothing by Thee, not of Thee, nor of any matter not Thine, or which was created before, but of concreated matter (that is, matter at the same time created by Thee), because without any interval of time Thou didst form its formlessness. For since the matter of heaven and earth is one thing, and the form of heaven and earth another, Thou hast made the matter indeed of almost nothing, but the form of the world Thou hast formed of formless matter; both, however, at the same time, so that the form should follow the matter with no interval of delay.

CHAPTER XXXIV

HE BRIEFLY REPEATS THE ALLEGORICAL INTERPRETATION OF GENESIS (CH. I.), AND CONFESSES THAT WE SEE IT BY THE DIVINE SPIRIT

We have also examined what Thou willedst to be shadowed forth, whether by the creation, or the description of things in such an order. And we have seen that things severally are good, and all things very good,[197] in Thy Word, in Thine Only-Begotten, both heaven and earth, the Head and the body of the Church, in Thy predestination before all times, without morning and evening. But when Thou didst begin to execute in time the things predestinated, that Thou mightest make manifest things hidden, and adjust our disorders (for our sins were over us, and we had sunk into profound darkness away from Thee, and Thy good Spirit was borne over us to help us in due season), Thou didst both justify the ungodly,[198] and didst divide them from the wicked; and madest firm the authority of Thy Book between those above, who would be docile unto Thee, and those under, who would be subject unto them; and Thou didst collect the society of unbelievers into one conspiracy, in order that the zeal of the faithful might appear, and that they might bring forth works of mercy unto Thee,

[197] Gen. i. 31 [198] Rom. iv. 5

even distributing unto the poor earthly riches, to obtain heavenly. And after this didst Thou kindle certain lights in the firmament, Thy holy ones, having the word of life, and shining with an eminent authority preferred by spiritual gifts; and then again, for the instruction of the unbelieving Gentiles, didst Thou out of corporeal matter produce the sacraments and visible miracles, and sounds of words according to the firmament of Thy Book, by which the faithful should be blessed. Next didst Thou form the living soul of the faithful, through affections ordered by the vigor of continency; and afterwards, the mind subjected to Thee alone, and needing to imitate no human authority, Thou didst renew after Thine image and likeness; and didst subject its rational action to the excellency of the understanding, as the woman to the man; and to all Thy ministries, necessary for the perfecting of the faithful in this life, Thou didst will that, for their temporal uses, good things, fruitful in the future time, should be given by the same faithful. We behold all these things, and they are very good, because Thou dost see them in us—Thou who hast given unto us Thy Spirit, whereby we might see them, and in them love Thee.

CHAPTER XXXV

HE PRAYS GOD FOR THAT PEACE OF REST WHICH HATH NO EVENING

O Lord God, grant Thy peace unto us—for Thou hast supplied us with all things—the peace of rest, the peace of the Sabbath, which hath no evening. For all this most beautiful order of things, "very good" (all their courses being finished), is to pass away, for in them there was morning and evening.

CHAPTER XXXVI

THE SEVENTH DAY, WITHOUT EVENING AND SETTING, THE IMAGE OF ETERNAL LIFE AND REST IN GOD

But the seventh day is without any evening, nor hath it any setting, because Thou hast sanctified it to an everlasting continuance; that that which Thou didst after Thy works, which were very good, resting on the seventh day, although in unbroken rest Thou madest them, that the voice of Thy Book may speak beforehand unto us, that we also after our works (therefore very good, because Thou hast given them unto us) may repose in Thee also in the Sabbath of eternal life.

CHAPTER XXXVII

OF REST IN GOD, WHO EVER WORKETH, AND YET IS EVER AT REST

For even then shalt Thou so rest in us, as now Thou dost work in us; and thus shall that be Thy rest through us, as these are Thy works through us. But Thou, O Lord, ever workest, and art ever at rest. Nor seest Thou in time, nor movest Thou in time, nor restest Thou in time; and yet Thou makest the scenes of time, and the times themselves, and the rest which results from time.

CHAPTER XXXVIII

OF THE DIFFERENCE BETWEEN THE KNOWLEDGE OF GOD AND OF MEN, AND OF THE REPOSE WHICH IS TO BE SOUGHT FROM GOD ONLY

We therefore see those things which Thou madest, because they are; but they are because Thou seest them. And we see without that they are, and within that they are good, but Thou didst see them there, when made, where Thou didst see them to be made. And we were at another time moved to do well, after our hearts had conceived of Thy Spirit; but in the former time, forsaking Thee, we were moved to do evil; but Thou, the One, the Good God, hast never ceased to do good. And we also have certain good works, of Thy gift, but not eternal; after these we hope to rest in Thy great hallowing. But Thou, being the Good, needing no good, art ever at rest, because Thou Thyself art Thy rest. And what man will teach man to understand this? Or what angel, an angel? Or what angel, a man? Let it be asked of Thee, sought in Thee, knocked for at Thee; so, even so shall it be received, so shall it be found, so shall it be opened.[199] *Amen.*

[199] Matt. vii. 7

SOLILOQUIES

SOLILOQUIES

Introductory Note

The *Soliloquies,* written in 387 A.D., is Saint Augustine's first work as a Christian. Critics agree that it was composed shortly after his baptism when he and his small group of friends had retired to the famous retreat in Cassiciacum. Though he was strong in his new faith, there were still matters upon which he was confused, and to a degree this confusion is reflected in the *Soliloquies* which is cast in the form of a dialogue between himself and Reason. It was at a later date that Saint Augustine finally reached his position concerning the relation of faith and reason which has had such a profound influence on subsequent Christian thought. Hence the *Soliloquies* becomes all the more interesting in that it reveals the preliminary introspective struggle out of which the mature solution was born. Furthermore, the work is important because in it are the first seeds of his famous doctrine of "Divine Illumination" which lies at the heart of Saint Augustine's thought. The present treatise thus provides invaluable insight into the state of mind of the writer at the very threshold of his great career, when apparently he had no inkling of his future work in the Church and believed that he and his friends were to devote themselves in seclusion only to the contemplation of God.

SOLILOQUIES

BOOK ONE

1. As I HAD been long revolving with myself matters many and various, and had been for many days sedulously inquiring both concerning myself and my chief good, or what of evil there was to be avoided by me: suddenly some one addresses me, whether I myself, or some other one, within me or without, I know not. For this very thing is what I chiefly toil to know. There says then to me, let us call it REASON—Behold, assuming that you had discovered somewhat, to whose charge would you commit it, that you might go on with other things? *A.* To the memory, no doubt. *R.* But is the force of memory so great as to keep safely everything that may have been wrought out in thought? *A.* It hardly could, nay indeed it certainly could not. *R.* Therefore you must write. But what are you to do, seeing that your health recoils from the labor of writing? nor will these things bear to be dictated, seeing they consent not but with utter solitude. *A.* True. Therefore I am wholly at a loss what to say. *R.* Entreat of God health and help, that you may the better compass your desires, and commit to writing this very petition, that you may be the more courageous in the offspring of your brain. Then, what you discover sum up in a few brief conclusions. Nor care just now to invite a crowd of readers; it will suffice if these things find audience among the few of thine own city.

2. O God, Framer of the universe, grant me first rightly to invoke Thee; then to show myself worthy to be heard by Thee; lastly, deign to set me free. God, through whom all things, which of themselves were not, tend to be. God, who withholdest from perishing even that which seems to be mutually destructive. God, who, out of nothing, hast created this world, which the eyes of all perceive to be most beautiful. God, who dost not cause evil, but causest that it be not most evil. God, who to the few that flee for refuge to that which truly is, showest evil to be nothing. God, through whom the universe, even taking in its sinister side, is perfect. God, from whom things most widely at variance with Thee effect no dissonance, since worser things are included in one plan with better. God, who art loved, wittingly or unwittingly, by everything that is capable of loving. God, in whom are all things, to whom nevertheless neither the vileness of any creature is vile, nor its wickedness harmful, nor its error erroneous. God, who hast not willed that any but the pure should know the truth. God, the Father of truth, the Father of wisdom, the Father of the true and crowning life, the Father of blessedness, the Father of that which is good

and fair, the Father of intelligible light, the Father of our awakening and illumination, the Father of the pledge by which we are admonished to return to Thee.

3. Thee I invoke, O God, the Truth, in whom and from whom and through whom all things are true which anywhere are true. God, the Wisdom, in whom and from whom and through whom all things are wise which anywhere are wise. God, the true and crowning Life, in whom and from whom and through whom all things live, which truly and supremely live. God, the Blessedness, in whom and from whom and through whom all things are blessed, which anywhere are blessed. God, the Good and Fair, in whom and from whom and through whom all things are good and fair, which anywhere are good and fair. God, the intelligible Light, in whom and from whom and through whom all things intelligibly shine, which anywhere intelligibly shine. God, whose kingdom is that whole world of which sense has no ken. God, from whose kingdom a law is even derived down upon these lower realms. God, from whom to be turned away, is to fall: to whom to be turned back, is to rise again: in whom to abide, is to stand firm. God, from whom to go forth, is to die: to whom to return, is to revive: in whom to have our dwelling, is to live. God, whom no one loses, unless deceived: whom no one seeks, unless stirred up: whom no one finds, unless made pure. God, whom to forsake, is one thing with perishing; towards whom to tend, is one thing with living: whom to see is one thing with having. God, towards whom faith rouses us, hope lifts us up, with whom love joins us. God, through whom we overcome the enemy, Thee I entreat. God, through whose gift it is, that we do not perish utterly. God, by whom we are warned to watch. God, by whom we distinguish good from ill. God, by whom we flee evil, and follow good. God, through whom we yield not to calamities. God, through whom we faithfully serve and benignantly govern. God, through whom we learn those things to be another's which aforetime we accounted ours, and those things to be ours which we used to account as belonging to another. God, through whom the baits and enticements of evil things have no power to hold us. God, through whom it is that diminished possessions leave ourselves complete. God, through whom our better good is not subject to a worse. God, through whom death is swallowed up in victory. God, who dost turn us to Thyself. God, who dost strip us of that which is not, and arrayest us in that which is. God, who dost make us worthy to be heard. God, who dost fortify us. God, who leadest us into all truth. God, who speakest to us only good, who neither terrifiest into madness nor sufferest another so to do. God, who callest us back into the way. God, who leadest us to the door of life. God, who causest it to be opened to them that knock. God, who givest us the bread of life. God, through whom we thirst for the draught, which being drunk we never thirst. God, who dost convince the world of sin, of righteousness, and of judgment. God, through whom it is that we are not commoved by those who refuse to be-

lieve. God, through whom we disapprove the error of those, who think that
there are no merits of souls before Thee. God, through whom it comes that
we are not in bondage to the weak and beggarly elements. God, who cleansest us, and preparest us for Divine rewards, to me propitious come Thou.

4. Whatever has been said by me, Thou the only God, do Thou come to my
help, the one true and eternal substance, where is no discord, no confusion,
no shifting, no indigence, no death. Where is supreme concord, supreme
evidence, supreme steadfastness, supreme fullness, and life supreme. Where
nothing is lacking, nothing redundant. Where Begetter and Begotten are
one. God, whom all things serve, that serve, to whom is compliant every
virtuous soul. By whose laws the poles revolve, the stars fulfill their courses,
the sun vivifies the day, the moon tempers the night: and all the frame-
work of things, day after day by vicissitude of light and gloom, month after
month by waxings and wanings of the moon, year after year by orderly
successions of spring and summer and fall and winter, cycle after cycle by
accomplished concurrences of the solar course, and through the mighty orbs
of time, folding and refolding upon themselves, as the stars still recur to
their first conjunctions, maintains, so far as this merely visible matter
allows, the mighty constancy of things. God, by whose ever-during laws the
stable motion of shifting things is suffered to feel no perturbation, the
thronging course of circling ages is ever recalled anew to the image of immovable quiet: by whose laws the choice of the soul is free, and to the good
rewards and to the evil pains are distributed by necessities settled throughout the nature of everything. God, from whom distil even to us all benefits,
by whom all evils are withheld from us. God, above whom is nothing, beyond whom is nothing, without whom is nothing. God, under whom is the
whole, in whom is the whole, with whom is the whole. Who hast made man
after Thine image and likeness, which he discovers, who has come to know
himself. Hear me, hear me, graciously hear me, my God, my Lord, my
King, my Father, my Cause, my Hope, my Wealth, my Honor, my House,
my Country, my Health, my Light, my Life. Hear, hear, hear me graciously, in that way, all Thine own, which though known to few is to those
few known so well.

5. Henceforth Thee alone do I love, Thee alone I follow, Thee alone I seek,
Thee alone am I prepared to serve, for Thou alone art Lord by a just title,
of Thy dominion do I desire to be. Direct, I pray, and command whatever
Thou wilt, but heal and open my ears, that I may hear Thine utterances.
Heal and open my eyes, that I may behold Thy significations of command.
Drive delusion from me, that I may recognize Thee. Tell me whither I must
tend, to behold Thee, and I hope that I shall do all things Thou mayest
enjoin. O Lord, most merciful Father, receive, I pray, Thy fugitive; enough
already, surely, have I been punished, long enough have I served Thine
enemies, whom Thou hast under Thy feet, long enough have I been a sport
of fallacies. Receive me fleeing from these, Thy house-born servant, for did

not these receive me, though another Master's, when I was fleeing from Thee? To Thee I feel I must return: I knock; may Thy door be opened to me; teach me the way to Thee. Nothing else have I than the will: nothing else do I know than that fleeting and falling things are to be spurned, fixed and everlasting things to be sought. This I do, Father, because this alone I know, but from what quarter to approach Thee I do not know. Do Thou instruct me, show me, give me my provision for the way. If it is by faith that those find Thee, who take refuge with Thee, then grant faith: if by virtue, virtue: if by knowledge, knowledge. Augment in me, faith, hope, and charity. O goodness of Thine, singular and most to be admired!

6. I beseech Thee and once again I beg of Thee the means to beseech Thee. For if Thou abandon me, I perish: but Thou dost not abandon me because Thou art the Supreme Good whom no one ever sought with justice and could not discover. And all have sought Thee rightly to whom Thou hast given to seek Thee rightly. Grant me, Father, that I may seek Thee; keep me from error. Let me find none but Thee, when I seek Thee. I beg Thee, Father. But if I have in me any trace of desire, do Thou make me clean and fit to behold Thee. And with regard to the health of this my mortal body, so long as I do not know what advantage it has for me, or those whom I love, I commit it to Thee, Father, most wise and most good; and I shall pray for it when Thou dost advise me. Only this I beg of Thy exceeding mercy,—that Thou turnest me wholly to Thee and grantest that nothing stand in my way when I come to Thee. And do Thou command me, so long as I move and wear this body, that I be pure and high of soul and just and prudent, that I be the perfect lover and perceiver of Thy wisdom and worthy of Thy dwelling-place; and grant me to dwell in Thy most blessed kingdom. Amen. Amen.

7. *A.* Behold I have prayed to God. *R.* What then wouldst thou know? *A.* All these things which I have prayed for. *R.* Sum them up in brief. *A.* God and the soul, that is what I desire to know. *R.* Nothing more? *A.* Nothing whatever. *R.* Therefore begin to inquire. But first explain how, if God should be set forth to thee, thou wouldst be able to say, It is enough. *A.* I know not how He is to be so set forth to me as that I shall say, It is enough: for I believe not that I know anything in such wise as I desire to know God. *R.* What then are we to do? Dost thou not judge that first thou oughtest to know, what it is to know God sufficiently, so that arriving at that point, thou mayst seek no farther? *A.* So I judge, indeed: but how that is to be brought about, I see not. For what have I ever understood like to God, so that I could say, As I understand this, so would I fain understand God? *R.* Not having yet made acquaintance with God, whence hast thou come to know that thou knowest nothing like to God? *A.* Because if I knew anything like God, I should doubtless love it: but now I love nothing else than God and the soul, neither of which I know. *R.* Do you then not love your friends? *A.* Loving them, how can I otherwise than love the soul? *R.* Do

you then love gnats and bugs similarly? *A.* The animating soul I said I loved, not animals. *R.* Men are then either not your friends, or you do not love them. For every man is an animal, and you say that you do not love animals. *A.* Men are my friends, and I love them, not in that they are animals, but in that they are men, that is, in that they are animated by rational souls, which I love even in highwaymen. For I may with good right in any man love reason, even though I rightly hate him, who uses ill that which I love. Therefore I love my friends the more, the more worthily they use their rational soul, or certainly the more earnestly they desire to use it worthily.

8. *R.* I allow so much: but yet if any one should say to thee, I will give thee to know God as well as thou dost know Alypius. wouldst thou not give thanks, and say, It is enough? *A.* I should give thanks indeed: but I should not say, It is enough. *R.* Why, I pray? *A.* Because I do not even know God so well as I know Alypius, and yet I do not know Alypius well enough. *R.* Beware then lest shamelessly thou wouldest fain be satisfied in the knowledge of God, who hast not even such a knowledge of Alypius as satisfies. *A. Non sequitur.* For, comparing it with the stars, what is of lower account than my supper? and yet what I shall sup on to-morrow I know not: but in what sign the moon will be, I need take no shame to profess that I know. *R.* Is it then enough for thee to know God as well as thou dost know in what sign the moon will hold her course to-morrow? *A.* It is not enough, for this I test by the senses. But I do not know whether or not either God, or some hidden cause of nature may suddenly change the moon's ordinary course, which if it came to pass, would render false all that I had presumed. *R.* And believest thou that this may happen? *A.* I do not believe. But I at least am seeking what I may know, not what I may believe. Now everything that we know, we may with reason perhaps be said to believe, but not to know everything which we believe. *R.* In this matter therefore you reject all testimony of the senses? *A.* I utterly reject it. *R.* That friend of yours then, whom you say you do not yet know, is it by sense that you wish to know him or by intellectual perception? *A.* Whatever in him I know by sense, if indeed anything is known by sense, is both mean and sufficiently known. But that part which bears affection to me, that is, the mind itself, I desire to know intellectually. *R.* Can it, indeed, be known otherwise? *A.* By no means. *R.* Do you venture then to call your friend, your inmost friend, unknown to you? *A.* Why not venture? For I account most equitable that law of friendship, by which it is prescribed, that as one is to bear no less, so he is to bear no more affection to his friend than to himself. Since then I know not myself, what injury does he suffer, whom I declare to be unknown to me, above all since (as I believe) he does not even know himself? *R.* If then these things which thou wouldst fain know, are of such a sort as are to be intellectually attained, when I said it was shameless in thee to crave to know God, when thou knowest not even

Alypius, thou oughtest not to have urged to me the similitude of thy supper and the moon, if these things, as thou hast said, appertain to sense.

9. But let that go, and now answer to this: if those things which Plato and Plotinus have said concerning God are true, is it enough for thee to know God as they knew him? *A.* Even allowing that those things which they have said are true, does it follow at once that they knew them? For many copiously utter what they do not know, as I myself have said that I desired to know all those things for which I prayed, which I should not desire if I knew them already: yet I was none the less able to enumerate them all. For I have enumerated not what I intellectually comprehended, but things which I have gathered from all sides and entrusted to my memory, and to which I yield as ample a faith as I am able: but to know is another thing. *R.* Tell me, I pray, do you at least know in geometry what a line is? *A.* So much I certainly know. *R.* Nor in professing so do you stand in awe of the Academicians? *A.* In no wise. For they, as wise men, would not run the risk of erring: but I am not wise. Therefore as yet I do not shrink from professing the knowledge of those things which I have come to know. But if, as I desire, I should ever have attained to wisdom, I will do what I may find her to suggest. *R.* I except not thereto: but, I had begun to inquire, as you know a line, do you also know a ball, or, as they say, a sphere? *A.* I do. *R.* Both alike, or one more, one less? *A.* Just alike. I am altogether certain of both. *R.* Have you grasped these by the senses or the intellect? *A.* Nay, I have essayed the senses in this matter as a ship. For after they had carried me to the place I was aiming for, and I had dismissed them, and was now, as it were, left on dry ground, where I began to turn these things over in thought, the oscillations of the senses long continued to swim in my brain. Wherefore it seems to me that it would be easier to sail on dry land, than to learn geometry by the senses, although young beginners seem to derive some help from them. *R.* Then you do not hesitate to call whatever acquaintance you have with such things, Knowledge? *A.* Not if the Stoics permit, who attribute knowledge only to the Wise Man. Certainly I maintain myself to have the perception of these things, which they concede even to folly: but neither am I at all in any great fear of the Stoics: unquestionably I hold those things which thou hast questioned me of in knowledge: proceed now till I see to what end thou questionest me of them. *R.* Be not too eager, we are not pressed for time. But give strict heed, lest you should make some rash concession. I would fain give thee the joy of things wherein thou fearest not to slip, and dost thou enjoin haste, as in a matter of no moment? *A.* God grant the event as thou forecastest it. Therefore question at thy will, and rebuke me more sharply if I err so again.

10. *R.* It is then plain to you that a line cannot possibly be longitudinally divided into two? *A.* Plainly so. *R.* What of a cross-section? *A.* This, of course, is possible to infinity. *R.* But is it equally apparent that if, beginning with the centre, you make any sections you please of a sphere, no two

resulting circles will be equal? *A*. It is equally apparent. *R*. What are a line and a sphere? Do they seem to you to be identical, or somewhat different? *A*. Who does not see that they differ very much? *R*. If then you know this and that equally well, while yet, as you acknowledge, they differ widely from each other, there must be an indifferent knowledge of different things. *A*. Who ever disputed it? *R*. You, a little while ago. For when I asked thee what way of knowing God was in thy desire, such that thou couldst say, It is enough, thou didst answer that thou couldst not explain this, because thou hadst no perception held in such a way as that in which thou didst desire to perceive God, for that thou didst know nothing like God. What then? Are a line and sphere alike? *A*. Absurd. *R*. But I had asked, not what you knew such as God, but what you knew so as you desire to know God. For you know a line in such wise as you know a sphere, although the properties of a line are not those of a sphere. Wherefore answer whether it would suffice you to know God in such wise as you know that geometrical ball; that is, to be equally without doubt concerning God as concerning that.

11. *A*. Pardon me, however vehemently thou urge and argue, yet I dare not say that I wish so to know God as I know these things. For not only the objects of the knowledge, but the knowledge itself appears to be unlike. First, because the line and the ball are not so unlike, but that one science includes the knowledge of them both: but no geometrician has ever professed to teach God. Then, if the knowledge of God and of these things were equivalent, I should rejoice as much to know them as I am persuaded that I should rejoice if God were known by me. But now I hold these things in the deepest disdain in comparison with Him, so that sometimes it seems to me that if I understood Him, and that in that manner in which He can be seen, all these things would perish out of my knowledge: since even now by reason of the love of Him they scarce come into my mind. *R*. Allow that thou wouldst rejoice more and much more in knowing God than in knowing these things, yet not by a different perception of the things; unless we are to say that thou beholdest with a different vision the earth and the serenity of the skies, although the aspect of this latter soothes and delights thee far more than of the former. But unless your eyes are deceived, I believe that, if asked whether you are as well assured that you see earth as heaven, you ought to answer yes, although you are not as much delighted by the earth and her beauty as by the beauty and magnificence of heaven. *A*. I am moved, I confess, by this similitude, and am brought to allow that by how much earth differs in her kind from heaven, so much do those demonstrations of the sciences, true and certain as they are, differ from the intelligible majesty of God.

12. *R*. Thou art moved to good effect. For the Reason which is talking with thee promises so to demonstrate God to thy mind, as the sun demonstrates himself to the eyes. For the senses of the soul are as it were the eyes of the

mind; but all the certainties of the sciences are like those things which are brought to light by the sun, that they may be seen, the earth, for instance, and the things upon it: while God is Himself the Illuminator. Now I, Reason, am that in the mind, which the act of looking is in the eyes. For to have eyes is not the same as to look; nor again to look the same as to see. Therefore the soul has need of three distinct things: to have eyes, such as it can use to good advantage, to look, and to see. Sound eyes, that means the mind pure from all stain of the body, that is, now remote and purged from the lusts of mortal things: which, in the first condition, nothing else accomplishes for her than Faith. For what cannot yet be shown forth to her stained and languishing with sins, because, unless sound, she cannot see, if she does not believe that otherwise she will not see, she gives no heed to her health. But what if she believes that the case stands as I say, and that, if she is to see at all, she can only see on these terms, but despairs of being healed; does she not utterly contemn herself and cast herself away, refusing to comply with the prescriptions of the physician? *A.* Beyond doubt, above all because by sickness remedies must needs be felt as severe. *R.* Then Hope must be added to Faith. *A.* So I believe. *R.* Moreover, if she both believes that the case stands so, and hopes that she could be healed, yet loves not, desires not the promised light itself, and thinks that she ought meanwhile to be content with her darkness, which now, by use, has become pleasant to her; does she not none the less reject the physician? *A.* Beyond doubt. *R.* Therefore Charity must needs make a third. *A.* Nothing so needful. *R.* Without these three things therefore no mind is healed, so that it can see, that is, understand its God.

13. When therefore the mind has come to have sound eyes, what next? *A.* That she look. *R.* The mind's act of looking is Reason; but because it does not follow that every one who looks sees, a right and perfect act of looking, that is, one followed by vision, is called Virtue; for Virtue is either right or perfect Reason. But even the power of vision, though the eyes be now healed, has not force to turn them to the light, unless these three things abide. Faith, whereby the soul believes that thing, to which she is asked to turn her gaze, is of such sort, that being seen it will give blessedness; Hope, whereby the mind judges that if she looks attentively, she will see; Charity, whereby she desires to see and to be filled with the enjoyment of the sight. The attentive view is now followed by the very vision of God, which is the end of looking; not because the power of beholding ceases, but because it has nothing further to which it can turn itself: and this is the truly perfect virtue, Virtue arriving at its end, which is followed by the life of blessedness. Now this vision itself is that apprehension which is in the soul, compounded of the apprehending subject and of that which is apprehended: as in like manner seeing with the eyes results from the conjunction of the sense and the object of sense, either of which being withdrawn, seeing becomes impossible.

14. Therefore when the soul has obtained to see, that is, to apprehend God, let us see whether those three things are still necessary to her. Why should Faith be necessary to the soul, when she now sees? Or Hope, when she already grasps? But from Charity not only is nothing diminished; but rather it receives large increase. For when the soul has once seen that unique and unfalsified Beauty, she will love it the more, and unless she shall with great love have fastened her gaze thereon, nor any way declined from the view, she will not be able to abide in that most blessed vision. But while the soul is in this body, even though she most fully sees, that is, apprehends God; yet, because the bodily senses still have their proper effect, if they have no prevalency to mislead, yet they are not without a certain power to call in doubt, therefore that may be called Faith whereby these dispositions are resisted, and the opposing truth affirmed. Moreover, in this life, although the soul is already blessed in the apprehension of God; yet, because she endures many irksome pains of the body, she has occasion of hope that after death all these incommodities will have ceased to be. Therefore neither does Hope, so long as she is in this life, desert the soul. But when after this life she shall have wholly collected herself in God, Charity remains whereby she is retained there. For neither can she be said to have Faith that those things are true, when she is solicited by no interruption of falsities; nor does anything remain for her to hope, whereas she securely possesses the whole. Three things therefore pertain to the soul, that she be sane, that she behold, that she see. And other three, Faith, Hope, Charity, for the first and second of those three conditions are always necessary: for the third in this life all; after this life, Charity alone.

15. Now listen, so far as the present time requires, while from that similitude of sensible things I now teach also something concerning God. Namely, God is intelligible, not sensible, intelligible also are those demonstrations of the schools; nevertheless they differ very widely. For as the earth is visible, so is light; but the earth, unless illumined by light, cannot be seen. Therefore those things also which are taught in the schools, which no one who understands them doubts in the least to be absolutely true, we must believe to be incapable of being understood, unless they are illuminated by somewhat else, as it were a sun of their own. Therefore as in this visible sun we may observe three things: that he is, that he shines, that he illuminates: so in that God most far withdrawn whom thou wouldst fain apprehend, there are these three things: that He is, that He is apprehended, and that He makes other things to be apprehended. These two, God and thyself, I dare promise that I can teach thee to understand. But give answer how thou receivest these things, as probable, or as true? *A.* As probable certainly; and, as I must own, I have been hoping more: for excepting those two illustrations of the line and the globe, nothing has been said by thee which I should dare to say that I know. *R.* It is not to be wondered at: for nothing has been yet so set forth, as that it exacts of thee perception.

16. But why do we delay? Let us set out: but first let us see (for this comes first) whether we are in a sound state. *A*. Do thou see to it, if either in thyself or in me that hast any discernment of what is to be found; I will answer, being inquired of, to my best knowledge. *R*. Do you love anything besides the knowledge of God and yourself? *A*. I might answer, that I love nothing besides, having regard to my present feelings; but I should be safer to say that I do not know. For it hath often chanced to me, that when I believed I was open to nothing else, something nevertheless would come into the mind which stung me otherwise than I had presumed. So often, when something, conceived in thought, disturbed me little, yet when it came in fact it disquieted me more than I supposed: but now I do not see myself sensible to perturbation except by three things; by the fear of losing those whom I love, by the fear of pain, by the fear of death. *R*. You love, therefore, both a life associated with those dearest to you, and your own good health, and your bodily life itself: or you would not fear the loss of these. *A*. It is so, I acknowledge. *R*. Now therefore, the fact that all your friends are not with you, and that your health is not very firm, occasions you some uneasiness of mind. For that I see to be implied. *A*. Thou seest rightly; I am not able to deny it. *R*. How if you should suddenly feel and find yourself sound in health, and should see all whom you love and who love each other, enjoying in your company liberal ease? would you not think it right to give way in reasonable measure even to transports of joy? *A*. In a measure, undoubtedly. Nay, if these things, as thou sayest, bechanced me suddenly, how could I contain myself? how could I possibly even dissemble joy of such a sort? *R*. As yet, therefore, you are tossed about by all the diseases and perturbations of the mind. What shamelessness, then, that with such eyes you should wish to see such a Sun! *A*. Thy conclusion then is, that I am utterly ignorant how far I am advanced in health, how far disease has receded, or how far it remains. Suppose me to grant this.

17. *R*. Do you not see that these eyes of the body, even when sound, are often so smitten by the light of this visible sun, as to be compelled to turn away and to take refuge in their own obscurity? Now you are proposing to yourself what you are moved to seek, but are not proposing to yourself what you desire to see: and yet I would discuss this very thing with you, what advance you think we have made. Are you without desire of riches? *A*. This at least no longer chiefly. For, being now three and thirty years of age, for almost these fourteen years last past I have ceased to desire them, nor have I sought anything from them, if by chance they should be offered, beyond the necessities of life and such a use of them as agrees with the state of a freeman. A single book of Cicero has thoroughly persuaded me, that riches are in no wise to be craved, but that if they come in our way, they are to be with the utmost wisdom and caution administered. *R*. What of honors? *A*. I confess that it is only lately, and as it were yesterday, that

I have ceased to desire these. *R.* What of a wife? Are you not sometimes charmed by the image of a beautiful, modest, complying maiden, well lettered, or of parts that can easily be trained by you, bringing you too (being a despiser of riches) just so large a dowry as will relieve your leisure of all burden on her account? It is implied, moreover, that you have good hope of coming to no grief through her. *A.* However much thou please to portray her and adorn her with all manner of gifts, I have determined that nothing is so much to be avoided by me as such a bed-fellow: I perceive that nothing more saps the citadel of manly strength, whether of mind or body, than female blandishments and familiarities. Therefore, if (which I have not yet discovered) it appertains to the office of a wise man to desire offspring, whoever for this reason only comes into this connection, may appear to me worthy of admiration, but in no wise a model for imitation: for there is more peril in the essay, than felicity in the accomplishment. Wherefore, I believe, I am contradicting neither justice nor utility in providing for the liberty of my mind by neither desiring, nor seeking, nor taking a wife. *R.* I inquire not now what thou hast determined, but whether thou dost yet struggle, or hast indeed already overcome desire itself. For we are considering the soundness of thine eyes. *A.* Nothing of the kind do I any way seek, nothing do I desire; it is even with horror and loathing that I recall such things to mind. What more wouldst thou? And day by day does this benefit grow upon me: for the more I grow in the hope of beholding that supernal Beauty with the desire of which I glow, the more my love and delight is wholly converted thereto. *R.* What of pleasant viands? How much do you care for them? *A.* Those things which I have determined not to eat, tempt me not. As to those which I have not cut off, I allow that I take pleasure in their present use, yet so that without any disturbance of mind, either the sight or the taste of them may be withdrawn. And when they are entirely absent, no craving of them dares intrude itself to the disturbance of my thoughts. But no need to inquire concerning food or drink, or baths: so much of these do I seek to have, as is profitable for the confirmation of health.

18. *R.* Thou hast made great progress: yet those things which remain in order to the seeing of that light, very greatly impede. But I am aiming at something which appears to me very easy to be shown; that either nothing remains to us to be subdued, or that we have made no advance at all, and that the taint of all those things which we believed cut away remains. For I ask of thee, if thou wert persuaded that thou couldst live with the throng of those dearest to thee in the study and pursuit of wisdom on no other terms than as possessed of an estate ample enough to meet all your joint necessities; would you not desire and seek for wealth? *A.* I should. *R.* How, if it should also be clear, that you would be to many a master of wisdom, if your authority in teaching were supported by civil honor, and that even these your familiars would not be able to put a bridle on their cravings ex-

cept as they too were in honor, and that this could only accrue to them through your honors and dignity? would not honor then be a worthy object of desire, and of strenuous pursuit? *A.* It is as thou sayest. *R.* I do not consider the question of a wife; for perhaps no such necessity could arise of marrying one: although if it were certain that by her ample patrimony all those could be sustained whom thou wouldst fain have live at ease with thee in one place, and that moreover with her cordial consent, especially if she were of a family of such nobility as that through her those honors which you have just granted, in our hypothesis, to be necessary, could easily be attained, I do not know that it would be any part of your duty to contemn these advantages, thus obtained. *A.* But how could I hope for such things? 19. *R.* You speak as if I were now inquiring what you hope. I am not inquiring what, denied, delights not, but what delights, obtained. For an extinguished plague is one thing, a dormant plague another. And, as some wise men say, all pools are so unsound, that they always smell of every foul thing, although you do not always perceive this, but only when you stir them up. And there is a wide difference whether a craving is suppressed by hopelessness of compassing it, or is expelled by saneness of soul. *A.* Although I am not able to answer thee, never wilt thou, for all this, persuade me that in this affection of mind in which I now perceive myself to be, I have advantaged nothing. *R.* This, doubtless, appears so to thee, because although thou mightest desire these things, yet they would not seem to thee objects of desire on their own account, but for ulterior ends. *A.* That is what I was endeavoring to say: for when I desired riches, I desired them for this reason, that I might be rich. And those honors, the lust of which I have declared myself to have but even now thoroughly overcome, I craved by a mere delight in some intrinsic splendor I imputed to them; and nothing else did I expect in a wife, when I expected, than the reputable enjoyment of voluptuousness. Then there was in me a veritable craving for those things; now I utterly contemn them all: but if I cannot except through these find a passage to those things which in effect I desire, I do not pursue them as things to be embraced, but accept them as things to be allowed. *R.* A thoroughly excellent distinction: for neither do I impute unworthiness to the desire of any lower things that are sought on account of something else. 20. But I ask of thee, why thou dost desire, either that the persons whom thou affectest should live, or that they should live with thee. *A.* That together and concordantly we might inquire out God and our souls. For so, whichever first discovers aught, easily introduces his companions into it. *R.* What if these will not inquire? *A.* I would persuade them into the love of it. *R.* What if you could not, be it that they suppose themselves to have already found, or think that such things are beyond discovery, or that they are entangled in cares and cravings of other things? *A.* We will use our best endeavors, I with them, and they with me. *R.* What if even their presence impedes you in your inquiries? would you not choose and endeavor that they should not be with you, rather than be with you on such terms? *A.* I own it is as thou sayest. *R.* It is not therefore on its own account that you crave either their life or presence, but as an auxiliary in the discovery of wisdom? *A.* I thoroughly agree to that. *R.* Further: if you were certain that your own life were an impediment to your comprehension of wisdom, should you desire its continuance? *A.* I should utterly eschew it. *R.* Furthermore: if thou wert taught, that either in this body or after leaving it thou couldst equally well attain unto wisdom, wouldst thou care whether it was in this or another life that thou didst enjoy that which thou supremely affectest? *A.* If I ascertained that I was to experience nothing worse, which would lead me back from the point to which I had made progress, I should not care. *R.* Then thy present dread of death rests on the fear of being involved in some worse evil, whereby the Divine cognition may be borne away from thee. *A.* Not solely such a possible loss do I dread, if I have any right understanding of the fact, but also lest access should be barred me into those things which I am now eager to explore; although what I already possess, I believe will remain with me. *R.* Therefore not for the sake of this life in itself, but for the sake of wisdom thou dost desire the continuance of this life. *A.* It is the truth.

21. *R.* We have pain of body left, which perhaps moves thee of its proper force. *A.* Nor indeed do I grievously dread even that for any other reason than that it impedes me in my research. For although of late I have been grievously tormented with attacks of toothache, so that I was not suffered to revolve aught in my mind except such things as I have been engaged in learning; while, as the whole intensity of my mind was requisite for new advances, I was entirely restrained from making these: yet it seemed to me, that if the essential refulgence of Truth would disclose itself to me, I should either not have felt that pain, or certainly would have made no account of it. But although I have never had anything severer to bear, yet, often reflecting how much severer the pains are which I might have to bear, I am sometimes forced to agree with Cornelius Celsus, who says that the supreme good is wisdom, and the supreme evil bodily pain. For since, says he, we are composed of two parts, namely, mind and body, of which the former part, the mind, is the better, the body the worse; the highest good is the best of the better part, and the chiefest evil the worst of the inferior; now the best thing in the mind is wisdom, and the worst thing in the body is pain. It is concluded, therefore, and as I fancy, most justly, that the chief good of man is to be wise, and his chief evil, to suffer pain. *R.* We will consider this later. For perchance Wisdom herself, towards which we strive, will bring us to be of another mind. But if she should show this to be true, we will then not hesitate to adhere to this your present judgment concerning the highest good and the deepest ill.

22. Now let us inquire concerning this, what sort of lover of wisdom thou art, whom thou desirest to behold with most chaste view and embrace, and to

grasp her unveiled charms in such wise as she affords herself to no one, except to her few and choicest votaries. For assuredly a beautiful woman, who had kindled thee to ardent love, would never surrender herself to thee, if she had discovered that thou hadst in thy heart another object of affection; and shall that most chaste beauty of Wisdom exhibit itself to thee, unless thou art kindled for it alone? *A.* Why then am I still made to hang in wretchedness, and put off with miserable pining? Assuredly I have already made it plain that I love nothing else, since what is not loved for itself is not loved. Now I at least love Wisdom for herself alone, while as to other things, it is for her sake that I desire their presence or absence, such as life, ease, friends. But what measure can the love of that beauty have in which I not only do not envy others, but even long for as many as possible to seek it, gaze upon it, grasp it and enjoy it with me; knowing that our friendship will be the closer, the more thoroughly conjoined we are in the object of our love?

23. *R.* Such lovers assuredly it is, whom Wisdom ought to have. Such lovers does she seek, the love of whom has in it nothing but what is pure. But there are various ways of approach to her. For it is according to our soundness and strength that each one comprehends that unique and truest good. It is a certain ineffable and incomprehensible light of minds. Let this light of the common day teach us, as well as it can, concerning the higher light. For there are eyes so sound and keen, that, as soon as they are first opened, they turn themselves unshrinkingly upon the sun himself. To these, as it were, the light itself is health, nor do they need a teacher, but only, perchance, a warning. For these to believe, to hope, to love is enough. But others are smitten by that very effulgence which they vehemently desire to see, and when the sight of it is withdrawn often return into darkness with delight. To whom, although such as that they may reasonably be called sound, it is nevertheless dangerous to insist on showing what as yet they have not the power to behold. These therefore should be first put in training, and their love for their good is to be nourished by delay. For first certain things are to be shown to them which are not luminous of themselves, but may be seen by the light, such as a garment, a wall, or the like. Then something which, though still not shining of itself, yet in the light flames out more gloriously, such as gold or silver, yet not so brilliantly as to injure the eyes. Then perchance this familiar fire of earth is to be cautiously shown, then the stars, then the moon, then the brightening dawn, and the brilliance of the luminous sky. Among which things, whether sooner or later, whether through the whole succession, or with some steps passed over, each one accustoming himself according to his strength, will at last without shrinking and with great delight behold the sun. In some such way do the best masters deal with those who are heartily devoted to Wisdom, and who, though seeing but dimly, yet have already eyes that see. For it is the office

of a wise training to bring one near to her in a certain graduated approach, but to arrive in her presence without these intermediary steps is a scarcely credible felicity. But to-day, I think we have written enough; regard must be had to health.

24. And, another day having come, *A*. Give now, I pray, if thou canst, that order. Lead by what way thou wilt, through what things thou wilt, how thou wilt. Lay on me things ever so hard, ever so strenuous, and, if only they are within my power, I doubt not that I shall perform them if only I may thereby arrive whither I long to be. *R*. There is only one thing which I can teach thee; I know nothing more. These things of sense are to be utterly eschewed, and the utmost caution is to be used, lest while we bear about this body, our pinions should be impeded by the viscous distilments of earth, seeing we need them whole and perfect, if we would fly from this darkness into that supernal Light: which deigns not even to show itself to those shut up in this cage of the body, unless they have been such that whether it were broken down or worn out it would be their native airs into which they escaped. Therefore, whenever thou shalt have become such that nothing at all of earthly things delights thee, at that very moment, believe me, at that very point of time thou wilt see what thou desirest. *A*. When shall that be, I entreat thee? For I think not that I am able to attain to this supreme contempt, unless I shall have seen that in comparison with which these things are worthless.

25. *R*. In this way too the bodily eye might say: I shall not love the darkness, when I shall have seen the sun. For this too seems, as it were, to pertain to the right order though it is far otherwise. For it loves darkness, for the reason that it is not sound; but the sun, unless sound, it is not able to see. And in this the mind is often at fault, that it thinks itself and boasts itself sound; and complains, as if with good right, because it does not yet see. But that supernal Beauty knows when she should show herself. For she herself discharges the office of physician, and better understands who are sound than the very ones who are rendered sound. But we, as far as we have emerged, seem to ourselves to see; but how far we were plunged in darkness, or how far we had made progress, we are not permitted either to think or feel, and in comparison with the deeper malady we believe ourselves to be in health. See you not how securely yesterday we had pronounced, that we were no longer detained by any evil thing, and loved nothing except Wisdom; and sought or wished other things only for her sake? To thee how low, how foul, how execrable those female embraces seemed, when we discoursed concerning the desire of a wife! Certainly in the watches of this very night, when we had again been discoursing together of the same things, thou didst feel how differently from what thou hadst presumed those imaginary blandishments and that bitter sweetness tickled thee; far, far less indeed, than is the wont, but also far otherwise

than thou hadst thought: so that that most confidential physician of thine set forth to thee each thing, both how far thou hast come on under his care, and what remains to be cured.

26. *A.* Peace, I pray thee, peace. Why tormentest thou me? Why diggest thou so remorselessly and descendest so deep? Now I weep intolerably, henceforth I promise nothing, I presume nothing; question me not concerning these things. Most true is what thou sayest, that He whom I burn to see Himself knows when I am in health; let Him do what pleaseth Him: when it pleaseth Him let Him show Himself; I now commit myself wholly to His clemency and care. Once for all do I believe that those so affected towards Him He faileth not to lift up. I will pronounce nothing concerning my health, except when I shall have seen that Beauty. *R.* Do nothing else, indeed. But now refrain from tears, and gird up thy mind. Thou hast wept most sore, and to the great aggravation of that trouble of thy breast. *A.* Wouldest thou set a measure to my tears, when I see no measure of my misery? or dost thou bid me consider the disease of my body, when I in my inmost self am wasted away with pining consumption? But, I pray thee, if thou availest aught over me, essay to lead me through some shorter ways, so that, at least by some neighbor nearness of that Light, such as, if I have made any advance whatever, I shall be able to endure, I may be made ashamed of withdrawing my eyes into that darkness which I have left; if indeed I can be said to have left a darkness which yet dares to dally with my blindness.

27. *R.* Let us conclude, if you will, this first volume, that in a second we may attempt some such way as may commodiously offer itself. For this disposition of yours must not fail to be cherished by reasonable exercise. *A.* I will in no wise suffer this volume to be ended, unless thou open to me at least a gleam from the nearness of that Light whither I am bound. *R.* Thy Divine Physician yields so far to thy wish. For a certain radiance seizes me, inviting me to conduct thee to it. Therefore be intent to receive it. *A.* Lead, I entreat thee, and snatch me away whither thou wilt. *R.* Thou art sure that thou art minded to know the soul, and God? *A.* That is all my desire. *R.* Nothing more? *A.* Nothing at all. *R.* What, do you not wish to comprehend Truth? *A.* As if I could know these things except through her. *R.* Therefore she first is to be known, through whom these things can be known. *A.* I refuse not. *R.* First then let us see this, whether, as Truth and True are two words, you hold that by these two words two things are signified, or one thing. *A.* Two things, I hold. For, as Chastity is one thing, and that which is chaste, another, and many things in this manner; so I believe that Truth is one thing, and that which, being declared, is true, is another. *R.* Which of these two do you esteem most excellent? *A.* Truth, as I believe. For it is not from that which is chaste that Chastity arises, but that which is chaste from Chastity. So also, if anything is true, it is assuredly from Truth that it is true.

28. *R.* What? When a chaste person dies, do you judge that Chastity dies also? *A.* By no means. *R.* Then, when anything perishes that is true, Truth perishes not. *A.* But how should anything true perish? For I see not. *R.* I marvel that you ask that question: do we not see thousands of things perish before our eyes? Unless perchance you think this tree, either to be a tree, but not a true one, or if so to be unable to perish. For even if you believe not your senses, and are capable of answering, that you are wholly ignorant whether it is a tree; yet this, I believe, you will not deny, that it is a true tree, if it is a tree: for this judgment is not of the senses, but of the intelligence. For if it is a false tree, it is not a tree; but if it is a tree, it cannot but be a true one. *A.* This I allow. *R.* Then as to the other proposition; do you not concede that a tree is of such a sort of things, as that it originates and perishes? *A.* I cannot deny it. *R.* It is concluded therefore, that something which is true perishes. *A.* I do not dispute it. *R.* What follows? Does it not seem to thee that when true things perish Truth does not perish, as Chastity dies not when a chaste person dies? *A.* I now grant this too, and eagerly wait to see what thou art laboring to show. *R.* Therefore attend. *A.* I am all attention.

29. *R.* Does this proposition seem to you to be true: Whatever is, is compelled to be somewhere? *A.* Nothing so entirely wins my consent. *R.* And you confess that Truth is? *A.* I confess it. *R.* Then we must needs inquire where it is; for it is not in a place, unless perchance you think there is something else in a place than a body, or think that Truth is a body. *A.* I think neither of these things. *R.* Where then do you believe her to be? For she is not nowhere, whom we have granted to be. *A.* If I knew where she was, perchance I should seek nothing more. *R.* At least you are able to know where she is not? *A.* If thou pass in review the places, perchance I shall be. *R.* It is not, assuredly, in mortal things. For whatever is, cannot abide in anything, if that does not abide in which it is: and that Truth abides, even though true things perish, has just been conceded. Truth, therefore, is not in mortal things. But Truth is, and is not nowhere. There are therefore things immortal. And nothing is true in which Truth is not. It results therefore that nothing is true, except those things which are immortal. And every false tree is not a tree, and false wood is not wood, and false silver is not silver, and everything whatever which is false, is not. Now everything which is not true, is false. Nothing therefore is rightly said to be, except things immortal. Do you diligently consider this little argument, lest there should be in it any point which you think impossible to concede. For if it is sound, we have almost accomplished our whole business, which in the other book will perchance appear more plainly.

30. *A.* I thank thee much, and will diligently and cautiously review these things in my own mind, and moreover with thee, when we are in quiet, if no darkness interfere, and, which I vehemently dread, inspire in me delight in itself. *R.* Steadfastly believe in God, and commit thyself wholly to Him

as much as thou canst. Be not willing to be as it were thine own and in thine own control; but profess thyself to be the bondman of that most clement and most profitable Lord. For so will He not desist from lifting thee to Himself, and will suffer nothing to occur to thee, except what shall profit thee, even though thou know it not. *A.* I hear, I believe, and as much as I can I yield compliance; and most intently do I offer a prayer for this very thing, that I may have the utmost power, unless perchance thou desirest something more of me. *R.* It is well meanwhile, thou wilt do afterwards what He Himself, being now seen, shall require of thee.

BOOK TWO

1. *A.* Long enough has our work been intermitted, and impatient is Love, nor have tears a measure, unless to Love is given what is loved: wherefore, let us enter upon the Second Book. *R.* Let us enter upon it. *A.* Let us believe that God will be present. *R.* Let us believe indeed, if even this is in our power. *A.* Our power He Himself is. *R.* Therefore pray most briefly and perfectly, as much as thou canst. *A.* God, always the same, let me know myself, let me know Thee. I have prayed. *R.* Thou who wilt know thyself, knowest thou that thou art? *A.* I know. *R.* Whence knowest thou? *A.* I know not. *R.* Feelest thou thyself to be simple, or manifold? *A.* I know not. *R.* Knowest thou thyself to be moved? *A.* I know not. *R.* Knowest thou thyself to think? *A.* I know. *R.* Therefore it is true that thou thinkest. *A.* True. *R.* Knowest thou thyself to be immortal? *A.* I know not. *R.* Of all these things which thou hast said that thou knowest not, which dost thou most desire to know? *A.* Whether I am immortal. *R.* Therefore thou lovest to live? *A.* I confess it. *R.* How will the matter stand when thou shalt have learned thyself to be immortal? Will it be enough? *A.* That will indeed be a great thing, but that to me will be but slight. *R.* Yet in this which is but slight how much wilt thou rejoice? *A.* Very greatly. *R.* For nothing then wilt thou weep? *A.* For nothing at all. *R.* What if this very life should be found such, that in it it is permitted thee to know nothing more than thou knowest? Wilt thou refrain from tears? *A.* Nay verily, I will weep so much that life should cease to be. *R.* Thou dost not then love to live for the mere sake of living, but for the sake of knowing. *A.* I grant the inference. *R.* What if this very knowledge of things should itself make thee wretched? *A.* I do not believe that that is in any way possible. But if it is so, no one can be blessed; for I am not now wretched from any other source than from ignorance of things. And therefore if the knowledge of things is wretchedness, wretchedness is everlasting. *R.* Now I see all which you desire. For since you believe no one to be wretched by knowledge, from which it is probable that intelligence renders blessed; but no one is blessed unless living, and no one lives who is not: thou wishest to be, to live and to have intelligence; but to be that thou mayest live, to live that thou mayest have intelligence. Therefore thou knowest that thou art, thou knowest that thou livest, thou knowest that thou dost exercise intelligence. But whether these things are to be always, or none of these things is to be, or something abides always, and something falls away, or whether these things can be diminished and increased, all things abiding, thou desirest to know. *A.* So it

is. *R.* If therefore we shall have proved that we are always to live, it will follow also that we are always to be. *A.* It will follow. *R.* It will then remain to inquire concerning intellection.

2. *A.* I see a very plain and compendious order. *R.* Let this then be the order, that you answer my questions cautiously and firmly. *A.* I attend. *R.* If this world shall always abide, it is true that this world is always to abide? *A.* Who doubts that? *R.* What if it shall not abide? is it not then true that the world is not to abide? *A.* I dispute it not. *R.* How, when it shall have perished, if it is to perish? will it not then be true, that the world has perished? For as long as it is not true that the world has come to an end, it has not come to an end: it is therefore self-contradictory, that the world is ended and that it is not true that the world is ended. *A.* This too I grant. *R.* Furthermore, does it seem to you that anything can be true, and not be Truth? *A.* In no wise. *R.* There will therefore be Truth, even though the frame of things should pass away. *A.* I cannot deny it. *R.* What if Truth herself should perish? will it not be true that Truth has perished? *A.* And even that who can deny? *R.* But that which is true cannot be, if Truth is not. *A.* I have just conceded this. *R.* In no wise therefore can Truth fail. *A.* Proceed as thou hast begun, for than this deduction nothing is truer.

3. *R.* Now I will have you answer me, does the soul seem to you to feel and perceive, or the body? *A.* The soul. *R.* And does the intellect appear to you to appertain to the soul? *A.* Assuredly. *R.* To the soul alone, or to something else? *A.* I see nothing else besides the soul, except God, in which I believe intellect to exist. *R.* Let us now consider that. If any one should tell you that wall was not a wall, but a tree, what would you think? *A.* Either that his senses or mine were astray, or that he called a wall by the name of a tree. *R.* What if he received in sense the image of a tree, and thou of a wall? may not both be true? *A.* By no means; because one and the same thing cannot be both a tree and a wall. For however individual things might appear different to us as individuals, it could not be but that one of us suffered a false imagination. *R.* What if it is neither tree nor wall, and you are both in error? *A.* That, indeed, is possible. *R.* This one thing therefore you had past by above. *A.* I confess it. *R.* What if you should acknowledge that anything seemed to you other than it is, are you then in error? *A.* No. *R.* Therefore that may be false which seems, and he not be in error to whom it seems. *A.* It may be so. *R.* It is to be allowed then that he is not in error who sees falsities, but he who assents to falsities. *A.* It is assuredly to be allowed. *R.* And this falsity, wherefore is it false? *A.* Because it is otherwise than it seems. *R.* If therefore there are none to whom it may seem, nothing is false. *A.* The inference is sound. *R.* Therefore the falsity is not in the things, but in the sense; but he is not beguiled who assents not to false things. It results that we are one thing, the sense another; since, when it is misled, we are able not to be misled. *A.* I have

nothing to oppose to this. *R.* But when the soul is misled, do you venture to say that you are not false? *A.* How should I venture? *R.* But there is no sense without soul, no falsity without sense. Either therefore the soul operates, or co-operates with the falsity. *A.* Our preceding reasonings imply assent to this.

4. *R.* Give answer now to this, whether it appears to you possible that at some time hereafter falsity should not be. *A.* How can that seem possible to me, when the difficulty of discovering truth is so great that it is absurder to say that falsity than that Truth cannot be. *R.* Do you then think that he who does not live, can perceive and feel? *A.* It cannot be. *R.* It results then, that the soul lives ever. *A.* Thou urgest me too fast into joys: more slowly, I pray. *R.* But, if former inferences are just, I see no ground of doubt concerning this thing. *A.* Too fast, I say. Therefore I am easier to persuade that I have made some rash concession, than to become already secure concerning the immortality of the soul. Nevertheless evolve this conclusion, and show how it has resulted. *R.* You have said that falsity cannot be without sense, and that falsity cannot but be: therefore there is always sense. But no sense without soul: therefore the soul is everlasting. Nor has it power to exercise sense, unless it lives. Therefore the soul always lives.

5. *A.* O leaden dagger! For thou mightest conclude that man is immortal if I had granted thee that this universe can never be without man, and that this universe is eternal. *R.* You keep a keen look-out. But yet it is no small thing which we have established, namely, that the frame of things cannot be without the soul, unless perchance in the frame of things at some time hereafter there shall be no falsity. *A.* This consequence indeed I allow to be involved. But now I am of opinion that we ought to consider farther, whether former inferences do not bend under pressure. For I see no small step to have been made towards the immortality of the soul. *R.* Have you sufficiently considered whether you may not have conceded something rashly? *A.* Sufficiently indeed, but I see no point at which I can accuse myself of rashness. *R.* It is therefore concluded that the frame of things cannot be without a living soul. *A.* So far as this, that in turn some souls may be born, and others die. *R.* What if from the frame of things falsity be taken away? will it not come to pass that all things are true? *A.* I admit the inference. *R.* Tell me whence this wall seems to thee to be true. *A.* Because I am not misled by its aspect. *R.* That is, because it is as it seems. *A.* Yes. *R.* If therefore anything is thereby false because it seems otherwise than it is, and thereby true because it is as it seems; take away him to whom it seems, and there is neither anything false, nor true. But if there is no falsity in the frame of things, all things are true. Nor can anything seem except to a living soul. There remains therefore soul in the frame of things, if falsity cannot be taken away; there remains, if it can. *A.* I see our former conclusions somewhat strengthened, indeed; but we have made no progress by this amplification. For none the less does that fact remain which chiefly

shakes me that souls are born and pass away, and that it comes about that they are not lacking to the world, not through their immortality, but by their succession.

6. *R.* Do any corporeal, that is, sensible things, appear to you to be capable of comprehension in the intellect? *A.* They do not. *R.* What then? does God appear to use senses for the cognition of things? *A.* I dare affirm nothing unadvisedly concerning this matter; but as far as there is room for conjecture, God in no wise makes use of senses. *R.* We conclude therefore that the only possible subject of sense is the soul. *A.* Conclude provisionally as far as probability permits. *R.* Well then; do you allow that this wall, if it is not a true wall, is not a wall? *A.* I could grant nothing more willingly. *R.* And that nothing, if it be not a true body, is a body? *A.* This likewise. *R.* Therefore if nothing is true, unless it be so as it seems; and if nothing corporeal can appear, except to the senses; and if the only subject of sense is the soul; and if no body can be, unless it be a true body: it follows that there cannot be a body, unless there has first been a soul. *A.* Thou dost urge too strongly, and means of resistance fail me.

7. *R.* Give now still greater heed. *A.* Behold me ready. *R.* Certainly this is a stone; and it is true on this condition, if it is not otherwise than it seems; and it is not a stone, if it is not true; and it cannot seem except to the senses. *A.* Yes. *R.* There are not therefore stones in the most secluded bosom of the earth, nor anywhere at all where there are not those who have the sense of them; nor would this be a stone, unless we saw it; nor will it be a stone when we shall have departed, and no one else shall be present to see it. Nor, if you lock your coffers well, however much you may have shut up in them, will they have anything. Nor indeed is wood itself wood interiorly. For that escapes all perceptions of sense which is in the depth of an absolutely opaque body, and so is in no wise compelled to be. For if it were, it would be true; nor is anything true, unless because it is so as it appears: but that does not appear; it is not therefore true: unless you have something to object to this. *A.* I see that this results from my previous concessions; but it is so absurd, that I would more readily deny any one of these, than concede that this is true. *R.* As you please. Consider then which you prefer to say: that corporeal things can appear otherwise than to the senses, or that there can be another subject of sense than the soul, or that there is a stone or something else but that it is not true, or that Truth itself is to be otherwise defined. *A.* Let us, I pray thee, consider this last position.

8. *R.* Define therefore the True. *A.* That is true which is so as it appears to the knower, if he will and can know. *R.* That therefore will not be true which no one can know? Then, if that is false which seems otherwise than it is; how if to one this stone should seem a stone, to another wood? will the same thing be both false and true? *A.* That former position disturbs me

more, how, if anything cannot be known, it results from that that it is not true. For as to this, that one thing is both true and false, I do not much care. For I see one thing, compared with diverse things, to be both greater and smaller. From which it results, that nothing is more or less of itself. For these are terms of comparison. *R.* But if you say that nothing is true of itself, do you not fear the inference, that nothing is of itself? For whereby this is wood, thereby is it also true wood. Nor can it be, that of itself, that is, without a knower, it should be wood, and should not be true wood. *A.* Therefore thus I say and so I define, nor do I fear lest my definition be disapproved on the ground of excessive brevity: for to me that seems to be true which is. *R.* Nothing then will be false, because whatever is, is true. *A.* Thou hast driven me into close straits, and I am wholly unprovided of an answer. So it comes to pass that whereas I am unwilling to be taught except by these questionings, I fear now to be questioned.

9. *R.* God, to whom we have commended ourselves, without doubt will render help, and set us free from these straits, if only we believe, and entreat Him most devoutly. *A.* Nothing, assuredly would I do more gladly in this place; for never have I been involved in so great a darkness. God, Our Father, who exhortest us to pray, who also bringest this about, that supplication is made to Thee; since when we make supplication to Thee, we live better, and are better: hear me groping in these glooms, and stretch forth Thy right hand to me. Shed over me Thy light, revoke me from my wanderings; bring Thyself into me that I may likewise return into Thee. Amen. *R.* Be with me now, as far as thou mayest, in most diligent attention. *A.* Utter, I pray, whatever has been suggested to thee, that we perish not. *R.* Give heed. *A.* Behold, I have neither eyes nor ears but for thee.

10. *R.* First let us again and yet again ventilate this question, What is falsity? *A.* I wonder if there will turn out to be anything, except what is not so as it seems. *R.* Give heed rather, and let us first question the senses themselves. For certainly what the eyes see, is not called false, unless it have some similitude of the true. For instance, a man whom we see in sleep, is not indeed a true man, but false, by this very fact that he has the similitude of a true one. For who, seeing a dog, would have a right to say that he had dreamed of a man? Therefore too that is thereby a false dog, that it is like a true one. *A.* It is as thou sayest. *R.* And moreover, if any one waking should see a horse and think he saw a man, is he not hereby misled, that there appears to him some similitude of a man? For if nothing should appear to him except the form of a horse, he cannot think that he sees a man. *A.* I fully concede this. *R.* We call that also a false tree which we see in a picture, and a false face which is reflected from a mirror, and a false motion of buildings to men that are sailing from them, and a false break in the oar when dipped, for no other reason than the verisimilitude in all these things. *A.* True. *R.* So we make mistakes between twins, so between

eggs, so between seals stamped by one ring, and other such things. *A*. I follow and agree to all. *R*. Therefore that similitude of things which pertains to the eyes, is the mother of falsity. *A*. I cannot deny it.

11. *R*. But all this forest of facts, unless I am mistaken, may be divided into two kinds. For it lies partly in equal, partly in inferior things. They are equal, when we say that this is as like to that as that to this, as is said of twins, or impressions of a ring. Inferior, when we say that the worse is like the better. For who, looking in a mirror, would dream of saying that he is like that image, and not rather that like him? And this class consists partly in what the soul undergoes, and partly in those things which are seen. And that again which the soul undergoes, it either undergoes in the sense, as the unreal motion of a building; or in itself from that which it has received from the senses, such as are the dreams of dreamers, and perhaps also of madmen. Furthermore, those things which appear in the things themselves which we see, are some of them from nature, and some expressed and framed by living creatures. Nature either by procreation or reflection effects inferior similitudes. By procreation, when to parents children like them are born; by reflection, as from mirrors of various kinds. For although it is men that make the most of the mirrors, yet it is not they that frame the images given back. On the other hand, the works of living creatures are seen in pictures, and creations of the like kind: in which may also be included (conceding their occurrence) those things which demons produce. But the shadows of bodies, because with but a slight stretch of language they may be described as like their bodies and a sort of false bodies, nor can be disputed to be submitted to the judgment of the eyes, may reasonably be placed in that class, which are brought about by nature through reflection. For every body exposed to the light reflects, and casts a shadow in the opposite direction. Or do you see any objection to be made? *A*. None. I am only awaiting anxiously the issue of these illustrations.

12. *R*. We must, however, wait patiently, until the remaining senses also make report to us that falsity dwells in the similitude of the true. For in the sense of hearing likewise there are almost as many sorts of similitudes: as when, hearing the voice of a speaker, whom we do not see, we think it some one else, whom in voice he resembles; and in inferior similitudes Echo is a witness, or that well-known roaring of the ears themselves, or in timepieces a certain imitation of thrush or crow, or such things as dreamers or lunatics imagine themselves to hear. And it is incredible how much false tones, as they are called by musicians, bear witness to the truth, which will appear hereinafter: yet they too (which will suffice just now) are not remote from a resemblance to those which men call true. Do you follow this? *A*. And most delightedly. For here I have no trouble to understand. *R*. Then, to press on, do you think it is easy, by the smell, to distinguish lily from lily, or by the taste honey from honey, gathered alike from

thyme, though brought from different hives, or by the touch to note the difference between the softness of the plumage of the goose and of the swan? *A.* It does not seem easy. *R.* And how is it when we dream that we either smell or taste, or touch such things? Are we not then deceived by a similitude of effects and images, inferior in proportion to its emptiness? *A.* Thou speakest truly. *R.* Therefore it appears that we, in all our senses, whether by equality or inferiority of likeness, are either misled by cozening similitude, or even if we are not misled, as suspending our consent, or discovering the difference, yet that we name those things false which we apprehend as like the true. *A.* I cannot doubt it.

13. *R.* Now give heed, while we run over the same things once more, that what we are endeavoring to show may come more plainly to view. *A.* Lo, here I am, speak what thou wilt. For I have once for all resolved to endure this circuitous course, nor will I be wearied out in it, hoping so ardently to arrive at length whither I perceive that we are tending. *R.* You do well. But take note whether it seems to you, when we see a resemblance in eggs, that we can justly say that any one of them is false. *A.* Far from it. For if all are eggs, they are true eggs. *R.* And when we see an image reflected from a mirror, by what signs do we apprehend it to be false? *A.* By the fact that it cannot be grasped, gives forth no sound, does not move independently, does not live, and by innumerable other properties, which it were tedious to detail. *R.* I see you are averse to delay, and regard must be borne to your haste. Then, not to recall every particular, if those men also whom we see in dreams, were able to live, speak, be grasped by waking men, and there were no difference between them and those whom when awake and sane we address and see, should we then have any reason to call them false? *A.* What possible right could we have to do so? *R.* Therefore if they were true, in exact proportion as they were likest the truth, and as no difference existed between them and the true and false so far as they were, by those or other differences, convicted of being dissimilar; must it not be confessed that similitude is the mother of truth, and dissimilitude of falsehood? *A.* I have no answer to make, and I am ashamed of my former so hasty assent.

14. *R.* It is ridiculous if you are ashamed, as if it were not for this very reason that we have chosen this mode of discourse: which, since we are talking with ourselves alone, I wish to be called and inscribed Soliloquies; a new name, it is true, and perhaps a grating one, but not ill suited for setting forth the fact. For since Truth can not be better sought than by asking and answering, and scarcely any one can be found who does not take shame to be worsted in debate, and so it almost always happens that when a matter is well brought into shape for discussion, it is exploded by some unreasonable clamor and petulance, and angry feeling, commonly dissembled, indeed, but sometimes plainly expressed; it has been, as I think, most advantageous, and most answerable to peace, that the resolution was

made by thee to seek truth in the way of question by me and answer by
thee: wherefore there is no reason why you should fear, if at any point
you have unadvisedly tied yourself up, to return and undo the knots; for
otherwise there is no escape from hence.

15. *A.* Thou speakest rightly; but what I have granted amiss I altogether
fail to see: unless perchance that that is rightly called false which has some
similitude of the true, since assuredly nothing else occurs to me worthy
of the name of false; and yet again I am compelled to confess that those
things which are called false are so called by the fact that they differ from
the true. From which it results that that very dissimilitude is the cause of
the falsity. Therefore I am disquieted; for I cannot easily call to mind
anything that is engendered by contrary causes. *R.* What if this is the one
and only kind in the universe of things which is so? Or are you ignorant,
that in running over the innumerable species of animals, the crocodile alone
is found to move its upper jaw in eating; especially as scarcely anything
can be discovered so like to another thing, that it is not also in some point
unlike it? *A.* I see that indeed; but when I consider that that which we
call false has both something like and something unlike the true, I am not
able to make out on which side it chiefly merits the name of false. For if I
say: on the side on which it is unlike; there will be nothing which cannot be
called false: for there is nothing which is not dissimilar to some thing, which
we concede to be true. And again, if I shall say, that it is to be called false
on that side on which it is similar; not only will those eggs cry out against
us which are true on the very ground of their excessive similarity, but even
so I shall not escape from his grasp who may compel me to confess that all
things are false, because I cannot deny that all things are on some side or
other similar to each other. But suppose me not afraid to give this answer,
that likeness and unlikeness alike give a right to call anything false; what
way of escape wilt thou give me? For none the less will the fatal necessity
hang over me of proclaiming all things false; since, as has been said above,
all things are found to be both similar, on some side, and dissimilar, on
some side, to each other. My only remaining resource would be to declare
nothing else false, except what was other than it seemed, unless I shrank
from again encountering all those monsters, which I flattered myself that
I had long since sailed away from. For a whirlpool again seizes me at unawares, and brings me round to own that to be true which is as it seems.
From which it results that without a knower nothing can be true: where I
have to fear a shipwreck on deeply hidden rocks, which are true, although
unknown. Or, if I shall say that that is true which is, it follows, let who
will oppose, that there is nothing false anywhere. And so I see the same
breakers before me again, and see that all my patience of thy delays has
helped me forward nothing at all.

16. *R.* Attend rather; for never can I be persuaded, that we have implored
the Divine aid in vain. For I see that, having tried all things as far as we

could, we found nothing to remain, which could rightly be called false, except what either feigns itself to be what it is not, or, to include all, tends to be and is not. But that former kind of falsity is either fallacious or mendacious. For that is rightly called fallacious which has a certain appetite of deceiving; which cannot be understood as without a soul: but this results in part from reason, in part from nature; from reason, in rational creatures, as in men; from nature, in beasts, as in the fox. But what I call mendacious, proceeds from those who utter falsehood. Who in this point differ from the fallacious, that all the fallacious seek to mislead; but not every one who utters falsehood, wishes to mislead; for both mimes and comedies and many poems are full of falsehoods, rather with the purpose of delighting than of misleading, and almost all those who jest utter falsehood. But he is rightly called fallacious, whose purpose is, that somebody should be deceived. But those who do not aim to deceive, but nevertheless feign somewhat, are mendacious only, or if not even this, no one at least doubts that they are to be called pleasant falsifiers: unless you have something to object.

17. *A.* Proceed, I pray; for now perchance thou hast begun to teach concerning falsities not falsely: but now I am considering of what sort that class of falsities may be, of which thou hast said, It tends to be, and is not. *R.* Why should you not consider? They are the same things, which already we have largely passed in review. Does not thy image in the mirror appear to will to be thou thyself, but to be therefore false, because it is not? *A.* This does, in very deed, seem so. *R.* And as to pictures, and all such expressed resemblances, every such thing wrought by the artist? Do they not press to be that, after whose similitude they have been made? *A.* I must certainly own this to be true. *R.* And you will allow, I believe, that the deceits under which dreamers or madmen suffer, are to be included in this kind. *A.* None more: for none tend more to be such things as the waking and the sane discern; and yet they are hereby false, because that which they tend to be they cannot be. *R.* Why need I now say more concerning the gliding towers, or the dipped oar, or the shadows of bodies? It is plain, as I think, that they are to be measured by this rule. *A.* Most evidently they are. *R.* I say nothing concerning the remaining senses; for no one by consideration will fail to find this, that in the various things which are subject to our sense, that is called false which tends to be anything and is not.

18. *A.* Thou speakest rightly; but I wonder why thou wouldst separate from this class those poems and jests, and other imitative trifles. *R.* Because forsooth it is one thing to will to be false, and another not to be able to be true. Therefore these works of men themselves, such as comedies or tragedies, or mimes, and other such things, we may include with the works of painters and sculptors. For a painted man cannot be so true, however much he may tend into the form of man, as those things which are written

in the books of the comic poets. For neither do they will to be false, nor
are they false by any appetite of their own; but by a certain necessity, so
far as they have been able to follow the mind of the author. But on the stage
Roscius in will was a false Hecuba, in nature a true man; but by that will
also a true tragedian, in that he was fulfilling the thing proposed: but a
false Priam, in that he made himself like Priam, but was not he. From
which now arises a certain marvellous thing, which nevertheless no one
doubts to be so. *A.* What, pray, is it? *R.* What think you, unless that all
these things are in certain aspects true, by this very thing that they are
in certain aspects false, and that for their quality of truth this alone avails
them, that they are false in another regard? Whence to that which they
either will or ought to be, they in no wise attain, if they avoid being false.
For how could he whom I have mentioned have been a true tragedian, had
he been unwilling to be a false Hector, a false Andromache, a false Her-
cules, and innumerable other things? or how would a picture, for instance,
be a true picture, unless it were a false horse? or how could there be in a
mirror a true image of a man, if it were not a false man? Wherefore, if it
avails some things that they be somewhat false in order that they may be
somewhat true; why do we so greatly dread falsity, and seek truth as the
greatest good? *A.* I know not, and I greatly marvel, unless because in these
examples I see nothing worthy of imitation. For not as actors, or specular
reflections, or Myron's brazen cows, ought we, in order that we may be
true in some character of our own, to be outlined and accommodated to
the personation of another; but to seek that truth, which is not, as if laid
out on a bifronted and self-repugnant plan, false on one side that it may
be true on the other. *R.* High and Divine are the things which thou re-
quirest. Yet if we shall have found them, shall we not confess that of these
things is Truth itself made up, and as it were brought into being from
their fusion—Truth, from which every thing derives its name which in any
way is called true? *A.* I yield no unwilling assent.

19. *R.* What then think you? Is the science of debate true, or false? *A.* True,
beyond controversy. But Grammar too is true. *R.* In the same sense as the
former? *A.* I do not see what is truer than the true. *R.* That assuredly
which has nothing of false: in view of which a little while ago thou didst
take umbrage at those things which, be it in this way or that, unless they
were false, could not be true. Or do you not know, that all those fabulous
and openly false things appertain to Grammar? *A.* I am not ignorant of
that indeed; but, as I judge, it is not through Grammar that they are false,
but through it, that whatever they may be, they are interpreted. Since a
drama is a falsehood composed for utility or delight. But Grammar is a
science which is the guardian and moderatrix of articulate speech: whose
profession involves the necessity of collecting even all the figments of the
human tongue, which have been committed to memory and letters, not
making them false, but teaching and enforcing concerning these certain prin

ciples of true interpretation. *R.* Very just: I care not now, whether or not these things have been well defined and distinguished by thee; but this I ask, whether it is Grammar itself, or that science of debate which shows this to be so. *A.* I do not deny that the force and skill of definition, whereby I have now endeavored to separate these things, is to be attributed to the art of disputation.

20. *R.* How as to Grammar itself? if it is true, is it not so far true as it is a discipline? For the name of Discipline signifies something to be learnt: but no one who has learned and who retains what he learns, can be said not to know; and no one knows falsities. Therefore every discipline and science is true. *A.* I see not what rashness there can be in assenting to this brief course of reasoning. But I am disturbed lest it should bring any one to suppose those dramas to be true; for these also we learn and retain. *R.* Was then our master unwilling that we should believe what he taught, and know it? *A.* Nay, he was thoroughly in earnest that we should know it. *R.* And did he, pray, ever set out to have us believe that Daedalus flew? *A.* That, indeed, never. But assuredly unless we remembered the poem, he took such order that we were scarcely able to hold anything in our hands. *R.* Do you then deny it to be true that there is such a poem, and that such a tradition is spread abroad concerning Daedalus? *A.* I do not deny this to be true. *R.* You do not then deny that you learned the truth, when you learned these things. For if it is true that Daedalus flew, and boys should receive and recite this as a feigning fable, they would be laying up falsities in mind by the very fact that the things were true which they recited. For from this results what we were admiring above, that there could not be a true fiction turning on the flight of Daedalus, unless it were false that Daedalus flew. *A.* I now grasp that; but what good is to come of it, I do not yet see. *R.* What, unless that that course of reasoning is not false, whereby we gather that a science, unless it is true, cannot be a science? *A.* And what does this signify? *R.* Because I wish to have you tell me on what the science of Grammar rests: for the truth of the science rests on that very principle which makes it a science. *A.* I know not what to answer thee. *R.* Does it not seem to you, that if nothing in it had been defined, and nothing distributed and distinguished into classes and parts, it could not in any wise be a true science? *A.* Now I grasp thy meaning: nor does the remembrance of any science whatever occur to me, in which definitions and divisions and processes of reasoning do not, inasmuch as it is declared what each thing is, as without confusion of parts its proper attributes are ascribed to each class, nothing peculiar to it being neglected, nothing alien to it admitted, perform that whole range of functions from which it has the name of Science. *R.* That whole range of functions therefore from which it has the name of true. *A.* I see this to be implied.

21. *R.* Tell me now what science contains the principles of definitions, divisions and partitions. *A.* It has been said above that these are contained

in the rules of disputation. *R*. Grammar therefore, both as a science, and as a true science, has been created by the same art which has above been defended from the charge of falsity. Which conclusion I am not required to confine to Grammar alone, but am permitted to extend to all sciences whatever. For you have said, and truly said, that no science occurs to you, in which the law of defining and distributing does not lie at the very foundation of its character as a science. But if they are true on that ground on which they are sciences, will any one deny that very thing to be truth through which all the sciences are true? *A*. Assuredly I find it hard to withhold assent: but this gives me pause, that we reckon highly to be commended: but you do not deny, I suppose, that it is true on the same ground on which it is a theory and science. *A*. Nay, that is my very ground of perplexity. For I have noted that it also is a science, and is on this account called true. *R*. What then? Do you think this could be a science on any other ground than that all things in it were defined and distributed? *A*. I have nothing else to say. *R*. But if this function appertains to it, it is in and of itself a true science. Why then should any one find it wonderful, if that truth whereby all things are true, should be through itself and in itself true? *A*. Nothing stands now in the way of my giving an unreserved assent to that opinion.

22. *R*. Attend therefore to the few things that remain. *A*. Bring forth whatever thou hast, if only it be such as I can understand, and I will willingly agree. *R*. We do not forget, that to say that anything is in anything, is capable of a double sense. It may mean that it is so in such a sense as that it can also be disjoined and be elsewhere, as this wood in this place, or the sun in the East. Or it may mean anything is so in a subject, that it cannot be separated from it, as in this wood the shape and visible appearance, as in the sun the light, as in fire heat, as in the mind discipline, and such like. Or seems it otherwise to thee? *A*. These distinctions are indeed most thoroughly familiar to us, and from early youth most studiously made an element of thought; wherefore, if asked about these, I must grant the position at once. *R*. But do you not concede that if the subject do not abide, that which is in the subject cannot inseparably abide? *A*. This also I see necessary: for, the subject remaining, that which is in the subject may possibly not remain, as any one with a little thought can perceive. Since the color of this body of mine may, by reason of health or age, suffer change, though the body has not yet perished. And this is not equally true of all things, but of those whose coexistence with the subject is not necessary to the existence of the subject. For it is not necessary that this wall, in order to be a wall, should be of this color, which we see in it; for even if, by some chance, it should become black or white, or should undergo some other change of color, it would nevertheless remain a wall and be so called. But if fire were without heat, it will not even be fire; nor can we call this snow unless it is white.

23. Indeed in regard to your question, who would grant, or to whom would it seem possible to occur, that that which is in the subject would endure while the subject perished? For it is monstrous and most utterly foreign to the truth, that what would not be unless it were in the subject, could be even when the subject itself was no more. *R.* Then that which we were seeking is found. *A.* What dost thou mean? *R.* What you hear. *A.* And is it then now clearly made out that the mind is immortal? *R.* If these things which you have granted are true, with most indisputable clearness: unless perchance you would say that the mind, even though it die, is still the mind. *A.* I, at least, will never say that; but by this very fact that it perishes it then comes about that it is not the mind, is what I do say. Nor am I shaken in this opinion because it has been said by great philosophers that that thing which, wherever it comes, affords life, cannot admit death into itself. For although the light wheresoever it has been able to gain entrance, makes that place luminous, and, by virtue of that memorable force of contrarieties, cannot admit darkness into itself; yet it is extinguished, and that place is by its extinction made dark. So that which resisted the darkness, neither in any way admitted the darkness into it, and yet made place for it by perishing, as it could have made place for it by departing. Therefore I fear lest death should befall the body in such wise as darkness a place, the mind, like light, sometimes departing, but sometimes being extinguished on the spot; so that now not concerning every death of the body is there security, but a particular kind of death is to be chosen, by which the soul may be conducted out of the body unharmed, and guided to a place, if there is any such place, where it cannot be extinguished. Or, if not even this may be, and the mind, as it were a light, is kindled in the body itself, nor has capacity to endure elsewhere, and every death is a sort of extinction of the soul in the body, or of the life; some sort is to be chosen by which, so far as man is allowed, life, while it is lived, may be lived in security and tranquillity, although I know not how that can come to pass if the soul dies. O greatly blessed they, who, whether from themselves, or from whom you will, have gained the persuasion, that death is not to be feared, even if the soul should perish! But, wretched me, no reasonings, no books, have hitherto been able to persuade of this.

24. *R.* Groan not, the human mind is immortal. *A.* How dost thou prove it? *R.* From those things which you have granted above, with great caution. *A.* I do not indeed recall to mind any want of vigilance in my admissions when questioned by thee: but now gather all into the sum, I pray thee; let us see at what point we have arrived after so many circuits, nor would I have thee in doing so question me. For if thou art about to enumerate concisely those things which I have granted, why is my response again desired? Or is it that thou wouldst wantonly torture me by delays of joy, if we have in fact achieved any solid result? *R.* I will do that which I see

that thou dost wish, but attend most diligently. *A.* Speak now, here I am; why slayest thou me? *R.* If everything which is in the subject always abides, it follows of necessity that the subject itself always abides. And every discipline is in the subject mind. It is necessary therefore that the mind should continue forever, if the science continues forever. Now Science is Truth, and always, as in the beginning of this book Reason hath convinced thee, doth Truth abide. Therefore the mind lasts forever, nor dead, could it be called the mind. He therefore alone can escape absurdity in denying the mind to be immortal, who can prove that any of the foregoing concessions have been made without reason.

25. *A.* And now I am ready to plunge into the expected joys, but yet I am held hesitating by two thoughts. For, first, it makes me uneasy that we have used so long a circuit, following out I know not what chain of reasonings, when the whole matter of discourse admitted of so brief a demonstration, as has now been shown. Wherefore, it renders me anxious that the discourse has so long held so wary a step, as if with some design of setting an ambush. Next, I do not see how a science is always in the mind, when, on the one hand, so few are familiar with it, and, on the other, whoever does know it, was during so long a time of early childhood unacquainted with it. For we can neither say that the minds of the untaught are not minds, nor that that science is in their mind of which they are ignorant. And if this is utterly absurd, it results that either the science is not always in the mind, or that that science is not Truth.

26. *R.* Thou mayest note that it is not for naught that our reasoning has taken so wide a round. For we were inquiring what is Truth, which not even now, in this very forest of thoughts and things, beguiling our steps into an infinity of paths, have we, as I see, been able to track out to the end. But what are we to do? Shall we desist from our undertaking, and wait in hope that some book or other may fall into our hands, which may satisfy this question? For many, I think, have written before our age, whom we have not read: and now, to give no guess at what we do not know, we see plainly that there is much writing upon this theme, both in verse and prose; and that by men whose writings cannot be unknown to us, and whose genius we know to be such, that we cannot despair of finding in their works what we require: especially when here before our eyes is he in whom we have recognized that eloquence for which we mourned as dead, to have revived in vigorous life. Will he suffer us, after having in his writings taught us the true manner of living, to remain ignorant of the true nature of living? *A.* I indeed do not think so, and hope much from thence, but one matter of grief I have, that we have not opportunity of opening to him our zealous affection either towards him or towards Wisdom. For assuredly he would pity our thirst, and would overflow much more quickly than now. For he is secure, because he has now won a full conviction of the immortality of the soul, and perhaps knows not that there are any, who have only

too well experienced the misery of this ignorance, and whom it is cruel not to aid, especially when they entreat it. But that other knows indeed from old familiarity our ardor of longing; but he is so far removed, and we are so circumstanced, that we have scarcely the opportunity of so much as sending a letter to him. Whom I believe to have lately in Transalpine retirement composed a spell, under whose ban the fear of death is compelled to flee, and the cold stupor of the soul, indurate with lasting ice, is expelled. But in the meantime, while these helps are leisurely making their way hither, a benefit which it is not in our power to command, is it not most unworthy that our leisure should be wasting, and our very mind hang wholly dependent on the uncertain decision of another's will?

27. What shall we say to this, that we have entreated God and do entreat, that He will show us a way, not to riches, not to bodily pleasures, not to popular honors and seats of state, but to the knowledge of our own soul, and that He will likewise disclose Himself to them that seek Him? Will He, indeed, forsake us, or shall He be forsaken by us? *R.* Most utterly foreign to Him is it indeed, that He should desert them who desire such things: whence also it ought to be strange to our thoughts that we should desert so great a Guide. Wherefore, if you will, let us briefly go over the considerations from which either proposition results, either that Truth always abides, or that Truth is the theory of argumentation. For you have said that these points wavered in your mind, so as to make us less secure of the final conclusion of the whole matter. Or shall we rather inquire this, how a science can be in an untrained mind, which yet we cannot deny to be a mind? For this seemed to give you uneasiness, so as to involve you again in doubt as to your previous concessions. *A.* Nay, let us first discuss the two former propositions, and then we will consider the nature of this latter fact. For so, as I judge, no controversy will remain. *R.* So be it, but attend with the utmost heed and caution. For I know what happens to you as you 'listen, namely, that while you are too intent upon the conclusion, and expecting that now, or now, it will be drawn, you grant the points implied in my questions without a sufficiently diligent scrutiny. *A.* Perchance thou speakest the truth; but I shall strive against this kind of disease as much as I can: only begin thou now to inquire of me, that we linger not over things superfluous.

28. *R.* From this truth, as I remember, that Truth cannot perish, we have concluded, that not only if the whole world should perish, but even if Truth itself should, it will still be true that both the world and Truth have perished. Now there is nothing true without truth: in no wise therefore does Truth perish. *A.* I acknowledge all this, and shall be greatly surprised if it turns out false. *R.* Let us then consider that other point. *A.* Suffer me, I pray thee, to reflect a little, lest I should soon come back in confusion. *R.* Will it therefore not be true that Truth has perished? If it will not be true, then Truth does not perish. If it were true, where, after the fall of Truth,

will be the true, when now there is no truth? *A.* I have no further occasion for thought and consideration; proceed to something else. Assuredly we will take order, so far as we may, that learned and wise men may read these musings, and may correct our unadvisedness, if they shall find any: for as to myself, I do not believe that either now or hereafter I shall be able to discover what can be said against this.

29. *R.* Is Truth then so called for any other reason than as being that by which everything is true which is true? *A.* For no other reason. *R.* Is it rightly called true for any ground than that it is not false? *A.* To doubt this were madness. *R.* Is that not false which is accommodated to the similitude of anything, yet is not that the likeness of which it appears? *A.* Nothing indeed do I see which I would more willingly call false. But yet that is commonly called false, which is far removed from the similitude of the true. *R.* Who denies it? But yet because it implies some imitation of the true. *A.* How? For when it is said, that Medea flew away with winged snakes harnessed to her car, that thing on no side imitates truth; inasmuch as the thing is naught, nor can that thing imitate aught, when itself is absolutely nothing. *R.* You say right; but you do not note that that thing which is absolutely nothing, cannot even be called false. For if it is false, it is: if it is not, it is not false. *A.* Shall we not then say that monstrous story of Medea is false? *R.* Assuredly not; for if it is false, how is it a monstrous story? *A.* Admirable! Then when I say

"The mighty winged snakes I fasten to my car,"

do I not say false? *R.* You do, assuredly: for that is which you say to be false. *A.* What, I pray? *R.* That sentence, forsooth, which is contained in the verse itself. *A.* And pray what imitation of truth has that? *R.* Because it would bear the same tenor, even if Medea had truly done that thing. Therefore in its very terms a false sentence imitates true sentences. Which, if it is not believed, in this alone does it imitate true ones, that it is expressed as they, and it is only false, it is not also misleading. But if it obtains faith, it imitates also those sentences which, being true, are believed true. *A.* Now I perceive that there is a great difference between those things which we say and those things concerning which we say aught; wherefore I now assent: for this proposition alone held me back, that whatever we call false is not rightly so called, unless it have an imitation of something true. For who, calling a stone false silver, would not be justly derided? Yet if any one should declare a stone to be silver, we say that he speaks falsely, that is, that he utters a false sentence. But it is not, I think, unreasonable that we should call tin or lead false silver, because the thing itself, as it were, imitates that: nor is our sentence declaring this therefore false, but that very thing concerning which it is pronounced.

30. *R.* You apprehend the matter well. But consider this, whether we can

also with propriety call silver by the name of false lead. *A.* Not in my opinion. *R.* Why so? *A.* I know not; except that I see that it would be altogether against my will to have it so called. *R.* Is it perchance for the reason that silver is the better, and such a name would be contemptuous of it; but it confers a certain honor, as it were, on lead, if it should be called false silver? *A.* Thou hast expressed exactly what I had in mind. And therefore I believe that it is with good right that those are held infamous and incapable of bearing witness, who flaunt themselves in female attire, whom I know not whether I should more reasonably call false women, or false men. True actors, however, and truly infamous, without doubt we can call them; or, if they lurk unseen, and if infamy implies an evil repute, we may call them not without truth, true specimens of worthlessness. *R.* We shall have another opportunity of discussing these things: for many things are done, which in the mere guise of them appear base, yet, done for some praiseworthy end, are shown to be honorable. And it is a great question whether one, for the sake of liberating his country, ought to put on a woman's garment to deceive the enemy, being, perhaps, by the very fact that he is a false woman, apt to be shown the truer man: and whether a wise man who in some way may have certainly ascertained that his life will be necessary to the interests of mankind, ought to choose rather to die of cold, than to indue himself in female vestments, if he can find no other. But concerning this, as has been said, we will consider hereafter. For unquestionably thou discernest how careful an inquisition it requires, how far such things can be carried, without falling into various inexcusable basenesses. But now—which suffices for the present question—I think it is now evident, and beyond doubt, that there is not anything false except by some imitation of the true.

31. *A.* Go on to what remains; for of this I am well convinced. *R.* Then I ask this, whether, besides the sciences in which we are instructed, and in which it is fitting that the study of wisdom itself should be included, we can find anything so true, that it is not, like that Achilles of the stage, false on one side, that it may be true on another? *A.* To me, indeed, many such things appear capable of being found. For no sciences contain this stone, nor yet, that it may be a true stone, does it imitate anything according to which it would be called false. Which one thing being mentioned, thou seest there is opportunity to dwell upon things innumerable, which of themselves occur to the thought. *R.* I see, I see. But do they not seem to thee to be included in the one name of Body? *A.* They might so seem, if either I had ascertained the inane to be nothing, or thought that the mind itself ought to be numbered among bodies, or believed that God also is a body. If all these things are, I see them not to be false and true in imitation of anything. *R.* You send us a long journey, but I will use all compendious speed. For certainly what you call the Inane is one thing, what you call Truth another. *A.* Widely diverse, indeed. For what more inane than I, if I think Truth

anything inane, or so greatly seek after aught inane? For what else than Truth do I desire to find? *R.* Therefore perchance you grant this too, that nothing is true which does not by Truth come to be true. *A.* This became manifest at an early stage. *R.* Do you doubt that nothing is inane except the Inane itself, or certainly that a body is not inane? *A.* I do not doubt it at all. *R.* I suppose therefore, you believe that Truth is some sort of body. *A.* In no wise. *R.* What is a body? *A.* I know not; no matter: for I think thou knowest that even that inane, if it is inane, is more completely so where there is no body. *R.* This assuredly is plain. *A.* Why then do we delay? *R.* Does it then seem to thee either that Truth made the inane, or that there is anything true where Truth is not? *A.* Neither seems true. *R.* The inane therefore is not true, because neither could it become inane by that which is not inane: and it is manifest that what is void of truth is not true; and, in fine, that very thing which is called inane, is so called because it is nothing. How therefore can that be true which is not? or how can that be which is absolutely nothing? *A.* Well then, let us desert the inane as being inane.

32. *R.* What sayest thou concerning the rest? *A.* What? *R.* Because you see how much stands on my side. For we have remaining the Soul and God. And if these two are true for the reason that Truth is in them, of the immortality of God no one doubts. But the mind is believed immortal, if Truth, which cannot perish, is proved to be in it. Wherefore let us consider this last point, whether the body be not truly true, that is, whether there be in it, not Truth, but a certain image of Truth. For if even in the body, which we know to be perishable, we find such an element of truth, as there is in the sciences, it does not then so certainly follow, that the art of discussion is Truth, whereby all sciences are true. For true is even the body, which does not seem to have been formed by the force of argument. But if even the body is true by a certain imitation, and is on this account, not absolutely and purely true, there will then, perchance, be nothing to hinder the theory of argument from being taught to be Truth itself. *A.* Meanwhile let us inspire concerning the body; for not even when this shall have been settled, do I see a prospect of ending this controversy. *R.* Whence knowest thou what God purposes? Therefore attend: for I at least think the body to be contained in a certain form and guise, which if it had not, it would not be the body; if it had it in truth, it would be the mind. Or does the fact stand otherwise? *A.* I assent in part, of the rest I doubt; for, unless some figure is maintained, I grant that it is not a body. But how, if it had it in truth, it would be the mind, I do not well understand. *R.* Do you then remember nothing concerning the exordium of this book, and that Geometry of yours? *A.* Thou hast mentioned it to purpose; I do indeed remember. and am most willing to do so. *R.* Are such figures found in bodies, as that science demonstrates? *A.* Nay, it is incredible how greatly inferior they are convicted of being. *R.* Which of them, therefore, do you think true? *A.* Do

not, I beg, think it necessary even to put that question to me. For who is so dull, as not to see that those figures which are taught in Geometry, dwell in Truth itself, or even Truth in these; but that those embodied figures, inasmuch as they seem, so to speak, to tend towards these, have I know not what imitation of truth, and are therefore false? For now that whole matter which thou wert laboring to show, I understand.

33. *R.* What need is there any longer than that we should inquire concerning the science of disputation? For whether the figures of Geometry are in the Truth, or the Truth is in them, that they are contained in our soul, that, is, in our intelligence, no one calls in question, and through this fact Truth also is compelled to be in our mind. But if every science whatever is so in the mind, as in the subject inseparably, and if Truth is not able to perish; why, I ask, do we doubt concerning the perpetual life of the mind through I know not what familiarity with death? Or have that line or squareness or roundness other things which they imitate that they may be true? *A.* In no way can I believe that, unless perchance a line be something else than length without breadth, and a circle something else than a circumscribed line everywhere verging equally to the centre. *R.* Why then do we hesitate? Or is not Truth where these things are? *A.* God avert such madness. *R.* Or is not the science in the mind? *A.* Who would say that? *R.* But is it possible, the subject perishing, that that which is in the subject should perdure? *A.* When could I imagine such a thing? *R.* It remains to suppose that Truth may fail. *A.* Whence could this be brought to pass? *R.* Therefore the soul is immortal: now at last yield to thine own arguments, believe the Truth; she cries out that she dwelleth in thee, and is immortal, and that her seat cannot be withdrawn from her by any possible death of the body. Turn away from thy shadow, return into thyself; of no meaning is the destruction thou fearest, except that thou hast forgotten that thou canst not be destroyed. *A.* I hear, I come to a better mind, I begin to recollect myself. But I beg thou wouldst expedite those things which remain; how, in an undisciplined mind, for a mortal one we cannot call it, Science and Truth are to be understood to be. *R.* That question requires another volume, if thou wouldst have it treated thoroughly: moreover also I see occasion for thee to review those things, which, after our best power, have been already examined; because if no one of those things which have been admitted is doubtful, I think that we have accomplished much, and with no small security may proceed to push our inquiries farther.

34. *A.* It is as thou sayest, and I willingly yield compliance with thine injunctions. But this at least I would entreat, before thou decreest a term to the volume, that thou wouldst summarily explain what the distinction is between the true figure, which is contained in the intelligence, and that which thought frames to itself, which in Greek is termed either Phantasia or Phantasma. *R.* Thou seekest that which no one except one of purest sight is able to see, and to the vision of which thing thou art but poorly

trained; nor have we now in these wide circuits anything else in view than to exercise thee, that thou mayest be competent to see: yet how it is possible to be taught that the difference is very great, perhaps I can, with a little pains, make clear. For suppose thou hadst forgotten something, and that others were wishing that thou shouldst recall it to memory. They therefore say: Is it this, or that? bringing forward things diverse from it as if similar to it. But thou neither seest that which thou desirest to recollect, and yet seest that it is not this which is suggested. Seems this to thee, when it happens, by any means equivalent to total forgetfulness? For this very power of distinguishing, whereby the false suggestions made to thee are repelled, is a certain part of recollection. *A.* So it seems. *R.* Such therefore do not yet see the truth; yet they cannot be misled and deceived; and what they seek, they sufficiently know. But if any one should say that thou didst laugh a few days after thou wast born, thou wouldst not venture to say it was false: and if he were an authority worthy of credit, thou art ready, not, indeed, to remember, but to believe; for to thee that whole time is buried in most authentic oblivion. Or thinkest thou otherwise? *A.* I thoroughly agree with this. *R.* This oblivion therefore differs exceedingly from that, but that stands midway. For there is another nearer and more closely neighboring to the recollection and rekindled vision of truth: the like of which is when we see something, and recognize for certain that we have seen it at some time, and affirm that we know it; but where, or when, or how, or with whom it came into our knowledge, we have enough to do to search our memory for an answer. As if this happens in regard to a man, we also inquire where we have known him: which when he has brought to mind, suddenly the whole thing flashes upon the memory like a light, and we have no more trouble to recollect. Is this sort of forgetfulness unknown to thee, or obscure? *A.* What plainer than this? or what is happening to me more frequently?

35. *R.* Such are those who are well instructed in the liberal arts; since they by learning disinter them, buried in oblivion, doubtless, within themselves, and, in a manner, dig them out afresh: nor yet are they content, nor refrain themselves until the whole aspect of Truth, of which, in those arts, a certain effulgence already gleams forth upon them, is by them most widely and most clearly beheld. But from this certain false colors and forms pour themselves as it were upon the mirror of thought, and mislead inquirers often, and deceive those who think that to be the whole which they know or which they inquire. Those imaginations themselves are to be avoided with great carefulness; which are detected as fallacious, by their varying with the varied mirror of thought, whereas that face of Truth abides one and immutable. For then thought portrays to itself, for instance, a square of this or that or the other magnitude, and, as it were, brings it before the eyes; but the inner mind which wishes to see the truth, applies itself rather to that general conception, if it can, according to which it

judges all these to be squares. *A.* What if some one should say to us that
the mind judges according to what it is accustomed to see with the eyes?
R. Why then does it judge, that is, if it is well trained, that a true sphere
of any conceivable size is touched by a true plane at a point? How has
eye ever seen, or how can eye ever see such a thing, when anything of this
kind cannot be bodied forth in the pure imagination of thought? Or do we
not prove this, when we describe even the smallest imaginary circle in our
mind, and from it draw lines to the centre? For when we have drawn two,
between which there is scarce room for a needle's point, we are no longer
able, even in imagination, to draw others between, so that they shall arrive
at the centre without any commixture; whereas reason exclaims that innumerable lines can be drawn, without being able to touch each other
except in the centre, so that in every interval between them even a circle
could be described. Since that Phantasy cannot accomplish this, and is
more deficient than the eyes themselves, since it is through them that it is
inflicted on the mind, it is manifest that it differs much from Truth, and
that that, when this is seen, is not seen.

36. These points will be treated with more pains and greater subtilty, when
we shall have begun to discuss the faculty of intelligence, which part of our
theme is proposed by us, as something which is to be developed and discussed by us, when anything gives anxiety concerning the life of the soul.
For I believe thee to stand in no slight fear lest the death of man, even if
it do not slay the soul, should nevertheless induce oblivion of all things,
and of Truth itself, if any shall have been discovered. *A.* It cannot be expressed how much this evil is to be feared. For of what sort will be that
eternal life, or what death is not to be preferred to it, if the soul so lives,
as we see it live in a child just born? to say nothing of that life which is
lived in the womb; for I do not think it to be none. *R.* Be of good courage;
God will be present, as we now feel, to us who seek, who promises a certain
most blessed body after this, and an utter plenitude of Truth without any
falsehood. *A.* May it be as we hope.

ON THE
IMMORTALITY OF THE SOUL

ON THE IMMORTALITY OF THE SOUL

Introductory Note

This treatise, which may be regarded as a sequel to the *Soliloquies,* was composed also in 387 A.D. and bears the same marks of the mind of the author while he was residing in Cassiciacum. As his thought was in a state of transition from Neo-Platonism to a fully developed Christianity, it is not strange that the writing of this period is still under a strong Platonic influence. In the treatise *On the Immortality of the Soul* Saint Augustine reproduces arguments that derive from Plato, though it is impossible to tell whether they came through direct contact or through the medium of Cicero or Plotinus. In any event, that he undertook to write on the problem of the soul's immortality indicates his interest at this period in developing a rational demonstration to support his own positive belief. In the *Rectractationes,* he refers to his early work in unfavorable terms, but for all its obscurity it remains an important document for this phase of Saint Augustine's thought.

ON THE IMMORTALITY OF THE SOUL*

CHAPTER I

THE FIRST REASON WHY THE SOUL IS IMMORTAL: IT IS THE SUBJECT OF SCIENCE WHICH IS ETERNAL

IF SCIENCE [*disciplina*] exists anywhere, and cannot exist except in that which lives; and if it is eternal, and nothing in which an eternal thing exists can be non-eternal; then that in which science exists lives eternally. If we exist who reason, that is, if our mind does, and if our mind cannot reason rightly without science, and if without science no mind can exist except as a mind without science, then science is in the mind of man. Science, moreover, is somewhere, for it exists, and whatever exists cannot be no-where. Further, science cannot exist except in that which lives. For nothing which is not alive learns anything, and science cannot be in a thing which does not learn.

Again, science is eternal. For what exists and is unchangeable must be eternal. But no one denies that science exists. And whoever admits that it is impossible that a line drawn through the midpoint of a circle is not greater than all lines which are not drawn through the midpoint, and admits that this is a part of science, does not deny that science is unchangeable. Further, nothing in which an eternal thing exists can be non-eternal. For nothing which is eternal ever allows to be taken from it that in which it exists eternally.

Now, truly, when we reason it is the mind which reasons. For only he who thinks reasons. Neither does the body think, nor does the mind receive the help of the body in thinking, since when the mind wishes to think it turns away from the body. For what is thought is thus eternal, and nothing pertaining to the body is thus eternal, therefore the body cannot help the mind as it strives to understand; for it is sufficient if the body does not hamper the mind. Again, without science [*disciplina*] nobody reasons rightly. For thought is right reasoning moving from things certain to the investigation of things uncertain, and there is nothing certain in an ignorant mind. All that the mind knows, moreover, it contains within itself, nor does knowledge consist in anything which does not pertain to some science. For science is the knowledge of any things whatsoever. Therefore the human mind always lives.

* Reprinted by permission from *St. Aurelius Augustine: Concerning the Teacher and On the Immortality of the Soul,* translated from the Latin with the addition of a preface by George G. Leckie. Copyright, 1938, by D. Appleton-Century Company, Inc.

CHAPTER II

ANOTHER REASON: IT IS THE SUBJECT OF REASON WHICH IS NOT CHANGED

Surely, reason either is the mind or is in the mind. Our reason, moreover, is better than our body, and body is a substance, and it is better to be a substance than to be nothing. Therefore, reason is not nothing.

Again, whatever the harmony of the body is, it must be in the body inseparably as in a subject; and nothing may be held to be in the harmony unless it is also necessarily in that body inseparably as in a subject. But the human body is mutable and reason is immutable. For all which does not exist always in the same mode is mutable, but that two and two are four exists always in the same mode, and also that four contains two and two exists always in the same mode, but two does not contain four, therefore two is not four. This sort of reasoning, then, is immutable. Therefore, reason is immutable.

Moreover, if the subject is changed, there is no way in which that which is in the subject remains unchanged. Hence, it follows that the mind is not a harmony of the body. Nor can death befall unchangeable things. Consequently, the mind always lives, and either the mind is reason itself or has reason in it inseparably.

CHAPTER III

MIND IS LIVING SUBSTANCE AND IMMUTABLE; AND IF IT IS IN SOME MODE MUTABLE, IT DOES NOT ON THAT ACCOUNT BECOME MORTAL

Some power [*virtus*] is constant, and all constancy is unchangeable, and all power can act, nor does it cease to be power when it acts. Further, all action is moved or moves. Therefore, not all which is moved, or surely not all which moves, is changeable. But all which is moved by another and does not move itself is a mortal thing. Nor is anything immutable which is mortal. Hence, certainly and without any disjunction, it is concluded that not all which moves is changed.

There is, moreover, no motion without substance, and any substance either is alive or is not alive, and all which does not live is inanimate. But no action is inanimate. Therefore, that which moves so as not to be changed can be only living substance. Any action, moreover, moves the body through a number of steps; therefore, not all which moves the body is changeable. The body, moreover, is not moved except in time; and to the body pertains being moved faster and slower; therefore, there is shown to be a certain thing which moves in time and is not changed. Moreover, every body which moves in time, although it tends towards one end, yet can neither accomplish simultaneously all the steps which lead to this end, nor can avoid the several steps. For by whatever impulse it is moved, a body cannot be perfectly one, because it can be divided into parts; and there is no body without parts, as there is no time without an interval of delay, even if it is expressed by a very short syllable of which you hear neither the beginning nor the end. Further, what occurs thus needs expectation that it may be accomplished and memory that it may be understood as much as possible. And expectation is of future things, while memory is of things past. But intention to act belongs to present time, through which the future moves into the past. And without memory we cannot expect the end of a motion which has begun. For how can that be expected to cease which forgets either that it has begun or that it is in motion? Again, the intention of accomplishing which is present cannot be without expectation of the end which is future: nor does anything exist which does not yet exist or which has already ceased to exist. Therefore, there can be something in acting which pertains to those things which do not yet exist. There can be several things simultaneously in the agent, although these several acts when executed cannot exist simultaneously. Likewise, they can exist simultaneously in the mover, although they cannot in the thing moved. But whatever things cannot exist simultaneously in time, and yet are transmitted from future into past, must of necessity be mutable.

From the above we have already gathered that there can be a certain thing which is not changed when it moves changeable things. For when the intention of the mover to bring the body which it moves to the end it desires is not changed, while the body which is acted upon is changed by this motion from moment to moment, and when that intention of accomplishment, which obviously remains unchanged, moves both the members of the artificer and the wood or stone which are subject to the artificer, who may doubt that what we have said follows as a logical consequence? Therefore, if any change in bodies be effected by the mind as mover, however intent upon the change the mind may be, we should not think that the mind is changed necessarily by this, or that the mind dies. For along with this intention it can have memory of past things and expectation of future things, none of which can exist without life. And even if there be no destruction without change, and no change without motion, yet not all change is engaged in destruction, nor is all motion engaged in change. For we can say that this body of ours has been for the most part moved by an action, and that it has undoubtedly been changed especially by age; still it has not yet perished, that is, is not without life. Therefore, from this it follows immediately that the mind is not deprived of life, even though some change does perchance occur to it through motion.

CHAPTER IV

ART AND THE UNCHANGEABLE PRINCIPLE OF NUMBERS, WHICH DO NOT INHERE IN THE MIND WITHOUT LIFE

For if there persists anything in the mind unchangeable, which cannot exist without life, then life must also remain in the mind eternally. For indeed the mind is so constituted that if the antecedent is true, the consequent is true. Moreover, the antecedent is true. For who dares say, not to mention other things, either that the principle [*ratio*] of number is changeable or that there is any art which does not depend upon this principle [*ratio*]; or that an art is not in the artist even if he be not applying it; or that it is in him other than as being in the mind; or that it can be where there is no life; or that what is unchangeable cannot be anywhere; or that art is other than a principle [*ratio*]? For although an art is said to be a sort of assemblage of many principles [*rationes*], yet an art can in truth be called one principle [*ratio*] and can be so thought. But whether it be the former or the latter, it follows none the less that art is unchangeable. Moreover, it is clear not only that an art is in the mind of the artist, but also that it is nowhere else except in the mind, and in it inseparably. For if art is separated from the mind it will be other than in the mind, or will be nowhere, or will pass immediately from the mind. But just as there is no seat of art without life, so there is no life according to a principle [*ratio*] anywhere except in the soul. Further, that which is cannot be nowhere nor can that which is immutable be non-existent at any time. But if art passes from mind to mind, it would leave one mind and abide in another; in this case nobody would teach an art except by losing it, or further, nobody would become skilled except through the forgetting of his teacher, or by the teacher's death. If these things are utterly absurd and false, as they are, then the human mind is immortal.

And if indeed art exists at some time, it does not so exist in a mind which is conspicuous for its forgetfulness and ignorance. The conclusion of this argument adds nothing to the mind's immortality unless the preceding be denied in the following way. Either there is something in the mind which is not in present thought or else the art of music is not in the educated mind when it thinks of geometry alone. And this latter is false. Hence the former is true. Moreover, the mind does not perceive that it contains anything except what comes into thought. Therefore, there can be something in the mind, which the mind itself does not perceive to be in it. But as long as it is there, this makes no difference. For if the mind has been occupied with other things too long to be able to turn its attention back to things thought of before, this is called forgetting or ignorance. But since, when we reason with ourselves or when we are skilfully questioned by another concerning certain liberal arts, we then discover the things which we discover nowhere else but in the mind; and since to discover is not to make or to cause, as otherwise the mind would cause eternal things through temporal discovery (for it often discovers eternal things, as the principle [*ratio*] of the circle, or anything else of this sort in the arts, which is not understood either to have been non-existent at some time or ever to be about to be); hence it is also evident that the human mind is immortal, and all true principles [*rationes*] are in its hidden places, although, either because of ignorance or forgetting, it seems not to contain them or to have lost them.

CHAPTER V

MIND IS NOT CHANGED SO THAT IT CEASES TO BE MIND

But now let us see to what extent we should accept the statement that the mind changes. For if the mind is the subject, with art existing in the subject, and if a subject cannot be changed unless that which is in it as in a subject be changed also, who can hold that art and principle [*ratio*] are unchangeable in the mind if the mind in which they exist is shown to be changeable? Moreover, where is there greater change than that in contraries? And who denies that the mind is, to say the least, at times stupid and at other times wise? Therefore, let us see in how many ways that which is called change of the soul may be taken. Of these I think there are found two genera quite evident or at least quite clear to us, though there are found several species. For the soul is said to be changed either according to passions of the body or according to its own passions. According to the passions of the body, as through age, disease, sorrow, work, hatred, or carnal desires; according to its own passions, however, as by desiring, enjoying, fearing, worrying, striving, or learning.

All these changes, if they are not necessarily proof that the soul dies, ought not to be feared at all taken separately each by each; but it should be seen whether they oppose our reasoning in which we said that when a subject is changed all which is in the subject is necessarily changed. But they do not oppose it. For this is said of a subject according to such a change as makes the name change entirely. For if wax changes to a black color from white, it is none the less wax; and also if it assumes a round shape after being square, becomes hard when it has been soft, cools after being hot. These are all in the subject, and wax is the subject. But wax remains not more or less wax when these things are changed. Therefore, some change of the things in the subject can occur, when the subject itself is not changed with regard to what it is and is called. But if so much change occurs in those things which are in the subject that that which was said to be the subject cannot any longer be so called, as, for example, when from the heat of fire wax disappears into the air, and suffers such change that it may rightly be understood that the subject is changed, since it was wax, and is no longer wax; then by no reasoning of any kind whatever would we think that any of those things would remain, which were in that subject because it was what it was.

Consequently, if, as we said above, the soul is a subject in which reason is inseparably (by that necessity also by which it is shown to be in the subject) neither can there be any soul except a living soul, nor can reason be in a soul without life, and reason is immortal; hence, the soul is immortal. For in absolutely no way could the soul remain immutable if its subject did not exist. This would happen if so great a change should befall the soul as would make it not a soul, that is, would compel it to die. Moreover, not one of those changes which occur to the soul, either through the body or through itself (although there is not a little question whether any occur through itself, that is, of which it is itself the cause) causes the soul not to be a soul. Therefore, they need not be feared *per se;* nor because they may oppose our reasoning.

CHAPTER VI

UNCHANGEABLE REASON, WHETHER IT BE IN THE MIND OR WITH THE MIND, OR WHETHER THE MIND BE IN IT, CANNOT BE SEPARATED FROM THE VERY SAME MIND

Hence I see that all men of reason ought to take pains to know what reason is and in how many ways it can be defined, so that it may remain firm according to all modes and with regard to the immortality of the soul. Reason is the aspect of the mind which perceives the true *per se* and not through the body; or it is the contemplation of the true, not through the body; or it is the true itself which is contemplated. Nobody doubts that the first of these is in the mind. There can be a question about the second and third; but even the second cannot exist without the mind. Concerning the third the great question is whether the true which is perceived by the mind without the instrument of the body exists *per se,* and is not in the mind, or whether it can exist without the mind. Moreover, in whatever mode the true may be, the mind cannot contemplate it *per se* except through some connection with it. For all that we contemplate we either perceive through cogitation [*cogitatio*], or through a sense or through the intellect. But those things which are perceived through sense we also sense to be outside us, and to be contained in places apart from which it is established that they cannot be perceived. But those things which are thought are not thought as being in another place other than the very mind which thinks them: for at the same time they also are thought as not being contained in any place.

Consequently, the connection between the mind which perceives and the true which it perceives is either such that the mind is the subject with the true in it as in a subject; or on the other hand the true is the subject with the mind in it as in a subject; or else each is a substance. Moreover, if the connection is of the first sort, the mind is as immortal as reason, according to the preceding argument, since reason can be in nothing but a living thing. The same necessity lies in the second sort of connection. For if the true, which is called reason, contains nothing which is changeable, as it appears, then nothing can be changed which is in it as in a subject. Therefore, all the struggle is left to the third. For if mind is one substance and reason another substance to which it is joined, he is not absurd who would think it possible for the former to remain while the latter perishes. But it is evident that as long as the mind is not separated from reason and remains connected with it, the mind necessarily survives and lives. But by what force can it be separated? By bodily force, whose power is weaker, whose origin is inferior, whose order is more disparate? Not at all. Then by animate strength? But how so? Cannot a more powerful mind contemplate reason without separating another mind from it? Reason is not lacking in any mind which contemplates, if all minds contemplate; and since nothing is more powerful than reason itself, than which nothing is more immutable, by no means will there be a mind not joined to reason and yet more powerful than one which is so joined. It remains that either reason separates itself from mind, or else the mind itself is separated by will. But there is no envy in that nature, and, therefore, it offers itself for mind's enjoyment; and, what is more, whatever it joins to itself it causes to be, which is contrary to destruction. Moreover, it is too absurd for someone to say that the mind is separated from reason by the mind's own will, provided there can be any mutual separation of things which space does not contain. Indeed this can be said in contradiction to all we have argued above in meeting other opposition. What then? Should it be concluded that the mind is immortal? Or, even though it cannot be separated, can it perhaps be extinguished? But if the very strength of reason affects the mind by its connection (and it cannot fail to affect it), then it at once causes being to be ascribed to mind. For it is in great measure reason itself in which the supreme immutability is thought. Therefore, that which reason affects by virtue of itself it causes to exist in a certain respect. Hence the mind cannot be extinguished unless it be separated from reason, and it cannot be separated, as we have proved above. Therefore it cannot perish.

CHAPTER VII

AND IF THE MIND TENDS THROUGH SUBSTANCE TOWARDS DEFECTION, STILL IT DOES NOT ON THIS ACCOUNT PERISH

But that very turning away from reason by which stupidity enters the mind cannot occur without a defect in the mind. For if the mind has more being when turned towards reason and inhering in it, thus adhering to the unchangeable thing which is truth, both greatest and first; so when turned away from reason it has less being, which constitutes a defection. Moreover, every defect tends towards nothing [non-being], nor do we ever speak more properly of destruction than when that which was something becomes nothing. Therefore, to tend towards nothing [non-being] is to tend towards destruction. It is hard to say why this does not occur to the soul in which defect occurs. We grant all the above, but we deny that it follows that what tends towards nothing [non-being] perishes, that is, that it reaches nothing. This can be observed in the body also. For any body is part of the sensible world, and for this reason the larger it is and the more space it occupies the nearer it is to the universe; and the more it does this, the greater it is. For the whole is greater than the part. Hence, necessarily, it is less when it is diminished; that is, it suffers a defect when it is lessened. Moreover, it is lessened when something is taken from it by cutting away, and it follows from this that because of such subtraction it tends to nothing. But no cutting away leads to nothing as such. For every part which remains is a body, and whatever is a body occupies a place in some space. Nor would this be possible unless it were to have parts into which it might be cut again and again. Therefore, it can be infinitely diminished through infinite division, and hence can suffer defection and tend towards nothing, although it can never reach nothing. Further, this can be said and understood of space itself and of any interval whatever. For by taking, let us say, a half part from the limits, and always a half part from what is left, the interval is diminished and approaches a limit which yet it can in no mode attain. Accordingly, even less should it be feared that the mind may become nothing, for the mind is indeed better and more lively than the body.

CHAPTER VIII

JUST AS THAT CANNOT BE TAKEN FROM BODY BY WHICH IT IS BODY, SO NEITHER CAN THAT BE TAKEN FROM MIND BY WHICH IT IS MIND

But if that which causes the body to be is not in the matter of the body but in the form (which point is established by quite irrefutable reasoning, for a body is greater according as it has better form and is more excellent, and it is less according as it is uglier and is more deformed, which defect occurs not from a taking away of matter, about which enough has been said, but from a privation of form), then this should be questioned and discussed, lest someone assert that mind perishes through defect of form; for seeing that when it is stupid mind is deprived of some of its form, it may be believed that this privation can be increased so much as to deprive the mind of form in every mode, by this misfortune reducing it to nothing and causing it to perish. Hence, if we can succeed in showing that not even the body can be deprived of that by virtue of which it is body, perhaps we shall rightly maintain that the mind can much less have that taken from it by virtue of which it is mind. For whoever considers carefully will admit that any kind of mind whatever must be preferred to every body.

Let this, then, be the beginning of our argument, namely, that no thing makes or begets itself, unless it was before it existed: if the latter is false, the former is true. Again, that which has not been made or begotten, and yet is, must be everlasting. Whoever attributes this nature and this excellence to any body, errs indeed greatly. But why do we dispute? For even were we to attribute it to body we should be forced to attribute it much more to the mind. Thus if any body is everlasting, there is no mind which is not everlasting; seeing that any mind is to preferred to any body and eternal things to non-eternal things. But if it is truly said that the body is made, it was made by some maker, nor was the maker inferior to body. For an inferior maker would not have power to give to that which he was making whatever it is that makes it what it is. But the maker and the body are not equals, since it is necessary for a maker to have something better for making than that which he makes. For we do not make the absurd statement that the begetter is that thing which is begotten by him. Therefore, a whole body has been made by some force which is more powerful and better, or at least not corporeal. For if a body be made by a body, it cannot be made whole; for it is very true, as we stated in the beginning of this argument, that no thing can be made by itself. Moreover, this force or incorporeal nature being the producer of the whole body preserves the whole by its abiding power. For it did not make a thing and then vanish and desert the thing made. Indeed that substance which is not body is not, if I may speak thus, moved in space so that it can be separated from that substance which is localized; and this effecting strength cannot be idle, but preserves that which it has made, and does not allow it to lack the form by virtue of which it is to whatever extent it is. For since the thing made does not exist *per se,* if it is abandoned by that through which it exists, it will immediately cease to exist, and we cannot say that when the body was made it received the power to be sufficient by virtue of itself when it is deserted by its maker.

And if this is so, the mind which clearly excels the body has power to a greater degree. And thus the mind is proved immortal, if it can exist *per se.* For whatever exists thus must be incorruptible, and therefore unable to perish, since nothing abandons itself. But the changeability of the body is manifest, which the whole motion of the entire body indicates adequately. Hence, it is found by those who investigate carefully, in so far as such a nature can be investigated, that ordered changeableness imitates that which is unchangeable. Moreover, that which exists *per se* has no need of anything, not even of motion, since it has all it needs existing in itself; for all motion is towards another thing which is that which is lacked by that which is moved. Therefore, form is present in the whole body while a better nature which made it provides for and sustains it, hence, that changeability does not take away from a body its being a body, but causes it to pass from one form to another by a well-ordered motion. For not one of its parts is allowed to be reduced to nothing, since that effective power with its force, neither striving nor inactive, aims at a whole, permitting the body to be all which through the power it is, in so far as it is. Consequently, there should be no one so devoid of reason as not to be certain that the mind is better than the body, or when this has been granted, to think that it does not happen to the body that the body is not body, yet happens to the mind that it is not mind. If this does not happen, and a mind cannot exist unless it lives, surely a mind can never die.

CHAPTER IX

MIND IS LIFE, AND THUS IT CANNOT LACK LIFE

If anyone asserts that the mind ought not to fear that destruction in which that which was something becomes nothing, but ought to fear that in which we call those things dead which lack life, let him notice that there is no thing which lacks itself. Moreover, mind is a certain life, so that all which is animated lives. But every inanimate thing which can be animated is understood to be dead, that is, deprived of life. Hence the mind cannot die. For if anything can lack life, this thing is not mind which animates, but a thing which has been animated. If this is absurd, this kind of destruction should be feared much less by the mind, since destruction of life is surely not to be feared. For if the mind dies wholly when life abandons it, that very life which deserts it is understood much better as mind, as now mind is not something deserted by life, but the very life itself which deserted. For whatever dead thing is said to be abandoned by life, is understood to be deserted by the soul. Moreover, this life which deserts the things which die is itself the mind, and it does not abandon itself; hence the mind does not die

CHAPTER X

MIND IS NOT THE ORGANIZATION OF BODY

Unless perhaps we ought to believe that life is some organization [*temperatio*] of the body, as some have held. It would never have seemed so to them if they had been able to see those things which exist truly and which remain unchangeable when the same mind has been freed from the habit of bodies and cleansed. For who has looked well within himself without having experienced that the more earnestly he had thought something, the more he was able to move and draw the attention of the mind away from the senses of the body? If the mind were an organization of the body, this would absolutely not happen. For a thing which did not have a nature of its own and was not a substance, but which like color and shape was in the body inseparably as in a subject, would not try in any way to turn itself away from that same body in order to perceive intelligible things; and only inasmuch as it could do this would it be able to look upon intelligible things and be made by this vision better and more excellent. Indeed, in no way can shape or color, or the very organization of the body, which is a certain mixture of four natures in which the same body consists, turn from the thing in which they are inseparably as in a subject. In comparison with these things, those things which the mind thinks when it turns away from the body are not wholly corporeal, and yet they exist, and that in great degree, for they maintain themselves always in the same mode. For nothing more absurd can be said than that those things which we see with the eyes exist, while those things which we perceive by the intellect do not; for it is mad to doubt that the intellect is incomparably superior to the eyes. Moreover, while these things which are thought maintain themselves in the same mode, when the mind sees them it shows well enough that it is joined to them in a certain miraculous and likewise incorporeal way, that is, not locally. For either they are in it, or it is in them. And whichever one of these is true, either the one is in the other as in a subject, or each one is a substance. But if the first is true, the mind is not in the body as in a subject, as color and shape are, since either it is substance itself or it is in another substance which is not body. Moreover, if the second is true, mind is not in body as in a subject, as color is in body, because the mind is a substance. Further, the organization of a body is in the body as in a subject, just as color is; therefore, mind is not the organization of the body, but the mind is life. No thing deserts itself, and that dies which is deserted by life. Therefore, the mind cannot die.

CHAPTER XI

EVEN THOUGH TRUTH IS THE CAUSE OF THE MIND, MIND DOES NOT PERISH THROUGH FALSEHOOD, THE CONTRARY OF TRUTH

And so again, if anything should be feared, it is that the mind may perish by defection, that is, may be deprived of the very form of existence. Although I think enough has been said about this, and it has been shown by clear reasoning that this cannot be done, yet it should also be observed that there is no other reason for this fear except that we have admitted that the stupid mind exists defectively, while the wise mind exists in more certain and fuller essence. But if, as nobody doubts, the mind is most wise when it looks upon truth which is always in the same mode, and clings immovable to it, joined by divine love; and if all things which exist in any mode whatever exist by that essence which exists in the highest and greatest degree; then either the mind exists by virtue of that essence, inasmuch as it does exist, or it exists *per se*. But if it exists *per se,* since it is itself the cause of its existing and never deserts itself, it never perishes, as we also argued above. But if we exist from that essence there is need to inquire carefully what thing can be contrary to it, which may rob the mind of being the mind which the essence causes. So, then, what is it? Falsity, perhaps, because the essence is truth? But it is manifest and clearly established to what extent falsity can harm the mind. For can it do more than deceive? And except he live is any deceived? Therefore, falsity cannot destroy the mind. But if what is contrary to truth cannot rob the mind of that being mind which truth gave it (for truth is thus unconquerable) what else may be found which may take from the mind that which is mind? Nothing, surely; for nothing is more able than a contrary to take away that which is made by its contrary.

CHAPTER XII

THERE IS NO CONTRARY TO THE TRUTH BY WHICH MIND EXISTS IN SO FAR AS IT EXISTS

But suppose we seek the contrary of truth, not inasmuch as it is truth as the contrary of falsity, but inasmuch as it exists in the greatest and highest degree (although truth exists thus to the extent that it is truth, if we call that truth by which all things are true, in whatever degree they may exist, they exist inasmuch as they are true); yet by no means shall I seek to avoid that which this suggests to me so clearly. For if there is no contrary to any essence inasmuch as it is an essence, then much less is there a contrary to that first essence inasmuch as it is essence. Moreover, the antecedent is true. For no essence exists for any other reason than that it exists. Being, moreover, has no contrary except non-being: hence nothing is the contrary of essence. Therefore, in no way can anything exist as a contrary to that substance which exists first and in highest degree. If the mind has its very essence from that essence (for since it does not have it from itself [ex se] it cannot have it otherwise than from that thing which is superior to the mind itself); then there is no thing by which it may lose its existence (being), because there is nothing contrary to that thing from which it has it. Hence the mind cannot cease to exist. But since the mind has wisdom because of turning to that by virtue of which it exists, so also when it turns away it can lose this wisdom. For turning away is the contrary of turning toward. But what it has from that to which there is no contrary is not a thing which it can lose. Therefore, it cannot perish.

CHAPTER XIII

NOR IS MIND CHANGED INTO BODY

Here perhaps some question may appear as to whether the mind which does not perish is not changed into a lower essence. For it can appear to some, and not unjustly, that this reasoning proves that the mind cannot

reach nothing, yet can be perhaps changed into body. For if what was formerly mind becomes body it will not yet be wholly non-existent. But this
is impossible unless the mind desires it or else is compelled by another. Yet
mind will not necessarily be able to be body, even if it desires it, or if it is
compelled. For if it is body it follows that it desires this or is compelled.
But it does not follow that if it desires or is compelled, it is body. Moreover, it will never desire to be body: for all the mind desires in regard to
body is that it may possess it, or make it live, or fashion it in a certain
manner, or look out for it in some way or other. Moreover, none of these
things is possible if mind is not better than body. But if mind is body, it
follows that it will not be better than body. Therefore, it will not wish to
be body. Nor is there any surer proof of this than when the mind questions
itself about this point. For thus the mind easily discovers that it has no
desire except for some action, either knowing or sensing, or only living to
the fullest extent of its power.

But if it is compelled to be body, by what, pray, is it compelled? Whatever it is it must surely be more powerful than mind, hence it cannot be
compelled by body itself; for no body can in any way be more powerful
than mind. Moreover, a more powerful mind compels only that which is set
under its power, and no mind can in any way be set under the power of
another mind except by the former's own desire. Hence, one mind does not
compel another mind more than the desires of the other allow. Moreover,
it has been said that mind cannot have desire to be body. Also it is clear
that the mind attains no satisfaction of its desire while it loses all desire,
which happens when it is made body. Therefore, a mind cannot be compelled to become body by one whose only right to compel lies in the desires
of the one compelled. Then whatever mind has another mind in its power
must prefer having it to having a body in its power, and must wish to pro-
mote its goodness or to have power over evil. Therefore, it will not wish it
to be body.

Finally, the mind which compels either is animal or it lacks body. But
if it lacks body it is not in this world. And if it is thus, it is supremely
good and cannot wish another to suffer such a wicked change. But if it is
animal, either the mind it compels is animal or it is not. But if it is not, it
cannot be compelled to anything by another. For none is more powerful
than that which exists in the greatest degree. On the other hand, if it is
body, again it is forced through body to whatever extent it is forced. But
who believes that in any way such a change can be made in mind through
body? For it would be made if the body were greater than it; although no
matter what it is to which it is compelled by body it is not compelled wholly
through body, but is compelled through its own desires, about which enough
has been said. Moreover, that which is better than a rational soul is God,
as all agree. He surely looks after the soul, and, therefore, the soul cannot
be forced by Him to be changed into body.

CHAPTER XIV

NOR IS THE STRENGTH OF THE MIND DIMINISHED BY SLEEP OR ANY OTHER SIMILAR AFFECTION OF THE BODY

Hence, if the mind does not suffer this change by its own will, or because it is compelled by another, by what means can it suffer it? Or, because sleep for the most part overtakes us against our will, should it be feared that by some such defect the mind may be changed to body? As if when our limbs are overwhelmed by sleep to say that the mind is made weaker in some sense. Sensible things only it does not sense, because whatever causes sleep pertains to the body and works in the body. Sleep lulls and shuts off the corporeal senses so soundly that the soul submits with pleasure to such a change of the body. Such a change is according to nature and refreshes the body after its labors, yet it does not take from the mind the power of sensing and thinking. For it still has images of sensible things at hand of such evident similarity that at the time they cannot be distinguished from the things of which they are the images. If the mind thinks anything, it is as true in sleeping as in waking. For, to give an example, if it should argue to itself in a dream, and following true principles in argument should learn something, when it is awakened the same principles remain immutable, although other things may be found false, such as the place where the argument seemed to have occurred, the person with whom it seemed to have been held, even, as far as sound is concerned, the words themselves by which it seemed the argument was made, and other things of this sort. Likewise when these things are perceived and discussed by those who are awake, they pass away and in no sense attain the eternal presence of true principles. From this it is inferred that when a body changes as in sleep the soul's use of that body can be diminished, but not its own life.

CHAPTER XV

AGAIN, MIND CANNOT BE CHANGED INTO BODY

Finally, however much the soul is joined to a body occupying space, still it is not joined locally. The soul is prior to the body in connection with those supreme and eternal principles which survive unchangeably and are not contained in space; and the soul's connection is not only prior but also greater; as much prior as it is nearer, and for the same reason as much greater as it is better than body. And this nearness is not in place but in the order of nature. According to this order it is understood that the supreme essence bestows form upon the body through the soul by which it exists in whatever degree it does exist. Therefore, the body subsists through the soul, and it exists to the extent that it is animated, whether universally, as the world, or particularly, as some animal or other within the world. Therefore, the conclusion was that a soul would become body through a soul, or else not at all. Since it does not become body, and the soul remains soul in that in which it is the soul, the body subsists through the soul which gives it form and does not take this form away; hence the soul cannot be changed into body. For if it does not give up the form which it takes from the Supreme Good, it does not become body through that form; and if it does not become body through that, either it does not become body at all, or else takes a form as near the Supreme Good as soul. But if, when it became body, it assumed a form as near the Supreme Good as soul, that form would be a soul; for this is important, that the soul is better to the extent to which it takes a form nearer the Supreme Good. Moreover, body would take a form of the corporeal order even if it did not take its form through soul. For if nothing intervened it would still take a form in this order. Nor is there found anything which exists between the Supreme Life which is wisdom and truth unchangeable and that remote thing which is made alive (that is, body) except the soul which makes the body live. If the soul gives form to body, so that body may exist to the extent that it does exist, it does not take the form away by giving. Moreover, it takes the soul into the body by transmutation. Therefore, the soul does not become body, either *per se,* because body is not made by soul unless the soul remains, or through another, because not except by giving form is body made through soul, and by taking away form soul would be changed into body, if it were changed.

CHAPTER XVI

NOR EVEN IS THE RATIONAL SOUL CHANGED INTO THE IRRATIONAL. THE WHOLE SOUL IS IN THE BODY AS A WHOLE AND IN EACH PART

Likewise it can be said that the rational soul is not changed into the irrational soul or life. For the irrational soul, even were it not held in a lower order by the rational soul, would nevertheless assume the same form it does assume and be moved as it is. Therefore, more powerful things receive form from the Supreme Excellence and give it to things in the natural order. And when they give, surely, they do not take away. And to whatever extent the things which are inferior exist, they exist because the form in which they exist is given to them by those more powerful than they. And, indeed, the more powerful are also better. For to these natures it has been granted, not that through greater mass they have more power over things of lesser mass, but that without any increase of local magnitude they are more powerful than and better than the lower forms. In this way the soul is better than and greater than the body. Therefore, since the body, as has been said, subsists through the soul, the soul can in no way be changed into body; for no body is made except by receiving its form from the soul. The soul, if it became body, would become body through losing form, not through receiving it; therefore, it is not possible, unless perhaps the soul be contained in a place and joined locally to the body. For if this were true, although the soul is more perfect in form, perhaps a greater mass could change the soul into its lower form, just as the greater air changes the lesser fire. But it is not true. Indeed, every mass which occupies a place is not a separate whole in each of its parts, but the whole consists of all the parts. Consequently, one part of such a whole is in one place, and another in another. But the soul is present as a whole not only in the entire mass of a body, but also in every least part of the body at the same time. For the soul senses the suffering of a part of the body as a whole, and yet not in the whole body. For when there is a pain in the foot the eye turns, the tongue speaks, the hand moves forward. This would not happen unless the soul which senses in these parts, also senses in the foot, nor could it while absent sense what was happening there. For it is not to be believed that it happens through any agent of communication which does not sense what it communicates; for the suffering which occurs does not run through the whole extent of the mass in such a way as to involve all the other parts of the soul which are elsewhere. Rather, the whole soul senses what happens to the foot in particular, and only senses it at the place at which it happens. The whole soul, therefore, is present simultaneously in each part, and simultaneously senses in each. Yet the soul is not wholly present in the way in which whiteness or any other quality of this sort is wholly present in each part of a body. For what a body suffers in one part by change of whiteness cannot pertain to the whiteness which is in another part. Hence, it is shown that a mass itself is differentiated according as its parts are differentiated. But we have proved above that this is not the case with the soul as it senses.

ON THE
MORALS OF THE CATHOLIC CHURCH

ON THE

MORALS OF THE CATHOLIC CHURCH

Introductory Note

Not long after Saint Augustine became a member of the Christian Church, he assumed the role of an active defender of the faith. The treatise *On the Morals of the Catholic Church*—which has a sequel or a second part, *On the Morals of the Manichaeans*—was written in Rome in 388 A.D. and hence is among the first of Saint Augustine's polemics against heresy. Because of his experience as a follower of Manicheism, he is master of his attack. In the work, he assails the Manichaean refusal to accept the authority of the *Old Testament*, as well as their false claim that they teach an asceticism. As Saint Augustine develops his argument he elucidates the Christian doctrine concerning the happy life, the harmony of the *Old* and *New Testaments*, and the moral teaching which is implicit in a true love of God. The treatise as a whole contains not only a clear statement of an important aspect of Christianity but also an enlightening picture of life within the Christian communion at the end of the fourth century.

MORALS OF THE CATHOLIC CHURCH

It is laid down at the outset that the customs of the holy life of the Church should be referred to the chief good of man, that is, God. We must seek after God with supreme affection; and this doctrine is supported in the Catholic Church by the authority of both Testaments. The four virtues get their names from different forms of this love. Then follow the duties of love to our neighbor. In the Catholic Church we find examples of continence and of true Christian conduct.

CHAPTER I

HOW THE PRETENSIONS OF THE MANICHAEANS ARE TO BE REFUTED. TWO MANICHAEAN FALSEHOODS

ENOUGH, probably, has been done in our other books in the way of answering the ignorant and profane attacks which the Manichaeans make on the law, which is called the Old Testament, in a spirit of vainglorious boasting, and with the approval of the uninstructed. Here, too, I may shortly touch upon the subject. For every one with average intelligence can easily see that the explanation of the Scriptures should be sought for from those who are the professed teachers of the Scriptures; and that it may happen, and indeed always happens, that many things seem absurd to the ignorant, which, when they are explained by the learned, appear all the more excellent, and are received in the explanation with the greater pleasure on account of the obstructions which made it difficult to reach the meaning. This commonly happens as regards the holy books of the Old Testament, if only the man who meets with difficulties applies to a pious teacher, and not to a profane critic, and if he begins his inquiries from a desire to find truth, and not in rash opposition. And should the inquirer meet with some, whether bishops or presbyters, or any officials or ministers of the Catholic Church, who either avoid in all cases opening up mysteries, or, content with simple faith, have no desire for more recondite knowledge, he must not despair of finding the knowledge of the truth in a case where neither are all able to teach to whom the inquiry is addressed, nor are all inquirers worthy of learning the truth. Diligence and piety are both necessary: on the one hand, we must have knowledge to find truth, and, on the other hand, we must deserve to get the knowledge.

But as the Manichaeans have two tricks for catching the unwary, so as to make them take them as teachers—one, that of finding fault with the

Scriptures, which they either misunderstand or wish to be misunderstood, the other, that of making a show of chastity and of notable abstinence—this book shall contain our doctrine of life and morals according to Catholic teaching, and will perhaps make it appear how easy it is to pretend to virtue, and how difficult to possess virtue. I will refrain, if I can, from attacking their weak points, which I know well, with the violence with which they attack what they know nothing of; for I wish them, if possible, to be cured rather than conquered. And I will quote such testimonies from the Scriptures as they are bound to believe, for they shall be from the New Testament; and even from this I will take none of the passages which the Manichaeans when hard pressed are accustomed to call spurious, but passages which they are obliged to acknowledge and approve. And for every testimony from apostolic teaching I will bring a similar statement from the Old Testament, that if they ever become willing to wake up from their persistent dreams, and to rise towards the light of Christian faith, they may discover both how far from being Christian is the life which they profess, and how truly Christian is the Scripture which they cavil at.

CHAPTER II

HE BEGINS WITH ARGUMENTS, IN COMPLIANCE WITH THE MISTAKEN METHOD OF THE MANICHAEANS

Where, then, shall I begin? With authority, or with reasoning? In the order of nature, when we learn anything, authority precedes reasoning. For a reason may seem weak, when, after it is given, it requires authority to confirm it. But because the minds of men are obscured by familiarity with darkness, which covers them in the night of sins and evil habits, and cannot perceive in a way suitable to the clearness and purity of reason, there is most wholesome provision for bringing the dazzled eye into the light of truth under the congenial shade of authority. But since we have to do with people who are perverse in all their thoughts and words and actions, and who insist on nothing more than on beginning with argument, I will, as a concession to them, take what I think a wrong method in discussion. For I like to imitate, as far as I can, the gentleness of my Lord Jesus Christ, who took on Himself the evil of death itself, wishing to free us from it.

CHAPTER III

HAPPINESS IS IN THE ENJOYMENT OF MAN'S CHIEF GOOD. TWO CONDITIONS OF THE CHIEF GOOD: 1ST, NOTHING IS BETTER THAN IT; 2D, IT CANNOT BE LOST AGAINST THE WILL

How then, according to reason, ought man to live? We all certainly desire to live happily; and there is no human being but assents to this statement almost before it is made. But the title happy cannot, in my opinion, belong either to him who has not what he loves, whatever it may be, or to him who has what he loves if it is hurtful, or to him who does not love what he has, although it is good in perfection. For one who seeks what he cannot obtain suffers torture, and one who has got what is not desirable is cheated, and one who does not seek for what is worth seeking for is diseased. Now in all these cases the mind cannot but be unhappy, and happiness and unhappiness cannot reside at the same time in one man; so in none of these cases can the man be happy. I find, then, a fourth case, where the happy life exists—when that which is man's chief good is both loved and possessed. For what do we call enjoyment but having at hand the objects of love? And no one can be happy who does not enjoy what is man's chief good, nor is there any one who enjoys this who is not happy. We must then have at hand our chief good, if we think of living happily.

We must now inquire what is man's chief good, which of course cannot be anything inferior to man himself. For whoever follows after what is inferior to himself, becomes himself inferior. But every man is bound to follow what is best. Wherefore man's chief good is not inferior to man. Is it then something similar to man himself? It must be so, if there is nothing above man which he is capable of enjoying. But if we find something which is both superior to man, and can be possessed by the man who loves it, who can doubt that in seeking for happiness man should endeavor to reach that which is more excellent than the being who makes the endeavor. For if happiness consists in the enjoyment of a good than which there is nothing better, which we call the chief good, how can a man be properly called happy who has not yet attained to his chief good? or how can that be the chief good beyond which something better remains for us to arrive at? Such, then, being the chief good, it must be something which cannot be lost against the will. For no one can feel confident regarding a good which he knows can be taken from him, although he wishes to keep and cherish it. But if a man feels no confidence regarding the good which he enjoys, how can he be happy while in such fear of losing it?

CHAPTER IV

MAN—WHAT?

Let us then see what is better than man. This must necessarily be hard to find, unless we first ask and examine what man is. I am not now called upon to give a definition of man. The question here seems to me to be —since almost all agree, or at least, which is enough, those I have now to do with are of the same opinion with me, that we are made up of soul and body—What is man? Is he both of these? or is he the body only, or the soul only? For although the things are two, soul and body, and although neither without the other could be called man (for the body would not be man without the soul, nor again would the soul be man if there were not a body animated by it), still it is possible that one of these may be held to be man, and may be called so. What then do we call man? Is he soul and body, as in a double harness, or like a centaur? Or do we mean the body only, as being in the service of the soul which rules it, as the word lamp denotes not the light and the case together, but only the case, yet it is on account of the light that it is so called? Or do we mean only the mind, and that on account of the body which it rules, as horseman means not the man and the horse, but the man only, and that as employed in ruling the horse? This dispute is not easy to settle; or, if the proof is plain, the statement requires time. This is an expenditure of time and strength which we need not incur. For whether the name man belongs to both, or only to the soul, the chief good of man is not the chief good of the body; but what is the chief good either of both soul and body, or of the soul only, that is man's chief good.

CHAPTER V

MAN'S CHIEF GOOD IS NOT THE CHIEF GOOD OF THE BODY ONLY, BUT THE CHIEF GOOD OF THE SOUL

Now if we ask what is the chief good of the body, reason obliges us to admit that it is that by means of which the body comes to be in its best state. But of all the things which invigorate the body, there is nothing better or greater than the soul. The chief good of the body, then, is not bodily pleasure, not absence of pain, not strength, not beauty, not swiftness, or whatever else is usually reckoned among the goods of the body, but simply the soul. For all the things mentioned the soul supplies to the body by its presence, and, what is above them all, life. Hence I conclude that the soul is not the chief good of man, whether we give the name of man to soul and body together, or to the soul alone. For as, according to reason, the chief good of the body is that which is better than the body, and from which the body receives vigor and life, so whether the soul itself is man, or soul and body both, we must discover whether there is anything which goes before the soul itself, in following which the soul comes to the perfection of good of which it is capable in its own kind. If such a thing can be found, all uncertainty must be at an end, and we must pronounce this to be really and truly the chief good of man.

If, again, the body is man, it must be admitted that the soul is the chief good of man. But clearly, when we treat of morals—when we inquire what manner of life must be held in order to obtain happiness—it is not the body to which the precepts are addressed, it is not bodily discipline which we discuss. In short, the observance of good *customs* belongs to that part of us which inquires and learns, which are the prerogatives of the soul; so, when we speak of attaining to virtue, the question does not regard the body. But if it follows, as it does, that the body which is ruled over by a soul possessed of virtue is ruled both bettter and more honorably, and is in its greatest perfection in consequence of the perfection of the soul which rightfully governs it, that which gives perfection to the soul will be man's chief good, though we call the body man. For if my coachman, in obedience to me, feeds and drives the horses he has charge of in the most satisfactory manner, himself enjoying the more of my bounty in proportion to his good conduct, can any one deny that the good condition of the horses, as well as that of the coachman, is due to me? So the question seems to me to be not, whether soul and body is man, or the soul only, or the body only, but what gives perfection to the soul; for when this is obtained, a man cannot but be either perfect, or at least much better than in the absence of this one thing.

CHAPTER VI

VIRTUE GIVES PERFECTION TO THE SOUL; THE SOUL OBTAINS VIRTUE BY FOLLOWING GOD; FOLLOWING GOD IS THE HAPPY LIFE

No one will question that virtue gives perfection to the soul. But it is a very proper subject of inquiry whether this virtue can exist by itself or only in the soul. Here again arises a profound discussion, needing lengthy treatment; but perhaps my summary will serve the purpose. God will, I trust, assist me, so that, notwithstanding our feebleness, we may give instruction on these great matters briefly as well as intelligibly. In either case, whether virtue can exist by itself without the soul, or can exist only in the soul, undoubtedly in the pursuit of virtue the soul follows after something, and this must be either the soul itself, or virtue, or something else. But if the soul follows after itself in the pursuit of virtue, it follows after a foolish thing; for before obtaining virtue it is foolish. Now the height of a follower's desire is to reach that which he follows after. So the soul must either not wish to reach what it follows after, which is utterly absurd and unreasonable, or, in following after itself while foolish, it reaches the folly which it flees from. But if it follows after virtue in the desire to reach it, how can it follow what does not exist? or how can it desire to reach what it already possesses? Either, therefore, virtue exists beyond the soul, or if we are not allowed to give the name of virtue except to the habit and disposition of the wise soul, which can exist only in the soul, we must allow that the soul follows after something else in order that virtue may be produced in itself; for neither by following after nothing, nor by following after folly, can the soul, according to my reasoning, attain to wisdom.

This something else then, by following after which the soul becomes possessed of virtue and wisdom, is either a wise man or God. But we have said already that it must be something that we cannot lose against our will. No one can think it necessary to ask whether a wise man, supposing we are content to follow after him, can be taken from us in spite of our unwillingness or our persistence. God then remains, in following after whom we live well, and in reaching whom we live both well and happily. If any deny God's existence, why should I consider the method of dealing with them, when it is doubtful whether they ought to be dealt with at all? At any rate, it would require a different starting-point, a different plan, a different investigation from what we are now engaged in. I am now addressing those who do not deny the existence of God, and who, moreover, allow that human affairs are not disregarded by Him. For there is no one, I suppose, who makes any profession of religion but will hold that divine Providence cares at least for our souls.

CHAPTER VII

THE KNOWLEDGE OF GOD TO BE OBTAINED FROM THE SCRIPTURE. THE PLAN AND PRINCIPAL MYSTERIES OF THE DIVINE SCHEME OF REDEMPTION

But how can we follow after Him whom we do not see? or how can we see Him, we who are not only men, but also men of weak understanding? For though God is seen not with the eyes but with the mind, where can such a mind be found as shall, while obscured by foolishness, succeed or even attempt to drink in that light? We must therefore have recourse to the instructions of those whom we have reason to think wise. Thus far argument brings us. For in human things reasoning is employed, not as of greater certainty, but as easier from use. But when we come to divine things, this faculty turns away; it cannot behold; it pants, and gasps, and burns with desire; it falls back from the light of truth, and turns again to its wonted obscurity, not from choice, but from exhaustion. What a dreadful catastrophe is this, that the soul should be reduced to greater helplessness when it is seeking rest from its toil! So, when we are hasting to retire into darkness, it will be well that by the appointment of adorable Wisdom we should be met by the friendly shade of authority, and should be attracted by the wonderful character of its contents, and by the utterances of its pages, which, like shadows, typify and attemper the truth.

What more could have been done for our salvation? What can be more gracious and bountiful than divine providence, which, when man had fallen from its laws, and, in just retribution for his coveting mortal things, had brought forth a mortal offspring, still did not wholly abandon him? For in this most righteous government, whose ways are strange and inscrutable, there is, by means of unknown connections established in the creatures subject to it, both a severity of punishment and a mercifulness of salvation. How beautiful this is, how great, how worthy of God, in fine, how true, which is all we are seeking for, we shall never be able to perceive, unless, beginning with things human and at hand, and holding by the faith and the precepts of true religion, we continue without turning from it in the way which God has secured for us by the separation of the patriachs, by the bond of the law, by the foresight of the prophets, by the witness of the apostles, by the blood of the martyrs, and by the subjugation of the Gentiles. From this point, then, let no one ask me for my opinion, but let us rather hear the oracles, and submit our weak inferences to the announcements of Heaven.

CHAPTER VIII

GOD IS THE CHIEF GOOD, WHOM WE ARE TO SEEK AFTER WITH SUPREME AFFECTION

Let us see how the Lord Himself in the gospel has taught us to live; how, too, Paul the apostle—for the Manichaeans dare not reject these Scriptures. Let us hear, O Christ, what chief end Thou dost prescribe to us; and that is evidently the chief end after which we are told to strive with supreme affection. "Thou shalt love," He says, "the Lord thy God." Tell me also, I pray Thee, what must be the measure of love; for I fear lest the desire enkindled in my heart should either exceed or come short in fervor. "With all thy heart," He says. Nor is that enough. "With all thy soul." Nor is it enough yet. "With all thy mind." [1] What do you wish more? I might, perhaps, wish more if I could see the possibility of more. What does Paul say on this? "We know," he says, "that all things issue in good to them that love God." Let him, too, say what is the measure of love. "Who then," he says, "shall separate us from the love of Christ? shall tribulation, or distress, or persecution, or famine, or nakedness, or peril, or the sword?" [2] We have heard, then, what and how much we must love; this we must strive after, and to this we must refer all our plans. The perfection of all our good things and our perfect good is God. We must neither come short of this nor go beyond it: the one is dangerous, the other impossible.

CHAPTER IX

HARMONY OF THE OLD AND NEW TESTAMENTS ON THE PRECEPTS OF CHARITY

Come now, let us examine, or rather let us take notice—for it is obvious and can be seen, at once—whether the authority of the Old Testament too agrees with those statements taken from the gospel and the apostle. What need to speak of the first statement, when it is clear to all that it is

---

[1] Matt. xxii. 37   [2] Rom. viii. 28, 35

a quotation from the law given by Moses? For it is there written, "Thou shalt love the Lord thy God with all thy heart, and with all thy soul, and with all thy mind." [3] And not to go farther for a passage of the Old Testament to compare with that of the apostle, he has himself added one. For after saying that no tribulation, no distress, no persecution, no pressure of bodily want, no peril, no sword, separates us from the love of Christ, he immediately adds, "As it is written, For Thy sake we are in suffering all the day long; we are accounted as sheep for the slaughter." [4] The Manichaeans are in the habit of saying that this is an interpolation— so unable are they to reply, that they are forced in their extremity to say this. But every one can see that this is all that is left for men to say when it is proved that they are wrong.

And yet I ask them if they deny that this is said in the Old Testament, or if they hold that the passage in the Old Testament does not agree with that of the apostle. For the first, the books will prove it; and as for the second, those prevaricators who fly off at a tangent will be brought to agree with me, if they will only reflect a little and consider what is said, or else I will press upon them the opinion of those who judge impartially. For what could agree more harmoniously than these passages? For tribulation, distress, persecution, famine, nakedness, peril, cause great suffering to man while in this life. So all these words are implied in the single quotation from the law, where it is said, "For Thy sake we are in suffering." [5] The only other thing is the sword, which does not inflict a painful life, but removes whatever life it meets with. Answering to this are the words, "We are accounted as sheep for the slaughter." And love could not have been more plainly expressed than by the words, "For Thy sake." Suppose, then, that this testimony is not found in the Apostle Paul, but is quoted by me, must you not prove, you heretic, either that this is not written in the old law, or that it does not harmonize with the apostle? And if you dare not say either of these things (for you are shut up by the reading of the manuscript, which will show that it is written, and by common sense, which sees that nothing could agree better with what is said by the apostle), why do you imagine that there is any force in accusing the Scriptures of being corrupted? And once more, what will you reply to a man who says to you, This is what I understand, this is my view, this is my belief, and I read these books only because I see that everything in them agrees with the Christian faith? Or tell me at once if you will venture deliberately to tell me to the face that we are not to believe that the apostles and martyrs are spoken of as having endured great sufferings for Christ's sake, and as having been accounted by their persecutors as sheep for the slaughter? If you cannot say this, why should you bring a charge against the book in which I find what you acknowledge I ought to believe?

[3] Deut. vi. 5   [4] Rom. viii. 36; cf. Ps. xliv. 22   [5] *Retract.* i. 7, 2

CHAPTER X

WHAT THE CHURCH TEACHES ABOUT GOD. THE TWO GODS OF THE MANICHAEANS

Will you say that you grant that we are bound to love God, but not the God worshipped by those who acknowledge the authority of the Old Testament? In that case you refuse to worship the God who made heaven and earth, for this is the God set forth all through these books. And you admit that the whole of the world, which is called heaven and earth, had God and a good God for its author and maker. For in speaking to you about God we must make a distinction. For you hold that there are two gods, one good and the other bad.

But if you say that you worship and approve of worshipping the God who made heaven and earth, but not the God supported by the authority of the Old Testament, you act impertinently in trying, though vainly, to attribute to us views and opinions altogether unlike the wholesome and profitable doctrine we really hold. Nor can your silly and profane discourses be at all compared with the expositions in which learned and pious men of the Catholic Church open up those Scriptures to the willing and worthy. Our understanding of the law and the prophets is quite different from what you suppose. Mistake us no longer. We do not worship a God who repents, or is envious, or needy, or cruel, or who takes pleasure in the blood of men or beasts, or is pleased with guilt and crime, or whose possession of the earth is limited to a little corner of it. These and such like are the silly notions you are in the habit of denouncing at great length. Your denunciation does not touch us. The fancies of old women or of children you attack with a vehemence that is only ridiculous. Any one whom you persuade in this way to join you shows no fault in the teaching of the Church, but only proves his own ignorance of it.

If, then, you have any human feeling—if you have any regard for your own welfare—you should rather examine with diligence and piety the meaning of these passages of Scripture. You should examine, unhappy beings that you are; for we condemn with no less severity and copiousness any faith which attributes to God what is unbecoming Him, and in those by whom these passages are literally understood we correct the mistake of ignorance, and look upon persistence in it as absurd. And in many other things which you cannot understand there is in the Catholic teaching a check on the belief of those who have got beyond mental childishness, not in years, but in knowledge and understanding—old in the progress towards wisdom. For we learn the folly of believing that God is bounded by any amount of space, even though infinite; and it is held unlawful to think of God, or any part of Him, as moving from one place to another. And should any one suppose that anything in God's substance or nature can suffer change or conversion, he will be held guilty of wild profanity. There are thus among us children who think of God as having a human form, which they suppose He really has, which is a most degrading idea; and there are many of full age to whose mind the majesty of God appears in its inviolableness and unchangeableness as not only above the human body, but above their own mind itself. These ages, as we said, are distinguished not by time, but by virtue and discretion. Among you, again, there is no one who will picture God in a human form; but neither is there one who sets God apart from the contamination of human error. As regards those who are fed like crying babies at the breast of the Catholic Church, if they are not carried off by heretics, they are nourished according to the vigor and capacity of each, and arrive at last, one in one way and another in another, first to a perfect man, and then to the maturity and hoary hairs of wisdom, when they may get life as they desire, and life in perfect happiness.

CHAPTER XI

GOD IS THE ONE OBJECT OF LOVE; THEREFORE HE IS MAN'S CHIEF GOOD. NOTHING IS BETTER THAN GOD. GOD CANNOT BE LOST AGAINST OUR WILL

Following after God is the desire of happiness; to reach God is happiness itself. We follow after God by loving Him; we reach Him, not by becoming entirely what He is, but in nearness to Him, and in wonderful and immaterial contact with Him, and in being inwardly illuminated and occupied by His truth and holiness. He is light itself; we get enlightenment from Him. The greatest commandment, therefore, which leads to happy life, and the first, is this: "Thou shalt love the Lord thy God with all thy heart, and soul, and mind." For to those who love the Lord all things issue in good. Hence Paul adds shortly after, "I am persuaded that neither death, nor life, nor angels, nor virtue, nor things present, nor things future, nor height, nor depth, nor any other creature, shall be able to separate us from the love of God, which is in Christ Jesus our Lord." [6] If, then, to those who love God all things issue in good, and if, as no one doubts, the chief or perfect good is not only to be loved, but to be loved so that nothing shall be loved better, as is expressed in the words, "With all thy soul, with all thy heart, and with all thy mind," who, I ask, will not at once conclude, when these things are all settled and most surely believed, that our chief good which we must hasten to arrive at in preference to all other things is nothing else than God? And then, if nothing can separate us from His love, must not this be surer as well as better than any other good?

But let us consider the points separately. No one separates us from this

[6] Rom. viii. 38, 39

by threatening death. For that with which we love God cannot die, except in not loving God; for death is not to love God, and that is when we prefer anything to Him in affection and pursuit. No one separates us from this in promising life; for no one separates us from the fountain in promising water. Angels do not separate us; for the mind cleaving to God is not inferior in strength to an angel. Virtue does not separate us; for if what is here called virtue is that which has power in this world, the mind cleaving to God is far above the whole world. Or if this virtue is perfect rectitude of our mind itself, this in the case of another will favor our union with God, and in ourselves will itself unite us with God. Present troubles do not separate us; for we feel their burden less the closer we cling to Him from whom they try to separate us. The promise of future things does not separate us; for both future good of every kind is surest in the promise of God, and nothing is better than God Himself, who undoubtedly is already present to those who truly cleave to Him. Height and depth do not separate us; for if the height and depth of knowledge are what is meant, I will rather not be inquisitive than be separated from God; nor can any instruction by which error is removed separate me from Him, by separation from whom it is that any one is in error. Or if what is meant are the higher and lower parts of this world, how can the promise of heaven separate me from Him who made heaven? Or who from beneath can frighten me into forsaking God, when I should not have known of things beneath but by forsaking Him? In fine, what place can remove me from His love, when He could not be all in every place unless He were contained in none?

CHAPTER XII

WE ARE UNITED TO GOD BY LOVE, IN SUBJECTION TO HIM

"No other creature," he says, separates us. O man of profound mysteries! He thought it not enough to say, no creature: but he says no other creature; teaching that that with which we love God and by which we cleave to God, our mind, namely, and understanding, is itself a creature. Thus the body is another creature; and if the mind is an object of intellectual perception, and is known only by this means, the other creature is all that is an object of sense, which as it were makes itself known through the eyes, or ears, or smell, or taste, or touch, and this must be inferior to what is perceived by the intellect alone. Now, as God also can be known by the worthy, only intellectually, exalted though He is above the intelligent mind as being its Creator and Author, there was danger lest the human mind, from being reckoned among invisible and immaterial things, should be thought to be of *the same* nature with Him who created it, and so should fall away by pride from Him to whom it should be united by love. For the mind becomes like God, to the extent vouchsafed by its subjection of itself to Him for information and enlightenment. And if it obtains the greatest nearness by that subjection which produces likeness, it must be far removed from Him by that presumption which would make the likeness greater. It is this presumption which leads the mind to refuse obedience to the laws of God, in the desire to be sovereign, as God is.

The farther, then, the mind departs from God, not in space, but in affection and lust after things below Him, the more it is filled with folly and wretchedness. So by love it returns to God—a love which places it not along with God, but under Him. And the more ardor and eagerness there is in this, the happier and more elevated will the mind be, and with God as sole governor it will be in perfect liberty. Hence it must know that it is a creature. It must believe what is the truth—that its Creator remains ever possessed of the inviolable and immutable nature of truth and wisdom, and must confess, even in view of the errors from which it desires deliverance, that it is liable to folly and falsehood. But then again, it must take care that it be not separated by the love of the other creature, that is, of this visible world, from the love of God Himself, which sanctifies it in order that it may abide most happy. No other creature, then—for we are ourselves a creature—separates us from the love of God which is in Christ Jesus our Lord.

CHAPTER XIII

WE ARE JOINED INSEPARATELY TO GOD BY CHRIST AND HIS SPIRIT

Let this same Paul tell us who is this Christ Jesus our Lord. "To them that are called," he says, "we preach Christ the virtue of God, and the wisdom of God." [7] And does not Christ Himself say, "I am the truth?" If, then, we ask what it is to live well—that is, to strive after happiness by living well—it must assuredly be to love virtue, to love wisdom, to love truth, and to love with all the heart, with all the soul, and with all the mind; virtue which is inviolable and immutable, wisdom which never gives place to folly, truth which knows no change or variation from its uniform character. Through this the Father Himself is seen; for it is said, "No man cometh unto the Father but by me." [8] To this we cleave by sanctification. For when sanctified we burn with full and perfect love, which is the only security for our not turning away from God, and for our being conformed to Him rather than to this world; for "He has predestinated us," says the same apostle, "that we should be conformed to the image of His Son." [9]

It is through love, then, that we become conformed to God; and by this conformation, and configuration, and circumcision from this world we are not confounded with the things which are properly subject to us. And this is done by the Holy Spirit. "For hope," he says, "does not confound us; for the love of God is shed abroad in our hearts by the Holy Spirit, which

[7] I Cor. i. 23, 24   [8] John xiv. 6   [9] Rom. viii. 29

is given unto us." [10] But we could not possibly be restored to perfection by the Holy Spirit, unless He Himself continued always perfect and immutable. And this plainly could not be unless He were of the nature and of the very substance of God, who alone is always possessed of immutability and invariableness. "The creature," it is affirmed, not by me but by Paul, "has been made subject to vanity." [11] And what is subject to vanity is unable to separate us from vanity, and to unite us to the truth. But the Holy Spirit does this for us. He is therefore no creature. For whatever is, must be either God or the creature.

CHAPTER XIV

WE CLEAVE TO THE TRINITY, OUR CHIEF GOOD, BY LOVE

We ought then to love God, the Trinity in unity, Father, Son, and Holy Spirit; for this must be said to be God Himself, for it is said of God, truly and in the most exalted sense, "Of whom are all things, by whom are all things, in whom are all things." Those are Paul's words. And what does he add? "To Him be glory." [12] All this is exactly true. He does not say, To them; for God is one. And what is meant by, To Him be glory, but to Him, be chief and perfect and wide-spread praise? For as the praise improves and extends, so the love and affection increase in fervor. And when this is the case, mankind cannot but advance with sure and firm step to a life of perfection and bliss. This, I suppose, is all we wish to find when we speak of the chief good of man, to which all must be referred in life and conduct. For the good plainly exists; and we have shown by reasoning, as far as we were able, and by the divine authority which goes beyond our reasoning, that it is nothing else but God Himself. For how can any thing be man's chief good but that in cleaving to which he is blessed? Now this is nothing but God, to whom we can cleave only by affection, desire, and love.

CHAPTER XV

THE CHRISTIAN DEFINITION OF THE FOUR VIRTUES

As to virtue leading us to a happy life, I hold virtue to be nothing else than perfect love of God. For the fourfold division of virtue I regard as taken from four forms of love. For these four virtues (would that all felt their influence in their minds as they have their names in their mouths!), I should have no hesitation in defining them: that temperance is love giving itself entirely to that which is loved; fortitude is love readily bearing all things for the sake of the loved object; justice is love serving only the loved object, and therefore ruling rightly; prudence is love distinguishing

---

[10] Rom. v. 5   [11] Rom. viii. 20   [12] Rom. xi. 36

with sagacity between what hinders it and what helps it. The object of this love is not anything, but only God, the chief good, the highest wisdom, the perfect harmony. So we may express the definition thus: that temperance is love keeping itself entire and incorrupt for God; fortitude is love bearing everything readily for the sake of God; justice is love serving God only, and therefore ruling well all else, as subject to man; prudence is love making a right distinction between what helps it towards God and what might hinder it.

CHAPTER XVI

HARMONY OF THE OLD AND NEW TESTAMENTS

I will briefly set forth the manner of life according to these virtues, one by one, after I have brought forward, as I promised, passages from the Old Testament parallel to those I have been quoting from the New Testament. For is Paul alone in saying that we should be joined to God so that there should be nothing between to separate us? Does not the prophet say the same most aptly and concisely in the words, "It is good for me to cleave to God"? [13] Does not this one word *cleave* express all that the apostle says at length about love? And do not the words, It is good, point to the apostle's statement, "All things issue in good to them that love God"? Thus in one clause and in two words the prophet sets forth the power and the fruit of love.

And as the apostle says that the Son of God is the virtue of God and the wisdom of God—virtue being understood to refer to action, and wisdom to teaching (as in the gospel these two things are expressed in the words, "All things were made by Him," which belongs to action and virtue; and then, referring to teaching and the knowledge of the truth, he says, "The life was the light of men" [14])—could anything agree better with these passages than what is said in the Old Testament [15] of wisdom, "She reaches from end to end in strength, and orders all things sweetly"? For reaching in strength expresses virtue, while ordering sweetly expresses skill and method. But if this seems obscure, see what follows: "And of all," he says, "God loved her; for she teaches the knowledge of God, and chooses His works." Nothing more is found here about action; for choosing works is not the same as working, so this refers to teaching. There remains action to correspond with the virtue, to complete the truth we wish to prove. Read then what comes next: "But if," he says, "the possession which is desired in life is honorable, what is more honorable than wisdom, which works all things?" Could anything be brought forward more striking or more distinct than this, or even more fully expressed? Or, if you wish more, hear another passage of the same meaning. "Wisdom," he says, "teaches sobriety, and justice, and

[13] Ps. lxxiii. 28   [14] John i. 3, 4   [15] Wisd. viii. 1, 4, 7

virtue." Sobriety refers, I think, to the knowledge of the truth, or to teaching; justice and virtue to work and action. And I know nothing comparable to these two things, that is, to efficiency in action and sobriety in contemplation, which the virtue of God and the wisdom of God, that is, the Son of God, gives to them that love Him, when the same prophet goes on to show their value; for it is thus stated: "Wisdom teaches sobriety, and justice, and virtue, than which nothing is more useful in life to man." [16]

Perhaps some may think that those passages do not refer to the Son of God. What, then, is taught in the following words: "She displays the nobility of her birth, having her dwelling with God"? [17] To what does birth refer but to parentage? And does not dwelling with the Father claim and assert equality? Again, as Paul says that the Son of God is the wisdom of God,[18] and as the Lord Himself says, "No man knoweth the Father save the only-begotten Son," [19] what could be more concordant than those words of the prophet: "With Thee is wisdom which knows Thy works, which was present at the time of Thy making the world, and knew what would be pleasing in Thine eyes"? [20] And as Christ is called the truth, which is also taught by His being called the brightness of the Father[21] (for there is nothing round about the sun but its brightness which is produced from it), what is there in the Old Testament more plainly and obviously in accordance with this than the words, "Thy truth is round about Thee"? [22] Once more, Wisdom herself says in the gospel, "No man cometh unto the Father but by me;" [23] and the prophet says, "Who knoweth Thy mind, unless Thou givest wisdom?" and a little after, "The things pleasing to Thee men have learned, and have been healed by wisdom." [24]

Paul says, "The love of God is shed abroad in our hearts by the Holy Spirit which is given unto us;" [25] and the prophet says, "The Holy Spirit of knowledge will shun guile." [26] For where there is guile there is no love. Paul says that we are "conformed to the image of the Son of God;" [27] and the prophet says, "The light of Thy countenance is stamped upon us." [28] Paul teaches that the Holy Spirit is God, and therefore is no creature; and the prophet says, "Thou sendest Thy Spirit from the highest." [29] For God alone is the highest, than whom nothing is higher. Paul shows that the Trinity is one God, when he says, "To Him be glory;" [30] and in the Old Testament it is said, "Hear, O Israel, the Lord thy God is one God." [31]

[16] *Retract.* i. 7, 3   [17] Wisd. viii. 3   [18] 1 Cor. i. 24   [19] Matt. xi. 27   [20] Wisd. ix. 9   [21] Heb. i. 3   [22] Ps. lxxxix. 8   [23] John xiv. 6   [24] Wisd. ix. 17-19   [25] Rom. v. 5   [26] Wisd. i. 5   [27] Rom. viii. 29   [28] Ps. iv. 6   [29] Wisd. ix. 17   [30] Rom. xi. 36   [31] Deut. vi. 4

CHAPTER XVII

APPEAL TO THE MANICHAEANS, CALLING ON THEM TO REPENT

What more do you wish? Why do you resist ignorantly and obstinately? Why do you pervert untutored minds by your mischievous teaching? The God of both Testaments is one. For as there is an agreement in the passages quoted from both, so is there in all the rest, if you are willing to consider them carefully and impartially. But because many expressions are undignified, and so far adapted to minds creeping on the earth, that they may rise by human things to divine, while many are figurative, that the inquiring mind may have the more profit from the exertion of finding their meaning, and the more delight when it is found, you pervert this admirable arrangement of the Holy Spirit for the purpose of deceiving and ensnaring your followers. As to the reason why divine Providence permits you to do this, and as to the truth of the apostle's saying, "There must needs be many heresies, that they which are approved may be made manifest among you," [32] it would take long to discuss these things, and you, with whom we have now to do, are not capable of understanding them. I know you well. To the consideration of divine things, which are far higher than you suppose, you bring minds quite gross and sickly, from being fed with material images.

We must therefore in your case try not to make you understand divine things, which is impossible, but to make you desire to understand. This is the work of the pure and guileless love of God, which is seen chiefly in the conduct, and of which we have already said much. This love, inspired by the Holy Spirit, leads to the Son, that is, to the wisdom of God, by which the Father Himself is known. For if wisdom and truth are not sought for with the whole strength of the mind, it cannot possibly be found. But when it is sought as it deserves to be, it cannot withdraw or hide itself from its lovers. Hence its words, which you too are in the habit of repeating, "Ask, and ye shall receive; seek, and ye shall find; knock, and it shall be opened unto you:" [33] "Nothing is hid which shall not be revealed." [34] It is love that asks, love that seeks, love that knocks, love that reveals, love, too, that gives continuance in what is revealed. From this love of wisdom, and this studious inquiry, we are not debarred by the Old Testament, as you always say most falsely, but are exhorted to this with the greatest urgency.

Hear, then, at length, and consider, I pray you, what is said by the prophet: "Wisdom is glorious, and never fadeth away; yea, she is easily seen of them that love her, and found of such as seek her. She preventeth them that desire her, in making herself first known unto them. Whoso seeketh her early shall have no great travail; for he shall find her sitting

[32] I Cor. xi. 19   [33] Matt. vii. 7   [34] Matt. x. 26

at his doors. To think, therefore, upon her is perfection of wisdom; and whoso watcheth for her shall quickly be without care. For she goeth about seeking such as are worthy of her, showeth herself favorably unto them in the ways, and meeteth them in every thought. For the very true beginning of her is the desire of discipline; and the care of discipline is love; and love is the keeping of her laws; and the giving heed unto her laws is the assurance of incorruption; and incorruption maketh us near unto God. Therefore the desire of wisdom bringeth to a kingdom." [35] Will you still continue in dogged hostility to these things? Do not things thus stated, though not yet understood, make it evident to every one that they contain something deep and unutterable? Would that you could understand the things here said! Forthwith you would abjure all your silly legends and your unmeaning material imaginations, and with great alacrity, sincere love, and full assurance of faith, would betake yourselves bodily to the shelter of the most holy bosom of the Catholic Church.

CHAPTER XVIII

ONLY IN THE CATHOLIC CHURCH IS PERFECT TRUTH ESTABLISHED ON THE HARMONY OF BOTH TESTAMENTS

I could, according to the little ability I have, take up the points separately, and could expound and prove the truths I have learned, which are generally more excellent and lofty than words can express; but this cannot be done while you bark at it. For not in vain is it said, "Give not that which is holy to dogs." [36] Do not be angry. I too barked and was a dog; and then, as was right, instead of the food of teaching, I got the rod of correction. But were there in you that love of which we are speaking, or should it ever be in you as much as the greatness of the truth to be known requires, may God vouchsafe to show you that neither is there among the Manichaeans the Christian faith which leads to the summit of wisdom and truth, the attainment of which is the true happy life, nor is it anywhere but in the Catholic teaching. Is not this what the Apostle Paul appears to desire when he says, "For this cause I bow my knees to the Father of our Lord Jesus Christ, from whom the whole family in heaven and earth is named, that He would grant unto you, according to the riches of His glory, to be strengthened with might by His Spirit in the inner man; that Christ may dwell in your hearts by faith; that ye, being rooted and grounded in love, may be able to comprehend with all saints what is the height, and length, and breadth, and depth, and to know the love of Christ, which passeth knowledge, that ye may be filled with all the fullness of God?" [37] Could anything be more plainly expressed?

Wake up a little, I beseech you, and see the harmony of both Testaments,

[35] Wisd. vi. 12-20   [36] Matt. vii. 6   [37] Eph. iii. 14-19

making it quite plain and certain what should be the manner of life in our conduct, and to what all things should be referred. To the love of God we are incited by the gospel, when it is said, "Ask, seek, knock;" [38] by Paul, when he says, "That ye, being rooted and grounded in love, may be able to comprehend;" [39] by the prophet also, when he says that wisdom can easily be known by those who love it, seek for it, desire it, watch for it, think about it, care for it. The salvation of the mind and the way of happiness is pointed out by the concord of both Scriptures; and yet you choose rather to bark at these things than to obey them. I will tell you in one word what I think. Do you listen to the learned men of the Catholic Church with as peaceable a disposition, and with the same zeal, that I had when for nine years I attended on you: [40] there will be no need of so long a time as that during which you made a fool of me. In a much, a very much, shorter time you will see the difference between truth and vanity.

CHAPTER XIX

DESCRIPTION OF THE DUTIES OF TEMPERANCE, ACCORDING TO THE SACRED SCRIPTURES

It is now time to return to the four virtues, and to draw out and prescribe a way of life in conformity with them, taking each separately. First, then, let us consider temperance, which promises us a kind of integrity and incorruption in the love by which we are united to God. The office of temperance is in restraining and quieting the passions which make us pant for those things which turn us away from the laws of God and from the enjoyment of His goodness, that is, in a word, from the happy life. For there is the abode of truth; and in enjoying its contemplation, and in cleaving closely to it, we are assuredly happy; but departing from this, men become entangled in great errors and sorrows. For, as the apostle says, "The root of all evils is covetousness; which some having followed, have made shipwreck of the faith, and have pierced themselves through with many sorrows." [41] And this sin of the soul is quite plainly, to those rightly understanding, set forth in the Old Testament in the transgression of Adam in Paradise. Thus, as the apostle says, "In Adam we all die, and in Christ we shall all rise again." [42] Oh, the depth of these mysteries! But I refrain; for I am now engaged not in teaching you the truth, but in making you unlearn your errors, if I can, that is, if God aid my purpose regarding you.

Paul then says that covetousness is the root of all evils; and by covetousness the old law also intimates that the first man fell. Paul tells us to put off the old man and put on the new.[43] By the old man he means Adam who sinned, and by the new man him whom the Son of God took to Himself

---

[38] Matt. vii. 7   [39] Eph. iii. 7   [40] From his 19th to his 28th year   [41] 1 Tim. vi. 10
[42] Col. iii. 9, 10   [43] 1 Cor. xv. 22

ın consecration for our redemption. For he says in another place, "The first man is of the earth, earthy; the second man is from heaven, heavenly. As is the earthy, such are they also that are earthy; and as is the heavenly, such are they also that are heavenly. And as we have borne the image of the earthy, let us also bear the image of the heavenly" [44]—that is, put off the old man, and put on the new. The whole duty of temperance, then, is to put off the old man, and to be renewed in God—that is, to scorn all bodily delights, and the popular applause, and to turn the whole love to things divine and unseen. Hence that following passage which is so admirable: "Though our outward man perish, our inward man is renewed day by day." [45] Hear, too, the prophet singing, "Create in me a clean heart, O God, and renew a right spirit within me." [46] What can be said against such harmony except by blind barkers?

CHAPTER XX

WE ARE REQUIRED TO DESPISE ALL SENSIBLE THINGS, AND TO LOVE GOD ALONE

Bodily delights have their source in all those things with which the bodily sense comes in contact, and which are by some called the objects of sense; and among these the noblest is light, in the common meaning of the word, because among our senses also, which the mind uses in acting through the body, there is nothing more valuable than the eyes, and so in the Holy Scriptures all the objects of sense are spoken of as visible things. Thus in the New Testament we are warned against the love of these things in the following words: "While we look not at the things which are seen, but at the things which are not seen; for the things which are seen are temporal, but the things which are not seen are eternal." [47] This shows how far from being Christians those are who hold that the sun and moon are to be not only loved but worshipped. For what is seen if the sun and moon are not? But we are forbidden to regard things which are seen. The man, therefore, who wishes to offer that incorrupt love to God must not love these things too. This subject I will inquire into more particularly elsewhere. Here my plan is to write not of faith, but of the life by which we become worthy of knowing what we believe. God then alone is to be loved; and all this world, that is, all sensible things, are to be despised—while, however, they are to be used as this life requires.

[44] I Cor. xv. 47-49   [45] 2 Cor. iv. 16   [46] Ps. li. 10   [47] 2 Cor. iv. 18

CHAPTER XXI

POPULAR RENOWN AND INQUISITIVENESS ARE CONDEMNED IN THE SACRED SCRIPTURES

Popular renown is thus slighted and scorned in the New Testament: "If I wished," says Saint Paul, "to please men, I should not be the servant of Christy." [48] Again, there is another production of the soul formed by imaginations derived from material things, and called the knowledge of things. In reference to this we are fitly warned against inquisitiveness to correct which is the great function of temperance. Thus it is said, "Take heed lest any one seduce you by philosophy." And because the word philosophy originally means the love and pursuit of wisdom, a thing of great value and to be sought with the whole mind, the apostle, with great prudence, that he might not be thought to deter from the love of wisdom, has added the words, "And the elements of this world." [49] For some people, neglecting virtues, and ignorant of what God is, and of the majesty of the nature which remains always the same, think that they are engaged in an important business when searching with the greatest inquisitiveness and eagerness into this material mass which we call the world. This begets so much pride, that they look upon themselves as inhabitants of the heaven of which they often discourse. The soul, then, which purposes to keep itself chaste for God must refrain from the desire of vain knowledge like this. For this desire usually produces delusion, so that the soul thinks that nothing exists but what is material; or if, from regard to authority, it confesses that there is an immaterial existence, it can think of it only under material images, and has no belief regarding it but that imposed by the bodily sense. We may apply to this the precept about fleeing from idolatry.

To this New Testament authority, requiring us not to love anything in this world, [50] especially in that passage where it is said, "Be not conformed to this world" [51]—for the point is to show that a man is conformed to whatever he loves—to this authority, then, if I seek for a parallel passage in the Old Testament, I find several; but there is one book of Solomon, called *Ecclesiastes,* which at great length brings all earthly things into utter contempt. The book begins thus: "Vanity of the vain, saith the Preacher, vanity of the vain; all is vanity. What profit hath a man of all his labor which he taketh under the sun?" [52] If all these words are considered, weighed, and thoroughly examined, many things are found of essential importance to those who seek to flee from the world and to take shelter in God; but this requires time and our discourse hastens on to other topics. But, after this beginning, he goes on to show in detail that the vain [53] are those who are deceived by things of this sort; and he calls this which de-

[48] Gal. i. 10   [49] Coll. ii. 8   [50] 1 John ii. 15   [51] Rom. xii. 2   [52] Eccles. i. 2, 3
[53] *Retract.* i. 7, 3

ceives them vanity—not that God did not create those things, but because men choose to subject themselves by their sins to those things, which the divine law has made subject to them in well-doing. For when you consider things beneath yourself to be admirable and desirable, what is this but to be cheated and misled by unreal goods? The man, then, who is temperate in such mortal and transient things has his rule of life confirmed by both Testaments, that he should love none of these things, nor think them desirable for their own sakes, but should use them as far as is required for the purposes and duties of life, with the moderation of an employer instead of the ardor of a lover. These remarks on temperance are few in proportion to the greatness of the theme, but perhaps too many in view of the task on hand.

CHAPTER XXII

FORTITUDE COMES FROM THE LOVE OF GOD

On fortitude we must be brief. The love, then, of which we speak, which ought with all sanctity to burn in desire for God, is called temperance, in not seeking for earthly things, and fortitude, in bearing the loss of them. But among all things which are possessed in this life, the body is, by God's most righteous laws, for the sin of old, man's heaviest bond, which is well known as a fact, but most incomprehensible in its mystery. Lest this bond should be shaken and disturbed, the soul is shaken with the fear of toil and pain; lest it should be lost and destroyed, the soul is shaken with the fear of death. For the soul loves it from the force of habit, not knowing that by using it well and wisely its resurrection and reformation will, by the divine help and decree, be without any trouble made subject to its authority. But when the soul turns to God wholly in this love, it knows these things, and so will not only disregard death, but will even desire it.

Then there is the great struggle with pain. But there is nothing, though of iron hardness, which the fire of love cannot subdue. And when the mind is carried up to God in this love, it will soar above all torture free and glorious, with wings beauteous and unhurt, on which chaste love rises to the embrace of God. Otherwise God must allow the lovers of gold, the lovers of praise, the lovers of women, to have more fortitude than the lovers of Himself, though love in those cases is rather to be called passion or lust. And yet even here we may see with what force the mind presses on with unflagging energy, in spite of all alarms, towards that it loves; and we learn that we should bear all things rather than forsake God, since those men bear so much in order to forsake Him.

CHAPTER XXIII

SCRIPTURE PRECEPTS AND EXAMPLES OF FORTITUDE

Instead of quoting here authorities from the New Testament, where it is said, "Tribulation worketh patience; and patience, experience and experience, hope;" [54] and where, in addition to these words, there is proof and confirmation of them from the example of those who spoke them; I will rather summon an example of patience from the Old Testament, against which the Manichaeans make fierce assaults. Nor will I refer to the man who, in the midst of great bodily suffering, and with a dreadful disease in his limbs, not only bore human evils, but discoursed of things divine. Whoever gives considerate attention to the utterances of this man, will learn from every one of them what value is to be attached to those things which men try to keep in their power, and in so doing are themselves brought by passion into bondage, so that they become the slaves of mortal things, while seeking ignorantly to be their masters. This man, in the loss of all his wealth, and on being suddenly reduced to the greatest poverty, kept his mind so unshaken and fixed upon God, as to manifest that these things were not great in his view, but that he was great in relation to them, and God to him.[55] If this mind were to be found in men in our day, we should not be so strongly cautioned in the New Testament against the possession of these things in order that we may be perfect; for to have these things without cleaving to them is much more admirable than not to have them at all.

But since we are speaking here of bearing pain and bodily sufferings, I pass from this man, great as he was, indomitable as he was: this is the case of a man. But these Scriptures present to me a woman of amazing fortitude, and I must at once go on to her case. This woman, along with seven children, allowed the tyrant and executioner to extract her vitals from her body rather than a profane word from her mouth, encouraging her sons by her exhortations, though she suffered in the tortures of their bodies, and was herself to undergo what she called on them to bear.[56] What patience could be greater than this? And yet why should we be astonished that the love of God, implanted in her inmost heart, bore up against tyrant, and executioner, and pain, and sex, and natural affection? Had she not heard, "Precious in the sight of the Lord is the death of His saints?" [57] Had she not heard, "A patient man is better than the mightiest?" [58] Had she not heard, "All that is appointed thee receive; and in pain bear it; and in abasement keep thy patience: for in fire are gold and silver tried?" [59] Had she not heard, "The fire tries the vessels of the potter, and for just men is the trial of tribulation?" [60] These she knew, and many other precepts of forti-

[54] Rom. v. 3, 4   [55] Job. i. 2   [56] 2 Mac. vii.   [57] Ps. cxvi. 15   [58] Prov. xvi. 32
[59] Ecclus. ii. 4, 5   [60] Ecclus. xxvii. 6

tude written in these books, which alone existed at that time, by the same divine Spirit who writes those in the New Testament.

CHAPTER XXIV

OF JUSTICE AND PRUDENCE

What of justice that pertains to God? As the Lord says, "Ye cannot serve two masters," [61] and the apostle denounces those who serve the creature rather than the Creator,[62] was it not said before in the Old Testament "Thou shalt worship the Lord thy God, and Him only shalt thou serve?" [63] I need say no more on this, for these books are full of such passages. The lover, then, whom we are describing, will get from justice this rule of life, that he must with perfect readiness serve the God whom he loves, the highest good, the highest wisdom, the highest peace; and as regards all other things, must either rule them as subject to himself, or treat them with a view to their subjection. This rule of life, is, as we have shown, confirmed by the authority of both Testaments.

With equal brevity we must treat of prudence, to which it belongs to discern between what is to be desired and what is to be shunned. Without this, nothing can be done of what we have already spoken of. It is the part of prudence to keep watch with most anxious vigilance, lest any evil influence should stealthily creep in upon us. Thus the Lord often exclaims, "Watch;" [64] and He says, "Walk while ye have the light, lest darkness come upon you." [65] And then it is said, "Know ye not that a little leaven leaveneth the whole lump?" [66] And no passage can be quoted from the Old Testament more expressly condemning this mental somnolence, which makes us insensible to destruction advancing on us step by step, than those words of the prophet, "He who despiseth small things shall fall by degrees." [67] On this topic I might discourse at length did our haste allow of it. And did our present task demand it, we might perhaps prove the depth of these mysteries, by making a mock of which profane men in their perfect ignorance fall, not certainly by degrees, but with a headlong overthrow.

CHAPTER XXV

FOUR MORAL DUTIES REGARDING THE LOVE OF GOD, OF WHICH LOVE THE REWARD IS ETERNAL LIFE AND THE KNOWLEDGE OF THE TRUTH

I need say no more about right conduct. For if God is man's chief good, which you cannot deny, it clearly follows, since to seek the chief good is to

---

[61] Matt. vi. 24   [62] Rom. i. 25   [63] Deut. vi. 13   [64] Matt. xxiv. 42   [65] John xii.
35   [66] I Cor. v. 6   [67] Ecclus. xix. 1

live well, that to live well is nothing else but to love God with all the heart, with all the soul, with all the mind; and, as arising from this, that this love must be preserved entire and incorrupt, which is the part of temperance; that it give way before no troubles, which is the part of fortitude; that it serve no other, which is the part of justice; that it be watchful in its inspection of things lest craft or fraud steal in, which is the part of prudence. This is the one perfection of man, by which alone he can succeed in attaining to the purity of truth. This both Testaments enjoin in concert; this is commended on both sides alike. Why do you continue to cast reproaches on Scriptures of which you are ignorant? Do you not see the folly of your attacks upon books which only those who do not understand them find fault with, and which only those who find fault fail in understanding? For neither can an enemy know them, nor can one who knows them be other than a friend to them.

Let us then, as many as have in view to reach eternal life, love God with all the heart, with all the soul, with all the mind. For eternal life contains the whole reward in the promise of which we rejoice; nor can the reward precede desert, nor be given to a man before he is worthy of it. What can be more unjust than this, and what is more just than God? We should not then demand the reward before we deserve to get it. Here, perhaps, it is not out of place to ask what is eternal life; or rather let us hear the Bestower of it: "This," He says, "is life eternal, that they should know Thee, the true God, and Jesus Christ whom Thou hast sent." [68] So eternal life is the knowledge of the truth. See, then, how perverse and preposterous is the character of those who think that their teaching of the knowledge of God will make us perfect, when this is the reward of those already perfect! What else, then, have we to do but first to love with full affection Him whom we desire to know? [69] Hence arises that principle on which we have all along insisted, that there is nothing more wholesome in the Catholic Church than using authority before argument.

CHAPTER XXVI

LOVE OF OURSELVES AND OF OUR NEIGHBOR

To proceed to what remains. It may be thought that there is nothing here about man himself, the lover. But to think this, shows a want of clear perception. For it is impossible for one who loves God not to love himself. For he alone has a proper love for himself who aims diligently at the attainment of the chief and true good; and if this is nothing else but God, as has been shown, what is to prevent one who loves God from loving himself? And then, among men should there be no bond of mutual love? Yea, verily; so that we can think of no surer step towards the love of God than the love of man to man.

[68] John xvii. 3   [69] *Retract.* i. 7, 4

Let the Lord then supply us with the other precept in answer to the question about the precepts of life; for He was not satisfied with one as knowing that God is one thing and man another, and that the difference is nothing less than that between the Creator and the thing created in the likeness of its Creator. He says then that the second precept is, "Thou shalt love thy neighbor as thyself." [70] Now you love yourself suitably when you love God better than yourself. What, then, you aim at in yourself you must aim at in your neighbor, namely, that he may love God with a perfect affection. For you do not love him as yourself, unless you try to draw him to that good which you are yourself pursuing. For this is the one good which has room for all to pursue it along with thee. From this precept proceed the duties of human society, in which it is hard to keep from error. But the first thing to aim at is, that we should be benevolent, that is, that we cherish no malice and no evil design against another. For man is the nearest neighbor of man.

Hear also what Paul says: "The love of our neighbor," he says, "worketh no ill." [71] The testimonies here made use of are very short, but, if I mistake not, they are to the point, and sufficient for the purpose. And every one knows how many and how weighty are the words to be found everywhere in these books on the love of our neighbor. But as a man may sin against another in two ways, either by injuring him or by not helping him when it is in his power, and as it is for these things which no loving man would do that men are called wicked, all that is required is, I think, proved by these words, "The love of our neighbor worketh no ill." And if we cannot attain to good unless we first desist from working evil, our love of our neighbor is a sort of cradle of our love to God, so that, as it is said, "the love of our neighbor worketh no ill," we may rise from this to these other words, "We know that all things issue in good to them that love God." [72]

But there is a sense in which these either rise together to fullness and perfection, or, while the love of God is first in beginning, the love of our neighbor is first in coming to perfection. For perhaps divine love takes hold on us more rapidly at the outset, but we reach perfection more easily in lower things. However that may be, the main point is this, that no one should think that while he despises his neighbor he will come to happiness and to the God whom he loves. And would that it were as easy to seek the good of our neighbor, or to avoid hurting him, as it is for one well trained and kind-hearted to love his neighbor! These things require more than mere good-will, and can be done only by a high degree of thoughtfulness and prudence, which belongs only to those to whom it is given by God, the source of all good. On this topic—which is one, I think, of great difficulty—I will try to say a few words such as my plan admits of, resting all my hope in Him whose gifts these are.

[70] Matt. xxii. 39   [71] Rom. xiii. 10   [72] Rom. viii. 28

CHAPTER XXVII

ON DOING GOOD TO THE BODY OF OUR NEIGHBOR

Man, then, as viewed by his fellowman, is a rational soul with a mortal and earthly body in its service. Therefore he who loves his neighbor does good partly to the man's body, and partly to his soul. What benefits the body is called medicine; what benefits the soul, discipline. Medicine here includes everything that either preserves or restores bodily health. It includes, therefore, not only what belongs to the art of medical men, properly so called, but also food and drink, clothing and shelter, and every means of covering and protection to guard our bodies against injuries and mishaps from without as well as from within. For hunger and thirst, and cold and heat, and all violence from without, produce loss of that health which is the point to be considered.

Hence those who seasonably and wisely supply all the things required for warding off these evils and distresses are called compassionate, although they may have been so wise that no painful feeling disturbed their mind in the exercise of compassion.[73] No doubt the word compassionate implies suffering in the heart of the man who feels for the sorrow of another. And it is equally true that a wise man ought to be free from all painful emotion when he assists the needy, when he gives food to the hungry and water to the thirsty, when he clothes the naked, when he takes the stranger into his house, when he sets free the oppressed, when, lastly, he extends his charity to the dead in giving them burial. Still the epithet compassionate is a proper one, although he acts with tranquillity of mind, not from the stimulus of painful feeling, but from motives of benevolence. There is no harm in the word compassionate when there is no passion in the case.

Fools, again, who avoid the exercise of compassion as a vice, because they are not sufficiently moved by a sense of duty without feeling also distressful emotion, are frozen into hard insensibility, which is very different from the calm of a rational serenity. God, on the other hand, is properly called compassionate; and the sense in which He is so will be understood by those whom piety and diligence have made fit to understand. There is a danger lest, in using the words of the learned, we harden the souls of the unlearned by leading them away from compassion instead of softening them with the desire of a charitable disposition. As compassion, then, requires us to ward off these distresses from others, so harmlessness forbids the infliction of them.

[73] *Retract.* i. 7, 4

CHAPTER XXVIII

ON DOING GOOD TO THE SOUL OF OUR NEIGHBOR. TWO PARTS OF
DISCIPLINE, RESTRAINT AND INSTRUCTION. THROUGH GOOD
CONDUCT WE ARRIVE AT THE KNOWLEDGE OF THE TRUTH

As regards discipline, by which the health of the mind is restored, without which bodily health avails nothing for security against misery, the subject is one of great difficulty. And as in the body we said it is one thing to cure diseases and wounds, which few can do properly, and another thing to meet the cravings of hunger and thirst, and to give assistance in all the other ways in which any man may at any time help another; so in the mind there are some things in which the high and rare offices of the teacher are not much called for—as, for instance, in advice and exhortation to give to the needy the things already mentioned as required for the body. To give such advice is to aid the mind by discipline, as giving the things themselves is aiding the body by our resources. But there are other cases where diseases of the mind, many and various in kind, are healed in a way strange and indescribable. Unless His medicine were sent from heaven to men, so heedlessly do they go on in sin, there would be no hope of salvation; and, indeed, even bodily health, if you go to the root of the matter, can have come to men from none but God, who gives to all things their being and their well-being.

This discipline, then, which is the medicine of the mind, as far as we can gather from the sacred Scriptures, includes two things, restraint and instruction. Restraint implies fear, and instruction love, in the person benefited by the discipline; for in the giver of the benefit there is the love without the fear. In both of these God Himself, by whose goodness and mercy it is that we are anything, has given us in the two Testaments a rule of discipline. For though both are found in both Testaments, still fear is prominent in the Old, and love in the New; which the apostle calls bondage in the one, and liberty in the other. Of the marvellous order and divine harmony of these Testaments it would take long to speak, and many pious and learned men have discoursed on it. The theme demands many books to set it forth and explain it as far as is possible for man. He, then, who loves his neighbor endeavors all he can to procure his safety in body and in soul, making the health of the mind the standard in his treatment of the body. And as regards the mind, his endeavors are in this order, that he should first fear and then love God. This is true excellence of conduct, and thus the knowledge of the truth is acquired which we are ever in the pursuit of.

The Manichaeans agree with me as regards the duty of loving God and our neighbor, but they deny that this is taught in the Old Testament. How greatly they err in this is, I think, clearly shown by the passages quoted above on both these duties. But, in a single word, and one which only stark madness can oppose, do they not see the unreasonableness of denying that these very two precepts which they commend are quoted by the Lord in the Gospel from the Old Testament, "Thou shalt love the Lord thy God with all thy heart, and with all thy soul, and with all thy mind;" and the other, "Thou shalt love thy neighbor as thyself?" [74] Or if they dare not deny this, from the light of truth being too strong for them, let them deny that these precepts are salutary; let them deny, if they can, that they teach the best morality; let them assert that it is not a duty to love God, or to love our neighbor; that all things do not issue in good to them that love God; that it is not true that the love of our neighbor worketh no ill (a two-fold regulation of human life which is most salutary and excellent). By such assertions they cut themselves off not only from Christians, but from mankind. But if they dare not speak thus, but must confess the divinity of the precepts, why do they not desist from assailing and maligning with horrible profanity the books from which they are quoted?

Will they say, as they often do, that although we find these precepts in the books, it does not follow that all is good that is found there? How to meet and refute this quibble I do not well see. Shall I discuss the words of the Old Testament one by one, to prove to stubborn and ignorant men their perfect agreement with the New Testament? But when will this be done? When shall I have time, or they patience? What, then, is to be done? Shall I desert the cause, and leave them to escape detection in an opinion which, though false and impious, is hard to disprove? I will not. God will Himself be at hand to aid me; nor will He suffer me in those straits to remain helpless or forsaken.

CHAPTER XXIX

OF THE AUTHORITY OF THE SCRIPTURES

Attend, then, ye Manichaeans, if perchance there are some of you of whom your superstition has hold so as to allow you yet to escape. Attend, I say, without obstinacy, without the desire to oppose, otherwise your decision will be fatal to yourselves. No one can doubt, and you are not so lost to the truth as not to understand that if it is good, as all allow, to love God and our neighbor, whatever hangs on these two precepts cannot rightly be pronounced bad. What it is that hangs on them it would be absurd to think of learning from me. Hear Christ Himself; hear Christ, I say; hear the Wisdom of God: "On these two commandments," He says, "hang all the law and the prophets." [75]

What can the most shameless obstinacy say to this? That these are not Christ's words? But they are written in the Gospel as His words. That the writing is false? Is not this most profane blasphemy? Is it not most pre-

[74] Deut. vi. 5; Lev. xix. 18; Matt. xxii. 37, 39   [75] Matt. xxii. 40

sumptuous to speak thus? Is it not most foolhardy? Is it not most criminal? The worshippers of idols, who hate even the name of Christ, never dared to speak thus against these Scriptures. For the utter overthrow of all literature will follow, and there will be an end to all books handed down from the past, if what is supported by such a strong popular belief and established by the uniform testimony of so many men and so many times, is brought into such suspicion, that it is not allowed to have the credit and the authority of common history. In fine, what can you quote from any writings of which I may not speak in this way, if it is quoted against my opinion and my purpose?

And is it not intolerable that they forbid us to believe a book widely known and placed now in the hands of all, while they insist on our believing the book which they quote? If any writing is to be suspected, what should be more so than one which has not merited notoriety, or which may be throughout a forgery, bearing a false name? If you force such a writing on me against my will, and make a display of authority to drive me into belief, shall I, when I have a writing which I see spread far and wide for a length of time, and sanctioned by the concordant testimony of churches scattered over all the world, degrade myself by doubting, and, worse degradation, by doubting at your suggestion? Even if you brought forward other readings, I should not receive them unless supported by general agreement; and this being the case, do you think that now, when you bring forward nothing to compare with the text except your own silly and inconsiderate statement, mankind are so unreasonable and so forsaken by divine Providence as to prefer to those Scriptures not others quoted by you in refutation, but merely your own words? You ought to bring forward another manuscript with the same contents, but incorrupt and more correct, with only the passage wanting which you charge with being spurious. For example, if you hold that the Epistle of Paul to the Romans is spurious, you must bring forward another incorrupt, or rather another manuscript with the same epistle of the same apostle, free from error and corruption. You say you will not, lest you be suspected of corrupting it. This is your usual reply, and a true one. Were you to do this, we should assuredly have this very suspicion; and all men of any sense would have it too. See then what you are to think of your own authority; and consider whether it is right to believe your words against these Scriptures, when the simple fact that a manuscript is brought forward by you makes it dangerous to put faith in it.

CHAPTER XXX

THE CHURCH APOSTROPHISED AS TEACHER OF ALL WISDOM. DOCTRINE OF THE CATHOLIC CHURCH

But why say more on this? For who but sees that men who dare to speak thus against the Christian Scriptures, though they may not be what they are suspected of being, are at least no Christians? For to Christians this rule of life is given, that we should love the Lord our God with all the heart, with all the soul, and with all the mind, and our neighbor as ourselves; for on these two commandments hang all the law and the prophets. Rightly, then, Catholic Church, most true mother of Christians, dost thou not only teach that God alone, to find whom is the happiest life, must be worshipped in perfect purity and chastity, bringing in no creature as an object of adoration whom we should be required to serve; and from that incorrupt and inviolable eternity to which alone man should be made subject, in cleaving to which alone the rational soul escapes misery, excluding everything made, everything liable to change, everything under the power of time; without confounding what eternity, and truth, and peace itself keeps separate, or separating what a common majesty unites: but thou dost also contain love and charity to our neighbor in such a way, that for all kinds of diseases with which souls are for their sins afflicted, there is found with thee a medicine of prevailing efficacy.

Thy training and teaching are childlike for children, forcible for youths, peaceful for the aged, taking into account the age of the mind as well as of the body. Thou subjectest women to their husbands in chaste and faithful obedience, not to gratify passion, but for the propagation of offspring, and for domestic society. Thou givest to men authority over their wives, not to mock the weaker sex, but in the laws of unfeigned love. Thou dost subordinate children to their parents in a kind of free bondage, and dost set parents over their children in a godly rule. Thou bindest brothers to brothers in a religious tie stronger and closer than that of blood. Without violation of the connections of nature and of choice, thou bringest within the bond of mutual love every relationship of kindred, and every alliance of affinity. Thou teachest servants to cleave to their masters from delight in their task rather than from the necessity of their position. Thou renderest masters forbearing to their servants, from a regard to God their common Master, and more disposed to advise than to compel. Thou unitest citizen to citizen, nation to nation, yea, man to man, from the recollection of their first parents, not only in society but in fraternity. Thou teachest kings to seek the good of their peoples; thou counsellest peoples to be subject to their kings. Thou teachest carefully to whom honor is due, to whom regard, to whom reverence, to whom fear, to whom consolation, to whom admonition, to whom encouragement, to whom discipline, to whom rebuke, to whom punishment; showing both how all are not due to all, and how to all love is due, and how injury is due to none.

Then, after this human love has nourished and invigorated the mind cleaving to thy breast, and fitted it for following God, when the divine majesty has begun to disclose itself as far as suffices for man while a dweller on the earth, such fervent charity is produced, and such a flame of divine love is kindled, that by the burning out of all vices, and by the purification and sanctification of the man, it becomes plain how divine are these words, "I am a consuming fire," [76] and, "I have come to send fire on the earth." [77] These two utterances of one God stamped on both Testaments, exhibit with harmonious testimony the sanctification of the soul, pointing forward to the accomplishment of that which is also quoted in the New Testament from the Old: "Death is swallowed up in victory. O death, where is thy sting? Where, O death, is thy contest?" [78] Could these heretics understand this one saying, no longer proud but quite reconciled, they would worship God nowhere but with thee and in thy bosom. In thee, as is fit, divine precepts are kept by widely-scattered multitudes. In thee, as is fit, it is well understood how much more heinous sin is when the law is known than when it is unknown. For "the sting of death is sin, and the strength of sin is the law," [79] which adds to the force with which the consciousness of disregard of the precept strikes and slays. In thee it is seen, as is fit, how vain is effort under the law, when lust lays waste the mind, and is held in check by fear of punishment, instead of being overborne by the love of virtue. Thine, as is fit, are the many hospitable, the many friendly, the many compassionate, the many learned, the many chaste, the many saints, the many so ardent in their love to God, that in perfect continence and amazing indifference to this world they find happiness even in solitude.

CHAPTER XXXI

THE LIFE OF THE ANACHORETES AND COENOBITES SET AGAINST THE CONTINENCE OF THE MANICHAEANS

What must we think is seen by those who can live without seeing their fellow-creatures, though not without loving them? It must be something transcending human things in contemplating which man can live without seeing his fellow-man. Hear now, ye Manichaeans, the customs and notable continence of perfect Christians, who have thought it right not only to praise but also to practise the height of chastity, that you may be restrained, if there is any shame in you, from vaunting your abstinence before uninstructed minds as if it were the hardest of all things. I will speak of things of which you are not ignorant, though you hide them from us. For who does not know that there is a daily increasing multitude of Christian men of absolute continence spread all over the world, especially in the East and in Egypt, as you cannot help knowing?

I will say nothing of those to whom I just now alluded, who, in complete seclusion from the view of men, inhabit regions utterly barren, content with simple bread, which is brought to them periodically, and with water, enjoying communion with God, to whom in purity of mind they cleave, and most

[76] Deut. iv. 24. *Retract.* i. 7, 5   [77] Luke xii. 49   [78] Hos. xiii. 14; 1 Cor. xv. 54, 55
[79] 1 Cor. xv. 56

blessed in contemplating His beauty, which can be seen only by the understanding of saints. I will say nothing of them, because some people think them to have abandoned human things more than they ought, not considering how much those may benefit us in their minds by prayer, and in their lives by example, whose bodies we are not permitted to see. But to discuss this point would take long, and would be fruitless; for if a man does not of his own accord regard this high pitch of sanctity as admirable and honorable, how can our speaking lead him to do so? Only the Manichaeans, who make a boast of nothing, should be reminded that the abstinence and continence of the great saints of the Catholic Church has gone so far, that some think it should be checked and recalled within the limits of humanity —so far above men, even in the judgment of those who disapprove, have their minds soared.

But if this is beyond our tolerance, who can but admire and commend those who, slighting and discarding the pleasures of this world, living together in a most chaste and holy society, unite in passing their time in prayers, in readings, in discussions, without any swelling of pride, or noise of contention, or sullenness of envy; but quiet, modest, peaceful, their life is one of perfect harmony and devotion to God, an offering most acceptable to Him from whom the power to do those things is obtained? No one possesses anything of his own; no one is a burden to another. They work with their hands in such occupations as may feed their bodies without distracting their minds from God. The product of their toil they give to the decans or tithesmen—so called from being set over the tithes—so that no one is occupied with the care of his body, either in food or clothes, or in anything else required for daily use or for the common ailments. These decans, again, arranging everything with great care, and meeting promptly the demands made by that life on account of bodily infirmities, have one called "father," to whom they give in their accounts. These fathers are not only more saintly in their conduct, but also distinguished for divine learning, and of high character in every way; and without pride they superintend those whom they call their children, having themselves great authority in giving orders, and meeting with willing obedience from those under their charge. At the close of the day they assemble from their separate dwellings before their meal to hear their father, assembling to the number of three thousand at least for one father; for one may have even a much larger number than this. They listen with astonishing eagerness in perfect silence, and give expression to the feelings of their minds as moved by the words of the preacher, in groans, or tears, or signs of joy without noise or shouting. Then there is refreshment for the body, as much as health and a sound condition of the body requires, every one checking unlawful appetite, so as not to go to excess even in the poor, inexpensive fare provided. So they not only abstain from flesh and wine, in order to gain the mastery over their passions, but also from those things which are only the more likely to whet the appetite of the palate and of the stomach, from what some call their greater cleanness, which often serves as a ridiculous and disgraceful excuse for an unseemly taste for exquisite viands, as distant from animal food. Whatever they possess in addition to what is required for their support (and much is obtained, owing to their industry and frugality), they distribute to the needy with greater care than they took in procuring it for themselves. For while they make no effort to obtain abundance, they make every effort to prevent their abundance remaining with them—so much so, that they send shiploads to places inhabited by poor people. I need say no more on a matter known to all.

Such, too, is the life of the women, who serve God assiduously and chastely, living apart and removed as far as propriety demands from the men, to whom they are united only in pious affection and in imitation of virtue. No young men are allowed access to them, nor even old men, however respectable and approved, except to the porch, in order to furnish necessary supplies. For the women occupy and maintain themselves by working in wool, and hand over the cloth to the brethren, from whom, in return, they get what they need for food. Such customs, such a life, such arrangements, such a system, I could not commend as it deserves, if I wished to commend it; besides, I am afraid that it would seem as if I thought it unlikely to gain acceptance from the mere description of it, if I considered myself obliged to add an ornamental eulogium to the simple narrative. Ye Manichaeans, find fault here if you can. Do not bring into prominence our tares before men too blind to discriminate.

CHAPTER XXXII

PRAISE OF THE CLERGY

There is not, however, such narrowness in the moral excellence of the Catholic Church as that I should limit my praise of it to the life of those here mentioned. For how many bishops have I known most excellent and holy men, how many presbyters, how many deacons, and ministers of all kinds of the divine sacraments, whose virtue seems to me more admirable and more worthy of commendation on account of the greater difficulty of preserving it amidst the manifold varieties of men, and in this life of turmoil! For they preside over men needing cure as much as over those already cured. The vices of the crowd must be borne with in order that they may be cured, and the plague must be endured before it is subdued. To keep here the best way of life and a mind calm and peaceful is very hard. Here, in a word, we are among people who are learning to live. There they live.

CHAPTER XXXIII

ANOTHER KIND OF MEN LIVING TOGETHER IN CITIES.
FASTS OF THREE DAYS

Still I would not on this account cast a slight upon a praiseworthy class of Christians—those, namely, who live together in cities, quite apart from common life. I saw at Milan a lodging-house of saints, in number not a few, presided over by one presbyter, a man of great excellence and learning. At Rome I knew several places where there was in each one eminent for weight of character, and prudence, and divine knowledge, presiding over all the rest who lived with him, in Christian charity, and sanctity, and liberty. These, too, are not burdensome to any one; but, in the Eastern fashion, and on the authority of the Apostle Paul, they maintain themselves with their own hands. I was told that many practised fasts of quite amazing severity, not merely taking only one meal daily towards night, which is everywhere quite common, but very often continuing for three days or more in succession without food or drink. And this among not men only, but women, who also live together in great numbers as widows or virgins, gaining a livelihood by spinning and weaving, and presided over in each case by a woman of the greatest judgment and experience, skilled and accomplished not only in directing and forming moral conduct, but also in instructing the understanding.

With all this, no one is pressed to endure hardships for which he is unfit; nothing is imposed on any one against his will; nor is he condemned by the rest because he confesses himself too feeble to imitate them: for they bear in mind how strongly Scripture enjoins charity on all: they bear in mind, "To the pure all things are pure," [80] and "Not that which entereth into your mouth defileth you, but that which cometh out of it." [81] Accordingly, all their endeavors are concerned not about the rejection of kinds of food as polluted, but about the subjugation of inordinate desire and the maintenance of brotherly love. They remember, "Meats for the belly, and the belly for meats; but God shall destroy both it and them;" [82] and again, "Neither if we eat shall we abound, nor if we refrain from eating shall we be in want;" [83] and, above all, this: "It is good, my brethren, not to eat flesh, nor drink wine, nor anything whereby thy brother is offended;" for this passage shows that love is the end to be aimed at in all these things. "For one man," he says, "believes that he can eat all things: another, who is weak, eateth herbs. He that eateth, let him not despise him that eateth not; and let not him that eateth not judge him that eateth: for God hath approved him. Who art thou that thou shouldest judge another man's servant? To his own master he stands or falls; but he shall stand: for God is

[80] Tit. i. 15   [81] Matt. xv. 11   [82] 1 Cor. vi. 13   [83] 1 Cor. viii. 8

able to make him to stand." And a little after: "He that eateth, to the Lord he eateth, and giveth God thanks; and he that eateth not, to the Lord he eateth not, and giveth God thanks." And also in what follows: "So every one of us shall give account of himself to God. Let us not, then, any more judge one another: but judge this rather, that ye place no stumbling-block, or cause of offence, in the way of a brother. I know, and am confident in the Lord Jesus, that there is nothing common in itself: but to him that thinketh anything to be common, to him it is common." Could he have shown better that it is not in the things we eat, but in the mind, that there is a power able to pollute it, and therefore that even those who are fit to think lightly of these things, and know perfectly that they are not polluted if they take any food in mental superiority, without being gluttons, should still have regard to charity? See what he adds: "For if thy brother be grieved with thy meat, now walkest thou not charitably." [84]

Read the rest: it is too long to quote all. You will find that those able to think lightly of such things—that is, those of greater strength and stability—are told that they must nevertheless abstain, lest those should be offended who from their weakness are still in need of such abstinence. The people I was describing know and observe these things; for they are Christians, not heretics. They understand Scripture according to the apostolic teaching, not according to the presumptuous and fictitious name of apostle. Him that eats not no one despises; him that eats no one judges; he who is weak eats herbs. Many who are strong, however, do this for the sake of the weak; with many the reason for so doing is not this, but that they may have a cheaper diet, and may lead a life of the greatest tranquillity, with the least expensive provision for the support of the body. "For all things are lawful for me," he says; "but I will not be brought under the power of any." [85] Thus many do not eat flesh, and yet do not superstitiously regard it as unclean. And so the same people who abstain when in health take it when unwell without any fear, if it is required as a cure. Many drink no wine; but they do not think that wine defiles them; for they cause it to be given with the greatest propriety and moderation to people of languid temperament, and, in short, to all who cannot have bodily health without it. When some foolishly refuse it, they counsel them as brothers not to let a silly superstition make them weaker instead of making them holier. They read to them the apostle's precept to his disciple to "take a little wine for his many infirmities." [86] Then they diligently exercise piety; bodily exercise, they know, profiteth for a short time, as the same apostle says.[87]

Those, then who are able, and they are without number, abstain both from flesh and from wine for two reasons: either for the weakness of their brethren, or for their own liberty. Charity is principally attended to. There is charity in their choice of diet, charity in their speech, charity in their

[84] Rom. xiv. 2-21   [85] I Cor. vi. 12   [86] I Tim. v. 23   [87] I Tim. iv. 8

dress, charity in their looks. Charity is the point where they meet, and the plan by whch they act. To transgress against charity is thought criminal, like transgressing against God. Whatever opposes this is attacked and expelled; whatever injures it is not allowed to continue for a single day. They know that it has been so enjoined by Christ and the apostles; that without it all things are empty, with it all are fulfilled.

CHAPTER XXXIV

THE CHURCH IS NOT TO BE BLAMED FOR THE CONDUCT OF BAD CHRISTIANS, WORSHIPPERS OF TOMBS AND PICTURES

Make objections against these, ye Manichaeans, if you can. Look at these people, and speak of them reproachfully, if you dare, without falsehood. Compare their fasts with your fasts, their chastity with yours; compare them to yourselves in dress, food, self-restraint, and, lastly, in charity. Compare, which is most to the point, their precepts with yours. Then you will see the difference between show and sincerity, between the right way and the wrong, between faith and imposture, between strength and inflatedness, between happiness and wretchedness, between unity and disunion; in short, between the sirens of superstition and the harbor of religion.

Do not summon against me professors of the Christian name, who neither know nor give evidence of the power of their profession. Do not hunt up the numbers of ignorant people, who even in the true religion are superstitious, or are so given up to evil passions as to forget what they have promised to God. I know that there are many worshippers of tombs and pictures. I know that there are many who drink to great excess over the dead, and who, in the feasts which they make for corpses, bury themselves over the buried, and give to their gluttony and drunkenness the name of religion. I know that there are many who in words have renounced this world, and yet desire to be burdened with all the weight of worldly things, and rejoice in such burdens. Nor is it surprising that among so many multitudes you should find some by condemning whose life you may deceive the unwary and seduce them from Catholic safety; for in your small numbers you are at a loss when called on to show even one out of those whom you call the elect who keeps the precepts, which in your indefensible superstition you profess. How silly those are, how impious, how mischievous, and to what extent they are neglected by most, nearly all of you, I have shown in another volume.

My advice to you now is this: that you should at least desist from slandering the Catholic Church, by declaiming against the conduct of men whom the Church herself condemns, seeking daily to correct them as wicked children. Then, if any of them by good will and by the help of God are corrected, they regain by repentance what they had lost by sin. Those, again, who with wicked will persist in their old vices, or even add to them others still worse, are indeed allowed to remain in the field of the Lord, and to grow along with the good seed; but the time for separating the tares will come. Or if, from their having at least the Christian name, they are to be placed among the chaff rather than among thistles, there will also come One to purge the floor and to separate the chaff from the wheat, and to assign to each part (according to its desert) the due reward.[88]

CHAPTER XXXV

MARRIAGE AND PROPERTY ALLOWED TO THE BAPTIZED
BY THE APOSTLES

Meanwhile, why do you rage? why does party spirit blind your eyes? Why do you entangle yourselves in a long defence of such great error? Seek for fruit in the field, seek for wheat in the floor: they will be found easily, and will present themselves to the inquirer. Why do you look so exclusively at the dross? Why do you use the roughness of the hedge to scare away the inexperienced from the fatness of the garden? There is a proper entrance, though known to but a few; and by it men come in, though you disbelieve it, or do not wish to find it. In the Catholic Church there are believers without number who do not use the world, and there are those who "use it," in the words of the apostle, "as not using it," [89] as was proved in those times when Christians were forced to worship idols. For then, how many wealthy men, how many peasant householders, how many merchants, how many military men, how many leading men in their own cities, and how many senators, people of both sexes, giving up all these empty and transitory things, though while they used them they were not bound down by them, endured death for the salutary faith and religion, and proved to unbelievers that instead of being possessed by all these things they really possessed them?

Why do you reproach us by saying that men renewed in baptism ought no longer to beget children, or to possess fields, and houses, and money? Paul allows it. For, as cannot be denied, he wrote to believers, after recounting many kinds of evil-doers who shall not possess the kingdom of God: "And such were you," he says: "but ye are washed, but ye are sanctified, but ye are justified in the name of the Lord Jesus Christ and by the Spirit of our God." By the washed and sanctified, no one, assuredly, will venture to think any are meant but believers, and those who have renounced this world. But, after showing to whom he writes, let us see whether he allows these things to them. He goes on: "All things are lawful for me, but all things are not expedient: all things are lawful for me, but I will not be brought under the power of any. Meat for the belly, and the belly for meats: but God will destroy both it and them. Now the body is not for fornication, but for the Lord, and the Lord for the body. But God

[88] Matt. iii. 13, and xiii. 24-43   [89] 1 Cor. vii. 31

raised up the Lord, and will raise us up also by His own power. Know ye not that your bodies are the members of Christ? shall I then take the members of Christ, and make them the members of an harlot? God forbid. Know ye not that he which is joined to an harlot is made one body? for the twain, saith He, shall be one flesh. But he that is joined to the Lord is one spirit. Flee fornication. Whatever sin a man doeth is without the body: but he that committeth fornication sinneth against his own body. Know ye not that your members are the temple of the Holy Spirit which is in you, which ye have of God, and ye are not your own? For ye are bought with a great price: glorify God, and carry Him in your body." [90] "But of the things concerning which ye wrote to me: it is good for a man not to touch a woman. Nevertheless, to avoid fornication, let every man have his own wife, and let every woman have her own husband. Let the husband render unto the wife due benevolence: and likewise also the wife unto the husband. The wife hath not power of her own body, but the husband: and likewise also the husband hath not power of his own body, but the wife. Defraud ye not one the other, except it be with consent for a time, that ye may have leisure for prayer; and come together again, that Satan tempt you not for your incontinency. But I speak this by permission, and not of commandment. For I would that all men were even as I myself: but every man hath his proper gift of God, one after this manner, and another after that." [91]

Has the apostle, think you, both shown sufficiently to the strong what is highest, and permitted to the weaker what is next best? Not to touch a woman he shows is highest when he says, "I would that all men were even as I myself." But next to this highest is conjugal chastity, that man may not be the prey of fornication. Did he say that these people were not yet believers because they were married? Indeed, by this conjugal chastity he says that those who are united are sanctified by one another, if one of them is an unbeliever, and that their children also are sanctified. "The unbelieving husband," he says, "is sanctified by the believing wife, and the unbelieving woman by the believing husband: otherwise your children would be unclean; but now are they holy." [92] Why do you persist in opposition to such plain truth? Why do you try to darken the light of Scripture by vain shadows?

Do not say that catechumens are allowed to have wives, but not believers; that catechumens may have money, but not believers. For there are many who use as not using. And in that sacred washing the renewal of the new man is begun so as gradually to reach perfection, in some more quickly, in others more slowly. The progress, however, to a new life is made in the case of many, if we view the matter without hostility, but attentively. As the apostle says of himself, "Though the outward man perish, the inward man is renewed day by day." [93] The apostle says that the inward man is

[90] I Cor. vi. 11-20   [91] I Cor. vii. 1-7   [92] I Cor. vii. 14   [93] 2 Cor. iv. 16

renewed day by day that it may reach perfection; and you wish it to begin with perfection! And it were well if you did wish it. In reality, you aim not at raising the weak, but at misleading the unwary. You ought not to have spoken so arrogantly, even if it were known that you are perfect in your childish precepts. But when your conscience knows that those whom you bring into your sect, when they come to a more intimate acquaintance with you, will find many things in you which nobody hearing you accuse others would suspect, is it not great impertinence to demand perfection in the weaker Catholics, to turn away the inexperienced from the Catholic Church, while you show nothing of the kind in yourself to those thus turned away? But not to seem to inveigh against you without reason, I will now close this volume, and will proceed at last to set forth the precepts of your life and your notable customs.

CONCERNING THE TEACHER

CONCERNING THE TEACHER

Introductory Note

In about 389 A.D. Saint Augustine composed his unusual treatise *Concerning the Teacher*. The work presumably grew out of conversations between himself and his son, Adeodatus, who, though only fifteen years old at the time, actually was responsible for the words that are attributed to him in the dialogue, as Saint Augustine himself records in the *Confessions* (ix. 16). Adeodatus, who died shortly afterwards, was evidently a youth of extraordinary powers, and the dialogue more than confirms the father's opinion of him. In the work the father and son address themselves to the question of the extent to which one can learn from a teacher. As they proceed, they discuss words as signs, engage in dialectical and rhetorical exercise, but all as a preliminary to perhaps the most concise statement of Saint Augustine's theory of Divine Illumination which is, of course, his basic theory of knowledge. The upshot of the treatise is that man refers all that he understands to the inner Truth which is implanted in his mind. The teacher at bottom only exhorts the learner to make that consultation.

CONCERNING THE TEACHER*

(A Dialogue)

Persons Represented: { AUGUSTINE
ADEODATUS, aged fifteen years, son of Augustine

CHAPTER I

THE PURPOSE OF SPEECH

Aug.—What does it seem to you that we wish to accomplish when we speak?

Ad.—As it occurs to me now, either to teach or to learn.

Aug.—I see, and I agree to one of these points. For it is evident that when we speak we wish to teach. But how do we learn?

Ad.—How, indeed, except by asking questions?

Aug.—Even then, as I understand it, we only wish to teach. For, I ask, do you question for any other reason except that you may teach what you wish to him you question?

Ad.—That is true.

Aug.—So now, you do see that in speaking we desire only that we may teach.

Ad.—That is not clear to me: for, if speaking is only expressing words, it is evident that we do that when we sing. And since we often sing when we are alone, with no one present to learn, it does not seem to me that we wish to teach anything.

Aug.—Ah, but I think there is a certain kind of teaching by means of reminding, indeed a very important kind, which will be revealed in this dialogue of ours. But if you do not think that we learn when we remember things, and that the man does not teach who reminds, I shall not object. And now I posit two reasons for speaking: either that we may teach, or that we may remind either others or ourselves; and the latter is what we do when we sing. Or does it not seem so to you?

Ad.—Not exactly. For it is quite seldom that I sing to remind myself; it is usually only to give myself pleasure.

Aug.—I see what you mean. But do you not see that what pleases you

---

* Reprinted by permission from *St. Aurelius Augustine: Concerning the Teacher and On the Immortality of the Soul,* translated from the Latin with the addition of a preface by George G. Leckie. Copyright, 1938, by D. Appleton-Century Company, Inc.

in singing is a certain modulation of sound. And, since this can be either added to or separated from the words, is not speaking one thing and singing another? For there are songs on pipes and on the cithara, and birds sing, and occasionally we, too, make musical sounds without words. This sound can be called singing, but it cannot be called speaking. Or have you any objection against this?

Ad.—None that matters.

Aug.—You do agree, then, that speaking is undertaken only for the sake of reminding or of teaching?

Ad.—It would seem so were I not troubled that while we are praying we are certainly speaking, and yet it is not right to believe that God is either taught anything by us or that He is reminded.

Aug.—It seems you do not know that we have been taught to pray in our secret closets,[1] by which is meant the inmost part of the mind, for the sole reason that God does not need to be reminded or taught by our speech in order that He may fulfil our desires. For he who speaks expresses the sign of his will by means of articulate sound. But God should be sought and entreated in the very secret places of the rational soul, which is called the interior man; for He wished this to be His temple. Have you not read in the Apostle: "Know ye not that ye are the temple of God, and that the spirit of God dwelleth in you?"[2] And also: "Christ dwells in the inner man."[3] And have you not observed, in the Psalm: "Commune with your own heart upon your bed, and be still. Offer the sacrifices of righteousness, and put your trust in the Lord."[4] Where, then, is a sacrifice of righteousness made, unless in the temple of the mind and in the chambers of the heart? And the place for sacrifice is also the place for prayer. Consequently, there is no need to speak when we pray, that is, with spoken words, unless perhaps for the sake of indicating, as the priests do, what is in our minds, not in order that God may hear, but that men may hear, and, through being reminded, may by their consent be lifted up to God. Or do you object?

Ad.—I entirely agree.

Aug.—Does it not trouble you that the Great Master, when He taught the disciples to pray, taught them certain words?[5] Such instruction seems only to have taught how we ought to speak in prayer.

Ad.—That does not disturb me at all. For He did not teach them words, but taught them things by means of the words in order that they might remind themselves to whom and for what purpose they ought to pray when they do so in those inner sanctuaries of the mind.

Aug.—You understand that correctly. For I believe that you observe, at the same time, that even when one formulates a statement, although we utter no sound, yet because we think words we speak within the mind. And so in all speech we only remind, since memory, within which words inhere,

[1] Matt. vi. 6   [2] 1 Cor. iii. 16   [3] Eph. iii. 17   [4] Ps. iv. 5, 6   [5] Matt. vi. 9

by revolving them causes to come into the mind the very things of which the words are signs.

Ad.—I understand and follow you.

CHAPTER II

MAN SHOWS THE MEANING OF WORDS ONLY THROUGH WORDS

Aug.—Then we agree that words are signs?

Ad.—We do agree.

Aug.—But what about this? Can a sign be a sign unless it signifies something?

Ad.—It cannot.

Aug.—How many words are in this line: *Si nihil ex tanta superis placet urbe relinqui?* [6]

Ad.—Eight.

Aug.—Then there are eight signs?

Ad.—That is so.

Aug.—I believe you understand this line.

Ad.—Quite well, I think.

Aug.—Then tell me what each word signifies.

Ad.—Indeed, I see what *si* [if] signifies, but I cannot find another word by which to explain it.

Aug.—Whatever may be signified by the word, at least you know where it is.

Ad.—It seems to me that *si* [if] signifies doubt, and where is doubt except in the mind?

Aug.—I accept that for the time being. Go on with the others.

Ad.—What does *nihil* [nothing] signify except that which is not?

Aug.—Perhaps you are right. But I cannot agree with you because of your recent admission, namely, that a sign is not a sign unless it signifies something. And that which is not cannot in any way be something. Accordingly, the second word in the line is not a sign because of the fact that it does not signify anything, which would mean that we have agreed falsely that all words are signs or that every sign signifies something.

Ad.—Indeed, you press too hard. But when we do not express what we signify, any word which we utter is simply nonsense. Yet I believe that as you are now speaking to me, you do not utter nonsense, but that by each word from your lips you give a sign to me in order that I may understand something. Consequently, you ought not to express the two syllables *nihil* [nothing] when you speak if you do not signify anything by means of them. But if you see that a necessary expression is made by means of them, and that we are taught or reminded of something when they strike the ear, then you likewise see just what I wish to say but cannot explain.

[6] *Aen.* ii. 659

Aug.—What shall we do? Since the mind does not see the thing and yet finds, or thinks that it finds, that it does not exist, can we not say that a certain affection of the mind is signified rather than a thing which is not?

Ad.—Perhaps that is just what I was trying to explain.

Aug.—Let us proceed then, be that matter as it may, lest a very silly thing happen to us.

Ad.—What, pray?

Aug.—Lest nothing should detain us, and we should suffer delay.

Ad.—That is indeed ridiculous; and yet I see that it can happen, although I do not know how. Ah, but indeed, I see clearly that it has happened.

Aug.—In due order, God willing, this sort of confusion will be clearer. Now go back to the line and try, as well as you can, to explain what the other words in it signify.

Ad.—The third is a preposition *ex* [from] for which we can, I think, say *de* [from].

Aug.—I am not asking you to replace one well known word with another equally well known word which means the same thing; granted indeed that it does mean the same thing, which for the present we shall allow. Surely, if the poet had not expressed it *ex tanta urbe*, but *de tanta*, and if I were to ask you what *de* means, you might say *ex*, and we should then have two words, or signs, signifying, as you think, the same one thing. But I am asking about that one thing itself, whatever it is, which is signified by these two words.

Ad.—It appears to mean a sort of separation from a thing in which something has been, though the thing no longer remains, as in this line, for example: although the city was destroyed, perhaps a few Trojans were left from the city [*ex illa*]; or, if the thing does remain, as when we say, for example, that there are traders in Africa from the city of Rome [*ex urbe Roma*].

Aug.—I admit that, and I prefer not to enumerate how many exceptions may be found to your rule. But, surely, you readily observe that you have expounded words with words, signs with signs, things well known by means of things likewise well known. I wish, however, that you would show me, if you can, the things themselves of which these are the signs.

CHAPTER III

WHETHER ANYTHING CAN BE SHOWN WITHOUT A SIGN

Ad.—I wonder that you do not know, or that you pretend not to know, that what you wish cannot be done by my answers as long as we are engaged in discussion, since while we are actually discussing I cannot answer except in words. You seek the things, however, which, whatever they are, are surely not words, and yet you also ask me about them by means of words. Do first ask me about them without the help of words, and I shall then reply in the same way.

Aug.—I admit that you are within your right. But if when *paries* [wall] is expressed, I should ask you what the three syllables mean, could you not point it out with your finger so that I might see the very thing itself of which the three-syllable word is a sign? You would show it to me, and yet you would not employ words.

Ad.—I admit that it can be done, but only in the case of nouns [names] by means of which bodies are signified, provided the bodies themselves are present.

Aug.—Do we not call color a certain quality of a body, rather than a body?

Ad.—That is so.

Aug.—Then why cannot this be shown by pointing the finger? Or do you also add to bodies the qualities of bodies, since, for example, when colors are present they can be shown quite as well without words?

Ad.—When I said bodies I meant all corporeal things, that is, all things which are sensed in bodies.

Aug.—But consider now: should you not make some exceptions?

Ad.—You advise me well. For I should not say all corporeal things, but all visible things. For I confess that sound, odor, taste, weight, and others of this sort which pertain to other senses, although they cannot be sensed without bodies, still they cannot be shown by pointing the finger.

Aug.—Have you not seen men when they discourse, so to speak, by means of gestures with those who are deaf, the deaf likewise using gestures? Do they not question and reply and teach and indicate everything they wish or at least a great many things? When they use gestures they do not merely indicate visible things, but also sounds and tastes and other things of this sort. For actors in the theatre present and exhibit entire dramas for the most part by means of pantomime without using words.

Ad.—I have no objection to make except that neither I nor even a pantomimic actor himself can show you without words what *ex* [from] signifies.

Aug.—Perhaps that is true. But let us fancy that he can. You do not doubt, I think, that whatever bodily movement the pantomimic actor may use in order to show me the thing signified by the word, the motion will not be the thing itself but a sign. Consequently the motion, though not indicating a word by means of a word, will nevertheless indicate a sign by a sign. The monosyllable *ex* and the gesture will both mean one and the same thing, which is what I wish to have shown me in some other way than by making a sign.

Ad.—How, I pray, can what you ask be done?

Aug.—In the same way in which the wall was shown.

Ad.—Not even a wall can be shown without a sign, as far as I can see from our discussion at this point. For the directing of the finger is certainly not the wall, but through it a sign is given by which the wall may be seen. I see nothing, therefore, which can be shown without signs.

Aug.—What if I were to ask you what walking is, and you should get up and walk. Would it not be shown me through the thing itself rather than through words, or would you use some other signs?

Ad.—I admit that point, and I am ashamed not to have seen so obvious a thing. From this thousands of other things now occur to me which can be shown through themselves [*per se*] and not through signs, as eating, drinking, sitting, standing, shouting and innumerable others.

Aug.—Come now, tell me; if I, knowing absolutely nothing of the meaning of the word, should ask you while you are in the act of walking what walking is, how would you teach me?

Ad.—I should walk somewhat more quickly in order that after your question your attention might be directed to something new. And yet I should do only what was to be shown.

Aug.—Do you know that walking is one thing and hurrying another? For he who walks need not immediately hurry, and he who hurries does not necessarily walk, since we speak of hurrying in writing and reading and in innumerable other things. Hence, if after my question you were to do more quickly what you were doing already, I should think walking to be merely hurrying. Hurrying would be the new thing added, and so I should be misled by that.

Ad.—I admit that we cannot show a thing without a sign if we are questioned while we are in the act of doing it. For if we add nothing, the questioner will think that we do not wish to show him and will suppose that, to ridicule him, we are continuing what we are doing. But if he asks about things which we are able to do, and yet does not ask while we are in the act of doing them, we can, by doing what he asks after his question, show him what he asks by means of the thing itself rather than by a sign. Unless perhaps the questioner should ask me what speaking is while I am in the act of speaking; since when I say anything in order to teach him the answer to this question it is necessary for me to speak. If this happens, I shall teach him until I make clear to him what he wants to know, adhering to the thing itself which he desires to have shown him and not casting about beyond the thing itself for some sign by which I may indicate it.

CHAPTER IV

WHETHER SIGNS ARE SHOWN BY SIGNS

Aug.—Very keen, indeed. Now, then, are we in agreement that those things can be shown without signs, which either we are not doing when we are asked but can do at once, or which themselves are signs (as in speaking). For when we speak we make signs, and this is called signifying.

Ad.—It is agreed.

Aug.—If certain signs are asked about, then these signs can be shown by means of signs. But when things which are not signs are asked about, they can be shown either by means of doing them after the question, if they can be done, or by giving signs by means of which they can be called to the attention.

Ad.—That is so.

Aug.—In this threefold division let us first consider this, namely, that signs are shown by means of signs. For words are not the only signs, are they?

Ad.—No.

Aug.—Now it seems to me that in speaking we signify by means of words either words themselves or other signs, as, for instance, when we say "gesture" or "letter" (for the things which are signified by the words *gesture* or *letter* are also signs); or we signify something else which is not a sign, as when we say "stone," for this word is a sign since it signifies something, but that which is signified in this case is not in turn a sign. But this genus, that is, the genus in which things which are not signs are signified by words, does not belong to the present part of our discussion. For we have undertaken to consider that genus in which signs are shown by means of signs, and in it we have discovered two parts, since through signs we teach or call to mind either the same signs or other signs. Or does it not seem so to you?

Ad.—It is obvious.

Aug.—Then tell me to what sense pertain the signs which are words.

Ad.—To hearing.

Aug.—And gesture?

Ad.—To sight.

Aug.—What do we find about written words? Are they not better understood as signs of words than as words? A word is that which is uttered by the articulate voice with some meaning, but the voice can be perceived only by the sense of hearing. It thus happens that when a word is read a sign is made in the eyes by which that sign which pertains to the ears comes into the mind.

Ad.—I agree entirely.

Aug.—I think you agree also when I say that the word *name* [noun] signifies something to us.

Ad.—Truly it does.

Aug.—What then?

Ad.—To be sure, that which something is called, as *Romulus, Rome, virtue, river,* and innumerable others.

Aug.—Do not these words signify things?

Ad.—Indeed they do signify things.

Aug.—Is there no difference between the names and the things which are signified by means of them?

Ad.—A great deal of difference.

Aug.—I should like to hear from you what it is.

Ad.—This, in the first place, that the former are signs, while the latter are not.

Aug.—Can we agree to call *signifiable* those things which can be signified by means of signs and yet are not signs, just as we call those things visible which can be seen, so that we may discuss these things more conveniently in proper order?

Ad.—It is quite agreeable.

Aug.—Are the four signs which you mentioned just above signified by no other signs?

Ad.—I am surprised you think I have forgotten that we found that written things are to things uttered by the voice as signs of signs.

Aug.—Tell me why they differ.

Ad.—Because the former are visible, the latter audible. For why should we not say audible if we say signifiable?

Aug.—I agree and thank you. But again, I ask, can these four signs be signified by no other audible signs, as you remember the visible signs can be?

Ad.—I also recall that this was said recently. For I answered that a noun [name] signifies something, and I had put the above four under its signification; both that [noun] and these things, if of course they be uttered by the voice, I understand to be audible.

Aug.—Now what is the difference between an audible sign and audible things signified which in turn are signs?

Ad.—Between what we call noun [name] and the four above which we put under its signification, I see this difference, that noun is an audible sign of audible signs, whereas those placed under its signification are audible signs of things: partly of visible things, as *Romulus* is, and *Rome*, and *river;* partly of intelligible things as *virtue* is.

Aug.—I accept and approve that. But do you know that all things which are uttered by the articulate voice with some signification are called words?

Ad.—I do.

Aug.—And so a noun [name] is a word, since we see that it is uttered with some signification by the articulate voice. And when we say that an eloquent man uses fair words, he also uses fair names, and when the slave in Terence's play said to the old lord, "I seek fair words," he had also expressed many nouns.[7]

Ad.—I agree.

Aug.—You grant, therefore, that by these two syllables which we pronounce when we say "verbum" [word] *name* [noun] is also signified, and that, accordingly, *word* is a sign of *name*.

Ad.—I agree.

[7] In *Andria,* act 1, scene 2, v. 33

Aug.—I also want you to answer this. Since *word* is a sign of *name*, and *name* is a sign of *river*, and *river* is a sign of a thing which can now be seen, so that between what can be seen and *river* which is its sign, and between this sign and the name which you have said to be its sign, there is a difference, what do you think is the difference between the sign of *name*, which we find to be *word*, and name itself of which it is the sign?

Ad.—I understand this difference, namely, that those things which are signified by *name* [noun] are also signified by *word*, for as *name* is a word, so also *river* is a word. Yet everything which is signified by means of a word is not signified by means of a noun. For *si* [if] which is at the inception of the line you mentioned, and *ex* [from], from the discussion of which we have been led by reason into these matters, are both words but not nouns; and many such are found. Consequently, since all nouns are words but not all words are nouns, it seems to me evident what I think the difference is between word and noun, that is, between the sign of that sign which signifies no other signs, and the sign of that sign which in turn signifies other signs.

Aug.—Do you grant that every horse is an animal, but that not every animal is a horse?

Ad.—Who doubts that?

Aug.—Then the difference between *noun* and *word* is the same as the difference between *horse* and *animal*. Perhaps, however, you are prevented from agreeing because we speak of *verbum* [verb] in another way in which it signifies words which are declined by tenses, and these words are obviously not nouns.

Ad.—That is precisely the point which made me doubtful.

Aug.—Do not let that trouble you. For speaking in a general sense, we call signs all those things which signify something, and words are included under this. Then, too, we say "military signs" or "banners," which are properly called signs, but words do not belong to this genus. And yet if I were to say that just as every horse is an animal but not every animal is a horse, so likewise every word is a sign but not every sign is a word, you would, I think, not doubt it.

Ad.—Now I understand and agree heartily that there is between *verbum* [word] used generally and *noun* the same difference which is between *animal* and *horse*.

Aug.—Do you also know that when we say "animal" this three-syllable word which is uttered by the voice is one thing and what it signifies is another?

Ad.—I have already agreed to that concerning all signs and things signifiable.

Aug.—Do all signs seem to you to signify something other than what they are, as when we say "animal" this three-syllable word in no way signifies what it is itself?

Ad.—Surely not, for when we say "sign" it signifies not only other signs, whatever they are, but it also signifies itself, for it is a word and all words certainly are signs.

Aug.—How then? When we say the two-syllable "verbum" [word], does not something of this sort happen? For if this two-syllable word signifies everything that is uttered by the articulate voice with some signification, it is also included in the genus.

Ad.—That is so.

Aug.—Is that not also true of *noun?* For it signifies nouns of all sorts, and *noun* [*nomen*] itself is a noun of the neuter gender. For if I should ask what part of speech a noun is, could you answer correctly anything except "noun"?

Ad.—That is true.

Aug.—Then there are signs which signify themselves along with the other things which they signify.

Ad.—There are.

Aug.—When we say "conjunctio" [conjunction], does it seem to you that this four-syllable word belongs to the above sort?

Ad.—Not at all, for those things which it signifies are not nouns, yet it is a noun.

CHAPTER V

RECRIPROCAL SIGNS

Aug.—You have been properly attentive. Now see whether signs are found which signify each other mutually, so that however the former may be signified by the latter, the latter is likewise signified by the former. For the four-syllable word *conjunctio* [conjunction] and the things which are signified by it, as, for example, *si* [if], *vel* [or], *nam* [for], *namque* [for indeed], *nisi* [except], *ergo* [therefore], *quoniam* [whereas], and the like, are not reciprocal, since the items enumerated are signified by *conjunctio*, but it in turn is not signified by any of them.

Ad.—I see, and I desire to know what signs do signify each other mutually.

Aug.—You do know that when we say "noun" and "word" we say two words.

Ad.—I know that.

Aug.—Do you know that when we say "noun" and "word" we also say two nouns?

Ad.—I know that also.

Aug.—Then you know that *noun* is signified by means of a word, and *word* by means of a noun.

Ad.—I agree.

Aug.—Can you say, aside from the fact that they are written and pronounced differently, what is the difference between them?

Ad.—Perhaps I can. For I see that the difference is the same as that which I determined above. For when we express words, we signify every-thing which is uttered by the articulate voice with some signification; hence, every noun and *noun* itself is a word. But not every word is a noun, although *word* itself is a noun.

Aug.—If anyone should assert and maintain that every noun is a word and every word is a noun, would you be able to find any difference between them except the differing sound of the letters?

Ad.—I could not, nor do I think there is any difference.

Aug.—What if all things which are uttered by the articulate voice with some significance are both words and nouns, but yet words for one reason and nouns for another. Will there be any difference between a noun and a word?

Ad.—I do not understand how.

Aug.—You understand this at least, namely, that everything colored is visible, and everything visible is colored, although the two words signify distinctly and differently.

Ad.—I do understand it.

Aug.—Well now, how will it be, if in this way every word is a noun and every noun is a word, although these two nouns, or two words, namely, *noun* and *word,* have different significations?

Ad.—I now see that this can happen. But I want you to explain to me how it happens.

Aug.—You observe, I think, that everything which is expressed by the articulate voice with some signification both strikes the ear so that it can be sensed and is committed to memory so that it can be known.

Ad.—I do observe it.

Aug.—Then two things happen when we utter something in that sort of voice.

Ad.—That is so.

Aug.—What if words be called such because of one fact and names be called names because of another, that is, words [*verba*] from the striking [*a verberando*] and nouns from the knowing [*a noscendo*]? As the first is called such with regard to the ears, should not the second be called such in reference to the soul?

Ad.—I shall agree when you have shown how all words may correctly be called nouns.

Aug.—That is easy. For I believe that you agree that a pronoun is so called because it stands for a noun and yet denotes a thing with less complete signification than does the noun. For I think that the rule you learned in grammar gave the definition thus: A pronoun is a part of speech which when put in place of a noun signifies the same thing, although less fully.

Ad.—I remember and I agree.

Aug.—You see, therefore, that according to this definition pronouns serve only nouns and can be substituted in place of these alone, as when we say: "this man, the ruler himself, the same woman, this gold, that silver." *This, himself, same, this, that* are pronouns. *Man, king, woman, gold,* and *silver* are nouns by which things are signified more fully than by pronouns.

Ad.—I see and agree.

Aug.—Now mention a few conjunctions, such as you please.

Ad.—*Et, que, at,* and *atque.*

Aug.—Do not all these things which you have expressed seem to you to be nouns?

Ad.—Not exactly.

Aug.—Did I not speak correctly when I said: "all these things which you have expressed"?

Ad.—Quite correctly. And I see with admiration that you have shown that I did express nouns, for otherwise the statement "all these things" could not have been said of them correctly. But still I fear you seem to me to speak correctly because I do not deny that the four conjunctions are words, so that "all these things" could be said of them correctly because "all these words" is said correctly. But if you ask me what part of speech *words* is, I can only say "noun." So that perhaps the pronoun modifies this noun, and thus your statement is correct.

Aug.—Indeed you are acutely mistaken. But in order that you may no longer be deceived, attend more closely to what I say, if indeed I am able to say it as I wish. For discussing words with words is as entangled as interlocking and rubbing the fingers with the fingers, in which case it may scarcely be distinguished, except by the one himself who does it, which fingers itch and which give aid to the itching.

Ad.—Your example has indeed aroused my sharpest attention.

Aug.—Surely I pronounce words, and they consist in letters.

Ad.—That is so.

Aug.—And so, in the first place, in order that we may use that authority which is quite dear to us, when the Apostle Paul said, "Non erat in Christo Est et Non, sed Est in illo erat" [8] ["There was not in Christ yea and nay, but in Him was yea"], I do not think that we should consider that the three letters which we express when we say "Est" were in Christ, but rather that which is signified by these three letters.

Ad.—That is true.

Aug.—You understand, therefore, that he who said, "Est in illo erat" said only that that which is in Him is called "Est." Similarly, if he had said, "Virtus in illo erat" ("Virtue was in Him"), he would be understood to have said only that what is in Him is called virtue, nor should we

[8] 2 Cor. i. 19

think that the two syllables expressed in saying "virtue" were in Him and not that which was signified by the two syllables.

Ad.—I understand and follow.

Aug.—Do you not also understand that it makes no difference whether one says "is called virtue" or "is named virtue"?

Ad.—It is obvious.

Aug.—Hence it is obvious in the same way that it makes no difference whether one says, "That which is in Him is called *Est*" or "That which is in Him is named *Est*."

Ad.—I see also that this makes no difference.

Aug.—Do you now see what I wish to show you?

Ad.—Not yet well enough.

Aug.—But you do see that a noun [name] is that by which something is called.

Ad.—That is very clear.

Aug.—Then you see that *Est* is a noun, if that which was in Him is named *Est*.

Ad.—I cannot deny it.

Aug.—And if I should ask you what part of speech, *Est* is, I think you would not say it is a noun [name] but a verb, although you have learned by reasoning that it is also a noun.

Ad.—That is exactly what I should say.

Aug.—Do you still doubt that other parts of speech are also nouns in the same way as has been shown?

Ad.—I do not doubt it, since I admit that they signify something. But if you ask what each one of the things which they signify is called or named, I can but answer those very parts of speech which we do not call nouns [names], but which are shown to be so called.

Aug.—Are you not at all disquieted lest there be someone who might weaken this reasoning of ours by saying that power over things should be ascribed to the Apostle, but not power over words, and that, therefore, the foundation of this statement is not as firm as we think; that it is possible that although Paul lived and taught with rectitude, yet that he spoke incorrectly when he said, "Est in illo erat," [9] especially since he confessed that he was unskilled in speaking? How then could this be refuted?

Ad.—I have no objection to make, and I beg you to find someone whose prestige is recognized among those who are skilled in words, that by his authority you may more ably effect what you wish.

Aug.—Indeed, because authority is lacking does that reasoning seem less qualified by means of which we have shown that something is signified by every part of speech, and if signified, then called; if called, then named; if named, then surely named by a noun [name]. This can

[9] 2 Cor. xi. 6

be easily determined by considering different languages. For anyone can see that if you ask what the Greeks call what we call *quis* [who], the the answer is τίς; what the Greeks call what we call *volo* [I wish], the answer is θέλω; what the Greeks call what we call *bene* [well], the answer is καλῶς; what the Greeks call what we call *scriptum* [text], the answer is τὸ γεγραμμένον; what the Greeks call what we call *et* [and], the answer is καί; what the Greeks call what we call *ab* [from], the answer is ἀπό; what the Greeks call what we call *hue* [alas], the answer is οἴ. And it seems that he who thus asks speaks correctly, which would not be possible unless the above parts of speech were nouns. And so since we can maintain that Paul spoke correctly, even if the authority of all orators be absent, why is there need to look for some individual by whom our decision may be substantiated?

But some duller or less cautious person might not grant this, and might assert that it ought not be granted without the authority of those who are by general consensus guardians of the rules of words; hence I ask, can there be anyone available who excels in the Latin language more than Cicero? But he, in those superb orations of his named Verrine, called the preposition *coram* (or in this case it may be an adverb) a noun. And yet since it is possible that I do not understand this context well enough and that it can be explained in different ways either by myself or by another, it is, I think, a thing to which no answer may be made. Now the noble masters of argument teach that a complete sentence is made up of a noun and a verb, which may be either affirmed or denied. Tullius in one place calls this a proposition. And when it is the third person of the verb, they say that the nominative case of the noun should accompany it, which is true, for if you consider with me as we say "homo sedet" [the man sits], "equus currit" [the horse runs], you will agree, I think, that they are two propositions.

Ad.—I do acknowledge that.

Aug.—You see there is a noun in each: in the first, *man,* and in the second, *horse;* and there is a verb in each: in the first, *sits,* and in the second, *runs.*

Ad.—I do see.

Aug.—Then if I were to say "sits" only or "runs" only, you would rightly ask me "who" or "what," and I should answer "man," or "horse," or "animal" or anything else, by which the noun can be restored to the verb and the proposition be completed, that is, the sentence which can be affirmed or denied.

Ad.—I understand.

Aug.—But attend to the rest. Suppose we see something remote and are uncertain whether it be an animal or a stone or something else, and suppose I say to you: "Because it is a man, it is an animal." Would I not speak rashly?

Ad.—Quite rashly, though not at all if you said: "If it is a man, then it is an animal."

Aug.—That is true. And what pleases me in your statement is *si* [if]. It pleases you too. But the *because* in my statement dissatisfies both of us.

Ad.—I agree.

Aug.—Now see whether these two statements are complete propositions: *if* pleases, *because* displeases.

Ad.—They are.

Aug.—Tell me now which are the verbs and which the nouns in those propositions.

Ad.—I see that *pleases* and *displeases* are the verbs, but what except *if* and *because* are the nouns?

Aug.—Then it is sufficiently proved that the two conjunctions are also nouns?

Ad.—Quite sufficiently.

Aug.—Can you treat other parts of speech in such a way that they will fall under the same rule?

Ad.—I can.

CHAPTER VI

SIGNS WHICH SIGNIFY THEMSELVES

Aug.—Then let us move on. Tell me whether, as we have found that all words [*verba*] are nouns and all nouns are words [*verba*], all nouns seem to you to be *vocabula* [words] and all *vocabula* [words] nouns?

Ad.—Clearly, I do not see what difference there is between them except in the sound of the syllables.

Aug.—At present I raise no objection, although some make a distinction in regard to the meaning, but we need not consider their opinion now. You surely note, however, that we have now discovered those signs which mutually signify each other, differing only in sound, and which signify themselves as well as all the other parts of speech.

Ad.—I do not understand.

Aug.—Do you not understand that a noun is signified by *vocabulum* [a word] and *vocabulum* by a noun, and that thus there is no difference between them beyond the sound of the letters in so far as *noun* in the general sense is concerned; for we also say "noun" in that special sense in which it is one of the eight parts of speech, so that it does not contain the other seven.

Ad.—I understand.

Aug.—But this is what I said, namely, that *vocabulum* and *noun* mutually signify each other.

Ad.—I grasp that, but I ask why you said: "since they signify themselves as well as the other parts of speech"?

Aug.—Did not our reasoning teach us that all parts of speech can be called nouns and *vocabula,* that is, can be signified by both *noun* and *vocabula?*

Ad.— That is so.

Aug.—What about *noun* itself, that is, that sound expressed by the two syllables [*nomen*]? If I ask what you call it, will you not correctly answer me with "noun"?

Ad.—Yes.

Aug.—Does the sign which we express when we say the four syllables "conjunctio" [conjunction] signify itself in this way? For this noun cannot be numbered with those things which it signifies.

Ad.—I quite accept that.

Aug.—That is because it has been said that *noun* signifies itself along with the other things which it signifies, and this, you may discern for yourself, also holds for *vocabulum.*

Ad.—That is now easy. But it has just occurred to me that *noun* is said both in a general sense and in a special sense, yet I do not take *vocabulum* to be among the eight parts of speech. It seems to me, therefore, that they differ in this respect in addition to the difference of sound between them.

Aug.—Do you think that *noun* [*nomen:* name] and ὄνομα differ otherwise than by the sound through which the Latin and Greek languages are distinguished?

Ad.—Indeed that is just what I understand.

Aug.—Then we have discovered those signs which (1) signify themselves, and (2) of which each is signified reciprocally by the other; (3) whatever is signified by one is signified by the other, (4) sound being the only difference between them. Of these only the fourth is a new discovery; for the three former are understood of *noun* and of *word* [*verbum*].

Ad.—It is entirely clear.

CHAPTER VII

CONCLUSION OF THE PRECEDING CHAPTERS

Aug.—Now I wish to review what we have discovered by means of this discussion.

Ad.—I shall do it in so far as I can. I remember that first of all we asked for what reason we speak. And it was found that we speak for the sake of teaching or reminding, since when we question we only do it that he who is asked may learn what we wish to hear; and that singing, which we seem to do for pleasure, is not properly speaking; that in praying to God whom we cannot suppose to be taught or reminded, words are for the purpose either of reminding ourselves or that others may be taught or reminded through us. Then, when it was clearly understood that words are only signs, you quoted a line in order that I might show what each word signified. And the line was: *Si nihil ex tanta superis placet urbe relinqui.* Although the second word was quite well known and very obvious, still I could not find what it means. And since it seemed to me that it is not used fecklessly in discourse, but that we use it in order to teach something by it to the hearer, you suggested that perhaps this word indicates an affection of the mind in which the mind seeks something and finds, or thinks it finds, that the something does not exist. Then, avoiding with a jest deep matters unknown to me, you put off the explanation until another time; and do not think that I have forgotten that you owe it me also. Then, when I was overtaxed to explain the third word in the line, you urged me not to substitute another word with the same meaning, but rather to indicate the thing itself which is signified by means of the word. And when we understood that this cannot be done in the act of speaking, we came to those things which are shown to the questioner by pointing the finger. I thought that these included all corporeal things, but we found that they are only the visible things. From here we went on, I do not know just how, to deaf men and actors who signify by gesture and without the use of words, not only things which can be seen, but also many others and almost everything that we say. Still we found that gestures themselves are signs. Then again we began to inquire how we can show without any signs the things themselves which are signified by the signs; since *wall,* and *color,* and everything visible that is shown by pointing the finger were all proved to be shown by a certain sign. I erred in having said that nothing of this sort could be found, and at length we agreed that those things can be shown without a sign, which we are not in the act of doing when we are asked about them and which we can do after being asked. But speaking does not belong to this genus. For if, while we are in the act of speaking, we are asked what speaking is, it is quite evident that it is easy to show it by means of itself.

By this we were reminded that either signs show signs, or they show other things which are not signs, or else without a sign are shown things which we can do after we are questioned. And we undertook to investigate and discuss the first of these three more thoroughly. In this discussion it was revealed that the signs are in part those which cannot in turn be signified by means of those signs which they signify, as in the four-syllable word *conjunctio* [conjuction]; in part, the signs are those which can in turn be signified by means of those signs which they signify, as when we say "sign," we also signify *word* [*verbum*], and when we say "word" we also signify *sign;* for *sign* and *word* are both two signs and two words. It was shown, moreover, that in this genus in which signs signify each other mutually, some mean not as much, some mean just as much, and some mean exactly the same thing. For the two-syllable word *sign* [*signum*] signifies absolutely everything by means of which anything is signified. *Word* [*verbum*] is not, however, a sign of all signs, but only of those which are uttered by the articulate voice; consequently, it is clear that although *word* [*verbum*] is signified by *sign* [*signum*] and *sign* by *word,* namely, the two former syllables by the latter two and the latter two by the former two, yet *sign* [*signum*] means more than *word* [*verbum*], for more things are signified by the former two syllables than by the latter two. But *word* in general means just as much as *noun* in general. For our reasoning taught us that all parts of speech are also nouns; for pronouns can be added to them, and it can be said of all that they name something; and there is none of them which cannot make a complete proposition when a verb is added to it. But although *word* [*verbum*] and *noun* [*nomen*] mean just the same amount because all things which are words are also names, yet they do not mean the same thing. It was argued, and with sufficient reason, that things are called words for one reason and nouns for another, since the former were found to be impressed on the vibration of the ear, but the latter on the memory of the mind; and this can be understood from the fact that in talking we correctly say "What is the name of this thing?" when we wish to commit it to memory, whereas we do not say "What is the word of this thing?" We found that *noun* and ὄνομα signify not only just as much but also the same thing exactly, and there is no difference between them except that of the differing sound in the letters. I had forgotten that in the genus in which signs signify each other mutually, we found no sign which does not signify itself as well as the other things which it signifies. I have recalled these things as best I could. Do you now, whom I believe to have spoken always with knowledge and certainty in this discussion, see whether I have set forth these things well and in good order.

CHAPTER VIII

THESE ARGUMENTS ARE NOT IN VAIN. LIKEWISE, WHEN SIGNS ARE HEARD, THE MIND MUST BE DIRECTED TOWARDS THE THINGS WHICH ARE SIGNIFIED, IN ORDER THAT THE QUESTIONER MAY BE ANSWERED

Aug.—You have recalled adequately all the things which I wanted, and now I acknowledge to you that these distinctions seem much clearer to me than they were when we unearthed them from unknown hiding places. But it is difficult at this point to say just where I am striving to lead you by so many circumlocutions. For it may seem that we are quibbling and so diverting the mind from earnest matters with naïve questions, or that we are seeking after some mean advantage. Or, if you suspect that this investigation tends towards some worthy object, you desire to know now what it is we strive after or at least you want it to be mentioned. But I want you to believe that I wish neither to have occupied myself with quibbles in this discussion, although we can afford to pun if the matter is not viewed naïvely; nor to have labored for petty or unimportant ends. Still if I say that there is a blessed life, to which I desire that we may be led under God's guidance, that is, by truth itself through stages of a degree suited to our weak progress, I fear to appear laughable because I have set out on such a road by considering not the things themselves which are signified, but signs. But be indulgent with this preparation, since it is not for amusement, but in order to exercise the strength and keenness of the mind by means of which we can not only bear the warmth and light of that region where the blessed life resides, but can also love the true.

Ad.—But do continue as you began, for I never think those things unimportant which you consider suitable to say or to do.

Aug.—Then come, and let us consider that case in which signs signify not other signs, but those things which we call signifiable. First, however, tell me whether a man is a man.

Ad.—But now you do seem to me to be jesting.

Aug.—Why so?

Ad.—Because you think that I should be asked whether man is anything other than man [*homo*].

Aug.—I believe that you would also think that you were being bantered if I should ask whether the first syllable of this word be other than *ho* and the second other than *mo?*

Ad.—Indeed I should.

Aug.—But these two syllables conjoined are man [*homo*], or do you object?

Ad.—Who could object to that?

Aug.—Now I ask whether you are these two conjoined syllables.

Ad.—Not at all, but your purpose is clear.

Aug.—Then tell me, and do not think me abusive.

Ad.—I infer that you think that I am not a man [*homo*].

Aug.—Why did you not think the same when you granted the truth of all the former inferences, from which this is derived?

Ad.—I shall not tell you what I think until I first hear from you whether, when you asked if man is man [*homo*], you were asking about the two syllables or about the thing itself which they signify.

Aug.—Do you rather tell me in what reference you take my questions; for if the reference is ambiguous you should have taken care not to answer me before making certain how I put the question.

Ad.—But how could the equivocation embarrass me, when I have answered both: for man is absolutely man [*homo*], and the two syllables are only the two syllables, and that which they signify is nothing other than that which it is.

Aug.—Of course you know this. But why have you only construed the word *homo* in two ways, and not also the other words which we have spoken?

Ad.—I am not at all certain that the others should not have been con-strued in this way.

Aug.—If you had construed my first question, not to mention the others, entirely in the sense in which the syllables sound, you would have made no answer, for I could not have seemed to ask anything. But just now when I pronounced the three words, one of which I reiterated in the center, saying "utrum homo homo sit" [whether man is man], you did not construe the first and last words as signs, but according to the things which are signified by them, and this is evident from the fact that you thought at once with certainty and confidence that my question should be answered.

Ad.—That is true.

Aug.—Then why did it seem suitable to you to construe the one I re-peated both according to the way in which it sounded and according to the thing which it signified?

Ad.—Ah, well, I now construe it entirely in the sense in which some-thing is signified, for I do agree with you that we cannot discuss at all un-less when we hear words we direct the mind to the things of which they are the signs. So now show me how that inference deceived me so that I concluded that I am not a man.

Aug.—No; rather, I shall question you again in order that you may dis-cover your error.

Ad.—Excellent.

Aug.—I shall not ask over again my first questions, for you have an-swered those already. Now, consider more carefully whether the syllable *ho* in *homo* is only the syllable *ho* and whether *mo* is only *mo*.

Ad.—I do not see any difference.

Aug.—See whether *homo* is not made by joining *ho* and *mo*.

Ad.—I do not agree at all. For we decided, and rightly so, when a sign is expressed to attend to that which is signified, and from the consideration of that to deny or affirm what is said. It has also been granted that, since the syllables uttered separately are expressed without any signification, they are just as they sound.

Aug.—It is agreed then and firmly established in your mind that answers ought to be made only to questions which are about things which are signified by words.

Ad.—It seems to me agreeable if the words are only words.

Aug.—Very well, but how would you refute that sophist of whom we hear, who asserted that when his opponent spoke a lion issued from his mouth? For first the sophist asked whether what we express proceeds from the mouth, which his opponent could not deny. Next he manipulated the conversation, which was easily done, so that his opponent pronounced "lion" in speaking. And when his opponent had done this, the sophist began to badger and heckle him, because his opponent had admitted that whatever we say comes forth from the mouth; nor was his opponent able to deny that he had spoken "lion," and the sophist asked the tormented victim if he who were seen to vomit such an enormous beast were not an evil fellow.

Ad.—It would be quite easy to refute this quibbler, for I should not admit that whatever we say proceeds from our mouth. For what we say we signify; and, in speaking, what issues from the mouth is not the thing itself which is signified, but the sign by means of which it is signified, except in that case in which signs themselves are signified, a genus which we previously discussed.

Aug.—Ah, in this way you would have held your own against him. Nevertheless, what will you say when I ask whether *man* is a noun?

Ad.—What indeed, but that it is a noun?

Aug.—And when I look at you do I see a noun?

Ad.—No.

Aug.—Do you wish me to say what follows?

Ad.—No, not at all, for I can answer myself that I am not that man which I have called a noun when you ask whether *man* is a noun; for it has been agreed that we are to affirm or to deny what is said according to the thing which is signified.

Aug.—But it seems to me not merely incidental that you made that answer, for your discrimination was ruled by the law of reason itself which has been placed within our minds. For if I should ask what man is, you would perhaps answer that he is an animal. But if I were to ask what part of speech *man* is, you could answer correctly only a noun. Accordingly, when *man* is found to be both a noun and an animal, the former is said in the sense in which it is a sign, the latter is said in the sense of the thing which is signified. And so when anyone asks whether *man* is a noun, I can only answer that it is, for the question thus put indicates clearly that the questioner wishes to be answered according to the sense in which *man* is a sign. But if he asks whether man is an animal, I may assent much more readily, since if he asked only what man is and indicated nothing in regard to *man* and to *animal,* my mind would fix itself according to the law of speaking towards that which is signified by the two syllables *homo* [man], and the answer would be "animal" only, or I might even give the full definition, namely, a rational, mortal animal. Do you understand the matter in this way?

Ad.—I do entirely. But when we have granted that *man* is a noun, how shall we avoid that absurd conclusion by which we are asserted not to be men?

Aug.—How indeed except by pointing out that the conclusion does not follow from the sense in which we agreed with the questioner? Or if he confesses to mean it not as a thing-reference but as a sign-reference, we need not be apprehensive, for why should one fear to admit that he is not a man [*homo*], namely, that he is not made up of three syllables.

Ad.—Very true. Why then is it offensive to us when it is said: "You, therefore, are not man [*homo*]," since according to our discussion that is quite true?

Aug.—Because one cannot help thinking that the conclusion bears a reference to that which is signified by the two syllables *homo* [man] as soon as the words are expressed, by virtue of that law which by nature is very strong, namely, that when signs are heard the attention is turned towards the things signified.

Ad.—I accept what you say.

CHAPTER IX

WHETHER ALL THINGS, AND ALSO THE COGNITION OF THEM, SHOULD BE PREFERRED TO THEIR SIGNS

Aug.—Now then, I wish you to understand that things which are signified are more to be depended upon than signs. For whatever exists because of another must of necessity be inferior to that because of which it exists, unless you think otherwise.

Ad.—It seems to me that assent should not be given too hastily. For when we say *coenum* [filth], this noun, I think, is far superior to that which it signifies. What offends us when we hear it does not pertain to the sound of the word itself, since *coenum* [filth] is changed by a single letter from *coelum* [heaven]. But we do see what a great difference there is between the things signified by these nouns. Hence I should not attribute to this sign what we so loathe in the thing signified. So for this reason I consider the sign superior to the thing, for we hear the sign with greater complaisance than we perceive the thing by means of any sense.

Aug.—Most watchful indeed. It is false, therefore, that all things are to be considered superior to their signs?

Ad.—It seems so.

Aug.—Then tell me what plan you think they followed who gave a name to this vile and despicable thing [*coenum:* filth]. Do you approve of them or not?

Ad.—Indeed, how should I dare to approve or to disapprove, for I do not know what plan they followed?

Aug.—At least you can determine what plan you follow when you utter the name.

Ad.—Clearly I can; for I wish to signify that which I think ought to be taught or reminded in order to teach or to remind him with whom I am speaking of the thing itself.

Aug.—The teaching or reminding, or the being taught or being reminded, which you either express suitably by means of the name or which is expressed to you—ought that not to be held superior to the name itself?

Ad.—I grant that the knowledge itself which results from the sign should be considered superior to the sign, but not for that reason, I think, the thing also.

Aug.—In this argument of ours, therefore, although it be false that all things ought to be considered superior to their signs, yet it is not false that everything which exists because of another is inferior to that because of which it exists. Surely, the cognition of filth because of which the noun [name] *filth* was determined ought to be considered superior to the noun itself which we found to be superior to filth itself. For the cognition is considered superior to the sign of which we spoke for the sole reason that it is proved conclusively that the sign exists because of the cognition and not the cognition because of the sign. Since, for example, when a certain glutton and servant of the belly, as the Apostle calls him,[10] said that he lived in order to eat, the temperate man who heard him chided him and said: "Would it not be better to eat in order to live?" This was clearly said in conformity with the rule that inferiors exist for the sake of superiors. And the Apostle was displeased only because the glutton's life should be of so little worth to him that he would have it degraded by the passion of gluttony as indicated by his saying that he lived for the sake of feasting. And this should be praised because the Apostle taught in these two distinctions that what ought to be done for the sake of something is that which should be subject to it, for it is understood that it is preferable to eat in order to live. Similarly you as well as other men who judge matters suitably would reply to a garrulous word-lover who said: "I teach in order to talk" with "Man, why not rather speak in order to teach?" For if these things are true, as you know they are, you truly see how much less words are to be esteemed than that for the sake of which we use words, since the use of words is superior to the words. For words exist in order that they may be used, and in addition we use them in order to teach. As teaching is superior to talking, in like degree speech is better than words. So of course doctrine is far superior to words. But I wish to hear whatever objections you have to offer.

Ad.—I agree indeed that doctrine is superior to words. But whether the rule that everything which exists for the sake of something else is inferior to that for the sake of which it exists has no exceptions is more than I am able to say.

Aug.—We shall discuss that more conveniently and more thoroughly at another time. For the present what you have granted is enough to prove what I now wish. For you grant that the cognition of things is superior to the signs of things. Consequently, the cognition of things which are signified is to be preferred to the cognition of signs by means of which they are signified. Do you agree?

Ad.—Did I admit that the cognition of things is superior to the cognition

[10] Rom. xvi. 18

of signs, and not just to signs themselves? Then I fear that I am not in agreement with you on this point. For if *coenum* [filth], the noun [name], is better than the thing it signifies, then the cognition of the noun [name] ought also to be preferred to the cognition of the thing, although the noun itself be inferior to the cognition. Indeed there are four considerations involved: (1) the noun, (2) the thing, (3) the cognition of the noun, (4) the cognition of the thing. Since the first is more excellent than the second, why is not the third better than the fourth? But if it is not better, must it therefore be considered as inferior?

Aug.—I see that you have very admirably retained what you conceded and understood what you thought. But you understand, I think, that the three-syllable word *vitium* [vice] is better than that which it signifies, though the cognition of the noun itself is far inferior to the knowledge of vices. Granted that you thus arrange and consider the four distinctions: (1) noun, (2) thing, (3) cognition of noun, (4) cognition of thing, we correctly place the first before the second. For the noun placed in the verse where Persius says,[11] "But he is drunk with vice," not only does not vitiate the verse but adds a certain ornament. But when the thing itself which is signified by this noun [*vitium*] is in anything it does vitiate it. So thus we see that the third does not excel the fourth, but the fourth the third. For the cognition of the noun *vitium* [vice] exists for the sake of the cognition [knowledge] of vices.

Ad.—Do you think that the cognition of vices is preferable even though it makes men more wretched? For among all the afflictions which man suffers, devised by the cruelty or cupidity of tyrants, this same Persius ranks first that torture which results when men are forced to acknowledge vices which they cannot avoid.

Aug.—Reasoning in this way, you can also deny that a knowledge [cognition] of virtues is preferable to the cognition of the word *virtue*. Because to see virtue but not to possess it is torture, and it was by this means that the satirist wished tyrants to be punished.[12]

Ad.—May God avert such madness. Now I do see that knowledge [the cognitions themselves] by which learning instructs the soul is not to be held as culpable, but that those men are to be judged the most pitiable of all, as I think Persius judged them, who are infected by such a malady that there is no remedy for it.

Aug.—You understand quite well. But then of what real moment is the opinion of Persius, the satirist, since in problems of the sort before us we are not subject to the authority of satirists? Well, if in some way one cognition is to be preferred to another, still that point is not easily explained just now. I am satisfied that it has been shown that the cognition of the thing which a sign signifies is more powerful than the sign itself, even if it is not superior to the cognition of a sign. Hence, let us discuss more thor-

[11] *Satira*, 3. 33   [12] *Satira*, 3. 35-38

oughly what the genus is of those things which we said can be shown through themselves [*per se*] without signs, as speaking, walking, sitting, throwing, etc.

Ad.—I recall now what you speak of.

CHAPTER X

WHETHER CERTAIN THINGS CAN BE TAUGHT WITHOUT SIGNS. THINGS ARE NOT LEARNED THROUGH WORDS THEMSELVES

Aug.—Does it seem to you that anything which may be immediately done when one asks a question about it can be shown without a sign, or do you see some exception?

Ad.—Running through the items of this whole genus time and again, I do not indeed find anything in it which can be taught without some sign, except perhaps speaking and also possibly teaching. For I see that whatever I do after his question in order that he may learn, the questioner does not learn from the thing itself which he desires to have shown him. For if I am asked what walking is when I am still, or doing something else, and if I, by walking immediately, try to teach without a sign what has been asked—all of which has been discussed earlier—then how shall I avoid having the asker think that walking consists in walking only so far as I walked? And if he did think that he would be misinformed, for if someone walked not so far or farther than I did the questioner would think that this individual had not walked. And what I have said about this one word will be true of all the others which we thought could be shown without a sign, except the ones we excluded (talking and teaching).

Aug.—I accept that, in truth; but does it not seem to you that speaking is one thing and teaching another?

Ad.—Surely it does, for if they were the same, none would teach without speaking, and since we teach many things by means of signs which are not words, who can doubt there is a difference?

Aug.—Are teaching and signifying the same or do they differ in some way?

Ad.—I think that they are the same.

Aug.—Is it not true that we signify in order to teach?

Ad.—That is true.

Aug.—What if it be said that we teach in order to signify? Is the assertion not easily refuted by the former statement?

Ad.—That is so.

Aug.—If then we signify that we may teach and do not teach in order to signify, teaching is one thing, signifying another.

Ad.—That is true, nor did I answer correctly that both are the same.

Aug.—Now tell me if he who teaches what teaching is does it by signifying or in some other way.

Ad.—I do not see that there is any other way.

Aug.—Therefore, what you said awhile ago is false, namely, that when someone asks what teaching is the thing itself can be taught without signs, since we see that not even this can be done without signifying. For you have granted that signifying is one thing, teaching another. And if, as it seems, they are different, and teaching is only by means of signifying, then teaching is not shown through itself [*per se*], as you thought. Consequently, nothing has yet been found which can be shown through itself except speaking which also signifies itself as well as other things. Yet since this is a sign also it is still not entirely clear what things can be taught without the aid of signs.

Ad.—I have no reason for disagreeing with you.

Aug.—It has been proved, therefore that nothing is taught without signs, and that cognition itself should be dearer to us than the signs by means of which we cognize, although all things which are signified cannot be greater than their signs.

Ad.—It seems so.

Aug.—Do you recall by what great circumlocutions we at length reached this slight point? For since we began this interchange of words which has occupied us for some time, we have labored to discover the following three points: 1. whether anything can be taught without signs, 2. whether certain signs ought to be preferred to the things which they signify, 3. whether the cognition of things is superior to their signs. But there is a fourth point which I wish to know briefly from you, namely, whether you think that these points are so clear and distinct that you cannot doubt them.

Ad.—I wish indeed to have arrived at certainty after such great doubts and complications, but your question disturbs me, although I do not know why, and keeps me from agreeing. For I see that you would not have asked me about this, if you did not have some objection to raise, and the problem is such a labyrinth that I am not able to explore it thoroughly or to answer with assurance, for I am disquieted lest something lie hidden in these windings which evades the keenness of my mind.

Aug.—I commend your hesitation. For it indicates a mind which is cautious and this is the greatest safeguard to equanimity. It is very difficult not to be perturbed when things we consider easily and readily provable are shaken by contrary arguments and, as it were, are wrenched from our hands. For just as it is proper to assent to things well explored and perused, so it is perilous to consider things known which are not known. Because there is a danger, when those things are often upset which we supposed would stand firmly and endure, lest we fall into such distrust and hatred of reason that it might seem that confidence in evident truth itself is not warranted.

But come, let us consider more diligently whether you think any of the points should be doubted. For consider, if someone unskilled in the art of bird-catching, which is done with reeds and bird-lime, should happen upon a fowler, carrying his instruments as he walked along though not fowling at the time, he would hasten to follow and in wonderment he would reflect and ask himself, as indeed he might, what the man's equipment meant. Now if the fowler, seeing himself watched, were to exhibit his art, and skilfully employ the reed, and then noting a little bird nearby, if he were to charm, approach, and capture it with his reed and hawk, would the fowler not teach his observer without the use of signification, but rather by means of the thing itself which the observer desired to know?

Ad.—I fear this observer of bird-catching is like the man whom I referred to above, who inquires about walking; for it does not seem that in this case the entire art of fowling is exhibited.

Aug.—It is easy to free you from that worry. For I suggest that an observer might be intelligent enough to recognize the whole complexity of the art from what he saw. It is enough for our purpose if certain men can be taught without signs about some things, if indeed not about all things.

Ad.—To that I can add that if the learner be very intelligent he will know what walking is fully when it has been shown by a few steps.

Aug.—That is agreeable. And I not only do not object, but I approve of your statement. For you see that the conclusion has been reached by both of us, namely, that some men can be taught certain things without signs, and that what we thought awhile back is false, that is, that there is nothing at all which can be shown without signs. For now of that sort, not one thing only or another, but thousands of things occur to the mind, which may be shown through themselves when no sign has been given. Why then do we hesitate, I pray you? For passing over the innumerable spectacles of men in every theatre where things are shown through themselves without signs, surely the sun and this light bathing and clothing all things, the moon and the other stars, the lands and the seas, and all things which are generated in them without number, are all exhibited and shown through themselves by God and nature to those who perceive them.

If we consider this more carefully, then perhaps you may find that there is nothing which is learned by means of signs. For when a sign is given me, if it finds me not knowing of what thing it is a sign, it can teach me nothing, but if it finds me knowing the thing of which it is the sign, what do I learn from the sign? For the word does not show me the thing which it signifies when I read: *Et saraballae eorum non sunt immutatae*[13] (And their *saraballae* are not changed). For if head-coverings of some sort are called by this name [*saraballae*], when I have heard it have I learned either what a head is or what coverings are? I knew these before, and it is not when someone names them, but when they are seen by me that knowledge of them is achieved for me. And indeed when the two syllables "caput" [head] were first expressed to me, I knew as little what they meant as

[13] Dan. iii. 94

when I first heard or read *saraballae*. But when "caput" was repeated over and over, as I observed and noticed when it was said, I found it to be the word of a thing which was already well known to me by sight. Before I discovered this the word was only a sound to me, and I learned that it is a sign when I found out of what thing it is a sign; which thing, indeed, I had learned, as I said above, not through its signification but by the sight of it. Therefore that the sign is learned after the thing is cognized is rather more the case than that the thing itself is learned after the sign is given.

That you may understand this more exactly, let us suppose that we now hear for the first time the word "caput" [head], and not knowing whether it is merely a meaningless sound or whether something is signified, we ask what "caput" [head] is. (Remember we want to have knowledge of the sign itself and not of the thing which it signifies, which knowledge we certainly lack as long as we do not know of what it is a sign.) And if, when we inquire, the thing itself is shown us by means of pointing the finger, when we have seen the thing we learn the sign which we had only heard before without knowing it. Since, however, two factors are involved with the sign, namely, sound and signification, we surely perceive the sound not through the sign but through the vibration when the ear is struck, while we learn the signification when the thing itself is shown. For the pointing of the finger can signify only that towards which the finger is pointed, but it was pointed not at the sign but at the member which is called the head; consequently, I have not learned by means of the pointing what the thing is, for I knew that already, nor did I learn the sign in that way since the pointing was not directed at the sign. But I do not wish to place too much emphasis on the pointing of the finger, because it seems to me that it is rather a sign of the demonstration itself rather than of the things demonstrated; as in the case of the adverb *ecce* [behold], for we are accustomed to point the finger with this adverb lest one sign of demonstration be not enough. And if I can, I shall try to prove to you above all that we learn nothing through those signs which are termed words. For it is more correct, as I have said, that we learn the meaning of the word, that is, the signification which is hidden in the sound when the thing itself which it signifies has been cognized, than that we perceive the thing through such signification.

And what I have said about *head*, I should say, too, of *coverings* [clothes] and of innumerable other things. And though I already know these, yet *saraballae* I do not know in the least. If someone were to indicate them by gesture or sketch them for me or show me something to which they are similar, I do not say that he would not teach me (which I could maintain if I wished to speak a little more fully). But I do say what is quite relevant to the point being discussed, namely, that he would not have taught me by means of words. If someone, seeing these *saraballae* while I was near, should bring them to my attention, saying "Ecce saraballas" [Here are the head-coverings], I would learn something unknown, not through the words which were spoken, but through its appearance, by means of which I was made to know and to retain the meaning of the name. For when I learned the thing itself I was not indebted to the words of others but to my eyes; yet perhaps I accepted their words in order to attend, that is, in order that I might find what was to be seen.

CHAPTER XI

WE DO NOT LEARN THROUGH THE WORDS WHICH SOUND OUTWARDLY, BUT THROUGH THE TRUTH WHICH TEACHES WITHIN US

To give them as much credit as possible, words possess only sufficient efficacy to remind us in order that we may seek things, but not to exhibit the things so that we may know them. He teaches me something, moreover, who presents to my eyes or to any other bodily sense or even to my mind itself those things which I wish to know. By means of words, therefore, we learn only words or rather the sound and vibration of words, for if those things which are not signs cannot be words, even though I have heard a word, I do not know that it is a word until I know what it signifies. So when things are known the cognition of the words is also accomplished, but by means of hearing words they are not learned. For we do not learn the words which we know, nor can we say that we learn those which we do not know unless their signification has been perceived; and this happens not by means of hearing words which are pronounced, but by means of a cognition of the things which are signified. For it is the truest reasoning and most correctly said that when words are uttered we either know already what they signify or we do not know; if we know, then we remember rather than learn, but if we do not know, then we do not even remember, though perhaps we are prompted to ask.

If you say this, we cannot know the head-coverings, the name of which is only a sound to us, unless we see them; and we cannot know the name itself more fully except by cognizing the things themselves. But we do accept the story of the boys, that they triumphed over the king and over the fires by faith and religion, that they sang praises to God, and that they won honor even from their very enemies. Has this been transmitted to us otherwise than by means of words? I answer that everything signified by these words was already in our knowledge. For I already grasp what three boys are, what a furnace is, and fire, and a king, what unhurt by fire is, and every thing else signified by those words. But Ananias and Azarias and Misael are as unknown to me as *saraballae;* these names do not help me at all to know these men, nor can they help me. I confess, moreover, that I believe rather than know that the things written in those stories were done at that time as they have been written; and those whom we believe knew the difference between believing and knowing. For the Prophet says: "If ye will not believe, ye shall not understand." [14] Surely he would not have said that, had he not thought that believing and understanding are different. Therefore, what I understand I also believe, but I do not understand everything that I believe; for all which I understand I know, but I do not know all that I believe. But still I am not unmindful of the utility of believing many things which are not known. I include in this utility the story about the three youths. And though the majority of things must remain unknown to me, yet I do know what is the utility of believing.

But, referring now to all things which we understand, we consult, not the speaker who utters words, but the guardian truth within the mind itself, because we have perhaps been reminded by words to do so. Moreover, He who is consulted teaches; for He who is said to reside in the interior man is Christ,[15] that is, the unchangeable excellence of God and His everlasting wisdom, which every rational soul does indeed consult. But there is revealed to each one as much as he can apprehend through his will according as it is more perfect or less perfect. And if sometimes one is deceived this is not due to a defect in the truth which he has consulted any more than it is a defect of external light that the eyes of the body are often deceived; yet we confess that we consult this external light about visible things in order that it may show them to us in so far as we have the power to discern.

CHAPTER XII

CHRIST THE TRUTH TEACHES WITHIN

If we consult light concerning color and other things which we sense through the body; if we consult the elements of this world and those bodies which we sense; if we consult the senses themselves which the mind uses as interpreters in recognizing things of this sort; and if we also consult the interior truth by means of reason about things which are understood: what can be said to indicate that we learn anything by means of words beyond that sound which strikes the ear? For all things which we perceive are perceived either through a sense of the body or by means of the mind. We call the former sensibles, the latter intelligibles; or to speak in the manner of our authorities, the former are carnal, the latter spiritual. If we are questioned about sensibles, we answer if the things sensed are at hand, as when we are questioned while gazing at the new moon as to where or of what sort it is. If the one who questions does not see, he believes words, and often he does not believe; but he learns nothing unless he also sees what is mentioned. If he does learn, he learns by means of the things themselves and from his own senses, but not through the articulated words. For the same words are heard by the man who sees and by the man who does not see. But if a question is not about things immediately sensed, although it is

[14] Isa. vii. 9   [15] Eph. iii. 16, 17

about things which we have sensed in the past, in this case we speak not of things themselves but of images impressed by things on the mind and committed to memory. I do not in the least know how we can speak of these as true when we see that they are false, unless it is because we do not speak of what we see or what we sense, but of what we have seen or have sensed. Thus we carry these images in the recesses of the memory as documents of things sensed before. Contemplating these in the mind, we say nothing that is false if we speak with good conscience. But these documents are our own, and he who hears of them, if he has been in their presence and sensed them, learns nothing from my words, but rather remembers [and confirms] what is said through the images hidden in himself. But if he has not perceived the things which are spoken of, it is clear that he believes [or accepts on trust] rather than learns through the words.

Indeed when things are discussed which we perceive through the mind, that is, by means of intellect and reason, these are said to be things which we see immediately in that interior light of truth by virtue of which he himself who is called the interior man is illumined, and upon this depends his joy. But then our hearer, if he also himself sees those things with his inner and pure eye, knows that of which I speak by means of his own contemplation, but not through my words. Accordingly, even though I speak about true things, I still do not teach him who beholds the true things, for he is taught not through my words but by means of the things themselves which God reveals within the soul. Hence, if he is questioned, he can answer about these. What could be more absurd than to think that he is taught by means of my speaking, when even before I speak he can express those very things if questioned? Now, if it often happens that he who is questioned denies something, and is driven by other questions to affirm that which he denied, this happens because of a defect in his discrimination in so far as he cannot consult that light about the whole matter. He is advised to do it part by part when he is questioned by one step after another about those very parts of which the whole consists, which he is unable to grasp in its entirety. If he is guided in this case by the words of the questioner, still he does not accomplish the grasp of the whole by means of verbal instruction, but by means of questions put in such a way that he who is questioned is able to teach himself through his inner power according to the measure of his ability. An apt example is found in our recent procedure, for when I asked you whether anything can be taught by words, the question at first seemed absurd to you, because you did not have an inclusive view of the problem. Thus, it was suitable for me to formulate my questions in such a way that your powers might be brought under the direction of the inner teacher. Accordingly, I should say things which as I spoke you would admit to be true, of which you would be certain, and about which you would declare that you had knowledge. From what source would you learn these things? You would perhaps answer that I had taught them to you. To that

I should reply: "What if I should say that I had seen a man flying?" Would my words carry the same certitude as if you should hear that wise men are superior to fools? You would immediately answer in the negative and assert that you do not believe the former statement, or if you do believe it, that you do not know it to be true, but that you do know the latter statement with great certainty. From this discussion you would understand clearly that you did not learn anything from me through words, neither about a man flying, of which you knew nothing though I did state it, nor about the relative worth of wise men and fools, which you did know quite well. If in addition you were also questioned about each word, you would state on oath that the latter is well known to you, while the former is not known. Then indeed you would admit all that you had denied, as you knew with clarity and certainty the things in which it consists. Whenever we say anything, either the hearer does not know whether what is said is false or true, or he knows that it is false, or he knows that it is true. In the first mode he will either believe (or accept in good confidence), or he will form an opinion, or he will hesitate; in the second mode he will resist the statement and reject it; in the third he merely confirms. In none of these three cases does the hearer learn anything from what is heard. For he who does not know about the thing after we have spoken, he who knows that what we said is false, and he who would be able upon being asked to state the same things without having heard them, are all three shown to have learned nothing through words.

CHAPTER XIII

THE POWER OF WORDS DOES NOT EVEN REVEAL THE MIND OF THE SPEAKER

From what has been said it follows, therefore, that in the case of those things which are grasped by the mind, anyone who is unable to grasp them hears to no purpose the words of him who does discern them; though we may make an exception in regard to the fact that where such things are unknown there is a certain utility in believing them until they are known. On the other hand, whoever can discern those things which are grasped by the mind is inwardly a pupil of truth and outwardly a judge of the speaker, or rather of his statements. For often he knows what has been said, though the speaker himself does not know; as if, for example, someone who is a follower of Epicurus and so thinks that the soul is mortal, should recite the arguments on the soul's immortality expounded by men of greater wisdom. If someone who is versed in spiritual things hears the speaker state the argument for the immortality of the soul, he will judge that true things have been said, but the speaker does not know that they are true; for, to the contrary, he thinks that they are quite false. Can he be understood as teaching what he does not know? He does use, however, the very same words which one who understood would use.

Now, therefore, not even this is left to words, namely, that at any rate they express the mind of the speaker, since a speaker may indeed not know the things about which he speaks. Consider also lying and deceiving, and you will easily understand from both of them that words not only do not disclose the true intention of the mind, but that they may serve to conceal it. For I by no means doubt that by words truthful men try, and to some extent do contrive, to disclose their minds, which would be accomplished, as all agree, if liars were not allowed to speak. And yet we have had the experience both in ourselves and in others of words being expressed which were not about the thing being thought. It seems to me that this can happen in two ways: (1) either when something which has been committed to memory and often repeated is expressed by one who is preoccupied with other things, as often happens to us when we sing a hymn, (2) or when against our will we make a slip in speech, for in this case, too, signs are expressed which are not of the things which we have in mind. For indeed those who lie also think of the things which they express, so that, although we do not know whether they tell the truth, we do yet know that they have in mind what they are saying, if they do not do one of the two things cited above. If anyone contends that this only happens now and then, and is apparent when it happens, I do not object, though frequently it is not observed and has often deceived me.

But among these there is another genus of words, one which is very prevalent and the cause of countless disagreements and battles, namely, that which is involved when he who speaks signifies the thing which he is thinking, but for the most part only to himself and certain others, while he does not signify the same thing to the one to whom he speaks nor to some others. For should someone say in our presence that man is surpassed in manly power [*virtus*] by certain large animals, we should not be able to brook such a statement; and we should deny this false and repugnant assertion with vehemence, though perhaps the speaker meant by *manly power* bodily strength. He may have expressed by the word what he had in mind, neither lying, nor making a mistake about the thing, nor linking together memorized words while turning other things over in his mind, nor saying by a slip of the tongue what he did not intend to say. He merely calls the thing about which he was thinking by a name which is other than the one by which we call it. We should agree with him at once if we could read his mind and see directly the thought which he was unable to express by the words spoken and the statement made. They say that definition can cure this error, so that in this case, if the speaker were to define what virtue is, it would be clear that the controversy is not about the thing but about the word. Now I may grant that this is so, but how often is it possible to find good definers? And yet many things have been charged against the science of defining, which are not approved by me in all respects, but it is not suitable to discuss this at present.

I pass over the fact that we hear many things imperfectly and yet wrangle long and forcefully as if we had heard perfectly; for example, you were saying but some time ago that you had heard that *piety* is signified by a certain Punic word which I had called *mercy,* and you had heard this from those who know the language well. But I objected and insisted that you had forgotten what you had heard, for you seemed to me to say "faith" rather than "piety," though you were sitting near me and the two words are by no means deceptive to the ear because of their similarity in sound. Yet for a long time I thought that you did not know what had been said to you, whereas it was I who did not know what you had said. If I had heard you well, it would not have seemed at all absurd to me that in Punic *piety* and *mercy* are called by one word. These things happen now and then, but, as I said, we shall overlook them lest I seem to bring false witness against words because of the negligence of the hearer or even because of human deafness. The points enumerated above are more distressing where, though we speak the same language as the speaker and the words are clearly heard and are Latin, we still are not able to understand the speaker.

But witness: I now relent and admit that when words are perceived in the hearing of him to whom they are known, the hearer may rest assured that the speaker has thought about the things which they signify. But we are now asking if for that reason he learns whether the speaker has told the truth?

CHAPTER XIV

CHRIST TEACHES WITHIN. MAN REMINDS BY MEANS OF WORDS SPOKEN OUTWARDLY

For do teachers profess that it is their thoughts which are perceived and grasped by the students, and not the sciences themselves which they convey through speaking? For who is so stupidly curious as to send his son to school in order that he may learn what the teacher thinks? But all those sciences which they profess to teach, and the science of virtue itself and wisdom, teachers explain through words. Then those who are called pupils consider within themselves whether what has been explained has been said truly; looking of course to that interior truth, according to the measure of which each is able. Thus they learn, and when the interior truth makes known to them that true things have been said, they applaud, but without knowing that instead of applauding teachers they are applauding learners, if indeed their teachers know what they are saying. But men are mistaken, so that they call those teachers who are not, merely because for the most part there is no delay between the time of speaking and the time of cognition. And since after the speaker has reminded them, the pupils quickly learn within, they think that they have been taught outwardly by him who prompts them.

But we shall, God willing, inquire at some other time about the utility of words, which if it is well considered is no mean matter. For the present I have warned you that we should not attribute more to words than is proper. So that now we may not only believe but also begin to understand that it has truly been written on divine authority that we are not to call anyone on earth our master because there is only one Master of all who is in heaven.[16] But what *in heaven* means He Himself will advertise to us by means of men, through signs and outwardly, so that we may by turning inwardly to Him be made wise; whom to know and to love is the blessed life which, though all claim to seek it, few indeed may rejoice that they have found. But now pray tell me what you think about this long disquisition of mine. For if you know that what I have said is true, then had you been questioned about each statement you would have said that you did know it. You see, therefore, from whom you have learned these matters. Surely, not from me to whom you would have given the correct answer if questioned. However, if you do not know that they are true, neither the inner man nor I have taught you; not I, because I can never teach; not the inner man, because you have it not yet in you to learn.

Ad.—But I have learned through being reminded by your words that man is only prompted by words in order that he may learn, and it is apparent that only a very small measure of what a speaker thinks is expressed in his words. Moreover, when He spoke among the people He reminded us that we learn whether things are true from that one only whose habitation is within us, whom now, by His grace, I shall so love more ardently as I progress in understanding. Nevertheless, I am most grateful to you for the discussion which you delivered without breaking the thread of your thought, because it anticipated and dissolved all the objections which occurred to me, and nothing which was causing me disquietude has been overlooked by you, nor is there anything about which the inner oracle does not tell me what your words stated.

[16] Matt. xxiii. 8-10

ON
THE PROFIT OF BELIEVING

ON

THE PROFIT OF BELIEVING

Introductory Note

In 391 A.D. Saint Augustine was ordained a priest in Hippo Regius and it was not long before he found himself completely and vigorously involved in the affairs and problems of the Church in that community. One of his first activities was to move against the strong group of Manichaeans who appeared to threaten the spiritual well-being of his parishioners. Hardly had he become established when he wrote the treatise *On the Profit of Believing*, addressing it to a friend, by name Honoratus, who had espoused the sect of Mani. Saint Augustine could bring his own powerful learning to bear upon the problem, could effectively compare Christianity with Manicheism, could show how the latter misrepresented Christ, and could point to the ways whereby he himself became free from the Manichaean grip. The resultant work is typical of the force which Saint Augustine could exert against this strange enemy of Christianity.

ON
THE PROFIT OF BELIEVING

1. IF, HONORATUS, a heretic, and a man trusting heretics seemed to me one and the same, I should judge it my duty to remain silent both in tongue and pen in this matter. But now, whereas there is a very great difference between these two: forasmuch as he, in my opinion, is an heretic, who, for the sake of some temporal advantage, and chiefly for the sake of his own glory and pre-eminence, either gives birth to, or follows, false and new opinions; but he, who trusts men of this kind, is a man deceived by a certain imagination of truth and piety. This being the case, I have not thought it my duty to be silent towards you, as to my opinions on the finding and retaining of truth: with great love of which, as you know, we have burned from our very earliest youth: but it is a thing far removed from the minds of vain men, who, having too far advanced and fallen into these corporeal things, think that there is nothing else than what they perceive by those five well-known reporters of the body; and what impressions and images they have received from these, they carry over with themselves, even when they essay to withdraw from the senses; and by the deadly and most deceitful rule of these think that they measure most rightly the unspeakable recesses of truth. Nothing is more easy, my dearest friend, than for one not only to say, but also to think, that he has found out the truth; but how difficult it is in reality, you will perceive, I trust, from this letter of mine. And that this may profit you, or at any rate may in no way harm you, and also all, into whose hands it shall chance to come, I have both prayed, and do pray, unto God; and I hope that it will be so, forasmuch as I am fully conscious that I have undertaken to write it, in a pious and friendly spirit, not as aiming at vain reputation, or trifling display.

2. It is then my purpose to prove to you, if I can, that the Manichees profanely and rashly inveigh against those, who, following the authority of the Catholic Faith, before they are able to gaze upon that Truth, which the pure mind beholds, are by believing forearmed, and prepared for God Who is about to give them light. For you know, Honoratus, that for no other reason we fell in with such men, than because they used to say, that, apart from all terror of authority, by pure and simple reason, they would lead within to God, and set free from all error those who were willing to be in their hearers. For what else constrained me, during nearly nine years, spurning the religion which had been set in me from a child by my parents,

to be a follower and diligent hearer of those men,[1] save that they said that
we are alarmed by superstition, and are commanded to have faith before
reason, but that they urge no one to have faith, without having first discussed and made clear the truth? Who would not be enticed by such promises, especially the mind of a young man desirous of the truth, and further
a proud and talkative mind by discussions of certain learned men in the
school? such as they then found me, disdainful forsooth as of old wives'
fables, and desirous to grasp and drink in, what they promised, the open
and pure Truth? But what reason, on the other hand, recalled me, not to
be altogether joined to them, so that I continued in that rank which they
call of Hearers, so that I resigned not the hope and business of this world;
save that I noticed that they also are rather eloquent and full in refutation
of others, than abide firm and sure in proof of what is their own. But of
myself what shall I say, who was already a Catholic Christian? Teats
which now, after very long thirst, I almost exhausted and dry, I have
returned to with all greediness, and with deeper weeping and groaning
have shaken together and wrung them out more deeply, that so there might
flow what might be enough to refresh me affected as I was, and to bring
back hope of life and safety. What then shall I say of myself? You, not yet
a Christian, who, through encouragement from me, execrating them greatly
as you did, were hardly led to believe that you ought to listen to them and
make trial of them, by what else, I pray you, were you delighted, call to
mind, I entreat you, save by a certain great presumption and promise of
reasons? But because they disputed long and much with very great copiousness and vehemence concerning the errors of unlearned men, a thing which
I learned too late at length to be most easy for any moderately educated
man; if even of their own they implanted in us any thing, we thought that
we were obliged to retain it, insomuch as there fell not in our way other
things, wherein to acquiesce. So they did in our case what crafty fowlers
are wont to do, who set branches smeared with bird-lime beside water to
deceive thirsty birds. For they fill up and cover anyhow the other waters
which are around, or fright them from them by alarming devices, that
they may fall into their snares, not through choice, but want.
3. But why do I not make answer to myself, that these fair and clever
similies, and charges of this nature may be poured forth against all who are
teachers of any thing by any adversary, with abundance of wit and sar-
casm? But I thought that I ought to insert something of this kind in my
letter, in order to admonish them to give over such proceedings; so that,
as he[2] says, apart from trifles of common-places, matter may contend with
matter, cause with cause, reason with reason. Wherefore let them give over
that saying, which they have in their mouths as though of necessity, when
any one, who has been for some long time a hearer, has left them; "The
Light hath made a passage through him." For you see, you who are my

[1] *Conf.* i. 11; v. 14   [2] Cicero

chief care (for I am not over anxious about them) how empty this is, and most easy for any one to find fault with. Therefore I leave this for your own wisdom to consider. For I have no fear that you will think me possessed by indwelling Light, when I was entangled in the life of this world, having a darkened hope, of beauty of wife, of pomp of riches, of emptiness of honors, and of all other hurtful and deadly pleasures. For all these, as is not unknown to you, I ceased not to desire and hope for, at the time when I was their attentive hearer. And I do not lay this to the charge of their teaching; for I also confess that they also carefully advise to shun these. But now to say that I am deserted by light, when I have turned myself from all these shadows of things, and have determined to be content with that diet merely which is necessary for health of body; but that I was enlightened and shining, at a time when I loved these things, and was wrapped up in them, is the part of a man, to use the mildest expression, wanting in a keen insight into matters, on which he loves to speak at length. But, if you please, let us come to the cause in hand.

4. For you well know that the Manichees move the unlearned by finding fault with the Catholic Faith, and chiefly by rending in pieces and tearing the Old Testament: and they are utterly ignorant, how far these things are to be taken, and how drawn out they descend with profit into the veins and marrows of souls as yet as it were but able to cry. And because there are in them certain things which are some slight offense to minds ignorant and careless of themselves (and there are very many such) they admit of being accused in a popular way: but defended in a popular way they cannot be, by any great number of persons, by reason of the mysteries that are contained in them. But the few, who know how to do this, do not love public and much talked of controversies and disputes: and on this account are very little known, save to such as are most earnest in seeking them out. Concerning then this rashness of the Manichees, whereby they find fault with the Old Testament and the Catholic Faith, listen, I entreat you, to the considerations which move me. But I desire and hope that you will receive them in the same spirit in which I say them. For God, unto Whom are known the secrets of my conscience, knows, that in this discourse I am doing nothing of evil craft; but, as I think it should be received, for the sake of proving the truth, for which one thing we have now long ago determined to live; and with incredible anxiety, lest it may have been most easy for me to err with you, but most difficult, to use no harder term, to hold the right way with you. But I venture to anticipate that, in this hope, wherein I hope that you will hold with us the way of wisdom, He will not fail me, unto Whom I have been consecrated; Whom day and night I endeavor to gaze upon: and since, by reason of my sins, and by reason of past habit, having the eye of the mind wounded by strokes of feeble opinions, I know that I am without strength, I often entreat with tears, and as, after long blindness and darkness the eyes being hardly opened, and

as yet, by frequent throbbing and turning away, refusing the light which yet they long after: specially if one endeavor to show to them the very sun; so it has now befallen me, who do not deny that there is a certain unspeakable and singular good of the soul, which the mind sees; and who with tears and groaning confess that I am not yet worthy of it. He will not then fail me, if I feign nothing, if I am led by duty, if I love truth, if I esteem friendship, if I fear much lest you be deceived.

5. All that Scripture therefore, which is called the Old Testament, is handed down fourfold to them who desire to know it, according to history, according to aetiology, according to analogy, according to allegory. Do not think me silly for using Greek words. In the first place, because I have so received, nor do I dare to make known to you otherwise than I have received. Next you yourself perceive, that we have not in use terms for such things: and had I translated and made such, I should have been indeed more silly: but, were I to use circumlocution, I should be less free in treating: this only I pray you to believe, that in whatever way I err, I am not inflated or swollen in any thing that I do. Thus (for example) it is handed down according to history, when there is taught what has been written, or what has been done; what not done, but only written as though it had been done. According to aetiology, when it is shown for what cause any thing has been done or said. According to analogy, when it is shown that the two Testaments, the Old and the New, are not contrary the one to the other. According to allegory, when it is taught that certain things which have been written are not to be taken in the letter, but are to be understood in a figure.

6. All these ways our Lord Jesus Christ and His Apostles used. For when it had been objected that His disciples had plucked the ears of corn on the sabbath-day, the instance was taken from history; "Have ye not read," said He, "what David did when he was an hungered, and they that were with him; how he entered into the house of God, and did eat the shewbread, which was not lawful for him to eat, neither for them that were with him, but only for the priests?" [3] But the instance pertains to aetiology, that, when Christ had forbidden a wife to be put away, save for the cause of fornication, and they, who asked Him, had alleged that Moses had granted permission after a writing of divorcement had been given, This, said He, "Moses did because of the hardness of your heart." [4] For here a reason was given, why that had been well allowed by Moses for a time; that this command of Christ might seem to show that now the times were other. But it is a long task to explain the changes of these times, and their order arranged and settled by a certain marvellous appointment of Divine Providence.

7. And further, analogy, whereby the agreement of both Testaments is plainly seen, why shall I say that all have made use of, to whose authority they yield; whereas it is in their power to consider with themselves, how

[3] Matt. xii. 3, 4   [4] Matt. xix. 8

many things they are wont to say have been inserted in the divine Scriptures by certain, I know not who, corrupters of truth? Which speech of theirs I always thought to be most weak, even at the time that I was their hearer: nor I alone, but you also (for I well remember) and all of us, who essayed to exercise a little more care in forming a judgment than the crowd of hearers. But now, after many things have been expounded and made clear to me, which used chiefly to move me: those, I mean, wherein their discourse for the most part boasts itself, and expatiates the more freely, the more safely it can do so as having no opponent; it seems to me that there is no assertion of their more shameless, or (to use a milder phrase) more careless and weak, than that the divine Scriptures have been corrupted; whereas there are no copies in existence, in a matter of so recent date, whereby they can prove it. For were they to assert, that they thought not that they ought thoroughly to receive them, because they had been written by persons, who they thought had not written the truth; any how their refusal would be more right, or their error more natural. For this is what they have done in the case of the Book which is inscribed the *Acts of the Apostles*. And this device of theirs, when I consider with myself, I cannot enough wonder at. For it is not the want of wisdom in the men that I complain of in this matter, but the want of ordinary understanding. For that book has so great matters, which are like what they receive, that it seems to me great folly to refuse to receive this book also, and if any thing offend them there to call it false and inserted. Or, if such language is shameless, as it is why in the *Epistles* of Paul, why in the four books of the *Gospel*, do they think that they are of any avail, in which I am not sure but that there are in proportion many more things, than could be in that book, which they will have believed to have been interpolated by falsifiers. But indeed this is what I believe to be the case, and I ask of you to consider it with me with as calm and serene a judgment as possible. For you know that, essaying to bring the person of their founder Manichaeus into the number of the Apostles, they say that the Holy Spirit, Whom the Lord promised His disciples that He would send, has come to us through him. Therefore, were they to receive *Acts of the Apostles,* in which the coming of the Holy Spirit is plainly set forth,[5] they could not find how to say that it was interpolated. For they will have it that there were some, I know not who, falsifiers of the divine Books before the times of Manichaeus himself; and that they were falsified by persons who wished to combine the Law of the Jews with the Gospel. But this they cannot say concerning the Holy Spirit, unless haply they assert that those persons divined, and set in their books what should be brought forward against Manichaeus, who should at some future time arise, and say that the Holy Spirit had been sent through him. But concerning the Holy Spirit we will speak somewhat more plainly in another place. Now let us return to my purpose.

[5] Acts ii. 2, 3, 4

8. For that both history of the Old Testament, and aetiology, and analogy are found in the New Testament, has been, as I think, sufficiently proved: it remains to show this of allegory. Our Redeemer Himself in the Gospel uses allegory out of the Old Testament. "This generation," said He, "seeketh a sign, and there shall not be given it save the sign of Jonas the prophet. For as Jonas was three days and three nights in the whale's belly, so also shall the Son of Man be three days and three nights in the heart of the earth." [6] For why should I speak of the Apostle Paul, who in his first *Epistle to the Corinthians* shows that even the very history of the Exodus was an allegory of the future Christian People. "But I would not that ye should be ignorant, brethren, how that all our fathers were under the cloud, and all passed through the sea, and were all baptized into Moses, in the cloud, and in the sea, and did all eat the same spiritual meat, and did all drink the same spiritual drink; for they drank of the spiritual Rock that followed with them; and that Rock was Christ. But in the more part of them God was not well pleased: for they were overthrown in the wilderness. But these things were figures of us, that we be not lustful of evil things, as they also lusted. Neither let us worship idols, as certain of them; as it is written, The people sat down to eat and drink, and rose up to play. Neither let us commit fornication, as certain of them committed, and fell in one day three and twenty thousand men. Neither let us tempt Christ, as certain of them tempted, and perished of serpents. Neither murmur we, as certain of them murmured, and perished of the destroyer. But all these things happened unto them in a figure. But they were written for our admonition, upon whom the ends of the world have come." [7] There is also in the Apostle a certain allegory, which indeed greatly relates to the cause in hand, for this reason that they themselves are wont to bring it forward, and make a display of it in disputing. For the same Paul says to the Galatians, "For it is written, that Abraham had two sons, one of a bond-maid, and one of a free woman. But he who was of the bond-maid was born after the flesh: but he who was of the free woman, by promise: which things were spoken by way of allegory. For these are the two Testaments, one of Mount Sinai gendering unto bondage, which is Agar: for Sinai is a mount in Arabia, which bordereth upon that Jerusalem which now is, and is in bondage with her children. But that Jerusalem which is above is free, which is the mother of us all." [8]

9. Here therefore these men too evil, while they essay to make void the Law, force us to approve these Scriptures. For they mark what is said, that they who are under the Law are in bondage, and they keep flying above the rest that last saying, "Ye are made empty of Christ, as many of you as are justified in the Law; ye have fallen from Grace." [9] We grant that all these things are true, and we say that the Law is not necessary, save for them unto whom bondage is yet profitable: and that the Law was on

[6] Matt. xii. 39, 40   [7] I Cor. x. 1-11   [8] Gal. iv. 22-26   [9] Gal. v. 4

this account profitably enacted, in that men, who could not be recalled from sins by reason, needed to be restrained by such a Law, that is to say, by the threats and terrors of those punishments which can be seen by fools: from which when the Grace of Christ sets us free, it condemns not that Law, but invites us at length to yield obedience to its love, not to be slaves to the fear of the Law. Itself is Grace, that is free gift, which they understand not to have come to them from God, who still desire to be under the bonds of the Law. Whom Paul deservedly rebukes as unbelievers, because they do not believe that now through our Lord Jesus they have been set free from that bondage, under which they were placed for a certain time by the most just appointment of God. Hence is that saying of the same Apostle, "For the Law was our schoolmaster in Christ." [10] He therefore gave to men a schoolmaster to fear, Who after gave a Master to love. And yet in these precepts and commands of the Law, which now it is not allowed Christians to use, such as either the Sabbath, or Circumcision, or Sacrifices, and if there be any thing of this kind, so great mysteries are contained, as that every pious person may understand, there is nothing more deadly than that whatever is there be understood to the letter, that is, to the word: and nothing more healthful than that it be unveiled in the Spirit. Hence it is: "The letter killeth, but the Spirit quickeneth." [11] Hence it is, "That same veil remaineth in the reading of the Old Testament, which veil is not taken away; since it is made void in Christ." [12] For there is made void in Christ, not the Old Testament, but its veil: that so through Christ that may be understood, and, as it were, laid bare, which without Christ is obscure and covered. Forasmuch as the same Apostle straightway adds, "But when thou shalt have passed over to Christ, the veil shall be taken away." [13] For he does not say the Law shall be taken away, or, the Old Testament. Not therefore through the Grace of the Lord, as though useless things were there hidden, have they been taken away; but rather the covering whereby useful things were covered. In this manner all they are dealt with, who earnestly and piously, not disorderly and shamelessly, seek the sense of those Scriptures, and they are carefully shown both the order of events, and the causes of deeds and words, and so great agreement of the Old Testament with the New, that there is left no jot that agrees not; and so great secrets of figures, that all the things that are drawn forth by interpretation force them to confess that they are wretched, who will to condemn these before they learn them.

10. But, passing over in the meanwhile the depth of knowledge, to deal with you as I think I ought to deal with my intimate friend; that is, as I have myself power, not as I have wondered at the power of very learned men; there are three kinds of error, whereby men err, when they read anything. I will speak of them one by one. The first kind is, wherein that which is false is thought true, whereas the writer thought otherwise. A second

[10] Gal. iii. 24   [11] cf. *Retract.* i. 14. 2 Cor. iii. 6   [12] 2 Cor. iii. 14   [13] 2 Cor. iii. 16

kind, although not so extensive, yet not less hurtful, when that, which is false, is thought true, yet the thought is the same as that of the writer. A third kind, when from the writing of another some truth is understood, whereas the writer understood it not. In which kind there is no little profit, rather, if you consider carefully, the whole entire fruit of reading. An instance of the first kind is, as if any one, for example, should say and believe that Rhadamanthus hears and judges the causes of the dead in the realms below, because he hath so read in the strain of Maro.[14] For this one errs in two ways: both in that he believes a thing not to be believed, and also in that he, whom he reads, is not to be thought to have believed it. The second kind may be thus noticed: if one, because Lucretius writes that the soul is formed of atoms, and that after death it is dissolved into the same atoms and perishes, were to think this to be true and what he ought to believe. For this one also is not less wretched, if, in a matter of so great moment, he has persuaded himself of that which is false, as certain; although Lucretius, by whose books he has been deceived, held this opinion. For what does it profit this one to be assured of the meaning of the author, whereas he has chosen him to himself not so as through him to escape error, but so as with him to err. An instance suited to the third kind is, if one, after having read in the books of Epicurus some place wherein he praises continence, were to assert that he had made the chief good to consist in virtue, and that therefore he is not to be blamed. For how is this man injured by the error of Epicurus, what though Epicurus believe that bodily pleasure is the chief good of man: whereas he has not surrendered up himself to so base and hurtful an opinion, and is pleased with Epicurus for no other reason, than that he thinks him not to have held sentiments which ought not to be held. This error is not only natural to man, but often also most worthy of a man. For what, if word were brought to me, concerning some one whom I loved, that, when now he was of bearded age, he had said, in the hearing of many, that he was so pleased with boyhood and childhood, as even to swear that he wished to live after the same fashion, and that that was so proved to me, as that should be shameless to deny it: I should not, should I, seem worthy of blame, if I thought that, in saying this, he wished to show, that he was pleased with the innocence, and with the temper of mind alien from those desires in which the race of man is wrapped up, and from this circumstance should love him yet more and more, than I used to love him before; although perhaps he had been foolish enough to love in the age of children a certain freedom in play and food, and an idle ease? For suppose that he had died after this report had reached me, and that I had been unable to make any inquiry of him, so as for him to open his meaning; would there be any one so shameless as to be angry with me, for praising the man's purpose and wish, through those very words which I had heard? What, that even a just judge of matters would

[14] Virg. *Aen.* vi. 566-569

not hesitate perhaps to praise my sentiment and wish, in that both I was pleased with innocence, and, as man of man, in a matter of doubt, preferred to think well, when it was in my power also to think ill?

11. And, this being so, hear also just so many conditions and differences of the same Scriptures. For it must be that just so many meet us. For either any one has written profitably, and is not profitably understood by some one: or both take place unprofitably: or the reader understands profitably, whereas he, who is read, has written contrariwise. Of these the first I blame not, the last I regard not. For neither can I blame the man, who without any fault of his own has been ill understood; nor can I be distressed at any one being read, who has failed to see the truth, when I see that the readers are no way injured. There is then one kind most approved, and as it were most cleansed, when both the things written are well, and are taken in a good sense by the readers. And yet that also is still further divided into two: for it does not altogether shut out error. For it generally comes to pass, that, when a writer has held a good sense, the reader also holds a good sense; still other than he, and often better, often worse, yet profitably. But when both we hold the same sense as he whom we read, and that is every way suited to right conduct of life, there is the fullest possible measure of truth, and there is no place opened for error from any other quarter. And this kind is altogether very rare, when what we read is matter of extreme obscurity: nor can it, in my opinion, be clearly known, but only believed. For by what proofs shall I so gather the will of a man who is absent or dead, as that I can swear to it: when, even if he were questioned being present, there might be many things, which, if he were no ill man, he would most carefully hide? But I think that it has nothing to do towards learning the matter of fact, of what character the writer was; yet is he most fairly believed good, whose writings have benefited the human race and posterity.

12. Wherefore I would that they would tell me, in what kind they place the, supposed, error of the Catholic Church. If in the first, it is altogether a grave charge; but it needs not a far-fetched defense: for it is enough to deny that we so understand, as the persons, who inveigh against us, suppose. If in the second, the charge is not less grave; but they shall be refuted by the same saying. If in the third, it is no charge at all. Proceed, and next consider the Scriptures themselves. For what objection do they raise against the books of (what is called) the Old Testament? Is it that they are good, but are understood by us in an ill sense? But they themselves do not receive them. Or is it that they are neither good, nor are well understood? But our defense above is enough to drive them from this position. Or is it this that they will say, although they are understood by you in a good sense, yet they are evil? What is this other than to acquit living adversaries, with whom they have to do, and to accuse men long ago dead, with whom they have no strife? I indeed believe that both those men profitably

delivered to memory all things, and that they were great and divine. And
that that Law was published, and framed by the command and will of
God: and of this, although I have but very slight knowledge of books of
that kind, yet I can easily persuade any, if there apply to me a mind fair
and no way obstinate: and this I will do, when you shall grant to me your
ears and mind well disposed: this however when it shall be in my power:
but now is it not enough for me, however that matter may stand, not to
have been deceived?

13. I call to witness, Honoratus, my conscience, and God Who hath His
dwelling in pure souls, that I account nothing more prudent, chaste, and
religious, than are all those Scriptures, which under the name of the Old
Testament the Catholic Church retains. You wonder at this, I am aware.
For I cannot hide that we were far otherwise persuaded. But there is indeed nothing more full of rashness (which at that time, being boys, we
had in us) than in the case of each several book, to desert expounders, who
profess that they hold them, and that they can deliver them to their
scholars, and to seek their meaning from those, who, I know not from what
cause compelling, have proclaimed a most bitter war against the framers
and authors of them. For who ever thought that the hidden and dark books
of Aristotle were to be expounded to him by one who was the enemy of
Aristotle; to speak of these systems of teaching, wherein a reader may perhaps err without sacrilege? Who, in fine, willed to read or learn the geometrical writings of Archimedes, under Epicurus as a master; against which
Epicurus used to argue with great obstinacy, so far as I judge, understanding them not at all? What are those Scriptures of the law most plain, against
which, as though set forth in public, these men make their attack in vain
and to no purpose? And they seem to me to be like that weak woman, whom
these same men are wont to mock at, who enraged at the sun being extolled
to her, and recommended as an object of worship by a certain female
Manichee, being as she was simple-minded and of a religious spirit, leaped
up in haste, and often striking with her foot that spot on which the sun
through the window cast light, began to cry out, Lo, I trample on the sun
and your God: altogether after a foolish and womanish manner; Who
denies it? But do not those men seem to you to be such, who, in matters
which they understand not, either wherefore, or altogether of what kind
they are, although like to matters cast in the way, yet to such as understand them exact and divine, rending them with great onset of speech and
reproaches, think that they are effecting something, because the unlearned
applaud them? Believe me, whatever there is in these Scriptures, it is lofty
and divine: there is in them altogether truth, and a system of teaching most
suited to refresh and renew minds: and clearly so ordered in measure, as
that there is no one but may draw thence, what is enough for himself, if
only he approach to draw with devotion and piety, as true religion demands.
To prove this to you, needs many reasons and a longer discourse. For first

I must so treat with you as that you may not hate the authors themselves; next, so as that you may love them: and this I must treat in any other way, rather than by expounding their meanings and words. For this reason, because in case we hated Virgil, nay, rather in case we loved him not, before understanding him, by the commendation of our forefathers, we should never be satisfied on those questions about him without number, by which grammarians are wont to be disquieted and troubled; nor should we listen willingly to one who solved these at the same time praising him; but should favor that one who by means of these essayed to show that he had erred and doted. But now, whereas many essay to open these, and each in a different way according to his capacity, we applaud these in preference, through whose exposition the poet is found better, who is believed, even by those who do not understand him, not only in nothing to have offended, but also to have sung nothing but what was worthy of praise. So that in some minute question, we are rather angry with the master who fails, and has not what to answer, than think him silent through any fault in Maro. And now, if, in order to defend himself, he should wish to assert a fault in so great an author, hardly will his scholars remain with him, even after they have paid his fee. How great matter were it, that we should show like good will towards them, of whom it has been confirmed by so long time of old that the Holy Spirit spake by them? But, indeed, we youths of the greatest understanding, and marvellous searchers out of reasons, without having at least unrolled these writings, without having sought teachers, without having somewhat chided our own dullness, lastly, without having yielded our heart even in a measure to those who have willed that writings of this kind be so long read, kept, and handled through the whole world; have thought that nothing in them is to be believed, moved by the speech of those who are unfriendly and hostile to them, with whom, under a false promise of reason, we should be compelled to believe and cherish thousands of fables.

14. But now I will proceed with what I have begun, if I can, and I will so treat with you, as not in the meanwhile to lay open the Catholic Faith, but, in order that they may search out its great mysteries, to show to those who have a care for their souls, hope of divine fruit, and of the discerning of truth. No one doubts of him who seeks true religion, either that he already believes that there is an immortal soul for that religion to profit, or that he also wishes to find that very thing in this same religion. Therefore all religion is for the sake of the soul; for howsoever the nature of the body may be, it causes no care or anxiety, especially after death, to him, whose soul possesses that whereby it is blessed. For the sake of the soul, therefore, either alone or chiefly, has true religion, if there be any such, been appointed. But this soul (I will consider for what reason, and I confess the matter to be most obscure) yet errs, and is foolish, as we see, until it attain to and perceive wisdom, and perhaps this very [wisdom] is true religion. I am not, am I, sending you to fables? I am not, am I, forcing you

to believe rashly? I say that our soul entangled and sunk in error and folly seeks the way of truth, if there be any such. If this be not your case, pardon me, I pray, and share with me your wisdom; but if you recognize in yourself what I say, let us, I entreat, together seek the truth.

15. Put the case that we have not as yet heard a teacher of any religion. Lo we have undertaken a new matter and business. We must seek, I suppose, them who profess this matter, if it have any existence. Suppose that we have found different persons holding different opinions, and through their difference of opinions seeking to draw persons each one to himself: but that, in the meanwhile, there are certain pre-eminent from being much spoken of, and from having possession of nearly all peoples. Whether these hold the truth, is a great question: but ought we not to make full trial of them first, in order that, so long as we err, being as we are men, we may seem to err with the human race itself?

16. But it will be said, the truth is with some few; therefore you already know what it is, if you know with whom it is. Said I not a little above, that we were in search of it as unlearned men? But if from the very force of truth you conjecture that few possess it, but know not who they are; what if it is thus, that there are so few who know the truth, as that they hold the multitude by their authority, whence the small number may set itself free, and, as it were, strain itself forth into those secrets? Do we not see how few attain the highest eloquence, whereas through the whole world the schools of rhetoricians are resounding with troops of young men? What, do they, as many as desire to turn out good orators, alarmed at the multitude of the unlearned, think that they are to bestow their labor on the orations of Caecilius, or Erucius, rather than those of Tullius? All aim at these, which are confirmed by authority of our forefathers. Crowds of unlearned persons essay to learn the same, which by the few learned are received as to be learned: yet very few attain, yet fewer practise, the very fewest possible become famous. What, if true religion be some such thing? What if a multitude of unlearned persons attend the Churches, and yet that be no proof, that therefore no one is made perfect by these mysteries? And yet, if they who studied eloquence were as few as the few who are eloquent, our parents would never believe that we ought to be committed to such masters. Whereas, then, we have been called to these studies by a multitude, which is numerous in that portion of it which is made up of the unlearned, so as to become enamored of that which few can attain unto; why are we unwilling to be in the same case in religion, which perhaps we despise with great danger to our soul? For if the truest and purest worship of God, although it be found with a few, be yet found with those, with whom a multitude, albeit wrapped up in lusts, and removed far from purity of understanding, agrees; (and who can doubt that this may happen?) I ask, if one were to charge us with rashness and folly, that we seek not diligently with them who teach it, that, which we are greatly anxious to discover, what can we

answer? [Shall we say,] I was deterred by numbers? Why from the pursuit of liberal arts, which hardly bring any profit to this present life; why from search after money? Why from attaining unto honor; why, in fine, from gaining and keeping good health; lastly, why from the very aim at a happy life; whereas all are engaged in these, few excel; were you deterred by no numbers?

17. "But they seemed there to make absurd statements." On whose assertion? Indeed on that of enemies, for whatever cause, for whatever reason, for this is not now the question, still enemies. Upon reading, I found it so of myself. Is it so? Without having received any instruction in poetry, you would not dare to essay to read Terentianus Maurus without a master: Asper, Cornutus, Donatus, and others without number are needed, that any poet whatever may be understood, whose strains seem to court even the applause of the theatre; do you in the case of those books, which, however they may be, yet of the confession of well-nigh the whole human race are commonly reported to be sacred and full of divine things, rush upon them without a guide, and dare to deliver an opinion on them without a teacher; and, if there meet you any matters, which seem absurd, do not accuse rather your own dullness, and mind decayed by the corruption of this world, such as is that of all that are foolish, than those [books] which haply cannot be understood by such persons! You should seek some one at once pious and learned, or who by consent of many was said to be such, that you might be both bettered by his advice, and instructed by his learning. Was he not easy to find? He should be searched out with pains. Was there no one in the country in which you lived? What cause could more profitably force to travel? Was he quite hidden, or did he not exist on the continent? One should cross the sea. If across the sea he was not found in any place near to us, you should proceed even as far as those lands, in which the things related in those books are said to have taken place. What, Honoratus, have we done of this kind? And yet a religion perhaps the most holy (for as yet I am speaking as though it were matter of doubt) the opinion whereof has by this time taken possession of the whole world, we wretched boys condemned at our own discretion and sentence. What if those things which in those same Scriptures seem to offend some unlearned persons, were so set there for this purpose, that when things were read of such as are abhorrent from the feeling of ordinary men, not to say of wise and holy men, we might with much more earnestness seek the hidden meaning. Perceive you not how the catamite of the *Bucolics*,[15] for whom the rough shepherd gushed forth into tears, men essay to interpret, and affirm that the boy Alexis, on whom Plato also is said to have composed a love strain, has some great meaning or other, but escapes the judgment of the unlearned; whereas without any sacrilege a poet however rich may seem to have published wanton songs?

[15] Virg. *Ecl*. ii.

18. But in truth was there either decree of any law, or power of gainsayers, or vile character of persons consecrated, or shameful report, or newness of institution, or hidden profession, to recall us from, and forbid us, the search? There is nothing of these. All laws divine and human allow us to seek the Catholic Faith; but to hold and exercise it is allowed us at any rate by human law, even if so long as we are in error there be a doubt concerning divine law; no enemy alarms our weakness (although truth and the salvation of the soul, in case being diligently sought it be not found where it may with most safety, ought to be sought at any risk); the degrees of all ranks and powers most devotedly minister to this divine worship; the name of religion is most honorable and most famous. What, I pray, hinders to search out and discuss with pious and careful inquiry, whether there be here that which it must needs be few know and guard in entire purity, although the goodwill and affection of all nations conspire in its favor?

19. The case standing thus, suppose, as I said, that we are now for the first time seeking unto what religion we shall deliver up our souls, for it to cleanse and renew them; without doubt we must begin with the Catholic Church. For by this time there are more Christians, than if the Jews and idolaters be added together. But of these same Christians, whereas there are several heresies, and all wish to appear Catholics, and call all others besides themselves heretics, there is one Church, as all allow: if you consider the whole world, more full filled in number; but, as they who know affirm, more pure also in truth than all the rest. But the question of truth is another; but, what is enough for such as are in search, there is one Catholic, to which different heresies give different names, whereas they themselves are called each by names of their own, which they dare not deny. From which may be understood, by judgment of umpires who are hindered by no favor, to which is to be assigned the name Catholic, which all covet. But, that no one may suppose that it is to be made matter of over garrulous or unnecessary discussion, this is at any rate one, in which human laws themselves also are in a certain way Christian. I do not wish any prejudgment to be formed from this fact, but I account it a most favorable commencement for inquiry. For we are not to fear lest the true worship of God, resting on no strength of its own, seem to need to be supported by them whom it ought to support: but, at any rate, it is perfect happiness, if the truth may be there found, where it is most safe both to search for it and to hold it: in case it cannot, then at length, at whatever risk, we must go and search some other where.

20. Having then laid down these principles, which, as I think, are so just that I ought to win this cause before you, let who will be my adversary, I will set forth to you, as I am able, what way I followed, when I was searching after true religion in that spirit, in which I have now set forth that it ought to be sought. For upon leaving you and crossing the sea, now delay-

ing and hesitating, what I ought to hold, what to let go; which delay rose upon me every day the more, from the time that I was a hearer of that man,[16] whose coming was promised to us, as you know, as if from heaven, to explain all things which moved us, and found him, with the exception of a certain eloquence, such as the rest; being now settled in Italy, I reasoned and deliberated greatly with myself, not whether I should continue in that sect, into which I was sorry that I had fallen, but in what way I was to find the truth, my sighs through love of which are known to no one better than to yourself. Often it seemed to me that it could not be found, and huge waves of my thoughts would roll toward deciding in favor of the Academics. Often again, with what power I had, looking into the human soul, with so much life, with so much intelligence, with so much clearness, I thought that the truth lay not hid, save that in it the way of search lay hid, and that this same way must be taken from some divine authority. It remained to inquire what was that authority, where in so great dissensions each promised that he would deliver it. Thus there met me a wood, out of which there was no way, which I was very loath to be involved in: and amid these things, without any rest, my mind was agitated through desire of finding the truth. However, I continued to unsew myself more and more from those whom now I had proposed to leave. But there remained nothing else, in so great dangers, than with words full of tears and sorrow to entreat the Divine Providence to help me. And this I was content to do: and now certain disputations of the Bishop of Milan[17] had almost moved me to desire, not without some hope, to inquire into many things concerning the Old Testament itself, which, as you know, we used to view as accursed, having been ill commended to us. And I had decided to be a catechumen in the Church, unto which I had been delivered by my parents, until such time as I should either find what I wished, or should persuade myself that it needed not to be sought. Therefore had there been one who could teach me, he would find me at a very critical moment most fervently disposed and very apt to learn. If you see that you too have been long affected in this way, therefore, and with a like care for your soul, and if now you seem to yourself to have been tossed to and fro enough, and wish to put an end to labors of this kind, follow the pathway of Catholic teaching, which has flowed down from Christ Himself through the Apostles even unto us, and will hereafter flow down to posterity.

21. This, you will say, is ridiculous, whereas all profess to hold and teach this: all heretics make this profession, I cannot deny it; but so, as that they promise to those whom they entice, that they will give them a reason concerning matters the most obscure: and on this account chiefly charge the Catholic [Church], that they who come to her are enjoined to believe; but they make it their boast, that they impose not a yoke of believing, but open a fount of teaching. You answer, What could be said, that should

[16] *i.e.* Faustus   [17] *i.e.* Saint Ambrose

pertain more to their praise? It is not so. For this they do, without being endued with any strength, but in order to conciliate to themselves a crowd by the name of reason: on the promise of which the human soul naturally is pleased, and, without considering its own strength and state of health, by seeking the food of the sound, which is ill entrusted save to such as are in health, rushes upon the poisons of them who deceive. For true religion, unless those things be believed, which each one after, if he shall conduct himself well and shall be worthy, attains unto and understands, and altogether without a certain weighty power of authority, can in no way be rightly entered upon.

22. But perhaps you seek to have some reason given you on this very point, such as may persuade you, that you ought not to be taught by reason before faith. Which may easily be done, if only you make yourself a fair hearer. But, in order that it may be done suitably, I wish you as it were to answer my questions; and, first, to tell me, why you think that one ought not to believe. Because, you say, credulity, from which men are called credulous, in itself, seems to me to be a certain fault: otherwise we should not use to cast this as a term of reproach. For if a suspicious man is in fault, in that he suspects things not ascertained; how much more a credulous man, who herein differs from a suspicious man, that the one allows some doubt, the other none, in matters which he knows not. In the meanwhile I accept this opinion and distinction. But you know that we are not wont to call a person even curious without some reproach; but we call him studious even with praise. Wherefore observe, if you please, what seems to you to be the difference between these two. This surely, you answer, that, although both be led by great desire to know, yet the curious man seeks after things that no way pertain to him, but the studious man, on the contrary, seeks after what pertain to him. But, because we deny not that a man's wife and children, and their health, pertain to him; if any one, being settled abroad, were to be careful to ask all comers, how his wife and children are and fare, he is surely led by great desire to know, and yet we call not this man studious, who both exceedingly wishes to know and that (in) matters which very greatly pertain to him. Wherefore you now understand that the definition of a studious person falters in this point, that every studious person wishes to know what pertain to himself, and yet not every one, who makes this his business, is to be called studious; but he who with all earnestness seeks those things which pertain to the liberal culture and adornment of the mind. Yet we rightly call him one who studies, especially if we add what he studies to hear. For we may call him even studious of his own (family) if he love only his own (family), we do not however, without some addition, think him worthy of the common name of the studious. But one who was desirous to hear how his family were I should not call studious of hearing, unless taking pleasure in the good report, he should wish to hear it again and again: but one who studied, even if only once.

Now return to the curious person, and tell me, if any one should be willing to listen to some tale, such as would no way profit him, that is, of matters that pertain not to him: and that not in an offensive way and frequently, but very seldom and with great moderation, either at a feast, or in some company, or meeting of any kind; would he seem to you curious? I think not: but at any rate he would certainly seem to have a care for that matter, to which he was willing to listen. Wherefore the definition of a curious person also must be corrected by the same rule as that of a studious person. Consider therefore whether the former statements also do not need to be corrected. For why should not both he, who at some time suspects something, be unworthy the name of a suspicious person; and he who at some time believes something, of a credulous person? Thus as there is very great difference between one who studies any matter, and the absolutely studious; and again between him who has a care and the curious; so is there between him who believes and the credulous.

23. But you will say, consider now whether we ought to believe in religion. For, although we grant that it is one thing to believe, another to be credulous, it does not follow that it is no fault to believe in matters of religion. For what if it be a fault both to believe and to be credulous, as (it is) both to be drunk and to be a drunkard? Now he who thinks this certain, it seems to me can have no friend; for, if it is base to believe any thing, either he acts basely who believes a friend, or in nothing believing a friend I see not how he can call either him or himself a friend. Here perhaps you may say, I grant that we must believe something at some time; now make plain, how in the case of religion it be not base to believe before one knows. I will do so, if I can. Wherefore I ask of you, which you esteem the graver fault, to deliver religion to one unworthy, or to believe what is said by them who deliver it. If you understand not whom I call unworthy, I call him, who approaches with feigned breast. You grant, as I suppose, that it is more blameable to unfold to such an one whatever holy secrets there are, than to believe religious men affirming any thing on the matter of religion itself. For it would be unbecoming you to make any other answer. Wherefore now suppose him present, who is about to deliver to you a religion, in what way shall you assure him, that you approach with a true mind, and that, so far as this matter is concerned, there is in you no fraud or feigning? You will say, your own good conscience that you are no way feigning, asserting this with words as strong as you can, but yet with words. For you cannot lay open man to man the hiding places of your soul, so that you may be thoroughly known. But if he shall say, Lo, I believe you, but is it not more fair that you also believe me, when, if I hold any truth, you are about to receive, I about to give, a benefit? what will you answer, save that you must believe?

24. But you say, Were it not better that you should give me a reason, that, wherever that shall lead me, I may follow without any rashness? Perhaps

it were: but, it being so great a matter, that you are by reason to come to the knowledge of God, do you think that all are qualified to understand the reasons, by which the human soul is led to know God, or many, or few? Few I think, you say. Do you believe that you are in the number of these? It is not for me, you say, to answer this. Therefore you think it is for him to believe you in this also: and this indeed he does: only do you remember, that he has already twice believed you saying things uncertain; that you are unwilling to believe him even once admonishing you in a religious spirit. But suppose that it is so, and that you approach with a true mind to receive religion, and that you are one of few men in such sense as to be able to take in the reasons by which the Divine Power is brought into certain knowledge; what? do you think that other men, who are not endued with so serene a disposition, are to be denied religion? or do you think that they are to be led gradually by certain steps unto those highest inner recesses? You see clearly which is the more religious. For you cannot think that any one whatever in a case where he desires so great a thing, ought by any means to be abandoned or rejected. But do you not think, that, unless he do first believe that he shall attain unto that which he purposes; and do yield his mind as a suppliant; and, submitting to certain great and necessary precepts, do by a certain course of life thoroughly cleanse it, that he will not otherwise attain the things that are purely true? Certainly you think so. What, then, is the case of those (of whom I already believe you to be the one) who are able most easily to receive divine secrets by sure reason, will it, I ask, be to them any hindrance at all, if they so come as they who at the first believe? I think not. But yet, you say, what need to delay them? Because although they will in no way harm themselves by what is done, yet they will harm the rest by the precedent. For there is hardly one who has a just notion of his own power: but he who has a less notion must be roused; he who has a greater notion must be checked: that neither the one be broken by despair, nor the other carried headlong by rashness. And this is easily done, if even they, who are able to fly (that they be not alluring the occasion of any into danger) are forced for a short time to walk where the rest also may walk with safety. This is the forethought of true religion: this the command of God: this what has been handed down from our blessed forefathers, this what has been preserved even unto us: to wish to distrust and overthrow this, is nothing else than to seek a sacrilegious way unto true religion. And whoso do this, not even if what they wish be granted to them are they able to arrive at the point at which they aim. For whatever kind of excellent genius they have, unless God be present, they creep on the ground. But He is then present, if they, who are aiming at God, have a regard for their fellow men. Than which step there can be found nothing more sure Heavenward. I for my part cannot resist this reasoning, for how can I say that we are to believe nothing without certain knowledge? whereas both there can be no friendship at all, unless there be believed something which cannot be proved by some reason, and often stewards, who are slaves, are trusted by their masters without any fault on their part. But in religion what can there be more unfair than that the ministers of God believe us when we promise an unfeigned mind, and we are unwilling to believe them when they enjoin us any thing. Lastly, what way can there be more healthful, than for a man to become fitted to receive the truth by believing those things, which have been appointed by God to serve for the previous culture and treatment of the mind? Or, if you be already altogether fitted, rather to make some little circuit where it is safest to tread, than both to cause yourself danger, and to be a precedent for rashness to other men?

25. Wherefore it now remains to consider, in what manner we ought not to follow these, who profess that they will lead by reason. For how we may without fault follow those who bid us to believe, has been already said: but to these who make promises of reason certain think that they come, not only without blame, but also with some praise: but it is not so. For there are two (classes of) persons, praiseworthy in religion; one of those who have already found, whom also we must judge most blessed; another of those who are seeking with all earnestness and in the right way. The first, therefore, are already in very possession, the other on the way, yet on that way whereby they are most sure to arrive.[18] There are three other kinds of men altogether to be disapproved of and detested. One is of those who hold an opinion, that is, of those who think that they know what they know not. Another is of those who are indeed aware that they know not, but do not so seek as to be able to find. A third is of those who neither think that they know, nor wish to seek. There are also three things, as it were bordering upon one another, in the minds of men well worth distinguishing; understanding, belief, opinion. And, if these be considered by themselves, the first is always without fault, the second sometimes with fault, the third never without fault. For the understanding of matters great, and honorable, and even divine, is most blessed.[19] But the understanding of things unnecessary is no injury; but perhaps the learning was an injury, in that it took up the time of necessary matters. But on the matters themselves that are injurious, it is not the understanding, but the doing or suffering them, that is wretched. For not, in case any understand how an enemy may be slain without danger to himself, is he guilty from the mere understanding, not the wish; and, if the wish be absent, what can be called more innocent? But belief is then worthy of blame, when either any thing is believed of God which is unworthy of Him, or any thing is over easily believed of man. But in all other matters if any believe aught, provided he understand that he knows it not, there is no fault. For I believe that very wicked conspirators were formerly put to death by the virtue of Cicero; but this I not only know not, but also I know for certain that I can by no

[18] cf. *Retract*. i. xiv. 2   [19] cf. *Retract*. i. xiv. 2

means know. But opinion is on two accounts very base; in that both he who has persuaded himself that he already knows, cannot learn; provided only it may be learnt; and in itself rashness is a sign of a mind not well disposed. For even if any suppose that he know what I said of Cicero (although it be no hindrance to him from learning, in that the matter itself is incapable of being grasped by any knowledge;) yet (in that he understands not that there is a great difference, whether any thing be grasped by sure reason of mind, which we call understanding, or whether for practical purposes it be entrusted to common fame or writing, for posterity to believe it) he assuredly errs, and no error is without what is base. What then we understand, we owe to reason; what we believe, to authority; what we have an opinion on, to error.[20] But every one who understands also believes, and also every one who has an opinion believes; not every one who believes understands, no one who has an opinion understands. Therefore if these three things be referred to the five kinds of men, which we mentioned a little above; that is, two kinds to be approved, which we set first, and three that remain faulty; we find that the first kind, that of the blessed, believe the truth itself; but the second kind, that of such as are earnest after, and lovers of, the truth, believe authority. In which kinds, of the two, the act of belief is praiseworthy. But in the first of the faulty kinds, that is, of those who have an opinion that they know what they know not, there is an altogether faulty credulity. The other two kinds that are to be disapproved believe nothing, both they who seek the truth despairing of finding it, and they who seek it not at all. And this only in matters which pertain to any system of teaching. For in the other business of life, I am utterly ignorant by what means a man can believe nothing. Although in the case of those also, they who say that in practical matters they follow probabilities, would seem rather to be unable to know than unable to believe. For who believes not what he approves? or how is what they follow probable, if it be not approved? Wherefore there may be two kinds of such as oppose the truth: one of those who assail knowledge alone, not faith; the other of those who condemn both: and yet again, I am ignorant whether these can be found in matters of human life. These things have been said, in order that we might understand, that, in retaining faith, even of those things which as yet we comprehend not, we are set free from the rashness of such as have an opinion. For they, who say that we are to believe nothing but what we know, are on their guard against that one name "opining," which must be confessed to be base and very wretched, but, if they consider carefully that there is a very great difference, whether one think that he knows, or moved by some authority believe that which he understands that he knows not, surely he will escape the charge of error, and inhumanity, and pride.

26. For I ask, if what is not known must not be believed, in what way may

[20] cf. *Retract.* i. xiv. 3

children do service to their parents, and love with mutual affection those whom they believe not to be their parents? For it cannot, by any means, be known by reason. But the authority of the mother comes in, that it be believed of the father; but of the mother it is usually not the mother that is believed, but midwives, nurses, servants. For she, from whom a son may be stolen and another put in his place, may she not being deceived deceive? Yet we believe, and believe without any doubt, what we confess we cannot know. For who but must see, that unless it be so, filial affection, the most sacred bond of the human race, is violated by extreme pride of wickedness? For what madman even would think him to be blamed who discharged the duties that were due to those whom he believed to be his parents, although they were not so? Who, on the other hand, would not judge him to deserve banishment, who failed to love those who were perhaps his true parents, through fear lest he should love pretended. Many things may be alleged, whereby to show that nothing at all of human society remains safe, if we shall determine to believe nothing, which we cannot grasp by full apprehension.

27. But now hear, what I trust I shall by this time more easily persuade you of. In a matter of religion, that is, of the worship and knowledge of God, they are less to be followed, who forbid us to believe, making most ready professions of reason. For no one doubts that all men are either fools or wise.[21] But now I call wise, not clever and gifted men, but those, in whom there is, so much as may be in man, the knowledge of man himself and of God most surely received, and a life and manners suitable to that knowlege; but all others, whatever be their skill or want of skill, whatever their manner of life, whether to be approved or disapproved, I would account in the number of fools. And, this being so, who of moderate understanding but will clearly see, that it is more useful and more healthful for fools to obey the precepts of the wise, than to live by their own judgment? For everything that is done, if it be not rightly done, is a sin, nor can that anyhow be rightly done which proceeds not from right reason. Further, right reason is very virtue. But to whom of men is virtue at hand, save to the mind of the wise? Therefore the wise man alone sins not. Therefore every fool sins, save in those actions, in which he has obeyed a wise man: for all such actions proceed from right reason, and, so to say, the fool is not to be accounted master of his own action, he being, as it were, the instrument and that which ministers to the wise man. Wherefore, if it be better for all men not to sin than to sin; assuredly all fools would live better, if they could be slaves of the wise. And, if no one doubts that this is better in lesser matters, as in buying and selling, and cultivating the ground, in taking a wife, in undertaking and bringing up children, lastly, in the management of household property, much more in religion. For both human matters are more easy to distinguish between, than divine; and in all mat-

[21] cf. *Retract*. i. xiv. 4

ters of greater sacredness and excellence, the greater obedience and service we owe them, the more wicked and the more dangerous is it to sin. Therefore you see henceforth that nothing else is left us, so long as we are fools, if our heart be set on an excellent and religious life, but to seek wise men, by obeying whom we may be enabled both to lessen the great feeling of the rule of folly, whilst it is in us, and at the last to escape from it.

28. Here again arises a very difficult question. For in what way shall we fools be able to find a wise man, whereas this name, although hardly any one dare openly, yet most men lay claim to indirectly: so disagreeing one with another in the very matters, in the knowledge of which wisdom consists, as that it must be that either none of them, or but some certain one be wise? But when the fool inquires, who is that wise man? I do not at all see, in what way he can be distinguished and perceived. For by no signs whatever can one recognize any thing, unless he shall have known that thing, whereof these are signs. But the fool is ignorant of wisdom. For not, as, in the case of gold and silver and other things of that kind, it is allowed both to know them when you see them, and not to have them, thus may wisdom be seen by the mind's eye of him who has it not. For whatever things we come into contact with by bodily sense, are presented to us from without; and therefore we may perceive by the eyes what belong to others, when we ourselves possess not any of them or of that kind. But what is perceived by the understanding is within in the mind, and to have it is nothing else than to see. But the fool is void of wisdom, therefore he knows not wisdom. For he could not see it with the eyes: but he cannot see it and not have it, nor have it and be a fool. Therefore he knows it not, and, so long as he knows it not, he cannot recognize it in another place. No one, so long as he is a fool, can by most sure knowledge find out a wise man, by obeying whom he may be set free from so great evil of folly.

29. Therefore this so vast difficulty, since our inquiry is about religion, God alone can remedy: nor indeed, unless we believe both that He is, and that He helps men's minds, ought we even to inquire after true religion itself. For what I ask do we with so great endeavor desire to search out? What do we wish to attain to? Whither do we long to arrive? Is it at that which we believe not exists or pertains to us? Nothing is more perverse than such a state of mind. Then, when you would not dare to ask of me a kindness, or at any rate would be shameless in daring, come you to demand the discovery of religion, when you think that God neither exists, nor, if He exist, has any care for us? What, if it be so great a matter, as that it cannot be found out, unless it be sought carefully and with all our might? What, if the very extreme difficulty of discovery be an exercise for the mind of the inquirer, in order to receive what shall be discovered? For what more pleasant and familiar to our eyes than this light? And yet men are unable after long darkness to bear and endure it. What more suited to the body exhausted by sickness than meat and drink? And yet we see that persons

who are recovering are restrained and checked, lest they dare to commit themselves to the fullness of persons in health, and so bring to pass by means of their very food their return to that disease which used to reject it. I speak of persons who are recovering. What, the very sick, do we not urge them to take something? Wherein assuredly they would not with so great discomfort obey us, if they believed not that they would recover from that disease. When then will you give yourself up to a search very full of pains and labor? When will you have the heart to impose upon yourself so great care and trouble as the matter deserves, when you believe not in the existence of that which you are in search of? Rightly therefore has it been ordained by the majesty of the Catholic system of teaching, that they who approach unto religion be before all things persuaded to have faith.

30. Wherefore that heretic (inasmuch as our discourse is of those who wish to be called Christians) I ask you, what reason he alleges to me? What is there whereby for him to call me back from believing, as if from rashness? If he bid me believe nothing; I believe not that this very true religion has any existence in human affairs; and what I believe not to exist, I seek not. But He, as I suppose, will show it to me seeking it: for so it is written, "He that seeketh shall find." [22] Therefore I should not come unto him, who forbids me to believe, unless I believed something. Is there any greater madness, than that I should displease him by faith alone, which is founded on no knowledge, which faith alone led me to him?

31. What, that all heretics exhort us to believe in Christ? Can they possibly be more opposed to themselves? And in this matter they are to be pressed in a twofold way. In the first place we must ask of them, where is the reason which they used to promise, where the reproof of rashness, where the assumption of knowledge? For, if it be disgraceful to believe any without reason, what do you wait for, what are you busied about, that I believe someone without reason, in order that I may the more easily be led by your reason? What, will your reason raise any firm superstructure on the foundation of rashness? I speak after their manner, whom we displease by believing. For I not only judge it most healthful to believe before reason, when you are not qualified to receive reason, and by the very act of faith thoroughly to cultivate the mind to receive the seeds of truth, but altogether a thing of such sort as that without it health cannot return to sick souls. And, in that this seems to them matter for mockery and full of rashness, surely they are shameless in making it their business that we believe in Christ. Next, I confess that I have already believed in Christ, and have convinced myself that what He hath said is true, although it be supported by no reason; is this, heretic, what you will teach me in the first place? Suffer me to consider a little with myself (since I have not seen Christ Himself, as He willed to appear unto men, Who is said to have been seen by them, even by common eyes) who they are that I have believed concerning

[22] Matt. vii. 8

Him, in order that I may approach you already furnished beforehand with such a faith. I see that there are none that I have believed, save the confirmed opinion and widely extended report of peoples and nations: and that the mysteries of the Church Catholic have in all times and places had possession of these peoples. Why therefore shall I not of these, in preference to others, inquire with all care, what Christ commanded, by whose authority I have been moved already to believe that Christ hath commanded something that is profitable? Are you likely to be a better expounder to me of what He said, Whose past or present existence I should not believe, if by you I were to be recommended to believe thus? This therefore I have believed, as I said, trusting to report strengthened by numbers, agreement, antiquity. But you, who are both so few, and so turbulent, and so new, no one doubts that ye bring forward nothing worthy of authority. What then is that so great madness? Believe them, that you are to believe in Christ, and learn from us what He said. Why, I pray you? For were they to fail and to be unable to teach me any thing with much greater ease could I persuade my self, that I am not to believe in Christ, than that I am to learn any thing concerning Him, save from those through whom I had believed in Him. O vast confidence, or rather absurdity! I teach you what Christ, in Whom you believe, commanded. What, in case I believed not in Him? You could not, could you, teach me any thing concerning Him? But says he, it behoves you to believe. You do not mean, do you, that I am (to believe) you when you commend Him to my faith? No, saith he, for we lead by reason them who believe in Him. Why then should I believe in Him? Because report hath been grounded. Whether is it through you, or through others? Through others, saith he. Shall I then believe them, in order that you may teach me? Perhaps I ought to do so, were it not that they gave me this chief charge, that I should not approach you at all; for they say that you have deadly doctrines. You will answer, They lie. How then shall I believe them concerning Christ, Whom they have not seen, (and) not believe them concerning you, whom they are unwilling to see? Believe the Scriptures, saith he. But every writing, if it be brought forward new and unheard of, or be commended by few, with no reason to confirm it, it is not it that is believed, but they who bring it forward. Wherefore, for those Scriptures, if you are they who bring them forward, you so few and unknown, I am not pleased to believe them. At the same time also you are acting contrary to your promise, in enforcing faith rather than giving a reason. You will recall me again to numbers and (common) report. Curb, I pray you, your obstinacy, and that untamed lust, I know not what, of spreading your name: and advise me rather to seek the chief men of this multitude, and to seek with all care and pains rather to learn something concerning these writings from these men, but for whose existence, I should not know that I had to learn at all. But do you return into your dens, and lay not any snares under the name of truth, which you endeavor to take from those, to whom you yourself grant authority.

32. But if they say that we are not even to believe in Christ, unless undoubted reason shall be given us, they are not Christians. For this is what certain pagans say against us, foolishly indeed, yet not contrary to, or inconsistent with, themselves. But who can endure that these profess to belong to Christ, who contend that they are to believe nothing, unless they shall bring forward to fools most open reason concerning God? But we see that He Himself, so far as that history, which they themselves believe, teaches, willed nothing before, or more strongly than, that He should be believed in: whereas they, with whom He had to do, were not yet qualified to receive the secret things of God. For, for what other purpose are so great and so many miracles, He Himself also saying, that they are done for no other cause, than that He may be believed in? He used to lead fools by faith, you lead by reason. He used to cry out, that He should be believed in, ye cry out against it. He used to praise such as believe in Him, ye blame them. But unless either He should change water into wine,[23] to omit other (miracles), if men would follow Him, doing no such, but (only) teaching; either we must make no account of that saying, "Believe ye God, believe also Me;"[24] or we must charge him with rashness, who willed not that He should come into his house, believing that the disease of his servant would depart at His mere command.[25] Therefore He bringing to us a medicine such as should heal our utterly corrupt manners, by miracles procured to Himself authority, by authority obtained Himself belief, by belief drew together a multitude, by a multitude possessed antiquity, by antiquity strengthened religion: so that not only the utterly foolish novelty of heretics dealing deceitfully, but also the inveterate error of the nations opposing with violence, should be unable on any side to rend it asunder.

33. Wherefore, although I am not able to teach, yet I cease not to advise, that (whereas many wish to appear wise, and it is no easy matter to discern whether they be fools) with all earnestness, and with all prayers, and lastly with groans, or even, if so it may be, with tears, you entreat of God to set you free from the evil of error; if your heart be set on a happy life. And this will take place the more easily, if you obey with a willing mind His commands, which He has willed should be confirmed by so great authority of the Catholic Church. For whereas the wise man is so joined to God in mind, as that there is nothing set between to separate; for God is Truth; and no one is by any means wise, unless his mind come into contact with the Truth; we cannot deny that between the folly of man, and the most pure Truth of God, the wisdom of man is set, as something in the middle. For the wise man, so far as it is given unto him, imitates God; but for a man who is a fool, there is nothing nearer to him, than a man who is

<hr>

[23] John ii. 7-9   [24] John xiv. 1   [25] Matt. viii. 8, 9

wise, for him to imitate with profit: and since, as has been said, it is not easy to understand this one by reason, it behoved that certain miracles be brought near to the very eyes, which fools use with much greater readiness than the mind, that, men being moved by authority, their life and habits might first be cleansed, and they thus rendered capable of receiving reason. Whereas, therefore, it needed both that man be imitated, and that our hope be not set in man, what could be done on the part of God more full of kindness and grace, than that the very pure, eternal, unchangeable Wisdom of God, unto Whom it behoves us to cleave, should deign to take upon Him (the nature of) man? That not only He might do what should invite us to follow God, but also might suffer what used to deter us from following God. For, whereas no one can attain to the most sure and chief good, unless he shall fully and perfectly love it; which will by no means take place, so long as the evils of the body and of fortune are dreaded; He by being born after a miraculous manner and working caused Himself to be loved; and by dying and rising again shut out fear. And, further, in all other matters, which it were long to go through, He showed Himself such, as that we might perceive unto what the clemency of God could be reached forth, and unto what the weakness of man be lifted up.

34. This is, believe me, a most wholesome authority, this a lifting up first of our mind from dwelling on the earth, this a turning from the love of this world unto the True God. It is authority alone which moves fools to hasten unto wisdom. So long as we cannot understand pure (truths), it is indeed wretched to be deceived by authority, but surely more wretched not to be moved. For, if the Providence of God preside not over human affairs, we have no need to busy ourselves about religion. But if both the outward form of all things, which we must believe assuredly flows from some fountain of truest beauty, and some, I know not what, inward conscience exhorts, as it were, in public and in private, all the better order of minds to seek God, and to serve God; we must not give up all hope that the same God Himself has appointed some authority, whereon, resting as on a sure step, we may be lifted up unto God. But this, setting aside reason, which (as we have often said) it is very hard for fools to understand pure, moves us two ways; in part by miracles, in part by multitude of followers: no one of these is necessary to the wise man; who denies it? But this is now the business in hand, that we may be able to be wise, that is, to cleave to the truth; which the filthy soul is utterly unable to do: but the filth of the soul, to say shortly what I mean, is the love of any things whatsoever save God and the soul: from which filth the more any one is cleansed, the more easily he sees the truth. Therefore to wish to see the truth, in order to purge your soul, when as it is purged for the very purpose that you may see, is surely perverse and preposterous. Therefore to man unable to see the truth, authority is at hand, in order that he may be made fitted for it, and may allow himself to be cleansed; and, as I said a little above, no one doubts

that this prevails, in part by miracles, in part by multitude. But I call that a miracle, whatever appears that is difficult or unusual above the hope of power of them who wonder. Of which kind there is nothing more suited for the people, and in general for foolish men, than what is brought near to the senses. But these, again, are divided into two kinds; for there are certain, which cause only wonder, but certain others procure also great favor and good-will. For, if one were to see a man flying, inasmuch as that matter brings no advantage to the spectator, beside the spectacle itself, he only wonders. But if any affected with grievous and hopeless disease were to recover straightway, upon being bidden, his affection for him who heals, will go beyond even his wonder at his healing. Such were done at that time at which God in True Man appeared unto men, as much as was enough. The sick were healed, the lepers were cleansed; walking was restored to the lame, sight to the blind, hearing to the deaf. The men of that time saw water turned into wine, five thousand filled with five loaves, seas passed on foot, dead rising again: thus certain provided for the good of the body by more open benefit, certain again for the good of the soul by more hidden sign, and all for the good of men by their witness to Majesty: thus, at that time, was the divine authority moving towards Itself the wandering souls of mortal man. Why, say you, do not those things take place now? because they would not move, unless they were wonderful, and, if they were usual, they would not be wonderful.[26] For the interchanges of day and night, and the settled order of things in Heaven, the revolution of years divided into four parts, the fall and return of leaves to trees, the boundless power of seeds, the beauty of light, the varieties of colors, sounds, tastes, and scents, let there be some one who shall see and perceive them for the first time, and yet such an one as we may converse with; he is stupefied and overwhelmed with miracles: but we contemn all these, not because they are easy to understand (for what more obscure than the causes of these?) but surely because they constantly meet our senses. Therefore they were done at a very suitable time, in order that, by these a multitude of believers having been gathered together and spread abroad, authority might be turned with effect upon habits.

35. But any habits whatever have so great power to hold possession of men's minds, that even what in them are evil, which usually takes place through excess of lusts, we can sooner disapprove of and hate, than desert or change. Do you think that little hath been done for the benefit of man, that not some few very learned men maintain by argument, but also an unlearned crowd of males and females in so many and different nations both believe and set forth, that we are to worship as God nothing of earth, nothing of fire, nothing, lastly, which comes into contact with the senses of the body, but that we are to seek to approach Him by the understanding only? that abstinence is extended even unto the slenderest food of bread

[26] cf. *Retract.* i. xiv. 5

and water, and fastings not only for the day, but also continued through several days together, that chastity is carried even unto the contempt of marriage and family; that patience even unto the setting light by crosses and flames; that liberality even unto the distribution of estates unto the poor; that, lastly, the contempt of this whole world even unto the desire of death? Few do these things, yet fewer do them well and wisely: but whole nations approve, nations hear, nations favor, nations, lastly, love. Nations accuse their own weakness that they cannot do these things, and that not without the mind being carried forward unto God, nor without certain sparks of virtue. This hath been brought to pass by the Divine Providence, through the prophecies of the Prophets, through the manhood and teaching of Christ, through the journeys of the Apostles, through the insults, crosses, blood, of the Martyrs, through the praiseworthy life of the Saints, and, in all these, according as times were seasonable, through miracles worthy of so great matters and virtues. When therefore we see so great help of God, so great progress and fruit, shall we doubt to hide ourselves in the bosom of that Church, which even unto the confession of the human race from [the] apostolic chair through successions of Bishops (heretics in vain lurking around her and being condemned, partly by the judgment of the very people, partly by the weight of councils, partly also by the majesty of miracles) has held the summit of authority. To be unwilling to grant to her the first place, is either surely the height of impiety, or is headlong arrogance. For, if there be no sure way unto wisdom and health of souls, unless where faith prepare them for reason, what else is it to be ungrateful for the Divine help and aid, than to wish to resist authority furnished with so great labor? And if every system of teaching, however mean and easy, requires, in order to its being received, a teacher or master, what more full of rash pride, than, in the case of books of divine mysteries, both to be unwilling to learn from such as interpret them, and to wish to condemn them unlearned?

36. Wherefore, if either our reasoning or our discourse has in any way moved you, and if you have, as I believe, a true care for yourself, I would you would listen to me, and with pious faith, lively hope, and simple charity, entrust yourself to good teachers of Catholic Christianity; and cease not to pray unto God Himself, by Whose goodness alone we were created, and suffer punishment by His justice, and are set free by His mercy. Thus there will be wanting to you neither precepts and treatises of most learned and truly Christian men, nor books, nor calm thoughts themselves, whereby you may easily find what you are seeking. For do you abandon utterly those wordy and wretched men (for what other milder name can I use?) who, while they seek to excess whence is evil, find nothing but evil. And on this question they often rouse their hearers to inquire; but after they have been roused, they teach them such lessons as that it were preferable even to sleep for ever, than thus to be awake. For in place of lethargic they make

them frantic, between which diseases, both being usually fatal, there is still this difference, that lethargic persons die without doing violence to others; but the frantic person many who are sound, and specially they who wish to help him, have reason to fear. For neither is God the author of evil, nor has it ever repented Him that He has done aught, nor is He troubled by storm of any passion of soul, nor is a small part of earth His Kingdom: He neither approves nor commands any sins or wickedness, He never lies. For these and such like used to move us, when they used them to make great and threatening assaults, and charged this as being the system of teaching of the Old Testament, which is most false. Thus then I allow that they do right in censuring these. What then have I learnt? What think you, save that, when these are censured, the Catholic system of teaching is not censured. Thus what I had learnt among them that is true, I hold, what is false that I had thought I reject. But the Catholic Church has taught me many other things also, which those men of bloodless bodies, but coarse minds, cannot aspire unto; that is to say, that God is not corporeal, that no part of Him can be perceived by corporeal eyes, that nothing of His Substance or Nature can any way suffer violence or change, or is compounded or formed; and if you grant me these (for we may not think otherwise concerning God) all their devices are overthrown. But how it is, that neither God begot or created evil, nor yet is there, or has there been ever, any nature and substance, which God either begot not or created not, and yet that He setteth us free from evil, is proved by reasons so necessary, that it cannot at all be matter of doubt; especially to you and such as you; that is, if to a good disposition there be added piety and a certain peace of mind, without which nothing at all can be understood concerning so great matters. And here there is no rumor concerning smoke, and I know not what Persian vain fable, to which it is enough to lend an ear, and soul not subtile, but absolutely childish. Far altogether, far otherwise is the truth, than as the Manichees dote. But since this discourse of ours has gone much further than I thought, here let us end the book; in which I wish you to remember, that I have not yet begun to refute the Manichees, and that I have not yet assailed that nonsense; and that neither have I unfolded any thing great concerning the Catholic Church itself, but that I have only wished to root out of you, if I could, a false notion concerning true Christians that was maliciously or ignorantly suggested to us, and to arouse you to learn certain great and divine things. Wherefore let this volume be as it is; but when your soul becomes more calmed, I shall perhaps be more ready in what remains.[27]

[27] cf. *Retract.* i. xiv. 6

CONCERNING THE NATURE OF GOOD

CONCERNING THE NATURE OF GOOD

Introductory Note

This short work, published in 405 A.D., is, as Dr. Newman the translator has pointed out, one of the most argumentative and abstruse of the writings against the Manichaeans. Though it repeats some of the earlier lines of attack which Saint Augustine has already employed, it contains extracts from Manichaean writings which not only are interesting in themselves but also by their very nature effectively undermine the Manichaean position. Even within its brief compass the treatise constitutes one of Saint Augustine's most powerful assaults upon the sect of Mani.

CONCERNING THE NATURE OF GOOD

CHAPTER I

GOD THE HIGHEST AND UNCHANGEABLE GOOD, FROM WHOM ARE ALL OTHER GOOD THINGS, SPIRITUAL AND CORPOREAL

THE highest good, than which there is no higher, is God, and consequently He is unchangeable good, hence truly eternal and truly immortal. All other good things are only from Him, not of Him. For what is of Him, is Himself. And consequently if He alone is unchangeable, all things that He has made, because He has made them out of nothing, are changeable. For He is so omnipotent, that even out of nothing, that is out of what is absolutely non-existent, He is able to make good things both great and small, both celestial and terrestrial, both spiritual and corporeal. But because He is also just, He has not put those things that He has made out of nothing on an equality with that which He begat out of Himself. Because, therefore, no good things whether great or small, through whatever gradations of things, can exist except from God; but since every nature, so far as it is nature, is good, it follows that no nature can exist save from the most high and true God: because all things even not in the highest degree good, but related to the highest good, and again, because all good things, even those of most recent origin, which are far from the highest good, can have their existence only from the highest good. Therefore every spirit, though subject to change, and every corporeal entity, is from God, and all this, having been made, is nature. For every nature is either spirit or body. Unchangeable spirit is God, changeable spirit, having been made, is nature, but is better than body; but body is not spirit, unless when the wind, because it is invisible to us and yet its power is felt as something not inconsiderable, is in a certain sense called spirit.

CHAPTER II

HOW THIS MAY SUFFICE FOR CORRECTING THE MANICHAEANS

But for the sake of those who, not being able to understand that all nature, that is, every spirit and every body, is naturally good, are moved by the iniquity of spirit and the mortality of body, and on this account endeavor to bring in another nature of wicked spirit and mortal body, which God did not make, we determine thus to bring to their understanding what we say can be brought. For they acknowledge that no good thing can exist

save from the highest and true God, which also is true and suffices for correcting them, if they are willing to give heed.

CHAPTER III

MEASURE, FORM, AND ORDER, GENERIC GOODS IN THINGS MADE BY GOD

For we Catholic Christians worship God, from whom are all good things
whether great or small; from whom is all measure great or small; from
whom is all form great or small; from whom is all order great or small. For
all things in proportion as they are better measured, formed, and ordered,
are assuredly good in a higher degree; but in proportion as they are measured, formed, and ordered in an inferior degree, are they the less good. These
three things, therefore, measure, form, and order—not to speak of innumerable other things that are shown to pertain to these three—these three
things, therefore, measure, form, order, are as it were generic goods in
things made by God, whether in spirit or in body. God is, therefore, above
every measure of the creature, above every form, above every order, nor is
He above by local spaces, but by ineffable and singular potency, from
whom is every measure, every form, every order. These three things, where
they are great, are great goods, where they are small, are small goods;
where they are absent, there is no good. And again where these things are
great, there are great natures, where they are small, there are small natures,
where they are absent, there is no nature. Therefore all nature is good.

CHAPTER IV

EVIL IS CORRUPTION OF MEASURE, FORM, OR ORDER

When accordingly it is inquired, whence is evil, it must first be inquired,
what is evil, which is nothing else than corruption, either of the measure, or
the form, or the order, that belong to nature. Nature therefore which has
been corrupted, is called evil, for assuredly when incorrupt it is good; but
even when corrupt, so far as it is nature it is good, so far as it is corrupted
it is evil.

CHAPTER V

THE CORRUPTED NATURE OF A MORE EXCELLENT ORDER SOMETIMES BETTER THAN AN INFERIOR NATURE EVEN UNCORRUPTED

But it may happen, that a certain nature which has been ranked as
more excellent by reason of natural measure and form, though corrupt,
is even yet better than another incorrupt which has been ranked lower by
reason of an inferior natural measure and form: as in the estimation of

men, according to the quality which presents itself to view, corrupt gold is assuredly better than incorrupt silver, and corrupt silver than incorrupt lead; so also in more powerful spiritual natures a rational spirit even corrupted through an evil will is better than an irrational though incorrupt, and better is any spirit whatever even corrupt than any body whatever though incorrupt. For better is a nature which, when it is present in a body, furnishes it with life, than that to which life is furnished. But however corrupt may be the spirit of life that has been made, it can furnish life to a body, and hence, though corrupt, it is better than the body though incorrupt.

CHAPTER VI

NATURE WHICH CANNOT BE CORRUPTED IS THE HIGHEST GOOD; THAT WHICH CAN, IS SOME GOOD

But if corruption take away all measure, all form, all order from corruptible things, no nature will remain. And consequently every nature which cannot be corrupted is the highest good, as is God. But every nature that can be corrupted is also itself some good; for corruption cannot injure it, except by taking away from or diminishing that which is good.

CHAPTER VII

THE CORRUPTION OF RATIONAL SPIRITS IS ON THE ONE HAND VOLUNTARY, ON THE OTHER PENAL

But to the most excellent creatures, that is, to rational spirits, God has offered this, that if they will not they cannot be corrupted; that is, if they should maintain obedience under the Lord their God, so should they adhere to his incorruptible beauty; but if they do not will to maintain obedience, since willingly they are corrupted in sins, unwillingly they shall be corrupted in punishment, since God is such a good that it is well for no one who deserts Him, and among the things made by God the rational nature is so great a good, that there is no good by which it may be blessed except God. Sinners, therefore, are ordained to punishment; which ordination is punishment for the reason that it is not conformable to their nature, but it is justice because it is conformable to their fault.

CHAPTER VIII

FROM THE CORRUPTION AND DESTRUCTION OF INFERIOR THINGS IS THE BEAUTY OF THE UNIVERSE

But the rest of things that are made of nothing, which are assuredly inferior to the rational soul, can be neither blessed nor miserable. But because in proportion to their fashion and appearance are things themselves good, nor could there be good things in a less or the least degree except from God, they are so ordered that the more infirm yield to the firmer, the weaker to the stronger, the more impotent to the more powerful; and so earthly things harmonize with celestial, as being subject to the things that are pre-eminent. But to things falling away, and succeeding, a certain temporal beauty in its kind belongs, so that neither those things that die, or cease to be what they were, degrade or disturb the fashion and appearance and order of the universal creation: as a speech well composed is assuredly beautiful, although in its syllables and all sounds rush past as it were in being born and in dying.

CHAPTER IX

PUNISHMENT IS CONSTITUTED FOR THE SINNING NATURE THAT IT MAY BE RIGHTLY ORDERED

What sort of punishment, and how great, is due to each fault, belongs to Divine judgment, not to human; which punishment assuredly when it is remitted in the case of the converted, there is great goodness on the part of God, and when it is deservedly inflicted, there is no injustice on the part of God; because nature is better ordered by justly smarting under punishment, than by rejoicing with impunity in sin; which nature nevertheless, even thus having some measure, form, and order, in whatever extremity there is as yet some good, which things, if they were absolutely taken away, and utterly consumed, there will be accordingly no good, because no nature will remain.

CHAPTER X

NATURES CORRUPTIBLE, BECAUSE MADE OF NOTHING

All corruptible natures therefore are natures at all only so far as they are *from* God, nor would they be corruptible if they were *of* Him; because they would be what He himself is. Therefore of whatever measure, of whatever form, of whatever order, they are, they are so because it is God by whom they were made; but they are not immutable, because it is nothing of which they were made. For it is sacrilegious audacity to make nothing and God equal, as when we wish to make what has been born of God such as what has been made by Him out of nothing.

CHAPTER XI

GOD CANNOT SUFFER HARM, NOR CAN ANY OTHER NATURE EXCEPT BY HIS PERMISSION

Wherefore neither can God's nature suffer harm, nor can any nature under God suffer harm unjustly: for when by sinning unjustly some do harm, an unjust will is imputed to them; but the power by which they are permitted to do harm is from God alone, who knows, while they themselves are ignorant, what they ought to suffer, whom He permits them to harm.

CHAPTER XII

ALL GOOD THINGS ARE FROM GOD ALONE

All these things are so perspicuous, so assured, that if they who introduce another nature which God did not make, were willing to give attention, they would not be filled with so great blasphemies, as that they should place so great good things in supreme evil, and so great evil things in God. For what the truth compels them to acknowledge, namely, that all good things are from God alone, suffices for their correction, if they were willing to give heed, as I said above. Not, therefore, are great good things from one, and small good things from another; but good things great and small are from the supremely good alone, which is God.

CHAPTER XIII

INDIVIDUAL GOOD THINGS, WHETHER SMALL OR GREAT, ARE FROM GOD

Let us, therefore, bring before our minds good things however great, which it is fitting that we attribute to God as their author, and these having been eliminated let us see whether any nature will remain. All life both great and small, all power great and small, all safety great and small, all memory great and small, all virtue great and small, all intellect great and small, all tranquillity great and small, all plenty great and small, all sensation great and small, all light great and small, all suavity great and small, all measure great and small, all beauty great and small, all peace great and small, and whatever other like things may occur, especially such as are found throughout all things, whether spiritual or corporeal, every measure, every form, every order both great and small, are from the Lord God. All which good things whoever should wish to abuse, pays the penalty by divine judgment; but where none of these things shall have been present at all, no nature will remain.

CHAPTER XIV

But in all these things, whatever are small are called by contrary names in comparison with greater things; as in the form of a man because the beauty is greater, the beauty of the ape in comparison with it is called deformity. And the imprudent are deceived, as if the former is good, and the latter evil, nor do they regard in the body of the ape its own fashion, the equality of members on both sides, the agreement of parts, the protection of safety, and other things which it would be tedious to enumerate.

CHAPTER XV

But that what we have said may be understood, and may satisfy those too slow of comprehension, or that even the pertinacious and those repugnant to the most manifest truth may be compelled to confess what is true, let them be asked, whether corruption can harm the body of an ape? But if it can, so that it may become more hideous, what diminishes but the good of beauty? Whence as long as the nature of the body subsists, so long something will remain. If, accordingly, good having been consumed, nature is consumed, the nature is therefore good. So also we say that slow is contrary to swift, but yet he who does not move at all cannot even be called slow. So we say that a heavy voice is contrary to a sharp voice, or a harsh to a musical; but if you completely remove any kind of voice, there is silence where there is no voice, which silence, nevertheless, for the simple reason that there is no voice, is usually opposed to voice as something contrary thereto. So also lucid and obscure are called as it were two contrary things, yet even obscure things have something of light, which being absolutely wanting, darkness is the absence of light in the same way in which silence is the absence of voice.

CHAPTER XVI

Yet even these privations of things are so ordered in the universe of nature, that to those wisely considering they not unfittingly have their vicissitudes. For by not illuminating certain places and times, God has also made the darkness as fittingly as the day. For if we by restraining the voice fittingly interpose silence in speaking, how much more does He, as the perfect framer of all things, fittingly make privations of things? Whence also in the hymn of the three children, light and darkness alike praise God,[1] that is, bring forth praise in the hearts of those who well consider.

CHAPTER XVII

NATURE, IN AS FAR AS IT IS NATURE, NO EVIL

No nature, therefore, as far as it is nature, is evil; but to each nature there is no evil except to be diminished in respect of good. But if by being diminished it should be consumed so that there is no good, no nature would be left; not only such as the Manichaeans introduce, where so great good things are found that their exceeding blindness is wonderful, but such as any one can introduce.

CHAPTER XVIII

HYLE, WHICH WAS CALLED BY THE ANCIENTS THE FORMLESS MATERIAL OF THINGS, IS NOT AN EVIL

For neither is that material, which the ancients called *Hyle,* to be called an evil. I do not say that which Manichaeus with most senseless vanity, not knowing what he says, denominates *Hyle,* namely, the former of corporeal beings; whence it is rightly said to him, that he introduces another god. For nobody can form and create corporeal beings but God alone; for neither are they created unless there subsist with them measure, form, and order, which I think that now even they themselves confess to be good things, and things that cannot be except from God. But by *Hyle* I mean a certain material absolutely formless and without quality, whence those qualities that we perceive are formed, as the ancients said. For hence also wood is called in Greek ὕλη, because it is adapted to workmen, not that itself may make anything, but that it is the material of which something may be made. Nor is that *Hyle,* therefore, to be called an evil which cannot be perceived through any appearance, but can scarcely be thought of through any sort of privation of appearance. For this has also a capacity of forms; for if it cannot receive the form imposed by the workman, neither assuredly may it be called material. Hence if form is some good, whence those who excel in it are called beautiful,[2] as from appearance they are called handsome,[3] even the capacity of form is undoubtedly something good. As because wisdom is a good, no one doubts that to be capable of wisdom is a good. And because every good is from God, no one ought to doubt that even matter, if there is any, has its existence from God alone.

[1] Dan. iii. 72   [2] *Forma—formosus*   [3] *Species—speciosus*

CHAPTER XIX

TO HAVE TRUE EXISTENCE IS AN EXCLUSIVE PREROGATIVE OF GOD

Magnificently and divinely, therefore, our God said to his servant: "I am that I am," and "Thou shalt say to the children of Israel, He who is sent me to you." [4] For He truly is because He is unchangeable. For every change makes what was not, to be: therefore He truly is, who is unchangeable; but all other things that were made by Him have received being from Him each in its own measure. To Him who is highest, therefore, nothing can be contrary, save what is not; and consequently as from Him everything that is good has its being, so from Him is everything that by nature exists; since everything that exists by nature is good. Thus every nature is good, and everything good is from God; therefore every nature is from God.

CHAPTER XX

PAIN ONLY IN GOOD NATURES

But pain which some suppose to be in an especial manner an evil, whether it be in mind or in body, cannot exist except in good natures. For the very fact of resistance in any being leading to pain, involves a refusal not to be what it was, because it was something good; but when a being is compelled to something better, the pain is useful, when to something worse, it is useless. Therefore in the case of the mind, the will resisting a greater power causes pain; in the case of the body, sensation resisting a more powerful body causes pain. But evils without pain are worse: for it is worse to rejoice in iniquity than to bewail corruption; yet even such rejoicing cannot exist save from the attainment of inferior good things. But iniquity is the desertion of better things. Likewise in a body, a wound with pain is better than painless putrescence, which is especially called the corruption which the dead flesh of the Lord did not see, that is, did not suffer, as was predicted in prophecy: "Thou shalt not suffer Thy Holy one to see corruption." [5] For who denies that He was wounded by the piercing of the nails, and that He was stabbed with the lance? [6] But even what is properly called by men corporeal corruption, that is, putrescence itself, if as yet there is anything left to consume, increases by the diminution of the good. But if corruption shall have absolutely consumed it, so that there is no good, no nature will remain, for there will be nothing that corruption may corrupt; and so there will not even be putrescence, for there will be nowhere at all for it to be.

[4] Ex. iii. 14   [5] Ps. xvi. 10   [6] John xix. 18, 34

CHAPTER XXI

FROM MEASURE THINGS ARE SAID TO BE MODERATE-SIZED [7]

Therefore now by common usage things small and mean are said to have measure, because some measure remains in them, without which they would no longer be moderate-sized, but would not exist at all. But those things that by reason of too much progress are called immoderate, are blamed for very excessiveness; but yet it is necessary that those things themselves be restrained in some manner under God who has disposed all things in extension, number, and weight.[8]

CHAPTER XXII

MEASURE IN SOME SENSE IS SUITABLE TO GOD HIMSELF

But God cannot be said to have measure, lest He should seem to be spoken of as limited. Yet He is not immoderate by whom measure is bestowed upon all things, so that they may in any measure exist. Nor again ought God to be called measured, as if He received measure from any one. But if we say that He is the highest measure, by chance we say something; if indeed in speaking of the highest measure we mean the highest good. For every measure in so far as it is a measure is good; whence nothing can be called measured, modest, modified, without praise, although in another sense we use *measure* for *limit*, and speak of no *measure* where there is no *limit*, which is sometimes said with praise as when it is said: "And of His kingdom there shall be no limit." [9] For it might also be said, "There shall be no measure," so that measure might be used in the sense of limit; for He who reigns in no measure, assuredly does not reign at all.

CHAPTER XXIII

WHENCE A BAD MEASURE, A BAD FORM, A BAD ORDER MAY SOMETIMES BE SPOKEN OF

Therefore a bad measure, a bad form, a bad order, are either so called because they are less than they should be, or because they are not adapted to those things to which they should be adapted; so that they may be called bad as being alien and incongruous; as if any one should be said not to have done in a good measure because he has done less than he ought, or because he has done in such a thing as he ought not to have done, or more than was fitting, or not conveniently; so that the very fact of that being reprehended which is done in a bad measure, is justly reprehended for no other cause than that the measure is not there maintained. Likewise a form is called bad either in comparison with something more handsome

[7] *Modus—modica*   [8] Wisd. xi. 21   [9] Luke i. 33

or more beautiful, this form being less, that greater, not in size but in comeliness; or because it is out of harmony with the thing to which it is applied, so that it seems alien and unsuitable. As if a man should walk forth into a public place naked, which nakedness does not offend if seen in a bath. Likewise also order is called bad when order itself is maintained in an inferior degree. Hence not order, but rather disorder, is bad; since either the ordering is less than it should be, or not as it should be. Yet where there is any measure, any form, any order, there is some good and some nature; but where there is no measure, no form, no order, there is no good, no nature.

CHAPTER XXIV

IT IS PROVED BY THE TESTIMONIES OF SCRIPTURE THAT GOD IS UNCHANGEABLE. THE SON OF GOD BEGOTTEN, NOT MADE

Those things which our faith holds and which reason in whatever way has traced out, are fortified by the testimonies of the divine Scriptures, so that those who by reason of feebler intellect are not able to comprehend these things, may believe the divine authority, and so may deserve to know. But let not those who understand, but are less instructed in ecclesiastical literature, suppose that we set forth these things from our own intellect rather than what are in those Books. Accordingly, that God is unchangeable is written in the *Psalms:* "Thou shalt change them and they shall be changed; but Thou thyself art the same." [10] And in the *Book of Wisdom,* concerning wisdom: "Remaining in herself, she renews all things." [11] Whence also the Apostle Paul: "To the invisible, incorruptible, only God." [12] And the Apostle James: "Every best giving and every perfect gift is from above, descending from the Father of light, with whom there is no changeableness, neither obscuring of influence." [13] Likewise because what He begat of Himself is what He Himself is, it is said in brief by the Son Himself: "I and the Father are one." [14] But because the Son was not made, since through Him were all things made, thus it is written: "In the beginning was the Word, and the Word was with God, and God was the Word; this was in the beginning with God. All things were made through Him, and without Him was made nothing;" [15] that is, without Him was not anything made.

[10] Ps. cii. 27   [11] Wisd. vii. 27   [12] 1 Tim. i. 17   [13] James i. 17   [14] John x. 30
[15] John i. 1-3

CHAPTER XXV

THIS LAST EXPRESSION MISUNDERSTOOD BY SOME

For no attention should be paid to the ravings of men who think that *nothing* should be understood to mean *something,* and moreover think to compel any one to vanity of this kind on the ground that *nothing* is placed at the end of the sentence. Therefore, they say, it was made, and because it was made, nothing is itself something. They have lost their senses by zeal in contradicting, and do not understand that it makes no difference whether it be said: "Without Him was made nothing," or "without Him nothing was made." For even if the order were the last mentioned, they could nevertheless say, that nothing is itself something because it was made. For in the case of what is in truth something, what difference does it make if it be said "Without him a house was made," so long as it is understood that something was made without him, which something is a house? So also because it is said: "Without Him was made nothing," since nothing is assuredly not anything, when it is truly and properly spoken, it makes no difference whether it be said: "Without Him was made nothing," or "Without Him nothing was made," or "nothing was made." But who cares to speak with men who can say of this very expression of mine "It makes no difference," "Therefore it makes some difference, for nothing itself is something?" But those whose brains are not addled, see it as a thing most manifest that this something is to be understood when it says "It makes no difference," as when I say "It matters in no respect." But these, if they should say to any one, "What hast thou done?" and he should reply that he has done nothing, would, according to this mode of disputation, falsely accuse him saying, "Thou hast done something, therefore, because thou hast done nothing; for nothing is itself something." But they have also the Lord Himself placing this word at the end of a sentence, when He says: "And in secret have I spoken nothing." [16] Let them read, therefore, and be silent.

CHAPTER XXVI

THAT CREATURES ARE MADE OF NOTHING

Because therefore God made all things which He did not beget of Himself, not of those things that already existed, but of those things that did not exist at all, that is, of nothing the Apostle Paul says: "Who calls the things that are not as if they are." [17] But still more plainly it is written in the *Book of Maccabees:* "I pray thee, son, look at the heaven and the earth and all the things that are in them; see and know that it was not

[16] John xviii. 20   [17] Rom. iv. 17

these of which the Lord God made us." [18] And from this that is written in the Psalm: "He spake, and they were made." [19] It is manifest, that not of Himself He begat these things, but that He made them by word and command. But what is not of Himself is assuredly of nothing. For there was not anything of which he should make them, concerning which the apostle says most openly: "For from Him, and through Him, and in Him are all things." [20]

CHAPTER XXVII

"FROM HIM" AND "OF HIM" DO NOT MEAN THE SAME THING

But "from Him" does not mean the same as "of Him." [21] For what is of Him may be said to be from Him; but not everything that is from Him is rightly said to be of Him. For from Him are heaven and earth, because He made them; but not of Him because they are not of His substance. As in the case of a man who begets a son and makes a house, from himself is the son, from himself is the house, but the son is of him, the house is of earth and wood. But this is so, because as a man he cannot make something even of nothing; but God of whom are all things, through whom are all things, in whom are all things, had no need of any material which He had not made to assist His omnipotence.

CHAPTER XXVIII

SIN NOT FROM GOD, BUT FROM THE WILL OF THOSE SINNING

But when we hear: "All things are from Him, and through Him, and in Him," we ought assuredly to understand all natures which naturally exist. For sins, which do not preserve but vitiate nature, are not from Him; which sins, Holy Scripture in many ways testifies, are from the will of those sinning, especially in the passage where the apostle says: "But dost thou suppose this, O man, that judgest those who do such things, and doest them, that thou shalt escape the judgment of God? Or dost thou despise the riches of His goodness, and patience, and long-suffering, not knowing that the patience of God leadeth thee to repentance? But according to the hardness of thy heart and thy impenitent heart, thou treasurest up for thyself wrath against the day of wrath and of the revelation of the just judgment of God, who will render unto every one according to his works." [22]

[18] Mac. vii. 28   [19] Ps. cxlviii. 5   [20] Rom. xi. 36   [21] *Ex ipso* and *de ipso*
[22] Rom. ii. 3-6

CHAPTER XXIX

THAT GOD IS NOT DEFILED BY OUR SINS

And yet, though all things that He established are in Him, those who sin do not defile Him, of whose wisdom it is said: "She touches all things by reason of her purity, and nothing defiled assails her." [23] For it behooves us to believe that as God is incorruptible and unchangeable, so also is He consequently undefilable.

CHAPTER XXX

THAT GOOD THINGS, EVEN THE LEAST, AND THOSE THAT ARE EARTHLY, ARE BY GOD

But that God made even the least things, that is, earthly and mortal things, must undoubtedly be understood from that passage of the apostle, where, speaking of the members of our flesh: "For if one member is glorified, all the members rejoice with it, and if one member suffers, all the members suffer with it;" also this he then says: "God has placed the members each one of them in the body as He willed;" and "God has tempered the body, giving to that to which it was wanting greater honor, that there should be no schism in the body, but that the members should have the same care one for another." [24] But what the apostle thus praises in the measure and form and order of the members of the flesh, you find in the flesh of all animals, alike the greatest and the least; for all flesh is among earthly goods, and consequently is esteemed among the least.

CHAPTER XXXI

TO PUNISH AND TO FORGIVE SINS BELONG EQUALLY TO GOD

Likewise because it belongs to divine judgment, not human, what sort of punishment and how great is due to every fault, it is thus written: "O the height of the riches of the wisdom and the knowledge of God! how inscrutable are His judgments and His ways past finding out!" [25] Likewise because by the goodness of God sins are forgiven to the converted, the very fact that Christ was sent sufficiently shows, who not in His own nature as God, but in our nature, which He assumed from a woman, died for us; which goodness of God with reference to us, and which love of God, the apostle thus sets forth: "But God commendeth His love toward us, in that while we were yet sinners Christ died for us; much more now being justified in His blood we shall be saved from wrath through Him. For if when we were enemies we were reconciled to God through the death of His Son,

[23] Wisd. vii. 24, 25   [24] 1 Cor. xii. 26, 18, 24, 25   [25] Rom. xi. 33

much more being reconciled we shall be saved in His life." [26] But because even when due punishment is rendered to sinners, there is no unrighteousness on God's part, he thus says: "What shall we say? Is God unrighteous who visiteth with wrath?" [27] But in one place he has briefly admonished that goodness and severity are alike from Him, saying: "Thou seest then the goodness and severity of God; toward them that have fallen, severity, but towards thee goodness, if thou shouldst continue in goodness.[28]

CHAPTER XXXII

FROM GOD ALSO IS THE VERY POWER TO BE HURTFUL

Likewise because the power even of those that are hurtful is from God alone, thus it stands written, Wisdom speaking: "Through me kings reign and tyrants hold the land through me." [29] The apostle also says: "For there is no power but of God." [30] But that it is worthily done is written in the *Book of Job:* "Who maketh to reign a man that is a hypocrite, on account of the perversity of the people." [31] And concerning the people of Israel God says: "I gave them a king in my wrath." [32] For it is not unrighteous, that the wicked receiving the power of being hurtful, both the patience of the good should be proved and the iniquity of the evil punished. For through power given to the Devil both Job was proved so that he might appear righteous,[33] and Peter was tempted lest he should be presumptuous,[34] and Paul was buffeted lest he should be exalted,[35] and Judas was damned so that he should hang himself.[36] When, therefore, through the power which He has given the Devil, God Himself shall have done all things righteously, nevertheless punishment shall at last be rendered to the Devil not for these things justly done, but for the unrighteous willing to be hurtful, which belonged to himself, when it shall be said to the impious who persevered in consenting to his wickedness, "Go ye into everlasting fire which my God has prepared for the Devil and his angels." [37]

CHAPTER XXXIII

THAT EVIL ANGELS HAVE BEEN MADE EVIL, NOT BY GOD, BUT BY SINNING

But because evil angels also were not constituted evil by God, but were made evil by sinning, Peter in his epistle says: "For if God spared not angels when they sinned, but casting them down into the dungeons of smoky hell, He delivered them to be reserved for punishment in judgment." [38]

---

[26] Rom. v. 8-10   [27] *Ibid*. iii. 5   [28] *Ibid*. xi. 22   [29] Prov. viii. 15   [30] Rom. xiii. 1
[31] Job xxxiv. 30   [32] Hos. xiii. 11   [33] Job i. and ii.   [34] Matt. xxvi. 31-35, 69-75
[35] 2 Cor. xii. 7   [36] Matt. xxvii. 5   [37] Matt. xxv. 41   [38] 2 Pet. ii. 4

Hence Peter shows that there is still due to them the penalty of the last judgment, concerning which the Lord says: "Go ye into everlasting fire, which has been prepared for the Devil and his angels." Although they have already penally received this hell, that is, an inferior smoky air as a prison, which nevertheless since it is also called heaven, is not that heaven in which there are stars, but this lower heaven by the smoke of which the clouds are conglobulated, and where the birds fly; for both a cloudy heaven is spoken of, and flying things are called heavenly. As when the Apostle Paul calls those evil angels, against whom as enemies by living piously we contend, "spiritual things of wickedness in heavenly places." [39] That this may not be understood of the upper heavens, he plainly says elsewhere: "According to the presence of the prince of this air, who now worketh in the sons of disobedience." [40]

CHAPTER XXXIV

THAT SIN IS NOT THE STRIVING FOR AN EVIL NATURE, BUT THE DESERTION OF A BETTER

Likewise because sin, or unrighteousness, is not the striving after evil nature but the desertion of better, it is thus found written in the Scriptures: "Every creature of God is good." [41] And accordingly every tree also which God planted in Paradise is assuredly good. Man did not therefore strive after an evil nature when he touched the forbidden tree; but by deserting what was better, he committed an evil deed. Since the Creator is better than any creature which He has made, His command should not have been deserted, that the thing forbidden, however good, might be touched; since the better having been deserted, the good of the creature was striven for, which was touched contrary to the command of the Creator. God did not plant an evil tree in Paradise; but He Himself was better who prohibited its being touched.

CHAPTER XXXV

THE TREE WAS FORBIDDEN TO ADAM NOT BECAUSE IT WAS EVIL, BUT BECAUSE IT WAS GOOD FOR MAN TO BE SUBJECT TO GOD

For besides, He had made the prohibition, in order to show that the nature of the rational soul ought not to be in its own power, but in subjection to God, and that it guards the order of its salvation through obedience, corrupting it through disobedience. Hence also He called the tree, the touching of which He forbade, the tree "of the knowledge of good and evil;" [42] because when man should have touched it in the face of the prohibition, he would experience the penalty of sin, and so would know the difference between the good of obedience, and the evil of disobedience.

[39] Eph. vi. 12 [40] *Ibid.* ii. 2 [41] I Tim. iv. 4 [42] Gen. ii. 9

CHAPTER XXXVI

NO CREATURE OF GOD IS EVIL, BUT TO ABUSE A CREATURE OF GOD IS EVIL

For who is so foolish as to think a creature of God, especially one planted in Paradise, blameworthy; when indeed not even thorns and thistles, which the earth brought forth, according to the judiciary judgment of God, for wearing out the sinner in labor, should be blamed? For even such herbs have their measure and form and order, which whoever considers soberly will find praiseworthy; but they are evil to that nature which ought thus to be restrained as a recompense for sin. Therefore, as I have said, sin is not the striving after an evil nature, but the desertion of a better, and so the deed itself is evil, not the nature which the sinner uses amiss. For it is evil to use amiss that which is good. Whence the apostle reproves certain ones as condemned by divine judgment, "Who have worshipped and served the creature more than the Creator." [43] He does not reprove the creature, which he who should do would act injuriously towards the Creator, but those who, deserting the better, have used amiss the good.

CHAPTER XXXVII

GOD MAKES GOOD USE OF THE EVIL DEEDS OF SINNERS

Accordingly, if all natures should guard their own proper measure and form and order, there would be no evil: but if any one should wish to misuse these good things, not even thus does he vanquish the will of God, who knows how to order righteously even the unrighteous; so that if they themselves through the iniquity of their will should misuse His good things, He through the righteousness of His power may use their evil deeds, rightly ordaining to punishment those who have perversely ordained themselves to sins.

CHAPTER XXXVIII

ETERNAL FIRE TORTURING THE WICKED, NOT EVIL

For neither is eternal fire itself, which is to torture the impious, an evil nature, since it has its measure, its form and its order depraved by no iniquity; but it is an evil torture for the damned, to whose sins it is due. For neither is yonder light, because it tortures the blear-eyed, an evil nature.

[43] Rom. i. 25

CHAPTER XXXIX

FIRE IS CALLED ETERNAL, NOT AS GOD IS, BUT BECAUSE WITHOUT END

But fire is eternal, not as God is eternal, because, though without end, yet it is not without beginning; but God is also without beginning. Then, although it may be employed perpetually for the punishment of sinners, yet it is mutable nature. But that is true eternity which is true immortality, that is that highest immutability, which cannot be changed at all. For it is one thing not to suffer change, when change is possible, and another thing to be absolutely incapable of change. Therefore, just as man is called good, yet not as God, of whom it was said, "There is none good save God alone;" [44] and just as the soul is called immortal, yet not as God, of whom it was said, "Who alone hath immortality;" [45] and just as a man is called wise, yet not as God, of whom it was said, "To God the only wise;" [46] so fire is called eternal, yet not as God, whose alone is immortality itself and true eternity.

CHAPTER XL

NEITHER CAN GOD SUFFER HURT, NOR ANY OTHER, SAVE BY THE JUST ORDINATION OF GOD

Since these things are so, according to the Catholic Faith, and wholesome doctrine, and truth perspicuous to those of good understanding, neither can any one hurt the nature of God, nor can the nature of God unrighteously hurt any one, or suffer any one to do hurt with impunity. "For he that doeth hurt shall receive," says the apostle, "according to the hurt that he has done; and there is no accepting of persons with God." [47]

CHAPTER XLI

HOW GREAT GOOD THINGS THE MANICHAEANS PUT IN THE NATURE OF EVIL, AND HOW GREAT EVIL THINGS IN THE NATURE OF GOOD

But if the Manichaeans were willing, without pernicious zeal for defending their error, and with the fear of God, to think, they would not most criminally blaspheme by supposing two natures, the one good, which they call God, the other evil, which God did not make: so erring, so delirious, nay so insane, are they that they do not see, that even in what they call the nature of supreme evil they place so great good things: life, power, safety, memory, intellect, temperance, virtue, plenty, sense, light, suavity, extensions, numbers, peace, measure, form, order; but in what they call

[44] Mark x. 18   [45] 1 Tim. vi. 16   [46] Rom. xvi. 27   [47] Col. iii. 25

supreme good, so many evil things: death, sickness, forgetfulness, foolishness, confusion, impotence, need, stolidity, blindness, pain, unrighteousness, disgrace, war, intemperance, deformity, perversity. For they say that the princes of darkness also have been alive in their own nature, and in their own kingdom were safe, and remembered and understood. For they say that the Prince of Darkness harangued in such a manner, that neither could he have said such things, nor could he have been heard by those by whom he was said to have been heard, without memory and understanding; and to have had a temper suitable to his mind and body, and to have ruled by virtue of power, and to have had abundance and fruitfulness with respect to his elements, and they are said to have perceived themselves mutually and the light as near at hand, and to have had eyes by which they could see the light afar off; which eyes assuredly could not have seen the light without some light (whence also they are rightly called light); and they are said to have enjoyed exceedingly the sweetness of their pleasures, and to have been determined by measured members and dwelling-places. But unless there had been some sort of beauty there, they would not have loved their wives, nor would their bodies have been steady by adaptation of parts; without which, those things could not have been done there which the Manichaeans insanely say were done. And unless some peace had been there, they would not have obeyed their Prince. Unless measure had been there, they would have done nothing else than eat or drink, or rage, or whatever they might have done, without any society: although not even those that did these things would have had determinate forms, unless measure had been there. But now the Manichaeans say that they did such things that they cannot be denied to have had in all their actions measures suitable to themselves. But if form had not been there, no natural quality would have there subsisted. But if there had been no order there, some would not have ruled, others been ruled; they would not have lived harmoniously in their elements; in fine, they would not have had their members adapted to their places, so that they could not do all those things that the Manichaeans vainly fable. But if they say that God's nature does not die, what according to their vanity does Christ raise from the dead? If they say that it does not grow sick, what does He cure? If they say that it is not subject to forgetfulness, what does He remind? If they say that it is not deficient in wisdom, what does He teach? If they say that it is not confused, what does He restore? If they say that it was not vanquished and taken captive, what does He liberate? If they say that it was not in need, to what does He minister aid? If they say that it did not lose feeling, what does He animate? If they say that it has not been blinded, what does He illuminate? If it is not in pain, to what does He give relief? If it is not unrighteous, what does He correct through precepts? If it is not in disgrace, what does He cleanse? If it is not in war, to what does He promise peace? If it is not deficient in moderation, upon what does

He impose the measure of law? If it is not deformed, what does He reform? If it is not perverse, what does He emend? For all these things done by Christ, they say, are to be attributed not to that thing which was made by God, and which has become depraved by its own free choice in sinning, but to the very nature, yea to the very substance of God, which is what God Himself is.

CHAPTER XLII

MANICHAEAN BLASPHEMIES CONCERNING THE NATURE OF GOD

What can be compared to those blasphemies? Absolutely nothing, unless the errors of other sectaries be considered; but if that error be compared with itself in another aspect, of which we have not yet spoken, it will be convicted of far worse and more execrable blasphemy. For they say that some souls, which they will have to be of the substance of God and of absolutely the same nature, which have not sinned of their own accord, but have been overcome and oppressed by the race of darkness, which they call evil, for combating which they descended not of their own accord, but at the command of the Father, are fettered forever in the horrible sphere of darkness. So according to their sacrilegious vaporings, God liberated Himself in a certain part from a great evil, but again condemned Himself in another part, which He could not liberate, and triumphed over the enemy itself as if it had been vanquished from above. O criminal, incredible audacity, to believe, to speak, to proclaim such things about God! Which when they endeavor to defend, that with their eyes shut they may rush headlong into yet worse things, they say that the commingling of the evil nature does these things, in order that the good nature of God may suffer so great evils: for that this good nature in its own sphere could or can suffer no one of these things. As if a nature were lauded as incorruptible, because it does not hurt itself, and not because it cannot suffer hurt from another. Then if the nature of God hurt the nature of darkness, and the nature of darkness hurt the nature of God, there are therefore two evil things which hurt each other in turn, and the race of darkness was the better disposed, because if it committed hurt it did it unwillingly; for it did not wish to commit hurt, but to enjoy the good which belonged to God. But God wished to extinguish it, as Manichaeus most openly raves forth in his epistle of the ruinous *Foundation*. For forgetting that he had shortly before said: "But His most resplendent realms were so founded upon the shining and happy land, that they could never be either moved or shaken by any one;" he afterwards said: "But the Father of the most blessed light, knowing that great ruin and desolation which would arise from the darkness, threaten his holy worlds, unless he should send in opposition a deity excellent and renowned, mighty in strength, by whom he might at the same time overcome and destroy the race of darkness, which having been extinguished, the inhabitants of light would enjoy perpetual rest." Behold, he feared ruin and desolation that threatened his worlds! Assuredly they were so founded upon the shining and happy land that they never could be either moved or shaken by any one? Behold, from fear he wished to hurt the neighboring race, which he endeavored to destroy and extinguish, in order that the inhabitants of light might enjoy perpetual rest. Why did he not add, and perpetual bondage? Were not these souls that he fettered forever in the sphere of darkness, the inhabitants of light, of whom he says plainly, that "they have suffered themselves to err from their former bright nature?" when against his will he is compelled to say, that they sinned by free will, while he wishes to ascribe sin only to the necessity of the contrary nature: everywhere ignorant what to say, and as if he were himself already in the sphere of darkness which he invented, seeking, and not finding, how he may escape. But let him say what he will to the seduced and miserable men by whom he is honored far more highly than Christ, that at this price he may sell to them such long and sacrilegious fables. Let him say what he will, let him shut up, as it were, in a sphere, as in a prison, the race of darkness, and let him fasten outside the nature of light, to which he promised perpetual rest on the extinction of the enemy: behold, the penalty of light is worse than that of darkness; the penalty of the divine nature is worse than that of the adverse race. But since although the latter is in the midst of darkness it pertains to its nature to dwell in darkness; but souls which are the very same thing that God is, cannot be received, he says, into those peaceful realms, and are alienated from the life and liberty of the holy light, and are fettered in the aforesaid horrible sphere: whence he says, "Those souls shall adhere to the things that they have loved, having been left in the same sphere of darkness, bringing this upon themselves by their own deserts." Is not this assuredly free voluntary choice? See how insanely he ignores what he says, and by making self-contradictory statements wages a worse war against himself than against the God of the race of darkness itself. Accordingly, if the souls of light are damned, because they loved darkness, the race of darkness, which loved light, is unjustly damned. And the race of darkness indeed loved light from the beginning, violently, it may be, but yet so as to wish for its possession, not its extinction: but the nature of light wished to extinguish in war the darkness; therefore when vanquished it loved darkness. Choose which you will: whether it was compelled by necessity to love darkness, or seduced by free will. If by necessity, wherefore is it damned? if by free will, wherefore is the nature of God involved in so great iniquity? If the nature of God was compelled by necessity to love darkness, it did not vanquish, but was vanquished: if by free will, why do the wretches hesitate any longer to attribute the will to sin to the nature which God made out of nothing, lest they should thereby attribute it to the light which He begat?

CHAPTER XLIII

MANY EVILS BEFORE HIS COMMINGLING WITH EVIL ARE ATTRIBUTED
TO THE NATURE OF GOD BY THE MANICHAEANS

What if we should also show that before the commingling of evil, which stupid fable they have most madly believed, great evils were in what they call the nature of light? what will it seem possible to add to these blasphemies? For before the conflict, there was the hard and inevitable necessity of fighting: here is truly a great evil, before evil is commingled with good. Let them say whence this is, when as yet no commingling had taken place? But if there was no necessity, there was therefore free will: whence also this so great evil, that God Himself should wish to hurt His own nature, which could not be hurt by the enemy, by sending it to be cruelly commingled, to be basely purged, to be unjustly damned? Behold, the great evil of a pernicious, noxious, and savage will, before any evil from the contrary nature was mingled with it! Or perchance he did not know that this would happen to his members, that they should love darkness and become hostile to holy light, as Manichaeus says, that is, not only to their own God, but also to the Father from whom they had their being? Whence therefore this so great evil of ignorance, before any evil from the nature of darkness was mingled with it? But if he knew that this would happen, either there was in him everlasting cruelty, if he did not grieve over the contamination and damnation of his own nature that was to take place, or everlasting misery, if he did so grieve: whence also this so great evil of your supreme good before any commingling with your supreme evil? Assuredly that part of the nature itself which was fettered in the eternal chain of that sphere, if it knew not that this fate awaited it, even so was there everlasting ignorance in the nature of God, but if it knew, then everlasting misery: whence this so great evil before any evil from the contrary nature was commingled? Or perchance did it, in the greatness of its love (charity), rejoice that through its punishment perpetual rest was prepared for the residue of the inhabitants of light? Let him who sees how abominable it is to say this, pronounce an anathema. But if this should be done so that at least the good nature itself should not become hostile to the light, it might be possible, perchance, not for the nature of God indeed, but for some man, as it were, to be regarded as praiseworthy, who for the sake of his country should be willing to suffer something of evil, which evil indeed could be only for a time, and not forever: but now also they speak of that fettering in the sphere of darkness as eternal, and not indeed of a certain thing but of the nature of God; and assuredly it were a most unrighteous, and execrable, and ineffably sacrilegious joy, if the nature of God rejoiced that it should love darkness, and should become hostile to holy light. Whence this so monstrous and abominable evil before any evil from the contrary nature was commingled? Who can endure insanity so perverse and so impious, as to attribute so great good things to supreme evil, and so great evils to supreme good, which is God?

CHAPTER XLIV

INCREDIBLE TURPITUDES IN GOD IMAGINED BY MANICHAEUS

But now when they speak of that part of the nature of God as everywhere mixed up in heaven, in earth, in all bodies dry and moist, in all sorts of flesh, in all seeds of trees, herbs, men, and animals: not as present by the power of divinity, for administering and ruling all things, undefilably, inviolably, incorruptibly, without any connection with them, which we say of God; but fettered, oppressed, polluted, to be loosed and liberated, as they say, not only through the running to and fro of the sun and the moon, and through the powers of light, but also through their Elect: what sacrilegious and incredible turpitudes this kind of error recommends to them even if it does not induce them to accept, it is horrible to speak of. For they say that the powers of light are transformed into beautiful males and are set over against the women of the race of darkness; and that the same powers again are transformed into beautiful females and are set over against the males of the race of darkness; that through their beauty they enkindle the foulest lust of the princes of darkness, and in this manner vital substance, that is, the nature of God, which they say is held fettered in their bodies, having been loosed from their members relaxed through lust, flies away, and when it has been taken up or cleansed, is liberated. This the wretches read, this they say, this they hear, this they believe, this they put as follows, in the seventh book of their *Thesaurus* (for so they call a certain writing of Manichaeus, in which these blasphemies stand written): "Then the blessed Father, who has bright ships, little apartments, dwellingplaces, or magnitudes, according to his indwelling clemency, brings the help by which he is drawn out and liberated from the impious bonds, straits, and torments of his vital substance. And so by his own invisible nod he transforms those powers of his, which are held in this most brilliant ship, and makes them to bring forth adverse powers, which have been arranged in the various tracts of the heavens. Since these consist of both sexes, male and female, he orders the aforesaid powers to bring forth partly in the form of beardless youths, for the adverse race of females, partly in the form of bright maidens, for the contrary race of males: knowing that all these hostile powers on account of the deadly and most foul lust innate in them, are very easily taken captive, delivered up to these most beautiful forms which appear, and in this manner they are dissolved. But you may know that this same blessed Father of ours is identical with his powers, which for a necessary reason he transforms into the undefiled likeness of youths and maidens. But these he uses as his own arms, and through them he accomplishes his will. But there are bright ships full of these divine powers, which are stationed after the likeness of marriage over against the infernal races, and who with alacrity and ease effect at the very moment what they have planned. Therefore, when reason demands that these same holy powers should appear to males, straightway also they show by their dress the likeness of most beautiful maidens. Again when females are to be dealt with, putting aside the forms of maidens, they show the forms of beardless youths. But by this handsome appearance of theirs, ardor and lust increase, and in this way the chain of their worst thoughts is loosed, and the living soul which was held by their members, relaxed by this occasion, escapes, and is mingled with its own most pure air; when the souls thoroughly cleansed ascend to the bright ships, which have been prepared for conveying them and for ferrying them over to their own country. But that which still bears the stains of the adverse race, descends little by little through billows and fires, and is mingled with trees and other plants and with all seeds, and is plunged into divers fires. And in what manner the figures of youths and maidens from that great and most glorious ship appear to the contrary powers which live in the heavens and have a fiery nature; and from that handsome appearance, part of the life which is held in their members having been released is conducted away through fires into the earth: in the same manner also, that most high power, which dwells in the ship of vital waters appears in the likeness of youths and holy maidens to those powers whose nature is cold and moist, and which are arranged in the heavens. And indeed to those that are females, among these the form of youths appears, but to the males, the form of maidens. By his changing and diversity of divine and most beautiful persons, the princes male and female of the moist and cold race are loosed, and what is vital in them escapes; but whatever should remain, having been relaxed, is conducted into the earth through cold, and is mingled with all the races of darkness." Who can endure this? Who can believe, not indeed that it is true, but that it could even be said? Behold those who fear to anathematize Manichaeus teaching these things, and do not fear to believe in a God doing them and suffering them!

CHAPTER LXV

CERTAIN UNSPEAKABLE TURPITUDES BELIEVED, NOT WITHOUT REASON, CONCERNING THE MANICHAEANS THEMSELVES

But they say, that through their own Elect that same commingled part and nature of God is purged, by eating and drinking forsooth (because they say that it is held fettered in all foods); that when they are taken up by the Elect for the nourishment of the body in eating and drinking, it is loosed, sealed, and liberated through their sanctity. Nor do the wretches pay heed to the fact that this is believed about them not without good reason, and they deny it in vain, so long as they do not anathematize the books of Manichaeus and cease to be Manichaeans. For if, as they say, a part of God is fettered in all seeds, and is purged by eating on the part of the Elect; who may not properly believe, that they do what they read in the *Thesaurus* was done among the powers of heaven and the princes of darkness; since indeed they say that their flesh is also from the race of darkness, and since they do not hesitate to believe and to affirm that the vital substance fettered in them is a part of God? Which assuredly if it is to be loosed, and purged by eating, as their lamentable error compels them to acknowledge; who does not see, who does not shudder at the greatness and the unspeakableness of what follows?

CHAPTER XLVI

THE UNSPEAKABLE DOCTRINE OF THE FUNDAMENTAL EPISTLE

For they even say that Adam, the first man, was created by certain princes of darkness so that the light might be held by them lest it should escape. For in the epistle which they call *Fundamental*, Manichaeus wrote as follows respecting the way in which the Prince of Darkness, whom they represent as the father of the first man, spoke to the rest of his allied princes of darkness, and how he acted: "Therefore with wicked inventions he said to those present: What does this huge light that is rising seem to you to be? See how the pole moves, how it shakes most of the powers. Wherefore it is right for me rather to ask you beforehand for whatever light you have in your powers: since thus I will form an image of that great one who has appeared in his glory, through which we may be able to rule, freed in some measure from the conversation of darkness. Hearing these things, and deliberating for a long time among themselves, they thought it most just to furnish what was demanded of them. For they did not have confidence in being able to retain the light that they had forever; hence they thought it better to offer it to their Prince, by no means without hope that in this way they would rule. It must be considered therefore how they furnished the light that they had. For this also is scattered throughout all the divine scriptures and the heavenly secrets; but to the wise it is easy enough to know how it was given: for it is known immediately and openly by him who should truly and faithfully wish to consider. Since there was a promiscuous throng of those who had come together, females and males of course, he impelled them to copulate among themselves: in which copulation the males emitted seed, the females were made pregnant. But the offspring were like those who had begotten them, the first obtaining as it were the largest portion of the parents' strength. Taking these as a special gift their Prince rejoiced. And just as even now we see take place, that the nature of evil taking thence strength forms the fashioner of bodies, so also the aforesaid Prince, taking the offspring of his companions, which had the senses of their parents, sagacity, light, procreated at the same time with themselves in the process of generation, devoured them; and very many powers having been taken from food of this kind, in which there was present not only fortitude, but much more astuteness and depraved sensibilities from the ferocious race of the progenitors, he called his own spouse to himself, springing from the same stock as himself, emitted, like the rest, the abundance of evils that he had devoured, himself also adding something from his own thought and power, so that his disposition became the former and arranger of all the things that he had poured forth; whose consort received these things as soil cultivated in the best way is accustomed to receive seed. For in her were constructed and woven together the images of all heavenly and earthly powers, so that what was formed obtained the likeness, so to speak, of a full orb."

CHAPTER XLVII

HE COMPELS TO THE PERPETRATION OF HORRIBLE TURPITUDES

O abominable monster! O execrable perdition and ruin of deluded souls! I am not speaking of the blasphemy of saying these things about the nature of God which is thus fettered. Let the wretches deluded and hunted by deadly error give heed to this at least, that if a part of their God is fettered by the copulation of males and females which they profess to loose and purge by eating it, the necessity of this unspeakable error compels them not only to loose and purge the part of God from bread and vegetables and fruits, which alone they are seen publicly to partake of, but also from that which might be fettered through copulation, if conception should take place. That they do this some are said to have confessed before a public tribunal, not only in Paphlagonia, but also in Gaul, as I heard in Rome from a certain Catholic Christian; and when they were asked by the authority of what writing they did these things, they betrayed this fact concerning the *Thesaurus* that I have just mentioned. But when this is cast in their teeth, they are in the habit of replying, that some enemy or other has withdrawn from their number, that is from the number of their Elect, and has made a schism, and has founded a most foul heresy of this kind. Whence it is manifest that even if they do not themselves practise this thing, some who do practise it do it on the basis of their books. Therefore let them reject the books, if they abhor the crime, which they are compelled to commit, if they hold to the books; or if they do not commit them, they endeavor in opposition to the books to live more purely. But what do they do when it is said to them, either purge the light from whatever seeds you can, so that you cannot refuse to do that which you assert that you do not do; or else anathematize Manichaeus, when he says that a part of God is in all seeds, and that it is fettered by copulation, but that whatever of light, that is, of the aforesaid part of God, should become the food of the Elect, is purged by being eaten. Do you see what he compels you to believe, and do you still hesitate to anathematize him? What do they do, I say, when this is said to them? To what subterfuges do they betake themselves, when either so nefarious a doctrine is to be anathematized, or so nefarious a turpitude committed, in comparison with which all those intolerable evils to which I have already called attention, seem tolerable, namely, that they say of the nature of God that it was pressed by necessity to wage war, that it was either secure by everlasting ignorance, or was disturbed by everlasting grief and fear, when the corruption of commingling and the chain of everlasting damnation should come upon it, that finally as a result of the conflict it should be taken captive, oppressed, polluted, that after a false victory it should be fettered forever in a horrible sphere and separated from its original blessedness, while if considered in themselves they cannot be endured?

CHAPTER XLVIII

AUGUSTINE PRAYS THAT THE MANICHAEANS MAY BE RESTORED TO THEIR SENSES

O great is Thy patience, Lord, full of compassion and gracious, slow to anger, and plenteous in mercy, and true;[48] who makest Thy sun to rise upon the good and the evil, and who sendest rain upon the just and the unjust;[49] who willest not the death of the sinner, so much as that he return and live;[50] who reproving in parts, dost give place to repentance, that wickedness having been abandoned, they may believe on Thee, O Lord;[51] who by Thy patience dost lead to repentance, although many according to the hardness of their heart and their impenitent heart treasure up for themselves wrath against the day of wrath and of the revelation of Thy righteous judgment, who wilt render to every man according to his works;[52] who in the day when a man shall have turned from his iniquity to Thy mercy and truth, wilt forget all his iniquities:[53] stand before us, grant unto us that through our ministry, by which Thou hast been pleased to refute this execrable and too horrible error, as many have already been liberated, many also may be liberated, and whether through the sacrament of Thy holy baptism, or through the sacrifice of a broken spirit and a contrite and humbled heart,[54] in the sorrow of repentance, they may deserve to receive the remission of their sins and blasphemies, by which through ignorance they have offended Thee. For nothing is of any avail, save Thy surpassing mercy and power, and the truth of Thy baptism, and the keys of the kingdom of heaven in Thy holy Church; so that we must not despair of

---

[48] Ps. ciii. 8   [49] Matt. v. 45   [50] Ezek. xxxiii. 11   [51] Wisd. xii. 2   [52] Rom. ii. 4-6
[53] Ezek. xviii. 21   [54] Ps. li. 17

men as long as by Thy patience they live on this earth, who even knowing how great an evil it is to think or to say such things about Thee, are detained in that malign profession on account of the use or the attainment of temporal or earthly convenience, if rebuked by Thy reproaches they in any way flee to Thy ineffable goodness, and prefer to all the enticements of the carnal life, the heavenly and eternal life.

ON THE SPIRIT AND THE LETTER

ON THE SPIRIT AND THE LETTER

Introductory Note

This treatise, the first in the present collection which represents Saint Augustine's share in the controversy against the Pelagians, was written in 412 A.D. Marcellinus, to whom it is addressed, was the Roman official who had been appointed by the emperor in the preceding year to preside over the great conference in Carthage between the Catholics and the Donatists. Saint Augustine had been extremely active in that conference and as a result became a friend of Marcellinus. As time passed, Marcellinus became absorbed in the questions raised by the writings of Pelagius and in Saint Augustine's answers to them. *On the Spirit and the Letter* is the reply to Marcellinus' puzzled query concerning the possibility of man's sinlessness in this life and the contrary assertion that no man ever was sinless, or ever would be. Saint Augustine does not stop with a simple answer to the question, but in effect writes a new treatise on the absolute need for the grace of God by man if he is in any sense to live well.

ON THE SPIRIT AND THE LETTER

ADDRESSED TO MARCELLINUS

Marcellinus, in a letter to Augustine, had expressed some surprise at having read, in the preceding work, of the possibility being allowed of a man continuing if he willed it, by God's help, without sin in the present life, although not a single human example anywhere of such perfect righteousness has ever existed. Augustine takes the opportunity of discussing, in opposition to the Pelagians, the subject of the aid of God's grace; and he shows that the divine help to the working of righteousness by us does not lie in the fact of God's having given us a law which is full of good and holy precepts; but in the fact that our will itself, without which we can do nothing good, is assisted and elevated by the spirit of grace being imparted to us, without the aid of which the teaching of the law is "the letter that killeth," because instead of justifying the ungodly, it rather holds them guilty of transgression. He begins to treat of the question proposed to him at the commencement of this work, and returns to it towards its conclusion; he shows that, as all allow, many things are possible with god's help, of which there occurs indeed no example; and then concludes that, although a perfect righteousness is unexampled among men, it is for all that not impossible.

CHAPTER I

THE OCCASION OF WRITING THIS WORK; A THING MAY BE CAPABLE OF BEING DONE, AND YET MAY NEVER BE DONE

AFTER reading the short treatises which I lately drew up for you, my beloved son Marcellinus, about the baptism of infants, and the perfection of man's righteousness—how that no one in this life seems either to have attained or to be likely to attain to it, except only the Mediator, who bore humanity in the likeness of sinful flesh, without any sin whatever—you wrote me in answer that you were embarrassed by the point which I advanced in the second book,[1] that it was possible for a man to be without sin, if he wanted not the will, and was assisted by the aid of God; and yet that except One in whom "all shall be made alive," [2] no one has ever lived or will live by whom this perfection has been attained while living here. It appeared to you absurd to say that anything was possible of which no example ever occurred—although I suppose you would not hesitate to admit that no camel ever passed through a needle's eye,[3] and yet He said that even this was possible with God; you may read, too, that twelve thousand legions[4] of angels could possibly have fought for Christ and rescued Him

---

[1] *On the Merits of Sins*, etc., ii. 6, 7, 20   [2] 1 Cor. xv. 22   [3] Matt. xix. 24, 26
[4] Matt. xxvi. 53, but observe the "thousand" inserted

from suffering, but in fact did not; you may read that it was possible for the nations to be exterminated at once out of the land which was given to the children of Israel,[5] and yet that God willed it to be gradually effected.[6] And one may meet with a thousand other incidents, the past or the future possibility of which we might readily admit, and yet be unable to produce any proofs of their having ever really happened. Accordingly, it would not be right for us to deny the possibility of a man's living without sin, on the ground that amongst men none can be found except Him who is in His nature not man only, but also God, in whom we could prove such perfection of character to have existed.

CHAPTER II

THE EXAMPLES APPOSITE

Here, perhaps, you will say to me in answer, that the things which I have instanced as not having been realized, although capable of realization, are *divine* works; whereas a man's being without sin falls in the range of a man's own work—that being indeed his very noblest work which effects a full and perfect righteousness complete in every part; and therefore that it is incredible that no man has ever existed, or is existing, or will exist in this life, who has achieved such a work, if the achievement is possible for a human being. But then you ought to reflect that, although this great work, no doubt, belongs to human agency to accomplish, yet it is also a divine gift, and therefore, not doubt that it is a divine work; "for it is God who worketh in you both to will and to do of His good pleasure." [7]

CHAPTER III

THEIRS IS COMPARATIVELY A HARMLESS ERROR, WHO SAY THAT A MAN LIVES HERE WITHOUT SIN

They therefore are not a very dangerous set of persons and they ought to be urged to show, if they are able, that they are themselves such, who hold that man lives or has lived here without any sin whatever. There are indeed passages of Scripture, in which I apprehend it is definitely stated that no man who lives on earth, although enjoying freedom of will, can be found without sin; as, for instance, the place where it is written, "Enter not into judgment with Thy servant, for in Thy sight shall no man living be justified." [8] If, however, anybody shall have succeeded in showing that this text and the other similar ones ought to be taken in a different sense from their obvious one, and shall have proved that some man or men have spent a sinless life on earth—whoever does not, not merely refrain from much opposing him, but also does not rejoice with him to the full, is afflicted

[5] Deut. xxxi. 3   [6] Judg. ii. 3   [7] Phil. ii. 13   [8] Ps. cxliii. 2

by extraordinary goads of envy. Moreover, if there neither is, has been, nor will be any man endowed with such perfection of purity (which I am more inclined to believe) and yet it is firmly set forth and thought there is or has been, or is to be—so far as I can judge, no great error is made, and certainly not a dangerous one, when a man is thus carried away by a certain benevolent feeling; provided that he who thinks so much of another, does not think himself to be such a being, unless he has ascertained that he really and clearly is such.

CHAPTER IV

THEIRS IS A MUCH MORE SERIOUS ERROR, REQUIRING A VERY VIGOROUS REFUTATION, WHO DENY GOD'S GRACE TO BE NECESSARY

They, however, must be resisted with the utmost ardor and vigor who suppose that without God's help, the mere power of the human will in itself, can either perfect righteousness, or advance steadily towards it; and when they begin to be hard pressed about their presumption in asserting that this result can be reached without the divine assistance, they check themselves, and do not venture to utter such an opinion, because they see how impious and insufferable it is. But they allege that such attainments are not made without God's help on this account, namely, because God both created man with the free choice of his will, and, by giving him commandments, teaches him, Himself, how man ought to live; and indeed assists him, in that He takes away his ignorance by instructing him in the knowledge of what he ought to avoid and to desire in his actions: and thus, by means of the free-will naturally implanted within him, he enters on the way which is pointed out to him, and by persevering in a just and pious course of life, deserves to attain to the blessedness of eternal life.

CHAPTER V

TRUE GRACE IS THE GIFT OF THE HOLY GHOST, WHICH KINDLES IN THE SOUL THE JOY AND LOVE OF GOODNESS

We, however, on our side affirm that the human will is so divinely aided in the pursuit of righteousness, that (in addition to man's being created with a free-will, and in addition to the teaching by which he is instructed how he ought to live) he receives the Holy Ghost, by whom there is formed in his mind a delight in, and a love of, that supreme and unchangeable good which is God, even now while he is still "walking by faith" and not yet "by sight;" [9] in order that by this gift to him of the earnest, as it were, of the free gift, he may conceive an ardent desire to cleave to his

[9] 2 Cor. v. 7

Maker, and may burn to enter upon the participation in that true light, that it may go well with him from Him to whom he owes his existence. A man's free-will, indeed, avails for nothing except to sin, if he knows not the way of truth; and even after his duty and his proper aim shall begin to become known to him, unless he also take delight in and feel a love for it, he neither does his duty, nor sets about it, nor lives rightly. Now, in order that such a course may engage our affections, God's "love is shed abroad in our hearts," not through the free-will which arises from ourselves, but "through the Holy Ghost, which is given to us." [10]

CHAPTER VI

THE TEACHING OF LAW WITHOUT THE LIFE-GIVING SPIRIT IS "THE LETTER THAT KILLETH"

For that teaching which brings to us the command to live in chastity and righteousness is "the letter that killeth," unless accompanied with "the spirit that giveth life." For that is not the sole meaning of the passage, "The letter killeth, but the spirit giveth life," [11] which merely prescribes that we should not take in the literal sense any figurative phrase which in the proper meaning of its words would produce only nonsense, but should consider what else it signifies, nourishing the inner man by our spiritual intelligence, since "being carnally-minded is death, while to be spiritually-minded is life and peace." [12] If, for instance, a man were to take in a literal and carnal sense much that is written in the Song of Solomon, he would minister not to the fruit of a luminous charity, but to the feeling of a libidinous desire. Therefore, the apostle is not to be confined to the limited application just mentioned, when he says, "The letter killeth, but the spirit giveth life;" [11] but this is also (and indeed especially) equivalent to what he says elsewhere in the plainest words: "I had not known lust, except the law had said, Thou shalt not covet;" [13] and again, immediately after: "Sin, taking occasion by the commandment, deceived me, and by it slew me." [14] Now from this you may see what is meant by "the letter that killeth." There is, of course, nothing said figuratively which is not to be accepted in its plain sense, when it is said, "Thou shalt not covet;" but this is a very plain and salutary precept, and any man who shall fulfil it will have no sin at all. The apostle, indeed, purposely selected this general precept, in which he embraced everything, as if this were the voice of the law, prohibiting us from all sin, when he says, "Thou shalt not covet;" for there is no sin committed except by evil concupiscence; so that the law which prohibits this is a good and praiseworthy law. But, when the Holy Ghost withholds His help, which inspires us with a good desire instead of this evil desire (in other words, diffuses love in our hearts) that law, however good

[10] Rom. v. 5   [11] 2 Cor. iii. 6   [12] Rom. viii. 6   [13] Rom. vii. 7   [14] Rom. vii. 11

in itself, only augments the evil desire by forbidding it. Just as the rush of water which flows incessantly in a particular direction, becomes more violent when it meets with any impediment, and when it has overcome the stoppage, falls in a greater bulk, and with increased impetuosity hurries forward in its downward course. In some strange way the very object which we covet becomes all the more pleasant when it is forbidden. And this is the sin which by the commandment deceives and by it slays, whenever transgression is actually added, which occurs not where there is no law.[15]

CHAPTER VII

WHAT IS PROPOSED TO BE HERE TREATED

We will, however, consider, if you please, the whole of this passage of the apostle and thoroughly handle it, as the Lord shall enable us. For I want, if possible, to prove that the apostle's words, "The letter killeth, but the spirit giveth life," do not refer to figurative phrases—although even in this sense a suitable signification might be obtained from them—but rather plainly to the law, which forbids whatever is evil. When I shall have proved this, it will more manifestly appear that to lead a holy life is the gift of God—not only because God has given a free-will to man, without which there is no living ill or well; nor only because He has given him a commandment to teach him how he ought to live; but because through the Holy Ghosts He sheds love abroad in the hearts[13] of those whom he foreknew, in order to predestinate them; whom He predestinated, that He might call them; whom He called, that he might justify them; and whom he justified, that He might glorify them.[16] When this point also shall be cleared, you will, I think, see how vain it is to say that those things only are unexampled possibilities, which are the works of God—such as the passage of the camel through the needle's eye, which we have already referred to, and other similar cases, which to us no doubt are impossible, but easy enough to God; and that man's righteousness is not to be counted in this class of things, on the ground of its being properly man's work, not God's; although there is no reason for supposing, without an example, that his perfection exists, even if it is possible. That these assertions are vain will be clear enough, after it has been also plainly shown that even man's righteousness must be attributed to the operation of God, although not taking place without man's will; and we therefore cannot deny that his perfection is possible even in this life, because all things are possible with God [17]—both those which He accomplishes of His own sole will, and those which He appoints to be done with the co-operation with Himself of His creature's will. Accordingly, whatever of such things He does not effect is no doubt without an example in the way of accomplished facts, although with God it possesses

---

[15] Rom. iv. 15   [16] Rom. viii. 29, 30   [17] Mark x. 27

both in His power the cause of its possibility, and in His wisdom the reason of its unreality. And should this cause be hidden from man, let him not forget that he is a man; nor charge God with folly simply because he cannot fully comprehend His wisdom.

CHAPTER VIII

ROMANS INTERPRETS CORINTHIANS

Attend, then, carefully, to the apostle while in his *Epistle to the Romans* he explains and clearly enough shows that what he wrote to the Corinthians, "The letter killeth, but the spirit giveth life," [18] must be understood in the sense which we have already indicated—that the letter of the law, which teaches us not to commit sin, kills, if the life-giving spirit be absent, forasmuch as it causes sin to be known rather than avoided, and therefore to be increased rather than diminished, because to an evil concupiscence there is now added the transgression of the law.

CHAPTER IX

THROUGH THE LAW SIN HAS ABOUNDED

The apostle, then, wishing to commend the grace which has come to all nations through Jesus Christ, lest the Jews should extol themselves at the expense of the other peoples on account of their having received the law, first says that sin and death came on the human race through one man, and that righteousness and eternal life came also through one, expressly mentioning Adam as the former, and Christ as the latter; and then says that "the law, however, entered, that the offence might abound: but where sin abounded, grace did much more abound: that as sin hath reigned unto death, even so might grace reign through righteousness unto eternal life by Jesus Christ our Lord." [19] Then, proposing a question for himself to answer, he adds, "What shall we say then? Shall we continue in sin, that grace may abound? God forbid." [20] He saw, indeed, that a perverse use might be made by perverse men of what he had said: "The law entered, that the offence might abound: but where sin abounded, grace did much more abound"—as if he had said that sin had been of advantage by reason of the abundance of grace. Rejecting this, he answers his question with a "God forbid!" and at once adds: "How shall we, that are dead to sin, live any longer therein?" [21] as much as to say, When grace has brought it to pass that we should die unto sin, what else shall we be doing, if we continue to live in it, than showing ourselves ungrateful to grace? The man who extols the virtue of a medicine does not contend that the diseases and wounds of which the medicine cures him are of advantage to him; on the contrary,

[18] 2 Cor. iii. 6   [19] Rom. v. 20, 21   [20] Rom. vi. 1, 2   [21] Rom. vi. 2

in proportion to the praise lavished on the remedy are the blame and horror which are felt of the diseases and wounds healed by the much-extolled medicine. In like manner, the commendation and praise of grace are vituperation and condemnation of offences. For there was need to prove to man how corruptly weak he was, so that against his iniquity, the holy law brought him no help towards good, but rather increased than diminished his iniquity; seeing that the law entered, that the offence might abound; that being thus convicted and confounded, he might see not only that he needed a physician, but also God as his helper so to direct his steps that sin should not rule over him, and he might be healed by betaking himself to the help of the divine mercy; and in this way, where sin abounded grace might much more abound—not through the merit of the sinner, but by the intervention of his Helper.

CHAPTER X

CHRIST THE TRUE HEALER

Accordingly, the apostle shows that the same medicine was mystically set forth in the passion and resurrection of Christ, when he says, "Know ye not, that so many of us as were baptized into Jesus Christ were baptized into His death? Therefore we were buried with Him by baptism into death; that like as Christ was raised up from the dead by the glory of the Father, even so we also should walk in newness of life. For if we have been planted together in the likeness of His death, we shall be also in the likeness of His resurrection: knowing this, that our old man is crucified with Him, that the body of sin might be destroyed, that henceforth we should not serve sin. For he that is dead is justified from sin. Now, if we be dead with Christ, we believe that we shall also live with Him: knowing that Christ, being raised from the dead, dieth no more; death hath no more dominion over Him. For in that He died, He died unto sin once; but in that He liveth, He liveth unto God. Likewise reckon ye also yourselves to be dead indeed unto sin, but alive unto God through Jesus Christ our Lord." [22] Now it is plain enough that here by the mystery of the Lord's death and resurrection is figured the death of our old sinful life, and the rising of the new; and that here is shown forth the abolition of iniquity and the renewal of righteousness. Whence then arises this vast benefit to man through the letter of the law, except it be through the faith of Jesus Christ?

CHAPTER XI

FROM WHAT FOUNTAIN GOOD WORKS FLOW

This holy meditation preserves "the children of men, who put their trust under the shadow of God's wings," [23] so that they are "drunken with the

[22] Rom. vi. 3-11   [23] Ps. xxxvi. 7

fatness of His house, and drink of the full stream of His pleasure. For with Him is the fountain of life, and in His light shall they see light. For He extendeth His mercy to them that know Him, and His righteousness to the upright in heart." [24] He does not, indeed, extend His mercy to them because they know Him, but that they may know Him; nor is it because they are upright in heart, but that they may become so, that He extends to them His righteousness, whereby He justifies the ungodly.[25] This meditation does not elevate with pride: this sin arises when any man has too much confidence in himself, and makes himself the chief end of living. Impelled by this vain feeling, he departs from that fountain of life, from the draughts of which alone is imbibed the holiness which is itself the good life—and from that unchanging light, by sharing in which the reasonable soul is in a certain sense inflamed, and becomes itself a created and reflected luminary; even as "John was a burning and a shining light," [26] who notwithstanding acknowledged the source of his own illumination in the words, "Of His fulness have all we received." [27] Whose, I would ask, but His, of course, in comparison with whom John indeed was no light at all? For "that was the true light, which lighteth every man that cometh into the world." [28] Therefore, in the same psalm, after saying, "Extend Thy mercy to them that know Thee, and Thy righteousness to the upright in heart," [29] he adds, "Let not the foot of pride come against me, and let not the hands of sinners move me. There have fallen all the workers of iniquity: they are cast out, and are not able to stand." [30] Since by that impiety which leads each to attribute to himself the excellence which is God's, he is cast out into his own native darkness, in which consist the works of iniquity. For it is manifestly these works which he does, and for the achievement of such alone is he naturally fit. The works of righteousness he never does, except as he receives ability from that fountain and that light, where the life is that wants for nothing, and where is "no variableness, nor the shadow of turning." [31]

CHAPTER XII

PAUL, WHENCE SO CALLED; BRAVELY CONTENDS FOR GRACE

Accordingly Paul, who, although he was formerly called Saul,[32] chose this new designation, for no other reason, as it seems to me, than because he would show himself *little*[33]—the "least of the apostles" [34]—contends with much courage and earnestness against the proud and arrogant, and such as plume themselves on their own works, in order that he may commend the grace of God. This grace, indeed, appeared more obvious and manifest in his case, inasmuch as, while he was pursuing such vehement measures of persecution against the Church of God as made him worthy of

---

[24] Ps. xxxvi. 8-10   [25] Rom. iv. 5   [26] John v. 35   [27] John i. 16   [28] John i. 9
[29] Ps. xxxvi. 10   [30] Ps. xxxvi. 11, 12   [31] Jas. i. 17   [32] Acts xiii. 9   [33] See *Confessions*, viii. 4   [34] 1 Cor. xv. 9

the greatest punishment, he found mercy instead of condemnation, and instead of punishment obtained grace. Very properly, therefore, does he lift voice and hand in defence of grace, and care not for the envy either of those who understood not a subject too profound and abstruse for them, or of those who perversely misinterpreted his own sound words; while at the same time he unfalteringly preaches that gift of God, whereby alone salvation accrues to those who are the children of the promise, children of the divine goodness, children of grace and mercy, children of the new covenant. In the salutation with which he begins every epistle, he prays: "Grace be to you, and peace, from God the Father, and from the Lord Jesus Christ;" [35] while this forms almost the only topic discussed for the Romans, and it is plied with so much persistence and variety of argument, as fairly to fatigue the reader's attention, yet with a fatigue so useful and salutary, that it rather exercises than breaks the faculties of the inner man.

CHAPTER XIII

KEEPING THE LAW; THE JEWS' GLORYING; THE FEAR OF PUNISHMENT; THE CIRCUMCISION OF THE HEART

Then comes what I mentioned above; then he shows what the Jew is, and says that he is called a Jew, but by no means fulfils what he promises to do. "But if," says he, "thou callest thyself a Jew, and restest in the law, and makest thy boast of God, and knowest His will, and triest the things that are different, being instructed out of the law; and art confident that thou art thyself a guide of the blind, a light of them that are in darkness, an instructor of the foolish, a teacher of babes, which hast the form of knowledge and of the truth in the law. Thou therefore who teachest another, teachest thou not thyself? thou that preachest a man should not steal, dost thou steal? thou that sayest a man should not commit adultery, dost thou commit adultery? thou that abhorrest idols, dost thou commit sacrilege? thou that makest thy boast of the law, through breaking the law dishonorest thou God? For the name of God is blasphemed among the Gentiles through you, as it is written. Circumcision verily profiteth, if thou keep the law; but if thou be a breaker of the law, thy circumcision is made uncircumcision. Therefore, if the uncircumcision keep the righteousness of the law, shall not his uncircumcision be counted for circumcision? And shall not uncircumcision which is by nature, if it fulfil the law, judge thee, who by the letter and circumcision dost transgress the law? For he is not a Jew who is one outwardly; neither is that circumcision which is outward in the flesh: but he is a Jew who is one inwardly; and circumcision is that of the heart, in the spirit, and not in the letter; whose praise is not of men, but of God." [36] Here he plainly showed in what sense he said, "Thou makest thy

[35] See Rom. i. 7, 1 Cor. i. 3, and Gal. i. 3   [36] Rom. ii. 17-29

boast of God." For undoubtedly if one who was truly a Jew made his boast of God in the way which grace demands (which is bestowed not for merit of works, but gratuitously) then his praise would be of God, and not of men. But they, in fact, were making their boast of God, as if they alone had deserved to receive His law, as the Psalmist said: "He did not the like to any nation, nor His judgments has He displayed to them." [37] And yet, they thought they were fulfilling the law of God by their righteousness, when they were rather breakers of it all the while! Accordingly, it "wrought wrath" [38] upon them, and sin abounded, committed as it was by them who knew the law. For whoever did even what the law commanded, without the assistance of the Spirit of grace, acted through fear of punishment, not from love of righteousness, and hence in the sight of God that was not in the will, which in the sight of men appeared in the work; and such doers of the law were held rather guilty of that which God knew they would have preferred to commit, if only it had been possible with impunity. He calls, however, "the circumcision of the heart" the will that is pure from all unlawful desire; which comes not from the *letter,* inculcating and threatening, but from the *Spirit,* assisting and healing. Such doers of the law have their praise therefore, not of men but of God, who by His grace provides the grounds on which they receive praise, of whom it is said, "My soul shall make her boast of the Lord;" [39] and to whom it is said, "My praise shall be of Thee;" [40] but those are not such who would have God praised because they are men; but themselves, because they are righteous.

CHAPTER XIV

IN WHAT RESPECT THE PELAGIANS ACKNOWLEDGE GOD AS THE AUTHOR OF OUR JUSTIFICATION

"But," say they, "we do praise God as the Author of our righteousness, in that He gave the law, by the teaching of which we have learned how we ought to live." But they give no heed to what they read: "By the law there shall no flesh be justified in the sight of God." [41] This may indeed be possible before men, but not before Him who looks into our very heart and inmost will, where He sees that, although the man who fears the law keeps a certain precept, he would nevertheless rather do another thing if he were permitted. And lest any one should suppose that, in the passage just quoted from him, the apostle had meant to say that none are justified by that law, which contains many precepts, under the figure of the ancient sacraments, and among them that circumcision of the flesh itself, which infants were commanded to receive on the eighth day after birth; he immediately adds what law he meant, and says, "For by the law is the knowledge of sin." [41] He refers then to that law of which he afterwards declares, "I had not

---

[37] Ps. cxlvii. 20　　[38] Rom. iv. 15　　[39] Ps. xxxiv. 2　　[40] Ps. xxii. 25　　[41] Rom. iii. 20

known sin but by the law; for I had not known lust except the law had said, Thou shalt not covet." [42] For what means this but that "by the law comes the knowledge of sin?"

CHAPTER XV

THE RIGHTEOUSNESS OF GOD MANIFESTED BY THE LAW
AND THE PROPHETS

Here, perhaps, it may be said by that presumption of man, which is ignorant of the righteousness of God, and wishes to establish one of its own, that the apostle quite properly said, "For by the law shall no man be justified," [41] inasmuch as the law merely shows what one ought to do, and what one ought to guard against, in order that what the law thus points out may be accomplished by the will, and so man be justified, not indeed by the power of the law, but by his free determination. But I ask your attention, O man, to what follows. "But now the righteousness of God," says he, "without the law is manifested, being witnessed by the law and the prophets." [43] Does this then sound a light thing in deaf ears? He says, "The righteousness of God is manifested." Now this righteousness they are ignorant of, who wish to establish one of their own; they will not submit themselves to it.[44] His words are, *"The righteousness of God* is manifested:" he does not say, the righteousness of man, or the righteousness of his own will, but the "righteousness *of God"*—not that whereby He is Himself righteous, but that with which He endows man when He justifies the ungodly. This is witnessed by the law and the prophets; in other words, the law and the prophets each afford it testimony. The law, indeed, by issuing its commands and threats, and by justifying no man, sufficiently shows that it is by God's gift, through the help of the Spirit, that a man is justified; and the prophets, because it was what they predicted that Christ at His coming accomplished. Accordingly he advances a step further, and adds, "But righteousness of God by faith of Jesus Christ," [45] that is, by the faith wherewith one believes in Christ; for just as there is not meant the faith with which Christ Himself believes, so also there is not meant the righteousness whereby God is Himself righteous. Both no doubt are ours, but yet they are called God's, and Christ's, because it is by their bounty that these gifts are bestowed upon us. The righteousness of God then is without the law, but not manifested without the law; for if it were manifested without the law, how could it be witnessed by the law? That righteousness of God, however, is without the law, which God by the Spirit of grace bestows on the believer without the help of the law—that is, when not helped by the law. When, indeed, He by the law discovers to a man his weakness, it is in order that by faith he may flee for refuge to His mercy, and be healed. And thus con-

[42] Rom. vii. 7   [43] Rom. iii. 21   [44] Rom. x. 3   [45] Rom. iii. 22

cerning His wisdom we are told, that "she carries law and mercy upon her tongue" [46]—the *"law,"* whereby she may convict the proud, the *"mercy,"* wherewith she may justify the humbled. "The righteousness of God," then, "by faith of Jesus Christ, is unto all that believe; for there is no difference, for all have sinned, and come short of the glory of God" [47]—not of their own glory. For what have they, which they have not received? Now if they received it, why do they glory as if they had not received it? [48] Well, then, they come short of the glory of God; now observe what follows: "Being justified freely by His grace." [49] It is not, therefore, by the law, nor is it by their own will, that they are justified; but they are justified *freely by His grace*—not that it is wrought without our will; but our will is by the law shown to be weak, that grace may heal its infirmity; and that our healed will may fulfill the law, not by compact under the law, nor yet in the absence of law.

CHAPTER XVI

HOW THE LAW WAS NOT MADE FOR A RIGHTEOUS MAN

Because "for a righteous man the law was not made;" [50] and yet "the law is good, if a man use it lawfully." [51] Now by connecting together these two seemingly contrary statements, the apostle warns and urges his reader to sift the question and solve it too. For how can it be that "the law is good, if a man use it lawfully," if what follows is also true: "Knowing this, that the law is not made for a righteous man?" [51] For who but a righteous man lawfully uses the law? Yet it is not for him that it is made, but for the unrighteous. Must then the unrighteous man, in order that he may be justified—that is, become a righteous man—lawfully use the law, to lead him, as by the schoolmaster's hand,[52] to that grace by which alone he can fulfil what the law commands? Now it is freely that he is justified thereby —that is, on account of no antecedent merits of his own works; "otherwise grace is no more grace," [53] since it is bestowed on us, not because we have done good works, but that we may be able to do them—in other words, not because we have fulfilled the law, but in order that we may be able to fulfil the law. Now He said, "I am not come to destroy the law, but to fulfil it," [54] of whom it was said, "We have seen His glory, the glory as of the only-begotten of the Father, full of grace and truth." [55] This is the glory which is meant in the words, "All have sinned, and come short of the glory of God;" [56] and this the grace of which he speaks in the next verse, "Being justified freely by His grace." [49] The unrighteous man therefore lawfully uses the law, that he may become righteous; but when he has become so, he must no longer use it as a chariot, for he has arrived at his journey's

[46] Prov. iii. 16   [47] Rom. iii. 22, 23   [48] 1 Cor. iv. 7   [49] Rom. iii. 24   [50] 1 Tim. i. 8   [51] 1 Tim. i. 9   [52] Gal. iii. 24   [53] Rom. xi. 6   [54] Matt. v. 17   [55] John i. 14   [56] Rom. iii. 23

end—or rather (that I may employ the apostle's own simile, which has been already mentioned) as a schoolmaster, seeing that he is now fully learned. How then is the law not made for a righteous man, if it is necessary for the righteous man too, not that he may be brought as an unrighteous man to the grace that justifies, but that he may use it lawfully, now that he is righteous? Does not the case perhaps stand thus—nay, not *perhaps*, but rather *certainly*—that the man who is become righteous thus lawfully uses the law, when he applies it to alarm the unrighteous, so that whenever the disease of some unusual desire begins in them, too, to be augmented by the incentive of the law's prohibition and an increased amount of transgression, they may in faith flee for refuge to the grace that justifies, and becoming delighted with the sweet pleasures of holiness, may escape the penalty of the law's menacing letter through the spirit's soothing gift? In this way the two statements will not be contrary, nor will they be repugnant to each other: even the righteous man may lawfully use a good law, and yet the law be not made for the righteous man; for it is not by the law that he becomes righteous, but by the law of faith, which led him to believe that no other resource was possible to his weakness for fulfilling the precepts which "the law of works" [57] commanded, except to be assisted by the grace of God.

CHAPTER XVII

THE EXCLUSION OF BOASTING

Accordingly he says, "Where is boasting then? It is excluded. By what law? of works? Nay; but by the law of faith." [57] He may either mean, the laudable boasting, which is in the Lord; and that it is *excluded,* not in the sense that it is driven off so as to pass away, but that it is clearly manifested so as to stand out prominently. Whence certain artificers in silver are called *"exclusores."* In this sense it occurs also in that passage in the *Psalms:* "That they may be *excluded,* who have been proved with silver" [58] —that is, that they may stand out in prominence, who have been tried by the word of God. For in another passage it is said: "The words of the Lord are pure words, as silver which is tried in the fire." [59] Or if this be not his meaning, he must have wished to mention that vicious boasting which comes of pride—that is, of those who appear to themselves to lead righteous lives, and boast of their excellence as if they had not received it— and further to inform us, that by the law of faith, not by the law of works, this boasting was *excluded,* in the other sense of shut out and driven away; because by the law of faith every one learns that whatever good life he leads he has from the grace of God, and that from no other source whatever can he obtain the means of becoming perfect in the love of righteousness.

[57] Rom. iii. 27   [58] Ps. lxviii. 30   [59] Ps. xii. 6

CHAPTER XVIII

PIETY IS WISDOM; THAT IS CALLED THE RIGHTEOUSNESS
OF GOD, WHICH HE PRODUCES

Now, this meditation makes a man godly, and this godliness is true wisdom. By godliness I mean that which the Greeks designate θεοσέβεια—that very virtue which is commended to man in the passage of Job, where it is said to him, "Behold, godliness is wisdom." [60] Now if the word θεοσέβεια be interpreted according to its derivation, it might be called *"the worship of God;"* and in this worship the essential point is, that the soul be not ungrateful to Him. Whence it is that in the most true and excellent sacrifice we are admonished to "give thanks unto our Lord God." Ungrateful, however, our soul would be, were it to attribute to itself that which it received from God, especially the righteousness, with the works of which (the especial property, as it were, of itself, and produced, so to speak, by the soul itself for itself) it is not puffed up in a vulgar pride, as it might be with riches, or beauty of limb, or eloquence, or those other accomplishments, external or internal, bodily or mental, which wicked men too are in the habit of possessing, but, if I may say so, in a wise complacency, as of things which constitute in an especial manner the good works of the good. It is owing to this sin of vulgar pride that even some great men have drifted from the sure anchorage of the divine nature, and have floated down into the shame of idolatry. Whence the apostle again in the same epistle, wherein he so firmly maintains the principle of grace, after saying that he was a debtor both to the Greeks and to the Barbarians, to the wise and to the unwise, and professing himself ready, so far as to him pertained, to preach the gospel even to those who lived in Rome, adds: "I am not ashamed of the Gospel of Christ: for it is the power of God unto salvation to every one that believeth; to the Jew first, and also to the Greek. For therein is the righteousness of God revealed from faith to faith: as it is written, The just shall live by faith." [61] This is the righteousness of God, which was veiled in the Old Testament, and is revealed in the New; and it is called *the righteousness of God,* because by His bestowal of it He makes us righteous, just as we read that "salvation is the Lord's," [62] because He makes us safe. And this is the faith "from which" and "to which" it is revealed— *from the faith* of them who preach it, *to the faith* of those who obey it. By this faith of Jesus Christ—that is, the faith which Christ has given to us— we believe it is from God that we now have, and shall have more and more, the ability of living righteously; wherefore we give Him thanks with that dutiful worship with which He only is to be worshipped.

[60] Job xxviii. 28   [61] Rom. i. 14-17   [62] Ps. iii. 8

CHAPTER XIX

THE KNOWLEDGE OF GOD THROUGH THE CREATION

And then the apostle very properly turns from this point to describe with detestation those men who, light-minded and puffed up by the sin which I have mentioned in the preceding chapter, have been carried away of their own conceit, as it were, through empty space where they could find no resting-place, only to fall shattered to pieces against the vain figments of their idols, as against stones. For, after he had commended the piety of that faith, whereby, being justified, we must needs be pleasing to God, he proceeds to call our attention to what we ought to abominate as the opposite. "For the wrath of God," says he, "is revealed from heaven against all ungodliness and unrighteousness of men, who hold down the truth in unrighteousness; because that which may be known of God is manifest in them: for God hath showed it unto them. For the invisible things of Him are clearly seen from the creation of the world, being understood through the things that are made, even His eternal power and divinity; so that they are without excuse: because, knowing God, they yet glorified Him not as God, neither were thankful; but became vain in their imaginations, and their foolish heart was darkened. Professing themselves to be wise, they became fools; and they changed the glory of the uncorruptible God into an image made like to corruptible man, and to birds, and to four footed beasts, and to creeping things." [63] Observe, he does not say that they were ignorant of the truth, but that they held down the truth in unrighteousness. For it occurred to him, that he would inquire whence the knowledge of the truth could be obtained by those to whom God had not given the law; and he was not silent on the source whence they could have obtained it: for he declares that it was through the visible works of creation that they arrived at the knowledge of the invisible attributes of the Creator. And, in very deed, as they continued to possess great faculties for searching, so they were able to find. Wherein then lay their impiety? Because "when they knew God, they glorified Him not as God, nor gave Him thanks, but became vain in their imaginations." Vanity is a disease especially of those who mislead themselves, and "think themselves to be something, when they are nothing." [64] Such men, indeed, darken themselves in that swelling pride, the foot of which the holy singer prays that it may not come against him,[65] after saying, "In Thy light shall we see light;" [66] from which very light of unchanging truth they turn aside, and "their foolish heart is darkened." [67] For theirs was not a wise heart, even though they knew God; but it was foolish rather, because they did not glorify Him as God, or give Him thanks; for "He said unto man, Behold, the fear of the Lord, that is wis-

---

[63] Rom. i. 18-23   [64] Gal. vi. 3   [65] Ps. xxxvi. 11   [66] Ps. xxxvi. 9   [67] Rom. i. 21

dom." [68] So by this conduct, while "professing themselves to be wise" (which can only be understood to mean that they attributed this to themselves), "they became fools." [69]

CHAPTER XX

THE LAW WITHOUT GRACE

Now why need I speak of what follows? For why it was that by this their impiety those men—I mean those who could have known the Creator through the creature—fell (since "God resisteth the proud" [70]) and whither they plunged, is better shown in the sequel of this epistle than we can here mention. For in this letter of mine we have not undertaken to expound this epistle, but only mainly on its authority, to demonstrate, so far as we are able, that we are assisted by divine aid towards the achievement of righteousness—not merely because God has given us a law full of good and holy precepts, but because our very will, without which we cannot do any good thing, is assisted and elevated by the importation of the Spirit of grace, without which help mere teaching is "the letter that killeth," [71] forasmuch as it rather holds them guilty of transgression, than justifies the ungodly. Now just as those who come to know the Creator through the creature received no benefit towards salvation, from their knowledge—because "though they knew God, they glorified Him not as God, nor gave Him thanks, although professing themselves to be wise" [67]—so also they who know from the law how man ought to live, are not made righteous by their knowledge, because, "going about to establish their own righteousness, they have not submitted themselves unto the righteousness of God." [72]

CHAPTER XXI

THE LAW OF WORKS AND THE LAW OF FAITH

The law, then, of deeds, that is, the law of works, whereby this boasting is not excluded, and the law of faith, by which it is excluded, differ from each other; and this difference it is worth our while to consider, if so be we are able to observe and discern it. Hastily, indeed, one might say that the law of works lay in Judaism, and the law of faith in Christianity; forasmuch as circumcision and the other works prescribed by the law are just those which the Christian system no longer retains. But there is a fallacy in this distinction, the greatness of which I have for some time been endeavoring to expose; and to such as are acute in appreciating distinctions, especially to yourself and those like you, I have possibly succeeded in my effort. Since, however, the subject is an important one, it will not be unsuitable, if with a view to its illustration, we linger over the many testi-

---

[68] Job. xxviii. 28   [69] Rom. i. 22   [70] Jas. iv. 6   [71] 2 Cor. iii. 6   [72] Rom. x. 3

monies which again and again meet our view. Now, the apostle says that
that law by which no man is justified,[73] entered in that the offence might
abound,[74] and yet in order to save it from the aspersions of the ignorant
and the accusations of the impious, he defends this very law in such words
as these: "What shall we say then? Is the law sin? God forbid. Nay, I had
not known sin but by the law: for I had not known concupiscence, except
the law had said, Thou shalt not covet. But sin, taking occasion, wrought,
by the commandment, in me all manner of concupiscence." [75] He says also:
"The law indeed is holy, and the commandment is holy, and just, and good;
but sin, that it might appear sin, worked death in me by that which is
good." [76] It is therefore the very letter that kills which says, "Thou shalt
not covet," and it is of this that he speaks in a passage which I have before
referred to: "By the law is the knowledge of sin. But now the righteousness
of God without the law is manifested, being witnessed by the law and the
prophets; even the righteousness of God, which is by faith of Jesus Christ
upon all them that believe; for there is no difference: seeing that all have
sinned, and come short of the glory of God: being justified freely by His
grace, through the redemption that is in Christ Jesus; whom God hath set
forth to be a propitiation through faith in His blood, to declare His righteousness for the remission of sins that are past, through the forbearance of
God; to declare His righteousness at this time; that He might be just, and
the justifier of him which believeth in Jesus." [77] And then he adds the
passage which is now under consideration: "Where, then, is your boasting?
It is excluded. By what law? of works? Nay; but by the law of faith." [78]
And so it is the very law of works itself which says, "Thou shalt not covet;"
because thereby comes the knowledge of sin. Now I wish to know, if anybody will dare to tell me, whether the law of faith does not say to us, "Thou
shalt not covet"? For if it does not say so to us, what reason is there why
we, who are placed under it, should not sin in safety and with impunity?
Indeed, this is just what those people thought the apostle meant, of whom
he writes: "Even as some affirm that we say, Let us do evil, that good may
come; whose damnation is just." [79] If, on the contrary, it too says to us,
"Thou shalt not covet" (even as numerous passages in the gospels and
epistles so often testify and urge), then why is not this law also called the
law of works? For it by no means follows that, because it retains not the
"works" of the ancient sacraments—even circumcision and the other ceremonies—it therefore has no "works" in its own sacraments, which are
adapted to the present age; unless, indeed, the question was about sacramental works, when mention was made of the law, just because by it is
the knowledge of sin, and therefore nobody is justified by it, so that it is
not by it that boasting is excluded, but by the law of faith, whereby the
just man lives. But is there not by it too the knowledge of sin, when even it
says, "Thou shalt not covet?"

[73] Rom. iii. 20   [74] Rom. v. 20   [75] Rom. vii. 7, 8   [76] Rom. vii. 12, 13   [77] Rom.
iii. 20-26   [78] Rom. iii. 27   [79] Rom. iii. 8

CHAPTER XXII

NO MAN JUSTIFIED BY WORKS

What the difference between them is, I will briefly explain. What the law of works enjoins by menace, that the law of faith secures by faith. The one says, "Thou shalt not covet;" [80] the other says, "When I perceived that nobody could be continent, except God gave it to him; and that this was the very point of wisdom, to know whose gift she was; I approached unto the Lord, and I besought Him." [81] This indeed is the very wisdom which is called *piety,* in which is worshipped "the Father of lights, from whom is every best giving and perfect gift." [82] This worship, however, consists in the sacrifice of praise and giving of thanks, so that the worshipper of God boasts not in himself, but in Him." [83] Accordingly, by the law of works, God says to us, Do what I command thee; but by the law of faith we say to God, Give me what Thou commandest. Now this is the reason why the law gives its command—to admonish us what faith ought to do, that is, that he to whom the command is given, if he is as yet unable to perform it, may know what to ask for; but if he has at once the ability, and complies with the command, he ought also to be aware from whose gift the ability comes. "For we have received not the spirit of this world," says again that most constant preacher of grace, "but the Spirit which is of God, that we might know the things that are freely given to us of God." [84] What, however, "is the spirit of this world," but the spirit of pride? By it their foolish heart is darkened, who, although knowing God, glorified Him not as God, by giving Him thanks.[85] Moreover, it is really by this same spirit that they too are deceived, who, while ignorant of the righteousness of God, and wishing to establish their own righteousness, have not submitted to God's righteousness.[86] It appears to me, therefore, that he is much more "a child of faith" who has learned from what source to hope for what he has not yet, than he who attributes to himself whatever he has; although, no doubt, to both of these must be preferred the man who both has, and at the same time knows from whom he has it, if nevertheless he does not believe himself to be what he has not yet attained to. Let him not fall into the mistake of the Pharisee, who, while thanking God for what he possessed, yet failed to ask for any further gift, just as if he stood in want of nothing for the increase or perfection of his righteousness.[87] Now, having duly considered and weighed all these circumstances and testimonies, we conclude that a man is not justified by the precepts of a holy life, but by faith in Jesus Christ—in a word, not by the law of works, but by the law of faith; not by the letter, but by the spirit; not by the merits of deeds, but by free grace.

[80] Ex. xx. 17   [81] Wisd. viii. 21   [82] Jas. i. 17   [83] 2 Cor. x. 17   [84] 1 Cor. ii. 12
[85] Rom. i. 21   [86] Rom. x. 3   [87] Luke xviii. 11, 12

CHAPTER XXIII

HOW THE DECALOGUE KILLS, IF GRACE BE NOT PRESENT

Although, therefore, the apostle seems to reprove and correct those who were being persuaded to be circumcised, in such terms as to designate by the word *"law"* circumcision itself and other similar legal observances, which are now rejected as shadows of a future substance by Christians who yet hold what those shadows figuratively promised; he at the same time nevertheless would have it to be clearly understood that the law, by which he says no man is justified, lies not merely in those sacramental institutions which contained promissory figures, but also in those works by which whosoever has done them lives holily, and amongst which occurs this prohibition: "Thou shalt not covet." Now, to make our statement all the clearer, let us look at the Decalogue itself. It is certain, then, that Moses on the mount received the law, that he might deliver it to the people, written on tables of stone by the finger of God. It is summed up in these ten commandments, in which there is no precept about circumcision, nor anything concerning those animal sacrifices which have ceased to be offered by Christians. Well, now, I should like to be told what there is in these ten commandments, except the observance of the Sabbath, which ought not to be kept by a Christian—whether it prohibit the making and worshipping of idols and of any other gods than the one true God, or the taking of God's name in vain; or prescribe honor to parents; or give warning against fornication, murder, theft, false witness, adultery, or coveting other men's property? Which of these commandments would any one say that the Christian ought not to keep? Is it possible to contend that it is not the law which was written on those two tables that the apostle describes as "the letter that killeth," but the law of circumcision and the other sacred rites which are now abolished? But then how can we think so, when in the law occurs this precept, "Thou shalt not covet," by which very commandment, notwithstanding its being holy, just, and good, "sin," says the apostle, "deceived me, and by it slew me?" [88] What else can this be than "the letter" that "killeth"?

CHAPTER XXIV

THE PASSAGE IN CORINTHIANS

In the passage where he speaks to the Corinthians about the letter that kills, and the spirit that gives life, he expresses himself more clearly, but he does not mean even there any other "letter" to be understood than the Decalogue itself, which was written on the two tables. For these are His

[88] See Rom. vii. 7-12

words: "Forasmuch as ye are manifestly declared to be the epistle of Christ ministered by us, written not with ink, but with the Spirit of the living God; not in tables of stone, but in fleshy tables of the heart. And such trust have we through Christ to God-ward: not that we are sufficient of ourselves to think anything as of ourselves; but our sufficiency is of God; who hath made us fit, as ministers of the New Testament; not of the letter, but of the spirit: for the letter killeth, but the spirit giveth life. But if the ministration of death, written and engraven in stones, was glorious, so that the children of Israel could not stedfastly behold the face of Moses for the glory of his countenance, which was to be done away; how shall not the ministration of the Spirit be rather glorious? For if the ministration of condemnation be glory, much more shall the ministration of righteousness abound in glory." [89] A good deal might be said about these words; but perhaps we shall have a more fitting opportunity at some future time. At present, however, I beg you to observe how he speaks of the letter that killeth, and contrasts therewith the spirit that giveth life. Now this must certainly be "the ministration of death written and engraven in stones," and "the ministration of condemnation," since the law entered that sin might abound. [90] But the commandments themselves are so useful and salutary to the doer of them, that no one could have life unless he kept them. Well, then, is it owing to the one precept about the Sabbath-day, which is included in it, that the Decalogue is called "the letter that killeth?" Because, forsooth, every man that still observes that day in its literal appointment is carnally wise, but to be carnally wise is nothing else than death? And must the other nine commandments, which are rightly observed in their literal form, not be regarded as belonging to the law of works by which none is justified, but to the law of faith whereby the just man lives? Who can possibly entertain so absurd an opinion as to suppose that "the ministration of death, written and engraven in stones," is not said equally of all the ten commandments, but only of the solitary one touching the Sabbath-day? In which class do we place that which is thus spoken of: "The law worketh wrath: for where no law is, there is no transgression?" [91] and again thus: "Until the law sin was in the world: but sin is not imputed when there is no law?" [92] and also that which we have already so often quoted: "By the law is the knowledge of sin?" [93] and especially the passage in which the apostle has more clearly expressed the question of which we are treating: "I had not known lust, except the law had said, Thou shalt not covet?" [94]

[89] 2 Cor. iii. 3-9   [90] Rom. v. 20   [91] Rom. iv. 15   [92] Rom. v. 13   [93] Rom. iii. 20   [94] Rom. vii. 7

CHAPTER XXV

THE PASSAGE IN ROMANS

Now carefully consider this entire passage, and see whether it says anything about circumcision, or the Sabbath, or anything else pertaining to a foreshadowing sacrament. Does not its whole scope amount to this, that the letter which forbids sin fails to give man life, but rather "killeth," by increasing concupiscence, and aggravating sinfulness by transgression, unless indeed grace liberates us by the law of faith, which is in Christ Jesus, when His love is "shed abroad in our hearts by the Holy Ghost, which is given to us?" [95] The apostle having used these words: "That we should serve in newness of spirit, and not in the oldness of the letter," [96] goes on to inquire, "What shall we say then? Is the law sin? God forbid. Nay; I had not known sin, but by the law: for I had not known lust, except the law had said, Thou shalt not covet. But sin, taking occasion by the commandment, wrought in me all manner of concupiscence. For without the law sin was dead. For I was alive without the law once; but when the commandment came, sin revived, and I died. And the commandment, which was ordained to life, I found to be unto death. For sin, taking occasion by the commandment deceived me, and by it slew me. Wherefore the law is holy, and the commandment holy, and just, and good. Was then that which is good made death unto me? God forbid. But sin, that it might appear sin, worked death in me by that which is good; that sin by the commandment might become exceeding sinful. For we know that the law is spiritual; whereas I am carnal, sold under sin. For that which I do I allow not: for what I would, that I do not; but what I hate, that I do. If then I do that which I would not, I consent unto the law that it is good. But then it is no longer I that do it, but sin that dwelleth in me. For I know that in me (that is, in my flesh) dwelleth no good thing. To will, indeed, is present with me; but how to perform that which is good I find not. For the good that I would, I do not; but the evil which I would not, that I do. Now, if I do that which I would not, it is no more I that do it, but sin that dwelleth in me. I find then a law, that, when I would do good, evil is present with me. For I delight in the law of God after the inward man: but I see another law in my members warring against the law of my mind, and bringing me into captivity to the law of sin which is in my members. O wretched man that I am! who shall deliver me from the body of this death? The grace of God, through Jesus Christ our Lord. So then with the mind I myself serve the law of God, but with the flesh the law of sin." [97]

[95] Rom. v. 5   [96] Rom. vii. 6   [97] Rom. vii. 7-25

CHAPTER XXVI

NO FRUIT GOOD EXCEPT IT GROW FROM THE ROOT OF LOVE

It is evident, then, that the oldness of the letter, in the absence of the newness of the spirit, instead of freeing us from sin, rather makes us guilty by the knowledge of sin. Whence it is written in another part of Scripture, "He that increaseth knowledge, increaseth sorrow" [98]—not that the law is itself evil, but because the commandment has its good in the demonstration of the letter, not in the assistance of the spirit; and if this commandment is kept from the fear of punishment and not from the love of righteousness, it is servilely kept, not freely, and therefore it is not kept at all. For no fruit is good which does not grow from the root of love. If, however, that faith be present which worketh by love,[99] then one begins to delight in the law of God after the inward man,[100] and this delight is the gift of the spirit, not of the letter; even though there is another law in our members still warring against the law of the mind, until the old state is changed, and passes into that newness which increases from day to day in the inward man, while the grace of God is liberating us from the body of this death through Jesus Christ our Lord.

CHAPTER XXVII

GRACE, CONCEALED IN THE OLD TESTAMENT, IS REVEALED IN THE NEW

This grace hid itself under a veil in the Old Testament, but it has been revealed in the New Testament according to the most perfectly ordered dispensation of the ages, forasmuch as God knew how to dispose all things. And perhaps it is a part of this hiding of grace, that in the Decalogue, which was given on Mount Sinai, only the portion which relates to the Sabbath was hidden under a prefiguring precept. The Sabbath is a day of sanctification; and it is not without significance that, among all the works which God accomplished, the first sound of sanctification was heard on the day when He rested from all His labors. On this, indeed, we must not now enlarge. But at the same time I deem it to be enough for the point now in question, that it was not for nothing that the nation was commanded on that day to abstain from all servile work, by which sin is signified; but because not to commit sin belongs to sanctification, that is, to God's gift through the Holy Spirit. And this precept alone among the others, was placed in the law, which was written on the two tables of stone, in a prefiguring shadow, under which the Jews observe the Sabbath, that by this very circumstance it might be signified that it was then the time for concealing the grace, which had to be revealed in the New Testament by the

---

[98] Eccles. i. 18   [99] Gal. v. 6   [100] Rom. vii. 22

death of Christ—the rending, as it were, of the veil.[101] "For when," says the apostle, "it shall turn to the Lord, the veil shall be taken away." [102]

CHAPTER XXVIII

WHY THE HOLY GHOST IS CALLED THE FINGER OF GOD

"Now the Lord is that Spirit: and where the Spirit of the Lord is, there is liberty." [103] Now this Spirit of God, by whose gift we are justified, whence it comes to pass that we delight not to sin—in which is liberty; even as, when we are without this Spirit, we delight to sin—in which is slavery, from the works of which we must abstain—this Holy Spirit, through whom love is shed abroad in our hearts, which is the fulfilment of the law, is designated in the gospel as "the finger of God." [104] Is it not because those very tables of the law were written by the finger of God, that the Spirit of God by whom we are sanctified is also *the finger of God*, in order that, living by faith, we may do good works through love? Who is not touched by this congruity, and at the same time diversity? For as fifty days are reckoned from the celebration of the Passover (which was ordered by Moses to be offered by slaying the typical lamb,[105] to signify, indeed, the future death of the Lord) to the day when Moses received the law written on the tables of stone by the finger of God,[106] so, in like manner, from the death and resurrection of Him who was led as a lamb to the slaughter,[107] there were fifty complete days up to the time when the finger of God— that is, the Holy Spirit—gathered together in one[108] perfect company those who believed.

CHAPTER XXIX

A COMPARISON OF THE LAW OF MOSES AND OF THE NEW LAW

Now, amidst this admirable correspondence, there is at least this very considerable diversity in the cases, in that the people in the earlier instance were deterred by a horrible dread from approaching the place where the law was given; whereas in the other case the Holy Ghost came upon them who were gathered together in expectation of His promised gift. *There* it was on tables of stone that the finger of God operated; *here* it was on the hearts of men. *There* the law was given outwardly, so that the unrighteous might be terrified;[109] *here* it was given inwardly, so that they might be justified.[110] For this, "Thou shalt not commit adultery, Thou shalt not kill, Thou shalt not covet; and if there be any other commandment"—such, of course, as was written on those tables—"it is briefly comprehended," says he, "in this saying, namely, Thou shalt love thy neighbor as thyself. Love

[101] Matt. xxvii. 51   [102] 2 Cor. iii. 16   [103] 2 Cor. iii. 17   [104] Luke xi. 20   [105] Ex. xii. 3   [106] Ex. xxxi. 18   [107] Isa. liii. 7   [108] Acts ii. 2   [109] Ex. xix. 12, 16   [110] Acts ii. 1-47

worketh no ill to his neighbor: therefore love is the fulfilling of the law." [111] Now this was not written on the tables of stone, but "is shed abroad in our hearts by the Holy Ghost, which is given unto us." [112] God's law, therefore, is love. "To it the carnal mind is not subject, neither indeed can be;" [113] but when the works of love are written on tables to alarm the carnal mind, there arises the law of works and "the letter which killeth" the transgressor; but when love itself is shed abroad in the hearts of believers, then we have the law of faith, and the spirit which gives life to him that loves.

CHAPTER XXX

THE NEW LAW WRITTEN WITHIN

Now, observe how consonant this diversity is with those words of the apostle which I quoted not long ago in another connection, and which I postponed for a more careful consideration afterwards: "Forasmuch," says he, "as ye are manifestly declared to be the epistle of Christ ministered by us, written not with ink, but with the Spirit of the living God; not in tables of stone, but in fleshy tables of the heart." [114] See how he shows that the one is written without man, that it may alarm him from without; the other within man himself, that it may justify him from within. He speaks of the "fleshy tables of the heart," not of the carnal mind, but of a living agent possessing sensation, in comparison with a stone, which is senseless. The assertion which he subsequently makes—that "the children of Israel could not look stedfastly on the end of the face of Moses," and that he accordingly spoke to them through a veil [115]—signifies that the letter of the law justifies no man, but that rather a veil is placed on the reading of the Old Testament, until it shall be turned to Christ, and the veil be removed—in other words, until it shall be turned to grace, and be understood that from Him accrues to us the justification, whereby we do what He commands. And He commands, in order that, because we lack in ourselves, we may flee to Him for refuge. Accordingly, after most guardedly saying, "Such trust have we through Christ to God-ward," [116] the apostle immediately goes on to add the statement which underlies our subject, to prevent our confidence being attributed to any strength of our own. He says: "Not that we are sufficient to ourselves to think anything as of ourselves; but our sufficiency is of God; who also hath made us fit to be ministers of the New Testament; not of the letter, but of the spirit: for the letter killeth, but the spirit giveth life." [117]

[111] Rom. xiii. 9, 10   [112] Rom. v. 5   [113] Rom. viii. 7   [114] 2 Cor. iii. 3   [115] 2 Cor. iii. 13   [116] 2 Cor. iii. 4   [117] 2 Cor. iii. 5, 6

CHAPTER XXXI

THE OLD LAW MINISTERS DEATH; THE NEW, RIGHTEOUSNESS

Now, since, as he says in another passage, "the law was added because of transgression," [118] meaning the law which is written externally to man, he therefore designates it both as "the ministration of death," [119] and "the ministration of condemnation;" [120] but the other, that is, the law of the New Testament, he calls "the ministration of the Spirit" [121] and "the ministration of righteousness," [120] because through the Spirit we work righteousness, and are delivered from the condemnation due to transgression. The one, therefore, vanishes away, the other abides; for the terrifying schoolmaster will be dispensed with, when love has succeeded to fear. Now "where the Spirit of the Lord is, there is liberty." [122] But that this ministration is vouchsafed to us, not on account of our deserving, but from His mercy, the apostle thus declares: "Seeing then that we have this ministry, as we have received mercy, let us faint not; but let us renounce the hidden things of dishonesty, not walking in craftiness, nor adulterating the word of God with deceit." [123] By this "craftiness" and "deceitfulness" he would have us understand the hypocrisy with which the arrogant would fain be supposed to be righteous. Whence in the psalm, which the apostle cites in testimony of this grace of God, it is said, "Blessed is the man to whom the Lord will not impute sin, and in whose mouth is no guile." [124] This is the confession of lowly saints, who do not boast to be what they are not. Then, in a passage which follows not long after, the apostle writes thus: "For we preach not ourselves, but Christ Jesus the Lord; and ourselves your servants for Jesus' sake. For God, who commanded the light to shine out of darkness, hath shined in our hearts, to give the light of the knowledge of the glory of God in the face of Jesus Christ." [125] This is the knowledge of His glory, whereby we know that He is the light which illumines our darkness. And I beg you to observe how he inculcates this very point: "We have," says he, "this treasure in earthen vessels, that the excellency of the power may be of God, and not of us." [126] When further on he commends in glowing terms this same grace, in the Lord Jesus Christ, until he comes to that vestment of the righteousness of faith, "clothed with which we cannot be found naked," and while longing for which "we groan, being burdened" with mortality, "earnestly desiring to be clothed upon with our house which is from Heaven," "that mortality might be swallowed up of life," [127]—observe what he says: "Now He that hath wrought us for the self-same thing is God, who also hath given unto us the earnest of the Spirit;" [128] and after a little he thus briefly draws the conclusion of the matter: "That we might

[118] Gal. iii. 19   [119] 2 Cor. iii. 7   [120] 2 Cor. iii. 9   [121] 2 Cor. iii. 8   [122] 2 Cor. iii. 17   [123] 2 Cor. iv. 1, 2   [124] Ps. xxxii. 2   [125] 2 Cor. iv. 5, 6   [126] 2 Cor. iv. 7   [127] See 2 Cor. v. 1-4   [128] 2 Cor. v. 5

be made the righteousness of God in Him." [129] This is not the righteousness whereby God is Himself righteous, but that whereby we are made righteous by Him.

CHAPTER XXXII

THE CHRISTIAN FAITH TOUCHING THE ASSISTANCE OF GRACE

Let no Christian then stray from this faith, which alone is the Christian one; nor let any one, when he has been made to feel ashamed to say that we become righteous through our own selves, without the grace of God working this in us—because he sees, when such an allegation is made, how unable pious believers are to endure it—resort to any subterfuge on this point, by affirming that the reason why we cannot become righteous without the operation of God's grace is this, that He gave the law, He instituted its teaching. He commanded its precepts of good. For there is no doubt that, without His assisting grace, the law is "the letter which killeth;" but when the life-giving spirit is present, the law causes that to be loved as written within, which it once caused to be feared as written without.

CHAPTER XXXIII

THE PROPHECY OF JEREMIAH CONCERNING THE NEW TESTAMENT

Observe this also in that testimony which was given by the prophet on this subject in the clearest way: "Behold, the days come, saith the Lord, that I will consummate a new covenant with the house of Israel, and with the house of Judah; not according to the covenant which I made with their fathers, in the day that I took them by the hand, to bring them out of the land of Egypt. Because they continued not in my covenant, I also have rejected them, saith the Lord. But this shall be the covenant that I will make with the house of Israel; After those days, saith the Lord, I will put my law in their inward parts, and write it in their hearts; and I will be their God, and they shall be my people. And they shall teach no more every man his neighbor, and every man his brother, saying, Know the Lord: for they shall all know me, from the least unto the greatest of them, saith the Lord: for I will forgive their iniquity, and I will remember their sin no more." [130] What say we to this? One nowhere, or hardly anywhere, except in this passage of the prophet, finds in the Old Testament Scriptures any mention so made of the New Testament as to indicate it by its very name. It is no doubt often referred to and foretold as about to be given, but not so plainly as to have its very name mentioned. Consider then carefully, what difference God has testified as existing between the two testaments—the old covenant and the new.

---

[129] 2 Cor. v. 21   [130] Jer. xxxi. 31-34

CHAPTER XXXIV

THE LAW; GRACE

After saying, "Not according to the covenant which I made with their fathers in the day that I took them by the hand, to bring them out of the land of Egypt," observe what He adds: "Because they continued not in my covenant." He reckons it as their own fault that they did not continue in God's covenant, lest the law, which they received at that time, should seem to be deserving of blame. For it was the very law that Christ "came not to destroy, but to fulfil." [131] Nevertheless, it is not by that law that the ungodly are made righteous, but by grace; and this change is effected by the life-giving Spirit, without whom the letter kills. "For if there had been a law given which could have given life, verily righteousness should have been by the law. But the Scripture hath concluded all under sin, that the promise by faith of Jesus Christ might be given to them that believe." [132] Out of this promise, that is, out of the kindness of God, the law is fulfilled, which without the said promise only makes men transgressors, either by the actual commission of some sinful deed, if the flame of concupiscence have greater power than even the restraints of fear, or at least by their mere will, if the fear of punishment transcend the pleasure of lust. In what he says, "The Scripture hath concluded all under sin, that the promise by faith of Jesus Christ might be given to them that believe," it is the benefit of this *"conclusion"* itself which is asserted. For what purposes *"hath it concluded,"* except as it is expressed in the next sentence: "Before, indeed, faith came, we were kept under the law, *concluded* for the faith which was afterwards revealed?" [133] The law was therefore given, in order that grace might be sought; grace was given, in order that the law might be fulfilled. Now it was not through any fault of its own that the law was not fulfilled, but by the fault of the carnal mind; and this fault was to be demonstrated by the law, and healed by grace. "For what the law could not do, in that it was weak through the flesh, God sending His own Son in the likeness of sinful flesh, and for sin, condemned sin in the flesh; that the righteousness of the law might be fulfilled in us, who walk not after the flesh, but after the Spirit." [134] Accordingly, in the passage which we cited from the prophet, he says, "I will consummate a new covenant with the house of Israel, and with the house of Judah" [135]—and what means *I will consummate* but *I will fulfil?*—"not, according to the covenant which I made with their fathers, in the day that I took them by the hand, to bring them out of the land of Egypt." [136]

---

[131] Matt. v. 17   [132] Gal. iii. 21, 22   [133] Gal. iii. 23   [134] Rom. viii. 3, 4   [135] Jer. xxxi. 31   [136] Jer. xxxi. 32

CHAPTER XXXV

THE OLD LAW; THE NEW LAW

The one was therefore old, because the other is new. But whence comes it that one is old and the other new, when the same law, which said in the Old Testament, "Thou shalt not covet," [137] is fulfilled by the New Testament? "Because," says the prophet, "they continued not in my covenant, I have also rejected them, saith the Lord." [138] It is then on account of the offence of the old man, which was by no means healed by the letter which commanded and threatened, that it is called the old covenant; whereas the other is called the new covenant, because of the newness of the spirit, which heals the new man of the fault of the old. Then consider what follows, and see in how clear a light the fact is placed, that men who have faith are unwilling to trust in themselves: "Because," says he, "this is the covenant which I will make with the house of Israel; After those days, saith the Lord, I will put my law in their inward parts, and write it in their hearts." [139] See how similarly the apostle states it in the passage we have already quoted: "Not in tables of stone, but in fleshy tables of the heart," [140] because "not with ink, but with the Spirit of the living God." [140] And I apprehend that the apostle in this passage had no other reason for mentioning "the New Testament" ("who hath made us able ministers of *the New Testament;* not of the letter, but of the spirit"), than because he had an eye to the words of the prophet, when he said, "Not in tables of stone, but in fleshy tables of the heart," inasmuch as in the prophet it runs: "I will write it in their hearts." [139]

CHAPTER XXXVI

THE LAW WRITTEN IN OUR HEARTS

What then is God's law written by God Himself in the hearts of men, but the very presence of the Holy Spirit, who is "the finger of God," and by whose presence is shed abroad in our hearts the love which is the fulfilling of the law,[141] and the end of the commandment? [142] Now the promises of the Old Testament are earthly; and yet (with the exception of the sacramental ordinances which were the shadow of things to come, such as circumcision, the Sabbath and other observances of days, and the ceremonies of certain meats,[143] and the complicated ritual of sacrifices and sacred things which suited "the oldness" of the carnal law and its slavish yoke) it contains such precepts of righteousness as we are even now taught to observe, which were especially expressly drawn out on

---

[137] Ex. xx. 17   [138] Jer. xxxi. 32   [139] Jer. xxxi. 33   [140] 2 Cor. iii. 3   [141] Rom. xiii. 10   [142] 1 Tim. i. 5   [143] See *Retract.*, ii. 37

the two tables without figure or shadow: for instance, "Thou shalt not commit adultery," "Thou shalt do no murder," "Thou shalt not covet," [144] "and whatsoever other commandment is briefly comprehended in the saying, Thou shalt love thy neighbor as thyself." [145] Nevertheless, whereas as in the said Testament earthly and temporal promises are, as I have said, recited, and these are goods of this corruptible flesh (although they prefigure those heavenly and everlasting blessings which belong to the New Testament), what is now promised is a good for the heart itself, a good for the mind, a good of the spirit, that is, an intellectual good; since it is said, "I will put my law in their inward parts, and in their hearts will I write them" [139]—by which He signified that men would not fear the law which alarmed them externally, but would love the very righteousness of the law which dwelt inwardly in their hearts.

CHAPTER XXXVII

THE ETERNAL REWARD

He then went on to state the reward: "I will be their God, and they shall be my people." [139] This corresponds to the Psalmist's words to God: "It is good for me to hold me fast by God." [146] "I will be," says God, "their God, and they shall be my people." What is better than this good, what happier than this happiness—to live to God, to live from God, with whom is the fountain of life, and in whose light we shall see light? [147] Of this life the Lord Himself speaks in these words: "This is life eternal, that they may know Thee the only true God, and Jesus Christ whom Thou hast sent" [148]—that is, "Thee and Jesus Christ whom Thou hast sent," the one true God. For no less than this did Himself promise to those who love Him: "He that loveth me, keepeth my commandments; and he that loveth me shall be loved of my Father, and I will love him, and will manifest myself unto him" [149]—in the form, no doubt, of God, wherein He is equal to the Father; not in the form of a servant, for in this He will display Himself even to the wicked also. Then, however, shall that come to pass which is written, "Let the ungodly man be taken away, that he see not the glory of the Lord." [150] Then also shall "the wicked go into everlasting punishment, and the righteous into life eternal." [151] Now this eternal life, as I have just mentioned, has been defined to be, that they may know the one true God.[148] Accordingly John again says: "Beloved, now are we the sons of God; and it doth not yet appear what we shall be: but we know that, when He shall appear, we shall be like Him; for we shall see Him as He is." [152] This likeness begins even now to be re-formed

---

[144] Ex. xx. 13, 14, 17   [145] Rom. xiii. 9   [146] Ps. lxxiii. 28   [147] Ps. xxxvi. 9
[148] John xvii. 3   [149] John xiv. 21   [150] Isa. xxvi. 10   [151] Matt. xxv. 46   [152] 1 John iii. 2

in us, while the inward man is being renewed from day to day, according to the image of Him that created him.[153]

CHAPTER XXXVIII

THE RE-FORMATION WHICH IS NOW BEING EFFECTED, COMPARED WITH THE PERFECTION OF THE LIFE TO COME

But what is this change, and how great, in comparison with the perfect eminence which is then to be realized? The apostle applies some sort of illustration, derived from well-known things to these indescribable things, comparing the period of childhood with the age of manhood. "When I was a child," says he, "I used to speak as a child, to understand as a child, to think as a child; but when I became a man, I put aside childish things." [154] He then immediately explains why he said this in these words: "For now we see by means of a mirror, darkly; but then face to face: now I know in part; but then shall I know even as also I am known." [155]

CHAPTER XXXIX

THE ETERNAL REWARD WHICH IS SPECIALLY DECLARED IN THE NEW TESTAMENT, FORETOLD BY THE PROPHET

Accordingly, in our prophet likewise, whose testimony we are dealing with, this is added, that in God is the reward, in Him the end, in Him the perfection of happiness, in Him the sum of the blessed and eternal life. For after saying, "I will be their God, and they shall be my people," he at once adds, "And they shall no more teach every man his neighbor, and every man his brother, saying, Know the Lord: for they shall all know me, from the least even unto the greatest of them." [156] Now, the present is certainly the time of the New Testament, the promise of which is given by the prophet in the words which we have quoted from his prophecy. Why then does each man still say even now to his neighbor and his brother, "Know the Lord?" Or is it not perhaps meant that this is everywhere said when the gospel is preached, and when this is its very proclamation? For on what ground does the apostle call himself "a teacher of the Gentiles," [157] if it be not that what he himself implies in the following passage becomes realized: "How shall they call on Him in whom they have not believed? and how shall they believe in Him of whom they have not heard? and how shall they hear without a preacher?" [158] Since, then, this preaching is now everywhere spreading, in what way is it the time of the New Testament of which the prophet spoke in the words, "And they shall not every man teach his neighbor, and every man his brother, saying, Know the Lord; for they shall all know me, from the least of them unto the greatest of them," [156]

[153] Col. iii. 10   [154] 1 Cor. xiii. 11   [155] 1 Cor. xiii. 12   [156] Jer. xxxi. 34   [157] 1 Tim. ii. 7   [158] Rom. x. 14

unless it be that he has included in his prophetic forecast the eternal reward of the said New Testament, by promising us the most blessed contemplation of God Himself?

CHAPTER XL

HOW THAT IS TO BE THE REWARD OF ALL; THE APOSTLE EARNESTLY DEFENDS GRACE

What then is the import of the *"All,* from the least unto the greatest of them,"* but all that belong spiritually to the house of Israel and to the house of Judah—that is, to the children of Isaac, to the seed of Abraham? For such is the promise, wherein it was said to him, "In Isaac shall thy seed be called; for they which are the children of the flesh are not the children of God: but the children of the promise are counted for the seed. For this is the word of promise, At this time will I come, and Sarah shall have a son. And not only this; but when Rebecca also had conceived by one, even by our father Isaac (for the children being not yet born, neither having done any good or evil, that the purpose of God according to election might stand, not of works, but of Him that calleth) it was said unto her, "The elder shall serve the younger." [159] This is the house of Israel, or rather the house of Judah, on account of Christ, who came of the tribe of Judah. This is the house of the children of promise —not by reason of their own merits, but of the kindness of God. For God promises what He Himself performs: He does not Himself promise, and another perform; which would no longer be promising, but prophesying. Hence it is "not of works, but of Him that calleth," [160] lest the result should be their own, not God's; lest the reward should be ascribed not to His grace, but to their due; and so grace should be no longer grace which was so earnestly defended and maintained by him who, though the least of the apostles, labored more abundantly than all the rest—yet not himself, but the grace of God that was with him.[161] "They shall all know me," [156] He says—*"All,"* the house of Israel and house of Judah. "All," however, "are not Israel which are of Israel," [162] but they only to whom it is said in "the psalm concerning the morning aid" [163] (that is, concerning the new refreshing light, meaning that of the New Testament), "All ye the seed of Jacob, glorify Him; and fear Him, all ye the seed of Israel." [164] All the seed, without exception, even the entire seed of the promise and of the called, but only of those who are the called according to His purpose.[165] "For whom He did predestinate, them He also called; and whom He called, them He also justified; and whom He justified; them He also glorified." [166] "Therefore it is of faith, that it might be by

---

[159] Rom. ix. 7-12   [160] Rom. ix. 11   [161] 1 Cor. xv. 9, 10   [162] Rom. ix. 6   [163] See title of Ps. xxii. (xxi. Sept.) in the Sept. and Latin   [164] Ps. xxii. 23   [165] Rom. viii. 28   [166] Rom. viii. 30

grace; to the end the promise might be sure to all the seed: not to that
only which is of the law"—that is, which comes from the Old Testament
into the New—"but to that also which is of faith," which was indeed
prior to the law, even "the faith of Abraham"—meaning those who imitate the faith of Abraham—"who is the father of us all; as it is written,
I have made thee the father of many nations." [167] Now all these predestinated, called, justified, glorified ones, shall know God by the grace
of the new testament, from the least to the greatest of them.

CHAPTER XLI

THE LAW WRITTEN IN THE HEART, AND THE REWARD OF THE ETERNAL CONTEMPLATION OF GOD, BELONG TO THE NEW COVENANT; WHO AMONG THE SAINTS ARE THE LEAST AND THE GREATEST

As then the law of works, which was written on the tables of stone,
and its reward, the land of promise, which the house of the carnal Israel
after their liberation from Egypt received, belonged to the Old Testament,
so the law of faith, written on the heart, and its reward, the beatific vision which the house of the spiritual Israel, when delivered from the
present world, shall perceive, belong to the New Testament. Then shall
come to pass what the apostle describes: "Whether there be prophecies,
they shall fail; whether there be tongues, they shall cease; whether there
be knowledge, it shall vanish away" [168]—even that imperfect knowledge
of "the child" [169] in which this present life is passed, and which is but
"in part," "by means of a mirror darkly." [170] Because of this, indeed,
"prophecy" is necessary, for still to the past succeeds the future; and
because of this, too, "tongues" are required—that is, a multiplicity of
expressions, since it is by different ones that different things are suggested
to him who does not as yet contemplate with a perfectly purified mind the
everlasting light of transparent truth. "When that, however, which is
perfect is come, then that which is in part shall be done away," [171] then,
what appeared to the flesh in assumed flesh shall display Itself as It is in
Itself to all who love It; then, there shall be eternal life for us to know
the one very God; [172] then shall we be like Him, [173] because "we shall
then know, even as we are known;" [174] then "they shall teach no more
every man his neighbor, and every man his brother, saying, Know the
Lord; for they shall all know me, from the least unto the greatest of
them." [175] Now this may be understood in several ways: Either, that in
that life the saints shall differ one from another in glory, as star from
star. It matters not how the expression runs—whether (as in the passage

[167] Rom. iv. 16, 17   [168] I Cor. xiii. 8   [169] *Ibid.* ver. 11   [170] *Ibid.* ver. 12   [171] I Cor.
xiii. 10   [172] John xvii. 3   [173] I John iii. 2   [174] I Cor. xiii. 12   [175] Jer. xxxi. 34

before us) it be, "From the least unto the greatest of them," or the other way, From the greatest unto the least. And, in like manner, it matters not even if we understand *"the least"* to mean those who simply believe, and *"the greatest"* those who have been further able to understand—so far as may be in this world—the light which is incorporeal and unchangeable. Or, *"the least"* may mean those who are later in time; while by *"the greatest"* he may have intended to indicate those who were prior in time. For they are all to receive the promised vision of God hereafter, since it was for us that they foresaw the future which would be better than their present, that they without us should not arrive at complete perfection.[176] And so the earlier are found to be the lesser, because they were less deferred in time; as in the case of the gospel "penny a day," which is given for an illustration.[177] This penny they are the first to receive who came last into the vineyard. Or, "the least and the greatest" ought perhaps to be taken in some other sense, which at present does not occur to my mind.

CHAPTER XLII

DIFFERENCE BETWEEN THE OLD AND THE NEW TESTAMENTS

I beg of you, however, carefully to observe, as far as you can, what I am endeavoring to prove with so much effort. When the prophet promised a new covenant, not according to the covenant which had been formerly made with the people of Israel when liberated from Egypt, he said nothing about a change in the sacrifices or any sacred ordinances although such change, too, was without doubt to follow, as we see in fact that it did follow, even as the same prophetic scripture testifies in many other passages; but he simply called attention to this difference, that God would impress His laws on the mind of those who belonged to this covenant, and would write them in their hearts,[178] whence the apostle drew his conclusion —"not with ink, but with the Spirit of the living God; not in tables of stone, but in fleshy tables of the heart;" [179] and that the eternal recompense of this righteousness was not the land out of which were driven the Amorites and Hittites, and other nations who dwelt there,[180] but God Himself, "to whom it is good to hold fast," [181] in order that God's good that they love, may be the God Himself whom they love, between whom and men nothing but sin produces separation; and this is remitted only by grace. Accordingly, after saying, "For all shall know me, from the least to the greatest of them," He instantly added, "For I will forgive their iniquity, and I will remember their sin no more." [175] By the law of works, then, the Lord says, "Thou shalt not covet:" [182] but by the law of faith He says, "Without me ye can do nothing;" [183] for He was treating

---

[176] Heb. xi. 40 [177] Matt. xx. 8 [178] Jer. xxxi. 32, 33 [179] 2 Cor. iii. 3 [180] Josh. xii. [181] Ps. lxxiii. 28 [182] Ex. xx. 17 [183] John xv. 5

of good works, even the fruit of the vine-branches. It is therefore apparent what difference there is between the old covenant and the new—that in the former the law is written on tables, while in the latter on hearts; so that what in the one alarms from without, in the other delights from within; and in the former man becomes a transgressor through the letter that kills, in the other a lover through the life-giving spirit. We must therefore avoid saying, that the way in which God assists us to work righteousness, and "works in us both to will and to do of His good pleasure," [184] is by externally addressing to our faculties precepts of holiness; for He gives His increase internally,[185] by shedding love abroad in our hearts by the Holy Ghost, which is given to us." [186]

CHAPTER XLIII

A QUESTION TOUCHING THE PASSAGE IN THE APOSTLE ABOUT THE
GENTILES WHO ARE SAID TO DO BY NATURE THE LAW'S
COMMANDS, WHICH THEY ARE ALSO SAID TO HAVE
WRITTEN ON THEIR HEARTS

Now we must see in what sense it is that the apostle says, "For when the Gentiles, which have not the law, do by nature the things contained in the law, these, having not the law, are a law unto themselves, which show the work of the law written in their hearts," [187] lest there should seem to be no certain difference in the new testament, in that the Lord promised that He would write His laws in the hearts of His people, inasmuch as the Gentiles have this done for them naturally. This question therefore has to be sifted, arising as it does as one of no inconsiderable importance. For some one may say, "If God distinguishes the new testament from the old by this circumstance, that in the old He wrote His law on tables but in the new He wrote them on men's hearts, by what are the faithful of the new testament discriminated from the Gentiles, which have the work of the law written on their hearts, whereby they do by nature the things of the law,[188] as if, forsooth, they were better than the ancient people, which received the law on tables, and before the new people, which has that conferred on it by the new testament which nature has already bestowed on them?"

CHAPTER XLIV

THE ANSWER IS, THAT THE PASSAGE MUST BE UNDERSTOOD OF
THE FAITHFUL OF THE NEW COVENANT

Has the apostle perhaps mentioned those Gentiles as having the law written in their hearts who belong to the new testament? We must look

[184] Phil. ii. 13   [185] 1 Cor. iii. 7   [186] Rom. v. 5   [187] Rom. ii. 14, 15   [188] Rom. ii. 14

at the previous context. First, then, referring to the gospel, he says, "It is the power of God unto salvation to every one that believeth; to the Jew first, and also to the Greek. For therein is the righteousness of God revealed from faith to faith: as it is written, The just shall live by faith." [189] Then he goes on to speak of the ungodly, who by reason of their pride profit not by the knowledge of God, since they did not glorify Him as God, neither were thankful.[190] He then passes to those who think and do the very things which they condemn—having in view, no doubt, the Jews, who made their boast of God's law, but as yet not mentioning them expressly by name; and then he says, "Indignation and wrath, tribulation and anguish, upon every soul of man that doeth evil, of the Jew first, and also of the Gentile: but glory, honor, and peace, to every soul that doeth good; to the Jew first, and also to the Gentile: for there is no respect of persons with God. For as many as have sinned without law, shall also perish without law; and as many as have sinned in the law, shall be judged by the law; for not the hearers of the law are just before God, but the doers of the law shall be justified." [191] Who they are that are treated of in these words, he goes on to tell us: "For when the Gentiles, which have not the law, do by nature the things contained in the law," [188] and so forth in the passage which I have quoted already. Evidently, therefore, no others are here signified under the name of Gentiles than those whom he had before designated by the name of "Greek" when he said, "To the Jew first, and also to the Greek," [192] Since then the gospel is "the power of God unto salvation to every one that believeth, to the Jew first, and also to the Greek;" [192] and since "indignation and wrath, tribulation and anguish, are upon every soul of man that doeth evil, of the Jew first, and also of the Greek: but glory, honor, and peace, to every man that doeth good; to the Jew first, and also to the Greek;" since, moreover, the Greek is indicated by the term "Gentiles" who do by nature the things contained in the law, and which have the work of the law written in their hearts: it follows that such Gentiles as have the law written in their hearts belong to the gospel, since to them, on their believing, it is the power of God unto salvation. To what Gentiles, however, would he promise glory, and honor, and peace, in their doing good works, if living without the grace of the gospel? Since there is no respect of persons with God,[193] and since it is not the hearers of the law, but the doers thereof, that are justified,[194] it follows that any man of any nation, whether Jew or Greek, who shall believe, will equally have salvation under the gospel. "For there is no difference," as he says afterwards; "for all have sinned, and come short of the glory of God: being justified freely by His grace." [195] How then could he say that any Gentile person, who was a doer of the law, was justified without the Saviour's grace?

[189] Rom. i. 16, 17   [190] Rom. i. 21   [191] Rom. ii. 8-13   [192] Rom. i. 16   [193] Rom. ii. 11   [194] Rom. ii. 13   [195] Rom. iii. 22-24

CHAPTER XLV

IT IS NOT BY THEIR WORKS, BUT BY GRACE, THAT THE DOERS OF THE LAW ARE JUSTIFIED; GOD'S SAINTS AND GOD'S NAME HALLOWED IN DIFFERENT SENSES

Now he could not mean to contradict himself in saying, "The doers of the law shall be justified," [196] as if their justification came through their works, and not through grace; since he declares that a man is justified freely by His grace without the works of the law,[197] intending by the term *"freely"* nothing else than that works do not precede justification. For in another passage he expressly says, "If by grace, then is it no more of works; otherwise grace is no longer grace." [198] But the statement that "the doers of the law shall be justified" [196] must be so understood, as that we may know that they are not otherwise doers of the law, unless they be justified, so that justification does not subsequently accrue to them as doers of the law, but justification precedes them as doers of the law. For what else does the phrase "being justified" signify than "being made righteous"—by Him, of course, who justifies the ungodly man, that he may become a godly one instead? For if we were to express a certain fact by saying, "The men will be liberated," the phrase would of course be understood as asserting that the liberation would accrue to those who were men already; but if we were to say, "The men will be created," we should certainly not be understood as asserting that the creation would happen to those who were already in existence, but that they became men by the creation itself. If in like manner it were said, "The doers of the law shall be honored," we should only interpret the statement correctly if we supposed that the honor was to accrue to those who were already doers of the law; but when the allegation is, "The doers of the law shall be justified," what else does it mean than that the just shall be justified? for of course the doers of the law are just persons. And thus it amounts to the same thing as if it were said, The doers of the law shall be created—not those who were so already, but that they may become such; in order that the Jews who were hearers of the law might hereby understand that they wanted the grace of the Justifier, in order to be able to become its doers also. Or else the term "They shall be justified" is used in the sense of, They shall be deemed, or reckoned as just, as it is predicted of a certain man in the Gospel, "But he, willing to justify himself" [199]—meaning that he wished to be thought and accounted just. In like manner, we attach one meaning to the statement, "God sanctifies His saints," and another to the words, "Sanctified be Thy name;" [200] for in the former case we suppose the words to mean that He makes those to be saints who

[196] Rom. ii. 13   [197] Rom. iii. 24, 28   [198] Rom. xi. 6   [199] Luke x. 29   [200] Matt. vi. 9

were not saints before, and in the latter, that the prayer would have that which is always holy in itself be also regarded as holy by men—in a word, be feared with a hallowed awe.

CHAPTER XLVI

HOW THE PASSAGE OF THE LAW AGREES WITH THAT OF THE PROPHET

If therefore the apostle, when he mentioned that the Gentiles do by nature the things contained in the law, and have the work of the law written in their hearts,[201] intended those to be understood who believed in Christ—who do not come to the faith like the Jews, through a precedent law—there is no good reason why we should endeavor to distinguish them from those to whom the Lord by the prophet promises the new covenant, telling them that He will write His laws in their hearts,[202] inasmuch as they too, by the grafting which he says had been made of the wild olive, belong to the self-same olive-tree[203]—in other words, to the same people of God. There is therefore a good agreement of this passage of the apostle with the words of the prophet; so that belonging to the new testament means having the law of God not written on tables, but on the heart— that is, embracing the righteousness of the law with innermost affection, where faith works by love.[204] Because it is by faith that God justifies the Gentiles;" and the Scripture foreseeing this, preached the gospel before to Abraham, saying, "In thy seed shall all nations be blessed," [205] in order that by this grace of promise the wild olive might be grafted into the good olive, and believing Gentiles might be made children of Abraham, "in Abraham's seed, which is Christ," [206] by following the faith of him who, without receiving the law written on tables, and not yet possessing even circumcision, "believed God, and it was counted to him for righteousness." [207] Now what the apostle attributed to Gentiles of this character —how that "they have the work of the law written in their hearts;" [208] must be some such thing as what he says to the Corinthians: "not in tables of stone, but in fleshy tables of the heart." [209] For thus do they become of the house of Israel, when their uncircumcision is accounted circumcision, by the fact that they do not exhibit the righteousness of the law by the excision of the flesh, but keep it by the charity of the heart. "If," says he, "the uncircumcision keep the righteousness of the law, shall not his uncircumcision be counted for circumcision?" [210] And therefore in the house of the true Israel, in which is no guile,[211] they are partakers of the new testament, since God puts His laws into their mind, and writes them in their hearts with his own finger, the Holy Ghost, by whom is shed abroad in them the love[212] which is the "fulfilling of the law." [213]

[201] Rom. ii. 14, 15   [202] Jer. xxxii. 32   [203] Rom. xi. 24   [204] Gal. v. 6   [205] Gal. iii. 8; Gen. xxii. 18   [206] Gal. iii. 16   [207] Gen. xv. 6; Rom. iv. 2   [208] Rom. ii. 15   [209] 2 Cor. iii. 3   [210] Rom. ii. 26   [211] See John i. 47   [212] Rom. v. 5   [213] Rom. xiii. 10

CHAPTER XLVII

THE LAW "BEING DONE BY NATURE" MEANS, DONE BY NATURE AS RESTORED BY GRACE

Nor ought it to disturb us that the apostle described them as doing that which is contained in the law *"by nature"*—not by the Spirit of God, not by faith, not by grace. For it is the Spirit of grace that does it, in order to restore in us the image of God, in which we were naturally created.[214] Sin, indeed, is contrary to nature, and it is grace that heals it—on which account the prayer is offered to God, "Be merciful unto me: heal my soul; for I have sinned against Thee." [215] Therefore it is by nature that men do the things which are contained in the law; [216] for they who do not, fail to do so by reason of their sinful defect. In consequence of this sinfulness, the law of God is erased out of their hearts; and therefore, when, the sin being healed, it is written there, the prescriptions of the law are done *"by nature"* —not that by nature grace is denied, but rather by grace nature is repaired. For "by one man sin entered into the world, and death by sin, and so death passed upon all men: in which all have sinned;" [217] wherefore "there is no difference: they all come short of the glory of God, being justified freely by His grace." [218] By this grace there is written on the renewed inner man that righteousness which sin had blotted out; and this mercy comes upon the human race through our Lord Jesus Christ. "For there is one God, and one Mediator between God and men, the Man Christ Jesus." [219]

CHAPTER XLVIII

THE IMAGE OF GOD IS NOT WHOLLY BLOTTED OUT IN THESE UNBELIEVERS; VENIAL SINS

According to some, however, they who do by nature the things contained in the law must not be regarded as yet in the number of those whom Christ's grace justifies, but rather as among those some of whose actions (although they are those of ungodly men, who do not truly and rightly worship the true God) we not only cannot blame, but even justly and rightly praise, since they have been done—so far as we read, or know, or hear—according to the rule of righteousness; though at the same time, were we to discuss the question with what motive they are done, they would hardly be found to be such as deserve the praise and defence which are due to righteous conduct. Still, since God's image has not been so completely erased in the soul of man by the stain of earthly affections, as to have left remaining there not even the merest lineaments of it whence it might be justly said

---

[214] Gen. i. 27   [215] Ps. xli. 4   [216] Rom. ii. 14   [217] Rom. v. 12   [218] Rom. iii. 22-24
[219] I Tim. ii. 5

that man, even in the ungodliness of his life, does, or appreciates, some
things contained in the law; if this is what is meant by the statement that
"the Gentiles, which have not the law" (that is, the law of God), "do by
nature the things contained in the law," [216] and that men of this character
"are a law to themselves," and "show the work of the law written in their
hearts"—that is to say, what was impressed on their hearts when they were
created in the image of God has not been wholly blotted out:—even in this
view of the subject, that wide difference will not be disturbed, which
separates the new covenant from the old, and which lies in the fact that by
the new covenant the law of God is written in the hearts of believers,
whereas in the old it was inscribed on tables of stone. For this writing in
the heart is effected by renovation, although it had not been completely
blotted out by the old nature. For just as that image of God is renewed
in the mind of believers by the new testament, which impiety had not
quite abolished (for there had remained undoubtedly that which the soul
of man cannot be except it be rational), so also the law of God, which had
not been wholly blotted out there by unrighteousness, is certainly written
thereon, renewed by grace. Now in the Jews the law which was written
on tables could not effect this new inscription, which is justification, but
only transgression. For they too were men, and there was inherent in them
that power of nature, which enables the rational soul both to perceive
and do what is lawful; but the godliness which transfers to another life
happy and immortal has "a spotless law, converting souls," [220] so that by
the light thereof they may be renewed, and that be accomplished in them
which is written, "There has been manifested over us, O Lord, the light of
Thy countenance." [221] Turned away from which, they have deserved to
grow old, while they are incapable of renovation except by the grace of
Christ—in other words, without the intercession of the Mediator; there
being "one God and one Mediator between God and men, the Man Christ
Jesus, who gave Himself a ransom for all." [222] Should those be strangers to
His grace of whom we are treating, and who (after the manner of which we
have spoken with sufficient fulness already) "do by nature the things contained in the law," [223] of what use will be their "excusing thoughts" to
them "in the day when God shall judge the secrets of men," [224] unless it be
perhaps to procure for them a milder punishment? For as, on the one hand,
there are certain venial sins which do not hinder the righteous man from
the attainment of eternal life, and which are unavoidable in this life, so,
on the other hand, there are some good works which are of no avail to an
ungodly man towards the attainment of everlasting life, although it would
be very difficult to find the life of any very bad man whatever entirely without them. But inasmuch as in the kingdom of God the saints differ in glory
as one star does from another,[225] so likewise, in the condemnation of ever-

---

[220] Ps. xix. 7   [221] Ps. iv. 6   [222] 1 Tim. ii. 5, 6   [223] Rom. ii. 14   [224] Rom. ii. 15,
16   [225] 1 Cor. xv. 41

lasting punishment, it will be more tolerable for Sodom than for that other city;[226] while some men will be twofold more the children of hell than others.[227] Thus in the judgment of God not even this fact will be without its influence—that one man will have sinned more, or less, than another, even when both are involved in the ungodliness that is worthy of damnation.

CHAPTER XLIX

THE GRACE PROMISED BY THE PROPHET FOR THE NEW COVENANT

What then could the apostle have meant to imply by—after checking the boasting of the Jews, by telling them that "not the hearers of the law are just before God, but the doers of the law shall be justified" [228]—immediately afterwards speaking of them "which, having not the law, do by nature the things contained in the law," [223] if in this description not they are to be understood who belong to the Mediator's grace, but rather they who, while not worshipping the true God with true godliness, do yet exhibit some good works in the general course of their ungodly lives? Or did the apostle perhaps deem it probable, because he had previously said that "with God there is no respect of persons," [229] and had afterwards said that "God is not the God of the Jews only, but also of the Gentiles" [230]—that even such scanty little works of the law, as are suggested by nature, were not discovered in such as received not the law, except as the result of the remains of the image of God; which He does not disdain when they believe in Him, with whom there is no respect of persons? But whichever of these views is accepted, it is evident that the grace of God was promised to the new testament even by the prophet, and that this grace was definitively announced to take this shape—God's laws were to be written in men's hearts; and they were to arrive at such a knowledge of God, that they were not each one to teach his neighbor and brother, saying, Know the Lord; for all were to know Him, from the least to the greatest of them.[231] This is the gift of the Holy Ghost, by which love is shed abroad in our hearts[232]— not, indeed, any kind of love, but the love of God, "out of a pure heart, and a good conscience, and an unfeigned faith," [233] by means of which the just man, while living in this pilgrim state, is led on, after the stages of "the glass," and "the enigma," and "what is in part," to the actual vision, that, face to face, he may know even as he is known.[234] For one thing has he required of the Lord, and that he still seeks after, that he may dwell in the house of the Lord all the days of his life, in order to behold the pleasantness of the Lord.[235]

[226] Luke x. 12   [227] Matt. xxiii. 15   [228] Rom. ii. 13   [229] Rom. ii. 11   [230] Rom. iii. 29   [231] Jer. xxxi. 33, 34   [232] Rom. v. 5   [233] 1 Tim. i. 5   [234] 1 Cor. xiii. 12   [235] Ps. xxvii. 4

CHAPTER L

RIGHTEOUSNESS IS THE GIFT OF GOD

Let no man therefore boast of that which he seems to possess, as if he had not received it;[236] nor let him think that he has received it merely because the external letter of the law has been either exhibited to him to read, or sounded in his ear for him to hear. For "if righteousness is by the law, then Christ has died in vain." [237] Seeing, however, that if He has not died in vain, He has ascended up on high, and has led captivity captive, and has given gifts to men,[238] it follows that whosoever has, has from this source. But whosoever denies that he has from Him, either has not, or is in great danger of being deprived of what he has.[239] "For it is one God which justifies the circumcision by faith, and the uncircumcision through faith;" [240] in which clauses there is no real difference in the sense, as if the phrase *"by faith"* meant one thing, and *"through faith"* another, but only a variety of expression. For in one passage, when speaking of the Gentiles— that is, of the uncircumcision—he says, "The Scripture, foreseeing that God would justify the heathen *by faith;*" [241] and again, in another, when speaking of the circumcision, to which he himself belonged, he says, "We who are Jews by nature, and not sinners of the Gentiles, knowing that a man is not justified by the works of the law, but *through faith* in Jesus Christ, even we believed in Jesus Christ." [242] Observe, he says that both the uncircumcision are justified by faith, and the circumcision through faith, if, indeed, the circumcision keep the righteousness of faith. For the Gentiles, which followed not after righteousness, have attained to righteousness, even the righteousness which is by faith [243]—by obtaining it of God, not by assuming it of themselves. But Israel, which followed after the law of righteousness, hath not attained to the law of righteousness. And why? Because they sought it not by faith, but as it were by works[244]—in other words, working it out as it were by themselves, not believing that it is God who works within them. "For it is God which worketh in us both to will and to do of His own good pleasure." [245] And hereby "they stumbled at the stumbling-stone." [246] For what he said, "not by faith, but as it were by works," [246] he most clearly explained in the following words: "They, being ignorant of God's righteousness, and going about to establish their own righteousness, have not submitted themselves unto the righteousness of God. For Christ is the end of the law for righteousness to every one that believeth." [247] Then are we still in doubt what are those works of the law by which a man is not justified, if he believes them to be his own works, as it were, without the help and gift of God, which is "by the faith of Jesus

---

[236] 1 Cor. iv. 7   [237] Gal. ii. 21   [238] Ps. lxviii. 18; Eph. iv. 8   [239] Luke viii. 18; xix. 26   [240] Rom. iii. 30   [241] Gal. iii. 8   [242] Gal. ii. 15, 16   [243] Rom. ix. 30 [244] Rom. ix. 31, 32   [245] Phil. ii. 13   [246] Rom. ix. 32   [247] Rom. x. 3, 4

Christ?" And do we suppose that they are circumcision and the other like ordinances, because some such things in other passages are read concerning these sacramental rites too? In this place, however, it is certainly not circumcision which they wanted to establish as their own righteousness, because God established this by prescribing it Himself. Nor is it possible for us to understand this statement, of those works concerning which the Lord says to them, "Ye reject the commandment of God, that ye may keep your own tradition;" [248] because, as the apostle says, Israel, which followed after the law of righteousness, hath not attained to the law of righteousness." [249] He did not say, Which followed after their own traditions, framing them and relying on them. This then is the sole distinction, that the very precept, "Thou shalt not covet," [250] and God's other good and holy commandments, they attributed to themselves; whereas, that man may keep them, God must work in him through faith in Jesus Christ, who is "the end of the law for righteousness to every one that believeth." [251] That is to say, every one who is incorporated into Him and made a member of His body, is able, by His giving the increase within, to work righteousness. It is of such a man's works that Christ Himself has said, "Without me ye can do nothing." [252]

CHAPTER LI

FAITH THE GROUND OF ALL RIGHTEOUSNESS

The righteousness of the law is proposed in these terms—that whosoever shall do it shall live in it; and the purpose is, that when each has discovered his own weakness, he may not by his own strength, nor by the letter of the law (which cannot be done), but by faith, conciliating the Justifier, attain, and do, and live in it. For the work in which he who does it shall live, is not done except by one who is justified. His justification, however, is obtained by faith; and concerning faith it is written, "Say not in thine heart, Who shall ascend into heaven? (that is, to bring down Christ therefrom); or, Who shall descend into the deep? (that is, to bring up Christ again from the dead). But what saith it? The word is nigh thee, even in thy mouth, and in thy heart: that is (says he), the word of faith which we preach: That if thou shalt confess with thy mouth the Lord Jesus, and shalt believe in thine heart that God hath raised Him from the dead, thou shalt be saved." [253] As far as he is saved, so far is he righteous. For by this faith we believe that God will raise even us from the dead—even now in the spirit, that we may in this present world live soberly, righteously, and godly in the renewal of His grace; and by and by in our flesh, which shall rise again to immortality, which indeed is the reward of the Spirit, who precedes it by a resurrection which is appropriate to Himself—that is, by justification. "For we are buried with Christ by baptism unto death, that like as

[248] Mark vii. 9   [249] Rom. ix. 31   [250] Ex. xx. 17   [251] Rom. x. 4   [252] John xv. 5
[253] Rom. x. 6-9

Christ was raised up from the dead by the glory of the Father, even so we also should walk in newness of life." [254] By faith, therefore, in Jesus Christ we obtain salvation—both in so far as it is begun within us in reality, and in so far as its perfection is waited for in hope; "for whosoever shall call on the name of the Lord shall be saved." [255] "How abundant," says the Psalmist, "is the multitude of Thy goodness, O Lord, which Thou hast laid up for them that fear Thee, and hast perfected for them that hope in Thee!" [256] By the law we fear God; by faith we hope in God: but from those who fear punishment grace is hidden. And the soul which labors under this fear, since it has not conquered its evil concupiscence, and from which this fear, like a harsh master, has not departed—let it flee by faith for refuge to the mercy of God, that He may give it what He commands, and may, by inspiring into it the sweetness of His grace through His Holy Spirit, cause the soul to delight more in what He teaches it, than it delights in what opposes His instruction. In this manner it is that the great abundance of His sweetness—that is, the law of faith—His love which is in our hearts, and shed abroad, is perfected in them that hope in Him, that good may be wrought by the soul, healed not by the fear of punishment, but by the love of righteousness.

CHAPTER LII

GRACE ESTABLISHES FREE WILL

Do we then by grace make void free will? God forbid! Nay, rather we establish free will. For even as the law by faith, so free will by grace, is not made void, but established.[257] For neither is the law fulfilled except by free will; but by the law is the knowledge of sin, by faith the acquisition of grace against sin, by grace the healing of the soul from the disease of sin, by the health of the soul freedom of will, by free will the love of righteousness, by love of righteousness the accomplishment of the law. Accordingly, as the law is not made void, but is established through faith, since faith procures grace whereby the law is fulfilled; so free will is not made void through grace, but is established, since grace cures the will whereby righteousness is freely loved. Now all the stages which I have here connected together in their successive links, have severally their proper voices in the sacred Scriptures. The law says: "Thou shalt not covet." [258] Faith says: "Heal my soul, for I have sinned against Thee." [259] Grace says: "Behold, thou art made whole: sin no more, lest a worse thing come unto thee." [260] Health says: "O Lord my God, I cried unto Thee, and Thou hast healed me." [261] Free will says: "I will freely sacrifice unto Thee." [262] Love of righteousness says: "Transgressors told me pleasant tales, but not ac-

---

[254] Rom. vi. 4   [255] Rom. x. 13; Joel ii. 32   [256] Ps. xxxi. 19   [257] Rom. iii. 31
[258] Ex. xx. 17   [259] Ps. xli. 4   [260] John v. 14   [261] Ps. xxx. 2   [262] Ps. liv. 6

cording to Thy law, O Lord." [263] How is it then that miserable men dare to be proud, either of their free will, before they are freed, or of their own strength, if they have been freed? They do not observe that in the very mention of free will they pronounce the name of liberty. But "where the Spirit of the Lord is, there is liberty." [264] If, therefore, they are the slaves of sin, why do they boast of free will? For by what a man is overcome, to the same is he delivered as a slave.[265] But if they have been freed, why do they vaunt themselves as if it were by their own doing, and boast, as if they had not received? Or are they free in such sort that they do not choose to have Him for their Lord who says to them: "Without me ye can do nothing;" [266] and "If the Son shall make you free, ye shall be free indeed?" [267]

CHAPTER LIII

VOLITION AND ABILITY

Some one will ask whether the faith itself, in which seems to be the beginning either of salvation, or of that series leading to salvation which I have just mentioned, is placed in our power. We shall see more easily, if we first examine with some care what "our power" means. Since, then, there are two things—will and ability; it follows that not every one that has the will has therefore the ability also, nor has every one that possesses the ability the will also; for as we sometimes will what we cannot do, so also we sometimes can do what we do not will. From the words themselves when sufficiently considered, we shall detect, in the very ring of the terms, the derivation of volition from willingness, and of *ability* from ableness. Therefore, even as the man who wishes has volition, so also the man who can has ability. But in order that a thing may be done by ability, the volition must be present. For no man is usually said to do a thing with ability if he did it unwillingly. Although, at the same time, if we observe more precisely, even what a man is compelled to do unwillingly, he does, if he does it, by his volition; only he is said to be an unwilling agent, or to act against his will, because he would prefer some other thing. He is compelled, indeed, by some unfortunate influence, to do what he does under compulsion, wishing to escape it or to remove it out of his way. For if his volition be so strong that he prefers not doing this to not suffering that, then beyond doubt he resists the compelling influence, and does it not. And accordingly, if he does it, it is not with a full and free will, but yet it is not without will that he does it; and inasmuch as the volition is followed by its effect, we cannot say that he lacked the ability to do it. If, indeed, he willed to do it, yielding to compulsion, but could not, although we should allow that a coerced will was present, we should yet say that ability was absent. But

[263] Ps. cxix. 85   [264] 2 Cor. iii. 17   [265] 2 Pet. ii. 19   [266] John xv. 5   [267] John viii. 36

when he did not do the thing because he was unwilling, then of course the ability was present, but the volition was absent, since he did it not, by his resistance to the compelling influence. Hence it is that even they who compel, or who persuade, are accustomed to say, Why don't you do what you have in your ability, in order to avoid this evil? While they who are utterly unable to do what they are compelled to do, because they are supposed to be able usually answer by excusing themselves, and say, I would do it if it were in my ability. What then do we ask more, since we call that ability when to the volition is added the faculty of doing? Accordingly every one is said to have that in his ability which he does if he likes, and does not if he dislikes.

CHAPTER LIV

WHETHER FAITH BE IN A MAN'S OWN POWER

Attend now to the point which we have laid down for discussion: whether faith is in our own power? We now speak of that faith which we employ when we believe anything, not that which we give when we make a promise; for this too is called *faith*. We use the word in one sense when we say, "He had no faith in me," and in another sense when we say, "He did not keep faith with me." The one phrase means, "He did not believe what I said;" the other, "He did not do what he promised." According to the faith by which we believe, we are faithful to God; but according to that whereby a thing is brought to pass which is promised, God Himself even is faithful to us; for the apostle declares, "God is faithful, who will not suffer you to be tempted above that ye are able." [268] Well, now, the former is the faith about which we inquire, Whether it be in our power? even the faith by which we believe God, or believe on God. For of this it is written, "Abraham believed God, and it was counted unto him for righteousness." [269] And again, "To him that believeth on Him that justifieth the ungodly, his faith is counted for righteousness." [270] Consider now whether anybody believes, if he be unwilling; or whether he believes not, if he shall have willed it. Such a position, indeed, is absurd (for what is believing but consenting to the truth of what is said? and this consent is certainly voluntary): faith, therefore, is in our own power. But, as the apostle says: "There is no power but comes from God," [271] what reason then is there why it may not be said to us even of this: "What hast thou which thou hast not received?" [272]—for it is God who gave us even to believe. Nowhere, however, in Holy Scripture do we find such an assertion as, There is no volition but comes from God. And rightly is it not so written, because it is not true: otherwise God would be the author even of sins (which Heaven forbid!), if there were no volition except what comes from Him; inasmuch as an evil volition alone is

[268] 1 Cor. x. 13   [269] Rom. iv. 3; comp. Gen. xv. 6   [270] Rom. iv. 5   [271] Rom. xiii. 1   [272] 1 Cor. iv. 7

already a sin, even if the effect be wanting—in other words, if it has not ability. But when the evil volition receives ability to accomplish its intention, this proceeds from the judgment of God, with whom there is no unrighteousness.[273] He indeed punishes after this manner; nor is His chastisement unjust because it is secret. The ungodly man, however, is not aware that he is being punished, except when he unwillingly discovers by an open penalty how much evil he has willingly committed. This is just what the apostle says of certain men: "God hath given them up to the evil desires of their own hearts, . . . to do those things that are not convenient." [274] Accordingly, the Lord also said to Pilate: "Thou couldest have no power at all against me, except it were given thee from above." [275] But still, when the ability is given, surely no necessity is imposed. Therefore, although David had received ability to kill Saul, he preferred sparing to striking him.[276] Whence we understand that bad men receive ability for the condemnation of their depraved will, while good men receive ability for trying of their good will.

CHAPTER LV

WHAT FAITH IS LAUDABLE

Since faith, then, is in our power, inasmuch as every one believes when he likes, and, when he believes, believes voluntarily; our next inquiry, which we must conduct with care, is, What faith it is which the apostle commends with so much earnestness? For indiscriminate faith is not good. Accordingly we find this caution: "Brethren, believe not every spirit, but try the spirits whether they are of God." [277] Nor must the clause in commendation of love, that it "believeth all things," [278] be so understood as if we should detract from the love of any one, if he refuses to believe at once what he hears. For the same love admonishes us that we ought not readily to believe anything evil about a brother; and when anything of the kind is said of him, does it not judge it to be more suitable to its character not to believe? Lastly, the same love, "which believeth all things," does not believe every spirit. Accordingly, charity *believes* all things no doubt, but it *believes in* God. Observe, it is not said, Believes *in* all things. It cannot therefore be doubted that the faith which is commended by the apostle is the faith whereby we believe in God.[279]

---

[273] Rom. ix. 14   [274] Rom. i. 24, 28   [275] John xix. 11   [276] 1 Sam. xxiv. 7, and xxvi. 9   [277] 1 John iv. 1   [278] 1 Cor. xiii. 7   [279] Rom. iv. 3

CHAPTER LVI

THE FAITH OF THOSE WHO ARE UNDER THE LAW DIFFERENT FROM THE FAITH OF OTHERS

But there is yet another distinction to be observed—since they who are under the law both attempt to work their own righteousness through fear of punishment, and fail to do God's righteousness, because this is accomplished by the love to which only what is lawful is pleasing, and never by the fear which is forced to have in its work the thing which is lawful, although it has something else in its will which would prefer, if it were only possible, that to be lawful which is not lawful. These persons also believe in God; for if they had no faith in Him at all, neither would they of course have any dread of the penalty of His law. This, however, is not the faith which the apostle commends. He says: "Ye have not received the spirit of bondage again to fear; but ye have received the spirit of adoption, whereby we cry, Abba, Father."[280] The fear, then, of which we speak is slavish; and therefore, even though there be in it a belief in the Lord, yet righteousness is not loved by it, but condemnation is feared. God's children, however, exclaim, "Abba, Father"—one of which words they of the circumcision utter; the other, they of the uncircumcision—the Jew first, and then the Greek;[281] since there is "one God, which justifieth the circumcision by faith, and the uncircumcision through faith."[282] When indeed they utter this call, they seek something; and what do they seek, but that which they hunger and thirst after? And what else is this but that which is said of them, "Blessed are they which do hunger and thirst after righteousness, for they shall be filled?"[283] Let, then, those who are under the law pass over hither, and become sons instead of slaves; and yet not so as to cease to be slaves, but so as, while they are sons, still to serve their Lord and Father freely. For even this have they received; for the Only-begotten "gave them power to become the sons of God, even to them that believe on His name;"[284] and He advised them to ask, to seek, and to knock, in order to receive, to find, and to have the gate opened to them,[285] adding by way of rebuke, the words: "If ye, being evil, know how to give good gifts to your children, how much more shall your Father which is in heaven give good things to them that ask Him?"[286] When, therefore, that strength of sin, the law,[287] inflamed the sting of death, even sin, to take occasion and by the commandment work all manner of concupiscence in them,[288] of whom were they to ask for the gift of continence but of Him who knows how to give good gifts to His children? Perhaps, however, a man, in his folly, is unaware that no one can be continent except God give

[280] Rom. viii. 15   [281] Rom. ii. 9   [282] Rom. iii. 30   [283] Matt. v. 6   [284] John i. 12
[285] See Matt. vii. 7   [286] Matt. vii. 11   [287] 1 Cor. xv. 56   [288] Rom. vii. 8

him the gift. To know this, indeed, he requires Wisdom herself.[289] Why, then, does he not listen to the Spirit of his Father, speaking through Christ's apostle, or even Christ Himself, who says in His gospel, "Seek and ye shall find;"[290] and who also says to us, speaking by His apostle: "If any one of you lack wisdom, let him ask of God, that giveth to all men liberally, and upbraideth not, and it shall be given to him. Let him, however, ask in faith, nothing wavering?"[291] This is the faith by which the just man lives;[292] this is the faith whereby he believes on Him who justifies the ungodly,[293] this is the faith through which boasting is excluded,[294] either by the retreat of that with which we become self-inflated, or by the rising of that with which we glory in the Lord. This, again, is the faith by which we procure that largess of the Spirit, of which it is said: "We indeed through the Spirit wait for the hope of righteousness by faith."[295] But this admits of the further question, Whether he meant by "the hope of righteousness" that by which righteousness hopes, or that whereby righteousness is itself hoped for? For the just man, who lives by faith, hopes undoubtedly for eternal life; and the faith likewise, which hungers and thirsts for righteousness, makes progress therein by the renewal of the inward man day by day,[296] and hopes to be satiated therewith in that eternal life, where shall be realized that which is said of God by the psalm: "Who satisfieth thy desire with good things."[297] This, moreover, is the faith whereby they are saved to whom it is said: "By grace are ye saved through faith; and that not of yourselves: it is the gift of God: not of works, lest any man should boast. For we are His workmanship, created in Christ Jesus unto good works, which God hath before ordained that we should walk in them."[298] This, in short, is the faith which works not by fear, but by love,[299] not by dreading punishment, but by loving righteousness. Whence, therefore, arises this love—that is to say, this charity—by which faith works, if not from the source whence faith itself obtained it? For it would not be within us, to what extent soever it is in us, if it were not diffused in our hearts by the Holy Ghost who is given to us.[300] Now *the love of God* is said to be shed abroad in our hearts, not because He loves us, but because He makes us lovers of Himself; just as *the righteousness of God*[301] is used in the sense of our being made righteous by His gift; and *the salvation of the Lord,*[302] in that we are saved by Him; and *the faith of Jesus Christ,*[303] because He makes us believers in Him. This is that righteousness of God, which He not only teaches us by the precept of His law, but also bestows upon us by the gift of His Spirit.

---

[289] Wisd. viii. 21   [290] Matt. vii. 7   [291] Jas. i. 5, 6   [292] Rom. i. 17   [293] Rom. iv. 5   [294] Rom. iii. 27   [295] Gal. v. 5   [296] 2 Cor. iv. 16   [297] Ps. ciii. 5   [298] Eph. ii. 8-10   [299] Gal. v. 6   [300] Rom. v. 5   [301] Rom. iii. 21   [302] Ps. iii. 8   [303] Gal. ii. 16

CHAPTER LVII

WHENCE COMES THE WILL TO BELIEVE?

But it remains for us briefly to inquire, Whether the will by which we believe be itself the gift of God, or whether it arise from that free will which is naturally implanted in us? If we say that it is not the gift of God, we must then incur the fear of supposing that we have discovered some answer to the apostle's reproachful appeal: "What hast thou that thou didst not receive? Now, if thou didst receive it, why dost thou glory, as if thou hadst not received it?"[304]—even some such an answer as this: 'See, we have the will to believe, which we did not receive. See in what we glory— even in what we did not receive!' If, however, we were to say that this kind of will is nothing but the gift of God, we should then have to fear lest unbelieving and ungodly men might not unreasonably seem to have some fair excuse for their unbelief, in the fact that God has refused to give them this will. Now this that the apostle says, "It is God that worketh in you both to will and to do of His own good pleasure," [305] belongs already to that grace which faith secures, in order that good works may be within the reach of man—even the good works which faith achieves through the love which is shed abroad in the heart by the Holy Ghost which is given to us. If we believe that we may attain this grace (and of course believe volun- tarily) then the question arises, whence we have this will?—if from nature, why it is not at everybody's command, since the same God made all men? if from God's gift, then again, why is not the gift open to all, since "He will have all men to be saved, and to come unto the knowledge of the truth?" [306]

CHAPTER LVIII

THE FREE WILL OF MAN IS AN INTERMEDIATE POWER

Let us then, first of all, lay down this proposition, and see whether it sat- isfies the question before us: that free will, naturally assigned by the Crea- tor to our rational soul, is such a neutral power, as can either incline towards faith, or turn towards unbelief. Consequently a man cannot be said to have even that will with which he believes in God, without having received it; since this rises at the call of God out of the free will which he received natu- rally when he was created. God no doubt wishes all men to be saved [306] and to come into the knowledge of the truth; but yet not so as to take away from them free will, for the good or the evil use of which they may be most righteously judged. This being the case, unbelievers indeed do contrary to the will of God when they do not believe His gospel; nevertheless they do

[304] 1 Cor. iv. 7   [305] Phil. ii. 13   [306] 1 Tim. ii. 4

not therefore overcome His will, but rob their own selves of the great, nay, the very greatest, good, and implicate themselves in penalties of punishment, destined to experience the power of Him in punishments whose mercy in His gifts they despised. Thus God's will is for ever invincible; but it would be vanquished, unless it devised what to do with such as despised it, or if these despises could in any way escape from the retribution which He has appointed for such as they. Suppose a master, for example, who should say to his servants, I wish you to labor in my vineyard, and, after your work is done, to feast and take your rest; but who, at the same time, should require any who refused to work to grind in the mill ever after. Whoever neglected such a command would evidently act contrary to the master's will; but he would do more than that—he would vanquish that will, if he also escaped the mill. This, however, cannot possibly happen under the government of God. Whence it is written, "God hath spoken once"—that is, irrevocably—although the passage may refer also to His one only Word.[307] He then adds what it is which He had irrevocably uttered, saying: "Twice have I heard this, that power belongeth unto God. Also unto Thee, O Lord, doth mercy belong: because Thou wilt render to every man according to his work." [308] He therefore will be guilty unto condemnation under God's power, who shall think too contemptuously of His mercy to believe in Him. But whosoever shall put his trust in Him, and yield himself up to Him, for the forgiveness of all his sins, for the cure of all his corruption, and for the kindling and illumination of his soul by His warmth and light, shall have good works by his grace; and by them[309] he shall be even in his body redeemed from the corruption of death, crowned, satisfied with blessings—not temporal, but eternal—above what we can ask or under stand.

CHAPTER LIX

MERCY AND PITY IN THE JUDGMENT OF GOD

This is the order observed in the psalm, where it is said: "Bless the Lord, O my soul, and forget not all His recompenses; who forgiveth all thine iniquities; who healeth all thy diseases; who redeemeth thy life from destruction; who crowneth thee with loving-kindness and tender mercy; who satisfieth thy desire with good things." [310] And lest by any chance these great blessings should be despaired of under the deformity of our old, that is, mortal condition, the Psalmist at once says, "Thy youth shall be renewed like the eagle's;" [311] as much as to say, All that you have heard belongs to the new man and to the new covenant. Now let us consider together briefly these things, and with delight contemplate the praise of mercy, that is, of the grace of God. "Bless the Lord, O my soul," he says,

---

[307] John i. 1   [308] Ps. lxii. 11, 12   [309] Ex quibus   [310] Ps. ciii. 2-5   [311] Ps. ciii. 5

"and forget not all His recompenses." Observe, he does not say blessings, but *recompenses;* because He recompenses evil with good. "Who forgiveth all thine iniquities:" this is done in the sacrament of baptism. "Who healeth all thy diseases:" this is effected by the believer in the present life, while the flesh so lusts against the spirit, and the spirit against the flesh, that we do not the things we would;[312] while also another law in our members wars against the law of our mind;[313] while to will is present indeed to us, but not how to perform that which is good.[314] These are the diseases of a man's old nature, which, however, if we only advance with persevering purpose, are healed by the growth of the new nature day by day, by the faith which operates through love.[315] "Who redeemeth thy life from destruction;" this will take place at the resurrection of the dead in the last day. "Who crowneth thee with loving-kindness and tender mercy;" this shall be accomplished in the day of judgment; for when the righteous King shall sit upon His throne to render to every man according to his works, who shall then boast of having a pure heart? or who shall glory of being clean from sin? It was therefore necessary to mention God's loving-kindness and tender mercy there, where one might expect debts to be demanded and deserts recompensed so strictly as to leave no room for mercy. He crowns, therefore, with loving-kindness and tender mercy; but even so according to works. For he shall be separated to the right hand, to whom it is said, "I was an hungered, and ye gave me meat." [316] There will, however, be also "judgment without mercy;" but it will be for him "that hath not showed mercy." [317] But "blessed are the merciful: for they shall obtain mercy" [318] of God. Then, as soon as those on the left hand shall have gone into eternal fire, the righteous, too, shall go into everlasting life,[319] because He says: "This is life eternal, that they may know Thee the only true God, and Jesus Christ whom Thou hast sent." [320] And with this knowledge, this vision, this contemplation, shall the desire of their soul be satisfied; for it shall be enough for it to have this and nothing else—there being nothing more for it to desire, to aspire to, or to require. It was with a craving after this full joy that his heart glowed who said to the Lord Christ, "Show us the Father, and it sufficeth us;" and to whom the answer was returned, "He that hath seen me hath seen the Father." [321] Because He is Himself the eternal life, in order that men may know the one true God, Thee and whom Thou hast sent, Jesus Christ. If, however, he that has seen the Son has also seen the Father, then assuredly he who sees the Father and the Son sees also the Holy Spirit of the Father and the Son. So we do not take away free will, while our soul blesses the Lord and forgets not all His recompenses;[322] nor does it, in ignorance of God's righteousness, wish to set up one of its own;[323] but it believes in Him who justifies the ungodly,[324] and until it

[312] Gal. v. 17 [313] Rom. vii. 23 [314] Rom. vii. 18 [315] Gal. v. 6 [316] Matt. xxv. 35 [317] Jas. ii. 13 [318] Matt. v. 7 [319] Matt. xxv. 46 [320] John xvii. 3 [321] John xiv. 8, 9 [322] Ps. ciii. 2 [323] Rom. x. 3 [324] Rom. iv. 5

arrives at sight, it lives by faith—even the faith which works by love.[315] And this love is shed abroad in our hearts, not by the sufficiency of our own will, nor by the letter of the law, but by the Holy Ghost who has been given to us.[325]

CHAPTER LX

THE WILL TO BELIEVE IS FROM GOD

Let this discussion suffice, if it satisfactorily meets the question we had to solve. It may be, however, objected in reply, that we must take heed lest some one should suppose that the sin would have to be imputed to God which is committed by free will, if in the passage where it is asked, "What hast thou which thou didst not receive?" [326] the very will by which we believe is reckoned as a gift of God, because it arises out of the free will which we received at our creation. Let the objector, however, attentively observe that this will is to be ascribed to the divine gift, not merely because it arises from our free will, which was created naturally with us; but also because God acts upon us by the incentives of our perceptions, to will and to believe, either externally by evangelical exhortations, where even the commands of the law also do something, if they so far admonish a man of his infirmity that he betakes himself to the grace that justifies by believing; or internally, where no man has in his own control what shall enter into his thoughts, although it appertains to his own will to consent or to dissent. Since God, therefore, in such ways acts upon the reasonable soul in order that it may believe in Him (and certainly there is no ability whatever in free will to believe, unless there be persuasion or summons towards some one in whom to believe), it surely follows that it is God who both works in man the willing to believe, and in all things prevents us with His mercy. To yield our consent, indeed, to God's summons, or to withhold it, is (as I have said) the function of our own will. And this not only does not invalidate what is said, "For what hast thou that thou didst not receive?" [326] but it really confirms it. For the soul cannot receive and possess these gifts, which are here referred to, except by yielding its consent. And thus whatever it possesses, and whatever it receives, is from God; and yet the act of receiving and having belongs, of course, to the receiver and possessor. Now, should any man be for constraining us to examine into this profound mystery, why this person is so persuaded as to yield, and that person is not, there are only two things occurring to me, which I should like to advance as my answer: "O the depth of the riches!" [327] and "Is there unrighteousness with God?" [328] If the man is displeased with such an answer, he must seek more learned disputants; but let him beware lest he find presumptuous ones.

---

[325] Rom. v. 5   [326] 1 Cor. iv. 7   [327] Rom. xi. 33   [328] Rom. ix. 14

CHAPTER LXI

CONCLUSION OF THE WORK

Let us at last bring our book to an end. I hardly know whether we have accomplished our purpose at all by our great prolixity. It is not in respect of you [my Marcellinus] that I have this misgiving, for I know your faith; but with reference to the minds of those for whose sake you wished me to write—who so much in opposition to my opinion, but (to speak mildly, and not to mention Him who spoke in His apostles) certainly against not only the opinion of the great Apostle Paul, but also his strong, earnest, and vigilant conflict, prefer maintaining their own views with tenacity to listening to him, when he "beseeches them by the mercies of God," and tells them, "through the grace of God which was given to him, not to think of themselves more highly than they ought to think, but to think soberly, according as God had dealt to every man the measure of faith." [329]

CHAPTER LXII

HE RETURNS TO THE QUESTION WHICH MARCELLINUS HAD PROPOSED TO HIM

But I beg of you to advert to the question which you proposed to me, and to what we have made out of it in the lengthy process of this discussion. You were perplexed how I could have said that it was possible for a man to be without sin, if his will were not wanting, by the help of God's aid, although no man in the present life had ever lived, was living, or would live, of such perfect righteousness. Now, in the books which I formerly addressed to you, I set forth this very question. I said: "If I were asked whether it be possible for a man to be without sin in this life, I should allow the possibility, by the grace of God, and his own free will; for I should have no doubt that the free will itself is of God's grace—that is, has its place among the gifts of God—not only as to its existence, but also in respect of its goodness; that is, that it applies itself to doing the commandments of God. And so, God's grace not only shows what ought to be done, but also helps to the possibility of doing what it shows." [330] You seemed to think it absurd, that a thing which was possible should be unexampled. Hence arose the subject treated of in this book; and thus did it devolve on me to show that a thing was possible although no example of it could be found. We accordingly adduced certain cases out of the gospel and of the law, at the beginning of this work—such as the passing of a camel through the eye of a needle; [331] and the twelve thousand legions of angels, who

---

[329] Rom. xii. 1, 3   [330] cf. De Peccat. Meritis, ii. 7   [331] Matt. xix. 24

could fight for Christ, if He pleased;[332] and those nations which God said He could have exterminated at once from the face of His people[333]—none of which possibilities were ever reduced to fact. To these instances may be added those which are referred to in the *Book of Wisdom*,[334] suggesting how many are the strange torments and troubles which God was able to employ against ungodly men, by using the creature which was obedient to His beck, which, however, He did not employ. One might also allude to that mountain, which faith could remove into the sea,[335] although, nevertheless, it was never done, so far as we have ever read or heard. Now you see how thoughtless and foolish would be the man who should say that any one of these things is impossible with God, and how opposed to the sense of Scripture would be his assertion. Many other cases of this kind may occur to anybody who reads or thinks, the possibility of which with God we cannot deny, although an example of them be lacking.

CHAPTER LXIII

AN OBJECTION

But inasmuch as it may be said that the instances which I have been quoting are divine works, whereas to live righteously is a work that belongs to ourselves, I undertook to show that even this too is a divine work. This I have done in the present book, with perhaps a fuller statement than is necessary, although I seem to myself to have said too little against the opponents of the grace of God. And I am never so much delighted in my treatment of a subject as when Scripture comes most copiously to my aid; and when the question to be discussed requires that "he that glorieth should glory in the Lord;" [336] and that we should in all things lift up our hearts and give thanks to the Lord our God, from whom, "as the Father of lights, every good and every perfect gift cometh down." [337] Now if a gift is not God's gift, because it is wrought by us, or because we act by His gift, then it is not a work of God that "a mountain should be removed into the sea," inasmuch as, according to the Lord's statement, it is by the faith of men that this is possible. Moreover, He attributes the deed to their actual operation: "If ye have faith in yourselves as a grain of mustard-seed, ye shall say unto this mountain, "Be thou removed, and be thou cast into the sea; and it shall be done, and nothing shall be impossible *to you*." [338] Observe how He said "to you," not "to Me" or "to the Father;" and yet it is certain that no man does such a thing without God's gift and operation. See how an instance of perfect righteousness is unexampled among men, and yet is not impossible. For it might be achieved if there were only applied so much of will as suffices for so great a thing. There would, however, be so

---

[332] Matt. xxvi. 53   [333] Deut. xxxi. 3; comp. Judg. ii. 3   [334] Wisd. xvi.   [335] Matt. xxi. 21   [336] 2 Cor. x. 17   [337] Jas. i. 17   [338] cf. Matt. xvii. 20, Mark xi. 23, Luke xvii. 6

much will, if there were hidden from us none of those conditions which pertain to righteousness; and at the same time these so delighted our mind, that whatever hindrance of pleasure or pain might else occur, this delight in holiness would prevail over every rival affection. And that this is not realized, is not owing to any intrinsic impossibility, but to God's judicial act. For who can be ignorant, that what he should know is not in man's power; nor does it follow that what he has discovered to be a desirable object is actually desired, unless he also feel a delight in that object, commensurate with its claims on his affection? This belongs to health of soul.

CHAPTER LXIV

WHEN THE COMMANDMENT TO LOVE IS FULFILLED

But somebody will perhaps think that we lack nothing for the knowledge of righteousness, since the Lord, when He summarily and briefly expounded His word on earth, informed us that the whole law and the prophets depend on two commandments;[339] nor was He silent as to what these were, but declared them in the plainest words: "Thou shalt love," said He, "the Lord thy God, with all thy heart, and with all thy soul, and with all thy mind;" and "Thou shalt love thy neighbor as thyself."[340] What is more surely true than that, if these be fulfilled, all righteousness is fulfilled? But the man who sets his mind on this truth must also carefully attend to another—in how many things we all of us offend,[341] while we suppose that what we do is pleasant, or, at all events, not unpleasing, to God whom we love; and afterwards, having (through His inspired word, or else by being warned in some clear and certain way) learned what is not pleasing to Him, we pray to Him that He would forgive us on our repentance. The life of man is full of examples of this. But whence comes it that we fall short of knowing what is pleasing to Him, if it be not that He is to that extent unknown to us? "For now we see through a glass, darkly; but then face to face."[342] Who, however, can make so bold, on arriving far enough, to say: "Then shall I know even as also I am known,"[342] as to think that they who shall see God will have no greater love towards Him than they have who now believe in Him? or that the one ought to be compared to the other, as if they were very near to each other? Now, if love increases just in proportion as our knowledge of its object becomes more intimate, of course we ought to believe that there is as much wanting now to the fulfilment of righteousness as there is defective in our love of it. A thing may indeed be known or believed, and yet not loved; but it is an impossibility that a thing can be loved which is neither known nor believed. But if the saints, in the exercise of their faith, could arrive at that great love, than which (as the Lord Himself testified) no greater can possibly be exhibited in the present life—

[339] Matt. xxii. 40   [340] Matt. xxii. 37, 39   [341] Jas. iii. 2   [342] 1 Cor. xiii. 12

even to lay down their lives for the faith, or for their brethren[343]—then after their pilgrimage here, in which their walk is by "faith," when they shall have reached the "sight" of that final happiness[344] which we hope for, though as yet we see is not, and wait for in patience,[345] then undoubtedly love itself shall be not only greater than that which we here experience, but far higher than all which we ask or think;[346] and yet it cannot be possibly more than "with all our heart, and with all our soul, and with all our mind." For there remains in us nothing which can be added to the whole; since, if anything did remain, there would not be the whole. Therefore the first commandment about righteousness, which bids us love the Lord with all our heart, and soul, and mind [347] (the next to which is, that we love our neighbor as ourselves) we shall completely fulfil in that life when we shall see face to face.[342] But even now this commandment is enjoined upon us, that we may be reminded what we ought by faith to require, and what we should in our hope look forward to, and, "forgetting the things which are behind, reach forth to the things which are before." [348] And thus, as it appears to me, that man has made a far advance, even in the present life, in the righteousness which is to be perfected hereafter, who has discovered by this very advance how very far removed he is from the completion of righteousness.

CHAPTER LXV

IN WHAT SENSE A SINLESS RIGHTEOUSNESS IN THIS LIFE CAN BE ASSERTED

Forasmuch, however, as an inferior righteousness may be said to be competent to this life, whereby the just man lives by faith[349] although absent from the Lord, and, therefore, walking by faith and not yet by sight [350]— it may be without absurdity said, no doubt, in respect of it, that it is free from sin; for it ought not to be attributed to it as a fault, that it is not as yet sufficient for so great a love to God as is due to the final, complete, and perfect condition thereof. It is one thing to fail at present in attaining to the fulness of love, and another thing to be swayed by no lust. A man ought therefore to abstain from every unlawful desire, although he loves God now far less than it is possible to love Him when He becomes an object of sight; just as in matters connected with the bodily senses, the eye can receive no pleasure from any kind of darkness, although it may be unable to look with a firm sight amidst refulgent light. Only let us see to it that we so constitute the soul of man in this corruptible body, that, although it has not yet swallowed up and consumed the motions of earthly lust in that supereminent perfection of the love of God, it nevertheless, in that inferior righteousness to which we have referred, gives no consent to the aforesaid lust

---

[343] John xv. 13   [344] 2 Cor. v. 7   [345] Rom. viii. 23   [346] Eph. iii. 20   [347] Matt. xxii. 37   [348] Phil. iii. 13   [349] Rom. i. 17   [350] 2 Cor. v. 7

for the purpose of effecting any unlawful thing. In respect, therefore, of that immortal life, the commandment is even now applicable: "Thou shalt love the Lord thy God with all thine heart, and with all thy soul, and with all thy might;" [351] but in reference to the present life the following: "Let not sin reign in your mortal body, that ye should obey it in the lusts thereof." [352] To the one, again, belongs, "Thou shalt not covet;" [353] to the other, "Thou shalt not go after thy lusts." [354] To the one it appertains to seek for nothing more than to continue in its perfect state; to the other it belongs actively to do the duty committed to it, and to hope as its reward for the perfection of the future life—so that in the one the just man may live forevermore in the sight of that happiness which in this life was his object of desire; in the other, he may live by that faith whereon rests his desire for the ultimate blessedness as its certain end. (These things being so, it will be sin in the man who lives by faith ever to consent to an unlawful delight—by committing not only frightful deeds and crimes, but even trifling faults; sinful, if he lend an ear to a word that ought not to be listened to, or a tongue to a phrase which should not be uttered; sinful, if he entertains a thought in his heart in such a way as to wish that an evil pleasure were a lawful one, although known to be unlawful by the commandment—for this amounts to a consent to sin, which would certainly be carried out in act, unless fear of punishment deterred.) Have such just men, while living by faith, no need to say: "Forgive us our debts, as we forgive our debtors?" [355] And do they prove this to be wrong which is written, "In Thy sight shall no man living be justified?" [356] and this: "If we say that we have no sin, we deceive ourselves, and the truth is not in us?" [357] and, "There is no man that sinneth not;" [358] and again, "There is not on the earth a righteous man, who doeth good and sinneth not" [359] (for both these statements are expressed in a general future sense—"sinneth not," "will not sin"—not in the past time, "has not sinned")?—and all other places of this purport contained in the Holy Scripture? Since, however, these passages cannot possibly be false, it plainly follows, to my mind, that whatever be the quality or extent of the righteousness which we may definitely ascribe to the present life, there is not a man living in it who is absolutely free from all sin; and that it is necessary for every one to give, that it may be given to him; [360] and to forgive, that it may be forgiven him; [361] and whatever righteousness he has, not to presume that he has it of himself, but from the grace of God, who justifies him, and still to go on hungering and thirsting for righteousness[362] from Him who is the living bread,[363] and with whom is the fountain of life;[364] who works in His saints, while laboring amidst temptation in this life, their justification in such

---

[351] Deut. vi. 5   [352] Rom. vi. 12   [353] Ex. xx. 17   [354] Ecclus. xviii. 30   [355] Matt. vi. 12   [356] Ps. cxliii. 2   [357] 1 John i. 8   [358] 1 Kings viii. 46   [359] Ecclus. vii. 21   [360] Luke vi. 30, 38   [361] Luke xi. 4   [362] Matt. v. 6   [363] John vi. 51   [364] Ps. xxxvi. 9

manner that He may still have somewhat to impart to them liberally when they ask, and something mercifully to forgive them when they confess.

CHAPTER LXVI

ALTHOUGH PERFECT RIGHTEOUSNESS BE NOT FOUND HERE ON EARTH, IT IS STILL NOT IMPOSSIBLE

But let objectors find, if they can, any man, while living under the weight of this corruption, in whom God has no longer anything to forgive; unless nevertheless they acknowledge that such an individual has been aided in the attainment of his good character not merely by the teaching of the law which God gave, but also by the infusion of the Spirit of grace—they will incur the charge of ungodliness itself, not of this or that particular sin. Of course they are not at all able to discover such a man, if they receive in a becoming manner the testimony of the divine writings. Still, for all that, it must not by any means be said that the possibility is lacking to God whereby the will of man can be so assisted, that there can be accomplished in every respect even now in a man, not that righteousness only which is of faith,[365] but that also in accordance with which we shall by and by have to live for ever in the very vision of God. For if he should now wish even that this corruptible in any particular man should put on incorruption,[366] and to command him so to live among mortal men (not destined himself to die) that his old nature should be wholly and entirely withdrawn, and there should be no law in his members warring against the law of his mind [367]— moreover, that he should discover God to be everywhere present, as the saints shall hereafter know and behold Him—who will madly venture to affirm that this is impossible? Men, however, ask why He does not do this; but they who raise the question consider not duly the fact that they are human. I am quite certain that, as nothing is impossible with God,[368] so also there is no iniquity with Him.[369] Equally sure am I that He resists the proud, and gives grace to the humble.[370] I know also that to him who had a thorn in the flesh, the messenger of Satan to buffet him, lest he should be exalted above measure, it was said, when he besought God for its removal once, twice, nay thrice: "My grace is sufficient for thee; for my strength is made perfect in weakness." [371] There is, therefore, in the hidden depths of God's judgments, a certain reason why every mouth even of the righteous should be shut in its own praise, and only opened for the praise of God. But what this certain reason is, who can search, who investigate, who know? So "unsearchable are His judgments, and His ways past finding out! For who hath known the mind of the Lord? or who hath been his counsellor? or who hath first given to Him, and it shall be recompensed unto him again? For of Him, and through Him, and to Him, are all things: to whom be glory for ever. Amen." [372]

[365] Rom. x. 6   [366] 1 Cor. xv. 53   [367] Rom. vii. 23   [368] Luke i. 37   [369] Rom. ix. 14   [370] Jas. iv. 6   [371] 2 Cor. xii. 7-9   [372] Rom. xi. 33-36

ON NATURE AND GRACE

ON NATURE AND GRACE

Introductory Note

The two young men, Timasius and Jacobus, to whom the treatise *On Nature and Grace* was addressed in the year 415 A.D., had been induced by the persuasion of Pelagius to enter upon an ascetic life. Pelagius had given them one of his own works for their instruction, but they in turn came in contact with some of Saint Augustine's writings, and soon realized the implications of Pelagius' position for the doctrine of grace. Hence they sent Pelagius' work to Saint Augustine with the request that he write in answer to it. The present treatise is Saint Augustine's reply, in which he does not mention Pelagius by name, but undertakes to refute the Pelagian doctrine. In the *Retractationes,* Saint Augustine says of his own treatise, that in it "I defend grace, not indeed as in opposition to nature, but as that which liberates and controls nature."

ON NATURE AND GRACE

CONTAINED IN ONE BOOK, ADDRESSED TO TIMASIUS AND JACOBUS

He begins with a statement of what is to be investigated concerning nature and grace; he shows that nature, as propagated from the flesh of the sinful Adam, being no longer what God made it at first—faultless and sound—requires the aid of grace, in order that it may be redeemed from the wrath of God and regulated for the perfection of righteousness: that the penal fault of nature leads to a most righteous retribution: whilst grace itself is not rendered to any deserts of ours, but is given gratuitously; and they who are not delivered by it are justly condemned. He afterwards refutes, with answers on every several point, a work by Pelagius, who supports this self-same nature in opposition to grace; among other things especially, in his desire to recommend the opinion that a man can live without sin, he contended that nature had not been weakened and changed by sin; for, otherwise, the matter of sin (which he thinks absurd) would be its punishment, if the sinner were weakened to such a degree that he committed more sin. He goes on to enumerate sundry righteous men both of the Old and of the New Testaments: deeming these to have been free from sin, he alleged the possibility of not sinning to be inherent in man; and this he attributed to God's grace, on the ground that God is the author of that nature in which is inseparably inherent this possibility of avoiding sin. Towards the end of this treatise there is an examination of sundry extracts from old writers, which Pelagius adduced in support of his views, and expressly from Hilary, Ambrose, and even Augustine himself.

CHAPTER I

THE OCCASION OF PUBLISHING THIS WORK;
WHAT GOD'S RIGHTEOUSNESS IS

THE book which you sent to me, my beloved sons, Timasius and Jacobus, I have read through hastily, but not indifferently, omitting only the few points which are plain enough to everybody; and I saw in it a man inflamed with most ardent zeal against those, who, when in their sins they ought to censure human will, are more forward in accusing the nature of men, and thereby endeavor to excuse themselves. He shows too great a fire against this evil, which even authors of secular literature have severely censured with the exclamation: "The human race falsely complains of its own nature!" [1] This same sentiment your author also has strongly insisted upon, with all the powers of his talent. I fear, however, that he will chiefly help those "who have a zeal for God, but not according to knowledge," who, "being ignorant of God's righteousness, and going about to establish their own righteousness, have not submitted themselves to the righteousness of

---

[1] See Sallust's Prologue to his *Jugurtha*

God." [2] Now, what the righteousness of God is, which is spoken of here, he immediately afterwards explains by adding: "For Christ is the end of the law for righteousness to every one that believeth." [3] This righteousness of God, therefore, lies not in the commandment of the law, which excites fear, but in the aid afforded by the grace of Christ, to which alone the fear of the law, as of a schoolmaster,[4] usefully conducts. Now, the man who understands this understands why he is a Christian. For "If righteousness came by the law, then Christ is dead in vain." [5] If, however, He did not die in vain, in Him only is the ungodly man justified, and to him, on believing in Him who justifies the ungodly, faith is reckoned for righteousness.[6] For all men have sinned and come short of the glory of God, being justified freely by His blood.[7] But all those who do not think themselves to belong to the "all who have sinned and fall short of the glory of God," have of course no need to become Christians, because "they that be whole need not a physician, but they that are sick;" [8] whence it is, that He came not to call the righteous, but sinners to repentance.[9]

CHAPTER II

FAITH IN CHRIST NOT NECESSARY TO SALVATION, IF A MAN WITHOUT IT CAN LEAD A RIGHTEOUS LIFE

Therefore the nature of the human race, generated from the flesh of the one transgressor, if it is self-sufficient for fulfilling the law and for perfecting righteousness, ought to be sure of its reward, that is, of everlasting life, even if in any nation or at any former time faith in the blood of Christ was unknown to it. For God is not so unjust as to defraud righteous persons of the reward of righteousness, because there has not been announced to them the mystery of Christ's divinity and humanity, which was manifested in the flesh.[10] For how could they believe what they had not heard of; or how could they hear without a preacher? [11] For "faith cometh by hearing, and hearing by the word of Christ." But I say (adds he): Have they not heard? "Yea, verily; their sound went out into all the earth, and their words unto the ends of the world." [12] Before, however, all this had been accomplished, before the actual preaching of the gospel reaches the ends of all the earth —because there are some remote nations still (although it is said they are very few) to whom the preached gospel has not found its way—what must human nature do, or what has it done—for it had either not heard that all this was to take place, or has not yet learnt that it was accomplished—but believe in God who made heaven and earth, by whom also it perceived by nature that it had been itself created, and lead a right life, and thus accomplish His will, uninstructed with any faith in the death and resurrection of

[2] Rom. x. 2, 3   [3] Rom. x. 4   [4] Gal. iii. 24   [5] Gal. ii. 21   [6] Rom. iv. 5
[7] Rom. iii. 23, 24   [8] Matt. ix. 12   [9] Matt. ix. 13   [10] 1 Tim. iii. 16   [11] Rom. x. 14   [12] Rom. x. 17, 18

Christ? Well, if this could have been done, or can still be done, then for my part I have to say what the apostle said in regard to the law: "Then Christ died in vain." [5] For if he said this about the law, which only the nation of the Jews received, how much more justly may it be said of the law of nature, which the whole human race has received, "If righteousness come by nature, then Christ died in vain." If, however, Christ did not die in vain, then human nature cannot by any means be justified and redeemed from God's most righteous wrath—in a word, from punishment—except by faith and the sacrament of the blood of Christ.

CHAPTER III

NATURE WAS CREATED SOUND AND WHOLE; IT WAS AFTERWARDS CORRUPTED BY SIN

Man's nature, indeed, was created at first faultless and without any sin; but that nature of man in which every one is born from Adam, now wants the Physician, because it is not sound. All good qualities, no doubt, which it still possesses in its make, life, senses, intellect, it has of the Most High God, its Creator and Maker. But the flaw, which darkens and weakens all those natural goods, so that it has need of illumination and healing, it has not contracted from its blameless Creator—but from that original sin, which it committed by free will. Accordingly, criminal nature has its part in most righteous punishment. For, if we are now newly created in Christ,[13] we were, for all that, children of wrath, even as others,[14] "but God, who is rich in mercy, for His great love wherewith He loved us, even when we were dead in sins, hath quickened us together with Christ, by whose grace we were saved." [15]

CHAPTER IV

FREE GRACE

This grace, however, of Christ, without which neither infants nor adults can be saved, is not rendered for any merits, but is given *gratis,* on account of which it is also called *grace.* "Being justified," says the apostle, "freely through His blood." [16] Whence they, who are not liberated through grace, either because they are not yet able to hear, or because they are unwilling to obey; or again because they did not receive, at the time when they were unable on account of youth to hear, that bath of regeneration, which they might have received and through which they might have been saved, are indeed justly condemned; because they are not without sin, either that which they have derived from their birth, or that which they have added

---

[13] 2 Cor. v. 17   [14] Eph. ii. 3   [15] Eph. ii. 4, 5   [16] Rom. iii. 24

from their own misconduct. "For all have sinned"—whether in Adam or in themselves—"and come short of the glory of God." [17]

CHAPTER V

IT WAS A MATTER OF JUSTICE THAT ALL SHOULD BE CONDEMNED

The entire mass, therefore, incurs penalty; and if the deserved punishment of condemnation were rendered to all, it would without doubt be righteously rendered. They, therefore, who are delivered therefrom by grace are called, not vessels of their own merits, but "vessels of mercy." [18] But of whose mercy, if not His who sent Christ Jesus into the world to save sinners, whom He foreknew, and foreordained, and called, and justified, and glorified? [19] Now, who could be so madly insane as to fail to give ineffable thanks to the Mercy which liberates whom it would? The man who correctly appreciated the whole subject could not possibly blame the justice of God in wholly condemning all men whatsoever.

CHAPTER VI

THE PELAGIANS HAVE VERY STRONG AND ACTIVE MINDS

If we are simply wise according to the Scriptures, we are not compelled to dispute against the grace of Christ, and to make statements attempting to show that human nature both requires no Physician—in infants, because it is whole and sound; and in adults, because it is able to suffice for itself in attaining righteousness, if it will. Men no doubt seem to urge acute opinions on these points, but it is only word-wisdom,[20] by which the cross of Christ is made of none effect. This, however, "is not the wisdom which descendeth from above." [21] The words which follow in the apostle's statement I am unwilling to quote; for we would rather not be thought to do an injustice to our friends, whose very strong and active minds we should be sorry to see running in a perverse, instead of an upright, course.

CHAPTER VII

HE PROCEEDS TO CONFUTE THE WORK OF PELAGIUS; HE REFRAINS AS YET FROM MENTIONING PELAGIUS' NAME

However ardent, then, is the zeal which the author of the book you have forwarded to me entertains against those who find a defence for their sins in the infirmity of human nature; not less, nay even much greater, should be our eagerness in preventing all attempts to render the cross of Christ of none effect. Of none effect, however, it is rendered, if it be contended that

[17] Rom. iii. 23   [18] Rom. ix. 23   [19] Rom. viii. 29, 30   [20] 1 Cor. i. 17   [21] Jas. iii. 15

by any other means than by Christ's own sacrament it is possible to attain to righteousness and everlasting life. This is actually done in the book to which I refer—I will not say by its author wittingly, lest I should express the judgment that he ought not to be accounted even a Christian, but, as I rather believe, unconsciously. He has done it, no doubt, with much power; I only wish that the ability he has displayed were sound and less like that which insane persons are accustomed to exhibit.

CHAPTER VIII

A DISTINCTION DRAWN BY PELAGIUS BETWEEN THE POSSIBLE AND ACTUAL

For he first of all makes a distinction: "It is one thing," says he, "to inquire whether a thing can be, which has respect to its possibility only; and another thing, whether or not it is." This distinction, nobody doubts, is true enough; for it follows that whatever is, was able to be; but it does not therefore follow that what is able to be, also is. Our Lord, for instance, raised Lazarus; He unquestionably was able to do so. But inasmuch as He did not raise up Judas, must we therefore contend that He was unable to do so? He certainly was able, but He would not. For if He had been willing, He could have effected this too. For the Son quickeneth whomsoever He will.[22] Observe, however, what he means by this distinction, true and manifest enough in itself, and what he endeavors to make out of it. "We are treating," says he, "of possibility only; and to pass from this to something else, except in the case of some certain fact, we deem to be a very serious and extraordinary process." This idea he turns over again and again, in many ways and at great length, so that no one would suppose that he was inquiring about any other point than the possibility of not committing sin. Among the many passages in which he treats of this subject, occurs the following: "I once more repeat my position: I say that it is possible for a man to be without sin. What do you say? That it is impossible for a man to be without sin? But I do not say," he adds, "that there is a man without sin; nor do you say, that there is not a man without sin. Our contention is about what is possible, and not possible; not about what is, and is not." He then enumerates certain passages of Scripture,[23] which are usually alleged in opposition to them, and insists that they have nothing to do with the question, which is really in dispute, as to the possibility or impossibility of a man's being without sin. This is what he says: "No man indeed is clean from pollution; and, There is no man that sinneth not; and, There is not a just man upon the earth; and, There is none that doeth good. There are these and similar passages in Scripture," says he, "but they testify to the point of not being, not of not being able; for by testimonies of this sort it is shown what kind of persons certain men were at such and such a time,

---

[22] John v. 21   [23] Job. xiv. 2; Kings viii. 46; Eccles. vii. 21; Ps. xiv. 1

not that they were unable to be something else. Whence they are justly found to be blameworthy. If, however, they had been of such a character, simply because they were unable to be anything else, they are free from blame."

CHAPTER IX

EVEN THEY WHO WERE NOT ABLE TO BE JUSTIFIED ARE CONDEMNED

See what he has said. I, however, affirm that an infant born in a place where it was not possible for him to be admitted to the baptism of Christ, and being overtaken by death, was placed in such circumstances, that is to say, died without the bath of regeneration, because it was not possible for him to be otherwise. He would therefore absolve him, and, in spite of the Lord's sentence, open to him the kingdom of heaven. The apostle, however, does not absolve him, when he says: "By one man sin entered into the world, and death by sin; by which death passed upon all men, for that all have sinned." [24] Rightly, therefore, by virtue of that condemnation which runs throughout the mass, is he not admitted into the kingdom of heaven, although he was not only not a Christian, but was unable to become one.

CHAPTER X

HE COULD NOT BE JUSTIFIED, WHO HAD NOT HEARD OF THE NAME OF CHRIST; RENDERING THE CROSS OF CHRIST OF NONE EFFECT

But they say: "He is not condemned; because the statement that all sinned in Adam, was not made because of the sin which is derived from one's birth, but because of imitation of him." If, therefore, Adam is said to be the author of all the sins which followed his own, because he was the first sinner of the human race, then how is it that Abel, rather than Christ, is not placed at the head of all the righteous, because he was the first righteous man? But I am not speaking of the case of an infant. I take the instance of a young man, or an old man, who has died in a region where he could not hear of the name of Christ. Well, could such a man have become righteous by nature and free will; or could he not? If they contend that he could, then see what it is to render the cross of Christ of none effect,[25] to contend that any man without it, can be justified by the law of nature and the power of his will. We may here also say, then is Christ dead in vain,[26] forasmuch as all might accomplish so much as this, even if He had never died; and if they should be unrighteous, they would be so because they wished to be, not because they were unable to be righteous. But even though a man could not be justified at all without the grace of Christ, he would absolve him, if he dared, in accordance with his words, to the effect

[24] Rom. v. 12   [25] I Cor. i. 1   [26] Gal. ii. 21

that, "if a man were of such a character, because he could not possibly have been of any other, he would be free from all blame."

CHAPTER XI

GRACE SUBTLY ACKNOWLEDGED BY PELAGIUS

He then starts an objection to his own position, as if, indeed, another person had raised it, and says: " 'A man,' you will say, 'may possibly be [without sin]; but it is by the grace of God.' " He then at once subjoins the following, as if in answer to his own suggestion: "I thank you for your kindness, because you are not merely content to withdraw your opposition to my statement, which you just now opposed, or barely to acknowledge it; but you actually go so far as to approve it. For to say, 'A man may possibly, but by this or by that,' is in fact nothing else than not only to assent to its possibility, but also to show the mode and condition of its possibility. Nobody, therefore, gives a better assent to the possibility of anything than the man who allows the condition thereof; because, without the thing itself, it is not possible for a condition to be." After this he raises another objection against himself: " 'But,' you will say, 'you here seem to reject the grace of God, inasmuch as you do not even mention it;' " and he then answers the objection: "Now, is it I that reject grace, who by acknowledging the thing must needs also confess the means by which it may be effected, or you, who by denying the thing do undoubtedly also deny whatever may be the means through which the thing is accomplished?" He forgot that he was now answering one who does not deny the thing, and whose objection he had just before set forth in these words: "A man may possibly be [without sin]; but it is by the grace of God." How then does that man deny the possibility, in defence of which his opponent earnestly contends, when he makes the admission to that opponent that "the thing is possible, but only by the grace of God?" That, however, after he is dismissed who already acknowledges the essential thing, he still has a question against those who maintain the impossibility of a man's being without sin, what is it to us? Let him ply his questions against any opponents he pleases, provided he only confesses this. which cannot be denied without the most criminal impiety, that without the grace of God a man cannot be without sin. He says, indeed: "Whether he confesses it to be by grace, or by aid, or by mercy, whatever that be by which a man can be without sin— every one acknowledges the thing itself."

CHAPTER XII

IN OUR DISCUSSIONS ABOUT GRACE, WE DO NOT SPEAK OF THAT WHICH RELATES TO THE CONSTITUTION OF OUR NATURE, BUT TO ITS RESTORATION

I confess to your love, that when I read those words I was filled with a sudden joy, because he did not deny the grace of God by which alone a man can be justified; for it is this which I mainly detest and dread in discussions of this kind. But when I went on to read the rest, I began to have my suspicions, first of all, from the similes he employs. For he says: "If I were to say, man is able to dispute; a bird is able to fly; a hare is able to run; without mentioning at the same time the instruments by which these acts can be accomplished—that is, the tongue, the wings, and the legs; should I then have denied the conditions of the various offices, when I acknowledged the very offices themselves?" It is at once apparent that he has here instanced such things as are by nature efficient; for the members of the bodily structure which are here mentioned are created with natures of such a kind—the tongue, the wings, the legs. He has not here posited any such thing as we wish to have understood by *grace*, without which no man is justified; for this is a topic which is concerned about the cure, not the constitution, of natural functions. Entertaining, then, some apprehensions, I proceeded to read all the rest, and I soon found that my suspicions had not been unfounded.

CHAPTER XIII

THE SCOPE AND PURPOSE OF THE LAW'S THREATENINGS; "PERFECT WAYFARERS"

But before I proceed further, see what he has said. When treating the question about the difference of sins, and starting as an objection to himself, what certain persons allege, "that some sins are light by their very frequency, their constant irruption making it impossible that they should be all of them avoided;" he thereupon denied that it was "proper that they should be censured even as light offences, if they cannot possibly be wholly avoided." He of course does not notice the Scriptures of the New Testament, wherein we learn[27] that the intention of the law in its censure is this, that, by reason of the transgressions which men commit, they may flee for refuge to the grace of the Lord, who has pity upon them—"the schoolmaster"[28] "shutting them up unto the same faith which should afterwards be revealed;"[29] that by it their transgressions may be forgiven, and then not again be committed, by God's assisting grace. The road indeed belongs

[27] We have read *discimus*, not *dicimus*   [28] Gal. iii. 24   [29] Gal. iii. 23

to all who are progressing in it; although it is they who make a good advance that are called "perfect travellers." That, however, is the height of perfection which admits of no addition, when the goal to which men tend has begun to be possessed.

CHAPTER XIV

REFUTATION OF PELAGIUS

But the truth is, the question which is proposed to him—"Are you even yourself without sin?"—does not really belong to the subject in dispute. What, however, he says—that "it is rather to be imputed to his own negligence that he is not without sin," is no doubt well spoken; but then he should deem it to be his duty even to pray to God that this faulty negligence get not the dominion over him—the prayer that a certain man once put up, when he said: "Order my steps according to Thy word, and let not any iniquity have dominion over me" [30]—lest, while relying on his own diligence as on strength of his own, he should fail to attain to the true righteousness either by this way, or by that other method in which, no doubt, perfect righteousness is to be desired and hoped for.

CHAPTER XV

NOT EVERYTHING [OF DOCTRINAL TRUTH] IS WRITTEN IN SCRIPTURE IN SO MANY WORDS

That, too, which is said to him, "that it is nowhere written in so many words, A man can be without sin," he easily refutes thus: "That the question here is not in what precise words each doctrinal statement is made." It is perhaps not without reason that, while in several passages of Scripture we may find it said that men are without excuse, it is nowhere found that any man is described as being without sin, except Him only, of whom it is plainly said, that "He knew no sin." [31] Similarly, we read in the passage where the subject is concerning priests: "He was in all points tempted like as we are, only without sin" [32]—meaning, of course, in that flesh which bore the likeness of sinful flesh, although it was not sinful flesh; a likeness, indeed, which it would not have borne if it had not been in every other respect the same as sinful flesh. How, however, we are to understand this: "Whosoever is born of God doth not commit sin; neither can he sin, for his seed remaineth in him;" [33] while the Apostle John himself, as if he had not been born of God, or else were addressing men who had not been born of God, lays down this position: "If we say that we have no sin, we deceive ourselves, and the truth is not in us" [34]—I have already explained, with such care as I was able, in those books which I wrote to Marcellinus on this

---

[30] Ps. cxix. 133   [31] 2 Cor. v. 21   [32] Heb. iv. 15   [33] 1 John iii. 9   [34] 1 John i. 8

very subject.[35] It seems, moreover, to me to be an interpretation worthy of acceptance to regard the clause of the above quoted passage: "Neither can he sin," as if it meant: *He ought not to commit sin.* For who could be so foolish as to say that sin ought to be committed, when, in fact, sin is sin, for no other reason than that it ought not to be committed?

CHAPTER XVI

PELAGIUS CORRUPTS A PASSAGE OF THE APOSTLE JAMES BY ADDING A NOTE OF INTERROGATION

Now that passage, in which the Apostle James says: "But the tongue can no man tame," [36] does not appear to me to be capable of the interpretation which he would put upon it, when he expounds it, "as if it were written by way of reproach; as much as to say: Can no man, then, tame the tongue? As if in a reproachful tone, which would say: You are able to tame wild beasts; cannot you tame the tongue? As if it were an easier thing to tame the tongue than to subjugate wild beasts." I do not think that this is the meaning of the passage. For, if he had meant such an opinion as this to be entertained of the facility of taming the tongue, there would have followed in the sequel of the passage a comparison of that member with the beasts. As it is, however, it simply goes on to say: "The tongue is an unruly evil, full of deadly poison"—such, of course, as is more noxious than that of beasts and creeping things. For while the one destroys the flesh, the other kills the soul. For, "The mouth that belieth slayeth the soul." [37] It is not, therefore, as if this is an easier achievement than the taming of beasts that Saint James pronounced the statement before us, or would have others utter it; but he rather aims at showing what a great evil in man his tongue is—so great, indeed, that it cannot be tamed by any man, although even beasts are tameable by human beings. And he said this, not with a view to our permitting, through our neglect, the continuance of so great an evil to ourselves, but in order that we might be induced to request the help of divine grace for the taming of the tongue. For he does not say: "None can tame the tongue;" but *"No man;"* in order that, when it is tamed, we may acknowledge it to be effected by the mercy of God, the help of God, the grace of God. The soul, therefore, should endeavor to tame the tongue, and while endeavoring should pray for assistance; the tongue, too, should beg for the taming of the tongue—He being the tamer who said to His disciples: "It is not ye that speak, but the Spirit of your Father which speaketh in you." [38] Thus, we are warned by the precept to do this—namely, to make the attempt, and, failing in our own strength, to pray for the help of God.

---

[35] See the *De Peccat. Meritis et Remissione,* ii. 8-10   [36] Jas. iii. 8   [37] Wisd. i. 11
[38] Matt. x. 20

CHAPTER XVII

EXPLANATION OF THIS TEXT CONTINUED

Accordingly, after emphatically describing the evil of the tongue—saying, among other things: "My brethren, these things ought not so to be" [39]—he at once, after finishing some remarks which arose out of his subject, goes on to add this advice, showing by what help those things would not happen, which (as he said) ought not: "Who is a wise man and endowed with knowledge among you? Let him show out of a good conversation his works with meekness of wisdom. But if ye have bitter envying and strife in your hearts, glory not and lie not against the truth. This wisdom descendeth not from above, but is earthly, sensual, devilish. For where there is envying and strife, there is confusion and every evil work. But the wisdom that is from above is first pure, then peaceable, gentle, and easy to be entreated, full of mercy and good fruits, without partiality, and without hypocrisy." [40] This is the wisdom which tames the tongue; it descends from above, and springs from no human heart. Will any one, then, dare to divorce it from the grace of God, and with most arrogant vanity place it in the power of man? Why should I pray to God that it be accorded me, if it may be had of man? Ought we not to object to this prayer lest injury be done to free will which is self-sufficient in the possibility of nature for discharging all the duties of righteousness? We ought, then, to object also to the Apostle James himself, who admonishes us in these words: "If any of you lack wisdom, let him ask of God, that giveth to all men liberally, and upbraideth not, and it shall be given him; but let him ask in faith, nothing doubting." [41] This is the faith to which the commandments drive us, in order that the law may prescribe our duty and faith accomplish it. For through the tongue, which no man can tame, but only the wisdom which comes down from above, "in many things we all of us offend." [42] For this truth also the same apostle pronounced in no other sense than that in which he afterwards declares: "The tongue no man can tame." [36]

CHAPTER XVIII

WHO MAY BE SAID TO BE IN THE FLESH

There is a passage which nobody could place against these texts with the similar purpose of showing the impossibility of not sinning: "The wisdom of the flesh is enmity against God; for it is not subject to the law of God, neither indeed can be; so then they that are in the flesh cannot please God;" [43] for he here mentions the wisdom of the flesh, not the

---

[39] Jas. iii. 10   [40] Jas. iii. 13–17   [41] Jas. i. 5, 6   [42] Jas. iii. 2   [43] Rom. viii. 7, 8

wisdom which cometh from above: moreover, it is manifest, that in this passage, by the phrase, "being in the flesh," are signified, not those who have not yet quitted the body, but those who live according to the flesh. The question, however, we are discussing does not lie in this point. But what I want to hear from him, if I can, is about those who live according to the Spirit, and who on this account are not, in a certain sense, in the flesh, even while they still live here—whether they, by God's grace, live according to the Spirit, or are sufficient for themselves, natural capability having been bestowed on them when they were created, and their own proper will besides. Whereas the fulfilling of the law is nothing else than love;[44] and God's love is shed abroad in our hearts, not by our own selves, but by the Holy Ghost which is given to us." [45]

CHAPTER XIX

SINS OF IGNORANCE; TO WHOM WISDOM IS GIVEN BY GOD ON THEIR REQUESTING IT

He further treats of sins of ignorance, and says that "a man ought to be very careful to avoid ignorance; and that ignorance is blameworthy for this reason, because it is through his own neglect that a man is ignorant of that which he certainly must have known if he had only applied diligence;" whereas he prefers disputing all things rather than to pray, and say: "Give me understanding, that I may learn Thy commandments." [46] It is, indeed, one thing to have taken no pains to know what sins of negligence were apparently expiated even through divers sacrifices of the law; it is another thing to wish to understand, to be unable, and then to act contrary to the law, through not understanding what it would have done. We are accordingly enjoined to ask of God wisdom, "who giveth to all men liberally;" [47] that is, of course, to all men who ask in such a manner, and to such an extent, as so great a matter requires in earnestness of petition.

CHAPTER XX

WHAT PRAYER PELAGIUS WOULD ADMIT TO BE NECESSARY

He confesses that "sins which have been committed do notwithstanding require to be divinely expiated, and that the Lord must be entreated because of them"—that is, for the purpose, of course, of obtaining pardon; "because that which has been done cannot," it is his own admission, "be undone," by that "power of nature and will of man" which he talks about so much. From this necessity, therefore, it follows that a man must pray to be forgiven. That a man, however, requires to be helped not to sin, he has nowhere admitted; I read no such admission in this passage; he keeps a

---

[44] Rom. xiii. 10   [45] Rom. v. 5   [46] Ps. cxix. 73   [47] Jas. i. 5

strange silence on this subject altogether; although the Lord's Prayer enjoins upon us the necessity of praying both that our debts may be remitted to us, and that we may not be led into temptation—the one petition entreating that past offences may be atoned for; the other, that future ones may be avoided. Now, although this is never done unless our will be assistant, yet our will alone is not enough to secure its being done; the prayer, therefore, which is offered up to God for this result is neither superfluous nor offensive to the Lord. For what is more foolish than to pray that you may do that which you have it in your own power to do.

CHAPTER XXI

PELAGIUS DENIES THAT HUMAN NATURE HAS BEEN DEPRAVED OR CORRUPTED BY SIN

You may now see (what bears very closely on our subject) how he endeavors to exhibit human nature, as if it were wholly without fault, and how he struggles against the plainest of God's Scriptures with that "wisdom of word" [48] which renders the cross of Christ of none effect. That cross, however, shall certainly never be made of none effect; rather shall such wisdom be subverted. Now, after we shall have demonstrated this, it may be that God's mercy may visit him, so that he may be sorry that he ever said these things: "We have," he says, "first of all to discuss the position which is maintained, that our nature has been weakened and changed by sin. I think," continues he, "that before all other things we have to inquire what sin is—some substance, or wholly a name without substance, whereby is expressed not a thing, not an existence, not some sort of a body, but the doing of a wrongful deed." He then adds: "I suppose that this is the case; and if so," he asks, "how could that which lacks all substance have possibly weakened or changed human nature?" Observe, I beg of you, how in his ignorance he struggles to overthrow the most salutary words of the remedial Scriptures: "I said, O Lord, be merciful unto me; heal my soul, for I have sinned against Thee." [49] Now, how can a thing be healed, if it is not wounded nor hurt, nor weakened and corrupted? But, as there is here something to be healed, whence did it receive its injury? You hear [the Psalmist] confessing the fact; what need is there of discussion? He says: "Heal my soul." Ask him how that which he wants to be healed became injured, and then listen to his following words: "Because I have sinned against Thee." Let him, however, put a question, and ask what he deemed a suitable inquiry, and say: "O you who exclaim, Heal my soul, for I have sinned against Thee! pray tell me what sin is? Some substance, or wholly a name without substance, whereby is expressed, not a thing, not an existence, not some sort of a

[48] I Cor. i. 17   [49] Ps. xli. 4

body, but merely the doing of a wrongful deed?" Then the other returns
for answer: "It is even as you say; sin is not some substance; but under
its name there is merely expressed the doing of a wrongful deed." But
he rejoins: "Then why cry out, Heal my soul, for I have sinned against
Thee? How could that have possibly corrupted your soul which lacks all
substance?" Then would the other, worn out with the anguish of his wound,
in order to avoid being diverted from prayer by the discussion, briefly
answer and say: "Go from me, I beseech you; rather discuss the point, if
you can, with Him who said: 'They that are whole need no physician, but
they that are sick; I am not come to call the righteous, but sinners' " [50]—
in which words, of course, He designated the righteous as the whole, and
sinners as the sick.

CHAPTER XXII

HOW OUR NATURE COULD BE VITIATED BY SIN, EVEN THOUGH IT
BE NOT A SUBSTANCE

Now, do you not perceive the tendency and direction of this controversy? Even to render of none effect the Scripture where it is said: "Thou
shalt call His name Jesus, for He shall save His people from their sins." [51]
For how is He to save where there is no malady? For the sins, from which
this gospel says Christ's people have to be saved, are not substances, and
according to this writer are incapable of corrupting. O brother, how good
a thing it is to remember that you are a Christian! To believe, might perhaps be enough; but still, since you persist in discussion, there is no harm,
nay there is even benefit, if a firm faith precede it; let us not suppose,
then, that human nature cannot be corrupted by sin, but rather, believing,
from the inspired Scriptures, that it is corrupted by sin, let our inquiry be
how this could possibly have come about. Since, then, we have already
learnt that sin is not a substance, do we not consider, not to mention any
other example, that not to eat is also not a substance? Because such abstinence is withdrawal from a substance, inasmuch as food is a substance. To
abstain, then, from food is not a substance; and yet the substance of our
body, if it does altogether abstain from food, so languishes, is so impaired
by broken health, is so exhausted of strength, so weakened and broken with
very weariness, that even if it be in any way able to continue alive, it is
hardly capable of being restored to the use of that food, by abstaining from
which it became so corrupted and injured. In the same way sin is not a substance; but God is a substance, yea the height of substance and only true
sustenance of the reasonable creature. The consequence of departing from
Him by disobedience, and of inability, through infirmity, to receive what
one ought really to rejoice in, you hear from the Psalmist, when he says:

[50] Matt. ix. 12, 13   [51] Matt. i. 21

"My heart is smitten and withered like grass, since I have forgotten to eat my bread." [52]

CHAPTER XXIII

ADAM DELIVERED BY THE MERCY OF CHRIST

But observe how, by specious arguments, he continues to oppose the truth of Holy Scripture. The Lord Jesus, who is called Jesus because He saves His people from their sins,[51] in accordance with this His merciful character, says: "They that be whole need not a physician, but they that are sick; I am come not to call the righteous, but sinners to repentance." [53] Accordingly, His apostle also says: "This is a faithful saying, and worthy of all acceptation, that Christ Jesus came into the world to save sinners." [54] This man, however, contrary to the "faithful saying, and worthy of all acceptation," declares that "this sickness ought not to have been contracted by sins, lest the punishment of sin should amount to this, that more sins should be committed." Now even for infants the help of the Great Physician is sought. This writer asks: "Why seek Him? They are whole for whom you seek the Physician. Not even was the first man condemned to die for any such reason, for he did not sin afterwards." As if he had ever heard anything of his subsequent perfection in righteousness, except so far as the Church commends to our faith that even Adam was delivered by the mercy of the Lord Christ. "As to his posterity also," says he, "not only are they not more infirm than he, but they actually fulfilled more commandments than he ever did, since he neglected to fulfil one"—this posterity which he sees so born (as Adam certainly was not made), not only incapable of commandment, which they do not at all understand, but hardly capable of sucking the breast, when they are hungry! Yet even these would He have to be saved in the bosom of Mother Church by His grace who saves His people from their sins; but these men gainsay such grace, and, as if they had a deeper insight into the creature than ever He possesses who made the creature, they pronounce [these infants] sound with an assertion which is anything but sound itself.

CHAPTER XXIV

SIN AND THE PENALTY OF SIN THE SAME

"The very matter," says he, "of sin is its punishment, if the sinner is so much weakened that he commits more sins." He does not consider how justly the light of truth forsakes the man who transgresses the law. When thus deserted, he of course becomes blinded, and necessarily offends more; and by so falling is embarrassed, and being embarrassed fails to rise, so

---

[52] Ps. cii. 4   [53] Matt. ix. 12   [54] 1 Tim. i. 15

as to hear the voice of the law, which admonishes him to beg for the Saviour's grace. Is no punishment due to them of whom the apostle says: "Because that, when they knew God, they glorified Him not as God, neither were thankful; but became vain in their imaginations, and their foolish heart was darkened?" [55] This darkening was, of course, already their punishment and penalty; and yet by this very penalty—that is, by their blindness of heart, which supervenes on the withdrawal of the light of wisdom— they fell into more grievous sins still. "For giving themselves out as wise, they became fools." This is a grievous penalty, if one only understands it; and from such a penalty only see to what lengths they ran: "And they changed," he says, "the glory of the uncorruptible God into an image made like to corruptible man, and to birds, and four-footed beasts, and creeping things." [56] All this they did owing to that penalty of their sin, whereby "their foolish heart was darkened." And yet, owing to these deeds of theirs, which, although coming in the way of punishment, were none the less sins (he goes on to say): "Wherefore God also gave them up to uncleanness, through the lusts of their own hearts." [57] See how severely God condemned them, giving them over to uncleanness in the very desires of their heart. Observe also the sins they commit owing to such condemnation: "To dishonor," says he, "their own bodies among themselves." [57] Here is the punishment of iniquity, which is itself iniquity; a fact which sets forth in a clearer light the words which follow: "Who changed the truth of God into a lie, and worshipped and served the creature more than the Creator, who is blessed for ever. Amen." "For this cause," says he, "God gave them up unto vile affections." [58] See how often God inflicts punishment; and out of the self-same punishment sins, more numerous and more severe, arise. "For even their women did change the natural use into that which is against nature; and likewise the men also, leaving the natural use of the woman, burned in their lust one toward another; men with men working that which is unseemly." [59] Then, to show that these things were so sins themselves, that they were also the penalties of sins, he further says: "And receiving in themselves that recompense of their error which was meet." [60] Observe how often it happens that the very punishment which God inflicts begets other sins as its natural offspring. Attend still further: "And even as they did not like to retain God in their knowledge," says he, "God gave them over to a reprobate mind, to do those things which are not convenient; being filled with all unrighteousness, fornication, wickedness, covetousness, maliciousness; full of envy, murder, debate, deceit, malignity; whisperers, backbiters, odious to God, despiteful, proud, boasters, inventors of evil things, disobedient to parents, without understanding, covenant-breakers, without natural affection, implacable, unmerciful." [61] Here, now, let our opponent say: "Sin ought not so to have been punished, that the sinner, through his punishment, should commit even more sins."

[55] Rom. i. 21   [56] Rom. i. 23   [57] Rom. i. 24   [58] Rom. i. 25, 26   [59] Rom. i. 26, 27   [60] Rom. i. 27   [61] Rom. i. 28-31

CHAPTER XXV

GOD FORSAKES ONLY THOSE WHO DESERVE TO BE FORSAKEN. WE ARE
SUFFICIENT OF OURSELVES TO COMMIT SIN; BUT NOT TO RETURN
TO THE WAY OF RIGHTEOUSNESS. DEATH IS THE PUNISHMENT,
NOT THE CAUSE OF SIN

Perhaps he may answer that God does not compel men to do these things, but only forsakes those who deserve to be forsaken. If he does say this, he says what is most true. For, as I have already remarked, those who are forsaken by the light of righteousness, and are therefore groping in darkness, produce nothing else than those works of darkness which I have enumerated, until such time as it is said to them, and they obey the command: "Awake thou that sleepest, and arise from the dead, and Christ shall give thee light." [62] The truth designates them as dead; whence the passage: "Let the dead bury their dead." The truth, then, designates as *dead* those whom this man declares to have been unable to be damaged or corrupted by sin, on the ground, forsooth, that he has discovered sin to be no substance! Nobody tells him that "man was so formed as to be able to pass from righteousness to sin, and yet not able to return from sin to righteousness." But that free will, whereby man corrupted his own self, was sufficient for his passing into sin; but to return to righteousness, he has need of a Physician, since he is out of health; he has need of a Vivifier, because he is dead. Now about such grace as this he says not a word, as if he were able to cure himself by his own will, since this alone was able to ruin him. We do not tell him that the death of the body is of efficacy for sinning, because it is only its punishment; for no one sins by undergoing the death of his body; but the death of the soul is conducive to sin, forsaken as it is by its life, that is, its God; and it must needs produce dead works, until it revives by the grace of Christ. God forbid that we should assert that hunger and thirst and other bodily sufferings necessarily produce sin. When exercised by such vexations, the life of the righteous only shines out with greater lustre, and procures a greater glory by overcoming them through patience; but then it is assisted by the grace, it is assisted by the Spirit, it is assisted by the mercy of God; not exalting itself in an arrogant will, but earning fortitude by a humble confession. For it had learnt to say unto God: "Thou art my hope; Thou art my trust." [63] Now, how it happens that concerning this grace, and help and mercy, without which we cannot live, this man has nothing to say, I am at a loss to know; but he goes further, and in the most open manner gainsays the grace of Christ whereby we are justified, by insisting on the sufficiency of nature to work righteousness, provided only the will be present. The reason, however, why, after

[62] Eph. v. 14   [63] Ps. lxxi. 5

sin has been released to the guilty one by grace, for the exercise of faith, there should still remain the death of the body, although it proceeds from sin, I have already explained, according to my ability, in those books which I wrote to Marcellinus of blessed memory.[64]

CHAPTER XXVI

CHRIST DIED OF HIS OWN POWER AND CHOICE

As to his statement, indeed, that "the Lord was able to die without sin;" His being born also was of the ability of His mercy, not the demand of His nature: so, likewise, did He undergo death of His own power; and this is our price which He paid to redeem us from death. Now, this truth their contention labors hard to make of none effect; for human nature is maintained by them to be such, that with free will it wants no such ransom in order to be translated from the power of darkness and of him who has the power of death,[65] into the kingdom of Christ the Lord.[66] And yet, when the Lord drew near His passion, He said, "Behold, the prince of this world cometh and shall find nothing in me" [67]—and therefore no sin, of course, on account of which he might exercise dominion over Him, so as to destroy Him. "But," added He, "that the world may know that I do the will of my Father, arise, let us go hence;" [68] as much as to say, I am going to die, not through the necessity of sin, but in voluntariness of obedience.

CHAPTER XXVII

EVEN EVILS, THROUGH GOD'S MERCY, ARE OF USE

He asserts that "no evil is the cause of anything good;" as if punishment, forsooth, were good, although thereby many have been reformed. There are, then, evils which are of use by the wondrous mercy of God. Did that man experience some good thing, when he said, "Thou didst hide Thy face from me, and I was troubled?" [69] Certainly not; and yet this very trouble was to him in a certain manner a remedy against his pride. For he had said in his prosperity, "I shall never be moved;" [70] and so was ascribing to himself what he was receiving from the Lord. "For what had he that he did not receive?" [71] It had, therefore, become necessary to show him whence he had received, that he might receive in humiilty what he had lost in pride. Accordingly, he says, "In Thy good pleasure, O Lord, Thou didst add strength to my beauty." [69] In this abundance of mine I once used to

<hr>

[64] The tribune Marcellinus had been put to death in the September of 413, "having, though innocent, fallen a victim to the cruel hatred of the tyrant Heraclius," as Jerome writes in his book iii. against the Pelagians

[65] Heb. ii. 14   [66] Col. i. 13   [67] John xiv. 30   [68] John xiv. 31   [69] Ps. xxx. 7   [70] Ps. xxx. 8   [71] 1 Cor. iv. 7

say, "I shall not be moved;" whereas it all came from Thee, not from my-self. Then at last Thou didst turn away Thy face from me, and I became troubled.

CHAPTER XXVIII

THE DISPOSITION OF NEARLY ALL WHO GO ASTRAY. WITH SOME
HERETICS OUR BUSINESS OUGHT NOT TO BE DISPUTATION,
BUT PRAYER

Man's proud mind has no relish at all for this; God, however, is great, in persuading even it how to find it all out. We are, indeed, more inclined to seek how best to reply to such arguments as oppose our error, than to experience how salutary would be our condition if we were free from error. We ought, therefore, to encounter all such, not by discussions, but rather by prayers both for them and for ourselves. For we never say to them, what this opponent has opposed to himself, that "sin was necessary in order that there might be a cause for God's mercy." Would there had never been misery to render that mercy necessary! But the iniquity of sin—which is so much the greater in proportion to the ease wherewith man might have avoided sin, while no infirmity did as yet beset him—has been followed closely up by a most righteous punishment; even that [of-fending man] should receive in himself a reward in kind of his sin, losing that obedience of his body which had been in some degree put under his own control, which he had despised when it was the right of his Lord. And, inasmuch as we are now born with the self-same law of sin, which in our members resists the law of our mind, we ought never to murmur against God, nor to dispute in opposition to the clearest fact, but to seek and pray for His mercy instead of our punishment.

CHAPTER XXIX

A SIMILE TO SHOW THAT GOD'S GRACE IS NECESSARY FOR DOING ANY
GOOD WORK WHATEVER. GOD NEVER FORSAKES THE JUSTIFIED MAN
IF HE BE NOT HIMSELF FORSAKEN[72]

Observe, indeed, how cautiously he expresses himself: "God, no doubt, applies His mercy even to this office, whenever it is necessary; because man after sin requires help in this way, not because God wished there should be a cause for such necessity." Do you not see how he does not say that God's grace is necessary to prevent us from sinning, but because we have sinned? Then he adds: "But just in the same way it is the duty of a physician to be ready to cure a man who is already wounded; although he ought not to wish for a man who is sound to be wounded." Now, if this

---

[72] See the treatise *De Peccatorum Meritis*, ii. 22

simile suits the subject of which we are treating, human nature is certainly incapable of receiving a wound from sin, inasmuch as sin is not a substance. As therefore, for example's sake, a man who is lamed by a wound is cured in order that his step for the future may be direct and strong, its past infirmity being healed, so does the Heavenly Physician cure our maladies, not only that they may cease any longer to exist, but in order that we may ever afterwards be able to walk aright—to which we should be unequal, even after our healing, except by His continued help. For after a medical man has administered a cure, in order that the patient may be afterwards duly nourished with bodily elements and aliments, for the completion and continuance of the said cure by suitable means and help, he commends him to God's good care, who bestows these aids on all who live in the flesh, and from whom proceeded even those means which [the physician] applied during the process of the cure. For it is not out of any resources which he has himself created that the medical man effects any cure, but out of the resources of Him who creates all things which are required by the whole and by the sick. God, however, whenever He—through "the one mediator between God and men, the man Christ Jesus"—spiritually heals the sick or raises the dead, that is, justifies the ungodly, and when He has brought him to perfect health, in other words, to the fulness of life and righteousness, does not forsake, if He is not forsaken, in order that life may be passed in constant piety and righteousness. For, just as the eye of the body, even when completely sound, is unable to see unless aided by the brightness of light, so also man, even when most fully justified, is unable to lead a holy life, if he be not divinely assisted by the eternal light of righteousness. God, therefore, heals us not only that He may blot out the sin which we have committed, but, furthermore, that He may enable us even to avoid sinning.

CHAPTER XXX

SIN IS REMOVED BY SIN

He no doubt shows some acuteness in handling, and turning over and exposing, as he likes, and refuting a certain statement, which is made to this effect, that "it was really necessary to man, in order to take from him all occasion for pride and boasting, that he should be unable to exist without sin." He supposes it to be "the height of absurdity and folly, that there should have been sin in order that sin might not be; inasmuch as pride is itself, of course, a sin." As if a sore were not attended with pain, and an operation did not produce pain, that pain might be taken away by pain. If we had not experienced any such treatment, but were only to hear about it in some parts of the world where these things had never happened, we might perhaps use this man's words, and say, It is the height of absurdity that pain should have been necessary in order that a sore should have no pain.

CHAPTER XXXI

THE ORDER AND PROCESS OF HEALING OUR HEAVENLY PHYSICIAN
DOES NOT ADOPT FROM THE SICK PATIENT, BUT DERIVES FROM
HIMSELF. WHAT CAUSE THE RIGHTEOUS HAVE FOR FEARING

"But God," they say, "is able to heal all things." Of course His purpose
in acting is to heal all things; but He acts on His own judgment, and does
not take His procedure in healing from the sick man. For undoubtedly it
was His wish to endow His apostle with very great power and strength, and
yet He said to him: "My strength is made perfect in weakness;" [73] nor
did He remove from him, though he so often entreated Him to do so, that
mysterious "thorn in the flesh," which He told him had been given to him
"lest he should be unduly exalted through the abundance of the revelation." [74] For all other sins only prevail in evil deeds; pride only has to
be guarded against in things that are rightly done. Whence it happens that
those persons are admonished not to attribute to their own power the gifts
of God, nor to plume themselves thereon, lest by so doing they should perish
with a heavier perdition than if they had done no good at all, to whom it
is said: "Work out your own salvation with fear and trembling, for it is
God which worketh in you, both to will and to do of His good pleasure." [75]
Why, then, must it be with fear and trembling, and not rather with security,
since God is working; except it be because there so quickly steals over our
human soul, by reason of our will (without which we can do nothing well),
the inclination to esteem simply as our own accomplishment whatever good
we do; and so each one of us says in his prosperity: "I shall never be
moved?" [76] Therefore, He who in His good pleasure had added strength
to our beauty, turns away His face, and the man who had made his boast
becomes troubled, because it is by actual sorrows that the swelling pride
must be remedied.

CHAPTER XXXII

GOD FORSAKES US TO SOME EXTENT THAT WE MAY NOT GROW PROUD

Therefore it is not said to a man: "It is necessary for you to sin that you
may not sin;" but it is said to a man: "God in some degree forsakes you,
in consequence of which you grow proud, that you may know that you are
'not your own,' but are His,[77] and learn not to be proud." Now even that
incident in the apostle's life, of this kind, is so wonderful, that were it not
for the fact that he himself is the voucher for it whose truth it is impious to
contradict, would it not be incredible? For what believer is there who is

[73] 2 Cor. xii. 9   [74] 2 Cor. xii. 7, 8   [75] Phil. ii. 12, 13   [76] Ps. xxx. 6   [77] 1 Cor.
vi. 19

ignorant that the first incentive to sin came from Satan, and that he is the
first author of all sins? And yet, for all that, some are "delivered over unto
Satan, that they may learn not to blaspheme." [78] How comes it to pass,
then, that Satan's work is prevented by the work of Satan? These and such
like questions let a man regard in such a light that they seem not to him
to be too acute; they have somewhat of the sound of acuteness, and yet
when discussed are found to be obtuse. What must we say also to our
author's use of similes whereby he rather suggests to us the answer which
we should give to him? "What" (asks he) "shall I say more than this, that
we may believe that fires are quenched by fires, if we may believe that
sins are cured by sins?" What if one cannot put out fires by fires: but yet
pains can, for all that, as I have shown, be cured by pains? Poisons can
also, if one only inquire and learn the fact, be expelled by poisons. Now, if
he observes that the heats of fevers are sometimes subdued by certain
medicinal warmths, he will perhaps also allow that fires may be extinguished by fires.

CHAPTER XXXIII

NOT EVERY SIN IS PRIDE. HOW PRIDE IS THE COMMENCEMENT OF EVERY SIN

"But how," asks he, "shall we separate pride itself from sin?" Now, why
does he raise such a question, when it is manifest that even pride itself is
a sin? "To sin," says he, "is quite as much to be proud, as to be proud is
to sin; for only ask what every sin is, and see whether you can find any sin
without the designation of pride." Then he thus pursues this opinion, and
endeavors to prove it thus: "Every sin," says he, "if I mistake not, is a
contempt of God, and every contempt of God is pride. For what is so proud
as to despise God? All sin, then, is also pride, even as Scripture says, Pride
is the beginning of all sin." [79] Let him seek diligently, and he will find in
the law that the sin of pride is quite distinguished from all other sins. For
many sins are committed through pride; but yet not all things which are
wrongly done are done proudly—at any rate, not by the ignorant, not by
the infirm, and not, generally speaking, by the weeping and sorrowful. And
indeed pride, although it be in itself a great sin, is of such sort in itself
alone apart from others, that, as I have already remarked, it for the most
part follows after and steals with more rapid foot, not so much upon sins as
upon things which are actually well done. However, that which he has
understood in another sense, is after all most truly said: "Pride is the commencement of all sin;" because it was this which overthrew the devil, from
whom arose the origin of sin; and afterwards, when his malice and envy
pursued man, who was yet standing in his uprightness, it subverted him in

---

[78] 1 Tim. i. 20   [79] Ecclus. x. 13

the same way in which he himself fell. For the serpent, in fact, only sought for the door of pride whereby to enter when he said, "Ye shall be as gods." [80] Truly then is it said, "Pride is the commencement of all sin;" [79] and, "The beginning of pride is when a man departeth from God." [81]

CHAPTER XXXIV

A MAN'S SIN IS HIS OWN, BUT HE NEEDS GRACE FOR HIS CURE

Well, but what does he mean when he says: "Then again, how can one be subjected to God for the guilt of that sin, which he knows is not his own? For," says he, "his own it is not, if it is necessary. Or, if it is his own, it is voluntary: and if it is voluntary, it can be avoided." We reply: It is unquestionably his own. But the fault by which sin is committed is not yet in every respect healed, and the fact of its becoming permanently fixed in us arises from our not rightly using the healing virtue; and so out of this faulty condition the man who is now growing strong in depravity commits many sins, either through infirmity or blindness. Prayer must therefore be made for him, that he may be healed, and that he may thenceforward attain to a life of uninterrupted soundness of health; nor must pride be indulged in, as if any man were healed by the self-same power whereby he became corrupted.

CHAPTER XXXV

WHY GOD DOES NOT IMMEDIATELY CURE PRIDE ITSELF. THE SECRET AND INSIDIOUS GROWTH OF PRIDE. PREVENTING AND SUBSEQUENT GRACE

But I would indeed so treat these topics, as to confess myself ignorant of God's deeper counsel, why He does not at once heal the very principle of pride, which lies in wait for man's heart even in deeds rightly done; and for the cure of which pious souls, with tears and strong crying, beseech Him that He would stretch forth His right hand and help their endeavors to overcome it, and somehow tread and crush it under foot. Now when a man has felt glad that he has even by some good work overcome pride, from the very joy he lifts up his head and says: "Behold, I live; why do you triumph? Nay, I live because you triumph." Premature, however, this forwardness of his to triumph over pride may perhaps be, as if it were now vanquished, whereas its last shadow is to be swallowed up, as I suppose, in that noontide which is promised in the scripture which says, "He shall bring forth thy righteousness as the light, and thy judgment as the noonday;" [82] provided that be done which was written in the preceding verse: "Commit thy way unto the Lord; trust also in Him, and He shall bring it to pass" [83]—not, as some suppose, that they themselves bring it to pass.

[80] Gen. iii. 5   [81] Ecclus. x. 12   [82] Ps. xxxvii. 6   [83] Ps. xxxvii. 5

Now, when he said, "And He shall bring it to pass," he evidently had none other in mind but those who say, We ourselves bring it to pass; that is to say, we ourselves justify our own selves. In this matter, no doubt, we do ourselves, too, work; but we are fellow-workers with Him who does the work, because His mercy anticipates us. He anticipates us, however, that we may be healed; but then He will also follow us, that being healed we may grow healthy and strong. He anticipates us that we may be called; He will follow us that we may be glorified. He anticipates us that we may lead godly lives; He will follow us that we may always live with Him, because without Him we can do nothing.[84] Now the Scriptures refer to both these operations of grace. There is both this: "The God of my mercy shall antici- pate me," [85] and again this: "Thy mercy shall follow me all the days of my life." [86] Let us therefore unveil to Him our life by confession, not praise it with a vindication. For if it is not His way, but our own, beyond doubt it is not the right one. Let us therefore reveal this by making our confession to Him; for however much we may endeavor to conceal it, it is not hid from Him. It is a good thing to confess unto the Lord.

CHAPTER XXXVI

PRIDE EVEN IN SUCH THINGS AS ARE DONE ARIGHT MUST BE AVOIDED. FREE WILL IS NOT TAKEN AWAY WHEN GRACE IS PREACHED

So will He bestow on us whatever pleases Him, that if there be anything displeasing to Him in us, it will also be displeasing to us. "He will," as the Scripture has said, "turn aside our paths from His own way," [87] and will make that which is His own to be our way; because it is by Himself that the favor is bestowed on such as believe in Him and hope in Him that we will do it. For there is a way of righteousness of which they are ignorant "who have a zeal for God, but not according to knowledge," [88] and who, wishing to frame a righteousness of their own, "have not submitted them- selves to the righteousness of God." [89] "For Christ is the end of the law for righteousness to every one that believeth;" [90] and He has said, "I am the way." [91] Yet God's voice has alarmed those who have already begun to walk in this way, lest they should be lifted up, as if it were by their own energies that they were walking therein. For the same persons to whom the apostle, on account of this danger, says, "Work out your own salvation with fear and trembling, for it is God that worketh in you, both to will and to do of His good pleasure," [92] are likewise for the self-same reason admon- ished in the psalm: "Serve the Lord with fear, and rejoice in Him with trembling. Accept correction, lest at any time the Lord be angry, and ye perish from the righteous way, when His wrath shall be suddenly kindled upon you." [93] He does not say, "Lest at any time the Lord be angry and

[84] John xv. 5   [85] Ps. lix. 10   [86] Ps. xxiii. 6   [87] See Ps. xliv. 18   [88] Rom. x. 2
[89] Rom. x. 3   [90] Rom. x. 4   [91] John xiv. 6   [92] Phil. ii. 12   [93] Ps. ii. 11, 12

refuse to show you the righteous way," or, "refuse to lead you into the way of righteousness;" but even after you are walking therein, he was able so to terrify as to say, "Lest ye perish from the righteous way." Now, whence could this arise if not from pride, which (as I have so often said, and must repeat again and again) has to be guarded against even in things which are rightly done, that is, in the very way of righteousness, lest a man, by regarding as his own that which is really God's, lose what is God's and be reduced merely to what is his own? Let us then carry out the concluding injunction of this same psalm, "Blessed are all they that trust in Him," [94] so that He may Himself indeed effect and Himself show His own way in us, to whom it is said, "Show us Thy mercy, O Lord;" [95] and Himself bestow on us the pathway of safety that we may walk therein, to whom the prayer is offered, "And grant us Thy salvation;" [95] and Himself lead us in the self-same way, to whom again it is said, "Guide me, O Lord, in Thy way, and in Thy truth will I walk;" [96] Himself, too, conduct us to those promises whither His way leads, to whom it is said, "Even there shall Thy hand lead me and Thy right hand shall hold me;" [97] Himself pasture therein those who sit down with Abraham, Isaac, and Jacob, of whom it is said, "He shall make them sit down to meat, and will come forth and serve them." [98] Now we do not, when we make mention of these things, take away freedom of will, but we preach the grace of God. For to whom are those gracious gifts of use, but to the man who uses, but humbly uses, his own will, and makes no boast of the power and energy thereof, as if it alone were sufficient for perfecting him in righteousness?

CHAPTER XXXVII

BEING WHOLLY WITHOUT SIN DOES NOT PUT MAN ON AN EQUALITY WITH GOD

But God forbid that we should meet him with such an assertion as he says certain persons advance against him: "That man is placed on an equality with God, if he is described as being without sin;" as if indeed an angel, because he is without sin, is put in such an equality. For my own part, I am of this opinion that the creature will never become equal with God, even when so perfect a holiness shall be accomplished in us, that it shall be quite incapable of receiving any addition. No; all who maintain that our progress is to be so complete that we shall be changed into the substance of God, and that we shall thus become what He is, should look well to it how they build up their opinion; for myself I must confess that I am not persuaded of this.

[94] Ps. ii. 12   [95] Ps. lxxxv. 7   [96] Ps. lxxxvi. 11   [97] Ps. cxxxix. 10   [98] Luke xii. 37

CHAPTER XXXVIII

I am favorably disposed, indeed, to the view of our author, when he resists those who say to him, "What you assert seems indeed to be reasonable,
but it is an arrogant thing to allege that any man can be without sin," with
this answer, that if it is at all true, it must not on any account be called an
arrogant statement; for with very great truth and acuteness he asks, "On
what side must humility be placed? No doubt on the side of falsehood, if
you prove arrogance to exist on the side of truth." And so he decides, and
rightly decides, that humility should rather be ranged on the side of truth,
not of falsehood. Whence it follows that he who said, "If we say that we
have no sin, we deceive ourselves, and the truth is not in us," [99] must without hesitation be held to have spoken the truth, and not be thought to have
spoken falsehood for the sake of humility. Therefore he added the words,
"And the truth is not in us;" whereas it might perhaps have been enough
if he merely said, "We deceive ourselves," if he had not observed that some
were capable of supposing that the clause "we deceive ourselves" is here
employed on the ground that the man who praises himself is even extolled
for a really good action. So that, by the addition of "the truth is not in us,"
he clearly shows (even as our author most correctly observes) that it is not
at all true if we say that we have no sin, lest humility, if placed on the side
of falsehood, should lose the reward of truth.

CHAPTER XXXIX

Beyond this, however, although he flatters himself that he vindicates the
cause of God by defending nature, he forgets that by predicating soundness of the said nature, he rejects the Physician's mercy. He, however, who
created him is also his Saviour. We ought not, therefore, so to magnify the
Creator as to be compelled to say, nay, rather as to be convicted of saying,
that the Saviour is superfluous. Man's nature indeed we may honor with
worthy praise, and attribute the praise to the Creator's glory; but at the
same time, while we show our gratitude to Him for having created us, let
us not be ungrateful to Him for healing us. Our sins which He heals we
must undoubtedly attribute not to God's operation, but to the wilfulness of
man, and submit them to *His* righteous punishment; as, however, we acknowledge that it was in our power that they should not be committed, so

[90] 1 John i. 8

let us confess that it lies in His mercy rather than in our own power that they should be healed. But this mercy and remedial help of the Saviour, according to this writer, consists only in this, that He forgives the transgressions that are past, not that He helps us to avoid such as are to come. Here he is most fatally mistaken; here, however unwittingly—here he hinders us from being watchful, and from praying that "we enter not into temptation," since he maintains that it lies entirely in our own control that this should not happen to us.

CHAPTER XL

WHY THERE IS A RECORD IN SCRIPTURE OF CERTAIN MEN'S SINS. RECKLESSNESS IN SIN ACCOUNTS IT TO BE SO MUCH LOSS WHENEVER IT FALLS SHORT IN GRATIFYING LUST

He who has a sound judgment says soundly, "that the examples of certain persons, of whose sinning we read in Scripture, are not recorded for this purpose, that they may encourage despair of not sinning, and seem somehow to afford security in committing sin"—but that we may learn the humility of repentance, or else discover that even in such falls salvation ought not to be despaired of. For there are some who, when they have fallen into sin, perish rather from the recklessness of despair, and not only neglect the remedy of repentance, but become the slaves of lusts and wicked desires, so far as to run all lengths in gratifying these depraved and abandoned dispositions—as if it were a loss to them if they failed to accomplish what their lust impelled them to, whereas all the while there awaits them a certain condemnation. To oppose this morbid recklessness, which is only too full of danger and ruin, there is great force in the record of those sins into which even just and holy men have before now fallen.

CHAPTER XLI

WHETHER HOLY MEN HAVE DIED WITHOUT SIN

But there is clearly much acuteness in the question put by our author, "How must we suppose that those holy men quitted this life—with sin, or without sin?" For if we answer, "With sin," condemnation will be supposed to have been their destiny, which it is shocking to imagine; but if it be said that they departed this life "without sin," then it would be a proof that man had been without sin in his present life, at all events, when death was approaching. But, with all his acuteness, he overlooks the circumstance that even righteous persons not without good reason offer up this prayer: "Forgive us our debts, as we forgive our debtors;" [100] and that the Lord Christ, after explaining the prayer in His teaching, most truly added: "For

[100] Matt. vi. 12

if ye forgive men their trespasses, your Father will also forgive you your trespasses." [101] Here, indeed, we have the daily incense, so to speak, of the Spirit, which is offered to God on the altar of the heart, which we are bidden "to lift up"—implying that, even if we cannot live here without sin, we may yet die without sin, when in merciful forgiveness the sin is blotted out which is committed in ignorance or infirmity.

CHAPTER XLII

THE BLESSED VIRGIN MARY MAY HAVE LIVED WITHOUT SIN. NONE OF THE SAINTS BESIDES HER WITHOUT SIN

He then enumerates those "who not only lived without sin, but are described as having led holy lives—Abel, Enoch, Melchizedek, Abraham, Isaac, Jacob, Joshua the son of Nun, Phinehas, Samuel, Nathan, Elijah, Joseph, Elisha, Micaiah, Daniel, Hananiah, Azariah, Mishael, Mordecai, Simeon, Joseph to whom the Virgin Mary was espoused, John." And he adds the names of some women—"Deborah, Anna the mother of Samuel, Judith, Esther, the other Anna, daughter of Phanuel, Elisabeth, and also the mother of our Lord and Saviour, for of her," he says, "we must needs allow that her piety had no sin in it." We must except the holy Virgin Mary, concerning whom I wish to raise no question when it touches the subject of sins, out of honor to the Lord; for from Him we know what abundance of grace for overcoming sin in every particular was conferred upon her who had the merit to conceive and bear Him who undoubtedly had no sin.[102] Well, then, if, with this exception of the Virgin, we could only assemble together all the forementioned holy men and women, and ask them whether they lived without sin while they were in this life, what can we suppose would be their answer? Would it be in the language of our author, or in the words of the Apostle John? I put it to you, whether, on having such a question submitted to them, however excellent might have been their sanctity in this body, they would not have exclaimed with one voice: "If we say we have no sin, we deceive ourselves, and the truth is not in us?" [103] But perhaps this their answer would have been more humble than true! Well, but our author has already determined, and rightly determined, "not to place the praise of humility on the side of falsehood." If, therefore, they spoke the truth in giving such an answer, they would have sin, and since they humbly acknowledged it, the truth would be in them; but if they lied in their answer, they would still have sin, because the truth would not be in them.

[101] Matt. vi. 14   [102] I John iii. 5   [103] I John i. 8

CHAPTER XLIII

WHY SCRIPTURE HAS NOT MENTIONED THE SINS OF ALL

"But perhaps," says he, "they will ask me: Could not the Scripture have mentioned sins of all of these?" And surely they would say the truth, who-ever should put such a question to him; and I do not discover that he has anywhere given a sound reply to them, although I perceive that he was unwilling to be silent. What he has said, I beg of you to observe: "This," says he, "might be rightly asked of those whom Scripture mentions neither as good nor as bad; but of those whose holiness it commemorates, it would also without doubt have commemorated the sins likewise, if it had perceived that they had sinned in anything." Let him say, then, that their great faith did not attain to righteousness in the case of those who comprised "the multitudes that went before and that followed" the colt on which the Lord rode, when "they shouted and said, Hosanna to the Son of David: Blessed is He that cometh in the name of the Lord," [104] even amidst the malignant men who with murmurs asked why they were doing all this! Let him then boldly tell us, if he can, that there was not a man in all that vast crowd who had any sin at all. Now, if it is most absurd to make such a statement as this, why has not the Scripture mentioned any sins in the persons to whom reference has been made, especially when it has carefully recorded the eminent goodness of their faith?

CHAPTER XLIV

PELAGIUS ARGUES THAT ABEL WAS SINLESS

This, however, even *he* probably observed, and therefore he went on to say: "But, granted that it has sometimes abstained, in a numerous crowd, from narrating the sins of all; still, in the very beginning of the world, when there were only four persons in existence, what reason (asks he) have we to give why it chose not to mention the sins of all? Was it in considera-tion of the vast multitude, which had not yet come into existence? or be-cause, having mentioned only the sins of those who had transgressed, it was unable to record any of him who had not yet committed sin?" And then he proceeds to add some words, in which he unfolds this idea with a fuller and more explicit illustration. "It is certain," says he, "that in the earliest age Adam and Eve, and Cain and Abel their sons, are mentioned as being the only four persons then in being. Eve sinned—the Scripture dis-tinctly says so much; Adam also transgressed, as the same Scripture does not fail to inform us; while it affords us an equally clear testimony that Cain also sinned: and of all these it not only mentions the sins, but also in-

---

[104] Matt. xxi. 9

dicates the character of their sins. Now if Abel had likewise sinned, Scripture would without doubt have said so. But it has not said so, therefore he committed no sin; nay, it even shows him to have been righteous. What we read, therefore, let us believe; and what we do not read, let us deem it wicked to add."

CHAPTER XLV

WHY CAIN HAS BEEN BY SOME THOUGHT TO HAVE HAD CHILDREN BY HIS MOTHER EVE. THE SINS OF RIGHTEOUS MEN, WHO CAN BE BOTH RIGHTEOUS, AND YET NOT WITHOUT SIN

When he says this, he forgets what he had himself said not long before: "After the human race had multiplied, it was possible that in the crowd the Scripture may have neglected to notice the sins of all men." If indeed he had borne this well in mind, he would have seen that even in one man there was such a crowd and so vast a number of slight sins, that it would have been impossible (or, even if possible, not desirable) to describe them. For only such are recorded as the due bounds allowed, and as would, by few examples, serve for instructing the reader in the many cases where he needed warning. Scripture has indeed omitted to mention concerning the few persons who were then in existence, either how many or who they were —in other words, how many sons and daughters Adam and Eve begat, and what names they gave them; and from this circumstance some, not considering how many things are quietly passed over in Scripture, have gone so far as to suppose that Cain cohabited with his mother, and by her had the children which are mentioned, thinking that Adam's sons had no sisters, because Scripture failed to mention them in the particular place, although it afterwards, in the way of recapitulation, implied what it had previously omitted—that "Adam begat sons and daughters," [105] without, however, dropping a syllable to intimate either their number or the time when they were born. In like manner it was unnecessary to state whether Abel, notwithstanding that he is rightly styled "righteous," ever indulged in immoderate laughter, or was ever jocose in moments of relaxation, or ever looked at an object with a covetous eye, or ever plucked fruit to extravagance, or ever suffered indigestion from too much eating, or ever in the midst of his prayers permitted his thoughts to wander and call him away from the purpose of his devotion; as well as how frequently these and many other similar failings stealthily crept over his mind. And are not these failings *sins*, about which the apostle's precept gives us a general admonition that we should avoid and restrain them, when he says: "Let not sin therefore reign in your mortal body, that ye should obey it in the lusts thereof?" [106] To escape from such an obedience, we have to struggle in a

[105] Gen. v. 4   [106] Rom. vi. 12

constant and daily conflict against unlawful and unseemly inclinations. Only let the eye be directed, or rather abandoned, to an object which it ought to avoid, and let the mischief strengthen and get the mastery, and adultery is consummated in the body, which is committed in the heart only so much more quickly as thought is more rapid than action and there is no impediment to retard and delay it. They who in a great degree have curbed this sin, that is, this appetite of a corrupt affection, so as not to obey its desires, nor to "yield their members to it as instruments of unrighteousness," [107] have fairly deserved to be called righteous persons, and this by the help of the grace of God. Since, however, sin often stole over them in very small matters, and when they were off their guard, they were both righteous, and at the same time not sinless. To conclude, if there was in righteous Abel that love of God whereby alone he is truly righteous who is righteous, to enable him, and to lay him under a moral obligation, to advance in holiness, still in whatever degree he fell short therein was of sin. And who indeed can help thus falling short, until he come to that mighty power thereof, in which man's entire infirmity shall be swallowed up?

CHAPTER XLVI

SHALL WE FOLLOW SCRIPTURE, OR ADD TO ITS DECLARATIONS?

It is, to be sure, a grand sentence with which he concluded this passage, when he says: "What we read, therefore, let us believe; and what we do not read, let us deem it wicked to add; and let it suffice to have said this of all cases." On the contrary, I for my part say that we ought not to believe even everything that we read, on the sanction of the apostle's advice: "Read all things; hold fast that which is good." [108] Nor is it wicked to add something which we have not read; for it is in our power to add something which we have *bona fide* experienced as witnesses, even if it so happens that we have not read about it. Perhaps he will say in reply: "When I said this, I was treating of the Holy Scriptures." Oh how I wish that he were never willing to add, I will not say anything but what he reads in the Scriptures, but in opposition to what he reads in them; that he would only faithfully and obediently hear that which is written there: "By one man sin entered into the world, and death by sin, and so death passed upon all men; in which all have sinned;" [109] and that he would not weaken the grace of the great Physician—all by his unwillingness to confess that human nature is corrupted! Oh how I wish that he would, as a Christian, read the sentence, "There is none other name under heaven given among men whereby we must be saved;" [110] and that he would not so uphold the possibility of human nature, as to believe that man can be saved by free will without that Name!

[107] Rom. vi. 13   [108] 1 Thess. v. 21   [109] Rom. v. 12   [110] Acts iv. 12

CHAPTER XLVII

FOR WHAT PELAGIUS THOUGHT THAT CHRIST IS NECESSARY TO US

Perhaps, however, he thinks the name of Christ to be necessary on this account, that by His gospel we may learn how we ought to live; but not that we may be also assisted by His grace, in order withal to lead good lives. Well, even this consideration should lead him at least to confess that there is a miserable darkness in the human mind, which knows how it ought to tame a lion, but knows not how to live. To know this, too, is it enough for us to have free will and natural law? This is that wisdom of word, whereby "the cross of Christ is rendered of none effect." [111] He, however, who said, "I will destroy the wisdom of the wise," [112] since that cross cannot be made of none effect, in very deed overthrows that wisdom by the foolishness of preaching whereby believers are healed. For if natural capacity, by help of free will, is in itself sufficient both for discovering how one ought to live, and also for leading a holy life, then "Christ died in vain," [113] and therefore also "the offence of the cross is ceased." [114] Why also may I not myself exclaim?—nay, I will exclaim, and chide them with a Christian's sorrow—"Christ is become of no effect unto you, whosoever of you are justified by nature; ye are fallen from grace;" [115] for, "being ignorant of God's righteousness, and wishing to establish your own righteousness, you have not submitted yourselves to the righteousness of God." [116] For even as "Christ is the end of the law," so likewise is He the Saviour of man's corrupted nature, "for righteousness to every one that believeth." [117]

CHAPTER XLVIII

HOW THE TERM "ALL" IS TO BE UNDERSTOOD

His opponents adduced the passage, "All have sinned," [118] and he met their statement founded on this with the remark that "the apostle was manifestly speaking of the then existing generation, that is, the Jews and the Gentiles;" but surely the passage which I have quoted, "By one man sin entered the world, and death by sin, and so death passed upon all men; in which all have sinned," [109] embraces in its terms the generations both of old and of modern times, both ourselves and our posterity. He adduces also this passage, whence he would prove that we ought not to understand all without exception, when "all" is used:—"As by the offence of one," he says, "upon all men to condemnation, even so by the righteousness of One, upon all men unto justification of life." [119] "There can be no doubt," he says, "that not all men are sanctified by the righteousness of Christ, but

---

[111] 1 Cor. i. 17   [112] 1 Cor. i. 19   [113] Gal. ii. 21   [114] Gal. v. 11   [115] Gal. v. 4
[116] Rom. x. 3   [117] Rom. x. 4   [118] Rom. iii. 23   [119] Rom. v. 18

only those who are willing to obey Him, and have been cleansed in the washing of His baptism." Well, but he does not prove what he wants by this quotation. For as the clause, "By the offence of one, upon all men to condemnation," is so worded that not one is omitted in its sense, so in the corresponding clause, "By the righteousness of One, upon all men unto justification of life," no one is omitted in its sense—not, indeed, because all men have faith and are washed in His baptism, but because no man is justified unless he believes in Christ and is cleansed by His baptism. The term *"all"* is therefore used in a way which shows that no one whatever can be supposed able to be saved by any other means than through Christ Himself. For if in a city there be appointed but one instructor, we are most correct in saying: That man teaches all in that place; not meaning, indeed, that all who live in the city take lessons of him, but that no one is instructed unless taught by him. In like manner no one is justified unless Christ has justified him.[120]

CHAPTER XLIX

A MAN CAN BE SINLESS, BUT ONLY BY THE HELP OF GRACE. IN THE SAINTS THIS POSSIBILITY ADVANCES AND KEEPS PACE WITH THE REALIZATION

"Well, be it so," says he, "I agree; he testifies to the fact that all were sinners. He says, indeed, what they have been, not that they might not have been something else. Wherefore," he adds, "if all men could be proved to be sinners, it would not by any means prejudice our own definite position, in insisting not so much on what men are, as on what they are able to be." He is right for once to allow that no man living is justified in God's sight. He contends, however, that this is not the question, but that the point lies in the possibility of a man's not sinning—on which subject it is unnecessary for us to take ground against him; for, in truth, I do not much care about expressing a definite opinion on the question, whether in the present life there ever have been, or now are, or ever can be, any persons who have had, or are having, or are to have, the love of God so perfectly as to admit of no addition to it (for nothing short of this amounts to a most true, full, and perfect righteousness). For I ought not too sharply to contend as to when, or where, or in whom is done that which I confess and maintain can be done by the will of man, aided by the grace of God. Nor do I indeed contend about the actual possibility, forasmuch as the possibility under dispute advances with the realization in the saints, their human will being healed and helped; while "the love of God," as fully as our healed and cleansed nature can possibly receive it, "is shed abroad in our hearts by the Holy Ghost, which is given to us." [121] In a better way, there-

---

[120] Cf. *De Peccatorum Meritis et Remissione*, i. 55   [121] Rom. v. 5

fore, is God's cause promoted (and it is to its promotion that our author professes to apply his warm defence of nature) when He is acknowledged as our Saviour no less than as our Creator, than when His succor to us as Saviour is impaired and dwarfed to nothing by the defence of the creature, as if it were sound and its resources entire.

CHAPTER L

GOD COMMANDS NO IMPOSSIBILITIES

What he says, however, is true enough, "that God is as good as just, and made man such that he was quite able to live without the evil of sin, if only he had been willing." For who does not know that man was made whole and faultless, and endowed with a free will and a free ability to lead a holy life? Our present inquiry, however, is about the man whom "the thieves" [122] left half dead on the road, and who, being disabled and pierced through with heavy wounds, is not so able to mount up to the heights of righteousness as he was able to descend therefrom; who, moreover, if he is now in "the inn," [123] is in process of cure. God therefore does not command impossibilities; but in His command He counsels you both to do what you can for yourself, and to ask His aid in what you cannot do. Now, we should see whence comes the possibility, and whence the impossibility. This man says: "That proceeds not from a man's will which he can do by nature." I say: A man is not righteous by his will if he can be by nature. He will, however, be able to accomplish by remedial aid what he is rendered incapable of doing by his flaw.

CHAPTER LI

STATE OF THE QUESTION BETWEEN THE PELAGIANS AND THE CATHOLICS. HOLY MEN OF OLD SAVED BY THE SELF-SAME FAITH IN CHRIST WHICH WE EXERCISE

But why need we tarry longer on general statements? Let us go into the core of the question, which we have to discuss with our opponents solely, or almost entirely, on one particular point. For inasmuch as he says that "as far as the present question is concerned, it is not pertinent to inquire whether there have been or now are any men in this life without sin, but whether they had or have the ability to be such persons;" so, were I even to allow that there have been or are any such, I should not by any means therefore affirm that they had or have the ability, unless justified by the grace of God through our Lord "Jesus Christ and Him crucified." [124] For the same faith which healed the saints of old now heals us—that is to say, faith "in the one Mediator between God and men, the man Christ Jesus" [125]

---

[122] Luke x. 30   [123] Luke x. 34   [124] I Cor. ii. 2   [125] I Tim. ii. 5

—faith in His blood, faith in His cross, faith in His death and resurrection. As we therefore have the same spirit of faith, we also believe, and on that account also speak.

CHAPTER LII

THE WHOLE DISCUSSION IS ABOUT GRACE

Let us, however, observe what our author answers, after laying before himself the question wherein he seems indeed so intolerable to Christian hearts. He says: "But you will tell me this is what disturbs a great many— that you do not maintain that it is by the grace of God that a man is able to be without sin." Certainly this is what causes us disturbance; this is what we object to him. He touches the very point of the case. This is what causes us such utter pain to endure it; this is why we cannot bear to have such points debated by Christians, owing to the love which we feel towards others and towards themselves. Well, let us hear how he clears himself from the objectionable character of the question he has raised. "What blindness of ignorance," he exclaims, "what sluggishness of an uninstructed mind, which supposes that that is maintained and held to be without God's grace which it only hears ought to be attributed to God!" Now, if we knew nothing of what follows this outburst of his, and formed our opinion on simply hearing these words, we might suppose that we had been led to a wrong view of our opponents by the spread of report and by the asseveration of some suitable witnesses among the brethren. For how could it have been more pointedly and truly stated that the possibility of not sinning, to whatever extent it exists or shall exist in man, ought only to be attributed to God? This too is our own affirmation. We may shake hands.

CHAPTER LIII

PELAGIUS DISTINGUISHES BETWEEN A POWER AND ITS USE

Well, are there other things to listen to? Yes, certainly; both to listen to, and correct and guard against. "Now, when it is said," he says, "that the very ability is not at all of man's will, but of the Author of nature— that is, God—how can that possibly be understood to be without the grace of God which is deemed especially to belong to God?" Already we begin to see what he means; but that we may not lie under any mistake, he explains himself with greater breadth and clearness: "That this may become still plainer, we must," says he, "enter on a somewhat fuller discussion of the point. Now we affirm that the possibility of anything lies not so much in the ability of a man's will as in the necessity of nature." He then proceeds to illustrate his meaning by examples and similes. "Take," says he, "for instance, my ability to speak. That I am able to speak is not my own;

but that I do speak is my own—that is, of my own will. And because the act of my speaking is my own, I have the power of alternative action—that is to say, both to speak and to refrain from speaking. But because my ability to speak is not my own, that is, is not of my own determination and will, it is of necessity that I am always able to speak; and though I wished not to be able to speak, I am unable, nevertheless, to be unable to speak, unless perhaps I were to deprive myself of that member whereby the function of speaking is to be performed." Many means, indeed, might be mentioned whereby, if he wish it, a man may deprive himself of the possibility of speaking, without removing the organ of speech. If, for instance, anything were to happen to a man to destroy his voice, he would be unable to speak, although the members remained; for a man's voice is of course no member. There may, in short, be an injury done to the member internally, short of the actual loss of it. I am, however, unwilling to press the argument for a word; and it may be replied to me in the contest, Why, even to injure is to lose. But yet we can so contrive matters, by closing and shutting the mouth with bandages, as to be quite incapable of opening it, and to put the opening of it out of our power, although it was quite in our own power to shut it while the strength and healthy exercise of the limbs remained.

CHAPTER LIV

THERE IS NO INCOMPATIBILITY BETWEEN NECESSITY AND FREE WILL

Now how does all this apply to our subject? Let us see what he makes out of it. "Whatever," says he, "is fettered by natural necessity is deprived of determination of will and deliberation." Well, now, here lies a question; for it is the height of absurdity for us to say that it does not belong to our will that we wish to be happy, on the ground that it is absolutely impossible for us to be unwilling to be happy, by reason of some indescribable but amiable coercion of our nature; nor dare we maintain that God has not the will but the necessity of righteousness, because He cannot will to sin.

CHAPTER LV

THE SAME CONTINUED

Mark also what follows. "We may perceive," says he, "the same thing to be true of hearing, smelling, and seeing—that to hear, and to smell, and to see is of our own power, while the ability to hear, and to smell, and to see is not of our own power, but lies in a natural necessity." Either I do not understand what he means, or he does not himself. For how is the possibility of seeing not in our own power, if the necessity of not seeing is in our own power because blindness is in our own power, by which we can deprive ourselves. if we will, of this very ability to see? How, moreover, is it in our own power to see whenever we will, when, without any loss whatever to our natural structure of body in the organ of sight, we are unable, even though we wish, to see—either by the removal of all external lights during the night, or by our being shut up in some dark place? Likewise, if our ability or our inability to hear is not in our own power, but lies in the necessity of nature, whereas our actual hearing or not hearing is of our own will, how comes it that he is inattentive to the fact that there are so many things which we hear against our will, which penetrate our sense even when our ears are stopped, as the creaking of a saw near to us, or the grunt of a pig? Although the said stopping of our ears shows plainly enough that it does not lie within our own power not to hear so long as our ears are open; perhaps, too, such a stopping of our ears as shall deprive us of the entire sense in question proves that even the ability not to hear lies within our own power. As to his remarks, again, concerning our sense of smell, does he not display no little carelessness when he says "that it is not in our own power to be able or to be unable to smell, but that it is in our own power"—that is to say, in our free will—"to smell or not to smell?" For let us suppose some one to place us, with our hands firmly tied, but yet without any injury to our olfactory members, among some bad and noxious smells; in such a case we altogether lose the power, however strong may be our wish, not to smell, because every time we are obliged to draw breath we also inhale the smell which we do not wish.

CHAPTER LVI

THE ASSISTANCE OF GRACE IN A PERFECT NATURE

Not only, then, are these similes employed by our author false, but so is the matter which he wishes them to illustrate. He goes on to say: "In like manner, touching the possibility of our not sinning, we must understand that it is of us not to sin, but yet that the ability to avoid sin is not of us." If he were speaking of man's whole and perfect nature, which we do not now possess ("for we are saved by hope: but hope that is seen is not hope. But if we hope for that we see not, then do we with patience wait for it" [126]), his language even in that case would not be correct to the effect that to avoid sinning would be of us alone, although to sin would be of us, for even then there must be the help of God, which must shed itself on those who are willing to receive it, just as the light is given to strong and healthy eyes to assist them in their function of sight. Inasmuch, however, as it is about this present life of ours that he raises the question, wherein our corruptible body weighs down the soul, and our earthly tabernacle depresses our sense with all its many thoughts, I am astonished that he can with any heart suppose that, even without the help of our Saviour's healing

[126] Rom. viii. 24, 25

balm, it is in our own power to avoid sin, and the ability not to sin is of nature, which gives only stronger evidence of its own corruption by the very fact of its failing to see its taint.

CHAPTER LVII

IT DOES NOT DETRACT FROM GOD'S ALMIGHTY POWER, THAT HE IS INCAPABLE OF EITHER SINNING, OR DYING, OR DESTROYING HIMSELF

"Inasmuch," says he, "as not to sin is ours, we are able to sin and to avoid sin." What, then, if another should say: "Inasmuch as not to wish for unhappiness is ours, we are able both to wish for it and not to wish for it?" And yet we are positively unable to wish for it. For who could possibly wish to be unhappy, even though he wishes for something else from which unhappiness will ensue to him against his will? Then again, inasmuch as, in an infinitely greater degree, it is God's not to sin, shall we therefore venture to say that He is able both to sin and to avoid sin? God forbid that we should ever say that He is able to sin! For He cannot, as foolish persons suppose, therefore fail to be almighty, because He is unable to die, or because He cannot deny Himself. What, therefore, does he mean? by what method of speech does he try to persuade us on a point which he is himself loth to consider? For he advances a step further, and says: "Inasmuch as, however, it is not of us to be able to avoid sin; even if we were to wish not to be able to avoid sin, it is not in our power to be unable to avoid sin." It is an involved sentence, and therefore a very obscure one. It might, however, be more plainly expressed in some such way as this: "Inasmuch as to be able to avoid sin is not of us, then, whether we wish it or do not wish it, we are able to avoid sin!" He does not say, "Whether we wish it or do not wish it, we do not sin"—for we undoubtedly do sin, if we wish—but yet he asserts that, whether we will or not, we have the capacity of not sinning—a capacity which he declares to be inherent in our nature. Of a man, indeed, who has his legs strong and sound, it may be said admissibly enough, "whether he will or not he has the capacity of walking;" but if his legs be broken, however much he may wish, he has not the capacity. The nature of which our author speaks is corrupted. "Why is dust and ashes proud?" [127] It is corrupted. It implores the Physician's help. "Save me, O Lord," [128] is its cry; "Heal my soul," [129] it exclaims. Why does he check such cries so as to hinder future health, by insisting, as it were, on its present capacity?

[127] Ecclus. x. 9   [128] Ps. xii. 1   [129] Ps. xli. 4

CHAPTER LVIII

EVEN PIOUS AND GOD-FEARING MEN RESIST GRACE

Observe also what remark he adds, by which he thinks that his position is confirmed: "No will," says he, "can take away that which is proved to be inseparably implanted in nature." Whence then comes that utterance: "So then ye cannot do the things that ye would?" [130] Whence also this: "For what good I would, that I do not; but what evil I hate, that do I?" [131] Where is that capacity which is proved to be inseparably implanted in nature? See, it is human beings who do not what they will; and it is about not sinning, certainly, that he was treating—not about not flying, because it was men, not birds, that formed his subject. Behold, it is man who does not the good which he would, but does the evil which he would not: "to will is present with him, but how to perform that which is good is not present." [132] Where is the capacity which is proved to be inseparably implanted in nature? For whomsoever the apostle represents by himself, if he does not speak these things of his own self, he certainly represents a man by himself. By our author, however, it is maintained that our human nature actually possesses an inseparable capacity of not at all sinning. Such a statement, however, even when made by a man who knows not the effect of his words (but this ignorance is hardly attributable to the man who suggests these statements for unwary though God-fearing men), causes the grace of Christ to be "made of none effect," [133] since it is pretended that human nature is sufficient for its own holiness and justification.

CHAPTER LIX

IN WHAT SENSE PELAGIUS ATTRIBUTED TO GOD'S GRACE THE CAPACITY OF NOT SINNING

In order, however, to escape from the odium wherewith Christians guard their salvation, he parries their question when they ask him, "Why do you affirm that man without the help of God's grace is able to avoid sin?" by saying, "The actual capacity of not sinning lies not so much in the power of will as in the necessity of nature. Whatever is placed in the necessity of nature undoubtedly appertains to the Author of nature, that is, God. How then," says he, "can that be regarded as spoken without the grace of God which is shown to belong in an especial manner to God?" Here the opinion is expressed which all along was kept in the background; there is, in fact, no way of permanently concealing such a doctrine. The reason why he attributes to the grace of God the capacity of not sinning is, that God is the Author of nature, in which, he declares, this capacity of avoiding sin

---

[130] Gal. v. 17   [131] Rom. vii. 15   [132] Rom. vii. 18   [133] 1 Cor. i. 17

is inseparably implanted. Whenever He wills a thing, no doubt He does it; and what He wills not, that He does not. Now, wherever there is this inseparable capacity, there cannot accrue any infirmity of the will; or rather, there cannot be both a presence of will and a failure in "performance." [132] This, then, being the case, how comes it to pass that "to will is present, but how to perform that which is good" is not present? Now, if the author of the work we are discussing spoke of that nature of man, which was in the beginning created faultless and perfect, in whatever sense his dictum be taken, "that it has an inseparable capacity"—that is, so to say, one which cannot be lost—then that nature ought not to have been mentioned at all which could be corrupted, and which could require a physician to cure the eyes of the blind, and restore that capacity of seeing which had been lost through blindness. For I suppose a blind man would like to see, but is unable; but, whenever a man wishes to do a thing and cannot, there is present to him the will, but he has lost the capacity.

CHAPTER LX

PELAGIUS ADMITS "CONTRARY FLESH" IN THE UNBAPTIZED

See what obstacles he still attempts to break through, if possible, in order to introduce his own opinion. He raises a question for himself in these terms: "But you will tell me that, according to the apostle, the flesh is contrary[130] to us;" and then answers it in this wise: "How can it be that in the case of any baptized person the flesh is contrary to him, when according to the same apostle he is understood not to be in the flesh? For he says, 'But ye are not in the flesh.'" [134] Very well; we shall soon see[135] whether it be really true that this says that in the baptized the flesh cannot be contrary to them; at present, however, as it was impossible for him quite to forget that he was a Christian (although his reminiscence on the point is but slight), he has quitted his defence of nature. Where then is that inseparable capacity of his? Are those who are not yet baptized not a part of human nature? Well, now, here by all means, here at this point, he might find his opportunity of awaking out of his sleep; and he still has it if he is careful. "How can it be," he asks, "that in the case of a baptized person the flesh is contrary to him?" Therefore to the unbaptized the flesh can be contrary! Let him tell us how; for even in these there is that nature which has been so stoutly defended by him. However, in these he does certainly allow that nature is corrupted, inasmuch as it was only among the baptized that the wounded traveller left his inn sound and well, or rather remains sound in the inn whither the compassionate Samaritan carried him that he might become cured.[136] Well, now, if he allows that the flesh is contrary even in these, let him tell us what has happened to occasion this, since the flesh

[134] Rom. viii. 9   [135] In the next chapter   [136] Luke x. 34

and the spirit alike are the work of one and the same Creator, and are therefore undoubtedly both of them good, because He is good—unless indeed it be that damage which has been inflicted by man's own will. And that this may be repaired in our nature, there is need of that very Saviour from whose creative hand nature itself proceeded. Now, if we acknowledge that this Saviour, and that healing remedy of His by which the Word was made flesh in order to dwell among us, are required by small and great— by the crying infant and the hoary-headed man alike—then, in fact, the whole controversy of the point between us is settled.

CHAPTER LXI

PAUL ASSERTS THAT THE FLESH IS CONTRARY EVEN IN THE BAPTIZED

Now let us see whether we anywhere read about the flesh being contrary in the baptized also. And here, I ask, to whom did the apostle say, "The flesh lusteth against the Spirit, and the Spirit against the flesh: and these are contrary the one to the other; so that ye do not the things that ye would?" [137] He wrote this, I apprehend, to the Galatians, to whom he also says, "He therefore that ministereth to you the Spirit, and worketh miracles among you, doeth he it by the works of the law or by the hearing of faith?" [138] It appears, therefore, that it is to Christians that he speaks, to whom, too, God had given His Spirit: therefore, too, to the baptized. Observe, therefore, that even in baptized persons the flesh is found to be contrary; so that they have not that capacity which, our author says, is inseparably implanted in nature. Where then is the ground for his assertion, "How can it be that in the case of a baptized person the flesh is contrary to him?" in whatever sense he understands the flesh? Because in very deed it is not its nature that is good, but it is the carnal defects of the flesh which are expressly named in the passage before us.[139] Yet observe, even in the baptized, how contrary is the flesh. And in what way contrary? So that, "They do not the things which they would." Take notice that the will is present in a man; but where is that "capacity of nature"? Let us confess that grace is necessary to us; let us cry out, "O wretched man that I am! who shall deliver me from the body of this death?" And let our answer be, "The grace of God, through Jesus Christ our Lord!" [140]

CHAPTER LXII

CONCERNING WHAT GRACE OF GOD IS HERE UNDER DISCUSSION. THE UNGODLY MAN, WHEN DYING, IS NOT DELIVERED FROM CONCUPISCENCE

Now, whereas it is most correctly asked in those words put to him, "Why do you affirm that man without the help of God's grace is able to avoid

[137] Gal. v. 17   [138] Gal. iii. 5   [139] See the context of Gal. v. 17, in verses 19-21
[140] Rom. vii. 24, 25

sin?" yet the inquiry did not concern that grace by which man was created, but only that whereby he is saved through Jesus Christ our Lord. Faithful men say in their prayer, "Lead us not into temptation, but deliver us from evil." [141] But if they already have capacity, why do they pray? Or, what is the evil which they pray to be delivered from, but, above all else, "the body of this death?" And from this nothing but God's grace alone delivers them, through our Lord Jesus Christ. Not of course from the substance of the body, which is good; but from its carnal offences, from which a man is not liberated except by the grace of the Saviour—not even when he quits the body by the death of the body. If it was this that the apostle meant to declare, why had he previously said, "I see another law in my members, warring against the law of my mind, and bringing me into captivity to the law of sin which is in my members?" [142] Behold what damage the disobedience of the will has inflicted on man's nature! Let him be permitted to pray that he may be healed! Why need he presume so much on the capacity of his nature? It is wounded, hurt, damaged, destroyed. It is a true confession of its weakness, not a false defence of its capacity, that it stands in need of. It requires the grace of God, not that it may be made, but that it may be re-made. And this is the only grace which by our author is proclaimed to be unnecessary; because of this he is silent! If, indeed, he had said nothing at all about God's grace, and had not proposed to himself that question for solution, for the purpose of removing from himself the odium of this matter,[143] it might have been thought that his view of the subject was consistent with the truth, only that he had refrained from mentioning it, on the ground that not on all occasions need we say all we think. He proposed the question of grace, and answered it in the way that he had in his heart; the question has been defined—not in the way we wished, but according to the doubt we entertained as to what was his meaning.

CHAPTER LXIII

DOES GOD CREATE CONTRARIES?

He next endeavors, by much quotation from the apostle, about which there is no controversy, to show "that the flesh is often mentioned by him in such a manner as proves him to mean not the substance, but the works of the flesh." What is this to the point? The defects of the flesh are contrary to the will of man; his nature is not accused; but a Physician is wanted for its defects. What signifies his question, "Who made man's spirit?" and his own answer thereto, "God, without a doubt?" Again he asks, "Who created the flesh?" and again answers, "The same God, I suppose." And yet a third question, "Is the God good who created both?" and the third answer, "Nobody doubts it." Once more a question, "Are not

---

[141] Matt. vi. 13   [142] Rom. vii. 23   [143] See above, ch. 59, *sub init.*

both good, since the good Creator made them?" and its answer, "It must be confessed that they are." And then follows his conclusion: "If, therefore, both the spirit is good, and the flesh is good, as made by the good Creator, how can it be that the two good things should be contrary to one another?" I need not say that the whole of this reasoning would be upset if one were to ask him, "Who made heat and cold?" and he were to say in answer, "God, without a doubt." I do not ask the string of questions. Let him determine himself whether these conditions of climate may either be said to be not good, or else whether they do not seem to be contrary to each other. Here he will probably object, "These are not substances, but the qualities of substances." Very true, it is so. But still they are natural qualities, and undoubtedly belong to God's creation; and substances, indeed, are not said to be contrary to each other in themselves, but in their qualities, as water and fire. What if it be so too with flesh and spirit? We do not affirm it to be so; but, in order to show that his argument terminates in a conclusion which does not necessarily follow, we have said so much as this. For it is quite possible for contraries not to be reciprocally opposed to each other, but rather by mutual action to temper health and render it good; just as, in our body, dryness and moisture, cold and heat—in the tempering of which altogether consists our bodily health. The fact, however, that "the flesh is contrary to the Spirit, so that we cannot do the things that we would," [144] is a defect, not nature. The Physician's grace must be sought, and their controversy must end.

CHAPTER LXIV

PELAGIUS' ADMISSION AS REGARDS THE UNBAPTIZED, FATAL

Now, as touching these two good substances which the good God created, how, against the reasoning of this man, in the case of unbaptized persons, can they be contrary the one to the other? Will he be sorry to have said this too, which he admitted out of some regard to the Christians' faith? For when he asked, "How, in the case of any person who is already baptized, can it be that his flesh is contrary to him?" he intimated, of course, that in the case of unbaptized persons it is possible for the flesh to be contrary. For why insert the clause, *"who is already baptized,"* when without such an addition he might have put his question thus: "How in the case of any person can the flesh be contrary?" and when, in order to prove this, he might have subjoined that argument of his, that as both body and spirit are good (made as they are by the good Creator), they therefore cannot be contrary to each other? Now, suppose unbaptized persons (in whom, at any rate, he confesses that the flesh is contrary) were to ply him with his own arguments, and say to him, Who made man's

[144] Gal. v. 17

spirit? he must answer, God. Suppose they asked him again, Who created the flesh? and he answers, The same God, I believe. Suppose their third question to be, Is the God good who created both? and his reply to be, Nobody doubts it. Suppose once more they put to him his yet remaining inquiry. Are not both good, since the good Creator made them? and he confesses it. Then surely they will cut his throat with his own sword, when they force home his conclusion on him, and say: Since therefore the spirit of man is good, and his flesh good, as made by the good Creator, how can it be that the two being good should be contrary to one another? Here, perhaps, he will reply: I beg your pardon, I ought not to have said that the flesh cannot be contrary to the spirit in any baptized person, as if I meant to imply that it is contrary in the unbaptized; but I ought to have made my statement general, to the effect that the flesh in no man's case is contrary. Now see into what a corner he drives himself. See what a man will say, who is unwilling to cry out with the apostle, "Who shall deliver me from the body of this death? The grace of God, through Jesus Christ our Lord." [145] "But why," he asks, "should I so exclaim, who am already baptized in Christ? It is for them to cry out thus who have not yet received so great a benefit, whose words the apostle in a figure transferred to himself—if indeed even they say so much." Well, this defence of nature does not permit even these to utter this exclamation! For in the baptized, there is no nature; and in the unbaptized, nature is not! Or if even in the one class it is allowed to be corrupted, so that it is not without reason that men exclaim, "O wretched man that I am! who shall deliver me from this body of death?" to the other, too, help is brought in what follows: "The grace of God, through Jesus Christ our Lord;" then let it at last be granted that human nature stands in need of Christ for its Physician.

CHAPTER LXV

"THIS BODY OF DEATH," SO CALLED FROM ITS DEFECT, NOT FROM ITS SUBSTANCE

Now, I ask, when did our nature lose that liberty, which he craves to be given to him when he says: "Who shall liberate me?" [146] For even he finds no fault with the substance of the flesh when he expresses his desire to be liberated from the body of this death, since the nature of the body, as well as of the soul, must be attributed to the good God as the author thereof. But what he speaks of undoubtedly concerns the offences of the body. Now from the body the death of the body separates us; whereas the offences contracted from the body remain, and their just punishment awaits them, as the rich man found in hell.[147] From these it

[145] Rom. vii. 24, 25   [146] Rom. vii. 24   [147] Luke xvi. 23

was that he was unable to liberate himself, who said: "Who shall liberate me from the body of this death?" [146] But whensoever it was that he lost this liberty, at least there remains that "inseparable capacity" of nature —he has the ability from natural resources—he has the volition from free will. Why does he seek the sacrament of baptism? Is it because of past sins, in order that they may be forgiven, since they cannot be undone? Well, suppose you acquit and release a man on these terms, he must still utter the old cry; for he not only wants to be mercifully let off from punishment for past offences, but to be strengthened and fortified against sinning for the time to come. For he "delights in the law of God, after the inward man; but then he sees another law in his members, warring against the law of his mind." [148] Observe, he sees that there *is,* not recollects that there *was.* It is a present pressure, not a past memory. And he sees the other law not only "warring," but even "bringing him into captivity to the law of sin, which *is*" (not which *was*) "in his members." [149] Hence comes that cry of his: "O wretched man that I am! who shall liberate me from the body of this death?" [146] Let him pray, let him entreat for the help of the mighty Physician. Why gainsay that prayer? Why cry down that entreaty? Why shall the unhappy suitor be hindered from begging for the mercy of Christ—and that too by Christians? For, it was even they who were accompanying Christ that tried to prevent the blind man, by clamoring him down, from begging for light; but even amidst the din and throng of the gainsayers He hears the suppliant; [150] whence the response: "The grace of God, through Jesus Christ our Lord." [151]

CHAPTER LXVI

THE WORKS, NOT THE SUBSTANCE, OF THE "FLESH" OPPOSED TO THE "SPIRIT"

Now if we secure even this concession from them, that unbaptized persons may implore the assistance of the Saviour's grace, this is indeed no slight point against that fallacious assertion of the self-sufficiency of nature and of the power of free will. For he is not sufficient to himself who says, "O wretched man that I am! who shall liberate me?" Nor can he be said to have full liberty who still asks for liberation. But let us, moreover, see to this point also, whether they who are baptized do the good which they would, without any resistance from the lust of the flesh. That, however, which we have to say on this subject, our author himself mentions, when concluding this topic he says: "As we remarked, the passage in which occur the words, 'The flesh lusteth against the Spirit' [152] must

[148] Rom. vii. 22, 23   [149] Rom. vii. 23   [150] Mark x. 46-52   [151] Rom. vii. 25
[152] Gal. v. 17

needs have reference not to the substance, but to the works of the flesh." We too allege that this is spoken not of the substance of the flesh, but of its works, which proceed from carnal concupiscence—in a word, from sin, concerning which we have this precept: "Not to let it reign in our mortal body, that we should obey it in the lusts thereof." [153]

CHAPTER LXVII

WHO MAY BE SAID TO BE UNDER THE LAW

But even our author should observe that it is to persons who have been already baptized that it was said: "The flesh lusteth against the Spirit, and the Spirit against the flesh, so that ye cannot do the things that ye would." [152] And lest he should makes them slothful for the actual conflict, and should seem by this statement to have given them laxity in sinning, he goes on to tell them: "If ye be led of the Spirit, ye are no longer under the law." [154] For that man is under the law, who, from fear of punishment which the law threatens, and not from any love for righteousness, obliges himself to abstain from the work of sin, without being as yet free and removed from the desire of sinning. For it is in his very will that he is guilty, whereby he would prefer, if it were possible, that what he dreads should not exist, in order that he might freely do what he secretly desires. Therefore he says, "If ye be led of the Spirit, ye are not under the law"—even the law which inspires fear, but gives not love. For this "love is shed abroad in our hearts," not by the letter of the law, but "by the Holy Ghost, which is given unto us." [155] This is the law of liberty, not of bondage; being the law of love, not of fear; and concerning it the Apostle James says: "Whoso looketh into the perfect law of liberty." [156] Whence he, too, no longer indeed felt terrified by God's law as a slave, but delighted in it in the inward man, although still seeing another law in his members warring against the law of his mind. Accordingly he here says: "If ye be led of the Spirit, ye are not under the law." So far, indeed, as any man is led by the Spirit, he is not under the law; because, so far as he rejoices in the law of God, he lives not in fear of the law, since "fear has torment," [157] not joy and delight.

CHAPTER LXVIII

DESPITE THE DEVIL, MAN MAY, BY GOD'S HELP, BE PERFECTED

If, therefore, we feel rightly on this matter, it is our duty at once to be thankful for what is already healed within us, and to pray for such further healing as shall enable us to enjoy full liberty, in that most absolute state of health which is incapable of addition, the perfect pleasure of God.[158]

[153] Rom. vi. 12   [154] Gal. v. 18   [155] Rom. v. 5   [156] Jas. i. 25   [157] 1 John iv. 18   [158] Ps. xvi. 11

For we do not deny that human nature can be without sin; nor ought we by any means to refuse to it the ability to become perfect, since we admit its capacity for progress—by God's grace, however, through our Lord Jesus Christ. By His assistance we aver that it becomes holy and happy, by whom it was created in order to be so. There is accordingly an easy refutation of the objection which our author says is alleged by some against him: "The devil opposes us." This objection we also meet in entirely identical language with that which he uses in reply: "We must resist him, and he will flee. 'Resist the devil,' says the blessed apostle, 'and he will flee from you.' [159] From which it may be observed, what his harming amounts to against those whom he flees; or what power he is to be understood as possessing, when he prevails only against those who do not resist him." Such language is my own also; for it is impossible to employ truer words. There is, however, this difference between us and them, that we, whenever the devil has to be resisted, not only do not deny, but actually teach, that God's help must be sought; whereas they attribute so much power to will, as to take away prayer from religious duty. Now it is certainly with a view to resisting the devil and his fleeing from us that we say when we pray, "Lead us not into temptation;" [160] to the same end also are we warned by our Captain, exhorting us as soldiers in the words: "Watch ye and pray, lest ye enter into temptation." [161]

CHAPTER LXIX

PELAGIUS PUTS NATURE IN THE PLACE OF GRACE

In opposition, however, to those who ask, "And who would be unwilling to be without sin, if it were put in the power of a man?" he rightly contends, saying "that by this very question they acknowledge that the thing is not impossible; because so much as this, many, if not all men, certainly desire." Well, then, let him only confess the means by which this is possible, and then our controversy is ended. Now the means is "the grace of God through our Lord Jesus Christ;" by which he nowhere has been willing to allow that we are assisted when we pray, for the avoidance of sin. If indeed he secretly allows this, he must forgive us if we suspect otherwise. For he himself works this result, who, though encountering so much obloquy on this subject, wishes to entertain the secret opinion, and yet is unwilling to confess or profess it. It would surely be no great matter were he to speak out, especially since he has undertaken to handle and open this point, as if it had been objected against him on the side of opponents. Why on such occasions did he choose only to defend nature, and assert that man was so created as to have it in his power not to sin if he wished not to sin; and, from the fact that he was so created, definitely

[159] Jas. iv. 17   [160] Matt. vi. 13   [161] Mark xiv. 38

say that the power was owing to God's grace which enabled him to avoid sin, if he was unwilling to commit it; and yet refuse to say anything concerning the fact that even nature itself is either, because disordered, healed by God's grace through our Lord Jesus Christ, or else assisted by it, because in itself it is so insufficient?

CHAPTER LXX

WHETHER ANY MAN IS WITHOUT SIN IN THIS LIFE

Now, whether there ever has been, or is, or ever can be, a man living so righteous a life in this world as to have no sin at all, may be an open question among true and pious Christians; but whoever doubts the possibility of this sinless state *after this present life,* is foolish. For my own part, indeed, I am unwilling to dispute the point even as respects this life. For although that passage seems to me to be incapable of bearing any doubtful sense, wherein it is written, "In thy sight shall no man living be justified" [162] (and so of similar passages) yet I could wish it were possible to show either that such quotations were capable of bearing a better signification, or that a perfect and plenary righteousness, to which it were impossible for any accession to be made, had been realized at some former time in some one while passing through this life in the flesh, or was now being realized, or would be hereafter. They, however, are in a great majority, who, while not doubting that to the last day of their life it will be needful to them to resort to the prayer which they can so truthfully utter, "Forgive us our trespasses, as we forgive those who trespass against us," [163] still trust that in Christ and His promises they possess a true, certain, and unfailing hope. There is, however, no method whereby any persons arrive at absolute perfection, or whereby any man makes the slightest progress to true and godly righteousness, but the assisting grace of our crucified Saviour Christ, and the gift of His Spirit; and whosoever shall deny this cannot rightly, I almost think, be reckoned in the number of any kind of Christians at all.

CHAPTER LXXI

AUGUSTINE REPLIES AGAINST THE QUOTATIONS WHICH PELAGIUS HAD ADVANCED OUT OF THE CATHOLIC WRITERS. LACTANTIUS

Accordingly, with respect also to the passages which he has adduced— not indeed from the canonical Scriptures, but out of certain treatises of Catholic writers—I wish to meet the assertions of such as say that the said quotations make for him. The fact is, these passages are so entirely neutral, that they oppose neither our own opinion nor his. Amongst them

[162] Ps. cxliii. 2   [163] Matt. vi. 12

he wanted to class something out of my own books, thus accounting me to be a person who seemed worthy of being ranked with them. For this I must not be ungrateful, and I should be sorry—so I say with unaffected friendliness—for him to be in error, since he has conferred this honor upon me. As for his first quotation, indeed, why need I examine it largely, since I do not see here the author's name, either because he has not given it, or because from some casual mistake the copy which you[164] forwarded to me did not contain it? Especially as in writings of such authors I feel myself free to use my own judgment (owing unhesitating assent to nothing but the canonical Scriptures) while in fact there is not a passage which he has quoted from the works of this anonymous author[165] that disturbs me. "It behooved," says he, "for the Master and Teacher of virtue to become most like to man, that by conquering sin He might show that man is able to conquer sin." Now, however this passage may be expressed, its author must see to it as to what explanation it is capable of bearing. We, indeed, on our part, could not possibly doubt that in Christ there was no sin to conquer—born as He was in *the likeness* of sinful flesh, not in sinful flesh itself. Another passage is adduced from the same author to this effect: "And again, that by subduing the desires of the flesh He might teach us that it is not of necessity that one sins, but of set purpose and will." [166] For my own part, I understand these desires of the flesh (if it is not of its unlawful lusts that the writer here speaks) to be such as hunger, thirst, refreshment after fatigue, and the like. For it is through these, however faultless they be in themselves, that some men fall into sin—a result which was far from our blessed Saviour, even though, as we see from the evidence of the gospel, these affections were natural to Him owing to His likeness to sinful flesh.

CHAPTER LXXII

HILARY. THE PURE IN HEART BLESSED. THE DOING AND PERFECTING OF RIGHTEOUSNESS

He quotes the following words from the blessed Hilary: "It is only when we shall be perfect in spirit, and changed in our immortal state, which blessedness has been appointed only for the pure in heart,[167] that we shall see that which is immortal in God." [168] Now I am really not aware what is here said contrary to our own statement, or in what respect this passage is of any use to our opponent, unless it be that it testifies to the possibility of a man's being "pure in heart." But who denies such possibility? Only it must be by the grace of God, through Jesus Christ our Lord, and not

[164] Timasius and Jacobus, to whom the treatise is addressed. See ch. 1
[165] Lactantius is the writer from whom Pelagius takes his first quotations here. See his *Instit. Divin,* iv. 24
[166] Lactantius, *Instit. Divin.* iv. 25   [167] See Matt. v. 8   [168] Hilary *in loco*

merely by our freedom of will. He goes on to quote also this passage: "This Job had so effectually read these Scriptures, that he kept himself from every wicked work, because he worshipped God purely with a mind un-mixed with offences: now such worship of God is the proper work of righteousness," [169] It is what Job had done which the writer here spoke of, not what he had brought to perfection in this world—much less what he had done or perfected without the grace of that Saviour whom he had actually foretold.[170] For that man, indeed, abstains from every wicked work, who does not allow the sin which he has within him to have do-minion over him; and who, whenever an unworthy thought stole over him, suffered it not to come to a head in actual deed. It is, however, one thing not to have sin, and another to refuse obedience to its desires. It is one thing to fulfil the command, "Thou shalt not covet;" [171] and another thing, by an endeavor at any rate after abstinence, to do that which is also written, "Thou shalt not go after thy lusts." [172] And yet one is quite aware that he can do nothing of all this without the Saviour's grace. It is to work righteousness, therefore, to fight in an internal struggle with the internal evil of concupiscence in the true worship of God; while to perfect it means to have no adversary at all. Now he who has to fight is still in danger, and is sometimes shaken, even if he is not overthrown; whereas he who has no enemy at all rejoices in perfect peace. He, moreover, is in the highest truth said to be without sin in whom no sin has an in-dwelling—not he who, abstaining from evil deeds, uses such language as "Now it is no longer I that do it, but the sin that dwelleth in me." [173]

CHAPTER LXXIII

HE MEETS PELAGIUS WITH ANOTHER PASSAGE FROM HILARY

Now even Job himself is not silent respecting his own sins; and your friend,[174] of course, is justly of opinion that humility must not by any means "be put on the side of falsehood." Whatever confession, therefore, Job makes, inasmuch as he is a true worshipper of God, he undoubtedly makes it in truth.[175] Hilary, likewise, while expounding that passage of the psalm in which it is written, "Thou hast despised all those who turn aside from Thy commandments," [176] says: "If God were to despise sinners, He would despise indeed all men, because no man is without sin; but it is those who turn away from Him, whom they call *apostates,* that He despises." You observe his statement: it is not to the effect that no man *was* without sin, as if he spoke of the past; but no man *is* without sin; and on this point, as I have already remarked, I have no contention with him. But if one refuses to submit to the Apostle John—who does not

[169] Hilary's *Fragments*   [170] Job xix. 25   [171] Ex. xx. 17   [172] Ecclus. xviii. 30   [173] Rom. vii. 20   [174] Pelagius, the friend of Timasius and Jacobus   [175] Job xl. 4, and xlii. 6   [176] Ps. cxix. 21, or 118

himself declare, "If we were to say we *have had* no sin," but "If we say we *have* no sin"[177]—how is he likely to show deference to Bishop Hilary? It is in defence of the grace of Christ that I lift up my voice, without which grace no man is justified—just as if natural free will were sufficient. Nay, He Himself lifts up His own voice in defence of the same. Let us submit to Him when He says: "Without me ye can do nothing."[178]

CHAPTER LXXIV

AMBROSE

Saint Ambrose, however, really opposes those who say that man cannot exist without sin in the present life. For, in order to support his statement, he avails himself of the instance of Zacharias and Elisabeth, because they are mentioned as "having walked in all the commandments and ordinances" of the law "blameless.[179] Well, but does he for all that deny that it was by God's grace that they did this through our Lord Jesus Christ? It was undoubtedly by such faith in Him that holy men lived of old, even before His death. It is He who sends the Holy Ghost that is given to us, through whom that love is shed abroad in our hearts whereby alone whosoever are righteous are righteous. This same Holy Ghost the bishop expressly mentioned when he reminds us that He is to be obtained by prayer (so that the will is not sufficient unless it be aided by Him); thus in his hymn he says:

> "Votisque praestat sedulis,
> Sanctum mereri Spiritum,"[180]

"To those who sedulously seek He gives to gain the Holy Spirit."

CHAPTER LXXV

AUGUSTINE ADDUCES IN REPLY SOME OTHER PASSAGES OF AMBROSE

I, too, will quote a passage out of this very work of Saint Ambrose, from which our opponent has taken the statement which he deemed favorable for citation: " 'It seemed good to me,' " he says; "but what he declares seemed good to him cannot have seemed good to him alone. For it is not simply to his human will that it seemed good, but also as it pleased Him, even Christ, who, says he, speaketh in me, who it is that causes that which is good in itself to seem good to ourselves also. For him on whom He has mercy He also calls. He, therefore, who follows Christ, when asked why he wished to be a Christian, can answer: 'It seemed good to me.' In

---

[177] I John i. 8   [178] John xv. 5   [179] Luke i. 6. See Ambrose *in loco* (Exp. 61, s. 17)   [180] Ambrose's *Hymns*, 3

saying this he does not deny that it also pleased God; for from God proceeds the preparation of man's will, inasmuch as it is by God's grace that God is honored by His saint." [181] See now what your author must learn, if he takes pleasure in the words of Ambrose, how that man's will is prepared by God, and that it is of no importance, or, at any rate, does not much matter, by what means or at what time the preparation is accomplished, provided no doubt is raised as to whether the thing itself be capable of accomplishment without the grace of Christ. Then, again, how important it was that he should observe one line from the words of Ambrose which he quoted! For after that holy man had said, "Inasmuch as the Church has been gathered out of the world, that is, out of sinful men, how can it be unpolluted when composed of such polluted material, except that, in the first place, it be washed of sins by the grace of Christ, and then, in the next place, abstain from sins through its nature of avoiding sin?"—he added the following sentence, which your author has refused to quote for a self-evident reason; for [Ambrose] says: "It was not from the first unpolluted, for that was impossible for human nature: but it is through God's grace and nature that because it no longer sins, it comes to pass that it seems unpolluted." [182] Now who does not understand the reason why your author declined adding these words? It is, of course, so contrived in the discipline of the present life, that the holy Church shall arrive at last at that condition of most immaculate purity which all holy men desire; and that it may in the world to come, and in a state unmixed with anything of evil men, and undisturbed by any law of sin resisting the law of the mind, lead the purest life in a divine eternity. Still he should well observe what Bishop Ambrose says—and his statement exactly tallies with the Scriptures: "It was not from the first unpolluted, for that condition was impossible for human nature." By his phrase, "from the first," he means indeed from the time of our being born of Adam. Adam no doubt was himself created immaculate; in the case, however, of those who are by nature children of wrath, deriving from him what in him was corrupted, he distinctly averred that it was an impossibility in human nature that they should be immaculate from the first.

CHAPTER LXXVI

JOHN OF CONSTANTINOPLE

He quotes also John, bishop of Constantinople, as saying "that sin is not a substance, but a wicked act." Who denies this? "And because it is not natural, therefore the law was given against it, and because it proceeds from the liberty of our will." [183] Who, too, denies this? However, the present question concerns our human nature in its corrupted state; it is

[181] Ambrose on Luke i. 3   [182] Ambrose on Luke i. 6   [183] Compare Chrysostom's *Homily on Eph.* ii. 3

a further question also concerning that grace of God whereby our nature is healed by the great Physician, Christ, whose remedy it would not need if it were only whole. And yet your author defends it as capable of not sinning, as if it were sound, or as if its freedom of will were self-sufficient.

CHAPTER LXXVII

XYSTUS

What Christian, again, is unaware of what he quotes the most blessed Xystus, bishop of Rome and martyr of Christ, as having said, "God has conferred upon men liberty of their own will, in order that by purity and sinlessness of life they may become like unto God?" [184] But the man who appeals to free will ought to listen and believe, and ask Him in whom he believes to give him His assistance not to sin. For when he speaks of "becoming like unto God," it is indeed through God's love that men are to be like unto God—even the love which is "shed abroad in our hearts," not by any ability of nature or the free will within us, but "by the Holy Ghost which is given unto us." [185] Then, in respect of what the same martyr further says, "A pure mind is a holy temple for God, and a heart clean and without sin is His best altar," who knows not that the clean heart must be brought to this perfection, while "the inward man is renewed day by day," [186] but yet not without the grace of God through Jesus Christ our Lord? Again, when he says, "A man of chastity and without sin has received power from God to be a son of God," he of course meant it as an admonition that on a man's becoming so chaste and sinless (without raising any question as to where and when this perfection was to be obtained by him—although in fact it is quite an interesting question among godly men, who are notwithstanding agreed as to the possibility of such perfection on the one hand, and on the other hand its impossibility except through "the one Mediator between God and men, the Man Christ Jesus")[187]—nevertheless, as I began to say, Xystus designed his words to be an admonition that, on any man's attaining such a high character, and thereby being rightly reckoned to be among the sons of God, the attainment must not be thought to have been the work of his own power. This indeed he, through grace, received from God, since he did not have it in a nature which had become corrupted and depraved—even as we read in the *Gospel,* "But as many as received Him, to them gave He power to become the sons of God;" [188] which they were not by nature, nor could at all become, unless by receiving Him they also received power through His grace. This is the power which is claimed for itself by the fortitude of

---

[184] This passage, which Pelagius had quoted as from Xystus the Roman bishop and martyr, Augustine subsequently ascertained to have had for its author Sextus, a Pythagorean philosopher. See *Retractations,* ii. 42

[185] Rom. v. 5   [186] 2 Cor. iv. 16   [187] 1 Tim. ii. 5   [188] John i. 12

that love which is only communicated to us by the Holy Ghost bestowed upon us.

CHAPTER LXXVIII

JEROME

We have next a quotation of some words of the venerable presbyter Jerome, from his exposition of the passage where it is written: " 'Blessed are the pure in heart; for they shall see God.' [189] These are they whom no consciousness of sin reproves," he says, and adds: "The pure man is seen by his purity of heart; the temple of God cannot be defiled." [190] This perfection is, to be sure, wrought in us by endeavor, by labor, by prayer, by effectual importunity therein that we may be brought to the perfection in which we may be able to look upon God with a pure heart, by His grace through our Lord Jesus Christ. As to his quotation, that the forementioned presbyter said, "God created us with free will; we are drawn by necessity neither to virtue nor to vice; otherwise, where there is necessity there is no crown" [191]—who would not allow this? Who would not cordially accept it? Who would deny that human nature was so created? The reason, however, why in doing a right action there is no bondage of necessity, is that liberty comes of love.

CHAPTER LXXIX

A CERTAIN NECESSITY OF SINNING

But let us revert to the apostle's assertion: "The love of God is shed abroad in our hearts by the Holy Ghost which is given unto us." [192] By whom given if not by Him who "ascended up on high, led captivity captive, and gave gifts unto men?" [193] Forasmuch, however, as there is, owing to the defects that have entered our nature, not to the constitution of our nature, a certain necessary tendency to sin, a man should listen, and in order that the said necessity may cease to exist, learn to say to God, "Bring Thou me out of my necessities;" [194] because in the very offering up of such a prayer there is a struggle against the tempter, who fights against us concerning this very necessity; and thus, by the assistance of grace through our Lord Jesus Christ, both the evil necessity will be removed and full liberty be bestowed.

[189] Matt. v. 8   [190] Jerome on Matt. v. 8 (*Comm.* Book i. c. 5)   [191] Jerome, *Against Jovinianus,* ii. 3   [192] Rom. v. 5   [193] Eph. iv. 8   [194] Ps. xxv. 17

CHAPTER LXXX

AUGUSTINE HIMSELF. TWO METHODS WHEREBY SINS, LIKE DISEASES, ARE GUARDED AGAINST

Let us now turn to our own case. "Bishop Augustine also," says your author, "in his books on Free Will has these words: 'Whatever the cause itself of volition is, if it is impossible to resist it, submission to it is not sinful; if, however, it may be resisted, let it not be submitted to, and there will be no sin. Does it, perchance, deceive the unwary man? Let him then beware that he be not deceived. Is the deception, however, so potent that it is not possible to guard against it? If such is the case, then there are no sins. For who sins in a case where precaution is quite impossible? Sin, however, is committed; precaution therefore is possible.' " [195] I acknowledge it, these are my words; but he, too, should condescend to acknowledge all that was said previously, seeing that the discussion is about the grace of God, which helps us as a medicine through the Mediator; not about the impossibility of righteousness. Whatever, then, may be the cause, it can be resisted. Most certainly it can. Now it is because of this that we pray for help, saying, "Lead us not into temptation," [196] and we should not ask for help if we supposed that resistance were quite impossible. It is possible to guard against sin, but by the help of Him who cannot be deceived.[197] For this very circumstance has much to do with guarding against sin that we can unfeignedly say, "Forgive us our debts, as we forgive our debtors." [198] Now there are two ways whereby, even in bodily maladies, the evil is guarded against—to prevent its occurrence, and, if it happen, to secure a speedy cure. To prevent its occurrence, we may find precaution in the prayer, "Lead us not into temptation;" to secure the prompt remedy, we have the resource in the prayer, "Forgive us our debts." Whether then the danger only threaten, or be inherent, it may be guarded against.

CHAPTER LXXXI

AUGUSTINE QUOTES HIMSELF ON FREE WILL

In order, however, that my meaning on this subject may be clear not merely to him, but also to such persons as have not read those treatises of mine on Free Will, which your author has read, and who have not only not read them, but perchance do read him; I must go on to quote out of my books what he has omitted, but which, if he had perceived and quoted in his book, no controversy would be left between us on this subject. For immediately after those words of mine which he has quoted, I expressly

---

[195] Augustine, *De Libero Arbitrio*, iii. 18 (50) [196] Matt. vi. 13 [197] Augustine gives a similar reply to the objection in his *Retractationes*, i. 9 [198] Matt. vi. 12

added, and (as fully as I could) worked out, the train of thought which might occur to any one's mind, to the following effect: "And yet some actions are disapproved of, even when they are done in ignorance, and are judged deserving of chastisement, as we read in the inspired authorities." After taking some examples out of these, I went on to speak also of infirmity as follows: "Some actions also deserve disapprobation, that are done from necessity; as when a man wishes to act rightly and cannot. For whence arise those utterances: 'For the good that I would, I do not; but the evil which I would not, that I do'?" [199] Then, after quoting some other passages of the Holy Scriptures to the same effect, I say: "But all these are the sayings of persons who are coming out of that condemnation of death; for if this is not man's punishment, but his nature, then those are no sins." Then, again, a little afterwards I add: "It remains, therefore, that this just punishment come of man's condemnation. Nor ought it to be wondered at, that either by ignorance man has not free determination of will to choose what he will rightly do, or that by the resistance of carnal habit (which by force of mortal transmission has, in a certain sense, become engrafted into his nature), though seeing what ought rightly to be done, and wishing to do it, he yet is unable to accomplish it. For this is the most just penalty of sin, that a man should lose what he has been unwilling to make good use of, when he might with ease have done so if he would; which, however, amounts to this, that the man who knowingly does not do what is right loses the ability to do it when he wishes. For, in truth, to every soul that sins there accrue these two penal consequences—ignorance and difficulty. Out of the ignorance springs the error which disgraces; out of the difficulty arises the pain which afflicts. But to approve of falsehoods as if they were true, so as to err involuntarily, and to be unable, owing to the resistance and pain of carnal bondage, to refrain from deeds of lust, is not the nature of man as he was created, but the punishment of man as under condemnation. When, however, we speak of a free will to do what is right, we of course mean that liberty in which man was created." Some men at once deduce from this what seems to them a just objection from the transfer and transmission of sins of ignorance and difficulty from the first man to his posterity. My answer to such objectors is this: "I tell them, by way of a brief reply, to be silent, and to cease from murmuring against God. Perhaps their complaint might have been a proper one, if no one from among men had stood forth a vanquisher of error and of lust, but when there is everywhere present One who calls off from himself, through the creature by so many means, the man who serves the Lord, teaches him when believing, consoles him when hoping, encourages him when loving, helps him when endeavoring, hears him when praying—it is not reckoned to you as a fault that you are involuntarily ignorant, but that you neglect to search out what you are ignorant of; nor is it imputed to you in censure

[199] Rom. vii. 19

that you do not bind up the limbs that are wounded, but that you despise him who wishes to heal them." [200] In such terms did I exhort them, as well as I could, to live righteously; nor did I make the grace of God of none effect, without which the now obscured and tarnished nature of man can neither be enlightened nor purified. Our whole discussion with them on this subject turns upon this, that we frustrate not the grace of God which is in Jesus Christ our Lord by a perverted assertion of nature. In a passage occurring shortly after the last quoted one, I said in reference to nature: "Of nature itself we speak in one sense, when we properly describe it as that human nature in which man was created faultless after his kind; and in another sense as that nature in which we are born ignorant and carnally minded, owing to the penalty of condemnation, after the manner of the apostle, 'We ourselves likewise were by nature children of wrath, even as others.' " [201]

CHAPTER LXXXII

HOW TO EXHORT MEN TO FAITH, REPENTANCE, AND ADVANCEMENT

If, therefore, we wish "to rouse and kindle cold and sluggish souls by Christian exhortations to lead righteous lives," [202] we must first of all exhort them to that faith whereby they may become Christians, and be subjects of His name and authority, without whom they cannot be saved. If, however, they are already Christians but neglect to lead holy lives, they must be chastised with alarms and be aroused by the praises of reward—in such a manner, indeed, that we must not forget to urge them to godly prayers as well as to virtuous actions, and furthermore to instruct them in such wholesome doctrine that they be induced thereby to return thanks for being able to accomplish any step in that holy life which they have entered upon, without difficulty, and whenever they do experience such "difficulty," that they then wrestle with God in most faithful and persistent prayer and ready works of mercy to obtain from Him facility. But provided they thus progress, I am not over-anxious as to the *where* and the *when* of their perfection in fulness of righteousness; only I solemnly assert, that wheresoever and whensoever they become perfect, it cannot be but by the grace of God through our Lord Jesus Christ. When, indeed, they have attained to the clear knowledge that they have no sin, let them not say they have sin, lest the truth be not in them;[203] even as the truth is not in those persons who, though they have sin, yet say that they have it not.

[200] *De Libero Arbitrio*, iii. 19   [201] Eph. ii. 3
[202] This passage, and others in this and the following chapters, are marked as quotations, apparently cited from Pelagius by Augustine   [203] 1 John i. 8

CHAPTER LXXXIII

GOD ENJOINS NO IMPOSSIBILITY, BECAUSE ALL THINGS ARE POSSIBLE AND EASY TO LOVE

But "the precepts of the law are very good," if we use them lawfully.[204] Indeed, by the very fact (of which we have the firmest conviction) "that the just and good God could not possibly have enjoined impossibilities," we are admonished both what to do in easy paths and what to ask for when they are difficult. Now all things are easy for love to effect, to which (and which alone) "Christ's burden is light" [205]—or rather, it is itself alone the burden which is light. Accordingly it is said, "And His commandments are not grievous;" [206] so that whoever finds them grievous must regard the inspired statement about their "not being grievous" as having been capable of only this meaning, that there may be a state of heart to which they are not burdensome, and he must pray for that disposition which he at present wants, so as to be able to fulfil all that is commanded him. And this is the purport of what is said to Israel in Deuteronomy, if understood in a godly, sacred, and spiritual sense, since the apostle, after quoting the passage, "The word is nigh thee, even in thy mouth and in thy heart" [207] (*and*, as the verse also has it, *in thine hands*, for in man's heart are his spiritual hands), adds in explanation, "This is the word of faith which we preach." [208] No man, therefore, who "returns to the Lord his God," as he is there commanded, "with all his heart and with all his soul," [209] will find God's commandment "grievous." How, indeed, can it be grievous, when it is the precept of love? Either, therefore, a man has not love, and then it is grievous; or he has love, and then it is not grievous. But he possesses love if he does what is there enjoined on Israel, by returning to the Lord his God with all his heart and with all his soul. "A new commandment," says He, "do I give unto you, that ye love one another;" [210] and "He that loveth his neighbor hath fulfilled the law;" [211] and again, "Love is the fulfilling of the law." [212] In accordance with these sayings is that passage, "Had they trodden good paths, they would have found, indeed, the ways of righteousness easy." [213] How then is it written, "Because of the words of Thy lips, I have kept the paths of difficulty," [214] except it be that both statements are true: These paths are paths of difficulty to fear; but to love they are easy?

[204] See 1 Tim. i. 8   [205] Matt. xi. 30   [206] 1 John v. 3   [207] Deut. xxx. 14, quoted Rom. x. 8   [208] Rom. x. 8   [209] Deut. xxx. 2   [210] John xiii. 34   [211] Rom. xiii. 8   [212] Rom. xiii. 10   [213] Prov. ii. 20   [214] Ps. xvii. 4

CHAPTER LXXXIV

THE DEGREES OF LOVE ARE ALSO DEGREES OF HOLINESS

Inchoate love, therefore, is inchoate holiness; advanced love is advanced holiness; great love is great holiness; "perfect love is perfect holiness"— but this "love is out of a pure heart, and of a good conscience, and of faith unfeigned," [215] "which in this life is then the greatest, when life itself is contemned in comparison with it." [216] I wonder, however, whether it has not a soil in which to grow after it has quitted this mortal life! But in what place and at what time soever it shall reach that state of absolute perfection, which shall admit of no increase, it is certainly not "shed abroad in our hearts" by any energies either of the nature or the volition that are within us, but "by the Holy Ghost which is given unto us," [217] and which both helps our infirmity and co-operates with our strength. For it is itself indeed the grace of God, through our Lord Jesus Christ, to whom, with the Father and the Holy Spirit, appertaineth eternity, and all goodness, for ever and ever. Amen.

[215] i Tim. i. 5
[216] See note at begining of ch. 82 for the meaning of this mark of quotation
[217] Rom. v. 5

ON THE GRACE OF CHRIST
AND
ON ORIGINAL SIN

ON THE GRACE OF CHRIST AND ON ORIGINAL SIN

Introductory Note

In the year 418 A.D. the heresy of Pelagius was condemned. Some months later Saint Augustine wrote the present two books at the request of two faithful Christians, Pinianus and Melania, a married couple, who had left Rome and ultimately separated, with the husband becoming a head of a monastery in Palestine while his wife entered a convent. Saint Augustine took advantage of this opportunity, amidst the pressure of his own great activity, to compose a complete and careful exposition of his views concerning grace and original sin, and at the same time to refute in detail the heretical doctrines of Pelagius himself and his close associate, Coelestius. The work, probably better than any other, illuminates the Augustinian position on these crucial problems.

ON THE GRACE OF CHRIST AND ON ORIGINAL SIN

WRITTEN AGAINST PELAGIUS AND COELESTIUS

BOOK ONE

ON THE GRACE OF CHRIST

Wherein he shows that Pelagius is disingenuous in his confession of grace, inasmuch as he places grace either in nature and free will, or in law and teaching; and, moreover, asserts that it is merely the "possibility" (as he calls it) of will and action, and not the will and action itself, which is assisted by divine grace; and that this assisting grace, too, is given by God according to men's merits; while he further thinks that they are so assisted for the sole purpose of being able the more easily to fulfil the Commandments. Augustine examines those passages of his writings in which he boasted that he had bestowed express commendation on the grace of God, and points out how they can be interpreted as referring to law and teaching—in other words, to the divine revelation and the example of Christ which are alike included in "the teaching"—or else to the remission of sins; nor do they afford any evidence whatever that Pelagius really acknowledged Christian grace, in the sense of help rendered for the performance of right action to natural faculty and instruction, by the inspiration of a most growing and luminous love; and he concludes with a request that Pelagius would seriously listen to Ambrose, whom he is so very fond of quoting, in his excellent eulogy in commendation of the grace of God.

CHAPTER I

INTRODUCTORY

How greatly we rejoice on account of your bodily, and, above all, your spiritual welfare, my most sincerely attached brethren and beloved of God, Albina, Pinianus, and Melania, we cannot express in words; we therefore leave all this to your own thoughts and belief, in order that we may now rather speak of the matters on which you consulted us. We have, indeed, had to compose these words to the best of the ability which God has vouchsafed to us, while our messenger was in a hurry to be gone, and amidst many occupations, which are much more absorbing to me at Carthage than in any other place whatever.

CHAPTER II

SUSPICIOUS CHARACTER OF PELAGIUS' CONFESSION AS TO THE NECESSITY OF GRACE FOR EVERY SINGLE ACT OF OURS

You informed me in your letter, that you had entreated Pelagius to express in writing his condemnation of all that had been alleged against him;

and that he had said, in the audience of you all: "I anathematize the man who either thinks or says that the grace of God, whereby 'Christ Jesus came into the world to save sinners,' [1] is not necessary not only for every hour and for every moment, but also for every act of our lives: and those who endeavor to disannul it deserve everlasting punishment." Now, whoever hears these words, and is ignorant of the opinion which he has clearly enough expressed in his books—not those, indeed, which he declares to have been stolen from him in an incorrect form, nor those which he repudiates, but those even which he mentions in his own letter which he forwarded to Rome—would certainly suppose that the views he holds are in strict accordance with the truth. But whoever notices what he openly declares in them, cannot fail to regard these statements with suspicion. Because, although he makes that grace of God whereby Christ came into the world to save sinners to consist simply in the remission of sins, he can still accommodate his words to this meaning, by alleging that the necessity of such grace for every hour and for every moment and for every action of our life, comes to this, that while we recollect and keep in mind the forgiveness of our past sins, we sin no more, aided not by any supply of power from without, but by the powers of our own will as it recalls to our mind, in every action we do, what advantage has been conferred upon us by the remission of sins. Then again, whereas they are accustomed to say that Christ has given us assistance for avoiding sin, in that He has left us an example by living righteously and teaching what is right Himself, they have it in their power here also to accommodate their words, by affirming that this is the necessity of grace to us for every moment and for every action, namely, that we should in all our conversation regard the example of the Lord's conversation. Your own fidelity, however, enables you clearly to perceive how such a profession of opinion as this differs from that true confession of grace which is now the question before us. And yet how easily can it be obscured and disguised by their ambiguous statements!

CHAPTER III

GRACE ACCORDING TO THE PELAGIANS

But why should we wonder at this? For the same Pelagius, who in the Proceedings of the episcopal synod unhesitatingly condemned those who say "that God's grace and assistance are not given for single acts, but consist in free will, or in law and teaching," [2] upon which points we were apt to think that he had expended all his subterfuges; and who also condemned such as affirm that the grace of God is bestowed in proportion to our merits: —is proved, notwithstanding, to hold, in the books which he has published on the freedom of the will, and which he mentions in the letter he sent to

[1] I Tim. i. 15   [2] cf. *De Gestis Pelagii*, 30

Rome, no other sentiments than those which he seemingly condemned. For that grace and help of God, by which we are assisted in avoiding sin, he places either in nature and free will, or else in the gift of the law and teaching; the result of which of course is this, that whenever God helps a man, He must be supposed to help him to turn away from evil and do good, by revealing to him and teaching him what he ought to do, but not with the additional assistance of His co-operation and inspiration of love, that he may accomplish that which he had discovered it to be his duty to do.

CHAPTER IV

PELAGIUS' SYSTEM OF FACULTIES

In his system, he posits and distinguishes three faculties, by which he says God's commandments are fulfilled:—*capacity, volition,* and *action:* meaning by "capacity," that by which a man is able to be righteous; by "volition," that by which he wills to be righteous; by "action," that by which he actually is righteous. The first of these, the capacity, he allows to have been bestowed on us by the Creator of our nature; it is not in our power, and we possess it even against our will. The other two, however, the volition and the action, he asserts to be our own; and he assigns them to us so strictly as to contend that they proceed simply from ourselves. In short, according to his view, God's grace has nothing to do with assisting those two faculties which he will have to be altogether our own, the volition and the action, but that only which is not in our own power and comes to us from God, namely the capacity; as if the faculties which are our own, that is, the volition and the action, have such avail for declining evil and doing good, that they require no divine help, whereas that faculty which we have of God, that is to say, the capacity, is so weak, that it is always assisted by the aid of grace.

CHAPTER V

PELAGIUS' OWN ACCOUNT OF THE FACULTIES, QUOTED

Lest, however, it should chance to be said that we either do not correctly understand what he advances, or malevolently pervert to another meaning what he never meant to bear such a sense, I beg of you to consider his own actual words: "We distinguish," says he, "three things, arranging them in a certain graduated order. We put in the first place 'ability;' in the second, 'volition;' and in the third, 'actuality.' The 'ability' we place in our nature, the 'volition' in our will, and the 'actuality' in the effect. The first, that is, the 'ability,' properly belongs to God, who has bestowed it on His creature; the other two, that is, the 'volition' and the 'actuality,' must be referred to man, because they flow forth from the fountain of the will. For his willing, therefore, and doing a good work, the praise belongs to man; or rather both to man, and to God who has bestowed on him the 'capacity' for his will and work, and who evermore by the help of His grace assists even this capacity. That a man is able to will and effect any good work, comes from God alone. So that this one faculty can exist, even when the other two have no being; but these latter cannot exist without that former one. I am therefore free not to have either a good volition or action; but I am by no means able not to have the capacity of good. This capacity is inherent in me, whether I will or no; nor does nature at any time receive in this point freedom for itself. Now the meaning of all this will be rendered clearer by an example or two. That we are able to see with our eyes is not of us; but it is our own that we make a good or a bad use of our eyes. So again (that I may, by applying a general case in illustration, embrace all) that we are able to do, say, think, any good thing, comes from Him who has endowed us with this 'ability,' and who also assists this 'ability;' but that we really do a good thing, or speak a good word, or think a good thought, proceeds from our own selves, because we are also able to turn all these into evil. Accordingly—and this is a point which needs frequent repetition, because of your calumniation of us—whenever we say that a man can live without sin, we also give praise to God by our acknowledgment of the capacity which we have received from Him, who has bestowed such 'ability' upon us; and there is here no occasion for praising the human agent, since it is God's matter alone that is for the moment treated of; for the question is not about 'willing,' or 'effecting,' but simply and solely about that which may possibly be."

CHAPTER VI

PELAGIUS AND PAUL OF DIFFERENT OPINIONS

The whole of this dogma of Pelagius, observe, is carefully expressed in these words, and none other, in the third book of his treatise in defence of the liberty of the will, in which he has taken care to distinguish with so great subtlety these three things—the "capacity," the "volition," and the "action," that is, the "ability," the "volition," and the "actuality"—that, whenever we read or hear of his acknowledging the assistance of divine grace in order to our avoidance of evil and accomplishment of good—whatever he may mean by the said assistance of grace, whether law and the teaching or any other thing—we are sure of what he says; nor can we run into any mistake by understanding him otherwise than he means. For we cannot help knowing that, according to his belief, it is not our "volition" nor our "action" which is assisted by the divine help, but solely our "capacity" to will and act, which alone of the three, as he affirms, we have of God. As if that faculty were infirm which God Himself placed in our nature; while the other two, which, as he would have it, are our own, are so strong and firm and self-sufficient as to require none of His help! so that He does not help us to will, nor help us to act, but simply helps us to the possibility of willing and acting. The apostle, however, holds the contrary, when he says, "Work out your own salvation with fear and trembling." [3] And that they might be sure that it was not simply in their being able to work (for this they had already received in nature and in teaching), but in their actual working, that they were divinely assisted, the apostle does not say to them, "For it is God that worketh in you to be able," as if they already possessed volition and operation among their own resources, without requiring His assistance in respect of these two; but he says, "For it is God which worketh in you both to will and to perform of His own good pleasure;" [4] or, as the reading runs in other copies, especially the Greek, "both to will and to operate." Consider, now, whether the apostle did not thus long before foresee by the Holy Ghost that there would arise adversaries of the grace of God; and did not therefore declare that God works within us those two very things, even "willing" and "operating," which this man so determined to be our own, as if they were in no wise assisted by the help of divine grace.

CHAPTER VII

PELAGIUS POSITS GOD'S AID ONLY FOR OUR "CAPACITY"

Let not Pelagius, however, in this way deceive incautious and simple persons, or even himself; for after saying, "Man is therefore to be praised for his willing and doing a good work," he added, as if by way of correcting himself, these words: "Or rather, this praise belongs to man *and to God.*" It was not, however, that he wished to be understood as showing any deference to the sound doctrine, that it is "God which worketh in us both to will and to do," that he thus expressed himself; but it is clear enough, on his own showing, why he added the latter clause, for he immediately subjoins: "Who has bestowed on him the 'capacity' for this very will and work." From his preceding words it is manifest that he places this capacity in our nature. Lest he should seem, however, to have said nothing about grace, he added these words: "And who evermore, by the help of His grace, assists this very capacity"—*"this very capacity,"* observe; not *"very will,"* or *"very action;"* for if he had said so much as this, he would clearly not be at variance with the teaching of the apostle. But there are his words: "this very capacity;" meaning that very one of the three faculties which he had placed in our nature. This God "evermore assists by the help of His grace." The result, indeed, is, that "the praise does not belong to man and to God," because man so wills that yet God also inspires his volition with the ardor of love, or that man so works that God nevertheless also cooperates with him—and without His help, what is man? But he has associated God in this praise in this wise, that were it not for the nature which

---

[3] Phil. ii. 12   [4] Phil. ii. 13

God gave us in our creation wherewith we might be able to exercise volition and action, we should neither will nor act.

CHAPTER VIII

GRACE, ACCORDING TO THE PELAGIANS, CONSISTS IN THE INTERNAL AND MANIFOLD ILLUMINATION OF THE MIND

As to this natural capacity which, he allows, is assisted by the grace of God, it is by no means clear from the passage either what grace he means, or to what extent he supposes our nature to be assisted by it. But, as is the case in other passages in which he expresses himself with more clearness and decision, we may here also perceive that no other grace is intended by him as helping natural capacity than the law and the teaching. For in one passage he says: "We are supposed by very ignorant persons to do wrong in this matter to divine grace, because we say that it by no means perfects sanctity in us without our will—as if God could have imposed any command on His grace, without also supplying the help of His grace to those on whom he imposed His commands, so that men might more easily accomplish through grace what they are required to do by their free will." Then, as if he meant to explain what grace he meant, he immediately went on to add these words: "And this grace we for our part do not, as you suppose, allow to consist merely in the law, but also in the help of God." Now who can help wishing that he would show us what grace it is that he would have us understand? Indeed, we have the strongest reason for desiring him to tell us what he means by saying that he does not allow grace merely to consist in the law. Whilst, however, we are in the suspense of our expectation, observe, I pray you, what he has further to tell us: "God helps us," says he, "by His teaching and revelation, whilst He opens the eyes of our heart; whilst He points out to us the future, that we may not be absorbed in the present; whilst He discovers to us the snares of the devil; whilst He enlightens us with the manifold and ineffable gift of heavenly grace." He then concludes his statement with a kind of absolution: "Does the man," he asks, "who says all this appear to you to be a denier of grace? Does he not acknowledge both man's free will and God's grace?" But, after all, he has not got beyond his commendation of the law and of teaching; assiduously inculcating this as the grace that helps us, and so following up the idea with which he had started, when he said, "We, however, allow it to consist in the help of God." God's help, indeed, he supposed must be recommended to us by manifold lures; by setting forth teaching and revelation, the opening of the eyes of the heart, the demonstration of the future, the discovery of the devil's wiles, and the illumination of our minds by the varied and indescribable gift of heavenly grace—all this, of course, with a view to our learning the commandments and promises of God. And what else is this than placing God's grace in "the law and the teaching"?

CHAPTER IX

THE LAW ONE THING, GRACE ANOTHER. THE UTILITY OF THE LAW

Hence, then, it is clear that he acknowledges that grace whereby God points out and reveals to us what we are bound to do; but not that whereby He endows and assists us to act, since the knowledge of the law, unless it be accompanied by the assistance of grace, rather avails for producing the transgression of the commandment. "Where there is no law," says the apostle, "there is no transgression;"[5] and again: "I had not known lust except the law had said, Thou shalt not covet."[6] Therefore so far are the law and grace from being the same thing, that the law is not only unprofitable, but it is absolutely prejudicial, unless grace assists it; and the utility of the law may be shown by this, that it obliges all whom it proves guilty of transgression to betake themselves to grace for deliverance and help to overcome their evil lusts. For it rather commands than assists; it discovers disease, but does not heal it; nay, the malady that is not healed is rather aggravated by it, so that the cure of grace is more earnestly and anxiously sought for, inasmuch as "The letter killeth, but the spirit giveth life."[7] "For if there had been a law given which could have given life, verily righteousness should have been by the law."[8] To what extent, however, the law gives assistance, the apostle informs us when he says immediately afterwards: "The Scripture hath concluded all under sin, that the promise by faith of Jesus Christ might be given to them that believe."[9] Wherefore, says the apostle, "the law was our schoolmaster in Christ Jesus."[10] Now this very thing is serviceable to proud men, to be more firmly and manifestly "concluded under sin," so that none may presumptuously endeavor to accomplish their justification by means of free will as if by their own resources; but rather "that every mouth may be stopped, and all the world may become guilty before God. Because by the deeds of the law there shall no flesh be justified in His sight: for by the law is the knowledge of sin. But now the righteousness of God without the law is manifested, being witnessed by the law and the prophets."[11] How then manifested without the law, if witnessed by the law? For this very reason the phrase is not, "manifested without the law," but "the righteousness without the law," because it is "the righteousness of God;" that is, the righteousness which we have not from the law, but from God—not the righteousness, indeed, which by reason of His commanding it, causes us fear through our knowledge of it; but rather the righteousness which by reason of His bestowing it, is held fast and maintained by us through our loving it—"so that he that glorieth, let him glory in the Lord."[12]

[5] Rom. iv. 15   [6] Rom. vii. 7   [7] 2 Cor. iii. 6   [8] Gal. iii. 21   [9] Gal. iii. 22
[10] Gal. iii. 24   [11] Rom. iii. 19-21   [12] 1 Cor. i. 31

CHAPTER X

WHAT PURPOSE THE LAW SUBSERVES

What object, then, can this man gain by accounting the law and the teaching to be the grace whereby we are helped to work righteousness? For, in order that it may help much, it must help us to feel our need of grace. No man, indeed, is able to fulfil the law through the law. "Love is the fulfilling of the law." [13] And the love of God is not shed abroad in our hearts by the law, but by the Holy Ghost, which is given unto us.[14] Grace, therefore, is pointed at by the law, in order that the law may be fulfilled by grace. Now what does it avail for Pelagius, that he declares the self-same thing under different phrases, that he may not be understood to place in law and teaching that grace which, as he avers, assists the "capacity" of our nature? So far, indeed, as I can conjecture, the reason why he fears being so understood is, because he condemned all those who maintain that God's grace and help are not given for a man's single actions, but exist rather in his freedom, or in the law and teaching. And yet he supposes that he escapes detection by the shifts he so constantly employs for disguising what he means by his formula of "law and teaching" under so many various phrases.

CHAPTER XI

PELAGIUS' DEFINITION OF HOW GOD HELPS US: "HE PROMISES US FUTURE GLORY"

For in another passage, after asserting at length that it is not by the help of God, but out of our own selves, that a good will is formed within us, he confronted himself with a question out of the apostle's epistle; and he asked this question: "How will this stand consistently with the apostle's words,[15] 'It is God that worketh in you both to will and to perfect'?" Then, in order to obviate this opposing authority, which he plainly saw to be most thoroughly contrasted with his own dogma, he went on at once to add: "He works in us to will what is good, to will what is holy, when He rouses us from our devotion to earthly desires, and from our love of the present only, after the manner of brute animals, by the magnitude of the future glory and the promise of its rewards; when by revealing wisdom to us He stirs up our sluggish will to a longing after God; when (what you are not afraid to deny in another passage) he persuades us to everything which is good." Now what can be plainer, than that by the grace whereby God works within us to will what is good, he means nothing else than the law and the teaching? For in the law and the teaching of the holy Scriptures are promised future

[13] Rom. xiii. 10   [14] Rom. v. 5   [15] Phil. ii. 13

glory and its great rewards. To the teaching also appertains the revelation of wisdom, while it is its further function to direct our thoughts to everything that is good. And if between teaching and persuading (or rather exhorting) there seems to be a difference, yet even this is provided for in the general term "teaching," which is contained in the several discourses or letters; for the holy Scriptures both teach and exhort, and in the processes of teaching and exhorting there is room likewise for man's operation. We, however, on our side would fain have him sometime confess that grace, by which not only future glory in all its magnitude is promised, but also is believed in and hoped for; by which wisdom is not only revealed, but also loved; by which everything that is good is not only recommended, but pressed upon us until we accept it. For all men do not possess faith,[16] who hear the Lord in the Scriptures promising the kingdom of heaven; nor are all men persuaded, who are counselled to come to Him, who says, "Come unto me, all ye that labor."[17] They, however, who have faith are the same who are also persuaded to come to Him. This He Himself set forth most plainly, when He said, "No man can come to me, except the Father, which hath sent me, draw him."[18] And some verses afterwards, when speaking of such as believe not, He says, "Therefore said I unto you, that no man can come unto me except it were given unto him of my Father."[19] This is the grace which Pelagius ought to acknowledge, if he wishes not only to be called a Christian, but to be one.

CHAPTER XII

THE SAME CONTINUED: "HE REVEALS WISDOM"

But what shall I say about the revelation of wisdom? For there is no man who can in the present life very well hope to attain to the great revelations which were given to the Apostle Paul; and of course it is impossible to suppose that anything was accustomed in these revelations to be made known to him but what appertained to wisdom. Yet for all this he says: "Lest I should be exalted above measure through the abundance of the revelations, there was given to me a thorn in the flesh, the messenger of Satan to buffet me. For this thing I besought the Lord thrice, that He would take it away from me. And He said unto me, My grace is sufficient for thee; for my strength is made perfect in weakness."[20] Now, undoubtedly, if there were already in the apostle that perfection of love which admitted of no further addition, and which could be puffed up no more, there could have been no further need of the messenger of Satan to buffet him, and thereby to repress the excessive elation which might arise from abundance of revelations. What means this elation, however, but a being puffed

---

[16] 2 Thess. iii. 2   [17] Matt. xi. 28   [18] John vi. 44   [19] John vi. 65   [20] 2 Cor. xii. 7-9

up? And of love it has been indeed most truly said, "Love vaunteth not itself, is not puffed up." [21] This love, therefore, was still in process of constant increase in the great apostle, day by day, as long as his "inward man was renewed day by day," [22] and would then be perfected, no doubt, when he was got beyond the reach of all further vaunting and elation. But at that time his mind was still in a condition to be inflated by an abundance of revelations before it was perfected in the solid edifice of love; for he had not arrived at the goal and apprehended the prize, to which he was reaching forward in his course.

CHAPTER XIII

GRACE CAUSES US TO DO

To him, therefore, who is reluctant to endure the troublesome process, whereby this vaunting disposition is restrained, before he attains to the ultimate and highest perfection of charity, it is most properly said, "My grace is sufficient for thee; for my strength is made perfect in weakness" [23] —in weakness, that is, not of the flesh only, as this man supposes, but both of the flesh and of the mind; because the mind, too, was, in comparison of that last stage of complete perfection, weak, and to it also was assigned, in order to check its elation, that messenger of Satan, the thorn in the flesh; although it was very strong, in contrast with the carnal or animal faculties, which as yet understand not the things of the Spirit of God.[24] Inasmuch, then, as strength is made perfect in weakness, whoever does not own himself to be weak, is not in the way to be perfected. This grace, however, by which strength is perfected in weakness, conducts all who are predestinated and called according to the divine purpose[25] to the state of the highest perfection and glory. By such grace it is effected, not only that we discover what ought to be done, but also that we do what we have discovered—not only that we believe what ought to be loved, but also that we love what we have believed.

CHAPTER XIV

THE RIGHTEOUSNESS WHICH IS OF GOD, AND THE RIGHTEOUSNESS WHICH IS OF THE LAW

If this grace is to be called "teaching," let it at any rate be so called in such wise that God may be believed to infuse it, along with an ineffable sweetness, more deeply and more internally, not only by *their* agency who plant and water from without, but likewise by His own too who ministers in secret His own increase—in such a way, that He not only exhibits truth,

---

[21] 1 Cor. xiii. 4   [22] 2 Cor. iv. 6   [23] 2 Cor. xii. 9   [24] 1 Cor. ii. 14   [25] Rom. viii. 28, 30

but likewise imparts love. For it is thus that God teaches those who have been called according to His purpose, giving them simultaneously both to know what they ought to do, and to do what they know. Accordingly, the apostle thus speaks to the Thessalonians: "As touching love of the brethren, ye need not that I write unto you; for ye yourselves are taught of God to love one another." [26] And then, by way of proving that they had been taught of God, he subjoined: "And indeed ye do it towards all the brethren which are in all Macedonia." [27] As if the surest sign that you have been taught of God, is that you put into practice what you have been taught. Of that character are all who are called according to God's purpose, as it is written in the prophets: "They shall be all taught of God." [28] The man, however, who has learned what ought to be done, but does it not, has not as yet been "taught of God" according to grace, but only according to the law—not according to the spirit, but only according to the letter. Although there are many who appear to do what the law commands, through fear of punishment, not through love of righteousness; and such righteousness as this the apostle calls "his own which is after the law"—a thing as it were commanded, not given. When, indeed, it has been given, it is not called our own righteousness, but God's; because it becomes our own only so that we have it from God. These are the apostle's words: "That I may be found in Him, not having mine own righteousness which is of the law, but that which is through the faith of Christ, the righteousness which is of God by faith." [29] So great, then, is the difference between the law and grace, that although the law is undoubtedly of God, yet the righteousness which is "of the law" is not "of God," but the righteousness which is consummated by grace is "of God." The one is designated "the righteousness of the law," because it is done through fear of the curse of the law; while the other is called "the righteousness of God," because it is bestowed through the beneficence of His grace, so that it is not a terrible but a pleasant commandment, according to the prayer in the psalm: "Good art Thou, O Lord, therefore in Thy goodness teach me Thy righteousness;" [30] that is, that I may not be compelled like a slave to live under the law with fear of punishment; but rather in the freedom of love may be delighted to live with law as my companion. When the freeman keeps a commandment, he does it readily. And whosoever learns his duty in this spirit, does everything that he has learned ought to be done.

[26] I Thess. iv. 9 [27] I Thess. iv. 10 [28] Isa. liv. 13; Jer. xxxi. 34; John vi. 45
[29] Phil. iii. 9 [30] Ps. cxix. 68

CHAPTER XV

HE WHO HAS BEEN TAUGHT BY GRACE ACTUALLY COMES TO CHRIST

Now as touching this kind of teaching, the Lord also says: "Every man that hath heard, and hath learned of the Father, cometh unto me." [31] Of the man, therefore, who has not come, it cannot be correctly said: "He has heard and has learned that it is his duty to come to Him, but he is not willing to do what he has learned." It is indeed absolutely improper to apply such a statement to that method of teaching, whereby God teaches by grace. For if, as the Truth says, "Every man that hath learned cometh," it follows, of course, that whoever does not come has not learned. But who can fail to see that a man's coming or not coming is by the determination of his will? This determination, however, may stand alone, if the man does not come; but if he does come, it cannot be without assistance; and such assistance, that he not only knows what it is he ought to do, but also actually does what he thus knows. And thus, when God teaches, it is not by the letter of the law, but by the grace of the Spirit. Moreover, He so teaches, that whatever a man learns, he not only sees with his perception, but also desires with his choice, and accomplishes in action. By this mode, therefore, of divine instruction, volition itself, and performance itself, are assisted, and not merely the natural "capacity" of willing and performing. For if nothing but this "capacity" of ours were assisted by this grace, the Lord would rather have said, "Every man that hath heard and hath learned of the Father *may possibly* come unto me." This, however, is not what He said; but His words are these: "Every man that hath heard and hath learned of the Father *cometh* unto me." Now *the possibility of coming* Pelagius places in nature, or even—as we found him attempting to say some time ago[32]—in grace (whatever that may mean according to him)—when he says, "whereby this very capacity is assisted;" whereas *the actual coming* lies in the will and act. It does not, however, follow that he who *may* come actually comes, unless he has also willed and acted for the coming. But every one who has learned of the Father not only has the possibility of coming, but *comes;* and in this result are already included the *motion* of the capacity, the *affection* of the will, and the *effect* of the action.[33]

CHAPTER XVI

WE NEED DIVINE AID IN THE USE OF OUR POWERS. ILLUSTRATION FROM SIGHT

Now what is the use of his examples, if they do not really accomplish his own promise of making his meaning clearer to us;[34] not, indeed, that we

---

[31] John vi. 45   [32] See above, ch. 7   [33] The technical gradation is here neatly expressed by *profectus, affectus,* and *effectus*   [34] See above, ch. 5

are bound to admit their sense, but that we may discover more plainly and openly what is his drift and purpose in using them? "That we are able," says he, "to see with our eyes is not of us; but it is of us that we make a good or a bad use of our sight." Well, there is an answer for him in the psalm, in which the psalmist says to God, "Turn Thou away mine eyes, that they behold not iniquity." [35] Now although this was said of the eyes of the mind, it still follows from it, that in respect of our bodily eyes there is either a good use or a bad use that may be made of them: not in the literal sense merely of a good sight when the eyes are sound, and a bad sight when they are bleared, but in the moral sense of a right sight when it is directed towards succoring the helpless, or a bad sight when its object is the indulgence of lust. For although both the pauper who is succored, and the woman who is lusted after, are seen by these external eyes; it is after all from the inner eyes that either compassion in the one case or lust in the other proceeds. How then is it that the prayer is offered to God, "Turn Thou away mine eyes, that they behold not iniquity"? Or why is that asked for which lies within our own power, if it be true that God does not assist the will?

CHAPTER XVII

DOES PELAGIUS DESIGNEDLY REFRAIN FROM OPENLY SAYING THAT ALL GOOD ACTION IS FROM GOD?

"That we are able to speak," says he, "is of God; but that we make a good or a bad use of speech is of ourselves." He, however, who has made the most excellent use of speech does not teach us so. "For," says He, "it is not ye that speak, but the Spirit of your Father that speaketh in you." [36] "So, again," adds Pelagius, "that I may, by applying a general case in illustration, embrace all—that we are able to do, say, think any good thing, comes from Him who has endowed us with this ability, and who also assists it." Observe how even here he repeats his former meaning—that of these three, capacity, volition, action, it is only the capacity which receives help. Then, by way of completely stating what he intends to say, he adds: "But that we really do a good thing, or speak a good word, or think a good thought, proceeds from our own selves." He forgot what he had before said by way of correcting, as it were, his own words; for after saying, "Man is to be praised therefore for his willing and doing a good work," he at once goes on to modify his statement thus: "Or rather, this praise belongs both to man, and to God who has given him the capacity of this very will and work." Now what is the reason why he did not remember this admission when giving his examples, so as to say this much at least after quoting them: "That we are able to do, say, think any good thing, comes from Him who

---

[35] Ps. cxix. 37   [36] Matt. x. 20

has given us this ability, and who also assists it. That, however, we really do a good thing, or speak a good word, or think a good thought, proceeds *both from ourselves and from Him!*" This, however, he has not said. But, if I am not mistaken, I think I see why he was afraid to do so.

CHAPTER XVIII

HE DISCOVERS THE REASON OF PELAGIUS' HESITATION SO TO SAY

For, when wishing to point out why this lies within our own competency, he says: "Because we are able to turn all these actions into evil." This, then, was the reason why he was afraid to admit that such an action proceeds *"both from ourselves and from God,"* lest it should be objected to him in reply: "If the fact of our doing, speaking, thinking anything good, is owing both to ourselves and to God, because He has endowed us with this ability, then it follows that our doing, thinking, speaking evil things, is due to ourselves and to God, because He has here also endowed us with ability of indifference; the conclusion from this being—and God forbid that we should admit any such—that just as God is associated with ourselves in the praise of good actions, so must He share with us the blame of evil actions." For that "capacity" with which He has endowed us makes us capable alike of good actions and of evil ones.

CHAPTER XIX

THE TWO ROOTS OF ACTION, LOVE AND CUPIDITY; AND EACH BRINGS FORTH ITS OWN FRUIT

Concerning this "capacity," Pelagius thus writes in the first book of his *Defence of Free Will:* "Now," says he, "we have implanted in us by God a capacity for either part. It resembles, as I may say, a fruitful and fecund root which yields and produces diversely according to the will of man, and which is capable, at the planter's own choice, of either shedding a beautiful bloom of virtues, or of bristling with the thorny thickets of vices." Scarcely heeding what he says, he here makes one and the same root productive both of good and evil fruits, in opposition to gospel truth and apostolic teaching. For the Lord declares that "a good tree cannot bring forth evil fruit, neither can a corrupt tree bring forth good fruit;" [37] and when the Apostle Paul says that covetousness is "the root of all evils," [38] he intimates to us, of course, that love may be regarded as the root of all good things. On the supposition, therefore, that two trees, one good and the other corrupt, represent two human beings, a good one and a bad, what else is the good man except one with a good will, that is, a tree with a good root? And what is the bad man except one with a bad will, that is, a tree with a bad

[37] Matt. vii. 18   [38] 1 Tim. vi. 10

root? The fruits which spring from such roots and trees are deeds, are words, are thoughts, which proceed, when good, from a good will, and when evil, from an evil one.

CHAPTER XX

HOW A MAN MAKES A GOOD OR A BAD TREE

Now a man makes a good tree when he receives the grace of God. For it is not by himself that he makes himself good instead of evil; but it is of Him, and through Him, and in Him who is always good. And in order that he may not only be a good tree, but also bear good fruit, it is necessary for him to be assisted by the self-same grace, without which he can do nothing good. For God Himself co-operates in the production of fruit in good trees, when He both externally waters and tends them by the agency of His servants, and internally by Himself also gives the increase.[39] A man, however, makes a corrupt tree when he makes himself corrupt, when he falls away from Him who is the unchanging good; for such a declension from Him is the origin of an evil will. Now this decline does not initiate some other corrupt nature, but it corrupts that which has been already created good. When this corruption, however, has been healed, no evil remains; for although nature no doubt had received an injury, yet nature was not itself a blemish.

CHAPTER XXI

LOVE THE ROOT OF ALL GOOD THINGS; CUPIDITY, OF ALL EVIL ONES

The "capacity," then, of which we speak is not (as he supposes) the one identical root both of good things and evil. For the love which is the root of good things is quite different from the cupidity which is the root of evil things—as different, indeed, as virtue is from vice. But without doubt this "capacity" is capable of either root: because a man is not only able to possess love, whereby the tree becomes a good one; but he is likewise able to have cupidity, which makes the tree evil. This human cupidity, however, which is a vice, has for its author man, or man's deceiver, but not man's Creator. It is indeed that "lust of the flesh, and the lust of the eyes, and the pride of life, which is not of the Father, but is of the world." [40] And who can be ignorant of the usage of the Scripture, which under the designation of *"the world"* is accustomed to describe those who inhabit the world?

[39] 1 Cor. iii. 7   [40] 1 John ii. 16

CHAPTER XXII

LOVE IS A GOOD WILL

That love, however, which is a virtue, comes to us from God, not from ourselves, according to the testimony of Scripture, which says: "Love is of God; and every one that loveth is born of God, and knoweth God: for God is love." [41] It is on the principle of this love that one can best understand the passage, "Whosoever is born of God doth not commit sin;" [42] as well as the sentence, "And he cannot sin." [43] Because the love according to which we are born of God "doth not behave itself unseemly," and "thinketh no evil." [44] Therefore, whenever a man sins, it is not according to love: but it is according to cupidity that he commits sin; and following such a disposition, he is not born of God. Because, as it has been already stated, "the capacity" of which we speak is capable of either root. When, therefore, the Scripture says, "Love is of God," or still more pointedly, "God is love;" when the Apostle John so very emphatically exclaims, "Behold what manner of love the Father hath bestowed upon us, that we should be called, and be, the sons of God!" [45] with what face can this writer, on hearing that "God is love," persist in maintaining his opinion, that we have of God one only of those three,[46] namely, "the capacity;" whereas it is of ourselves that we have "the good will" and "the good action"? As if, indeed, this good will were a different thing from that love which the Scripture so loudly proclaims to have come to us from God, and to have been given to us by the Father, that we might become His children.

CHAPTER XXIII

PELAGIUS' DOUBLE DEALING CONCERNING THE GROUND
OF THE CONFERRENCE OF GRACE

Perhaps, however, our own antecedent merits caused this gift to be bestowed upon us; as this writer has already suggested in reference to God's grace, in that work which he addressed to a holy virgin,[47] whom he mentions in the letter sent by him to Rome. For, after adducing the testimony of the Apostle James, in which he says, "Submit yourselves unto God; but resist the devil, and he will flee from you," [48] he goes on to say: "He shows us how we ought to resist the devil, if we submit ourselves indeed to God and by doing His will merit His divine grace, and by the help of the Holy Ghost more easily withstand the evil spirit." Judge, then, how sincere was his condemnation in the Palestine Synod of those who say that God's grace is conferred on us according to our merits! Have we any doubt as to his

[41] 1 John iv. 7, 8   [42] 1 John iii. 9   [43] Same verse   [44] 1 Cor. xiii. 5   [45] 1 John iii. 1   [46] See above, ch. 4   [47] *Epistola ad Demetriadem*, c. 25   [48] Jas. iv. 7

still holding this opinion, and most openly proclaiming it? Well, how could that confession of his before the bishops have been true and real? Had he already written the book in which he most explicitly alleges that grace is bestowed on us according to our deserts—the very position which he without any reservation condemned at that Synod in the East? Let him frankly acknowledge that he once held the opinion, but that he holds it no longer; so should we most frankly rejoice in his improvement. As it is, however, when, besides other objections, this one was laid to his charge which we are now discussing, he said in reply: "Whether these are the opinions of Coelestius or not, is the concern of those who affirm that they are. For my own part, indeed, I never entertained such views; on the contrary, I anathematize every one who does entertain them." [49] But how could he "never have entertained such views," when he had already composed this work? Oh how does he still "anathematize everybody who entertains these views," if he afterwards composed this work?

CHAPTER XXIV

PELAGIUS PLACES FREE WILL AT THE BASIS OF ALL TURNING
TO GOD FOR GRACE

But perhaps he may meet us with this rejoinder, that in the sentence before us he spoke of our "meriting the divine grace by doing the will of God," in the sense that grace is added to those who believe and lead godly lives, whereby they may boldly withstand the tempter; whereas their very first reception of grace was, that they might do the will of God. Lest, then, he make such a rejoinder, consider some other words of his on this subject: "The man," says he, "who hastens to the Lord, and desires to be directed by Him, that is, who makes his own will depend upon God's, who moreover cleaves so closely to the Lord as to become (as the apostle says) 'one spirit' with him,[50] does all this by nothing else than by his freedom of will." Observe how great a result he has here stated to be accomplished only by our freedom of will; and how, in fact, he supposes us to cleave to God without the help of God: for such is the force of his words, "by nothing else than by his own freedom of will." So that, after we have cleaved to the Lord without His help, we even then, because of such adhesion of our own, deserve to be assisted. For he goes on to say: "Whosoever makes a right use of this" (that is, rightly uses his freedom of will), "does so entirely surrender himself to God, and does so completely mortify his own will, that he is able to say with the apostle, 'Nevertheless it is already not I that live, but Christ liveth in me;' [51] and 'He placeth his heart in the hand of God, so that He turneth it whithersoever He willeth.' " [52] Great indeed is the help of the grace of God, so that He turns our heart in whatever direction

---

[49] See the *De Gestis Pelagii*, 30   [50] 1 Cor. vi. 17   [51] Gal. ii. 20   [52] Prov. xxi. 1

He pleases. But according to this writer's foolish opinion, however great the help may be, we deserve it all at the moment when, without any assistance beyond the liberty of our will, we hasten to the Lord, desire His guidance and direction, suspend our own will entirely on His, and by close adherence to Him become one spirit with Him. Now all these vast courses of goodness we (according to him) accomplish, forsooth, simply by the freedom of our own free will; and by reason of such antecedent merits we so secure His grace, that He turns our heart which way soever He pleases. Well, now, how is *that* grace which is not gratuitously conferred? How can it be grace, if it is given in payment of a debt? How can that be true which the apostle says, "It is not of yourselves, but it is the gift of God; not of works, lest any man should boast;" [53] and again, "If it is of grace, then is it no more of works, otherwise grace is no more grace:" [54] how, I repeat, can this be true, if such meritorious works precede as to procure for us the bestowal of grace? Surely, under the circumstances, there can be no gratuitous gift, but only the recompense of a due reward. Is it the case, then, that in order to find their way to the help of God, men run to God without God's help? And in order that we may receive God's help while cleaving to Him, do we without His help cleave to God? What greater gift, or even what similar gift, could grace itself bestow upon any man, if he has already without grace been able to make himself one spirit with the Lord by no other power than that of his own free will?

CHAPTER XXV

GOD BY HIS WONDERFUL POWER WORKS IN OUR HEARTS GOOD DISPOSITIONS OF OUR WILL

Now I want him to tell us whether that king of Assyria,[55] whose holy wife Esther "abhorred his bed," [56] while sitting upon the throne of his kingdom, and clothed in all his glorious apparel, adorned all over with gold and precious stones, and dreadful in his majesty, when he raised his face, which was inflamed with anger, in the midst of his splendor, and beheld her, with the glare of a wild bull in the fierceness of his indignation; and the queen was afraid, and her color changed as she fainted, and she bowed herself upon the head of the maid that went before her[57]—I want him to tell us whether this king had yet "hastened to the Lord, and had desired to be directed by Him, and had subordinated his own will to His, and had, by cleaving fast to God, become one spirit with Him, simply by the force of his own free will." Had he surrendered himself wholly to God, and entirely mortified his own will, and placed his heart in the hand of God? I suppose that anybody who should think this of the king, in the state he was then

[53] Eph. ii. 8, 9   [54] Rom. xi. 6
[55] The reading *"Assyrius"* is replaced in some editions by the more suitable word *"Assuerus"*   [56] Esth. iv., Septuagint   [57] Esth. v. 1

in, would be not foolish only, but even mad. And yet God converted him, and turned his indignation into gentleness. Who, however, can fail to see how much greater a task it is to change and turn wrath completely into gentleness, than to bend the heart to something, when it is not preoccupied with either affection, but is indifferently poised between the two? Let them therefore read and understand, observe and acknowledge, that it is not by law and teaching uttering their lessons from without, but by a secret, wonderful, and ineffable power operating within, that God works in men's hearts not only revelations of the truth, but also good dispositions of the will.

CHAPTER XXVI

THE PELAGIAN GRACE OF "CAPACITY" EXPLODED. THE SCRIPTURE TEACHES THE NEED OF GOD'S HELP IN DOING, SPEAKING, AND THINKING, ALIKE

Let Pelagius, therefore, cease at last to deceive both himself and others by his disputations against the grace of God. It is not on account of only one of these three[58]—that is to say, of the "capacity" of a good will and work—that the grace of God towards us ought to be proclaimed; but also on account of the good "will" and "work" themselves. This "capacity," indeed, according to his definition, avails for both directions; and yet our sins must not also be attributed to God in consequence, as our good actions, according to his view, are attributed to Him owing to the same capacity. It is not only, therefore, on this account that the help of God's grace is maintained, because it assists our natural capacity. He must cease to say, "That we are able to do, say, think any good, is from Him who has given us this ability, and who also assists this ability; whereas that we really do a good thing, or speak a good word, or think a good thought, proceeds from our own selves." He must, I repeat, cease to say this. For God has not only given us the ability and aids it, but He further works in us "to will and to do." [59] It is not because we do not will, or do not do, that we will and do nothing good, but because we are without His help. How can he say, "That we are able to do good is of God, but that we actually do it is of ourselves," when the apostle tells us that he "prays to God" in behalf of those to whom he was writing, "that they should do no evil, but that they should do that which is good?" [60] His words are not, "We pray that ye *be able* to do nothing evil;" but, "that ye do no evil." Neither does he say, "that *ye be able* to do good;" but, "that ye do good." Forasmuch as it is written, "As many as are led by the Spirit of God, they are the sons of God," [61] it follows that, in order that they may do that which is good, they must be led by Him who is good. How can Pelagius say, "That we are able to make a good

---

[58] See above, ch. 4   [59] Phil. ii. 13   [60] See 2 Cor. xiii. 7   [61] Rom. viii. 14

use of speech comes from God; but that we do actually make this good use of speech proceeds from ourselves," when the Lord declares, "It is the Spirit of your Father which speaketh in you"? [62] He does not say, "It is not you who have given to yourselves the power of speaking well;" but His words are, "It is not ye that speak." [62] Nor does He say, "It is the Spirit of your Father which *giveth, or hath given, you the power* to speak well;" but He says, "which speaketh in you." He does not allude to the motion[63] of "the capacity," but He asserts the effect of the co-operation. How can this arrogant asserter of free will say, "That we are able to think a good thought comes from God, but that we actually think a good thought proceeds from ourselves"? He has his answer from the humble preacher of grace, who says, "Not that we are sufficient of ourselves to think anything as of ourselves, but our sufficiency is of God." [64] Observe he does not say, *"to be able* to think anything;" but, "to think anything."

CHAPTER XXVII

WHAT TRUE GRACE IS, AND WHEREFORE GIVEN.
MERITS DO NOT PRECEDE GRACE

Now even Pelagius should frankly confess that this grace is plainly set forth in the inspired Scriptures; nor should he with shameless effrontery hide the fact that he has too long opposed it, but admit it with salutary regret; so that the holy Church may cease to be harassed by his stubborn persistence, and rather rejoice in his sincere conversion. Let him distinguish between knowledge and love, as they ought to be distinguished; because "knowledge puffeth up, but love edifieth." [65] And then knowledge no longer puffeth up when love builds up. And inasmuch as each is the gift of God (although one is less, and the other greater), he must not extol our righteousness above the praise which is due to Him who justifies us, in such a way as to assign to the lesser of these two gifts the help of divine grace, and to claim the greater one for the human will. And should he consent that we receive love from the grace of God, he must not suppose that any merits of our own preceded our reception of the gift. For what merits could we possibly have had at the time when we loved not God? In order, indeed, that we might receive that love whereby we might love, we were loved while as yet we had no love ourselves. This the Apostle John most expressly declares: "Not that we loved God," says he, "but that He loved us;" [66] and again, "We love Him, because He first loved us." [67] Most excellently and truly spoken! For we could not have wherewithal to love Him, unless we received it from Him in His first loving us. And what good could we possibly do if we possessed no love? Or how could we help doing good if we have love? For although God's commandment appears sometimes to be

[62] Matt. x. 20   [63] See ch. 15 at the end   [64] 2 Cor. iii. 5   [65] 1 Cor. viii. 1   [66] 1 John iv. 10   [67] 1 John iv. 19

kept by those who do not love Him, but only fear Him; yet where there is no love, no good work is imputed, nor is there any good work, rightly so called; because "whatsoever is not of faith is sin," [68] and "faith worketh by love." [69] Hence also that grace of God, whereby "His love is shed abroad in our hearts through the Holy Ghost, which is given unto us," [70] must be so confessed by the man who would make a true confession, as to show his undoubting belief that nothing whatever in the way of goodness pertaining to godliness and real holiness can be accomplished without it. Not after the fashion of him who clearly enough shows us what he thinks of it when he says, that "grace is bestowed in order that what God commands may be the more easily fulfilled;" which of course means, that even without grace God's commandments may, although less easily, yet actually, be accomplished.

CHAPTER XXVIII

PELAGIUS TEACHES THAT SATAN MAY BE RESISTED WITHOUT THE HELP OF THE GRACE OF GOD

In the book which he addressed to a certain holy virgin, there is a passage which I have already mentioned,[71] wherein he plainly indicates what he holds on this subject; for he speaks of our "deserving the grace of God, and by the help of the Holy Ghost *more easily* resisting the evil spirit." Now why did he insert the phrase "more easily"? Was not the sense already complete: "And by the help of the Holy Ghost resisting the evil spirit"? But who can fail to perceive what an injury he has done by this insertion? He wants it, of course, to be supposed, that so great are the powers of our nature, which he is in such a hurry to exalt, that even without the assistance of the Holy Ghost the evil spirit can be resisted—less easily it may be, but still in a certain measure.

CHAPTER XXIX

WHEN HE SPEAKS OF GOD'S HELP, HE MEANS IT ONLY TO HELP US DO WHAT WITHOUT IT WE STILL COULD DO

Again, in the first book of his *Defence of the Freedom of the Will,* he says: "But while we have within us a free will so strong and so stedfast against sinning, which our Maker has implanted in human nature generally, still, by His unspeakable goodness, we are further defended by His own daily help." What need is there of such help, if free will is so strong and so stedfast against sinning? But here, as before, he would have it understood that the purpose of the alleged assistance is, that that may be more

---

[68] Rom. xiv. 23   [69] Gal. v. 6   [70] Rom. v. 5   [71] Quoted above, ch. 23, from the *Epistola ad Demetriadem*

easily accomplished by grace which he nevertheless supposes may be effected, less easily, no doubt, but yet actually, without grace.

CHAPTER XXX

WHAT PELAGIUS THINKS IS NEEDFUL FOR EASE OF PERFORMANCE IS REALLY NECESSARY FOR THE PERFORMANCE

In like manner, in another passage of the same book, he says: "In order that man may more easily accomplish by grace that which they are commanded to do by free will." Now, expunge the phrase *"more easily,"* and you leave not only a full, but also a sound sense, if it be regarded as meaning simply this: "That men may accomplish through grace what they are commanded to do by free will." The addition of the words "more easily," however, tacitly suggests the possibility of accomplishing good works even without the grace of God. But such a meaning is disallowed by Him who says, "Without me ye can do nothing." [72]

CHAPTER XXXI

PELAGIUS AND COELESTIUS NOWHERE REALLY ACKNOWLEDGE GRACE

Let him amend all this, that if human infirmity has erred in subjects so profound, he may not add to the error diabolical deception and wilfulness, either by denying what he has really believed, or by maintaining what he has rashly believed, after he has once discovered, on recollecting the light of truth, that he ought never to have so believed. As for that grace, indeed, by which we are justified—in other words, whereby "the love of God is shed abroad in our hearts by the Holy Ghost, which is given unto us" [70]—I have nowhere, in those writings of Pelagius and Coelestius which I have had the opportunity of reading, found them acknowledging it as it ought to be acknowledged. In no passage at all have I observed them recognising "the children of the promise," concerning whom the apostle thus speaks: "They which are children of the flesh, these are not the children of God; but the children of the promise are counted for the seed." [73] For that which God promises we do not ourselves bring about by our own choice or natural power, but He Himself effects it by grace.

CHAPTER XXXII

WHY THE PELAGIANS DEEMED PRAYERS TO BE NECESSARY. THE LETTER WHICH PELAGIUS DESPATCHED TO POPE INNOCENT WITH AN EXPOSITION OF HIS BELIEF

Now I will say nothing at present about the works of Coelestius, or those tracts of his which he produced in those ecclesiastical proceedings, copies

[72] John xv. 5　　[73] Rom. ix. 8

of the whole of which we have taken care to send to you, along with another letter which we deemed it necessary to add. If you carefully examine all these documents, you will observe that he does not posit the grace of God, which helps us whether to avoid evil or to do good, beyond the natural choice of the will, but only in the law and teaching. Thus he even asserts that their very prayers are necessary for the purpose of showing men what to desire and love. All these documents, however, I may omit further notice of at present; for Pelagius himself has lately forwarded to Rome both a letter and an exposition of his belief, addressing it to Pope Innocent, of blessed memory, of whose death he was ignorant. Now in this letter he says that "there are certain subjects about which some men are trying to vilify him. One of these is, that he refuses to infants the sacrament of baptism, and promises the kingdom of heaven to some, independently of Christ's redemption. Another of them is, that he so speaks of man's ability to avoid sin as to exclude God's help, and so strongly confides in free will that he repudiates the help of divine grace." Now, as touching the perverted opinion he holds about the baptism of infants (although he allows that it ought to be administered to them), in opposition to the Christian faith and Catholic truth, this is not the place for us to enter on an accurate discussion, for we must now complete our treatise on the assistance of grace, which is the subject we undertook. Let us see what answer he makes out of this very letter to the objection which he has proposed concerning this matter. Omitting his invidious complaints about his opponents, we approach the subject before us; and find him expressing himself as follows.

CHAPTER XXXIII

PELAGIUS PROFESSES NOTHING ON THE SUBJECT OF GRACE WHICH MAY NOT BE UNDERSTOOD OF THE LAW AND TEACHING

"See," he says, "how this epistle will clear me before your Blessedness; for in it we clearly and simply declare, that we possess a free will which is unimpaired for sinning and for not sinning; and this free will is in all good works *always* assisted by divine help." Now you perceive, by the understanding which the Lord has given you, that these words of his are inadequate to solve the question. For it is still open to us to inquire what the help is by which he would say that the free will is assisted; lest perchance he should, as is usual with him, maintain that law and teaching are meant. If, indeed, you were to ask him why he used the word *"always,"* he might answer: Because it is written, "And in His law will he meditate day and night." [74] Then, after interposing a statement about the condition of man, and his natural capacity for sinning and not sinning, he added the following words: "Now this power of free will we declare to reside generally in all

[74] Ps. i. 2

alike—in Christians, in Jews, and in Gentiles. In all men free will exists equally by nature, but in Christians alone is it assisted by grace." We again ask: "By what grace?" And again he might answer: "By the law and the Christian teaching."

CHAPTER XXXIV

PELAGIUS SAYS THAT GRACE IS GIVEN ACCORDING TO MEN'S MERITS. THE BEGINNING, HOWEVER, OF MERIT IS FAITH; AND THIS IS A GRATUITOUS GIFT, NOT A RECOMPENSE FOR OUR MERITS

Then, again, whatever it is which he means by "grace," he says is given even to Christians according to their merits, although (as I have already mentioned above[75]), when he was in Palestine, in his very remarkable vindication of himself, he condemned those who hold this opinion. Now these are his words: "In the one," says he, "the good of their created condition is naked and defenceless;" meaning in those who are not Christians. Then adding the rest: "In these, however, who belong to Christ, there is defence afforded by Christ's help." You see it is still uncertain what the help is, according to the remark we have already made on the same subject. He goes on, however, to say of those who are not Christians: "Those deserve judgment and condemnation, because, although they possess free will whereby they could come to have faith and deserve God's grace, they make a bad use of the freedom which has been granted to them. But these deserve to be rewarded, who by the right use of free will merit the Lord's grace, and keep His commandments." Now it is clear that he says grace is bestowed according to merit, whatever and of what kind soever the grace is which he means, but which he does not plainly declare. For when he speaks of those persons as deserving reward who make a good use of their free will, and as therefore meriting the Lord's grace, he asserts in fact that a debt is paid to them. What, then, becomes of the apostle's saying, "Being justified freely by His grace"? [76] And what of his other statement too, "By grace are ye saved"? [77]—where, that he might prevent men's supposing that it is by works, he expressly added, *"by faith."* [78] And yet further, lest it should be imagined that faith itself is to be attributed to men independently of the grace of God, the apostle says: "And that not of yourselves; for it is the gift of God." [78] It follows, therefore, that we receive, without any merit of our own, that from which everything which, according to them, we obtain because of our merit, has its beginning—that is, faith itself. If, however, they insist on denying that this is freely given to us, what is the meaning of the apostle's words: "According as God hath dealt to every man the measure of faith"? [79] But if it is contended that faith is so bestowed as to be a recompense for merit, not a free gift, what then

[75] In ch. 23   [76] Rom. iii. 24   [77] Eph. ii. 8   [78] Eph. ii. 8   [79] Rom. xii. 3

becomes of another saying of the apostle: "Unto you it is given in the behalf of Christ, not only to believe in Him, but also to suffer for His sake"? [80] Each is by the apostle's testimony made a gift—both that he believes in Christ, and that each suffers for His sake. These men, however, attribute faith to free will in such a way as to make it appear that grace is rendered to faith not as a gratuitous gift, but as a debt—thus ceasing to be grace any longer, because that is not grace which is not gratuitous.

CHAPTER XXXV

PELAGIUS BELIEVES THAT INFANTS HAVE NO SIN TO BE REMITTED IN BAPTISM

But Pelagius would have the reader pass from this letter to the book which states his belief. This he has made mention of to yourselves, and in it he has discoursed a good deal on points about which no question was raised as to his views. Let us, however, look simply at the subjects about which our own controversy with them is concerned. Having, then, terminated a discussion which he had conducted to his heart's content—from the Unity of the Trinity to the resurrection of the flesh, on which nobody was questioning him—he goes on to say: "We hold likewise one baptism, which we aver ought to be administered to infants in the same sacramental formula as it is to adults." Well, now, you have yourselves affirmed that you heard him admit at least as much as this in your presence. What, however, is the use of his saying that the sacrament of baptism is administered to children "in the same words as it is to adults," when our inquiry concerns the thing, not merely the words? It is a more important matter, that (as you write) with his own mouth he replied to your own question, that "infants receive baptism for the remission of sins." For he did not say here, too, "in words of remission of sins," but he acknowledged that they are baptized for the remission itself; and yet for all this, if you were to ask him what the sin is which he supposes to be remitted to them, he would contend that they had none whatever.

CHAPTER XXXVI

COELESTIUS OPENLY DECLARES INFANTS TO HAVE NO ORIGINAL SIN

Who would believe that, under so clear a confession, there is concealed a contrary meaning, if Coelestius had not exposed it? He who in that book of his, which he quoted at Rome in the ecclesiastical proceedings there,[81] distinctly acknowledged that "infants too are baptized for the remission of sins," also denied "that they have any original sin." But let us now observe what Pelagius thought, not about the baptism of infants, but rather about

[80] Phil. i. 29   [81] See above, ch. 32, compare *De Pecc. Orig.* chs. 5, 6

the assistance of divine grace, in this exposition of his belief which he forwarded to Rome. "We confess," says he, "free will in such a sense that we
declare ourselves to be always in need of the help of God." Well, now, we
ask again, what the help is which he says we require; and again we find
ambiguity, since he may possibly answer that he meant the law and the
searching of Christ, whereby that natural "capacity" is assisted. We, however, on our side require them to acknowledge a grace like that which the
apostle describes, when he says: "For God hath not given us the spirit of
fear; but of power, and of love, and of a sound mind;" [82] although it does
not follow by any means that the man who has the gift of knowledge,
whereby he has discovered what he ought to do, has also the grace of love
so as to do it.

CHAPTER XXXVII

PELAGIUS NOWHERE ADMITS THE NEED OF DIVINE HELP
FOR WILL AND ACTION

I also have read those books or writings of his which he mentions in the
letter which he sent to Pope Innocent, of blessed memory, with the exception of a brief epistle which he says he sent to the holy Bishop Constantius;
but I have nowhere been able to find in them that he acknowledges such a
grace as helps not only that "natural capacity of willing and acting" (which
according to him we possess, even when we neither will a good thing nor
do it), but also the will and the action itself, by the ministration of the
Holy Ghost.

CHAPTER XXXVIII

A DEFINITION OF THE GRACE OF CHRIST BY PELAGIUS

"Let them read," says he, "the epistle which we wrote about twelve years
ago to that holy man Bishop Paulinus: its subject throughout in some three
hundred lines is the confession of God's grace and assistance alone, and
our own inability to do any good thing at all without God." Well, I have
read this epistle also, and found him dwelling throughout it on scarcely any
other topic than the faculty and capacity of nature, while he makes God's
grace consist almost entirely in this. Christ's grace, indeed, he treats with
great brevity, simply mentioning its name, so that his only aim seems to
have been to avoid the scandal of ignoring it altogether. It is, however, absolutely uncertain whether he means Christ's grace to consist in the remission of sins, or even in the teaching of Christ, including also the example
of His life (a meaning which he asserts in several passages of his treatises);
or whether he believes it to be a help towards good living, in addition to

[82] 2 Tim. i. 7

nature and teaching, through the inspiring influence of a burning and shining love.

CHAPTER XXXIX

A LETTER OF PELAGIUS UNKNOWN TO AUGUSTINE

"Let them also read," says he, "my epistle to the holy Bishop Constantius, wherein I have—briefly no doubt, but yet plainly—conjoined the grace and help of God with man's free will." This epistle, as I have already stated,[83] I have not read; but if it is not unlike the other writings which he mentions, and with which I am acquainted, even this work does nothing for the subject of our present inquiry.

CHAPTER XL

THE HELP OF GRACE PLACED BY PELAGIUS IN THE MERE REVELATION OF TEACHING

"Let them read, moreover," says he, "what I wrote,[84] when I was in the East, to Christ's holy virgin Demetrias, and they will find that we so commend the nature of man as always to add the help of God's grace." Well, I read this letter too; and it had almost persuaded me that he did acknowledge therein the grace about which our discussion is concerned, although he did certainly seem in many passages of this work to contradict hmself. But when there also came to my hands those other treatises which he afterwards wrote for more extensive circulation, I discovered in what sense he must have intended to speak of grace—concealing what he believed under an ambiguous generality, but employing the term "grace" in order to break the force of obloquy, and to avoid giving offence. For at the very commencement of this work (where he says: "Let us apply ourselves with all earnestness to the task which we have set before us, nor let us have any misgiving because of our own humble ability; for we believe that we are assisted by the mother's faith and her daughter's merit" [85]) he appeared to me at first to acknowledge the grace which helps us to individual action; nor did I notice at once the fact that he might possibly have made this grace consist simply in the revelation of teaching.

CHAPTER XLI

RESTORATION OF NATURE UNDERSTOOD BY PELAGIUS AS FORGIVENESS OF SINS

In this same work he says in another passage: "Now, if even without God men show of what character they have been made by God, see what Christians have it in their power to do, whose nature has been through

[83] See above, ch. 37 [84] See above, ch. 23 [85] Epistle to Demetrias, ch. 1

Christ restored to a better condition, and who are, moreover, assisted by the help of divine grace." [86] By this restoration of nature to a better state he would have us understand the remission of sins. This he has shown with sufficient clearness in another passage of this epistle, where he says: "Even those who have become in a certain sense obdurate through their long practice of sinning, can be restored through repentance." [87] But he may even here too make the assistance of divine grace consist in the revelation of teaching.

CHAPTER XLII

GRACE PLACED BY PELAGIUS IN THE REMISSION OF SINS AND THE EXAMPLE OF CHRIST

Likewise in another place in this epistle of his he says: "Now, if even before the law, as we have already remarked, and long previous to the coming of our Lord and Saviour, some men are related to have lived righteous and holy lives; how much more worthy of belief is it that we are capable of doing this since the illumination of His coming, who have been restored by the grace of Christ, and born again into a better man? How much better than they, who lived before the law, ought we to be, who have been reconciled and cleansed by His blood, and by His example encouraged to the perfection of righteousness!" [88] Observe how even here, although in different language, he has made the assistance of grace to consist in the remission of sins and the example of Christ. He then completes the passage of adding these words: "Better than they were even who lived under the law; according to the apostle, who says, 'Sin shall not have dominion over you: for ye are not under the law, but under grace.' [89] Now, inasmuch as we have," says he, "said enough, as I suppose, on this point, let us describe a perfect virgin, who shall testify the good at once of nature and of grace by the holiness of her conduct, evermore warmed with the virtues of both." [90] Now you ought to notice that in these words also he wished to conclude what he was saying in such a way that we might understand the good of nature to be that which we received when we were created; but the good of grace to be that which we receive when we regard and follow the example of Christ—as if sin were not permitted to those who were or are under the law, on this account, because they either had not Christ's example, or else do not believe in Him.

[86] Epistle to Demetrias, ch. 3   [87] Epistle to Demetrias, ch. 17   [88] Epistle to Demetrias, ch. 8   [89] Rom. vi. 14   [90] Epistle to Demetrias, ch. 9

CHAPTER XLIII

THE FORGIVENESS OF SINS AND EXAMPLE OF CHRIST HELD BY PELAGIUS ENOUGH TO SAVE THE MOST HARDENED SINNER

That this, indeed, is his meaning, other words also of his show us—not contained in this work, but in the third book of his *Defence of Free Will,* wherein he holds a discussion with an opponent, who had insisted on the apostle's words when he says, "For what I would, that do I not;" [91] and again, "I see another law in my members, warring against the law of my mind." [92] To this he replied in these words: "Now that which you wish us to understand of the apostle himself, all Church writers assert that he spoke in the person of the sinner, and of one who was still under the law—such a man as was, by reason of a very long custom of vice, held bound, as it were, by a certain necessity of sinning, and who, although he desired good with his will, in practice indeed was hurried headlong into evil. In the person, however, of one man," he continues, "the apostle designates the people who still sinned under the ancient law. This nation he declares was to be delivered from this evil of custom through Christ, who first of all remits all sins in baptism to those who believe in Him, and then urges them by an imitation of Himself to perfect holiness, and by the example of His own virtues overcomes the evil custom of their sins." Observe in what way he supposes them to be assisted who sin under the law: they are to be delivered by being justified through Christ's grace, as if the law alone were insufficient for them, without some reinforcement from Christ, owing to their long habit of sinning; not the inspiration of love by His Holy Spirit, but the contemplation and copy of His example in the inculcation of virtue by the gospel. Now here, at any rate, there was the very greatest call on him to say plainly what grace he meant, seeing that the apostle closed the very passage which formed the ground of discussion with these telling words: "O wretched man that I am, who shall deliver me from the body of this death? The grace of God, through Jesus Christ our Lord." [93] Now, when he places this grace, not in the aid of His power, but in His example for imitation, what further hope must we entertain of him, since everywhere the word "grace" is mentioned by him under an ambiguous generality?

CHAPTER XLIV

PELAGIUS ONCE MORE GUARDS HIMSELF AGAINST THE NECESSITY OF GRACE

Then, again, in the work addressed to the holy virgin,[94] of which we have spoken already, there is this passage: "Let us submit ourselves to God, and by doing His will let us merit the divine grace; and let us the more easily, by the help of the Holy Ghost, resist the evil spirit." Now, in these words

[91] Rom. vii. 15   [92] Rom. vii. 23   [93] Rom. vii. 25   [94] The nun Demetrias

of his, it is plain enough that he regards us as assisted by the grace of the Holy Ghost, not because we are unable to resist the tempter without Him by the sheer capacity of our nature, but in order that we may resist *more easily*. With respect, however, to the quantity and quality, whatever these might be, of this assistance, we may well believe that he made them consist of the additional knowledge which the Spirit reveals to us through teaching, and which we either cannot, or scarcely can, possess by nature. Such are the particulars which I have been able to discover in the book which he addressed to the virgin of Christ, and wherein he seems to confess grace. Of what purport and kind these are, you of course perceive.

CHAPTER XLV

TO WHAT PURPOSE PELAGIUS THOUGHT PRAYERS OUGHT TO BE OFFERED

"Let them also read," says he, "my recent little treatise which we were obliged to publish a short while ago in defence of free will, and let them acknowledge how unfair is their determination to disparage us for a denial of grace, when we throughout almost the whole work acknowledge fully and sincerely both free will and grace." There are four books in this treatise, all of which I read, marking such passages as required consideration, and which I proposed to discuss: these I examined as well as I was able, before we came to that epistle of his which was sent to Rome. But even in these four books, that which he seems to regard as the grace which helps us to turn aside from evil and to do good, he describes in such a manner as to keep to his old ambiguity of language, and thus have it in his power so to explain to his followers, that they may suppose the assistance which is rendered by grace, for the purpose of helping our natural capacity, consists of nothing else than the law and the teaching. Thus our very prayers (as, indeed, he most plainly affirms in his writings) are of no other use, in his opinion, than to procure for us the explanation of the teaching by a divine revelation, not to procure help for the mind of man to perfect by love and action what it has learned should be done. The fact is, he does not in the least relinquish that very manifest dogma of his system in which he sets forth those three things, capacity, volition, action; maintaining that only the first of these, the capacity, is favored with the constant assistance of divine help, but supposing that the volition and the action stand in no need of God's assistance. Moreover, the very help which he says assists our natural capacity, he places in the law and teaching. This teaching, he allows, is revealed or explained to us by the Holy Ghost, on which account it is that he concedes the necessity of prayer. But still this assistance of law and teaching he supposes to have existed even in the days of the prophets; whereas the help of grace, which is properly so called he will have to lie simply in the example of Christ. But this example, you can plainly see, pertains after all to "teaching"—even that which is preached to us as the gospel. The general result, then, is the pointing out, as it were, of a road to us by which we are bound to walk, by the powers of our free will, and needing no assistance from any one else, may suffice to ourselves not to faint or fail on the way. And even as to the discovery of the road itself, he contends that nature alone is competent for it; only the discovery will be *more* easily effected if grace renders assistance.

CHAPTER XLVI

PELAGIUS PROFESSES TO RESPECT THE CATHOLIC AUTHORS

Such are the particulars which, to the best of my ability, I have succeeded in obtaining from the writings of Pelagius, whenever he makes mention of grace. You perceive, however, that men who entertain such opinions as we have reviewed are "ignorant of God's righteousness, and desire to establish their own," [95] and are far off from "the righteousness which we have of God" [96] and not of ourselves; and this they ought to have discovered and recognised in the very holy canonical Scriptures. Forasmuch, however, as they read these Scriptures in a sense of their own, they of course fail to observe even the most obvious truths therein. Would that they would but turn their attention in no careless mood to what might be learned concerning the help of God's grace in the writings, at all events, of Catholic authors; for they freely allow that the Scriptures were correctly understood by these, and that they would not pass them by in neglect, out of an overweening fondness for their own opinions. For note how this very man Pelagius, in that very treatise of his so recently put forth, and which he formally mentions in his self-defence (that is to say, in the third book of his *Defence of Free Will*), praises Saint Ambrose.

CHAPTER XLVII

AMBROSE MOST HIGHLY PRAISED BY PELAGIUS

"The blessed Bishop Ambrose," says he, "in whose writings the Roman faith shines forth with especial brightness, and whom the Latins have always regarded as the very flower and glory of their authors, and who has never found a foe bold enough to censure his faith or the purity of his understanding of the Scripture." Observe the sort as well as the amount of the praises which he bestows; nevertheless, however holy and learned he is, he is not to be compared to the authority of the canonical Scripture. The reason of this high commendation of Ambrose lies in the circumstance, that Pelagius sees proper to quote a certain passage from his writings to prove that man is able to live without sin.[97] This, however, is not the question before us. We are at present discussing that assistance of grace which helps us towards avoiding sin, and leading holy lives.

[95] Rom. x. 3   [96] Phil. iii. 9   [97] See *On Nature and Grace*, ch. 74

CHAPTER XLVIII

AMBROSE IS NOT IN AGREEMENT WITH PELAGIUS

I wish, indeed, that he would listen to the venerable bishop when, in the second book of his *Exposition of the Gospel according to Luke*,[98] he expressly teaches us that the Lord co-operates also with our wills. "You see, therefore," says he, "because the power of the Lord co-operates everywhere with human efforts, that no man is able to build without the Lord, no man to watch without the Lord, no man to undertake anything without the Lord. Whence the apostle thus enjoins: 'Whether ye eat, or whether ye drink, do all to the glory of God.' "[99] You observe how the holy Ambrose takes away from men even their familiar expressions—such as, "We undertake, but God accomplishes"—when he says here that "no man is able to undertake anything without the Lord." To the same effect he says, in the sixth book of the same work,[100] treating of the two debtors of a certain creditor: "According to men's opinions, he perhaps is the greater offender who owed most. The case, however, is altered by the Lord's mercy, so that he loves the most who owes the most, if he yet obtains grace." See how the Catholic doctor most plainly declares that the very love which prompts every man to an ampler love appertains to the kindly gift of grace.

CHAPTER XLIX

AMBROSE TEACHES WITH WHAT EYE CHRIST TURNED AND LOOKED UPON PETER

That repentance, indeed, itself, which beyond all doubt is an action of the will, is wrought into action by the mercy and help of the Lord, is asserted by the blessed Ambrose in the following passage in the ninth book of the same work:[101] "Good," says he, "are the tears which wash away sin. They upon whom the Lord at last turns and looks, bewail. Peter denied Him first, and did not weep, because the Lord had not turned and looked upon him. He denied Him a second time, and still wept not, because the Lord had not even yet turned and looked upon him. The third time also he denied Him, Jesus turned and looked, and then he wept most bitterly." Let these persons read the Gospel; let them consider how the Lord Jesus was at that moment within, having a hearing before the chief of the priests; while the Apostle Peter was outside,[102] and down in the hall,[103] sitting at one time with the servants at the fire,[104] at another time standing,[105] as

---

[98] Book ii. c. 84, on Luke iii. 22. Compare *Against Two Letters of the Pelagians*, iv. ch. 30 [99] 1 Cor. x. 31 [100] Book vi. c. 25, on Luke vii. 41 [101] The reference is to Book x. of the editions, c. 89, on Luke xxii. 61 [102] Matt. xxvi. 69, 71 [103] Mark xiv. 66 [104] Luke xxii. 55 [105] John xviii. 16

the most accurate and consistent narrative of the evangelists shows. It cannot therefore be said that it was with His bodily eyes that the Lord turned and looked upon him by a visible and apparent admonition. That, then, which is described in the words, "The Lord turned and looked upon Peter,"[106] was effected internally; it was wrought in the mind, wrought in the will. In mercy the Lord silently and secretly approached, touched the heart, recalled the memory of the past, with His own internal grace visited Peter, stirred and brought out into external tears the feelings of his inner man. Behold in what manner God is present with His help to our wills and actions; behold how "He worketh in us both to will and to do."

CHAPTER L

AMBROSE TEACHES THAT ALL MEN NEED GOD'S HELP

In the same book the same Saint Ambrose says again:[107] "Now if Peter fell, who said, 'Though all men shall be offended, yet will I never be offended,' who else shall rightly presume concerning himself? David, indeed, because he had said, 'In my prosperity I said, I shall never be moved,' confesses how injurious his confidence had proved to himself: 'Thou didst turn away Thy face,' he says, 'and I was troubled.' "[108] Pelagius ought to listen to the teaching of so eminent a man, and should follow his faith, since he has commended his teaching and faith. Let him listen humbly; let him follow with fidelity; let him indulge no longer in obstinate presumption, lest he perish. Why does Pelagius choose to be sunk in that sea whence Peter was rescued by the Rock?[109]

CHAPTER LI

AMBROSE TEACHES THAT IT IS GOD THAT DOES FOR MAN WHAT PELAGIUS ATTRIBUTES TO FREE WILL

Let him lend an ear also to the same godly bishop, who says, in the sixth book of this same book:[110] "The reason why they would not receive Him is mentioned by the evangelist himself in these words, 'Because His face was as though He would go to Jerusalem.'[111] But His disciples had a strong wish that He should be received into the Samaritan town. God, however, calls whomsoever He deigns, and whom He wills He makes religious." What wise insight of the man of God, drawn from the very fountain of God's grace! "God," says he, "calls whomsoever He deigns, and whom He wills He makes religious." See whether this is not the prophet's own declaration: "I will have mercy on whom I will have mercy, and will show pity on whom

---

[106] Luke xxii. 61   [107] Book x. c. 89   [108] Ps. xxx. 7

[109] It is impossible to preserve the paronomasia of the original, which plays on the meaning of the names *Pelagius* (*pelago*, sea) and *Petrus* (*petra*, rock)

[110] It is the *seventh* book in the editions, c. 27, on Luke ix. 53   [111] Luke ix. 53

I will be pitiful;" [112] and the apostle's deduction therefrom: "So then," says he, "it is not of him that willeth, nor of him that runneth, but of God that showeth mercy." [113] Now, when even his model man of our own times says, that "whomsoever God deigns He calls, and whom He wills He makes religious," will any one be bold enough to contend that that man is not yet religious "who hastens to the Lord, and desires to be directed by Him, and makes his own will depend upon God's; who, moreover, cleaves so closely to the Lord, that he becomes (as the apostle says) 'one spirit' with Him?" [114] Great, however, as is this entire work of a "religious man," Pelagius maintains that "it is effected only by the freedom of the will." But his own blessed Ambrose, whom he so highly commends in word, is against him, saying, "The Lord God calls whomsoever He deigns, and whom He wills He makes religious." It is God, then, who makes religious whomsoever He pleases, in order that he may "hasten to the Lord, and desire to be directed by Him, and make his own will depend upon God's, and cleave so closely to the Lord as to become (as the apostle says) 'one spirit' with Him;" and all this none but a religious man does. Who, then, ever does so much, unless he be made by God to do it?

CHAPTER LII

IF PELAGIUS AGREES WITH AMBROSE, AUGUSTINE HAS NO CONTROVERSY WITH HIM

Inasmuch, however, as the discussion about free will and God's grace has such difficulty in its distinctions, that when free will is maintained, God's grace is apparently denied; while when God's grace is asserted, free will is supposed to be done away with—Pelagius can so involve himself in the shades of this obscurity as to profess agreement with all that we have quoted from Saint Ambrose, and declare that such is, and always has been, his opinion also; and endeavor so to explain each, that men may suppose his opinion, to be in fair accord with Ambrose's. So far, therefore, as concerns the questions of God's help and grace, you are requested to observe the three things which he has distinguished so very plainly, under the terms "ability," "will," and "actuality," that is, "capacity," "volition," and "action." [115] If, then, he has come round to an agreement with us, then not the "capacity" alone in man, even if he neither wills nor performs the good, but the volition and the action also—in other words, our willing well and doing well—things which have no existence in man, except when he has a good will and acts rightly:—if, I repeat, he thus consents to hold with us, that even the volition and the action are assisted by God, and so assisted that we can neither will nor do any good thing without such help; if, too,

---

[112] Ex. xxxiii. 19   [113] Rom. ix. 16
[114] 1 Cor. vi. 17. These are the words of Pelagius, which have been already quoted above, in ch. 24   [115] See above, ch. 4

he believes that this is that very grace of God through our Lord Jesus Christ which makes us righteous through His righteousness, and not our own, so that our true righteousness is that which we have of Him—then, so far as I can judge, there will remain no further controversy between us concerning the assistance we have from the grace of God.

CHAPTER LIII

IN WHAT SENSE SOME MEN MAY BE SAID TO LIVE WITHOUT SIN IN THE PRESENT LIFE

But in reference to the particular point in which he quoted the holy Ambrose with so much approbation—because he found in that author's writings, from the praises he accorded to Zacharias and Elisabeth, the opinion that a man might possibly in this life be without sin;[116] although this cannot be denied if God wills it, with whom all things are possible, yet he ought to consider more carefully *in what sense* this was said, Now, so far as I can see, this statement was made in accordance with a certain standard of conduct, which is among men held to be worthy of approval and praise, and which no human being could justly call in question for the purpose of laying accusation or censure. Such a standard Zacharias and his wife Elisabeth are said to have maintained in the sight of God, for no other reason than that they, by walking therein, never deceived people by any dissimulation; but as they in their sincerity appeared to men, so were they known in the sight of God.[117] The statement, however, was not made with any reference to that perfect state of righteousness in which we shall one day live truly and absolutely in a condition of spotless purity. The Apostle Paul, indeed, has told us that he was "blameless, as touching the righteousness which is of the law;" [118] and it was in respect of the same law that Zacharias also lived a blameless life. This righteousness, however, the apostle counted as "dung" and "loss," in comparison with the righteousness which is the object of our hope,[119] and which we ought to "hunger and thirst after," [120] in order that hereafter we may be satisfied with the vision thereof, enjoying it now by faith, so long as "the just do live by faith." [121]

CHAPTER LIV

AMBROSE TEACHES THAT NO ONE IS SINLESS IN THIS WORLD

Lastly, let him give good heed to his venerable bishop, when he is expounding the Prophet Isaiah,[122] and says that "no man in this world

[116] Ambrose on St. Luke, Book i. c. 17   [117] Luke i. 6; compare *De Perfect. Just.* ch. 38   [118] Phil. iii. 6   [119] Phil. iii. 8   [120] Matt. v. 6   [121] Rom. i. 17   [122] This work of Ambrose is no longer extant

can be without sin." Now nobody can pretend to say that by the phrase *"in this world"* he simply meant, in the love of this world. For he was speaking of the apostle, who said, "Our conversation is in heaven;" [123] and while unfolding the sense of these words, the eminent bishop expressed himself thus: "Now the apostle says that many men, even while living in the present world, are perfect with themselves, who could not possibly be deemed perfect, if one looks at true perfection. For he says himself: 'We now see through a glass, darkly; but then face to face: now I know in part; but then shall I know, even as also I am known.' [124] Thus, there are those who are spotless in this world, there are those who will be spotless in the kingdom of God; although, of course, if you sift the thing minutely, no one could be spotless, because no one is without sin." That passage, then, of the holy Ambrose, which Pelagius applies in support of his own opinion, was either written in a qualified sense, probable, indeed, but not expressed with minute accuracy; or if the holy and lowly-minded author did think that Zacharias and Elisabeth lived according to the highest and absolutely perfect righteousness, which was incapable of increase or addition, he certainly corrected his opinion on a minuter examination of it.

CHAPTER LV

AMBROSE WITNESSES THAT PERFECT PURITY IS IMPOSSIBLE TO HUMAN NATURE

He ought, moreover, carefully to note that, in the very same context from which he quoted that passage of Ambrose's, which seemed so satisfactory for his purpose, he also said this: "To be spotless from the beginning is an impossibility to human nature." [125] In this sentence the venerable Ambrose does undoubtedly predicate feebleness and infirmity of that natural "capacity," which Pelagius refuses faithfully to regard as corrupted by sin, and therefore boastfully extols. Beyond question, this runs counter to this man's will and inclination, although it does not contravene the truthful confession of the apostle, wherein he says: "We too were once by nature the children of wrath, even as others." [126] For through the sin of the first man, which came from his free will, our nature became corrupted and ruined; and nothing but God's grace alone, through Him who is the Mediator between God and men, and our Almighty Physician, succors it. Now, since we have already prolonged this work too far in treating of the assistance of the divine grace towards our justification, by which God co-operates in all things for good with those who love Him,[127] and whom He first loved [128]—giving to them that He might receive from them: we must commence another treatise, as the Lord shall enable us, on

---

[123] Phil. iii. 20   [124] 1 Cor. xiii. 13   [125] See Augustine, *De Natura et Gratia*, c. 75
[126] Eph. ii. 3   [127] Rom. viii. 28   [128] 1 John iv. 19

the subject of sin also, which by one man has entered into the world, along with death, and so has passed upon all men,[129] setting forth as much as shall seem needful and sufficient, in opposition to those persons who have broken out into violent and open error, contrary to the truth here stated.

[129] Rom. v. 12

BOOK TWO

ON ORIGINAL SIN

Wherein Augustine shows that Pelagius really differs in no respect, on the question of original sin and the baptism of infants, from his follower Coelestius, who, refusing to acknowledge original sin and even daring to deny the doctrine in public, was condemned in trials before the bishops—first at Carthage, and afterwards at Rome; for this question is not, as these heretics would have it, one wherein persons might err without danger to the faith. Their heresy, indeed, aimed at nothing else than the very foundations of Christian belief. He afterwards refutes all such as maintained that the blessing of matrimony is disparaged by the doctrine of original depravity, and an injury done to God himself, the creator of man who is born by means of matrimony.

CHAPTER I

CAUTION NEEDED IN ATTENDING TO PELAGIUS' DELIVERANCES ON INFANT BAPTISM

Next I beg of you [1] carefully to observe with what caution you ought to lend an ear, on the question of the baptism of infants, to men of this character, who dare not openly deny the laver of regeneration and the forgiveness of sins to this early age, for fear that Christian ears would not bear to listen to them; and who yet persist in holding and urging their opinion, that the carnal generation is not held guilty of man's first sin, although they seem to allow infants to be baptized for the remission of sins. You have, indeed, yourselves informed me in your letter, that you heard Pelagius say in your presence, reading out of that book of his which he declared that he had also sent to Rome, that they maintain that "infants ought to be baptized with the same formula of sacramental words as adults." [2] Who, after that statement, would suppose that one ought to raise any question at all on this subject? Or if he did, to whom would he not seem to indulge a very calumnious disposition—previous to the perusal of their plain assertions, in which they deny that infants inherit original sin, and contend that all persons are born free from all corruption?

CHAPTER II

COELESTIUS, ON HIS TRIAL, AT CARTHAGE, REFUSES TO CONDEMN HIS ERROR; THE WRITTEN STATEMENT WHICH HE GAVE TO ZOSIMUS

Coelestius, indeed, maintained this erroneous doctrine with less restraint. To such an extent did he push his freedom as actually to refuse, when on

[1] For the persons addressed, see above, in Book i. c. i, of *On the Grace of Christ*
[2] See *On the Grace of Christ*, ch. 35

trial before the bishops at Carthage,[3] to condemn those who say, "That Adam's sin injured only Adam himself, and not the human race; and that infants at their birth are in the same state that Adam was in before his transgression."[4] In the written statement, too, which he presented to the most blessed Pope Zosimus at Rome, he declared with especial plainness, "that original sin binds no single infant." Concerning the ecclesiastical proceedings at Carthage we copy the following account of his words.

CHAPTER III

PART OF THE PROCEEDINGS OF THE COUNCIL OF CARTHAGE AGAINST COELESTIUS

"The bishop Aurelius said: 'Let what follows be recited.' It was accordingly recited, 'That the sin of Adam was injurious to him alone, and not to the human race.' Then, after the recital, Coelestius said: 'I said that I was in doubt about the transmission of sin,[5] but so as to yield assent to any man whom God has gifted with the grace of knowledge; for I have heard different opinions from those who have been even appointed presbyters in the Catholic Church.' The deacon Paulinus[6] said: 'Tell us their names.' Coelestius answered: 'The holy presbyter Rufinus,[7] who lived at Rome with the holy Pammachius. I have heard him declare that there is no transmission of sin.' The deacon Paulinus then asked: 'Is there any one else?' Coelestius replied: 'I have heard more say the same.' The deacon Paulinus rejoined: 'Tell us their names.' Coelestius said: 'Is not

[3] See *Concerning the Proceedings of Pelagius*, ch. 23

[4] Pelagius, at Diospolis, condemned this position of Coelestius. Hence the comparative restraint of Pelagius, and the greater freedom in holding the error which is here attributed to Coelestius

[5] *De traduce peccati*, the technical phrase to express the conveyance by birth of original sin

[6] This Paulinus, according to Mercator (*Commonit. super nomine Coelestii*), was the deacon of Ambrose, Bishop of Milan, and the author of his biography, which he wrote at the instance of Augustine. According to his own showing, he lived in Africa, and wrote the *Life of Ambrose* when John was pretorian prefect, *i.e.* either in the year 412, or 413, or 422. The trial mentioned in the text took place about the commencement of the year 412, according to Augustine's letter to Pope Innocent (see Augustine's letter, 175, 1. 6). See *On the Proceedings of Pelagius*, 23

[7] Mercator (*Commonit. adv. Haeres. Pelagii*) informs us that a certain Syrian called Rufinus introduced the discussion against original sin and its transmission into Rome in the pontificate of Anastasius. According to some, this was the Rufinus of Aquileia, whom Jerome (*in Epist. ad Ctesiphont.*) notices as the precursor of Pelagius in his error about the sinless nature of man; according, however, to others, it is the other Rufinus, mentioned by Jerome in his 66th Epistle, who is possibly the same as he who rejects the transmission of original sin in a treatise *On Faith*, which J. Sismondi published as the work of Rufinus, a presbyter of the province of Palestine. It is, at any rate, hardly possible to suppose that the Aquileian Rufinus either went to Rome, or lodged there with Pammachius, in the time of Pope Anastasius

one priest enough for you?' " Then afterwards in another place we read: "The bishop Aurelius said: 'Let the rest of the accusation be read.' It then was recited 'That infants at their birth are in the same state that Adam was before the transgression;' and they read to the very end of the brief accusation which had been previously put in. The bishop Aurelius inquired: 'Have you, Coelestius, taught at any time, as the deacon Paulinus has stated, that infants are at their birth in the same state that Adam was before his transgression?' Coelestius answered: 'Let him explain what he meant when he said, *"before the transgression."* ' The deacon Paulinus then said: 'Do you on your side deny that you ever taught this doctrine? It must be one of two things: he must either say that he never so taught, or else he must now condemn the opinion.' Coelestius rejoined: 'I have already said, Let him explain the words he mentioned, *"before the transgression."* ' The deacon Paulinus then said: 'You must deny ever having taught this.' The bishop Aurelius said: 'I ask, What conclusion I have on my part to draw from this man's obstinacy; my affirmation is, that although Adam, as created in Paradise, is said to have been made immortal at first, he afterwards became corruptible through transgressing the commandment. Do you say this, brother Paulinus?' 'I do, my lord,' answered the deacon Paulinus. Then the bishop Aurelius said: 'As regards the condition of infants before baptism at the present day, the deacon Paulinus wishes to be informed whether it is such as Adam's was before the transgression; and whether it derives the guilt of transgression from the same origin of sin from which it is born?' The deacon Paulinus asked: 'Let him deny whether he taught this, or not.' Coelestius answered: 'As touching the transmission of sin, I have already asserted, that I have heard many persons of acknowledged position in the Catholic Church deny it altogether; and on the other hand, others affirm it: it may be fairly deemed a matter for inquiry, but not a heresy. I have always maintained that infants require baptism, and ought to be baptized. What else does he want?' "

CHAPTER IV

COELESTIUS CONCEDES BAPTISM FOR INFANTS, WITHOUT AFFIRMING ORIGINAL SIN

You, of course, see that Coelestius here conceded baptism for infants only in such a manner as to be unwilling to confess that the sin of the first man, which is washed away in the laver of regeneration, passes over to them, although at the same time he did not venture to deny this; and on account of this doubt he refused to condemn those who maintain "That Adam's sin injured only himself, and not the human race;" and "that infants at their birth are in the same condition wherein Adam was before the transgression."

CHAPTER V

But in the book which he published at Rome, and produced in the proceedings before the church there, he so speaks on this question as to show that he really believes what he had professed to be in doubt about. For these are his words:[8] "That infants, however, ought to be baptized for the remission of sins, according to the rule of the Church universal, and according to the meaning of the Gospel, we confess. For the Lord has determined that the kingdom of heaven should only be conferred on baptized persons;[9] and since the resources of nature do not possess it, it must necessarily be conferred by the gift of grace." Now if he had not said anything elsewhere on this subject, who would not have supposed that he acknowledged the remission of original sin even in infants at their baptism, by saying that they ought to be baptized for the remission of sins? Hence the point of what you have stated in your letter, that Pelagius' answer to you was on this wise, "That infants are baptized with the same words of sacramental formula as adults," and that you were rejoiced to hear the very thing which you were desirous of hearing, and yet that you preferred holding a consultation with us concerning his words.

CHAPTER VI

Carefully observe, then, what Coelestius has advanced so very openly, and you will discover what amount of concealment Pelagius has practised upon you. Coelestius goes on to say as follows: "That infants, however, must be baptized for remission of sins, was not admitted by us with the view of our seeming to affirm sin by transmission. This is very alien from the Catholic meaning, because sin is not born with a man—it is subsequently committed by the man: for it is shown to be a fault, not of nature, but of the will. It is fitting, therefore, to confess this, lest we should seem to make different kinds of baptism; it is, moreover, necessary to lay down this preliminary safeguard, lest by the occasion of this mystery evil should, to the disparagement of the Creator, be said to be conveyed to man by nature, before it has been committed by man." Now Pelagius was either afraid or ashamed to avow this to be his own opinion before you; although his disciple experienced neither a qualm nor a blush in openly professing it to be his, without any obscure subterfuges, in presence of the Apostolic See.

[8] See *On the Grace of Christ*, ch. 36   [9] John iii. 5

CHAPTER VII

POPE ZOSIMUS KINDLY EXCUSES HIM

The bishop, however, who presides over this See, upon seeing him hurrying headlong in so great presumption like a madman, chose in his great compassion, with a view to the man's repentance, if it might be, rather to bind him tightly by eliciting from him answers to questions proposed by himself, than by the stroke of a severe condemnation to drive him over the precipice, down which he seemed to be even now ready to fall. I say advisedly, "down which he seemed to be ready to fall," rather than "over which he had actually fallen," because he had already in this same book of his forecast the subject with an intended reference to questions of this sort in the following words: "If it should so happen that any error of ignorance has stolen over us human beings, let it be corrected by your decisive sentence."

CHAPTER VIII

COELESTIUS CONDEMNED BY ZOSIMUS

The venerable Pope Zosimus, keeping in view this deprecatory preamble, dealt with the man, puffed up as he was with the blasts of false doctrine, so as that he should condemn all the objectionable points which had been alleged against him by the deacon Paulinus, and that he should yield his assent to the rescript of the Apostolic See which had been issued by his predecessor of sacred memory. The accused man, however, refused to condemn the objections raised by the deacon, yet he did not dare to hold out against the letter of the blessed Pope Innocent; indeed, he went so far as to "promise that he would condemn all the points which the Apostolic See condemned." Thus the man was treated with gentle remedies, as a delirious patient who required rest; but, at the same time, he was not regarded as being yet ready to be released from the restraints of excommunication. The interval of two months being granted him, until communications could be received from Africa, a place for recovery was conceded to him, under the mild restorative of the sentence which had been pronounced. For in truth, if he would have laid aside his vain obstinacy, and be now willing to carry out what he had undertaken, and would carefully read the very letter to which he had replied by promising submission, he would yet come to a better mind. But after the rescripts were duly issued from the council of the African bishops, there were very good reasons why the sentence should be carried out against him, in strictest accordance with equity. What these reasons were you may read for yourselves, for we have sent you all the particulars.

CHAPTER IX

PELAGIUS DECEIVED THE COUNCIL IN PALESTINE, BUT WAS UNABLE TO DECEIVE THE CHURCH AT ROME

Wherefore Pelagius, too, if he will only reflect candidly on his own position and writings, has no reason for saying that he ought not to have been banned with such a sentence. For although he deceived the council in Palestine, seemingly clearing himself before it, he entirely failed in imposing on the church at Rome (where, as you well know, he is by no means a stranger), although he went so far as to make the attempt, if he might somehow succeed. But, as I have just said, he entirely failed. For the most blessed Pope Zosimus recollected what his predecessor, who had set him so worthy an example, had thought of these very proceedings. Nor did he omit to observe what opinion was entertained about this man by the trusty Romans, whose faith deserved to be spoken of in the Lord,[10] and whose consistent zeal in defence of Catholic truth against this heresy he saw prevailing amongst them with warmth, and at the same time most perfect harmony. The man had lived among them for a long while, and his opinions could not escape their notice; moreover, they had so completely found out his disciple Coelestius, as to be able at once to adduce the most trustworthy and irrefragable evidence on this subject. Now what was the solemn judgment which the holy Pope Innocent formed respecting the proceedings in the Synod of Palestine, by which Pelagius boasts of having been acquitted, you may indeed read in the letter which he addressed to me. It is duly mentioned also in the answer which was forwarded by the African Synod to the venerable Pope Zosimus, and which, along with the other instructions, we have despatched to your loving selves. But it seems to me, at the same time, that I ought not to omit producing the particulars in the present work.

CHAPTER X

THE JUDGMENT OF INNOCENT RESPECTING THE PROCEEDINGS IN PALESTINE

Five bishops, then, of whom I was one, wrote him a letter,[11] wherein we mentioned the proceedings in Palestine, of which the report had already reached us. We informed him that in the East, where this man lived, there had taken place certain ecclesiastical proceedings, in which he was thought to have been acquitted on all the charges. To this communication from us Innocent replied in a letter which contains the following among other words: "There are," says he, "sundry positions, as stated in these very Proceedings, which, when they were objected against him, he partly sup-

[10] Rom. i. 8   [11] *Epistle* 177

pressed by avoiding them, and partly confused in absolute obscurity, by wresting the sense of many words; while there are other allegations which he cleared off—not, indeed, in the honest way which he might seem at the time to use, but rather by methods of sophistry, meeting some of the objections with a flat denial, and tampering with others by a fallacious interpretation. Would, however, that he would even now adopt what is the far more desirable course of turning from his own error back to the true ways of Catholic Faith; that he would also, duly considering God's daily grace, and acknowledging the help thereof, be willing and desirous to appear, amidst the approbation of all men, to be truly corrected by the method of open conviction—not, indeed, by judicial process, but by a hearty conversion to the Catholic Faith. We are therefore unable either to approve of or to blame their proceedings at that trial; for we cannot tell whether the proceedings were true, or even, if true, whether they do not really show that the man escaped by subterfuge, rather than that he cleared himself by entire truth." [12] You see clearly from these words, how that the most blessed Pope Innocent without doubt speaks of this man as of one who was by no means unknown to him. You see what opinion he entertained about his acquittal. You see, moreover, what his successor the holy Pope Zosimus was bound to recollect—as in truth he did—so as to confirm without hesitation the judgment of his predecessor in this case.

CHAPTER XI

HOW PELAGIUS DECEIVED THE SYNOD OF PALESTINE

Now I pray you carefully to observe by what evidence Pelagius is shown to have deceived his judges in Palestine, not to mention other points, on this very question of the baptism of infants, lest we should seem to any one to have used calumny and suspicion, rather than to have ascertained the certain fact, when we alleged that Pelagius concealed the opinion which Coelestius expressed with greater frankness, while at the same time he actually entertained the same views. Now, from what has been stated above, it has been clearly seen that Coelestius refused to condemn the assertion that "Adam's sin injured only himself, and not the human race, and that infants at their birth are in the same state that Adam was before the transgression," because he saw that, if he condemned these propositions, he would affirm that there was in infants a transmission of sin from Adam. When, however, it was objected to Pelagius that he was of one mind with Coelestius on this point, he condemned the words without hesitation. I am quite aware that you have read all this before. Since, however, we are not writing this account for you alone, we proceed to transcribe the very words of the synodal acts, lest the reader should be unwilling either to turn to the

[12] Innocent's letter occurs amongst *The Epistles of Augustine,* letter 183. 3, 4

record for himself, or if he does not possess it, take the trouble to procure a copy. Here, then, are the words:—

CHAPTER XII

A PORTION OF THE PROCEEDINGS OF THE SYNOD OF PALESTINE IN THE CAUSE OF PELAGIUS

"The synod said:[13] Now, forasmuch as Pelagius has pronounced his anathema on this uncertain utterance of folly, rightly replying that a man by God's help and grace is able to live ἀναμάρτητος, that is to say, without sin, let him give us his answer on other articles also. Another particular in the teaching of Coelestius, disciple of Pelagius, selected from the heads which were mentioned and heard at Carthage before the holy Aurelius bishop of Carthage, and other bishops, was to this effect: 'That Adam was made mortal, and that he would have died, whether he sinned or did not sin; that Adam's sin injured himself alone, and not the human race; that the law no less than the gospel leads us to the kingdom; that before the coming of Christ there were persons without sin; that newborn infants are in the same condition that Adam was before the transgression; that, on the one hand, the entire human race does not die on account of Adam's death and transgression, nor, on the other hand, does the whole human race rise again through the resurrection of Christ; that the holy bishop Augustine wrote a book in answer to his followers in Sicily, on articles which were subjoined, and in this book, which was addressed to Hilary, are contained the following statements: That a man is able to be without sin if he wishes; that infants, even if they are unbaptized, have eternal life; that rich men, even if they are baptized, unless they renounce and give up all, have, whatever good they may seem to have done, nothing of it reckoned unto them, neither can they possess the kingdom of heaven.' Pelagius then said: As regards man's ability to be without sin, my opinion has been already spoken. With respect, however, to the allegation that there were even before the Lord's coming persons who lived without sin, we also on our part say, that before the coming of Christ there certainly were persons who passed their lives in holiness and righteousness, according to the accounts which have been handed down to us in the Holy Scriptures. As for the other points, indeed, even on their own showing, they are not of a character which obliges me to be answerable for them; but yet, for the satisfaction of the sacred Synod, I anathematize those who either now hold or have ever held these opinions."

[13] Compare *On the Proceedings of Pelagius*, chs. 16, 23

CHAPTER XIII

COELESTIUS THE BOLDER HERETIC; PELAGIUS THE MORE SUBTLE

You see, indeed, not to mention other points, how that Pelagius pronounced his anathema against those who hold that "Adam's sin injured only himself, and not the human race; and that infants are at their birth in the same condition in which Adam was before the transgression." Now what else could the bishops who sat in judgment on him have possibly understood him to mean by this, but that the sin of Adam is transmitted to infants? It was to avoid making such an admission that Coelestius refused to condemn this statement, which this man on the contrary anathematized. If, therefore, I shall show that he did not really entertain any other opinion concerning infants than that they are born without any contagion of a single sin, what difference will there remain on this question between him and Coelestius, except this, that the one is more open, the other more reserved; the one more pertinacious, the other more mendacious; or, at any rate, that the one is more candid, the other more astute? For, the one before the church of Carthage refused to condemn what he afterwards in the church at Rome publicly confessed to be a tenet of his own; at the same time professing himself "ready to submit to correction if an error had stolen over him, considering that he was but human;" whereas the other both condemned this dogma as being contrary to the truth lest he should himself be condemned by his Catholic judges, and yet kept it in reserve for subsequent defence, so that either his condemnation was a lie, or his interpretation a trick.

CHAPTER XIV

HE SHOWS THAT, EVEN AFTER THE SYNOD OF PALESTINE, PELAGIUS HELD THE SAME OPINIONS AS COELESTIUS ON THE SUBJECT OF ORIGINAL SIN

I see, however, that it may be most justly demanded of me, that I do not defer my promised demonstration, that he actually entertains the same views as Coelestius. In the first book of his more recent work, written in defence of free will (which work he mentions in the letter he despatched to Rome) he says: "Everything good, and everything evil, on account of which we are either laudable or blameworthy, is not born with us but done by us: for we are born not fully developed, but with a capacity for either conduct; and we are procreated as without virtue, so also without vice; and previous to the action of our own proper will, that alone is in man which God has formed." Now you perceive that in these words of Pelagius, the dogma of both these men is contained, that infants are born without the contagion of any sin from Adam. It is therefore not astonishing that Coelestius refused to condemn such as say that Adam's sin injured only himself, and not the human race; and that infants are at their birth in the same state in which Adam was before the transgression. But it is very much to be wondered at, that Pelagius had the effrontery to anathematize these opinions. For if, as he alleges, "evil is not born with us, and we are procreated without fault, and the only thing in man previous to the action of his own will is what God has formed," then of course the sin of Adam did only injure himself, inasmuch as it did not pass on to his offspring. For there is not any sin which is not an evil; or a sin that is not a fault; or else sin was created by God. But he says: "Evil is not born with us, and we are procreated without fault; and the only thing in men at their birth is what God has formed." Now, since by this language he supposes it to be most true, that, according to the well-known sentence of his: "Adam's sin was injurious to himself alone, and not to the human race," why did Pelagius condemn this, if it were not for the purpose of deceiving his Catholic judges? By parity of reasoning, it may also be argued: "If evil is not born with us, and if we are procreated without fault, and if the only thing found in man at the time of his birth is what God has formed," it follows beyond a doubt that "infants at their birth are in the same condition that Adam was before the transgression," in whom no evil or fault was inherent, and in whom that alone existed which God had formed. And yet Pelagius pronounced anathema on all those persons "who hold now, or have at any time held, that newborn babes are placed by their birth in the same state that Adam was in before the transgression"—in other words, are without any evil, without any fault, having that only which God had formed. Now, why again did Pelagius condemn this tenet also, if it were not for the purpose of deceiving the Catholic Synod, and saving himself from the condemnation of an heretical innovator?

CHAPTER XV

PELAGIUS BY HIS MENDACITY AND DECEPTION STOLE HIS ACQUITTAL FROM THE SYNOD IN PALESTINE

For my own part, however, I, as you are quite aware, and as I also stated in the book which I addressed to our venerable and aged Aurelius on the proceedings in Palestine, really felt glad that Pelagius in that answer of his had exhausted the whole of this question.[14] To me, indeed, he seemed most plainly to have acknowledged that there is original sin in infants, by the anathema which he pronounced against those persons who supposed that by the sin of Adam only himself, and not the human race, was injured, and who entertained the opinion that infants are in the same state in which

[14] See *On the Proceedings of Pelagius*, ch. 24

the first man was before the transgression. When, however, I had read his four books (from the first of which I copied the words which I have just now quoted), and discovered that he was still cherishing thoughts which were opposed to the Catholic Faith touching infants, I felt all the greater surprise at a mendacity which he so unblushingly maintained in a synod of the Church, and on so great a question. For if he had already written these books, how did he profess to anathematize those who had ever entertained the opinions alluded to? If he purposed, however, afterwards to publish such a work, how could he anathematize those who at the time were holding the opinions? Unless, to be sure, by some ridiculous subterfuge he meant to say that the objects of his anathema were such persons as had in some previous time held, or were then holding, these opinions; but that in respect of the future—that is, as regarded those persons who were about to take up with such views—he felt that it would be impossible for him to prejudge either himself or other people, and that therefore he was guilty of no lie when he was afterwards detected in the maintenance of similar errors. This plea, however, he does not advance, not only because it is a ridiculous one, but because it cannot possibly be true; because in these very books of his he both argues against the transmission of sin from Adam to infants, and glories in the proceedings of the Synod in Palestine, where he was supposed to have sincerely anathematized such as hold the opinions in dispute, and where he, in fact, stole his acquittal by practising deceit.

CHAPTER XVI

PELAGIUS' FRAUDULENT AND CRAFTY EXCUSES

For what is the significance to the matter with which we now have to do of his answers to his followers, when he tells them that "the reason why he condemned the points which were objected against him, is because he himself maintains that that primal sin was injurious not only to the first man, but to the whole human race, not by transmission, but by example;" in other words, not because those who have been propagated from him have derived any fault from him, but because all who afterwards have sinned, have imitated him who committed the first sin? Or when he says that "the reason why infants are not in the same state in which Adam was before the transgression, is because they are not yet able to receive the commandment, whereas he was able; and because they do not yet make use of that choice of a rational will which he certainly made use of, since otherwise no commandment would have been given to him"? How does such an exposition as this of the points alleged against him justify him in thinking that he rightly condemned the propositions, "Adam's sin injured only himself, and not the whole race of man;" and "infants at their birth are in the self-same state in which Adam was before he sinned;" and that by the said condemnation he is not guilty of deceit in holding such opinions as are found in his subsequent writings, how that "infants are born without any evil or fault, and that there is nothing in them but what God has formed"—no wound, in short, inflicted by an enemy?

CHAPTER XVII

HOW PELAGIUS DECEIVED HIS JUDGES

Now, is it by making such statements as these, meeting objections which are urged in one sense with explanations which are meant in another, that he designs to prove to us that he did not deceive those who sat in judgment on him? Then he utterly fails in his purpose. In proportion to the craftiness of his explanations, was the stealthiness with which he deceived them. For, just because they were Catholic bishops, when they heard the man pouring out anathemas upon those who maintained that "Adam's sin was injurious to none but himself, and not to the human race," they understood him to assert nothing but what the Catholic Church has been accustomed to declare, on the ground of which it truly baptizes infants for the remission of sins—not, indeed, sins which they have committed by imitation owing to the example of the first sinner, but sins which they have contracted by their very birth, owing to the corruption of their origin. When, again, they heard him anathematizing those who assert that "infants at their birth are in the same state in which Adam was before the transgression," they supposed him to refer to none others than those persons who "think that infants have derived no sin from Adam, and that they are accordingly in that state that he was in before his sin." For, of course, no other objection would be brought against him than that on which the question turned. When, therefore, he so explains the objection as to say that infants are not in the same state that Adam was in before he sinned, simply because they have not yet arrived at the same firmness of mind or body, not because of any propagated fault that has passed on to them, he must be answered thus: "When the objections were laid against you for condemnation, the Catholic bishops did not understand them in this sense; therefore, when you condemned them, they believed that you were a Catholic. That, accordingly, which they supposed you to maintain, deserved to be released from censure; but that which you really maintained was worthy of condemnation. It was not you, then, that were acquitted, who held tenets which ought to be condemned; but that opinion was freed from censure which you ought to have held and maintained. You could only be supposed to be acquitted by having been believed to entertain opinions worthy to be praised; for your judges could not suppose that you were concealing opinions which merited condemnation. Rightly have you been adjudged an accomplice of Coelestius, in whose opinions you prove yourself to be a sharer. And though you kept your books shut during your trial, you published them to the world after it was over."

CHAPTER XVIII

THE CONDEMNATION OF PELAGIUS

This being the case, you of course feel that episcopal councils, and the Apostolic See, and the whole Roman Church, and the Roman Empire itself,[15] which by God's gracious favor has become Christian, has been most righteously moved against the authors of this wicked error, until they repent and escape from the snares of the devil. For who can tell whether God may not give them repentance to discover, and acknowledge, and even proclaim His truth,[16] and to condemn their own damnable error? But whatever may be the bent of their own will, we cannot doubt that the merciful kindness of the Lord has sought the good of many persons who followed them, for no other reason than because they saw them associated in communion with the Catholic Church.

CHAPTER XIX

PELAGIUS' ATTEMPT TO DECEIVE THE APOSTOLIC SEE; HE INVERTS THE BEARINGS OF THE CONTROVERSY

But I would have you carefully observe the way in which Pelagius endeavored by deception to overreach even the judgment of the bishop of the Apostolic See on this very question of the baptism of infants. He sent a letter to Rome to Pope Innocent of blessed memory; and when it found him not in the flesh, it was handed to the holy Pope Zosimus, and by him directed to us. In this letter he complains of being "defamed by certain persons for refusing the sacrament of baptism to infants, and promising the kingdom of heaven irrespective of Christ's redemption." The objections, however, are not urged against them in the manner he has stated. For they neither deny the sacrament of baptism to infants, nor do they promise the kingdom of heaven to any irrespective of the redemption of Christ. As regards, therefore, his complaint of being defamed by sundry persons, he has set it forth in such terms as to be able to give a ready answer to the alleged charge against him, without injury to his own dogma. The real objection against them is, that they refuse to confess that unbaptized infants are liable to the condemnation of the first man, and that original sin has been transmitted to them and requires to be purged by regeneration; their contention being that infants must be baptized solely for being admitted

---

[15] Possidius, in his *Life of Augustine*, ch. 18, says: "Even the most pious Emperor Honorius, upon hearing that the weighty sentence of the Catholic Church of God had been pronounced against them, in pursuance of the same, determined that they should be regarded as heretics, under condemnation by his own laws." These enactments are printed by the Benedictine editors in the second part of their Appendix.

[16] 2 Tim. ii. 25, 26

into the kingdom of heaven, as if they could only have eternal death apart from the kingdom of heaven, who cannot have eternal life without partaking of the Lord's body and blood. This, I would have you know, is the real objection to them respecting the baptism of infants; and not as he has represented it, for the purpose of enabling himself to save his own dogmas while answering what is actually a proposition of his own, under color of meeting an objection.

CHAPTER XX

PELAGIUS PROVIDES A REFUGE FOR HIS FALSEHOOD IN AMBIGUOUS SUBTERFUGES

And then observe how he makes his answer, how he provides in the obscure mazes of his double sense retreats for his false doctrine, quenching the truth in his dark mist of error; so that even we, on our first perusal of his words, almost rejoiced at their propriety and correctness. But the fuller discussions in his books, in which he is generally forced, in spite of all his efforts at concealment, to explain his meaning, have made even his better statements suspicious to us, lest on a closer inspection of them we should detect them to be ambiguous. For, after saying that "he had never heard even an impious heretic say this" (namely, what he set forth as the objection) "about infants," he goes on to ask: "Who indeed is so unacquainted with Gospel lessons, as not only to attempt to make such an affirmation, but even to be able lightly to say it or even let it enter his thought? And then who is so impious as to wish to exclude infants from the kingdom of heaven, by forbidding them to be baptized and to be born again in Christ?"

CHAPTER XXI

PELAGIUS AVOIDS THE QUESTION AS TO WHY BAPTISM IS NECESSARY FOR INFANTS

Now it is to no purpose that he says all this. He does not clear himself thereby. Not even they have ever denied the impossibility of infants entering the kingdom of heaven without baptism. But this is not the question; what we are discussing concerns the obliteration of original sin in infants. Let him clear himself on this point, since he refuses to acknowledge that there is anything in infants which the laver of regeneration has to cleanse. On this account we ought carefully to consider what he has afterwards to say. After adducing, then, the passage of the Gospel which declares that "whosoever is not born again of water and the Spirit cannot enter into the kingdom of heaven" [17] (on which matter, as we have said, they raise no question), he goes on at once to ask: "Who indeed is so impious as to

[17] John iii. 5

have the heart to refuse the common redemption of the human race to an infant of any age whatever?" But this is ambiguous language; for what *redemption* does he mean? Is it from evil to good? or from good to better? Now even Coelestius, at Carthage, allowed a redemption for infants in his book; although, at the same time, he would not admit the transmission of sin to them from Adam.

CHAPTER XXII

ANOTHER INSTANCE OF PELAGIUS' AMBIGUITY

Then, again, observe what he subjoins to the last remark: "Can any one," says he, "forbid a second birth to an eternal and certain life, to him who has been born to this present uncertain life?" In other words: "Who is so impious as to forbid his being born again to the life which is sure and eternal, who has been born to this life of uncertainty?" When we first read these words, we supposed that by the phrase "uncertain life" he meant to designate this present temporal life; although it appeared to us that he ought rather to have called it "mortal" than "uncertain," because it is brought to a close by certain death. But for all this, we thought that he had only shown a preference for calling this mortal life an *uncertain* one, because of the general view which men take that there is undoubtedly not a moment in our lives when we are free from this uncertainty. And so it happened that our anxiety about him was allayed to some extent by the following consideration, which rose almost to a proof, notwithstanding the fact of his unwillingness openly to confess that infants incur eternal death who depart this life without the sacrament of baptism. We argued: "If, as he seems to admit, eternal life can only accrue to them who have been baptized, it follows of course that they who die unbaptized incur everlasting death. This destiny, however, cannot by any means justly befall those who never in this life committed any sins of their own, unless on account of original sin."

CHAPTER XXIII

WHAT HE MEANS BY OUR BIRTH TO AN "UNCERTAIN" LIFE

Certain brethren, however, afterwards failed not to remind us that Pelagius possibly expressed himself in this way, because on this question he is represented as having his answer ready for all inquirers, to this effect: "As for infants who die unbaptized, I know indeed whither they go not; yet whither they go, I know not;" that is, I know they do not go into the kingdom of heaven. But as to whither they go, he was (and for the matter of that, *still is*) in the habit of saying that he knew not, because he dared not say that those went to eternal death, who he was persuaded had never committed sin in this life, and whom he would not admit to have inherited original sin. Consequently those very words of his which were forwarded to Rome to secure his absolute acquittal, are so steeped in ambiguity that they afford a shelter for their doctrine, out of which may sally forth an heretical sense to entrap the unwary straggler; for when no one is at hand who can give the answer, any solitary man may find himself weak.

CHAPTER XXIV

PELAGIUS' LONG RESIDENCE AT ROME

The truth indeed is, that in the book of his faith which he sent to Rome with this very letter[18] to the before-mentioned Pope Innocent, to whom also he had written the letter, he only the more evidently exposed himself by his efforts at concealment. He says:[19] "We hold one baptism, which we say ought to be administered in the same sacramental words in the case of infants as in the case of adults." He did not, however, say, "in the same sacrament" (although if he had so said, there would still have been ambiguity), but "in the same sacramental words"—as if remission of sins in infants were declared by the sound of the words, and not wrought by the effect of the acts. For the time, indeed, he seemed to say what was agreeable with the Catholic Faith; but he had it not in his power permanently to deceive that see. Subsequent to the rescript of the African Council, into which province this pestilent doctrine had stealthily made its way—without, however, spreading widely or sinking deeply—other opinions also of this man were by the industry of some faithful brethren discovered and brought to light at Rome, where he had dwelt for a very long while, and had already engaged in sundry discourses and controversies. In order to procure the condemnation of these opinions, Pope Zosimus, as you may read, annexed them to his letter, which he wrote for publication throughout the Catholic world. Among these statements, Pelagius, pretending to expound the Apostle Paul's *Epistle to the Romans,* argues in these words: "If Adam's sin injured those who have not sinned, then also Christ's righteousness profits those who do not believe." He says other things, too, of the same purport; but they have all been refuted and answered by me with the Lord's help in the books which I wrote, *On the Baptism of Infants.* But he had not the courage to make those objectionable statements in his own person in the fore-mentioned so-called exposition. This particular one, however, having been enunciated in a place where he was so well known, his words and their meaning could not be disguised. In those books, from the first of which I have already before quoted,[20] he treats this point without any suppression of his views. With all the energy of which he is capable, he most plainly asserts that human nature in infants cannot in any wise be supposed to be corrupted by propagation; and by claiming salvation for them as their due, he does despite to the Saviour.

[18] See above, ch. 19   [19] See above, ch. 1, and *On the Grace of Christ,* ch. 35   [20] In ch. 14

CHAPTER XXV

THE CONDEMNATION OF PELAGIUS AND COELESTIUS

These things, then, being as I have stated them, it is now evident that there has arisen a deadly heresy, which, with the Lord's help, the Church by this time guards against more directly—now that those two men, Pelagius and Coelestius, have been either offered repentance, or on their refusal been wholly condemned. They are reported, or perhaps actually proved, to be the authors of this perversion; at all events, if not the authors (as having learnt it from others), they are yet its boasted abettors and teachers, through whose agency the heresy has advanced and grown to a wider extent. This boast, too, is made even in their own statements and writings, and in unmistakable signs of reality, as well as in the fame which arises and grows out of all these circumstances. What, therefore, remains to be done? Must not every Catholic, with all the energies wherewith the Lord endows him, confute this pestilential doctrine, and oppose it with all vigilance; so that whenever we contend for the truth, compelled to answer, but not fond of the contest, the untaught may be instructed, and that thus the Church may be benefited by that which the enemy devised for her destruction; in accordance with that word of the apostle's, "There must be heresies, that they which are approved may be made manifest among you"? [21]

CHAPTER XXVI

THE PELAGIANS MAINTAIN THAT RAISING QUESTIONS ABOUT ORIGINAL SIN DOES NOT ENDANGER THE FAITH

Therefore, after the full discussion with which we have been able to rebut in writing this error of theirs, which is so inimical to the grace of God bestowed on small and great through our Lord Jesus Christ, it is now our duty to examine and explode that assertion of theirs, which in their desire to avoid the odious imputation of heresy they astutely advance, to the effect that "calling this subject into question produces no danger to the faith"— in order that they may appear, forsooth, if they are convicted of having deviated from it, to have erred not criminally, but only, as it were, courteously. This, accordingly, is the language which Coelestius used in the ecclesiastical process at Carthage:[22] "As touching the transmission of sin," he said, "I have already said that I have heard many persons of acknowledged position in the Catholic Church deny it, and on the other hand many affirm it; it may fairly, indeed, be deemed a matter for inquiry, but not a heresy. I have always maintained that infants require baptism, and ought to be

[21] 1 Cor. xi. 19   [22] See above, ch. 3

baptized. What else does he want?" He said this, as if he wanted to intimate that only then could he be deemed chargeable with heresy, if he were
to assert that they ought not to be baptized. As the case stood, however,
inasmuch as he acknowledged that they ought to be baptized, he thought
that he had not erred [criminally], and therefore ought not to be adjudged
a heretic, even though he maintained the reason of their baptism to be
other than the truth holds, or the faith claims as its own. On the same principle, in the book which he sent to Rome, he first explained his belief, so
far as it suited his pleasure, from the Trinity of the One Godhead down
to the kind of resurrection of the dead that is to be; on all which points,
however, no one had ever questioned him, or been questioned by him. And
when his discourse reached the question which was under consideration, he
said: "If, indeed, any questions have arisen beyond the compass of the
faith, on which there might be perhaps dissension on the part of a great
many persons, in no case have I pretended to pronounce a decision on any
dogma, as if I possessed a definitive authority in the matter myself; but
whatever I have derived from the fountain of the prophets and the apostles,
I have presented for approbation to the judgment of your apostolic office;
so that if any error has crept in among us, human as we are, through our
ignorance, it may be corrected by your sentence." [23] You of course clearly
see that in this action of his he used all this deprecatory preamble in order
that, if he had been discovered to have erred at all, he might seem to have
erred not on a matter of faith, but on questionable points outside the faith;
wherein, however necessary it may be to correct the error, it is not corrected
as a heresy; wherein also the person who undergoes the correction is declared indeed to be in error, but for all that is not adjudged a heretic.

CHAPTER XXVII

ON QUESTIONS OUTSIDE THE FAITH—WHAT THEY ARE, AND INSTANCES OF THE SAME

But he is greatly mistaken in this opinion. The questions which he supposes to be outside the faith are of a very different character from those in
which, without any detriment to the faith whereby we are Christians, there
exists either an ignorance of the real fact, and a consequent suspension of
any fixed opinion, or else a conjectural view of the case, which, owing to
the infirmity of human thought, issues in conceptions at variance with
truth: as when a question arises about the description and locality of that
Paradise where God placed man whom He formed out of the ground, without any disturbance, however, of the Christian belief that there undoubtedly is such a Paradise; or as when it is asked where Elijah is at the
present moment, and where Enoch—whether in this Paradise or in some

[23] See above, ch. 6

other place, although we doubt not of their existing still in the same bodies in which they were born; or as when one inquires whether it was in the body or out of the body that the apostle was caught up to the third heaven—an inquiry, however, which betokens great lack of modesty on the part of those who would fain know what he who is the subject of the mystery itself expressly declares his ignorance of,[24] without impairing his own belief of the fact; or as when the question is started, how many are those heavens, to the "third" of which he tells us that he was caught up; or whether the elements of this visible world are four or more; what it is which causes those eclipses of the sun or the moon which astronomers are in the habit of foretelling for certain appointed seasons; why, again, men of ancient times lived to the age which Holy Scripture assigns to them; and whether the period of their puberty, when they begat their first son, was postponed to an older age, proportioned to their longer life; or where Methuselah could possibly have lived, since he was not in the Ark, inasmuch as (according to the chronological notes of most copies of the Scripture, both Greek and Latin) he is found to have survived the deluge; or whether we must follow the order of the fewer copies—and they happen to be extremely few—which so arrange the years as to show that he died before the deluge. Now who does not feel, amidst the various and innumerable questions of this sort, which relate either to God's most hidden operations or to most obscure passages of the Scriptures, and which it is difficult to embrace and define in any certain way, that ignorance may on many points be compatible with sound Christian faith, and that occasionally erroneous opinions may be entertained without any room for the imputation of heretical doctrine?

CHAPTER XXVIII

THE HERESY OF PELAGIUS AND COELESTIUS AIMS AT THE VERY FOUNDATIONS OF OUR FAITH

This is, however, in the matter of the two men by one of whom we are sold under sin,[25] by the other redeemed from sins—by the one have been precipitated into death, by the other are liberated unto life; the former of whom has ruined us in himself, by doing his own will instead of His who created him; the latter has saved us in Himself, by not doing His own will, but the will of Him who sent Him:[26] and it is in what concerns these two men that the Christian faith properly consists. For "there is one God, and one Mediator between God and men, the man Christ Jesus;"[27] since "there is none other name under heaven given to men, whereby we must be saved;"[28] and "in Him hath God defined unto all men their faith, in that He hath raised Him from the dead."[29] Now without this faith, that is to say, without a belief in the one Mediator between God and men, the man

[24] 2 Cor. xii. 2 [25] Rom. vii. 14 [26] John iv. 34, v. 30 [27] 1 Tim. ii. 5 [28] Acts iv. 12 [29] Acts xvii. 31

Christ Jesus; without faith, I say, in His resurrection, by which God has given assurance to all men, and which no man could of course truly believe, were it not for His incarnation and death; without faith, therefore, in the incarnation and death and resurrection of Christ, the Christian verity unhesitatingly declares that the ancient saints could not possibly have been cleansed from sin, so as to have become holy, and justified by the grace of God. And this is true both of the saints who are mentioned in Holy Scripture, and of those also who are not indeed mentioned therein, but must yet be supposed to have existed—either before the deluge, or in the interval between that event and the giving of the law, or in the period of the law itself —not merely among the children of Israel, as the prophets, but even outside that nation, as for instance Job. For it was by the self-same faith in the one Mediator that the hearts of these, too, were cleansed, and there also was "shed abroad in them the love of God by the Holy Ghost," [30] "who bloweth where He listeth," [31] not following men's merits, but even producing these very merits Himself. For the grace of God will in no wise exist unless it be wholly free.

CHAPTER XXIX

THE RIGHTEOUS MEN WHO LIVED IN THE TIME OF THE LAW WERE FOR ALL THAT NOT UNDER THE LAW, BUT UNDER GRACE. THE GRACE OF THE NEW TESTAMENT HIDDEN UNDER THE OLD

Death indeed reigned from Adam until Moses,[32] because it was not possible even for the law given through Moses to overcome it: it was not given, in fact, as something able to give life;[33] but as something that ought to show those that were dead and for whom grace was needed to give them life, that they were not only prostrated under the propagation and domination of sin, but also convicted by the additional guilt of breaking the law itself: not in order that any one might perish who in the mercy of God understood this even in that early age; but that, destined though he was to punishment, owing to the dominion of death, and manifested, too, as guilty through his own violation of the law, he might seek God's help, and so where sin abounded, grace might much more abound,[34] even the grace which alone delivers from the body of this death.[35] Yet, notwithstanding this, although not even the law which Moses gave was able to liberate any man from the dominion of death, there were even then, too, at the time of the law, men of God who were not living under the terror and conviction and punishment of the law, but under the delight and healing and liberation of grace. Some there were who said, "I was shapen in iniquity, and in sin did my mother conceive me;" [36] and, "There is no rest in my bones, by rea-

---

[30] Rom. v. 5   [31] John iii. 8   [32] Rom. v. 14   [33] Gal. iii. 21   [34] Rom. v. 20
[35] Rom. vii. 24, 25   [36] Ps. li. 5

son of my sins;" [37] and, "Create in me a clean heart, O God; and renew a right spirit in my inward parts;" [38] and, "Stablish me with Thy directing Spirit;" [39] and, "Take not Thy Holy Spirit from me." [40] There were some, again, who said: "I believed, therefore have I spoken." [41] For they too were cleansed with the self-same faith with which we ourselves are. Whence the apostle also says: "We having the same spirit of faith, according as it is written, I believe, and therefore have I spoken; we also believe, and therefore speak." [42] Out of very faith was it said, "Behold, a virgin shall conceive and bear a son, and they shall call His name Emmanuel," [43] "which is, being interpreted, God with us." [44] Out of very faith too was it said concerning Him: "As a bridegroom He cometh out of His chamber; as a giant did He exult to run His course. His going forth is from the extremity of heaven, and His circuit runs to the other end of heaven; and no one is hidden from His heat." [45] Out of very faith, again, was it said to Him: "Thy throne, O God, is for ever and ever; a sceptre of righteousness is the sceptre of Thy kingdom. Thou hast loved righteousness, and hated iniquity; therefore God, Thy God, hath anointed Thee with the oil of gladness above Thy fellows." [46] By the self-same Spirit of faith were all these things foreseen by them as to happen, whereby they are believed by us as having happened. They, indeed, who were able in faithful love to foretell these things to us were not themselves partakers of them. The Apostle Peter says, "Why tempt ye God to put a yoke upon the neck of the disciples, which neither our fathers nor we were able to bear? But we believe that through the grace of the Lord Jesus Christ we shall be saved, even as they." [47] Now on what principle does he make this statement, if it be not because even they were saved through the grace of the Lord Jesus Christ, and not the law of Moses, from which comes not the cure, but only the knowledge of sin? [48] Now, however, the righteousness of God without the law is manifested, being witnessed by the law and the prophets.[49] If, therefore, it is now manifested, it even then existed, but it was hidden. This concealment was symbolized by the veil of the temple. When Christ was dying, this veil was rent asunder,[50] to signify the full revelation of Him. Even of old, therefore, there existed amongst the people of God this grace of the one Mediator between God and men, the man Christ Jesus; but like the rain in the fleece which God sets apart for His inheritance,[51] not of debt, but of His own will, it was latently present, but is now patently visible amongst all nations as its "floor," the fleece being dry—in other words, the Jewish people having become reprobate.[52]

[37] Ps. xxxviii. 3   [38] Ps. li. 10   [39] Ps. li. 12   [40] Ps. li. 11   [41] Ps. cxvi. 10   [42] 2 Cor. iv. 13   [43] Isa. vii. 14   [44] Matt. i. 23   [45] Ps. xix. 5, 6   [46] Ps. xlv. 6, 7   [47] Acts xv. 10, 11   [48] Rom. iii. 20   [49] Rom. iii. 21   [50] Matt. xxvii. 51   [51] Ps. lxviii. 9   [52] Judg. vi. 36-40

CHAPTER XXX

PELAGIUS AND COELESTIUS DENY THAT THE ANCIENT SAINTS WERE SAVED BY CHRIST

We must not therefore divide the times, as Pelagius and his disciples do, who say that men first lived righteously by nature, then under the law, thirdly under grace—by nature meaning all the long time from Adam before the giving of the law. "For then," say they, "the Creator was known by the guidance of reason; and the rule of living rightly was carried written in the hearts of men, not in the law of the letter, but of nature. But men's manners became corrupt; and then," they say, "when nature now tarnished began to be insufficient, the law was added to it, whereby as by a moon the original lustre was restored to nature after its blush was impaired. But after the habit of sinning had too much prevailed among men, and the law was unequal to the task of curing it, Christ came; and the Physician Himself, through His own self, and not through His disciples, brought relief to the malady at its most desperate development."

CHAPTER XXXI

CHRIST'S INCARNATION WAS OF AVAIL TO THE FATHERS, EVEN THOUGH IT HAD NOT YET HAPPENED

By disputation of this sort, they attempt to exclude the ancient saints from the grace of the Mediator, as if the man Christ Jesus were not the Mediator between God and *those men;* on the ground that, not having yet taken flesh of the Virgin's womb, He was not yet man at the time when those righteous men lived. If this, however, were true, in vain would the apostle say: "By man came death, by man came also the resurrection of the dead; for as in Adam all die, even so in Christ shall all be made alive." [53] For inasmuch as those ancient saints, according to the vain conceits of these men, found their nature self-sufficient, and required not the man Christ to be their Mediator to reconcile them to God, so neither shall they be made alive in Him, to whose body they are shown not to belong as members, according to the statement that it was on man's account that He became man. If, however, as the Truth says through His apostles, even as all die in Adam, even so shall all be made alive in Christ; forasmuch as the resurrection of the dead comes through the one man, even as death comes through the other man; what Christian man can be bold enough to doubt that even those righteous men who pleased God in the more remote periods of the human race are destined to attain to the resurrection of eternal life, and not eternal death, because they shall be made alive in Christ? that they

[53] 1 Cor. xv, 21, 22

are made alive in Christ, because they belong to the body of Christ? that
they belong to the body of Christ, because Christ is the head even to
them? [54] and that Christ is the head even to them, because there is but one
Mediator between God and men, the man Christ Jesus? But this He
could not have been to them, unless through His grace they had believed in
His resurrection. And how could they have done this, if they had been ignorant that He was to come in the flesh, and if they had not by this faith
lived justly and piously? Now, if the incarnation of Christ could be of no
concern to them, on the ground that it had not yet come about, it must follow that Christ's judgment can be of no concern to us, because it has not
yet taken place. But if we shall stand at the right hand of Christ through
our faith in His judgment, which has not yet transpired, but is to come
to pass, it follows that those ancient saints are members of Christ through
their faith in His resurrection, which had not in their day happened, but
which was one day to come to pass.

CHAPTER XXXII

HE SHOWS BY THE EXAMPLE OF ABRAHAM THAT THE ANCIENT
SAINTS BELIEVED IN THE INCARNATION OF CHRIST

For it must not be supposed that those saints of old only profited by
Christ's divinity, which was ever existent, and not also by the revelation
of His humanity, which had not yet come to pass. What the Lord Jesus
says, "Abraham desired to see my day, and he saw it, and was glad," [55]
meaning by the phrase *his day* to understand *his time*, affords of course a
clear testimony that Abraham was fully imbued with belief in His incarnation. It is in respect of this that He has a "time;" for His divinity exceeds
all time, for it was by IT that all times were created. If, however, any one
supposes that the phrase in question must be understood of that eternal
"day" which is limited by no morrow, and preceded by no yesterday—in
a word, of the very eternity in which He is co-eternal with the Father
—how would Abraham really desire this, unless he was aware that there
was to be a future mortality belonging to Him whose eternity he wished
for? Or, perhaps, some one would confine the meaning of the phrase so far
as to say, that nothing else is meant in the Lord's saying, "He desired to
see my day," than "He desired to see me," who am the never-ending Day,
or the unfailing Light, as when we mention the life of the Son, concerning
which it is said in the Gospel: "So hath He given to the Son to have life
in Himself." [56] Here the life is nothing less than Himself. So we understand the Son Himself to be the life, when He said, "I am the way, the
truth, and the life;" [57] of whom also it was said, "He is the true God, and
eternal life." [58] Supposing, then, that Abraham desired to see this equal

---

[54] 1 Cor. xi. 3   [55] John viii. 56   [56] John v. 26   [57] John xiv. 6   [58] 1 John v. 20

divinity of the Son's with the Father, without any precognition of His coming in the flesh—as certain philosophers sought Him, who knew nothing of His flesh—can that other act of Abraham, when he orders his servant to place his hand under his thigh, and to swear by the God of heaven,[59] be rightly understood by any one otherwise than as showing that Abraham well knew that the flesh in which the God of heaven was to come was the offspring of that very thigh?

CHAPTER XXXIII

HOW CHRIST IS OUR MEDIATOR

Of this flesh and blood Melchizedek also, when he blessed Abram himself,[60] gave the testimony which is very well known to Christian believers, so that long afterwards it was said to Christ in the *Psalms:* "Thou art a Priest for ever, after the order of Melchizedek." [61] This was not then an accomplished fact, but was still future; yet that faith of the fathers, which is the self-same faith as our own, used to chant it. Now, to all who find death in Adam, Christ is of this avail, that He is the Mediator for life. He is, however, not a Mediator, because He is equal with the Father; for in this respect He is Himself as far distant from us as the Father; and how can there be any medium where the distance is the very same? Therefore the apostle does not say, "There is one Mediator between God and men, even Jesus Christ;" but his words are, "The MAN Christ Jesus." [62] He is the Mediator, then, in that He is man—inferior to the Father, by so much as He is nearer to ourselves, and superior to us, by so much as He is nearer to the Father. This is more openly expressed thus: "He is inferior to the Father, because in the form of a servant;" [63] superior to us, because without spot of sin.

CHAPTER XXXIV

NO MAN EVER SAVED SAVE BY CHRIST

Now, whoever maintains that human nature at any period required not the second Adam for its physician, because it was not corrupted in the first Adam, is convicted as an enemy to the grace of God; not in a question where doubt or error might be compatible with soundness of belief, but in that very rule of faith which makes us Christians. How happens it, then, that the human nature, which first existed, is praised by these men as being so far less tainted with evil manners? How is it that they overlook the fact that men were even then sunk in so many intolerable sins, that, with the exception of one man of God and his wife, and three sons and their wives,

---

[59] Gen. xxiv. 2, 3   [60] Gen. xiv. 18-20   [61] Ps. cx. 4   [62] 1 Tim. ii. 5   [63] Phil. ii. 7

the whole world was in God's just judgment destroyed by the flood, even as the little land of Sodom was afterwards with fire? [64] From the moment, then, when "by one man sin entered into the world, and death by sin, and so death passed upon all men, in whom all sinned," [65] the entire mass of our nature was ruined beyond doubt, and fell into the possession of its destroyer. And from him no one—no, not one—has been delivered, or is being delivered, or ever will be delivered, except by the grace of the Redeemer.

CHAPTER XXXV

WHY THE CIRCUMCISION OF INFANTS WAS ENJOINED UNDER PAIN OF SO GREAT A PUNISHMENT

The Scripture does not inform us whether before Abraham's time righteous men or their children were marked by any bodily or visible sign. Abraham himself, indeed, received the sign of circumcision, a seal of the righteousness of faith.[66] And he received it with this accompanying injunction: All the male infants of his household were from that very time to be circumcised, while fresh from their mother's womb, on the eighth day from their birth;[67] so that even they who were not yet able with the heart to believe unto righteousness, should nevertheless receive the seal of the righteousness of faith. And this command was imposed with so fearful a sanction, that God said: "That soul shall be cut off from his people, whose flesh of his foreskin is not circumcised on the eighth day." [68] If inquiry be made into the justice of so terrible a penalty, will not the entire argument of these men about free will, and the laudable soundness and purity of nature, however cleverly maintained, fall to pieces, struck down and fractured to atoms? For, pray tell me, what evil has an infant committed of his own will, that, for the negligence of another in not circumcising him, he himself must be condemned, and with so severe a condemnation, that the soul must be cut off from his people? It was not of any temporal death that this fear was inflicted, since of righteous persons, when they died, it used rather to be said, "And he was gathered unto his people;" [69] or, "He was gathered to his fathers:" [70] for no attempt to separate a man from his people is long formidable to him, when his own people is itself the people of God.

CHAPTER XXXVI

THE PLATONISTS' OPINION ABOUT THE EXISTENCE OF THE SOUL PREVIOUS TO THE BODY REJECTED

What, then, is the purport of so severe a condemnation, when no wilful sin has been committed? For it is not as certain Platonists have thought,

---

[64] See Gen. vii. and xix.   [65] Rom. v. 12   [66] Rom. iv. 11   [67] Gen. xvii. 10
[68] Gen. xvii. 14   [69] Gen. xxv. 17   [70] 1 Macc. ii. 69

because every such infant is thus requited in his soul for what it did of its own wilfulness previous to the present life, as having possessed previous to its present bodily state a free choice of living either well or ill; since the Apostle Paul says most plainly, that before they were born they did neither good nor evil.[71] On what account, therefore, is an infant rightly punished with such ruin, if it be not because he belongs to the mass of perdition, and is properly regarded as born of Adam, condemned under the bond of the ancient debt unless he has been released from the bond, not according to debt, but according to grace? And what grace but God's, through our Lord Jesus Christ? Now there was a forecast of His coming undoubtedly contained not only in other sacred institutions of the ancient Jews, but also in their circumcision of the foreskin. For the eighth day, in the recurrence of weeks, became the Lord's day, on which the Lord arose from the dead; and Christ was the rock [72] whence was formed the stony blade for the circumcision;[73] and the flesh of the foreskin was the body of sin.

CHAPTER XXXVII

IN WHAT SENSE CHRIST IS CALLED "SIN"

There was a change of the sacramental ordinances made after the coming of Him whose advent they prefigured; but there was no change in the Mediator's help, who, even previous to His coming in the flesh, all along delivered the ancient members of His body by their faith in His incarnation; and in respect of ourselves too, though we were dead in sins and in the uncircumcision of our flesh, we are quickened together in Christ, in whom we are circumcised with the circumcision not made with the hand,[74] but such as was prefigured by the old manual circumcision, that the body of sin might be done away[75] which was born with us from Adam. The propagation of a condemned origin condemns us, unless we are cleansed by the likeness of sinful flesh, in which He was sent without sin, who nevertheless concerning sin condemned sin, having been made sin for us.[76] Accordingly the apostle says "We beseech you in Christ's stead, be ye reconciled unto God. For He hath made Him to be sin for us, who knew no sin; that we might be made the righteousness of God in Him." [77] God, therefore, to whom we are reconciled, has made Him to be sin for us—that is to say, a sacrifice by which our sins may be remitted; for by sins are designated the sacrifices for sins. And indeed He was sacrificed for our sins, the only one among men who had no sins, even as in those early times one was sought for among the flocks to prefigure the Faultless One who was to come to heal our offences. On whatever day, therefore, an infant may be baptized after his birth, he is as if circumcised on the eighth day; inasmuch as he is cir-

[71] Rom. ix. 11   [72] 1 Cor. x. 4   [73] Ex. iv. 25   [74] Col. ii. 11, 13   [75] Rom. vi. 6
[76] Rom. viii. 3 and Gal. iii. 13   [77] 2 Cor. v. 20, 21

cumcised in Him who rose again the third day indeed after He was crucified, but the eighth according to the weeks. He is circumcised for the
putting off of the body of sin; in other words, that the grace of spiritual regeneration may do away with the debt which the contagion of carnal generation contracted. "For no one is pure from uncleanness" (what uncleanness,
pray, but that of sin?) "not even the infant, whose life is but that of a
single day upon the earth." [78]

CHAPTER XXXVIII

ORIGINAL SIN DOES NOT RENDER MARRIAGE EVIL

But they argue thus, saying: "Is not, then, marriage an evil, and the
man that is produced by marriage not God's work?" As if the good of the
married life were that disease of concupiscence with which they who know
not God love their wives—a course which the apostle forbids; [79] and not
rather that conjugal chastity, by which carnal lust is reduced to the good
purposes of the appointed procreation of children. Or as if, forsooth, a man
could possibly be anything but God's work, not only when born in wedlock,
but even if he be produced in fornication or adultery. In the present inquiry, however, when the question is not for what a Creator is necessary,
but for what a Saviour, we have not to consider what good there is in the
procreation of nature, but what evil there is in sin, whereby our nature
has been certainly corrupted. No doubt the two are generated simultaneously—both nature and nature's corruption; one of which is good, the
other evil. The one comes to us from the bounty of the Creator, the other
is contracted from the condemnation of our origin; the one has its cause
in the good-will of the Supreme God, the other in the depraved will of the
first man; the one exhibits God as the maker of the creature, the other exhibits God as the punisher of disobedience: in short, the very same Christ
was the *maker* of man for the creation of the one, and was *made* man for
the healing of the other.

CHAPTER XXXIX

THREE THINGS GOOD AND LAUDABLE IN MATRIMONY

Marriage, therefore, is a good in all the things which are proper to the
married state. And these are three: it is the ordained means of procreation,
it is the guarantee of chastity, it is the bond of union. In respect of its ordination for generation the Scripture says, "I will therefore that the younger
women marry, bear children, guide the house;" [80] as regards its guarantee-
ing chastity, it is said of it, "The wife hath not power of her own body,
but the husband; and likewise also the husband hath not power of his own

---

[78] Job xiv. 4, 5   [79] i Thess. iv. 5   [80] i Tim. v. 14

body, but the wife;" [81] and considered as the bond of union: "What God hath joined together, let not man put asunder." [82] Touching these points, we do not forget that we have treated at sufficient length, with whatever ability the Lord has given us, in other works of ours, which are not unknown to you.[83] In relation to them all the Scripture has this general praise: "Marriage is honorable in all, and the bed undefiled." [84] For, inasmuch as the wedded state is good, insomuch does it produce a very large amount of good in respect of the evil of concupiscence; for it is not lust, but reason, which makes a good use of concupiscence. Now lust lies in that law of the "disobedient" members which the apostle notes as "warring against the law of the mind;" [85] whereas reason lies in that law of the wedded state which makes good use of concupiscence. If, however, it were impossible for any good to arise out of evil, God could not create man out of the embraces of adultery. As, therefore, the damnable evil of adultery, whenever man is born in it, is not chargeable on God, who certainly amidst man's evil work actually produces a good work; so, likewise, all which causes shame in that rebellion of the members which brought the accusing blush on those who after their sin covered these members with the fig-tree leaves,[86] is not laid to the charge of marriage, by virtue of which the conjugal embrace is not only allowable, but is even useful and honorable; but it is imputable to the sin of that disobedience which was followed by the penalty of man's finding his own members emulating against himself that very disobedience which he had practised against God. Then, abashed at their action, since they moved no more at the bidding of his rational will, but at their own arbitrary choice as it were, instigated by lust, he devised the covering which should conceal such of them as he judged to be worthy of shame. For man, as the handiwork of God, deserved not confusion of face; nor were the members which it seemed fit to the Creator to form and appoint by any means designed to bring the blush to the creature. Accordingly, that simple nudity was displeasing neither to God nor to man: there was nothing to be ashamed of, because nothing at first accrued which deserved punishment.

CHAPTER XL

MARRIAGE EXISTED BEFORE SIN WAS COMMITTED. HOW GOD'S BLESSING OPERATED IN OUR FIRST PARENTS

There was, however, undoubtedly marriage, even when sin had no prior existence; and for no other reason was it that woman, and not a second man, was created as a help for the man. Moreover, those words of God, "Be fruitful and multiply," [87] are not prophetic of sins to be condemned, but a benediction upon the fertility of marriage. For by these ineffable words of His, I mean by the divine methods which are inherent in the

---

[81] 1 Cor. vii. 4   [82] Matt. xix. 6   [83] *De Bono Conjugali*, 3 ff.   [84] Heb. xiii. 4
[85] Rom. vii. 23   [86] Gen. iii. 7   [87] Gen. i. 28

truth of His wisdom by which all things were made, God endowed the primeval pair with their seminal power. Suppose, however, that nature had not been dishonored by sin, God forbid that we should think that marriages in Paradise must have been such, that in them the procreative members would be excited by the mere ardor of lust, and not by the command of the will for producing offspring—as the foot is for walking, the hand for labor, and the tongue for speech. Nor, as now happens, would the chastity of virginity be corrupted to the conception of offspring by the force of a turbid heat, but it would rather be submissive to the power of the gentlest love; and thus there would be no pain, no blood-effusion of the concumbent virgin, as there would also be no groan of the parturient mother. This, however, men refuse to believe, because it has not been verified in the actual condition of our mortal state. Nature, having been vitiated by sin, has never experienced an instance of that primeval purity. But we speak to faithful men, who have learnt to believe the inspired Scriptures, even though no examples are adduced of actual reality. For how could I now possibly *prove* that a man was made of the dust, without any parents, and a wife formed for him out of his own side? [88] And yet faith takes on trust what the eye no longer discovers.

CHAPTER XLI

LUST AND TRAVAIL, COME FROM SIN. WHENCE OUR MEMBERS BECAME A CAUSE OF SHAME

Granted, therefore, that we have no means of showing both that the nuptial acts of that primeval marriage were quietly discharged, undisturbed by lustful passion, and that the motion of the organs of generation, like that of any other members of the body, was not instigated by the ardor of lust, but directed by the choice of the will (which would have continued such with marriage had not the disgrace of sin intervened); still, from all that is stated in the sacred Scriptures on divine authority, we have reasonable grounds for believing that such was the original condition of wedded life. Although, it is true, I am not told that the nuptial embrace was unattended with prurient desire; as also I do not find it on record that parturition was unaccompanied with groans and pain, or that actual birth led not to future death; yet, at the same time, if I follow the verity of the Holy Scriptures, the travail of the mother and the death of the human offspring would never have supervened if sin had not preceded. Nor would that have happened which abashed the man and woman when they covered their loins; because in the same sacred records it is expressly written that the sin was first committed, and then immediately followed this hiding of their shame.[89] For unless some indelicacy of motion had announced to their eyes

[88] Gen. ii. 7, 22   [89] Gen. iii. 7

—which were of course not closed, though not open to this point, that is, not attentive—that those particular members should be corrected, they would not have perceived anything on their own persons, which God had entirely made worthy of all praise, that called for either shame or conceal-ment. If, indeed, the sin had not first occurred which they had dared to commit in their disobedience, there would not have followed the disgrace which their shame would fain conceal.

CHAPTER XLII

THE EVIL OF LUST OUGHT NOT TO BE ASCRIBED TO MARRIAGE. THE
THREE GOOD RESULTS OF THE NUPTIAL ORDINANCE: OFFSPRING,
CHASTITY, AND THE SACRAMENTAL UNION

It is then manifest that that must not be laid to the account of marriage, even in the absence of which, marriage would still have existed. The good of marriage is not taken away by the evil, although the evil is by marriage turned to a good use. Such, however, is the present condition of mortal men, that the connubial intercourse and lust are at the same time in action; and on this account it happens, that as the lust is blamed, so also the nuptial commerce, however lawful and honorable, is thought to be reprehensible by those persons who either are unwilling or unable to draw the distinction be-tween them. They are, moreover, inattentive to that good of the nuptial state which is the glory of matrimony; I mean offspring, chastity, and the pledge.[90] The evil, however, at which even marriage blushes for shame is not the fault of marriage, but of the lust of the flesh. Yet because without this evil it is impossible to effect the good purpose of marriage, even the procreation of children, whenever this process is approached, secrecy is sought, witnesses removed, and even the presence of the very children which happen to be born of the process is avoided as soon as they reach the age of observation. Thus it comes to pass that marriage is permitted to effect all that is lawful in its state, only it must not forget to conceal all that is improper. Hence it follows that infants, although incapable of sin-ning, are yet not born without the contagion of sin—not, indeed, because of what is lawful, but on account of that which is unseemly: for from what is lawful nature is born; from what is unseemly, sin. Of the nature so born, God is the Author, who created man, and who united male and female under the nuptial law; but of the sin the author is the subtlety of the devil who deceives, and the will of the man who consents.

[90] Sacramentum

CHAPTER XLIII

HUMAN OFFSPRING, EVEN PREVIOUS TO BIRTH, UNDER CONDEMNATION AT THE VERY ROOT. USES OF MATRIMONY UNDERTAKEN FOR MERE PLEASURE NOT WITHOUT VENIAL FAULT

Where God did nothing else than by a just sentence to condemn the man who wilfully sins, together with his stock; there also, as a matter of course, whatsoever was even not yet born is justly condemned in its sinful root. In this condemned stock carnal generation holds every man; and from it nothing but spiritual regeneration liberates him. In the case, therefore, of regenerate parents, if they continue in the same state of grace, it will undoubtedly work no injurious consequence, by reason of the remission of sins which has been bestowed upon them, unless they make a perverse use of it—not alone all kinds of lawless corruptions, but even in the marriage state itself, whenever husband and wife toil at procreation, not from the desire of natural propagation of their species, but are mere slaves to the gratification of their lust out of very wantonness. As for the permission which the apostle gives to husbands and wives, "not to defraud one another, except with consent for a time, that they may have leisure for prayer," [91] he concedes it by way of indulgent allowance, and not as a command; but this very form of the concession evidently implies some degree of fault. The connubial embrace, however, which marriage-contracts point to as intended for the procreation of children, considered in itself simply, and without any reference to fornication, is good and right; because, although it is by reason of this body of death (which is unrenewed as yet by the resurrection) impracticable without a certain amount of bestial motion, which puts human nature to the blush, yet the embrace is not after all a sin in itself, when reason applies the concupiscence to a good end, and is not overmastered to evil.

CHAPTER XLIV

EVEN THE CHILDREN OF THE REGENERATE BORN IN SIN. THE EFFECT OF BAPTISM

This concupiscence of the flesh would be prejudicial, just in so far as it is present in us, if the remission of sins were not so beneficial that while it is present in men, both as born and as born again, it may in the former be prejudicial as well as present, but in the latter present simply but never prejudicial. In the unregenerate it is prejudicial to such an extent indeed, that, unless they are born again, no advantage can accrue to them from being born of regenerate parents. The fault of our nature remains in our

[91] I Cor. vii. 5

offspring so deeply impressed as to make it guilty, even when the guilt of the self-same fault has been washed away in the parent by the remission of sins—until every defect which ends in sin by the consent of the human will is consumed and done away in the last regeneration. This will be identical with that renovation of the very flesh itself which is promised in its future resurrection, when we shall not only commit no sins, but be even free from those corrupt desires which lead us to sin by yielding consent to them. To this blessed consummation advances are even now made by us, through the grace of that holy laver which we have put within our reach. The same regeneration which now renews our spirit, so that all our past sins are remitted, will by and by also operate, as might be expected, to the renewal to eternal life of that very flesh, by the resurrection of which to an incorruptible state the incentives of all sins will be purged out of our nature. But this salvation is as yet only accomplished in hope; it is not realized in fact; it is not in present possession, but it is looked forward to with patience. And thus there is a whole and perfect cleansing, in the self-same baptismal laver, not only of all the sins remitted now in our baptism, which make us guilty owing to the consent we yield to wrong desires, and to the sinful acts in which they issue; but of these said wrong desires also, which, if not consented to by us, would contract no guilt of sin, and which, though not in this present life removed, will yet have no existence in the life beyond.

CHAPTER XLV

MAN'S DELIVERANCE SUITED TO THE CHARACTER OF HIS CAPTIVITY

The guilt, therefore, of that corruption of which we are speaking will remain in the carnal offspring of the regenerate, until in them also it be washed away in the laver of regeneration. A regenerate man does not regenerate, but generates, sons according to the flesh; and thus he transmits to his posterity, not the condition of the regenerated, but only of the generated. Therefore, be a man guilty of unbelief, or a perfect believer, he does not in either case beget faithful children, but sinners; in the same way that the seeds, not only of a wild olive, but also of a cultivated one, produce not cultivated olives, but wild ones. So, likewise, his first birth holds a man in that bondage from which nothing but his second birth delivers him. The devil holds him, Christ liberates him: Eve's deceiver holds him, Mary's Son frees him: he holds him, who approached the man through the woman; He frees him, who was born of a woman that never approached a man: he holds him, who injected into the woman the cause of lust; He liberates him, who without any lust was conceived in the woman. The former was able to hold all men in his grasp through one; nor does any deliver them out of his power but One, whom he was unable to grasp. The very sacraments indeed of the Church, which she administers with due ceremony, according to the authority of very ancient tradition (so that these men, notwithstanding their opinion that the sacraments are imitatively rather than really used in the case of infants, still do not venture to reject them with open disapproval)—the very sacraments, I say, of the holy Church show plainly enough that infants, even when fresh from the womb, are delivered from the bondage of the devil through the grace of Christ. For, to say nothing of the fact that they are baptized for the remission of sins by no fallacious, but by a true and faithful mystery, there is previously wrought on them the exorcism and the exsufflation of the hostile power, which they profess to renounce by the mouth of those who bring them to baptism. Now, by all these consecrated and evident signs of hidden realities, they are shown to pass from their worst oppressor to their most excellent Redeemer, who, by taking on Himself our infirmity in our behalf, has bound the strong man, that He may spoil his goods;[92] seeing that the weakness of God is stronger, not only than men, but also than angels. While, therefore, God delivers small as well as great, He shows in both instances that the apostle spoke under the direction of the Truth. For it is not merely adults, but little babes too, whom He rescues from the power of darkness, in order to transfer them to the kingdom of God's dear Son.[93]

CHAPTER XLVI

DIFFICULTY OF BELIEVING ORIGINAL SIN. MAN'S VICE IS A BEAST'S NATURE

No one should feel surprise, and ask: "Why does God's goodness create anything for the devil's malignity to take possession of?" The truth is, God's gift is bestowed on the seminal elements of His creature with the same bounty wherewith "He maketh His sun to rise on the evil and on the good, and sendeth rain on the just and on the unjust." [94] It is with so large a bounty that God has blessed the very seeds, and by blessing has constituted them. Nor has this blessing been eliminated out of our excellent nature by a fault which puts us under condemnation. Owing, indeed, to God's justice, who punishes, this fatal flaw has so far prevailed, that men are born with the fault of original sin; but yet its influence has not extended so far as to stop the birth of men. Just so does it happen in persons of adult age: whatever sins they commit, do not eliminate his manhood from man; nay, God's work continues still good, however evil be the deeds of the impious. For although "man being placed in honor abideth not; and being without understanding, is compared with the beasts, and is like them," [95] yet the resemblance is not so absolute that he becomes a beast. There is a comparison, no doubt, between the two; but it is not by reason of nature, but through vice—not vice in the beast, but in nature. For so excellent is a man in comparison with a beast, that man's vice is beast's nature; still

---

[92] Matt. xii. 29   [93] Col. i. 13   [94] Matt. v. 45   [95] Ps. xlix. 12

man's nature is never on this account changed into beast's nature. God, therefore, condemns man because of the fault wherewithal his nature is disgraced, and not because of his nature, which is not destroyed in consequence of its fault. Heaven forbid that we should think beasts are obnoxious to the sentence of condemnation! It is only proper that they should be free from our misery, inasmuch as they cannot partake of our blessedness. What, then, is there surprising or unjust in man's being subjected to an impure spirit—not on account of nature, but on account of that impurity of his which he has contracted in the stain of his birth, and which proceeds, not from the divine work, but from the will of man—since also the impure spirit itself is a good thing considered as spirit, but evil in that it is impure? For the one is of God, and is His work, while the other emanates from man's own will. The stronger nature, therefore, that is, the angelic one, keeps the lower, or human, nature in subjection, by reason of the association of vice with the latter. Accordingly the Mediator, who was stronger than the angels, became weak for man's sake.[96] So that the pride of the Destroyer is destroyed by the humility of the Redeemer; and he who makes his boast over the sons of men of his angelic strength, is vanquished by the Son of God in the human weakness which He assumed.

CHAPTER XLVII

SENTENCES FROM AMBROSE IN FAVOR OF ORIGINAL SIN

And now that we are about to bring this book to a conclusion, we think it proper to do on this subject of *Original Sin* what we did before in our treatise *On Grace*—adduce in evidence against the injurious talk of these persons that servant of God, the Archbishop Ambrose, whose faith is proclaimed by Pelagius to be the most perfect among the writers of the Latin Church; for *grace* is more especially honored in doing away with *original sin.* In the work which the saintly Ambrose wrote, *Concerning the Resurrection,* he says: "I fell in Adam, in Adam was I expelled from Paradise, in Adam I died; and He does not recall me unless He has found me in Adam— so as that, as I am obnoxious to the guilt of sin in him, and subject to death, I may be also justified in Christ." [97] Then, again, writing against the Novatians, he says: "We men are all of us born in sin; our very origin is in sin; as you may read when David says, 'Behold, I was shapen in iniquity, and in sin did my mother conceive me.' [98] Hence it is that Paul's flesh is 'a body of death;' [99] even as he says himself, 'Who shall deliver me from the body of this death?' Christ's flesh, however, has condemned sin, which He experienced not by being born, and which by dying He crucified, that in our flesh there might be justification through grace, where previously there was impurity through sin." [100] The same holy man also, in his *Exposition of*

[96] 2 Cor. viii. 9   [97] Ambrose's *De Exec. Sal.* ii. 6   [98] Ps. li. 5   [99] Rom. vii. 24
[100] Ambrose's *De Paenitentia,* i. 2, 3

Isaiah, speaking of Christ, says: "Therefore as man He was tried in all things, and in the likeness of men He endured all things; but as born of the Spirit, He was free from sin. For every man is a liar, and no one but God alone is without sin. It is therefore an observed and settled fact, that no man born of a man and a woman, that is, by means of their bodily union, is seen to be free from sin. Whosoever, indeed, is free from sin, is free also from a conception and birth of this kind." [101] Moreover, when expounding the Gospel according to Luke, he says: "It was no cohabitation with a husband which opened the secrets of the Virgin's womb; rather was it the Holy Ghost which infused immaculate seed into her unviolated womb. For the Lord Jesus alone of those who are born of woman is holy, inasmuch as He experienced not the contact of earthly corruption, by reason of the novelty of His immaculate birth; nay, He repelled it by His heavenly majesty." [102]

CHAPTER XLVIII

PELAGIUS RIGHTLY CONDEMNED AND REALLY OPPOSED BY AMBROSE

These words, however, of the man of God are contradicted by Pelagius, notwithstanding all his commendation of his author, when he himself declares that "we are procreated, as without virtue, so without vice." What remains, then, but that Pelagius should condemn and renounce this error of his; or else be sorry that he has quoted Ambrose in the way he has? Inasmuch, however, as the blessed Ambrose, Catholic bishop as he is, has expressed himself in the above-quoted passages in accordance with the Catholic Faith, it follows that Pelagius, along with his disciple Coelestius, was justly condemned by the authority of the Catholic Church, for having turned aside from the true way of faith, since he repented not for having bestowed commendation on Ambrose, and for having at the same time entertained opinions in opposition to him. I know full well with what insatiable avidity you read whatever is written for edification and in confirmation of the faith; but yet, notwithstanding its utility as contributing to such an end, I must at last bring this treatise to a conclusion.

[101] Quoted from a work by Saint Ambrose, *On Isaiah,* not now extant
[102] See Book ii. 56 of this *Commentary on St. Luke,* ch. ii

THE ENCHIRIDION ON FAITH, HOPE AND LOVE

THE ENCHIRIDION

Introductory Note

In 421 A.D., in response to a request by a certain Laurentianus that he might have a short work on the manner in which God is to be worshipped, Saint Augustine composed *The Enchiridion,* to which he usually refers by its sub-title *On Faith, Hope and Love.* The treatise is among the most remarkable in the Augustinian corpus. Within very brief compass the author has given a compact yet complete expression to his whole position, beginning with a discussion of the Apostle's Creed, followed by an exposition of the Lord's Prayer, and concluding with a disquisition on Christian love. The work is truly a "hand-book" in the best sense of the word and it is little wonder that it has been widely read through the centuries.

THE ENCHIRIDION
ON FAITH, HOPE AND LOVE

ARGUMENT

Laurentius having asked Augustine to furnish him with a handbook of Christian doctrine, containing in brief compass answers to several questions which he had proposed, Augustine shows him that these questions can be fully answered by any one who knows the proper objects of faith, hope, and love. He then proceeds, in the first part of the work (Chap. IX-CXIII), to expound the objects of faith, taking as his text the Apostles' Creed; and in the course of this exposition, besides refuting divers heresies, he throws out many observations on the conduct of life. The second part of the work (Chap. CXIV-CXVI) treats of the objects of hope, and consists of a very brief exposition of the several petitions in the Lord's Prayer. The third and concluding part (Chap. CXVII-CXXII) treats of the objects of love, showing the pre-eminence of this grace in the gospel system, that it is the end of the commandment and the fulfilling of the law, and that God Himself is love.

CHAPTER I

THE AUTHOR DESIRES THE GIFT OF TRUE WISDOM
FOR LAURENTIUS

I CANNOT express, my beloved son Laurentius, the delight with which I witness your progress in knowledge, and the earnest desire I have that you should be a wise man: not one of those of whom it is said, "Where is the wise? where is the scribe? where is the disputer of this world? hath not God made foolish the wisdom of this world?" [1] but one of those of whom it is said, "The multitude of the wise is the welfare of the world," [2] and such as the apostles wishes those to become, whom he tells, "I would have you wise unto that which is good, and simple concerning evil." [3] Now, just as no one can exist of himself, so no one can be wise of himself, but only by the enlightening influence of Him of whom it is written, "All wisdom cometh from the Lord." [4]

CHAPTER II

THE FEAR OF GOD IS MAN'S TRUE WISDOM

The true wisdom of man is piety. You find this in the book of holy Job. For we read there what wisdom itself has said to man: "Behold, the fear of the Lord [*pietas*], that is wisdom." [5] If you ask further what is meant

[1] I Cor. i. 20   [2] Wisd. vi. 24   [3] Rom. xvi. 19   [4] Ecclus. i. 1   [5] Job xxviii. 28

in that place by *pietas*, the Greek calls it more definitely θεοσέβεια, that is, the worship of God. The Greeks sometimes call piety εὐσέβεια, which signifies right worship, though this, of course, refers specially to the worship of God. But when we are defining in what man's true wisdom consists, the most convenient word to use is that which distinctly expresses the fear of God. And can you, who are anxious that I should treat of great matters in few words, wish for a briefer form of expression? Or perhaps you are anxious that this expression should itself be briefly explained, and that I should unfold in a short discourse the proper mode of worshipping God?

CHAPTER III

GOD IS TO BE WORSHIPPED THROUGH FAITH, HOPE, AND LOVE

Now if I should answer, that God is to be worshipped with faith, hope, and love, you will at once say that this answer is too brief, and will ask me briefly to unfold the objects of each of these three graces, *viz.*, what we are to believe, what we are to hope for, and what we are to love. And when I have done this, you will have an answer to all the questions you asked in your letter. If you have kept a copy of your letter, you can easily turn it up and read it over again: if you have not, you will have no difficulty in recalling it when I refresh your memory.

CHAPTER IV

THE QUESTIONS PROPOUNDED BY LAURENTIUS

You are anxious, you say, that I should write a sort of handbook for you, which you might always keep beside you, containing answers to the questions you put, *viz.*: what ought to be man's chief end in life; what he ought, in view of the various heresies, chiefly to avoid; to what extent religion is supported by reason; what there is in reason that lends no support to faith, when faith stands alone; what is the starting-point, what the goal, of religion; what is the sum of the whole body of doctrine; what is the sure and proper foundation of the Catholic Faith. Now, undoubtedly, you will know the answers to all these questions, if you know thoroughly the proper objects of faith, hope, and love. For these must be the chief, nay, the exclusive objects of pursuit in religion. He who speaks against these is either a total stranger to the name of Christ, or is a heretic. These are to be defended by reason, which must have its starting-point either in the bodily senses or in the intuitions of the mind. And what we have neither had experience of through our bodily senses, nor have been able to reach through the intellect, must undoubtedly be believed on the testimony of those witnesses by whom the Scriptures, justly called divine, were written; and who by divine assistance were enabled, either through bodily sense or intellectual perception, to see or to foresee the things in question.

CHAPTER V

BRIEF ANSWERS TO THESE QUESTIONS

Moreover, when the mind has been imbued with the first elements of that faith which worketh by love,[6] it endeavors by purity of life to attain unto sight, where the pure and perfect in heart know that unspeakable beauty, the full vision of which is supreme happiness. Here surely is an answer to your question as to what is the starting-point, and what the goal: we begin in faith, and are made perfect by sight. This also is the sum of the whole body of doctrine. But the sure and proper foundation of the Catholic Faith is Christ. "For other foundation," says the apostle, "can no man lay than that is laid, which is Jesus Christ."[7] Nor are we to deny that this is the proper foundation of the Catholic Faith, because it may be supposed that some heretics hold this in common with us. For if we carefully consider the things that pertain to Christ, we shall find that, among those heretics who call themselves Christians, Christ is present in name only: in deed and in truth He is not among them. But to show this would occupy us too long, for we should require to go over all the heresies which have existed, which do exist, or which could exist, under the Christian name, and to show that this is true in the case of each—a discussion which would occupy so many volumes as to be all but interminable.

CHAPTER VI

CONTROVERSY OUT OF PLACE IN A HANDBOOK LIKE THE PRESENT

Now you ask of me a handbook, that is, one that can be carried in the hand, not one to load your shelves. To return, then, to the three graces through which, as I have said, God should be worshipped—faith, hope, and love: to state what are the true and proper objects of each of these is easy. But to defend this true doctrine against the assaults of those who hold an opposite opinion, requires much fuller and more elaborate instruction. And the true way to obtain this instruction is not to have a short treatise put into one's hands, but to have a great zeal kindled in one's heart.

CHAPTER VII

THE CREED AND THE LORD'S PRAYER DEMAND THE EXERCISE OF FAITH, HOPE, AND LOVE

For you have the Creed and the Lord's Prayer. What can be briefer to hear or to read? What easier to commit to memory? When, as the result of sin, the human race was groaning under a heavy load of misery, and was

[6] Gal. v. 6   [7] 1 Cor. iii. 11

in urgent need of the divine compassion, one of the prophets, anticipating the time of God's grace, declared: "And it shall come to pass, that whosoever shall call on the name of the Lord shall be delivered." [8] Hence the Lord's Prayer. But the apostle, when, for the purpose of commending this very grace, he had quoted this prophetic testimony, immediately added: "How then shall they call on Him in whom they have not believed?" [9] Hence the Creed. In these two you have those three graces exemplified: faith believes, hope and love pray. But without faith the two last cannot exist, and therefore we may say that faith also prays. Whence it is written: "How shall they call on Him in whom they have not believed?"

CHAPTER VIII

THE DISTINCTION BETWEEN FAITH AND HOPE, AND THE MUTUAL DEPENDENCE OF FAITH, HOPE, AND LOVE

Again, can anything be hoped for which is not an object of faith? It is true that a thing which is not an object of hope may be believed. What true Christian, for example, does not believe in the punishment of the wicked? And yet such an one does not hope for it. And the man who believes that punishment to be hanging over himself, and who shrinks in horror from the prospect, is more properly said to fear than to hope. And these two states of mind the poet carefully distinguishes, when he says: "Permit the fearful to have hope." [10] Another poet, who is usually much superior to this one, makes a wrong use of the word, when he says: "If I have been able to hope for so great a grief as this." [11] And some grammarians take this case as an example of impropriety of speech, saying, "He said *sperare* [to hope] instead of *timere* [to fear]." Accordingly, faith may have for its object evil as well as good; for both good and evil are believed, and the faith that believes them is not evil, but good. Faith, moreover, is concerned with the past, the present, and the future, all three. We believe, for example, that Christ died—an event in the past; we believe that He is sitting at the right hand of God—a state of things which is present; we believe that He will come to judge the quick and the dead—an event of the future. Again, faith applies both to one's own circumstances and those of others. Every one, for example, believes that his own existence had a beginning, and was not eternal, and he believes the same both of other men and other things. Many of our beliefs in regard to religious matters, again, have reference not merely to other men, but to angels also. But hope has for its object only what is good, only what is future, and only what affects the man who entertains the hope. For these reasons, then, faith must be distinguished from hope, not merely as a matter of verbal propriety, but because they are essentially different. The fact that we do not see either what we believe or

[8] Joel ii. 32   [9] Rom. x. 14   [10] Lucan, *Phars.* ii. 15   [11] Virgil, *Aen.* iv. 419

what we hope for, is all that is common to faith and hope. In the *Epistle to the Hebrews,* for example, faith is defined (and eminent defenders of the Catholic Faith have used the definition as a standard) "the evidence of things not seen." [12] Although, should any one say that he believes, that is, has grounded his faith, not on words, nor on witnesses, nor on any reasoning whatever, but on the direct evidence of his own senses, he would not be guilty of such an impropriety of speech as to be justly liable to the criticism, "You saw, therefore you did not believe." And hence it does not follow that an object of faith is not an object of sight. But it is better that we should use the word "faith" as the Scriptures have taught us, applying it to those things which are not seen. Concerning hope, again, the apostle says: "Hope that is seen is not hope; for what a man seeth, why doth he yet hope for? But if we hope for that we see not, then do we with patience wait for it." [13] When, then, we believe that good is about to come, this is nothing else but to hope for it. Now what shall I say of love? Without it, faith profits nothing; and in its absence, hope cannot exist. The Apostle James says: "The devils also believe, and tremble" [14]—that is, they, having neither hope nor love, but believing that what we hope and hope for is about to come, are in terror. And so the Apostle Paul approves and commends the "faith that worketh by love;" [15] and this certainly cannot exist without hope. Wherefore there is no love without hope, no hope without love, and neither love nor hope without faith.

CHAPTER IX

WHAT WE ARE TO BELIEVE. IN REGARD TO NATURE IT IS NOT NECESSARY FOR THE CHRISTIAN TO KNOW MORE THAN THAT THE GOODNESS OF THE CREATOR IS THE CAUSE OF ALL THINGS

When, then, the question is asked what we are to believe in regard to religion, it is not necessary to probe into the nature of things, as was done by those whom the Greeks call *physici;* nor need we be in alarm lest the Christian should be ignorant of the force and number of the elements— the motion, and order, and eclipses of the heavenly bodies; the form of the heavens; the species and the natures of animals, plants, stones, fountains, rivers, mountains; about chronology and distances; the signs of coming storms; and a thousand other things which those philosophers either have found out, or think they have found out. For even these men themselves, endowed though they are with so much genius, burning with zeal, abounding in leisure, tracking some things by the aid of human conjecture, searching into others with the aids of history and experience, have not found out all things; and even their boasted discoveries are oftener mere guesses than certain knowledge. It is enough for the Christian to believe that the only

---

[12] Heb. xi. 1   [13] Rom. viii. 24, 25   [14] Jas. ii. 19   [15] Gal. v. 6

cause of all created things, whether heavenly or earthly, whether visible or invisible, is the goodness of the Creator, the one true God; and that nothing exists but Himself that does not derive its existence from Him; and that He is the Trinity—to wit, the Father, and the Son begotten of the Father, and the Holy Spirit proceeding from the same Father, but one and the same Spirit of Father and Son.

CHAPTER X

THE SUPREMELY GOOD CREATOR MADE ALL THINGS GOOD

By the Trinity, thus supremely and equally and unchangeably good, all things were created; and these are not supremely and equally and unchangeably good, but yet they are good, even taken separately. Taken as a whole, however, they are very good, because their *ensemble* constitutes the universe in all its wonderful order and beauty.

CHAPTER XI

WHAT IS CALLED EVIL IN THE UNIVERSE IS BUT THE ABSENCE OF GOOD

And in the universe, even that which is called evil, when it is regulated and put in its own place, only enhances our admiraton of the good; for we enjoy and value the good more when we compare it with the evil. For the Almighty God, who, as even the heathen acknowledge, has supreme power over all things, being Himself supremely good, would never permit the existence of anything evil among His works, if He were not so omnipotent and good that He can bring good even out of evil. For what is that which we call evil but the absence of good? In the bodies of animals, disease and wounds mean nothing but the absence of health; for when a cure is effected, that does not mean that the evils which were present—namely, the diseases and wounds—go away from the body and dwell elsewhere: they altogether cease to exist; for the wound or disease is not a substance, but a defect in the fleshly substance—the flesh itself being a substance, and therefore something good, of which those evils—that is, privations of the good which we call health—are accidents. Just in the same way, what are called vices in the soul are nothing but privations of natural good. And when they are cured, they are not transferred elsewhere: when they cease to exist in the healthy soul, they cannot exist anywhere else.

CHAPTER XII

ALL BEINGS WERE MADE GOOD, BUT NOT BEING MADE PERFECTLY GOOD, ARE LIABLE TO CORRUPTION

All things that exist, therefore, seeing that the Creator of them all is supremely good, are themselves good. But because they are not, like their

Creator, supremely and unchangeably good, their good may be diminished and increased. But for good to be diminished is an evil, although, however much it may be diminished, it is necessary, if the being is to continue, that some good should remain to constitute the being. For however small or of whatever kind the being may be, the good which makes it a being cannot be destroyed without destroying the being itself. An uncorrupted nature is justly held in esteem. But if, still further, it be incorruptible, it is undoubtedly considered of still higher value. When it is corrupted, however, its corruption is an evil, because it is deprived of some sort of good. For if it be deprived of no good, it receives no injury; but it does receive injury, therefore it is deprived of good. Therefore, so long as a being is in process of corruption, there is in it some good of which it is being deprived; and if a part of the being should remain which cannot be corrupted, this will certainly be an incorruptible being, and accordingly the process of corruption will result in the manifestation of this great good. But if it do not cease to be corrupted, neither can it cease to possess good of which corruption may deprive it. But if it should be thoroughly and completely consumed by corruption, there will then be no good left, because there will be no being. Wherefore corruption can consume the good only by consuming the being. Every being, therefore, is a good; a great good, if it can not be corrupted; a little good, if it can: but in any case, only the foolish or ignorant will deny that it is a good. And if it be wholly consumed by corruption, then the corruption itself must cease to exist, as there is no being left in which it can dwell.

CHAPTER XIII

THERE CAN BE NO EVIL WHERE THERE IS NO GOOD; AND AN EVIL MAN IS AN EVIL GOOD

Accordingly, there is nothing of what we call evil, if there be nothing good. But a good which is wholly without evil is a perfect good. A good, on the other hand, which contains evil is a faulty or imperfect good; and there can be no evil where there is no good. From all this we arrive at the curious result: that since every being, so far as it is a being, is good, when we say that a faulty being is an evil being, we just seem to say that what is good is evil, and that nothing but what is good can be evil, seeing that every being is good, and that no evil can exist except in a being. Nothing, then, can be evil except something which is good. And although this, when stated, seems to be a contradiction, yet the strictness of reasoning leaves us no escape from the conclusion. We must, however, beware of incurring the prophetic condemnation: "Woe unto them that call evil good, and good evil: that put darkness for light, and light for darkness: that put bitter for sweet, and sweet for bitter." [16] And yet our Lord says: "An evil man out

[16] Isa. v. 20

of the evil treasure of his heart bringeth forth that which is evil." [17] Now, what is an evil man but an evil being? for a man is a being. Now, if a man is a good thing because he is a being, what is an evil man but an evil good? Yet, when we accurately distinguish these two things, we find that it is not because he is a man that he is an evil, or because he is wicked that he is a good; but that he is a good because he is a man, and an evil because he is wicked. Whoever, then, says, "To be a man is an evil," or, "To be wicked is a good," falls under the prophetic denunciation: "Woe unto them that call evil good, and good evil!" For he condemns the work of God, which is the man, and praises the defect of man, which is the wickedness. Therefore every being, even if it be a defective one, in so far as it is a being is good, and in so far as it is defective is evil.

CHAPTER XIV

GOOD AND EVIL ARE AN EXCEPTION TO THE RULE THAT CONTRARY ATTRI-
BUTES CANNOT BE PREDICATED OF THE SAME SUBJECT. EVIL SPRINGS
UP IN WHAT IS GOOD, AND CANNOT EXIST EXCEPT IN WHAT IS GOOD

Accordingly, in the case of these contraries which we call good and evil, the rule of the logicians, that two contraries cannot be predicated at the same time of the same thing, does not hold. No weather is at the same time dark and bright: no food or drink is at the same time sweet and bitter: no body is at the same time and in the same place black and white: none is at the same time and in the same place deformed and beautiful. And this rule is found to hold in regard to many, indeed nearly all, contraries, that they cannot exist at the same time in any one thing. But although no one can doubt that good and evil are contraries, not only can they exist at the same time, but evil cannot exist without good, or in anything that is not good. Good, however, can exist without evil. For a man or an angel can exist without being wicked; but nothing can be wicked except a man or an angel: and so far as he is a man or an angel, he is good; so far as he is wicked, he is an evil. And these two contraries are so far co-existent, that if good did not exist in what is evil, neither could evil exist; because corruption could not have either a place to dwell in, or a source to spring from, if there were nothing that could be corrupted; and nothing can be corrupted except what is good, for corruption is nothing else but the destruction of good. From what is good, then, evils arose, and except in what is good they do not exist; nor was there any other source from which any evil nature could arise. For if there were, then, in so far as this was a being, it was certainly a good: and a being which was incorruptible would be a great good; and even one which was corruptible must be to some extent a good, for only by corrupting what was good in it could corruption do it harm.

[17] Luke vi. 45

CHAPTER XV

THE PRECEDING ARGUMENT IS IN NO WISE INCONSISTENT WITH THE
SAYING OF OUR LORD: "A GOOD TREE CANNOT BRING FORTH EVIL FRUIT"

But when we say that evil springs out of good, let it not be thought that this contradicts our Lord's saying: "A good tree cannot bring forth evil fruit." [18] For, as He who is the Truth says, you cannot gather grapes of thorns,[19] because grapes do not grow on thorns. But we see that on good soil both vines and thorns may be grown. And in the same way, just as an evil tree cannot bring forth good fruit, so an evil will cannot produce good works. But from the nature of man, which is good, may spring either a good or an evil will. And certainly there was at first no source from which an evil will could spring, except the nature of angel or of man, which was good. And our Lord Himself clearly shows this in the very same place where He speaks about the tree and its fruit. For He says: "Either make the tree good, and his fruit good; or else make the tree corrupt, and his fruit corrupt" [20]—clearly enough warning us that evil fruits do not grow on a good tree, nor good fruits on an evil tree; but that nevertheless the ground itself, by which He meant those whom He was then addressing, might grow either kind of trees.

CHAPTER XVI

IT IS NOT ESSENTIAL TO MAN'S HAPPINESS THAT HE SHOULD KNOW
THE CAUSES OF PHYSICAL CONVULSIONS; BUT IT IS, THAT
HE SHOULD KNOW THE CAUSES OF GOOD AND EVIL

Now, in view of these considerations, when we are pleased with that line of Maro, "Happy the man who has attained to the knowledge of the causes of things," [21] we should not suppose that it is necessary to happiness to know the causes of the great physical convulsions, causes which lie hid in the most secret recesses of nature's kingdom, "whence comes the earthquake whose force makes the deep seas to swell and burst their barriers, and again to return upon themselves and settle down." [22] But we ought to know the causes of good and evil as far as man may in this life know them, in order to avoid the mistakes and troubles of which this life is so full. For our aim must always be to reach that state of happiness in which no trouble shall distress us, and no error mislead us. If we must know the causes of physical convulsions, there are none which it concerns us more to know than those which affect our own health. But seeing that, in our ignorance of these, we are fain to resort to physicians, it would seem that we might

[18] Matt. vii. 18   [19] Matt. vii. 16   [20] Matt. xii. 33   [21] Virgil, *Georgics,* ii. 490
[22] *Ibid.*

bear with considerable patience our ignorance of the secrets that lie hid in the earth and heavens.

CHAPTER XVII

THE NATURE OF ERROR. ALL ERROR IS NOT HURTFUL, THOUGH IT IS MAN'S DUTY AS FAR AS POSSIBLE TO AVOID IT

For although we ought with the greatest possible care to avoid error, not only in great but even in little things, and although we cannot err except through ignorance, it does not follow that, if a man is ignorant of a thing, he must forthwith fall into error. That is rather the fate of the man who thinks he knows what he does not know. For he accepts what is false as if it were time, and that is the essence of error. But it is a point of very great importance what the subject is in regard to which a man makes a mistake. For on one and the same subject we rightly prefer an instructed man to an ignorant one, and a man who is not in error to one who is. In the case of different subjects, however—that is, when one man knows one thing, and another a different thing, and when what the former knows is useful, and what the latter knows is not so useful, or is actually hurtful—who would not, in regard to the things the latter knows, prefer the ignorance of the former to the knowledge of the latter? For there are points on which ignorance is better than knowledge. And in the same way, it has sometimes been an advantage to depart from the right way—in travelling, however, not in morals. It has happened to myself to take the wrong road where two ways met, so that I did not pass by the place where an armed band of Donatists lay in wait for me. Yet I arrived at the place whither I was bent, though by a roundabout route; and when I heard of the ambush, I congratulated myself on my mistake, and gave thanks to God for it. Now, who would not rather be the traveller who made a mistake like this, than the highwayman who made no mistake? And hence, perhaps, it is that the prince of poets puts these words into the mouth of a lover in misery:[23] "How I am undone, how I have been carried away by an evil error!" for there is an error which is good, as it not merely does no harm, but produces some actual advantage. But when we look more closely into the nature of truth, and consider that to err is just to take the false for the true, and the true for the false, or to hold what is certain as uncertain, and what is uncertain as certain, and that error in the soul is hideous and repulsive just in proportion as it appears fair and plausible when we utter it, or assent to it, saying, "Yea, yea; Nay, nay"—surely this life that we live is wretched indeed, if only on this account, that sometimes, in order to preserve it, it is necessary to fall into error. God forbid that such should be that other life, where truth itself is the life of the soul, where no one deceives, and no one is deceived. But here men deceive and are deceived, and they are more to be

[23] Virgil, *Eclog.* viii. 41

pitied when they lead others astray than when they are themselves led astray by putting trust in liars. Yet so much does a rational soul shrink from what is false, and so earnestly does it struggle against error, that even those who love to deceive are most unwilling to be deceived. For the liar does not think that he errs, but that he leads another who trusts him into error. And certainly he does not err in regard to the matter about which he lies, if he himself knows the truth; but he is deceived in this, that he thinks his lie does him no harm, whereas every sin is more hurtful to the sinner than to the sinned against.

CHAPTER XVIII

IT IS NEVER ALLOWABLE TO TELL A LIE; BUT LIES DIFFER VERY MUCH IN GUILT, ACCORDING TO THE INTENTION AND THE SUBJECT

But here arises a very difficult and very intricate question, about which I once wrote a large book, finding it necessary to give it an answer. The question is this: whether at any time it can become the duty of a good man to tell a lie? For some go so far as to contend that there are occasions on which it is a good and pious work to commit perjury even, and to say what is false about matters that relate to the worship of God, and about the very nature of God Himself. To me, however, it seems certain that every lie is a sin, though it makes a great difference with what intention and on what subject one lies. For the sin of the man who tells a lie to help another is not so heinous as that of the man who tells a lie to injure another; and the man who by his lying puts a traveller on the wrong road, does not do so much harm as the man who by false or misleading representations distorts the whole course of a life. No one, of course, is to be condemned as a liar who says what is false, believing it to be true, because such an one does not consciously deceive, but rather is himself deceived. And, on the same principle, a man is not to be accused of lying, though he may sometimes be open to the charge of rashness, if through carelessness he takes up what is false and holds it as true; but, on the other hand, the man who says what is true, believing it to be false, is, so far as his own consciousness is concerned, a liar. For in saying what he does not believe, he says what to his own conscience is false, even though it should in fact be true; nor is the man in any sense free from lying who with his mouth speaks the truth without knowing it, but in his heart wills to tell a lie. And, therefore, not looking at the matter spoken of, but solely at the intention of the speaker, the man who unwittingly says what is false, thinking all the time that it is true, is a better man than the one who unwittingly says what is true, but in his conscience intends to deceive. For the former does not think one thing and say another; but the latter, though his statements may be true in fact, has one thought in his heart and another on his lips: and that is the very essence of lying. But when we come to consider truth and falsehood in respect to the subjects spoken of, the point on which one deceives or is deceived becomes a matter of the utmost importance. For although, as far as a man's own conscience is concerned, it is a greater evil to deceive than to be deceived, nevertheless it is a far less evil to tell a lie in regard to matters that do not relate to religion, than to be led into error in regard to matters the knowledge and belief of which are essential to the right worship of God. To illustrate this by example: suppose that one man should say of some one who is dead that he is still alive, knowing this to be untrue; and that another man should, being deceived, believe that Christ shall at the end of some time (make the time as long as you please) die; would it not be incomparably better to lie like the former, than to be deceived like the latter? and would it not be a much less evil to lead some man into the former error, than to be led by any man into the latter?

CHAPTER XIX

MEN'S ERRORS VARY VERY MUCH IN THE MAGNITUDE OF THE EVILS THEY PRODUCE; BUT YET EVERY ERROR IS IN ITSELF AN EVIL

In some things, then, it is a great evil to be deceived; in some it is a small evil; in some no evil at all; and in some it is an actual advantage. It is to his grievous injury that a man is deceived when he does not believe what leads to eternal life, or believes what leads to eternal death. It is a small evil for a man to be deceived, when, by taking falsehood for truth, he brings upon himself temporal annoyances; for the patience of the believer will turn even these to a good use, as when, for example, taking a bad man for a good, he receives injury from him. But one who believes a bad man to be good, and yet suffers no injury, is nothing the worse for being deceived, nor does he fall under the prophetic denunciation: "Woe to those who call evil good!" [24] For we are to understand that this is spoken not about evil man, but about the things that make men evil. Hence the man who calls adultery good, falls justly under that prophetic denunciation. But the man who calls the adulterer good, thinking him to be chaste, and not knowing him to be an adulterer, falls into no error in regard to the nature of good and evil, but only makes a mistake as to the secrets of human conduct. He calls the man good on the ground of believing him to be what is undoubtedly good; he calls the adulterer evil, and the pure man good; and he calls this man good, not knowing him to be an adulterer, but believing him to be pure. Further, if by making a mistake one escape death, as I have said above once happened to me, one even derives some advantage from one's mistake. But when I assert that in certain cases a man may be deceived without any injury to himself, or even with some advantage to himself, I do not mean that the mistake in itself is no evil, or is in any sense a good; I refer only to the evil that is avoided, or the advantage that

[24] Isa. v. 20

is gained, through making the mistake. For the mistake, considered in itself, is an evil: a great evil if it concern a great matter, a small evil if it concern a small matter, but yet always an evil. For who that is of sound mind can deny that it is an evil to receive what is false as if it were true, and to reject what is true as if it were false, or to hold what is uncertain as certain, and what is certain as uncertain? But it is one thing to think a man good when he is really bad, which is a mistake; it is another thing to suffer no ulterior injury in consequence of the mistake, supposing that the bad man whom we think good inflicts no damage upon us. In the same way, it is one thing to think that we are on the right road when we are not; it is another thing when this mistake of ours, which is an evil, leads to some good, such as saving us from an ambush of wicked men.

CHAPTER XX

EVERY ERROR IS NOT A SIN. AN EXAMINATION OF THE OPINION OF THE ACADEMIC PHILOSOPHERS, THAT TO AVOID ERROR WE SHOULD IN ALL CASES SUSPEND BELIEF

I am not sure whether mistakes such as the following—when one forms a good opinion of a bad man, not knowing what sort of man he is; or when, instead of the ordinary perceptions through the bodily senses, other appearances of a similar kind present themselves, which we perceive in the spirit, but think we perceive in the body, or perceive in the body, but think we perceive in the spirit (such a mistake as the Apostle Peter made when the angel suddenly freed him from his chains and imprisonment, and he thought he saw a vision[25]); or when, in the case of sensible objects themselves, we mistake rough for smooth, or bitter for sweet, or think that putrid matter has a good smell; or when we mistake the passing of a carriage for thunder; or mistake one man for another, the two being very much alike, as often happens in the case of twins (hence our great poet calls it "a mistake pleasing to parents"[26]—whether these, and other mistakes of this kind, ought to be called sins. Nor do I now undertake to solve a very knotty question, which perplexed those very acute thinkers, the Academic philosophers: whether a wise man ought to give his assent to anything, seeing that he may fall into error by assenting to falsehood: for all things, as they assert, are either unknown or uncertain. Now I wrote three volumes shortly after my conversion, to remove out of my way the objections which lie, as it were, on the very threshold of faith. And assuredly it was necessary at the very outset to remove this utter despair of reaching truth, which seems to be strengthened by the arguments of these philosophers. Now in their eyes every error is regarded as a sin, and they think that error can only be avoided by entirely suspending belief. For they say that the man who as-

[25] Acts xii. 9   [26] Virgil, *Aen.* x. 392

sents to what is uncertain falls into error; and they strive by the most acute, but most audacious arguments, to show that, even though a man's opinion should by chance be true, yet that there is no certainty of its truth, owing to the impossibility of distinguishing truth from falsehood. But with us, "the just shall live by faith." [27] Now, if assent be taken away, faith goes too; for without assent there can be no belief. And there are truths, whether we know them or not, which must be believed if we would attain to a happy life, that is, to eternal life. But I am not sure whether one ought to argue with men who not only do not know that there is an eternal life before them, but do not know whether they are living at the present moment; nay, say that they do not know what it is impossible they can be ignorant of. For it is impossible that any one should be ignorant that he is alive, seeing that if he be not alive it is impossible for him to be ignorant; for not knowledge merely, but ignorance too, can be an attribute only of the living. But, forsooth, they think that by not acknowledging that they are alive they avoid error, when even their very error proves that they are alive, since one who is not alive cannot err. As, then, it is not only true, but certain, that we are alive, so there are many other things both true and certain; and God forbid that it should ever be called wisdom, and not the height of folly, to refuse assent to these.

CHAPTER XXI

ERROR, THOUGH NOT ALWAYS A SIN, IS ALWAYS AN EVIL

But as to those matters in regard to which our belief or disbelief, and indeed their truth or supposed truth or falsity, are of no importance whatever, so far as attaining the kingdom of God is concerned: to make a mistake in such matters is not to be looked on as a sin, or at least as a very small and trifling sin. In short, a mistake in matters of this kind, whatever its nature and magnitude, does not relate to the way of approach to God, which is the faith of Christ that "worketh by love." [28] For the "mistake pleasing to parents" in the case of the twin children was no deviation from this way; nor did the Apostle Peter deviate from this way, when, thinking that he saw a vision, he so mistook one thing for another, that, till the angel who delivered him had departed from him, he did not distinguish the real objects among which he was moving from the visionary objects of a dream;[29] nor did the patriarch Jacob deviate from this way, when he believed that his son, who was really alive, had been slain by a beast.[30] In the case of these and other false impressions of the same kind, we are indeed deceived, but our faith in God remains secure. We go astray, but we do not leave the way that leads us to Him. But yet these errors, though they are not sinful, are to be reckoned among the evils of this life, which is so far made subject to vanity, that we receive what is false as if it were true, reject

[27] Rom. i. 17   [28] Gal. v. 6   [29] Acts xii. 9-11   [30] Gen. xxxvii. 33

what is true as if it were false, and cling to what is uncertain as if it were certain. And although they do not trench upon that true and certain faith through which we reach eternal blessedness, yet they have much to do with that misery in which we are now living. And assuredly, if we were now in the enjoyment of the true and perfect happiness that lies before us, we should not be subject to any deception through any sense, whether of body or of mind.

CHAPTER XXII

A LIE IS NOT ALLOWABLE, EVEN TO SAVE ANOTHER FROM INJURY

But every lie must be called a sin, because not only when a man knows the truth, but even when, as a man may be, he is mistaken and deceived, it is his duty to say what he thinks in his heart, whether it be true, or whether he only think it to be true. But every liar says the opposite of what he thinks in his heart, with purpose to deceive. Now it is evident that speech was given to man, not that men might therewith deceive one another, but that one man might make known his thoughts to another. To use speech, then, for the purpose of deception, and not for its appointed end, is a sin. Nor are we to suppose that there is any lie that is not a sin, because it is sometimes possible, by telling a lie, to do service to another. For it is possible to do this by theft also, as when we steal from a rich man who never feels the loss, to give to a poor man who is sensibly benefited by what he gets. And the same can be said of adultery also, when, for instance, some woman appears likely to die of love unless we consent to her wishes, while if she lived she might purify herself by repentance; but yet no one will assert that on this account such an adultery is not a sin. And if we justly place so high a value upon chastity, what offense have we taken at truth, that, while no prospect of advantage to another will lead us to violate the former by adultery, we should be ready to violate the latter by lying? It cannot be denied that they have attained a very high standard of goodness who never lie except to save a man from injury; but in the case of men who have reached this standard, it is not the deceit, but their good intention, that is justly praised, and sometimes even rewarded. It is quite enough that the deception should be pardoned, without its being made an object of laudation, especially among the heirs of the new covenant, to whom it is said: "Let your communication be, Yea, yea; Nay, nay: for whatsoever is more than these cometh of evil." [31] And it is on account of this evil, which never ceases to creep in while we retain this mortal vesture, that the co-heirs of Christ themselves say, "Forgive us our debts." [32]

[31] Matt. v. 37   [32] Matt. vi. 12

CHAPTER XXIII

SUMMARY OF THE RESULTS OF THE PRECEDING DISCUSSION

As it is right that we should know the causes of good and evil, so much of them at least as will suffice for the way that leads us to the kingdom, where there will be life without the shadow of death, truth without any alloy of error, and happiness unbroken by any sorrow, I have discussed these subjects with the brevity which my limited space demanded. And I think there cannot now be any doubt, that the only cause of any good that we enjoy is the goodness of God, and that the only cause of evil is the falling away from the unchangeable good of a being made good but changeable, first in the case of an angel, and afterwards in the case of man.

CHAPTER XXIV

THE SECONDARY CAUSES OF EVIL ARE IGNORANCE AND LUST

This is the first evil that befell the intelligent creation—that is, its first privation of good. Following upon this crept in, and now even in opposition to man's will, *ignorance* of duty, and *lust* after what is hurtful: and these brought in their train *error* and *suffering*, which, when they are felt to be imminent, produce that shrinking of the mind which is called *fear*. Further, when the mind attains the objects of its desire, however hurtful or empty they may be, error prevents it from perceiving their true nature, or its perceptions are overborne by a diseased appetite, and so it is puffed up with a *foolish joy*. From these fountains of evil, which spring out of defect rather than superfluity, flows every form of misery that besets a rational nature.

CHAPTER XXV

GOD'S JUDGMENTS UPON FALLEN MEN AND ANGELS. THE DEATH OF THE BODY IS MAN'S PECULIAR PUNISHMENT

And yet such a nature, in the midst of all its evils, could not lose the craving after happiness. Now the evils I have mentioned are common to all who for their wickedness have been justly condemned by God, whether they be men or angels. But there is one form of punishment peculiar to man —the death of the body. God had threatened him with this punishment of death if he should sin,[33] leaving him indeed to the freedom of his own will, but yet commanding his obedience under pain of death; and He placed him amid the happiness of Eden, as it were in a protected nook of life, with the intention that, if he preserved his righteousness, he should thence ascend to a better place.

[33] Gen. ii. 17

CHAPTER XXVI

THROUGH ADAM'S SIN HIS WHOLE POSTERITY WERE CORRUPTED, AND WERE BORN UNDER THE PENALTY OF DEATH, WHICH HE HAD INCURRED

Thence, after his sin, he was driven into exile, and by his sin the whole race of which he was the root was corrupted in him, and thereby subjected to the penalty of death. And so it happens that all descended from him, and from the woman who had led him into sin, and was condemned at the same time with him—being the offspring of carnal lust on which the same punishment of disobedience was visited—were tainted with the original sin, and were by it drawn through divers errors and sufferings into that last and endless punishment which they suffer in common with the fallen angels, their corrupters and masters, and the partakers of their doom. And thus "by one man sin entered into the world, and death by sin; and so death passed upon all men, for that all have sinned." [34] By "the world" the apostle, of course, means in this place the whole human race.

CHAPTER XXVII

THE STATE OF MISERY TO WHICH ADAM'S SIN REDUCED MANKIND, AND THE RESTORATION EFFECTED THROUGH THE MERCY OF GOD

Thus, then, matters stood. The whole mass of the human race was under condemnation, was lying steeped and wallowing in misery, and was being tossed from one form of evil to another, and, having joined the faction of the fallen angels, was paying the well-merited penalty of that impious rebellion. For whatever the wicked freely do through blind and unbridled lust, and whatever they suffer against their will in the way of open punishment, this all evidently pertains to the just wrath of God. But the goodness of the Creator never fails either to supply life and vital power to the wicked angels (without which their existence would soon come to an end); or, in the case of mankind, who spring from a condemned and corrupt stock, to impart form and life to their seed, to fashion their members, and through the various seasons of their life, and in the different parts of the earth, to quicken their senses, and bestow upon them the nourishment they need. For He judged it better to bring good out of evil, than not to permit any evil to exist. And if He had determined that in the case of men, as in the case of the fallen angels, there should be no restoration to happiness, would it not have been quite just, that the being who rebelled against God, who in the abuse of his freedom spurned and transgressed the command of his Creator when he could so easily have kept it, who defaced in himself the image of his Creator by stubbornly turning away from His light, who by

[34] Rom. v. 12

an evil use of his free-will broke away from his wholesome bondage to the Creator's laws—would it not have been just that such a being should have been wholly and to all eternity deserted by God, and left to suffer the everlasting punishment he had so richly earned? Certainly so God would have done, had He been only just and not also merciful, and had He not designed that His unmerited mercy should shine forth the more brightly in contrast with the unworthiness of its objects.

CHAPTER XXVIII

WHEN THE REBELLIOUS ANGELS WERE CAST OUT, THE REST REMAINED IN THE ENJOYMENT OF ETERNAL HAPPINESS WITH GOD

While some of the angels, then, in their pride and impiety rebelled against God, and were cast down from their heavenly abode into the lowest darkness, the remaining number dwelt with God in eternal and unchanging purity and happiness. For all were not sprung from one angel who had fallen and been condemned, so that they were not all, like men, involved by one original sin in the bonds of an inherited guilt, and so made subject to the penalty which one had incurred; but when he, who afterwards became the devil, was with his associates in crime exalted in pride, and by that very exaltation was with them cast down, the rest remained steadfast in piety and obedience to their Lord, and obtained, what before they had not enjoyed, a sure and certain knowledge of their eternal safety, and freedom from the possibility of falling.

CHAPTER XXIX

THE RESTORED PART OF HUMANITY SHALL, IN ACCORDANCE WITH THE PROMISES OF GOD, SUCCEED TO THE PLACE WHICH THE REBELLIOUS ANGELS LOST

And so it pleased God, the Creator and Governor of the universe, that, since the whole body of the angels had not fallen into rebellion, the part of them which had fallen should remain in perdition eternally, and that the other part, which had in the rebellion remained steadfastly loyal, should rejoice in the sure and certain knowledge of their eternal happiness; but that, on the other hand, mankind, who constituted the remainder of the intelligent creation, having perished without exception under sin, both original and actual, and the consequent punishments, should be in part restored, and should fill up the gap which the rebellion and fall of the devils had left in the company of the angels. For this is the promise to the saints, that at the resurrection they shall be equal to the angels of God.[35] And thus the Jerusalem which is above, which is the mother of us all, the city

---

[35] Luke xx. 36

of God, shall not be spoiled of any of the number of her citizens, shall perhaps reign over even a more abundant population. We do not know the number either of the saints or of the devils; but we know that the children of the holy mother who was called barren on earth shall succeed to the place of the fallen angels, and shall dwell for ever in that peaceful abode from which they fell. But the number of the citizens, whether as it now is or as it shall be, is present to the thoughts of the great Creator, who calls those things which are not as though they were,[36] and ordereth all things in measure, and number, and weight.[37]

CHAPTER XXX

MEN ARE NOT SAVED BY GOOD WORKS, NOR BY THE FREE DETERMINATION
OF THEIR OWN WILL, BUT BY THE GRACE OF GOD THROUGH FAITH

But this part of the human race to which God has promised pardon and a share in His eternal kingdom, can they be restored through the merit of their own works? God forbid. For what good work can a lost man perform, except so far as he has been delivered from perdition? Can they do anything by the free determination of their own will? Again I say, God forbid. For it was by the evil use of his free-will that man destroyed both it and himself. For, as a man who kills himself must, of course, be alive when he kills himself, but after he has killed himself ceases to live, and cannot restore himself to life; so, when man by his own free-will sinned, then sin being victorious over him, the freedom of his will was lost. "For of whom a man is overcome, of the same is he brought in bondage." [38] This is the judgment of the Apostle Peter. And as it is certainly true, what kind of liberty, I ask, can the bond-slave possess, except when it pleases him to sin? For he is freely in bondage who does with pleasure the will of his master. Accordingly, he who is the servant of sin is free to sin. And hence he will not be free to do right, until, being freed from sin, he shall begin to be the servant of righteousness. And this is true liberty, for he has pleasure in the righteous deed; and it is at the same time a holy bondage, for he is obedient to the will of God. But whence comes this liberty to do right to the man who is in bondage and sold under sin, except he be redeemed by Him who has said, "If the Son shall make you free, ye shall be free indeed?" [39] And before this redemption is wrought in a man, when he is not yet free to do what is right, how can he talk of the freedom of his will and his good works, except he be inflated by that foolish pride of boasting which the apostle restrains when he says, "By grace are ye saved, through faith." [40]

[36] Rom. iv. 17   [37] Wisd. xi. 20   [38] 2 Pet. ii. 19   [39] John viii. 36   [40] Eph. ii. 8

CHAPTER XXXI

FAITH ITSELF IS THE GIFT OF GOD; AND GOOD WORKS
WILL NOT BE WANTING IN THOSE WHO BELIEVE

And lest men should arrogate to themselves the merit of their own faith at least, not understanding that this too is the gift of God, this same apostle, who says in another place that he had "obtained mercy of the Lord to be faithful," [41] here also adds: "and that not of yourselves; it is the gift of God: not of works, lest any man should boast." [42] And lest it should be thought that good works will be wanting in those who believe, he adds further: "For we are His workmanship, created in Christ Jesus unto good works, which God hath before ordained that we should walk in them." [43] We shall be made truly free, then, when God fashions us, that is, forms and creates us anew, not as men—for He has done that already—but as good men, which His grace is now doing, that we may be a new creation in Christ Jesus, according as it is said: "Create in me a clean heart, O God." [44] For God had already created his heart, so far as the physical structure of the human heart is concerned; but the psalmist prays for the renewal of the life which was still lingering in his heart.

CHAPTER XXXII

THE FREEDOM OF THE WILL IS ALSO THE GIFT OF GOD, FOR GOD
WORKETH IN US BOTH TO WILL AND TO DO

And further, should any one be inclined to boast, not indeed of his works, but of the freedom of his will, as if the first merit belonged to him, this very liberty of good action being given to him as a reward he had earned, let him listen to this same preacher of grace, when he says: "For it is God which worketh in you, both to will and to do of His own good pleasure;" [45] and in another place: "So, then, it is not of him that willeth, nor of him that runneth, but of God that showeth mercy." [46] Now as, undoubtedly, if a man is of the age to use his reason, he cannot believe, hope, love, unless he will to do so, nor obtain the prize of the high calling of God unless he voluntarily run for it; in what sense is it "not of him that willeth, nor of him that runneth, but of God that showeth mercy," except that, as it is written, "the preparation of the heart is from the Lord?" [47] Otherwise, if it is said, "It is not of him that willeth, nor of him that runneth, but of God that showeth mercy," because it is of both, that is, both of the will of man and of the mercy of God, so that we are to understand the saying, "It is not of him that willeth, nor of him that runneth, but of God that showeth

[41] I Cor. vii. 25   [42] Eph. ii. 8, 9   [43] Eph. ii. 10   [44] Ps. li. 10   [45] Phil. ii. 13
[46] Rom. ix. 16   [47] Prov. xvi. I

mercy," as if it meant the will of man alone is not sufficient, if the mercy of God go not with it—then it will follow that the mercy of God alone is not sufficient, if the will of man go not with it; and therefore, if we may rightly say, "it is not of man that willeth, but of God that showeth mercy," because the will of man by itself is not enough, why may we not also rightly put it in the converse way: "It is not of God that showeth mercy, but of man that willeth," because the mercy of God by itself does not suffice? Surely, if no Christian will dare to say this, "It is not of God that showeth mercy, but of man that willeth," lest he should openly contradict the apostle, it follows that the true interpretation of the saying, "It is not of him that willeth, nor of him that runneth, but of God that showeth mercy," is that the whole works belongs to God, who both makes the will of man righteous, and thus prepares it for assistance, and assists it when it is prepared. For the man's righteousness of will precedes many of God's gifts, but not all; and it must itself be included among those which it does not precede. We read in Holy Scripture, both that God's mercy "shall meet me," [48] and that His mercy "shall follow me." [49] It goes before the unwilling to make him willing; it follows the willing to make his will effectual. Why are we taught to pray for our enemies,[50] who are plainly unwilling to lead a holy life, unless that God may work willingness in them? And why are we ourselves taught to ask that we may receive,[51] unless that He who has created in us the wish, may Himself satisfy the wish? We pray, then, for our enemies, that the mercy of God may prevent them, as it has prevented us: we pray for ourselves that His mercy may follow us.

CHAPTER XXXIII

MEN, BEING BY NATURE THE CHILDREN OF WRATH, NEEDED A MEDIATOR. IN WHAT SENSE GOD IS SAID TO BE ANGRY

And so the human race was lying under a just condemnation, and all men were the children of wrath. Of which wrath it is written: "All our days are passed away in Thy wrath; we spend our years as a tale that is told." [52] Of which wrath also Job says: "Man that is born of a woman is of few days, and full of trouble." [53] Of which wrath also the Lord Jesus says: "He that believeth on the Son hath everlasting life: and he that believeth not the Son shall not see life; but the wrath of God abideth on him." [54] He does not say it will come, but it "abideth on him." For every man is born with it; wherefore the apostle says: "We were by nature the children of wrath, even as others." [55] Now, as men were lying under this wrath by reason of their original sin, and as this original sin was the more heavy and deadly in proportion to the number and magnitude of the actual sins which

[48] Ps. lix. 10   [49] Ps. xxiii. 6   [50] Matt. v. 44   [51] Matt. vii. 7   [52] Ps. xc. 9
[53] Job xiv. 1   [54] John iii. 36. These words, attributed by the author to Christ, were really spoken by John the Baptist   [55] Eph. ii. 3

were added to it, there was need for a Mediator, that is, for a reconciler, who, by the offering of one sacrifice, of which all the sacrifices of the law and the prophets were types, should take away this wrath. Wherefore the apostle says: "For if, when we were enemies, we were reconciled to God by the death of His Son, much more, being reconciled, we shall be saved by His life." [56] Now when God is said to be angry, we do not attribute to Him such a disturbed feeling as exists in the mind of an angry man; but we call His just displeasure against sin by the name "anger," a word transferred by analogy from human emotions. But our being reconciled to God through a Mediator, and receiving the Holy Spirit, so that we who were enemies are made sons ("For as many as are led by the Spirit of God, they are the sons of God" [57]): this is the grace of God through Jesus Christ our Lord.

CHAPTER XXXIV

THE INEFFABLE MYSTERY OF THE BIRTH OF CHRIST THE MEDIATOR THROUGH THE VIRGIN MARY

Now of this Mediator it would occupy too much space to say anything at all worthy of Him; and, indeed, to say what is worthy of Him is not in the power of man. For who will explain in consistent words this single statement, that "the Word was made flesh, and dwelt among us," [58] so that we may believe on the only Son of God the Father Almighty, born of the Holy Ghost and the Virgin Mary? The meaning of the Word being made flesh, is not that the divine nature was changed into flesh, but that the divine nature assumed our flesh. And by "flesh" we are here to understand "man," the part being put for the whole, as when it is said: "By the deeds of the law that no flesh be justified," [59] that is, no man. For we must believe that no part was wanting in that human nature which He put on, save that it was a nature wholly free from every taint of sin—not such a nature as is conceived between the two sexes through carnal lust, which is born in sin, and whose guilt is washed away in regeneration; but such as it behoved a virgin to bring forth, when the mother's faith, not her lust, was the condition of conception. And if her virginity had been marred even in bringing Him forth, He would not have been born of a virgin; and it would be false (which God forbid) that He was born of the Virgin Mary, as is believed and declared by the whole Church, which, in imitation of His mother, daily brings forth members of His body, and yet remains a virgin. Read, if you please, my letter on the virginity of the holy Mary which I sent to that eminent man, whose name I mention with respect and affection, Volusianus.[60]

---

[56] Rom. v. 10   [57] Rom. viii. 14   [58] John i. 14   [59] Rom. iii. 20   [60] Ep. 137

CHAPTER XXXV

JESUS CHRIST, BEING THE ONLY SON OF GOD, IS AT THE SAME TIME MAN

Wherefore Christ Jesus, the Son of God, is both God and man; God before all worlds; man in our world: God, because the Word of God (for "the Word was God" [61]); and man, because in His one person the Word was joined with a body and a rational soul. Wherefore, so far as He is God, He and the Father are one; so far as He is man, the Father is greater than He. For when He was the only Son of God, not by grace, but by nature, that He might be also full of grace, He became the Son of man; and He Himself unites both natures in His own identity, and both natures constitute one Christ; because, "being in the form of God, He thought it not robbery to be," what He was by nature, "equal with God." [62] But He made Himself of no reputation, and took upon Himself the form of a servant, not losing or lessening the form of God. And, accordingly, He was both made less and remained equal, being both in one, as has been said: but He was one of these as Word, and the other as man. As Word, He is equal with the Father; as man, less than the Father. One Son of God, and at the same time Son of man; one Son of man, and at the same time Son of God; not two Sons of God, God and man, but one Son of God: God without beginning; man with a beginning, our Lord Jesus Christ.

CHAPTER XXXVI

THE GRACE OF GOD IS CLEARLY AND REMARKABLY DISPLAYED IN RAISING THE MAN CHRIST JESUS TO THE DIGNITY OF THE SON OF GOD

Now here the grace of God is displayed with the greatest power and clearness. For what merit had the human nature in the man Christ earned, that it should in this unparalleled way be taken up into the unity of the person of the only Son of God? What goodness of will, what goodness of desire and intention, what good works, had gone before, which made this man worthy to become one person with God? Had He been a man previously to this, and had He earned this unprecedented reward, that He should be thought worthy to become God? Assuredly nay; from the very moment that He began to be man, He was nothing else than the Son of God, the only Son of God, the Word who was made flesh, and therefore He was God; so that just as each individual man unites in one person a body and a rational soul, so Christ in one person unites the Word and man. Now wherefore was this unheard of glory conferred on human nature—a glory which, as there was no antecedent merit, was of course

[61] John i. 1   [62] Phil. ii. 6

wholly of grace—except that here those who looked at the matter soberly and honestly might behold a clear manifestation of the power of God's free grace, and might understand that they are justified from their sins by the same grace which made the man Christ Jesus free from the possibility of sin? And so the angel, when he announced to Christ's mother the coming birth, saluted her thus: "Hail, thou that art full of grace;" [63] and shortly afterwards, "Thou hast found grace with God." [64] Now she was said to be full of grace, and to have found grace with God, because she was to be the mother of her Lord, nay, of the Lord of all flesh. But, speaking of Christ Himself, the evangelist John, after saying, "The Word was made flesh, and dwelt among us," adds, "and we behold His glory, the glory as of the only-begotten of the Father, full of grace and truth." [65] When he says, "The Word was made flesh," this is "full of grace;" when he says, "the glory of the only-begotten of the Father," this is "full of truth." For the Truth Himself, who was the only-begotten of the Father, not by grace, but by nature, by grace took our humanity upon Him, and so united it with His own person that He Himself became also the Son of man.

CHAPTER XXXVII

THE SAME GRACE IS FURTHER CLEARLY MANIFESTED IN THIS, THAT THE BIRTH OF CHRIST ACCORDING TO THE FLESH IS OF THE HOLY GHOST

For the same Jesus Christ who is the only-begotten, that is, the only Son of God, our Lord, was born of the Holy Ghost and of the Virgin Mary. And we know that the Holy Spirit is the gift of God, the gift being Himself indeed equal to the Giver. And therefore the Holy Spirit also is God, not inferior to the Father and the Son. The fact, therefore, that the nativity of Christ in His human nature was by the Holy Spirit, is another clear manifestation of grace. For when the Virgin asked the angel how this which he had announced should be, seeing she knew not a man, the angel answered, "The Holy Ghost shall come upon thee, and the power of the Highest shall overshadow thee: therefore also that holy thing which shall be born of thee shall be called the Son of God." [66] And when Joseph was minded to put her away, suspecting her of adultery, as he knew she was not with child by himself, he was told by the angel, "Fear not to take unto thee Mary thy wife; for that which is conceived in her is of the Holy Ghost:" [67] that is, what thou suspectest to be begotten of another man is of the Holy Ghost.

[63] Luke i. 28　　[64] Luke i. 30　　[65] John i. 14　　[66] Luke i. 35　　[67] Matt. i. 20

CHAPTER XXXVIII

JESUS CHRIST, ACCORDING TO THE FLESH, WAS NOT BORN OF THE
HOLY SPIRIT IN SUCH A SENSE THAT THE HOLY SPIRIT
IS HIS FATHER

Nevertheless, are we on this account to say that the Holy Ghost is the father of the man Christ, and that as God the Father begat the Word, so God the Holy Spirit begat the man, and that these two natures constitute the one Christ; and that as the Word He is the Son of God the Father, and as man the Son of God the Holy Spirit, because the Holy Spirit as His father begat Him of the Virgin Mary? Who will dare to say so? Nor is it necessary to show by reasoning how many other absurdities flow from this supposition, when it is itself so absurd that no believer's ears can bear to hear it. Hence, as we confess, "Our Lord Jesus Christ, who of God is God, and as man was born of the Holy Ghost and of the Virgin Mary, having both natures, the divine and the human, is the only Son of God the Father Almighty, from whom proceedeth the Holy Spirit." [68] Now in what sense do we say that Christ was born of the Holy Spirit, if the Holy Spirit did not beget Him? Is it that He made Him, since our Lord Jesus Christ, though as God "all things were made by Him," [69] yet as man was Himself made; as the apostle says, "who was made of the seed of David according to the flesh?" [70] But as that created thing which the Virgin conceived and brought forth, though it was united only to the person of the Son, was made by the whole Trinity (for the works of the Trinity are not separable), why should the Holy Spirit alone be mentioned as having made it? Or is it that, when one of the Three is mentioned as the author of any work, the whole Trinity is to be understood as working? That is true, and can be proved by examples. But we need not dwell longer on this solution. For the puzzle is, in what sense it is said, "born of the Holy Ghost," when He is in no sense the Son of the Holy Ghost? For though God made this world, it would not be right to say that it is the Son of God, or that it was born of God; we would say that it was created, or made, or framed, or ordered by Him, or whatever form of expression we can properly use. Here, then, when we make confession that Christ was born of the Holy Ghost and of the Virgin Mary, it is difficult to explain how it is that He is not the Son of the Holy Ghost and is the Son of the Virgin Mary, when He was born both of Him and of her. It is clear beyond a doubt that He was not born of the Holy Spirit as His father, in the same sense that He was born of the Virgin as His mother.

[68] A quotation from a form of the Apostles' Creed anciently in use in the Latin Church   [69] John i. 3   [70] Rom. i. 3

CHAPTER XXXIX

NOT EVERYTHING THAT IS BORN OF ANOTHER IS TO BE CALLED A SON OF THAT OTHER

We need not therefore take for granted, that whatever is born of a thing is forthwith to be declared the son of that thing. For, to pass over the fact that a son is born of a man in a different sense from that in which a hair or a louse is born of him, neither of these being a son; to pass over this, I say, as too mean an illustration for a subject of so much importance: it is certain that those who are born of water and of the Holy Spirit cannot with propriety be called sons of the water, though they are called sons of God the Father, and of the Church their mother. In the same way, then, He who was born of the Holy Spirit is the Son of God the Father, not of the Holy Spirit. For what I have said of the hair and the other things is sufficient to show us that not everything which is born of another can be called the son of that of which it is born, just as it does not follow that all who are called a man's sons were born of him, for some sons are adopted. And some men are called sons of hell, not as being born of hell, but as prepared for it, as the sons of the kingdom are prepared for the kingdom.

CHAPTER XL

CHRIST'S BIRTH THROUGH THE HOLY SPIRIT MANIFESTS TO US THE GRACE OF GOD

And, therefore, as one thing may be born of another, and yet not in such a way as to be its son, and as not every one who is called a son was born of him whose son he is called, it is clear that this arrangement by which Christ was born of the Holy Spirit, but not as His son, and of the Virgin Mary as her son, is intended as a manifestation of the grace of God. For it was by this grace that a man, without any antecedent merit, was at the very commencement of His existence as man, so united in one person with the Word of God, that the very person who was Son of man was at the same time Son of God, and the very person who was Son of God was at the same time Son of man; and in the adoption of His human nature into the divine, the grace itself became in a way so natural to the man, as to leave no room for entrance of sin. Wherefore this grace is signified by the Holy Spirit; for He, though in His own nature God, may also be called the gift of God. And to explain all this sufficiently, if indeed it could be done at all, would require a very lengthened discussion.

CHAPTER XLI

CHRIST, WHO WAS HIMSELF FREE FROM SIN WAS MADE SIN FOR US, THAT WE MIGHT BE RECONCILED TO GOD

Begotten and conceived, then, without any indulgence of carnal lust, and therefore bringing with Him no original sin, and by the grace of God joined and united in a wonderful and unspeakable way in one person with the Word, the Only-begotten of the Father, a son by nature, not by grace, and therefore having no sin of His own; nevertheless, on account of the likeness of sinful flesh in which He came, He was called sin, that He might be sacrificed to wash away sin. For, under the Old Covenant, sacrifices for sin were called sins.[71] And He, of whom all these sacrifices were types and shadows, was Himself truly made sin. Hence the apostle, after saying, "We pray you in Christ's stead, be ye reconciled to God," forthwith adds: "for He hath made Him to be sin for us who knew no sin; that we might be made the righteousness of God in Him." [72] He does not say, as some incorrect copies read, "He who knew no sin did sin for us," as if Christ had Himself sinned for our sakes; but he says, "Him who knew no sin," that is, Christ, God, to whom we are to be reconciled, "hath made to be sin for us," that is, hath made Him a sacrifice for our sins, by which we might be reconciled to God. He, then, being made sin, just as we are made righteousness (our righteousness being not our own, but God's, not in ourselves, but in Him); He being made sin, not His own, but ours, not in Himself, but in us, showed, by the likeness of sinful flesh in which He was crucified, that though sin was not in Him, yet that in a certain sense He died to sin, by dying in the flesh which was the likeness of sin; and that although He Himself had never lived the old life of sin, yet by His resurrection He typified our new life springing up out of the old death in sin.

CHAPTER XLII

THE SACRAMENT OF BAPTISM INDICATES OUR DEATH WITH CHRIST TO SIN, AND OUR RESURRECTION WITH HIM TO NEWNESS OF LIFE

And this is the meaning of the great sacrament of baptism which is solemnized among us, that all who attain to this grace should die to sin, as He is said to have died to sin, because He died in the flesh, which is the likeness of sin; and rising from the font regenerate, as He arose alive from the grave, should begin a new life in the Spirit, whatever may be the age of the body?

---

[71] Hos. iv. 8   [72] 2 Cor. v. 20, 21

CHAPTER XLIII

BAPTISM AND THE GRACE WHICH IT TYPIFIES ARE OPEN TO ALL, BOTH INFANTS AND ADULTS

For from the infant newly born to the old man bent with age, as there is none shut out from baptism, so there is none who in baptism does not die to sin. But infants die only to original sin; those who are older die also to all the sins which their evil lives have added to the sin which they brought with them.

CHAPTER XLIV

IN SPEAKING OF SIN, THE SINGULAR NUMBER IS OFTEN PUT FOR THE PLURAL, AND THE PLURAL FOR THE SINGULAR

But even these latter are frequently said to die to sin, though undoubtedly they die not to one sin, but to all the numerous actual sins they have committed in thought, word, or deed: for the singular number is often put for the plural, as when the poet says, "They fill its belly with the armed soldier," [73] though in the case here referred to there were many soldiers concerned. And we read in our own Scriptures: "Pray to the Lord, that He take away the serpent from us." [74] He does not say *serpents*, though the people were suffering from many; and so in other cases. When, on the other hand, the original sin is expressed in the plural number, as when we say that infants are baptized for the remission of *sins*, instead of saying for the remission of *sin*, this is the converse figure of speech, by which the plural number is put in place of the singular; as in the Gospel it is said of the death of Herod, "for they are dead which sought the young child's life," [75] instead of saying, "he is dead." And in *Exodus:* "They have made them," Moses says, "gods of gold," [76] though they had made only one calf, of which they said: "These be thy gods, O Israel, which brought thee up out of the land of Egypt" [77]—here, too, putting the plural in place of the singular.

CHAPTER XLV

IN ADAM'S FIRST SIN, MANY KINDS OF SIN WERE INVOLVED

However, even in that one sin, which "by one man entered into the world, and so passed upon all men," [78] and on account of which infants are baptized, a number of distinct sins may be observed, if it be analyzed as it were into its separate elements. For there is in it pride, because man

[73] "Uterumque armato milite complent."—Virgil, *Aen.* ii. 20   [74] Num. xxi. 7
[75] Matt. ii. 20   [76] Ex. xxxii. 31   [77] Ex. xxxii. 4   [78] Rom. v. 12

chose to be under his own dominion, rather than under the dominion of God; and blasphemy, because he did not believe God; and murder, for he brought death upon himself; and spiritual fornication, for the purity of the human soul was corrupted by the seducing blandishments of the serpent; and theft, for man turned to his own use the food he had been forbidden to touch; and avarice, for he had a craving for more than should have been sufficient for him; and whatever other sin can be discovered on careful reflection to be involved in this one admitted sin.

CHAPTER XLVI

IT IS PROBABLE THAT CHILDREN ARE INVOLVED IN THE GUILT NOT ONLY OF THE FIRST PAIR, BUT OF THEIR OWN IMMEDIATE PARENTS

And it is said, with much appearance of probability, that infants are involved in the guilt of the sins not only of the first pair, but of their own immediate parents. For that divine judgment, "I shall visit the iniquities of the fathers upon the children," [79] certainly applies to them before they come under the new covenant by regeneration. And it was this new covenant that was prophesied of, when it was said by Ezekiel, that the sons should not bear the iniquity of the fathers, and that it should no longer be a proverb in Israel, "The fathers have eaten sour grapes, and the children's teeth are set on edge." [80] Here lies the necessity that each man should be born again, that he might be freed from the sin in which he was born. For the sins committed afterwards can be cured by penitence, as we see is the case after baptism. And therefore the new birth would not have been appointed only that the first birth was sinful, so sinful that even one who was legitimately born in wedlock says: "I was shapen in iniquities, and in sins did my mother conceive me." [81] He did not say in *iniquity*, or in *sin*, though he might have said so correctly; but he preferred to say "iniquities" and "sins," because in that one sin which passed upon all men, and which was so great that human nature was by it made subject to inevitable death, many sins, as I showed above, may be discriminated; and further, because there are other sins of the immediate parents, which, though they have not the same effect in producing a change of nature, yet subject the children to guilt unless the divine grace and mercy interpose to rescue them.

[79] Ex. xx. 5; Deut. v. 9   [80] Ezek. xviii. 2   [81] Ps. li. 5

CHAPTER XLVII

IT IS DIFFICULT TO DECIDE WHETHER THE SINS OF A MAN'S OTHER PROGENITORS ARE IMPUTED TO HIM

But about the sins of the other progenitors who intervene between Adam and a man's own parents, a question may very well be raised. Whether every one who is born is involved in all their accumulated evil acts, in all their multiplied original guilt, so that the later he is born, so much the worse is his condition; or whether God threatens to visit the iniquity of the fathers upon the children unto the third and fourth generations because in His mercy He does not extend His wrath against the sins of the progenitors further than that, lest those who do not obtain the grace of regeneration might be crushed down under too heavy a burden if they were compelled to bear as original guilt all the sins of all their progenitors from the very beginning of the human race, and to pay the penalty due to them; or whether any other solution of this great question may or may not be found in Scripture by a more diligent search and a more careful interpretation, I dare not rashly affirm.

CHAPTER XLVIII

THE GUILT OF THE FIRST SIN IS SO GREAT THAT IT CAN BE WASHED AWAY ONLY IN THE BLOOD OF THE MEDIATOR, JESUS CHRIST

Nevertheless, that one sin, admitted into a place where such perfect happiness reigned, was of so heinous a character, that in one man the whole human race was originally, and as one may say, radically, condemned; and it cannot be pardoned and blotted out except through the one Mediator between God and men, the man Christ Jesus, who only has had power to be so born as not to need a second birth.

CHAPTER XLIX

CHRIST WAS NOT REGENERATED IN THE BAPTISM OF JOHN, BUT SUBMITTED TO IT TO GIVE US AN EXAMPLE OF HUMILITY, JUST AS HE SUBMITTED TO DEATH, NOT AS THE PUNISHMENT OF SIN, BUT TO TAKE AWAY THE SIN OF THE WORLD

Now, those who were baptized in the baptism of John, by whom Christ was Himself baptized,[82] were not regenerated; but they were prepared through the ministry of His forerunner, who cried, "Prepare ye the way of the Lord," [83] for Him in whom only they could be regenerated. For His baptism is not with water only, as was that of John, but with the

[82] Matt. iii. 13-15   [83] Matt. iii. 3

Holy Ghost also;[84] so that whoever believes in Christ is regenerated by that Spirit, of whom Christ being generated, He did not need regeneration. Whence that announcement of the Father which was heard after His baptism, "This day have I begotten Thee," [85] referred not to that one day of time on which He was baptized, but to the one day of an unchangeable eternity, so as to show that this man was one in person with the Only-begotten. For when a day neither begins with the close of yesterday, nor ends with the beginning of to-morrow, it is an eternal to-day. Therefore He asked to be baptized in water by John, not that any iniquity of His might be washed away, but that He might manifest the depth of His humility. For baptism found in Him nothing to wash away, as death found in Him nothing to punish; so that it was in the strictest justice, and not by the mere violence of power, that the devil was crushed and conquered: for, as he had most unjustly put Christ to death, though there was no sin in Him to deserve death, it was most just that through Christ he should lose his hold of those who by sin were justly subject to the bondage in which he held them. Both of these, then, that is, both baptism and death, were submitted to by Him, not through a pitiable necessity, but of His own free pity for us, and as part of an arrangement by which, as one man brought sin into the world, that is, upon the whole human race, so one man was to take away the sin of the world.

CHAPTER L

CHRIST TOOK AWAY NOT ONLY THE ONE ORIGINAL SIN, BUT ALL THE OTHER SINS THAT HAVE BEEN ADDED TO IT

With this difference: the first man brought one sin into the world, but this man took away not only that one sin, but all that He found added to it. Hence the apostle says: "And not as it was by one that sinned, so is the gift: for the judgment was by one to condemnation, but the free gift is of many offenses unto justification." [86] For it is evident that the one sin which we bring with us by nature would, even if it stood alone, bring us under condemnation; but the free gift justifies man from many offenses: for each man, in addition to the one sin which, in common with all his kind, he brings with him by nature, has committed many sins that are strictly his own.

[84] Matt. iii. 11
[85] Ps. ii. 7; Heb. i. 5, v. 5. It is by a mistake that Augustine quotes these words as pronounced at our Lord's baptism   [86] Rom. v. 16

CHAPTER LI

ALL MEN BORN OF ADAM ARE UNDER CONDEMNATION, AND ONLY IF NEW BORN IN CHRIST ARE FREED FROM CONDEMNATION

But what he says a little after, "Therefore, as by the offense of one judgment came upon all men to condemnation; even so by the righteousness of one the free gift came upon all men unto justification of life," [87] shows clearly enough that there is no one born of Adam but is subject to condemnation, and that no one, unless he be new born in Christ, is freed from condemnation.

CHAPTER LII

IN BAPTISM, WHICH IS THE SIMILITUDE OF THE DEATH AND RESURRECTION OF CHRIST, ALL, BOTH INFANTS AND ADULTS, DIE TO SIN THAT THEY MAY WALK IN NEWNESS OF LIFE

And after he has said as much about the condemnation through one man, and the free gift through one man, as he deemed sufficient for that part of his epistle, the apostle goes on to speak of the great mystery of holy baptism in the cross of Christ, and to explain clearly to us that baptism in Christ is nothing else than a similitude of the death of Christ, and that the death of Christ on the cross is nothing but a similitude of the pardon of sin: so that just as real as is His death, so real is the remission of our sins; and just as real as is His resurrection, so real is our justification. He says: "What shall we say, then? Shall we continue in sin, that grace may abound?" [88] For he had said previously, "But where sin abounded, grace did much more abound." [89] And therefore he proposes to himself the question, whether it would be right to continue in sin for the sake of the consequent abounding grace. But he answers, "God forbid;" and adds, "How shall we, that are dead to sin, live any longer therein?" Then, to show that we are dead to sin, "Know ye not," he says, "that so many of us as were baptized into Jesus Christ, were baptized into His death?" If, then, the fact that we were baptized into the death of Christ proves that we are dead to sin, it follows that even infants who are baptized into Christ die to sin, being baptized into His death. For there is no exception made: "So many of us as were baptized into Jesus Christ, were baptized into His death." And this is said to prove that we are dead to sin. Now, to what sin do infants die in their regeneration but that sin which they bring with them at birth? And therefore to these also applies what follows: "Therefore we are buried with Him by baptism into death; that, like as Christ was raised up

[87] Rom. v. 18   [88] Rom. vi. 1   [89] Rom. v. 20

from the dead by the glory of the Father, even so we also should walk in newness of life. For if we have been planted together in the likeness of His death, we shall be also in the likeness of His resurrection: knowing this, that our old man is crucified with Him, that the body of sin might be destroyed, that henceforth we should not serve sin. For he that is dead is freed from sin. Now if we be dead with Christ, we believe that we shall also live with Him: knowing that Christ, being raised from the dead, dieth no more; death hath no more dominion over Him. For in that He died, He died unto sin once; but in that He liveth, He liveth unto God. Likewise reckon ye also yourselves to be dead indeed unto sin, but alive unto God through Jesus Christ our Lord." Now he had commenced with proving that we must not continue in sin that grace may abound, and had said: "How shall we that are dead to sin live any longer therein?" And to show that we are dead to sin, he added: "Know ye not, that so many of us as were baptized into Jesus Christ, were baptized into His death?" And so he concludes this whole passage just as he began it. For he has brought in the death of Christ in such a way as to imply that Christ Himself also died to sin. To what sin did He die if not to the flesh, in which there was not sin, but the likeness of sin, and which was therefore called by the name of sin? To those who are baptized into the death of Christ, then—and this class includes not adults only, but infants as well—he says: "Likewise reckon ye also yourselves to be dead indeed unto sin, but alive unto God through Jesus Christ our Lord." [90]

CHAPTER LIII

CHRIST'S CROSS AND BURIAL, RESURRECTION, ASCENSION, AND SITTING DOWN AT THE RIGHT HAND OF GOD, ARE IMAGES OF THE CHRISTIAN LIFE

All the events, then, of Christ's crucifixion, of His burial, of His resurrection the third day, of His ascension into heaven, of His sitting down at the right hand of the Father, were so ordered, that the life which the Christian leads here might be modelled upon them, not merely in a mystical sense, but in reality. For in reference to His crucifixion it is said: "They that are Christ's have crucified the flesh, with the affections and lusts." [91] And in reference to His burial: "We are buried with Him by baptism into death." [92] In reference to His resurrection: "That, like as Christ was raised up from the dead by the glory of the Father, even so we also should walk in newness of life." [93] And in reference to His ascension into heaven and sitting down at the right hand of the Father: "If ye then be risen with Christ, seek those things which are above, where Christ sitteth on the right hand of God. Set your affection on things above, not on things on the earth. For ye are dead, and your life is hid with Christ in God." [94]

[90] Rom. vi. 1-11   [91] Gal. v. 24   [92] Rom. vi. 4   [93] Rom. vi. 5   [94] Col. iii. 1-3

CHAPTER LIV

But what we believe as to Christ's action in the future, when He shall come from heaven to judge the quick and the dead, has no bearing upon the life which we now lead here; for it forms no part of what He did upon earth, but is part of what He shall do at the end of the world. And it is to this that the apostle refers in what immediately follows the passage quoted above: "When Christ, who is our life shall appear, then shall ye also appear with Him in glory." [95]

CHAPTER LV

Now the expression, "to judge the quick and the dead," may be interpreted in two ways: either we may understand by the "quick" those who at His advent shall not yet have died, but whom He shall find alive in the flesh, and by the "dead" those who have departed from the body, or who shall have departed before His coming; or we may understand the "quick" to mean the righteous, and the "dead" the unrighteous; for the righteous shall be judged as well as others. Now the judgment of God is sometimes taken in a bad sense, as, for example, "They that have done evil unto the resurrection of judgment;" [96] sometimes in a good sense, as, "Save me, O God, by Thy name, and judge me by Thy strength." [97] This is easily understood when we consider that it is the judgment of God which separates the good from the evil, and sets the good at His right hand, that they may be delivered from evil, and not destroyed with the wicked; and it is for this reason that the Psalmist cried, "Judge me, O God," and then added, as if in explanation, "and distinguish my cause from that of an ungodly nation." [98]

CHAPTER LVI

And now, having spoken of Jesus Christ, the only Son of God, our Lord, with the brevity suitable to a confession of our faith, we go on to say that we believe also in the Holy Ghost—thus completing the Trinity which constitutes the Godhead. Then we mention the Holy Church. And thus we are

[95] Col. iii. 4   [96] John v. 29   [97] Ps. liv. 1   [98] Ps. xliii. 1

made to understand that the intelligent creation, which constitutes the free Jerusalem,[99] ought to be subordinate in the order of speech to the Creator, the Supreme Trinity: for all that is said of the man Christ Jesus has reference, of course, to the unity of the person of the Only-begotten. Therefore the true order of the Creed demanded that the Church should be made subordinate to the Trinity, as the house to Him who dwells in it, the temple to God who occupies it, and the city to its builder. And we are here to understand the whole Church, not that part of it only which wanders as a stranger on the earth, praising the name of God from the rising of the sun to the going down of the same, and singing a new song of deliverance from its old captivity; but that part also which has always from its creation remained steadfast to God in heaven, and has never experienced the misery consequent upon a fall. This part is made up of the holy angels, who enjoy uninterrupted happiness; and (as it is bound to do) it renders assistance to the part which is still wandering among strangers: for these two parts shall be one in the fellowship of eternity, and now they are one in the bonds of love, the whole having been ordained for the worship of the one God. Wherefore, neither the whole Church, nor any part of it, has any desire to be worshipped instead of God, nor to be God to any one who belongs to the temple of God—that temple which is built up of the saints who were created by the uncreated God. And therefore the Holy Spirit, if a creature, could not be the Creator, but would be a part of the intelligent creation. He would simply be the highest creature, and therefore would not be mentioned in the Creed before the Church; for He Himself would belong to the Church, to that part of it which is in the heavens. And He would not have a temple, for He Himself would be part of a temple. Now He has a temple, of which the apostle says: "Know ye not that your body is the temple of the Holy Ghost, which is in you, which ye have of God?" [100] Of which body he says in another place: "Know ye not that your bodies are the members of Christ?" [101] How, then, is He not God, seeing that He has a temple? and how can He be less than Christ, whose members are His temple? Nor has He one temple, and God another, seeing that the same apostle says: "Know ye not that ye are the temple of God?" [102] and adds, as proof of this, "and that the Spirit of God dwelleth in you." [103] God, then, dwells in His temple: not the Holy Spirit only, but the Father also, and the Son, who says of His own body, through which He was made Head of the Church upon earth ("that in all things He might have the pre-eminence"):[104] "Destroy this temple, and in three days I will raise it up." [105] The temple of God, then, that is, of the Supreme Trinity as a whole, is the Holy Church, embracing in its full extent both heaven and earth.

[99] Gal. iv. 26   [100] 1 Cor. vi. 19   [101] 1 Cor. vi. 15   [102] 1 Cor. iii. 16   [103] 1 Cor. iii. 16   [104] Col. i. 18   [105] John ii. 19

CHAPTER LVII

THE CONDITION OF THE CHURCH IN HEAVEN

But of that part of the Church which is in heaven what can we say, except that no wicked one is found in it, and that no one has fallen from it, or shall ever fall from it, since the time that "God spared not the angels that sinned," as the Apostle Peter writes, "but cast them down to hell, and delivered them into chains of darkness, to be reserved unto judgment?" [106]

CHAPTER LVIII

WE HAVE NO CERTAIN KNOWLEDGE OF THE ORGANIZATION OF THE ANGELIC SOCIETY

Now, what the organization is of that supremely happy society in heaven: what the differences of rank are, which explain the fact that while all are called by the general name *angels*, as we read in the *Epistle to the Hebrews*, "but to which of the angels said God at any time, Sit on my right hand?" [107] (this form of expression being evidently designed to embrace all the angels without exception) we yet find that there are some called *archangels;* and whether the archangels are the same as those called *hosts*, so that the expression, "Praise ye Him, all His angels: praise ye Him, all His hosts," [108] is the same as if it had been said, "Praise ye Him, all His angels: praise ye Him, all His archangels;" and what are the various significations of those four names under which the apostle seems to embrace the whole heavenly company without exception, "whether they be thrones, or dominions, or principalities, or powers:" [109]—let those who are able answer these questions, if they can also prove their answers to be true; but as for me, I confess my ignorance. I am not even certain upon this point: whether the sun, and the moon, and all the stars, do not form part of this same society, though many consider them merely luminous bodies, without either sensation or intelligence.

CHAPTER LIX

THE BODIES ASSUMED BY ANGELS RAISE A VERY DIFFICULT, AND NOT VERY USEFUL, SUBJECT OF DISCUSSION

Further, who will tell with what sort of bodies it was that the angels appeared to men, making themselves not only visible, but tangible; and again, how it is that, not through material bodies, but by spiritual power, they present visions not to the bodily eyes, but to the spiritual eyes of the mind, or speak something not into the ear from without, but from within

---

[106] 2 Pet. ii. 4   [107] Heb. i. 13   [108] Ps. cxlviii. 2   [109] Col. i. 16

the soul of the man, they themselves being stationed there too, as it is written in the prophet, "And the angel that spake in me said unto me" [110] (he does not say, "that spake *to* me," but "that spake *in* me"); or appear to men in sleep, and make communications through dreams, as we read in the Gospel, "Behold, the angel of the Lord appeared unto him in a dream, saying"? [111] For these methods of communication seem to imply that the angels have not tangible bodies, and make it a very difficult question to solve how the patriarchs washed their feet,[112] and how it was that Jacob wrestled with the angel in a way so unmistakeably material.[113] To ask questions like these, and to make such guesses as we can at the answers, is a useful exercise for the intellect, if the discussion be kept within proper bounds, and if we avoid the error of supposing ourselves to know what we do not know. For what is the necessity for affirming, or denying, or defining with accuracy on these subjects, and others like them, when we may without blame be entirely ignorant of them?

CHAPTER LX

IT IS MORE NECESSARY TO BE ABLE TO DETECT THE WILES OF SATAN WHEN HE TRANSFORMS HIMSELF INTO AN ANGEL OF LIGHT

It is more necessary to use all our powers of discrimination and judgment when Satan transforms himself into an angel of light,[114] lest by his wiles he should lead us astray into hurtful courses. For, while he only deceives the bodily senses, and does not pervert the mind from that true and sound judgment which enables a man to lead a life of faith, there is no danger to religion; or if, feigning himself to be good, he does or says the things that befit good angels, and we believe him to be good, the error is not one that is hurtful or dangerous to Christian faith. But when, through these means, which are alien to his nature, he goes on to lead us into courses of his own, then great watchfulness is necessary to detect, and refuse to follow, him. But how many men are fit to evade all his deadly wiles, unless God restrains and watches over them? The very difficulty of the matter, however, is useful in this respect, that it prevents men from trusting in themselves or in one another, and leads all to place their confidence in God alone. And certainly no pious man can doubt that this is most expedient for us.

CHAPTER LXI

THE CHURCH ON EARTH HAS BEEN REDEEMED FROM SIN BY THE BLOOD OF A MEDIATOR

This part of the Church, then, which is made up of the holy angels and the hosts of God, shall become known to us in its true nature, when, at the

---

[110] Zech. i. 9   [111] Matt. i. 20   [112] Gen. xviii. 4, xix. 2   [113] Gen. xxxii. 24, 25
[114] 2 Cor. xi. 14

end of the world, we shall be united with it in the common possession of everlasting happiness. But the other part, which, separated from it, wanders as a stranger on the earth, is better known to us, both because we belong to it, and because it is composed of men, and we too are men. This section of the Church has been redeemed from all sin by the blood of a Mediator who had no sin, and its song is: "If God be for us, who can be against us? He that spared not His own Son, but delivered Him up for us all." [115] Now it was not for the angels that Christ died. Yet what was done for the redemption of man through His death was in a sense done for the angels, because the enmity which sin had put between men and the holy angels is removed, and friendship is restored between them, and by the redemption of man the gaps which the great apostasy left in the angelic host are filled up.

CHAPTER LXII

BY THE SACRIFICE OF CHRIST ALL THINGS ARE RESTORED, AND PEACE IS MADE BETWEEN EARTH AND HEAVEN

And, of course, the holy angels, taught by God, in the eternal contemplation of whose truth their happiness consists, know how great a number of the human race are to supplement their ranks, and fill up the full tale of their citizenship. Wherefore the apostle says, that "all things are gathered together in one in Christ, both which are in heaven and which are on earth." [116] The things which are in heaven are gathered together when what was lost therefrom in the fall of the angels is restored from among men; and the things which are on earth are gathered together, when those who are predestined to eternal life are redeemed from their old corruption. And thus, through that single sacrifice in which the Mediator was offered up, the one sacrifice of which the many victims under the law were types, heavenly things are brought into peace with earthly things, and earthly things with heavenly. Wherefore, as the same apostle says: "For it pleased the Father that in Him should all fullness dwell: and, having made peace through the blood of His cross, by Him to reconcile all things to Himself: by Him, I say, whether they be things in earth, or things in heaven." [117]

CHAPTER LXIII

THE PEACE OF GOD, WHICH REIGNETH IN HEAVEN, PASSETH ALL UNDERSTANDING

This peace, as Scripture saith, "passeth all understanding," [118] and cannot be known by us until we have come into the full possession of it. For in what sense are heavenly things reconciled, except they be reconciled to

[115] Rom. viii. 31   [116] Eph. i. 10   [117] Col. i. 19, 20   [118] Phil. iv. 7

us, *viz.* by coming into harmony with us? For in heaven there is unbroken peace, both between all the intelligent creatures that exist there, and between these and their Creator. And this peace, as is said, passeth all understanding; but this, of course, means our understanding, not that of those who always behold the face of their Father. We now, however great may be our human understanding, know but in part, and see through a glass darkly.[119] But when we shall be equal unto the angels of God [120] then we shall see face to face, as they do; and we shall have as great peace towards them as they have towards us, because we shall love them as much as we are loved by them. And so their peace shall be known to us: for our own peace shall be like to theirs, and as great as theirs, nor shall it then pass our understanding. But the peace of God, the peace which He cherisheth towards us, shall undoubtedly pass not our understanding only, but theirs as well. And this must be so: for every rational creature which is happy derives its happiness from Him; He does not derive His from it. And in this view it is better to interpret "all" in the passage, "The peace of God passeth all understanding," as admitting of no exception even in favor of the understanding of the holy angels: the only exception that can be made is that of God Himself. For, of course, His peace does not pass His own understanding.

CHAPTER LXIV

PARDON OF SIN EXTENDS OVER THE WHOLE MORTAL LIFE OF THE SAINTS, WHICH, THOUGH FREE FROM CRIME, IS NOT FREE FROM SIN

But the angels even now are at peace with us when our sins are pardoned. Hence, in the order of the Creed, after the mention of the Holy Church is placed the remission of sins. For it is by this that the Church on earth stands: it is through this that what had been lost, and was found, is saved from being lost again. For, setting aside the grace of baptism, which is given as an antidote to original sin, so that what our birth imposes upon us, our new birth relieves us from (this grace, however, takes away all the actual sins also that have been committed in thought, word, and deed): setting aside, then, this great act of favor, whence commences man's restoration, and in which all our guilt, both original and actual, is washed away, the rest of our life from the time that we have the use of reason provides constant occasion for the remission of sins, however great may be our advance in righteousness. For the sons of God, as long as they live in this body of death, are in conflict with death. And although it is truly said of them, "As many as are led by the Spirit of God, they are the sons of God," [121] yet they are led by the Spirit of God, and as the sons of God ad-

[119] 1 Cor. xiii. 12   [120] Luke xx. 36   [121] Rom. viii. 14

vance towards God under this drawback, that they are led also by their own spirit, weighted as it is by the corruptible body;[122] and that, as the sons of men, under the influence of human affections, they fall back to their old level, and so sin. There is a difference, however. For although every crime is a sin, every sin is not a crime. And so we say that the life of holy men, as long as they remain in this mortal body, may be found without crime; but, as the Apostle John says, "If we say that we have no sin, we deceive ourselves, and the truth is not in us."[123]

CHAPTER LXV

GOD PARDONS SINS, BUT ON CONDITION OF PENITENCE, CERTAIN TIMES FOR WHICH HAVE BEEN FIXED BY THE LAW OF THE CHURCH

But even crimes themselves, however great, may be remitted in the Holy Church; and the mercy of God is never to be despaired of by men who truly repent, each according to the measure of his sin. And in the act of repentance, where a crime has been committed of such a nature as to cut off the sinner from the body of Christ we are not to take account so much of the measure of time as of the measure of sorrow; for a broken and a contrite heart God doth not despise.[124] But as the grief of one heart is frequently hid from another, and is not made known to others by words or other signs, when it is manifest to Him of whom it is said, "My groaning is not hid from Thee,"[125] those who govern the Church have rightly appointed times of penitence, that the Church in which the sins are remitted may be satisfied; and outside the Church sins are not remitted. For the Church alone has received the pledge of the Holy Spirit, without which there is no remission of sins—such, at least, as brings the pardoned to eternal life.

CHAPTER LXVI

THE PARDON OF SIN HAS REFERENCE CHIEFLY TO THE FUTURE JUDGMENT

Now the pardon of sin has reference chiefly to the future judgment. For, as far as this life is concerned, the saying of Scripture holds good: "A heavy yoke is upon the sons of Adam, from the day that they go out of their mother's womb, till the day that they return to the mother of all things."[126] So that we see even infants, after baptism and regeneration, suffering from the infliction of divers evils: and thus we are given to understand, that all that is set forth in the sacraments of salvation refers rather to the hope of future good, than to the retaining or attaining of present blessings. For

---

[122] Wisd. ix. 15   [123] I John i. 8   [124] Ps. li. 17   [125] Ps. xxxviii. 9   [126] Ecclus. xl. 1

many sins seem in this world to be overlooked and visited with no punishment, whose punishment is reserved for the future (for it is not in vain that the day when Christ shall come as Judge of quick and dead is peculiarly named the day of judgment); just as, on the other hand, many sins are punished in this life, which nevertheless are pardoned, and shall bring down no punishment in the future life. Accordingly, in reference to certain temporal punishments, which in this life are visited upon sinners, the apostle, addressing those whose sins are blotted out, and not reserved for the final judgment, says: "For if we would judge ourselves, we should not be judged. But when we are judged, we are chastened of the Lord, that we should not be condemned with the world." [127]

CHAPTER LXVII

FAITH WITHOUT WORKS IS DEAD, AND CANNOT SAVE A MAN

It is believed, moreover, by some, that men who do not abandon the name of Christ, and who have been baptized in the Church by His baptism, and who have never been cut off from the Church by any schism or heresy, though they should live in the grossest sin, and never either wash it away in penitence nor redeem it by almsgiving, but persevere in it persistently to the last day of their lives, shall be saved by fire: that is, that although they shall suffer a punishment by fire, lasting for a time proportionate to the magnitude of their crimes and misdeeds, they shall not be punished with everlasting fire. But those who believe this, and yet are Catholics, seem to me to be led astray by a kind of benevolent feeling natural to humanity. For Holy Scripture, when consulted, gives a very different answer. I have written a book on this subject, entitled *Of Faith and Works*, in which, to the best of my ability, God assisting me, I have shown from Scripture, that the faith which saves us is that which the Apostle Paul clearly enough describes when he says: "For in Jesus Christ neither circumcision availeth anything, nor uncircumcision, but faith which worketh by love." [128] But if it worketh evil, and not good, then without doubt, as the Apostle James says, "it is dead, being alone." [129] The same apostle says again, "What doth it profit, my brethren, though a man say he hath faith, and have not works? Can faith save him?" [130] And further, if a wicked man shall be saved by fire on account of his faith alone, and if this is what the blessed Apostle Paul means when he says, "But he himself shall be saved, yet so as by fire;" [131] then faith without works *can* save a man, and what his fellow-apostle James says must be false. And that must be false which Paul himself says in another place: "Be not deceived: neither fornicators, nor idolaters, nor adulterers, nor effeminate, nor abusers of themselves with mankind, nor thieves, nor covetous, nor drunkards, nor revilers, nor extortioners,

[127] I Cor. xi. 31, 32   [128] Gal. v. 6   [129] Jas. ii. 17   [130] Jas. ii. 14   [131] I Cor. iii. 15

shall inherit the kingdom of God." [132] For if those who persevere in these wicked courses shall nevertheless be saved on account of their faith in Christ, how can it be true that they shall not inherit the kingdom of God?

CHAPTER LXVIII

THE TRUE SENSE OF THE PASSAGE (I COR. III. 11-15) ABOUT THOSE WHO ARE SAVED, YET SO AS BY FIRE

But as these most plain and unmistakable declarations of the apostles cannot be false, that obscure saying about those who build upon the foundation, Christ, not gold, silver, and precious stones, but wood, hay, and stubble (for it is these who, it is said, shall be saved, yet so as by fire, the merit of the foundation saving them[133]), must be so interpreted as not to conflict with the plain statements quoted above. Now wood, hay, and stubble may, without incongruity, be understood to signify such an attachment to worldly things, however lawful these may be in themselves, that they cannot be lost without grief of mind. And though this grief burns, yet if Christ hold the place of foundation in the heart—that is, if nothing be preferred to Him, and if the man, though burning with grief, is yet more willing to lose the things he loves so much than to lose Christ—he is saved by fire. If, however, in time of temptation, he prefer to hold by temporal and earthly things rather than by Christ, he has not Christ as his foundation; for he puts earthly things in the first place, and in a building nothing comes before the foundation. Again, the fire of which the apostle speaks in this place must be such a fire as both men are made to pass through, that is, both the man who builds upon the foundation, gold, silver, precious stones, and the man who builds wood, hay, stubble. For he immediately adds: "The fire shall try every man's work, of what sort it is. If any man's work abide which he hath built thereupon, he shall receive a reward. If any man's work shall be burned, he shall suffer loss; but he himself shall be saved, yet so as by fire." [134] The fire then shall prove, not the work of one of them only, but of both. Now the trial of adversity is a kind of fire which is plainly spoken of in another place: "The furnace proveth the potter's vessels: and the furnace of adversity just men." [135] And this fire does in the course of this life act exactly in the way the apostle says. If it come into contact with two believers, one "caring for the things that belong to the Lord, how he may please the Lord," [136] that is, building upon Christ the foundation, gold, silver, precious stones; the other "caring for the things that are of the world, how he may please his wife," that is, building upon the same foundation wood, hay, stubble—the work of the former is not burned, because he has not given his love to things whose loss can cause him grief; but the work of the latter is burned, because things that are en-

---

[132] I Cor. vi. 9, 10   [133] I Cor. iii. 11-15   [134] I Cor. iii. 13-15   [135] Ecclus. xxvii. 5, ii. 5   [136] I Cor. vii. 32

joyed with desire cannot be lost without pain. But since, by our supposition, even the latter prefers to lose these things rather than to lose Christ, and since he does not desert Christ out of fear of losing them, though he is grieved when he does lose them, he is saved, but it is so as by fire; because the grief for what he loved and has lost burns him. But it does not subvert nor consume him; for he is protected by his immovable and incorruptible foundation.

CHAPTER LXIX

IT IS NOT IMPOSSIBLE THAT SOME BELIEVERS MAY PASS THROUGH A PURGATORIAL FIRE IN THE FUTURE LIFE

And it is not impossible that something of the same kind may take place even after this life. It is a matter that may be inquired into, and either ascertained or left doubtful, whether some believers shall pass through a kind of purgatorial fire, and in proportion as they have loved with more or less devotion the goods that perish, be less or more quickly delivered from it. This cannot, however, be the case of any of those of whom it is said, that they "shall not inherit the kingdom of God," [137] unless after suitable repentance their sins be forgiven them. When I say "suitable," I mean that they are not to be unfruitful in almsgiving; for Holy Scripture lays so much stress on this virtue, that our Lord tells us beforehand, that He will ascribe no merit to those on His right hand but that they abound in it, and no defect to those on His left hand but their want of it, when He shall say to the former, "Come, ye blessed of my Father, inherit the kingdom," and to the latter, "Depart from me, ye cursed, into everlasting fire." [138]

CHAPTER LXX

ALMSGIVING WILL NOT ATONE FOR SIN UNLESS THE LIFE BE CHANGED

We must beware, however, lest any one should suppose that gross sins, such as are committed by those who shall not inherit the kingdom of God, may be daily perpetrated, and daily atoned for by almsgiving. The life must be changed for the better; and almsgiving must be used to propitiate God for past sins, not to purchase impunity for the commission of such sins in the future. For He has given no man license to sin,[139] although in His mercy He may blot out sins that are already committed, if we do not neglect to make proper satisfaction.

[137] I Cor. vi. 10   [138] Matt. xxv. 31-46   [139] Ecclus. xv. 20

CHAPTER LXXI

THE DAILY PRAYER OF THE BELIEVER MAKES SATISFACTION FOR THE TRIVIAL SINS THAT DAILY STAIN HIS LIFE

Now the daily prayer of the believer makes satisfaction for those daily sins of a momentary and trivial kind which are necessary incidents of this life. For he can say, "Our Father which art in heaven," [140] seeing that to such a Father he is now born again of water and of the Spirit.[141] And this prayer certainly takes away the very small sins of daily life. It takes away also those which at one time made the life of the believer very wicked, but which, now that he is changed for the better by repentance, he has given up, provided that as truly as he says, "Forgive us our debts" (for there is no want of debts to be forgiven), so truly does he say, "as we forgive our debtors;" [142] that is, provided he does what he says he does: for to forgive a man who asks for pardon, is really to give alms.

CHAPTER LXXII

THERE ARE MANY KINDS OF ALMS, THE GIVING OF WHICH ASSISTS TO PROCURE PARDON FOR OUR SINS

And on this principle of interpretation, our Lord's saying, "Give alms of such things as ye have, and, behold, all things are clean unto you," [143] applies to every useful act that a man does in mercy. Not only, then, the man who gives food to the hungry, drink to the thirsty, clothing to the naked, hospitality to the stranger, shelter to the fugitive, who visits the sick and the imprisoned, ransoms the captive, assists the weak, leads the blind, comforts the sorrowful, heals the sick, puts the wanderer on the right path, gives advice to the perplexed, and supplies the wants of the needy—not this man only, but the man who pardons the sinner also gives alms; and the man who corrects with blows, or restrains by any kind of discipline one over whom he has power, and who at the same time forgives from the heart the sin by which he was injured, or prays that it may be forgiven, is also a giver of alms, not only in that he forgives, or prays for forgiveness for the sin, but also in that he rebukes and corrects the sinner: for in this, too, he shows mercy. Now much good is bestowed upon unwilling recipients, when their advantage and not their pleasure is consulted; and they themselves frequently prove to be their own enemies, while their true friends are those whom they take for their enemies, and to whom in their blindness they return evil for good. (A Christian, indeed, is not permitted to return evil even for evil.[144]) And thus there are many kinds of alms, by giving of which we assist to procure the pardon of our sins.

[140] Matt. vi. 9   [141] John iii. 5   [142] Matt. vi. 12   [143] Luke xi. 41   [144] Rom. xii. 17; Matt. v. 44

CHAPTER LXXIII

THE GREATEST OF ALL ALMS IS TO FORGIVE OUR DEBTORS AND TO LOVE OUR ENEMIES

But none of those is greater than to forgive from the heart a sin that has been committed against us. For it is a comparatively small thing to wish well to, or even to do good to, a man who has done no evil to you. It is a much higher thing, and is the result of the most exalted goodness, to love your enemy, and always to wish well to, and when you have the opportunity, to do good to, the man who wishes you ill, and, when he can, does you harm. This is to obey the command of God: "Love your enemies, do good to them that hate you, and pray for them which persecute you." [145] But seeing that this is a frame of mind only reached by the perfect sons of God, and that though every believer ought to strive after it, and by prayer to God and earnest struggling with himself endeavor to bring his soul up to this standard, yet a degree of goodness so high can hardly belong to so great a multitude as we believe are heard when they use this petition, "Forgive us our debts, as we forgive our debtors;" in view of all this, it cannot be doubted that the implied undertaking is fulfilled if a man, though he has not yet attained to loving his enemy, yet, when asked by one who has sinned against him to forgive him his sin, does forgive him from his heart. For he certainly desires to be himself forgiven when he prays, "as we forgive our debtors," that is, Forgive us our debts when we beg forgiveness, as we forgive our debtors when they beg forgiveness from us.

CHAPTER LXXIV

GOD DOES NOT PARDON THE SINS OF THOSE WHO DO NOT FROM THE HEART FORGIVE OTHERS

Now, he who asks forgiveness of the man against whom he has sinned, being moved by his sin to ask forgiveness, cannot be counted an enemy in such a sense that it should be as difficult to love him now as it was when he was engaged in active hostility. And the man who does not from his heart forgive him who repents of his sin, and asks forgiveness, need not suppose that his own sins are forgiven of God. For the Truth cannot lie. And what reader or hearer of the Gospel can have failed to notice, that the same person who said, "I am the Truth," [146] taught us also this form of prayer; and in order to impress this particular petition deeply upon our minds, said, "For if ye forgive men their trespasses, your heavenly Father will also forgive you; but if ye forgive not men their trespasses, neither will your Father forgive your trespasses"? [147] The man whom the thunder of this

[145] Matt. v. 44   [146] John xiv. 6   [147] Matt. vi. 14, 15

warning does not awaken is not asleep, but dead; and yet so powerful is that voice, that it can awaken even the dead.

CHAPTER LXXV

THE WICKED AND THE UNBELIEVING ARE NOT MADE CLEAN BY THE GIVING OF ALMS, EXCEPT THEY BE BORN AGAIN

Assuredly, then, those who live in gross wickedness, and take no care to reform their lives and manners, and yet amid all their crimes and vices do not cease to give frequent alms, in vain take comfort to themselves from the saying of our Lord: "Give alms of such things as ye have; and, behold, all things are clean unto you." [148] For they do not understand how far this saying reaches. But that they may understand this, let them hear what He says. For we read in the Gospel as follows: "And as He spake, a certain Pharisee besought Him to dine with him; and He went in, and sat down to meat. And when the Pharisee saw it, he marvelled that He had not first washed before dinner. And the Lord said unto him, Now do ye Pharisees make clean the outside of the cup and the platter; but your inward part is full of ravening and wickedness. Ye fools, did not he that made that which is without, make that which is within also? But rather give alms of such things as ye have; and, behold, all things are clean unto you." [149] Are we to understand this as meaning that to the Pharisees who have not the faith of Christ all things are clean, if only they give alms in the way these men count almsgiving, even though they have never believed in Christ, nor been born again of water and of the Spirit? But the fact is, that all are unclean who are not made clean by the faith of Christ, according to the expression, "purifying their hearts by faith;" [150] and that the apostle says, "Unto them that are defiled and unbelieving is nothing pure; but even their mind and conscience is defiled." [151] How, then, could all things be clean to the Pharisees, even though they gave alms, if they were not believers? And how could they be believers if they were not willing to have faith in Christ, and to be born again of His grace? And yet what they heard is true: "Give alms of such things as ye have; and, behold, all things are clean unto you."

CHAPTER LXXVI

TO GIVE ALMS ARIGHT, WE SHOULD BEGIN WITH OURSELVES, AND HAVE PITY UPON OUR OWN SOULS

For the man who wishes to give alms as he ought, should begin with himself, and give to himself first. For almsgiving is a work of mercy; and most truly is it said, "To have mercy on thy soul is pleasing to God." [152] And

---

[148] Luke xi. 41   [149] Luke xi. 37-41   [150] Acts xv. 9   [151] Tit. i. 15   [152] Ecclus. xxx. 24

for this end are we born again, that we should be pleasing to God, who is justly displeased with that which we brought with us when we were born. This is our first alms, which we give to ourselves when, through the mercy of a pitying God, we find that we are ourselves wretched, and confess the justice of His judgment by which we are made wretched, of which the apostle says, "The judgment was by one to condemnation;" [153] and praise the greatness of His love, of which the same preacher of grace says, "God commendeth His love toward us, in that, while we were yet sinners, Christ died for us:" [154] and thus, judging truly of our own misery, and loving God with the love which He has Himself bestowed, we lead a holy and virtuous life. But the Pharisees, while they gave as alms the tithe of all their fruits, even the most insignificant, passed over judgment and the love of God, and so did not commence their almsgiving at home, and extend their pity to themselves in the first instance. And it is in reference to this order of love that it is said, "Love thy neighbor as thyself." [155] When, then, our Lord had rebuked them because they made themselves clean on the outside, but within were full of ravening and wickedness, He advised them, in the exercise of that charity which each man owes to himself in the first instance, to make clean the inward parts. "But rather," He says, "give alms of such things as ye have; and, behold, all things are clean unto you." [156]

Then, to show what it was that He advised, and what they took no pains to do, and to show that He did not overlook or forget their almsgiving, "But woe unto you, Pharisees!" [156] He says; as if He meant to say: I indeed advise you to give alms which shall make all things clean unto you; "but woe unto you! for ye tithe mint, and rue, and all manner of herbs;" as if He meant to say: I know these alms of yours, and ye need not think that I am now admonishing you in respect of such things; "and pass over judgment and the love of God," and alms by which ye might have been made clean from all inward impurity, so that even the bodies which ye are now washing would have been clean to you. For this is the import of "all things," both inward and outward things, as we read in another place: "Cleanse first that which is within, that the outside may be clean also." [157] But lest He might appear to despise the alms which they were giving out of the fruits of the earth, He says: "These ought ye to have done," referring to judgment and the love of God, "and not to leave the other undone," referring to the giving of the tithes.

---

[153] Rom. v. 16   [154] Rom. v. 8   [155] Luke x. 27   [156] Luke xi. 42   [157] Matt. xxiii. 26

CHAPTER LXXVII

IF WE WOULD GIVE ALMS TO OURSELVES, WE MUST FLEE INIQUITY;
FOR HE WHO LOVETH INIQUITY HATETH HIS SOUL

Those, then, who think that they can by giving alms, however profuse, whether in money or in kind, purchase for themselves the privilege of persisting with impunity in their monstrous crimes and hideous vices, need not thus deceive themselves. For not only do they commit these sins, but they love them so much that they would like to go on forever committing them, if only they could do so with impunity. Now, he who loveth iniquity hateth his own soul;[158] and he who hateth his own soul is not merciful but cruel towards it. For in loving it according to the world, he hateth it according to God. But if he desired to give alms to it which should make all things clean unto him, he would hate it according to the world, and love it according to God. Now no one gives alms unless he receive what he gives from one who is not in want of it. Therefore it is said, "His mercy shall meet me." [159]

CHAPTER LXXVIII

WHAT SINS ARE TRIVIAL AND WHAT HEINOUS IS A MATTER FOR
GOD'S JUDGMENT

Now, what sins are trivial and what heinous is not a matter to be decided by man's judgment, but by the judgment of God. For it is plain that the apostles themselves have given an indulgence in the case of certain sins: take, for example, what the Apostle Paul says to those who are married: "Defraud ye not one the other, except it be with consent for a time, that ye may give yourselves to fasting and prayer: and come together again, that Satan tempt you not for your incontinency." [160] Now it is possible that it might not have been considered a sin to have intercourse with a spouse, not with a view to the procreation of children, which is the great blessing of marriage, but for the sake of carnal pleasure, and to save the incontinent from being led by their weakness into the deadly sin of fornication, or adultery, or another form of uncleanness which it is shameful even to name, and into which it is possible that they might be drawn by lust under the temptation of Satan. It is possible, I say, that this might not have been considered a sin, had the apostle not added: "But I speak this by permission, and not of commandment." [161] Who, then, can deny that it is a sin, when confessedly it is only by apostolic authority that permission is granted to those who do it? Another case of the same kind is where he says: "Dare any of you, having a matter against another, go to law before the unjust

---

[158] Ps. xi. 5   [159] Ps. lix. 10   [160] 1 Cor. vii. 5   [161] 1 Cor. vii. 6

and not before the saints?" [162] And shortly afterwards: "If then ye have judgments of things pertaining to this life, set them to judge who are least esteemed in the Church. I speak to your shame. Is it so, that there is not a wise man among you? no, not one that shall be able to judge between his brethren? But brother goeth to law with brother, and that before the unbelievers." [163] Now it might have been supposed in this case that it is not a sin to have a quarrel with another, that the only sin is in wishing to have it adjudicated upon outside the Church, had not the apostle immediately added: "Now therefore there is utterly a fault among you, because ye go to law with one another." [164] And lest any one should excuse himself by saying that he had a just cause, and was suffering wrong, and that he only wished the sentence of the judges to remove his wrong, the apostle immediately anticipates such thoughts and excuses, and says: "Why do ye not rather take wrong? Why do ye not rather suffer yourselves to be defrauded?" Thus bringing us back to our Lord's saying, "If any man will sue thee at the law, and take away thy coat, let him have thy cloak also;" [165] and again, "Of him that taketh away thy goods, ask them not again." [166] Therefore our Lord has forbidden His followers to go to law with other men about worldly affairs. And carrying out this principle, the apostle here declares that to do so is "altogether a fault." But when, notwithstanding, he grants his permission to have such cases between brethren decided in the Church, other brethren adjudicating, and only sternly forbids them to be carried outside the Church, it is manifest that here again an indulgence is extended to the infirmities of the weak. It is in view, then, of these sins, and others of the same sort, and of others again more trifling still, which consist of offenses in words and thought (as the Apostle James confesses, "In many things we offend all" [167]) that we need to pray every day and often to the Lord, saying, "Forgive us our debts," and to add in truth and sincerity, "as we forgive our debtors."

CHAPTER LXXIX

SINS WHICH APPEAR VERY TRIFLING, ARE SOMETIMES IN REALITY VERY SERIOUS

Again, there are some sins which would be considered very trifling, if the Scriptures did not show that they are really very serious. For who would suppose that the man who says to his brother, "Thou fool," is in danger of hell-fire, did not He who is the Truth say so? To the wound, however, He immediately applies the cure, giving a rule for reconciliation with one's offended brother: "Therefore, if thou bring thy gift to the altar, and there rememberest that thy brother hath ought against thee; leave there thy gift

---

[162] I Cor. vi. 1 [163] I Cor. vi. 4-6 [164] I Cor. vi. 7 [165] Matt. v. 40 [166] Luke vi. 30 [167] Jas. iii. 2

before the altar, and go thy way: first be reconciled to thy brother, and then come and offer thy gift." [168] Again, who would suppose that it was so great a sin to observe days, and months, and times, and years, as those do who are anxious or unwilling to begin anything on certain days, or in certain months or years, because the vain doctrines of men lead them to think such times lucky or unlucky, had we not the means of estimating the greatness of the evil from the fear expressed by the apostle, who says to such men, "I am afraid of you, lest I have bestowed upon you labor in vain"? [169]

CHAPTER LXXX

SINS, HOWEVER GREAT AND DETESTABLE, SEEM TRIVIAL WHEN WE ARE ACCUSTOMED TO THEM

Add to this, that sins, however great and detestable they may be, are looked upon as trivial, or as not sins at all, when men get accustomed to them; and so far does this go, that such sins are not only not concealed, but are boasted of, and published far and wide; and thus, as it is written, "The wicked boasteth of his heart's desire, and blesseth the covetous, whom the Lord abhorreth." [170] Iniquity of this kind is in Scripture called a *cry*. You have an instance in the prophet Isaiah, in the case of the evil vineyard: "He looked for judgment, but behold oppression; for righteousness, but behold a cry." [171] Whence also the expression in *Genesis:* "The cry of Sodom and Gomorrah is great," [172] because in these cities crimes were not only not punished, but were openly committed, as if under the protection of the law. And so in our own times: many forms of sin, though not just the same as those of Sodom and Gomorrah, are now so openly and habitually practised, that not only dare we not excommunicate a layman, we dare not even degrade a clergyman, for the commission of them. So that when, a few years ago, I was expounding the *Epistle to the Galatians*, in commenting on that very place where the apostle says, "I am afraid of you, lest I have bestowed labor upon you in vain," I was compelled to exclaim, "Woe to the sins of men! for it is only when we are not accustomed to them that we shrink from them: when once we are accustomed to them, though the blood of the Son of God was poured out to wash them away, though they are so great that the kingdom of God is wholly shut against them, constant familiarity leads to the toleration of them all, and habitual toleration leads to the practice of many of them. And grant, O Lord, that we may not come to practise all that we have not the power to hinder." But I shall see whether the extravagance of grief did not betray me into rashness of speech.

[168] Matt. v. 22, 23   [169] Gal. iv. 10, 11   [170] Ps. x. 3   [171] Isa. v. 7   [172] Gen. xviii. 20

CHAPTER LXXXI

THERE ARE TWO CAUSES OF SIN, IGNORANCE AND WEAKNESS; AND WE NEED DIVINE HELP TO OVERCOME BOTH

I shall now say this, which I have often said before in other places of my works. There are two causes that lead to sin: either we do not yet know our duty, or we do not perform the duty that we know. The former is the sin of ignorance, the latter of weakness. Now against these it is our duty to struggle; but we shall certainly be beaten in the fight, unless we are helped by God, not only to see our duty, but also, when we clearly see it, to make the love of righteousness stronger in us than the love of earthly things, the eager longing after which, or the fear of losing which, leads us with our eyes open into known sin. In the latter case we are not only sinners, for we are so even when we err through ignorance, but we are also transgressors of the law; for we leave undone what we know we ought to do, and we do what we know we ought not to do. Wherefore not only ought we to pray for pardon when we have sinned, saying, "Forgive us our debts, as we forgive our debtors;" but we ought to pray for guidance, that we may be kept from sinning, saying, "and lead us not into temptation." And we are to pray to Him of whom the Psalmist says, "The Lord is my light and my salvation:" [173] my light, for He removes my ignorance; my salvation, for He takes away my infirmity.

CHAPTER LXXXII

THE MERCY OF GOD IS NECESSARY TO TRUE REPENTANCE

Now even penance itself, when by the law of the Church there is sufficient reason for its being gone through, is frequently evaded through infirmity; for shame is the fear of losing pleasure when the good opinion of men gives more pleasure than the righteousness which leads a man to humble himself in penitence. Wherefore the mercy of God is necessary not only when a man repents, but even to lead him to repent. How else explain what the apostle says of certain persons: "if God peradventure will give them repentance"? [174] And before Peter wept bitterly, we are told by the evangelist, "The Lord turned, and looked upon him." [175]

CHAPTER LXXXIII

THE MAN WHO DESPISES THE MERCY OF GOD IS GUILTY OF THE SIN AGAINST THE HOLY GHOST

Now the man who, not believing that sins are remitted in the Church, despises this great gift of God's mercy, and persists to the last day of his

[173] Ps. xxvii. 1   [174] 2 Tim. ii. 25   [175] Luke xxii. 61

life in his obstinacy of heart, is guilty of the unpardonable sin against the Holy Ghost, in whom Christ forgives sins.[176] But this difficult question I have discussed as clearly as I could in a book devoted exclusively to this one point.

CHAPTER LXXXIV

THE RESURRECTION OF THE BODY GIVES RISE TO NUMEROUS QUESTIONS

Now, as to the resurrection of the body—not a resurrection such as some have had, who came back to life for a time and died again, but a resurrection to eternal life, as the body of Christ Himself rose again—I do not see how I can discuss the matter briefly, and at the same time give a satisfactory answer to all the questions that are ordinarily raised about it. Yet that the bodies of all men—both those who have been born and those who shall be born, both those who have died and those who shall die—shall be raised again, no Christian ought to have the shadow of a doubt.

CHAPTER LXXXV

THE CASE OF ABORTIVE CONCEPTIONS

Hence in the first place arises a question about abortive conceptions, which have indeed been born in the mother's womb, but not so born that they could be born again. For if we shall decide that these are to rise again, we cannot object to any conclusion that may be drawn in regard to those which are fully formed. Now who is there that is not rather disposed to think that unformed abortions perish, like seeds that have never fructified? But who will dare to deny, though he may not dare to affirm, that at the resurrection every defect in the form shall be supplied, and that thus the perfection which time would have brought shall not be wanting, any more than the blemishes which time did bring shall be present: so that the nature shall neither want anything suitable and in harmony with it that length of days would have added, nor be debased by the presence of anything of an opposite kind that length of days has added; but that what is not yet complete shall be completed, just as what has been injured shall be renewed.

CHAPTER LXXXVI

IF THEY HAVE EVER LIVED, THEY MUST OF COURSE HAVE DIED, AND THEREFORE SHALL HAVE A SHARE IN THE RESURRECTION OF THE DEAD

And therefore the following question may be very carefully inquired into and discussed by learned men, though I do not know whether it is in man's power to resolve it: At what time the infant begins to live in the womb:

[176] Matt. xii. 32

whether life exists in a latent form before it manifests itself in the motions of the living being. To deny that the young who are cut out limb by limb from the womb, lest if they were left there dead the mother should die too, have never been alive, seems too audacious. Now, from the time that a man begins to live, from that time it is possible for him to die. And if he die, wheresoever death may overtake him, I cannot discover on what principle he can be denied an interest in the resurrection of the dead.

CHAPTER LXXXVII

THE CASE OF MONSTROUS BIRTHS

We are not justified in affirming even of monstrosities, which are born and live, however quickly they may die, that they shall not rise again, nor that they shall rise again in their deformity, and not rather with an amended and perfected body. God forbid that the double-limbed man who was lately born in the East, of whom an account was brought by most trust-worthy brethren who had seen him—an account which the presbyter Jerome, of blessed memory, left in writing[177]—God forbid, I say, that we should think that at the resurrection there shall be one man with double limbs, and not two distinct men, as would have been the case had twins been born. And so other births, which, because they have either a super-fluity or a defect, or because they are very much deformed, are called *monstrosities,* shall at the resurrection be restored to the normal shape of man; and so each single soul shall possess its own body; and no bodies shall cohere together even though they were born in cohesion, but each separately shall possess all the members which constitute a complete human body.

CHAPTER LXXXVIII

THE MATERIAL OF THE BODY NEVER PERISHES

Nor does the earthly material out of which men's mortal bodies are cre-ated ever perish; but though it may crumble into dust and ashes, or be dissolved into vapors and exhalations, though it may be transformed into the substance of other bodies, or dispersed into the elements, though it should become food for beasts or men, and be changed into their flesh, it returns in a moment of time to that human soul which animated it at the first, and which caused it to become man, and to live and grow.

[177] Jerome, in his *Epistle to Vitalis:* "Or because in our times a man was born at Lydda with two heads, four hands, one belly, and two feet, does it necessarily follow that all men are so born?"

CHAPTER LXXXIX

BUT THIS MATERIAL MAY BE DIFFERENTLY ARRANGED
IN THE RESURRECTION BODY

And this earthly material, which when the soul leaves it becomes a corpse, shall not at the resurrection be so restored as that the parts into which it is separated, and which under various forms and appearances become parts of other things (though they shall all return to the same body from which they were separated) must necessarily return to the same parts of the body in which they were originally situated. For otherwise, to suppose that the hair recovers all that our frequent clippings and shavings have taken away from it, and the nails all that we have so often pared off, presents to the imagination such a picture of ugliness and deformity, as to make the resurrection of the body all but incredible. But just as if a statue of some soluble metal were either melted by fire, or broken into dust, or reduced to a shapeless mass, and a sculptor wished to restore it from the same quantity of metal, it would make no difference to the completeness of the work what part of the statue any given particle of the material was put into, as long as the restored statue contained all the material of the original one; so God, the Artificer of marvellous and unspeakable power, shall with marvellous and unspeakable rapidity restore our body, using up the whole material of which it originally consisted. Nor will it affect the completeness of its restoration whether hairs return to hairs, and nails to nails, or whether the part of these that had perished be changed into flesh, and called to take its place in another part of the body, the great Artist taking careful heed that nothing shall be unbecoming or out of place.

CHAPTER XC

IF THERE BE DIFFERENCES AND INEQUALITIES AMONG THE BODIES
OF THOSE WHO RISE AGAIN, THERE SHALL BE NOTHING
OFFENSIVE OR DISPROPORTIONATE IN ANY

Nor does it necessarily follow that there shall be differences of stature among those who rise again, because they were of different statures during life; nor is it certain that the lean shall rise again in their former leanness, and the fat in their former fatness. But if it is part of the Creator's design that each should preserve his own peculiarities of feature, and retain a recognizable likeness to his former self, while in regard to other bodily advantages all should be equal, then the material of which each is composed may be so modified that none of it shall be lost, and that any defect may be supplied by Him who can create at His will out of nothing. But if in the bodies of those who rise again there shall be a well-ordered inequality, such as there is in the voices that make up a full harmony, then the material of each man's body shall be so dealt with that it shall form a man fit for the assemblies of the angels, and one who shall bring nothing among them to jar upon their sensibilities. And assuredly nothing that is unseemly shall be there; but whatever shall be there shall be graceful and becoming: for if anything is not seemly, neither shall it be.

CHAPTER XCI

THE BODIES OF THE SAINTS SHALL AT THE RESURRECTION BE SPIRITUAL BODIES

The bodies of the saints, then, shall rise again free from every defect, from every blemish, as from all corruption, weight, and impediment. For their ease of movement shall be as complete as their happiness. Whence their bodies have been called *spiritual,* though undoubtedly they shall be bodies and not spirits. For just as now the body is called *animate,* though it is a body, and not a soul [*anima*], so then the body shall be called spiritual, though it shall be a body, not a spirit.[178] Hence, as far as regards the corruption which now weighs down the soul, and the vices which urge the flesh to lust against the spirit,[179] it shall not then be flesh, but body; for there are bodies which are called celestial. Wherefore it is said, "Flesh and blood cannot inherit the kingdom of God;" and, as if in explanation of this, "neither doth corruption inherit incorruption." [180] What the apostle first called "flesh and blood," he afterwards calls "corruption;" and what he first called "the kingdom of God," he afterwards calls "incorruption." But as far as regards the substance, even then it shall be flesh. For even after the resurrection the body of Christ was called flesh.[181] The apostle, however, says: "It is sown a natural body; it is raised a spiritual body;" [182] because so perfect shall then be the harmony between flesh and spirit, the spirit keeping alive the subjugated flesh without the need of any nourishment, that no part of our nature shall be in discord with another; but as we shall be free from enemies without, so we shall not have ourselves for enemies within.

CHAPTER XCII

THE RESURRECTION OF THE LOST

But as for those who, out of the mass of perdition caused by the first man's sin, are not redeemed through the one Mediator between God and man, they too shall rise again, each with his own body, but only to be punished with the devil and his angels. Now, whether they shall rise again with

---

[178] I Cor. xv. 44   [179] Wisd. ix. 15; Gal. v. 17   [180] I Cor. xv. 50   [181] Luke xxiv.
39   [182] I Cor. xv. 44

712 712 THE ENCHIRIDION

all their diseases and deformities of body, bringing with them the diseased and deformed limbs which they possessed here, it would be labor lost to inquire. For we need not weary ourselves speculating about their health or their beauty, which are matters uncertain, when their eternal damnation is a matter of certainty. Nor need we inquire in what sense their body shall be incorruptible, if it be susceptible of pain; or in what sense corruptible, if it be free from the possibility of death. For there is no true life except where there is happiness in life, and no true incorruption except where health is unbroken by any pain. When, however, the unhappy are not permitted to die, then, if I may so speak, death itself dies not; and where pain without intermission afflicts the soul, and never comes to an end, corruption itself is not completed. This is called in Holy Scripture "the second death." [183]

CHAPTER XCIII

BOTH THE FIRST AND THE SECOND DEATHS ARE THE CONSEQUENCE OF SIN. PUNISHMENT IS PROPORTIONED TO GUILT

And neither the first death, which takes place when the soul is compelled to leave the body, nor the second death, which takes place when the soul is not permitted to leave the suffering body, would have been inflicted on man had no one sinned. And, of course, the mildest punishment of all will fall upon those who have added no actual sin, to the original sin they brought with them; and as for the rest who have added such actual sins, the punishment of each will be the more tolerable in the next world, according as his iniquity has been less in this world.

CHAPTER XCIV

THE SAINTS SHALL KNOW MORE FULLY IN THE NEXT WORLD THE BENEFITS THEY HAVE RECEIVED BY GRACE

Thus, when reprobate angels and men are left to endure everlasting punishment, the saints shall know more fully the benefits they have received by grace. Then, in contemplation of the actual facts, they shall see more clearly the meaning of the expression in the psalms, "I will sing of mercy and judgment;" [184] for it is only of unmerited mercy that any is redeemed, and only in well-merited judgment that any is condemned.

[183] Rev. ii. 2   [184] Ps. ci. 1

CHAPTER XCV

GOD'S JUDGMENTS SHALL THEN BE EXPLAINED

Then shall be made clear much that is now dark. For example, when of two infants, whose cases seem in all respects alike, one is by the mercy of God chosen to Himself, and the other is by His justice abandoned (wherein the one who is chosen may recognize what was of justice due to himself, had not mercy intervened); why, of these two, the one should have been chosen rather than the other, is to us an insoluble problem. And again, why miracles were not wrought in the presence of men who would have repented at the working of the miracles, while they were wrought in the presence of others who, it was known, would not repent. For our Lord says most distinctly: "Woe unto thee, Chorazin! woe unto thee, Bethsaida! for if the mighty works, which were done in you, had been done in Tyre and Sidon, they would have repented long ago in sackcloth and ashes." [185] And assuredly there was no injustice in God's not willing that they should be saved, though they could have been saved had He so willed it. Then shall be seen in the clearest light of wisdom what with the pious is now a faith, though it is not yet a matter of certain knowledge, how sure, how unchangeable, and how effectual is the will of God; how many things He can do which He does not will to do, though willing nothing which He cannot perform; and how true is the song of the psalmist, "But our God is in the heavens; He hath done whatsoever He hath pleased." [186] And this certainly is not true, if God has ever willed anything that He has not performed; and, still worse, if it was the will of man that hindered the Omnipotent from doing what He pleased. Nothing, therefore, happens but by the will of the Omnipotent, He either permitting it to be done, or Himself doing it.

CHAPTER XCVI

THE OMNIPOTENT GOD DOES WELL EVEN IN THE PERMISSION OF EVIL

Nor can we doubt that God does well even in the permission of what is evil. For He permits it only in the justice of His judgment. And surely all that is just is good. Although, therefore, evil, in so far as it is evil, is not a good; yet the fact that evil as well as good exists, is a good. For if it were not a good that evil should exist, its existence would not be permitted by the omnipotent God, who without doubt can as easily refuse to permit what He does not wish, as bring about what He does wish. And if we do not believe this, the very first sentence of our creed is endangered, wherein we profess to believe in God the Father Almighty. For He is not truly called Almighty if He cannot do whatsoever He pleases, or if the power of His almighty will is hindered by the will of any creature whatsoever .

[185] Matt. xi. 21   [186] Ps. cxv. 3

CHAPTER XCVII

IN WHAT SENSE DOES THE APOSTLE SAY THAT "GOD WILL HAVE ALL MEN TO BE SAVED," WHEN, AS A MATTER OF FACT, ALL ARE NOT SAVED?

Hence we must inquire in what sense is said of God what the apostle has most truly said: "Who will have all men to be saved." [187] For, as a matter of fact, not all, nor even a majority, are saved: so that it would seem that what God wills is not done, man's will interfering with, and hindering the will of God. When we ask the reason why all men are not saved, the ordinary answer is: "Because men themselves are not willing." This, indeed, cannot be said of infants, for it is not in their power either to will or not to will. But if we could attribute to their will the childish movements they make at baptism, when they make all the resistance they can, we should say that even they are not willing to be saved. Our Lord says plainly, however, in the Gospel, when upbraiding the impious city: "How often would I have gathered thy children together, even as a hen gathereth her chickens under her wings, and ye would not!" [188] as if the will of God had been overcome by the will of men, and when the weakest stood in the way with their want of will, the will of the strongest could not be carried out. And where is that omnipotence which hath done all that it pleased on earth and in heaven, if God willed to gather together the children of Jerusalem, and did not accomplish it? or rather, Jerusalem was not willing that her children should be gathered together? But even though she was unwilling, He gathered together as many of her children as He wished: for He does not will some things and do them, and will others and do them not; but "He hath done all that He pleased in heaven and in earth."

CHAPTER XCVIII

PREDESTINATION TO ETERNAL LIFE IS WHOLLY OF GOD'S FREE GRACE

And, moreover, who will be so foolish and blasphemous as to say that God cannot change the evil wills of men, whichever, whenever, and wheresoever He chooses, and direct them to what is good? But when He does this, He does it of mercy; when He does it not, it is of justice that He does it not; for "He hath mercy on whom He will have mercy, and whom He will He hardeneth." [189] And when the apostle said this, he was illustrating the grace of God, in connection with which he had just spoken of the twins in the womb of Rebecca, "who being not yet born, neither having done any good or evil, that the purpose of God according to election might stand, not of works, but of Him that calleth, it was said unto her, The elder shall serve the younger." [190] And in reference to this matter he quotes another pro-

[187] I Tim. ii. 4   [188] Matt. xxiii. 37   [189] Rom. ix. 18   [190] Rom. ix. 12

phetic testimony: "Jacob have I loved, but Esau have I hated." [191] But perceiving how what he had said might affect those who could not penetrate by their understanding the depth of this grace: "What shall we say then?" he says: "Is there unrighteousness with God? God forbid." [192] For it seems unjust that, in the absence of any merit or demerit, from good or evil works, God should love the one and hate the other. Now, if the apostle had wished us to understand that there were future good works of the one, and evil works of the other, which of course God foreknew, he would never have said, "not of works," but, "of future works," and in that way would have solved the difficulty, or rather there would then have been no difficulty to solve. As it is, however, after answering, "God forbid;" that is, God forbid that there should be unrighteousness with God; he goes on to prove that there is no unrighteousness in God's doing this, and says: "For He saith to Moses, I will have mercy on whom I will have mercy, and I will have compassion on whom I will have compassion." [193] Now, who but a fool would think that God was unrighteous, either in inflicting penal justice on those who had earned it, or in extending mercy to the unworthy? Then he draws his conclusion: "So then it is not of him that willeth, nor of him that runneth, but of God that showeth mercy." [194] Thus both the twins were born children of wrath, not on account of any works of their own, but because they were bound in the fetters of that original condemnation which came through Adam. But He who said, "I will have mercy on whom I will have mercy," loved Jacob of His undeserved grace, and hated Esau of His deserved judgment. And as this judgment was due to both, the former learnt from the case of the latter that the fact of the same punishment not falling upon himself gave him no room to glory in any merit of his own, but only in the riches of the divine grace; because "it is not of him that willeth, nor of him that runneth, but of God that showeth mercy." And indeed the whole face, and, if I may use the expression, every lineament of the countenance of Scripture conveys by a very profound analogy this wholesome warning to every one who looks carefully into it, that he who glories should glory in the Lord.[195]

CHAPTER XCIX

AS GOD'S MERCY IS FREE, SO HIS JUDGMENTS ARE JUST, AND CANNOT BE GAINSAID

Now after commending the mercy of God, saying, "So it is not of him that willeth, nor of him that runneth, but of God that showeth mercy," that he might commend His justice also (for the man who does not obtain mercy finds, not iniquity, but justice, there being no iniquity with God) he im-

[191] Rom. ix. 13; Mal. i. 2, 3   [192] Rom. ix. 14   [193] Rom. ix. 15; Ex. xxxiii. 19
[194] Rom. ix. 16   [195] cf. 1 Cor. i. 31

mediately adds: "For the scripture saith unto Pharoah, Even for this same purpose have I raised thee up, that I might show my power in thee, and that my name might be declared throughout all the earth." [196] And then he draws a conclusion that applies to both, that is, both to His mercy and His justice: "Therefore hath He mercy on whom He will have mercy, and whom He will He hardeneth." [197] "He hath mercy" of His great goodness, "He hardeneth" without any injustice; so that neither can he that is pardoned glory in any merit of his own, nor he that is condemned complain of anything but his own demerit. For it is grace alone that separates the redeemed from the lost, all having been involved in one common perdition through their common origin. Now if any one, on hearing this, should say, "Why doth He yet find fault? for who hath resisted His will?" [198] as if a man ought not to be blamed for being bad, because God hath mercy on whom He will have mercy, and whom He will He hardeneth, God forbid that we should be ashamed to answer as we see the apostle answered: "Nay, but, O man, who art thou that repliest against God? Shall the thing formed say to Him that formed it, Why hast Thou made me thus? Hath not the potter power over the clay, of the same lump to make one vessel unto honor, and another unto dishonor?" [199] Now some foolish people think that in this place the apostle had no answer to give; and for want of a reason to render, rebuked the presumption of his interrogator. But there is great weight in this saying: "Nay, but, O man, who art thou?" and in such a matter as this it suggests to a man in a single word the limits of his capacity, and at the same time does in reality convey an important reason. For if a man does not understand these matters, who is he that he should reply against God? And if he does understand them, he finds no further room for reply. For then he perceives that the whole human race was condemned in its rebellious head by a divine judgment so just, that if not a single member of the race had been redeemed, no one could justly have questioned the justice of God; and that it was right that those who are redeemed should be redeemed in such a way as to show, by the greater number who are unredeemed and left in their just condemnation, what the whole race deserved, and whither the deserved judgment of God would lead even the redeemed, did not His undeserved mercy interpose, so that every mouth might be stopped of those who wish to glory in their own merits, and that he that glorieth might glory in the Lord.[200]

---

[196] Rom. ix. 17; Ex. ix. 16   [197] Rom. ix. 18   [198] Rom. ix. 19   [199] Rom. ix. 20, 21
[200] Rom. iii. 19; 1 Cor. i. 31

CHAPTER C

THE WILL OF GOD IS NEVER DEFEATED, THOUGH MUCH IS DONE THAT IS CONTRARY TO HIS WILL

These are the great works of the Lord, sought out according to all His pleasure,[201] and so wisely sought out, that when the intelligent creation, both angelic and human, sinned, doing not His will but their own, He used the very will of the creature which was working in opposition to the Creator's will as an instrument for carrying out His will, the supremely Good thus turning to good account even what is evil, to the condemnation of those whom in His justice He has predestined to punishment, and to the salvation of those whom in His mercy He has predestined to grace. For, as far as relates to their own consciousness, these creatures did what God wished not to be done: but in view of God's omnipotence, they could in no wise effect their purpose. For in the very fact that they acted in opposition to His will, His will concerning them was fulfilled. And hence it is that "the works of the Lord are great, sought out according to all His pleasure," because in a way unspeakably strange and wonderful, even what is done in opposition to His will does not defeat His will. For it would not be done did He not permit it (and of course His permission is not unwilling, but willing); nor would a Good Being permit evil to be done only that in His omnipotence He can turn evil into good.

CHAPTER CI

THE WILL OF GOD, WHICH IS ALWAYS GOOD, IS SOMETIMES FULFILLED THROUGH THE EVIL WILL OF MAN

Sometimes, however, a man in the goodness of his will desires something that God does not desire, even though God's will is also good, nay, much more fully and more surely good (for His will never can be evil): for example, if a good son is anxious that his father should live, when it is God's good will that he should die. Again, it is possible for a man with evil will to desire what God wills in His goodness: for example, if a bad son wishes his father to die, when this is also the will of God. It is plain that the former wishes what God does not wish, and that the latter wishes what God does wish; and yet the filial love of the former is more in harmony with the good will of God, though its desire is different from God's, than the want of filial affection of the latter, though its desire is the same as God's. So necessary is it, in determining whether a man's desire is one to be approved or disapproved, to consider what it is proper for man, and what it is proper for God, to desire, and what is in each case the real motive of the will. For

[201] Ps. cxi. 2 (LXX.)

God accomplishes some of His purposes, which of course are all good, through the evil desires of wicked men: for example, it was through the wicked designs of the Jews, working out the good purpose of the Father, that Christ was slain; and this event was so truly good, that when the Apostle Peter expressed his unwillingness that it should take place, he was designated Satan by Him who had come to be slain.[202] How good seemed the intentions of the pious believers who were unwilling that Paul should go up to Jerusalem lest the evils which Agabus had foretold should there befall him! [203] And yet it was God's purpose that he should suffer these evils for preaching the faith of Christ, and thereby become a witness for Christ. And this purpose of His, which was good, God did not fulfill through the good counsels of the Christians, but through the evil counsels of the Jews; so that those who opposed His purpose were more truly His servants than those who were the willing instruments of its accomplishment.

CHAPTER CII

THE WILL OF THE OMNIPOTENT GOD IS NEVER DEFEATED, AND IS NEVER EVIL

But however strong may be the purposes either of angels or of men, whether of good or bad, whether these purposes fall in with the will of God or run counter to it, the will of the Omnipotent is never defeated; and His will never can be evil; because even when it inflicts evil it is just, and what is just is certainly not evil. The omnipotent God, then, whether in mercy He pitieth whom He will, or in judgment hardeneth whom He will, is never unjust in what He does, never does anything except of His own free-will, and never wills anything that He does not perform.

CHAPTER CIII

INTERPRETATION OF THE EXPRESSION IN I TIM. II. 4: "WHO WILL HAVE ALL MEN TO BE SAVED"

Accordingly, when we hear and read in Scripture that He "will have all men to be saved," [204] although we know well that all men are not saved, we are not on that account to restrict the omnipotence of God, but are rather to understand the Scripture, "Who will have all men to be saved," as meaning that no man is saved unless God wills his salvation: not that there is no man whose salvation He does not will, but that no man is saved apart from His will; and that, therefore, we should pray Him to will our salvation, because if He will it, it must necessarily be accomplished. And it was of prayer to God that the apostle was speaking when he used this expression. And on the same principle we interpret the expression in the Gospel: "The true light which lighteth every man that cometh into the world:" [205]

---

[202] Matt. xvi. 21-23   [203] Acts xxi. 10-12   [204] I Tim. ii. 4   [205] John i. 9

not that there is no man who is not enlightened, but that no man is enlightened except by Him. Or, it is said, "Who will have all men to be saved;" not that there is no man whose salvation He does not will (for how, then, explain the fact that He was unwilling to work miracles in the presence of some who, He said, would have repented if He had worked them?), but that we are to understand by "all men," the human race in all its varieties of rank and circumstances—kings, subjects; noble, plebeian, high, low, learned, and unlearned; the sound in body, the feeble, the clever, the dull, the foolish, the rich, the poor, and those of middling circumstances; males, females, infants, boys, youths; young, middle-aged, and old men; of every tongue, of every fashion, of all arts, of all professions, with all the innumerable differences of will and conscience, and whatever else there is that makes a distinction among men. For which of all these classes is there out of which God does not will that men should be saved in all nations through His only-begotten Son, our Lord, and therefore does save them; for the Omnipotent cannot will in vain, whatsoever He may will? Now the apostle had enjoined that prayers should be made for all men, and had especially added, "For kings, and for all that are in authority," who might be supposed, in the pride and pomp of worldly station, to shrink from the humility of the Christian faith. Then saying, "For this is good and acceptable in the sight of God our Saviour," that is, that prayers should be made for such as these, he immediately adds, as if to remove any ground of despair, "Who will have all men to be saved, and to come unto the knowledge of the truth." [206] God, then, in His great condescension has judged it good to grant to the prayers of the humble the salvation of the exalted; and assuredly we have many examples of this. Our Lord, too, makes use of the same mode of speech in the Gospel, when He says to the Pharisees: "Ye tithe mint, and rue, and every herb." [207] For the Pharisees did not tithe what belonged to others, nor all the herbs of all the inhabitants of other lands. As, then, in this place we must understand by "every herb," every kind of herbs, so in the former passage we may understand by "all men," every sort of men. And we may interpret it in any other way we please, so long as we are not compelled to believe that the omnipotent God has willed anything to be done which was not done: for, setting aside all ambiguities, if "He hath done all that He pleased in heaven and in earth," [208] as the psalmist sings of Him, He certainly did not will to do anything that He hath not done.

[206] 1 Tim. ii. 1-4   [207] Luke xi. 42   [208] Ps. cxv. 3

CHAPTER CIV

GOD, FOREKNOWING THE SIN OF THE FIRST MAN,
ORDERED HIS OWN PURPOSES ACCORDINGLY

Wherefore, God would have been willing to preserve even the first man in that state of salvation in which he was created, and after he had begotten sons to remove him at a fit time, without the intervention of death, to a better place, where he should have been not only free from sin, but free even from the desire of sinning, if He had foreseen that man would have the steadfast will to persist in the state of innocence in which he was created. But as He foresaw that man would make a bad use of his free-will, that is, would sin, God arranged His own designs rather with a view to do good to man even in his sinfulness, that thus the good will of the Omnipotent might not be made void by the evil will of man, but might be fulfilled in spite of it.

CHAPTER CV

MAN WAS SO CREATED AS TO BE ABLE TO CHOOSE EITHER GOOD OR EVIL:
IN THE FUTURE LIFE, THE CHOICE OF EVIL WILL BE IMPOSSIBLE

Now it was expedient that man should be at first so created, as to have it in his power both to will what was right and to will what was wrong; not without reward if he willed the former, and not without punishment if he willed the latter. But in the future life it shall not be in his power to will evil; and yet this will constitute no restriction on the freedom of his will. On the contrary, his will shall be much freer when it shall be wholly impossible for him to be the slave of sin. We should never think of blaming the will, or saying that it was no will, or that it was not to be called free, when we so desire happiness, that not only do we shrink from misery, but find it utterly impossible to do otherwise. As, then, the soul even now finds it impossible to desire unhappiness, so in future it shall be wholly impossible for it to desire sin. But God's arrangement was not to be broken, according to which He willed to show how good is a rational being who is able even to refrain from sin, and yet how much better is one who cannot sin at all; just as that was an inferior sort of immortality, and yet it was immortality, when it was possible for man to avoid death, although there is reserved for the future a more perfect immortality, when it shall be impossible for man to die.

CHAPTER CVI

THE GRACE OF GOD WAS NECESSARY TO MAN'S SALVATION
BEFORE THE FALL AS WELL AS AFTER IT

The former immortality man lost through the exercise of his free-will; the latter he shall obtain through grace, whereas, if he had not sinned, he should have obtained it by desert. Even in that case, however, there could have been no merit without grace; because, although the mere exercise of man's free-will was sufficient to bring in sin, his free-will would not have sufficed for his maintenance in righteousness, unless God had assisted it by imparting a portion of His unchangeable goodness. Just as it is in man's power to die whenever he will (for, not to speak of other means, any one can put an end to himself by simple abstinence from food), but the mere will cannot preserve life in the absence of food and the other means of life; so man in paradise was able of his mere will, simply by abandoning righteousness, to destroy himself; but to have maintained a life of righteousness would have been too much for his will, unless it had been sustained by the Creator's power. After the fall, however, a more abundant exercise of God's mercy was required, because the will itself had to be freed from the bondage in which it was held by sin and death. And the will owes its freedom in no degree to itself, but solely to the grace of God which comes by faith in Jesus Christ; so that the very will, through which we accept all the other gifts of God which lead us on to His eternal gift, is itself prepared of the Lord, as the Scripture says.[209]

CHAPTER CVII

ETERNAL LIFE, THOUGH THE REWARD OF GOOD WORKS,
IS ITSELF THE GIFT OF GOD

Wherefore, even eternal life itself, which is surely the reward of good works, the apostle calls the gift of God. "For the wages of sin," he says, "is death; but the gift of God is eternal life through Jesus Christ our Lord." [210] Wages is paid as a recompense for military service; it is not a gift: wherefore he says, "the *wages* of sin is death," to show that death was not inflicted undeservedly, but as the due recompense of sin. But a gift, unless it is wholly unearned, is not a gift at all.[211] We are to understand, then, that man's good deserts are themselves the gift of God, so that when these obtain the recompense of eternal life, it is simply grace given for grace. Man, therefore, was thus made upright that, though unable to remain in his uprightness without divine help, he could of his own mere will depart from it. And whichever of these courses he had chosen, God's will would have been done, either by him, or concerning him. Therefore, as he chose to do his own will rather than God's, the will of God is fulfilled concerning him; for God, out of one and the same heap of perdition which constitutes the race of man, makes one vessel to honor, another to dishonor; to honor in mercy, to dishonor in judgment;[212] that no one may glory in man, and consequently not in himself.

CHAPTER CVIII

A MEDIATOR WAS NECESSARY TO RECONCILE US TO GOD; AND UNLESS THIS MEDIATOR HAD BEEN GOD, HE COULD NOT HAVE BEEN OUR REDEEMER

For we could not be redeemed, even through the one Mediator between God and men, the man Christ Jesus, if He were not also God. Now when Adam was created, he, being a righteous man, had no need of a mediator. But when sin had placed a wide gulf between God and the human race, it was expedient that a Mediator, who alone of the human race was born, lived, and died without sin, should reconcile us to God, and procure even for our bodies a resurrection to eternal life, in order that the pride of man might be exposed and cured through the humility of God; that man might be shown how far he had departed from God, when God became incarnate to bring him back; that an example might be set to disobedient man in the life of obedience of the God-Man; that the fountain of grace might be opened by the Only-begotten taking upon Himself the form of a servant, a form which had no antecedent merit; that an earnest of that resurrection of the body which is promised to the redeemed might be given in the resurrection of the Redeemer; that the devil might be subdued by the same nature which it was his boast to have deceived, and yet man not glorified, lest pride should again spring up; and, in fine, with a view to all the advantages which the thoughtful can perceive and describe, or perceive without being able to describe, as flowing from the transcendent mystery of the person of the Mediator.

CHAPTER CIX

THE STATE OF THE SOUL DURING THE INTERVAL BETWEEN DEATH AND THE RESURRECTION

During the time, moreover, which intervenes between a man's death and the final resurrection, the soul dwells in a hidden retreat, where it enjoys rest or suffers affliction just in proportion to the merit it has earned by the life which it led on earth.

[212] Rom. ix. 21

CHAPTER CX

THE BENEFIT TO THE SOULS OF THE DEAD FROM THE SACRAMENTS AND ALMS OF THEIR LIVING FRIENDS

Nor can it be denied that the souls of the dead are benefited by the piety of their living friends, who offer the sacrifice of the Mediator, or give alms in the church on their behalf. But these services are of advantage only to those who during their lives have earned such merit, that services of this kind can help them. For there is a manner of life which is neither so good as not to require these services after death, nor so bad that such services are of no avail after death; there is, on the other hand, a kind of life so good as not to require them; and again, one so bad that when life is over they render no help. Therefore, it is in this life that all the merit or demerit is acquired, which can either relieve or aggravate a man's sufferings after this life. No one, then, need hope that after he is dead he shall obtain merit with God which he has neglected to secure here. And accordingly it is plain that the services which the church celebrates for the dead are in no way opposed to the apostle's words: "For we must all appear before the judgment-seat of Christ; that every one may receive the things done in his body, according to that he hath done, whether it be good or bad;" [213] for the merit which renders such services as I speak of profitable to a man, is earned while he lives in the body. It is not to every one that these services are profitable. And why are they not profitable to all, except because of the different kinds of lives that men lead in the body? When, then, sacrifices either of the altar or of alms are offered on behalf of all the baptized dead, they are thank-offerings for the very good, they are propitiatory offerings for the not very bad, and in the case of the very bad, even though they do not assist the dead, they are a species of consolation to the living. And where they are profitable, their benefit consists either in obtaining a full remission of sins, or at least in making the condemnation more tolerable.

CHAPTER CXI

AFTER THE RESURRECTION THERE SHALL BE TWO DISTINCT KINGDOMS, ONE OF ETERNAL HAPPINESS, THE OTHER OF ETERNAL MISERY

After the resurrection, however, when the final, universal judgment has been completed, there shall be two kingdoms, each with its own distinct boundaries, the one Christ's, the other the devil's; the one consisting of the good, the other of the bad—both, however, consisting of angels and men. The former shall have no will, the latter no power, to sin, and neither shall

[213] 2 Cor. v. 10; cf. Rom. xiv. 10

have any power to choose death; but the former shall live truly and happily in eternal life, the latter shall drag a miserable existence in eternal death without the power of dying; for the life and the death shall both be without end. But among the former there shall be degrees of happiness, one being more pre-eminently happy than another; and among the latter there shall be degrees of misery, one being more endurably miserable than another.

CHAPTER CXII

THERE IS NO GROUND IN SCRIPTURE FOR THE OPINION OF THOSE WHO DENY THE ETERNITY OF FUTURE PUNISHMENTS

It is in vain, then, that some, indeed very many, make moan over the eternal punishment, and perpetual, unintermitted torments of the lost, and say they do not believe it shall be so; not, indeed, that they directly oppose themselves to Holy Scripture, but, at the suggestion of their own feelings, they soften down everything that seems hard, and give a milder turn to statements which they think are rather designed to terrify than to be received as literally true. For "Hath God," they say, "forgotten to be gracious? hath He in anger shut up His tender mercies?" [214] Now, they read this in one of the holy psalms. But without doubt we are to understand it as spoken of those who are elsewhere called "vessels of mercy," [215] because even they are freed from misery not on account of any merit of their own, but solely through the pity of God. Or, if the men we speak of insist that this passage applies to all mankind, there is no reason why they should therefore suppose that there will be an end to the punishment of those of whom it is said, "These shall go away into everlasting punishment;" for this shall end in the same manner and at the same time as the happiness of those of whom it is said, "but the righteous unto life eternal." [216] But let them suppose, if the thought gives them pleasure, that the pains of the damned are, at certain intervals, in some degree assuaged. For even in this case the wrath of God, that is, their condemnation (for it is this, and not any disturbed feeling in the mind of God that is called His wrath) abideth upon them; [217] that is, His wrath, though it still remains, does not shut up His tender mercies; though His tender mercies are exhibited, not in putting an end to their eternal punishment, but in mitigating, or in granting them a respite from, their torments; for the psalm does not say, "to put an end to His anger," or, "when His anger is passed by," but "in His anger." [218] Now, if this anger stood alone, or if it existed in the smallest conceivable degree, yet to be lost out of the kingdom of God, to be an exile from the city of God, to be alienated from the life of God, to have no share in that great goodness which God hath laid up for them that fear Him, and hath

[214] Ps. lxxvii. 9   [215] Rom. ix. 23   [216] Matt. xxv. 46   [217] John iii. 36   [218] Ps lxxviii.

wrought out for them that trust in Him,[219] would be a punishment so great, that, supposing it to be eternal, no torments that we know of, continued through as many ages as man's imagination can conceive, could be compared with it.

CHAPTER CXIII

THE DEATH OF THE WICKED SHALL BE ETERNAL IN THE SAME SENSE AS THE LIFE OF THE SAINTS

This perpetual death of the wicked, then, that is, their alienation from the life of God, shall abide for ever, and shall be common to them all, whatever men, prompted by their human affections, may conjecture as to a variety of punishments, or as to a mitigation or intermission of their woes; just as the eternal life of the saints shall abide for ever, and shall be common to them all, whatever grades of rank and honor there may be among those who shine with an harmonious effulgence.

CHAPTER CXIV

HAVING DEALT WITH FAITH, WE NOW COME TO SPEAK OF HOPE. EVERYTHING THAT PERTAINS TO HOPE IS EMBRACED IN THE LORD'S PRAYER

Out of this confession of *faith,* which is briefly comprehended in the Creed, and which, carnally understood, is milk for babies, but, spiritually apprehended and studied, is meat for strong men, springs the good *hope* of believers; and this is accompanied by a holy *love.* But of these matters, all of which are true objects of faith, those only pertain to hope which are embraced in the Lord's Prayer. For, "Cursed is the man that trusteth in man" [220] is the testimony of holy writ; and, consequently, this curse attaches also to the man who trusteth in himself. Therefore, except from God the Lord we ought to ask for nothing either that we hope to do well, or hope to obtain as a reward of our good works.

CHAPTER CXV

THE SEVEN PETITIONS OF THE LORD'S PRAYER, ACCORDING TO MATTHEW

Accordingly, in the *Gospel according to Matthew* the Lord's Prayer seems to embrace seven petitions, three of which ask for eternal blessings, and the remaining four for temporal; these latter, however, being necessary antecedents to the attainment of the eternal. For when we say, "Hallowed be Thy name: Thy Kingdom come: Thy will be done in earth, as it is in heaven" [221] (which some have interpreted, not unfairly, in body as well as

[219] Ps. xxxi. 19   [220] Jer. xvii. 5   [221] Matt. vi. 9, 10

in spirit) we ask for blessings that are to be enjoyed for ever; which are indeed begun in this world, and grow in us as we grow in grace, but in their perfect state, which is to be looked for in another life, shall be a possession for evermore. But when we say, "Give us this day our daily bread: and forgive us our debts, as we forgive our debtors: and lead us not into temptation, but deliver us from evil," [222] who does not see that we ask for blessings that have reference to the wants of this present life? In that eternal life, where we hope to live for ever, the hallowing of God's name, and His kingdom, and His will in our spirit and body, shall be brought to perfection, and shall endure to everlasting. But our daily bread is so called because there is here constant need for as much nourishment as the spirit and the flesh demand, whether we understand the expression spiritually, or carnally, or in both senses. It is here too that we need the forgiveness that we ask, for it is here that we commit the sins; here are the temptations which allure or drive us into sin; here, in a word, is the evil from which we desire deliverance: but in that other world there shall be none of these things.

CHAPTER CXVI

LUKE EXPRESSES THE SUBSTANCE OF THESE SEVEN PETITIONS MORE BRIEFLY IN FIVE

But the Evangelist Luke in his version of the Lord's Prayer embraces not seven, but five petitions: not, of course, that there is any discrepancy between the two evangelists, but that Luke indicates by his very brevity the mode in which the seven petitions of Matthew are to be understood. For God's name is hallowed in the spirit; and God's kingdom shall come in the resurrection of the body. Luke, therefore, intending to show that the third petition is a sort of repetition of the first two, has chosen to indicate that by omitting the third altogether. Then he adds three others: one for daily bread, another for pardon of sin, another for immunity from temptation. And what Matthew puts as the last petition, "but deliver us from evil," Luke has omitted, to show us that it is embraced in the previous petition about temptation. Matthew, indeed, himself says, *"but* deliver," not *"and* deliver," as if to show that the petitions are virtually one: do not this, but this; so that every man is to understand that he is delivered from evil in the very fact of his not being led into temptation.

[222] Matt. vi. 11-13

CHAPTER CXVII

LOVE, WHICH IS GREATER THAN FAITH AND HOPE, IS SHED
ABROAD IN OUR HEARTS BY THE HOLY GHOST

And now as to *love,* which the apostle declares to be greater than the other two graces, that is, than faith and hope,[223] the greater the measure in which it dwells in a man, the better is the man in whom it dwells. For when there is a question as to whether a man is good, one does not ask what he believes, or what he hopes, but what he loves. For the man who loves aright no doubt believes and hopes aright; whereas the man who has not love believes in vain, even though his beliefs are true; and hopes in vain, even though the objects of his hope are a real part of true happiness; unless, indeed, he believes and hopes for this, that he may obtain by prayer the blessing of love. For, although it is not possible to hope without love, it may yet happen that a man does not love that which is necessary to the attainment of his hope; as, for example, if he hopes for eternal life (and who is there that does not desire this?) and yet does not love righteousness, without which no one can attain to eternal life. Now this is the true faith of Christ which the apostle speaks of, "which worketh by love;" [224] and if there is anything that it does not yet embrace in its love, asks that it may receive, seeks that it may find, and knocks that it may be opened unto it.[225] For faith obtains through prayer that which the law commands. For without the gift of God, that is, without the Holy Spirit, through whom love is shed abroad in our hearts,[226] the law can command, but it cannot assist; and, moreover, it makes a man a transgressor, for he can no longer excuse himself on the plea of ignorance. Now carnal lust reigns where there is not the love of God.

CHAPTER CXVIII

THE FOUR STAGES OF THE CHRISTIAN'S LIFE, AND THE FOUR
CORRESPONDING STAGES OF THE CHURCH'S HISTORY

When, sunk in the darkest depths of ignorance, man lives according to the flesh, undisturbed by any struggle of reason or conscience, this is his first state. Afterwards, when through the law has come the knowledge of sin, and the Spirit of God has not yet interposed His aid, man, striving to live according to the law, is thwarted in his efforts and falls into conscious sin, and so, being overcome of sin, becomes its slave ("for of whom a man is overcome, of the same is he brought in bondage" [227]); and thus the effect produced by the knowledge of the commandment is this, that sin worketh

[223] 1 Cor. xiii. 13   [224] Gal. v. 6   [225] Matt. vii. 7   [226] Rom. v. 5   [227] 2 Pet. ii. 19

in man all manner of concupiscence, and he is involved in the additional guilt of willful transgression, and that is fulfilled which is written: "The law entered that the offense might abound." [228] This is man's second state. But if God has regard to him, and inspires him with faith in God's help, and the Spirit of God begins to work in him, then the mightier power of love strives against the power of the flesh; and although there is still in the man's own nature a power that fights against him (for his disease is not completely cured), yet he lives the life of the just by faith, and lives in righteousness so far as he does not yield to evil lust, but conquers it by the love of holiness. This is the third state of a man of good hope; and he who by steadfast piety advances in this course, shall attain at last to peace, that peace which, after this life is over, shall be perfected in the repose of the spirit, and finally in the resurrection of the body. Of these four different stages the first is before the law, the second is under the law, the third is under grace, and the fourth is in full and perfect peace. Thus, too, has the history of God's people been ordered according to His pleasure who disposeth all things in number, and measure, and weight.[229] For the church existed at first before the law; then under the law, which was given by Moses; then under grace, which was first made manifest in the coming of the Mediator. Not, indeed, that this grace was absent previously, but, in harmony with the arrangements of the time, it was veiled and hidden. For none, even of the just men of old, could find salvation apart from the faith of Christ; nor unless He had been known to them could their ministry have been used to convey prophecies concerning Him to us, some more plain, and some more obscure.

CHAPTER CXIX

THE GRACE OF REGENERATION WASHES AWAY ALL PAST SIN AND ALL ORIGINAL GUILT

Now in whichever of these four stages (as we may call them) the grace of regeneration finds any particular man, all his past sins are there and then pardoned, and the guilt which he contracted in his birth is removed in his new birth; and so true is it that "the wind bloweth where it listeth," [230] that some have never known the second stage, that of slavery under the law, but have received the divine assistance as soon as they received the commandment.

[228] Rom. v. 20   [229] Wisd. xi. 20   [230] John iii. 8

CHAPTER CXX

DEATH CANNOT INJURE THOSE WHO HAVE RECEIVED
THE GRACE OF REGENERATION

But before a man can receive the commandment, it is necessary that he should live according to the flesh. But if once he has received the grace of regeneration, death shall not injure him, even if he should forthwith depart from this life; "for to this end Christ both died, and rose, and revived, that He might be Lord both of the dead and the living;" [231] nor shall death retain dominion over him for whom Christ freely died.

CHAPTER CXXI

LOVE IS THE END OF ALL THE COMMANDMENTS,
AND GOD HIMSELF IS LOVE

All the commandments of God, then, are embraced in love, of which the apostle says: "Now the end of the commandment is charity, out of a pure heart, and of a good conscience, and of faith unfeigned." [232] Thus the end of every commandment is charity, that is, every commandment has love for its aim. But whatever is done either through fear of punishment or from some other carnal motive, and has not for its principle that love which the Spirit of God sheds abroad in the heart, is not done as it ought to be done, however it may appear to men. For this love embraces both the love of God and the love of our neighbor, and "on these two commandments hang all the law and the prophets," [233] we may add the Gospel and the apostles. For it is from these that we hear this voice: The end of the commandment is charity, and God is love.[234] Wherefore, all God's commandments, one of which is, "Thou shalt not commit adultery," [235] and all those precepts which are not commandments but special counsels, one of which is, "It is good for a man not to touch a woman," [236] are rightly carried out only when the motive principle of action is the love of God, and the love of our neighbor in God. And this applies both to the present and the future life. We love God now by faith, then we shall love Him through sight. Now we love even our neighbor by faith; for we who are ourselves mortal know not the hearts of mortal men. But in the future life, the Lord "both will bring to light the hidden things of darkness, and will make manifest the counsels of the hearts, and then shall every man have praise of God;" [237] for every man shall love and praise in his neighbor the virtue which, that it may not be hid, the Lord Himself shall bring to light. Moreover, lust diminishes as love grows, till the latter grows to such a height that it can

[231] Rom. xiv. 9   [232] 1 Tim. i. 5   [233] Matt. xxii. 40; Rom. v. 5   [234] 1 Tim. i. 5; 1 John iv. 16   [235] Matt. v. 27 and Rom. xiii. 9   [236] 1 Cor. vii. 1   [237] 1 Cor. iv. 5

grow no higher here. For "greater love hath no man than this, that a man lay down his life for his friends." [238] Who then can tell how great love shall be in the future world, when there shall be no lust for it to restrain and conquer? for that will be the perfection of health when there shall be no struggle with death.

CHAPTER CXXII

CONCLUSION

But now there must be an end at last to this volume. And it is for yourself to judge whether you should call it a *hand-book*, or should use it as such. I, however, thinking that your zeal in Christ ought not to be despised, and believing and hoping all good of you in dependence on our Redeemer's help, and loving you very much as one of the members of His body, have, to the best of my ability, written in this book for you on *Faith, Hope, and Love*. May its value be equal to its length.

[238] John xv. 13

ON GRACE AND FREE WILL

ON GRACE AND FREE WILL

Introductory Note

Towards the close of Saint Augustine's life in the years 426 and 427 A.D., an incident occurred which indicates the extent to which his work operated as a powerful force within the Church. Some years before, he had written a long letter on the problems of grace and predestination. Because of its scope and importance it was copied and came to the hands of some monks in a monastery at Adrumetum. The monks were seriously divided in the theological debate which the document precipitated, with some assuming an all but complete Pelagian position in reaction to Saint Augustine's apparently overwhelming emphasis upon grace. Finally, in order to settle the dispute, two monks, by name Cresconius and Felix, came to receive direct instruction from Saint Augustine himself. Not only did he give them several documents in which he had already dealt with the problem, but also asked them to study the present treatise, *On Grace and Free Will*, in which he attempts to show that a strong doctrine of grace by no means denies the validity of free will.

ON GRACE AND FREE WILL

ADDRESSED TO VALENTINUS AND THE MONKS OF ADRUMETUM

In this treatise Augustine teaches us to beware of maintaining grace by denying free will, or free will by denying grace; for that it is evident from the testimony of Scripture that there is in man a free choice of will; and there are also in the same Scriptures inspired proofs given of that very grace of God without which we can do nothing good. Afterwards, in opposition to the Pelagians, he proves that grace is not bestowed according to our merits. He explains how eternal life, which is rendered to good works, is really of grace. He then goes on to show that the grace which is given to us through our Lord Jesus Christ is neither the knowledge of the law, nor nature, nor simply remission of sins; but that it is grace that makes us fulfil the law, and causes nature to be liberated from the dominion of sin. He demolishes that vain subterfuge of the Pelagians, to the effect that "grace, although it is not bestowed according to the merits of good works, is yet given according to the merits of the antecedent good-will of the man who believes and prays." He incidentally touches the question, why God commands what He means Himself to give, and whether He imposes on us any commands which we are unable to perform. He clearly shows that the love which is indispensable for fulfilling the commandments is only within us from God Himself. He points out that God works in men's hearts to incline their wills whithersoever He willeth, either to good works according to His mercy, or to evil ones in return for their deserving; His judgment, indeed, being sometimes manifest, sometimes hidden, but always righteous. Lastly, he teaches us that a clear example of the gratuitousness of grace, not given in return for our deserts, is supplied to us in the case of those infants which are saved, while others perish though their case is identical with that of the rest.

CHAPTER I

THE OCCASION AND ARGUMENT OF THIS WORK

WITH reference to those persons who so preach and defend man's free will, as boldly to deny, and endeavor to do away with, the grace of God which calls us to Him, and delivers us from our evil deserts, and by which we obtain the good deserts which lead to everlasting life: we have already said a good deal in discussion, and committed it to writing, so far as the Lord has vouchsafed to enable us. But since there are some persons who so defend God's grace as to deny man's free will, or who suppose that free will is denied when grace is defended, I have determined to write somewhat on this point to your Love,[1] my brother Valentinus, and the rest of you, who are serving God together under the impulse of a mutual love. For it has been told me concerning you, brethren, by some members of your brotherhood who have visited us, and are the bearers of this communica-

---

[1] A form of address, like "your Honor."

tion of ours to you, that there are dissensions among you on this subject. This, then, being the case, dearly beloved, that you be not disturbed by the obscurity of this question, I counsel you first to thank God for such things as you understand; but as for all which is beyond the reach of your mind, pray for understanding from the Lord, observing, at the same time, peace and love among yourselves; and until He Himself lead you to perceive what at present is beyond your comprehension, walk firmly on the ground of which you are sure. This is the advice of the Apostle Paul, who, after saying that he was not yet perfect,[2] a little later adds, "Let us, therefore, as many as are perfect, be thus minded"[3]—meaning perfect to a certain extent, but not having attained to a perfection sufficient for us; and then immediately adds, "And if, in any thing, ye be otherwise minded, God shall reveal even this unto you. Nevertheless, whereunto we have already attained, let us walk by the same rule."[4] For by walking in what we have attained, we shall be able to advance to what we have not yet attained— God revealing it to us if in anything we are otherwise minded—provided we do not give up what He has already revealed.

CHAPTER II

HE PROVES THE EXISTENCE OF FREE WILL IN MAN FROM THE PRECEPTS ADDRESSED TO HIM BY GOD

Now He has revealed to us, through His Holy Scriptures, that there is in a man a free choice of will. But how He has revealed this I do not recount in human language, but in divine. There is, to begin with, the fact that God's precepts themselves would be of no use to a man unless he had free choice of will, so that by performing them he might obtain the promised rewards. For they are given that no one might be able to plead the excuse of ignorance, as the Lord says concerning the Jews in the gospel: "If I had not come and spoken unto them, they would not have sin; but now they have no excuse for their sin."[5] Of what sin does He speak but of that great one which He foreknew, while speaking thus, that they would make their own—that is, the death they were going to inflict upon Him? For they did not have "no sin" before Christ came to them in the flesh. The apostle also says: "The wrath of God is revealed from heaven against all ungodliness and unrighteousness of men who hold back the truth in unrighteousness; because that which may be known of God is manifest in them; for God hath showed it unto them. For the invisible things of Him are from the creation of the world clearly seen—being understood by the things that are made—even His eternal power and Godhead, so that they are inexcusable."[6] In what sense does he pronounce them to be "inexcusable," except with reference to such excuse as human pride is apt to allege

[2] Phil. iii. 12   [3] Phil. iii. 15   [4] Phil .iii. 16   [5] John xv. 22   [6] Rom. i. 18-20

in such words as, "If I had only known, I would have done it; did I not fail to do it because I was ignorant of it?" or, "I would do it if I knew how; but I do not know, therefore I do not do it"? All such excuse is removed from them when the precept is given them, or the knowledge is made manifest to them how to avoid sin.

CHAPTER III

SINNERS ARE CONVICTED WHEN ATTEMPTING TO EXCUSE THEMSELVES BY BLAMING GOD, BECAUSE THEY HAVE FREE WILL

There are, however, persons who attempt to find excuse for themselves even from God. The Apostle James says to such: "Let no man say when he is tempted, I am tempted of God; for God cannot be tempted with evil, neither tempteth He any man. But every man is tempted when he is drawn away of his own lust, and enticed. Then, when lust hath conceived, it bringeth forth sin; and sin, when it is finished, bringeth forth death." [7] Solomon, too, in his book of *Proverbs*, has this answer for such as wish to find an excuse for themselves from God Himself: "The folly of a man spoils his ways; but he blames God in his heart." [8] And in the book of *Ecclesiasticus* we read: "Say not thou, It is through the Lord that I fell away; for thou oughtest not to do the things that He hateth: nor do thou say, He hath caused me to err; for He hath no need of the sinful man. The Lord hateth all abomination, and they that fear God love it not. He Himself made man from the beginning, and left him in the hand of His counsel. If thou be willing, thou shalt keep His commandments, and perform true fidelity. He hath set fire and water before thee: stretch forth thine hand unto whither thou wilt. Before man is life and death, and whichsoever pleaseth him shall be given to him." [9] Observe how very plainly is set before our view the free choice of the human will.

CHAPTER IV

THE DIVINE COMMANDS WHICH ARE MOST SUITED TO THE WILL ITSELF ILLUSTRATE ITS FREEDOM

What is the import of the fact that in so many passages requires all His commandments to be kept and fulfilled? How does He make this requisition, if there is no free will? What means "the happy man," of whom the Psalmist says that "his will has been the law of the Lord"? [10] Does he not clearly enough show that a man by his own will takes his stand in the law of God? Then again, there are so many commandments which in some way are expressly adapted to the human will; for instance, there is, "Be not overcome of evil," [11] and others of similar import, such as,

[7] Jas. i. 13-15   [8] Prov. xix. 3   [9] Ecclus. xv. 11-17   [10] Ps. i. 2   [11] Rom. xii. 1

"Be not like a horse or a mule, which have no understanding;" [12] and, "Reject not the counsels of thy mother;" [13] and, "Be not wise in thine own conceit;" [14] and, "Despise not the chastening of the Lord;" [15] and, "Forget not my law;" [16] and, "Forbear not to do good to the poor;" [17] and, "Devise not evil against thy friend;" [18] and, "Give no heed to a worthless woman;" [19] and, "He is not inclined to understand how to do good;" [20] and, "They refused to attend to my counsel;" [21] with numberless other passages of the inspired Scriptures of the Old Testament. And what do they all show us but the free choice of the human will? So, again, in the evangelical and apostolic books of the New Testament what other lesson is taught us? As when it is said, "Lay not up for yourselves treasures upon earth;" [22] and, "Fear not them which kill the body;" [23] and, "If any man will come after me, let him deny himself;" [24] and again, "Peace on earth to men of good will." [25] So also that the Apostle Paul says: "Let him do what he willeth; he sinneth not if he marry. Nevertheless, he that standeth stedfast in his heart, having no necessity, but hath power over his own will, and hath so decreed in his heart that he will keep his virgin, doeth well." [26] And so again, "If I do this willingly, I have a reward;" [27] while in another passage he says, "Be ye sober and righteous, and sin not;" [28] and again, "As ye have a readiness to will, so also let there be a prompt performance;" [29] then he remarks to Timothy about the younger widows, "When they have begun to wax wanton against Christ, they choose to marry." So in another passage, "All that will to live godly in Christ Jesus shall suffer persecution;" [30] while to Timothy himself he says, "Neglect not the gift that is in thee." [31] Then to Philemon he addresses this explanation: "That thy benefit should not be as it were of necessity, but of thine own will." [32] Servants also he advises to obey their masters "with a good will." [33] In strict accordance with this, James says: "Do not err, my beloved brethren . . . and have not the faith of our Lord Jesus Christ with respect to persons;" [34] and, "Do not speak evil one of another." [35] So also John in his *Epistle* writes, "Do not love the world," [36] and other things of the same import. Now wherever it is said, "Do not do this," and "Do not do that," and wherever there is any requirement in the divine admonitions for the work of the will to do anything, or to refrain from doing anything, there is at once a sufficient proof of free will. No man, therefore, when he sins, can in his heart blame God for it, but every man must impute the fault to himself. Nor does it detract at all from a man's own will when he performs any act in accordance with

---

[12] Ps. xxxii. 9   [13] Prov. i. 8   [14] Prov. iii. 7   [15] Prov. iii. 11   [16] Prov. iii. 1
[17] Prov. iii. 27   [18] Prov. iii. 29   [19] Prov. v. 2   [20] Ps. xxxvi. 3   [21] Prov. i. 30
[22] Matt. vi. 19   [23] Matt. x. 28   [24] Matt. xvi. 24   [25] Luke ii. 14   [26] 1 Cor. vii.
36, 37   [27] 1 Cor. ix. 17   [28] 1 Cor. xv. 34   [29] 2 Cor. viii. 11   [30] 2 Tim. iii. 12
[31] 1 Tim. iv. 14   [32] Philemon 14   [33] Eph. vi. 7   [34] Jas. i. 16, and ii. 1   [35] Jas.
iv. 11   [36] 1 John ii. 15

God. Indeed, a work is then to be pronounced a good one when a person does it willingly; then, too, may the reward of a good work be hoped for from Him concerning whom it is written, "He shall reward every man according to his works." [37]

CHAPTER V

HE SHOWS THAT IGNORANCE AFFORDS NO SUCH EXCUSE AS SHALL FREE THE OFFENDER FROM PUNISHMENT; BUT THAT TO SIN WITH KNOWLEDGE IS A GRAVER THING THAN TO SIN IN IGNORANCE

The excuse such as men are in the habit of alleging from ignorance is taken away from those persons who know God's commandments. But neither will those be without punishment who know not the law of God. "For as many as have sinned without law shall also perish without law; and as many as have sinned in the law shall be judged by the law." [38] Now the apostle does not appear to me to have said this as if he meant that they would have to suffer something worse who in their sins are ignorant of the law than they who know it. It is seemingly worse, no doubt, "to perish" than "to be judged;" but inasmuch as he was speaking of the Gentiles and of the Jews when he used these words, because the former were without the law, but the latter had received the law, who can venture to say that the Jews who sin in the law will not perish, since they refused to believe in Christ, when it was of them that the apostle said, "They shall be judged by the law"? For without faith in Christ no man can be delivered; and therefore they will be so judged that they perish. If, indeed, the condition of those who are ignorant of the law of God is worse than the condition of those who know it, how can that be true which the Lord says in the gospel: "The servant who knows not his lord's will, and commits things worthy of stripes, shall be beaten with few stripes; whereas the servant who knows his lord's will, and commits things worthy of stripes, shall be beaten with many stripes"? [39] Observe how clearly He here shows that it is a graver matter for a man to sin with knowledge than in ignorance. And yet we must not on this account betake ourselves for refuge to the shades of ignorance, with the view of finding our excuse therein. It is one thing to be ignorant, and another thing to be unwilling to know. For the will is at fault in the case of the man of whom it is said, "He is not inclined to understand, so as to do good." [40] But even the ignorance, which is not theirs who refuse to know, but theirs who are, as it were, simply ignorant, does not so far excuse any one as to exempt him from the punishment of eternal fire, though his failure to believe has been the result of his not having at all heard what he should believe; but probably

---

[37] Matt. xvi. 27   [38] Rom. ii. 12   [39] Luke xii. 47, 48   [40] Ps. xxxvi. 3

only so far as to mitigate his punishment. For it was not said without reason: "Pour out Thy wrath upon the heathen that have not known Thee;" [41] nor again according to what the apostle says: "When He shall come from heaven in a flame of fire to take vengeance on them that know not God." [42] But yet in order that we may have that knowledge that will prevent our saying, each one of us, "I did not know," "I did not hear," "I did not understand;" the human will is summoned, in such words as these: "Wish not to be as the horse or as the mule, which have no understanding;" [43] although it may show itself even worse, of which it is written, "A stubborn servant will not be reproved by words; for even if he understand, yet he will not obey." [44] But when a man says, "I cannot do what I am commanded, because I am mastered by my concupiscence," he has no longer any excuse to plead from ignorance, nor reason to blame God in his heart, but he recognises and laments his own evil in himself; and still to such an one the apostle says: "Be not overcome by evil, but overcome evil with good;" [45] and of course the very fact that the injunction, "Consent not to be overcome," is addressed to him, undoubtedly summons the determination of his will. For to consent and to refuse are functions proper to will.

CHAPTER VI

GOD'S GRACE TO BE MAINTAINED AGAINST THE PELAGIANS; THE PELAGIAN HERESY NOT AN OLD ONE

It is, however, to be feared lest all these and similar testimonies of Holy Scripture (and undoubtedly there are a great many of them) in the maintenance of free will, be understood in such a way as to leave no room for God's assistance and grace in leading a godly life and a good conversation, to which the eternal reward is due; and lest poor wretched man, when he leads a good life and performs good works (or rather thinks that he leads a good life and performs good works) should dare to glory in himself and not in the Lord, and to put his hope of righteous living in himself alone; so as to be followed by the prophet Jeremiah's malediction when he says, "Cursed is the man who has hope in man, and maketh strong the flesh of his arm, and whose heart departeth from the Lord." [46] Understand, my brethren, I pray you, this passage of the prophet. Because the prophet did not say, "Cursed is the man who has hope in his own self," it might seem to some that the passage, "Cursed is the man who has hope in man," was spoken to prevent man having hope in any other man but himself. In order, therefore, to show that his admonition to man was not to have hope in himself, after saying, "Cursed is the man who has

---

[41] Ps. lxix. 6   [42] 2 Thess. i. 7, 8   [43] Ps. xxxii. 9   [44] Prov. xxix. 19   [45] Rom. xii. 21   [46] Jer. xvii. 5

hope in man," he immediately added, "And maketh strong the flesh of his arm." He used the word *"arm"* to designate *power in operation*. By the term *"flesh,"* however, must be understood *human frailty*. And therefore he makes strong the flesh of his arm who supposes that a power which is frail and weak (that is, human) is sufficient for him to perform good works, and therefore puts not his hope in God for help. This is the reason why he subjoined the further clause, "And whose heart departeth from the Lord." Of this character is the Pelagian heresy, which is not an ancient one, but has only lately come into existence. Against this system of error there was first a good deal of discussion; then, as the ultimate resource, it was referred to sundry episcopal councils, the proceedings of which, not, indeed, in every instance, but in some, I have despatched to you for your perusal. In order, then, to our performance of good works, let us not have hope in man, making strong the flesh of our arm; nor let our heart ever depart from the Lord, but let it say to him, "Be Thou my helper; forsake me not, nor despise me, O God of my salvation." [47]

CHAPTER VII

GRACE IS NECESSARY ALONG WITH FREE WILL TO LEAD A GOOD LIFE

Therefore, my dearly beloved, as we have now proved by our former testimonies from Holy Scripture that there is in man a free determination of will for living rightly and acting rightly; so now let us see what are the divine testimonies concerning the grace of God, without which we are not able to do any good thing. And first of all, I will say something about the very profession which you make in your brotherhood. Now your society, in which you are leading lives of continence, could not hold together unless you despised conjugal pleasure. Well, the Lord was one day conversing on this very topic, when His disciples remarked to Him, "If such be the case of a man with his wife, it is not good to marry." He then answered them, "All men cannot receive this saying, save they to whom it is given." [48] And was it not to Timothy's free will that the apostle appealed, when he exhorted him in these words: "Keep thyself continent"? [49] He also explained the power of the will in this matter when He said, "Having no necessity, but possessing power over his own will, to keep his virgin." [50] And yet "all men do not receive this saying, except those to whom the power is given." Now they to whom this is not given either are unwilling or do not fulfil what they will; whereas they to whom it is given so will as to accomplish what they will. In order, therefore, that this saying, which is not received by all men, may yet be received by some, there are both the gift of God and free will.

[47] Ps. xxvii. 9   [48] Matt. xix. 10   [49] I Tim. v. 22   [50] I Cor. vii. 37

CHAPTER VIII

CONJUGAL CHASTITY IS ITSELF THE GIFT OF GOD

It is concerning conjugal chastity itself that the apostle treats, when he says, "Let him do what he will, he sinneth not if he marry;" [51] and yet this too is God's gift, for the Scripture says, "It is by the Lord that the woman is joined to her husband." Accordingly the teacher of the Gentiles, in one of his discourses, commends both conjugal chastity, whereby adulteries are prevented, and the still more perfect continence which foregoes all cohabitation, and shows how both one and the other are severally the gift of God. Writing to the Corinthians, he admonished married persons not to defraud each other; and then, after his admonition to these, he added: "But I could wish that all men were even as I am myself" [52]—meaning, of course, that he abstained from all cohabitation; and then proceeded to say: "But every man hath his own gift of God, one after this manner, and another after that." [52] Now, do the many precepts which are written in the law of God, forbidding all fornication and adultery, indicate anything else than free will? Surely such precepts would not be given unless a man had a will of his own, wherewith to obey the divine commandments. And yet it is God's gift which is indispensable for the observance of the precepts of chastity. Accordingly, it is said in the *Book of Wisdom:* "When I knew that no one could be continent, except God gives it, then this became a point of wisdom to know whose gift it was." [53] "Every man," however, "is tempted when he is drawn away of his own lust, and enticed" [54] not to observe and keep these holy precepts of chastity. If he should say in respect of these commandments, "I wish to keep them, but am mastered by my concupiscence," then the Scripture responds to his free will, as I have already said: "Be not overcome of evil, but overcome evil with good." [55] In order, however, that this victory may be gained, grace renders its help; and were not this help given, then the law would be nothing but the strength of sin. For concupiscence is increased and receives greater energies from the prohibition of the law, unless the spirit of grace helps. This explains the statement of the great Teacher of the Gentiles, when he says, "The sting of death is sin, and the strength of sin is the law." [56] See, then, I pray you, whence originates this confession of weakness, when a man says, "I desire to keep what the law commands, but am overcome by the strength of my concupiscence." And when his will is addressed, and it is said, "Be not overcome of evil," of what avail is anything but the succor of God's grace to the accomplishment of the precept? This the apostle himself afterwards stated; for after saying, "The strength of sin is the law," he immediately subjoined, "But thanks

[51] I Cor. vii. 36   [52] I Cor. vii. 7   [53] Wisd. viii. 21   [54] Jas. i. 14   [55] Rom. xii. 21   [56] I Cor. xv. 56

be to God, who giveth us the victory, through our Lord Jesus Christ." [57]
It follows, then, that the victory in which sin is vanquished is nothing
else than the gift of God, who in this contest helps free will.

CHAPTER IX

ENTERING INTO TEMPTATION. PRAYER IS A PROOF OF GRACE

Wherefore, our Heavenly Master also says: "Watch and pray, that ye enter not into temptation." [58] Let every man, therefore, when fighting against
his own concupiscence, pray that he enter not into temptation; that is, that
he be not drawn aside and enticed by it. But he does not enter into temptation if he conquers his evil concupiscence by good will. And yet the
determination of the human will is insufficient, unless the Lord grant it
victory in answer to prayer that it enter not into temptation. What, indeed,
affords clearer evidence of the grace of God than the acceptance of prayer
in any petition? If our Saviour had only said, "Watch that ye enter not
into temptation," He would appear to have done nothing further than
admonish man's will; but since He added the words, "and pray," He
showed that God helps us not to enter into temptation. It is to the free
will of man that the words are addressed: "My son, remove not thyself
from the chastening of the Lord." [59] And the Lord said: "I have prayed
for thee, Peter, that thy faith fail not." [60] So that a man is assisted by
grace, in order that his will may not be uselessly commanded.

CHAPTER X

FREE WILL AND GOD'S GRACE ARE SIMULTANEOUSLY COMMENDED

When God says, "Turn ye unto me, and I will turn unto you," [61] one
of these clauses—that which invites our return to God—evidently belongs
to our will; while the other, which promises His return to us, belongs to
His grace. Here, possibly, the Pelagians think they have a justification for
their opinion which they so prominently advance, that God's grace is
given according to our merits. In the East, indeed, that is to say, in the
province of Palestine, in which is the city of Jerusalem, Pelagius, when examined in person by the bishop,[62] did not venture to affirm this. For it
happened that among the objections which were brought up against him,
this in particular was objected, that he maintained that the grace of God
was given according to our merits—an opinion which was so diverse from
Catholic doctrine, and so hostile to the grace of Christ, that unless he had
anathematized it, as laid to his charge, he himself must have been anathematized on its account. He pronounced, indeed, the required anathema

---

[57] I Cor. xv. 57   [58] Matt. xxvi. 41   [59] Prov. iii. 11   [60] Luke xxii. 32   [61] Zech.
i. 3   [62] See *On the Proceedings of Pelagius,* xiv. 30-37

upon the dogma, but how insincerely his later books plainly show; for
in them he maintains absolutely no other opinion than that the grace of
God is given according to our merits. Such passages do they collect out of
the Scriptures—like the one which I just now quoted, "Turn ye unto me,
and I will turn unto you"—as if it were owing to the merit of our turning
to God that His grace were given us, wherein He Himself even turns unto
us. Now the persons who hold this opinion fail to observe that, unless our
turning to God were itself God's gift, it would not be said to Him in prayer,
"Turn us again, O God of hosts;" [63] and, "Thou, O God, wilt turn and
quicken us;" [64] and again, "Turn us, O God of our salvation" [65]—with
other passages of similar import, too numerous to mention here. For,
with respect to our coming unto Christ, what else does it mean than our
being turned to Him by believing? And yet He says: "No man can come
unto me, except it were given unto him of my Father." [66]

CHAPTER XI

OTHER PASSAGES OF SCRIPTURE WHICH THE PELAGIANS ABUSE

Then, again, there is the Scripture contained in the second book of the
Chronicles: "The Lord is with you when ye are with Him: and if ye shall
seek Him ye shall find Him; but if ye forsake Him, He also will forsake
you." [67] This passage, no doubt, clearly manifests the choice of the will.
But they who maintain that God's grace is given according to our merits,
receive these testimonies of Scripture in such a manner as to believe that
our merit lies in the circumstance of our "being with God," while His
grace is given according to this merit, so that He too may be with us. In
like manner, that our merit lies in the fact of "our seeking God," and then
His grace is given according to this merit, in order that we may find Him.
Again, there is a passage in the first book of the same *Chronicles* which
declares the choice of the will: "And thou, Solomon, my son, know thou
the God of thy father, and serve Him with a perfect heart and with a
willing mind, for the Lord searcheth all hearts, and understandeth all the
imaginations of the thoughts; if thou seek Him, He will be found of thee;
but if thou forsake Him, He will cast thee off for ever." [68] But these people
find some room for human merit in the clause, "If thou seek Him," and
then the grace is thought to be given according to this merit in what is
said in the ensuing words, "He will be found of thee." And so they labor
with all their might to show that God's grace is given according to our
merits—in other words, that grace is not grace. For, as the apostle most
expressly says, to them who receive reward according to merit "the recompense is not reckoned of grace but of debt." [69]

[63] Ps. lxxx. 7   [64] Ps. lxxxv. 6   [65] Ps. lxxxv. 4   [66] John vi. 65   [67] 2 Chron.
xv. 2   [68] 1 Chron. xxviii. o   [69] Rom. iv. 4

CHAPTER XII

HE PROVES OUT OF SAINT PAUL THAT GRACE IS NOT GIVEN ACCORDING TO MEN'S MERITS

Now there was, no doubt, a decided merit in the Apostle Paul, but it was an *evil* one, while he persecuted the Chruch, and he says of it: "I am not meet to be called an apostle, because I persecuted the Church of God." [70] And it was while he had this evil merit that a good one was rendered to him instead of the evil; and, therefore, he went on at once to say, "But by the grace of God I am what I am." [71] Then, in order to exhibit also his free will, he added in the next clause, "And His grace within me was not in vain, but I have labored more abundantly than they all." This free will of man he appeals to in the case of others also, as when he says to them, "We beseech you that ye receive not the grace of God in vain." [72] Now, how could he so enjoin them, if they received God's grace in such a manner as to lose their own will? Nevertheless, lest the will itself should be deemed capable of doing any good thing without the grace of God, after saying, "His grace within me was not in vain, but I have labored more abundantly than they all," he immediately added the qualifying clause, "Yet not I, but the grace of God which was with me." [71] In other words, Not I alone, but the grace of God with me. And thus, neither was it the grace of God alone, nor was it he himself alone, but it was the grace of God with him. For his call, however, from heaven and his conversion by that great and most effectual call, God's grace was alone, because his merits, though great, were yet evil. Then, to quote one passage more, he says to Timothy: "But be thou a co-laborer with the gospel, according to the power of God, who saveth us and calleth us with His holy calling—not according to our works, but according to His own purpose and grace, which was given us in Christ Jesus." [73] Then, elsewhere, he enumerates his merits, and gives us this description of their evil character: "For we ourselves also were formerly foolish, unbelieving, deceived, serving divers lusts and pleasures, living in malice and envy, hateful, and hating one another." [74] Nothing to be sure, but punishment was due to such a course of evil desert! God, however, who returns good for evil by His grace, which is not given according to our merits, enabled the apostle to conclude his statement and say: "But when the kindness and love of our Saviour God shone upon us—not of works of righteousness which we have done, but according to His mercy He saved us, by the laver of regeneration and renewal of the Holy Ghost, whom He shed upon us abundantly through Jesus Christ our Saviour; that, being justified by His grace, we should be made heirs according to the hope of eternal life." [75]

[70] 1 Cor. xv. 9   [71] 1 Cor. xv. 10   [72] 2 Cor. vi. 1   [73] 2 Tim. i. 8, 9   [74] Titus iii. 3   [75] Titus iii. 4-7

CHAPTER XIII

THE GRACE OF GOD IS NOT GIVEN ACCORDING TO MERIT, BUT ITSELF MAKES ALL GOOD DESERT

From these and similar passages of Scripture, we gather the proof that God's grace is not given according to our merits. The truth is, we see that it is given not only where there are no good, but even where there are many evil merits preceding: and we see it so given daily. But it is plain that when it has been given, also our good merits begin to be—yet only by means of it; for, were that only to withdraw itself, man falls, not raised up, but precipitated by free will. Wherefore no man ought, even when he begins to possess good merits, to attribute them to himself, but to God, who is thus addressed by the Psalmist: "Be Thou my helper, forsake me not." [76] By saying, "Forsake me not," he shows that if he were to be forsaken, he is unable of himself to do any good thing. Wherefore also he says: "I said in my abundance, I shall never be moved," [77] for he thought that he had such an abundance of good to call his own that he would not be moved. But in order that he might be taught whose that was, of which he had begun to boast as if it were his own, he was admonished by the gradual desertion of God's grace, and says: "O Lord, in Thy good pleasure Thou didst add strength to my beauty. Thou didst, however, turn away Thy face, and then I was troubled and distressed." [78] Thus, it is necessary for a man that he should be not only justified when unrighteous by the grace of God—that is, be changed from unholiness to righteousness—when he is re-quited with good for his evil; but that, even after he has become justified by faith, grace should accompany him on his way, and he should lean upon it, lest he fall. On this account it is written concerning the Church herself in the book of *Canticles:* "Who is this that cometh up in white raiment, leaning upon her kinsman?" [79] Made white is she who by herself alone could not be white. And by whom has she been made white except by Him who says by the prophet, "Though your sins be as purple, I will make them white as snow"? [80] At the time, then, that she was made white, she deserved nothing good; but now that she is made white, she walketh well—but it is only by her continuing ever to lean upon Him by whom she was made white. Wherefore, Jesus Himself, on whom she leans that was made white, said to His disciples, "Without me ye can do nothing." [81]

[76] Ps. xxvii. 9   [77] Ps. xxx. 6   [78] Ps. xxx. 7   [79] Cant. viii. 5   [80] Isa. i. 18
[81] John xv. 5

CHAPTER XIV

PAUL FIRST RECEIVED GRACE THAT HE MIGHT WIN THE CROWN

Let us return now to the Apostle Paul, who, as we have found, obtained God's grace, who recompenses good for evil, without any good merits of his own, but rather with many evil merits. Let us see what he says when his final sufferings were approaching, writing to Timothy: "I am now ready to be offered, and the time of my departure is at hand. I have fought a good fight; I have finished my course; I have kept the faith." [82] He enumerates these as, of course, now his good merits; so that, as after his evil merits he obtained grace, so now, after his good merits, he might receive the crown. Observe, therefore, what follows: "There is henceforth laid up for me," he says, "a crown of righteousness, which the Lord, the righteous Judge, shall give me at that day." [83] Now, to whom should the righteous Judge award the crown, except to him on whom the merciful Father had bestowed grace? And how could the crown be one "of righteousness," unless the grace had preceded which "justifieth the ungodly"? How, moreover, could these things now be awarded as of debt, unless the other had been before given as a free gift?

CHAPTER XV

THE PELAGIANS PROFESS THAT THE ONLY GRACE WHICH IS NOT GIVEN ACCORDING TO OUR MERITS IS THAT OF THE FORGIVENESS OF SINS

When, however, the Pelagians say that the only grace which is not given according to our merits is that whereby his sins are forgiven to man, but that that which is given in the end, that is, eternal life, is rendered to our preceding merits: they must not be allowed to go without an answer. If, indeed, they so understand our merits as to acknowledge them, too, to be the gifts of God, then their opinion would not deserve reprobation. But inasmuch as they so preach human merits as to declare that a man has them of his own self, then most rightly the apostle replies: "Who maketh thee to differ from another? And what hast thou, that thou didst not receive? Now, if thou didst receive it, why dost thou glory as if thou hadst not received it?" [84] To a man who holds such views, it is perfect truth to say: It is His own gifts that God crowns, not your merits—if, at least, your merits are of your own self, not of Him. If, indeed, they are such, they are evil; and God does not crown them; but if they are good, they are God's gifts, because, as the Apostle James says, "Every good gift and every perfect gift is from above, and cometh down from the Father of lights." [85]

[82] 2 Tim. iv. 6, 7   [83] 2 Tim. iv. 8   [84] 2 Cor. iv. 7   [85] Jas. i. 17

In accordance with which John also, the Lord's forerunner, declares: "A man can receive nothing except it be given him from heaven" [86]—from heaven, of course, because from thence came also the Holy Ghost, when Jesus ascended up on high, led captivity captive, and gave gifts to men.[87] If, then, your good merits are God's gifts, God does not crown your merits as your merits, but as His own gifts.

CHAPTER XVI

PAUL FOUGHT, BUT GOD GAVE THE VICTORY: HE RAN, BUT GOD SHOWED MERCY

Let us, therefore, consider those very merits of the Apostle Paul which he said the Righteous Judge would recompense with the crown of righteousness; and let us see whether these merits of his were really his own—I mean, whether they were obtained by him of himself, or were the gifts of God. "I have fought," says he, "the good fight; I have finished my course; I have kept the faith." [88] Now, in the first place, these good works were nothing, unless they had been preceded by good thoughts. Observe, therefore, what he says concerning these very thoughts. His words, when writing to the Corinthians, are: "Not that we are sufficient of ourselves to think anything as of ourselves; but our sufficiency is of God." [89] Then let us look at each several merit. "I have fought the good fight." Well, now, I want to know by what power he fought. Was it by a power which he possessed of himself, or by strength given to him from above? It is impossible to suppose that so great a teacher as the apostle was ignorant of the law of God, which proclaims the following in *Deuteronomy:* "Say not in thine heart, My own strength and energy of hand hath wrought for me this great power; but thou shalt remember the Lord thy God, how it is He that giveth thee strength to acquire such power." [90] And what avails "the good fight," unless followed by victory? And who gives the victory but He of whom the apostle says himself, "Thanks be to God, who giveth us the victory through our Lord Jesus Christ"? [91] Then, in another passage, having quoted from the Psalm these words: "Because for Thy sake we are killed all the day long; we are accounted as sheep for slaughter," [92] he went on to declare: "Nay, in all these things we are more than conquerors, through Him that loved us." [93] Not by ourselves, therefore, is the victory accomplished, but by Him who hath loved us. In the second clause he says, "I have finished my course." Now, who is it that says this, but he who declares in another passage, "So then it is not of him that willeth, nor of him that runneth, but of God that showeth mercy." [94] And this senence can by no means be transposed, so that it could be said: It is not of

[86] John iii. 27   [87] Ps. lxviii. 18, and Eph. iv. 8   [88] 2 Tim. iv. 7   [89] 2 Cor. iii. 5
[90] Deut. viii. 17   [91] 1 Cor. xv. 57   [92] Ps. xliv. 22   [93] Rom. viii. 37   [94] Rom. ix. 16

God, who showeth mercy, but of the man who willeth and runneth. If any person be bold enough to express the matter thus, he shows himself most plainly to be at issue with the apostle.

CHAPTER XVII

THE FAITH THAT HE KEPT WAS THE FREE GIFT OF GOD

His last clause runs thus: "I have kept the faith." But he who says this is the same who declares in another passage, "I have obtained mercy that I might be faithful." [95] He does not say, "I obtained mercy because I was faithful," but "in order that I might be faithful," thus showing that even faith itself cannot be had without God's mercy, and that it is the gift of God. This he very expressly teaches us when he says, "For by grace are ye saved through faith, and that not of yourselves; it is the gift of God." [96] They might possibly say, "We received grace because we believed;" as if they would attribute the faith to themselves, and the grace to God. Therefore, the apostle having said, "Ye are saved through faith," added, "And that not of yourselves, but it is the gift of God." And again, lest they should say they deserved so great a gift by their works, he immediately added, "Not of works, lest any man should boast." [97] Not that he denied good works, or emptied them of their value, when he says that God renders to every man according to his works; [98] but because works proceed from faith, and not faith from works. Therefore it is from Him that we have works of righteousness, from whom comes also faith itself, concerning which it is written, "The just shall live by faith." [99]

CHAPTER XVIII

FAITH WITHOUT GOOD WORKS IS NOT SUFFICIENT FOR SALVATION

Unintelligent persons, however, with regard to the apostle's statement: "We conclude that a man is justified by faith without the works of the law," [100] have thought him to mean that faith suffices to a man, even if he lead a bad life, and has no good works. Impossible is it that such a character should be deemed "a vessel of election" by the apostle, who, after declaring that "in Christ Jesus neither circumcision availeth anything, nor uncircumcision," [101] adds at once, "but faith which worketh by love." It is such faith which severs God's faithful from unclean demons—for even these "believe and tremble," [102] as the Apostle James says; but they do not do well. Therefore they possess not the faith by which the just man lives—the faith which works by love in such wise, that God recompenses it according to its works with eternal life. But inasmuch as we have even our good works

---

[95] I Cor. vii. 25   [96] Eph. ii. 8   [97] Eph. ii. 9   [98] Rom. ii. 6   [99] Habak. ii. 4
[100] Rom. iii. 28   [101] Gal. v. 6   [102] Jas. ii. 19

from God, from whom likewise comes our faith and our love, therefore the self-same great teacher of the Gentiles has designated "eternal life" itself as His gracious "gift." [103]

CHAPTER XIX

HOW IS ETERNAL LIFE BOTH A REWARD FOR SERVICE AND A FREE GIFT OF GRACE?

And hence there arises no small question, which must be solved by the Lord's gift. If eternal life is rendered to good works, as the Scripture most openly declares: "Then He shall reward every man according to his works:" [104] how can eternal life be a matter of grace, seeing that grace is not rendered to works, but is given gratuitously, as the apostle himself tells us: "To him that worketh is the reward not reckoned of grace, but of debt;" [105] and again: "There is a remnant saved according to the election of grace;" with these words immediately subjoined: "And if of grace, then is it no more of works; otherwise grace is no more grace"? [106] How, then, is eternal life by grace, when it is received from works? Does the apostle perchance not say that eternal life is a grace? Nay, he has so called it, with a clearness which none can possibly gainsay. It requires no acute intellect, but only an attentive reader, to discover this. For after saying, "The wages of sin is death," he at once added, "The grace of God is eternal life through Jesus Christ our Lord." [103]

CHAPTER XX

THE QUESTION ANSWERED. JUSTIFICATION IS GRACE SIMPLY AND ENTIRELY. ETERNAL LIFE IS REWARD AND GRACE

This question, then, seems to me to be by no means capable of solution, unless we understand that even those good works of ours, which are recompensed with eternal life, belong to the grace of God, because of what is said by the Lord Jesus: "Without me ye can do nothing." [107] And the apostle himself, after saying, "By grace are ye saved through faith; and that not of yourselves, it is the gift of God: not of works, lest any man should boast;" [108] saw, of course, the possibility that men would think from this statement that good works are not necessary to those who believe, but that faith alone suffices for them; and again, the possibility of men's boasting of their good works, as if they were of themselves capable of performing them. To meet, therefore, these opinions on both sides, he immediately added, "For we are His workmanship, created in Christ Jesus unto good works, which God hath before ordained that we should walk in them." [109]

[103] Rom. vi. 23   [104] Matt. xvi. 27   [105] Rom. iv. 4   [106] Rom. xi. 5, 6   [107] John xv. 5   [108] Eph. ii. 8, 9   [109] Eph. ii. 10

What is the purport of his saying, "Not of works, lest any man should boast," while commending the grace of God? And then why does he afterwards, when giving a reason for using such words, say, "For we are His workmanship, created in Christ Jesus unto good works"? Why, therefore, does it run, "Not of works, lest any man should boast"? Now, hear and understand. "Not of works" is spoken of the works which you suppose have their origin in yourself alone; but you have to think of works for which God has moulded (that is, has formed and created) you. For of these he says, "We are His workmanship, created in Christ Jesus unto good works." Now he does not here speak of that creation which made us human beings, but of that in reference to which one said who was already in full manhood, "Create in me a clean heart, O God;" [110] concerning which also the apostle says, "Therefore, if any man be in Christ, he is a new creature: old things are passed away; behold, all things are become new. And all things are of God." [111] We are framed, therefore, that is, formed and created, "in the good works which" we have not ourselves prepared, but "God hath before ordained that we should walk in them." It follows, then, dearly beloved, beyond all doubt, that as your good life is nothing else than God's grace, so also the eternal life which is the recompense of a good life is the grace of God; moreover it is given gratuitously, even as that is given gratuitously to which it is given. But that to which it is given is solely and simply grace; this therefore is also that which is given to it, because it is its reward—grace is for grace, as if remuneration for righteousness; in order that it may be true, because it is true, that God "shall reward every man according to his works." [112]

CHAPTER XXI

ETERNAL LIFE IS "GRACE FOR GRACE"

Perhaps you ask whether we ever read in the Sacred Scriptures of *"grace for grace."* Well, you possess the *Gospel according to John,* which is perfectly clear in its very great light. Here John the Baptist says of Christ: "Of His fulness have we all received, even *grace for grace.*" [113] So that out of His fulness we have received, according to our humble measure, our particles of ability as it were for leading good lives—"according as God hath dealt to every man his measure of faith;" [114] because "every man hath his proper gift of God; one after this manner, and another after that." [115] And this is grace. But, over and above this, we shall also receive "grace for grace," when we shall have awarded to us eternal life, of which the apostle said: "The grace of God is eternal life through Jesus Christ our Lord," [116] having just said that "the wages of sin is death." Deservedly did he call

---

[110] Ps. li. 12   [111] 2 Cor. v. 17, 18   [112] Matt. xvi. 27; Ps. lxii. 12; Rev. xxii. 12
[113] John i. 16   [114] Rom. xii. 3   [115] 1 Cor. vii. 7   [116] Rom. vi. 23

it *"wages,"* because everlasting death is awarded as its proper due to diabolical service. Now, when it was in his power to say, and rightly to say:
"But the wages of righteousness is eternal life," he yet preferred to say:
"The grace of God is eternal life;" in order that we may hence understand
that God does not, for any merits of our own, but from His own divine
compassion, prolong our existence to everlasting life. Even as the Psalmist
says to his soul, "Who crowneth thee with mercy and compassion." [117] Well,
now, is not a crown given as the reward of good deeds? It is, however, only
because He works good works in good men, of whom it is said, "It is God
which worketh in you both to will and to do of His good pleasure," [118]
that the Psalm has it, as just now quoted: "He crowneth thee with mercy
and compassion," since it is through His mercy that we perform the good
deeds to which the crown is awarded. It is not, however, to be for a moment supposed, because he said, "It is God that worketh in you both to
will and to do of his own good pleasure," that free will is taken away. If
this, indeed, had been his meaning, he would not have said just before,
"Work out your own salvation with fear and trembling." [119] For when
the command is given "to work," their free will is addressed; and when it
is added, "with fear and trembling," they are warned against boasting of
their good deeds as if they were their own, by attributing to themselves the
performance of anything good. It is pretty much as if the apostle had this
question put to him: "Why did you use the phrase, 'with fear and trembling'?" And as if he answered the inquiry of his examiners by telling
them, "For it is God which worketh in you." Because if you fear and
tremble, you do not boast of your good works—as if they were your own,
since it is God who works within you.

CHAPTER XXII

WHO IS THE TRANSGRESSOR OF THE LAW? THE OLDNESS OF ITS
LETTER. THE NEWNESS OF ITS SPIRIT

Therefore, brethren, you ought by free will not do evil but do good; this,
indeed, is the lesson taught us in the law of God, in the Holy Scriptures—
both Old and New. Let us, however, read, and by the Lord's help understand, what the apostle tells us: "Because by the deeds of the law there
shall no flesh be justified in His sight; for by the law is the knowledge of
sin." [120] Observe, he says *"the knowledge,"* not "the destruction," of sin.
But when a man knows sin, and grace does not help him to avoid what he
knows, undoubtedly the law works wrath. And this the apostle explicitly
says in another passage. His words are: "The law worketh wrath." [121] The
reason of this statement lies in the fact that God's wrath is greater in the
case of the transgressor who by the law knows sin, and yet commits it;

---

[117] Ps. ciii. 4   [118] Phil. ii. 13   [119] Phil. ii. 12   [120] Rom. iii. 20   [121] Rom. iv. 15

such a man is thus a transgressor of the law, even as the apostle says in another sentence, "For where no law is, there is no transgression." [121] It is in accordance with this principle that he elsewhere says, "That we may serve in newness of spirit, and not in the oldness of the letter;" [122] wishing *the law* to be here understood by "the oldness of the letter," and what else by "newness of spirit" than *grace?* Then, that it might not be thought that he had brought any accusation, or suggested any blame, against the law, he immediately takes himself to task with this inquiry: "What shall we say, then? Is the law sin? God forbid." He then adds the statement: "Nay, I had not known sin but by the law;" [123] which is of the same import as the passage above quoted: "By the law is the knowledge of sin." [124] Then: "For I had not known lust," he says, "except the law had said, 'Thou shalt not covet.' [125] But sin, taking occasion by the commandment, wrought in me all manner of concupiscence. For without the law sin was dead. For I was alive without the law once; but when the commandment came, sin revived, and I died. And the commandment, which was ordained to life, I found to be unto death. For sin, taking occasion by the commandment, deceived me, and by it slew me. Wherefore the law is holy; and the commandment holy, just, and good. Was, then, that which is good made death unto me? God forbid. But sin, that it might appear sin, worked death in me by that which is good—in order that the sinner, or the sin, might by the commandment become beyond measure." [126] And to the Galatians he writes: "Knowing that a man is not justified by the works of the law, except through faith in Jesus Christ, even we have believed in Jesus Christ, that we might be justified by the faith of Christ, and not by the works of the law; for by the works of the law shall no flesh be justified." [127]

CHAPTER XXIII

THE PELAGIANS MAINTAIN THAT THE LAW IS THE GRACE OF GOD WHICH HELPS US NOT TO SIN

Why, therefore, do those very vain and perverse Pelagians say that the law is the grace of God by which we are helped not to sin? Do they not, by making such an allegation, unhappily and beyond all doubt contradict the great apostle? He, indeed, says, that by the law sin received strength against man; and that man, by the commandment, although it be holy, and just, and good, nevertheless dies, and that death works in him through that which is good, from which death there is no deliverance unless the Spirit quickens him, whom the letter had killed—as he says in another passage, "The letter killeth, but the Spirit giveth life." [128] And yet these obstinate persons, blind to God's light, and deaf to His voice, maintain that the let-

---

[122] Rom. vii. 6   [123] Rom. vii. 6, 7   [124] Rom. iii. 20   [125] Ex. xx. 17   [126] Rom. vii. 7-13   [127] Gal. ii. 16   [128] 2 Cor. iii. 6

ter which kills gives life, and thus gainsay the quickening Spirit. "Therefore, brethren" (that I may warn you with better effect in the words of the apostle himself), "we are debtors not to the flesh, to live after the flesh; for if ye live after the flesh ye shall die; but if ye through the Spirit do mortify the deeds of the body, ye shall live." [129] I have said this to deter your free will from evil, and to exhort it to good by apostolic words; but yet you must not therefore glory in man—that is to say, in your own selves—and not in the Lord, when you live not after the flesh, but through the Spirit mortify the deeds of the flesh. For in order that they to whom the apostle addressed this language might not exalt themselves, thinking that they were themselves able of their own spirit to do such good works as these, and not by the Spirit of God, after saying to them, "If ye through the Spirit do mortify the deeds of the flesh, ye shall live," he at once added, "For as many as are led by the Spirit of God, they are the sons of God." [130] When, therefore, you by the Spirit mortify the deeds of the flesh, that you may have life, glorify Him, praise Him, give thanks to Him by whose Spirit you are so led as to be able to do such things as show you to be the children of God; "for as many as are led by the Spirit of God, they are the sons of God."

CHAPTER XXIV

WHO MAY BE SAID TO WISH TO ESTABLISH THEIR OWN RIGHTEOUSNESS. "GOD'S RIGHTEOUSNESS," SO CALLED, WHICH MAN HAS FROM GOD

As many, therefore, as are led by their own spirit, trusting in their own virtue, with the addition merely of the law's assistance, without the help of grace, are not the sons of God. Such are they of whom the same apostle speaks as "being ignorant of God's righteousness, and wishing to establish their own righteousness, who have not submitted themselves to the righteousness of God." [131] He said this of the Jews, who in their self-assumption rejected grace, and therefore did not believe in Christ. Their own righteousness, indeed, he says, they wish to establish; and this righteousness is of the law—not that the law was established by themselves, but that they had constituted their righteousness in the law which is of God, when they supposed themselves able to fulfil that law by their own strength, ignorant of God's righteousness—not indeed that by which God is Himself righteous, but that which man has from God. And that you may know that he designated as *theirs* the righteousness which is of the law, and as *God's* that which man receives from God, hear what he says in another passage, when speaking of Christ: "For whose sake I counted all things not only as loss, but I deemed them to be dung, that I might win Christ, and be found in Him—not having my own righteousness, which is of the law, but that

---

[129] Rom. viii. 12-13   [130] Rom. viii. 14   [131] Rom. x. 3

which is through the faith of Christ, which is of God." [132] Now what does he mean by "not having my own righteousness, which is of the law," when the law is really not his at all, but God's—except this, that he called it his own righteousness, although it was of the law, because he thought he could fulfil the law by his own will, without the aid of grace which is through faith in Christ? Wherefore, after saying, "Not having my own righteousness, which is of the law," he immediately subjoined, "But that which is through the faith of Christ, which is of God." This is what they were ignorant of, of whom he says, "Being ignorant of God's righteousness"—that is, the righteousness which is of God (for it is given not by the letter, which kills, but by the life-giving Spirit), "and wishing to establish their own righteousness," which he expressly described as the righteousness of the law, when he said, "Not having my own righteousness, which is of the law;" they were not subject to the righteousness of God—in other words, they submitted not themselves to the grace of God. For they were under the law, not under grace, and therefore sin had dominion over them, from which a man is not freed by the law, but by grace. On which account he elsewhere says, "For sin shall not have dominion over you; because ye are not under the law, but under grace." [133] Not that the law is evil; but because they are under its power, whom it makes guilty by imposing commandments, not by aiding. It is by grace that any one is a doer of the law; and without this grace, he who is placed under the law will be only a hearer of the law. To such persons he addresses these words: "Ye who are justified by the law are fallen from grace." [134]

CHAPTER XXV

AS THE LAW IS NOT, SO NEITHER IS OUR NATURE ITSELF THAT GRACE BY WHICH WE ARE CHRISTIANS

Now who can be so insensible to the words of the apostle, who so foolishly, nay, so insanely ignorant of the purport of his statement, as to venture to affirm that the law is grace, when he who knew very well what he was saying emphatically declares, "Ye who are justified by the law are fallen from grace"? Well, but if the law is not grace, seeing that in order that the law itself may be kept, it is not the law, but only grace which can give help, will not nature at any rate be grace? For this, too, the Pelagians have been bold enough to aver, that grace is the nature in which we were created, so as to possess a rational mind, by which we are enabled to understand—formed as we are in the image of God, so as to have dominion over the fish of the sea, and over the fowl of the air, and over every living thing that creepeth upon the earth. This, however, is not the grace which the apostle commends to us through the faith of Jesus Christ. For it is certain

[132] Phil. iii. 8, 9   [133] Rom. vi. 14   [134] Gal. v. 4

that we possess this nature in common with ungodly men and unbelievers; whereas the grace which comes through the faith of Jesus Christ belongs only to them to whom the faith itself appertains. "For all men have not faith." [135] Now, as the apostle, with perfect truth, says to those who by wishing to be justified by the law have fallen from grace, "If righteousness come by the law, then Christ is dead in vain;" [136] so likewise, to those who think that the grace which he commends and faith in Christ receives, is nature, the same language is with the same degree of truth applicable: if righteousness come from nature, then Christ is dead in vain. But the law was in existence up to that time, and it did not justify; and nature existed too, but it did not justify. It was not, then, in vain that Christ died, in order that the law might be fulfilled through Him who said, "I am come not to destroy the law, but to fulfil it;" [137] and that our nature, which was lost through Adam, might through Him be recovered, who said that "He was come to seek and to save that which was lost;" [138] in whose coming the old fathers likewise who loved God believed.

CHAPTER XXVI

THE PELAGIANS CONTEND THAT THE GRACE, WHICH IS NEITHER THE LAW NOR NATURE, AVAILS ONLY TO THE REMISSION OF PAST SINS, BUT NOT TO THE AVOIDANCE OF FUTURE ONES

They also maintain that God's grace, which is given through the faith of Jesus Christ, and which is neither the law nor nature, avails only for the remission of sins that have been committed, and not for the shunning of future ones, or the subjugation of those which are now assailing us. Now if all this were true, surely after offering the petition of the Lord's Prayer, "Forgive us our debts, as we forgive our debtors," we could hardly go on and say, "And lead us not into temptation." [139] The former petition we present that our sins may be forgiven; the latter, that they may be avoided or subdued—a favor which we should by no means beg of our Father who is in heaven if we were able to accomplish it by the virtue of our human will. Now I strongly advise and earnestly require your Love to read attentively the book of the blessed Cyprian which he wrote *On the Lord's Prayer*. As far as the Lord shall assist you, understand it, and commit it to memory. In this work you will see how he so appeals to the free will of those whom he edifies in his treatise, as to show them, that whatever they have to fulfil in the law, they must ask for in the prayer. But this, of course, would be utterly empty if the human will were sufficient for the performance without the help of God.

[135] 2 Thess. iii. 2   [136] Gal. ii. 21   [137] Matt. v. 17   [138] Matt. xviii. 11; Luke xix. 10   [139] Matt. vi. 12, 13

CHAPTER XXVII

GRACE EFFECTS THE FULFILMENT OF THE LAW, THE DELIVERANCE
OF NATURE, AND THE SUPPRESSION OF SIN'S DOMINION

It has, however, been shown to demonstration, that instead of really maintaining free will, they have only inflated a theory of it, which, having no stability, has fallen to the ground. Neither the knowledge of God's law, nor nature, nor the mere remission of sins is that grace which is given to us through our Lord Jesus Christ; but it is this very grace which accomplishes the fulfilment of the law, and the liberation of nature, and the removal of the dominion of sin. Being, therefore, convicted on these points, they resort to another expedient, and endeavor to show in some way or other that the grace of God is given us according to our merits. For they say: "Granted that it is not given to us according to the merits of good works, inasmuch as it is through it that we do any good thing, still it is given to us according to the merits of a good will; for," say they, "the good will of him who prays precedes his prayer, even as the will of the believer preceded his faith, so that according to these merits the grace of God who hears, follows."

CHAPTER XXVIII

FAITH IS THE GIFT OF GOD

I have already discussed [140] the point concerning faith, that is, concerning the will of him who believes, even so far as to show that it appertains to grace—so that the apostle did not tell us, "I have obtained mercy because I was faithful;" but he said, "I have obtained mercy in order to be faithful." [141] And there are many other passages of similar import—among them that in which he bids us "think soberly, according as God hath dealt out to every man the proportion of faith;" [142] and that which I have already quoted: "By grace are ye saved through faith; and that not of yourselves; it is the gift of God;" [143] and again another in the same *Epistle to the Ephesians:* "Peace be to the brethren, and love with faith, from God the Father, and the Lord Jesus Christ;" [144] and to the same effect that passage in which he says, "For unto you it is given in the behalf of Christ not only to believe on Him, but also to suffer for His sake." [145] Both alike are therefore due to the grace of God—the faith of those who believe, and the patience of those who suffer, because the apostle spoke of both as *given.* Then, again, there is the passage, especially noticeable, in which he says, "We, having the same spirit of faith," [146] for his phrase is not *"the knowledge of faith,"* but *"the spirit of faith;"* and he expressed himself thus in order that

[140] See above, 16, 17, 18   [141] 1 Cor. vii. 25   [142] Rom. xii. 3   [143] Eph. ii. 8
[144] Eph. vi. 23   [145] Phil. i. 29   [146] 2 Cor. iv. 13

we might understand how that faith is given to us, even when it is not sought, so that other blessings may be granted to it at its request. For "how," says he, "shall they call upon Him in whom they have not believed?" [147] The spirit of grace, therefore, causes us to have faith, in order that through faith we may, on praying for it, obtain the ability to do what we are commanded. On this account the apostle himself constantly puts faith before the law; since we are not able to do what the law commands unless we obtain the strength to do it by the prayer of faith.

CHAPTER XXIX

GOD IS ABLE TO CONVERT OPPOSING WILLS, AND TO TAKE AWAY FROM THE HEART ITS HARDNESS

Now if faith is simply of free will, and is not given by God, why do we pray for those who will not believe, that they may believe? This it would be absolutely useless to do, unless we believe, with perfect propriety, that Almighty God is able to turn to belief wills that are perverse and opposed to faith. Man's free will is addressed when it is said, "To-day, if ye will hear His voice, harden not your hearts." [148] But if God were not able to remove from the human heart even its obstinacy and hardness, He would not say, through the prophet, "I will take from them their heart of stone, and will give them a heart of flesh." [149] That all this was foretold in reference to the New Testament is shown clearly enough by the apostle when he says, "Ye are our epistle, . . . written not with ink, but with the Spirit of the living God; not in tables of stone, but in fleshly tables of the heart." [150] We must not, of course, suppose that such a phrase as this is used as if those might live in a fleshly way who ought to live spiritually; but inasmuch as a stone has no feeling, with which man's hard heart is compared, what was there left Him to compare man's intelligent heart with but the flesh, which possesses feeling? For this is what is said by the prophet Ezekiel: "I will give them another heart, and I will put a new spirit within you; and I will take the stony heart out of their flesh, and will give them a heart of flesh; that they may walk in my statutes, and keep mine ordinances, and do them: and they shall be my people, and I will be their God, saith the Lord." [151] Nor can we possibly, without extreme absurdity, maintain that there previously existed in any man the good merit of a good will, to entitle him to the removal of his stony heart, when all the while this very heart of stone signifies nothing else than a will of the hardest kind and such as is absolutely inflexible against God? For where a good will precedes, there is, of course, no longer a heart of stone.

[147] Rom. x. 14   [148] Ps. xcv. 7, 8   [149] Ezek. xi. 19   [150] 2 Cor. iii. 2, 3   [151] Ezek. xi. 19, 20

CHAPTER XXX

THE GRACE BY WHICH THE STONY HEART IS REMOVED
IS NOT PRECEDED BY GOOD DESERTS, BUT BY EVIL ONES

In another passage, also, by the same prophet, God, in the clearest language, shows us that it is not owing to any good merits on the part of men, but for His own name's sake, that He does these things. This is His language: "This I do, O house of Israel, [not for your sakes] but for mine holy name's sake, which ye have profaned among the heathen, whither ye went. And I will sanctify my great name, which was profaned among the heathen, which ye have profaned in the midst of them; and the heathen shall know that I am the Lord, saith the Lord God, when I shall be sanctified in you before their eyes. For I will take you from among the heathen, and gather you out of all countries, and will bring you into your own land. Then will I sprinkle you with clean water, and ye shall be clean: from all your own filthiness, and from all your idols will I cleanse you. A new heart also will I give you, and a new spirit will I put within you; and the stony heart shall be taken away out of your flesh, and I will give you a heart of flesh. And I will put my Spirit within you, and will cause you to walk in my statutes, and ye shall keep my judgments, and do them." [152] Now who is so blind as not to see, and who so stone-like as not to feel, that this grace is not given according to the merits of a good will, when the Lord declares and testifies, "It is I, O house of Israel, who do this, but for my holy name's sake"? Now why did He say "It is I that do it, but for my holy name's sake," were it not that they should not think that it was owing to their own good merits that these things were happening, as the Pelagians hesitate not unblushingly to say? But there were not only no good merits of theirs, but the Lord shows that evil ones actually preceded; for He says, "But for my holy name's sake, *which ye have profaned among the heathen.*" Who can fail to observe how dreadful is the evil of profaning the Lord's own holy name? And yet, for the sake of this very name of mine, says He, which ye have profaned, I, even I, will make you good, but not for your own sakes; and, as He adds, "I will sanctify my great name, which was profaned among the heathen, which ye have profaned in the midst of them." He says that He sanctifies His name, which He had already declared to be holy. Therefore, this is just what we pray for in the Lord's Prayer—"Hallowed be Thy name." [153] We ask for the hallowing among men of that which is in itself undoubtedly always holy. Then it follows, "And the heathen shall know that I am the Lord, saith the Lord God, when I shall be sanctified in you." Although, then, He is Himself always holy, He is, nevertheless, sanctified in those on whom He bestows His grace, by

[152] Ezek. xxxvi. 22-27   [153] Matt. vi 9

taking from them that stony heart by which they profaned the name of the Lord.

CHAPTER XXXI

FREE WILL HAS ITS FUNCTION IN THE HEART'S CONVERSION; BUT GRACE TOO HAS ITS

Lest, however, it should be thought that men themselves in this matter do nothing by free will, it is said in the Psalm, "Harden not your hearts;" [154] and in Ezekiel himself, "Cast away from you all your transgressions, which ye have impiously committed against me; and make you a new heart and a new spirit; and keep all my commandments. For why will ye die, O house of Israel, saith the Lord? for I have no pleasure in the death of him that dieth, saith the Lord God: and turn ye, and live." [155] We should remember that it is He who says, "Turn ye and live," to whom it is said in prayer, "Turn us again, O God." [156] We should remember that He says, "Cast away from you all your transgressions," when it is even He who justifies the ungodly. We should remember that He says, "Make you a new heart and a new spirit," who also promises, "I will give you a new heart, and a new spirit will I put within you." [157] How is it, then, that He who says, "Make you," also says, "I will give you"? Why does He command, if He is to give? Why does He give if man is to make, except it be that He gives what He commands when He helps him to obey whom He commands? There is, however, always within us a free will—but it is not always good; for it is either free from righteousness when it serves sin— and then it is evil—or else it is free from sin when it serves righteousness— and then it is good. But the grace of God is always good; and by it it comes to pass that a man is of a good will, though he was before of an evil one. By it also it comes to pass that the very good will, which has now begun to be, is enlarged, and made so great that it is able to fulfil the divine commandments which it shall wish, when it shall once firmly and perfectly wish. This is the purport of what the Scripture says: "If thou wilt, thou shalt keep the commandments;" [158] so that the man who wills but is not able knows that he does not yet fully will, and prays that he may have so great a will that it may suffice for keeping the commandments. And thus, indeed, he receives assistance to perform what he is commanded. Then is the will of use when we have ability; just as ability is also then of use when we have the will. For what does it profit us if we will what we are unable to do, or else do not will what we are able to do?

[154] Ps. xcv. 8   [155] Ezek. xviii. 31, 32   [156] Ps. lxxx. 3   [157] Ezek. xxxvi. 26
[158] Ecclus. xv. 15

CHAPTER XXXII

IN WHAT SENSE IT IS RIGHTLY SAID THAT, IF WE LIKE, WE MAY KEEP GOD'S COMMANDMENTS

The Pelagians think that they know something great when they assert that "God would not command what He knew could not be done by man." Who can be ignorant of this? But God commands some things which we cannot do, in order that we may know what we ought to ask of Him. For this is faith itself, which obtains by prayer what the law commands. He, indeed, who said, "If thou wilt, thou shalt keep the commandments," did in the same book of *Ecclesiasticus* afterwards say, "Who shall give a watch before my mouth, and a seal of wisdom upon my lips, that I fall not suddenly thereby, and that my tongue destroy me not." [159] Now he had certainly heard and received these commandments: "Keep thy tongue from evil, and thy lips from speaking guile." [160] Forasmuch, then, as what he said is true: "If thou wilt, thou shalt keep the commandments," why does he want a watch to be given before his mouth, like him who says in the Psalm, "Set a watch, O Lord, before my mouth"? [161] Why is he not satisfied with God's commandment and his own will; since, if he has the will, he shall keep the commandments? How many of God's commandments are directed against pride! He is quite aware of them; if he will, he may keep them. Why, therefore, does he shortly afterwards say, "O God, Father and God of my life, give me not a proud look"? [162] The law had long ago said to him, "Thou shalt not covet;" [163] let him then only will, and do what he is bidden, because, if he has the will, he shall keep the commandments. Why, therefore, does he afterwards say, "Turn away from me concupiscence"? [164] Against luxury, too, how many commandments has God enjoined! Let a man observe them; because, if he will, he may keep the commandments. But what means that cry to God, "Let not the greediness of the belly nor lust of the flesh take hold on me!"? [165] Now, if we were to put this question to him personally, he would very rightly answer us and say, From that prayer of mine, in which I offer this particular petition to God, you may understand in what sense I said, "If thou wilt, thou mayest keep the commandments." For it is certain that we keep the commandments if we will; but because the will is prepared by the Lord, we must ask of Him for such a force of will as suffices to make us act by the willing. It is certain that it is we that *will* when we will, but it is He who makes us will what is good, of whom it is said (as he has just now expressed it), "The will is prepared by the Lord." [166] Of the same Lord it is said, "The steps of a man are ordered by the Lord, and his way doth He will." [167] Of the same

---

[159] Ecclus. xxii. 27   [160] Ps. xxxiv. 13   [161] Ps. cxli. 3   [162] Ecclus. xxiii. 4   [163] Ex. xx. 17   [164] Ecclus. xxiii. 5   [165] Ecclus. xxiii. 6   [166] Prov. viii. 35   [167] Ps. xxxvii. 23

Lord again it is said, "It is God who worketh in you, even to will!" [168] It is certain that it is we that act when we act; but it is He who makes us act, by applying efficacious powers to our will, who has said, "I will make you to walk in my statutes, and to observe my judgments, and to do them." [169] When he says, "I will make you . . . to do them," what else does He say in fact than, "I will take away from you your heart of stone," [170] from which used to arise your inability to act, "and I will give you a heart of flesh," [171] in order that you may act? And what does this promise amount to but this: I will remove your hard heart, out of which you did not act, and I will give you an obedient heart, out of which you shall act? It is He who causes us to act, to whom the human suppliant says, "Set a watch, O Lord, before my mouth." [161] That is to say: Make or enable me, O Lord, to set a watch before my mouth—a benefit which he has already obtained from God who thus described its influence: "I set a watch upon my mouth." [172]

CHAPTER XXXIII

A GOOD WILL MAY BE SMALL AND WEAK; AN AMPLE WILL, GREAT LOVE. OPERATING AND CO-OPERATING GRACE

He, therefore, who wishes to do God's commandment, but is unable, already possesses a good will, but as yet a small and weak one; he will, however, become able when he shall have acquired a great and robust will. When the martyrs did the great commandments which they obeyed, they acted by a great will—that is, with great love. Of this love the Lord Himself thus speaks: "Greater love hath no man than this, that a man lay down his life for his friends." [173] In accordance with this, the apostle also says, "He that loveth his neighbor hath fulfilled the law. For this: Thou shalt not commit adultery, Thou shalt not kill, Thou shalt not steal, Thou shalt not covet; and if there be any other commandment, it is briefly comprehended in this saying, namely, Thou shalt love thy neighbor as thyself.[174] Love worketh no ill to his neighbor: therefore love is the fulfilling of the law." [175] This love the Apostle Peter did not yet possess, when he for fear thrice denied the Lord.[176] "There is no fear in love," says the Evangelist John in his first *Epistle*, "but perfect love casteth out fear." [177] But yet, however small and imperfect his love was, it was not wholly wanting when he said to the Lord, "I will lay down my life for Thy sake;" [178] for he supposed himself able to effect what he felt himself willing to do. And who was it that had begun to give him his love, however small, but He who prepares the will, and perfects by His co-operation what He initiates by His operation? Forasmuch as in beginning He works in us that we may have

[168] Phil. ii. 13   [169] Ezek. xxxvi. 27   [170] Ezek. xi. 19, and xxxvi. 26   [171] Ezek. xxxvi. 26   [172] Ps. xxxix. 1   [173] John xv. 13   [174] Lev. xix. 18   [175] Rom. xiii. 8-10   [176] Matt. xxvi. 69-75   [177] 1 John iv. 18   [178] John xiii. 37

the will, and in perfecting works with us when we have the will.[179] On which account the apostle says, "I am confident of this very thing, that He which hath begun a good work in you will perform it until the day of Jesus Christ." [180] He operates, therefore, without us, in order that we may will; but when we will, and so will that we may act, He co-operates with us. We can, however, ourselves do nothing to effect good works of piety without Him either working that we may will, or co-working when we will. Now, concerning His working that we may will, it is said: "It is God which worketh in you, even to will." [181] While of His co-working with us, when we will and act by willing, the apostle says, "We know that in all things there is co-working for good to them that love God." [182] What does this phrase, "all things," mean, but the terrible and cruel sufferings which affect our condition? That burden, indeed, of Christ, which is heavy for our infirmity, becomes light to love. For to such did the Lord say that His burden was light,[183] as Peter was when he suffered for Christ, not as he was when he denied Him.

CHAPTER XXXIV

THE APOSTLE'S EULOGY OF LOVE. CORRECTION
TO BE ADMINISTERED WITH LOVE

This charity, that is, this will glowing with intensest love, the apostle eulogizes with these words: "Who shall separate us from the love of Christ? shall tribulation, or distress, or persecution, or famine, or nakedness, or peril, or the sword? (As it is written, For Thy sake we are killed all the day long; we are accounted as sheep for the slaughter.) Nay, in all these things we are more than conquerors, through Him that loved us. For I am persuaded, that neither death, nor life, nor angels, nor principalities, nor things present, nor things to come, nor height, nor depth, nor any other creature, shall be able to separate us from the love of God, which is in Christ Jesus our Lord." [184] And in another passage he says, "And yet I show unto you a more excellent way. Though I speak with the tongues of men and of angels, and have not love, I am become as sounding brass, or a tinkling cymbal. And though I have the gift of prophecy, and understand all mysteries, and all knowledge; and though I have all faith, so that I could remove mountains, and have not love, I am nothing. And though I bestow all my goods to feed the poor, and though I give my body to be burned, and have not love, it profiteth me nothing. Love suffereth long, and is kind; love envieth not; love vaunteth not itself, is not puffed up, doth not behave itself unseemly, seeketh not her own, is not easily provoked, thinketh no evil; rejoiceth not in iniquity, but rejoiceth in the truth; beareth all things, believ-

---

[179] compare Art. X of the Church of England   [180] Phil. i. 6   [181] Phil. ii. 13
[182] Rom. viii. 28   [183] Matt. xi. 30   [184] Rom. viii. 35-39

eth all things, hopeth all things, endureth all things. Love never faileth." [185] And a little afterwards he says, "And now abideth faith, hope, love, these three; but the greatest of these is love. Follow after love." [186] He also says to the Galatians, "For, brethren, ye have been called unto liberty; only use not liberty for an occasion to the flesh, but by love serve one another. For all the law is fulfilled in one word, even in this, Thou shalt love thy neighbor as thyself." [187] This is the same in effect as what he writes to the Romans: "He that loveth another hath fulfilled the law." [188] In like manner he says to the Colossians, "And above all these things, put on love, which is the bond of perfectness." [189] And to Timothy he writes, "Now the end of the commandment is love;" and he goes on to describe the quality of this grace, saying, "Out of a pure heart, and of a good conscience, and of faith unfeigned." [190] Moreover, when he says to the Corinthians, "Let all your things be done with love," [191] he shows plainly enough that even those chastisements which are deemed sharp and bitter by those who are corrected thereby, are to be administered with love. Accordingly, in another passage, after saying, "Warn them that are unruly, comfort the feebleminded, support the weak, be patient toward all men," he immediately added, "See that none render evil for evil unto any man." [192] Therefore, even when the unruly are corrected, it is not rendering evil for evil, but contrariwise, good. However, what but love worketh all these things?

CHAPTER XXXV

COMMENDATIONS OF LOVE

The Apostle Peter, likewise, says, "And, above all things, have fervent love among yourselves: for love shall cover the multitude of sins." [193] The Apostle James also says, "If ye fulfil the royal law, according to the Scripture, Thou shalt love thy neighbor as thyself, ye do well." [194] So also the Apostle John says, "He that loveth his brother abideth in the right;" [195] again, in another passage, "Whosoever doeth not righteousness is not of God, neither he that loveth not his brother; for this is the message which we have heard from the beginning, that we should love one another." [196] Then he says again, "This is His commandment, that we should believe on the name of His Son Jesus Christ, and love one another." [197] Once more: "And this commandment have we from Him, that he who loveth God love his brother also." [198] Then shortly afterwards he adds, "By this we know that we love the children of God, when we love God, and keep His commandments; for this is the love of God, that we keep His commandments:

---

[185] I Cor. xii. 31, xiii. 8　　[186] I Cor. xiii. 13, and xiv. 1　　[187] Gal. v. 13, 14, and Lev. xix. 18　　[188] Rom. xiii. 8　　[189] Col. iii. 14　　[190] I Tim. i. 5　　[191] I Cor. xvi. 14 [192] I Thess. v. 14, 15　　[193] I Pet. iv. 8　　[194] Jas. ii. 8　　[195] I John ii. 10　　[196] I John iii. 10, 11　　[197] I John iii. 23　　[198] I John iv. 21

and His commandments are not grievous." [199] While, in his second *Epistle*, it is written, "Not as though I wrote a new commandment unto thee, but that which we had from the beginning, that we love one another." [200]

CHAPTER XXXVI

LOVE COMMENDED BY OUR LORD HIMSELF

Moreover, the Lord Jesus Himself teaches us that the whole law and the prophets hang upon the two precepts of love to God and love to our neighbor. Concerning these two commandments the following is written in the *Gospel according to St. Mark:* "And one of the scribes came, and having heard them reasoning together, and perceiving that He had answered them well, asked Him: Which is the first commandment of all? And Jesus answered him: The first of all the commandments is, Hear, O Israel! the Lord our God is one Lord; and thou shalt love the Lord thy God with all thine heart, and with all thy soul, and with all thy mind, and with all thy strength.[201] This is the first commandment. And the second is like unto it: Thou shalt love thy neighbor as thyself.[202] There is none other commandment greater than these." [203] Also, in the *Gospel according to St. John,* He says, "A new commandment I give unto you, that ye love one another; as I have loved you, that ye also love one another. By this shall all men know that ye are my disciples, if ye have love to one another." [204]

CHAPTER XXXVII

THE LOVE WHICH FULFILS THE COMMANDMENTS IS NOT OF OURSELVES, BUT OF GOD

All these commandments, however, respecting love or charity[205] (which are so great, and such that whatever action a man may think he does well is by no means well done if done without love) would be given to men in vain if they had not free choice of will. But forasmuch as these precepts are given in the law, both old and new (although in the new came the grace which was promised in the old, but the law without grace is the letter which killeth, but in grace the Spirit which giveth life) from what source is there in men the love of God and of one's neighbor but from God Himself? For indeed, if it be not of God but of men, the Pelagians have gained the victory; but if it come from God, then we have vanquished the Pelagians. Let, then, the Apostle John sit in judgment between us; and let him say to us,

[199] 1 John v. 2, 3   [200] 2 John ver. 5   [201] Deut. vi. 4, 5   [202] Lev. xix. 18   [203] Mark xii. 28-31   [204] John xiii. 34, 35

[205] "Love *or* charity," the disjunctive being intended to *identify*, not *distinguish*, the two. The word *amor* is distinguishable from the pair (*dilectio* and *charitas*) here used, though even this must not be pressed too far. See Augustine's *City of God*, xiv. 7

"Beloved, let us love one another." [206] Now, when they begin to extol themselves on these words of John, and to ask why this precept is addressed to us at all if we have not of our own selves to love one another, the same apostle proceeds at once, to their confusion, to add, "For love is of God." [206] It is not of ourselves, therefore, but it is of God. Wherefore, then, is it said, "Let us love one another, for love is of God," unless it be as a precept to our free will, admonishing it to seek the gift of God? Now, this would be indeed a thoroughly fruitless admonition if the will did not previously receive some donation of love, which might seek to be enlarged so as to fulfil whatever command was laid upon it. When it is said, "Let us love one another," it is law; when it is said, "For love is of God," it is grace. For God's "wisdom carries law and mercy upon her tongue." [207] Accordingly, it is written in the *Psalm,* "For He who gave the law will give blessings." [208]

CHAPTER XXXVIII

WE WOULD NOT LOVE GOD UNLESS HE FIRST LOVED US. THE APOSTLES CHOSE CHRIST BECAUSE THEY WERE CHOSEN; THEY WERE NOT CHOSEN BECAUSE THEY CHOSE CHRIST

Let no one, then, deceive you, my brethren, for we should not love God unless He first loved us. John again gives us the plainest proof of this when he says, "We love Him because He first loved us." [209] Grace makes us lovers of the law; but the law itself, without grace, makes us nothing but breakers of the law. And nothing else than this is shown us by the words of our Lord when He says to His disciples, "Ye have not chosen me, but I have chosen you." [210] For if we first loved Him, in order that by this merit He might love us, then we first chose Him that we might deserve to be chosen by Him. He, however, who is the Truth says otherwise, and flatly contradicts this vain conceit of men. "You have not chosen me," He says. If, therefore, you have not chosen me, undoubtedly you have not loved me (for how could they choose one whom they did not love?). "But I," says He, "have chosen you." And then could they possibly help choosing Him afterwards, and preferring Him to all the blessings of this world? But it was because they had been chosen, that they chose Him; not because they chose Him that they were chosen. There could be no merit in men's choice of Christ, if it were not that God's grace was prevenient in His choosing them. Whence the Apostle Paul pronounces in the *Thessalonians* this benediction: "The Lord make you to increase and abound in love one toward another, and toward all men." [211] This benediction to love one another He gave us, who had also given us a law that we should love each other. Then, in another passage addressed to the same church, seeing that there now

[206] I John iv. 7   [207] Prov. iii. 16   [208] Ps. lxxxiv. 6   [209] I John iv. 19   [210] John xv. 16   [211] I Thess. iii. 12

existed in some of its members the disposition which he had wished them to cultivate, he says, "We are bound to thank God always for you, brethren, as it is meet, because that your faith groweth exceedingly, and the charity of every one of you all toward each other aboundeth." [212] This he said lest they should make a boast of the great good which they were enjoying from God, as if they had it of their own mere selves. Because, then, your faith has so great a growth (this is the purport of his words), and the love of every one of you all toward each other so greatly abounds, we ought to thank God concerning you, but not to praise you, as if you possessed these gifts of yourselves.

CHAPTER XXXIX

THE SPIRIT OF FEAR A GREAT GIFT OF GOD

The apostle also says to Timothy, "For God hath not given to us the spirit of fear, but of power, and of love, and of a sound mind." [213] Now in respect of this passage of the apostle, we must be on our guard against supposing that we have not received the spirit of the fear of God, which is undoubtedly a great gift of God, and concerning which the prophet Isaiah says, "The Spirit of the Lord shall rest upon thee, the spirit of wisdom and understanding, the spirit of counsel and might, the spirit of knowledge and piety, the spirit of the fear of the Lord." [214] It is not the fear with which Peter denied Christ that we have received the spirit of, but that fear concerning which Christ Himself says, "Fear Him who hath power to destroy both soul and body in hell; yea, I say unto you, Fear Him." [215] This, indeed, He said, lest we should deny Him from the same fear which shook Peter; for such cowardice he plainly wished to be removed from us when He, in the preceding passage, said, "Be not afraid of them that kill the body, and after that have no more that they can do." [216] It is not of this fear that we have received the spirit, but of power, and of love, and of a sound mind. And of this spirit the same Apostle Paul discourses to the Romans: "We glory in tribulations, knowing that tribulation worketh patience; and patience, experience; and experience, hope; and hope maketh not ashamed; because the love of God is shed abroad in our hearts by the Holy Ghost, which is given unto us." [217] Not by ourselves, therefore, but by the Holy Ghost which is given to us, does it come to pass that, through that very love, which he shows us to be the gift of God, tribulation does not do away with patience, but rather produces it. Again, he says to the Ephesians, "Peace be to the brethren, and love with faith." [218] Great blessings these! Let him tell us, however, whence they come. "From God the Father," says he immediately afterwards, "and the Lord Jesus Christ." [219] These great blessings, therefore, are nothing else than God's gifts to us.

[212] 2 Thess. i. 3   [213] 2 Tim. i. 7   [214] Isa. xi. 2   [215] Luke xii. 5   [216] Luke xii. 4
[217] Rom. v. 3, 4, 5   [218] Eph. vi. 23   [219] John i. 5

CHAPTER XL

THE IGNORANCE OF THE PELAGIANS IN MAINTAINING THAT THE KNOWLEDGE OF THE LAW COMES FROM GOD, BUT THAT LOVE COMES FROM OURSELVES

It is no wonder that light shineth in darkness, and the darkness comprehendeth it not.[219] In John's *Epistle* the Light declares, "Behold what manner of love the Father hath bestowed upon us, that we should be called the sons of God." [220] And in the Pelagian writings the darkness says, "Love comes to us of our own selves." Now, if they only possessed the true, that is, Christian love, they would also know whence they obtained possession of it; even as the apostle knew when he said, "But we have received not the spirit of the world, but the Spirit which is of God, that we might know the things that are freely given to us of God." [221] John says, "God is love." [222] And thus the Pelagians affirm that they actually have God Himself, not from God, but from their own selves! and although they allow that we have the knowledge of the law from God, they will yet have it that love is from our very selves. Nor do they listen to the apostle when he says, "Knowledge puffeth up, but love edifieth." [223] Now what can be more absurd, nay, what more insane and more alien from the very sacredness of love itself, than to maintain that from God proceeds the knowledge which, apart from love, puffs us up, while the love which prevents the possibility of this inflation of knowledge springs from ourselves? And again, when the apostle speaks of "the love of Christ as surpassing knowledge," [224] what can be more insane than to suppose that the knowledge which must be subordinated to love comes from God, while the love which surpasses knowledge comes from man? The true faith, however, and sound doctrine declare that both graces are from God; the Scripture says, "From His face cometh knowledge and understanding;" [225] and another Scripture says, "Love is of God." [226] We read of "the Spirit of wisdom and understanding." [227] Also of "the Spirit of power, and of love, and of a sound mind." [228] But love is a greater gift than knowledge; for whenever a man has the gift of knowledge, love is necessary by the side of it, that he be not puffed up. For "love envieth not, vaunteth not itself, is not puffed up." [229]

[220] 1 John iii. 1   [221] 1 Cor. ii. 12   [222] 1 John iv. 16   [223] 1 Cor. viii. 1   [224] Eph. iii. 19   [225] Prov. ii. 6   [226] 1 John iv. 7   [227] Isa. xi. 2   [228] 2 Tim. i. 7   [229] 1 Cor. xiii. 4

CHAPTER XLI

THE WILLS OF MEN ARE SO MUCH IN THE POWER OF GOD, THAT HE CAN TURN THEM WHITHERSOEVER IT PLEASES HIM

I think I have now discussed the point fully enough in opposition to those who vehemently oppose the grace of God, by which, however, the human will is not taken away, but changed from bad to good, and assisted when it is good. I think, too, that I have so discussed the subject that it is not so much I myself as the inspired Scripture which has spoken to you, in the clearest testimonies of truth; and if this divine record be looked into carefully, it shows us that not only men's good wills, which God Himself converts from bad ones, and, when converted by Him, directs to good actions and to eternal life, but also those which follow the world are so entirely at the disposal of God, that He turns them whithersoever He wills, and whensoever He wills—to bestow kindness on some, and to heap punishment on others, as He Himself judges right by a counsel most secret to Himself, indeed, but beyond all doubt most righteous. For we find that some sins are even the punishment of other sins, as are those "vessels of wrath" which the apostle describes as "fitted to destruction;" [230] as is also that hardening of Pharaoh, the purpose of which is said to be to set forth in him the power of God; [231] as, again, is the flight of the Israelites from the face of the enemy before the city of Ai, for fear arose in their heart so that they fled, and this was done that their sin might be punished in the way it was right that it should be; by reason of which the Lord said to Joshua the son of Nun, "The children of Israel shall not be able to stand before the face of their enemies." [232] What is the meaning of, "They shall not be able to stand"? Now, why did they not stand by free will, but, with a will perplexed by fear, took to flight, were it not that God has the lordship even over men's wills, and when He is angry turns to fear whomsoever He pleases? Was it not of their own will that the enemies of the children of Israel fought against the people of God, as led by Joshua, the son of Nun? And yet the Scripture says, "It was of the Lord to harden their hearts, that they should come against Israel in battle, that they might be exterminated." [233] And was it not likewise of his own will that the wicked son of Gera cursed King David? And yet what says David, full of true, and deep, and pious wisdom? What did he say to him who wanted to smite the reviler? "What," said he, "have I to do with you, ye sons of Zeruiah? Let him alone and let him curse, because the Lord hath said unto him, Curse David. Who, then, shall say, Wherefore hast thou done so?" [234] And then the inspired Scripture, as if it would confirm the king's profound utterance

---

[230] Rom. ix. 22   [231] Ex. vii. 3, and x. 1   [232] Josh. vii. 4, 12   [233] Josh. xi. 20
[234] 2 Sam. xvi. 9, 10

by repeating it once more, tells us: "And David said to Abishai, and to all his servants, Behold, my son, which came forth from my bowels, seeketh my life: how much more may this Benjamite do it! Let him alone, and let him curse; for the Lord hath bidden him. It may be that the Lord will look on my humiliation, and will requite me good for his cursing this day." [235] Now what prudent reader will fail to understand in what way the Lord bade this profane man to curse David? It was not by a command that He bade him, in which case his obedience would be praiseworthy; but He inclined the man's will, which had become debased by his own perverseness, to commit this sin, by His own just and secret judgment. Therefore it is said, "The Lord said unto him." Now if this person had obeyed a command of God, he would have deserved to be praised rather than punished, as we know he was afterwards punished for this sin. Nor is the reason an obscure one why the Lord told him after this manner to curse David. "It may be," said the humbled king, "that the Lord will look on my humiliation, and will requite me good for his cursing this day." See, then, what proof we have here that God uses the hearts of even wicked men for the praise and assistance of the good. Thus did He make use of Judas when betraying Christ; thus did He make use of the Jews when they crucified Christ. And how vast the blessings which from these instances He has bestowed upon the nations that should believe in Him! He also uses our worst enemy, the devil himself, but in the best way, to exercise and try the faith and piety of good men—not for Himself indeed, who knows all things before they come to pass, but for our sakes, for whom it was necessary that such a discipline should be gone through with us. Did not Absalom choose by his own will the counsel which was detrimental to him? And yet the reason of his doing so was that the Lord had heard his father's prayer that it might be so. Wherefore the Scripture says that "the Lord appointed to defeat the good counsel of Ahithophel, to the intent that the Lord might bring all evils upon Absalom." [236] It called Ahithophel's counsel *"good,"* because it was for the moment of advantage to his purpose. It was in favor of the son against his father, against whom he had rebelled; and it might have crushed him, had not the Lord defeated the counsel which Ahithophel had given, by acting on the heart of Absalom so that he rejected this counsel, and chose another which was not expedient for him.

CHAPTER XLII

GOD DOES WHATSOEVER HE WILLS IN THE HEARTS OF EVEN WICKED MEN

Who can help trembling at those judgments of God by which He does in the hearts of even wicked men whatsoever He wills, at the same time rendering to them according to their deeds? Rehoboam, the son of Solomon,

---

[235] 2 Sam. xvi. 11, 12   [236] 2 Sam. xvii. 14

rejected the salutary counsel of the old men, not to deal harshly with the people, and preferred listening to the words of the young men of his own age, by returning a rough answer to those to whom he should have spoken gently. Now whence arose such conduct, except from his own will? Upon this, however, the ten tribes of Israel revolted from him, and chose for themselves another king, even Jeroboam, that the will of God in His anger might be accomplished which He had predicted would come to pass.[237] For what says the Scripture? "The king hearkened not unto the people; for the turning was from the Lord, that He might perform His saying, which the Lord spake to Ahijah the Shilonite concerning Jeroboam the son of Nebat." [238] All this, indeed, was done by the will of man, although the turning was from the Lord. Read the books of the *Chronicles,* and you will find the following passage in the second book: "Moreover, the Lord stirred up against Jehoram the spirit of the Philistines, and of the Arabians, that were neighbors to the Ethiopians; and they came up to the land of Judah, and ravaged it, and carried away all the substance which was found in the king's house." [239] Here it is shown that God stirs up enemies to devastate the countries which He adjudges deserving of such chastisement. Still, did these Philistines and Arabians invade the land of Judah to waste it with no will of their own? Or were their movements so directed by their own will that the Scripture lies which tells us that "the Lord stirred up their spirit" to do all this? Both statements to be sure are true, because they both came by their own will, and yet the Lord stirred up their spirit; and this may also with equal truth be stated the other way: The Lord both stirred up their spirit, and yet they came of their own will. For the Almighty sets in motion even in the innermost hearts of men the movement of their will, so that He does through their agency whatsoever He wishes to perform through them—even He who knows not how to will anything in unrighteousness. What, again, is the purport of that which the man of God said to King Amaziah: "Let not the army of Israel go with thee; for the Lord is not with Israel, even with all the children of Ephraim: for if thou shalt think to obtain with these, the Lord shall put thee to flight before thine enemies: for God hath power either to strengthen or to put to flight"? [240] Now, how does the power of God help some in war by giving them confidence, and put others to flight by injecting fear into them, except it be that He who has made all things according to His own will, in heaven and on earth,[241] also works in the hearts of men? We read also what Joash, king of Israel, said when he sent a message to Amaziah, king of Judah, who wanted to fight with him. After certain other words, he added, "Now tarry at home; why dost thou challenge me to thine hurt, that thou shouldest fall, even thou, and Judah with thee?" [242] Then the Scripture has added this sequel: "But Amaziah would not hear; for it came of God, that he

[237] i Kings xii. 8-14   [238] i Kings xii. 15   [239] 2 Chron. xxi. 16, 17   [240] 2 Chron. xxv. 7, 8   [241] Ps. cxxxv. 6   [242] 2 Kings xiv. 10

might be delivered into their hands, because they sought after the gods of Edom." [243] Behold, now, how God, wishing to punish the sin of idolatry, wrought this in this man's heart, with whom He was indeed justly angry, not to listen to sound advice, but to despise it, and go to the battle, in which he with his army was routed. God says by the prophet Ezekiel, "If the prophet be deceived when he hath spoken a thing, I the Lord have deceived that prophet: I will stretch out my hand upon him, and will destroy him from the midst of my people Israel." [244] Then there is the book of Esther, who was a woman of the people of Israel, and in the land of their captivity became the wife of the foreign King Ahasuerus. In this book it is written, that, being driven by necessity to interpose in behalf of her people, whom the king had ordered to be slain in every part of his dominions, she prayed to the Lord. So strongly was she urged by the necessity of the case, that she even ventured into the royal presence without the king's command, and contrary to her own custom. Now observe what the Scripture says: "He looked at her like a bull in the vehemence of his indignation; and the queen was afraid, and her color changed as she fainted; and she bowed herself upon the head of her delicate maiden which went before her. But God turned the king, and transformed his indignation into gentleness." [245] The Scripture says in the *Proverbs* of Solomon, "Even as the rush of water, so is the heart of a king in God's hand; He will turn it in whatever way He shall choose." [246] Again, in the 104th *Psalm,* in reference to the Egyptians, one reads what God did to them: "And He turned their heart to hate His people, to deal subtilly with His servants." [247] Observe, likewise, what is written in the letters of the apostles. In the *Epistle to the Romans* of Paul, the Apostle, occur these words: "Wherefore God gave them up to uncleanness, through the lusts of their own hearts;" [248] and a little afterwards: "For this cause God gave them up unto vile affections;" [249] again, in the next passage: "And even as they did not like to retain God in their knowledge, God gave them over to a reprobate mind, to do those things which are not convenient." [250] So also in his second *Epistle to the Thessalonians,* the apostle says of sundry persons, "Inasmuch as they received not the love of the truth, that they might be saved; therefore also God shall send them strong delusion, that they should believe a lie; that they all might be judged who believed not the truth, but had pleasure in unrighteousness." [251]

[243] 2 Chron. xxv. 20   [244] Ezek. xiv. 9   [245] Esther v. (according to the *Sept.*) [246] Prov. xxi. 1   [247] Ps. cv. 25   [248] Rom. i. 24   [249] Rom. i. 26   [250] Rom. i. 28 [251] 2 Thess. ii. 10-12

CHAPTER XLIII

GOD OPERATES ON MEN'S HEARTS TO INCLINE THEIR WILLS WHITHERSOEVER HE PLEASES

From these statements of the inspired word, and from similar passages which it would take too long to quote in full, I think, sufficiently clear that God works in the hearts of men to incline their wills whithersoever He wills, whether to good deeds according to His mercy, or to evil after their own deserts; His own judgment being sometimes manifest, sometimes secret, but always righteous. This ought to be the fixed and immovable conviction of your heart, that there is no unrighteousness with God. Therefore, whenever you read in the Scriptures of Truth, that men are led aside, or that their hearts are blunted and hardened by God, never doubt that some ill deserts of their own have first occurred, so that they justly suffer these things. Thus you will not run counter to that proverb of Solomon: "The foolishness of a man perverteth his ways, yet he blameth God in his heart." [252] Grace, however, is not bestowed according to men's deserts; otherwise grace would no longer be grace.[253] For grace is so designated because it is given gratuitously. Now if God is able, either through the agency of angels (whether good ones or evil), or in any other way whatever, to operate in the hearts even of the wicked, in return for their deserts—whose wickedness was not made by Him, but was either derived originally from Adam, or increased by their own will—what is there to wonder at if, through the Holy Spirit, He works good in the hearts of the elect, who has wrought it that their hearts become good instead of evil?

CHAPTER XLIV

GRATUITOUS GRACE EXEMPLIFIED IN INFANTS

Men, however, may suppose that there are certain good deserts which they think are precedent to justification through God's grace; all the while failing to see, when they express such an opinion, that they do nothing else than deny grace. But, as I have already remarked, let them suppose what they like respecting the case of adults, in the case of infants, at any rate, the Pelagians find no means of answering the difficulty. For these in receiving grace have no will, from the influence of which they can pretend to any precedent merit. We see, moreover, how they cry and struggle when they are baptized, and feel the divine sacraments. Such conduct would, of course, be charged against them as a great impiety, if they already had free will in use; and notwithstanding this, grace cleaves to them even in their resisting struggles. But most certainly there is no

[252] Prov. xix. 3   [253] Rom. xi. 6

prevenient merit, otherwise the grace would be no longer grace. Sometimes, too, this grace is bestowed upon the children of unbelievers, when they happen by some means or other to fall, by reason of God's secret providence, into the hands of pious persons; but, on the other hand, the children of believers fail to obtain grace, some hindrance occurring to prevent the approach of help to rescue them in their danger. These things, no doubt, happen through the secret providence of God, whose judgments are unsearchable, and His ways past finding out. These are the words of the apostle; and you should observe what he had previously said, to lead him to add such a remark. He was discoursing about the Jews and Gentiles, when he wrote to the Romans—themselves Gentiles—to this effect: "For as ye, in times past, have not believed God, yet have now obtained mercy, through their unbelief; even so have these also now not believed, that through your mercy they also may obtain mercy; for God hath concluded them all in unbelief, that He might have mercy upon all." [254] Now, after he had thought upon what he said, full of wonder at the certain truth of his own assertion, indeed, but astonished at its great depth, how God concluded all in unbelief that He might have mercy upon all—as if doing evil that good might come—he at once exclaimed, and said, "O the depth of the riches both of the wisdom and knowledge of God! how unsearchable are His judgments, and His ways past finding out;" [255] Perverse men, who do not reflect upon these unsearchable judgments and untraceable ways, indeed, but are ever prone to censure, being unable to understand, have supposed the apostle to say, and censoriously gloried over him for saying, "Let us do evil, that good may come!" God forbid that the apostle should say so! But men, without understanding, have thought that this was in fact said, when they heard these words of the apostle: "Moreover, the law entered, that the offence might abound; but where sin abounded, grace did much more abound." [256] But grace, indeed, effects this purpose—that good works should now be wrought by those who previously did evil; not that they should persevere in evil courses and suppose that they are recompensed with good. Their language, therefore, ought not to be: "Let us do evil, that good may come;" but: "We have done evil, and good has come; let us henceforth do good, that in the future world we may receive good for good, who in the present life are receiving good for evil." Wherefore it is written in the *Psalm,* "I will sing of mercy and judgment unto Thee, O Lord." [257] When the Son of man, therefore, first came into the world, it was not to judge the world, but that the world through Him might be saved.[258] And this dispensation was for mercy; by and by, however, He will come for judgment—to judge the quick and the dead. And yet even in this present time salvation itself does not eventuate without judgment—although it be a hidden one; there-

[254] Rom. xi. 30-32   [255] Rom. xi. 33   [256] Rom. v. 20   [257] Ps. ci. 1   [258] John iii. 17

fore He says, "For judgment I am come into this world, that they which see not may see, and that they which see may be made blind." [259]

CHAPTER XLV

THE REASON WHY ONE PERSON IS ASSISTED BY GRACE, AND ANOTHER IS NOT HELPED, MUST BE REFERRED TO THE SECRET JUDGMENTS OF GOD

You must refer the matter, then, to the hidden determinations of God, when you see, in one and the same condition, such as all infants unquestionably have—who derive their hereditary evil from Adam—that one is assisted so as to be baptized, and another is not assisted, so that he dies in his very bondage; and again, that one baptized person is left and forsaken in his present life, who God foreknew would be ungodly, while another baptized person is taken away from this life, "lest that wickedness should alter his understanding;" [260] and be sure that you do not in such cases ascribe unrighteousness or unwisdom to God, in whom is the very fountain of righteousness and wisdom, but, as I have exhorted you from the commencement of this treatise, "whereto you have already attained, walk therein," [261] and "even this shall God reveal unto you" [262] —if not in this life, yet certainly in the next, "for there is nothing covered that shall not be revealed." [263] When, therefore, you hear the Lord say, "I the Lord have deceived that prophet," [264] and likewise what the apostle says: "He hath mercy on whom He will have mercy, and whom He will He hardeneth," [265] believe that, in the case of him whom He permits to be deceived and hardened, his evil deeds have deserved the judgment; whilst in the case of him to whom He shows mercy, you should loyally and unhesitatingly recognise the grace of the God who "rendereth not evil for evil; but contrariwise blessing." [266] Nor should you take away from Pharaoh free will, because in several passages God says, "I have hardened Pharaoh;" or, "I have hardened or I will harden Pharaoh's heart;" [267] for it does not by any means follow that Pharaoh did not, on this account, harden his own heart. For this, too, is said of him, after the removal of the fly-plague from the Egyptians, in these words of the Scripture: "And Pharaoh hardened his heart at this time also; neither would he let the people go." [268] Thus it was that both God hardened him by His just judgment, and Pharaoh by his own free will. Be ye then well assured that your labor will never be in vain, if, setting before you a good purpose, you persevere in it to the last. For God, who fails to render, according to their deeds, only to those whom He liberates, will then "recompense every-

---

[259] John ix. 39   [260] Wisd. iv. 11   [261] Phil. iii. 16   [262] Phil. iii. 15   [263] Matt. x. 26   [264] Ezek. xiv. 9   [265] Rom. ix. 18   [266] 1 Pet. iii. 9   [267] Ex. iv. 21, vii. 3, xiv. 4   [268] Ex. viii. 32

man according to his works." [269] God will, therefore, certainly recompense both evil for evil, because He is just; and good for evil, because He is good; and good for good, because He is good and just; only, evil for good He will never recompense, because He is not unjust. He will, therefore, recompense evil for evil—punishment for unrighteousness; and He will recompense good for evil—grace for unrighteousness; and He will recompense good for good—grace for grace.

CHAPTER XLVI

UNDERSTANDING AND WISDOM MUST BE SOUGHT FROM GOD

Peruse attentively this treatise, and if you understand it, give God the praise; but where you fail to understand it, pray for understanding, for God will give you understanding. Remember what the Scriptures say: "If any of you lack wisdom, let him ask of God, who giveth to all men liberally, and upbraideth not; and it shall be given to him." [270] Wisdom itself cometh down from above, as the Apostle James himself tells us.[271] There is, however, another wisdom, which you must repel from you, and pray against its remaining in you; this the same apostle expressed his detestation of when he said, "But if ye have bitter envying and strife in your hearts, . . . this is not the wisdom which descendeth from above, but is earthly, sensual, devilish. For wherever there is envying and strife, there is also confusion, and every evil work. But the wisdom which is from above is first pure, then peaceable, gentle, and easy to be entreated, full of mercy and good works, without partiality, and without hypocrisy." [272] What blessing, then, will that man not have who has prayed for this wisdom and obtained it of the Lord? And from this you may understand what grace is; because if this wisdom were of ourselves, it would not be from above; nor would it be an object to be asked for of the God who created us. Brethren, pray ye for us also, that we may live "soberly, righteously, and godly in this present world; looking for that blessed hope, and the glorious appearing of our Lord and Saviour Jesus Christ," [273] to whom belong the honor, and the glory, and the kingdom, with the Father and the Holy Ghost, for ever and ever. Amen.

[269] Matt. xvi. 27   [270] Jas. i. 5   [271] Jas. i. 17, and iii. 17   [272] Jas. iii. 14-17
[273] Titus ii. 12

ON THE PREDESTINATION OF SAINTS

ON THE PREDESTINATION OF THE SAINTS

Introductory Note

Almost the last of his completed works, the treatise *On the Predestination of the Saints* appeared in 428 or 429 A.D. Written in order to stem a sudden up-surge of semi-Pelagianism, it perhaps better than any document, reveals the calm and ripe wisdom of Saint Augustine as he opposes this subtle variant of the Pelagianism which in the past he had attacked with such unrestrained violence. It is fitting that the concluding treatise in the present group of selections should deal with semi-Pelagianism, for it constitutes one of the Church's central and perennial problems upon which new light must always be thrown.

ON THE PREDESTINATION OF THE SAINTS

ADDRESSED TO PROSPER AND HILARY

Wherein the truth of predestination and grace is defended against the semi-Pelagians —those people, to wit, who by no means withdraw altogether from the Pelagian heresy, in that they contend that the beginning of salvation and of faith is of ourselves; so that in virtue, as it were, of this precedent merit, the other good gifts of God are attained. Augustine shows that not only the increase, but the very beginning also of faith, is in God's gift. On this matter he does not disavow that he once thought differently, and that in some small works, written before his episcopate, he was in error, as in that exposition, which they object to him, of propositions from the Epistle to the Romans. But he points out that he was subsequently convinced chiefly by this testimony, "But what hast thou that thou hast not received?" which he proves is to be taken as a testimony concerning faith itself also. He says that faith is to be counted among other works, which the apostle denies to anticipate God's grace when he says, "not of works." He declares that the hardness of the heart is taken away by grace, and that all come to Christ who are taught to come by the Father; but that those whom He teaches, He teaches in mercy, while those whom He teaches not, in judgment He teaches not. That the passage from his hundred and second epistle, question 2, "concerning the time of the Christian religion," which is alleged by the semi-Pelagians, may rightly be explained without detriment to the doctrine of grace and predestination. He teaches what is the difference between grace and predestination. Further, he says that God in His predestination foreknew what He had purposed to do. He marvels greatly that the adversaries of predestination, who are said to be unwilling to be dependent on the uncertainty of God's will, prefer rather to trust themselves to their own weakness than to the strength of God's promise. He clearly points out that they abuse this authority, "if thou believest, thou shalt be saved." That the truth of grace and perseverance shines forth in the case of infants that are saved, who are distinguished by no merits of their own from others who perish. For that there is no difference between them arising from the foreknowledge of merits which they would have had if they had lived longer. That that testimony is wrongfully rejected by the adversaries as being uncanonical, which he adduced for the purpose of this discussion, "he was taken away lest wickedness," etc. That the most illustrious instance of predestination and grace is the Saviour Himself, in whom a man obtained the privilege of being the Saviour and the only-begotten son of God, through being assumed into oneness of person by the word co-eternal with the Father, on account of no precedent merits, either of works or of faith. That the predestinated are called by some certain calling peculiar to the elect, and that they have been elected before the foundation of the world; not because they were foreknown as men who would believe and would be holy, but in order that by means of that very election of grace they might be such, etc.

CHAPTER I

INTRODUCTION

WE KNOW that in the *Epistle to the Philippians* the apostle said, "To write the same things to you to me indeed is not grievous, but for you it is safe;"[1] yet the same apostle, writing to the Galatians, when he saw that he had done enough among them of what he regarded as being needful for them, by the ministry of his preaching, said, "For the rest let no man cause me labor,"[2] or as it is read in many codices, "Let no one be troublesome to me." But although I confess that it causes me trouble that the divine word in which the grace of God is preached (which is absolutely no grace if it is given according to our merits) great and manifest as it is, is not yielded to, nevertheless my dearest sons, Prosper and Hilary, your zeal and brotherly affection—which makes you so reluctant to see any of the brethren in error, as to wish that, after so many books and letters of mine on this subject, I should write again from here—I love more than I can tell, although I do not dare to say that I love it as much as I ought. Wherefore, behold, I write to you again. And although not with you, yet through you I am still doing what I thought I had done sufficiently.

CHAPTER II

TO WHAT EXTENT THE MASSILIANS [3] WITHDRAW FROM THE PELAGIANS

For on consideration of your letters, I seem to see that those brethren on whose behalf you exhibit a pious care that they may not hold the poetical opinion in which it is affirmed, "Every one is a hope for himself,"[4] and so fall under that condemnation which is, not poetically, but prophetically, declared, "Cursed is every man that hath hope in man,"[5] must be treated in that way wherein the apostle dealt with those to whom he said, "And if in anything ye be otherwise minded, God shall reveal even this unto you."[6] For as yet they are in darkness on the question concerning the predestination of the saints, but they have that whence, "if in anything they are otherwise minded, God will reveal even this unto them," if they are walking in that to which they have attained. For which reason the apostle, when he had said, "If ye are in anything otherwise minded, God shall reveal even this unto you," says, "Nevertheless, whereunto we have attained, let us walk in the same."[7] And those brethren of ours, on whose behalf your pious love is solicitous, have attained with Christ's Church to the belief that the human race is born obnoxious to the sin of the first man, and that none can be delivered from that evil save by the righteousness of the Second Man. Moreover, they have attained to the confession that men's wills are anticipated by God's grace; and to the agreement that no one can suffice to himself either for beginning or for completing any good work. These things, therefore, unto which they have

---

[1] Phil. iii. 1   [2] Gal. vi. 17

[3] The party which Augustine is here opposing had its chief centre in Marseilles, and hence is called "Massilians." Prosper in his letter called them *reliquiae Pelagianorum*, i.e., "the remnants of the Pelagians." They are now most commonly called "Semi-Pelagians"   [4] Virg. *Aeneid*, xi, 309   [5] Jer. xvii. 5   [6] Phil. iii. 15   [7] Phil. iii. 16

attained, being held fast, abundantly distinguish them from the error of the Pelagians. Further, if they walk in them, and beseech Him who giveth understanding, if in anything concerning predestination they are otherwise minded, He will reveal even this unto them. Yet let us also spend upon them the influence of our love, and the ministry of our discourse, according to His gift, whom we have asked that in these letters we might say what should be suitable and profitable to them. For whence do we know whether by this our service, wherein we are serving them in the free love of Christ, our God may not perchance will to effect that purpose?

CHAPTER III

EVEN THE BEGINNING OF FAITH IS OF GOD'S GIFT

Therefore I ought first to show that the faith by which we are Christians is the gift of God, if I can do that more thoroughly than I have already done in so many and so large volumes. But I see that I must now reply to those who say that the divine testimonies which I have adduced concerning this matter are of avail for this purpose, to assure us that we have faith itself of ourselves, but that its increase is of God; as if faith were not given to us by Him, but were only increased in us by Him, on the ground of the merit of its having begun from us. Thus there is here no departure from that opinion which Pelagius himself was constrained to condemn in the judgment of the bishops of Palestine, as is testified in the same Proceedings, "That the grace of God is given according to our merits," [8] if it is not of God's grace that we begin to believe, but rather that on account of this beginning an addition is made to us of a more full and perfect belief; and so we first give the beginning of our faith to God, that His supplement may also be given to us again, and whatever else we faithfully ask.

CHAPTER IV

CONTINUATION OF THE PRECEDING

But why do we not, in opposition to this, rather hear the words, "Who hath first given to Him and it shall be recompensed to him again? since of Him, and through Him, and in Him, are all things"? [9] And from whom, then, is that very beginning of our faith if not from Him? For this is not excepted when other things are spoken of as of Him; but "of Him, and through Him, and in Him, are *all* things." But who can say that he who has already begun to believe deserves nothing from Him in whom he has believed? Whence it results that, to him who already deserves, other things are said to be added by a divine retribution, and thus that God's grace is given according to our merits. And this assertion when put before him,

---

[8] *On the Proceedings of Pelagius*, ch. 30   [9] Rom. xi. 35

Pelagius himself condemned, that he might not be condemned. Whoever, then, wishes on every side to avoid this condemnable opinion, let him understand that what the apostle says is said with entire truthfulness, "Unto you it is given in the behalf of Christ not only to believe on Him, but also to suffer for His sake." [10] He shows that both are the gifts of God, because he said that both were given. And he does not say, "to believe on Him more fully and perfectly," but, "to believe on Him." Neither does he say that he himself had obtained mercy to be more faithful, but "to be faithful," [11] because he knew that he had not first given the beginning of his faith to God, and had its increase given back to him again by Him; but that he had been made faithful by God, who also had made him an apostle. For the beginnings of his faith are recorded, and they are very well known by being read in the church on an occasion calculated to distinguish them: [12] how, being turned away from the faith which he was destroying, and being vehemently opposed to it, he was suddenly by a more powerful grace converted to it, by the conversion of Him, to whom as One who would do this very thing it was said by the prophet, "Thou wilt turn and quicken us;" [13] so that not only from one who refused to believe he was made a willing believer, but, moreover, from being a persecutor, he suffered persecution in defence of that faith which he persecuted. Because it was given him by Christ "not only to believe on Him, but also to suffer for His sake."

CHAPTER V

TO BELIEVE IS TO THINK WITH ASSENT

And, therefore, commending that grace which is not given according to any merits, but is the cause of all good merits, he says, "Not that we are sufficient to think anything as of ourselves, but our sufficiency is of God." [14] Let them give attention to this, and well weigh these words, who think that the beginning of faith is of ourselves, and the supplement of faith is of God. For who cannot see that that thinking is prior to believing? For no one believes anything unless he has first thought that it is to be believed. For however suddenly, however rapidly, some thoughts fly before the will to believe, and this presently follows in such wise as to attend them, as it were, in closest conjunction, it is yet necessary that everything which is believed should be believed after thought has preceded; although even belief itself is nothing else than to think with assent. For it is not every one who thinks that believes, since many think in order that they may not believe; but everybody who believes, thinks—both thinks in believing, and believes in thinking. Therefore in what pertains to religion and piety (of which the apostle was speaking) if we are not capable of thinking anything

---

[10] Phil. i. 29   [11] 1 Cor. vii. 25   [12] The *Acts of the Apostles* were read during Easter   [13] Ps. lxxxv. 6   [14] 2 Cor. iii. 5

as of ourselves, but our sufficiency is of God, we are certainly not capable of believing anything as of ourselves, since we cannot do this without thinking; but our sufficiency, by which we begin to believe, is of God. Wherefore, as no one is sufficient for himself, for the beginning or the completion of any good work whatever—and this those brethren of yours, as what you have written intimates, already agree to be true, whence, as well in the beginning as in the carrying out of every good work, our sufficiency is of God—so no one is sufficient for himself, either to begin or to perfect faith; but our sufficiency is of God. Because if faith is not a matter of thought, it is of no account; and we are not sufficient to think anything as of ourselves, but our sufficiency is of God.

CHAPTER VI

PRESUMPTION AND ARROGANCE TO BE AVOIDED

Care must be taken, brethren, beloved of God, that a man do not lift himself up in opposition to God, when he says that he does what God has promised. Was not the faith of the nations promised to Abraham, "and he, giving glory to God, most fully believed that what He promised He is able also to perform"? [15] He therefore makes the faith of the nations, who is able to do what He has promised. Further, if God works our faith, acting in a wonderful manner in our hearts so that we believe, is there any reason to fear that He cannot do the whole; and does man on that account arrogate to himself its first elements, that he may merit to receive its last from God? Consider if in such a way any other result be gained than that the grace of God is given in some way or other, according to our merits, and so grace is no more grace. For on this principle it is rendered as debt, it is not given gratuitously; for it is due to the believer that his faith itself should be increased by the Lord, and that the increased faith should be the wages of the faith begun; nor is it observed when this is said, that this wage is assigned to believers, not of grace, but of debt. And I do not at all see why the whole should not be attributed to man—as he who could originate for himself what he had not previously, can himself increase what he had originated—except that it is impossible to withstand the most manifest divine testimony, by which faith, whence piety takes its beginning, is shown also to be the gift of God: such as is that testimony that "God hath dealt to every man the measure of faith;" [16] and that one, "Peace be to the brethren, and love with faith, from God the Father, and the Lord Jesus Christ," [17] and other similar passages. Man, therefore, unwilling to resist such clear testimonies as these, and yet desiring himself to have the merit of believing, compounds as it were with God to claim a portion of faith for himself, and to leave a portion for Him; and, what is still more

[15] Rom. iv. 20   [16] Rom. xii. 3   [17] Eph. vi. 23

arrogant, he takes the first portion for himself, and gives the subsequent to Him; and so in that which he says belongs to both, he makes himself the first, and God the second!

CHAPTER VII

AUGUSTINE CONFESSES THAT HE HAD FORMERLY BEEN IN ERROR CONCERNING THE GRACE OF GOD

It was not thus that that pious and humble teacher thought—I speak of the most blessed Cyprian—when he said "that we must boast in nothing, since nothing is our own." [18] And in order to show this, he appealed to the apostle as a witness, where he said, "For what hast thou that thou hast not received? And if thou hast received it, why boastest thou as if thou hadst not received it?" [19] And it was chiefly by this testimony that I myself also was convinced when I was in a similar error, thinking that faith whereby we believe on God is not God's gift, but that it is in us from ourselves, and that by it we obtain the gifts of God, whereby we may live temperately and righteously and piously in this world. For I did not think that faith was preceded by God's grace, so that by its means would be given to us what we might profitably ask, except that we could not believe if the proclamation of the truth did not precede; but that we should consent when the gospel was preached to us I thought was our own doing, and came to us from ourselves. And this my error is sufficiently indicated in some small works of mine written before my episcopate. Among these is that which you have mentioned in your letters,[20] wherein is an exposition of certain propositions from the *Epistle to the Romans*. Eventually, when I was retracting all my small works, and was committing that retraction to writing—of which task I had already completed two books before I had taken up your more lengthy letters—when in the first volume I had reached the retractation of this book, I then spoke thus—"Also discussing, I say, 'what God could have chosen in him who was as yet unborn, whom He said that the elder should serve; and what in the same elder, equally as yet unborn, He could have rejected; concerning whom, on this account, the prophetic testimony is recorded, although declared long subsequently, "Jacob have I loved, and Esau have I hated," ' [21] I carried out my reasoning to the point of saying: 'God did not therefore choose the works of any one in foreknowledge of what He Himself would give them, but he chose the faith, in the foreknowledge that He would choose that very person whom He foreknew would believe on Him—to whom He would give the Holy Spirit, so that by doing good works he might obtain eternal life also.' I had not yet very carefully sought, nor had I as yet found, what is the nature of the

[18] Cpyrian, *Testimonies to Quirinus*, Book iii. ch. 4; *The Ante-Nicene Fathers*, vol. v, p. 528   [19] 1 Cor. iv. 7   [20] Hilary's Letter, No. 226 in the collection of Augustine's *Letters*   [21] Mal. i. 2, 3. Cf. Rom. ix. 13

election of grace, of which the apostle says, 'A remnant are saved according to the election of grace.' [22] Which assuredly is not grace if any merits precede it; lest what is now given, not according to grace, but according to debt, be rather paid to merits than freely given. And what I next subjoined: 'For the same apostle says, "The same God which worketh all in all;" [23] but it was never said, God believeth all in all;' and then added, 'Therefore what we believe is our own, but what good thing we do is of Him who giveth the Holy Spirit to them that believe:' I certainly could not have said, had I already known that faith itself also is found among those gifts of God which are given by the same Spirit. Both, therefore, are ours on account of the choice of the will, and yet both are given by the spirit of faith and love. For faith is not alone, but, as it is written, 'Love with faith, from God the Father, and our Lord Jesus Christ.' [24] And what I said a little after—'For it is ours to believe and to will, but it is His to give to those who believe and will, the power of doing good works through the Holy Spirit, by whom love is shed abroad in our hearts'—is true indeed; but by the same rule both are also God's, because God prepares the will; and both are ours too, because they are only brought about with our good wills. And thus what I subsequently said also: 'Because we are not able to will unless we are called; and when, after our calling, we would will, our willing is not sufficient, nor our running, unless God gives strength to us that run, and leads us whither He calls us;' and thereupon added: 'It is plain, therefore, that it is not of him that willeth, nor of him that runneth, but of God that showeth mercy, that we do good works'—this is absolutely most true. But I discovered little concerning the calling itself, which is according to God's purpose; for not such is the calling of all that are called, but only of the elect. Therefore what I said a little afterwards: 'For as in those whom God elects it is not works but faith that begins the merit so as to do good works by the gift of God, so in those whom He condemns, unbelief and impiety begin the merit of punishment, so that even by way of punishment itself they do evil works'—I spoke most truly. But that even the merit itself of faith was God's gift, I neither thought of inquiring into, nor did I say. And in another place I say: 'For whom He has mercy upon, He makes to do good works, and whom He hardeneth He leaves to do evil works; but that mercy is bestowed upon the preceding merit of faith, and that hardening is applied to preceding iniquity.' And this indeed is true; but it should further have been asked, whether even the merit of faith does not come from God's mercy—that is, whether that mercy is manifested in man only because he is a believer, or whether it is also manifested that he may be a believer? For we read in the apostle's words: 'I obtained mercy to be a believer.' [25] He does not say, 'Because I was a believer.' Therefore, although it is given to the believer, yet it has been given also that he may be a believer. Therefore, also, in another place

[22] Rom. xi. 5   [23] 1 Cor. xii. 6   [24] Eph. vi. 23   [25] 1 Cor. vii. 25

in the same book I most truly said: 'Because, if it is of God's mercy, and not of works, that we are even called that we may believe, and it is granted to us who believe to do good works, that mercy must not be grudged to the heathen'—although I there discoursed less carefully about that calling which is given according to God's purpose." [26]

CHAPTER VIII

WHAT AUGUSTINE WROTE TO SIMPLICIANUS, THE SUCCESSOR OF AMBROSE, BISHOP OF MILAN

You see plainly what was at that time my opinion concerning faith and works, although I was laboring in commending God's grace; and in this opinion I see that those brethren of ours now are, because they have not been as careful to make progress with me in my writings as they were in reading them. For if they had been so careful, they would have found that question solved in accordance with the truth of the divine Scriptures in the first book of the two which I wrote in the very beginning of my episcopate to Simplicianus, of blessed memory, Bishop of the Church of Milan, and successor to Saint Ambrose. Unless, perchance, they may not have known these books; in which case, take care that they do know them. Of this first of those two books, I first spoke in the second book of the *Retractationes;* and what I said is as follows: "Of the books, I say, on which, as a bishop, I have labored, the first two are addressed to Simplicianus, president of the Church of Milan, who succeeded the most blessed Ambrose— concerning divers questions, two of which I gathered into the first book from the *Epistle of Paul the Apostle to the Romans.* The former of them is about what is written: 'What shall we say, then? Is the law sin? By no means;' [27] as far as the passage where he says, 'Who shall deliver me from the body of this death? The grace of God through Jesus Christ our Lord.' [28] And therein I have expounded those words of the apostle: 'The law is spiritual; but I am carnal,' [29] and others in which the flesh is declared to be in conflict against the Spirit, in such a way as if a man were there described as still under law, and not yet established under grace. For, long afterwards, I perceived that those words might even be (and probably were) the utterance of a spiritual man. The latter question in this book is gathered from that passage where the apostle says, 'And not only this, but when Rebecca also had conceived by one act of intercourse, even by our father Isaac,' [30] as far as that place where he says, 'Except the Lord of Sabaoth had left us a seed, we should be as Sodoma, and should have been like unto Gomorrah.' [31] In the solution of this question I labored indeed on behalf of the free choice of the human will, but God's grace overcame, and I could only reach that point where the apostle is perceived to have said with the

[26] *Retractationes*, i. 23. Nos. 3, 4   [27] Rom. vii. 7   [28] Rom. vii. 24   [29] Rom. vii. 14
[30] Rom. ix. 10   [31] Rom. ix. 29

most evident truth, 'For who maketh thee to differ? and what hast thou that thou hast not received? Now, if thou hast received it, why dost thou glory as if thou receivedst it not?'[32] And this the martyr Cyprian was also desirous of setting forth when he compressed the whole of it in that title: 'That we must boast in nothing, since nothing is our own.' "[33] This is why I previously said that it was chiefly by this apostolic testimony that I myself had been convinced, when I thought otherwise concerning this matter; and this God revealed to me as I sought to solve this question when I was writing, as I said, to the Bishop Simplicianus. This testimony, therefore, of the apostle, when for the sake of repressing man's conceit he said, "For what hast thou which thou hast not received?"[32] does not allow any believer to say, I have faith which I received not. All the arrogance of this answer is absolutely repressed by these apostolic words. Moreover, it cannot even be said, "Although I have not a perfected faith, yet I have its beginning, whereby I first of all believed in Christ." Because here also is answered: "But what hast thou that thou hast not received? Now, if thou hast received it, why dost thou glory as if thou receivedst it not?"

CHAPTER IX

THE PURPOSE OF THE APOSTLE IN THESE WORDS

The notion, however, which they entertain, "that these words, 'What hast thou that thou hast not received?' cannot be said of this faith, because it has remained in the same nature, although corrupted, which at first was endowed with health and perfection,"[34] is perceived to have no force for the purpose that they desire, if it be considered why the apostle said these words. For he was concerned that no one should glory in man, because dissensions had sprung up among the Corinthian Christians, so that every one was saying, "I, indeed, am of Paul, and another, I am of Apollos, and another, I am of Cephas;"[35] and thence he went on to say: "God hath chosen the foolish things of the world to confound the wise; and God hath chosen the weak things of the world to confound the strong things; and God hath chosen the ignoble things of the world, and contemptible things, and those things which are not, to make of no account things which are; that no flesh should glory before God."[36] Here the intention of the apostle is of a certainty sufficiently plain against the pride of man, that no one should glory in man; and thus, no one should glory in himself. Finally, when he had said "that no flesh should glory before God," in order to show in what man ought to glory, he immediately added, "But it is of Him that ye are in Christ Jesus, who is made unto us wisdom from God, and righteousness, and sanctification, and redemption: that according as it is

[32] I Cor. iv. 7

[33] Cypr. *Test.* Book iii. ch. 4; see *The Ante-Nicene Fathers*, p. 528. Augustine's *Retractationes*, II. i. 1   [34] See Epistle of Hilary (Augustine's *Epistles*, 226)   [35] I Cor. i. 12   [36] I Cor. i. 27

written, He that glorieth, let him glory in the Lord." [37] Thence that intention of his progressed, till afterwards rebuking them he says, "For ye are yet carnal; for whereas there are among you envying and contention, are ye not carnal, and walk according to man? For while one saith I am of Paul, and another, I am of Apollos, are ye not men? What, then, is Apollos, and what Paul? Ministers by whom you believed; and to every one as the Lord has given. I have planted, and Apollos watered; but God gave the increase. Therefore, neither is he that planteth anything, nor he that watereth, but God that giveth the increase." [38] Do you not see that the sole purpose of the apostle is that man may be humbled, and God alone exalted? Since in all those things, indeed, which are planted and watered, he says that not even are the planter and the waterer anything, but God who giveth the increase: and the very fact, also, that one plants and another waters he attributes not to themselves, but to God, when he says, "To every one as the Lord hath given; I have planted, Apollos watered." Hence, therefore, persisting in the same intention he comes to the point of saying, "Therefore let no man glory in man," [39] for he had already said, "He that glorieth, let him glory in the Lord." After these and some other matters which are associated therewith, that same intention of his is carried on in the words: "And these things, brethren, I have in a figure transferred to myself and to Apollos for your sakes, that ye might learn in us that no one of you should be puffed up for one against another above that which is written. For who maketh thee to differ? And what hast thou which thou hast not received? Now, if thou hast received it, why dost thou glory as if thou receivedst it not?" [40]

CHAPTER X

IT IS GOD'S GRACE WHICH SPECIALLY DISTINGUISHES ONE MAN FROM ANOTHER

In this the apostle's most evident intention, in which he speaks against human pride, so that none should glory in man but in God, it is too absurd, as I think, to suppose God's natural gifts, whether man's entire and perfected nature itself, as it was bestowed on him in his first state, or the remains, whatever they may be, of his degraded nature. For is it by such gifts as these, which are common to all men, that men are distinguished from men? But here he first said, "For who maketh thee to differ?" and then added, "And what hast thou that thou hast not received?" Because a man, puffed up against another, might say, "My faith makes me to differ," or "My righteousness," or anything else of the kind. In reply to such notions, the good teacher says, "But what hast thou that thou hast not received?" And from whom but from Him who maketh thee to

---

[37] 1 Cor. i. 30   [38] 1 Cor. iii. 3 ff.   [39] 1 Cor. iii. 21   [40] 1 Cor. iv. 6

differ from another, on whom He bestowed not what He bestowed on thee? "Now if," says he, "thou hast received it, why dost thou glory as if thou receivedst it not?" Is he concerned, I ask, about anything else save that he who glorieth should glory in the Lord? But nothing is so opposed to this feeling as for any one to glory concerning his own merits in such a way as if he himself had made them for himself, and not the grace of God— a grace, however, which makes the good to differ from the wicked, and is not common to the good and the wicked. Let the grace, therefore, whereby we are living and reasonable creatures, and are distinguished from cattle, be attributed to nature; let that grace also by which, among men themselves, the handsome are made to differ from the ill-formed, or the intelligent from the stupid, or anything of that kind, be ascribed to nature. But he whom the apostle was rebuking did not puff himself up as contrasted with cattle, nor as contrasted with any other man, in respect of any natural endowment which might be found even in the worst of men. But he ascribed to himself, and not to God, some good gift which pertained to a holy life, and was puffed up therewith when he deserved to hear the rebuke, "Who hath made thee to differ? and what hast thou that thou receivedst not?" For though the capacity to have faith is of nature, is it also of nature to have it? "For all men have not faith," [41] although all men have the capacity to have faith. But the apostle does not say, "And what hast thou capacity to have, the capacity to have which thou receivedst not?" but he says, "And what hast thou which thou receivedst not?" Accordingly, the capacity to have faith, as the capacity to have love, belongs to men's nature; but to have faith, even as to have love, belongs to the grace of believers. That nature therefore, in which is given to us the capacity of having faith, does not distinguish man from man, but faith itself makes the believer to differ from the unbeliever. And thus, when it is said, "For who maketh thee to differ? and what hast thou that thou receivedst not?" if any one dare to say, "I have faith of myself, I did not, therefore, receive it," he directly contradicts this most manifest truth—not because it is not in the choice of man's will to believe or not to believe, but because in the elect the will is prepared by the Lord. Thus, morover, the passage, "For who maketh thee to differ? and what hast thou that thou receivedst not?" refers to that very faith which is in the will of man.

CHAPTER XI

THAT SOME MEN ARE ELECTED IS OF GOD'S MERCY

"Many hear the word of truth; but some believe, while others contradict. Therefore, the former will to believe; the latter do not will." Who does not know this? Who can deny this? But since in some the will is prepared by

[41] 2 Thess. iii. 2

the Lord, in others it is not prepared, we must assuredly be able to distinguish what comes from God's mercy, and what from His judgment. "What Israel sought for," says the apostle, "he hath not obtained, but the election hath obtained it; and the rest were blinded, as it is written, God gave to them the spirit of compunction—eyes that they should not see, and ears that they should not hear, even to this day. And David said, Let their table be made a snare, a retribution, and a stumblingblock to them; let their eyes be darkened, that they may not see; and bow down their back always." [42] Here is mercy and judgment—mercy towards the election which has obtained the righteousness of God, but judgment to the rest which have been blinded. And yet the former, because they willed, believed; the latter, because they did not will believed not. Therefore mercy and judgment were manifested in the very wills themselves. Certainly such an election is of grace, not at all of merits. For he had before said, "So, therefore, even at this present time, the remnant has been saved by the election of grace. And if by grace, now it is no more of works; otherwise grace is no more grace." [43] Therefore the election obtained what it obtained gratuitously; there preceded none of those things which they might first give, and it should be given to them again. He saved them for nothing. But to the rest who were blinded, as is there plainly declared, it was done in recompense. "All the paths of the Lord are mercy and truth." [44] But His ways are unsearchable. Therefore the mercy by which He freely delivers, and the truth by which He righteously judges, are equally unsearchable.

CHAPTER XII

WHY THE APOSTLE SAID THAT WE ARE JUSTIFIED BY FAITH AND NOT BY WORKS

But perhaps it may be said: "The apostle distinguishes faith from works; he says, indeed, that grace is not of works, but he does not say that it is not of faith." This, indeed, is true. But Jesus says that faith itself also is the work of God, and commands us to work it. For the Jews said to Him, "What shall we do that we may work the work of God? Jesus answered, and said unto them, This is the work of God, that ye believe on Him whom He hath sent." [45] The apostle, therefore, distinguishes faith from works, just as Judah is distinguished from Israel in the two kingdoms of the Hebrews, although Judah is Israel itself. And he says that a man is justified by faith and not by works, because faith itself is first given, from which may be obtained other things which are specially characterized as works, in which a man may live righteously. For he himself also says, "By grace ye are saved through faith; and this not of yourselves; but it is the gift of God" [46]—that is to say, "And in saying, 'through faith,' even faith it-

[42] Rom. xi. 7   [43] Rom. xi. 5   [44] Ps. xxv. 10   [45] John vi. 28   [46] Eph. ii. 8

self is not of yourselves, but is God's gift." "Not of works," he says, "lest any man should be lifted up." For it is often said, "He deserved to believe, because he was a good man even before he believed." Which may be said of Cornelius,[47] since his alms were accepted and his prayers heard before he had believed on Christ; and yet without some faith he neither gave alms nor prayed. For how did he call on Him on whom he had not believed? But if he could have been saved without the faith of Christ, the Apostle Peter would not have been sent as an architect to build him up; although, "Except the Lord build the house, they labor in vain who build it." [48] And we are told, Faith is of ourselves; other things which pertain to works of righteousness are of the Lord; as if faith did not belong to the building— as if, I say, the foundation did not belong to the building. But if this primarily and especially belongs to it, he labors in vain who seeks to build up the faith by preaching, unless the Lord in His mercy builds it up from within. Whatever, therefore, of good works Cornelius performed, as well before he believed in Christ as when he believed and after he had believed, are all to be ascribed to God, lest, perchance any man be lifted up.

CHAPTER XIII

THE EFFECT OF DIVINE GRACE

Accordingly, our only Master and Lord Himself, when He had said what I have above mentioned—"This is the work of God, that ye believe on Him whom He hath sent"—says a little afterwards in that same discourse of His, "I said unto you that ye also have seen me and have not believed. All that the Father giveth me shall come to me." [49] What is the meaning of "shall come to me," but, "shall believe in me"? But it is the Father's gift that this may be the case. Moreover, a little after He says, "Murmur not among yourselves. No one can come to me, except the Father which hath sent me draw him; and I will raise him up at the last day. It is written in the prophets, And they shall be all teachable of God. Every man that hath heard of the Father, and hath learned, cometh unto me." [50] What is the meaning of, "Every man that hath heard from the Father, and nath learned, cometh unto me," except that there is none who hears from the Father, and learns, who cometh not to me? For if every one who has heard from the Father, and has learned, comes, certainly every one who does not come has not heard from the Father; for if he had heard and learned, he would come. For no one has heard and learned, and has not come; but every one, as the Truth declares, who has heard from the Father, and has learned, comes. Far removed from the senses of the flesh is this teaching in which the Father is heard, and teaches to come to the Son. Engaged herein is also the Son Himself, because He is His Word by which He thus teaches;

---

[47] Acts x.   [48] Ps. cxxvii. 1   [49] John vi. 36   [50] John vi. 43 ff.

and He does not do this through the ear of the flesh, but of the heart. Herein engaged, also, at the same time, is the Spirit of the Father and of the Son; and He, too, teaches, and does not teach separately, since we have learned that the workings of the Trinity are inseparable. And that is certainly the same Holy Spirit of whom the apostle says, "We, however, having the same Spirit of faith." [51] But this is especially attributed to the Father, for the reason that of Him is begotten the Only Begotten, and from Him proceeds the Holy Spirit, of which it would be tedious to argue more elaborately; and I think that my work in fifteen books on the Trinity which God is, has already reached you. Very far removed, I say, from the senses of the flesh is this instruction wherein God is heard and teaches. We see that many come to the Son because we see that many believe on Christ, but when and how they have heard this from the Father, and have learned, we see not. It is true that that grace is exceedingly secret, but who doubts that it is grace? This grace, therefore, which is hiddenly bestowed in human hearts by the Divine gift, is rejected by no hard heart, because it is given for the sake of first taking away the hardness of the heart. When, therefore, the Father is heard within, and teaches, so that a man comes to the Son, He takes away the heart of stone and gives a heart of flesh, as in the declaration of the prophet He has promised. Because He thus makes them children and vessels of mercy which He has prepared for glory.

CHAPTER XIV

WHY THE FATHER DOES NOT TEACH ALL THAT THEY MAY COME TO CHRIST

Why, then, does He not teach all that they may come to Christ, except because all whom He teaches, He teaches in mercy, while those whom He teaches not, in judgment He teaches not? Since, "On whom He will He has mercy, and whom He will He hardeneth." [52] But He has mercy when He gives good things. He hardens when He recompenses what is deserved. Or if, as some would prefer to distinguish them, those words also are his to whom the apostle says, "Thou sayest then unto me," so that he may be regarded as having said, "Therefore hath He mercy on whom He will, and whom He will He hardeneth," as well as those which follow—to wit, "What is it that is still complained of? for who resists His will?" does the apostle answer, "O man, what thou hast said is false?" No; but he says, "O man, who art thou that repliest against God? Doth the thing formed say to him that formed it, Why hast thou made me thus? Hath not the potter power over the clay of the same lump?" [53] and what follows, which you very well know. And yet in a certain sense the Father teaches all men to come to His Son. For it was not in vain that it was written in the prophets, "And they

[51] 2 Cor. iv. 13   [52] Rom. ix. 18   [53] Rom. ix. 18 ff.

shall all be teachable of God." [54] And when He too had premised this testimony, He added, "Every man, therefore, who has heard of the Father, and has learned, cometh to me." As, therefore, we speak justly when we say concerning any teacher of literature who is alone in a city, He teaches literature here to everybody—not that all men learn, but that there is none who learns literature there who does not learn from him—so we justly say, God teaches all men to come to Christ, not because all come, but because none comes in any other way. And why He does not teach all men the apostle explained, as far as he judged that it was to be explained, because, "willing to show His wrath, and to exhibit His power, He endured with much patience the vessels of wrath which were perfected for destruction; and that He might make known the riches of His glory on the vessels of mercy which He has prepared for glory." [55] Hence it is that the "word of the cross is foolishness to them that perish; but unto them that are saved it is the power of God." [56] God teaches all such to come to Christ, for He wills all such to be saved, and to come to the knowledge of the truth. And if He had willed to teach even those to whom the word of the cross is foolishness to come to Christ, beyond all doubt these also would have come. For He neither deceives nor is deceived when He says, "Every one that hath heard of the Father, and hath learned, cometh to me." Away, then, with the thought that any one cometh not, who has heard of the Father and has learned.

CHAPTER XV

IT IS BELIEVERS THAT ARE TAUGHT OF GOD

"Why," say they, "does He not teach all men?" If we should say that they whom He does not teach are unwilling to learn, we shall be met with the answer: And what becomes of what is said to Him, "O God, Thou wilt turn us again, and quicken us"? [57] Or if God does not make men willing who were not willing, on what principle does the Church pray, according to the Lord's commandment, for her persecutors? For thus also the blessed Cyprian[58] would have it to be understood that we say, "Thy will be done, as in heaven so in earth"—that is, as in those who have already believed, and who are, as it were, *heaven,* so also in those who do not believe, and on this account are still *the earth.* What, then, do we pray for on behalf of those who are unwilling to believe, except that God would work in them to will also? Certainly the apostle says, "Brethren, my heart's good will, indeed, and my prayer to God for them, is for their salvation." [59] He prays for those who do not believe—for what, except that they may believe? For in no other way do they obtain salvation. If, then, the faith of the petitioners precede the grace of God, does the faith of them on whose behalf

[54] John vi. 45   [55] Rom. ix. 22   [56] I Cor. i. 18   [57] Ps. lxxx. 7   [58] Cypr. *Treatise on the Lord's Prayer.*   [59] Rom. x. 1

prayer is made that they may believe precede the grace of God?—since this is the very thing that is besought for them, that on them that believe not—that is, who have not faith—faith itself may be bestowed? When, therefore, the gospel is preached, some believe, some believe not; but they who believe at the voice of the preacher from without, hear of the Father from within, and learn; while they who do not believe, hear outwardly, but inwardly do not hear nor learn—that is to say, to the former it is given to believe; to the latter it is not given. Because "no man," says He, "cometh to me, except the Father which sent me draw him." [60] And this is more plainly said afterwards. For after a little time, when He was speaking of eating His flesh and drinking His blood, and some even of His disciples said, "This is a hard saying, who can hear it? Jesus, knowing in Himself that His disciples murmured at this, said unto them, Doth this offend you?" [61] And a little after He said, "The words that I have spoken unto you are spirit and life; but there are some among you which believe not." [62] And immediately the evangelist says, "For Jesus knew from the beginning who were the believers, and who should betray Him; and He said, There-fore said I unto you, that no man can come unto me except it were given him of my Father." Therefore, to be drawn to Christ by the Father, and to hear and learn of the Father in order to come to Christ, is nothing else than to receive from the Father the gift by which to believe in Christ. For it was not the hearers of the gospel that were distinguished from those who did not hear, but the believers from those who did not believe, by Him who said, "No man cometh to me except it were given him of my Father."

CHAPTER XVI

WHY THE GIFT OF FAITH IS NOT GIVEN TO ALL

Faith, then, as well in its beginning as in its completion, is God's gift; and let no one have any doubt whatever, unless he desires to resist the plainest sacred writings, that this gift is given to some, while to some it is not given. But why it is not given to all ought not to disturb the believer, who believes that from one all have gone into a condemnation, which un-doubtedly is most righteous; so that even if none were delivered therefrom, there would be no just cause for finding fault with God. Whence it is plain that it is a great grace for many to be delivered, and to acknowledge in those that are not delivered what would be due to themselves; so that he that glorieth may glory not in his own merits, which he sees to be equalled in those that are condemned, but in the Lord. But why He delivers one rather than another—"His judgments are unsearchable, and His ways past finding out." [63] For it is better in this case for us to hear or to say, "O man, who art thou that repliest against God?" [64] than to dare to speak

[60] John vi. 44   [61] John vi. 60 ff   [62] John vi. 63 ff   [63] Rom. xi. 33   [64] Rom. ix. 20

as if we could know what He has chosen to be kept secret. Since, moreover, He could not will anything unrighteous.

CHAPTER XVII

HIS ARGUMENT IN HIS LETTER AGAINST PORPHYRY, AS TO WHY THE GOSPEL CAME SO LATE INTO THE WORLD

But that which you remember my saying in a certain small treatise of mine against Porphyry, under the title of *The Time of the Christian Religion*, I so said for the sake of escaping this more careful and elaborate argument about grace; although its meaning, which could be unfolded elsewhere or by others, was not wholly omitted, although I had been unwilling in that place to explain it. For, among other matters, I spoke thus in answer to the question proposed, why it was after so long a time that Christ came: "Accordingly, I say, since they do not object to Christ that all do not follow His teaching (for even they themselves feel that this could not be objected at all with any justice, either to the wisdom of the philosophers or even to the deity of their own gods), what will they reply, if—leaving out of the question that depth of God's wisdom and knowledge where perchance some other divine plan is far more secretly hidden, without prejudging also other causes, which cannot be traced out by the wise— we say to them only this, for the sake of brevity in the arguing of this question, that Christ willed to appear to men, and that His doctrine should be preached among them, at that time when He knew, and at that place where He knew, that there were some who would believe on Him. For at those times, and in those places, at which His gospel was not preached, He foreknew that all would be in His preaching such as, not indeed all, but many were in His bodily presence, who would not believe on Him, even when the dead were raised by Him; such as we see many now, who, although the declarations of the prophets concerning Him are fulfilled by such manifestations, are still unwilling to believe, and prefer to resist by human astuteness, rather than yield to divine authority so clear and perspicuous, and so lofty, and sublimely made known, so long as the human understanding is small and weak in its approach to divine truth. What wonder is it, then, if Christ knew the world in former ages to be so full of unbelievers, that He should reasonably refuse to appear, or to be preached to them, who, as He foreknew, would believe neither His words nor His miracles? For it is not incredible that all at that time were such as from His coming even to the present time we marvel that so many have been and are. And yet from the beginning of the human race, sometimes more hiddenly, sometimes more evidently, even as to Divine Providence the times seemed to be fitting, there has neither been a failure of prophecy, nor were there wanting those who believed on Him; as well from Adam to Moses, as in the people of Israel itself, which by a certain special mystery was a prophetic people; and in other nations before He had come in the flesh. For as some are mentioned in the sacred Hebrew books, as early as the time of Abraham—neither of his fleshly race nor of the people of Israel, nor of the foreign society among the people of Israel—who were, nevertheless, sharers in their sacrament, why may we not believe that there were others elsewhere among other people, here and there, although we do not read any mention of them in the same authorities? Thus the salvation of this religion, by which only true one true salvation is truly promised, never failed him who was worthy of it; and whoever it failed was not worthy of it. And from the very beginning of the propagation of man, even to the end, the gospel is preached, to some for a reward, to some for judgment; and thus also those to whom the faith was not announced at all were foreknown as those who would not believe; and those to whom it was announced, although they were not such as would believe, are set forth as an example for the former; while those to whom it is announced who should believe, are prepared for the kingdom of heaven, and the company of the holy angels." [65]

CHAPTER XVIII

THE PRECEDING ARGUMENT APPLIED TO THE PRESENT TIME

Do you not see that my desire was, without any prejudgment of the hidden counsel of God, and of other reasons, to say what might seem sufficient about Christ's foreknowledge, to convince the unbelief of the pagans who had brought forward this question? For what is more true than that Christ foreknew who should believe on Him, and at what times and places they should believe? But whether by the preaching of Christ to themselves by themselves they were to have faith, or whether they would receive it by God's gift—that is, whether God only foreknew them, or also predestinated them, I did not at that time think it necessary to inquire or to discuss. Therefore what I said, "that Christ willed to appear to men at that time, and that His doctrine should be preached among them when He knew, and where He knew, that there were those who would believe on Him," may also thus be said, "That Christ willed to appear to men at that time, and that His gospel should be preached among those, whom He knew, and where He knew, that there were those who had been elected in Himself before the foundation of the world." But since, if it were so said, it would make the reader desirous of asking about those things which now by the warning of Pelagian errors must of necessity be discussed with greater copiousness and care, it seemed to me that what at that time was sufficient should be briefly said, leaving to one side, as I said, the depth of the wisdom and knowledge of God, and without prejudging other reasons, concern-

[65] Augustine's *Epistles*, 102, 14, 15

ing which I thought that we might more fittingly argue, not then, but at some other time.

CHAPTER XIX

IN WHAT RESPECTS PREDESTINATION AND GRACE DIFFER

Moreover, that which I said, "That the salvation of this religion has never been lacking to him who was worthy of it, and that he to whom it was lacking was not worthy"—if it be discussed and it be asked whence any man can be worthy, there are not wanting those who say—by human will. But we say, by divine grace or predestination. Further, between grace and predestination there is only this difference, that predestination is the preparation for grace, while grace is the donation itself. When, therefore, the apostle says, "Not of works, lest any man should boast. For we are His workmanship, created in Christ Jesus in good works," [66] it is grace; but what follows—"which God hath prepared that we should walk in them"—is predestination, which cannot exist without foreknowledge, although foreknowledge may exist without predestination; because God foreknew by predestination those things which He was about to do, whence it was said, "He made those things that shall be." [67] Moreover, He is able to foreknow even those things which He does not Himself do—as all sins whatever. Because, although there are some which are in such wise sins as that they are also the penalties of sins, whence it is said, "God gave them over to a reprobate mind, to do those things which are not convenient," [68] it is not in such a case the sin that is God's, but the judgment. Therefore God's predestination of good is, as I have said, the preparation of grace; which grace is the effect of that predestination. Therefore when God promised to Abraham in his seed the faith of the nations, saying, "I have established thee a father of many nations," [69] whence the apostle says, "Therefore it is of faith, that the promise, according to grace, might be established to all the seed," [70] He promised not from the power of our will, but from His own predestination. For He promised what He Himself would do, not what men would do. Because, although men do those good things which pertain to God's worship, He Himself makes them to do what He has commanded; it is not they that cause Him to do what He has promised. Otherwise the fulfilment of God's promises would not be in the power of God, but in that of men; and thus what was promised by God to Abraham would be given to Abraham by men themselves. Abraham, however, did not believe thus, but "he believed, giving glory to God, that what He promised He is able also to do." [71] He does not say, "to foretell"—he does not say, "to foreknow;" for He can foretell and foreknow the doings of strangers

---

[66] Eph. ii. 9, 10   [67] Isa. xlv. 11   [68] Rom. i. 28   [69] Gen. xvii. 5   [70] Rom. iv. 16
[71] Rom. iv. 21

also; but he says, "He is able also to do;" and thus he is speaking not of the doings of others, but of His own.

CHAPTER XX

DID GOD PROMISE THE GOOD WORKS OF THE NATIONS, AND NOT THEIR FAITH, TO ABRAHAM

Did God, perchance, promise to Abraham in his seed the good works of the nations, so as to promise that which He Himself does, but did not promise the faith of the Gentiles, which men do for themselves; but so as to promise what He Himself does, did He foreknow that men would effect that faith? The apostle, indeed, does not speak thus, because God promised children to Abraham, who should follow the footsteps of his faith, as he very plainly says. But if He promised the works, and not the faith of the Gentiles, certainly since they are not good works unless they are of faith (for "the righteous lives of faith," [72] and, "Whatsoever is not of faith is sin," [73] and, "Without faith it is impossible to please" [74]) it is nevertheless in man's power that God should fulfil what He has promised. For unless man should do what without the gift of God pertains to man, he will not cause God to give—that is, unless man have faith of himself. God does not fulfil what He has promised, that works of righteousness should be given by God. And thus that God should be able to fulfil His promises is not in God's power, but in man's. And if truth and piety do not forbid our believing this, let us believe with Abraham, that what He has promised He is able also to perform. But He promised children to Abraham; and this men cannot be unless they have faith, therefore He gives faith also.

CHAPTER XXI

IT IS TO BE WONDERED AT THAT MEN SHOULD RATHER TRUST TO THEIR OWN WEAKNESS THAN TO GOD'S STRENGTH

Certainly, when the apostle says, "Therefore it is of faith that the promise may be sure according to grace," [70] I marvel that men would rather entrust themselves to their own weakness, than to the strength of God's promise. But sayest thou, God's will concerning myself is to me uncertain? What then? Is thine own will concerning thyself certain to thee? and dost thou not fear—"Let him that thinketh he standeth take heed lest he fall"? [75] Since, then, both are uncertain, why does not man commit his faith, hope, and love to the stronger will, rather than to the weaker?

[72] Hab. ii. 4   [73] Rom. xiv. 23   [74] Heb. xi. 6   [75] 1 Cor. x. 12

CHAPTER XXII

GOD'S PROMISE IS SURE

"But," say they, "when it is said, 'If thou believest, thou shalt be saved,' one of these things is required; the other is offered. What is required is in man's power; what is offered is in God's." [76] Why are not both in God's, as well what He commands as what He offers? For He is asked to give what He commands. Believers ask that their faith may be increased; they ask on behalf of those who do not believe, that faith may be given to them; therefore both in its increase and in its beginnings, faith is the gift of God. But it is said thus: "If thou believest, thou shalt be saved," in the same way that it is said, "If by the Spirit ye shall mortify the deeds of the flesh, ye shall live." [77] For in this case also, of these two things one is required, the other is offered. It is said, "If by the Spirit ye shall mortify the deeds of the flesh, ye shall live." Therefore, that we mortify the deeds of the flesh is required, but that we may live is offered. Is it, then, fitting for us to say, that to mortify the deeds of the flesh is not a gift of God, and not to confess it to be a gift of God, because we hear it required of us, with the offer of life as a reward if we shall do it? Away with this being approved by the partakers and champions of grace! This is the condemnable error of the Pelagians, whose mouths the apostle immediately stopped when he added, "For as many as are led by the Spirit of God, they are the sons of God;" [78] lest we should believe that we mortify the deeds of the flesh, not by God's Spirit, but by our own. And of this Spirit of God, moreover, he was speaking in that place where he says, "But all these worketh that one and the self-same Spirit, dividing unto every man what is his own, as He will;" [79] and among all these things, as you know, he also named faith. As, therefore, although it is the gift of God to mortify the deeds of the flesh, yet it is required of us, and life is set before us as a reward; so also faith is the gift of God, although when it is said, "If thou believest, thou shalt be saved," faith is required of us, and salvation is proposed to us as a reward. For these things are both commanded us, and are shown to be God's gifts, in order that we may understand both that we do them, and that God makes us to do them, as He most plainly says by the prophet Ezekiel. For what is plainer than when He says, "I will cause you to do"? [80] Give heed to that passage of Scripture, and you will see that God promises that He will make them to do those things which He commands to be done. He truly is not silent as to the merits but as to the evil deeds, of those to whom He shows that He is returning good for evil, by the very fact that He causeth them thenceforth to have good works, in causing them to do the divine commands.

[76] See Hilary's Letter in Augustine's *Letters*, 226, ch. 2   [77] Rom. viii. 13   [78] Rom. viii. 14   [79] I Cor. xii. 11   [80] Ezek. xxxvi. 27

CHAPTER XXIII

REMARKABLE ILLUSTRATIONS OF GRACE AND PREDESTINATION IN
INFANTS, AND IN CHRIST

But all this reasoning, whereby we maintain that the grace of God through Jesus Christ our Lord is truly grace, that is, is not given according to our merits, although it is most manifestly asserted by the witness of the divine declarations, yet, among those who think that they are withheld from all zeal for piety unless they can attribute to themselves something, which they first give that it may be recompensed to them again, involves somewhat of a difficulty in respect of the condition of grown-up people, who are already exercising the choice of will. But when we come to the case of infants, and to the Mediator between God and man Himself, the man Christ Jesus, there is wanting all assertion of human merits that precede the grace of God, because the former are not distinguished from others by any preceding good merits that they should belong to the Deliverer of men; any more than He Himself, being Himself a man, was made the Deliverer of men by virtue of any precedent human merits.

CHAPTER XXIV

THAT NO ONE IS JUDGED ACCORDING TO WHAT HE WOULD HAVE
DONE IF HE HAD LIVED LONGER

For who can hear that infants, baptized in the condition of mere infancy, are said to depart from this life by reason of their future merits, and that others not baptized are said to die in the same age because their future merits are foreknown—but as evil; so that God rewards or condemns in them not their good or evil, but no life at all? [81] The apostle, indeed, fixed a limit which man's incautious suspicion, to speak gently, ought not to transgress, for he says, "We shall all stand before the judgment-seat of Christ; that every one may receive according to the things which he has done by means of the body, whether it be good or evil." [82] "Has done," he said; and he did not add, "or would have done." But I know not whence this thought should have entered the minds of such men, that infants' future merits (which shall not be) should be punished or honored. But why is it said that a man is to be judged according to those things which he has done by means of the body, when many things are done by the mind alone, and not by the body, nor by any member of the body; and for the most part things of such importance, that a most righteous punishment would be due to such thoughts, such as—to say nothing of others—that "The fool hath said in his heart there is no God"? [83] What, then, is the

---

[81] See Prosper's Letter in Augustine's *Letters*, 225, ch. 5   [82] 2 Cor. v. 10   [83] Ps. xiv. 1

meaning of, "According to those things that he hath done by means of the body," except according to those things which he has done during that time in which he was in the body, so that we may understand "by means of the body" as meaning "throughout the season of bodily life"? But after the body, no one will be in the body except at the last resurrection— not for the purpose of establishing any claims of merit, but for the sake of receiving recompenses for good merits, and enduring punishments for evil merits. But in this intermediate period between the putting off and the taking again of the body, the souls are either tormented or they are in repose, according to those things which they have done during the period of the bodily life. And to this period of the bodily life moreover pertains, what the Pelagians deny, but Christ's Church confesses, original sin; and according to whether this is by God's grace loosed, or by God's judgment not loosed, when infants die, they pass, on the one hand, by the merit of regeneration from evil to good, or on the other, by the merit of their origin from evil to evil. The Catholic Faith acknowledges this, and even some heretics, without any contradiction, agree to this. But in the height of wonder and astonishment I am unable to discover whence men, whose intelligence your letters show to be by no means contemptible, could entertain the opinion that any one should be judged not according to the merits that he had as long as he was in the body, but according to the merits which he would have had if he had lived longer in the body; and I should not dare to believe that there were such men, if I could venture to disbelieve you. But I hope that God will interpose, so that when they are admonished they may at once perceive, that if those sins which, as is said, would have been, can rightly be punished by God's judgment in those who are not baptized, they may also be rightly remitted by God's grace in those who are baptized. For whoever says that future sins can only be punished by God's judgment, but cannot be pardoned by God's mercy, ought to consider how great a wrong he is doing to God and His grace; as if future sin could be foreknown, and could not be foregone. And if this is absurd, it is the greater reason that help should be afforded to those who would be sinners if they lived longer, when they die in early life, by means of that laver wherein sins are washed away.

CHAPTER XXV

POSSIBLY THE BAPTIZED INFANTS WOULD HAVE REPENTED IF THEY HAD LIVED, AND THE UNBAPTIZED NOT

But if, perchance, they say that sins are re-remitted to penitents, and that those who die in infancy are not baptized because they are foreknown as not such as would repent if they should live, while God has foreknown that those who are baptized and die in infancy would have repented if they had lived, let them observe and see that if it be so it is not in this case original sins which are punished in infants that die without baptism, but what would have been the sins of each one had he lived; and also in baptized infants, that it is not original sins that are washed away, but their own future sins if they should live, since they could not sin except in more mature age; but that some were foreseen as such as would repent, and others as such as would not repent, therefore some were baptized, and others departed from this life without baptism. If the Pelagians should dare to say this, by their denial of original sin they would thus be relieved of the necessity of seeking, on behalf of infants outside of the kingdom of God, for some place of I know not what happiness of their own; especially since they are convinced that they cannot have eternal life because they have not eaten the flesh nor drunk the blood of Christ; and because in them who have no sin at all, baptism, which is given for the remission of sins, is falsified. For they would go on to say that there is no original sin, but that those who as infants are released are either baptized or not baptized according to their future merits if they should live, and that according to their future merits they either receive or do not receive the body and blood of Christ, without which they absolutely cannot have life; and are baptized for the true remission of sins although they derived no sins from Adam, because the sins are remitted unto them concerning which God foreknew that they would repent. Thus with the greatest ease they would plead and would win their cause, in which they deny that there is any original sin, and contend that the grace of God is only given according to our merits. But that the future merits of men, which merits will never come into existence, are beyond all doubt no merits at all, it is certainly most easy to see: for this reason even the Pelagians were not able to say this; and much rather these ought not to say it. For it cannot be said with what pain I find that they who with us on Catholic authority condemn the error of those heretics, have not seen this, which the Pelagians themselves have seen to be most false and absurd.

CHAPTER XXVI

REFERENCE TO CYPRIAN'S TREATISE "ON THE MORTALITY"

Cyprian wrote a work *On the Mortality*,[84] known with approval to many and almost all who love ecclesiastical literature, wherein he says that death is not only not disadvantageous to believers, but that it is even found to be advantageous, because it withdraws men from the risks of sinning, and establishes them in a security of not sinning. But wherein is the advantage of this, if even future sins which have not been committed are punished? Yet he argues most copiously and well that the risks of sinning are not wanting in this life, and that they do not continue after this life is

---

[84] Cyprian, Works in *The Ante-Nicene Fathers*, vol. v. p 469

done; where also he adduces that testimony from the *Book of Wisdom:* "He was taken away, lest wickedness should alter his understanding." [85] And this was also adduced by me, though you said that those brethren of yours had rejected it on the ground of its not having been brought forward from a canonical book; as if, even setting aside the attestation of this book, the thing itself were not clear which I wished to be taught therefrom. For what Christian would dare to deny that the righteous man, if he should be prematurely laid hold of by death, will be in repose? Let who will, say this, and what man of sound faith will think that he can withstand it? Moreover, if he should say that the righteous man, if he should depart from his righteousness in which he has long lived, and should die in that impiety after having lived in it, I say not a year, but one day, will go hence into the punishment due to the wicked, his righteousness having no power in the future to avail him—will any believer contradict this evident truth? Further, if we are asked whether, if he had died then at the time that he was righteous, he would have incurred punishment or repose, shall we hesitate to answer, repose? This is the whole reason why it is said—whoever says it—"He was taken away, lest wickedness should alter his understanding." For it was said in reference to the risks of this life, not with reference to the foreknowledge of God, who foreknew that which was to be, not that which was not to be—that is, that He would bestow on him an untimely death in order that he might be withdrawn from the uncertainty of temptations; not that he would sin, since he was not to remain in temptation. Because, concerning this life, we read in the *Book of Job,* "Is not the life of man upon earth a temptation?" [86] But why it should be granted to some to be taken away from the perils of this life while they are righteous, while others who are righteous until they fall from righteousness are kept in the same risks in a more lengthened life—who has known the mind of the Lord? And yet it is permitted to be understood from this, that even those righteous people who maintain good and pious characters, even to the maturity of old age and to the last day of this life, must not glory in their own merits, but in the Lord, since He who took away the righteous man from the shortness of life, lest wickedness should alter his understanding, Himself guards the righteous man in any length of life, that wickedness may not alter his understanding. But why He should have kept the righteous man here to fall, when He might have withdrawn him before— His judgments, although absolutely righteous, are yet unsearchable.

[85] Wisd. iv. 11   [86] Job vii. 1

CHAPTER XXVII

THE BOOK OF WISDOM OBTAINS IN THE CHURCH THE AUTHORITY OF CANONICAL SCRIPTURE

And since these things are so, the judgment of the *Book of Wisdom* ought not to be repudiated, since for so long a course of years that book has deserved to be read in the Church of Christ, from the station of the readers of the Church of Christ, and to be heard by all Christians, from bishops downwards, even to the lowest lay believers, penitents, and catechumens, with the veneration paid to divine authority. For assuredly, if, from those who have been before me in commenting on the divine Scriptures, I should bring forward a defence of this judgment, which we are now called upon to defend more carefully and copiously than usual against the new error of the Pelagians—that is, that God's grace is not given according to our merits, and that it is given freely to whom it is given, because it is neither of him that willeth, nor of him that runneth, but of God that showeth mercy; but that by righteous judgment it is not given to whom it is not given, because there is no unrighteousness with God—if, therefore, I should put forth a defence of this opinion from Catholic commentators on the divine oracles who have preceded us, assuredly these brethren for whose sake I am now discoursing would acquiesce, for this you have intimated in your letters. What need is there, then, for us to look into the writings of those who, before this heresy sprang up, had no necessity to be conversant in a question so difficult of solution as this, which beyond a doubt they would have done if they had been compelled to answer such things? Whence it arose that they touched upon what they thought of God's grace briefly in some passages of their writings, and cursorily; but on those matters which they argued against the enemies of the Church, and in exhortations to every virtue by which to serve the living and true God for the purpose of attaining eternal life and true happiness, they dwelt at length. But the grace of God, what it could do, shows itself artlessly by its frequent mention in prayers; for what God commands to be done would not be asked for from God, unless it could be given by Him that it should be done.

CHAPTER XXVIII

CYPRIAN'S TREATISE "ON THE MORTALITY"

But if any wish to be instructed in the opinions of those who have handled the subject, it behoves them to prefer to all commentators the *Book of Wisdom*, where it is read, "He was taken away, that wickedness should not alter his understanding;" because illustrious commentators, even in the times nearest to the apostles, preferred it to themselves, seeing that when they made use of it for a testimony, they believed that they were making use of nothing but a divine testimony; and certainly it appears that the most blessed Cyprian, in order to commend the advantage of an earlier death, contended that those who end this life, wherein sin is possible, are taken away from the risks of sins. In the same treatise, among other things, he says, "Why, when you are about to be with Christ, and are secure of the divine promise, do you not embrace being called to Christ, and rejoice that you are free from the devil?" [87] And in another place he says, "Boys escape the peril of their unstable age." And again, in another place, he says, "Why do we not hasten and run, that we may see our country, that we may hail our relatives? A great number of those who are dear to us are expecting us there—a dense and abundant crowd of parents, brethren, sons, are longing for us; already secure of their own safety, but still anxious about our salvation." By these and such like sentiments, that teacher sufficiently and plainly testifies, in the clearest light of the Catholic Faith, that perils of sin and trials are to be feared even until the putting off of this body, but that afterwards no one shall suffer any such things. And even if he did not testify thus, when could any manner of Christian be in doubt on this matter? How, then, should it not have been of advantage to a man who has lapsed, and who finishes his life wretchedly in that same state of lapse, and passes into the punishment due to such as he—how, I say, should it not have been of the greatest and highest advantage to such an one to be snatched by death from this sphere of temptations before his fall?

CHAPTER XXIX

GOD'S DEALING DOES NOT DEPEND UPON
ANY CONTINGENT MERITS OF MEN

And thus, unless we indulge in reckless disputation, the entire question is concluded concerning him who is taken away lest wickedness should alter his understanding. And the *Book of Wisdom,* which for such a series of years has deserved to be read in Christ's Church, and in which this is read, ought not to suffer injustice because it withstands those who are mistaken on behalf of men's merits, so as to come in opposition to the most manifest grace of God: and this grace chiefly appears in infants, and while some of these baptized, and some not baptized, come to the end of this life, they sufficiently point to God's mercy and His judgment—His mercy, indeed, gratuitous, His judgment, of debt. For if men should be judged according to the merits of their life, which merits they have been prevented by death from actually having, but would have had if they had lived, it would be of no advantage to him who is taken away lest wickedness should

---

[87] Cyprian, *On the Mortality,* as above

alter his understanding; it would be of no advantage to those who die in a state of lapse if they should die before. And this no Christian will venture to say. Wherefore our brethren, who with us on behalf of the Catholic Faith assail the pest of the Pelagian error, ought not to such an extent to favor the Pelagian opinion, wherein they conceive that God's grace is given according to our merits, as to endeavor (which they cannot dare) to invalidate a true sentiment, plainly and from ancient times Christian—"He was taken away, lest wickedness should alter his understanding;" and to build up that which we should think, I do not say, no one would believe, but no one would dream—to wit, that any deceased person would be judged according to those things which he would have done if he had lived for a more lengthened period. Surely thus what we say manifests itself clearly to be incontestable—that the grace of God is not given according to our merits; so that ingenious men who contradict this truth are constrained to say things which must be rejected from the ears and from the thoughts of all men.

CHAPTER XXX

THE MOST ILLUSTRIOUS INSTANCE OF PREDESTINATION IS CHRIST JESUS

Moreover, the most illustrious Light of predestination and grace is the Saviour Himself—the Mediator Himself between God and men, the man Christ Jesus. And, pray, by what preceding merits of its own, whether of works or of faith, did the human nature which is in Him procure for itself that it should be this? Let this have an answer, I beg. The man, whence did He deserve this—to be assumed by the Word co-eternal with the Father into unity of person, and be the only-begotten Son of God? Was it because any kind of goodness in Him preceded? What did He do before? What did He believe? What did He ask, that He should attain to this unspeakable excellence? Was it not by the act and the assumption of the Word that that man, from the time He began to be, began to be the only Son of God? Did not that woman, full of grace, conceive the only Son of God? Was He not born the only Son of God, of the Holy Spirit and the Virgin Mary—not of the lust of the flesh, but by God's peculiar gift? Was it to be feared that as age matured this man, He would sin of free will? Or was the will in Him not free on that account? and was it not so much the more free in proportion to the greater impossibility of His becoming the servant of sin? Certainly, in Him human nature—that is to say, our nature —specially received all those specially admirable gifts, and any others that may most truly be said to be peculiar to Him, by virtue of no preceding merits of its own. Let a man here answer to God if he dare, and say, Why was it not I also? And if he should hear, "O man, who art thou that repliest against God?" [88] let him not at this point restrain himself, but increase his

[88] Rom. ix. 10

impudence and say, "How is it that I hear, Who art thou, O man? since I am what I hear—that is, a man, and He of whom I speak is but the same? Why should not I also be what He is? For it is by grace that He is such and so great; why is grace different when nature is common? Assuredly, there is no respect of persons with God." I say, not what Christian man, but what madman will say this?

CHAPTER XXXI

CHRIST PREDESTINED TO BE THE SON OF GOD

Therefore in Him who is our Head let there appear to be the very fountain of grace, whence, according to the measure of every man, He diffuses Himself through all His members. It is by that grace that every man from the beginning of his faith becomes a Christian, by which grace that one man from His beginning became Christ. Of the same Spirit also the former is born again of which the latter was born. By the same Spirit is effected in us the remission of sins, by which Spirit it was effected that He should have no sin. God certainly foreknew that He would do these things. This, therefore, is the same predestination of the saints which most especially shone forth in the Saint of saints; and who is there of those who rightly understand the declarations of the truth that can deny this predestination? For we have learned that the Lord of glory Himself was predestinated in so far as the man was made the Son of God. The teacher of the Gentiles exclaims, in the beginning of his epistles, "Paul, a servant of Jesus Christ, called to be an apostle, separated unto the gospel of God (which He had promised afore by His prophets in the Holy Scriptures) concerning His son, which was made of the seed of David according to the flesh, who was predestinated the Son of God in power, according to the Spirit of sanctification by the resurrection of the dead." [89] Therefore Jesus was predestinated, so that He who was to be the Son of David according to the flesh should yet be in power the Son of God, according to the Spirit of sanctification, because He was born of the Holy Spirit and of the Virgin Mary. This is that ineffably accomplished sole taking up of man by God the Word, so that He might truly and properly be called at the same time the Son of God and the Son of man—Son of man on account of the man taken up, and the Son of God on account of the God only-begotten who took Him up, so that a Trinity and not a Quaternity might be believed in. Such a transporting of human nature was predestinated, so great, so lofty, and so sublime that there was no exalting it more highly—just as on our behalf that divinity had no possibility of more humbly putting itself off, than by the assumption of man's nature with the weakness of the flesh, even to the death of the cross. As, therefore, that one man was predestinated to be

[89] Rom. i. 1 ff.

our Head, so we being many are predestinated to be His members. Here let human merits which have perished through Adam keep silence, and let that grace of God reign which reigns through Jesus Christ our Lord, the only Son of God, the one Lord. Let whoever can find in our Head the merits which preceded that peculiar generation, seek in us His members for those merits which preceded our manifold regeneration. For that generation was not recompensed to Christ, but given; that He should be born, namely, of the Spirit and the Virgin, separate from all entanglement of sin. Thus also our being born again of water and the Spirit is not recompensed to us for any merit, but freely given; and if faith has brought us to the laver of regeneration, we ought not therefore to suppose that we have first given anything, so that the regeneration of salvation should be recompensed to us again; because He made us to believe in Christ, who made for us a Christ on whom we believe. He makes in men the beginning and the completion of the faith in Jesus who made the man Jesus the beginner and finisher of faith;[90] for thus, as you know, He is called in the epistle which is addressed to the Hebrews.

CHAPTER XXXII

THE TWOFOLD CALLING

God indeed calls many predestinated children of His, to make them members of His only predestinated Son—not with that calling with which they were called who would not come to the marriage, since with that calling were called also the Jews, to whom Christ crucified is an offence, and the Gentiles, to whom Christ crucified is foolishness; but with that calling He calls the predestinated which the apostle distinguished when he said that he preached Christ, the wisdom of God and the power of God, to them that were called, Jews as well as Greeks. For thus he says, "But unto them which are called," [91] in order to show that there were some who were not called; knowing that there is a certain sure calling of those who are called according to God's purpose, whom He has foreknown and predestinated before to be conformed to the image of His Son. And it was this calling he meant when he said, "Not of works, but of Him that calleth; it was said unto her, That the elder shall serve the younger." [92] Did he say, "Not of works, but of him that believeth"? Rather, he actually took this away from man, that he might give the whole to God. Therefore he said, "But of Him that calleth"—not with any sort of calling whatever, but with that calling wherewith a man is made a believer.

[90] Heb. xii. 2   [91] 1 Cor. i. 24   [92] Rom. ix. 12

CHAPTER XXXIII

IT IS IN THE POWER OF EVIL MEN TO SIN; BUT TO DO THIS OR THAT
BY MEANS OF THAT WICKEDNESS IS IN GOD'S POWER ALONE

Moreover, it was this that he had in view when he said, "The gifts and calling of God are without repentance." [93] And in that saying also consider for a little what was its purport. For when he had said, "For I would not, brethren, that ye should be ignorant of this mystery, that ye may not be wise in yourselves, that blindness in part is happened to Israel, until the fulness of the Gentiles be come in, and so all Israel should be saved; as it is written, There shall come out of Sion one who shall deliver, and turn away impiety from Jacob: and this is the covenant to them from me, when I shall take away their sins;" [94] he immediately added, what is to be very carefully understood, "As concerning the gospel, indeed, they are enemies for your sakes: but as concerning the election, they are beloved for their fathers' sakes." [95] What is the meaning of, "as concerning the gospel, indeed, they are enemies for your sakes," but that their enmity wherewith they put Christ to death was, without doubt, as we see, an advantage to the gospel? And he shows that this came about by God's ordering, who knew how to make a good use even of evil things; not that the vessels of wrath might be of advantage to Him, but that by His own good use of them they might be of advantage to the vessels of mercy. For what could be said more plainly than what is actually said, "As concerning the gospel, indeed, they are enemies for your sakes"? It is, therefore, in the power of the wicked to sin; but that in sinning they should do this or that by that wickedness is not in their power, but in God's, who divides the darkness and regulates it; so that hence even what they do contrary to God's will is not fulfilled except it be God's will. We read in the *Acts of the Apostles* that when the apostles had been sent away by the Jews, and had come to their own friends, and shown them what great things the priests and elders said to them, they all with one consent lifted up their voices to the Lord, and said, "Lord, Thou art God, which hast made heaven, and earth, and the sea, and all things that are therein; who, by the mouth of our father David, Thy holy servant, hast said, Why did the heathen rage, and the peoples imagine vain things? The kings of the earth stood up, and the princes were gathered together against the Lord, and against His Christ. For in truth, there have assembled together in this city against Thy holy child Jesus, whom Thou hast anointed, Herod and Pilate, and the people of Israel, to do whatever Thy hand and counsel predestinated to be done." [96] See what

[93] Rom. xi. 29   [94] Rom. xi. 25 ff.   [95] Rom. xi. 28   [96] Acts iv. 24 ff.

is said: "As concerning the gospel, indeed, they are enemies for your sakes." Because God's hand and counsel predestinated such things to be done by the hostile Jews as were necessary for the gospel, for our sakes. But what is it that follows? "But as concerning the election, they are beloved for their fathers' sakes." For are those enemies who perished in their enmity, and those of the same people who still perish in their opposition to Christ—are those chosen and beloved? Away with the thought! Who is so utterly foolish as to say this? But both expressions, although contrary to one another—that is, "enemies" and "beloved"—are appropriate, though not to the same men, yet to the same Jewish people, and to the same carnal seed of Israel, of whom some belonged to the falling away, and some to the blessing of Israel himself. For the apostle previously explained this meaning more clearly when he said, "That which Israel wrought for, he hath not obtained; but the election hath obtained it, and the rest were blinded." [97] Yet in both cases it was the very same Israel. Where, therefore, we hear, "Israel hath not obtained," or, "The rest were blinded," there are to be understood the enemies for our sakes; but where we hear, "that the election hath obtained it," there are to be understood the beloved for their fathers' sakes, to which fathers those things were assuredly promised; because "the promises were made to Abraham and his seed," [98] whence also in that olive-tree is grafted the wild olive-tree of the Gentiles. Now subsequently we certainly ought to fall in with the election, of which he says that it is according to grace, not according to debt, because "there was made a remnant by the election of grace." [99] This election obtained it, the rest being blinded. As concerning this election, the Israelites were beloved for the sake of their fathers. For they were not called with that calling of which it is said, "Many are called," but with that whereby the chosen are called. Whence also after he had said, "But as concerning the election, they are beloved for the fathers' sakes," he went on to add those words whence this discussion arose: "For the gifts and calling of God are without repentance"—that is, they are firmly established without change. Those who belong to this calling are all teachable by God; nor can any of them say, "I believed in order to being thus called," because the mercy of God anticipated him, because he was so called in order that he might believe. For all who are teachable of God come to the Son because they have heard and learned from the Father through the Son, who most clearly says, "Every one who has heard of the Father, and has learned, cometh unto me." [100] But of such as these none perishes, because "of all that the Father hath given Him, He will lose none." [101] Whoever, therefore, is of these does not perish at all; nor was any who perishes ever of these. For which reason it is said, "They went out from among us, but they were not of us; for if they had been of us, they would certainly have continued with us." [102]

[97] Rom. xi. 7   [98] Gal. iii. 16   [99] Rom. xi. 5   [100] John vi. 45   [101] John vi. 39
[102] John ii. 19

CHAPTER XXXIV

THE SPECIAL CALLING OF THE ELECT IS NOT BECAUSE THEY HAVE BELIEVED, BUT IN ORDER THAT THEY MAY BELIEVE

Let us, then, understand the calling whereby they become elected—not those who are elected because they have believed, but who are elected that they may believe. For the Lord Himself also sufficiently explains this calling when He says, "Ye have not chosen me, but I have chosen you." [103] For if they had been elected because they had believed, they themselves would certainly have first chosen Him by believing in Him, so that they should deserve to be elected. But He takes away this supposition altogether when He says, "Ye have not chosen me, but I have chosen you." And yet they themselves, beyond a doubt, chose Him when they believed on Him. Whence it is not for any other reason that He says, "Ye have not chosen me, but I have chosen you," than because they did not choose Him that He should choose them, but He chose them that they might choose Him; because His mercy preceded them according to grace, not according to debt. Therefore He chose them out of the world while He was wearing flesh, but as those who were already chosen in Himself before the foundation of the world. This is the changeless truth concerning predestination and grace. For what is it that the apostle says, "As He hath chosen us in Himself before the foundation of the world"? [104] And assuredly, if this were said because God foreknew that they would believe, not because He Himself would make them believers, the Son is speaking against such a foreknowledge as that when He says, "Ye have not chosen me, but I have chosen you;" when God should rather have foreknown this very thing, that they themselves would have chosen Him, so that they might deserve to be chosen by Him. Therefore they were elected before the foundation of the world with that predestination in which God foreknew what He Himself would do; but they were elected out of the world with that calling whereby God fulfilled that which He predestinated. For whom He predestinated, them He also called, with that calling, to wit, which is according to the purpose. Not others, therefore, but those whom He predestinated, them He also called; nor others, but those whom He so called, them He also justified; nor others, but those whom He predestinated, called, and justified, them He also glorified; assuredly to that end which has no end. Therefore God elected believers; but He chose them that they might be so, not because they were already so. The Apostle James says: "Has not God chosen the poor in this world, rich in faith, and heirs of the kingdom which God hath promised to them that love Him?" [105] By choosing them, therefore, He makes them rich in faith, as He makes them heirs of the

---

[103] John xv. 16   [104] Eph. i. 4   [105] Jas. ii. 5

kingdom; because He is rightly said to choose that in them, in order to make which in them He chose them. I ask, who can hear the Lord saying, "Ye have not chosen me, but I have chosen you," and can dare to say that men believe in order to be elected, when they are rather elected to believe; lest against the judgment of truth they be found to have first chosen Christ to whom Christ says, "Ye have not chosen me, but I have chosen you"? [106]

CHAPTER XXXV

ELECTION IS FOR THE PURPOSE OF HOLINESS

Who can hear the apostle saying, "Blessed be the God and Father of our Lord Jesus Christ, who hath blessed us in all spiritual blessing in the heavens in Christ; as He has chosen us in Him before the foundation of the world, that we should be holy and without spot in His sight; in love predestinating us to the adoption of children by Jesus Christ to Himself according to the good pleasure of His will, wherein He hath shown us favor in His beloved Son; in whom we have redemption through His blood, the remission of sins according to the riches of His grace, which hath abounded to us in all wisdom and prudence; that He might show to us the mystery of His will according to His good pleasure, which He hath purposed in Himself, in the dispensation of the fulness of times, to restore all things in Christ, which are in heaven, and in the earth, in Him: in whom also we have obtained a share, being predestinated according to the purpose; who worketh all things according to the counsel of His will, that we should be to the praise of his glory" [107]—who, I say, can hear these words with attention and intelligence, and can venture to have any doubt concerning a truth so clear as this which we are defending? God chose Christ's members in Him before the foundation of the world; and how should He choose those who as yet did not exist, except by predestinating them? Therefore He chose us by predestinating us. Would he choose the unholy and the unclean? Now if the question be proposed, whether He would choose such, or rather the holy and unstained, who can ask which of these he may answer, and not give his opinion at once in favor of the holy and pure?

CHAPTER XXXVI

GOD CHOSE THE RIGHTEOUS; NOT THOSE WHOM HE FORESAW AS BEING OF THEMSELVES, BUT THOSE WHOM HE PREDESTINATED FOR THE PURPOSE OF MAKING SO

"Therefore," says the Pelagian, "He foreknew who would be holy and immaculate by the choice of free will, and on that account elected them before the foundation of the world in that same foreknowledge of His in

[106] John xvi. 16   [107] Eph. i. 3 ff.

which He foreknew that they would be such. Therefore He elected them," says he, "before they existed, predestinating them to be children whom He foreknew to be holy and immaculate. Certainly He did not make them so; nor did He foresee that He would make them so, but that they would be so." Let us, then, look into the words of the apostle and see whether He chose us before the foundation of the world because we were going to be holy and immaculate, or in order that we might be so. "Blessed," says he, "be the God and Father of our Lord Jesus Christ, who hath blessed us in all spiritual blessing in the heavens in Christ; even as He hath chosen us in Himself before the foundation of the world, that we should be holy and unspotted." [108] Not, then, because we were to be so, but that we might be so. Assuredly it is certain—assuredly it is manifest. Certainly we were to be such for the reason that He has chosen us, predestinating us to be such by His grace. Therefore "He blessed us with spiritual blessing in the heavens in Christ Jesus, even as He chose us in Him before the foundation of the world, that we should be holy and immaculate in His sight, predestinating us in love to the adoption of children through Jesus Christ to Himself." Attend to what he then adds: "According to the good pleasure," he says, "of His will;" in order that we might not in so great a benefit of grace glory concerning the good pleasure of our will. "In which," says he, "He hath shown us favor in His beloved Son"—in which, certainly, His own will, He hath shown us favor. Thus, it is said, He hath shown us grace by grace, even as it is said, He has made us righteous by righteousness. "In whom," he says, "we have redemption through His blood, the forgiveness of sins, according to the riches of His grace, which has abandoned to us in all wisdom and prudence; that He might show to us the mystery of His will, according to His good pleasure." In this mystery of His will, He placed the riches of His grace, according to His good pleasure, not according to ours, which could not possibly be good unless He Himself, according to His own good pleasure, should aid it to become so. But when he had said, "According to His good pleasure," he added, "which He purposed in Him," that is, in His beloved Son, "in the dispensation of the fulness of times to restore all things in Christ, which are in heaven, and which are in earth, in Him: in whom also we too have obtained a lot, being predestinated according to His purpose who worketh all things according to the counsel of His will; that we should be to the praise of His glory."

CHAPTER XXXVII

WE WERE ELECTED AND PREDESTINATED, NOT BECAUSE WE WERE GOING TO BE HOLY, BUT IN ORDER THAT WE MIGHT BE SO

It would be too tedious to argue about the several points. But you see without doubt, you see with what evidence of apostolic declaration this

[108] Eph. i. 3

grace is defended, in opposition to which human merits are set up, as if man should first give something for it to be recompensed to him again. Therefore God chose us in Christ before the foundation of the world, pre-destinating us to the adoption of children, not because we were going to be of ourselves holy and immaculate, but He chose and predestinated us that we might be so. Moreover, He did this according to the good pleasure of His will, so that nobody might glory concerning his own will, but about God's will towards himself. He did this according to the riches of His grace, according to His good-will, which He purposed in His beloved Son, in whom we have obtained a share, being predestinated according to the purpose, not ours, but His, who worketh all things to such an extent as that He worketh in us to will also. Moreover, He worketh according to the counsel of His will, that we may be to the praise of His glory.[109] For this reason it is that we cry that no one should glory in man, and, thus, not in himself; but whoever glorieth let him glory in the Lord, that he may be for the praise of His glory. Because He Himself worketh according to His purpose that we may be to the praise of His glory, and, of course, holy and immaculate, for which purpose He called us, predestinating us before the foundation of the world. Out of this, His purpose, is that special calling of the elect for whom He co-worketh with all things for good, because they are called according to His purpose, and "the gifts and calling of God are without repentance."[110]

CHAPTER XXXVIII

WHAT IS THE VIEW OF THE PELAGIANS, AND WHAT OF THE SEMI-PELAGIANS, CONCERNING PREDESTINATION

But these brethren of ours, about whom and on whose behalf we are now discoursing, say, perhaps, that the Pelagians are refuted by this apostolical testimony in which it is said that we are chosen in Christ and predestinated before the foundation of the world, in order that we should be holy and immaculate in His sight in love. For they think that "having received God's commands we are of ourselves by the choice of our free will made holy and immaculate in His sight in love; and since God foresaw that this would be the case," they say, "He therefore chose and predestinated us in Christ before the foundation of the world." Although the apostle says that it was not because He foreknew that we should be such, but in order that we might be such by the same election of His grace, by which He showed us favor in His beloved Son. When, therefore, He predestinated us, He foreknew His own work by which He makes us holy and immaculate. Whence the Pelagian error is rightly refuted by this testimony. "But we say," say they, "that God did not foreknow anything as

---

[109] Phil. ii. 13   [110] Rom. xi. 29

ours except that faith by which we begin to believe, and that He chose and predestinated us before the foundation of the world, in order that we might be holy and immaculate by His grace and by His work." But let them also hear in this testimony the words where he says, "We have obtained a lot, being predestinated according to His purpose who worketh all things." [111] He, therefore, worketh the beginning of our belief who worketh all things; because faith itself does not precede that calling of which it is said: "For the gifts and calling of God are without repentance;" [112] and of which it is said: "Not of works, but of Him that calleth" [113] (although He might have said, "of Him that believeth"); and the election which the Lord signified when He said: "Ye have not chosen me, but I have chosen you." [114] For He chose us, not because we believed, but that we might believe, lest we should be said first to have chosen Him, and so His word be false (which be it far from us to think possible), "Ye have not chosen me, but I have chosen you." Neither are we called because we believed, but that we may believe; and by that calling which is without repentance it is effected and carried through that we should believe. But all the many things which we have said concerning this matter need not be repeated.

CHAPTER XXXIX

THE BEGINNING OF FAITH IS GOD'S GIFT

Finally, also, in what follows this testimony, the apostle gives thanks to God on behalf of those who have believed—not, certainly, because the gospel has been declared to them, but because they have believed. For he says, "In whom also after ye had heard the word of truth, the gospel of your salvation; in whom also, after that ye believed, ye were sealed with the Holy Spirit of promise, which is the pledge of our inheritance, to the redemption of the purchased possession unto the praise of His glory. Wherefore I also, after I had heard of your faith in Christ Jesus and with reference to all the saints, cease not to give thanks for you." [115] Their faith was new and recent on the preaching of the gospel to them, which faith when he hears of, the apostle gives thanks to God on their behalf. If he were to give thanks to man for that which he might either think or know that man had not given, it would be called a flattery or a mockery, rather than a giving of thanks. "Do not err, for God is not mocked;" [116] for His gift is also the beginning of faith, unless the apostolic giving of thanks be rightly judged to be either mistaken or fallacious. What then? Does that not appear as the beginning of the faith of the Thessalonians, for which, nevertheless, the same apostle gives thanks to God when he says, "For this cause also we thank God without ceasing, because when ye had received from us the word of the hearing of God, ye received it not as the word of

[111] Eph. i. 11   [112] Rom. xi. 29   [113] Rom. ix. 12   [114] John xv. 16   [115] Eph. i. 13 ff.   [116] Gal. vi. 7

men, but as it is in truth the word of God, which effectually worketh in you and which ye believed"? [117] What is that for which he here gives thanks to God? Assuredly it is a vain and idle thing if He to whom he gives thanks did not Himself do the thing. But, since this is not a vain and idle thing, certainly God, to whom he gave thanks concerning this work, Himself did it; that when they had received the word of the hearing of God, they received it not as the word of men, but as it is in truth the word of God. God, therefore, worketh in the hearts of men with that calling according to His purpose, of which we have spoken a great deal, that they should not hear the gospel in vain, but when they heard it, should be converted and believe, receiving it not as the word of men, but as it is in truth the word of God.

CHAPTER XL

APOSTOLIC TESTIMONY TO THE BEGINNING OF FAITH BEING GOD'S GIFT

Moreover, we are admonished that the beginning of men's faith is God's gift, since the apostle signifies this when, in the *Epistle to the Colossians,* he says, "Continue in prayer, and watch in the same in giving of thanks. Withal praying also for us that God would open unto us the door of His word, to speak the mystery of Christ, for which also I am in bonds, that I may so make it manifest as I ought to speak." [118] How is the door of His word opened, except when the sense of the hearer is opened so that he may believe, and, having made a beginning of faith, may admit those things which are declared and reasoned, for the purpose of building up wholesome doctrine, lest, by a heart closed through unbelief, he reject and repel those things which are spoken? Whence, also, he says to the Corinthians: "But I will tarry at Ephesus until Pentecost. For a great and evident door is opened unto me, and there are many adversaries." [119] What else can be understood here, save that, when the gospel had been first of all preached there by him, many had believed, and there had appeared many adversaries of the same faith, in accordance with that saying of the Lord, "No one cometh unto me, unless it were given him of my Father;" [120] and, "To you it is given to know the mysteries of the kingdom of heaven, but to them it is not given"? [121] Therefore, there is an open door in those to whom it is given, but there are many adversaries among those to whom it is not given.

---

[117] 1 Thess. ii. 13　　[118] Col. iv. 2 ff.　　[119] 1 Cor. xvi. 8　　[120] John vi. 66　　[121] Luke viii. 10

CHAPTER XLI

FURTHER APOSTOLIC TESTIMONIES

And again, the same apostle says to the same people, in his second Epistle: "When I had come to Troas for the gospel of Christ, and a door had been opened unto me in the Lord, I had no rest in my spirit, because I found not Titus, my brother: but, making my farewell to them, I went away into Macedonia." [122] To whom did he bid farewell but to those who had believed—to wit, in whose hearts the door was opened for his preaching of the gospel? But attend to what he adds, saying, "Now thanks be unto God, who always causes us to triumph in Christ, and maketh manifest the savor of His knowledge by us in every place: because we are unto God a sweet savor of Christ in them who are saved, and in them who perish: to some, indeed, we are the savor of death unto death, but to some the savor of life unto life." [123] See concerning what this most zealous soldier and invincible defender of grace gives thanks. See concerning what he gives thanks—that the apostles are a sweet savor of Christ unto God, both in those who are saved by His grace, and in those who perish by His judgment. But in order that those who little understand these things may be less enraged, he himself gives a warning when he adds the words: "And who is sufficient for these things?" [124] But let us return to the opening of the door by which the apostle signified the beginning of faith in his hearers. For what is the meaning of, "Withal praying also for us that God would open unto us a door of the word," [125] unless it is a most manifest demonstration that even the very beginning of faith is the gift of God? For it would not be sought for from Him in prayer, unless it were believed to be given by Him. This gift of heavenly grace had descended to that seller of purple[126] for whom, as Scripture says in the *Acts of the Apostles,* "The Lord opened her heart, and she gave heed unto the things which were said by Paul;" for she was so called that she might believe. Because God does what He will in the hearts of men, either by assistance or by judgment; so that, even through their means, may be fulfilled what His hand and counsel have predestinated to be done.

CHAPTER XLII

OLD TESTAMENT TESTIMONIES

Therefore also it is in vain that objectors have alleged, that what we have proved by Scripture testimony from the books of *Kings* and *Chronicles* is not pertinent to the subject of which we are discoursing:[127] such, for

[122] 2 Cor. ii. 12, 13   [123] 2 Cor. ii. 14 ff.   [124] 2 Cor. ii. 16   [125] Col. iv. 3   [126] Acts xvi. 14   [127] Hilary's Letter in Augustine's *Letters,* 226, sec. 7

instance, as that when God wills that to be done which ought only to be done by the willing men, their hearts are inclined to will this—inclined, that is to say, by His power, who, in a marvellous and ineffable manner, worketh in us also to will. What else is this than to say nothing, and yet to contradict? Unless, perchance, they have given some reason to you for the view that they have taken, which reason you have preferred to say nothing about in your letters. But what that reason can be I do not know. Whether, possibly, since we have shown that God has so acted on the hearts of men, and has induced the wills of those whom He pleased to this point, that Saul or David should be established as king—do they not think that these instances are appropriate to this subject, because to reign in this world temporally is not the same thing as to reign eternally with God? And so do they suppose that God inclines the wills of those whom He pleases to the attainment of earthly kingdoms, but does not incline them to the attainment of a heavenly kingdom? But I think that it was in reference to the kingdom of heaven, and not to an earthly kingdom, that it was said, "Incline my heart unto Thy testimonies;" [128] or, "The steps of a man are ordered by the Lord, and He will will His way;" [129] or, "The will is prepared by the Lord;" [130] or, "Let our Lord be with us as with our fathers; let Him not forsake us, nor turn Himself away from us; let Him incline our hearts unto Him, that we may walk in all His ways;" [132] or, "I will give them a heart to know me, and ears that hear;" [133] or, "I will give them another heart, and a new spirit will I give them." [133] Let them also hear this, "I will give my Spirit within you, and I will cause you to walk in my righteousnesses; and ye shall observe my judgments, and do them." [134] Let them hear, "Man's goings are directed by the Lord, and how can a man understand His ways?" [135] Let them hear, "Every man seemeth right to himself, but the Lord directeth the hearts." [136] Let them hear, "As many as were ordained to eternal life believed." [137] Let them hear these passages, and whatever others of the kind I have not mentioned in which God is declared to prepare and to convert men's wills, even for the kingdom of heaven and for eternal life. And consider what sort of a thing it is to believe that God worketh men's wills for the foundation of earthly kingdoms, but that men work their own wills for the attainment of the kingdom of heaven.

CHAPTER XLIII

CONCLUSION

I have said a great deal, and, perchance, I could long ago have persuaded you what I wished, and am still speaking this to such intelligent minds as if they were obtuse, to whom even what is too much is not enough. But

---

[128] Ps. cxix. 36   [129] Ps. xxxvii. 23   [130] Prov. viii. [see LXX]   [131] 1 Kings viii. 57
[132] Baruch ii. 31   [133] Ezek. xi. 19   [134] Ezek. xxxvi. 27   [135] Prov. xx. 24   [136] Prov. xxi. 2   [137] Acts xiii. 48

let them pardon me, for a new question has compelled me to this. Because, although in my former little treatises I had proved by sufficiently appropriate proofs that faith also was the gift of God, there was found this ground of contradiction, *viz.*, that those testimonies were good for this purpose, to show that the increase of faith was God's gift, but that the beginning of faith, whereby a man first of all believes in Christ, is of the man himself, and is not the gift of God—but that God requires this, so that when it has preceded, other gifts may follow, as it were on the ground of this merit, and these are the gifts of God; and that none of them is given freely, although in them God's grace is declared, which is not grace except as being gratuitous. And you see how absurd all this is. Wherefore I determined, as far as I could, to set forth that this very beginning also is God's gift. And if I have done this at a greater length than perhaps those on whose account I did it might wish, I am prepared to be reproached for it by them, so long as they nevertheless confess that, although at greater length than they wished, although with the disgust and weariness of those that understand, I have done what I have done: that is, I have taught that even the beginning of faith, as continence, patience, righteousness, piety, and the rest, concerning which there is no dispute with them, is God's gift. Let this, therefore, be the end of this treatise, lest too great length in this one may give offence.

APPENDIX

AN ANALYSIS OF THE TREATISE *ON FREE WILL*

Book One: "In which, after the question 'Whence evil' is raised, the problem of evil-doing is unfolded. Then it is pointed out that the evil deeds of men arise from the free choice of the will; to be sure, since the mind is compelled by no one to be a slave of that desire which rules in every evil deed."

Chapter 1: After distinguishing between doing and suffering evil, Saint Augustine shows that the evil man is the author of his own evil deeds. Learning is ruled out as a source of evil.

Chapter 2: The problem is restated by asking why, if God, as Creator of all, creates souls which are in turn the sources of evil, He is not ultimately responsible for evil.

Chapter 3: In the light of God's absolute supremacy, the discussion turns to the precise nature of evil-doing. This is discovered to be in desire (*libido*).

Chapter 4: Desire (*libido*) is established as a desire for things one can lose unwillingly.

Chapter 5: The discussion centers on the limitations of man-made law, which leaves many things unpunished, with which Divine Providence will deal.

Chapter 6: Eternal law is described as that by which "it is just that all things be most perfectly ordered," and all "just" temporal law is derived therefrom.

Chapter 7: Man lives and, by reason, knows he lives. Beasts, whom man controls by virtue of reason or intelligence, lack this power, and in turn the knowledge that they live. By understanding, men lead a more perfect life, through the light of the mind. Knowledge, except when the word is used metaphorically, can only be good.

Chapter 8: Man shares with plants the capacity to grow, and the powers of the senses with animals. He has the power to joke and laugh, the lowest of strictly human qualities. A man is well ordered when reason dominates, which state is a reflection of eternal law.

Chapter 9: Man, whose mind or spirit can use reason, and in whom mind rules, is properly called wise.

Chapter 10: Mind has more power than desire since it can dominate desire rightly and justly. Soul is superior to body, and there is nothing more excellent than a rational and wise mind.

Chapter 11: Whatever excels a mind potent in its virtue cannot be unjust. Even though this nature might have the power to make a mind a slave to lust or desire, it will never do so. No other things, therefore, can cause a mind to consort with desire than its will and free choice. The will justly pays the penalty for such a great sin. Man by his own will fell to a life subservient to desire.

Chapter 12: But, Saint Augustine asks, why do we, who are stupid and have never been wise, and thus really have never surrendered to desire, have to suffer these penalties? This raises the question whether we really have never been wise, which in turn raises the problem of the pre-existence of the soul. This difficult question must be deferred. The existence of the will is established on the simple ground of the desire or will to know. A good will is that by which we seek to live rightly and honorably, and to attain to the highest wisdom. Such a good will is man's priceless possession, —which needs only to be willed, that it may be possessed.

Chapter 13: Prudence tells us what to seek and what to avoid; Fortitude enables us to endure hardship and the loss of those things not in our power; Temperance checks our desire for things we should not seek. Justice is that virtue by which his own is returned to each. A man who possesses a good will must embrace this justice, and hold nothing as more excellent; it cannot be taken from him against his will, and he will always oppose anything that is hostile to it. Prudence instructs him, Fortitude sustains him, Temperance helps him control his desires, and Justice makes him oppose all that is harmful to good will. A man who delights in his own good will is happy, and this delighting in one's own good will is in itself a good will.—And the man oppositely disposed will be unhappy. Therefore by will we are either happy or unhappy

Chapter 14: All men want a happy life, but why do not all attain it? Only by willing that which is ordained by eternal law as right can men reach happiness. When we say that men are miserable by will, we do not maintain that they will to be miserable, but that their will is so disposed that unhappiness follows it necessarily, even though they themselves don't want it.

Chapter 15: He who lives by the eternal law and by good will adheres to it is happy. Men who love temporal things are unhappy, and upon them the temporal law is imposed. But those who are subservient to the temporal law cannot be free from the eternal law for the temporal law is derived therefrom. Those who cleave through good will to the eternal law have no need of the temporal law. The temporal law can be just, and permits us to possess rightly those things which can be called ours in time. By that right, peace and human associations are maintained insofar as they can be. Such possessions are health, human liberty, relatives and friends, the state and money. The temporal law operates through fear and can rightly be enforced on those who make a bad use of these possessions.

Chapter 16: There are two laws, eternal and temporal, two classes of things, eternal and temporal, and two classes of men, those who love things eternal, and those who love things temporal. The mind is removed from its citadel of domination by nothing except the will. Only he who misuses the will can be charged with its misuse. But has God given us the free choice of the will?

Book Two: "In which, when the difficulty arises from the fact that the liberty whereby man sins is given by God, these three points are investigated: By what rational process is it manifest that God exists? Do all goods come from Him? Is free will to be considered among goods?"

Chapter 1: If God had not given man free will, he could not have sinned. In answer to this question, Saint Augustine points out that God would not give to man what He ought not to have given. All good is from God; all that is just is good; it is just that sinners pay the penalty and that the righteous be rewarded. Hence God brings it about that sinners are wretched and the righteous are happy. But this leads to the question how we know we are from Him. The answer lies in the admitted fact that God punishes sins, for all justice comes from Him. It is clear that we belong to Him, because He is most kind in bestowing goods upon us, as He is most just in punishing us. All good is from God; man is from God. Man *qua* man is good, because he can live rightly when he wills. Man must have free will without which he would be incapable of right action. We should not believe that because man sins through free will God gave it to him for that purpose. It should suffice to realize that without it man cannot live rightly.

Chapter 2: It is admitted that God has given man free will. Why is it perverted? To answer this, Saint Augustine suggests that the problem be approached as if all points were unproved or uncertain. This in turn raises the question of the existence of God.

Chapter 3: Man's existence is proved on the basis of the *si fallor, sum* argument. Therefore man lives and has understanding (*intelligentia*) which is the most excellent of the three (*i.e.*, existence, life, and intelligence). Man knows he possesses the five senses: by the eyes we apprehend color, by the ears sound, by the sense of smell odors, by taste flavors, the soft and the hard, etc., by touch. Some objects are apprehended by more than one sense. By reason we comprehend that there is an interior sense to which everything is referred by the five senses. This "interior sense" is not reason, for beasts evidently have it, but we comprehend it by reason. The following in the phenomenon of sense perception can be distinguished: a) the object; b) the sense impression in the sense organ; c) the interior sense in the soul; and d) the reason by which they are defined and enumerated.

Chapter 4: The manifest facts thus far established are: a) corporeal things are perceived by a bodily sense; b) this same sense cannot be perceived by the same sense; c) by the interior sense *both* corporeal things perceived by a bodily sense *and* the bodily sense itself are perceived; d) by reason all these as well as reason itself become known and are comprehended in knowledge.

Chapter 5: That which corporeal sense apprehends falls, in the hierarchy of existence, life, and understanding, in the category of that which *is*. The bodily sense falls in the class of that which *lives*, and is thus superior to its object which merely *is*. The interior sense is in the class of that which *lives*, and is to be preferred as a kind of judge of the other bodily senses.

Chapter 6: Reason in turn judges the interior sense. Reason, or the rational mind, is in the class of that which *is, lives*, and *understands*, than which there is nothing more excellent in man. God is the only entity superior to reason, to whom nothing is superior. Nothing can be above man's reason except what is eternal and unchanging, *viz.*, God. Bodies change, life does not lack mutability, and even reason itself, as it struggles more or less successfully towards truth, is shown clearly to be changeable. If reason through no other instrumentality than itself concludes that there is something eternal and immutable, and concludes that it itself is inferior, this entity reason must admit to be its God. If that which is above reason can be proved to exist, then God will be proved to exist.

Chapter 7: As each man has his own bodily senses and his own interior sense, so each has his own rational mind (*rationalis mens*). Though each has his own senses, one object may be perceived simultaneously by more than one person.

Chapter 8: The truth of number is seen in common by men through reason and mind, and is something which does not change. This truth of number is not grasped by the senses, but by the light of the mind. The objects of sense perception change, but seven and three are ten not only now but always. *One* is not perceived by the bodily senses, for all objects of bodily sense are made up of innumerable parts, but by interior light *one* is perceived and all the truths of number. There are other things which can be apprehended in common by the mind and reason which are and remain immutable.

Chapter 9: What is the nature of wisdom? Does each man possess his own wisdom, or is it common to all, with one being wiser than another in proportion to the extent to which he participates in it? Wisdom is nothing other than the truth in which the highest good is apprehended and held. To the extent that all men seek a happy life, they do not err. Since we all will to be happy, it is demonstrated that we all will to be wise. No one is happy without wisdom; that is, no one is happy without the highest good which is apprehended and held in that truth which we call wisdom. Wisdom or knowing, like the rationale of number and truth, presents itself in common to all who reason, and thus the highest good is one for all men. Even though there are apparently many goods, still the light of wisdom, whereby these can be seen, may be common to all wise men.

Chapter 10: That which is true is seen by our minds and is common to all of us. It is true that we must strive for wisdom—and this truth is grasped by the mind of each man. Each man in this way discovers such truths as these: that we should live justly, that the less excellent should give place to the more excellent, that the incorrupt is better than the corrupt, the eternal than the temporal. The recognition of all these belongs to wisdom. Like the rules of numbers, so these are the true and immutable rules of wisdom, available and present in common to all.

Chapter 11: The truth of number and the truth of wisdom are marvelous, and are conjoined in the Holy Scriptures. Why should the majority of men look down upon number? Perhaps we do so since number is imposed upon things that are below us. And yet when we turn our gaze upwards, we see that numbers transcend our minds, and remain immutable in truth itself. Learned men observe that both number and wisdom are in truth itself.

Chapter 12: The existence of immutable truth is established, according to Saint Augustine's argument. If this truth were inferior, we would pass judgment upon it as we do upon bodies which are inferior to us. Upon our souls we pass judgments in terms of the inner rules of truth, but no one judges of the rules themselves. As we see the truth more plainly or less plainly, we see that our minds change while truth does not, and thus our minds are not equal to truth. If truth is neither inferior nor equal to our minds, it follows that it is superior and more excellent.

Chapter 13: Therefore that which is superior to our mind and our reason has been revealed, *viz.,* truth. In comparison to all else, our happiness and joy are to be found in truth. Since in truth the highest good is known and held, and since this truth is wisdom, let us behold and grasp in it the highest good. This is our liberty when we subordinate ourselves to the truth. This is the meaning of "You shall know the truth and the truth shall make you free."

Chapter 14: No one against his will loses the truth and wisdom, and we may all enjoy them equally and in common. The truth is not difficult to approach, and has no flaw in it. It is near to all, eternal for all; it is in no particular place, yet nowhere is it lacking. It admonishes from without, it teaches from within. It makes better those who see it. No one can make it worse. No man can judge it, yet no man judges well without it. Thus it is clear that it is superior and more potent than our minds.

Chapter 15: It was agreed that if anything could be shown to be superior to our minds, this entity would be God, but on the further condition that nothing could be shown to be superior to it. If there is something more excellent than truth, that superior entity is God. If not, truth itself is God. Whether truth is or is not God, one cannot deny that God exists. We have reached this conclusion by a process of reason, but we must remember that we reach and hold the same conclusion by faith. Even though we may not declare ourselves completely wise with respect to this truth, yet we want to be wise, a desire we could not have unless there inhered in our minds a conception of wisdom.

Chapter 16: The desire to be wise leads us to the contemplation of that which is unaffected by time and place—that which is one and the same always. As the soul is the whole life of the body, so God is the happy life of the soul. While we are in this life, we are on the way towards this goal. Wisdom leads one on, no matter where one turns one's gaze. All bodies are seen to have number imposed upon them. One has within one certain laws of beauty, which are norms for the beautiful objects of sense. The forms of objects in nature derive from number, as do the objects made by the artisan, and hence are from the source of number. Number is in time and place. As wisdom is the sweetest light of the purified mind, woe to those who abandon her leadership and stray from her paths.

Chapter 17: Everything that is mutable must be capable of being formed. No thing can form itself, since it cannot give itself what it has not. As both body and soul are mutable, they must be formed by a certain immutable and ever enduring form. Thus one can say that all things are governed by Providence whence they derive form. Body and life (by these two terms one can express that which is, lives, and understands) are formable, and hence derive from that form which always exists, *i.e.*, from God.

Chapter 18: That God is, and that all good things come from Him, have been demonstrated. As for the third question, whether the free choice of the will is to be counted as a good, it can also be regarded as solved. Earlier it was urged that, since there can be no right action without the free choice of the will, for this reason God gave it. But this led to the rational proof of the existence of God, during the course of which it became apparent that we must count free will among things good. The nature of the body is on a lower level than the nature of the soul. The soul therefore is a greater good than the body. Among the goods of the body are things which man can misuse. Yet we do not insist that therefore they should not have been given, for we admit that they are good. It is no wonder then that the soul has certain goods which can be misused, but since they are good, they can be given only by the Giver of all goods. Hands, feet, and eyes, which are all goods, can be misused. So in the soul, free will is a good which can be misused. That it is a good cannot be doubted, for without it man is incapable of living rightly.

Chapter 19: The great goods, the virtues of justice, prudence, fortitude and temperance, as well as the least goods, are from God. The virtues are the great goods; bodies, without which one can live rightly, are the least goods, while the powers of the soul, without which one cannot live rightly, are between the two. No one can use virtue wrongly, whereas it is possible to misuse the other two types of goods. As we know reason by the use of reason, so we use free will by the will. So memory not only remembers things, but also through itself remembers itself. When the will, a medium good, cleaves to the immutable good, then is man's life happy. The virtues are in him, which he gets not from the virtues of another man, but from immutable truth which is common to all. The will, a medium good, can by cleaving to the immutable good gain for man the great goods, *i.e.*, the virtues. When the will is not thus oriented, man sins. Neither the goods that are sought by wrong-doers, nor free will itself, are evil in any way. Evil is the turning away from the immutable good, and turning towards mutable goods. This turning is not done under compulsion, but is a matter of the will, and the just penalty of unhappiness follows it.

Chapter 20: Whence then is that movement, that turning away from God? This we cannot know, for what is nothing cannot be known. Where there are measure, number and order in a thing, they are all attributed to God as artificer. But if these are *completely* taken away, nothing will remain. All good is from God. There is no nature, therefore, which is not from God. That motion of turning away from Him, *i.e.,* sin, is a defective motion. Every defect is from nothing, hence it cannot belong to God. This defect, since it is voluntary, is in our power. If you fear, it is necessary that you not will it. If you don't will it, it will not be. But since, as man fell of his own will, let us hold by faith that the right hand of God is stretched out to us from above, our Lord Jesus Christ.

Book Three: "In which is investigated the source of that motion whereby the will turns away from the immutable good; is there a conflict between the foreknowledge of God concerning the sins of men, and the liberty of men themselves in sinning? Presently it is shown that it is in vain to impute to the Creator that which must take place in the creature with the result that it happens by the will of sinners. And directly concerning the production of a creature who is liable to sin and in his punishment, God is to be praised. Hence when the discussion is turned to the sins of our origin, it is declared how these by no means unjustly descend to the posterity of Adam; how on account of these facts unjustly sinners plead an excuse. Thereafter some difficulties pertaining thereto are elucidated."

Chapter 1: The movement of the will away from the immutable good can not be attributed to a natural or necessary movement of the soul. This movement is not natural but voluntary. It is like the downward movement of a stone, because, just as this is proper to a stone, so is that proper to the soul. But whereas the stone cannot stop its motion downward, the soul can stop its motion by the will.

Chapter 2: Saint Augustine asks, how can it be: how both God can have foreknowledge and we sin through no necessity? How is the will free, when so inevitable a necessity is apparent? Many men are tortured by this question because they do not approach it in an attitude of piety. They either limit God's providence or maintain that it is weak, unjust and evil. They rather should believe that the goodness, justice and power of God are greater than anything the human mind can conceive. Thus they would be grateful to God, would be led by the sure ways of divine wisdom, neither inflated by what they have found, nor distraught by what they have not found.

Chapter 3: God foreknows all. But even though He does this, it does not result that we will anything not by the means of the will. For example, God's foreknowledge does not take away one's will for happiness. Our will would not be will unless it were in our power. If it is in our power, for us it is free. Thus it comes about that we do not deny that God foreknows all that is future and nevertheless that we will what we will.

Chapter 4: Does God's foreknowledge of our sins contradict our free choice in sinning? One's foreknowledge that another will sin does not compel him to sin; so it is with God's foreknowledge which does not compel those who will sin through their own will. God has foreknowledge of all things of which He is the author, but nevertheless He is not the author of all things of which He has foreknowledge. Yet He is the just avenger of those things of which he is not the evil author. If God ought not to punish sinners because He foresees that they will sin, then He ought not to give rewards to those who act rightly because He foresees no less that they will so act.

Chapter 5: We ought not to impute to the Creator that which is done of necessity in His creature. This problem should recall to us that rule of piety whereby we should give thanks to Him, even if He had created us on a lower level. We are better than this visible light, even though we sin. Yet we praise God for this light, even though sullied by sin; yet souls are of greater worth than the light for which God is justly praised. Don't say that things ought to have been made other than they are. Whatever you conceive to be better through true reason, this you may know to have been made by God. For example, if a creature is a source of delight who through a steadfast will does not sin, through right reason you prefer that creature to one who sins; just as you prefer him by a process of thought, so has the Creator by His decree placed him higher. Things are arranged in hierarchic order. Thus a creature who sins through free will is more excellent than one who does not sin because he does not have free will. As even the least souls are worth more than bodies, is not God for this reason to be praised? Reason, which proceeds in the light of truth, can determine the worth of things far better than use.

Chapter 6: Thus the sins of the creature cannot be imputed to the Creator, even though He has foreknowledge. It is a lie to say, "I would prefer not to exist rather than to be unhappy." The important point is that you will to be happy. From ingratitude for that which you will to be, you are compelled to be that which you do not will to be, *i.e.,* unhappy. God is to be praised because you have the will to be happy, and He is likewise to be praised if He justly compels you to endure the unhappiness which you do not will. If you will not be master of yourself, then either someone stronger or weaker will have you in his power. If a weaker, then it is your own fault, and your unhappiness is just. But if a stronger has you in his power, you cannot think that this is unjust. If this is unjust, you will not be unhappy. If it is just, you will be unhappy, and we should praise Him whose laws have so decreed.

Chapter 7: Since being itself is a great good, it is preferable to be even if you are unhappy. Actually you are unhappy to the extent that you do not come near to God, who in the highest sense *is*. Therefore one must love in oneself the will to be, and the more one does this, the closer he will come to God, the highest Being. All things are to be praised because they *are*. And by the fact of their existence, they are good. The more one yearns to be, the more he will desire eternal life. One should love temporal things, then, in so far as they are, and if he so views things temporal, he will be firm in his love of the eternal. When he starts along the way of being perfectly, then he will not be unhappy.

Chapter 8: To prefer not to be than to be unhappy is absurd, for *not to be* is *nothing*. There is no choice when one of the things to be chosen does not exist. Furthermore, suicides should not influence our judgment in this question. Even if a suicide insists that he is choosing *nothing*, this very answer shows that we should not be moved. No man really believes that he will not live after death, and therefore really wishes to die. The notion that death involves complete obliteration results from an error of opinion. The desire is to be at rest, which is not non-being, but *being* in a fuller sense.

Chapter 9: Why has God not decreed that no creature should be unhappy? As we cannot say that no creature should be, so we cannot say that a creature should be of such and such a sort. The hierarchic order of things in the perfect universe means that some things are greater and some lesser. Among souls, which are greater than bodies, those which are unhappy are so because they have willed to sin. Sin and unhappiness are not necessary to the perfection of the universe, but souls *qua* souls are, and souls *qua* souls may sin if they so will. Sin and punishment are not natures, but affections of natures. The punishment of sin corrects the disgrace of sin, so that even the sinning soul contributes to the order and perfection of the universe. The first man brought sin, and the adornment of the penalty suited to the sin, and Christ brought the adornment of mercy to grant freedom from sin. The immortality of the saints can be gained, not by the way of the proud, but by the humility revealed by Jesus Christ.

Chapter 10: There are two origins of sins, one from one's own thinking, the second from the persuasion of another, and both are voluntary. It is worse to sin of one's own volition and to persuade another than to yield to the persuasion of another. This latter is as it is with the prince of this world, the prince of all sinners and the one who presides over death. Man who fears, is uncertain, a prey to illicit pleasures and to pride, is wont to break. Who needs mercy more and who is more undeserving of it? But it is Christ who extends us this mercy. Man must struggle by conjectures derived from visible things to reach an understanding of things invisible, of the Word among men who overcame the devil.

Chapter 11: God created all natures, whether they were to sin or not, to adorn the universe. Without souls the creation would be defective. Rational souls are in their functions unequal to the celestial and supercelestial powers, but in nature they are equal.

Chapter 12: The will to sin is the only defect in the creation. The angelic nature does not sin by free will. Yet even if it did, God would still rule all. The corporeal nature, though inferior to the angelic nature, still was created out of lavish bounty, so great that no one can look upon it without owning that God is the artificer of all, the most excellent maker and most just ruler of all natures.

Chapter 13: Every nature that can be made less good is good. Every nature *qua* nature is good. If it is incorruptible it will be superior to a corruptible nature. If corruptible, while it is being corrupted, it becomes less good, but still without doubt it is good. So if every nature is either corruptible or incorruptible, every nature is good. Nature is usually called substance. Every substance is either God or from God, because every good is either God or from God. Every rational nature, endowed with free will, if it maintains itself in the enjoyment of immutable good, must be praised. The rational nature which is contrarily disposed must be blamed. In either case, God the creator is to be praised—for how can we blame Him if a rational nature does not will to enjoy the immutable good? Not nature, but only a fault of nature can be blamed—and since a fault is opposed to the nature, when the fault is blamed, implicitly the nature is praised.

Chapter 14: Is it true that a nature can be corrupted by the fault of another without adding any fault of its own? There can be no doubt that if this happens, it is a result of a combined fault in the wills of both.

Chapter 15: If the blaming of faults has implicit in it the praise of natures, how great should be the praise of God, the creator of natures, in whose faults their very goodness can be seen. A sinful nature ought to act rightly. God gave it the power so to act if so it wills. God also grants unhappiness if it does not act rightly, and happiness if it does.

Chapter 16: God does not owe anything to anyone, because He stands above all and does so gratuitously. Nothing is lacking to Him if you will not turn to Him. It is you who lose. All is owing to Him, first of all the very existence of natures in so far as they are natures. Natures with free will owe its proper use. If anyone thinks that he is forced to sin and thus owes this, that he ought to sin, is in error, for his own nature compels no one to sin.

Chapter 17: What is the cause of the will? If you answer this in some way, you will ask for the cause of the cause, and be led into an infinite regression. If you take avarice to be cupidity, then cupidity is wrong will, and wrong will is the cause of all evils. Wrong will is opposed to nature and is destructive of it. Thus it is wrong, and it is fair to say that the root of all evils is not according to nature. The will itself must therefore be the first cause of sin.

Chapter 18: Can compulsion against the will be the first cause? If the will cannot resist, there is no sin in yielding. But if it can, and it does not give in, there is no sin. This shows that the will is the first cause of sin. Man, being what he is, is not good nor does he have it in his power to be good; he sins, and is punished by the omnipotent justice of God. This is a description of fallen man. When we speak of man's free will to act rightly, we are speaking of that will in which man was made.

Chapter 19: Next comes the question why men should suffer for the original sin of Adam and Eve. The answer is the presence of the Lord who teaches the believer, who consoles the hopeful, encourages him who loves, helps him who tries, and hears him who prays.

Chapter 20: After the first sin, God's justice in punishing sin was apparent, and then His mercy as He freed man from sin. After the first sin, it was not right that man should produce a better posterity than himself. But man by right will can overcome the lot of his birth. If one soul is the origin of all souls, if this first soul sins, who can deny sin to the rest? If souls are created one by one for each man, it seems correct that the ill merit of the former should be the nature of the one that follows, and that the good merit of the one that follows should be the nature of the former. The Creator thus reveals the greater value of the soul than the body by making it possible for the soul to rise above the level of its fallen state. Ignorance and difficulty in which souls are born will not be a punishment for sin, but rather an admonition to move forward and a start on the road to perfection. If preexisting souls are sent to rule men's bodies, then, by ruling well, the incorruption of heaven may be reached. If souls enter bodies of their own volition, then ignorance and difficulty come as a result of this volition, and blame cannot be imputed to the Creator.

Chapter 21: There are four theories concerning the origin of the soul: a) they are propagated by the first soul; b) they are created individually; c) they pre-exist and are sent into human bodies; d) they pre-exist and enter human bodies of their own volition. No one of these should be accepted heedlessly. Either Catholic scholars have not yet elucidated the problem, or else if they have their works are not yet available. In this question we must hold to nothing that is false or untrue concerning the nature of the Creator. Things revealed to us must be held by faith, but many things, however, are beyond human intelligence. Against unbelievers, the weight of authority may be used, but also it must be shown in so far as possible, first how it is not stupid to believe, and next how stupid it is not to believe. We should refute the false by things immutable, and in so far as possible by transparent reasoning. The past should be used for its bearing on the future, and in preparing for the future. Such is the attitude in which the problem concerning the origin of the soul should be studied.

Chapter 22: Whatever may be the solution to the problem, still it is by God's justice that the souls of sinners pay the penalty for their sins. It is all a matter of will, and the soul has the will to move forward, and the soul may ask God's help.

Chapter 23: What of the problem of the death and bodily suffering of little children? The answer is that there is nothing superfluous in God's creation. What good is child baptism? The faith of those who offer them for baptism is an advantage to them. The authority of the Church commends this, for faith begets faith in others. But what of the bodily suffering of children? The elders are tried and made better, or if they do not sustain the trial, they will not have an excuse in the face of the punishment of the future judgment. But who knows what good God may have in store for these children? What of the suffering of animals? Men who are troubled by this do not use right reason concerning the highest good. The pain of animals reveals the presence in them of a marvelous force of soul; it reveals its desire for unity, for pain merely is an evidence of resistance to that which disrupts unity. We would not be aware of this desire for unity in the lower creatures, were it not for the suffering of animals. Thus we would not be so well aware of the fact that all things are constituted by the ineffable unity of the Creator. All things—the beauty of physical creation, the reaction to pleasure and pain, the rational nature's desire for knowledge, its flight from error—point to the unity of the Creator.

Chapter 24: The question as to the nature and character of the first man is more to be investigated than the manner in which his posterity was propagated. If wise, how was he seduced? If stupid, why is God not responsible? Man is rather in a mean state between wisdom and stupidity. Through the will he moves towards stupidity. By reason man is capable of a command, and can obey the command. A rational nature receives a command, and the will is for the purpose of obeying it. A rational nature is deserving to receive a command, but when this command is obeyed, it deserves to receive wisdom. And wisdom comes from him who gives illumination, as the command comes from the commander, not from the one who is commanded. For all this, the Creator of man should be praised.

Chapter 25: Man chooses by his will among things seen, either those from God or from the devil. There are two classes of things seen. One comes from the will of a persuader, *e.g.,* the devil. The other class derives from that which comes to the notice of the mind or the senses of the body. What comes to the attention of the mind first of all is the mind itself. It observes, as it contemplates the highest Wisdom, how it differs from God, yet is something which pleases after God. The mind is better when it is forgetful of itself as compared with the love of God or when it contemns itself wholly in comparison with Him. If it pleases itself wrongly, this is pride, the beginning of all sin. An evil will was added to the pride of the devil, who persuaded man. As the devil submitted himself for the imitation of pride, so our Lord submitted himself for the imitation of humility, through Whom eternal life is promised to us. Let us cleave to our Liberator so that nothing can separate us from Him. One day in the beauty of justice and the joy of eternal light would make us contemn innumerable years of the delights of this life and of temporal goods.

NOTE ON THE ANALYSIS OF THE TREATISE *ON FREE WILL*

It was originally intended that the full text of the treatise *On Free Will* should be included in this volume. However, the prolix character of certain portions of the text led to the decision to prepare a detailed summary of this important statement of Saint Augustine's earlier thought. An attempt is here made to give the substance of the work, chapter by chapter, by using condensation, paraphrase, and, at more significant points, complete translation, in the hope that a clear impression of the argument will be apparent. Obviously for the general understanding of Saint Augustine no one can overlook his views expressed in the treatise *On Free Will* concerning the origin of moral evil, the nature of free will, the rational proof of God's existence, and the relation of God's foreknowledge to man's free will. Written as it was between 388-395 A.D., the document antedates his controversy with the Pelagians, and hence came before he had given a full expression to his doctrine of grace which that controversy necessitated. It is noteworthy that the Pelagians used this work against Saint Augustine, who towards the end of his life, in the *Retractationes* (426 A.D.), took pains to clarify his meaning. In his review of his earlier work he pointed out with precision how the Pelagians had misconceived his argument and doctrine.

The only complete text and translation of *De Libro Arbitrio* available in the United States was prepared by F. S. Tourscher, S.T.M., O.S.A. and published by the Peter Reilly Company, Philadelphia, 1937.

INDEX TO *THE CONFESSIONS*